WORLD DIRECTORY OF MINORITIES

MINORITY RIGHTS GROUP INTERNATIONAL

Minority Rights Group works to secure rights and justice for ethnic, linguistic and religious minorities. It is dedicated to the cause of cooperation and understanding between communities.

Founded in the 1960s, MRG is a small international non-governmental organization that informs and warns governments, the international community, non-governmental organizations and the wider public about the situation of minorities around the world. This work is based on the publication of well-researched reports, books and papers; direct advocacy on behalf of minority rights in international fora; the development of a global network of like-minded organizations and minority communities to collaborate on these issues; and **the challenging of prejudice and promotion of public understanding** through information and education projects.

MRG believes that the best hope for a peaceful world lies in **identifying and monitoring conflict** between communities, **advocating preventive measures** to avoid the escalation of conflict and **encouraging positive action** to build trust between majority and minority communities.

MRG has consultative status with the United Nations Economic and Social Council and has a worldwide network of partners. Its international headquarters are in London. Legally it is registered both as a charity and as a limited company under United Kingdom Law with an International Governing Council.

WORLD DIRECTORY OF MINORITIES

Edited by
Minority Rights Group

Project Director
Miles Litvinoff

Legal Consultant
Patrick Thornberry

Preface by
Alan Phillips
Executive Director, MRG International

Contributors
Bridget Anderson, James Chin, John Connell, Patrick Costello, Lindsey Crickmay, Chris Dammers, James Ferguson, David Hawk, David McDowall, Anna Matveeva, Julia Maxted, Neil Melvin, Peter O'Neill, Suzanne Pattle, Martyn Rady, Javaid Rehman, Alex Roslin, Nikhil Roy, David Sogge, Bogdan Szajkowski, Carl Wilson, Abebe Zegeye

Minority Rights Group International

lom in 1997 by
ıal

British Library Cataloguing in Publication Data
A CIP catalogue record of this book is available from the British Library.

ISBN 1 873194 36 6

Library of Congress Cataloguing in Publication Data
CIP Data available from the Library of Congress.

Typeset by The Midlands Book Typesetting Company, Loughborough, Leics., UK.
Printed and Bound by Mateu Cromo, Madrid, Spain.

This Directory has been commissioned and is published by Minority Rights Group as a contribution to public understanding of minority rights issues. The text does not necessarily represent, in every detail and in all its aspects, the collective view of Minority Rights Group.

CONTENTS

PREFACE

The large majority of violent conflicts in the world today are conflicts within states, with groups polarized across ethnic and religious divides and not across borders. Ethnic, religious and linguistic minorities are often among the poorest of the poor, suffer discrimination and are frequently the victims of human rights abuses. Time and time again in the past, the United Nations system, governments and even non-governmental organizations (NGOs) working in the field of 'conflict prevention' have failed to promote the human rights of minorities or to take early action to promote cooperation between communities. Early action may have prevented the loss of millions of lives in many countries, ranging from Rwanda to the former Yugoslavia, and from Sri Lanka to Guatemala. It is also significant that the Nobel Peace Prize was awarded to the Dalai Lama in 1989 and to José Ramos-Horta and Bishop Carlos Belo in1996 as a result of their peaceful campaigns to promote the rights of their people.

The situation of minorities is, then, a matter of major concern, and it is essential that accurate, objective and up-to-date information is made available. This *Directory* contributes to that process.

It is difficult to assess accurately what proportion of the world's population identify themselves as belonging to minority communities. Conservative estimates place this above 10 per cent, and some suggest that more than 20 per cent of the world's population belongs to several thousand different minority groups and subgroups. National statistics are often skewed for political reasons, and there is no universally accepted definition of 'minorities'. The word has different interpretations in different societies throughout the world, while the United Nations General Assembly has not sought to reach a definition beyond that implied in the title of the UN Declaration on the Rights of Persons belonging to National or Ethnic, Religious and Linguistic Minorities adopted in December 1992. Minority Rights Group focuses its work on non-dominant ethnic, religious and linguistic communities, whether or not they are numerical minorities. The concept thus relates to any self-identified community that is marginalized, without power, unable to take decisions over its destiny and often experiencing high levels of illiteracy, under-education and overt or covert discrimination. The basic rights of such communities need protection and promotion.

There is, however, a danger of generalizing about minorities and forgetting the complexity of their social composition, including the rural poor, urban migrants, older people, women and children. These groups may be considered as doubly vulnerable. What makes their situation particularly problematic is that there is often a deliberate political policy on the part of majorities and states not to give due regard to the legitimate interests of minorities, while members of minorities see their identity as central to their social and economic situation. They are often excluded from political power and decision-making in the development process, without equal opportunities to secure a better quality of life.

One further danger may lie in regarding ethnicities as fixed, rather than as the potentially fluid phenomena that they often are. 'Situational ethnicity' does occur, and individuals and groups do modify their self-identifications depending on circumstances.

Minorities, development and democracy

Few minorities seek to be assimilated through insensitive 'mono-ethnic' state policies. Yet states commonly fail to include sensitivity to minority needs in their development programmes presented to investors and aid donors. Banks and donors find these issues difficult to raise with majoritarian-ruled 'emerging' democracies, despite the donor framework of 'good governance conditionality'. Often, the inter-governmental community ignores minority rights and is insensitive to minority needs, until violence erupts or there are development disasters. Conversely, few companies appreciate how a multi-ethnic workforce can open up new business opportunities among different communities and can help build bridges across society. This has been dangerous for stability and short-sighted for development, and it perpetuates injustice.

The United Nations has now recognized that intercommunity tensions and conflicts are serious threats to the peace and stability of a region and go beyond the exclusive concern of the state in which the communities in question reside. Conflict resolution and minorities are now high-priority issues on the international agenda. Long-term donor strategies are needed to enhance equitable development of societies and to prevent the escalation of tensions. The continuing human cost of failure is immense, although economists appear slow to interrelate the vast and growing costs of conflicts and the need for pre-emptive development action. Organization for Economic Cooperation and Development (OECD) assistance to the poorest countries fell by $5 billion between 1992 and 1994, a reduction of 6 per cent in real terms, and may be set to fall further. Ironically, an investment in targeted aid to improve intercommunity relations and true democratization processes would have safeguarded past aid investment and reduced the prospects and costs of conflicts.

There is recognition that the marginalization of minorities is a human rights issue irrespective of the conflict-resolution perspective. The UN Declaration on the Rights of Minorities of 1992 recognizes that developmental responses are essential. In Article 5 it states: 'National policies and programmes shall be planned and implemented with due regard for the legitimate interests of persons belonging to minorities' (5.1); and 'Programmes of cooperation and assistance among States should be planned and implemented with due regard for the legitimate interests of persons belonging to minorities' (5.2). These two basic rights should be axiomatic in any coherent development strategy.

It is crucial to ensure that, as a minimum, minorities are protected from ill-considered and sometimes hostile aid programmes. A multitude of programmes have been promoted in the name of development but, often unwittingly, have damaged vulnerable communities. Examples include hydroelectric dam projects such as the Sardar Sarovar in India and others in the Chittagong Hill Tracts of Bangladesh, in Sri Lanka and in Iraq; oil extraction projects in the Caucasus, in the delta coastal region of Nigeria, in Siberia and Ecuador; population transfers in the name of development in Tibet, Kurdish Iraq and Turkey, Kalimantan, West Papua, East Timor and Ethiopia; national parks projects affecting the Veddhas (Waaniy-a-Laato) in Sri Lanka, the Masai in Kenya and the Basarwa (San) in Botswana; and, last but not least, logging and other forestry developments impacting severely on minorities in Brazil, Burma, Thailand and Malaysia, among other countries.

There is a danger in implying that poorly conceived development programmes and a lack of participation exclusively affect minorities. This is clearly not the case. Nevertheless, certain kinds of programmes are more likely than most to have an adverse effect on minorities in isolated communities. A broad development principle is clear: all communities affected by development programmes should be formally consulted at the design stage and should be involved throughout the programme as participants and evaluators. On the more positive side, development failures are increasingly recognized as such. The World Bank has a new approach towards indigenous peoples (though not yet towards all minorities), and donor governments are beginning to recognize the importance of minority-sensitive aid strategies, and to relate human rights policies to development practices.

There is a manifest need for more dialogue between donors, recipient governments, non-governmental organizations (NGOs) and others with regard to the inclusion of minority concerns in aid strategies. The objective should be both to target some of the poorest and most vulnerable in society while also contributing to long-term conflict prevention. (These objectives are not necessarily mutually complementary; it would be possible to prevent violent conflicts by massive repression within states or by seeking political agreements between political elites.) Aid officials sometimes admit that they find it difficult to raise ethnicity as an issue during project identification and appraisal; it is often the great unmentionable. Research into, and documentation of, the successes and failures of development projects with regard to minority communities are a neglected area; this should be redressed to learn lessons from the past.

The notion that democracy is brought about by elections where the winner – the largest parliamentary party – takes all is unacceptable from a minority rights perspective. On a number of occasions, such as in Angola, a winner-takes-all view of democracy has contributed to the beginning or renewal of conflict. This contrasts with Zimbabwe, where power-sharing between the leadership of different communities helped avoid an escalating civil war in the 1980s. Democracy should involve the effective participation and cooperation of all communities at all levels. The broadening and deepening of the democratization process is crucial for minority rights, minority participation and stable development. The strengthening of civil society is a lengthy and complex process yet an essential part of creating pluralist democracies where people can be involved in creating their own future.

Strategies should seek to promote the identity of minorities, while also avoiding increasing areas of conflict arising from ethnic differences. These apparently contradictory objectives can only be achieved with experience, care and subtlety. When reviewing the situation of minorities in such fields as education, employment and access to resources – issues that are more fully explored in MRG's thematic reports – the minimum standards of the UN Declaration on the Rights of Minorities should act as a comparator.

Implementing minimum standards for minorities

Education

A state may query whether minorities should have special educational rights at all. It may see the purpose of its education system as being the inculcation of a sense of national unity and identity; and therefore, when it makes declarations about the educational rights of all its citizens, these may not include the rights of minorities. This approach is often in conflict with the idea of special rights for minorities in respect of language, religion and curricula. Minorities see education as crucial, both for their future prospects and also for transmitting their values and culture. It is important to consider who defines minority groups. Is it the majority or the minorities themselves? Different educational provision may result from whose definition is used. At its most extreme, a state does not even need to consider any special provision for a minority which it does not define as officially existing – for example, the historic approach of Turkey towards its Kurdish community.

Language issues

One of the critical ways in which minorities define themselves is through language. Language is an essential part of an individual's identity, and for minority groups it is a significant part of group identity. The minority language transmits cultural norms and values. In most states, however, minority language does not have equal status with the majority language. From the position of the state, language is one of the bonds that hold the state together. It can be argued that the cultural identity and political and social unity of a state will be promoted if everyone is educated in the same national language. In addition, the cost of providing minority language teaching can be prohibitive, especially in states with many languages. It is not in dispute that minority groups need to be taught the national language of the state in which they live so that they may participate fully in that society. However, there are also strong arguments for teaching minority languages, as well as the majority language. A child's first language is normally the best medium for learning, especially in the early stages of education. Minority language teaching is necessary for the development of a positive self-image and for children to know about their history and culture. In addition, mother-tongue teaching, as well as being important in its own right, actually enhances second language learning rather than detracting from it. Teaching minority languages prevents language loss and helps prevent forced linguistic and cultural assimilation: cultural and linguistic pluralism can thus be seen as enriching society as a whole.

Religion and secularism

Religion and religious education are, like language, a key area in the education of minorities. Since education is provided by the state, it belongs to the public domain, while religion in a secular state belongs to the private domain. However, for many minorities, if their religion remains in the private domain it may become invisible and low status – both in educational terms and to society at large. Another difficulty is that secular values may not satisfy the religious longings and needs of minorities, who may then argue for separate schools. There is often a real tension between the values of a secular society and the religious values that minorities may wish their children to learn. If religious minorities establish their own separate schools through disenchantment with state schooling, then mutual understanding between minority and majority is more difficult to achieve. The rise of fundamentalism in secular states may be a reflection of how those states have failed to provide a safe and secure framework for different religious minorities.

Employment

Throughout the world, direct and indirect discriminatory practices exist in employment. Sometimes, although rarely, affirmative action (positive discrimination) policies are implemented as special temporary measures to redress inequalities and poverty among minority communities. More often than not, however, adverse discrimination takes place, reflecting the prejudice within society and the lack of confidence of the majority group in employing members of minority communities. In the more extreme cases, there exists racial or religious discrimination, leading state or private employers to apply strict language tests which are unnecessary for particular posts. The UN committee monitoring the International Convention on the Elimination of All Forms of Racial Discrimination and International Labour Organization officials reporting on the implementation of ILO 111 on non-discrimination in the workplace have produced numerous well-documented country reports, but this remains a crucial issue. It should not be forgotten that Dr Boutros Boutros-Ghali, a Copt, was never able to rise above the position of Deputy Foreign Minister in Egypt and yet became Secretary-General of the United Nations.

Land rights and natural resources

Land is a key issue underlying minority claims for protection. Some minorities claim restoration of lands of which they were dispossessed long ago; others seek to avert further dispossession or demand genuine equality of rights with dominant majorities. For many minorities, territory is synonymous with identity and the ability to survive as an entity. The best-known examples are those indigenous peoples for whom the relationship with land represents an entire way of life – history, ancestors, respect for the environment, community organization and relationships with outsiders.

Important land and natural resources issues also arise for other minorities. The way that water is used or diverted, for example, can have an immense impact on a rural society, as has been demonstrated by the redirecting of rivers and draining of marshes in Iraq, which have had such a dramatic effect on the Marsh Arabs. Dam projects, mentioned earlier, have had devastating effects on millions of people within minorities, in the name of development. Related issues include fishing rights in rivers and coastal waters, pollution of water by outside industry and even the use of waterways for tourism.

Often the most contentious debates are about resources under the ground, where governments and investors see the opportunity for substantial returns and significant foreign exchange earning. Mining for minerals has devastated many areas, frequently through pollution and the construction of infrastructure. In recent years, the ownership of oil has been a flashpoint for violence in the Caucasus and in the delta areas of Nigeria. Time and time again, the local minority community receives little benefit and many disadvantages from such 'developments', while outsiders accrue enormous financial profits.

One of the most intractable land-and-minority issues has been redressing the problems of the past, particularly the repressive policies of population movement into and out of an area to strengthen the control of a state by central government. The experiences of the deported peoples of the former Soviet Union, including the Crimean Tatars, and the presence of Russians in the periphery of the former Soviet Union today both create animosity that provides opportunities for exploitation by politicians. Currently, too, Tibet is experiencing major movements of Chinese into the area with drastic consequences for the demographic and cultural composition of the country.

Land rights have begun to receive considerable attention in the United Nations and its agencies and in national constitutions. The main focus has been on the rights of indigenous and tribal peoples. However, the UN Declaration on the Rights of Minorities makes no reference to land rights, and this is undoubtedly one of its weaknesses. The strong recognition of indigenous land rights under international law and the absence of recognition of minorities' land rights are an anomaly. States are often reluctant to accept devolution or autonomy arrangements, believing that they will weaken the fabric of the state. History has shown the converse to be true.

Protection of indigenous peoples

The territorial claims of indigenous peoples may be rooted far back in history. They are underpinned by the notion of their special claims to the land, because their unique relationship with the environment is crucial to their survival, and their land and resource rights may never be ceded. The first international legal instrument to codify indigenous and tribal peoples' rights was the ILO Convention concerning the Protection and Integration of Indigenous and other Tribal and semi-Tribal Populations in Independent Countries, No. 107 (1957). By the mid-1980s, this convention was out of tune with current realities and aspirations; the ILO adopted a new Indigenous and Tribal Peoples Convention in 1989 (No. 169), emphasizing recognition of such peoples' rights to control their own development. Land rights are also central to the Draft Declaration on Indigenous Rights issued by the UN Working Group on Indigenous Populations (established in 1982).

Demands for protection of indigenous and tribal land rights have influenced the policies of international financial institutions, whose past efforts have been criticized for their devastating impact on traditional land security. A 1991 World Bank operational directive requires an indigenous people's development plan to be adopted, with the informed participation of indigenous people, before project appraisal. New concepts thus arise beyond equality of treatment and access. States should recognize indigenous and tribal peoples' special relationship with, and prior ownership of, traditional lands; they should render this ownership effective and establish adequate claims and disputes procedures.

Programmes to promote good intercommunity relations

In many situations, there is the need for special programmes to tackle the multiple needs of minorities: literacy and language disadvantages; their concentration in the poorest regions and the worst slums; denial of land and resources; and high levels of employment. To avoid further polarization, on occasions such activities may not be identified explicitly as ethnic minority programmes, but targeted at specific areas. These are crucial areas of minority rights which are elaborated on in MRG reports. Initiatives to counter disadvantage play a significant role in addressing the underlying causes of ethnic conflicts and discriminatory practices. These include programmes of research into the economic, social and political environment of inter-ethnic relations, which need to be undertaken before any programming or advocacy. Support for civil society institutions researching, documenting, reporting and informing on minority rights is essential, while practical experience shows that these are often the springboard for other intercommunity actions transcending ethnic identities. Education programmes on inter-racial justice, equality and the empowerment of minority communities can play a crucial catalytic role, particularly at times of change. Educational and media programmes can help promote attitudes of tolerance and mutual respect in multi-ethnic societies.

Information flows and technical assistance to promote political development including constitutional reform, the building of new institutions such as language commissions, minority commissions, minority round tables and the design of autonomy or devolutionary arrangements – all can make valuable contributions. Additionally, there can be minority programmes to strengthen the formal institutions of the state, such as the composition of the legal system and its sensitivity to minority communities, and the access of minorities to, and their participation in, governmental programmes and institutions. The application and monitoring of international standards and of equal opportunity policies in both state and private sectors – supported by contract compliance and the targeting of aid – are equally important.

Minority rights have to be achieved within states. Lasting responses have to be based on local and national initiatives. Local initiatives on their own can easily be isolated and marginalized, and it is here that the synergy and solidarity of international partnerships and networks are crucial. These need to be real partnerships and not based on external actors dominating through funding or coordination locally. MRG's own project partners insist on a solid understanding of agreed international standards and of how they have been implemented in practice. This ensures that the 'minority rights' wheel does not have to be reinvented. Donor governments and international monitoring bodies can usefully learn much from NGO research and experience.

The *World Directory of Minorities*

The objective of this *World Directory* is therefore to provide an authoritative and concise reference book on the contemporary situation of minorities worldwide. Minorities and indigenous people have frequently captured the news in the 1990s, and there has been a spate of academic research on specific minorities and minority themes. MRG and others have published numerous books and reports on individual minority groups. However, this *Directory* is arguably unique; its entries, covering more than 200 states and dependent territories, provide a coherent and wide-ranging introduction to the situation of the world's minority groups, complete with key bibliographical references and listings of active NGOs involved with minority and related issues. The *Directory* also features a substantial legal essay by Professor Patrick Thornberry, who has acted as mentor to MRG throughout this publication, and an appendix to place country entries within a broader global context of legal instruments for the protection of minorities.

The *Directory* aims to provide insight into the conditions of minority communities throughout the world – reflecting, where appropriate, issues of gender and impacts on children and other vulnerable groups – and to indicate major areas of intercommunity tension. Relationships between communities do not, as a rule, change rapidly; they are usually deep rooted within society and within states. Thus we hope that the book will remain a valuable reference work for a number of years to come. The previous edition of the *Directory*, published in 1990, was often used to establish a *prima facie* case on whether individuals might have a well-founded fear of persecution. This new edition – expanded to cover a wider range of countries and minorities than its predecessor – should therefore be of considerable use to refugee agencies and the like, as well as to scholars, educationalists, human rights bodies, media workers, government and UN officials, those working in development agencies and members of minorities themselves.

Twenty-two regional specialist writers and a further fifty consultant readers have contributed to this book – all of them acknowledged scholars and practitioners in the field of minorities. I would like to thank them and the project's legal consultant, Patrick Thornberry, alongside the MRG staff, ably led by Miles Litvinoff, who have successfully brought this publication to completion.

The International Council of Minority Rights Group had the courage to initiate this project, like many other MRG projects, without being certain of where the funding would come from. It was confident that a major publication such as this was needed to fill a crucial information gap, and that in due course it would be able to convince donors of the merits of this. This confidence was well placed, because a range of donors have contributed to the project, without whose help publication of this *Directory* would not have been possible. Substantial financial contributions have been made by Bilance, the European Human Rights Foundation, the Norwegian Foreign Ministry, the UK Overseas Development Administration and the US Institute of Peace, to all of which bodies we are pleased to express our gratitude. Responsibility for this publication rests exclusively with Minority Rights Group.

Alan Phillips
Director

INTRODUCTION TO THE *DIRECTORY*

With this second edition of the *World Directory of Minorities*, Minority Rights Group seeks to build on the success of the first edition, which was published in 1990. Like its predecessor, the new *Directory* is arranged by geographical region, although within each section the material is now organized country by country, rather than minority by minority. Because some minorities, such as the Kurds and the Roma, reside in several countries, readers may need to refer to more than one country entry for a full account of the minority in question. Cross-references in the text, and the index at the end of the book, should help here.

By drawing on the work of a large and international team of experienced specialist writers, and on the advice of numerous expert and independent referees and reviewers, it is hoped that every significant minority issue for which information is generally available is accounted for. As far as possible, the viewpoints of minorities themselves are well represented. As with all MRG's publications, the text has been subject to rigorous checking and independent criticism.

Organization of the *Directory*

Each of the *Directory*'s eleven regional sections begins with a general introduction and is accompanied by a map. The maps, provided by Oxford Cartographers, are based on the Peters Projection, which corrects the Eurocentric distortions of traditional maps; country names are printed broadly in proportion to land area and available space, and their size is not intended to imply relative 'importance'. The maps do not imply a position on the part of MRG regarding international boundaries of the status of any territory.

Country entries follow alphabetically, with each country represented by a brief 'profile' of facts and figures, and further text. Where few or no significant minority rights issues have been identified, country entries are short. Space is broadly allocated according to the availability of information and the size of populations affected.

The profile for each country provides information on languages spoken, religions practised and population statistics for the main minority groups – both absolute numbers and percentages of the country total. Real per capita GDP (gross domestic product) in 1993 (unless otherwise indicated) US dollars is also shown, as is the country's Human Development Index number and rank (UNDP HDI/rank), both the latter drawn from the United Nations Development Programme's *Human Development Report 1996*.

Dates given in the text are frequently accompanied by the abbreviation BCE (Before the Christian or Common Era) or CE (Christian or Common Era).

Minority groups are, as a rule, listed in the statistical profile and discussed in the text in descending order of population size; exceptions to this include instances where one minority has been identified as a subgroup of another larger group, and cases where different kinds of minorities – such as ethnic groups on the one hand, and religious groups on the other – are differentiated. The case-by-case discussion of minorities in the text varies considerably, largely as a result of the huge diversity of situations examined and much variance in the information obtained. It is nevertheless hoped that many of the accounts of minorities will be broadly comparable. A useful basis for analysis of similarities and differences in terms of both legal and constitutional provision and *de facto* experience is provided by the United Nations Declaration on the Rights of Persons belonging to National or Ethnic, Religious and Linguistic Minorities of 1992. For a discussion of the Declaration, see p.694; for the text of the Declaration, see p.755. Lists of further reading and of minority-based and advocacy organizations at the end of the country entries are intended to provide access to further information and to facilitate contacts.

The regional sections and country entries are followed by Professor Patrick Thornberry's essay on 'Contemporary Legal Standards on Minority Rights' and, in the appendix, the texts of key international instruments. A full list of acknowledgements appears on p.802, notes on the main contributors on p.805 and the index on p.808.

Definition and methodology

How is 'minority' to be defined? This *Directory* bases its definition on a formulation offered by F. Capotorti, Special Rapporteur for the UN Sub-Commission on the Prevention of Discrimination and Protection of Minorities, in his *Study on the Rights of Persons belonging to Ethnic, Religious and Linguistic Minorities*: a minority must be a 'non-dominant' group; its members must 'possess ethnic, religious or linguistic characteristics differing from those of the rest of the population'; and they must also 'show, if only implicitly, a sense of solidarity, directed towards preserving their culture, traditions, religion or language' (1979, reprinted 1991, para. 568).

Unlike Capotorti, however, we include as minorities non-dominant groups that may be a numerical majority in a state, and those who are not necessarily nationals or citizens of the state where they reside. In a few exceptional cases, dominant groups have been included – mainly in the section on the Middle East, where their inclusion is considered necessary for completeness of coverage. The general principle has been to refer to minority groups using their own preferred names and self-descriptions; for example, 'Roma/Gypsies' is the preferred term in Western Europe, but Central and Eastern European Roma reject the name 'Gypsies'.

This focus on ethnic, religious and linguistic groups, while fully in keeping with the UN Declaration on Minorities, excludes other types of minority, such as sexual minorities and people with disabilities. These latter groups are considered to be beyond the scope of this *Directory*.

A number of indigenous peoples included in the *Directory* reject the term 'minority', concerned that it may imply a lack of entitlement to the self-determination to which they aspire. Inclusion here does not mean that MRG considers such peoples not to be indigenous. Nor should any discussion of self-determination be interpreted as advocacy by MRG of a group's secession from a state.

Population statistics can be controversial. Governments may in their statistical analysis or reporting minimize the size of minority populations, while some minorities may inflate the figure. Besides, group boundaries may be variously understood and interpreted; individuals – children of mixed parentage, for example – may cross quickly from one group to another, either temporarily or permanently. Contributors have taken population data from a range of sources, including international yearbooks, UN publications and official censuses. Sources are not always specified; and in many cases an estimate (signified by the abbreviation 'est.') or range of possible figures is given. The temptation to update total country population figures using the most recent data has generally been resisted, because this would tend to reduce the comparative value of the minority population statistics and percentages, the majority of which cannot easily be updated from one year to the next.

Details of minority-based and advocacy organizations have not always been easy to obtain, select or verify. The general rule has been to include organizations located in the region in question and considered to have an active interest in minority rights or related issues relevant to the country concerned. These criteria exclude Northern-based international and solidarity organizations concerned with Southern minority rights (such groups are likely to be better known than many of those listed in the book). Exceptionally, for the Middle East, where civil society is severely restricted in many countries, organizations based outside the region have been included.

The listings generally comprise non-governmental bodies rather than governmental ones, although here too readers may identify exceptions. University specialist institutes and departments, as well as minority-based political parties, are sometimes included. Every effort has been made to check the details given, but MRG cannot accept liability for the consequence of any errors that may appear. The inclusion of an organization does not imply endorsement of its aims, policies, methods or statements.

MRG is indebted to the writers, consultant readers and many others who have given their time, knowledge and expertise to this book, as it is to the donors whose financial assistance has made the project possible. A special debt of gratitude is owed to Patrick Thornberry, who acted as the project's legal adviser from inception to publication.

During the time it has taken to complete the *Directory*, the situation of many minorities has changed relatively little, although in other cases significant developments have occurred. Every possible effort has been made to ensure that the text is up to date at the time of going to press. However, MRG will welcome information that may enable inaccuracies or omissions to be corrected for a subsequent edition.

Miles Litvinoff
Project Director

ABBREVIATIONS

ASEAN	Association of South-East Asian Nations
ASSR	Autonomous Soviet Socialist Republic
BCE	Before Christian (Common) Era
CE	Christian (Common) Era
CIS	Commonwealth of Independent States
CSCE	Conference on Security and Cooperation in Europe
ECOWAS	Economic Community of West African States
EFTA	European Free Trade Area
est.	estimate
EU	European Union
GATT	General Agreement on Tariffs and Trade
GDP	gross domestic product
HDI	Human Development Index
ILO	International Labour Organization
IMF	International Monetary Fund
NAFTA	North American Free Trade Organization
NGO	non-governmental organization
OAU	Organization of African Unity
OECD	Organization for Economic Cooperation and Development
OECS	Organization of Eastern Caribbean States
OSCE	Organization for Security and Cooperation in Europe
SP HDI	South Pacific Human Development Index
UN	United Nations
UNDP	United Nations Development Programme
UNESCO	United Nations Educational, Scientific and Cultural Organization
UNHCR	United Nations High Commissioner for Refugees

NORTH AMERICA

Alex Roslin and Carl Wilson

Canada, Mexico and the USA were each established through the dispossession of indigenous peoples who had settled there thousands of years before. In each case, the initial colonizers were different: Spanish in Mexico; French and British in Canada; British, French and Dutch in the USA. But the outcome was similar. Millions of indigenous people were killed; millions more died of disease and starvation; and survivors were forcibly removed from their lands to make way for development. In Canada and the USA, Native peoples were moved to reservations. Indigenous cultures and ways of life were deprived of their subsistence bases, and in many cases Native people were subjected to 're-education' and other attempts at assimilation. In Mexico, where there was more intermarriage, complex social structures based on landownership, degree of European or indigenous ethnicity and elite power developed. But indigenous and *mestizo* (mixed) people generally maintained longer-standing autonomy outside of major centres. Despite such differences, all three countries were built on minorities' low-wage or slave labour. The legacy of slavery exerts special force in the United States, where it is the bedrock grievance of the country's largest minority, African Americans.

Treatment and protection of minorities

Although tied by geography, overlapping histories and, in recent years, a series of economic pacts, the three North American countries have significantly different political, economic and demographic profiles. These differences are reflected in their treatment of minorities. The USA is a very diverse society, but its minority groups have been pressured to 'melt' into mainstream culture and to uphold US patriotism and global ambitions. However, US minorities have benefited from traditions of self-assertion and non-conformity, and have made major gains thanks to organization, outspoken leaders and judicial action.

Despite increasing immigration, Canada still has a more homogeneous population than the USA. However, because Canada is also less populated and less urbanized, the differences among what Canadians now call their 'three founding peoples' – Native, French and British – remain prominent. Native people have made solid gains in influence in the past decade; the settlement of outstanding land claims and measures for Native self-government are now recognized as political necessities. These demands put additional pressure on the dispute between the descendants of British and French colonists, principally between the federal government and the Quebecers. The need to balance Quebec's demands with other regional issues colours every aspect of Canadian politics and has produced a much more decentralized federation than in the USA. Besides, in its desire to retain an independent identity from the United States, Canada has embraced an official policy of multiculturalism, advocating a 'cultural mosaic' rather than a US-style 'melting pot' approach to ethnic difference. But many minority critics say this goal is more rhetorical than real.

Mexico does not fall into the same category. It is a much less industrialized and prosperous nation than its continental neighbours, and its social structure is based less on ethnic competition for middle-class status than on elite-vs-mass dynamics. Mexico also takes far fewer immigrants than do Canada and the USA; in fact, large numbers of Mexicans have migrated, legally and otherwise, to work in the USA. However, political change in Mexico, from the Mexican Revolution to the 1994 Zapatista uprising, has often originated with indigenous peoples who see their rights trampled in the course of government-driven 'modernization'.

Despite their differences, all three countries provide guarantees of minority rights and liberties in their constitutions. US-originated thinking on integration, affirmative action, equality and non-discrimination has been adapted to the Mexican and Canadian contexts and has been incorporated in human rights law internationally. In practice, though, such guarantees are not evenly applied.

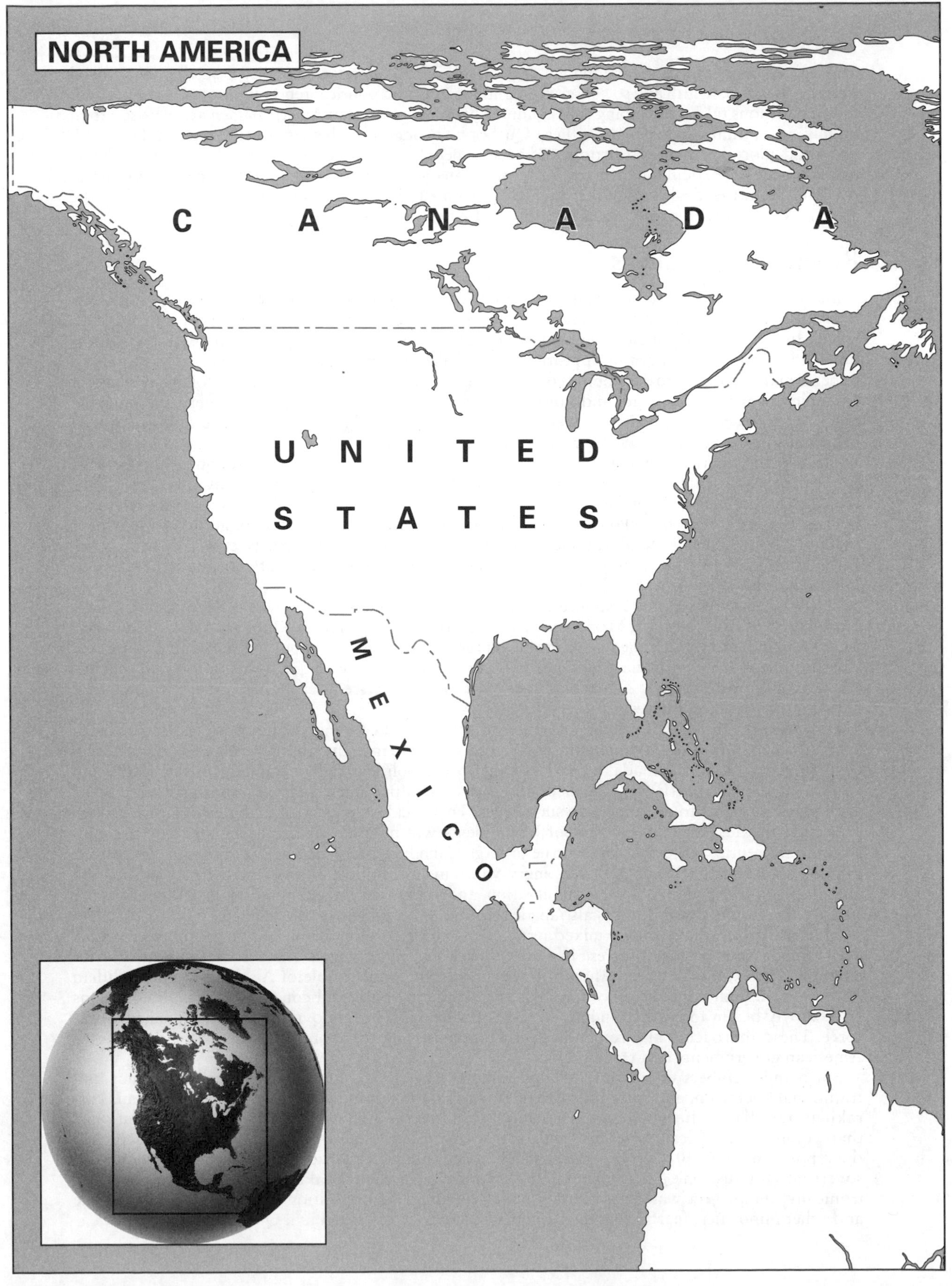
NORTH AMERICA
C A N A D A
U N I T E D
S T A T E S
M E X I C O

Through economic inequity and malign neglect, minorities often lack equality in justice, jobs, social status, education, health and social services, public safety and political representation. On the ground, these conditions take a disturbing toll on human lives. More African American men are in prison than in university; Inuit teenagers in northern Quebec have one of the highest suicide rates in the world; and child mortality among Mexican indigenous people is as high as 20 per cent. Prejudiced law enforcement is a particular barrier to North American minorities enjoying the rights they are promised. All three countries dealt with police and military corruption scandals in the early 1990s, while the agencies charged with protecting and enforcing human rights were comparatively inactive.

Recent developments

While legal and political reform from the Second World War to the end of the 1970s tended to bolster recognition of minority claims, today's changing economic and political patterns pose difficult challenges. In the USA and Canada, well-paying manufacturing jobs for people without extensive education and training have been disappearing, as globalization permits multinational corporations to relocate manufacturing to developing countries. The average wage has fallen in real dollars; permanent unemployment is widespread; and government cutbacks due to high levels of debt have removed much of the 'social safety net' of the welfare state, especially in urban centres in the declining industrial heartlands of the northern USA or central and eastern Canada.

The North American Free Trade Agreement (NAFTA) and the Uruguay round of the General Agreement on Tariffs and Trade (GATT) have heightened these trends. Many businesses have relocated to low-wage, unregulated areas such as the Mexican *maquiladora* factory regions – relatively lawless border zones that allow for unsafe, environmentally toxic and exploitative employment practices. For Mexicans, NAFTA undermines local production for local needs, especially subsistence agriculture, and limits the ability of the government to control price and interest rate trends, as was reflected in the 1994–5 peso collapse.

Perhaps the most striking response to the new global economy came when the indigenous Zapatista rebels of Chiapas state, Mexico, launched an armed insurgency on 1 January 1994, the day that NAFTA came into effect. The rebellion was repressed by the military, but the Mexican government was still negotiating with the Zapatistas two years later. These events have demonstrated that the Mexican authorities cannot simply expect minorities to acquiesce to economic restructuring when it runs contrary to their interests.

However, this rebellion was the exception to the norm. Economic change has generally reduced sympathies to minorities, as dominant groups become more insecure about their own continued success. In the USA and Canada, a marked shift to the political right beginning in the 1980s and consolidated in the mid-1990s propelled conservatives to office and led parties traditionally concerned with minority rights to de-emphasize such issues. This backlash coincided with demographic change – at current rates, over 50 per cent of US residents will be minority group members by the mid-twenty-first century, and the same is true of large Canadian cities such as Toronto and Vancouver. Pundits spoke of the 'revenge of the angry white males'. Politicians competed to see who could eliminate social spending, lower immigration and repeal anti-discrimination programmes more quickly. Economic instability has also made reform more problematic in Mexico.

Minority groups have shown mixed responses to these developments. Native peoples in the USA and Canada took a great interest in indigenous Mexicans' struggles, and some minorities – for example, Afro-Canadians and African Americans, or the Inuit people of Alaska and the Canadian Arctic – have built contacts on common political and environmental concerns. Some labour unions have slowly begun to react to industrial restructuring, high unemployment and a diversified workforce. These approaches also respond directly to intensifying collaboration between the three North American governments as a trading bloc.

But many members of minority groups have become cynical about ecumenical democracy and traditional liberalism, and some have turned towards nationalism for political sustenance. Louis Farrakhan, the Black Muslim self-determinationist and cultural conservative, is far more isolationist than comparable African American leaders of the past. Nationalists in Quebec have also hardened their positions. On 30 October 1995, Quebecois pro-independence forces lost a referendum on sovereignty by just one percentage point. A majority of French-speakers voted for separation and, ironically, the project was defeated only by near-unanimous opposition from First Nations people and other minorities, fearful that their rights would not be respected in a Quebecois country.

The potential for renewal may rest with the next generation. More people are growing up in multiracial families and ethnically mixed classrooms than ever before in North American history, especially in large cities. New coalitions, hybrids and forms of intercultural consciousness are emerging, and these forces promise to alter the ethnic, social and political landscapes of North America in years to come.

Further reading

Bethell, L. (ed.), *Mexico since Independence*, Cambridge, Cambridge University Press, 1991.

Caplan, R. and Feffer, J. (eds), *State of the Union 1994: The Clinton Administration and the Nation in Profile*, Boulder, CO, Westview Press, 1994.

Carnoy, M., *Faded Dreams: The Politics and Economics of Race in America*, New York, Cambridge University Press, 1994.

Gedicks, A., *The New Resource Wars: Native and Environmental Struggles against Multinational Corporations*, Boston, MA, South End Press, 1993.

International Work Group for Indigenous Affairs, *The Indigenous World 1995–96*, Copenhagen, IWGIA, 1996.

Jaimes, A.M. (ed.), *The State of Native America: Genocide, Colonization and Resistance*, Boston, MA, South End Press, 1992.

Miller, M.S. and Cultural Survival (eds), *State of the Peoples: A Global Human Rights Report on Societies in Danger*, Boston, MA, Beacon Press, 1993.

Petras, J. and Morris, M., *Empire or Republic? American Global Power and Domestic Decay*, New York, Routledge, 1995.

Richardson, B. (ed.), *Drum Beat: Anger and Renewal in Indian Country*, Toronto, Assembly of First Nations, 1989.

Canada

Land area:	9,958,319 sq km
Population:	29.2 million (1994)
Main languages:	English and French (both official), 53 indigenous languages (some with official status in Native-majority territories)
Main religions:	Roman Catholicism, United Church, Anglicanism
Main minority groups:	French Canadians 6.1 million (20.9%), Eastern European Canadians 1.5 million (5.1%), Asian Canadians 1.5 million (5.1%), First Nations (including *métis* and Inuit) 1–1.2 million (3–4.1%), African Canadians 340,000 (1.2%)
Real per capita GDP:	$20,950
UNDP HDI/rank:	0.951 (1)

Canada is an immense country, with most of its population squeezed into a narrow strip along its southern border with the USA. When European settlement got under way in the 1600s, the entirety of the territory that was to become Canada had already been settled by millions of indigenous people, divided into hundreds of nations each with a distinct language, culture, social structure and political tradition.

The 'founder' of Canada is sometimes said to have been French explorer Jacques Cartier, who reached the Gulf of St Lawrence in 1534.

European settlement was pioneered by the French, who established Quebec City in 1608 and Montreal in 1642, and declared New France a colony in 1663. Britain acquired these territories from the French in a succession of military victories between 1759 and 1763. Canada achieved independence from Britain in 1867.

Canada is often described as 'a country of immigrants', perhaps implying that it is by definition a racially tolerant country. However, members of certain ethnic groups and First Nations people face widespread discrimination and endure poorer-than-average living standards in Canada. As a general rule, the relative position of minorities is determined by factors such as the darkness of skin colour, popular pressures, political expedience and economic conditions. Language is also a dividing line, especially between the English-speaking majority and French Canadian minority. Many English-speakers in the French-majority province of Quebec consider themselves disempowered.

Initial relations between Europeans and the First Nations ranged from cordial trade exchanges and military alliances, to mutual indifference, to outright hostility and armed conflict. Many aboriginal nations were decimated through deliberate campaigns of extermination; a small number have been able, with difficulty, to maintain their traditional ways of life.

Inter-ethnic tensions also divide non-Native ethnic groups, particularly English and French Canadians. Many of the 6.1 million Francophones, most of whom live in the province of Quebec, are critical of the provisions of the Canadian federation. In 1994, a provincial government was elected in Quebec dedicated to achieving independence for the province. It held a referendum the next year, which the pro-independence movement lost very narrowly.

Nominally, minority groups may appeal to the Canadian Charter of Rights and Freedoms (Part I of the Constitution Act of 1982) and to similar provincial charters to defend themselves from discrimination. Certain aboriginal rights, like the right to hunt, trap and fish, were also enshrined in the constitution, as were all existing treaties signed between the federal government and First Nations. Practically, however, the enshrinement of these rights has often meant gains on paper only.

An individual who claims his or her rights were violated can appeal to both federal and provincial government human rights commissions, which rule on complaints. The commissions have helped many complainants seeking redress, but they are understaffed and lack resources. Rights cases commonly take two or three years to be resolved and are frequently dropped by the complainant before this is done. Moreover, the codification of various rights has often been accompanied by government policies which have eroded those same rights. Minority activists complain that while the commission process may solve individual cases of abuse, little has been done to dismantle systemic patterns of discrimination. On affirmative action, for instance, Canada lags far behind the USA, with only an ineffective voluntary employment equity law at the federal level.

Religious minorities in Canada include the quarter-million-strong Jewish Canadian community. Largely concentrated in Montreal and Toronto, Jewish people have strong community institutions and are active in promoting minority rights at a political level. In the past, they have faced discriminatory policies and still face some intolerance. Jewish organizations have documented incidents of anti-Semitism, including vandalism of synagogues and hate propaganda from extremist organizations. Fortunately, such incidents have been quickly denounced by public officials. In late 1995, a Quebec judge was roundly condemned by government officials and the legal community for suggesting in a courtroom that Jews did not suffer during the Holocaust.

Today, despite a strong popular desire for ethnic harmony, race relations in Canada have been strained by a prolonged economic crisis which has exacerbated social and political divisions. White racist organizations have engaged in campaigns of violence and hate propaganda, and some mainstream political parties have pandered to white racist sentiment. In such a climate, minority leaders are discouraged that successive federal governments have increasingly restricted immigration and still resist efforts to institute an effective employment equity policy.

French Canadians

French Canadians are by far Canada's largest minority, numbering 6.1 million people in the 1991 census, and are considered to be one of the country's three founding nations, along with English Canadians and Native people. Most are Catholic and trace their heritage to French colonists who settled in the Atlantic region and along the St Lawrence River in the 1600s and 1700s. French is one of Canada's two official languages, along with English, and it enjoys special protection under the Canadian constitution. Many French-speakers consider the homeland of French culture in North America to be the province of Quebec, where French-speakers constitute 80 per cent of the population. About 1 million other French Canadians live outside Quebec, the most cohesive single community being the Acadians of New Brunswick.

In 1993, for the first time, Quebecers overwhelmingly voted for a pro-independence party to represent them in Canada's Parliament. So many were elected, in fact, that they formed the official opposition and second biggest caucus of any party in the national legislature. A year later, a separatist party, the Parti Québécois (PQ), was elected to the provincial legislature of Quebec on a platform favouring independence from Canada. A referendum was held on 30 October 1995, and the pro-independence movement lost by the narrowest of margins – just one percentage point.

The PQ expresses the grievances of many French Canadians who feel they are in a subordinate position in the country they helped found. Outside Quebec, many French-speakers feel marginalized, ignored and under pressure to assimilate into English Canadian culture. Within Quebec, many see independence from Canada as the culmination of more than 200 years of resistance to the British conquest of French Canada between 1759 and 1763. After this conquest, attempts were made to assimilate the French. They were forced to swear allegiance to the Crown; British authorities refused to recognize the Roman Catholic religion; and French administrative structures were eliminated.

Within a few years, however, this policy was muted as the American War of Independence broke out in the British colonies to the south. Desperate for French support, British officials passed the Quebec Act of 1774, restoring the power of the Roman Catholic Church and permitting use of the French civil code, which is still in place today. When the war ended, thousands of Americans who had sided with the British – the so-called United Empire Loyalists – flooded north and threatened to reduce the French to minority status. Most settled in what became known as Upper Canada (the southern part of the present-day province of Ontario).

Difficult economic conditions and political discontent prompted a major rebellion by French Canadians in 1837–8. British forces defeated the rebels in a bloody military campaign, executing many of their leaders and deporting others. An inquiry for the British government by Lord Durham found 'two nations at war within one state'. Durham viewed French Canadians with contempt and recommended that they be assimilated. The resulting Union Act of 1840 curtailed what limited political power French Canadians had won back; the French language was not permitted in the colony's legislative assembly; British immigration was encouraged and, within a decade, the descendants of the French settlers were in the minority.

Under these conditions, the French worked to attain limited rights within the colonial political system. Years later, they regained recognition of their language. On a social level, their institutions became conservative and the people devoted themselves to preserving the Roman Catholic faith, the French language and a rural-based way of life in the face of powerful assimilationist pressures.

In the federal system, provinces have power over certain areas – health care, education – while the national government controls defence and foreign affairs. Jurisdictional disputes have frequently pitted the provinces against the federal government. The country's founding constitution guaranteed certain language rights to the Francophone minority such as the right to use French in Parliament, federal courts and courts in Quebec.

But French Canadians, despite a high birth rate, found themselves increasingly outnumbered by English-speakers due to the federal government's preference for immigrants from English-speaking countries. The addition of new western provinces to the federation meant a further erosion of the French Canadian position. French Canadians grew particularly incensed over Canadian support for British foreign policy. During both world wars, major rioting occurred when conscription was forced upon Quebec. As French Canadians in Quebec became more urbanized, resentment grew against their economic domination by the Montreal-based Anglophone elite and the stifling nature of the old Roman Catholic institutions that still controlled the schools, social and cultural life.

The 'quiet revolution'

In the early 1960s, the resentments burst into the open, ushering in a 30-year period of social, cultural, economic and political transformation known as the 'quiet revolution'. All levels of Quebec society experienced sweeping change. Government was democratized, measures were taken to strengthen the French language and Quebecois culture, the provincial government took over the running of education, health care and social services from the Roman Catholic Church and French was promoted in the workplace.

Another key development was the birth of 'Quebec Inc.' – a vast project to strengthen

Francophone-owned private businesses, develop a Quebecois middle class and build strong public companies that would play an interventionist role in the Quebec economy. The creation of a provincial-owned electrical utility, Hydro-Québec, was a key part of this process. Today, it is one of the world's largest power companies. A network of credit unions, the Caisses Populaires, was formed that today has tens of billions of dollars in assets. Hydro-Québec and a vastly expanded civil service provided the growing Francophone middle class with new job opportunities. The government created a new network of colleges and universities accessible to Francophones. Quebecois culture flourished.

These changes were forced by widespread social unrest within Quebec. Trade union militancy reached unprecedented levels. A strike called by the 'Common Front' in 1972 briefly brought the provincial economy to a halt. Some 10,000 students marched in Montreal demanding that McGill University, the Anglophone elite's bastion, be turned into a Francophone institution. Through the 1960s, a bombing campaign was conducted by the Front de Libération du Québec (FLQ), an urban guerrilla organization that professed a blend of nationalist and left-wing ideology. In October 1970, the FLQ provoked an international crisis by abducting the British Consul and then murdering the provincial Labour Minister. At the request of the Quebec government, Canada invoked the 1914 War Measures Act, sent federal troops into Quebec and arrested hundreds of political activists across the country, most of whom were later found to have had no FLQ links. The harsh state response encouraged sympathy for the FLQ and Quebecers attended large rallies in support of the organization's demands.

In 1976, the fledgling Parti Québécois under the leadership of nationalist intellectual René Lévesque was elected to Quebec's National Assembly in a surprise victory. The party did not favour outright separation from Canada, but a form of sovereignty-association in which a nominally independent Quebec would retain strong formal ties with Canada. In 1980, the PQ held Quebec's first referendum on sovereignty-association. Quebecers rejected it by a 60–40 margin: 52 per cent of Francophones voted No to sovereignty, along with 95 per cent of non-French-speakers.

The PQ also continued efforts of previous governments to transform Quebec society, further promoting small and medium Francophone-owned businesses, democratizing the state and strengthening use of the French language in schools and the workplace. The party's initiatives were popular enough that, despite its 1980 referendum loss, it won a second term as the provincial government in the 1981 election.

Despite the political and social advances made in Quebec during the 1960s and 1970s, alarm still grew among many Quebecers about the weak state of the French language and culture. Their fears were fuelled by a falling birth rate in Quebec and growing numbers of non-French-speaking immigrants who usually preferred learning English to French. In 1968, the provincial government established a commission into the French language and ways of promoting it. The commission recommended in its report of 1972 that French be made Quebec's official language and that measures be taken to increase the use of French at work and in schools. In 1974, the Liberal government of Robert Bourassa adopted a new and controversial language law that made French the official language and placed severe restrictions on parents' right to choose their children's language of education.

Further measures were put in place by the PQ government, which issued a French Language Charter in 1977, known as Bill 101, and created a watchdog body to monitor the status of French in Quebec. The PQ also ruled that French was to be the language of government administration, government contracts and collective bargaining agreements. Bill 101 is often credited with improving the position of French in the province. The 1981 census showed that the number of Anglophone Quebecers dropped by nearly 12 per cent, from 800,000 to 706,000, in the five previous years.

The 'quiet revolution' also saw the disappearance of a large wage gap between Anglophones and Francophones in Quebec. In 1970, Quebec's Anglophones were the highest income earners in the province. Today, bilingual Francophones earn an average 3.5 per cent more than bilingual Anglophones. Economists point to two reasons for the changes: a surge in education among Francophones and the exodus of educated Anglophones from Quebec. Another trend has emerged. While Francophones have improved their lot, non-English minorities in Quebec have watched their relative living standards fall dramatically. One reason for the trend is that allophones are vastly under-represented in the provincial and municipal civil services, which is about 97 per cent white and francophone.[1]

The new laws helped Francophones, but they have also been widely condemned as being repressive and punitive by minorities within Quebec, who are also alarmed by frequent outbursts of extremist anti-minority sentiment by some white Francophones. Starting in the mid-1970s, thousands of English-speakers and other Quebec minorities left the province for other parts of Canada, complaining of restrictive language laws and the prospect of sovereignty.

In 1988, part of the French Language Charter was struck down by the Supreme Court of Canada as a violation of the human rights of Quebec's non-Francophone minorities. But the provincial government, controlled at the time by the federalist Liberal Party, was able to maintain key sections of the charter by invoking the so-called 'notwithstanding clause' of the Canadian constitution. The clause gives provinces a loophole they can temporarily use to allow provincial laws to stand, even when in violation of constitutional rights.

The Liberal government's invocation of this clause provoked great division in Quebec. Three English-speaking Liberal cabinet ministers resigned in protest. Anglophone-rights activists and dissident Liberals formed the Equality Party, which won four seats from the Liberals in the 1989 provincial election. With time, however, tensions over language gave way to tensions over the more explosive issue of sovereignty, which is opposed by 90–95 per cent of Anglophones and allophones and is divisive even among Francophones. Equality lost all its seats in the 1994 election, as Anglophone voters concerned by the PQ's sovereignty plans rallied back to the Liberals. Their concerns were further fuelled by remarks of pro-independence leaders during and after the latest referendum exercise. Most dramatic was a comment Premier Parizeau made in a speech immediately after the vote, bitterly blaming the loss on 'money and the ethnic vote'. This comment was widely condemned, and Parizeau resigned as premier the next day.

Tensions have also escalated between Quebecois and First Nations in the province over two key issues – Quebec sovereignty and natural resource development. The PQ has claimed Quebec can separate from Canada, taking with it vast traditional Native territories, but that the First Nations do not have a similar right to separate from an independent Quebec, or even to remain within Canada should Quebec leave. This position has angered Native people, who point to United Nations declarations on the right of all peoples to self-determination and to choose their own political status. Native people in Quebec worry that their rights would suffer in an independent Quebec and express concern that the PQ cabinet includes ministers who have made racist remarks against Natives.

Disputes over Native land claims have been at the centre of a number of civil disturbances in Quebec. Due to relatively lax environmental protection regulations, resource companies have devastated large tracts of traditional First Nations land in Quebec. The Quebec government's own entities, particularly Hydro-Québec, have been conspicuous among the culprits.

Recent developments

The PQ's 1980 referendum defeat threw the project of separation into disarray and forced the party to re-evaluate its priorities. It dedicated itself to being a left-of-centre party that promised good government and would work for Quebec's rights within the Canadian federation. The PQ lent its political machine to candidates of federal parties perceived to be favourable to Quebec interests. But the party appeared to have lost its *raison d'être*, especially when it dropped its long-standing goal of sovereignty in 1985, the same year it finally lost office to the Liberal Party. In the 1980s, sovereignty was widely thought to be a spent force.

But the seeds of a new discontent were sown in 1982, when Prime Minister Pierre Trudeau repatriated the Canadian constitution from Britain. Quebec, at the time still ruled by the PQ, refused to sign the new constitutional document, claiming it promoted greater centralization of power in Ottawa and weakened the provinces. In the 1984 federal election, Trudeau's Liberal government was replaced by the Progressive Conservative Party, led by Quebec lawyer Brian Mulroney. Mulroney campaigned on a promise to bring Quebec back into the constitution. He orchestrated two attempts to do so, both of which failed and set the stage for the PQ's second referendum campaign in 1995.

The first attempt, the Meech Lake Accord, would have recognized Quebec's distinctive identity and culture and its powers to protect the French language. Meech Lake failed after not receiving the consent of all ten provinces within a required period of time. Another effort quickly followed, the Charlottetown Accord of 1992, which would have granted Quebec most of the powers in Meech Lake. It was placed before the Canadian public in a referendum, but despite the endorsement of every major federal party and all ten premiers, a majority of both Quebecers and of Canadians in the rest of the country voted it down. Many Quebecers felt they were not given enough, while many Canadians felt they had given too much.

The defeat of the Charlottetown Accord caused separatist sentiment to surge as many Quebecers came to believe constitutional change was impossible. Anti-French incidents in other provinces further inflamed Quebecers. In federal elections in 1993, a new federal party favouring Quebec independence, the Bloc Québécois, won a majority of the province's share of seats in Parliament. The next year, the PQ swept into power in Quebec promising a second chance for separation.

The 30 October 1995 referendum on the sovereignty of Quebec almost removed Canada's geographically largest province from the country. The sovereignty option was favoured by 49.4 per cent of voters, compared to 50.6 per cent who voted against it. Restricted to Francophones only, the sovereigntists would have won the referendum by a 60–40 margin. But Quebec's 1-million-strong non-Francophone minority voted overwhelmingly against separation and expressed concerns during the campaign about xenophobic tendencies in the PQ government. Both sides called the result a victory – federalists because they had won the vote in absolute numbers, separatists because English Canada had been sent a resounding message: Canada has to change or it will fall apart.

French-speakers outside Quebec

About 1 million French Canadians live in provinces other than Quebec. The most cohesive communities exist in the largest province, Ontario, where there are about 500,000 Francophones, and in New Brunswick, which is home to about a quarter-million Acadians. The Acadian people make up about a third of the population of New Brunswick, which is the only officially bilingual province in Canada. It has special legislation to protect the French language and French has official status as a language of education. Acadians are concentrated in forestry and fishing sectors, and are the poorest section of the New Brunswick population. When the British first conquered the Acadian lands, known as L'Acadie, from the French in the eighteenth century, they attempted to deport most of the population because they were considered a security risk in a militarily strategic area. The ancestors of Acadians were dispersed as far away as Louisiana, although many were able to return. Today, some Acadians are trying to obtain redress for the traumas suffered by their ancestors.

In Ontario, efforts by French Canadians to have French recognized as an official language by the provincial government have run into heavy opposition. Not all French Canadians speak their mother tongue fluently and many have become assimilated into the majority culture.

French Canadians once formed a majority of the province of Manitoba. Today, they are about 6 per cent of the population and only two-thirds speak fluent French. The protection of French has been a thorny issue in Manitoba for over 100 years. In 1980 a Supreme Court ruling overturned the previous English-only policy of the Manitoba government. But much of the public appears to oppose recognition of French as an official language and a 1984 attempt to make French and English official languages failed.

Eastern European Canadians

Eastern Europeans made up the first large wave of immigration into Canada that was not of English or French origin. Tens of thousands of peasants arrived in the late 1800s and early 1900s lured by promises of cheap land in the western prairies. Ukrainians form the largest and most prominent Eastern European community in Canada, but smaller numbers from other countries also arrived. The 1991 census puts the number of Ukrainian Canadians at 407,000, two-thirds of whom live in the three prairie provinces – Alberta, Manitoba and Saskatchewan. This figure is considered to be low by the Ukrainian community, which estimates its own numbers at about 1 million.

Poles form the next largest group with 273,000, according to the census; Hungarians are next with 101,000, followed by Czechs and Slovaks (59,000), Lithuanians, Estonians and Latvians (40,000) and Russians (38,000). Since the census was taken, numbers of all these groups have risen due to the opening up of the Iron Curtain and easing of Cold-War era emigration restrictions. Today, Eastern European communities in Canada are undergoing a renaissance due to the influx of new members, and none more so than the Ukrainian Canadian community, which was rejuvenated by the 1991 proclamation of Ukraine's independence from the Soviet Union.

The largest numbers of early Eastern European arrivals came from the western Ukrainian region of Halychyna, then occupied by the Austrian Empire. Conditions for the new arrivals in Canada were miserable, the climate and land harsher than expected and the reception was far from welcoming. Anti-Ukrainian sentiment was widespread. An 1897 editorial in Winnipeg's *Daily Nor-Wester* stated:

'The dumping down of these filthy, penniless and ignorant foreigners into progressive and intelligent communities is a serious hardship to such a community. These people bring with them disease in almost every consignment . . . and their dirty habits render the stamping out of infection among them a very difficult matter.'

It was only with the passage of time, as Ukrainians proved to be expert farmers and hard workers, that public hostility eased.

As the First World War engulfed Canada, anti-Ukrainian sentiment reached unprecedented and explosive proportions. Since most had arrived on passports from Austria, a country with which Canada was at war, they were indiscriminately declared enemy aliens and nearly 100,000 Canadian citizens of Ukrainian descent were stripped of all their rights as citizens, including their right to vote. The irony is that Ukrainians despised the Austrian occupation, a reason many had fled their homeland in the first place. But the Canadian government, facing ferocious anti-Ukrainian sentiment, refused to heed an official assurance from the British government that Ukrainian immigrants could be trusted. The Canadian authorities were motivated partly by political considerations: Ukrainians, many of them radicalized by the difficult conditions of peasant life under Austria, had developed strong community organizations and were taking a lead in forming trade unions and other organizations dedicated to improving their living conditions, including political parties.

Thousands of Ukrainians who were politically active or simply unemployed were arrested, stripped of their belongings and interned in isolated forced labour camps for the duration of the war. In the camps, they were paid little or nothing for their work, kept under heavy guard and lived in abominable conditions. They had little to eat or wear and were often interned in worse facilities than German prisoners of war held in the same camp. Beatings and torture were commonly reported, and several Ukrainian internees committed suicide or were killed trying to escape. After the war, the government refused to return their belongings.

Today, after nearly 80 years, the federal government continues to reject efforts by the Ukrainian Canadian community to seek redress. Ottawa refuses to apologize for the internments, rejects the idea of compensation to the families of internees and throws obstacles in front of efforts to build commemorative monuments at the site of each internment camp. In a 1991 letter, Environment Minister Jean Charest rejected the monument campaign saying the internments were not of 'national significance'.

Asian Canadians

People of Asian origin are Canada's fastest growing minority. The 1991 census reveals a total of 1.46 million Canadians reporting an Asian background, but it is likely the numbers are somewhat higher. About half live in the province of Ontario and a quarter in British Columbia (BC). About a third are Chinese Canadians, who number 587,000. The next largest groups are Indians (325,000), Filipinos (157,000), West Asians (82,000), Japanese (49,000) and Koreans (44,000). The largely French-speaking Vietnamese Canadians are the only Asian community with large numbers in Quebec.

Asian Canadians were first lured to Canada in 1858 by the gold rush on the Pacific coast. At the time, Canada's west coast was inhabited only by a handful of fur traders and Native people. Suddenly, 25,000 white miners flooded into the area, along with 4,000 Chinese migrant labourers hired as menial workers.

From the outset, white attitudes towards Asian immigrants were hostile. Testimony at the 1885 Royal Commission on Chinese Immigration reveals numerous highly offensive and demeaning comments expressed by ordinary Canadians and public officials. Newspapers at the time also published pieces displaying startling ignorance and hostility towards people of Chinese origin.

The Chinese population of BC reached a peak of 4,000 in 1860, fell to 1,500 by the decade's end as mining activity fell off, and steadily rose after that to 20,000 by the early 1920s. White numbers grew much faster, but Chinese people generally made up between 15 and 40 per cent of the province's population until Asian immigration was halted in 1908. By 1921, they fell to around 6 per cent. Most of the immigrants were peasants schooled in the intensive wet-rice agriculture of the province of Guangdong south-west of Canton and were fleeing acute poverty and social disorder. Most apparently intended to return home once they had accumulated some savings.

Anti-Chinese agitation grew steadily, prompting the provincial legislature to ban Chinese employment on public works projects and levy a $40 per year fee on all Chinese people over age 12 in 1878. The tax was struck down by the BC Supreme Court, but the agitation only grew, fuelled by the coming of 15,000 new Chinese immigrants between 1881 and 1885 to work on the first Canadian transcontinental railway. Associations formed to oppose the immigration and one of the most vocal leaders was elected mayor of the province's capital, Victoria, and later a federal member of parliament. In 1883, a pitched battle broke out between white and Chinese workers on the rail line and whites returned that night to burn the Chinese camp to the ground and beat nine Chinese men unconscious, killing two more. Mass anti-Chinese protests drew thousands.

In 1885, the federal government yielded to white pressure in BC and imposed a $50 fee on all Chinese immigrants. The fee was later hiked to $100, but racist sentiment only increased, further fuelled by an influx of Japanese immigrants at the turn of the century. In 1903, the Chinese entry tax was upped again to $500 and efforts were made to segregate Asian children. Japan's imperial ambitions quickly became the new focus for anti-Asian agitation, which culminated in a 1907 riot by 8,000–9,000 white protesters who rampaged through Vancouver's Chinatown and Japanese district.

After the riot, Ottawa set up another Royal Commission on immigration, this time headed by W.L. Mackenzie King, then Deputy Labour Minister and later to become Prime Minister. On his recommendation, the government imposed harsh new restrictions that effectively eliminated all Asian immigration. White immigrants were required to pay a $25 entry fee while the Asian fee was set at $200. Asian immigration was reduced to virtually nothing until the 1950s when the restrictions were slowly lifted. The new policy also cut off immigration from India, a move that proved contentious because 3,000–4,000 ex-Indian Army veterans had immigrated to BC in the early 1900s. On an official visit to explain the new policy to the colonial government of India in 1909, Mackenzie King wrote in his diary that he had come to the conclusion that Canada should be kept racially pure, even if it meant the country would be weakened economically.

Anti-Japanese sentiment reached new proportions during the Second World War. In 1942, Japanese Canadians were removed from the west coast where most lived and forcibly relocated to 'exclusion centres'. This was supposedly done for national security reasons, but the Prime Minister of the day admitted in the House of Commons in 1944 that 'no person of Japanese race born in Canada has been charged with any act of sabotage or disloyalty during the years of war'. Japanese Canadian property was impounded and sold at low prices, and the costs of internment were deducted from the proceeds. Japanese people were not allowed to return to the west coast until 1949. Some were deported and exiled after the war. In recent years, after sustained pressure from the Japanese Canadian community, the federal government finally conferred compensation and an apology on the estimated 12,000 survivors of the relocation.

The last restrictions on Asian immigration were removed in 1962, prompting a great expansion of the Asian Canadian population. Currently, a new wave of immigration is occurring from Hong Kong. Asian Canadians today do not face the acute racism of the past, but a level of intolerance continues, including violent attacks by racist skinheads, discrimination in the workplace, stereotyping and police harassment. Although Asians have done well in certain fields, they continue to be under-represented in the media, police departments, political office and the public service.

As in the past, tensions are particularly high on the west coast where many immigrants from Hong Kong have settled. Asian Canadian leaders have criticized the mainstream media for fostering misunderstandings. This most recent wave of Asian immigration has been spurred by the impending Chinese take-over of Hong Kong and by generous immigration rules encouraging immigrants willing to invest money in Canada. The resulting immigration has transformed the face of the Pacific north-west and is a key reason British Columbia experienced an economic boom in the early 1990s while the rest of the country limped through a recession.

First Nations

Some 1–1.2 million Native people inhabit Canada, approximately 4 per cent of the population. They live in every area of the country and form a majority of the population in most northern regions. The 1991 census found 470,600 individuals who identified themselves as aboriginal, including 75,000 *métis* or mixed-race people and 30,000 Inuit, who are ethnically, culturally and linguistically distinct from the more southerly Natives. The census figures are widely recognized to be low, since many First Nations governments and individuals did not participate in the survey.

When European explorers first arrived in the territory that is now Canada, they encountered indigenous peoples who had established numerous distinct societies thousands of years before. European traders marvelled about the prosperity, good health, tall stature and lack of disease among the indigenous people they met. By some estimates, two times more First Nations people lived in Canada when the Europeans arrived than do today. Only one-quarter of First Nations people still live in their own original territories.

Many migrated to urban centres as life in their own communities became difficult due to poor living standards, development of their traditional territories and government suppression of traditional ways. Nevertheless, the traditional hunting, fishing and trapping way of life continues to be at the core of life in many First Nations communities, especially those further north where up to a third of individuals still live off the land full-time and most others go hunting or fishing at least during part of the year.

Spirituality, religion and strong values of community play a major role among most Native people and a revival of traditional beliefs is under way, especially among the youth. Among older people, Christianity is important. While some First Nations languages are now spoken only by a few hundred individuals, others remain very strong and continue to be used in daily life. Many languages are now being revived, and some have official status in Native-majority territories. When the Europeans first arrived, they found new names for each of the individual peoples. Eeyou and Eenou were renamed Crees; Kanienekaha were called Kanienkehakas, Inuit were called Eskimos, and Innu were called Montagnais. In their own languages, all these terms mean 'the people'. Today, the original inhabitants prefer to be called First Nations, aboriginal or Native people.

Since the arrival of the Europeans, the First Nations have been central and at times decisive actors in the development of the territory that is now Canada. Following initial contact, they entered strategic alliances with various European powers, supplying trade goods and permitting access to abundant natural resources. At crucial points in history, various aboriginal nations agreed to lend their armed might to the protection of French and British interests. Historians note that the first European expeditions to Canada would have been lost to starvation were it not for the assistance provided by First Nations people. An abundance of fur in the vast Hudson's Bay watershed made First Nations hunters and trappers willing to give up valuable pelts at highly profitable rates to the Hudson's Bay Company, then a British Crown charter.

In the areas first settled by the French in the 1600s and 1700s, the Kanienkehaka were one of the most militarily formidable aboriginal nations and acted as regional powerbrokers well into the 1800s. They are the northernmost member of the Iroquois Confederacy, an alliance of six First Nations whose territory spans from what today is southern Quebec into the US Midwest. Traditionally, the Kanienkehaka led an agricultural life, living in large, well-organized communities which still exist today. To the north and north-east of the Kanienkehaka live the Algonquin, Inuit, Innu, Naskapi and Eeyou (Crees) – nations of hunters and trappers with whom the Europeans traded for fur and continue to do so today.

In general, aboriginal nations' social and political structures across the country were and continue to be heavily influenced by the way of life that can be sustained in the local environment. Some are more hierarchical and at one time kept slaves; others are more egalitarian and democratic. Their traditional ways of life follow a seasonal cycle. Among the Eeyou of James Bay hunters gather in settlements during the summer to trade and socialize, then depart in groups of four or five families for winter hunting grounds as the water freezes in the fall, returning to their settlements as the ice thaws in spring-time. Traditionally, the Native diet varies by season: the Eeyou primarily hunt moose in the fall and winter, geese in the spring and fall, beaver in winter, and catch fish in summer.

Approximately 100,000 First Nations hunters and trappers still pursue a traditional way of life in Canada. Most of them use traditionally made hunting implements in conjunction with store-bought equipment such as rifles and all-terrain vehicles. To afford the latter, most engage in selling fur, over 70 per cent of which is exported to Europe. Today, this trade is in jeopardy because of a ban on fur imports from Canada promoted by the European animal rights movement, which Native leaders say will have a devastating effect on First Nations economies.

Development and colonization

As European settlement progressed in the 1800s, intensive development spread into the interior in the form of railways, roads, mines, urban growth, farmland, logging and later hydroelectric development. Private business interests and public officials viewed development as incompatible with a strong First Nations attachment to vast tracts of resource-rich land. The removal of indigenous peoples from their lands – a practice since known elsewhere as 'ethnic cleansing' – became government doctrine and, even today, some aspects of this basic policy remain in place. The removals were achieved through a variety of policy instruments, including assimilation, compulsory schooling by extremist religious orders, forced relocations to Native 'reserves' and the destruction of equipment and animals used by Native hunters. When these efforts were not effective, the colonizing authorities relied on more forceful measures, including the intentional spread of diseased blankets, massacres and other atrocities.

Although, in some remote areas, thousands of Native people continued living their way of life unchanged and some did not see a white person until the twentieth century, the combination of the colonizing efforts succeeded in virtually wiping out entire communities and even some nations by the early 1900s.

Assimilation of Native people was and continues to be a key method of freeing up land for development. A key element of the assimilation policy was compulsory schooling in church-run institutions established by often fanatical missionaries during the mid-1800s. The stated goal was to 'civilize' the Natives and mould them into God-fearing Canadian citizens, preferably nowhere near their ancestral lands. In these so-called 'residential schools', many of which remained open until the 1970s, thousands of Native children endured brutal treatment, sexual, physical and emotional abuse, deprivation and loneliness. Students were severely punished for speaking Native languages and other misdeeds, in some cases by having pins driven through their tongues or their mouths washed out with lye soap. In a typical incident, an Eeyou boy who dropped a glass of milk was forced to lick it up with his tongue off an unfinished wood floor.

The quality of the schools these children had been forcibly brought to, often from hundreds of kilometres away, was notoriously poor. They saw their families only two months each year and were taught to be ashamed of Native traditions and cultures. Parents who refused to hand over their children lost government benefits and food rations, a necessity on the many reserves that were devoid of game. After spending their childhoods in such schools, many Natives could or would no longer speak their own languages, had lost touch with their communities and had not learnt the skills needed to survive on the land. Many left for the growing cities, often deeply troubled by their experiences.

The abuse has caused great social problems for First Nations peoples. It has led to continuing cycles of suicide, sexual and physical abuse, addictions and loss of language and traditional skills. Native organizations and some church leaders have called on the government to launch an inquiry into residential school abuse, but so far politicians have stalled.

When the schools were initially set up, federal officials were quite open about the objectives. 'It is considered by many that the ultimate destiny of the Indian will be to lose his identity as an Indian, so that he will take his place fairly and evenly beside his white brother', wrote an agent of the Indian Affairs Department in an official report in 1913. 'It is only by systematically building from one generation to another that this will be accomplished. The ex-pupils merely form the second link in a chain between barbarism and civilization.'[2]

In 1920, when the Indian Act of 1880 was amended to make education compulsory for Native children, a top Indian Affairs policy-maker summarized the intent. 'Our object is to continue until there is not a single Indian in Canada that has not been absorbed into the body politic, and there is no Indian question, and no Indian department, and that is the whole object of this Bill', said Duncan Campbell Scott, Deputy Superintendent General of Indian Affairs.[3]

In the same amendment came another change to the Indian Act, the law that still regulates Native peoples today. Ottawa was given the power to force Natives to give up their legal status as 'Indians', which meant they lost federal benefits and exemption from taxes. Those who wanted to attend university faced enormous pressure to give up their status. In 1930, the Indian Act was amended again to permit the government to jail or fine Native parents if their children did not attend. The federal government had greater power over Native children than the provinces had over non-Native students.

The Indian Act also gives the federal government near absolute control over life on reserves. It defines a reserve as 'a tract of land, the legal title to which is vested in Her Majesty, that has been set apart by Her Majesty for the use and benefit of the band'.[4] Reserves are legally controlled by Ottawa, which merely allows Native people to 'use' the land, but retains the authority to transfer this land to a provincial or municipal government or to a private corporation, without obtaining the consent of the local inhabitants. Most of Canada's 2,200 reserves were set up in the mid-1800s, often carved out of the worst land available and out of the path of any foreseeable development. All are a fraction of the size of the ancestral land traditionally used to sustain the community. Today, the total area of reserves is one-fifth as large as the amount of land set aside for national parks – less than 0.2 per cent of Canada's total area. In the USA, the proportion set aside for Natives is 20 times larger.

Until 1960, the Indian Act prevented Natives from voting in federal elections unless they agreed to give up their official status as Natives in a formal, irrevocable process known as enfranchisement. Some provinces took even longer, with Quebec granting Natives the vote only in 1969.

The Indian Act still effectively prevents Natives from mortgaging their land, thus removing an important instrument for entrepreneurs to raise funds for economic ventures. The Indian Affairs Minister is also given extraordinary powers to overrule any decision made by elected Native officials. Band Councils are given authority to pass by-laws over only minor matters, such as 'the destruction and control of noxious weeds' and 'the regulation of bee-keeping and poultry-raising'. As recently as 1979, Indian Affairs disallowed one Band Council's by-law to enforce speed limits on its reserve, stating that the by-law exceeded 'the scope of the powers enumerated in Section 81 of the Indian Act'.[5]

Native women fared particularly badly under the Act. If they married a non-Native man, they immediately lost their Indian status. Many had to leave their communities. The reverse did not apply to Native men. This clause was finally removed in 1986. But since then, many First Nations communities have refused to accept back Native women, arguing that the federal government did not provide them with any additional resources to meet the needs of the new members. Thousands of Native women are still waiting to be welcomed home and have had to go to court to force acceptance.

Until the 1960s, the provisions of the Indian Act were enforced by so-called 'Indian agents', government-appointed officials who wielded near-absolute powers over the Native people in their charge. In the Prairies, Natives needed a special permit from the agents to sell their crops or cattle. They could prosecute Natives for offences, preside over Band Council meetings and prohibit Natives from leaving reserves without a pass. Traditional ceremonies, such as the potlatch and sun dance, were suppressed. Today, most First Nations communities are ruled by a foreign system of governance that was forcibly imposed by the federal government and replaced traditional systems more suited to the local people's needs. In some cases, these Native governments have been criticized for a lack of accountability and openness, as well as corruption.

The Indian Act and other aspects of the government's aboriginal policy have had substantial and devastating impacts on Native societies. They created difficult living conditions in Native communities, succeeded in controlling Native resistance to the government and put overwhelming pressure on Natives to migrate to cities. Today, only about a quarter of all Native people in Canada still live on their ancestral lands. Of the 1 million or more Native people, about 336,000 have official 'Indian status' granted them by the government, which means they qualify for rights conferred on Natives under the Indian Act. An additional 750,000 Natives without official status live in cities. Many of the surviving Native languages in Canada are in danger of extinction. Thirteen languages are considered extremely endangered because they are spoken by fewer than 100 individuals.

Extinguishment is another central aspect of the federal government's aboriginal policy. As Native nations were relocated to reserves, they were and continue to be obliged to sign treaties or land agreements in which they agree to 'extinguish' or surrender all future claims to their ancestral lands in exchange for certain benefits – for example, the payment to the band of Canadian (Cdn) $5 per member once a year. Treaties, usually signed under duress or impending development of their lands, have also exempted Natives from paying taxes and guaranteed them federally provided health care, social services, education and housing. The so-called 'extinguishment policy' is widely recognized by scholars of international law as a violation of human rights, but continues to be enforced.

The treaties did grant First Nations important benefits and services, but their quality has generally been inferior to that of the same services received by other Canadians and is generally so poor as to further encourage the exodus of Natives to cities. Health care and social services are poorly funded and hampered by inadequate training and a lack of Native personnel. They have struggled to deal with the difficult health and social conditions in Native communities. The suicide rate among Natives is six times the Canadian average and much higher in some communities.

The housing problem, according to Native leaders, has reached crisis proportions. In the Eeyou (Cree) community of Wemindji in northern Quebec, one small house has four families sharing it. In the Eenou community of Mistissini, one house of 832 sq ft has 16 people living in it, and in nearby Waswanipi, 60 per cent of families live in overcrowded homes, according to government standards. Existing housing stock is poorly constructed, susceptible to fire and in need of repair. To rectify the problems, Ottawa needs to build or repair 40,000 homes in Native communities at a cost of Cdn $3 billion, according to the Assembly of First Nations, the body that represents status Indians. Yet, the federal government has made repeated cutbacks to funding for Native housing.

Recent developments

In recent years, First Nations peoples across the country have experienced a resurgence of community spirit and pride, organizing activity and political will. One of the most dramatic triumphs came in 1994, when the Eeyou (Cree) of northern Quebec declared victory in a six-year international campaign against the Quebec provincial government's proposed Cdn $13.3 billion Great Whale hydroelectric project, which would have flooded an area the size of Connecticut. Newly elected Quebec Premier Jacques Parizeau indefinitely postponed the project, citing a lack of energy demand and the desire to make peace with Natives.

First Nations peoples have taken control over schools, health care, social services and policing – both on reserves and in urban settings, where a well-organized network of 111 Native Friendship Centres has been established to provide services to aboriginal people. Healing programmes for survivors of abuse and addictions have been initiated. Native people have taken a new pride in their languages and cultures, prompting a renewal of Native traditions like pow wows, a rapid increase in Native-language courses, new Native periodicals, television programmes and radio stations. Efforts are under way to reform the operation of federal and provincial justice systems as they affect Native people. In some jurisdictions, the recommendations of Elders' Circles are now accepted by the courts.

Since 1990 protests over land disputes have pitted Native people against police more and more frequently. In the summer of 1995 gunfire was reportedly exchanged in British Columbia, where local Aboriginal people blockaded land they were claiming. In September 1995 two unarmed Chippewa protesters were shot by Ontario Provincial Police at Ipperwash Park. One died of his wounds, and police were reportedly drunk during the attack. Ontario has rejected calls for an inquiry. Aboriginal leaders warn that, if Native concerns are not heard, such confrontations will grow in frequency and blemish Canada's international reputation.

In November 1996 the five-year Royal Commission on Aboriginal Peoples issued its final 5,000-page report, which calls for a profound rebalancing of the Canadian federation to remedy and end the centuries of government neglect, abuse and oppression of the First Nations. The commission says that Canada's record is not in keeping with domestic and international standards and constitutes its single most serious and pressing human rights issue. 'There cannot be harmony unless there is justice,' the commission states. 'Our central conclusion can be summarized simply: The main policy direction, pursued for more than 150 years, first by colonial then by Canadian governments, has been wrong.'

Inuit

The 1991 Canadian census reported 30,000 Inuit living in Canada – 18,000 in the Northwest Territories, 7,000 in Quebec and nearly 4,000 in the Yukon Territory. But these numbers are widely acknowledged to be low and Inuit organizations estimate that 41,000 Inuit live in Canada. Other Inuit communities survive in Siberian Russia, Greenland and the US state of Alaska. Great changes have transformed the Canadian Arctic, often to the disadvantage of the Inuit people. After decades of seeing changes forced on them, today the Inuit have embarked on a cultural and political renaissance and are working to take back power over their lands, communities, institutions and future.

Britain granted the vast Canadian Arctic to the Hudson's Bay Company in 1670, but the first recorded contact between modern European explorers and the Inuit did not occur until the nineteenth century. The explorers brought back reports of a seemingly primitive and inferior people with none of the advantages of European civilization. Some explorers paid dearly for their mistaken perception when they were shipwrecked and refused to entertain the idea that the Inuit could help them.

At the time of the first contacts, the Inuit people had developed a sophisticated technology for surviving in a harsh environment that provided them with a rich and secure economy. Inhabiting the entire north from the coast of Alaska to Labrador, they lived in groups of families in temporary camps, moving according to the seasons and the availability of game. Travel was by skin boat, dog team or on foot. They were mostly a maritime people, depending for food and clothing on marine mammals – bowhead whale, beluga, narwhal, walrus and seal – although caribou and fish were also important. A small group of people known as Caribou Inuit lived in the Keewatin region in the central Canadian Arctic, dependent for food, clothing and summer shelter on caribou and taking no sea animals.

Inuit were hard-hit by initial contact with Europeans, particularly the American and Scottish whalers who decimated this vital element of Inuit survival in a few short decades starting in the 1850s. Ironically, the Europeans made extensive use of Inuit knowledge of the water and of the whales in order to make their catches, pressing local Inuit into service on their ships. The whaling industry also brought with it diseases and alcohol, which had enormous impacts on the Inuit. By 1910, the number of Inuit in the Mackenzie River Delta in the western Canadian Arctic had fallen from 2,000 to about 130.

In 1870, the Hudson's Bay Company sold the land of the Inuit to the Canadian government, which renamed it the Northwest Territories (NWT) and parcelled it out to existing provinces. All this was done without any consultation with the Inuit people, much less their consent. In 1912, again without consulting local Inuit, the federal government extended the boundary of the province of Quebec northward to include the 'Ungava' district (known by the Inuit as Nunavik). At this time, the Arctic held no intrinsic value for the Canadian government. But as other countries, especially the United States, became interested in the area in the late 1800s, Canada was forced to establish its sovereignty.

Between 1953 and 1955, Canada forcibly relocated 92 Inuit from the northern Quebec village of Inukjuak to the High Arctic in a bid to assert its sovereignty over the area. They endured hunger and cold, and were not warned about the long months of darkness that awaited them. They were also not provided with warm clothing. In 1994, the federally appointed Royal Commission on Aboriginal Peoples called the move 'paternalistic' and 'illegal' because it was financed with money intended for Inuit economic development. The Commission also said that Canada never gave the Inuit a choice in whether to move or stay, echoing calls for compensation and an apology already made by the Inuit Tapirisat of Canada (the political body representing Canada's Inuit), the Canadian Human Rights Commission and a House of Commons committee. The federal government has expressed regret about the relocations, but has yet to issue a formal apology or compensation.

The Inuit people of northern Quebec have experienced some of the worst effects of European contact. In the mid-1970s, they entered a period of falling life expectancy that still continues. This new trend coincided with the signing of the James Bay and Northern Quebec Agreement of 1975, in which Inuit and their southern neighbours, the Cree, were forced to sign away their aboriginal rights and agree to a vast series of hydroelectric projects in exchange for monetary compensation. Today, Quebec Inuit life expectancy is 60 years, according to a survey by the Quebec health department, while average Canadian life expectancy is 77 years. A major reason for the falling life expectancy rate is the fact that Inuit aged 15–19 have a suicide rate of 480 per 100,000 people, nearly 25 times the Quebec average. Among other indicators, Inuit infant mortality is four times the Canadian average; and Inuit are six times more likely to die of respiratory diseases than Quebecers and almost 50 per cent more likely to die of cancer.[7]

Alarmed by the changes in their environment and the social problems in their communities, Inuit people have formed movements to regain power over their lives from government bureaucrats and developers. Years of sustained pressure by Inuit in the eastern Arctic obliged the federal government to agree to carve a new territory, Canada's third, out of the eastern NWT, known as Nunavut. Its capital, Iqaluit, was chosen by referendum in December 1995. Unlike in the NWT, where non-natives dominated much of the government bureaucracy, Inuit will form 80 per cent of Nunavut's population and will have substantial control over health and social services, education, economic development, tourism and resource exploitation. The territory will officially come into existence in 1999, and Inuit officials are now collaborating with the federal and NWT governments to work out details. The process of creating the new territory and transferring powers has been slow, but Inuit leaders are optimistic about the possibilities and other First Nations are looking at Nunavut as a model for their own strivings towards self-government.

Canada's Inuit leaders have been instrumental in setting up the Inuit Circumpolar Conference, with representatives from all countries where there are Inuit people. Inuit people have renewed pride in their culture, and are strengthening it through innovative locally-designed television programmes and a network of radio stations. Well-organized and outspoken youth councils have been forming in Inuit communities across the Canadian Arctic. They have raised questions not only about government paternalism and environmental destruction but lack of accountability among the Inuit leadership. A new generation of Inuit have also broken down barriers to higher education, enrolling in record numbers in post-secondary institutions.

African Canadians

About 345,000 people of African origin live in Canada, according to the 1991 census. Most live in two cities, Toronto and Montreal. About 26,000 identified themselves as Africans, 94,400 as Caribbeans and another 225,000 simply as black. About 60 per cent live in the country's most populous province, Ontario. Montreal, in the French-majority province of Quebec, is home to a sizeable and dynamic Haitian community. Most African Canadians immigrated since the 1960s, when immigration rules were eased for non-white individuals. But black people have been in Canada since the days of the earliest European settlement, and black community leaders argue that Canadians have not sufficiently acknowledged the rich contributions of the country's pioneering black citizens.

Mattieu da Costa, an African translator and navigator fluent in the Mi'gmaq Native language, arrived in Canada in 1606 and served as an interpreter for French explorer Samuel de Champlain. Later, thousands of freed black slaves remained loyal to the British, fighting alongside British forces against the Americans in the War of Independence and again during the war of 1812. In the mid-1800s, a black militia unit, the Victoria Pioneer Rifle Company, was the only organized defence force in British Columbia's capital city.

Canada was also a base of operations for the organizers of the 'underground railway', a clandestine network that assisted black slaves attempting to flee the USA. In 1853, Mary Ann Shadd, a black teacher, was the first woman in North America to start a newspaper, the *Provincial Freeman*, which she used to fight slavery. The famous American novel, *Uncle Tom's Cabin*, is believed to be a depiction of the life of Josiah Henson, a black man born into slavery in the USA in 1789 who faithfully served his master for years until he escaped to southern Ontario. There, he helped found the Dawn Settlement, a colony where black people could study and live.

Until Britain abolished slavery in 1834, Canada had its share of slaves, too, many owned by prominent Canadians. One of the most famous was Marie-Joseph Angélique, who in 1734 set her mistress's house on fire in an attempt to escape. The fire spread, causing fire damage to half of Montreal, Canada's largest city at the time. Angélique was caught, tortured and hanged.

Until the 1960s, the number of people of African descent in Canada did not exceed 25,000 due to white pressure on the government to restrict immigration of black people and other minorities. When these policies were changed, the black population expanded more than tenfold in the space of two decades.

For the most part, Canadians of African descent have been marginalized in poorly remunerated and insecure sectors of the economy. Unemployment and poverty rates among African Canadians are much higher than the national average, and black people remain under-represented in higher education institutions, professional fields, police departments, the civil service and politics. A 1995 study found that black men born in Canada earn 16 per cent less than Anglo-Saxon men; black men born outside Canada earn 21 per cent less. Until changes were made in the 1960s, school officials, employers and landlords were legally permitted to discriminate and segregate on the basis of race. Today, *de jure* discrimination has in most cases been eradicated, but more subtle *de facto* discrimination is still prevalent. Federal and provincial charters of rights that outlawed racial and other forms of discrimination have often proved ineffective.

In certain fields, such as law enforcement, the representation of black people is so low it has contributed to social unrest. A lack of black officers in all major police departments across Canada has contributed to a problem of police racism against black people, particularly against black youth. Fatal police shootings of young black men appear to be occurring more frequently in large urban centres like Montreal and Toronto, often in questionable circumstances and amid evidence of police negligence and cover-ups, and even police racism. Effective independent monitoring of police procedures has not been instituted.

Economic difficulties and political turmoil have contributed to a rise of intolerance in Canada, resulting in a growing number of racist incidents affecting black people and other minorities and support for a clamp-down on immigration. A new generation of young African Canadians is responding to this challenge. These individuals are renewing pride in their community's accomplishments, taking leadership roles inside and outside their communities, renewing Black cultural forms and media, and moving into fields where people of African descent have been under-represented.

Conclusions and future prospects

A cultural, social and political revival is occurring among many minority groups and First Nations in Canada that has strengthened their communities, cultures, institutions and languages. Especially involved are minority and First Nations youth. However, difficult challenges lie ahead for minorities and Native people as Canada struggles with a period of economic and political dislocation. Despite a strong desire among ordinary Canadians to accommodate Quebec, communal divisions remain marked. The recent Quebec referendum, which pro-independence forces nearly won, indicates that the federal government and other provinces will need to yield special autonomy to Quebec to preserve national unity. First Nations and African Canadians continue to find themselves at the bottom of Canada's social ladder. Despite a rebirth of pride among Native and black people, and their efforts to improve their living conditions, Canadian society has been slow to change long-standing patterns of discrimination, marginalization and subjugation. Significant improvements will be required in the future if Canada's majority and minority populations are to benefit from their coexistence.

Further reading

Creery, I., *The Inuit (Eskimo) of Canada*, London, MRG report, 1993; also in MRG (ed.), *Polar Peoples: Self Determination and Development*, London, Minority Rights Publications, 1994.

Goodleaf, D., *Entering the War Zone: A Mohawk Perspective on Resisting Invasions*, Penticton, BC, Theytus Books, 1995.

Hill, L., *Trials and Triumphs: The Story of African Canadians*, Toronto, Umbrella Press, 1993.

Joffe, P., *Sovereign Injustice: Forcible Inclusion of the James Bay Crees and Cree Territory into a Sovereign Quebec*, Montreal, Grand Council of the Crees, 1995.

Keywan, Z. and Coles, M., *Greater Than Kings: Ukrainian Pioneer Settlement in Canada*, Montreal, Harvest House, 1977.

Richardson, B. (ed.), *Drum Beat: Anger and Renewal in Indian Country*, Toronto, Assembly of First Nations, 1989.

York, G., *The Dispossessed: Life and Death in Native Canada*, London, Vintage, 1990.

Wilson, J., *Canada's Indians*, London, MRG report, 1992.

Minority-based and advocacy organizations

Amnesty International (English), 214 Montreal Road, Suite 401, Vanier, Ontario KIL 8L8, Canada; tel. 1 613 744 7667, fax 1 613 746 2411; (French) 6250 Boulevard Monk, Montreal, Quebec H4E 3H7, Canada; tel. 1 514 766 9766, fax 1 514 766 2088.

Assembly of First Nations, 1 Nicholas Street, Suite 1002, Ottawa, Ontario K1N 7B7, Canada; tel. 1 613 241 6789, fax 1 613 241 5808.

Canadian Alliance in Solidarity with Native Peoples, PO Box 574, Stn P, Toronto, Ontario M5S 2TI, Canada.

Canadian Helsinki Watch Group, 205 Edmonton Street, 2nd Floor, Winnipeg, Manitoba R3C 1R4, Canada; tel. 1 204 944 1831, fax 1 204 956 2819; and c/o McGill University, Faculty of Law, 3644 Peel Street, Montreal, Quebec H3A 1W9, Canada; tel. 1 514 398 6622, fax 1 514 398 4659.

Canadian Jewish Congress, Edifice Samuel Bronfman House, 1590 Ave Docteur Penfield, Montreal, Quebec H3G 1C5, Canada; tel. 1 514 931 7531.

Centre de Recherches Action sur les Relations Raciales, 3465 Cote-des-Neiges, # 801, Montreal, Quebec H3H 1T7, Canada; tel. 1 514 939 3342, fax 1 514 939 9763.

Chinese Canadian National Council, 119 Spadina Avenue, Suite 605, Toronto, Ontario M5V 2L1, Canada; tel. 1 416 977 9871, fax 1 514 977 1630.

Confederacy of Treaty Six First Nations, Louis Bull First Nation, Treaty Six Territory, PO Box 130, Hobbema, Alberta T0C 1N0, Canada; tel. 1 403 585 3978, fax 1 403 585 3799.

Congress of Black Women, c/o Ethnic Origins Bookstore, 2725 Notre Dame Street W., Montreal, Quebec H3J 1N9, Canada; tel. 1 514 938 1188, fax 1 514 938 1229.

Fédération des Communautés Francophones et Acadiens du Canada, 1 Nicholas Street, Suite 1404, Ottawa, Ontario K1N 7D7, Canada; tel. 1 613 241 7600, fax 1 613 241 6046.

Grand Council of the Crees (of Quebec), 2 Lakeshore Road, Nemaska, Quebec J0Y 3B0, Canada; tel. 1 819 673 2600, fax 1 819 673 2606.

International Human Rights Association of American Minorities, Suite 253, 919 Albert Street, Regina, Saskatchewan S4R 2P6, Canada; tel./fax 1 306 924 1285.

Inuit Circumpolar Conference, 170 Laurier Ave W., Suite 504, Ottawa, Ontario K1P 5V6, Canada; tel. 1 613 563 2642.

Inuit Tapirisat of Canada, 170 Laurier Ave W., Suite 501, Ottawa, Ontario K1P 5V5, Canada; tel. 1 613 238 8181, fax 1 613 234 1991.

Minority Rights Group Canada, 3 Glenshaw Crescent, Toronto, Ontario M4B 2C8, Canada; tel. 1 416 759 4739, fax 1 613 545 6509.

The Nation Cree magazine, 5678 Parc Ave, PO Box 48036, Montreal, Quebec H2V 4S8, Canada; tel. 1 514 272 3077, fax 1 514 278 9914.

National Organization of Immigrant and Visible Minority Women of Canada, 251 Bank Street, Suite 504, Ottawa, Ontario K2P 1X3, Canada; tel. 1 613 232 0689, fax 1 613 232 0988.

Société St Jean Baptiste du Québec, 82 Sherbrooke Street W., Montreal, Quebec H2X 1X3, Canada; tel. 1 514 843 8851, fax 1 514 844 6369.

Ukrainian Canadian Congress, 456 Main Street, Winnipeg, Manitoba R3B 1B6, Canada; tel. 1 204 942 4627, fax 1 204 947 3882.

Vietnamese Canadian Federation, 249 Rochester Street, Ottawa, Ontario K1R 7M9, Canada; tel./fax 1 613 230 8282.

World Council of Indigenous Peoples, 555 King Edward Avenue, Ottawa, Ontario, K1N 6N5, Canada; tel. 1 613 230 9030, fax 1 613 230 9340.

Mexico

Land area:	1,958,201 sq km
Population:	92.4 million (1994)
Main languages:	Spanish (official), about 50 indigenous languages
Main religions:	Roman Catholicism, indigenous religions
Main minority groups:	56 indigenous peoples 10–20 million (10.8–23.8%), African Mexicans 460,000–4.7 million (0.5–5%)
Real per capita GDP:	$7,010
UNDP HDI/rank:	0.845 (48)

Mexico borders the USA to the north and Guatemala and Belize to the south. Although it is the largest and northernmost country of the Central American isthmus, it is today widely considered part of North America. Its climate ranges from the hot, wet tropical southern region and coastal lowlands, to the more temperate central highlands, to the arid desert of the north and west.

Mexico has been inhabited for at least 11,000 years. Beginning centuries before the European conquest, a sequence of major indigenous civilizations flourished in the region, culminating with the militarily powerful Aztec empire, which arose in the early fifteenth century. Spanish colonization began in 1519 with the explorations and campaigns of Hernán Cortés. Cortés quickly ascertained that the Aztec empire was not a monolithic entity and that some subjugated nations could be turned to the Spanish side. Large numbers of indigenous troops supported his decisive attack on the Aztec capital of Tenochtitlán.

Spanish colonialism had many different impacts on the pre-existing societies after the conquest. Forcible conversion to Christianity was the rule. Disease epidemics previously unknown in the Americas, against which the indigenous population had no immunity, resulted in millions of deaths. The Spanish colonial authorities relocated indigenous communities into fewer, larger towns where they could be more effectively controlled, and on to the least fertile lands. The Europeans themselves took possession of the rich soils that had provided bountiful and reliable harvests of maize, beans and squash for the indigenous communities.

Mexico achieved independence from Spain in 1821. The establishment of a republic in 1824 was followed by a period of political instability, and war with Britain, France and the USA. Mexico ceded much of its territory to the USA after the war of 1846. Stability was regained in 1876 under the dictator Porfirio Díaz. The following decades witnessed significant growth in Mexico's economy and the consolidation of landownership in the form of huge *haciendas* (estates) in the hands of a small and wealthy Spanish-descended elite. Tricked into debt-bondage, large numbers of indigenous Mexicans worked on the *haciendas* as virtual slaves. Severe poverty was rampant among both the indigenous and the *mestizo* (ethnically mixed) population.

The exploitation and impoverishment of the rural and urban masses, combined with a lack of democracy, led to the revolution of 1910–20. Among other reforms, the subsequent constitution of 1917 revised landownership and drafted a labour code. Indigenous rights were ignored. Established in the wake of these events, the Partido Revolucionario Institucional (PRI) has maintained since that time a virtual monopoly on political power, despite accusations of electoral irregularities and corruption. The PRI was from its early years instrumental in setting up workers' and peasant groups that remain strong supporters of the government.

A concerted effort to industrialize and modernize Mexico's infrastructure took place from the later 1940s onwards. The establishment of *ejidos* – communal peasant farms on state-owned land – through the expropriation of large capitalist farms was a central project of the government of President Lázaro Cárdenas (1934–40). However, subsequent administrations favoured capital-intensive export agriculture and neglected the *ejido* sector where most of the country's corn producers, including the majority of indigenous farmers, were concentrated. This led to a loss of self-sufficiency in basic grains and greater reliance on imports in the 1970s.

Economic crisis was temporarily overcome in the second half of the 1970s, when large oilfields were discovered and high world prices for oil allowed the government to increase revenue and attract massive foreign loans. The oil-debt boom came to an abrupt end in 1982 as a result of the simultaneous fall in oil prices and rising interest rates of international creditor banks. A period of austerity and economic restructuring followed, culminating in Mexico's decision to approve the North American Free Trade Agreement (NAFTA), which came into force on 1 January 1994.

Indigenous people and *mestizos* form a numerical majority of the population, but most power in Mexican society continues to be in the hands of the white elite. Indigenous peoples and *mestizos*, as well as African Mexicans, remain largely on the margins of a fast-changing society struggling to keep up with economic globalization. Minorities have been especially hurt by the country's struggles to rid itself of severe economic problems and inequality. Despite Mexico's adoption of a range of administrative measures for the protection of human rights, indigenous peasants are frequently subjected to human rights violations, particularly in the impoverished southern states. In January 1994 the armed Zapatista rebellion in Chiapas gained international attention for the plight of Mexico's rural poor but has yet to achieve significant and lasting improvements in their situation.

This entry does not include a discussion of Mexico's *mestizo* population, who comprise some 55 million people (60 per cent of the national total) but do not self-identify as an ethnic or cultural community in the same way as the indigenous peoples do.

Indigenous peoples

Mexico has the largest indigenous population of any Latin American country.[1] Its 56 indigenous peoples, numbering between 10 million and 20 million, comprise a wide range of culturally distinct groups. They include the Tarahumara of the upland forests of northern Chihuahua state, the Maya of the southern highlands, the Lacandones of the jungles of Chiapas state, the Zapotec and the Nahua. Some of these peoples have retained local forms of organization to defend their culture and livelihoods. Others have witnessed the collapse of their traditions under the burden of poverty, and believe that they must reject their ethnic identity and integrate into *mestizo* society if they are to improve their living conditions.

Indigenous populations are concentrated in south and south-central Mexico. Almost 90 per cent of those who speak an indigenous language live in 10 of Mexico's 31 states or the Federal District; in rank order, these are Oaxaca, Veracruz, Chiapas, Yucatán, Puebla, State of Mexico, Hidalgo, Guerrero, Federal District, San Luis Potosí and Michoacán. The government now recognizes 49 indigenous 'ethnic groups' (indigenous organizations prefer the term 'peoples'). The 1990 census showed that 7.5 per cent of Mexicans aged over five spoke an indigenous language. Of this figure, 80 per cent also speak Spanish and 16 per cent are monolingual. The five predominant languages are Nahuatl, followed by Maya, Mixtec, Zapotec and Otomi.

Official data underestimate the true size of Mexico's indigenous populations, being based on purely linguistic criteria and excluding children under five years of age. However, although such figures solely refer to those who speak one of the indigenous languages, they give a useful indication of the comparative size of different populations. Thus, according to 1990 census statistics, the larger linguistic groups are: Nahuatl, 1,197,328 (located in Veracruz, Hidalgo, San Luis Potosí, Guerrero, Oaxaca, Puebla and Morelos); Maya 713,520 (in Quintana Roo, Campeche and Yucatán); Mixtec 383,544 (in Oaxaca and Guerrero); Zapotec 380,690 (in Oaxaca); Otomi

280,238 (in Hidalgo); Tzeltal 261,084 (in Chiapas); Tzotzil 229,203 (in Chiapas); Totonaca 207,876 (in Puebla and Veracruz); Mazateco 168,374 (in Oaxaca).

Indigenous culture is considered to be at the heart of Mexican society. Mexico is proud of its ancient Maya and Aztec monuments, and its indigenous dances, crafts and markets, which contribute significantly to the country's appeal to tourists. Since the revolution of 1910–20, successive governments have professed a desire to integrate indigenous people into Mexican society. The Independent Department of Native Affairs, set up in 1946 under the Ministry of Education, began a programme of teaching Spanish to indigenous children.

Officially Mexico's indigenous communities are protected by human rights legislation. The government's National Indigenous Institute has offices throughout the country to facilitate consultation with indigenous communities, and government statements are careful to recognize the principle of cultural diversity. However, there have been complaints that the institute is patronizing in its attitude to indigenous people and simply a token effort of the government, although its personnel have at times been energetic defenders of indigenous communities and have even been persecuted as a result.

Basic protections against human rights abuses also include the National Commission of Human Rights, established in 1990, and human rights commissions established in each state, to which complainants can appeal for redress. The National Commission is known for its silence on cases of grievous rights violations, leading many indigenous leaders and rights activists to question its credibility. Nevertheless, the Commission produces reports and publications drawing attention to Mexico's human rights record.

The government has also ratified International Labour Organization (ILO) Convention No. 169 of 1989 on the rights of indigenous and tribal peoples, although it is argued that constitutional changes during the 1990s have undermined land rights guaranteed under the Convention.

Despite these provisions, indigenous people in Mexico experience a double form of discrimination – both because of their low economic standing and poor levels of formal education, and also on grounds of language, dress and other cultural manifestations. What little land they own is generally insufficient to support them, so many seek waged work from white and *mestizo* employers, who generally treat them disrespectfully. Sixty per cent of indigenous people over age 12 lack formal paid employment, and most live from subsistence farming and informal work. The majority of those who have jobs earn less than the minimum daily wage (US $2.50 in mid-1995).[2]

An estimated two-thirds of indigenous people live in small peasant communities where they are the majority population, mostly located in the poorest, least developed parts of the country. Although conditions vary considerably, half such communities lack electricity and running water. Housing is often substandard and overcrowded. Many indigenous communities regularly experience shortages of medicines and food. Child malnutrition is rife in many communities; child mortality is as high as 20 per cent, and illiteracy is considerably higher than the Mexican average.

Indigenous farmers have been harassed or attacked by paramilitary groups as they work their land. Police brutality and mistreatment by the justice system are commonly reported. Some indigenous communities have been prevented from electing their customary representatives. Attempts by communities to defend their lands against illegal loggers or to campaign for their rights have met with violence on the part of armed groups who appear to operate with impunity. Leaders who speak out for political change are singled out for persecution by powerful landowners who wield inordinate influence over the local police, political and judicial systems. The repression can range from incarceration and expulsion from communities to torture and murder. 'Disappearances' and massacres of unarmed peasants have been reported.

Indigenous people are also over-represented in the country's prison system, languishing in jail as proceedings stagnate and often spending more time behind bars than a sentence would require were they actually convicted and sentenced. In many cases, they are not provided with interpreters even though one in six indigenous people speak no Spanish and despite guarantees of such basic protection under the law. Courts often accept confessions extracted under duress as the main evidence for sentencing.

Indigenous women are particularly marginalized in many communities. Their illiteracy levels are 20 per cent higher than those of indigenous men, and they suffer considerable violence at the hands of their men. Male migration in search of work often means that women experience abandonment and increased economic hardship. Alcoholism, child abuse and incest are also reported as significant problems affecting indigenous families.

Conditions have been exacerbated by a structural economic crisis that has left indigenous people, who sustain themselves mainly in the agricultural sector, especially subject to increasing privation. The government has moved to erode the rights of indigenous peoples to communal lands, and the impact of Mexico's joining of NAFTA – effective from 1994 – is also likely to prove largely negative for the indigenous minority.

Many indigenous organizations have arisen to press for better living conditions. They have campaigned for schools, health care, water, credits, low prices, fair wages, political representation and consultation, the protection of local environments, and official recognition of their languages and traditional skills as healers. Such groups often work in collaboration with local non-governmental organizations and human rights bodies. In the early 1990s there were an estimated 500–600 indigenous organizations ranging from small community-based groups to national bodies. Indigenous Mexicans are also active within the large national peasant unions. Where their basic needs are met, they have shown themselves adept at making use of literacy and a knowledge of modern technology.

Environmental protection has been central to much of the indigenous struggle of recent years. In the early 1990s, for example, the Nahua of Guerrero state successfully opposed the construction of a hydroelectric dam that would have flooded archaeological sites and affected the lives of 17 communities. Widespread, often illegal, logging of communally owned forests has been reported, with few benefits going to local indigenous communities.

The situation of Mexico's indigenous communities gained worldwide attention on 1 January 1994 when Mayan and other indigenous peasants, taking the name of Emiliano Zapata, a popular leader murdered by the military in 1919, launched an armed uprising on the day that the North American Free Trade Agreement came into effect. Occupying four towns in Chiapas – where the situation of indigenous people has long been worse than in other states – the Ejercito Zapatista de Liberacion Nacional (EZLN) stated its opposition to indignities faced by indigenous people and others in modern Mexico. They called for better conditions for indigenous peoples, protection of communal land and an end to government corruption and human rights abuses. After the initial fighting, the government declared a ceasefire, promised to address rebel concerns and released prisoners. Negotiations were started between a government-appointed mediator and the rebels but broke down when the government proved unwilling to accept most of the rebel demands. At the height of the uprising government forces shot, execution-style, eight suspected members of the EZLN; and, according to human rights observers, dozens of critics of the regime have been killed or have 'disappeared', reportedly at the hands of death squads organized by government forces working in collusion with private interests. The brutal torture and rape of indigenous women in Chiapas is also documented; perpetrators are rarely brought to trial.

In the elections of August 1994 the PRI candidate, Eduardo Robledo Rincón, officially won the governor's race in Chiapas, but the EZLN and opposition leaders insisted that progressive candidate Amado Avendado was the rightful winner. They created a parallel government, seized government offices, took over radio stations, mounted roadblocks and the EZLN eventually took over 38 towns in the state. The parallel authority permitted peasants to expropriate large estates, liquidated existing state structures and instituted new laws favouring indigenous people and the poor. Large demonstrations were held in cities across Mexico in support of the rebels.

The Mexican government was forced to devalue the peso by 50 per cent in the last two weeks of December 1994, precipitating a loss of business confidence in the new adminstration of President Ernesto Zedillo. In an attempt to regain investors' support, Zedillo implemented harsh austerity measures designed to control government spending and inflation. In February 1995 he also ordered a military offensive against the EZLN bases, forcing the rebels to retreat into the mountains. During 1995 social protest increased throughout the country as the public reacted to a painful economic downturn, government corruption and austerity measures demanded by foreign debt holders. The situation in Chiapas and elsewhere in the country remains tense as indigenous people and impoverished *mestizos* see further deterioration in their living conditions.

Negotiations resumed in Chiapas in April 1995 but proceeded slowly until the end of the year, when some advances were made in the area of indigenous rights and culture. A minimal accord was signed in February 1996 which recommended that reforms be made to Article 4 of the constitution. These reforms would lay the basis for a greater degree of self-government for indigenous communities, although the precise details remained to be defined. The EZLN and indigenous organizations represented in the Asamblea Nacional Indígena Plural por la Autonomía had been demanding constitutional reforms to allow for the creation of pluri-ethnic autonomous regions in areas of significant indigenous population. In effect, this would establish a fourth level of government at a regional level, which would coexist with the existing municipal, state and federal government authorities. Regional autonomy would also allow indigenous peoples greater control over their land and resources in accordance with ILO Convention No. 169. Government negotiators refused to accept these demands, preferring a concept of autonomy limited to communities rather than peoples.

African Mexicans

There have been no official figures on the numbers of Mexicans of African descent since 1810, when a census found that black people made up 10.1 per cent of the population.[3] Most estimates now place their numbers at between 474,000 and 4.7 million, although one US researcher estimates that as many as 75 per cent of Mexicans have some African ancestry. A mass forced migration of perhaps 250,000 or more African slaves occurred during the three centuries of Spanish conquest and rule. Many died *en route* in the ships' holds, while many others perished in the dire conditions of slave labour. By the early 1600s Mexico had more African slaves than any other country in the Americas, and during the colonial period there were as many Africans as Spanish in the population, while by the late eighteenth century there were twice as many African-*mestizos* as Spanish.

African slaves escaped from early times, establishing *palenques* or slave communities in the mountains and other remote places. African Mexican soldiers helped overthrow Spanish rule in the War of Independence, and the *ejercito moreno* (dark army) of Father Hidalgo is said to have initiated the independence struggle. In other ways too, people of African descent made a marked contribution to Mexico's development. They developed and cultivated farmland, provided skilled labour in the silver mines, worked on cattle ranches and sugar plantations. A black revolutionary, General Vincente Guerrero, became the country's second President after independence. African traditions and culture were adopted into Mexico's national culture. Traditional Mexican music has been described as a mixture of the country's Spanish, indigenous and African elements. Mexico's well-known 'La Bamba' dance is African in origin.

Despite this contribution, most African Mexicans live in poverty, often in isolated rural communities with negligible sanitation, health or education services. Their primary sources of income are fishing, farming and domestic work. The vast majority are unable to enter higher-education institutions. The African presence in Mexico is often denied or trivialized, and where popular culture depicts black people they tend to be caricatured and ridiculed. Some observers suggest nevertheless that Mexico's African heritage is slowly emerging as an issue of concern and interest.

Guatemalan refugees

Approximately 150,000 Mayan refugees fled into Chiapas to avoid the Guatemalan army's counter-insurgency campaign in the early 1980s. Few have returned to their homes, and more than 50,000 have taken up residence in rural and urban areas as 'illegal aliens'. There have been calls for the government to declare an amnesty for those Guatemalan refugees now integrated into Mexican society.

Conclusions and future prospects

Mexico has taken some notable steps towards reform in recent years. Likewise its indigenous peoples and African Mexicans have made important strides in organizing themselves to improve their living conditions and gain acceptance for their rights. Yet without more genuine representation, consultation and impartial justice, lasting stability in relations between the country's majority and minority populations will remain elusive. Resistance from those in power continues to be formidable, although a positive sign is the degree to which indigenous peoples in Chiapas have been able to mobilize popular support across the country for their demands. There are indications that the PRI's grip on power is weakening, and in this climate indigenous peoples and others may have an opportunity to press for change. The main political debates will revolve around the concept of autonomy, with indigenous organizations pressing for a regionally defined unit of self-government together with increased representation in national, state and local decision-making bodies. The Chiapas uprising provided an impetus for national and international networking, and it is likely that regional movements will seek legal and institutional reforms with their respective state governments. On the other hand, the federal government will attempt to limit claims for autonomy to individual communities in order to maintain centralized jurisdiction over the use of land and natural resources.

Further reading

Aguirre Beltrán, G., *La población negra de México: estudio etnohistorica*, Xalapa, Universidad Veracruzana, 1989.

Bonfil Batalla, G., *Mexico profundo: una civilización negada*, Mexico, Grijalbo, 1990.

Castillo, R.A.H., *et al.*, *La experiencia de refugio en Chiapas: nuevas relaciones en la frontera sur mexicana*, Academia Mexicana de Derechos Humanos, Centros de Investigaciones y Estudios Superiores en Antropología Social, Consejería en Proyectos para Refugiados Latinoamericanos, OXFAM and UNRISD, n.d.

Collier, G. with Lowery Quaratiello, E., *Basta! Land and the Zapatista Rebellion in Chiapas*, Oakland, CA, Institute for Food and Development Policy, 1994.

Jordan, P.R., *Poblaciones indígenas de America Latina y el Caribe*, Mexico City, FAO and Inter-American Indigenous Institute, 1990.

Lloyd, J-D. and Perez Rosales, L. (eds), *Paisajes rebeldes: una larga noche de rebelión indígena*, Mexico City, Universidad Iberoamericana, 1995.

MacLeod, M.J. and Wasserstrom, R. (eds), *Spaniards and Indians in Southeastern Mesoamerica*, Lincoln, NE, University of Nebraska Press, 1983.

Mejia Píñeros, M.C. and Sarmiento Silva, S., *La lucha indígena: un reto a la ortodoxia*, Mexico City, Siglo XXI Editores and Instituto de Investigaciones Sociales, UNAM, 1987.

Muhammad, Jameelah S., 'Mexico', in MRG (ed.), *No Longer Invisible: Afro-Latin Americans Today*, London, Minority Rights Publications, 1995; and in MRG (ed.), *Afro-Central Americans*, London, MRG report, 1996.

Minority-based and advocacy organizations

Amnesty International, Calle Anicet Ortega 624, Colonia del Valle, Mexico DF, Mexico; tel. 52 5 559 8413, fax 52 5 559 8413.

Centro de Derechos Humanos 'Fray Francisco de Vitoria OP', Odontología 35, Colonia Copilco – Universidad, Mexico DF 04360, Mexico; tel. 52 5 658 9000.

Comisión Mexicana de Defensa y Promoción de los Derechos Humanos, Calle Tabasco no. 262 – despacho 201, Colonia Roma, Mexico DF 06700, Mexico; tel. 52 5 682 2014, fax 52 5 669 4076.

Consejo General de las Regiones Autonomas Plurietnicas de Chiapas, Lazaro Cardenas 71, Casa 3, La Cabana, Barrio Mexicanos, San Cristóbal de las Casas, Chiapas, Mexico.

Consejo Guerrerense 500 Años de Resistencia Indígena, Avenida Insurgentes 5, Colonia Electricistas, Chilpancingo, Guerrero 39010, Mexico; e-mail: cg500ari@laneta.apc.org

Filo Rojo (human rights journal), Cuauhtemoc 16, MZ, Colonia Doctores, Mexico DF 06720, Mexico; tel. 52 5 761 0806.

Frente Independiente de Pueblos Indios, Apartado Postal 28–145, Mexico DF 06080, Mexico; tel./fax 52 5 712 6954.

Instituto Nacional Indigenista, Ave Revolucíon 1279, 2 Piso, Colonia Tlacopac, Mexico DF 01040, Mexico; tel. 52 5 651 3199/593 5781.

National Commission for Human Rights, Periférico Sur No. 3469, 4 Piso, Colonia San Jerónimo/Lidice, Del. Magdalena Contreras, Mexico DF 10200, Mexico; tel. 52 5 681 8125, fax 52 5 681 6581.

Ojarasca (journal of indigenous affairs), Epigmenio Ibarra 53, Romero de Terreros, Mexico DF 04310, Mexico; tel./fax 52 5 659 8652.

United States of America

Land area:	9,809,000 sq km
Population:	248.7 million (1990; official est. 1994, 260.3 million)
Main languages:	English, Spanish
Main religions:	Christianity, Judaism, Islam
Main minority groups:	African Americans 30 million (12.1%), Latinos 22.1 million (8.9%) including 2.5 million US Puerto Ricans (1%), Asian-Pacific Americans 7.3 million (2.9%), Arab and other Middle Eastern Americans, approx. 3 million (1.2%), Native Americans 1.96 million (0.79%) including 240,000 Native Hawai'ians and 80,000 Inuit and Alaska Natives[1]
Real per capita GDP:	$24,680
UNDP HDI/rank:	0.940 (2)

The USA presents a minority situation of unusual diversity and complexity. Largely, although not entirely, a nation of immigrants, its concepts of civil rights, integration, universal equality and independence have influenced human rights around the globe. Dominance by the 'white' Christian majority has been a constant since North America was colonized in the sixteenth century. Since US independence in 1776, government policy has evolved from a basis in slavery and conquest, through segregation and exploitation, into an official stance favouring minority integration and even self-determination. Yet reality often belies the rhetoric. Many US minorities suffer high rates of unemployment, poverty, infant mortality, disease, social alienation and low political participation. The conditions of the worst-off minorities render them a nation apart. Inner-city African Americans and reservation Native Americans, for example, live with health and economic levels more readily comparable to life in low-income developing countries than to the suburban USA. Meanwhile, minorities that do achieve some social mobility (notably Asian-Pacific Americans and Arab Americans) face resentment, random violence and organized hate groups, as well as pressure for total assimilation to 'the American way'.

Minority rights instruments

The USA was founded in 1776 with the American Declaration of Independence, including the basic tenets that the equality of all people is 'self-evident' and that human rights including 'life, liberty and the pursuit of happiness' are 'inalienable'. The US constitution's first ten amendments, or the Bill of Rights, provide for equal access to a broad range of civil rights and liberties. The thirteenth amendment prohibits slavery; the fourteenth entrenches the due process of law and equal protection for all.

Until the mid-twentieth century, however, these provisions were consciously misinterpreted to allow for disenfranchizement of women and minority groups, dispossession of indigenous peoples, official segregation, discrimination in education, employment and housing, and unequal access to public services. The US Supreme Court repeatedly endorsed these practices as legal and acceptable.

After the Second World War, the Supreme Court shifted its stance radically. The *Brown* case (1954) ended official school segregation, a symbolic blow for general social integration. This landmark case was broadened by later rulings extending desegregation into other areas and requiring governments to take a proactive stance in integrating 'racial' groups and providing equal opportunity.

These decisions were both the product and the engine of an extraordinary period of minority activism for civil and political rights. Eventually, minority demands were recognized in new legislation. The Civil Rights Act of 1964 outlawed discrimination on the basis of race, colour and creed in voting, employment, federal programmes and public facilities. The Voting Rights Act of 1965 included a series of measures intended to short-circuit racist attempts to exclude minorities from political life. At the same time, the Johnson administration launched the Great Society anti-poverty campaign, including expanded social welfare programmes and equal employment opportunity laws. Over the next decade, governments and courts entrenched these new laws in policy, and the USA recognized (limited) indigenous sovereignty rights for the first time since the colonial period.

However, the USA has been reluctant to make international commitments to internal minority rights. It has often delayed ratifying UN accords for decades after signing them. Only in the early 1990s did the USA finally ratify the Torture Convention, the Convention on the Elimination of Racial Discrimination, and the International Covenant on Civil and Political Rights. The USA is also party to the American Declaration on the Rights of Man, which contains a general statement against discrimination.

Recent legal developments

New methods of registering voters have been promoted as a way to bolster minority electoral participation. The National Voter Registration Act was finally passed in 1994, after long resistance from the Republican Party. By allowing voters to register when they obtain drivers' licences or at social service offices, this 'Motor Voter Act' more than tripled the pace of registrations in 1995. However, other measures intended to ensure minority political representation are in peril. The 1965 Voting Rights Act mandated the redrawing of voting districts to benefit minorities. These 'racially gerrymandered' districts, which did help return a higher proportion of minorities to office, are now in question. The Supreme Court's 1995 ruling that the state of Georgia could not draw districts on the basis of race could ultimately end the practice.

Critics charge that the Supreme Court of the 1980s and 1990s generally abandoned the role of minority advocate. Five significant cases in the 1988–9 term narrowed protection against discrimination and opened the way to white employees or students successfully challenging affirmative action, although the Civil Rights Act of 1991 restored weaker versions of the provisions the Court had struck down. The *Hicks* case of 1993 shifted the burden of proof to complainants rather than defendants in discrimination cases. Another series of decisions in the 1994–5 term established that affirmative action could be considered reverse discrimination, that set-aside federal contracts for minority-based companies were unconstitutional unless patterns of discrimination could be proven to the highest standard, and that states were not justified in taking expensive and elaborate measures to promote school desegregation. The Court also refused to hear an appeal of a lower court decision prohibiting the University of Maryland from providing scholarships for minority students.

Affirmative action became a pivotal issue in the 1990s. California Governor Pete Wilson launched a suit against the federal government in 1995 protesting against mandatory affirmative-action programmes for state governments. A referendum was planned on the issue in California for 1996, and several Republican candidates for the 1996 US presidential election nomination made loud and clear attacks on 'quotas' and 'reverse discrimination'.

It has become almost a truism that the US legal system discriminates against non-whites, especially in criminal cases. The 1992 police beating of Rodney King and the 1995 trial of O.J. Simpson were particular flashpoints. Other frequently cited examples include: the wildly disparate sentencing patterns in convictions for possession of crack cocaine (associated with non-white users) and powder cocaine (used mostly by whites); the disproportionate imprisonment of black, Latino and Native American convicts compared to whites; and the more frequent use of the death sentence against non-whites, especially when convicted of killing a white victim.

Minority issues

This entry focuses on seven key minority groupings: African Americans, Latinos (including Puerto Ricans), Asian-Pacific Americans, Arab and other Middle Eastern Americans, Native Americans, Native Hawai'ians, and Inuit and Alaska Natives. In most cases, these groupings include several distinct subgroups that nonetheless have enough in common to be discussed under a single heading. However, the indigenous peoples of Hawai'i and Alaska are dealt with separately from other Native American groups, mostly because of differences in legal circumstances caused by the relatively recent addition of those states to the American Union. Puerto Ricans are discussed slightly apart from other Latino groups because the island of Puerto Rico has a unique political relationship to the continental United States, making Puerto Ricans' problems and concerns distinct from those of Mexicans and Latin Americans in the USA. Their situation is closer to that of Native Hawai'ians', for example.

Each group has been selected for detailed examination according to a combination of criteria: size, current and historic levels of systemic discrimination, political presence as a vocal interest group, and self-definition as a minority.

Significant portions of each group chosen face entrenched obstacles to educational, economic, legal and social equality directly attributable to their minority status.

Besides the minorities discussed in detail, there are dozens of other distinctive ethnic and religious groups in the USA. While some are small immigrant groups that do not yet have sufficient numbers and history to attract notice, others have been relatively successful in reaching accommodation with the dominant population and cannot be said to suffer significant discrimination as minorities in the USA today. Irish, Italian, Polish and other Roman Catholic European immigrants, for example, encountered serious prejudice prior to the Second World War, but have now integrated as 'whites'. Often these groups have maintained their cultural cohesion while achieving economic advancement. Some anti-Roman Catholic sentiment remains, but not to a severe degree. More recent immigrants from Europe (notably from Ireland and the former Soviet sphere) often earn less than other Americans, but this is better explained by immigrant status and the time needed for adjustment to a new country than by discrimination.

Jewish people – 2.5 per cent of the US population – are a special case. Anti-Semitism in the USA was widespread and embedded in social and economic structures as recently as the mid-1960s. Today, however, Jews partake in every aspect of life: 7 per cent of the Senate and Congress are Jewish, Jews are accepted in social organizations, and American Jewish income is above average. Jewish participation in religious and cultural institutions has decreased, however, and Jewish communities are arguably less cohesive than in the past. Organized anti-Semitic violence occurs through hate-group activity, and some conservative politicians (both white and African American) have spoken in veiled terms about Jewish conspiracies. If these elements continue to gain ground, the Jewish situation in the United States could become less secure.

Other religious minorities – including Amish, Quaker, Dukhobor and Bruderhoffer Christians, Mormons, Muslims (especially Black Muslims), Christian Scientists, Hare Krishnas, Native American spiritualists and Scientologists – have encountered barriers to the free practice of their faith in the past. However, jurisprudence has affirmed these groups' constitutional rights to freedom of religion, including tax exemption. The pacifist Amish and Quakers were guaranteed freedom from compulsory service under the 1950s and 1960s military draft, and the Amish and other traditionalist religious groups have prevailed against pressures to abandon their rural, independent lifestyles.

However, the 1990 *Smith* decision of the Supreme Court condemning the use of peyote by the Native American Church raised concerns about whether religious freedom would continue to take priority over other state imperatives. The Christian fundamentalist population in the USA has burgeoned over the past decade, resulting in political trends that trouble religious liberty advocates. For example, there have been popular (if so far unsuccessful) conservative campaigns on compulsory prayer in public schools and for 'family values' policies generally. Some operations against religious 'cults' have been criticized for blurring the line between enforcing the law and enforcing moral and religious conformity.

Finally, people of 'mixed race' make up a growing proportion of US society. Mixed-race births rose from 1 per cent to 3.4 per cent between 1968 and 1989, according to US government statistics (which often undercount by slotting mixed-race people into one category or another). Mixed-race people face particular emotional and social challenges in the rigid grid of US race relations, although they may possess the personal experience and insight needed to challenge social norms. Their increasing numbers indicate that separation and retrenchment are not the sole and inevitable trend in US race relations today.

African Americans

African Americans make up 12.1 per cent of the US population, the largest minority group, numbering approximately 30 million. Once called Negroes, and now often called 'black' Americans or (evoking solidarity with other non-white minorities around the world) 'people of colour', they are mainly descendants of slaves brought from Africa between the seventeenth and nineteenth centuries. Their history of forced immigration to the United States is unique among US minorities, and compared to slaves elsewhere African Americans were uniquely de-cultured and dehumanized, their misery treated as 'natural' and benign.[2] Today, they are the most important minority in a nation with a singular degree of world influence. Much of the USA's vitality can be credited to African Americans, but white–black conflict remains a definitive, often *sotto voce* reality.

Slavery to civil rights and beyond

Blacks arrived with British and Dutch settlers in the early colonial period, and officially enjoyed equal rights with whites, although impoverished blacks and whites alike were subject to indentured servitude. Soon, however, African slaves were imported in large numbers as labourers by seafaring entrepreneurs, and by the 1670s statutes enforcing slavery were adopted by each of the Thirteen Colonies.

Although slavery was instituted mostly for economic reasons, racist beliefs became entrenched as slavery and African Americans became linked in the white colonial mind. During the Revolutionary War, both slaves and free blacks fought for the Colonies, but the subsequent 1787 constitution included three clauses reinforcing slavery. Blacks were designated as property and counted as 'three-fifths of a person'. All told, slavery was an important part of the US economy for more than two centuries, despite slave revolts, an elaborate 'underground railroad' network for escaped slaves, and consistent protest from white and black abolitionists.

Between 1777 and 1804, each of the northern states responded to changing moralities and urban labour shortages by abolishing slavery. But in the south, slaves were key to the enormous plantation system. The issue became part of the growing North–South antipathy that culminated in the mid-nineteenth century civil war. Towards the end of the war, in 1863, President Abraham Lincoln signed the Emancipation Proclamation, ending slavery in most states.

During the 'Reconstruction' period after the civil war, the thirteenth, fourteenth and fifteenth amendments to the US constitution finally guaranteed African Americans the rights of freedom and full citizenship, including the vote. Soon, African Americans were elected to Congress, were admitted to schools and began to integrate and even intermarry with whites. The first Civil Rights Act, passed in 1875, guaranteed access to public facilities and accommodation without regard to race, colour or previous servitude.

The optimism of the time did not last long. White bigots in many states bent the rules to restrict voting rights, and enforced segregation through fear and intimidation. From 1883 to 1952, 'lynchings' (mob executions) of African Americans were reported every year, often with tacit official approval. This period also saw the advent of white supremacist groups like the Ku Klux Klan, many of which persist to this day. At the same time, state and federal courts were forging the 'Jim Crow' system (named after an archetypal figure in the African American minstrel tradition), an apartheid doctrine in which blacks and whites were described as 'separate-but-equal'. In 1883, the Civil Rights Act was deemed unconstitutional, and in 1896 the Supreme Court upheld the separate-but-equal rule in *Plessy v. Ferguson*.

Riots and protest did little to stem the tide, and the African American condition did not improve visibly in the first half of the twentieth century. However, many African American musicians, artists and poets came to prominence in the 'Harlem Renaissance' of the 1930s, and black athletes began to break colour bars in the Olympics and professional team sports. The African American community was developing autonomous institutions like the National Association for the Advancement of Colored People (NAACP) (1901), the National Urban League (1911) and Caribbean-born Marcus Garvey's United Negro Improvement Association, which promoted black self-determination and the idea that blacks should go 'back to Africa', culturally or even physically (1920s). African American colleges and universities became popular. The Supreme Court slowly eroded the bases of Jim Crow, deciding one by one against state laws that segregated interstate bus travel, housing and neighbourhoods, or withheld voting rights.

The watershed Supreme Court ruling for African American civil rights came in 1954. *Brown v. Topeka Board of Education* held that racial segregation in public schools was unconstitutional, and that 'separate' was inherently unequal. The main legal plank of Jim Crow was demolished.

Energized by *Brown* and led by coalitions of black organizations with the inspiration of Dr Martin Luther King Jr, the Civil Rights Movement used nonviolent resistance to shatter segregation in the early 1960s. Civil Rights activists held sit-ins in segregated establishments, boycotted segregated buses, and held 'Freedom Rides' into segregated areas. Voter registration drives all over the south helped ensure that black voters would be represented. In 1963, 250,000 Americans – blacks, whites and others, including major religious leaders – participated in the March on Washington for civil rights. Dr King, awarded the Nobel Peace Prize, was assassinated by a white man in 1968. (In 1986 a public holiday was instituted to commemorate his life, the first time a black American has been thus honoured.)

Support from Jewish organizations, church and labour groups, students and others gave the civil rights movement an inter-racial character, which made it much more effective. Still, some whites fought back. Lynchings were the most dramatic form of retaliation. Riots broke out in many urban centres, and police brutality against protesters was widespread. Many African Americans, especially youth, thought the nonviolent style championed by King an inadequate response.

The Nation of Islam, a militant Black Muslim organization founded in the 1930s by dissenters from the Garvey movement and the mystical Moorish Science Temple, established temples throughout the north in the 1960s. It recruited many followers through the charismatic, controversial leadership of Malcolm X, although Malcolm later broke with the Nation. The Black Power movement was launched in 1966, advocating African American block voting and community control of institutions, organizations and resources. The Black Panther Party, both a community renewal programme and a Marxist revolutionary force, was also formed in 1966. These militant groups terrified governments and were opposed by many moderate blacks. In the late 1960s, like Martin Luther King, Malcolm X was assassinated. Over the next decade, many other activists died in suspicious circumstances, were imprisoned, succumbed to fatigue or went into exile.

However, in the early 1960s the shift towards equal rights gained support in the upper levels of government. The Voting Rights Act broke down entrenched and Byzantine regulations that prevented blacks from exercising their franchise. Blacks began to make gains in Congress and the Senate, and even bigger gains in regional and municipal politics. Affirmative action measures helped establish a sizeable African American middle class for the first time.

In the late 1960s and early 1970s, white and black children were 'bussed' to schools outside their immediate neighbourhoods to promote school desegregation. Resentment and resistance to change came to focus on this issue. There were heated protests, and many white children were removed from the public system. During the 1970s and 1980s, 'white flight' from many more-integrated cities to all-white suburbs left blacks and other minorities isolated in inner-city ghettos, whose tax bases and government infrastructure funding gradually declined. This was just one of the factors that the Civil Rights Movement could not anticipate, which would set back many of the victories of the 1960s.

The three decades after the advent of the Civil Rights Movement saw more progress by African Americans than the whole of the previous century combined. However, the living conditions of poorer African Americans – more than 40 per cent of the black population – have declined further. The writer Andrew Hacker describes the situation as tantamount to once again having two nations in the United States, 'black and white, separate, hostile, unequal' (a reference to Gunnar Myrdal's watershed 1940s race study).[3]

Anger over this situation exploded in 1992 with the 'Rodney King riots' in Los Angeles and other US cities. Rodney King was a black motorist arrested after a high-speed chase on 3 March 1991. An amateur videotape of the arrest showed several police officers beating a prone, helpless King dozens of times with batons, while other police officers stood by. The tape was broadcast worldwide on the Cable News Network. When on 29 April 1992 an all-white jury found the officers not guilty of brutality, blacks in Los Angeles took to the streets in fury. Latinos and some whites joined in the riot, which was echoed in unrest in other cities. Over the next three days, 60 people were killed in Los Angeles (LA), 3,000 injured and 15,000 arrested. Thousands of buildings were burned and stores were looted, mostly in minority neighbourhoods. The Rodney King verdict was widely compared to the Supreme Court's 1857 ruling in the *Dred Scott* case that 'black people have no rights that white people are bound to respect'. The federal government later retried four police officers on civil rights grounds, convicting three of the four and giving them minimum-security prison sentences.

Political and socioeconomic indicators and issues

The fundamental right of US democracy is the right to vote. Though granted in Reconstruction, the black vote has always been an elusive matter. Black registration is still low, as is participation of registered voters. Racially based redistricting has helped increase the clout of the black vote, but its future is now in doubt. On the other hand, the surge in voter registration brought about by the 1994 National Voter Registration Act may significantly increase black participation. African Americans remain massively under-represented in office, currently holding about 2 per cent of political offices across the country, and fewer at the highest levels.

While in the past many African Americans were loyal to the Republican Party, the party of Lincoln, today they overwhelmingly vote Democrat since Republicans are seen as a right-wing force, generally unconcerned with black voters. Some critics say blacks are now effectively unrepresented, because Democrats know they can count on black votes whether or not they advocate African American interests. However, individual African Americans have made gains on the national scene, most notably Jesse Jackson and Colin Powell. In

1991, Republican President George Bush chose the neo-conservative African American Justice Clarence Thomas for the Supreme Court.

Many major US cities, including New York, Chicago, Washington and Los Angeles, have had black mayors. African Americans are also well-represented on most large cities' councils. However, politics and funding have limited their attempts to make significant changes in the conditions of urban African Americans, and polls show that African Americans believe politicians from their community still face harsher treatment from their opposition and the media than do whites.

In non-electoral politics, the picture is bleaker. The NAACP has been plagued by internal divisions, and few new organizations or leaders have made an impact. The programme of separatism and black self-determination advocated by the Nation of Islam has galvanized some African Americans and alienated others. The Nation's outspoken leader, Louis Farrakhan, has been criticized for anti-Jewish and anti-Asian American remarks, sexism and homophobia, but the Nation has also had unmatched success in organizing community action and public protest among the black middle class. Farrakhan was the driving force behind the Million Man March on Washington of October 1995, a 'day of atonement' for black male responsibility, pride and self-determination that attracted around 900,000 supporters despite its open exclusion of women and gay men. Perhaps the most politically potent vehicles for African American protest and politics in the 1980s and 1990s have been rap music (or 'hip-hop') and the films of black directors. However, both have come under fire for glamourizing violence and drug abuse, as well as for misogyny, homophobia and obscenity.

Turning to socioeconomic indicators and issues, the statistics on black education are not promising.[4] The number of black males attending institutions of higher education has decreased significantly, and 1990 studies showed that under 16 per cent of African Americans had completed four or more years of college, compared to nearly 30 per cent of whites. One out of every three black children entering high school drops out, a rate twice as high as for white children. Although illiteracy among African Americans has consistently declined, at 1.6 per cent it is still four times higher than the white rate.

In many urban areas today public schools remain almost entirely black or white. Approximately two-thirds of African American children attend schools where pupils are predominantly from minority groups. Most of these schools are underfunded and overcrowded. Few African American families can afford the costs of private education, so black children are still faced with the prospect of inadequate education. Efforts at further desegregating schools or providing viable alternatives – for example high-quality 'magnet' schools that emphasize specialist subjects to attract both black and white students – have been set back by Supreme Court decisions ruling that states could not compel such efforts or be required to fund them.

In higher education, the 1960s saw African Americans gain greater access to colleges and universities, and to courses and programmes on black American and African cultures. However, these programmes have come under attack, as hostility to so-called 'political correctness' has mounted. Recent Supreme Court rulings have raised the spectre of 'reverse discrimination' in minority set-asides and scholarships for university admissions, and the University of California abolished affirmative action in admissions and hirings in July 1995. Government loans and scholarships have also been cut back. Along with the abandonment of employment equity legislation, declining access to education could result in fewer African Americans entering the middle classes in the future.

However, the 'Afrocentric' history and cultural movement of the 1980s promoted new enthusiasm for scholarship within the black community, focusing on black people's contributions to US and world history and civilization. A group of 'new black intellectuals' has also emerged in publishing and the media as spokespeople for African American thought and scholarship.

Approximately one-third of the black American population live at or below the poverty level, and one out of two African American children grows up in poverty. The unemployment rate for African Americans has consistently been at least twice that of whites since the Second World War. In 1990, blacks made up 11 per cent of the workforce and 22 per cent of the unemployed. Young black men, especially teenagers, encounter an even worse situation: 32 per cent were unemployed in 1990. The teenage motherhood rate is higher among young African American women than any other group, and 64 per cent of black children were born to single mothers in 1992. The black poverty rate is highest among single women with children.

Real income for black families has decreased by 20 per cent over the past ten years, with average black family income at about half the white level in 1995. A 1991 Urban Institute study found that African Americans are three times more likely than whites to encounter barriers to employment – including being refused the right to apply. Yet the Supreme Court has made a series of decisions since the late 1980s that make such discrimination difficult to challenge.

Some political leaders have put an emphasis on African American independent business and self-sufficiency as a way out of economic stagnation. Black businesses have been growing, but they are fragile and concentrated in service sectors (retail and restaurant). The black-run banks and savings institutions that have been important to community economic development were hard hit by the 1980s Savings and Loans crisis. Black businesses have difficulty getting loans from white-owned banks due to the practice of 'red-lining' – systematically refusing loans to minority districts. Even the wealthiest blacks were less likely in 1991 to receive loans than the poorest whites, despite federal regulations to the contrary.

Red-lining has also been exposed as common practice among mortgage bankers, real estate agents and insurance companies. Partially as a result, segregated housing and discrimination in rentals prevail across the USA, more than two decades after the 1968 Fair Housing Act. Urban sprawl has exacerbated the situation, and despite federal studies that said in 1991 African Americans encountered housing discrimination at least 56 per cent of the time, less than one-half of 1 per cent of all discrimination cases filed in the early 1990s were prosecuted by authorities. Public housing is mostly segregated by race, and for African American families this housing is consistently worse-maintained than for whites. Estimates also indicate that between 40 and 50 per cent of America's 3 million homeless are African American, meaning that about 4 per cent of the African American population is homeless. Shelters are few, and in many places their health and safety conditions, due to overcrowding, are intolerable.

In 1990, the life expectancy for African Americans was 69.7 years, while for white Americans it was 75.9. Infant mortality is particularly high, but in general health care for African Americans is disproportionately poor, a fact recognized in the Disadvantaged Minority Health Improvement Act of 1990. Due to poverty and high unemployment, African Americans are also under-insured for health care. African Americans are also at high risk for environmentally related sickness. Toxic waste dumping, waste incinerators, mixed industrial zoning, poor public sanitation and air pollution are all higher in black-dominated residential areas. African American children are two to three times more likely than their white counterparts to suffer from lead poisoning, and many African Americans work in unsafe conditions.

African Americans have higher rates of drug abuse than the general population, although as individuals they are more likely to abstain altogether than whites. They are also at high risk for mental illness, heart disease, cancer, AIDS and other major diseases, due to a cluster of factors, including level of education, poverty, stress, poor health care, pollution and family instability. During the 1980s and 1990s, addiction to crack (a smokeable cocaine derivative) has been one of the most severe and destabilizing health problems in the African American community. The cocaine use rate has been as high as 3 per cent among African Americans, and the intense high and quick addictive action of the drug is partially blamed for increases in prostitution, robbery, violence, pregnancy, urban decay and disease.

Violence is perhaps the greatest threat to African American health. Homicide is the leading cause of death for black males between 15 and 24 years old, mostly from gunshot wounds. One in 21 black men will be murdered, according to 1990 statistics. Black women are three times more likely to be killed than white women.[5]

African Americans are not only disproportionately victimized by crime; they also offend disproportionately. In the most serious crime, homicide, 54.7 per cent of the perpetrators identified in 1990 were black, and 'black-on-black' violence is a serious concern. Black crime rates, higher still than the already unusually high crime rate in the United States, have been exacerbated by teenage gang activity and drug-dealing in inner cities. Analysts generally concur that this is caused by the myriad social conditions discussed above. Partially as a result, but also due to the more severe application of the law to African Americans, blacks are imprisoned in numbers significantly out of proportion to their general numbers. For example, African Americans make up 15 per cent of users of crack cocaine, but 50 per cent of those incarcerated on crack-related charges. Penalties for crack use (more common in the black community) are more severe than those for cocaine use (more often a white phenomenon).

In 1995, 54 per cent of the US prison population was African American, compared to 13 per cent of the general population. One in three African American males between 20 and 29 years old was under penal supervision on any given day, and in some areas the rate was closer to one in two. A 1991 study found that 85 per cent of African American men could expect to be arrested at some point in their lives. For this reason, human rights abuses in the prison system – including overcrowding, which is endemic, violence at the hands of guards or between prisoners, segregation and other extreme punishments and high rates of AIDS and tuberculosis – have a disproportionate effect on African Americans.

Police abuse is another critical issue. The Rodney King case served as a flashpoint for a problem that was already much on the mind of African Americans. The case of ex-football player O.J. Simpson, charged by Los Angeles police with the murder of his wife, aroused similar sympathies. Many African Americans saw his acquittal as a vindication, especially after a key police investigator in the case was revealed as a racist.

Anti-black bias also affects the application of the death penalty. Killers of white victims are three times more likely to be sentenced to death than killers of black victims, and in 1995, 39 per cent of the Death Row population was black. In the early 1990s, the case of Mumia Abu-Jamal, an African American activist and journalist sentenced to death for the murder of a police officer in 1982, came to symbolize this issue. Jamal's supporters have objected that evidence was excluded from his trial and that his anti-police politics were used in the case against him. Mass protests and petitions from artists, writers, politicians and others around the world called for a new trial.

Poverty rates among African American women are more severe than among black men. Black women have also encountered discrimination and marginalization in white-dominated feminist movements.

Haitians

Besides the traditional African American community, the United States has been home in recent years to an increasing number of other black immigrants. Some come from war-torn African nations like Somalia; others, seeking economic improvement, come from Jamaica or Guyana and other Caribbean nations. Haitian refugees have endured particular troubles in the 1980s and 1990s that set them apart from other black Americans.

Because Haitian governments historically have been sponsored by the United States, Haitians have seldom been accepted as refugees. In 1981, President Ronald Reagan authorized the US coastguard to intercept and repatriate Haitians encountered on the high seas *en route* to the USA as illegal immigrants. The screening process admitted only 0.1 per cent as legitimate asylum seekers. In 1991 Haitian advocates filed suit, challenging this process under the Act and international law. The suit was but resulted in the screening process being to Guantanamo Bay military base in Cuba.

In 1992, because of a false scare over high AIDS rates in Haiti, HIV testing was added to the screening process. Those found positive were held without procedure for release or repatriation. A further suit in 1992 challenged conditions in the Guantanamo Bay camp – where ill refugees were held without medical treatment or adequate nutrition – as well as the discrimination represented by the fact that non-Haitian applicants were not detained according to HIV status. In May 1992, President George Bush shut down the screening process and ordered all interdicted Haitians repatriated, in contravention of the Refugee Act.

When Bill Clinton was elected later that year, he promised to re-examine the case, as Haitian boat people continued to arrive in huge numbers. After a series of reversals on the issue, in 1994 he agreed to process Haitians like other asylum seekers, and sought to relieve immigration pressure instead through US military intervention against the illegitimate government of Haiti. Some Haitians returned home after President Jean-Bertrand Aristide's reinstatement, while others applied to stay in the USA for economic reasons and out of fear of the continuing strength of military and terrorist forces in Haiti.

Haitians who fled their homeland because of opposition to the military junta have faced retribution from Haitian military-sponsored death squads operating in the USA. Despite appeals from the Haitian community, US officials have done little to investigate or prosecute offenders, and connections between these squads and the US Central Intelligence Agency have been exposed.

Some Haitians, like some Afro-Cubans, have also faced persecution for their practice of the Santeria faith, which involves ritual animal sacrifice. However, in 1993 the Supreme Court reversed a lower court ruling against Santeria practitioners saying that the government's legitimate concern for public health and animal welfare 'could be addressed by restrictions stopping far short of a flat prohibition of all Santeria practices'.

Haitians have also been particularly affected by the under-scrutinized practices of the US Immigration and Naturalization Service (INS). Even after the Guantanamo Bay refugee camps were closed, Haitians have been held in inadequate facilities in the USA with no clear indication of how long they would be detained. Some of these detention centres have been leased out to private contractors, who allowed conditions to degenerate to the point that riots ensued. Inmates of INS

...ecourse and are often ...mily and legal counsel.

... fastest-growing minorities ...90 census counted over 22 ...aking 8.9 per cent of the ...on, up from 19.5 million (5 per ... both figures probably undercount u... ...ted immigrants. About 61 per cent of Latinos are Mexican Americans, while 5 per cent come from Cuba, 13 per cent from Central and South America, 12 per cent from Puerto Rico and 9 per cent from other origins. Each of these groups favours nationally specific names over any general term, but 'Latino' has emerged as the most popular alternative. Most are Roman Catholic by upbringing, and a majority are bilingual Spanish-speakers.

Latinos have lived in what is now the southwestern USA for centuries. Over half of Mexican Americans live either in California or Texas, and most Cubans live in Florida, but there are now large groups in every urban centre. Mexican Americans are descended mostly from *mestizo* people of mixed Spanish and indigenous heritage, plus other European and African influences, as is the case for most of the population in Mexico. As individuals and as a group, Latinos are in part an indigenous minority, in part a conquered European minority and in part an immigrant group. Nevertheless, they are sometimes classified as 'white' in the black-and-white grid that makes up US racial politics and have thus experienced misunderstanding, and in some sense an identity crisis.

The Chicano movement of the 1960s was one response, as are current concepts of 'border consciousness' and 'living on the hyphen', a sort of internal multiculturalism. The move towards new syntheses has had political impact. Latinos joined with Native Americans to protest against the celebration of the 1992 quincentenary of Columbus's arrival in the Americas, and have joined with African Americans to protest against urban poverty and discrimination. New concepts of identity have had an energizing effect on Latino writers, artists and performers in recent decades, but political and economic successes have been fewer.

Mexican Americans

During the sixteenth century, many *mestizo* and some other Mexicans settled to farm and ranch in the mountain slopes and desert valleys of Texas, California, New Mexico and Arizona. Eventually much of the frontier was granted to settlers by royal decree, a decision confirmed by the Mexican government after its independence from Spain in 1821. The USA annexed Texas in 1845, then captured the remainder of the southwest in the Mexican–American War of 1846–8. Annexation was followed by the gold rush in California, which brought hordes of Anglo settlers. Conflict and discrimination became widespread. In several states, after initial peaceful coexistence, Spanish education and voting rights were cut off and were not restored until well into the twentieth century. The 1848 Treaty of Guadalupe Hidalgo guaranteed the safety of Mexican land grants, but 80 per cent of grant lands were lost to force, debt or legal manipulation.

Mexican Americans had to cope with becoming a dispossessed minority in their own lands, but the community remained fairly stable. The majority of the rural population was Spanish-speaking, and almost all Mexican Americans lived in rural areas in isolated and self-reliant *pueblos* (towns). The forces of the Mexican Revolution, in the early twentieth century, brought a flood of immigrants and new political currents to the USA. At the end of the Second World War, rural Mexicans (legal and illegal) flocked to the cities to take advantage of plentiful industrial jobs. They created *pueblos* within cities, called *barrios*. *Barrio* Latinos have benefited from strong social and family networks, but have been under-served by government services and outside employers, as well as suffering from internal rivalries that have undermined political unity.

In the early 1960s, unsuccessful efforts were made to reclaim the lands guaranteed in the Treaty of Guadalupe Hidalgo. The United Farm Workers union, led by Cesar Chávez, mounted innovative and effective campaigns against low wages, abuse and pesticide contamination of Mexican American workers in the fruit and vegetable farms of California. Later in the 1960s, the Chicano movement was born. Chicano, once a pejorative for 'Mexicano', was used by high school and college students in the *barrios* of California as a symbol of defiance against discrimination. The Chicano youth movement – including the militant Brown Berets – began to unite the *barrios* for improved living conditions, bilingual education and cultural pride. The movement led to an upsurge in cultural activity and new national organizations like the National Council of La Raza and the Mexican American Legal Defense and Education Fund. The Southwest

Voter Registration and Education Project helped to increase Latino participation in elections, leading to a small increase in Latino representation.

Cuban Americans

Cuban Americans are seen stereotypically as a powerful, conservative community, quite different from every other Latino group. While it is true that the first Cuban refugees after Fidel Castro's 1959 revolution were mostly upper class anti-communists given generous settlement aid by the US government, subsequent immigrants have not had the same advantages.

In the early 1980s, Fidel Castro began to permit small numbers of people to leave Cuba as a safety valve to political and economic tensions (partially caused by the US embargo). At the same time, the USA passed the 1980 Refugee Act, which severely limited the number of Cubans who could legally enter the county and put them on an equal footing with other prospective immigrants. In April 1980 Castro authorized the Mariel Boat Lift, and within months nearly 125,000 Cubans – 40 per cent of them Afro-Cubans – left Cuba. The Reagan and Bush administrations refused the 'Marielitos' immigration processing and thousands, including children, were placed in administrative detention by the Immigration and Naturalization Service (INS) for years after their arrival. A few were eventually deported and the rest remained 'on parole', their residency status indeterminate. Another exodus in 1994 forced President Bill Clinton to negotiate with Castro to allow 20,000 Cuban refugees to enter the USA annually, provided that the tide of migrants was stemmed.

Each group of Cuban refugees has been poorer than the last. Although they sometimes benefit from the prosperity of Cuban enclaves, especially in Miami, they have also been exploited by employers, even within the Cuban community. In 1990, 16.9 per cent of Cuban Americans lived below the poverty line, with women refugees in especially dire straits. In addition, those who disagree with the Miami establishment's hard-right anti-Castro position have a difficult time. Assaults, bombings, censorship and blackmail have been used as weapons against such dissidents. However, the Cuban American population is changing to include more economic and fewer political refugees, and there are signs that the boundaries of accepted opinion within it may widen.

Central and South Americans

Growing numbers of Central and South Americans have joined the US Latino community since the mid-1970s, including Peruvians and Colombians. Dominicans have also come in significant numbers, as have many Salvadorans and Guatemalans seeking refuge from repression. The latter groups have not been accepted as bona fide refugees because of US support for Central American military regimes. These people have been subjected to INS detention, or must work and live as undocumented residents. Most are poor and without political rights. Refugees who attempt to speak out or otherwise aid the opposition in their home countries have found themselves under police investigation. During the 1980s, for example, the Committee in Support of the People of El Salvador was infiltrated and undermined by the Federal Bureau of Investigation.

Political and socioeconomic indicators and issues

Numbers, visibility and Chicano consciousness brought Latinos into the spotlight in the late 1970s. Yet during the 1980s many prominent Latinos (including city mayors and two state governors) slipped from prominence due to scandal and opposition. Latino electoral participation has remained low and Latino interests have been represented by a select few political figures nationally. Although there is a Congressional Hispanic Caucus, and there have been a small number of high-level Latino appointments under the Reagan, Bush and Clinton administrations, Latino officials number less than 1 per cent of the national total.

The Latino population is on average 10 years younger than the general population, and the average household is larger. Latinos in general have very low rates of education (fewer than 60 per cent graduate from high school, according to 1991 figures), and health services to Latino communities are ranked the poorest in the USA. Workplaces and communities of low-waged Latinos tend to have more hazardous environmental and safety conditions than the average. Latinos are now 90 per cent urban (compared with 75 per cent of all Americans) and are often lumped in with African Americans as part of the urban 'underclass'; on most measures they register somewhere between whites and blacks in socio-economic status. However, the extended family and social networks of the *barrios*, while they may hinder social mobility, have kept Latino neighbourhoods from eroding to the same level of anomie and illegality found in African American ghettos.

Anti-immigrant sentiments, the shift from manufacturing to service jobs and urban decay have undermined Latino economic and social stability. In 1990, 28 per cent lived below the poverty line, compared to 13 per cent of whites. The growth rate of the Latino population has led to conflict with other communities over urban space and influence. Deadly wars between Latino and African American youth gangs are one symptom of these conflicts, and more Latinos than blacks participated in the 1992 Los Angeles riots. Latinos experience many of the same problems with police that African Americans do, as well as high levels of unfounded persecution by immigration agents.[6]

Latinas (Latino women) tend to work, marry and bear children younger than their white counterparts. As a result, there is a smaller wage gap between men and women in the Latino community than in the workforce overall, but there are also many teenage Latina mothers, many exploited Latina sweatshop workers, and many Latinas with health problems, including AIDS. Chicana activists have criticized the Latino male culture of *machismo* as institutionalized sexism, analyzing Latina problems as a nexus of class, race and gender issues. Partly as a result, over the past twenty years, Latina organizers, members of Congress and artists have emerged in equal numbers to men. Latinas still face pressure to fulfil traditional roles, but there may be greater recognition now of their right to participate in public and economic life.

Along with immigration, language is one of the issues most commonly used to raise educational, occupational and political barriers against Latinos. The vast majority of Latinos in the USA speak English, and many second- or third-generation Latinos speak only English. Those who simply prefer Spanish or speak with strong accents may face discrimination. Spanish is widely used in schools, business, advertising and media, but language rights are not protected by the US constitution. Recognition of language barriers in the 1960s and 1970s motivated federal legislation for bilingual ballots and bilingual education in areas where numbers warrant, and it is now possible in many areas to use Spanish in courts and other government services. But there is no guaranteed right to these services except in criminal proceedings. When employer discrimination against Spanish-speakers is challenged, courts have generally ruled that employers are within their rights.

Latino communities have debated the goals of bilingualism, but this debate has been eclipsed in recent years by an Anglo backlash. By 1995, 22 states had passed laws declaring English their official language – including California, which was 40 per cent Spanish-speaking – and 38 members of Congress were sponsoring official English legislation nationally. The grassroots 'English Only' or 'US English' movement has had a chilling effect on Anglo–Latino relations, and threatens to eliminate bilingual ballots and education or require English proficiency tests before naturalization. In 1992 the writer Carlos Fuentes commented that declaring English the official language of a state like California 'means only one thing': that English is no longer the official language.[7]

Immigration and the Mexican border

Throughout the twentieth century, workers have flooded from rural (and later urban) Mexico and Central and South America to the US south-west, legally and illegally, across the Mexican border. Some are 'commuters', others temporary residents, and others stay permanently. These people have made up a huge cheap labour force for US employers, often working for less than the minimum wage. The Bracero programme (1942–64) brought in Mexicans for seasonal agriculture; many absconded to work in industry. During the recession after the Korean War, the government launched 'Operation Wetback' (*wetback* is derogatory slang for Mexican immigrants), which deported some 2 million people in 1954 and 1955. In recent decades, the human traffic has exceeded 9 million people a year – though many of these are the same people crossing back and forth – and 1 million 'undocumenteds' are deported each year.

By the 1980s, an anti-immigration fever was building, despite evidence that immigrants create more jobs and revenue than they drain. The Federation for American Immigration Reform led the demand to close the border. In Texas and California, vigilante groups prowled the border to apprehend and assault migrants. INS agents became more brutal, often concentrating on language and appearance more than on documentation. In 1986, the Simpson-Rodino Immigration Reform and Control Act greatly expanded the size and powers of the Border Patrol and imposed heavy sanctions against employers of illegal labour. (It also granted amnesty to a certain number of undocumented workers, although their chances of achieving citizenship depend on a screening process that will take years to complete.) A General Accounting Office 1990 study found that 20 per cent of employers responded by instituting anti-Latino hiring practices, and two 1992 studies found that beatings, unjustified shootings, torture and sexual abuse by border guards have escalated unchecked.[8]

A steel wall has been constructed along parts of the border and there have been calls for a national identity card and other measures that would put all Americans' civil rights at risk, especially Latinos'. The passage of Proposition 187 in California in a 1994 referendum has deprived illegal immigrants of rights to education, social assistance and medical services. None of these measures have decreased immigration. They have only increased the misery of undocumented immigrants, 66 per cent of them Latinos, and the racial polarization of the southwestern USA.

Puerto Ricans

Small numbers of Puerto Ricans started moving to the US mainland at the beginning of the twentieth century (see also **Puerto Rico** in **CENTRAL AND SOUTH AMERICA AND THE CARIBBEAN**). Migration expanded after the Second World War, encouraged by both governments to even out labour markets. The migrant population quadrupled between 1940 and 1950, and by 1960 it was 887,000, with about a quarter born on the mainland. Return migration became an important factor in the 1970s, with tens of thousands of USA-based Puerto Ricans going back to the island to retire, work or raise children without the burden of discrimination. With cutbacks in federal aid, the flow reversed again in the 1980s. Although there were many second- and third-generation Puerto Ricans among the 2.5 million in the USA in 1990, two-thirds were island-born. Initially concentrated in New York, Puerto Ricans still form a large part of the population there, but now at least half of the Puerto Rican population has spread out across the north-east (especially to Chicago and the state of New Jersey) and into southern states such as Texas, California and Florida. Pre-1950s Puerto Rican migrants tended to be skilled male workers, but since then most have been unskilled labourers, evenly split between men and women.

Puerto Ricans are US citizens but face racial and language barriers that prevent their enjoyment of an advantage over other immigrants. They only recently gained access to bilingual education, and the future of these programmes is in question. For this reason – as well as discrimination, low-quality schools, family poverty and resistance to assimilation – the Puerto Rican education level in the USA is worse than that of almost any other urban group. In the 1950s and 1960s, Puerto Rican migrant employment rates were better than the US average, but by 1990 (male) factory and (female) garment-industry mainstay opportunities were reduced by structural change and competition from new immigrant groups. Puerto Ricans' employment in New York dropped between 1970 and 1990 more than any other group's. The average wage of employed Puerto Rican men also dropped. In 1990, nearly 40 per cent of US Puerto Ricans lived in poverty. This minority also has the highest rate of single motherhood of any group in the United States. Only 52 per cent of Puerto Rican families are headed by married couples, compared with 83 per cent of whites' and 74 per cent of Mexican Americans'. Single motherhood is the single greatest risk category for family poverty in the USA, as opposed to Puerto Rico where common-law marriage is the norm.

Puerto Ricans have also been hurt by legislative changes. The Immigration Reform and Control Act produced hiring discrimination against all Latinos in the USA by employers who feared immigration service raids. Further, from 1976 to 1990, federal contributions to New York's budget dropped from 22 per cent to 9 per cent. The concomitant reduction in community services eliminates aid Puerto Ricans could have used to cope with social breakdown. Political redistricting based on the 1990 census may help Puerto Ricans gain more of a voice in these decisions, if it is not reversed by recent Supreme Court decisions. So far, however, Puerto Rican migrants' voting and electoral success rates are very low. Groups like the Puerto Rican Legal Defense and Education Fund and the National Council of La Raza have organized to enhance Puerto Ricans' political clout. Representation, bilingualism, education, community development, housing, jobs, childcare and health are among their prime concerns.

Asian-Pacific Americans

'Asian-Pacific American' or 'Asian American' are pan-ethnic terms designating the many communities of Asian immigrants and their descendants in the USA. These terms have arisen in response to the common discrimination and immigrant experiences the different communities share, although specific group designations, such as 'Korean American', are also used. Asian-Pacific Americans are the fastest growing group in the USA, due mostly to immigration. The 1990 census counted over 7 million Asian-Pacific Americans, making up 2.9 per cent of the US population. This is up from only 877,934 in 1960 and an increase of more than 100 per cent since 1980. By the year 2000, the Asian-Pacific American population is expected to reach nearly 10 million.

The longest-established Asian-Pacific American communities are Chinese, Japanese, Filipino and Asian Indian, with the first two predominant. The first wave of immigrants came in the 1840s, when young men from China, Japan and the Philippines were recruited as cheap manual labour on the west coast and in Hawai'i. Chinese and Filipinos worked on sugar plantations in Hawai'i, and all three groups worked as miners, railroad workers, agricultural labour, fishery workers and light industrial labour in California and the northwest. Many went on to run small businesses and to run their own farms, until they were prohibited from owning land by the Alien Land Act of 1913.

Early Asian-Pacific Americans faced slander, exploitative working conditions, segregation laws and political disenfranchisement. When the need for extra workers receded, bills like the Chinese Exclusion Act of 1882 and the Asian exclusionary zone legislation of 1917 cut off immigration from China and India. The Filipino and Japanese American populations continued to grow, however, and despite discrimination many achieved a modest prosperity over the next several decades.

With the outbreak of the Second World War, Japanese Americans – even citizens with deep family roots in the USA – became suspect as spies or saboteurs. There was no substance to these charges, yet Japanese American communities of the western states were subjected to an internment order in February 1942 and moved to prison camps in the interior. Conditions in the camps were harsh, with a total of 110,000–120,000 people interned, two-thirds of them US citizens. In December 1944 the Supreme Court belatedly ruled internment unconstitutional, and most detainees were released in 1945, although the camps were not closed until early 1946.

While Japanese Americans suffered greatly during the war, the positions of other Asian-Pacific communities improved because their countries were allied with the USA. The virulent racism of earlier decades abated somewhat, paving the way for a 1965 revision of immigration law that led to a massive intake of Vietnamese and other Indochinese refugees after 1975. Before long over 40 per cent of new US immigrants were Asian-Pacific applicants. Asian-Pacific Americans became a majority-immigrant populace, while for much of the century most Asians in the USA had been born there. By 1990, there was near-parity between numbers of Filipino Americans and Chinese Americans (with larger numbers from Hong Kong and Taiwan than in the past), with Indochinese, Korean and Asian Indian groups gradually overtaking the Japanese in numbers and youthfulness. The Korean and Indochinese populations are now the fastest growing, while the Japanese and Chinese proportion of the community is decreasing.

Although there are large Asian-Pacific communities across the USA, the majority are located in the west, particularly Hawai'i (where they are the largest single group) and California. Asian Indians are concentrated in New York. Ninety per cent of all Asian-Pacific groups live in large cities, making them the most urban population in the USA.

Socioeconomic indicators

Asian-Pacific Americans are visible in all strata of American society, except perhaps the highest elites. Some live in enclaves, for example New York and San Francisco's 'Chinatowns' or Los Angeles's 'Little Tokyo', although Koreans, Indians and Japanese tend to be more dispersed than other Asian-Pacific communities. Apart from the Indochinese, they have high marriage rates, and most except the Japanese are youthful populations. Asian-Pacific Americans are active in all occupations in the USA, usually with average-or-better rates of employment. Koreans run many convenience stores in large cities, and have entered medicine in large numbers. Asian Indians are prominent in academia, technical professions and the grocery and motel businesses. Many Japanese Americans work in sales and management. The Chinese and Filipino populations are split between the skilled professions and low-wage manual labour and service jobs, though many Chinese now also work in small businesses. The first group of Vietnamese refugees in 1975 have generally done well educationally and in business. Later refugees, mostly farmers, fishers and small traders, have lacked the language, skills and capital to reach the same levels. Probably the worst off are the smaller communities from Samoa, Laos and Cambodia.

Today's image of Asian-Pacific Americans as an educationally and economically successful 'model minority' is based in reality but distorts the truth. In 1990, the median family income for Asian-Pacific Americans was US $42,250, the highest for any US group (the median for whites was US $36,920). High school and college completion rates for Asian-Pacific Americans were 82 and 35 per cent, respectively, compared to 80 and 22 per cent for non-Hispanic whites.

This success is usually explained in cultural terms – a high premium put on education by Asian families, a strong family-based work ethic, powerful group support networks, and so on.[9]

However, these images conceal several other facts. The family median income rate is deceptive because Asian-Pacific American families tend to have more family members in the workforce than other groups. The per capita income of Asian-Pacific Americans in 1990 was less than for whites: US $13,420 compared to US $15,260; and their poverty rate was 11 per cent, 3 per cent higher than whites'. Many poorer Asians – often Chinese, Thai or Indochinese illegals – work in urban sweatshops at below minimum wage. In 1995, it was discovered that clothing companies were being supplied by a compound-style factory complex staffed by illegal Thai women secretly held as slaves. In addition, wide gaps occur between different Asian-Pacific groups. Indochinese communities, dominated by refugees, have a high-school completion rate of only 35 per cent. Incomes follow much the same pattern – in Los Angeles in 1993, 25 per cent of Vietnamese and 45 per cent of other Indochinese lived below the poverty line, as did 24 per cent of Pacific Islanders, while few Japanese or Koreans did.

The 'model minority' image seems positive, but many Asian-Pacific Americans object that it denies their diversity and tends to pit Asians against other minorities. Even to the extent that the stereotype is accurate, it comes at the price of high pressure and long hours of study or work that may lead to depression and anxiety, especially for young people. The success myth also implies that Asians do not experience disadvantage and discrimination, which is patently untrue. For example, Asians are admitted to higher education at a lower rate than whites with the same qualifications, and when they graduate they are paid less than whites with the same education. Asian-Pacific students who have language troubles seldom receive bilingual education or remedial help, which is one reason they gravitate to scientific disciplines. A 'glass ceiling' also seems to limit the earnings and promotion opportunities of Asian-Pacific Americans in large companies; they hold less than 0.5 per cent of top management positions. Asians are also the targets of more bias-related harassment and violence than other urban minorities.

Increasing immigration has also left Asians open to the vagaries of US refugee policy. Although the USA has sometimes been generous to refugees – for example, Vietnamese and Indochinese after 1975, and Chinese students who had been involved in Tiananmen Square – the Clinton administration in 1993 enlisted Mexican and Honduran officials in a campaign to intercept Chinese 'boat people' who were leap-frogging from China to Pacific islands to the USA. Hundreds were repatriated and several died in the process. Though the operation was legal (because neither Mexico nor Honduras is a signatory to the Geneva Convention on Refugees) it contradicted the spirit of the USA's international commitments and angered the Chinese American community. Several of those deported were known to have credible asylum claims. Asian-Pacific Americans, like Latinos, have also been subject to immigration department raids on their workplaces.

Political and social developments

In the late 1960s, Asian-Pacific Americans became involved in the civil rights and student movements. This generation formed professional organizations, community service agencies and political interest groups that fought for bilingual education, Asian Studies programmes in universities, multilingual voting ballots and better working conditions in the garment and restaurant sectors where poorer Asians worked.

The other major issue was Japanese Americans' fight for redress for internment. Though some compensation had been given to victims of internment after the war, and over the next decade Japanese Americans were restored to all the normal rights of citizenship, Japanese Americans felt that the racism and injustice of the action had never been fully recognized. They formed political organizations, lobbied, filed court cases and appealed to public sympathy for decades. In August 1988, Congress and President Ronald Reagan offered a formal apology and US $20,000 per person to each of the 60,000 surviving internees – about US $1.25 billion in all.

The murder of Vincent Chin, a Chinese American man, in a Detroit bar in 1982 has become the archetypal case of violence against Asian-Pacific Americans. His assailants were white auto workers who took Chin for Japanese, accused Chin's 'people' of destroying the American auto industry and beat him to death with a baseball bat. They were sentenced to probation and a fine. This case, along with later attacks by gangs and individuals against Asians, rallied Asian-Pacific Americans to campaign against bigotry and racist violence. Some of the backlash against increasing Asian-Pacific American visibility has come from other minorities. The Los Angeles riots and controversies in New York in the early 1990s illustrated that resentment against Korean storekeepers and other Asian business people, expressed in attacks on and boycotts of Asian businesses by African American and Latino consumers, had became commonplace.

To counter the misunderstanding that leads to violence, Asian-Pacific Americans are increasingly organizing in concert with other minority groups around immigration, racism, sexism, the environment and other issues. Asian-Pacific organizations have also been formed to protest against misrepresentation and exclusion in media and the arts. Electoral representation is another issue. Although some Asian-Pacific American politicians in the north-west have triumphed at state and local levels (especially in Hawai'i), only the Japanese have fared well in the Senate and Congress. With increasing numbers and 'Pan-Asian' politicization, this situation may change.

Arab and other Middle Eastern Americans

No single term encompasses the several million Americans of Middle Eastern/West Asian descent. Although they share broadly similar histories of immigration and reception in the USA, their origins, faiths, languages and cultures are diverse. Many would not necessarily consider themselves a 'minority', preferring to see themselves as part of the mainstream, but are concerned about recognition of their communities. Some have proposed that an official Arab American category be used by the US Census and other agencies.

There were reportedly between 1 million and 3 million Arab Americans in the USA in 1995, 82 per cent of them US citizens and 63 per cent born in the USA. (The 1990 census counted some 870,000, widely believed to be an undercount.) They resided across the country, but one-third lived either in Michigan (especially the Detroit area), New York or California. Immigrants from the Arabic-speaking countries arrived in the USA in three distinct waves. The first, between 1890 and 1920, brought over 250,000 people from what was then Greater Syria and other regions, mostly Christian peasants seeking economic opportunity. The second wave came after the Second World War and the creation of Israel, when tens of thousands of Palestinians emigrated to the USA. After 1965, when prejudicial immigration laws were reformed, there was a third wave of Arab immigrants, numbering about 250,000. The second and third waves were about 60 per cent Muslim and often highly educated, constituting a 'brain drain' from Palestine, Egypt, North Africa, Iraq, Yemen and other parts of the Arab world. North African Arab Americans, Muslim and non-Muslim, are increasing in number, and share concerns both with other Arab Americans and with African Americans.

By the late 1980s, the USA cut back the number of Middle Eastern immigrants it accepted. Many recent immigrants are alienated by prevailing attitudes and have limited contact with longer-established, more assimilated Arab American communities. Linguistic barriers have also blocked their social and economic advancement. On average, however, Arab Americans in the 1990s are better educated, more prosperous and more politically active than the average American.[10]

In the 1980s, Iran became one of the top 10 source countries of US immigration, although by the early 1990s it had become more difficult for Iranians to obtain visas. Many came as students in the 1960s and 1970s, but most arrived after the Iranian Revolution. A plurality are Muslims and supporters of the former Shah, but many left because they were members of leftist opposition movements, non-Islamic faiths or oppressed ethnic groups. The total number of Iranian Americans is unclear: estimates in 1993 ranged from 200,000 to over 1 million. The largest Iranian population centre is in Los Angeles, but New York City and Washington DC also have large communities. Many of the immigrants were members of the upper classes in Iran, and on average they are extremely well educated. Half the US Iranian population is self-employed. However, many were never wealthy, and the process of moving to the USA has caused considerable financial hardship and personal pain.[11] Open hostility between the US and Iranian governments has also raised problems for the Iranian American community. The 1979–80 hostage crisis at the US embassy in Iran, in particular, led to widespread harassment, violence and discrimination.

Armenians fled in significant numbers to the USA in reaction to the genocide of 1915–23, and immigrants from Armenia and its diaspora continue to arrive. Estimates of their total numbers ranged up to one million in 1992. Turkey was also a significant source of immigrants in the early twentieth century, and several thousand people came to the USA from Turkey each year after 1960, many of them Kurdish. Since the mid-1960s, some 80,000 US immigrants have arrived from Israel, and many more Israelis have come as students. They have not been entirely welcomed by US Jewish communities, among whom leaving Israel is sometimes seen as a betrayal. Other migrants during the 1980s and 1990s, often seeking US refugee status, have included Afghans, Azerbaijanis and Bosnians, of whom only a small portion have been admitted.

Political and social issues

Middle Eastern immigrant communities are often lumped together by US politicians and the general public as 'Arabs'. Persians and even non-Middle East groups like South Indians and Pakistanis have shared the brunt of widespread anti-Arab (and anti-Iranian) prejudice. Arab Americans and other Middle Eastern people have been the targets of repeated FBI investigation and random violence since the early 1970s, and each US confrontation with a Middle Eastern country is followed by an outbreak of hatred. During the 1991 Gulf War, hundreds of anti-Arab actions, including arson, bombings, assault and attempted murder, took place across the country. In 1985, Alex Odeh, a regional director of the American-Arab Anti-Discrimination Committee (ADC) was killed by a bomb trip-wired to his office door, to little government or media reaction. In 1995, when a federal building in Oklahoma was bombed, government officials and media blamed the event on Arabs or Muslims for days, causing a rash of violence, until the FBI charged members of a white anti-government militia. Few attackers have ever been prosecuted for anti-Arab acts.

Since the late 1970s, Arab Americans and Arab Canadians have sometimes been subject to harassment at border crossings, and the USA has repeatedly sought to deport politically active Arab visitors or immigrants as 'terrorist supporters', even though they have not been convicted of any crime. Negative stereotypes of Middle Eastern characters and of Islam are common in US film and television, and in radio and newspaper commentaries. Civil rights groups have drawn attention to these representations, with some success, but the stereotypes persist in popular US culture.

The ADC and several other Arab groups have been highly visible in recent years as critics of bias in US foreign and domestic policy, as well as in public life. Many Arab American individuals have achieved political prominence, mostly from the assimilated 'first wave', including members of Congress, senators, cabinet members, state governors and municipal officials. Non-Arab groups have organized more around internal professional, academic and religious ties.

Middle Eastern women are politically and professionally engaged, but in some groups, particularly Muslim ones, their workforce participation is limited by cultural tradition. However, the US government and anti-Arab interests have exaggerated both the 'oppression' of Muslim women and the 'liberation' of American women, particularly as a political tool during the Gulf War. Muslim women have been harassed for wearing traditional dress, and in some schools and other institutions it is prohibited. Middle Eastern American women have complained of marginalization in such debates, particularly in feminist forums, but have gained visibility, for example at the 1994 Cairo Conference on Population and Development and at the 1995 Beijing World Conference on Women.[12]

Native Americans

Native Americans, the indigenous people of what is now the mainland USA, are not a homogeneous group but members of hundreds of nations with different linguistic, social, cultural and economic traits. The 1990 census counted 1,959,000 Native Americans (including Native Hawai'ians, Inuit and Alaska Natives), or 0.79 per cent of the population, although not all of these people are recognized as Native by the US government. Native Americans live throughout the USA, especially in the rural west, and most often speak English or their own traditional language. The majority were converted to Christianity in early colonial times, but some have always maintained traditional religious practices, and traditional spirituality has experienced a revival in recent decades. Native Americans are also commonly called American Indians (a misnomer of historic proportions but a prevalent one), or by specific national designations such as Mohawk, Creek, Chippewa and Hopi. Recognized nations ('tribes' in official parlance) live on reserved lands of wildly varying sizes and populations.

The Bureau of Indian Affairs (BIA), the federal department supervising Native Americans, deals with over 500 reservations in mainland USA, but more than a hundred other groups identify themselves as Native American and are not officially recognized, a question of survival for some groups. Many people who consider themselves Native have less than the BIA's 'blood quantum' of one-quarter Native ancestry, and so are not included in population counts or BIA services. Further, half of the Native American population do not receive direct BIA service, because they live in cities and towns, largely integrated with the general population. The US government has a financial interest in keeping the numbers of recognized Native Americans low, but critics say the right of self-identification is evident in other minorities' treatment and essential to Native sovereignty. In the past quarter-century, though the US government has restored limited recognition of Native sovereignty, government–Native relations are perhaps best described as those of internal neo-colonialism.[13]

From conquest to 'termination' to self-determination

Native American nations were established in the present-day United States for thousands of years before European colonization. Estimates of the pre-contact population range between 3 million and 12 million people, living in over 600 different societies. Each region had nations with distinct cultures, languages and lifestyles – from nomadic hunting bands in arid regions to large agricultural settlements on the coasts. Common elements included complex social structures based on ceremonial and subsistence roles, communal stewardship of resources, collective decision-making (one of the models for US democracy) and a visionary spiritual tradition that emphasized history, ancestry and reverence for the land.

The first European conquerors were the Spanish, who invaded Mexico and the south-west in the late sixteenth century and for a time enslaved indigenous people there. The French and Dutch arrived in the seventeenth century, followed by the British. In most cases, initial relations were friendly, but with increased immigration and self-sufficiency by the 1630s, colonists began to covet and invade Native land, and attempt to impose European religion and culture on Native Americans. The Europeans had a devastating effect, bringing previously unknown diseases that wiped out whole Native American populations, including smallpox, syphilis and influenza. Over-hunting and land depletion caused famines. When negotiation was inconvenient, the Europeans used their superior weapons to force Natives off their own land. Native bands were divided and manipulated during wars between colonial powers.

After independence, Congress signed treaties with the surviving nations, recognizing and guaranteeing their title to lands remaining – the core of the 'nation to nation' relationship Native Americans still struggle to revitalize today. The constitution grants the federal government exclusive jurisdiction over relations with Native Americans. From that point until 1975, government policy alternated between eradicating the 'Indian Problem' through extermination/assimilation, and paternalistic programmes providing services and limited autonomy to reservation dwellers.

In the nineteenth century, Natives were herded from their lands to reservations, sometimes hundreds of miles away. Thousands died in such forced marches. Broken treaties, land frauds and military attacks were common. Some tribes responded with armed resistance, particularly in the 'Indian Wars' of the 1880s, but at best achieved temporary stalemates. In 1887, the General Allotment Act (or 'Dawes Act') nulled tribal land holdings, assigning each Native American 160 acres 'in trust', while the rest was sold. In all, 90 million acres of land were seized and the communal property system was destroyed. As documented in the Meriam Report of 1928, Native Americans on and off reservations were left destitute and prone to suicide, alcoholism and mental illness; housing and health conditions were abysmal. Cultures, languages and families were lost. In 1900, the total Native American population of the USA had fallen from several million to 237,000. This figure is often cited as evidence that policy on Native American peoples through most of US history was ethnocidal.

Outrage over the Meriam Report prompted the administration of President Franklin Roosevelt to attempt an 'Indian New Deal'. The Indian Reorganization Act (IRA) became law in 1934 and was accepted by 191 tribes. It recognized limited sovereignty for Native American tribes and mandated elected councils to assume partial control over reservations. Monetary aid accompanied the new structures, as did on-reserve education and health care. Native religions were decriminalized. In 1946, the Indian Claims Commission was established to deal with outstanding land claims. Critics such as the American Indian Movement (AIM) point out that IRA reforms were imposed, often by underhanded manipulation of the referendum process, regardless of tribes' own traditional systems. (Several councils' first acts were to provide US companies with access to their resources.) Later, IRA structures fostered conflicts and even violence between council supporters and traditionalists. But they were the first step made in decades towards greater self-determination.

In the 1950s, Congress ordered that Native Americans should be cut off as soon as possible from all federal responsibility and forced to assimilate into white society. By 1960, 61 Native American tribes had been 'terminated'. Development projects were dropped, loans frozen and federal services cut off. Termination threats spurred the first national Native organization, the National Congress of American Indians, and many new Native American leaders who had gained some experience of white politics in military service. They pressured government to halt the termination process, and by 1960 it unofficially stopped. In 1964, the Economic

Opportunity Act gave Natives access to funds not controlled by the BIA, which helped launch businesses on some reservations. In 1968, the Indian Civil Rights Act ceased the termination policy, removed Native Americans from the jurisdiction of states, and set out the intention of involving Natives more directly as BIA employees.

Native American cultural nationalism had begun to emerge by the mid-1960s. The Native American Rights Fund organized tribes to pursue land claims and federal recognition. The National Indian Youth Council and, later, AIM exposed broken treaties and corruption among BIA agents and IRA-style councils, advocating traditionalist politics and Native civil rights. AIM's demonstrations, occupations and armed militancy were met with brutal repression by BIA and FBI agents, with tragic results in standoffs at Pine Ridge and Wounded Knee. But this upsurge in Native visibility did much to raise US and international awareness of Native American rights and to put sovereignty on top of the Native agenda. In 1970, partly to head off AIM and its supporters, President Richard Nixon began to promote self-determination for Native American nations. The Indian Self-Determination Act of 1975 affirmed the rights of recognized tribes and allowed tribal governments to contract for federal funding to run former BIA services (education, health care, economic development and child welfare), although it did not provide for new programmes and standards defined by Natives themselves.

The history of Native America since 1975 is more fractured. By 1980, more than half the Native population had been urbanized, and to some degree assimilated, under the 1956 Relocation Act funds administered by the BIA. Meanwhile, political battles were fought to arrest or reverse the damage done by centuries of marginalization, and urban Natives advanced 'pan-Indianism'. The revival of traditionalism and new self-determination structures have facilitated an unprecedented unity among Native Americans, and unprecedented support from non-Natives – especially during Native-led protests against the 1992 Columbus quincentennial ('500 Years of Oppression') and in the environmentalist movement. Native Americans have also emerged as leaders defending indigenous rights worldwide, with an active role in the establishment of the UN Working Group on Indigenous Populations in 1982 and in the formulation of the Draft Declaration on the Rights of Indigenous Peoples.

Socioeconomic, legal and cultural issues

While Native American income relative to whites' has risen dramatically in recent decades, they still have the highest unemployment rate of any minority group – usually about twice the national average – and nearly 60 per cent of those with jobs work for tribal or US government agencies. On some reservations the unemployment rate is as high as 90 per cent. One-third of the Native population lives in poverty. Reserve housing is still substandard, often without electricity, indoor plumbing or refrigeration, except in the wealthiest nations. Although Native life expectancy has risen dramatically in recent decades, it is still the lowest of any group in the USA. The Native American population has a high incidence of communicable diseases, including tuberculosis and AIDS, and fatal infectious illnesses. The ratio of health-care providers to patients is lower on reserves than in any other community. Violence, drunkenness and despair are commonplace. Suicide and accidents (often drug or alcohol related) are the two biggest causes of Native American deaths. Reservations are also used as dumping grounds for toxic or nuclear waste. Lead poisoning, landfill sites, water pollution from nearby industries, cancers caused by nuclear weapons testing (nearly all of it on Native lands) and many more environmental problems plague Native communities.

Natives also have the lowest high school and university graduation rates in the USA, partly because education has been an assimilationist tool since colonial times. Programmes such as bicultural education and Native-run schools under the Indian Education Act of the early 1970s have improved the situation, but only marginally – in part because of a shortage of qualified Native American teachers. Most Native children attend public schools. The Tribally Controlled Community College Assistance Act of 1978 was partially successful, establishing Native-run colleges and increasing grants for Native students, but its funding has been drastically cut back over the 1980s and 1990s. In 1995 the Office of Indian Education was threatened with closure by Congress.

Economic development efforts on reservations have been limited by issues like jurisdiction, financing, training and isolation, by internal disputes over direction and sometimes by obstruction by non-Native opponents and governments. Nevertheless, the 1980s and 1990s saw an upsurge in programmes for economic self-sufficiency, including mineral exploration, industrial parks, forestry, fisheries, hotels, agriculture, tobacco sales, casinos and high-stakes gambling on reserves. These enterprises could dramatically alter Natives' economic position, if they are allowed sufficient control over their administration, land and resources. However, each Native economic success is likely to meet with local resentment, especially when Native Americans use the legal benefits of tribal sovereignty to their advantage. Hunting and fishing disputes in the north-west and controversies over casino operations in the north-east are typical mid-1990s examples.

Poverty, dispossession and drug abuse have made crimes of violence 10 times more frequent on reservations than among the population as a whole. The Native population in prisons is twice their proportion in the general population. Attempts at Native policing and reconciliation models have had some success at coping with Native offenders, but have been obstructed by jurisdictional issues. Suspicion of unfair law enforcement is widespread, and there are indications of political motives at work. The case of Leonard Peltier, a Native activist convicted of involvement in the deaths of two FBI agents in a confrontation at Ogala reservation in 1973, is indicative. Over the years, the evidence against Peltier has been discredited, and Native Americans widely believe that the AIM leader was framed for his political activities, but he has consistently been refused a new trial. Several other reserves have complained of the same kind of police harassment that led to Peltier's arrest, and other prisoners have asserted that they are persecuted by police and prison authorities for their political or religious beliefs. Prohibitions in prisons include restriction on Native prisoners' hair length, sweat lodges, peace pipes, drums, headbands and other elements of traditional spirituality. Justice for Peltier would be a major step forward in USA–Native relations.

In 1978, the American Indian Religious Freedom Act was passed to 'preserve and protect' the rights of Native Americans to pursue their traditional spiritual paths. But the act has no real enforcement mechanisms, and while it has sometimes helped Natives protect sacred sites and religious practices, courts have deprived plaintiffs of protection under the act in all but four cases. The Supreme Court ruled in the *Lyng* case of 1988 that the US Forest Service was free to cut roads and timber in the sacred high country of Siskyou Mountain, saying that the government could not compel religious observance or deliberately interdict a religion for its own sake, but was under no obligation to *protect* anyone's religious practices. The Clinton administration was at work in 1995 on an Executive Order that would mandate stronger protections for sacred sites, but again there were no guarantees that the order would be interpreted as outweighing economic interests of business and government.

The persecution of the Native American Church's use of peyote – a controlled hallucinogen whose sacramental use by Natives dates back at least 1400 years – is another case of the inadequacy of the Act. The Supreme Court ruled in *Employment Division v. Smith* (1990) that an employer was within his rights in firing two Native workers for their religious practice of using peyote, and that the decision of whether to bring criminal prosecution against Native American Church members would be left up to the states. This was a clear reversal of usual religious protection in the USA and touched off a rash of marginal prosecutions against other groups.

Natives also protest against stereotypical or offensive appropriations of their culture, beginning with mid-century 'cowboys and Indians' movies, and today including 'Crazy Horse' malt liquor, the frequent use of Native names or pejoratives for sports teams, inaccurate museum displays and so on. There is concern about non-Native 'New Age shamans', men's and women's movement groups, gay activists, environmentalists and anthropologists who mystify and caricature Native culture, especially spiritual practices, for their own ideological and/or therapeutic ends. Traditionalists also worry about the effects of businesses like mining, casinos and tobacco smuggling on Native values and culture.

Self-determination, land resources

Although the official policy of the United States is now to encourage Native Americans' self-determination, in reality the power of Native communities is severely limited. The self-determination process has also forced Native Americans to adopt structures foreign to their own traditions – including the current reconfiguration of traditional structures as 'nations' comparable to the European nation-state, a process described by legal scholar R.L. Barsh as 'simulated state building'.[14] Even with this modification, Native nations are not viewed within US law as independent entities to which the USA has historically derived responsibilities, but as internal dependent nations or 'wards'. Native Americans possess only 'residual sovereignty' – power over what is not already regulated. US policy towards Native self-determination allows not much more autonomy than is given to a municipality or, at best, one of the states in the Union.

Tribal courts are often forbidden to deal with events on reservations involving non-tribal members, especially non-Natives (making jurisdiction racial rather than political or territorial), and cannot mete out sentences of more than one year's imprisonment. Native nations' ability to enforce their own land use and environmental regulations is not respected by the legal system. Their powers of taxation are also restricted. The BIA maintains ultimate control over Native American nations' constitutions, the composition of their governments, their power to make contracts, the disposition of their property and the funding and implementation of most programmes that affect them. It has authority to veto decisions made by the tribal councils. The concept of distributing self-determination funds for tribes to use at their discretion has been floated but never adopted.

Congress has always reserved 'plenary power' over Native Americans, and the Supreme Court ruled in 1978 that tribal sovereignty exists 'only at the sufferance of Congress', which at any time could 'limit, modify or eliminate' it. There is also the fear that the current policy is 'termination in disguise', and that once Natives achieve a certain degree of autonomy, Congress will cut off all aid. Both the BIA and the Indian Health Service have volunteered to dismantle services in the name of self-government, without proposing exactly how tribes would replace them; only Native protest forced Congress to forbid programme termination or contracting out without tribes' consent. Budget cuts have also severely impaired Native Americans' pursuit of self-sufficiency. In fiscal 1996, for example, the budget allocation for the BIA was cut 15 per cent from the previous year.

The BIA has frequently been negligent and abused its function and authority, usually by contracting on Native Americans' behalf to lease land to resource companies, often at less than 2 per cent of the resources' real value. Political pressures make this rarer now – instead government simply pressures the tribal council to make the same decisions – but government has been reluctant to compensate for past admitted extortions of peoples like the Cheyenne and Navajo. In 1977, the American Indian Policy Review Commission called such leases 'among the poorest agreements ever made'. It is now seen as politically correct to employ large numbers of Native Americans within the BIA, and in recent years it has been headed by Natives; but aside from the direct employment benefits the results of such affirmative action are debatable.

US government actions have had other negative repercussions, for example when the Reagan administration adopted a policy of discouraging Native-run businesses in favour of contracts between tribes and resource companies. It was also suggested that tribes voluntarily relinquish their legal jurisdiction in civil disputes to encourage companies to locate on reserves.

In 1988, amendments to the Indian Self-Determination Act allowed pilot projects for tribes to revise government structures away from the IRA model. By 1995, about half the reservations in the USA had somehow modified their systems to make them more compatible with traditional values. (However, conflicts over forms of government and economic direction at reserves like the Akwesasne Mohawk reservation on the New York/Ontario border still cause severe tensions.) The most forward-looking policy direction coming from the US government was proposed in Hawai'i Senator Daniel Inouye's report from the Senate Select Committee on Indian Affairs in 1989. Documenting BIA mismanagement, Inouye and his colleagues suggest that every tribe adopt a democratically approved constitution, on the basis of which new treaties would be negotiated to transfer full governmental power and moneys *in toto* for use at tribal governments' discretion. The sole caveat was that tribal governments – which have sometimes been caught in scandals – remain subject to federal corruption laws.

These proposals are the closest the US government has come to the demands of such Native platforms as AIM's Twenty Point Programme or the National Congress of American Indians' 1974 American Indian Declaration of Sovereignty. While they have not yet been enacted, US policy has slowly drifted in this direction. Many Native American activists and scholars argue that social justice can only be achieved with full sovereignty – complete control of land, resources and law in Native jurisdictions – perhaps through Native nations negotiating agreements for Commonwealth-type status within the USA. However, since the majority of Native Americans now live in cities, self-determination in Native territories may not by itself guarantee full equality for all the people affected by the legacy of colonization.

The Dawes Act forced Native Americans to part with 64 per cent of the land that they retained at the end of the Native American wars of the 1880s and today less than 215,000 square kilometres remain. Reservations often include the poorest agricultural land, with severe water shortages and limited economic potential. At least 25 per cent of these lands are currently occupied by non-Natives, and on some reserves as much as 90 per cent of the land is held by outsiders. Meanwhile, the Native American population has increased nearly seven-fold over the last century and the land base is unable to sustain them.

From 1946 to 1978, the Indian Claims Commission adjudicated Native land claims, but could provide only monetary, not territorial compensation, and estimated land value based not on current market value but on its worth at the time of taking. Many nations, for example in New York State, were compensated at derisory levels for their lost land. Not until 1974 did the Supreme Court rule that Native Americans had the right to pursue land restoration. Thousands of square kilometres and millions of dollars have since been transferred, though an act of Congress is required for each such settlement. In some cases, often due to the sacred significance of a particular site, Native nations have refused to accept monetary settlements. The most dramatic case of this has been the 'Black Hills Are Not for Sale' campaign by the Lakota of South Dakota, who turned down over US $100 million in compensation for their lands and sacred sites in the late 1970s, a case still in dispute today.

Other pending claims include: the Papago Nation of Arizona's claim on the sacred Baboquivari Mountain Range, where mining has taken place; suits by the landless Schaghticoke and Mohegan peoples of Connecticut and Catawbas of South Carolina for recovery of their former reservations; the Western Shoshone's land claims, covering 80 per cent of Nevada; the San Carlos Apache of Arizona's attempt to block construction of the Mount Graham International Observatory on their ceremonial mountain grounds; and the several-sided dispute between traditional Dineh and Hopi, the Navajo and Hopi tribal councils, the federal government and the Peabody Coal Company over the Big Mountain/Black Mesa lands in Arizona, a case that perhaps better than any other indicates the complexity of Native land and sovereignty issues.

The sheer number of disputes reveals the inadequacy of US government mechanisms. These conflicts have been sharpened by the recent realization that Native land is one of the few untapped sources of natural resources left in the United States. Again, much of the richest land was stolen (for example by oil companies in Texas and Arizona) in years past, but large amounts remain. In 1975, 25 Native American tribes in the northwest joined together to form the Council of Energy Resource Tribes, modelled on the Organization of Petroleum Exporting Countries (OPEC), and some of these tribes have grown rich from mineral and oil profits. However, a 1989 Supreme Court ruling that tribal councils could not limit land uses by non-Natives on reservation land has hampered attempts to control development.

In 1982, 240 out of 300 federally recognized tribes had some energy resources, amounting to 25 per cent of US mineral wealth. Nearly all the uranium in the USA is under Native land. In addition, other valuable forest and mining land is directly adjacent to reservation land, sometimes on traditional hunting and fishing or ceremonial grounds, and its use tends to pollute water tables, rivers, lakes, air and other life sources of Native peoples. For example, the Gros Ventre and Assiniboine peoples in Montana are threatened by the Zortman-Landusky gold mine expansion that could release over 1,000 million gallons of cyanide solution into the local watershed and also disrupt traditional religious and medical uses of the Little Rocky Mountains. Natives have had little success in disputing such corporate incursions, and have often not received the due financial benefits of their own holdings. Water diversion, pollution and damming around Native lands, as well as pollution of groundwater, has been sanctioned by the courts. The separation of land and water rights is contrary to international standards, besides being socially, economically and environmentally destructive.

Native Hawai'ians

Native Hawai'ians are the descendants of the original Polynesian settlers of Hawai'i, an eastern Pacific island chain. Formerly an independent kingdom and later a US territory, Hawai'i became the fiftieth US state in 1959. Of the state's population, 240,000 people (20 per cent) are Native Hawai'ian. The colonial experience of Native Hawai'ians is comparable to the plight of indigenous peoples worldwide, with the added tragedy of colonization-by-*kitsch*. The burgeoning Hawai'ian tourism industry brings six times more visitors to the island every year than there are permanent residents. It has marketed the islands to the world as an ahistorical '*hula-hula* girl' paradise.

Pre-contact Hawai'i was governed by a system of family groups and hierarchies, cultivating land on a communal basis. The natural world was regarded as a polytheistic, animistic network of familial relations. A rich culture of music, chant, poetry, dance, story and ritual supported this worldview. When white Europeans (*haole*) arrived in 1778 with Captain James Cook of Great Britain, they introduced a host of diseases that, within a century, reduced Hawai'i from a pre-contact population of over 800,000 to an indigenous population of under 39,000.

Hawai'i was recognized internationally as an independent kingdom from 1779 to 1893. But by the mid-nineteenth century, the 'big five' US sugar companies dominated the Hawai'ian economy. To the anguish of the Hawai'ian people, Queen Lili'uokalani was forcefully overthrown by US marines in 1893, and Congress completed the process with the annexation of Hawai'i as a territory in 1898. Large numbers of Asian and US mainland labourers were imported to work the plantations; the USA imposed tight economic control and established military bases. The Hawai'ian language was banned from schools, while traditional religious practices were marginalized or forbidden. During the Second World War, Hawai'i was placed under martial law by territorial governors. In the immediate postwar period, Japanese and Hawai'ian activists began to assume prominent roles in the local Democratic Party, which was instrumental in gaining statehood for Hawai'i in 1959. Today, no ethnic group in Hawai'i forms a majority. Institutional racism and US influence have preserved the dominance of the *haole* 30 per cent, but Japanese and Chinese residents have recovered from severe discrimination to assume powerful roles. Most Hawai'ians welcomed statehood as preferable to territorial status, but few benefits have flowed to the indigenous people.

Aside from a few middle-class professionals and politicians, most Native Hawai'ians are concentrated in low-wage service sectors, with high levels of unemployment. They have the worst death and disease rate of any ethnic group in the USA and high rates of school failure, substance abuse, suicide, homelessness, welfare dependency and incarceration. Thirty-one per cent of Native Hawai'ians have annual incomes below US $4,000. In their struggle to recover the integrity of Hawai'ian cultures, Native Hawai'ians have created a renaissance in politically charged versions of traditional arts, established immersion schools, made Hawai'ian an official state language, and gained a constitutional guarantee of religious rights.[15]

The US Congress allocated just over 800 sq km for Native Hawai'ians in the 1921 Homestead Land Act, and another 5,666 sq km in 1959 as 'ceded' lands. A series of state agencies has leased much of this land to industrial, resort or military interests and most of the rest has never been provided the infrastructure necessary for homesteading. By 1996, there were 27,000 Hawai'ian families on the homelands waiting list. In 1993, President Clinton proclaimed Public Law 103–150, a public apology for the US role in the overthrow of the monarchy, but no new rights or reparations accompanied this gesture. Attempts to resolve questions of state and federal trustees' misappropriation of lands and resources in court are frustrated by Hawai'ians' status as 'wards of the state' – making Native Hawai'ians the only US group unable to sue the federal government or state for breach of trust.

In the late 1970s, the state Democratic Party attempted to placate Native Hawai'ian pressure by establishing the Office of Hawai'ian Affairs (OHA), a semi-autonomous self-government device. Many Hawai'ians believe that as a state agency the OHA has an inherent conflict of interest. The past two decades have seen the development of a large, radical Hawai'ian nationalist movement, led mostly by Hawai'ian women. The largest of about 40 groups opposed to the OHA approach is Ka Lahui Hawai'i (Hawai'ian Nation), founded in 1987 and with an enrolment of 23,000 'citizens' (1995). On 17 January 1993, over 15,000 people marched in support of Native Hawai'ian sovereignty. Ka Lahui Hawai'i opposed a state plebiscite initiative for 1996 designed to ratify wardship.

The Hawai'ian nationalist movement has generated protest and discussion of a large number of related issues, including: the crowding, economic exploitation, pollution, land misuse and, in particular, commodification and misrepresentation of Hawai'ian culture caused by the state's leading industry, tourism; the US military presence, which brings economic dependency, occupies and pollutes thousands of square kilometres of homelands, and may serve as a launching pad for aggression abroad; violation of sacred grounds through geothermal power extraction in the sacred Kilauea volcano on Big Island, the H-3 highway in the Halawa Valley, the disinterment of bodies from Hawai'ian burial grounds by developers and anthropologists, and the test bombing of Kaho'olawe Island; the arrest and imprisonment without bail in August 1995 of Ka Lahui Hawai'i's official Head of State, Pu'uhonua B. Kanahele, for interfering with the arrest of a Hawai'ian protester.

US influence is heavy, and the ethnically based balance of voter power may discourage politicians from going far to accommodate Hawai'ian rights. Other minorities, notably Filipinos, fear that gains for Native Hawai'ian sovereignty will impede their own progress, while the *haole* minority continues to resist concrete action to compensate the islands' indigenous peoples for colonization and to break down corporate power.

Inuit and Alaska Natives

Indigenous peoples of Alaska include at least 20 language groups and several hundred villages and tribal groups. Inuit are the largest group (mistakenly sometimes called 'Eskimos' by southerners). Others include Aleuts and Athabaskan, Tlingit, Haida and Tsimshian Natives. In 1990, their population numbered 85,000 throughout the state of Alaska, working in every sector from traditional hunting to corporate management.

Before European contact, Inuit lived in extended family groups as semi-nomadic hunter-fisher-gatherers. Aleuts also hunted and trapped, but lived in more permanent, partly subterranean homes on the Aleutian Islands. Native groups further south had large permanent settlements and trade networks. The first Europeans to land in Alaska were Russian explorers, and the territory was occupied by the Russian Empire from 1741 until 1867, when it was sold to the USA. The USA imposed restrictions on indigenous Alaskans' education, religious and voting rights similar to those experienced by Native Americans in more southerly states. Alaska became the forty-ninth and largest US state in 1959. In 1966, the Alaska Federation of Natives was formed and filed land claims covering the entire state. Oil was discovered in Alaska in 1968, and in 1971 the US Congress passed the Alaskan Native Claims Settlement Act (ANCSA). It extinguished aboriginal titles and created for-profit corporations in each region to administer an award totalling US $962.5 million and 178,068 square kilometres. Corporate shares, which could not be sold until 1991, were granted exclusively to indigenous Alaskans born before December 1971.

The treatment of Alaskan aboriginal peoples by European-descended Americans parallels the history of dispossession of other indigenous peoples in North America, with many of the same effects: dependency on government income transfers, poverty (Inuit and Natives earn on average less than half of white Alaskans' income per capita), educational failure, health problems, teenage suicide, poverty, language loss, alcoholism and violence. However, because of Alaska's relative isolation and long territorial status, the principle of Native sovereignty is less well-entrenched there. The state government maintains that historically indigenous Alaskans have always been treated as individuals, not peoples. No treaties and only a few reservation lands exist.

Alaska Natives widely criticized the ANCSA for imposing a corporate structure over their traditional forms of governance. Its provisions provided only weak protection of aboriginal title, leaving lands open to eventual corporate or government take-over, and gave no recognition to traditional subsistence hunting and fishing rights. In February 1988, Congress passed amendments to the act that extended the stock sale restrictions and tax exemptions indefinitely, but allowed corporations to issue new stock to younger people and non-aboriginals. These amendments split the Alaska Federation of Natives (AFN). Some members welcomed the amendments as a way to resolve the dispute and encourage economic development. Others objected that not enough had been done to safeguard traditional lifestyles and rights.

In 1980, the Alaska National Interest Lands Conservation Act set aside lands for national parks and wildlife refuges and recognized the priority of traditional uses of resources. But the Conservation Act is administered mostly by state government, which leans towards commercial interests, and the situation has never been clarified. However, in October 1993 the federal Bureau of Indian Affairs quietly confirmed 225 Alaskan villages as recognized tribes. Several regional corporations have now transferred their lands to tribal governments to protect against state appropriation. Ironically, indigenous Alaskans might ultimately achieve self-determination only by obtaining federal government support.

Indigenous Alaskans' rights, like those of other circumpolar peoples, are closely linked to environmental concerns, particularly in connection with oil. Oil companies provide 85 per cent of the state revenue of Alaska, but oil drilling is highly disruptive to subsistence life. Thus, oil exploration is controversial both inside and outside Native communities. In 1988, in 1991 and again in 1995, Congress proposed opening the coastal plain of the Arctic National Wildlife Refuge to oil development. President Bill Clinton considered vetoing the measure if passed by Congress in the 1996 budget. Oil spills, including the 11 million gallon *Exxon-Valdez* spill in 1989 and the up to 80 million gallon Russian spill in 1994, pollute the Arctic Sea and disrupt indigenous wildlife, culture and economies; in 1994, Native villagers were paid US $20 million on top of Exxon's 1991 thousand-million-dollar settlement with Alaska, and litigation is ongoing. Other current environmental issues include anti-fur activism and whaling conservation efforts, which threaten Native livelihoods. The Inuit Circumpolar Conference's alternative whaling commission argues that Native hunting should not be included in the US quota, but should be protected as a separate category. In addition, dumping and international control failures make the Arctic

Circle a 'sink' for greenhouse gases, chlorofluorocarbons, DDT, heavy metals, hydrocarbons, radionucleotides and nuclear wastes. These substances may alter the climate of the region, and toxins accumulate in the bodies of Alaska Natives and other polar peoples, causing unknown health risks.

Since the 1987 split over the ANCSA amendments, the United Tribes of Alaska and the Alaska Native Coalition have joined the AFN and Alaska Inter-Tribal Council in representing Alaska Native interests, along with tribal and village governments. In 1977, Inuit from Alaska, Greenland and Canada created a common forum in the Inuit Circumpolar Conference (ICC), which meets yearly and in 1983 gained non-governmental organization status at the United Nations. Inuit of the former Soviet Union joined the ICC in 1993. There is also an initiative, led by Canada, for an Arctic Council with indigenous and governmental representatives from the seven countries on the Arctic Circle: Canada, the USA, Russia, Norway, Finland, Iceland and Denmark. The Council would extend and enforce the Arctic Environmental Protection Strategy, which is not yet a legally binding treaty.

Conclusions and future prospects

US minorities have generally shared a common pattern of experience since the 1960s. Civil rights movements brought cultural awareness, community organization and political participation. A small percentage of each group entered the middle class – often leaving traditional ethnic neighbourhoods for the suburbs – but the less well-educated and financially secure saw their communities and personal fortunes sink. By the 1990s, the expansion of minority middle classes had also stagnated. This pattern was accompanied by the decline of US economic competitiveness globally, which provoked growing domestic inequities during the 1980s and 1990s. The average US worker's wage (in constant dollars) decreased, while upper class incomes rose. Minority workers often lost more than others, in spite of affirmative action programmes, and government programmes for the poor were cut back significantly. Open hostility towards immigrants and inner-city minority groups intensified, even among elected officials. As a result, many people became disilliusioned with the integrationist ideals and welfare state programmes of the 1960s. In the 1990s, nationalist and separatist movements among minorities have proliferated, and many insecure middle class whites have succumbed to suburban protectionism, whose extremes are manifested in the growing number of 'gated communities' with protective walls and private security forces.

The 1992 election of Bill Clinton's Democratic administration raised hopes for improved representation, especially among African Americans. Superficially, the Clinton cabinet was the most diverse in US history, but few of its policies fulfilled its promises of urban economic renewal. In 1994, Congress was taken over by a Republican majority whose agenda (the 'Contract with America') included dismantling anti-poverty programmes and ending programmes that favour minority candidates for positions in employment or education. Economic hardship coincided with a crisis of purpose. The end of the Cold War meant the USA was no longer united against the common Soviet enemy, but the expected 'peace dividend' of guns-into-butter conversion failed to materialize. Increasingly, there was talk of the 'domestic enemy', a non-white criminal 'underclass' locked in a cycle of social breakdown. Fear of crime became the most powerful US issue in the early 1990s, expressed in the 'drug war' and increased law enforcement programmes. Such measures targeted inner-city minorities disproportionately.

In the mid-1990s, police ranks and prison populations were swelling at unprecedented rates. 'Police abuse is one of the most pressing human rights issues facing the USA,' according to a 1993 Human Rights Watch/American Civil Liberties Union report. This study documented excessive force, harassment of racial minorities and unjustifiable shootings by police across the USA. With the USA one of the few Western democracies that still employs the death penalty, a 1990 General Accounting Office investigation found that in 82 per cent of studies made on the issue race was identified as influencing sentencing in capital crimes.[16] The combination of decreased urban aid, increased policing and cultural misunderstanding is potentially explosive. Riots in Los Angeles and Miami in the early 1990s were touched off by police brutality in economically deprived communities. Meanwhile, the 1995 bombing of a federal building in Oklahoma by members of white-supremacist 'citizen militias' – along with continuing evidence of neo-Nazi, Ku Klux Klan and other organized racist activity – hinted at the extremes of white backlash. While the USA still provides better opportunities and legal rights to minorities than many other nations, it no longer leads the way. Yet, at current rates of demographic change, white Americans will be in the minority by the second quarter of the twenty-first century.

Without a credible governmental or oppositional agenda for unity, ethnic division poses a serious threat to all US communities.

Besides the problems of white racism and government relations, conflicts between minorities are becoming more frequent. African Americans in particular, because of their numbers and a history of oppression that reaches back to the beginning of US colonial history, are often wary of newer groups. Some African Americans have come into serious conflict with Jewish and Asian-Pacific Americans in recent years. Louis Farrakhan of the Nation of Islam has been widely condemned as an anti-Semite, and his ideas have been reinforced by 'Afrocentric' scholars like Leonard Jeffries, who accuses Jews of leading the slave trade and expresses doubt about the Holocaust. However, even more mainstream black leaders like Jesse Jackson have been accused of making anti-Semitic remarks, while some Jewish public figures have made disparaging comments about African Americans. Black anti-Semitism and Jewish racism came to a head in Brooklyn, New York, in 1992. After a Hasidic Jewish driver killed an African American child in a hit-and-run accident, the neighbourhood boiled over in rioting, retaliatory beatings on both sides, boycotts and recriminations, arguably marking the death of a century-long fragile tradition of solidarity between African Americans and liberal Jews.

African American complaints about Asian-Pacific Americans have centred on Asian immigrants' successes in business and particularly the presence of Asian-run shops in black neighbourhoods. The simmering antipathy became critical in 1991 when a Korean storekeeper in Los Angeles shot an African American child whom he believed was shoplifting. Pickets, boycotts and hate crimes followed, with the end result that Korean businesses were particularly targeted for destruction in the Los Angeles riots. Similarly, Native Hawai'ians often complain that Asian-Pacific Americans have made political gains at their expense. Enmity between Arab Americans and Jewish Americans has centred on US policy in the Middle East, a conflict that has included espionage, bombing and assassinations. The assumed convergence of interests between African Americans and Latinos has been belied by increasing economic and political rivalries, as well as gang violence, especially in California and New York City. Beliefs that some minorities conspire with whites to keep other minorities down – along with new immigrants' tendency to internalize local bigotries as part of the assimilation process – pose formidable barriers to multicultural peace in the USA.

Further reading

Barringer, H.R., Gardner, R.W. and Levin, M.J., *Asians and Pacific Islanders in the United States*, New York, Russell Sage Foundation, 1993.

Claiborne, L., *et al.*, *Race and Law in Britain and the United States*, London, MRG report, 1983.

Green, D.E. and Tonnesen, T.V. (eds), *American Indians: Social Justice and Public Policy*, Madison, WI, University of Wisconsin System Institute on Race and Ethnicity, 1991.

Haas, M., *Institutional Racism: The Case of Hawai'i*, Westport, CT, Praeger, 1992.

Human Rights Watch and American Civil Liberties Union, *Human Rights Violations in the United States: A Report on U.S. Compliance with the International Covenant on Civil and Political Rights*, New York, 1993.

Korsmo, F.L., 'The Alaska Natives', in Minority Rights Group (ed.), *Polar Peoples*, London, Minority Rights Publications, 1994, pp. 81–104.

Meier, M.S. and Ribera, F., *Mexican Americans/American Mexicans: From Conquistadors to Chicanos*, New York, Hill &Wang, 1993.

Olson, J.S. and Olson, J.E., *Cuban Americans: From Trauma to Triumph*, New York, Twayne, 1995.

Pinkney, A., *Black Americans,* 4th edn, Englewood Cliffs, NJ, Prentice Hall, 1993.

Reimers, D.M., *Still the Golden Door: The Third World Comes to America*, New York, Columbia University Press, 1992.

Seltzer, R.M. and Cohen, N.J., *The Americanization of the Jews*, New York, New York University Press, 1995.

Steiner, S., *Mexican Americans*, London, MRG report, 1979.

Stepick, A., *Haitian Refugees in the USA*, London, MRG report, 1986.

Trask, H.K., *From a Native Daughter: Nationalism and Sovereignty in Hawai'i*, Monroe, ME, Common Courage Press, 1989.

Wagenheim, K., *Puerto Ricans in the United States*, London, MRG report, 1989.

Wilson, J., *Original Americans: USA Indians*, London, MRG report, 1986.

Zack, N. (ed.), *American Mixed Race: The Culture of Microdiversity*, Lanham, MD, Rowman & Littlefield, 1995.

Zogby, J. (ed.), *Taking Root, Bearing Fruit: The Arab American Experience*, Washington, DC, ADC Reports, 1984.

Minority-based and advocacy organizations

Alaskan Intertribal Council, 4201 Tudor Centre Drive, Suite 300, Anchorage, AK 99508, USA.

American-Arab Anti-Discrimination Committee, 4201 Connecticut Avenue NW, Suite 500, Washington, DC 2008, USA; tel. 1 202 244 2990.

Amnesty International, 322 8th Avenue, New York, NY 10001, USA; tel. 1 212 807 8400, fax 1 212 463 9193/627 1451; 304 Pennsylvania Avenue SE, Washington, DC 20003, USA; tel. 1 202 544 0200, fax 1 202 546 7142.

Armenian National Committee of America, 888 17th Street NW, Suite 905, Washington, DC 20006, USA; tel. 1 202 775 1918, fax 1 202 775 5648, e-mail: anca-dc@ix.netcom.com

Asian-American Legal Defense and Education Fund, 99 Hudson Street, 12th Floor, New York, NY 10013, USA; tel. 1 212 996 5932, fax 1 212 966 4303.

Coordinating Committee of Hungarian Organizations in North America, 4101 Blackpool Road, Rockville, MD 20853, USA; tel. 1 301 871 7018.

Cultural Survival, 46 Brattle Street, Cambridge, MA 02138, USA; tel. 1 617 441 5400, fax 1 617 441 5417.

Human Rights Watch/Americas, 485 Fifth Avenue, New York, NY 10017, USA; tel. 1 212 972 8400, fax 1 212 972 0905.

International Indian Treaty Council, 54 Mint Street, Suite 400, San Francisco, CA 94103, USA; tel. 1 415 512 1501, fax 1 415 512 1507.

Ka Lahui Hawai'i (Sovereign Nation of Hawai'i), PO Box 4964, Hilo, HI 96720, USA; tel. 1 808 961 2888, fax 1 808 935 8854.

Minority Rights Group USA, 169 East 78th Street, New York, NY 10021, USA; tel. 1 212 879 4924, fax 1 212 879 5489.

Minority Rights Group Washington, 444 North Capitol Street, Suite 712, Washington, DC 20001, USA; tel. 202 347 4805, fax 202 393 7006.

National Association for the Advancement of Colored People (NAACP), 4805 Mount Hope Drive, Baltimore, MD 21215, USA; tel. 1 410 358 8900, fax 1 410 358 3818.

National Council of La Raza, 810 First Street NE, Suite 300, Washington, DC 20002, USA; tel. 1 202 785 1670, fax 1 202 776 1792.

Native American Rights Fund, 1506 Broadway, Boulder, CO 8032, USA; tel. 1 303 447 8760, fax 1 303 443 7776.

Organization of Africans in the Americas, 1931 Quaker Lane, Alexandria, VA 22305, USA; tel. 1 703 820 8853/845 0753.

Notes

Contributions to this regional section are as follows. Alex Roslin: entries on Canada and Mexico; Carl Wilson: regional introduction and entry on the United States of America

Canada

1 'Allophones suffer as English–French wage gap closes', *Montreal Gazette*, 20 September 1995.

2 Quoted by York, G., *The Dispossessed*, London, Vintage UK, 1990, p. 32.

3 Quoted, ibid., p. 23.

4 Quoted, ibid., p. 58.

5 Ibid., p. 59.

6 Interview with Wapachee, B., *The Nation* Cree magazine, vol. 1, no. 20, pp. 10–13, 26.

7 Roslin, A., 'Inuit teen suicide soars in Quebec', *Montreal Gazette*, 16 February 1995.

Mexico

1 This account draws significantly from Stocker, P., 'Indigenous peoples in Mexico', unpublished research report for MRG, 1993; and from information provided in 1996 by Neil Harvey, Department of Government, New Mexico State University, Las Cruces, NM.

2 Minnesota Advocates for Human Rights, 'Racism in Mexico', *Human Rights Observer*, vol. 8, no. 5, July 1995.

3 This account is based on Muhammad, J.S., 'Mexico', in MRG (ed.), *No Longer Invisible: Afro-Latin Americans Today*, London, Minority Rights Publications; and on information provided by Neil Harvey (see note 1).

USA

1 Minority populations and percentages from the 1990 US census.

2 See Pinkney, A., *Black Americans*, Englewood Cliffs, NJ, Prentice Hall, 1993.

3 Hacker, A., *Two Nations: Black and White, Separate, Hostile, Unequal,* 2nd edn, New York, Ballantine, 1995.

4 Statistics on African Americans drawn mainly from Human Rights Watch and American Civil Liberties Union, *Human Rights Violations in the United States: A Report on US Compliance with the International Covenant on Civil and Political Rights*, New York, 1993; also from Pinkney, op. cit., Jackson, J.S. (ed.), *Life in Black America*, Newbury Park, CA, Sage Publications, 1991; and US Census data and news reports.

5 Pinkney, op. cit., pp. 111–21, 141.

6 General statistics on Latinos drawn mainly from Moore, J. and Pinderhughes, R. (eds), *In the Barrios*, New York, Russell Sage Foundation, 1993; Morales, R. and Bonilla, F. (eds), *Latinos in a Changing US Economy*, Newbury Park, CA, Sage Publications, 1993; and HRW and ACLU, op. cit.

7 Fuentes, C., 'Hispanic USA: the mirror of the other', *The Nation*, 30 March 1992.

8 American Friends Service Committee, *Sealing Our Borders: The Human Toll*, New York, AFSC, 1992; Americas Watch, *Brutality Unchecked: Human Rights Abuses Along the US Border with Mexico*, New York, Human Rights Watch, 1992.

9 Statistics on Asian-Pacific Americans, and related insights, drawn mainly from Chan, K.S. and Hune, S., 'Racialization and panethnicity: from Asians in America to Asian Americans', in Hawley, W.D. and Jackson, A.W. (eds), *Towards a Common Destiny: Improving Race and Ethnic Relations in America*, San Francisco, CA, Jossey-Bass, 1955, pp. 205–33.

10 El-Badry, S., 'The Arab American market', *American Demographics*, January 1994, pp. 22–30.

11 Kelly, R. *et al.* (eds), *Irangeles: Iranians in Los Angeles*, Los Angeles, CA, University of California Press, 1993.

12 See Kadi, J. (ed.), *Food for our Grandmothers: Writings by Arab American and Arab Canadian Feminists*, Boston, MA, South End Press, 1994.

13 Gedicks, A., *The New Resource Wars: Native and Environmental Struggles Against Multinational Corporations,* Boston, MA, South End Press, 1993, p. 42; Churchill, W., *Struggle for the Land: Indigenous Resistance to Genocide, Ecocide and Expropriation in Contemporary North America*, Monroe, ME, Common Courage Press, 1993.

14 See Green, D.E. and Tonnesen, T.V. (eds), *American Indians: Social Justice and Public Policy*, Madison, WI, University of Wisconsin System Institute on Race and Ethnicity, 1991.

15 Haas, M., *Institutional Racism: The Case of Hawai'i*, Westport, CT, Praeger, 1992.

16 HRW and ACLU, op. cit., pp. 120–6.

CENTRAL AND SOUTH AMERICA AND THE CARIBBEAN

Patrick Costello, Lindsey Crickmay and James Ferguson

Central America

In pre-Columbian America, the area now known as Central America was divided in two. Mesoamerica in the north was dominated by the Maya and, later, Aztec societies extending their control southwards. In the south, nomadic peoples predominated who had migrated northwards from the Amazon basin. Thus, while the indigenous peoples of Guatemala, Belize, El Salvador and part of Honduras are descendants of the agricultural societies of the pre-Columbian Maya, further south the populations were much more dispersed, consisting of large numbers of smaller groups of peoples.

Following the conquest, Central America was a peripheral region of the Spanish empire and, as such, it was regarded largely as a source of forced labour for the more lucrative areas, in particular, the silver mines of the Andes. Large areas of what are now the central plains of Honduras, El Salvador and Nicaragua were virtually depopulated during the first century of the conquest. The few people who remained formed the mixed race (*mestizo*) cultures which remain dominant in most of the countries of the isthmus today. Where significant indigenous cultures survived, this tended to be because of the relative remoteness of the terrain, either because of mountains (in the case of the Guatemalan Maya) or jungle (in the case of the Miskitu and Sumu of Honduras and Nicaragua).

In the only country where the indigenous population remains a majority, Guatemala, the population has continued to suffer genocide and massacre. Elsewhere, indigenous groups have been assimilated into peasant culture or kept at arm's length in isolated reserves, usually on poor land. The only exception is the Kuna in Panama who have used their isolation to their own benefit. More recently, the award of the 1992 Nobel Peace Prize to the Guatemalan Maya Rigoberta Menchú is both a cause and an effect of a growing indigenous self-consciousness. The revolutionary movements of Central America have been guilty of marginalizing indigenous rights; but a good deal of re-evaluation has taken place, both in Guatemala, where the strength of the new indigenous movements has forced government and guerrillas to take them seriously within the peace negotiations, and in Nicaragua, where the autonomy process introduced by the Sandinistas has proved a unique experiment in the implementation of indigenous rights.

The other major group of minorities in the region are Afro-Central Americans. A century and a half of US political and economic domination of the region, as well as the prior British involvement on the Caribbean coast, has involved the importing of migrant workers from both Africa and the Caribbean. This has resulted in the development of some unique composite cultures (the Garífuna and the Miskitu) as well as adding another layer of complexity to the ethnicity of the region. While in certain cases (such as Honduras and Panama) black and indigenous groups have united over common struggles for land and civil rights, in other countries the relation has been more fraught (such as Guatemala). The continental campaign to oppose celebration of the quincentennial of Columbus's arrival in the Americas, the '500 Years of Resistance Campaign', acknowledged the presence of African culture only on the last day of the Continental Congress in Guatemala in 1991. As a result, the campaign was dominated by indigenous and class issues which marginalized the English-speaking Caribbean when a greater level of unity could have been promoted.

BERMUDA
BAHAMAS
TURKS & CAICOS IS.
CUBA
CAYMAN IS.
DOMINICAN REPUBLIC
HAITI
JAMAICA
PUERTO RICO
BRITISH VIRGIN IS.
U.S. VIRGIN IS.
ANTIGUA & BARBUDA
ST. KITTS & NEVIS
MONTSERRAT
GUADELOUPE
DOMINICA
MARTINIQUE
ST LUCIA
BARBADOS
GRENADA
TRINIDAD & TOBAGO
NETHERLANDS ANTILLES & ARUBA
ST. VINCENT & THE GRENADINES
BELIZE
GUATEMALA
HONDURAS
EL SALVADOR
NICARAGUA
COSTA RICA
PANAMA
VENEZUELA
GUYANA
SURINAME
FR. GUIANA
COLOMBIA
ECUADOR
PERU
BRAZIL
BOLIVIA
PARAGUAY
CHILE
ARGENTINA
URUGUAY
CENTRAL AND SOUTH AMERICA AND THE CARIBBEAN

South America

South America's minorities are primarily indigenous and tribal peoples who have been continually subjected to political, social, economic and religious oppression since they were first colonized by the Spanish, Portuguese, Dutch, French or British. Indigenous peoples in South America increasingly refer to themselves as nations and are concerned that their claims, as original inhabitants of the land, be seen as distinct from those of other minorities. For a variety of reasons, figures on indigenous populations have until now been approximate. However, legislation on indigenous rights brings into question how the term can and should be defined; neither ethnicity nor language can be conclusive factors. This is because not all those eligible on ethnic grounds may wish to be considered indigenous; nor do all those who self-identify as indigenous speak an indigenous language.

South America also has a significant Afro-Latin American population, especially in Brazil and Colombia. In general, this group is recognized neither as a minority nor, despite its long-term presence, as having claims to the land comparable to those of the indigenous population. Emerging Afro-Latin American political consciousness takes its inspiration from the US Civil Rights Movement and from an awareness of exclusion from the achievements of the growing number of indigenous rights movements which became a focus of international attention in 1992, the 500th anniversary of the European 'discovery' of the Americas. Afro-Latin American aims – political autonomy and improved economic conditions, including rights to land – are similar to those of indigenous peoples.

Immigrants and their descendants make up a third group of minorities. Although they suffer varying degrees of ethnic discrimination, they are far less numerous than other minorities, economically better established and primarily urban. They have consequently fewer claims, although language policy is an issue with some.

Many Latin American governments see the future position of both indigenous and Afro-Latin American peoples as one in which they become part of a single *mestizo* state; thus national identity is exacted as the price of economic and political equality. Brazil's initial policy of miscegenation has been put forward as evidence of its lack of racial discrimination, and other countries besides Brazil have publicly claimed that they have no minorities. Where indigenous peoples are perceived as having a cultural identity, it is often considered 'backward' or 'childish'. Forest peoples are frequently seen as incapable of taking decisions about their future, and highland people's cultures as having to 'progress' into modern, urban society.

The main issues of indigenous politics are the claims to inalienable territorial rights, nationhood and self-determination. While governments may fail to live up to their promises of land demarcation, it is self-determination which is raising most problems for indigenous legislation. Governments often mistakenly assume that self-determination and autonomy automatically imply secession from, rather than existence within, the state. At the recent twelfth session of the UN Working Group preparing the Draft Declaration on the Rights of Indigenous Peoples, the proposal to append to Article 3, which recognizes indigenous rights to self-determination, and Article 31, which attempts to define self-determination, caused heated debate. While some see this proposal as dangerously limiting the extent to which minorities may exercise this right, its supporters see it as safeguarding a minimum level of autonomy where this may be interpreted as threatening the sovereignty of the state.[1]

In some cases what appears to be acceptance of indigenous nationhood in reality merely admits them to be 'ethno-linguistic groups'. In Peru, where Quechua and Aymara are spoken by almost half the population, these are recognized as official languages, but official documents and official proceedings are carried on in the dominant language – Spanish. Other countries only recognize indigenous languages 'within their (indigenous peoples') own territory'. This linguistic policy automatically bars many indigenous peoples from fully understanding or taking part in legal debate on their future. In spite of the clause guaranteeing intercultural bilingual education which is included in the 1989 International Labour Organization (ILO) Convention 169 on Indigenous and Tribal Rights to which several Latin American governments are signatories, in practice, apart from larger projects organized by European countries, it is more often the minorities themselves who organize these programmes.

In the very broadest terms indigenous South American peoples can be divided into those of the *altiplano* (high plain) and warm upland valleys, and the tribal peoples inhabiting the lowland forests of Amazonia. In pre-colonial times, highland peoples maintained isolated communities in lowland and coastal areas. A predominant feature of the highland economy is still its 'vertical' nature, and the complementary relationship between the products of the *puna* (high plateau) and those of the lower, more temperate valleys. In the lowlands the contrast is between the fertile flood plains, which are capable of supporting sedentary populations, and those lands which are less fertile and were traditionally the home of hunter-gatherers. Each area, however, includes a wide variety of ecological niches whose inhabitants make use of them through relationships of exchange and complementarity comparable to those of the Andean highlands.[2]

Many forest tribes are semi-nomadic; their land needs are different from those of highland farmers; their problems are also different. Forest peoples are threatened by colonists seeking fresh land, and by logging and mining concerns eager to exploit untapped resources. Highland groups have difficulty proving their inherited territorial right to land misappropriated by large landholders in the nineteenth and twentieth centuries. For both groups, rights to their lands are a spiritual as well as an economic necessity.

The complex ecology of the tropical rainforest makes it particularly vulnerable to large-scale exploitation. Forest peoples are increasingly requesting the help of outside agencies and are travelling abroad to make their position known internationally. Since the early 1980s the focus of international interest and support and the resulting pressure put on South American governments have shifted. Not all ecological pressure groups now try to preserve parks without people. Forest tribes (other than those of Brazil, where land titles are not recognized) have recently had, theoretically at least, considerable success in the attainment of land titles. Land rights now include environmental rights, which should include the right to administer the land's resources and entitlement to restitution for environmental damage due to commercial exploitation and to relocation on similar territory whilst this damage is being repaired.

In the 1970s and 1980s national governments welcomed development projects in the name of progress. For the many forest tribes, however, roads opening up the interior, such as the Transamazonian highway and Polonoroeste project in Brazil, spell disaster. Road construction destroys the forest and frightens its game. Moreover, colonists introduce diseases to which tribal peoples have no resistance; even influenza can become an epidemic. Following the access roads come coal-mining, oil and timber companies, cattle ranchers and agriculturalists. The forest is further reduced, its shallow soils eroded, and its air and water polluted by mining wastes and by agricultural pesticides and herbicides. The flooding caused by the damming of rivers for hydroelectric projects can create malarial zones, and has left many indigenous peoples homeless; resettlement provision is inadequate or non-existent. Tourist agencies offer package tours to the diminishing area which remains 'untouched'. Many colonists are urban poor whose settlement is encouraged by governments anxious to reduce the shanty-town population. Ironically, tribes who attempt to escape violent confrontation with colonists by moving closer to towns are forced into similar conditions of poverty.

Development agencies are now taking the potentially detrimental effects of large-scale projects into account. However, even where legislation intended to protect both people and environment exists, economic pressures mean that it is often disregarded by governments willing to capitalize on all available resources. Legislation on reparation cannot guarantee the impossible; it is questionable to what extent a damaged habitat can regenerate. Payment of damages cannot reverse the effects on those forced to live in contaminated surroundings.

Lack of recognition of territorial and cultural rights can be a real threat to survival, but many South American governments also have a poor human rights record. This affects the whole population, but minority groups can become particularly vulnerable when they are caught up in the violence between government forces and guerrilla movements. While the violence surrounding Sendero Luminoso in Peru is the most extreme case, in which more than 27,000 are estimated dead or 'disappeared' and many others tortured and imprisoned without trial, comparable situations have provoked killings in Colombia, Ecuador and Suriname. The clash of interests between cocaine dealers and guerrilla movements, and usurpation of land by colonists, oil companies, agribusiness and gold miners, have all resulted in lethal violence against indigenous groups, such as the massacre of Yanomami on the Venezuelan border in 1993.Yet perpetrators are seldom brought to trial. In Bolivia the US coca-eradication programme has destroyed the livelihood of many small farmers while the imported crop strains and inappropriate techniques recommended as alternatives by foreign 'experts' also cause ecological damage.

Although in most South American countries Roman Catholicism is the state religion, the practice of traditional beliefs, in which women often play a significant role, continues to be a source of strength in the reaffirmation of national identity for both indigenous and Afro-Latin Americans. Degrees of syncretism vary from country to country and in some cases the two religions are carried on simultaneously. Besides its initial role in the colonization of the Americas, the church has traditionally played a major part in the administration of indigenous and Afro-Latin American populations, and in many parts of South America today it works in favour of indigenous people's rights. The Indigenist Missionary Council (CIMI) in Brazil and the Amazonian Centre for Anthropology and Applied Practice (CAAAP) in Peru actively help indigenous peoples and publish their material. However, missionary presence also has a negative aspect. Missionary work is divided between Roman Catholic orders, mainly from Europe, and Protestant sects mainly from the USA. Their conflicting approaches to life can cause division and confusion in the indigenous communities where they work.

In many areas, Roman Catholic missionaries attract indigenous peoples to their mission stations. Although this has changed under the influence of liberation theology, Roman Catholic missions formerly disregarded traditional indigenous ways of life and enforced the use of Western clothing and the Spanish language.

In the Andes, prohibition of tobacco, drugs (such as coca leaf) and particularly alcohol prevent converts to some Protestant sects from taking part in, and more significantly taking responsibility for, community festivals. While it may be welcomed as a means of avoiding crippling financial outlay, lack of participation also threatens to fragment social organization in the community. Protestant missions often work within the communities. The most active is the Summer Institute of Linguistics, a linguistic and cultural institution, which presents another face as the Wycliffe Bible Translators. Its fieldworkers proselytize the evangelical and fundamentalist traditions of Protestantism and have been known to favour government and commercial interests to the disadvantage of indigenous communities. They are no longer permitted to work in Colombia and were previously expelled from Ecuador. The fundamentalist New Tribes Mission, active in Paraguay, Brazil and Venezuela, actively hunts down tribal peoples from the air, and forces its 'converts' to live in settlements, where they are often used as a source of cheap labour,[3] as they are by a non-proselytizing religious minority, the Mennonites.

South American minorities, whether indigenous peoples or descendants of African slaves, have a long history of resistance to oppression. Maintaining continuity with past traditions and inventing new ones is a source of inspiration in their struggle to claim an equal place in a world still refusing its full acknowledgement.

Indigenous political awareness in South America is still evolving, and while the term 'nation' has been adopted by more politically conscious peoples, some would not choose to describe themselves in this way, while others prefer *comunidad nativa* (native community). Information on particular South American indigenous minorities is often limited, but similar problems affect many groups and the discussion in much of this section can be taken as reasonably representative of issues affecting them today.[4] Issues affecting women are described in the context of the relevant indigenous, Afro-Latin or other minority group. Accounts of the minority situation in each South American country are intended to summarize the problems they experience, the legislation regarding them, and the extent to which, individually or together, minorities are acting to achieve self-determination.

The Caribbean

The issue of minorities in the Caribbean (here defined as the islands of the Caribbean Sea, plus Bermuda) is inseparable from the processes of colonization, enslavement, production and labour migration which has moulded the region's history. Every territory has undergone a pattern of dramatic ethnic transformation, because colonizing powers, for the most part European, removed or destroyed indigenous populations and replaced them with imported workforces, the forebears of most Caribbean people today.

Only isolated survivors of the Caribbean's original peoples remain. The Arawaks who inhabited the larger islands of the present-day Greater Antilles were exterminated within a century of Columbus's arrival in 1492. The Caribs of the Lesser Antilles, however, successfully resisted European colonization, and thanks to the inaccessible landscape and limited agricultural potential of islands such as Dominica and St Vincent, as well as their own resistance, escaped extermination. Compared to the indigenous populations of South and Central America, their numbers are tiny and their future far from certain.

The development of the plantation economy, with sugar-cane at its centre, created societies where numerical minorities wielded exclusive economic and political power. Slavery was the first form of coercive labour used to fuel the plantation system, followed by apprenticeship, indentureship and low-paid wage labour. In each instance, the great majority of Caribbean people were effectively excluded from economic and political participation. Even with the advent of formal political independence, there has been a tendency for a small minority or elite to control the levers of government and the economy. This elite is generally, although by no means always, lighter-skinned than the majority.

In the Hispanic Caribbean countries of Cuba, the Dominican Republic and Puerto Rico, the large-scale migration and settlement of Europeans has meant that the ethnic balance is different from that of the English- and French-speaking Caribbean. Black people in these territories do not constitute a large majority, as they do in many other islands, and they may reasonably be seen as minorities, a position reinforced by their social and economic status.

The Caribbean has been a region built on migration. After approximately three centuries of African slavery, the planters and colonial authorities turned to the Indian sub-continent to meet their labour needs, and thousands of 'East Indians' arrived in Trinidad and in smaller numbers in Guadeloupe, Martinique, Jamaica and other islands. Their distinct cultural identity makes them a recognizable minority (although technically a numerical majority in Trinidad) throughout the region. They were joined by Chinese, Madeirans and people from throughout the Middle East in a constant stream of migration.

While migrants have come to the Caribbean from every continent, movement within the region has always been a feature of economic and social life. Unemployment and poverty have spurred the great migratory waves to Europe and North America, but equally from one territory to another. This mobility of labour has encouraged significant cultural exchanges and a sense of regional identity. Yet it has also led to the formation of particular minorities, characterized by low economic status and non-assimilation into broader society. However, not all migrants are poor and marginalized. Middle-class professionals and entrepreneurs also move from one territory to another, but with a greater tendency towards social assimilation.

In the latter half of the twentieth century, the phenomenon of migration has taken on complex political dimensions, especially with the recurrent crisis in Haiti and the resulting outflow of Haitian refugees. Haitians have formed significant communities in the Dominican Republic, the Bahamas and other islands. With their distinct linguistic and cultural identity, they are recognizable minorities and often vulnerable to racism and harassment.

Further reading

Beckles, H. and Shepherd, V. (eds), *Caribbean Freedom: Economy and Society from Emancipation to the Present*, London, James Currey, 1993.

Boff, L. and Elizondo, V., *Concillium (1990/6) 1492–1992: The Voice of the Victims*, London, SCM Press, 1990.

Cuppers, G., *Compañeras: Voices from the Latin American Women's Movement*, London, Latin America Bureau, 1994.

Davis, D.J. (ed.), *Slavery and Beyond: The African Impact on Latin America and the Caribbean,* Wilmington, DE, Scholarly Resources/Jaguar Books, 1995.

Davis, S.H., *Land Rights and Indigenous Peoples: The Role of the Inter-American Commission on Human Rights*, Cambridge, MA, Cultural Survival, 1988.

Dunbar Ortiz, R., *Indians of the Americas: Human Rights and Self-Determination*, London, Zed Books, 1984.

Ferguson, J., *Far from Paradise: An Introduction to Caribbean Development,* London, Latin America Bureau, 1990.

Gray, A., *Amerindians of South America*, London, MRG report, 1987.

Harris, O., *Latin American Women*, London, MRG report, 1983.

International Work Group for Indigenous Affairs, *The Indigenous World 1995–6*, Copenhagen, IWGIA, 1996.

Miller, M.S. and Cultural Survival (eds), *State of the Peoples: A Global Human Rights Report on Societies in Danger*, Boston, MA, Beacon Press, 1993.

MRG (ed.), *No Longer Invisible: Afro-Latin Americans Today*, London, Minority Rights Publications, 1995.

MRG (ed.), *Afro-Central Americans: Rediscovering the African Heritage*, London, MRG report, 1996.

NACLA, 'The Black Americas 1492–1992', *NACLA Report on the Americas,* vol. 25, no. 4, 1992.

NACLA, 'The First Nations 1492–1992', *NACLA Report on the Americas*, vol. 25, 1991.

Payne, A. and Sutton, P. (eds), *Modern Caribbean Politics*, Baltimore, MD, Johns Hopkins University Press, 1993.

Sale, K., *The Conquest of Paradise: Christopher Columbus and the Columbian Legacy*, London, Hodder & Stoughton, 1990.

Stavenhagen, R., 'La situación y los derechos de los pueblos indígenas de América', *América Indígena*, 1/2, 1992, pp. 63–119.

Sunshine, C., *The Caribbean: Survival, Struggle and Sovereignty,* Washington, DC, EPICA, 1988.

Urban, J. and Sherzer, J. (eds), *Nation-States and Indians in Latin America*, Austin, University of Texas Press, 1994.

Wearne, P., *Return of the Indian*, London, Cassell and Latin America Bureau, 1996.

Antigua-Barbuda

Land area:	441.6 sq km
Population:	64,000 (1991)
Main languages:	English
Main religions:	Christianity (majority Anglican)
Main minority groups:	—
Real per capita GDP:	$5,369
UNDP HDI/rank:	0.866 (40)

The twin-island state of Antigua-Barbuda lies in the Leeward Island chain in the Caribbean. The country gained its independence as a unitary state from Britain in 1984. It is almost entirely dependent on tourism. The country's population is estimated to be about 85 per cent of African descent. No minority rights issues have been identified.

Argentina

Land area:	2,766,889 sq km
Population:	33.5 million (est., 1993)
Main languages:	Spanish, indigenous languages, Welsh, Japanese
Main religions:	Christianity (majority Roman Catholic), Judaism, indigenous religions
Main minority groups:	indigenous peoples including Guaraní/Mbyá, Quechua, Aymara, Mapuche, Toba, Wichi/Mataco and Chiriguano 373,000 (2%), Jews 211,000 (0.6%), Japanese 50,000 (0.15%), Welsh, 10,000 (0.03%), small Afro-Argentinian, Arab and Asian populations
Real per capita GDP:	$8,350
UNDP HDI/rank:	0.885 (30)

Although Argentina was colonized by Spain, other European countries, including Britain, have played an important role in its development since the conquest. Indigenous communities were the victims of extermination campaigns in the eighteenth and nineteenth centuries on the part of those wishing to claim savanna lands. Argentina's fifteen indigenous peoples, who include Guaraní/Mbyá, Quechua, Aymara, Mapuche, Toba, Wichi/Mataco and Chiriguano, now live mainly on the country's northern and western fringes. Other minorities include Jews (mainly in Buenos Aires), Welsh (in Chubut) and Japanese, as well as Arab, Asian and Afro-Argentinian populations.

Until 1983 the indigenous population had no legal status in Argentine law. A federal act of 1985 now provides that indigenous communities should receive sufficient land for their needs; this land should be unseizable. Although Argentina is a party to the United Nations Educational Scientific and Cultural Organization (UNESCO) convention on discrimination in education, a recent case in which a Quechua-speaking family was unable to register a child with a Quechua name, because it is not considered a 'civilized' language, calls into question how far this clause is being implemented.[1] Indigenous peoples continue to be threatened by colonization as well as by logging interests and tourism.

Toba

Colonization of Toba land in the Chaco region has been a persistent problem since a reserve was originally granted in 1923. Since then their territory has been reduced by 25 per cent. While sugar plantations and cotton and timber industries provide the Toba with work, conditions are poor and often result in debt peonage. Toba in the northern province of Bermejo, however, have successfully reacquired lands previously occupied by a sugar refinery.

Wichi/Mataco

Traditionally Wichi are hunter gatherers, planting gardens and gathering honey as well as fishing. In 1987, contrary to national and international legislation, the provincial government of Salta passed a law which recognized settlers as having legal right to Wichi land. Settlers forbade Wichi to hunt and took gratuitous violent action against them. The non-traditional herding of cattle and goats on scrubby Chaco forest is reducing previously fertile grassland to a sandy desert. Colonization has created a vicious circle in which the settlers have forced Wichi into the same situation of urban poverty that the settlers hope to escape.[2]

Guaraní/Mbyá

About 6,000 Guaraní/Mbyá inhabit the north-eastern province of Misiones. The revocation of Law 2435, which gave some degree of autonomy to indigenous peoples and the passing of the New Aboriginal Law 2727 in December 1988, has placed all Guaraní under the direct control of the state. In spite of denunciation by the UN, in 1993 the Governor of Misiones was still obliging Guaraní to abandon their lands. In September 1993 Guaraní gathered in the provincial capital of Posadas to demand restitution of Law 2435 and to protest against destruction of their unique forest ecosystem by logging, mining and tourist interests, and against the construction of a hydroelectric dam on their lands. Guaraní communities have been destroyed by illegal logging companies, and protestors beaten and imprisoned.[3]

Mapuche

Argentinian Mapuche are asserting their sociocultural identity in spite of outside pressures. Driven from the pampas in the nineteenth century they now inhabit the western area of Argentina, divided from their relatives in Chile by an international boundary (see **Chile**). Free access across this frontier is an issue with both halves of the nation.[4] In April 1993, Mapuche united to discuss the implementation of educational programmes in the Mapuche language and pledged themselves to autonomy and self-determination. Mapuche have their own organizations such as Taiñ Kiñegetuam 'to return to being one', in which women, who traditionally play a major role in Mapuche ritual, are prominent.[5]

Other minorities

Welsh immigration to Chubut region in Patagonia took place mainly between 1865 and 1914. Historical conflict over linguistic and political autonomy led to an unsuccessful attempt at secession at the turn of the century. As a result the state has encouraged non-Welsh settlement of the area; tax incentives have brought many non-Welsh enterprises, with whom the still predominantly Welsh agricultural community, which previously functioned as a cooperative, is forced to compete. Break-up of the cooperatives and other community organizations, as well as the lack of Welsh teaching in schools, has meant Welsh is spoken less. Furthermore, since it is associated with low status it may be rejected by younger members of the community. Welsh suffer minimal ethnic discrimination, although Welsh first names are not permitted, and token support is given to demonstrations of ethnicity such as their annual *eisteddfod*.[6]

Large-scale Jewish immigration between 1890 and 1930 provoked disapproval from the Roman Catholic Church and provoked a pogrom in 1919. Anti-Semitism among Argentinian elites, particularly the armed forces, derived from French right-wing, Falangist, Fascist and Nazi sources. In the postwar period Argentina became an international centre for anti-Semitic publications and neo-Nazi activity. During the military dictatorship of 1976–83, a large number of the disappeared were Jews but Carlos Menem's government appears committed to combatting anti-Semitism. The car-bombing of the Jewish Mutual Society of Argentina in 1994, in which 76 people were killed, provoked demonstrations of solidarity with the Jewish community.[7]

Afro-Argentinians have played a significant role in the country's history; many, both free people and slaves, died fighting for Argentina in the Cisplatine War and War of Independence. Although it is not possible to give an exact figure, Argentina reportedly has a small but politically aware Afro-Argentinian population, living mainly in Buenos Aires, who continue to preserve their heritage.

The majority of some 2,000 Japanese who settled in Argentina prior to 1920 were immigrants who had re-emigrated from either Brazil or Peru. Early migrants worked in a variety of occupations as unskilled labourers but subsequently concentrated on laundry and dry-cleaning or market gardening. Most of the 50,000 immigrants and their descendants are located in and around Buenos Aires; their assimilation and acculturation are advanced.[8] Koreans and other Asian groups are subject to the same kind of racial discrimination as indigenous groups.

Conclusions and future prospects

Indigenous peoples are now taking action both individually and collectively to protest against their lack of land titles and the damage caused to their environment by colonization and industrial interests. Bilingual intercultural education is an issue which recently united members of Toba, Wichi Pilagua, Chiriguano, Mbyá and Mocoví nations for a three-day conference and one which is also relevant to non-indigenous linguistic minorities. The issue of access contested by Mapuche also affects Quechua, Aymara and Guaraní.

Further reading

América Indígena, vols. 1–2, 4, 1993.

Gray, A., *Amerindians of South America*, London, MRG report, 1987.

Maybury-Lewis, D., 'Becoming Indian in lowland South America', in G. Urban and J. Sherzer (eds), *Nation States and Indians in Latin America*, Austin, University of Texas Press, 1994, pp. 207–36.

Minority-based and advocacy organizations

Amnesty International, 25 de Mayo 67, 4 Piso, 1002 Capital Federal, Buenos Aires, Argentina; tel. 54 1 331 2370, fax 54 1 334 2826.

Asociación Indígena de la República Argentina, Balbastro 1790, 1406 Capital Federal, Buenos Aires, Argentina; tel. 54 1 977 308, fax 54 1 613 4992.

Casa de la Cultura Indo-Afro-Americana, Casa de Correo 155, 3000 Santa Fé, Argentina.

Confederación de Organizaciones Mapuches 'Taiñ Kiñegetuam', CC No. 88–8300, Neuquen, Argentina.

Mapuche de Puelmapu, Batilana 315, Barrio Islas Malvinas, 8300 Neuquen, Argentina.

Bahamas

Land area:	13,939 sq km
Population:	262,000 (1992)
Main languages:	English
Main religions:	Christianity (majority Anglican)
Main minority groups:	Haitians 20,000–70,000 (8–27%)
Real per capita GDP:	$16,180
UNDP HDI/rank:	0.895 (26)

The Bahamas are comprised of almost 700 islands and 2,000 uninhabited cays which stretch 1,220 kilometres south-eastwards from a point only 80 kilometres from Florida. Independent since 1973, the country's economy has been interlinked with that of the USA for most of the twentieth century.

Haitians

A significant minority of migrant Haitian workers live in the Bahamas, principally in the islands of New Providence, Grand Bahama and Great Abaco. Fleeing poverty and repression at home, their number is calculated between 20,000 and 70,000. Haitians have been migrating since the 1960s, but numbers increased dramatically in the late 1980s and 1990s. Of these, most are illegal immigrants. The majority work in service-sector jobs, in hotels and construction, on farms and as gardeners, labourers and domestic workers. Mostly speaking Creole and often living in squatter camps, Haitians are conspicuous and have frequently been targets for harassment and forced repatriations. Since the Bahamian economy went into recession in the early 1990s and the Free National Movement took power in the 1992 elections, incidents of violent eviction have grown.[1]

Conclusions and future prospects

Promising a 'Bahamianization process', the government is currently committed to the 'detention and early repatriation of all illegal immigrants'. It has offered resident status to those who have lived in the Bahamas for ten years or more on payment of a US $2,500 fee; others are to be deported. In May 1994 the Bahamian government insisted that it would not accept even bona fide 'political' refugees; this was on grounds of 'national security'.[2]

Minority-based and advocacy organizations

Grand Bahama Human Rights Association, Regent Centre North, PO Box F-2562, Freepost, Bahamas; tel. 1 809 352 5195, fax 1 809 353 5225.

Barbados

Land area:	430 sq km
Population:	269,000 (1993)
Main languages:	English
Main religions:	Christianity (majority Anglican)
Main minority groups:	'poor whites' 400 (est., 0.15%)
Real per capita GDP:	$10,570
UNDP HDI/rank:	0.906 (25)

After independence from Britain in 1966, Barbados enjoyed twenty years of political stability and economic growth until recession hit in the late 1980s. Based on sugar production and tourism, the island's economy is vulnerable to uncertain markets and unpredictable prices. However, the UN Development Programme has ranked Barbados among the very highest countries in the developing world in terms of social indicators. There is a small minority of so-called 'poor whites' (also pejoratively known as 'redlegs'), numbering no more than several hundred. These are the descendants of indentured labourers sent from Britain in the seventeenth and eighteenth centuries.[1] Traditionally marginalized and engaged in subsistence agriculture, this community is mainly to be found in St John parish on the east coast of the island. After centuries of deliberate separation from wider society, the 'poor whites' have now almost disappeared as a distinct minority.

Belize

Land area:	22,960 sq km
Population:	200,000 (1992)
Main languages:	English (official), English Creole, Spanish, Mayan (Kekchi, Mopan), Garífuna
Main religions:	Christianity (majority Roman Catholic, Anglican and Methodist), Mayan religions (largely hidden)
Main minority groups:	Maya 20,000 (10%), Garífuna (Garinagu) 13,200 (6.6%), Mennonites 6,000 (3%)
Real per capita GDP:	$4,610
UNDP HDI/rank:	0.754 (67)

Belize is the most culturally diverse nation in Central America. Its British colonial history in a Spanish-dominated region and its difficult border relations with Guatemala, which until 1991 maintained a constitutional claim on the territory, have dominated the country's history. This is reflected in the population. The Afro-Belizean Creoles, mainly descendants of British settlers and African slaves, are concentrated in the Belize district including Belize City. Due to their relations with the British, who ruled what was formerly British Honduras until 1981, they are the dominant group in most social and political institutions.

Spanish-speaking *mestizos*, mostly the descendants of mixed-race Mexican Maya who fled from the War of the Castes in the mid-1800s, settled in the northern lowlands, introducing agriculture to a society largely based on the sale of timber to British traders. The *mestizo* population grew significantly during the 1980s due to a continuing flow of refugees, economic migrants and seasonal farm workers from Guatemala, El Salvador and Honduras; by 1991 they formed 41 per cent of the population, the largest group in the country. In addition, there are a number of small minorities, including Maya, Garífuna and Mennonites.

Maya

Mayan communities remain in Belize, surviving on subsistence agriculture in the Toledo region, even though most were driven out of the country by the British. The Mopan Maya have managed to maintain small settlements. In addition, there are 30 small Kekchi Maya settlements. The Kekchi are descended from people who migrated from the coffee farms of Guatemala in the 1870s and 1880s. They are the country's poorest and most neglected minority. During the 1980s, the Mayan population expanded due to the exodus of Maya from Guatemala. A recent development of cultural revivalism has led to plans to create a Maya Institute of Belize.

Garinagu

The Garífuna of Belize, who refer to themselves as Garinagu, initially came to the area from the Bay Islands of Honduras (see **Honduras**). Several coastal towns and villages are predominantly Garífuna while others are mixed Creole/Garífuna. Under colonial rule in the nineteenth century, they were prohibited from owning land, in order to create a cheap and available labour force for the logging industry. However, they managed to resist these attempts at assimilation. Today, the struggle to maintain their community is largely a cultural one as they have retained a number of Afro-Caribbean traditions in addition to their language. The Garinagu have traditionally been discriminated against and demonized by some.

Mennonites

Mennonites, members of a Swiss Protestant sect, began arriving in Belize in 1958. They own large areas of farming land and control their own schools and financial institutions. They mainly live in six communities in northern Belize and are divided into a progressive wing, who believe that the church should be more involved in the world, and a traditional wing, who believe that the modern world contaminates their faith.

Conclusions and future prospects

While there is no institutionalized discrimination in Belize, colonial history has tended to favour people with lighter skins, who, among the Creoles, form most of the dominant political and economic class. Poverty and unemployment have exacerbated racial tensions, particularly between Creoles and *mestizos*. However, the geographic distribution of different minorities has prevented major problems of this kind. Belize's major problems are non-ethnic, centring on the country's severe economic dependency on the USA, which has replaced Britain as the major economic and cultural influence.

Further reading

Barry, T. and Vernon, D., *Inside Belize*, Albuquerque, N. Mex., Resource Center Press, 1995.

Ewens, D., 'Belize', in MRG (ed.), *No Longer Invisible: Afro-Latin Americans Today*, London, Minority Rights Publications, 1995; and in MRG (ed.) *Afro-Central Americans*, London, MRG report, 1996.

Minority-based and advocacy organizations

Society for the Promotion of Education and Research (SPEAR), PO Box 1766, Belmopan, Belize; tel. 501 22779.

Bermuda

Land area:	53 sq km
Population:	60,000 (1993)
Main languages:	English
Main religions:	Christianity (majority Anglican)
Main minority groups:	—
Real per capita GDP:	—
UNDP HPI/rank:	—

Bermuda is a Crown Colony of the United Kingdom and has been a colonial possession since 1684. Situated 1,450 kilometres north-east of the Bahamas, it comprises over 150 small islands, most of which are uninhabited. Its economy is almost entirely based upon tourism and offshore financial services, and these sectors have brought considerable prosperity to many Bermudans. About 60 per cent of the population is regarded as of African descent, and during the 1970s there were serious racial tensions when the mainly black, pro-independence Progressive Labour Party (PLP) was denied power, claiming gerrymandering. The PLP continues to press for independence, while the more conservative multiracial United Bermuda Party (UBP), which won elections in 1993, favours the retention of dependent status. A referendum in 1995 produced 73 per cent against independence, but with a low turn-out. No minority rights issues have been identified.

Bolivia

Land area:	1,084,391 sq km
Population:	6.3 million (1992)
Main languages:	Spanish, Quechua, Aymara, other indigenous languages
Main religions:	Christianity (majority Roman Catholic), indigenous religions
Main minority groups:	indigenous groups including Aymara, Quechua, Chiquitano, Guaraní and Moxeño 4.1 million (65%), Afro-Bolivians 158,000 (est., 2%), small communities of Japanese and Europeans including Germans (Mennonites)
Real per capita GDP:	$2,510
UNDP HDI/rank:	0.584 (111)

During the 1970s and 1980s Bolivia was governed by a series of harsh military dictatorships with little regard for human rights. Its return to democracy has been hampered by economic crises and the escalation in the production and traffic of cocaine. Highland Quechua (pop. 2.3 million) and Aymara (1.6 million) make up more than 50 per cent of the population. Lowland groups include Chiquitano (40,000), Guaraní (38,000), Moxeño (30,000) and Ayoreo. There is also an Afro-Bolivian population and small communities of Japanese and people of European origin including Germans. The recently established government Department of Ethnic Affairs is conducting a census of lowland ethnic minorities and intends to do the same with Afro-Bolivians.

In Bolivia land rights have until recently been governed by the 1953 Agrarian Reform Law, which is mostly applicable to highland regions. A resolution enacted in 1989 considered as indigenous territory the areas traditionally occupied by indigenous groups, and prohibited the allocation of this land for colonization, ranching or forestry. In 1990, in response to mobilization by indigenous organizations, a five-year ecological pause was declared to allow for a review of policies that could have a potentially adverse impact on the environment, and several decrees recognized the ownership of specific areas of land by forest-dwelling groups.[1]

Highland groups

The majority of Aymara are small farmers living in the departments of La Paz, Oruro and North Potosí. Many maintain lands in both highland and lowland zones, a practice which has its roots in the pre-Incaic period. Women in particular may be monolingual in Aymara. Rural Quechua life is very similar. Aymaras have long been active in the peasant movement; the Katarista movement, named after the Aymara leader of the eighteenth-century Indian uprising, Tupac Katari, began in La Paz with the creation of a cultural centre and its own radio programme. Kataristas saw Bolivia's problem as being those of exploited social classes and of oppressed peoples within a common state.[2] There is now a Katarista political party whose Aymara leader holds the post of Vice-President. Aymaras have their own Institute of Aymara Language and Culture, which, with Aymara participation, publishes material in Aymara about Aymara culture. After 1953 Aymara migrated to La Paz in increasing numbers. Young girls found employment as live-in servants, older women became street vendors and have forged a special place for themselves in La Paz society. A few have achieved greater economic and social standing than middle class 'whites'.[3]

Many Quechua worked in the mines of Oruro and Potosí. The fall in the price of agricultural products and the collapse of the world tin market means that Quechua are increasingly migrating to the cities where men find work as cargo carriers; women, who join the ranks of street vendors, are often subjected to discrimination by better established Quechua and Aymara colleagues. A more lucrative, but also more risky, alternative is to work as a *pisado*r (treader) in one of the cocaine producing zones.[4] Since 1952 tens of thousands of Quechua and Aymara have migrated to the lowlands where they work and live as small farmers under precarious conditions.

Lowland groups

Cattle ranching and colonization are a major threat to tribes of the department of Beni such as the Chiman and Moxeño. In September 1990, 800 members of the lowland groups walked to La Paz from the Amazonian town of Trinidad to demand recognition of land rights. As a result of that march more than 1.5 million hectares of land in northern Bolivia were recognized as indigenous territory.[5] The relevant decrees have not, however, been properly implemented.

Lowland groups are also menaced by logging and mining concerns. Timber companies are supposed to pay a tax of 11 per cent to compensate for environmental destruction; Chiquitano are owed millions of dollars and the Quebrada Azul company which is robbing precious woods from Amboró National Park has threatened to kill Chiquitano leaders. American anti-drug agents are reported by inhabitants of Isiboro Sécuré National Park to have wrecked homes on the pretext of drug eradication. Large landowners use toxic chemicals such as parathion and heptachloride which leach into the water supply. Intensive agriculture is unsuitable for the area and results in soil erosion. Lowland groups are now demanding territorial rights and legal recognition of their political organizations.[6] During the 1990s the Confederación de los Pueblos Indígenas del Oriente, Chacó y Amazonia Boliviana has played an important role in achieving bilingual education and preliminary recognition of indigenous territory.

Afro-Bolivians

Bolivia's Afro-Latin population is descended from slaves who first arrived in 1535 to work in the royal mint at Potosí and on haciendas in the warmer climate of Yungas where the main Afro-Bolivian communities are today.[7] Those born in Africa were not numerous enough to form 'nations', which may account for the extent to which present day Afro-Bolivians have adopted Aymara language and culture. Afro-Bolivians are bilingual in Aymara and Spanish and their religion shares the Roman Catholic Andean syncretism.

Afro-Bolivians are usually referred to as *negros*; they are distinguished from 'whites' and *mestizos* in economic rather than racial terms, and many think of themselves as Bolivian rather than African. The Afro-Bolivian Spanish dialect and their music and dance have been becoming less distinctive, but lately this trend has been reversed with the revival of the *saya* dance. 'Afro-Bolivian' has recently been adopted as a self-description with the emergence of a black consciousness movement; but the movement faces organizational problems as well as a split between the interests of urban intellectuals and rural peasant farmers.

Environmental deterioration, low prices for agricultural produce and US-sponsored demands for the eradication of coca cultivation are problems shared with other inhabitants of the region and can best be confronted by participating in the peasant federation and the association of coca producers.

Other minorities

In the past Ayoreo of the Chaco region have been harassed by the New Tribes Mission (NTM) (see **Paraguay**); reports now indicate that NTM are adopting similar tactics with the Yuki. Ayoreo have been 'deported' to the town of Santa Cruz, where they are reduced to begging.[8]

About 150 Uru still live around Lake Titicaca, using traditional reed boats for their fishing but in other respects adopting Aymara lifestyle. Around 2,000 Chipaya live in the high plateau to the south-west of Bolivia close to the Chilean frontier. Their weaving is distinctive as are their round, thatched houses and they maintain a determined independence.

Japanese initially migrated from Peru and Brazil to the forests of eastern Bolivia during the rubber boom of 1900–15. Today's Japanese population is distributed mainly in La Paz and the lowland departments of Beni and Santa Cruz; the majority are farmers well assimilated into Bolivian society. Those who received free land in the Santa Cruz area by the Migration Agreement of 1956 are mechanized farmers and assimilated to a lesser degree.[9]

There are several Mennonite communities (see **Paraguay**) in the Santa Cruz area, where they are involved in agriculture and cattle ranching.

Conclusions and future prospects

Bolivia's constitution now recognizes the country's multi-ethnic character and includes clauses on land claims and bilingual education. There is a possibility that television programmes by indigenous peoples will be used in education.[10] However, indigenous lands in the east are not yet officially demarcated, nor is the extent of the land holdings of settlers and church within that territory described. Logging in the forests of the Chimán, due to end by 1990, appears to continue. With the 1994 legislation regarding *participación popular*, political power is shifting to the countryside. It remains to be seen whether this change, which undermines traditional indigenous social and political systems, will bring positive results.

Further reading

Albó, X., *Bolivia plurilingue: guía para planificadores y educadores*, La Paz, CIPCA/ UNICEF, 1994.

Latin America Bureau, *Bolivia in Focus*, London, LAB, 1994.

Rivera Cusicanqui, S., *Oppressed but Not Defeated: Peasant Struggles among the Aymara and Quechua in Bolivia, 1900–1980*, Geneva, UN Research Institute for Social Development, 1987.

Spedding, A., 'Bolivia', in MRG (ed.), *No Longer Invisible: Afro-Latin Americans Today*, London, Minority Rights Publications, 1995.

Stern, S. (ed.), *Resistance, Rebellion and Consciousness in the Andean Peasant World: 18th to 20th Centuries*, Madison, University of Wisconsin Press, 1987.

Minority-based and advocacy organizations

Asamblea Permanente de los Derechos Humanos, Casilla 8678, La Paz, Bolivia.

Confederación de los Pueblos Indígenas de Bolivia (CIDOB), Villa 1ro. de Mayo, Casilla 4213, Santa Cruz de la Sierra, Bolivia; tel. 591 3 460714, fax 591 3 460714.

Frente Indio Amautico del Tawantinsuyu, Casilla 8825, La Paz, Bolivia; tel 591 2 811032.

Instituto de Lengua y Cultura Aymara, La Paz, Bolivia.

Organización de Mujeres Aymaras del Kollasuyo (OMAK), Casilla 13195, La Paz, Bolivia; tel. 591 2 69 38625, fax 591 2 66 52818.

Brazil

Land area:	8,511,996 sq km
Population:	162.2 million (est., 1994)
Main languages:	Portuguese, indigenous languages
Main religions:	Christianity (majority Roman Catholic, also Pentecostal), Afro-Brazilian religions (Candomblé, Umbanda), Judaism, indigenous religions
Main minority groups:	Afro-Brazilians 65 million–120 million (40–75%), Japanese 1.7 million (1%), indigenous groups including Yanomami, Tukano, Urueu-Wau-Wau, Awá, Arara, Guaraní, Nambiquara, Tikuna, Makuxi, Wapixana and Kayapó 254,000 (0.16%), Jews 100,000 (0.06%)
Real per capita GDP:	$5,500
UNDP HDI/rank:	0.796 (58)

Unlike most of Latin America, Brazil was colonized by the Portuguese. Initial relations with the indigenous population were friendly but colonists eager to exploit trade in wood and sugar soon provoked conflict. The massacre and slavery which almost exterminated the coastal Tupi initiated a pattern repeated over the next 500 years. Rival colonial powers, France and the Netherlands, exploited existing hostilities between indigenous groups. Colonists introduced dysentery, smallpox, influenza and plague. Epidemics of these European diseases swept through the *reduções* (settlements) instituted by Jesuit missionaries, killing many thousands of indigenous and tribal peoples within a few decades.

In the early nineteenth century, Brazil increased its traditional exports of cotton, sugar and coffee, encroaching still further on indigenous lands. A reported eighty-seven indigenous groups were exterminated in the first half of the twentieth century through contact with expanding colonial frontiers. Between 1964 and 1984 foreign companies and international lending banks tightened control over Brazil's economic structure, continuing to push back the colonizing frontier. Roads stretching across the Amazon basin forced the removal of twenty-five indigenous groups.

Brazil now has 197 forest-dwelling indigenous groups, including Yanomami, Tukano, Urueu-Wau-Wau, Awá, Arara, Guaraní, Nambiquara, Tikuna, Makuxi, Wapixana and Kayapó, living either on reservations or in one of four national parks. Besides its large Afro-Brazilian population there are also significant Japanese and Jewish minorities. Brazilian policy in general is to assimilate all populations of foreign origin in the Brazilian 'melting pot'. Those unable to express themselves in the national language are banned from voting.

The 1988 Brazilian constitution guarantees indigenous forest peoples rights to inhabit their ancestral lands, though not their legal right to own it; it made no provision for land reform. Environmental issues dominated the latter part of 1988 and much of 1989 when the murder of Francisco (Chico) Mendes, the leader of the rubber tappers' union, brought Brazil's environmental problems to international attention. International concern was expressed that large-scale development projects – together with cattle ranching, industrial logging, the 'slash and burn' farming techniques of peasant smallholders and the release of large amounts of mercury into the environment by an estimated 60,000 gold prospectors (*garimpeiros*) in the Amazon region – presented a serious threat to the indigenous population and the rain-forest. International criticism of the government's poor response to the threat to the environment persisted throughout the early 1990s. Of particular concern to many international observers was the plight of the Yanomami. The National Indian Foundation (FUNAI) was heavily criticized for failing to provide effective protection and support for Brazil's indigenous population. A new cabinet post of Minister with Special Responsibility for the Brazilian Amazon was created after the Yanomami massacre at Haximú in 1993 (see **Venezuela**), which was at first believed to have taken place in Brazil. In June 1992 Brazil hosted the UN Conference on Environment and Development, the Earth Summit.[1]

Afro-Brazilians

After the decimation of the local indigenous population in the seventeenth century an estimated 3,650,000 African slaves were imported to Brazil, many of them to Brazil's first capital, Salvador da Bahia. Urban slave labour differed from plantation life; slaves were not passive victims of the system and many escaped to found their own *quilombos* or 'republics'. Africans preserved their cultural heritage and religions despite the lack of a common language. Brazilian Portuguese was richly influenced by the speech of African peoples, and a new Afro-Brazilian vocabulary developed. African religions survive in Brazil today. Brazil did not abolish slavery until 1888. Initially the Portuguese authorities promoted miscegenation as a population policy in underpopulated regions. But, fearing to become a black nation, Brazil subsequently opened its country to white immigrants, who were given preference to black people in jobs, housing and education.

The Portuguese attitude towards miscegenation is often offered as proof of their open-mindedness on race, and the term 'people of colour' has also contributed to the myth of racial democracy. The Brazilian sociologist Gilberto Freyre has been quoted as saying that negritude, black consciousness, is a 'mysticism that has no place in Brazil'. Racism is, however, an issue of importance in Brazil; although in law all Brazilians enjoy equality, and racial or colour discrimination is a criminal offence, for many years advertisements for jobs included the phrase 'boa aparência' (good appearance), meaning that only light-skinned people need to apply. By the time of the 1980 census Brazilians had coined 136 terms to define themselves and avoid categorization with those of a darker skin colour. It is argued that prejudice is not directed against darker people on the basis of their colour but on that of their socioeconomic standing. Most Afro-Brazilians lack economic power, political influence and effective representation and have been led to believe that *embranquecimento* (whitening) offers the only route to socioeconomic improvement. The policy of miscegenation was intended to stress the importance of assimilating the African into the broader *mestiça* society. Despite their distinctive ethnicity and religion, Brazil's estimated 65–120 million people of African ancestry (65 million was the official 1991 census figure), including *caboclos* (people of mixed Afro- and indigenous ancestry), are not officially recognized as a minority.

Afro-Brazilian religions constitute powerful sources of inner strength, enabling believers to reaffirm their African identity. A loose association of Roman Catholic saints with African deities, rather than syncretism, Candomblé is central to the lives of many Afro-Brazilians. Umbanda, along with Pentecostalism, is one of the fastest growing religions in Brazil today. The music, dance and lyrics of samba are also rich with the history and experience of Afro-Brazil.

Many Brazilians of colour themselves accept the myth of non-racialism in Brazil, yet others are becoming aware of the degree to which their cultural, religious, socioeconomic and political identities have been suppressed. Many hundreds of black consciousness and civil rights organizations are actively at work today. A community-based press acts as a catalyst for organizing, claiming rights and fighting racism. The Frente Negra Brasileira, founded in 1930 and the first national civil rights organization in Brazil, saw race and gender rights as intimately related; the women's movement obtained the right to vote in 1932. Women played an important role in the escaped slave communities and are still important leaders in the Candomblé religion today. They play an active role in the Movimento Negro Nacional whose ties with the Worker and Democratic Workers' parties have encouraged Afro-Brazilians to stand as election candidates. In 1994, Brazil's first black woman senator, Benedita da Silva, was elected.

While some Afro-Brazilians see racism as primarily a cultural problem to be solved through the development of black identity, others believe the struggle against racism must seek to change economic, social and political structures. For all its achievements the Afro-Brazilian movement has far to go before it can mobilize the majority of Brazilians of colour.[3]

Yanomami[2]

Yanomami are one of the largest groups (est. 9,000) of hunter gatherers living in the Amazonian rain forest of Roraima and Amazonas States which straddles the Brazil-Venezuela border. Since the illegal invasion of their lands by *garimpeiros* an estimated 20 per cent have been exterminated through disease. A major campaign by national and international support groups in 1991 resulted in the signing of a presidential decree creating an indigenous 'park' which covered all Yanomami lands in Brazil. Nevertheless, in August 1993 international attention was again focused on the region following the slaughter of 16 Yanomami of the village of Haximú by *garimpeiros* in the territorial dispute prompted by the miners' attempts to exploit the rich mineral deposits of Yanomami land. Yanomami spokesperson Davi Kopenawa requested the military evacuation of gold prospectors and the blowing up of their illegally-constructed runways. FUNAI stressed the need for permanent vigilance of the reserve and confirmed that despite pressure from Roraima state politicians, the extent of the Yanomami reserve would not be diminished.

Tukano

Tukano are river-dwelling agriculturalists living on the Upper Rio Negro. A number of government proposals regarding demarcation of their land has resulted in a 75 per cent reduction of the 'indigenous areas' proposed by FUNAI. Land close to the Colombian border on which Tukano have been carrying out small scale, environmentally sound gold mining operations is recognized by FUNAI as belonging to Tukano but is now wanted for strategic defence purposes by the military. This has led to harassment and accusations of illegal dealing in gold and drugs.

Urueu-Wau-Wau

Urueu-Wau-Wau are hunter gatherers in the state of Rondonia. They were contacted by FUNAI in 1981 when the area was opened up by the road building and colonization promoted by the World Bank-funded Polonoroeste project. Since then their population has decreased dramatically to less than 1,000. Besides conflict with invading settlers and miners, it is estimated that more than half the population has fallen victim to diseases introduced by outsiders. Rubber interests have prevented the acceptance of demarcation of their lands decreed by FUNAI. In 1991, one of the largest deposits of tin in the world was discovered in this already intensively mined area which has recently been invaded by gold miners expelled from Yanomami lands. In addition the Institute of Colonization and Land Reform is granting lands to illegal colonists. Urueu-Wau-Wau now have a single continuous area demarcated as a reserve.

Awá (Awá-Guajá)

Awá are a nomadic tribe of hunter gatherers referred to by other groups as Guajá, or Wazaiara, 'the owners of the hair garments'. They live in small groups in the hilly Gurupi region of Maranhão state; about 150 remain uncontacted. Since the 1950s their lands have been drastically reduced by government policy to an area too small to permit them to follow their traditional way of life. The sometimes violent invasions of settlers, ranchers, loggers, miners and charcoal burners, and the diseases they inevitably bring, have severely affected numbers. Some Awá have been resettled by FUNAI on neighbouring Guajajara land, causing inter-tribal tension. In spite of international protest Awá-Guajá continued to be the victims of violent attacks in 1993; government delay in demarcating Awá land due to lobbying of local politicians threatens this group with extinction.

Arara

Arara were first contacted in a series of violent encounters during the construction of the Transamazonian highway in the 1970s. Arara land has been sold by FUNAI to cattle ranchers; illegal mahogany logging is bringing an increased number of settlers; in 1992 remaining land was threatened by flooding from the proposed Babaquara dam on the Xingu river and its tributaries. This dam has now been shelved. Contacted Arara are forced to live in three villages and FUNAI have allowed fundamentalist missionaries to come in, bringing rapid and profound changes to the Arara way of life.

Nambiquara

Nambiquara are primarily hunter gatherers. In 1960 the BR-364 highway, part of the Polonoroeste project, was bulldozed straight through Nambiquara land, and the tribe relocated to a tiny, arid reserve, where they suffer malnutrition and imported diseases such as typhoid and yellow fever. In 1985 the remaining 1,200 Nambiquara led protests against the invasion and the proposed construction of a hydroelectric dam on their lands. In September 1993 the logging company Anilton Antonio Pompermayer was ordered to pay an indemnity of $200,000 to a group of Nambiquara for illegal invasion and logging in their Guaporé reserve.

Tikuna

In 1988, fourteen Tikuna living on the Solimões in western Amazonas were murdered. The trial of the loggers responsible, to be heard in Manaus by the federal rather than the state court, was originally scheduled for December 1994, but in 1995 was still liable to postponement.

Makuxi and Wapixana

Makuxi and Wapixana groups live in the Raposa-Serra do Sul area of Roraima state. This region has been opened up for cattle ranching. Since 1988 these groups have been the victims of lethal attacks by ranchers on several occasions. In 1992 it was proposed that their land be officially recognized. In 1994 continued delay in the demarcation of their lands led these groups, together with Ingarikó and Taurepang, to take direct action against illegal gold prospectors by setting up road blockades to cut off their supplies. Police destroyed their villages in retaliation. Makuxi and Ingarikó who protested against the construction of a hydroelectric dam on reserve lands were illegally removed from the proposed site.

Kayapó

In 1989 Kayapó organized a successful protest against the construction of a dam which would have flooded a vast area of Amazon territory. Kayapó visited the headquarters of the World Bank and secured mass media coverage of their plight. The resulting international protest led the World Bank to withdraw its funding, and the Brazilian government was forced to abandon the project. In October 1992 the Kayapó Menkragnotí were finally decreed nearly five million hectares in the Xingu and Altamira area of the rain forest. It is hoped that an innovative system of fire-breaks indicating the extent of the reserve will facilitate vigilance of its boundaries from the air. These clearings will be planted with species intended to provide a micro-ecosystem capable of resisting the pressure of the natural vegetation.

Other indigenous groups

Tapeba and Tremenbe from the northern coast were among the first to be colonized and 'acculturated'. Their struggle for identity has had to be undertaken from the suburbs of Fortaleza. In 1993 the court ruling which expelled Kaiowá and Nandevi Guarani from the state of Mato Grosso do Sul to make way for cattle ranchers was overruled by a regional tribunal; it recognized their original right to the land and ruled that FUNAI should demarcate it. In September 1994 this had still not been carried out and the groups were reported to be returning to their lands in spite of death threats from bandits hired by local farmers. More than 150 Kaiowá have committed suicide in the last decade.

Other minorities

Excluding the period 1941–50, Japanese migration to Brazil has continued uninterrupted since 1908. By the 1980s it had reached 750,000. Prior to 1914 the majority of Japanese immigrants were contract labourers. Later, efforts were made to establish agricultural colonies. Many also worked on coffee plantations. Although they have been the subject of popular protest in the past, Japanese and their descendants have blended well into the Brazilian scene; trends in social mobility, industrialization and urbanization contribute constantly to this process. First generation immigrants (Issei) generally, and second (Nisei) and third-generation (Sansei) in rural areas, remain Japanese in spirit and loyalty and consciously resist any racial and cultural losses. Mixed marriages among Issei are almost unknown.[4]

Brazil's Jewish population lives mainly in São Paulo, Rio de Janeiro and Porto Alegre. Since 1945 Jews have served in all areas of Brazilian political, economic and military life. Anti-Semitism has never been a major social problem in independent Brazil. Modern anti-Semitism dates from the 1930s and the creation of the Integralist Party. Explicit anti-Semitic movements are small, although some anti-Semitic attacks were made during the 1994 political campaigns.[5]

Conclusions and future prospects

International financial institutions are now more aware of the implications of development projects for indigenous and tribal peoples and it should be possible to avoid repeating Polonoroeste. Demarcation of indigenous land, which the government undertook to complete by 1993, is still being carried out; however, recent debate on constitutional amendments may modify the decree (22/91) defining demarcation of indigenous land and make it easier for outside mining and logging interests to usurp it. FUNAI's activities have been severely curtailed due to funding problems. Where land has been demarcated, the exclusive rights of indigenous peoples to its resources, recognized under Article 231 of the constitution, have not been protected; many peoples continue to be threatened by illegal exploitation and colonization. Lengthy campaigning has achieved the demarcation of a reserve to Yanomami but no governmental action is taken to uphold the integrity of the reserve; in 1993 Yanomami continued to be the victims of premeditated attacks by illegal gold prospectors.

In the face of government failure indigenous peoples are themselves organizing to defend their territory and, as accurate census figures are needed for land demarcation, to carry out their own census. Yucca and banana flour are being marketed by indigenous peoples in the Xingu National Park and it is hoped that marketing these goods to more distant and more objective markets will prevent nearby villages from obtaining them at unfavourable rates of exchange.

With regard to Brazil's African-descended populations, while the international community has a part to play in such urgent issues as the protection of street children, the full participation of Afro-Brazilians themselves is needed if they are to become the protagonists of their own liberation.

Further reading

Burdick, J., 'Brazil's black consciousness movement' and 'The myth of racial democracy', in NACLA, *Report on the Americas: The Black Americas 1492–1992*, vol. 25, no. 4. 1992, pp. 23–27 and 40–44.

Davis, D.J. (ed.), *Slavery and Beyond: The African Impact on Latin America and the Caribbean*, Wilmington, DE, Scholarly Resources/Jaguar Books, 1995.

Dzidzienyo, A. and Casal, L., *The Position of Blacks in Brazilian and Cuban Society*, London, MRG report, 1971, 1979.

Hill, J. (ed.), *Rethinking History and Myth: Indigenous South American Perspectives on the Past*, Chicago, University of Illinois Press, 1988.

Survival International, *Yanomami*, London, Survival International, 1990.

Urban, G. and Sherzer, J. (eds), *Nation-States and Indians in Latin America*, Austin, University of Texas Press, 1994.

Vieira, R.M., 'Brazil', in MRG (ed.), *No Longer Invisible: Afro-Latin Americans Today*, London, Minority Rights Publications, 1995.

Minority-based and advocacy organizations

Amnesty International, Rua dos Andradas 1560, Sala 2525, 90020–010 Porto Alegre RS, Brazil; tel./fax 55 51 228 8634.

Council of Indigenous Peoples and Organizations in Brazil (CAPOIB), Brasília, Brazil; tel. 55 61 322 4133.

Coordenação das Organizações Indígenas da Amazônia Brasileira, Av. Ayrão 235, Matinha, Caixa Postal 3264, 69025–290 Manaus, Brazil; tel. 55 92 233 0548, fax 55 92 233 0209.

Human Rights and Indigenous Rights in Brazil, Rua Dias Vieira 81, 05632 São Paulo, Brazil.

Geledés – Instituto da Mulher Negra, Praça Carlos Gomes 67, 20° Andar, Conj. 'J', Liberdade, São Paulo, Brazil; tel. 55 11 605 3869, fax 55 11 606 9901.

Movimento do Negro Unificado, Caixa Postal 2201, 90001–970 Porto Alegre, Brazil.

Núcleo de Estudos Interdisciplinares do Negro Brasileiro, São Paulo, Brazil; tel. 55 11 262 7526, fax 55 11 263 3657.

União da Nações Indígenas, Rua Ministro Godoy 1484, Sala 57, São Paulo SP 04015, Brazil.

British Virgin Islands

Land area:	153 sq km
Population:	17,000 (1993)
Main languages:	English
Main minority groups:	—
Main religions:	Christianity (majority Protestant)
Real per capita GDP:	—
UNDP HDI rank:	—

Comprising forty islands, the British Virgin Islands are a British Dependent Territory with a large degree of internal self-government. About 50 per cent of the islands' income is provided by tourism, and there is a growing offshore financial sector. The recent growth in tourism and related construction has encouraged considerable immigration from poorer neighbouring islands. The majority of the population is of African descent, although there is also a large white expatriate community. No minority rights issues have been identified.

Cayman Islands

Land area:	259 sq km
Population:	29,000 (1993)
Main languages:	English
Main religions:	Christianity
Main minority groups:	—
Real per capita GDP:	—
UNDP HPI/rank:	—

The Cayman Islands are a British Dependent Territory. The islands' main sources of income are offshore financial services and tourism, which have replaced traditional turtle fishing and agriculture. There is a substantial migrant workforce, estimated at 40 per cent of the population, drawn from Haiti, Jamaica and other islands. In 1994 and 1995 the islands were involved in the Cuban refugee crisis, when several thousand Cubans arrived in search of political asylum. Most were sent on to the US military base in Guantánamo, Cuba, while some were granted political asylum. No minority rights issues have been identified.

Chile

Land area:	756,626 sq km
Population:	13.3 million (1992)
Main languages:	Spanish, Polynesian, indigenous languages
Main religions:	Christianity (majority Roman Catholic), Judaism, indigenous religions
Main minority groups:	indigenous nations including Mapuche, Aymara and Rapanui 990,000 (7%), Jews 15,000 (0.11%), small Asian, German and Arab communities
Real per capita GDP:	$8,900
UNDP HDI/rank:	0.882 (33)

Like most of South America, Chile was conquered by Spain and achieved independence in the nineteenth century. During Augusto Pinochet's military regime (1973–90) Chile's human rights record was one of the worst in South America. Democratic rule was restored in 1990. Chile's indigenous minorities, numbering almost one million people, are Mapuche, Aymara, Polynesian Rapanui of Easter Island and the few remaining survivors of several Fuegian nations. There is a significant Jewish population in Santiago. Immigration by Japanese has been limited, but other Asian groups, such as Koreans, are now coming to Chile in increasing numbers. The Special Commission for Indigenous People, created in 1989, is pledged to bilingual cultural education and land rights. All indigenous groups are represented in the National Corporation for Indigenous Development. In October 1994, a new law (no. 19.253) was passed regarding indigenous rights.

Mapuche

The Mapuche people now possess only 1.5 per cent of the lands they had at the time of the Spanish invasion. At the end of the nineteenth century they were removed to reservations after being decimated by the Chilean army. The frontier with Argentina now forms an artificial boundary between the two halves of the nation and access is a major issue (see **Argentina**). The government of Salvador Allende (1970–3) began to restore Mapuche territory, but this process was harshly reversed under Pinochet's dictatorship, which called for 'division of the reserves and the liquidation of the Indian communities'. Since the passing of decree 2568 in 1979 the number of communities has fallen by 25 per cent. During the Pinochet regime paramilitary forces murdered Mapuche leaders; others were threatened with imprisonment or exiled. The violation of Mapuche rights escalated during the state of siege in 1986.

Mapuche give their active support to indigenous groups from outside Chile, such as the Kuna (or Cuna) of Colombia and Panama. Not all support the Mapuche commando, Mapuche Lautaro, or the Council of all Lands, which actively reoccupies lands. In a declaration made at the unofficial gathering in Santiago which marked the commemoration of the 500th anniversary of the European arrival in the Americas, Mapuche denied wanting to establish an independent state and reaffirmed their aims of cultural autonomy and territorial rights while remaining 'obligatory' Chilean citizens.[1] The year 1993 saw the founding of the Mapuche Inter-regional Council. At the July 1994 meeting of the UN Working Group on Indigenous Peoples its delegates, while admitting the benefits of law 19.253, which recognizes indigenous cultural and territorial rights and the need for bilingual education, urged that Chile ratify ILO Convention 169.

Pehuenche, a subgroup of Mapuche, continue to live under the threat of the Bio-Bio river hydroelectric project, funded by the World Bank and the Chilean electricity company ENDESA. International protests caused this project to be frozen, but the decision has since been reversed. Deforestation and flooding caused by dams on the Bio-Bio would irreversibly destroy more than half of the already much reduced Pehuenche territory.[2]

Rapanui (Easter Islanders)

Although they are represented on mainland bodies such as the National Corporation for Indigenous Development, the majority of the 3,090 Rapanui live on Easter Island, a small Pacific island far to the west of the Chilean mainland. Rapanui are a

Polynesian people who for the past century have lived under Chilean administration. Easter Island was first occupied over 1,000 years ago but this was followed by only sporadic contact. When Peruvian slavers took 1,500 people to the mainland, those Rapanui who escaped and returned to the island carried diseases which by 1877 had reduced the population from several thousand to 110.

Under a treaty of 1888, Chile assumed administrative responsibility for the island in return for respecting Rapanui lands and culture. This guarantee has not been honoured. In 1985 Rapanui opposition to the extension of the island's airstrip for use by the North American space agency NASA was ignored by the Pinochet government and the extension was opened in 1987. At present the governor of the island receives instructions from Santiago, and has been known to assume personal control over much of the island's resources. Rapanui are now being given grants to study in mainland Chile; many students, including women, study engineering and plan to return to the island on graduation. While this will initially benefit the island economy, opportunities for the professionally qualified will inevitably remain limited. Rapanui reportedly do not seek independence from Chile but aspire to a degree of cultural autonomy and control over land and cultural resources.[3]

Other indigenous groups

In 1987 the last 50 of the Yamana who live at Ukika, just north of Cape Horn, and the Qawasqar, who live on Wellington Island, were in a critical condition. Without motorboats, their fishing is undercut by colonists, and medical assistance is virtually non-existent, with a nurse visiting them once or twice a year. In the north Aymara have experienced difficulties obtaining title to lands. Due partly to the activities of Pentecostal sects, and partly to large scale migration to the cities, they have been losing cultural identity, a trend which was being reversed by the mid-1990s.

Other minorities

The first Jewish immigrants to Chile came from Russia and Eastern Europe at the end of the nineteenth century. A second wave, in the 1920s, came from Greece and the Balkans, followed by thousands from Germany, Poland and Hungary. The Chilean Jewish community is primarily middle class and professional and has achieved a high degree of assimilation. Latent anti-Semitism and stereotyping are found in most sectors; overt anti-Semitism may be on the increase among skinhead and other neo-Nazi groups.[4]

Japanese migration to Chile has not been significant. Only about 500 Japanese entered Chile during the period 1903–25. The major factor limiting Japanese settlement in Chile prior to 1925 was the lack of agricultural opportunities. At present most Japanese have small shops in Santiago and its suburbs, although a few have market gardens. Marriage into the Chilean community is unusual.[5]

Chile has a German minority from immigration in the nineteenth century; many live in the southern provinces of Valdivia and Osorno. Some Arab migration took place during the early part of the twentieth century. There is a degree of intolerance towards smaller racial ethnic minority groups such as the Koreans, who have recently been migrating to Chile in increasing numbers.

Conclusions and future prospects

Since Chile's return to democracy, indigenous groups have been successful in claiming their rights to bilingual education. Mapuche plans for the opening of a bilingual primary school with a Mapuche teacher were under way in 1992; a similar project for Aymara children in the north of the country is now in action. Although law 19.253 does not fulfil all the demands of the indigenous movement, it has introduced substantial changes, providing a legislative framework for the future relationship of Chile's indigenous peoples and the state. As a result of the government's positive efforts regarding human rights, it seems likely that it may be asked to chair the new Human Rights Commission drafting the United Nations Declaration on the Rights of Indigenous Peoples.

Further reading

Alwyn, J., 'Nueva legislación indígena: avance hacia una nueva relación entre el Estado y los pueblos indígenas de Chile', *Anuario Indigenista*, vol. 32, 1993, pp. 9–22.

Bergland, S., *The National Integration of Mapuche*, Stockholm, Almquist & Wiksell, 1977.

Gray, A., *Amerindians of South America*, London, MRG report, 1987.

'Rapanui of Easter Island', in MRG (ed.), *World Directory of Minorities*, 1st edn, London, Longman, 1990.

Urban, G. and Sherzer, J. (eds), *Nation-States and Indians in Latin America*, Austin, University of Texas Press, 1994.

Minority-based and advocacy organizations

Amnesty International, Casilla 4062, Santiago, Chile; tel. 56 2 672 0307, fax 56 2 671 2619.

Comisión Chilena de Derechos Humanos, Huérfanos 1805, Casilla 10144, Santiago, Chile.

Consejo Interregional Mapuche, Casilla 1872, Temuco, Chile; tel./fax 56 45 239 305.

Folil-che Aflaiai, Avenida Irarrázaval 2220, Ñuñoa, Santiago, Chile; tel. 56 45 223 2479.

Colombia

Land area:	1,141,748 sq km
Population:	35.6 million (1992)
Main languages:	Spanish, indigenous languages
Main religions:	Christianity (majority Roman Catholic), Judaism, indigenous religions
Main minority groups:	Afro-Colombians 4.9–15 million (14–42%), indigenous groups including Arhuaco, Embera, Guambiano, Wayúu, Nukak, Kuna, Kogi, Paez and Zenu 620,000 (1.7%), Jews 7,000 (0.02%)
Real per capita GDP:	$5,790
UNDP HDI/rank:	0.840 (49)

Political and drugs-related violence in Colombia has escalated since the 1970s, with frequent clashes between left-wing guerrilla movements, government forces and paramilitary groups. Terrorism and the revelation of the numerous human rights abuses perpetrated by the military have recently led to international pressure on the government to respect human rights. Colombia has more than eighty indigenous peoples living in a variety of ecological zones, including Arhuaco, Embera, Guambiano, Wayúu, Nukak, Kuna, Kogi, Paez and Zenu. Colombia also has a large black population and a significant Jewish minority. During the 1980s there was large-scale titling of forest lands in indigenous communities. The government recognized the territorial rights of indigenous groups over some 1.8 million square kilometres of its Amazon area. The legal entity in which these rights are vested is the *resguardo*, a concept of Spanish colonial origin. Until the late 1980s it applied only to the lands of indigenous groups outside the forest areas who could base their claims on ancient title. Colombia's 1991 constitution recognizes the concept of territorial rights for indigenous peoples, together with the right to self-government and management of their internal resources; a National Commission on Indigenous Rights was established in 1992. In 1993 traditional indigenous councils and organizations were recognized as legal entities, and there is a National Indigenous Policy Council.

Colombia was one of the leaders in the creation of indigenous organizations; the Indigenous Regional Council for Cauca was founded by the Paez and Guambiano in 1971, and in the early 1970s indigenous consciousness increased throughout Colombia. Regional indigenous rights groups were established in many departments in order to reclaim usurped lands. The movement aimed at reclaiming land and reinforcing community structure through a return to the colonial *resguardo* system of communal lands, with individuals having only user rights to their plots. It was based on earlier attempts at indigenous solidarity and particularly on those made between 1910 and 1940 by the Paez farmer Manuel Quintin Lame.[1]

Afro-Colombians

African slaves were first landed at Cartegena in the sixteenth century. Estimates of Colombia's present black population, who live on the Caribbean islands of San Andrés, Providencia and

Santa Catalina, on the Pacific coast and in the cities of Buenaventura, Popayán, Calí and Medellín, range between 10 per cent and 30 per cent, and are as high as 90 per cent for the northern region of Chocó.

In this fragile northern ecosystem Afro-Colombians practise crop diversity while delegating animal husbandry and other agricultural tasks to the indigenous Embera, a relationship which has led to tension as pressure on available land increases. The relative autonomy of this group came to a violent end in the 1970s when their lands were usurped for cultivation of soya beans, and more recently this peaceful region has been the scene of guerrilla action, causing many Afro-Colombians to leave. Both they and the Embera are threatened by the incursions of logging interests. Afro-Colombian farmers are classed officially as squatters but in 1993 lobbying of the constitutional reform process carried out in alliance with indigenous organizations resulted in law 70, which promises land titles for 'black communities'.

Afro-Colombian political consciousness, inspired by the US Black Power movement, began as a reaction to the emergence of indigenous minority organizations from which they felt themselves excluded. Whereas in the 1950s the term *mestizo* was used indiscriminately in an attempt to obliterate social differences, 'negro' is now being reclaimed by the politically aware minority. Afro-Colombians, both men and women, are being elected to the senate.[2]

Paez and Guambiano

The Cauca valley is the home of 200,000 Paez and Guambiano. Guambianos have been active in the reclamation of their lands since at least 1980 when they joined with Paez and Cumbales from the department of Nariño to form the Indigenous Authorities of the South-west movement. They aimed to create an autonomous nation within the Colombian state, with the right to make their claims to Colombian authorities directly rather than through the traditional intermediaries. Although *resguardo* legislation theoretically protected their lands from usurpation, in the past this legislation has been ignored or bypassed through the falsification of titles and the declaration of *resguardos* as public land. The Colombian indigenous movement is pledged to *recuperación*, reclaiming land through repossession.

Paez and Guambiano lands have been extensively usurped for coffee plantations. While indigenous communities have always been active in reclaiming lands through judicial channels, land occupation enables them to reverse the process of land loss on a much larger scale. Retaliation against this method has been violent. In December 1991, 20 Paez, including four children, were killed and as many wounded. A gang working for local landowners or drug dealers are suspected of the crime. These and other killings led to the founding of the indigenous guerrilla group Comando Quintin Lame, which has now been disbanded. Paez land is wanted for growing the opium poppy which is replacing cocaine in the Cauca area.[3]

Wayúu (Guajiro)

Wayúu lands on the border with Venezuela have been granted to mining interests and to the Colombian Tourist Agency. The Colombian constitution recognizes indigenous rights to management of the resources found on their territories but whereas private concessions to extract salt on Wayúu land have been granted, Wayúu have been denied the right to do so. Coal mining which has been undertaken on their lands also appears to be in contravention of constitutional law. The presence of multinational mining companies in their territory not only takes land but spreads pollution; the ILO has requested information on the suitability of the lands on which, owing to the resulting contamination, the Wayúu were relocated, and as to whether damages for this contamination have been paid. There is also a report of the assassination of a Wayúu leader by the military.[4]

Arhuaco

Arhuaco, related to the Kogi and Arsario peoples, live in the mountains of the Sierra Nevada where they have firmly but peacefully resisted interference with their culture. In 1982 they took action to evict a Roman Catholic mission which was attempting to prohibit use of national dress and language. In 1990 Colombian military tortured and killed Arhuaco leaders. This unprovoked violence seems to have been generated in response to the activities of the leftist guerrilla group FARC.

Nukak and Tukano

One of Colombia's last nomadic peoples, the Nukak branch of the Maku people, spend several months of each year working for another indigenous group, Tukano. Subjected to lethal attacks by colonists during the rubber boom, twenty Nukak were killed by colonists in 1987. Survivors of the attack who were taken to the New Tribes Mission station were subsequently returned to the forest with no medication against the diseases they carried with them. Between 1988 and 1991 Nukak, who now number only a few hundred, were decimated by imported diseases such as influenza. Nukak are also caught up in the violence surrounding the Colombian drug traffic. They are attacked both by coca growers and by the military, whose pilots apparently mistake them for coca growers or left-wing guerrillas.

Tukano are among the most politically active of lowland groups, although not all are members of the Regional Council of Vaupés Indians (CRIVA), a federation founded in 1973 with members from some 35 different ethnic groups. Many Tukano are hostile to CRIVA, considering it an organization created by whites, and one which has had little influence.

Other indigenous groups

In the northern coastal rainforests Kuna struggle to retain cultural identity in the face of vastly reduced lands and invasion by colonists and oil companies (see **Panama**). In 1905 Zenu lands were declared officially 'empty' and their reserves abolished. Since 1974 Zenu have struggled to regain their land in the face of violent action by paramilitary groups. In March 1994 four of their leaders were killed by unknown bandits, making a total of 24 such killings since 1974.

Other minorities

Colombia's Jewish population resides mainly in Bogotá, Barranquilla, Calí and Medellín, where Jews have become integrated at the professional level. Religious anti-Semitism has been part of Colombian culture since the sixteenth century, but the prohibition of all foreign immigration in 1939, which meant that comparatively few Jews migrated to Colombia during this period, also meant that Colombian governments were less influenced by Nazism. Although anti-Semitic attitudes and stereotypes exist among the upper class, neo-Nazi skinhead groups appear to have been a passing phenomenon in Colombian society.[5]

Conclusions and future prospects

Since 1991 Colombian law ostensibly recognizes indigenous rights to land but the Colombian Institute of Agrarian Reform, INCORA, has granted reservation land to private individuals; other lands have been appropriated by the state for use as military bases and in the attempt to stem the drug traffic. In August 1993 ONIC, the National Colombian Indian Organization, issued a region by region protest concerning government failure to provide land titles, and against continuing invasion by colonists. ONIC sees the granting of land to forest peoples under the *resguardo* system as an advantage, but this land is subsequently being declared 'empty' and therefore the property of the state. Indigenous peoples other than forest peoples still experience difficulty in obtaining land titles. Among Afro-Colombians, law 70 only applies to the Pacific communities, and while it limits the use these communities make of natural resources, no such limitations are set on the activities of national and international logging companies. Laws regarding indigenous peoples need to be implemented and more legislation is necessary regarding the large Afro-Colombian population. It remains to be seen how effectively existing legislation stands up to the onslaught by development interests.

Further reading

Friedemann, N.S. de and Arocha, J., 'Colombia', in MRG (ed.), *No Longer Invisible: Afro-Latin Americans Today*, London, Minority Rights Publications, 1995.

Mosquera, J. de D., *Las comunidades negras de Colombia*, Bogotá, Movimiento Nacional Cimarrón, 1993.

Pearce, J., *Colombia: Inside the Labyrinth*, London, Latin America Bureau, 1990.

Rappaport, J., *The Politics of Memory: Native Historical Interpretation in the Colombian Andes*, Cambridge, Cambridge University Press, 1990.

Urban, G. and Sherzer, J. (eds), *Nation-States and Indians in Latin America*, Austin, University of Texas Press, 1994.

Minority-based and advocacy organizations

Amnesty International (do not mention Amnesty on envelope), Señores, AA 76350, Bogotá, Colombia; tel. 57 1 334 5632.

Instituto Latinoamericano de Servicios Legales Alternativos, AA 077844 Bogotá, Colombia.

Movimiento Nacional Afrocolombiano Cimarrón, Calle 13 Num. 5 63 Of. 403, AA 894, Bogotá, Colombia.

Organización de Barrios Populares y Comunidades Negras de la Costa Pacífica del Chocó, AA 273, Quibdo, Chocó, Colombia.

Organización Nacional Indígena de Colombia, AA 32395, Bogotá, Colombia; tel. 57 1 284 6815, fax 57 1 284 3465.

Costa Rica

Land area:	51,100 sq km
Population:	3.2 million (1992)
Main languages:	Spanish, English Creole, indigenous languages
Main religions:	Christianity (majority Roman Catholic)
Main minority groups:	Afro-Costa Ricans 64,000 (2%), indigenous Costa Ricans 25,000 (0.78%)
Real per capita GDP:	$5,680
UNDP HDI/rank:	0.884 (31)

Costa Rica is the richest of the Central American republics, a wealth based on coffee and banana exports. Its wealth has promoted a relative degree of social and political stability. It has a century-long tradition of multi-party democracy and from 1948 until the end of the 1980s it had the most developed welfare state in Central America. In recent years, its export revenues have been hit by falling international prices and the drop in European Union banana quotas. The country is a largely *mestizo* society with the exception of the Afro-Costa Ricans of the Atlantic Coast and the small numbers of indigenous Costa Ricans, most of whom live in twenty-two reserves established by the government. These groups have been historically excluded from the wealth of the country. It was not until 1949 that Afro-Costa Ricans obtained full citizenship. Many indigenous peoples were undocumented until the early 1990s. Currently no formal discrimination against minorities exists but the socioeconomic inequalities remain.

Afro-Costa Ricans[1]

The Spanish began to ship Africans to the area in the eighteenth century to substitute for indigenous labour. However, the main influx of Afro-Costa Ricans arrived, as in Panama, as migrant workers from the Caribbean. Initially involved in the construction of railways, they also worked on plantations and, this century, within the United Fruit Company (UFC) enclaves. Few Afro-Costa Ricans travelled to the capital and they retained their English Creole language.

Following the collapse of the UFC plantations in the 1920s and 1930s, the largely black labour force either set up as independent farmers or migrated to the cities and gradually adapted to Costa Rican society. While in Limón, where a third of the population is Afro-Costa Rican, the community has remained separate, in the rest of the country, considerable ethnic mixing has taken place. In Limón, English remains the dominant language, although the new generation is bilingual since they now go to Spanish-language schools. Despite political participation (since 1949), the economic position of Afro-Costa Ricans has changed little. Only a small minority has achieved financial success.

Indigenous peoples

Most of Costa Rica's indigenous peoples live in isolated stretches of jungle near the Panamanian border. Not only are they isolated in their reserves from the dominant society, they are isolated from each other by geographical separation and cultural differences. Twelve ethnic groups exist, although only six languages have survived. They often lack access to schools, health care, electricity and drinking water. In 1977, the government passed the Indigenous Law which created the reserves and authorized measures to preserve indigenous language and culture. Indigenous peoples now participate in the management of their own affairs through the National Indigenous Commission (CONAI), and indigenous leaders continue to urge the government to devote more resources to helping their communities. However, many community leaders have complained that the government has not adequately protected indigenous land rights. On many reserves, most of the land has fallen into the hands of non-indigenous Costa Rican ranchers and farmers. In other areas, the reserves are threatened by mining and petroleum exploration, moves which have been sanctioned by successive amendments to the 1977 law.

Conclusions and future prospects

Despite an apparently progressive policy towards minorities, Afro-Costa Ricans and the indigenous peoples in the country have always been the poorest sectors, excluded from the country's relative wealth. The recent pressures on the economy could exacerbate this change and it seems likely that the exclusion of Costa Rica's minorities will continue.

Further reading

Lara, S., with Barry, T. and Simonson, P., *Inside Costa Rica*, Albuquerque, N. Mex., Resource Center Press, 1995.

Sawyers Royal, K. and Perry, F., 'Costa Rica', in MRG (ed.), *No Longer Invisible: Afro-Latin Americans Today*, London, MRG Publications, 1995; and in MRG (ed.), *Afro-Central Americans*, London, MRG report, 1996.

Minority-based and advocacy organizations

Asociación Cultural Sejekto de Costa Rica, Apdo 1293–2150 Moravia, San José, Costa Rica; tel. 506 234 7115, fax 506 240 8373.

CODEHUCA, Apdo Postal 189, Paseo de los Estudiantes, San José, Costa Rica.

Comisión Costarricense de Derechos Humanos, Apdo 379, Y Griega 1011, San José, Costa Rica; tel. 506 230 531.

Proyecto Caribe, PO Box 2387–100, San José, Costa Rica; tel./fax 506 226 7390.

Cuba

Land area:	110,860 sq km
Population:	10.8 million (1992)
Main languages:	Spanish
Main religions:	Christianity (Roman Catholic, Protestant), syncretic African religions
Main minority groups:	Afro-Cubans 3.6–6.5 million (34–62%)
Real per capita GDP:	$3,000
UNDP HDI/rank:	0.726 (79)

Cuba is the largest of the Greater Antilles in the Caribbean, lying only 150 kilometres south of the tip of Florida. Under Spanish colonial rule and later US tutelage, Cuba was a major sugar-exporting territory. After the revolution of 1959, relations with the USA deteriorated and since 1960 the island has been subject to an economic embargo by the USA. The collapse of Eastern bloc communism in 1989 signalled the end of Cuba's preferential trading relationship with the Soviet Union and led to a severe economic crisis. As one of the last centrally planned economies in the world, Cuba is currently introducing market reforms while attempting to preserve its existing political system. Besides the large number of Cubans of African descent, there is a small

Chinese minority. The existence of strongly Taino-Arawak-influenced partly indigenous communities in parts of rural Cuba is disputed.

Afro-Cubans

Since 1989 and the so-called 'special period in peacetime', statistics and analysis concerning social trends in Cuba have been almost unavailable. This compounds a more long-standing problem of information concerning race relations and minorities in the island. An objective assessment of the situation of Afro-Cubans remains problematic due to 'scant records and a paucity of systematic studies both pre- and post-revolution'.[1]

Estimates of the percentage of people of African descent in the Cuban population vary enormously, ranging from 33.9 per cent to 62 per cent.[2] This is partly a question of self-perception, as census figures are based on how Cubans define themselves. As in many Latin American and Caribbean countries, there is also a large 'mulatto' or ethnically mixed population, and colour, class and social status are closely interlinked. Few Cubans are either 'pure' white or black. Definitions of 'colour' are as much the result of social criteria as of somatic classification. Afro-Cubans are most prevalent in the eastern part of the island and in districts of Havana.

Africans first arrived in Cuba in the fifteenth century to work on the island's sugar plantations. By the nineteenth century Cuba was the largest sugar plantation economy in the Caribbean; it was also the last Caribbean country to abolish slavery, in 1886. Afro-Cubans played a prominent role in the War of Independence (1895–8) which ended Spanish colonial rule. The constitution of 1901 guaranteed formal equality for all Cubans, but at the same time a policy of *blanqueamiento* (whitening) was pursued whereby 400,000 Spanish immigrants arrived in Cuba between 1902 and 1919, making it 'the most Spanish of Latin American countries'.[3]

The 1959 revolution outlawed all forms of formal discrimination and institutional racism. Its wide-reaching economic and social reforms clearly benefited the majority of Afro-Cubans who were the lowest on the social scale. Access to housing, education and health services improved dramatically, as did the representation of black people among a wider range of professions. Afro-Cuban women have been particular beneficiaries of the revolution's progressive social legislation, gaining much-improved employment opportunities.

Yet, however radical the assault on institutional racism, 'progress towards elimination of the more subtle and damaging forms of racism . . . moved at a snail's pace'.[4] Attempts by intellectuals to raise the issue of racism in revolutionary Cuba were harshly dealt with in the 1960s, and the government insisted that it had eliminated racial discrimination. On various occasions, Fidel Castro has explicitly condemned racism and affirmed his government's commitment to equality. However, critics of official policy allege that educational policy and official culture are still strongly Eurocentric. Afro-Cubans are not, for example, widely represented in the higher echelons of the ruling Communist Party nor in the upper levels of the civil service or state industries. And, with few exceptions, Afro-Cuban women have not yet reached the highest professional strata. Such exclusion is accompanied by a range of popular prejudices.

The marginalization of Afro-Cubans today takes various forms. The limited statistics suggest that they live in the most neglected urban areas, especially in Havana. Of Cuba's large prison population of 100,000, approximately 70 per cent are estimated to be black.[5] Blacks are disproportionately involved in informal sector activities and in the 'underground' economy which surrounds the tourist industry.

The recent move towards free-market reforms and tourism-led growth has further disadvantaged most Afro-Cubans. The tourism boom has tended to benefit wealthier Cubans who own property and vehicles, while the enclave nature of Cuban tourism means that black people are often prevented from entering hotels or going to certain beaches. They tend to be restricted to work on the fringes of the tourist industry such as prostitution and other forms of 'hustling'. Nor has the arrival of foreign businesses in search of joint ventures improved conditions for Afro-Cubans, since the emerging capitalist sector is largely dominated by 'white' Cubans. As a result, blacks receive little of the hard currency nowadays essential for buying basic consumer items.

Conclusions and future prospects

The shortages and draconian rationing which have accompanied the 'special period' have hit Afro-Cubans hard. It is symptomatic of their particular vulnerability within Cuba's economic crisis that during the 1980s and 1990s the proportion of blacks among the 'boat people' seeking to flee Cuba has grown significantly. Nevertheless, in an uncertain future, many Afro-Cubans feel that they have more to fear from the return of the largely 'white' Miami-based exiles than from the continuation, in whatever form, of the present social system.

Further reading

Dzidzienyo, A. and Casal, L., *The Position of Blacks in Brazilian and Cuban Society*, London, MRG report, 1971, 1979.

McGarrity, G. and Cárdenas, O., 'Cuba', in MRG (ed.), *No Longer Invisible: Afro-Latin Americans Today*, London, Minority Rights Publications, 1995.

Stubbs, J. and Perez Sarduy, P. (eds), *Afro-Cuba: An Anthology of Cuban Writing on Race, Politics and Culture*, London, Latin America Bureau, 1993.

Minority-based and advocacy organizations

Centre Félix Varela, Apdo 4041, Plaza 10400, Havana, Cuba; tel. 53 7 303 900, fax 53 7 333 328; e-mail: cfv@ceniai.cu.

Dominica

Land area:	749.8 sq km
Population:	73,000 (1993)
Main languages:	English, Creole
Main religions:	Christianity (Roman Catholic, Anglican, Methodist)
Main minority groups:	Caribs 2,500 (est., 3.4%)
Real per capita GDP:	$3,810
UNDP HDI/rank:	0.764 (65)

Dominica is the most northerly of the four English-speaking Windward Islands, lying between Martinique and Guadeloupe. It is not a major tourist destination and is largely dependent on banana cultivation for its export earnings. Formerly a British colony, Dominica became independent in 1978. During the late 1970s and early 1980s Dominica's small Rastafarian community was the object of harassment by the authorities, which linked them with marijuana production and alleged subversion. Caribs represent the only sizeable minority on the island.

Caribs

Caribs (Kwaib in Creole) are an indigenous minority in Dominica and are unique in being the last community claiming direct descent from the indigenous Carib people. There is some debate as to how many 'pure' Caribs remain, but a population of about 2,500 people inhabit the Carib Territory on the east of the island, of whom only 70 define themselves as 'pure'.[1]

Today's Caribs are the descendants of male migrants from mainland South America, who arrived in about CE 1200, and the indigenous Arawak women with whom they intermarried, after killing the men. Up until the early twentieth century, Carib men in Dominica spoke Carib and women Arawak languages. Columbus landed on the island of Wai'tukubuli in 1493 and named it Dominica, but fierce Carib resistance kept European colonizers at bay for 200 years. While indigenous communities were destroyed elsewhere in the Caribbean, the Caribs of Dominica survived.

In the eighteenth century, African slaves – from whom the majority of today's population is descended – were imported. As the island was settled, the Caribs were driven north to the least accessible land. In 1903 the British colonial administration set aside 3,700 acres as a Carib Territory, which remains today.

The Carib Territory is among the poorest districts in Dominica. Caribs farm their land collectively and have also developed handicrafts for the small tourist market. They elect a chief for a five-year term and are also entitled to elect a parliamentary representative for the national parliament. In 1991 Chief Irvince Auguiste announced that Dominica's Caribs did not wish to be involved in proposed celebrations for the quincentenary of Columbus' arrival in the Caribbean, stressing the legacy of suffering experienced by the region's indigenous peoples.[2]

Conclusions and future prospects

Traditional income-generating activities such as fishing and canoe-building are being supplanted by the modernizing effects of tourism. As integration with the majority Afro-Dominican population continues, albeit gradually, the long-term future of a distinct Carib community seems doubtful. Although the Dominican Caribs have a dance and drama group and have established links with other indigenous groups in Belize, Guyana and St Vincent, their sense of identity is under threat. There are no longer any surviving speakers of indigenous languages in Dominica.

Minority-based and advocacy organization

Carib Council, Carib Territory, Salybia, Dominica.

Dominican Republic

Land area:	48,422 sq km
Population:	7.6 million (1992)
Main languages:	Spanish
Main religions:	Christianity, (Roman Catholic), syncretic African religions
Main minority groups:	Haitians 550,000 (est. 7.2%)
Real per capita GDP:	$3,690
UNDP HDI/rank:	0.701 (87)

The Dominican Republic shares the island of Hispaniola with Haiti. Despite attempts in the last thirty years to diversify its economy into tourism and light manufacturing, the Dominican Republic remains heavily dependent on sugar production. Many of the sugar workers are Haitians or of Haitian origin. The relationship between the Dominican Republic and Haiti has long been a troubled one. Modern Dominican perceptions of Haiti as a threat to national sovereignty are still coloured by a previous 22-year occupation by Haitian troops. The independent state of the Dominican Republic was declared in 1844.

In 1916 US forces occupied the Dominican Republic and the arrival of large-scale US investment propelled the Dominican sugar industry into a major boom. Most Dominicans, however, regarded plantation labour as too arduous, badly paid and associated with slavery. In the 1930s the first Haitian *braceros* or cane-cutters were brought across the border, the 1935 census recording a Haitian population of 50,000. The depression and a precipitous drop in sugar prices created a crisis in the industry. In October 1937, the Dominican dictator, General Rafael Trujillo, ordered the massacre of Haitian migrants in the Dominican Republic: between 10,000 and 20,000 Haitians were murdered by the Dominican armed forces.[1]

Despite the massacre, subsequent Haitian governments signed contracts with the Dominican authorities, notably the State Sugar Council (CEA), allowing the recruitment of Haitian *braceros* in return for a per capita fee. Since the overthrow of the dictatorship of François and Jean-Claude Duvalier (1957–86), these agreements have ceased.

Haitians

Haitians constitute a significant minority within the Dominican Republic. Although reliable statistics are not easily available, it is estimated that approximately 500,000 Haitians live permanently but illegally in the country.[2] Of these many work in the agricultural sector, in sugar, coffee and cocoa production, but others also work in construction and informal sector industries in urban centres. There is continual migration between the two countries, depending on a complex series of political and economic factors. Generally, however, Haitians go to seek work in the Dominican Republic, driven by high unemployment and low wages at home.

Since the 1980s international human rights campaigning has focused on the plight of Haitians who work in the Dominican sugar industry. The great majority of these live in work camps known as *bateyes* which are notorious for their poor conditions. Anti-Slavery International, in particular, has criticized the Dominican authorities for tolerating and even encouraging coercive forms of labour. There are considerable numbers of long-term Haitian residents in the Dominican Republic. Many of the men, known as *viejos*, have married Dominican women and have families, but few Dominican-Haitians are entitled to Dominican citizenship. They are joined by temporary migrants, illegal and undocumented, known as *ambafiles* (literally 'under the wire'), who are recruited by Dominican agents (*buscones*) with promises of well-paid work. The number of Haitians recruited varies from year to year, but it has been estimated that approximately 40,000 *braceros* work on CEA plantations.

There is long-standing anti-Haitian racism in many sectors of Dominican society, and the Dominican government has frequently exploited such sentiments. Several thousand Haitians were expelled, in June 1991, after a series of critical human rights reports about Haitian migrants. A further 15,000 fled to avoid the Dominican military, the Haitian Foreign Ministry claimed in August. The coup which overthrew President Aristide in September, however, resulted in 70,000 Haitians escaping to the Dominican Republic, of whom fewer than 100 were recognized as political refugees by the Dominican government.[3]

Conclusions and future prospects

Haitians form a distinct cultural and linguistic group within the Dominican Republic, yet many Dominicans have Haitian ancestors and connections. While anti-black racism is not widespread in the Dominican Republic, anti-Haitian xenophobia is rife. This is partly a legacy of the two countries' troubled history and also a reflection of Haitians' low economic status. Despite a hostile political environment, some degree of organization has taken place among Haitian workers in the Dominican Republic with the forming of two trade unions, SIPICAIBA in the Barahona region and SINATRAPLASI in San Pedro de Macorís. So far, these unions have been tolerated by the Dominican government, under pressure from foreign agencies and liberal opinion in the US Congress.

Further reading

Ferguson, J., *Dominican Republic: Beyond the Lighthouse*, London, Latin America Bureau, 1992.

Plant, R., *Sugar and Modern Slavery: A Tale of Two Countries*, London, Zed Books, 1987.

Torres-Saillant, S., 'The Dominican Republic', in MRG (ed.), *No Longer Invisible: Afro-Latin Americans Today*, London, Minority Rights Publications, 1995.

Wilhelms, S.K.S., *Haitian and Dominican Sugarcane Workers in Dominican Bateyes: Patterns and Effects of Prejudice, Stereotypes and Discrimination*, Boulder, CO, Westview, 1995.

Minority-based and advocacy organizations

Comité de Coordinación de las Instituciones Haitianas, PO Box 764, Santo Domingo, Dominican Republic.

Instituto de Investigaciones, Documentación y Derechos Humanos, Arzbispo Nouel No. 2, Zona Colonial, Apdo de Correos No. 21424, Santo Domingo, Dominican Republic; tel. 1 809 688 9715, fax 1 809 682 6744, e-mail: rb.martinez@codetel.net.do.

Red de Mujeres Afrocaribeñas y Afrolatinoamericanas, Socorro Sanchez No. 64, Gazcue, Santo Domingo, Dominican Republic; tel. 1 809 682 9721, fax 1 809 682 9844.

Ecuador

Land area:	275,341 sq km
Population:	10.6 million (1992)
Main languages:	Spanish, indigenous languages
Main religions:	Christianity (majority Roman Catholic), indigenous religions
Main minority groups:	indigenous peoples including Quichua, Achuar, Shuar, Waorani, Cofán, Siona, Secoya, Tsáchila and Chachí 2,634,000 (25%), Afro-Ecuadorians 573,000–1.1 million (5.4–10%).
Real per capita GDP:	$4,400
UNDP HDI/rank:	0.764 (64)

Ecuador has been a democracy since 1979, but the political situation remains unstable due to the worsening recession that has followed the oil boom of the 1970s and 1980s and to increasingly active peasant movements. The country has twelve indigenous peoples living in three distinct habitats; these groups include highland and lowland Quichua (the same linguistic group as the Quechua of Bolivia and Peru), lowland Cofán, Secoya, Siona, Waorani, Achuar and Shuar, and coastal Tsáchila and Chachí. The 1973 Agrarian Reform Law emphasized individual land titles, which indigenous peoples reject as divisive. The Institute for Agrarian Reform and Colonization has supported both colonization and the Protestant missionary sect the Summer Institute of Linguistics. Between 1968 and 1972 these missionaries cooperated with government and oil companies in the removal of Waorani peoples from their oil rich territories.

The highland Quichua organization ECUARUNARI was founded in 1972; since 1979 it has promoted a programme of land revindication. The Confederation of Indigenous Nationalities of the Ecuadorian Amazon, founded in 1980, has successfully resisted penetration of indigenous territory. In 1986 these organizations gave birth to the Confederation of the Indigenous Nations of Ecuador (CONAIE) which organized a pan-indigenous uprising demanding land restitution in May 1990. CONAIE envisages a national economy based on territorial autonomy. Its sixteen-point demands include the right to practise traditional medicine, to bilingual education and to indigenous control of archaeological sites and the (re)expulsion of the Summer Institute.[1]

Although other oil subsidiaries have been active in the Orient, it was Texaco's arrival, followed by the Ecuadorian military, evangelical missionaries and land hungry settlers, which devastated the Siona, Secoya, Cofán, Waorani and lowland Quichua. For some it was their first experience of contact; the Tetete, who lived at the site of Texaco's first well, are now extinct. Since Texaco came, rivers have turned black with oil. When medical studies showed that some 30,000 people had been affected by cancer and skin diseases caused by unsafe petroleum extraction, indigenous communities and local ecological groups united to sue the company for one billion dollars. In 1995 Texaco attempted to avoid payment of damages by claiming bankruptcy at the time the damage was done.[2]

Waorani

The successful claim made in 1990 by the lowland Waorani to 600,000 hectares of territory was subject to the condition that they would not interfere with oil companies drilling there. As part of the government's strategy for developing resources even in restricted areas, the Maxus Energy Oil Company, whose claim lies within a national park of great biological diversity, has been given permission to construct a pipeline and a narrow access road. Due to more stringent US legislation in the face of the devastation left by Texaco, Maxus proposes a model project and the policing by Quichuas of illegal entry of colonists who always follow the opening of access roads. International human rights agencies are concerned that controls proposed by Maxus may be insufficient and that their claim to discuss procedures with Waorani representatives fails to take into account that few Waorani speak Spanish. In 1993 Waorani and Maxus were reported to be in agreement, although further to the east the Tagieri remain hostile.[3]

Cofán, Siona, Secoya

Cofán, Siona and Secoya peoples are opposing action by the Ecuadorian company PetroEcuador which has begun cutting trees in the hitherto untouched forest of Cuyabero. They demand that the environmental effect of such work be monitored. According to CONAIE more than 400 indigenous communities – Quichua, Shuar, Siona, Secoya and Cofán – are located in the area of recent border conflict with Peru and have been directly affected by the military confrontation.[4]

Shuar

The Shuar Federation, founded in 1964, was one of the earliest resistance organizations, and one whose substantial achievements have made it a model for other groups. Since Shuar perceive Western education, with its emphasis on book-learning, as fostering the belief in white superiority, the federation has concentrated on promoting bilingual/bicultural education, which will preserve the Shuar language and give Shuar children a sense of the importance of their culture. In 1993 it began operating its own system of radio schools based on its own radio station; it transmits on several channels 16 hours a day to local schools programmes aimed at both children and adults. In the local schools, teaching is done alternately in Shuar and Spanish, using textbooks prepared by Shuar. The teaching schedule is adapted to the routine of the family.The Federation publishes books, periodicals and a bilingual newspaper.[5]

Other indigenous groups

Coastal Tsáchila and Chachi, living on small reserves, are threatened by settlers. In the highlands, Quichua farmers are increasingly compelled by the worsening economic situation to earn their livelihood as day labourers in commercial agriculture or as seasonal migrant workers. Otavalo Quichua are an exception. Their textile industry, notable in the Incaic period, was maintained by the colonial administration to produce clothes for slaves working in the mines of Bolivia and Peru. The growing success of today's Otavaleños began in the 1920s and has since created a model of indigenous capitalism. Successful weavers, who continue to wear the traditional blue poncho and white cotton trousers, now sell their products in the international market and reinvest their profits in the purchase of farmland.[6]

Afro-Ecuadorians

Slave ships first arrived in Ecuadorian ports in 1553 and slaves worked on plantations or in the gold mines. In the Amazon region there are black-skinned Quichua-speaking people, some of whom migrated westwards from Peru and Bolivia during the rubber boom. However, the majority of Afro-Ecuadorians now live in the coastal province of Esmereldas, in Imbabura in the Northern Andes and in Loja to the south. The cities of Guayaquil, Quito and Ibarra also have black populations.

Afro-Ecuadorians are estimated at between 573,000 and 1.1 million, or 5–10 per cent of the population, but there is little recognition of their contribution to Ecuadorian culture. Afro-Ecuadorian musical tradition is strong; their cosmology reflects a fusion of Catholic and African religions; they speak a dialect of Spanish. There is significant racial discrimination and, as in Colombia and Venezuela, upward mobility is achieved largely by *blanqueamiento* on an individual basis. A wide variety of colour-based terms are used to describe them; 'Afro-Ecuadorian' is used by intellectuals.

Afro-Ecuadorian consciousness emerged in 1992 as a response to the 500th anniversary of the European arrival in the Americas, and to interest in indigenous peoples, from which Afro-Ecuadorians see themselves as excluded. The Afro-Ecuadorian association ASONE was founded in 1988. Like indigenous peoples, Afro-Ecuadorians are considered to live on 'empty' lands, which can be appropriated for colonization and development. ASONE aims to reassert Afro-Ecuadorian dignity and to reverse the ecological destruction caused by lumber companies and by shrimp farms which are destroying the mangrove swamps vital to the coastal region.[7]

Conclusions and future prospects

Ecologists are sceptical about Maxus Oil's good intentions of 'exploitation without destruction' and doubt whether Quichua 'police' will be able to prevent illegal colonization. Lowland Quichua have put the growing demand for 'eco-tourism', which is still mostly run by international companies without indigenous representation, to their own use, organizing communally based indigenous-operated eco-tourism.[8] Their education programme has enabled Shuar to reassert themselves and take pride in their cultural inheritance. Strategic adaptation to changing realities gives them an improved chance of long-term survival as a people and their initiative may be followed by other groups. Educational opportunities for the Afro-Ecuadorian population also appear to be on the increase, but they would benefit from receiving some of the international attention which has so far tended to focus on indigenous or ecological issues.

Further reading

Corkill, D. and Cubitt, D., *Ecuador: Fragile Democracy*, London, Latin America Bureau, 1988.

Field, L., 'Ecuador's pan-Indian uprising', NACLA *Report on the Americas*, vol. 25, no. 3, December 1991, pp. 39–44.

Urban, G. and Sherzer, J. (eds), *Nation-States and Indians in Latin America*, Austin, University of Texas Press, 1994, pp. 53–71.

Whitten, N.E. and Quiroga, D., 'Ecuador', in MRG (ed.), *No Longer Invisible: Afro-Latin Americans Today*, London, Minority Rights Publications, 1995.

Minority-based and advocacy organizations

Amnesty International, Casilla 15–17, 240 C, Quito, Ecuador; tel./fax. 593 2 507 414.

Asociación Latinoamericana para los Derechos Humanos, Apartado 9296–7, Avenida Colon 196, Quito, Ecuador.

Consejo Nacional de Coordinación de las Nacionalidades Indígenas del Ecuador, Casilla Postal 92-c, Sucursal 15, Los Granados 2553 y 6 de Diciembre (Batau), Quito, Ecuador; tel. 593 2 248 930, fax 593 2 442 271, e-mail: ccc@conaie.ec.

Organizaciones Indígenas de la Cuenca Amazonica, Calle Joaquín Pinto No. 241, entre Diego de Almagro y Reina Victoria, Casilla Postal 17–21–752, Quito, Ecuador; tel./fax 593 2 564 012, e-mail: COICA@ecuanex.ec.

Organización de Pueblos Indígenas de Pastaza, Tnte. Ortiz General Villemil, Apdo 790, Puyo-Pastaza, Ecuador.

El Salvador

Land area:	21,040 sq km
Population:	5.4 million (1992)
Main languages:	Spanish, Nahuatl, Lenca
Main religions:	Christianity (Roman Catholic, Protestant/Evangelical)
Main minority groups:	indigenous (Pipil, Pocomam, Lenca) 324,000–1,080,000 (est., 6–20%)
Real per capita GDP:	$2,360
UNDP HPI/rank:	0.576 (115)

El Salvador is the smallest and most densely populated country in Central America. While it was never a centre of indigenous civilization, the Spanish conquistadors found a sizeable indigenous population. Many died during the conquest, but the last census of indigenous Salvadoreans, in 1930, still showed 80,000, 5.6 per cent of the population.[1]

The concentration of land in the hands of a small, Spanish-descended landowning elite has been at the root of the conflict faced by the country at different times this century. In 1932, between 10,000 and 50,000 people were killed by the government of General Maximiliano Hernandez Martínez following an abortive uprising. During the *matanza* (massacres) anyone wearing indigenous dress or having indigenous physical features might be deemed guilty of participating in the uprising and murdered. In the face of this repression, most of the remaining indigenous peoples adopted Spanish customs and assimilated into the general population; this was the virtual end of a distinctive indigenous culture. However, apart from the small numbers of indigenous communities still remaining, many of the Salvadorean poor continue to identify themselves as descendants of the original inhabitants in talking about 500 years of oppression.[2]

Pressures on the land and widespread poverty were the causes of the country's second major conflict, during the 1980s. The army, financed, trained and backed by the USA, waged a war against the FMLN guerrillas for twelve years, during which a further 75,000 people lost their lives. However, since peace accords were signed on 16 January 1992, land issues have once again become a source of tension.

Indigenous peoples

The current constitution states that all people are equal before the law and prohibits discrimination based on nationality, race, sex, or religion. A few very small communities of indigenous peoples exist who still wear traditional dress, speak their native languages and maintain traditional customs without repression or interference. These include the Pipils (Nahuatl-speaking people related to Aztecs who migrated from Mexico in the eleventh century), Pocomam (the original settlers related to the Maya) and Lenca (living north and east of the river Lempa). The Salvadorean National Indigenous Association (ANIS), promotes indigenous culture and language. Nahuatl and Lenca are still spoken although the number of mother-tongue Nahuatl-speakers has been declining. Indigenous affairs are coordinated by the Ministry of Culture and the possibility of providing bilingual education in indigenous areas such as Sonsonate is being discussed.

Despite the participation of indigenous organizations in the peace process, none of the peace accords mentioned raises questions of indigenous rights or issues of self-determination. Equally, in the 1994 elections, none of the electoral programmes included proposals for solving indigenous peoples' demands. While certain advances in indigenous rights, such as the creation of a sub-secretary of indigenous affairs, may be possible, the more sensitive questions, such as land rights, look unlikely to be resolved in the near future.

Conclusions and future prospects

El Salvador's peace accords have not resolved the causes of the armed conflict. Human rights violations are on the rise and the growth of organized crime and vigilante squads is a reminder of the failure to dismantle the structures of repression during the war. Meanwhile, further pressure will be put on the land by the return of thousands of Salvadorean exiles from the USA. Despite a growing cultural consciousness, the situation of the Pipil, Pocomam and Lenca seems to be tied to the fate of the Salvadorean population as a whole. It is unlikely that questions of indigenous land rights will be solved unless the land question in the whole country is settled more equitably.

Further reading

Catholic Institute of International Relations, *El Salvador: Wager for Peace*, London, CIIR, 1993.

Gatehouse, M. and Macdonald, M., *In the Mountains of Morazán*, London, Latin America Bureau, 1994.

Macdonald, T., 'El Salvador's Indians', *Cultural Survival Quarterly*, vol. 6, no. 1, Winter 1982.

Murray, K., with Barry, T., *Inside El Salvador*, Albuquerque, N. Mex., Resource Center Press, 1995.

US Department of State, *Country Reports on Human Rights Practices for 1994, El Salvador*, Washington, DC, US Government Printing Office, 1995.

Minority-based and advocacy organizations

Asociación Nacional Indígena Salvadoreña (ANIS), Calle Obispo Marroquín, Oficina Antigua Aduana Maritima, Casa 5–1, Sonsonate, El Salvador.

CALMUS, Apartado Postal 1703, San Salvador, El Salvador.

Popular Education Collective (CIAZO), Colonia La Centroaméricana, Avenida A No. 127, Calle A San Antonio Abad, San Salvador, El Salvador; tel./fax 503 225 1288.

French Guiana

Land area:	91,000 sq km
Population:	115,000 (1990)
Main languages:	French, Creole
Main religions:	Christianity (majority Roman Catholic), African-derived and indigenous religions
Main minority groups:	indigenous minorities totalling 4,000 (3.6%), Maroons (no data)
Real per capita GDP:	—
UNDP HDI/rank:	—

French occupation of what is now French Guiana began in the early seventeenth century. Large parts of the country are accessible only by river and after a brief period of prosperity due to the discovery of gold in the interior it was used as a penal colony. In 1946 it became a *département d'outre mer* (overseas department) of France. The 1970s were marked by increased tensions between the resident population and immigrant workers and a growing demand for independence. Greater autonomy is still an issue. The proposal for joint exploitation of Guianan gold mines by France and a South African company led to accusations of colonialism and was subsequently withdrawn. In 1986–7 French Guiana's relationship with neighbouring Suriname deteriorated as increasing numbers of Surinamese refugees fled over the border to escape the violence between rebel groups and Surinamese government forces. Increased military patrols on the border led Suriname to accuse French Guiana of preparing an invasion.

French Guiana's 4,000 indigenous peoples include the coastal-dwelling Arawak, Galibi and Palikur and Emerillon, Oyampi and Wayana of the interior. A considerable number of Maroons or 'Bush Negroes' also live in the interior.

Minority groups

Maroons (see also **Suriname**) are descendants of escaped slave populations, and retain an identity based on their West African origins. Until recently, international borders have meant little to them and they maintain contact with Maroons in Suriname. During 1986 both indigenous peoples and Maroons from Suriname fled across the border into French Guiana to escape from government retaliation for guerrilla activities. This placed a severe strain on the infrastructure of French Guiana and the French government refused them recognition as refugees although it provided food and medical care.

Conclusions and future prospects

Under the Inini Statute indigenous people could live as they liked, but in 1969 the statute was abolished, bringing them abruptly under French sociocultural rule. Traditional land claims are not recognized and the indigenous population is threatened with invasion by French colonists and Brazilian gold prospectors. Democratic parliamentary government in Suriname was restored at the beginning of 1988, and under the Portal Agreement refugees were guaranteed a safe return. Repatriation was supposed to be completed by September 1992; in July of that year about half the officially registered refugees had accepted French government incentives to return to Suriname.

Further reading

'La question amerindienne en Guyane Française', *Ethnies (Survival France)*, vol. 1, no. 1–2, June/September 1985.

'French Guiana' and 'Maroons of Suriname', in MRG (ed.), *World Directory of Minorities*, 1st edn, London, Longman, 1990.

Minority-based and advocacy organizations

Association des Amérindiens de Guyane Française, Rue Charles Claude, 97360 Awala, Yalimapo, French Guiana.

Grenada

Land area:	344.5 sq km
Population:	95,000 (1991)
Main languages:	English, French-based patois
Main religions:	Christianity (Roman Catholic)
Main minority groups:	—
Real per capita GDP:	$3,118
UNDP HDI/rank:	0.729 (77)

Independent from Britain since 1974 and a member of the Organization of Eastern Caribbean States (OECS), Grenada was invaded by the USA in October 1983 after a putsch within the ruling People's Revolutionary Government (PRG) resulted in the death of Prime Minister Maurice Bishop. Most Grenadians are of African descent, but there is also a small community descended from East Indian indentured labourers. No minority rights issues have been identified.

Guadeloupe

Land area:	1,780 sq km
Population:	387,000 (1990)
Main languages:	French, French Creole
Main religions:	Christianity (Roman Catholic)
Main minority group:	East Indians 65,000 (est., 17%)
Real per capita GDP:	—
UNDP HDI/rank:	—

Since 1946 Guadeloupe has been a *département d'outre mer* (overseas department) of France, with its population enjoying full French citizenship. Although the standard of living is high, racial tension is prevalent in Guadeloupe. This is largely because a small minority of whites, some the descendants of colonial planters (known as *békés*) and other more recent arrivals, dominate the economy and administration. There is a significant community of East Indian descent, estimated at one in six of the population. These are the descendants of indentured labourers brought to Guadeloupe in the aftermath of the abolition of slavery in 1848. There are also estimated to be approximately 45,000 illegal immigrants from Haiti, Dominica and St Lucia who are popularly believed to work for wages much lower than the French minimum.

Further reading

Burton, R.D.E. and Reno, F. (eds), *French and West Indian: Martinique, Guadeloupe and French Guiana Today*, Basingstoke, Macmillan, 1995.

Guatemala

Land area:	108,890 sq km
Population:	9.8 million (1992 est., 1994 census figures currently disputed)
Main languages:	Spanish (national language), 21 Mayan languages
Main religions:	Christianity (majority Roman Catholic), some practice of Mayan religions (largely hidden), Judaism
Main minority groups:	Maya 5,782,000 (59%), Garífuna 5,500 (0.05%)
Real per capita GDP:	$3,400
UNDP HPI/rank.:	0.580 (112)

Guatemala is the most populated of the Central American republics. Estimates vary but the majority of Guatemalans are indigenous, descendants of the pre-Columbian Maya civilization. Most of the rest of the population are *ladino*, a term referring to white Europeans, mixed-race Guatemalans and Mayans who have adopted a European culture. In addition, there is a small Garífuna population on the Atlantic seaboard and a tiny, but powerful, Jewish community in the capital, Guatemala City. Economic and political power has been in the hands of *ladinos* since the dispossession of the indigenous population by the Spanish conquest in the sixteenth century. The Maya have suffered a history of discrimination, marginalization and periodic genocide ever since.

Recent history has been dominated by the distribution of land which is the most unequal in the whole of Latin America. Nearly 90 per cent of farms are not large enough to provide subsistence for a family, while 2.2 per cent of farms cover 65 per cent of the land.[1] Large plantations cover most of the fertile coastal strips, where large landowners grow coffee, sugar, bananas and cotton for export. Small farmers, mainly Mayan, try to grow subsistence crops (maize, beans, rice) on stony land in the mountains while many are forced to migrate yearly to work on the large plantations on starvation wages. Since 1954, when a US-supported coup overthrew a government committed to social reform and the redistribution of land, Guatemala's history has been characterized by military rule, the repression of legal opposition and civil war. Since the 1970s, when many Mayans joined the guerrilla movements, the Maya have made up most of the 150,000 victims of the armed conflict. A particularly brutal counter-insurgency campaign launched by General Ríos Montt in 1982 involved the complete destruction of 440 Mayan villages in areas where the guerrillas were strong.

In 1985, the army restored civilian rule but maintained political control over a series of weak civilian governments. Following significant pressure from the international community since 1993, agreements have been signed between the government and the Guatemalan National Revolutionary Unity (URNG) guerrillas on human rights, refugees and displaced persons, and indigenous rights, leading up to the signing of a formal peace accord between the government and the URNG in December 1996.

Maya

The 21 different Maya peoples of Guatemala make up an estimated 59 per cent of the population.[2] While the Mayan civilization was in decline when the Spanish arrived in the sixteenth century, the conquest accelerated the process through the dispossession of lands and the use of Mayans for forced labour on the farms. Mayan leaders today refer to the massacres of the 1980s as the 'third holocaust' they have suffered since the conquest, following the aftermath of the conquest itself and the land dispossession during the Liberal revolution of the nineteenth century. However, a self-identified Mayan majority remains in the country, partly due to an ability to assimilate cultural and religious influences and partly because of the internal coherence and secrecy of Mayan communities in their approach to the outside world.

The 1960s saw the rise of social movements demanding land and fair wages in the Mayan highlands and the large farms of the south coast. The repression which the movement faced, exemplified by the burning down of the Spanish Embassy on 31 January 1980 while a group of 39 Mayan leaders were taking refuge inside, created fertile ground for recruitment to the armed insurgency.

The response, in the form of the counter-insurgency campaigns of General Ríos Montt and the subsequent militarization of the area, destroyed these movements and created over 200,000 refugees in Mexico and a million internally displaced within the country.

The return to civilian rule created a state with no formal discrimination; however *de facto* discrimination excludes the Mayan communities from the legal, political, economic and social systems of the country. In many Mayan areas, the militarization as a consequence of the civil war has left the army as the only visible institution of the state. Of 116 members of Congress, only eight represent the indigenous population and of 330 municipalities, only 97 have Mayan mayors.[3] Article 66 of the 1985 constitution recognizes the existence of Mayan groups and provides for the state to respect their rights to use their languages, traditional dress, customs and forms of social organization. Article 70 calls for a law to establish regulations relating to indigenous questions.

However, 10 years after the introduction of the constitution, the necessary law had not been enacted. In addition, under the existing electoral law, the Maya have no opportunity to organize politically. During 1992, there was some hope that Congress might ratify the ILO Convention 169 relating to indigenous peoples, but a series of delays and a short-lived coup in 1993 put an end to the process. Mayan culture continues to be denigrated by a political elite which is implicated in their massacre. Where concessions have been made, as in the limited government bilingual education programme, they are designed to integrate Maya into a non-Mayan culture, in this case by integrating Mayan children into the existing Spanish education system.

Yet despite the levels of discrimination and the fact that Maya suffered the most from the civil war, the decade since 1985 has seen the flowering of a new movement of Mayan organizations. Locally based development organizations have appeared, some of which are also involved in political struggles in national coalitions. Social organizations are struggling for material rights including the rights to land, civil and cultural rights, such as those to bilingual education and the recognition of local Mayan authorities. Mayan academic institutions and research institutes are beginning to bring together the documentary history of Mayan civilization. A symbol of this new movement was the award of the 1992 Nobel Peace Prize to Rigoberta Menchú, a Mayan exile whose autobiography documented the plight of her people, and who had raised indigenous rights within a number of UN bodies. The award gave the new Mayan organizations increased international recognition and a level of protection from repression by the security forces.

The existence of this movement has forced both the government and the URNG guerrillas to radically alter their positions regarding the Maya. A significant step forward was taken in March 1995 with the signing of an accord on indigenous rights between the government and the guerrillas, which has been cautiously welcomed by the Council of Guatemalan Mayan Organizations (COPMAGUA), the umbrella organization representing most of the different sectors. The accord defines the Guatemalan nation as 'multi-ethnic, pluri-cultural and multilingual', a definition which will be incorporated into the constitution. It promises the introduction of anti-discriminatory legislation and the congressional approval of ILO Convention 169. It also agrees a number of measures to increase Mayan participation in society. Bilingual education at all levels of the state education system is to be promoted. The official use of indigenous languages within the legal system is to be sanctioned through indigenous legal aid organizations, the training of bilingual judges and interpreters and the provision of special legal defence services for indigenous women. In addition, commitment to the principle of municipal autonomy is made through an agreement to reform the municipal code and to strengthen Mayan authorities.

Other minorities

The Garífuna are a small group concentrated on the Atlantic Coast. They are descended from the African and Carib peoples on the island of St Vincent in the Lesser Antilles who were deported to Roatán Island in Honduras by the British in 1796 (see **Honduras**). The 4,500 Garífuna in Guatemala have largely escaped the violence that has affected the Maya. Historically, they have been wage labourers in the logging and shipping industries. The greatest threat to their survival as a distinct minority within Guatemala is large scale permanent migration to Belize and the USA in the face of limited economic opportunities.

A small Jewish community exists in Guatemala City. It is influential within the Guatemalan business community. Despite its small size in comparison to the larger Roman Catholic and evangelical religious communities, the Jewish community's importance was recognized in its participation as a religious community in talks between the URNG and religious leaders in 1990.

Conclusions and future prospects

The 1995 indigenous rights accord was an important step forward, but subsequent accords, particularly the socioeconomic accord signed in early 1996, have so far proved a disappointment to those hoping for a serious response to the land problem. In September 1996 a further accord was signed on demilitarization, and peace was signed on 29 December 1996 between the government of President Arzu and the URNG. Issues such as the freedom of the refugees and displaced to return to their homes without repression are dependent on demilitarization and the implementation of a lasting peace. While the prospects for peace are good, much depends on the commitment of President Arzu's government to turn the accords into a process of structural change for the Mayan people of Guatemala. Nonetheless, Mayan rights have come to the fore of the national agenda for the first time since the Spanish conquest. The presence of a UN Human Rights Verification Mission in Guatemala (MINUGUA) since October 1994 has already made a contribution to removing the culture of fear from the Mayan highlands by allowing the Mayan movement to make its voice heard without fear of repression.

Further reading

Barry, T., *Inside Guatemala*, Albuquerque, N. Mex., Resource Center Press, 1992.

Manz, B., *Refugees of a Hidden War: The Aftermath of Counterinsurgency in Guatemala*, Albany, State University of New York Press, 1988.

Menchú, R. (ed. E. Burgos Debray), *'I . . . Rigoberta Menchú': An Indian Woman in Guatemala*, London, Verso, 1984.

Wearne, P., *The Maya of Guatemala*, London, MRG report, 1994.

Wilson, R., *Maya Resurgence in Guatemala: Q'eqchi' Experiences*, Norman, University of Oklahoma Press, 1995.

Minority-based and advocacy organizations

Academy of Mayan Languages (ALMG), 13 Calle 11–52, Zona 1, Guatemala City, Guatemala.

Arzobispado de Guatemala, Office of Human Rights, 7A Avenida 6–21, Zona 1, Apdo Postal 723, Guatemala City, Guatemala.

CEDIM, 14 Calle A 10–35, Zona 1, Guatemala City, Guatemala.

Defensoria Maya, 32 Avenida 1–56, Zona 7, Col. Residencialies Acuario, Guatemala City, Guatemala; tel./fax 502 2 946575.

Fundación Rigoberta Menchú Tum, Avenida Elena 3–53, Zona 1, Guatemala City, Guatemala; tel. 502 2 230 3948, fax 502 2 81356.

Majawil Q'ij, 32 Avenida 1–56, Zona 7, Guatemala City, Guatemala.

Mayan Documentation and Research Centre (CEDIM), 14 Calle A 10–35, Zona 1, Guatemala City, Guatemala.

Guyana

Land area:	214,969 sq km
Population:	806,000 (1992)
Main languages:	English, Hindi/Urdu dialect, indigenous languages
Main religions:	Christianity, Hinduism, Islam, indigenous religions
Main minority groups:	East Indians (Indo-Caribbeans) 400,000 (49.6%), indigenous Carib and Arawak 46,000 (5.6%), small Portuguese and Chinese populations
Real per capita GDP:	$2,140
UNDP HDI/rank:	0.633 (103)

Guyana, formerly a British colony, became independent in 1966 and since 1970 has functioned as an independent cooperative republic. Due to the shortage of arable land, 90 per cent of Guyana's population live on its alluvial coastal strip. In the nineteenth century competition over land led to racial antagonism between East Indians and the Afro-Guyanese population who saw the incomers replacing them on estates and later buying what little land there was. Areas of conflict were sharpened in the latter half of this century as Indians moved into the towns; over 150 died in widespread racial violence between Indians and Afro-Guyanese in 1962–4.

The People's National Congress (PNC) won the elections of 1968 and 1973 although the latter, like subsequent polls, was disputed. Opposition to the PNC grew in the 1970s and 1980s and in 1981 government relations with the church and human rights movements deteriorated after opposition leaders were arrested. In the late 1980s social unrest and industrial disruption, including a six-week strike in the sugar and bauxite industries, hampered government attempts at reform. Deposition of the PNC in the 1992 election led to serious riots by their mainly Afro-Guyanese supporters.[1]

East Indians comprise approximately 50 per cent of the total population, and there is an indigenous community in the interior. The Hinterland Department of the Ministry of Regional Development deals with indigenous affairs and the Amerindian Act of 1978 allows for titling of land to both individuals and communities, although little has been carried out.

East Indians

Guyana's East Indians are the descendants of immigrants from the Indian sub-continent who were first brought to the Caribbean in the mid-1840s; they soon came to dominate the labour market on the plantations. They also established small rice farms but have since become an increasingly urban population. Many Indians now study abroad before entering the medical and legal professions. While the position of East Indians is not that of a 'beleaguered' minority, the racial tensions and disparaging stereotypes which originated in the colonial period have survived into the present. East Indians have not become integrated into the Creole way of life and some communities have been terrorized by Afro-Guyanese gangs. East Indians also perceive Afro-Guyanese political power as a threat.

Other minorities

On the coast the indigenous population has adopted a Western life style but in the interior both Arawak- and Carib-speaking groups maintain their own way of life. The main threats are from logging, notably by south-east Asian companies, and from mining. In August 1995, 300 million gallons of cyanide and milling waste from the Omai gold mine spilled into the Omai and Essequibo rivers and may contaminate other rivers which are home to many indigenous communities.[2] The Omai spill was predicted and could easily have been avoided. Omai Gold Mines now promise to provide affected communities with safe drinking water, yet in view of their repeated assurance of the safety of their plant in the face of warnings from within the company, it is questionable whether they will honour this commitment. Small Portuguese and Chinese minorities dominate the retail trade in the urban centres.

Conclusions and future prospects

The Guyanese government has shown no interest in honouring the treaty of independence with Britain which stipulated that indigenous lands should be titled. To avoid possible repetition of disasters such as that which occurred at Omai, the granting of large scale concessions to mining and logging companies should be suspended, at least until adequate surveys to assess the impact on the environment and on the livelihood and lifestyles of the peoples of Guyana's interior have been carried out.

Further reading

Colchester, M., *Guyana: Fragile Frontier*, London, Latin American Bureau, 1996.

Cross, M., *The East Indians of Guyana and Trinidad*, London, MRG report, 1987.

'East Indians of the Caribbean', in MRG (ed.), *World Directory of Minorities*, 1st edn, London, Longman, 1990.

Minority rights and advocacy organizations

Amerindian Peoples' Association and Guyana Human Rights Association, PO Box 10720, c/o 71 Quamina Street, Georgetown, Guyana; tel./fax 592 2 61 789.

Amnesty International, c/o PO Box 10720, Palm Court Building, 35 Main Street, Georgetown, Guyana.

Haiti

Land area:	27,750 sq km
Population:	6.9 million (1993)
Main languages:	Creole, French
Main religions:	Christianity (Roman Catholic), syncretic African religions (voodoo)
Main minority group:	—
Real per capita GDP:	$1,050
UNDP HDI/rank:	0.359 (145)

Haiti is the poorest country in the Western hemisphere. Since the slave revolution which ended French colonial rule in 1804, the country has suffered from a succession of dictatorships and foreign intervention. A small light-skinned elite controls most of Haiti's economy, while the black majority is for the most part excluded from political and economic participation. The government of former radical priest Jean-Bertrand Aristide, overthrown by the Haitian military but restored by US diplomatic-military pressure in 1994, brought about some reforms, but Haiti remains the victim of poverty, social inequality and ecological degradation. During recent civilian and military dictatorships its human rights record has been among the worst in the Americas. For these reasons, many Haitians try to leave the country to seek work in the USA, Canada or other Caribbean territories. In some states they constitute recognizable minorities (see **Bahamas, Dominican Republic**). No specific minority rights issues have been identified.

Further reading

Ridgeway, J. (ed.), *The Haiti Files: Decoding the Crisis*, London, Latin America Bureau, 1994.

Honduras

Land area:	112,090 sq km
Population:	5.8 million (1994)
Main languages:	Spanish, Garífuna, English Creole, indigenous languages
Main religions:	Christianity (Roman Catholic, Evangelical)
Main minority groups:	Afro-Hondurans 100,000–320,000 (1.82–5.81%), Lenca 90,000 (1.64%), Miskitu 35,000 (0.64%), Xicaque (Tolupan) 10,000 (0.18%), Chortí 3,500 (0.06%) Pech 2,000 (0.03%), Tawahka (Sumu) 500 (0.01%),
Real per capita GDP:	$2,100
UNDP HDI/rank:	0.576 (114)

The current territory of Honduras cuts across what was a pre-Columbian boundary between Mesoamerica and the more dispersed indigenous communities to the south. In the north and west of the country, Aztec and Mayan groups based their communities around agriculture. The Chortí and Lenca are descendants of these populations. The rest of the territory was made up of nomadic migrants, including the Sumu, Xicaque and Pech from South America. The division was largely maintained following the conquest. In the west, tens of thousands died and as many as 150,000 were enslaved and exported to mines and estates in other countries. The less accessible jungle areas were less affected by the conquest, while on the Atlantic Coast the Miskitu population formed around the areas of British trading posts (see **Nicaragua**) and the Garífuna society developed.

Modern Honduran history has been dominated by the struggle to forge a national identity from two disparate halves. US companies developed fruit plantations on the Atlantic Coast and a complete infrastructure of railways and roads to service them. Until 1970 there was not even a road to these areas from the capital in the west. In response, the culture of national unity forged by the state has been on the basis of the *mestizo* culture dominant in the west of the country, part of an attempt to integrate the diverse cultures of the Atlantic Coast. As a consequence, minority populations have historically been ignored or discriminated against.

Indigenous organizations have been working at a national level since the 1950s. However, over the last decade, there has been a rising consciousness of minority rights which has focused on struggles against the expulsion from traditional lands. Land conflicts sharpened with the Law on the Modernization of the Agricultural Sector which brought indigenous groups into conflict with investors in tourism and agro-industry. President Callejas (1989–93) pledged to demarcate territory and issue land titles. In the case of the Xicaque, a presidential order to follow this up was issued. However, hopes for change were crushed when one of their leaders, Vicente Matute, was assassinated in May 1992.

Afro-Hondurans

Most black Hondurans belong to the Garífuna Afro-Carib group. While there are significant Garífuna populations in the cities, most are located among coastal communities along the Atlantic Coast. It is generally agreed that they are the descendants of African and Carib populations from the Caribbean islands of St Vincent and Dominica. Slaves who survived a shipwreck in the mid-seventeenth century took refuge on St Vincent where they mixed with the local Carib population. In 1775, the British conquered St Vincent and evicted the Garífuna. War ensued and in 1797 the remaining 3,000–5,000 Garífuna were expelled to the Honduran island of Roatán. They remained in Honduras, although a new exodus to Nicaragua, Guatemala and Belize occurred following their support for the ultimately defeated Conservative forces against Liberal reformers in the first half of the nineteenth century.

Garífuna communities today live on subsistence agriculture and fishing. Unemployment is high and many men emigrate periodically in search of work, reinforcing the traditional matriarchal structure of the Garífuna family. Garífuna are one of the most economically disadvantaged peoples in Honduras and social struggles have centred on the holding of scarce land resources and fishing rights. These struggles have strengthened their links with indigenous groups.

Lenca and Chortí

Lenca are found in the mountains of the departments of La Paz, Intibucá and Lempira. The communities are fairly acculturated and the Lenca language was lost at the end of the last century although a few older Lencas remember Lenca words. Communities survive on subsistence agriculture supplemented by seasonal work in the coffee plantations. Production of artefacts is largely oriented towards domestic use. Land in the region is unequally distributed and the struggle for land has been the focus of Lenca organizing in recent years.

Chortí are a Maya-Quiché group mostly found in the Guatemalan department of Chiquimula. There is a small Honduran population in Copán department. Unlike in Guatemala, Honduran Chortís have lost their language and their traditional dress.

Miskitu, Tawahka, Pech and Xicaque

As in Nicaragua, the Honduran Miskitu were recruited by the British as a buffer class to defend the area from Spanish incursions and those by other indigenous groups (see **Nicaragua**). In Honduras, they are largely concentrated in the department of Gracias a Dios and survived from the export economy, providing forest products to exporters. Moravian missionaries promoted the formation of settled communities, and the decline of British influence has left Miskitu communities relying on agriculture, fishing and some cattle raising. Many Miskitu work in the dangerous Honduran fishing industry.

As yet, the forests of the region have not been over-exploited; this is mostly due, in large part, to the lack of roads in the region. However, Decree-Law 103, through which a state forestry organization was created in 1974, creates no special rights for the Miskitu. The Tawahka, like the Sumu in Nicaragua, had less contact with the European trading posts. However, many communities have abandoned their language to avoid harassment. Both Miskitu and the few remaining Tawahka communities suffered disruption by the Contra war of the 1980s through the flow of Miskitu refugees from Nicaragua.

Pech are now confined to a few small communities in Olancho, Colón, and Gracias a Dios. They have resisted the national education curriculum and have developed Pech language courses and Pech teachers.

Xicaque are found in 28 communities in Yoro department and two in Francisco Morazán department. They have lost much of their traditional culture and values through contact with the Spanish which has affected the language (Tol), although in some communities, Tol is still spoken. Struggles over traditional land rights by Xicaque organizations resulted in the assassination of Vicente Matute. It is a sign of the continuing lack of power of minorities that no investigation into the murder has been completed to date.

Conclusions and future prospects

The international focus on the 500th anniversary of the arrival of the Spanish in the Americas in 1992 has facilitated awareness of indigenous peoples in Honduras. In July 1994, in an unprecedented demonstration by Honduran indigenous groups, 3,000 indigenous activists camped outside the legislative assembly in Tegucigalpa for five days. Their demands included indigenous rights, protection of the environment and the release of indigenous leaders jailed in land disputes. In response, the new government of President Carlos Reina set up an emergency commission to attend to the demands. Since then, some logging concessions in indigenous areas have been cancelled and, in 1995, ILO Convention 169 on indigenous rights was implemented. While the government is broadly in favour of indigenous rights, it has yet to demonstrate the political will to enforce those rights.

Further reading

Hogdahl, K., 'Honduras', in *Human Rights in Developing Countries Yearbook 1994*, Deventer, Kluwer, 1994.

Norsworthy, K. and Barry, T., *Inside Honduras*, Albuquerque, N. Mex., Resource Center Press, 1995.

Rivas, R.D., *Pueblos indígenas y Garífuna de Honduras*, Tegucigalpa, Guayamuras, 1993.

Sieder, R., 'Honduras', in MRG (ed.), *No Longer Invisible: Afro-Latin Americans Today*, London, Minority Rights Publications, 1995; and in MRG (ed.), *Afro-Central Americans*, London, MRG report, 1996.

Minority-based and advocacy organizations

Comisión de Derechos Humanos en Honduras (CODEH), Apdo Postal 1256, Tegucigalpa, Honduras; tel./fax 504 37 5368.

Comité para la Defensa de los Derechos Humanos en Honduras (CODEH), Apdo Postal 3189, Tegucigalpa, Honduras; tel. 504 37 7825, fax 504 37 9238, e mail: codehuhon@igc.apc.org

Organización Negra de Centro América, Honduras; tel./fax 504 43 3651.

Jamaica

Land area:	10,990 sq km
Population:	2.5 million (1993)
Main languages:	English, patois
Main religions:	Christianity (Anglican, Roman Catholic, Presbyterian), Rastafarianism
Main minority groups:	Rastafarians 10,000 (est., 0.4%)
Real per capita GDP:	$3,180
UNDP HDI/rank:	0.702 (86)

Jamaica was formerly a British colony and became independent in 1962. Despite its relatively diversified economy which includes bauxite, tourism and sugar, the island is vulnerable to unstable commodity prices and recession in the industrialized North. The legacy of slavery is evident in the existence of three small communities of Maroons, the descendants of runaway slaves who established settlements in isolated rural districts.[1]

Rastafarians

Rastafarians make up a distinct religious-cultural minority within Jamaican society. Rastafarianism traces its roots back to the influence of Jamaican-born Marcus Garvey (1887–1940) and his vision of reuniting the world's black diaspora with the African 'homeland'. The 'back-to-Africa' movement coincided with the crowning of Haile Selassie, also known as Ras Tafari, as Emperor of Ethiopia in 1930. This gave rise to the belief that Selassie was the 'God of Ethiopia' whose reign presaged the end of white domination and black suffering throughout the world. Drawing upon biblical interpretation, the Rastafarians came largely from poor, marginal communities in Jamaica, attracted by the movement's message of redemption.

Rastafarians encountered strong disapproval and frequent hostility from the authorities and mainstream Jamaican society. Their distinctive dreadlocks and their use of *ganja* (marijuana) as a religious sacrament led to harassment and arrests in the 1960s. The Rastafarians constituted a 'cult of outcasts'.[2] In the 1970s, however, the emergence of a distinctive 'rasta' culture in the form of successful and respected musicians such as Bob Marley led to greater tolerance.

Conclusions and future prospects

Rastafarianism has spread to other Caribbean islands and to communities in Britain, the USA, Canada and other countries where there is a significant Afro-Caribbean population.[3] It is difficult to estimate how many 'true' Rastafarians exist since many people adopt the outward trappings of the religion as a fashion gesture. The movement has also undergone various theological modifications over time, and many adherents now see the return to Africa as a symbolic rather than literal phenomenon.

Further reading

Barrett, L., *The Rastafarians*, London, Heinemann, 1977.

Cashmore, E.E. *The Rastafarians*, London, MRG report, 1992.

Owens, J., *Dread*, London, Heinemann, 1977.

Minority-based and advocacy organizations

Jamaica Council for Human Rights, PO Box 8850, CSO Kingston 8, Jamaica; tel./fax 1 809 922 5012.

Martinique

Land area:	1,100 sq km
Population:	359,579 (1990)
Main languages:	French, French Creole
Main religions:	Christianity (Roman Catholic)
Main minority group:	East Indians 10,000 (est., 3%)
Real per capita GDP:	—
UNDP HDI/rank:	—

Like Guadeloupe, Martinique has been a *département d'outre mer* of France since 1946, and its economy also depends to a large degree on subsidies from Paris. Most Martinicans are of African descent, although there is also a small white minority, who are alleged to monopolize areas of the economy and public services. The black majority in Martinique has traditionally been reinforced by illegal immigrants from Haiti, Dominica and St Lucia, although precise information on these communities is not available. The East Indian community is much smaller than in Guadeloupe and is estimated at 3 per cent of the population.

Further reading

Burton, R.D.E. and Reno, F. (eds), *French and West Indian: Martinique, Guadeloupe and French Guiana Today,* Basingstoke, Macmillan, 1995.

Montserrat

Land area:	102 sq km
Population:	12,000 (1990)
Main languages:	English
Main religions:	Christianity (Anglican)
Main minority groups:	—
Real per capita GDP:	—
UNDP HDI/rank:	—

Montserrat is a British Dependent Territory and a member of the Organization of Eastern Caribbean States. Its economy is now dominated by tourism and the financial service sector. A large majority of Montserratians are of African origin. No minority issues have been identified.

Netherlands Antilles and Aruba

Land area:	800 sq km (Aruba 193 sq km)
Population:	189,000 (1992) (Aruba 72,000 [1993])
Main languages:	Dutch, Papiamento, English
Main religions:	Christianity
Main minority groups:	—
eal per capita GDP:	—
UNDP HDI/rank:	—

The six islands of the Netherlands Dependencies (Aruba, Bonaire, Curaçao, St Maarten, St Eustatius and Saba) range in population and economic importance from Curaçao, with its 150,000 inhabitants and important petroleum refinery, to Saba (1,100 population). The islands' economies are mostly dependent on tourism, financial services and aid and remittances sent from the Netherlands. In 1986 Aruba seceded from the Netherlands Antilles federation. The ethnic cultural composition of the islands varies; the so-called 'ABC' islands are extremely cosmopolitan, with the oil industry attracting workers from throughout the region. Until the development of the tourist industry in St Maarten the 'three S's' were more isolated, with a predominantly European-descended population. No minority rights issues have been identified.

Nicaragua

Land area:	130,000 sq km
Population:	4 million (1992)
Main languages:	Spanish, English Creole, Miskitu, Sumu, Rama
Main religions:	Christianity (Roman Catholic, Protestant/Moravian)
Main minority groups:	Miskitu 67,000–160,000 (1.67–4%), Creoles 36,000 (0.9%), Sumu 5,000 (0.12%), Garífuna 3,000 (0.08%), Rama <600 (<0.01%)
Real per capita GDP:	$2,280
UNDP HDI/rank:	0.568 (117)

Nicaragua's minorities are largely confined to the jungles and lagoons of the Atlantic Coast region. On the Pacific plains, where over 90 per cent of the people and the centres of government are located, the indigenous population of Aztec Nahua-speaking communities was largely eliminated in the first few decades of Spanish rule. One Spanish official estimated that, out of a population of 600,000 at the time of the conquest (1523), 30,000 remained in Nicaragua by 1544.[1] Those who disappeared were mostly shipped as slaves to mine the 'metal mountains' of South America. The remaining population formed a *mestizo* culture, Nicaragua's dominant culture today. In addition, there are a few Pacific Coast Sumu communities.

The Atlantic Coast peoples escaped most of the early depopulation as the dense jungle was never fully colonized by the Spanish. These people were mostly Chibcha, who lived by hunting and fishing and had migrated northwards from coastal areas of Colombia and Panama. One group began trading with European pirates at trading posts on the coastal seaboard and became known as the

Miskitu. Subsequently, British traders brought Africans to the area as slaves in order to extract timber more effectively. The Miskitu, who mixed freely with Africans and Europeans, developed a unique composite culture owing something to all of these roots. Used by the British as a buffer class to control any disturbances from slaves, other indigenous groups and incursions by the Spanish that would interfere with their trade, Miskitu gained an ascendancy over other groups on the coast during the period of the British Protectorate (1687–1787). The Chibcha who had little to do with the Europeans became known as Sumu, and a third group, the Rama, maintained their small communities.

After the British left, the African former slaves, many of whom had interbred with their masters, inherited economic and political roles previously occupied by the British and formed independent communities which became the Creole population centres in the southern Atlantic Coast, in particular around the town of Bluefields. The penetration of US companies, from 1880 to 1950, strengthened the position of the Creoles since their English-based education qualified them for white collar work in the companies' economic enclaves and in government. However, following the coming to power of President Zelaya in 1893, who was determined to bring the Atlantic Coast area under the control of central government in Managua, *mestizos* replaced Creoles in government.

Under the dynastic Somoza dictatorship, the region was largely neglected as foreign companies were given free reign to exploit its gold, silver, woods and seafoods. But following the triumph of the Sandinista Revolution in 1979, the rights of the coast's diverse peoples became a centre of attention, both for the revolutionary government and for the US-backed 'contra' forces.

Indigenous peoples (Miskitu, Sumu, Rama)

Under the Sandinistas, for the first time in the Atlantic Coast's history, the opportunities existed for Nicaragua's minorities to campaign for their rights. However, the troubled history between the two coasts meant that the Sandinista plans for revolution in the Atlantic Coast were met with distrust. For many, the revolution simply meant a change of government in the 'Spanish' part of the country. This was compounded by a lack of understanding of the region by the new government. The Sandinistas recognized MISURASATA (the Miskitu, Sumu and Rama Sandinista Alliance), a Miskitu-dominated popular organization, as the only link between the indigenous communities and the Sandinista government. However, few MISURASATA leaders and activists were Sandinistas and some of the Miskitu leaders used Sandinista initiatives, such as the literacy crusade in indigenous languages, to promote demands for the legalizing of Miskitu communal lands based on a map which would have given 48 per cent of national territory to the Miskitu alone.[2] This was unacceptable to the Sandinistas who were worried that the demand would be exploited by the USA in its plans to overthrow the government.

In February 1981, war broke out. Around 40,000 Miskitu went into exile in Honduras during the fighting and some joined the US-backed 'Contras'. The threat of large scale Miskitu participation in the civil war forced a major rethink by the national government which led to an initial ceasefire in 1985. Over the following two years, discussions with community representatives produced the 1987 Autonomy Law of the Atlantic Coast. This remarkable piece of legislation guarantees not only cultural, linguistic and religious rights but also economic rights to land, trade and a share in the exploitation of natural resources. In addition, it provides for political representation through two independently financed Autonomous Regional Councils (RAAN Council for the north and RAAS Council for the south). The councils were intended to control all of the coast's finances and its development. The principles of the law were also incorporated into the 1987 constitution which was designed to prevent any of the ethnic groups on the coast from gaining ascendancy, since the rights were granted to individuals free to determine their own cultural identity.

Most of the refugees had returned from Honduras by 1989. In essence, the indigenous peoples of the coast had implemented a minority rights agenda by using the already existing civil war to force the hand of the revolutionary government. Certain of the autonomy programmes, in particular the bilingual-bicultural education programme, were implemented immediately. However, they were restricted by the economic crisis, caused by the war and US economic embargo, and the delays in the elections to the new regional councils. This which led many to adopt a wait-and-see approach to the autonomy process.

Paradoxically, the national elections in 1990 did the most to undermine the autonomy process. While the autonomous councils were elected, the Violeta Chamorro government reasserted central control through the Managua-based

Regional Development Institute (INDERA) which took over the functions and also the funding of the region from the new councils. The area's future was being largely determined by the UNO government's policies. At a national level, the only indigenous representatives are two Miskitu members of the National Assembly.

Creoles[3]

The Creoles of the Atlantic Coast were equally mistrustful of the Sandinistas. Sandinista economic policies, designed to reduce economic inequality and economic dependency, undermined Creole status in the ethnic hierarchy and therefore their identity. The legitimation of MISURASATA by the Sandinistas as the sole representative for the coast also undermined Creole organizations, such as the Southern Indigenous and Caribbean Community (SICC).

In 1980, SICC organized strikes and demonstrations against the arrival of Cuban teachers and technicians to work in Bluefields. Some of these escalated into the first ethnic violence of the revolution and were forcibly repressed by the government. The autonomy process increased Creole confidence in the revolution with a revival of black consciousness and the Creole language through the bilingual education programme. In the elections for the regional council, two currents appeared: a 'black internationalist' tendency, running on a Sandinista ticket, and a 'pragmatic Creole' ticket running as the regional version of UNO.

In both the 1990 and 1994 regional elections, Creoles have taken key posts on the executive board of the RAAS Council. However they have been unable to advance either regional or ethnic rights due to the marginalization of regional government by the Chamorro government. In addition, the political divisions within the Creole community gave UNO an effective majority within the RAAS Council which undermined their ability to oppose central government's policies.

Garífuna

Garífuna, who had entered Nicaragua in the 1830s after siding with the loyalists in the independence war in Honduras (see **Honduras**), worked as seasonal loggers in US-owned mahogany camps and earned positions of responsibility within the company hierarchies. This earned them resentment from Creoles and Miskitu. However, the decline of the foreign enclaves forced Garífuna communities, located in Orinoco and La Fé in the southern region, to depend on subsistence agriculture. Many assimilated, linguistically and culturally, into the dominant Creole culture in Bluefields and since the 1950s, the Garífuna language has been little used.

Unlike the other minorities of the Atlantic Coast, Garífuna saw the Sandinista Revolution as an opportunity to resolve long-standing struggles over land rights with Creole and Miskitu communities. As a result of their support for the Sandinistas, Garífuna villages suffered 'Contra' attacks during the war, and in 1985, Orinoco became a Sandinista military base. In 1986, Orinoco became the centre of an autonomy pilot project with international non-governmental organization (NGO) assistance. However, following the defeat of the Sandinistas, they became marginalized once again and have suffered discrimination from other people in the region for supporting the Spanish-speaking Sandinistas. Their land rights are unresolved and under attack and they have only one representative within the RAAS Council with its now limited powers.

Conclusions and future prospects

Nicaragua's autonomy process is a remarkable experiment, unique in the history of the Americas. However, its implementation has so far been seriously undermined. The statutory instruments, which would fully elaborate the provisions of the Autonomy Law, have yet to be laid. Central government control of resources through INDERA has minimized the role of the RAAN and RAAS councils. In addition, ethnic tensions are on the rise again: the appointment to INDERA of Brooklyn Rivera and Steadman Fagoth, both of whom had led factions of the Miskitu 'contra', has furthered Creole resentment, creating tension between the RAAN and RAAS councils.

However, even if the political will existed in Managua to promote autonomy in the Atlantic Coast, the severity of Nicaragua's economic crisis would probably prevent any significant advances. In such circumstances, what is remarkable is that the autonomy process has survived at all. International NGO assistance has been crucial in keeping certain projects alive. A number of dedicated workers in both RAAN and RAAS have managed to extend the bilingual education programme. Perhaps most remarkably, the University of the Autonomous Regions of the Atlantic Coast began its first year in March 1995. It aims to create and maintain the necessary human resources for a genuinely autonomous development. Alta Hooker, president of the RAAN Council, pinpointed the importance of the process for minority rights struggles in the Americas: 'If [autonomy] succeeds, it will set indigenous and other ethnic struggles ahead by twenty-five years. If it fails, or is made to fail, it will set those struggles back just as far.'[4]

Further reading

Archer, D. and Costello, P., *Literacy and Power: The Latin American Battleground*, London, Earthscan, 1990, ch. 10.

Dunbar Ortiz, R., *The Miskitu Indians of Nicaragua*, London, MRG report, 1988.

Freeland, J., *A Special Place in History: The Atlantic Coast in the Nicaraguan Revolution*, London, Nicaragua Solidarity Campaign/ War on Want, 1988.

Freeland, J., 'Nicaragua', in MRG (ed.), *No Longer Invisible: Afro-Latin Americans Today*, London, Minority Rights Publications, 1995.

Hale, C.R., *Miskitu Indians and the Nicaraguan State 1894–1987*, Stanford, CA, Stanford University Press, 1994.

Norsworthy, K. with Barry, T., *Nicaragua: A Country Guide*, Albuquerque, N. Mex., Resource Center Press, 1990.

Minority-based and advocacy organizations

CIDCA (Investigation Centre for the Atlantic Coast), Apdo Postal A-189, Managua, Nicaragua; tel. 505 2 780854/784930, fax 505 2 784089, e-mail: cidca@nicarao.apc.org

URACCAN (University of the Autonomous Regions of the Caribbean Coast of Nicaragua), Canal 4 1c al sur, Edificio El Carmen, Managua, Nicaragua; tel. 505 2 682143/682144, fax 505 2 682145.

Panama

Land area:	77,080 sq km
Population:	2.5 million (1992)
Main languages:	Spanish, English Creole, indigenous languages
Main religions:	Christianity (Roman Catholic, Protestant/Evangelical), indigenous religions, Judaism, Islam, Hinduism, Baha'i faith
Main minority groups:	Afro-Panamanians 325,000 (13%), Ngobe-Bugle 54,000–145,000 (2.16–5.8%), Kuna 30,000 (1.2%), Chocó 25,000 (1%)
Real per capita GDP:	$5,890
UNDP HDI/rank:	0.859 (43)

As the narrowest part of the American continent, Panama's modern history has been largely determined by its strategic importance for imperial powers. The area almost immediately became a crossroads for intercontinental travel following the arrival of the Spanish in 1501. In 1903, the USA supported the secession of Panama from Colombia in order to gain control over an 8 kilometre strip of land, the Canal Zone, either side of the construction site of an intercontinental canal. In exchange for a US guarantee of Panamanian freedom from reincorporation into Colombia, the new state granted the USA the right to build and own the canal 'in perpetuity'. The canal was opened in 1914 and US involvement in the creation of Panama set a precedent for regular interference in Panamanian affairs.

In 1939, the country's protectorate status was ended in a revision of the canal treaty which explicitly recognized Panamanian sovereignty. However, the USA continued to control the Canal Zone. It was not until the 1970s, under the government of Omar Torrijos, that a new form of Panamanian nationalism and a desire for sovereignty brought Afro-Panamanians and the dominant *mestizo* Spanish-speakers together. A concrete result of this process was the revision of the canal treaty in 1977 which gave Panama sovereignty over the Canal Zone and affirmed that full operational control would pass into Panamanian hands in December 1999.

The US removal of Panamanian leader General Manuel Noriega, through a military operation in December 1989 marked a blow to Panamanian sovereignty and a return to a period of US interference in the country's affairs. More than 2,000 died, many more 'disappeared' and 20,000 lost their homes during the first days of the invasion.[1] Since the invasion, Panamanian political parties have been more cautious about promoting an anti-US nationalism. The 1994 elections were won by Ernesto Balladares and the PRD, the party of Noriega. The new government has toned down the party's previous anti-US views.

Afro-Panamanians

The first Afro-Panamanians arrived as slaves from Africa. Their descendants are found in small communities along the Atlantic Coast and in small villages within the Darién jungle. A second group arrived as migrants from the Caribbean. From the 1820s onwards, people migrated to work on construction projects and in commercial agricultural enterprises. The migration was accelerated by the construction of the Panama canal. Three-quarters of the workforce during the US-run construction came from the British West Indies. By the 1930s, this migration had changed the demographics of Panama City, and Colón City around the canal.

Black Panamanians have faced a double racism, despite being more integrated than in other Central American countries. First, they have suffered US discrimination. During the construction of the canal, black workers were paid in silver while their white counterparts were paid in gold. Within the Canal Zone, segregation was practised by US government social services and, in the 1950s, the canal administrators expelled Afro-Panamanians from the Canal Zone to avoid civil rights protests, creating a form of apartheid.

Second, they have suffered discrimination within Panama's *mestizo* society. Panamanian nationalism attempts to co-opt black people born in Panama while encouraging Caribbeans to identify with Hispanic values. Panamanians often distinguish between Caribbean black people (*antillanos*) and those who predate the Caribbean migrations (*negros nativos*). The distinction is related to the resentment of English-speakers. This was challenged by Torrijos' more encompassing nationalism, and the predominantly white Panamanian oligarchy's opposition to Manuel Noriega had racial overtones since Noriega himself is of mixed race.

The US invasion proved disastrous for Afro-Panamanians. The poor neighbourhoods which suffered most of the casualties from US artillery fire were disproportionately inhabited by Afro-Panamanians. In addition, the invasion exacerbated the existing crisis in social services.

However, since the 1980s, when Afro-Panamanian activists organized a series of national congresses to discuss issues of race and ethnicity, there has been a growing pan-African consciousness. This is reflected in the leading involvement of Afro-Panamanians in community education, the labour movement, human rights groups and campaigns with indigenous groups to promote minority rights.

Indigenous peoples (Ngobe-Bugle, Kuna, Chocó)

The constitution seeks to protect the ethnic identity and native languages of Panama's population, requiring the government to provide bilingual literacy programmes in indigenous communities. The Ministry of Government and Justice also maintains a Directorate of Indigenous Policy. However, despite legal protection and formal equality, indigenous peoples generally have relatively higher levels of poverty, disease, malnutrition, and illiteracy than the rest of the population. The biggest campaigning issue for Panama's indigenous peoples has been the struggle for land rights in the form of autonomous land reserves.

The Ngobe-Bugle, the most numerous group, who live in the western provinces of Bocas del Toro, Veraguas and Chiriquí, have organized over the past two decades to protect their land and culture. Their society has been disrupted by the spread of banana plantations, the construction of the Inter-American Highway through their territory, and the appropriation of their communal lands by *mestizo* peasants and cattle ranchers. The erosion of their lands has caused many to leave and join Panama's migrant workforce where they are generally given the lowest paid and most physically damaging jobs. Most recently, there has been a struggle over the government's granting of mining concessions to international companies on Ngobe-Bugle land.

The Kuna, who now live mainly on the San Blas islands and in some settlements on the Colombian border, have been the most successful at preserving their land and culture. Three national chiefs, chosen by the Kuna General Congress, act as the Kuna spokespersons to the Panamanian government. The relative isolation of the Kuna and successful resistance to encroachment by European traders and agricultural colonists during the early part of this century, led to the partial autonomy of the San Blas region through a 1930 treaty and the formation of the Kuna *comarca* (semi-autonomous region) eight years later. The Kuna have maintained a stable, successful economy based on tourism, crafts and fishing. In 1985, they were the first indigenous group to establish an internationally recognized forest reserve. They are exceptional among indigenous groups in Central America in that they have not only survived the conquest but have since thrived and maintained an important level of autonomy from the post-colonial state. However, problems arising from squatter incursions into their traditional lands have led to demands for another Kuna reserve.

The Chocó consider themselves as two distinct peoples: the Embera and Wounan. They are hunter gatherers who migrated to the Pacific jungle lowlands in the late eighteenth century from western Colombia. They were brought to the region by the Spanish in order to break Kuna control over the Darién region. In the 1960s, they began to organize themselves into self-governing communities and to demand recognition of their land rights. In 1983, the government recognized the *Comarca* Embera-Drua, a 300,000 hectare reserve. However, the area is under threat from the encroachment of lumber companies and agricultural colonists.

Conclusions and future prospects

In November 1993, following a successful national strike with the support of other social movements, the National Coordination of Indigenous Peoples of Panama, made up of Kuna, Embera and Ngobe-Bugle leaders, sponsored a national convention to demand the creation of a high-level government commission to implement greater investment in indigenous areas. President Endara endorsed the proposals and incorporated the Convention on the Indigenous Peoples' Development Fund into domestic law. These are important steps; however, the Ngobe-Bugle experience of fighting the mining concessions has shown that the government will only allow the participation of indigenous groups in decisions when it is forced to by civil protests. The same applies to the struggles of Afro-Panamanians. There are some hopes that the new President may initiate an era of reconciliation. However, minority rights will only be safeguarded when the contribution of all of Panama's minorities to its history and culture have been recognized.

Further reading

Barry, T., Lindsay-Poland, J., et al., *Inside Panama*, Albuquerque, N. Mex., Resource Center Press, 1995.

Davis, D.J., 'Panama', in MRG (ed.), *No Longer Invisible: Afro-Latin Americans Today*, London, Minority Rights Publications, 1995; and in MRG (ed.), *Afro-Central Americans*, London, MRG report, 1996.

US Department of State, *Country Reports on Human Rights Practices for 1994, Panama*, Washington, DC, US Government Printing Office, 1995.

Minority-based and advocacy organizations

Aiban Wagua (Kuna), Apdo 87–1610, Panama 7, Panama City, Panama.

Asociación Cultural Ngobe (ACUN), Apdo 807, Panama 1, Panama City, Panama.

Centro de Capacitación Social de Panama, Apdo Postal 192, Zona 9A, Panama; tel. 507 229 1542, fax 507 261 0215, e-mail: ccs@nicarao.apc.org.

Centro de Estudios y Acción Social Panameña (CEASPA), Apdo 6–133, El Dorado, Panama City, Panama; tel. 507 266 602, fax 507 265 320.

Centro de Orientación y Desarrollo Integral Ngäbé – Buglé (CODEI), Distrito de San Felix, Provincia de Chiriquí, Panama.

Comité Tierra y Cultura (CTC), Alberto Montezuma, San Felix Chiriquí, Panama.

Consejo Nacional de Derechos Humanos en Panama (CONADEHUPA), Apdo 6–567, El Dorado, Panama City, Panama; tel./fax 507 269 0670.

Coordinadora Nacional de Pastoral Indígena (CONAPI), Apdo 807, Panama 1, Panama City, Panama.

Movimiento de la Juventud Kuna, Apdo 536, Panama 1, Panama City, Panama.

Paraguay

Land area:	406,752 sq km
Population:	4.1 million (1992)
Main languages:	Spanish, Guaraní, other indigenous languages
Main religions:	Christianity (majority Roman Catholic), indigenous religions
Main minority groups:	indigenous peoples including Guaraní, Ayoreo, Toba-Maskoy, Aché and Sanapan 95,000 (2.3%), Germans (Mennonites) 12,000 (0.3%), Japanese 8,000 (est., 0.2%)
Real per Capita GDP:	$3,340
UNDP HDI/rank:	0.704 (85)

Geographically, Paraguay is divided into forests to the east and the vast Gran Chaco scrubland plain to the west. It has eighteen indigenous peoples, many of them nomadic, and significant German (Mennonite) and Japanese minorities.

From 1954 to 1989 Paraguay was ruled by the military dictatorship of General Alfredo Stroessner. During this period the indigenous population was deprived of more land than at any other period in Paraguay's history.[1] Paraguay has recently ratified ILO Convention 169 (1989) on indigenous and tribal populations but land claims fail to be recognized. Paraguay is unusual in that an indigenous language, Guaraní, is spoken by 90 per cent of the population. Although it has now been recognized as an official language, there is little evidence of bilingual/bicultural education being made available.

Indigenous affairs in Paraguay are controlled by the National Indigenous Institute (INDI) which co-exists with the Indigenist Affairs Department. Individual groups such as the Mbyá are also forming their own organizations.[2]

Human rights abuses against Paraguay's indigenous population under the Stroessner regime were appalling. Indigenous communities are still threatened by logging and cattle ranching, by hydroelectric projects, by diseases brought by outsiders and notably by the activities of missionary groups such as the New Tribes Mission, who have 'hunted' Aché and Ayoreo.

Maskoy and Enxet

The Maskoy linguistic group inhabits the Paraguayan Chaco region.[3] There have been several instances of an indigenous group having its land claims upheld. In 1987 a group of Maskoy were reported as living in unhealthy and poverty stricken conditions on land now held by the Argentine firm Carlos Casado.[4] They have recently been awarded 30,000 hectares.

Enxet, a subgroup of the Maskoy, live in an area known as the Anglican zone, in four small 'colonies' purchased for them by the Anglican Church, while the rest of their extensive lands have been taken over for cattle ranching. Enxet work under poor conditions for white ranchers. Recent attempts by them to claim legal right to a small part of their land resulted in continued harassment including the burning of their homes.[5]

Enxet have become increasingly politically conscious in their dealings with the missions and other white outsiders. Like other South American indigenous peoples such as the Brazilian Kayapó, they are 'reinventing' the history of the colonization of their territory so as to support their land claims; this has led to increased confidence in themselves as a group. One hundred Enxet recently travelled to Asunción where they performed traditional dances in front of the Parliament buildings; their leader then addressed the House of Deputies in Enxet, making clear their claim to 160,000 hectares of their traditional territory.

Ayoreo

The Ayoreo are made up of a number of subgroups which have traditionally been hostile to each other. Many of the Totobiegosode group had not been contacted until, with the help of the Guidaigosode group, they were forcibly settled by the New Tribes Mission in 1979 and again in 1986; many died of malnutrition and disease. Ayoreo also work for Mennonites for less than the minimum wage. Around two dozen of the group remain uncontacted but are in imminent danger of violent confrontation with the outside world since their village was accidentally 'discovered' by a Mennonite worker. In 1993, after enduring years of settlement existence, Ayoreo asked for their ownership of almost 1,000,000 hectares of Chaco territory to be recognized but this claim remains unresolved.[6]

Other minorities

Mennonites are a group of German-speaking Anabaptists who emigrated to the Chaco in 1928–31 and 1946–7 to escape religious persecution. They own more than 1,000,000 hectares of Chaco land and their economy is based on cattle ranching and commercial agriculture. Mennonites employ indigenous workers such as Enxet and Ayoreo, often paying them less than the minimum wage or obliging them to accept notes of credit which can only be exchanged for goods in Mennonite stores, thus drawing them into debt peonage.[7]

Paraguay's 1903 immigration law banning 'persons of the yellow race' was modified in 1924. Since 1935 four colonies have been set up with Japanese from northern and central Japan as well as Brazil; cotton has been the dominant crop. In 1959 a migration agreement with Paraguay provided for 85,000 Japanese immigrants over a 30-year period; many of the original immigrants have, however, returned to Japan.[8]

Conclusions and future prospects

Indigenous groups in Paraguay are acting increasingly to inform the international community of their situation. As a result, human rights groups have recently been successful in convincing the World Bank to withdraw from projects such as that to develop the Caazapá area where many indigenous communities would have lost their lands. The European Union has also made its project 'Sustainable Development in the Paraguayan Chaco' conditional upon land claims by Ayoreo and Enxet being satisfactorily resolved, and the Italians withdrew from a joint project which would have moved hundreds of settlers onto Enxet and Sanapaná land.

Further reading

Kidd, S., 'Land, politics and benevolent shamanism: the Enxet in a democratic Paraguay', *Journal of Latin American Studies*, vol. 17, part 1, 1995, pp. 43–76.

Gray, A., *Amerindians of South America*, London, MRG report, 1987.

Minority-based and advocacy organizations

Asociación de Parcialidades Indígenas (API), Casilla Postal 2512, Asunción, Paraguay.

Defensa del Patrimonio Indígena (ADEPI), Independencia Nacional y Comuneros, Universidad Católica Ntra Sra de la Asunción, Asunción, Paraguay; tel. 595 21 495517, fax 595 21 445429.

Peru

Land area:	1,280,000 sq km
Population:	22.5 million (est., 1992)
Main languages:	Spanish, Quechua, Aymara, other indigenous languages
Main religions:	Christianity (majority Roman Catholic), indigenous religions
Main minority groups:	indigenous peoples including Aguaruna, Ashaninka, Huambisa, Quechua and Aymara 8.8 million (39.2%), Afro-Peruvians 1.4–2.2 million (6–10%), Japanese 48,000 (est., 0.2%)
Real per capita GDP:	$3,320
UNDP HDI/rank:	0.694 (91)

In 1968 General Juan Velasco's radical military dictatorship implemented a wide-ranging agrarian reform for the highlands, based on the breaking-up of the hacienda system and the establishment of cooperatives. Subsequent changes in government and the closing of the pro-indigenous government-run agency SINAMOS destroyed most of the reform's benefits. A comparable law for the Amazonian communities was passed in 1974 but was repealed in 1978 by one which limited indigenous rights to those lands unsuitable for forestry and agribusiness. In 1987 the Peruvian congress introduced a new agrarian law which threatened to expropriate 'unused' communal land in the highlands and make it available for business and development. The clause was, however, withdrawn after a major protest by national farming organizations and international support groups.[1] In 1976 an official alphabet was developed for the Quechua language, and according to the 1994 constitution Quechua and Aymara are recognized as official languages in areas where they predominate.

Since 1980 the Maoist guerrilla group Sendero Luminoso (Shining Path) has been active in Peru. Initially active in the province of Ayacucho, its gradual spread reduced more than half the country to a state of emergency. Action by Sendero and by government forces seriously violated human rights. By 1990 the war between guerrillas and government forces had claimed more than 15,000 lives. Sendero's economic and political ideology disregarded and destroyed distinctive features of Andean life. Many of the victims came from isolated villages and communities and were targeted simply because they lived in zones of conflict. Despite the capture of Sendero's founder, Abimael Guzmán, in 1992, Sendero remains active under new leadership and the number of dead is estimated at over 27,000.[2]

There are fifty-one indigenous peoples in Peru. Aymara and Quechua inhabit the high valleys; lowland groups include Aguaruna, Ashaninka, Huambisa and Quechua. Other minorities include significant Afro-Peruvian and Japanese populations.

Aymara and highland Quechua

Highland Quechua make up more than one-third of Peru's total population. The great majority live in small towns, villages and rural communities and are primarily small farmers who may also work elsewhere as day labourers for part of the year. While in the countryside most men speak Spanish, many women, who seldom have occasion to travel to town, may be monolingual in Aymara or Quechua. Language and dress are seen as significant in preserving traditional culture. The Quechua concept of *pachakuti*, a turning over of world/time (*pacha*), holds the possibility of a time when the pre-colonial order, at present below the earth, will return (*kuti*) to power. This belief is a source of inspiration for both Quechua and Aymara indigenous organizations. The majority of Peru's 600,000 Aymara live in the southern department of Puno. Their way of life is in many ways similar to the Quechua but they have suffered less at the hands of Sendero.

Quechua were among those worst affected during the *manchay tiempo*, the 'time of fear' initiated by Sendero Luminoso in the Quechua village of Chuschi, one of the few places where initially they were well received. Subsequently Chuschí and many other Quechua villages were burnt. Quechua were executed for suspected 'collaboration' with government forces, and for failing to follow Senderista ideology which took no account of the traditional patterns of marketing and exchange between highland and lowland groups, nor of the problems confronting indigenous minorities in adapting these and other traditions in the face of growing urbanization and mass communication. Migration to towns is increasing as children choose to leave home, but many thousands of Quechua were forced to move to the shanty towns of Lima and Ayacucho by Sendero's activities. Although the danger persists many are now returning to their homes.[3]

Women are active in shanty town organizations and Puno has an Aymara and Cusco a Quechua radio programme directed by women. Aimed primarily at migrants, these discuss topics such as terrorism, domestic violence and economic discrimination and warn about the sale of unsafe contraceptives and agricultural fertilizer. In 1977 a bilingual education programme was begun in Puno for both Quechua and Aymara using specially produced and culturally relevant primary school material.

Ashaninka

Ashaninka, members of the Arawak linguistic group, inhabit the Peruvian Amazonian rain forests. They have had a long and difficult relationship with missionaries and other external agents. Earlier in the century they were colonized by rubber tappers; in the 1970s and 1980s their lands were usurped for the production of sugar and palm oil, for cattle ranching and forestry, by gold prospectors and a new wave of colonists. In addition almost 700,000 hectares of forest have been destroyed to provide extra coca growing areas and for the construction of airstrips for its illegal transportation. Violence has intensified over the past two years due to the combined pressures of drug traffickers, terrorists and colonists. In 1989 Sendero Luminoso invaded Ashaninka territory seeking control of the lucrative drug trade; following a massacre in six Ashaninka villages in August 1993 a delegation of Ashaninka travelled to Lima to ask for economic aid and arms. In response to coercion from government forces they have attempted to organize their own defence groups, thus becoming further involved in the conflict. Those who tried to defend their communities during a further attack by Sendero in September 1993 were arrested on charges of terrorism. According to the Asociación Interetnica para el Desarrollo de la Selva Peruana (Interethnic Association for the Development of the Peruvian Forest, AIDESEP), which represents all indigenous Peruvians of the Amazon region, four still remained imprisoned in July 1994.[4]

Other indigenous minorities

Amazonian Aguaruna and Huambisa have formed their own organization to protest against oil company invasion and to demand government recognition of their territorial rights. According to AIDESEP Aguaruna have successfully reclaimed land invaded by settlers for production of cocoa and coffee.

Afro-Peruvians

The first slaves arrived in Peru in the sixteenth century. Many came via the Caribbean or Brazil and had already lost touch with their African identity. The majority lived in Lima. Afro-Peruvians now live primarily in the southern coastal region and have contributed a special blend of religion, language and cuisine. They suffer urban poverty and its accompanying problems of alcohol and drug abuse. The poor relationship which has existed in the past between the country's Afro-Peruvian and indigenous urban populations can be partly accounted for by the marginalized situation of both groups.

Until recently Afro-Peruvians have had little sense of ethnic identity. Since 1950 the situation has changed somewhat. There has been a reaffirmation of Afro-Peruvian culture with the emergence of dance and theatre groups. Influenced by the US Civil Rights Movement, groups formed to trace their African roots. Although these groups were short-lived, other groups have taken their place, including the Afro-Peruvian Research Institute, INAPE, and the Movimiento Negro Francisco Congo. The Asociación pro Derechos Humanos del Negro provides legal aid and human rights support.[5]

Other minorities

Peru was among the first Latin American republics to establish diplomatic relations with the Japanese empire in 1877 and issued a decree authorising the immigration of contract labourers in 1898. Manual labour at sugar plantations and mills was the principal work; 95 per cent of the Japanese are now located in the department of Lima. By the 1980s they totalled 48,000. Japanese have gained notable economic success in Peru. In 1990 a Japanese agronomist, Alberto Fujimori, became President. Many Japanese are owners or operators of small shops and bars, and have made a significant contribution to the Peruvian economy.[6]

Conclusions and future prospects

Many national NGOs have been able to assist Peru's indigenous groups in demarcation and titling of their lands. However, lowland groups continue to be threatened by colonists and industrial concerns. Sendero Luminoso are still a major threat in many areas, as is the violence surrounding the cocaine traffic. Although the use of fear and terror in counter-insurgency has diminished since Guzmán's capture, reports indicate that the country still falls far short of international standards in its commitment to human rights.

Further reading

Allen, C.J., *The Hold Life Has: Coca and Cultural Identity in an Andean Community*, Washington, DC, Smithsonian Institution, 1988.

Luciano, J. and Rodriguez Pastor, H., 'Peru', in MRG (ed.), *No Longer Invisible: Afro-Latin Americans Today*, London, Minority Rights Publications, 1995.

Poole, D. and Renique, G., *Peru: Time of Fear*. London, Latin America Bureau, 1992.

Starn, O., Degregori, C.I. and Kirk, R. (eds), *The Peru Reader: History, Culture, Politics*, London, Latin America Bureau, 1996.

Minority-based and advocacy organizations

Amnesty International (do not mention Amnesty on envelope), Señores, Casilla 659, Lima 18, Peru; tel. 51 1 447 1360, fax 51 1 447 1360.

Asociación Interetnica para el Desarrollo de la Selva Peruana, Apdo Postal 14–0267, Lima 14, Peru; tel. 51 1 472661, fax 51 1 724805.

Association of the Families of Disappeared in Ayacucho, Apdo 196, Ayacucho, Peru.

Centre for Research and Action for Peace, Costa Rica 150, Lima 11, Peru.

Centro Amauta de Estudios y Promoción de la Mujer, Av. Infancia 541, Cuzco, Peru; tel. 51 84 240572, fax 51 84 239736.

Centro de Communicación, Capacitación y Cultura Arunakasa, Apdo Postal 348, Puno, Peru; tel. 51 54 352559, fax 51 54 353559.

Comisión Andina de Jurista, Los Sauces 285, San Isidro, Lima 27, Peru.

Comisión Juridica de los Pueblos de Integración Tawantinsuyana, Casilla 230, Arequipa, Peru; tel. 51 54 238 383.

Comité de Defensa de los Derechos Humanos, San Andres 270, Oficina 5, Apdo 477, Cuzco, Peru.

Committee for the Defence of Human Rights in Apurimac, Apdo 26, Abancay, Cuzco, Peru; tel. 51 84 321276.

Consejo Indio de Sud-America, Jr. Camana No. 780, Oficina 309, Lima, Peru; tel./fax 51 1 282719.

Movimiento pro Derechos Humanos del Negro, Jr. Camana No. 280, Of. 211, Lima 1, Peru; tel. 51 1 275423, fax 51 1 275423.

Sankay Pankara, c/o Centro de Educación y Comunicación, Illa Géron No. 540, Puno, Peru.

Warmikuna Rimanchis, c/o Centro Amauta de Estudios y Promoción de la Mujer, Apdo 167, Avenida Infancia 541, Cuzco, Peru; tel. 51 84 240572, fax 51 84 239736, e-mail: postmaster@camauta.org.pe

Puerto Rico

Land area:	8,959 sq km
Population:	3.7 million (1994)
Main languages:	Spanish (official), English
Main religions:	Christianity (Roman Catholic)
Main minority group:	Afro-Puerto Ricans 800,000–2.4 million (22–65%), Dominicans 60,000 (est., 1.69)
Real per capita GDP:	—
UNDP HDI/rank:	—

Puerto Rico is the smallest of the Greater Antilles, lying some 1,600 kilometres south-east of Miami. As inhabitants of a 'free and associated state' of the USA, Puerto Ricans have US citizenship and are free to travel and work in the USA. Since the 1950s Puerto Rico has developed as an offshore manufacturing enclave for US companies, and while wages are lower than in the USA the standard of living is high in comparison to other Caribbean territories.

Afro-Puerto Ricans

According to the Bill of Rights, discrimination on grounds of race or colour is illegal. Since 1950 censuses on the island have not included ethnic classifications, and it is therefore difficult to quantify Afro-Puerto Ricans as a percentage of the population. Moreover, as with other Hispanic Caribbean societies, ethnicity is closely interlinked with income, education and social status. The 'official' national ideology of *mestizaje* stresses the Spanish indigenous heritage, and there is 'little, if any, "national" emphasis on the African component of Puerto Rican heritage'.[1] Yet a history of slavery (abolished in 1873) and plantation agriculture has left a significant population of African descent in Puerto Rico, sometimes referred to as *gente de color* (people of colour). Persistent inequalities reinforce their low social status. Sociological studies from the 1950s onwards have suggested that Afro-Puerto Ricans are disproportionately present in deprived urban neighbourhoods, low-paid informal-sector employment and youth detention centres.[2]

Dominicans

Approximately 60,000 Dominicans live in Puerto Rico, of whom about 20,000 are thought to be illegal immigrants.[3] The flow of migration began in the mid-1960s but accelerated in the 1980s when the Dominican Republic suffered economic recession and high unemployment. Some Dominicans are en route to the USA, using Puerto Rico as a staging post, but most remain, forming a distinct enclave minority on the island. Although racist sterotypes in Puerto Rico portray Dominican migrants as poor, illiterate peasants, most are relatively well-educated and previously worked in white-collar urban employment. In Puerto Rico, however, Dominicans mostly work in the informal sector as street vendors, domestic workers and in assembly work, although there is a small professional class.

There is considerable hostility towards Dominicans in Puerto Rico, and their numbers and effect on wage levels are frequently exaggerated in the media.[4] Racism also identifies Dominicans as overwhelmingly black and 'mulatto'. The Puerto Rican authorities often arrest Afro-Puerto Ricans without identification, assuming them to be illegal Dominican migrants. Supported by a system of community links and reciprocal help, however, many Dominicans prefer to stay in a cultural and linguistic environment similar to that at home rather than to travel further to join the estimated 300,000 Dominicans in New York.

Conclusions and future prospects

The prospects for Afro-Puerto Ricans and Dominicans in Puerto Rico are not encouraging, especially as the authorities target these communities in a context of economic recession and mounting concerns about crime.

Further reading

Alvárez, L.M., *La tercera raíz: presencia africana en Puerto Rico*, San Juan, Centro de Estudios de la Realidad Puertoriqueña, 1992.

Meléndez, E. and Edgardo, D. (eds), *Colonial Dilemma: Critical Perspectives on Contemporary Puerto Rico*, Boston, MA, South End Press, 1993.

Santiago-Valles, K.A., 'Puerto Rico', in MRG (ed.), *No Longer Invisible: Afro-Latin Americans Today*, London, Minority Rights Publications, 1995.

Minority-based and advocacy organizations

Amnesty International, Calle El Roble #54, Oficina 11, Rio Piedras, Puerto Rico 00925; tel. 1 809 751 7073, fax 1 809 767 7095.

Proyecto Caribeño de Justicia y Paz, PO Box 13241, San Juan 00928–3241, Puerto Rico; tel. 1 809 722 1640/722 2680, fax 1 809 754 5789, e-mail: caribdoc.igc.apc.org

St Kitts-Nevis

Land area:	261.6 sq km
Population:	42,000 (1993)
Main languages:	English
Main religions:	Christianity (Anglican)
Main minority groups:	—
Real per capita GDP:	$9,340
UNDP HDI/rank:	0.858 (45)

St Kitts-Nevis (officially St Christopher and Nevis) became independent from Britain in 1983 after the island of Anguilla, formerly part of the territory under associated statehood, broke away to remain a British dependency. Still largely reliant on its sugar industry, St Kitts has recently developed its tourist industry. Ninety per cent of Kittitians define themselves as of African descent, the rest being mixed European–African or East Indian. No minority rights issues have been identified.

St Lucia

Land area:	616.3 sq km
Population:	140,000 (1993)
Main languages:	English, French-based Creole
Main religions:	Christianity (Roman Catholic)
Main minority groups:	—
Real per capita GDP:	$3,795
UNDP HDI/ rank:	0.733 (76)

One of the Windward Islands and a member of the Organization of Eastern Caribbean States (OECS), St Lucia became independent from Britain in 1979. The island depends to a large degree on banana exports and is highly vulnerable to changes to its protected market in Britain. Approximately 90 per cent of its population is estimated to be of African descent, the rest of mixed African–European parentage. No minority rights issues have been identified.

St Vincent and the Grenadines

Land area:	389.3 sq km
Population:	108,000 (1993)
Main languages:	English
Main religions:	Christianity (Anglican, Roman Catholic, Methodist)
Main minority groups:	Caribs 3,000 (est., 2.8%)
Real per capita GDP:	$3,552
UNDP HDI/rank:	0.738 (73)

Independent from Britain since 1979, St Vincent and the Grenadines has a primarily agricultural economy, in which banana exports play a central part. Tourism is undeveloped in comparison to neighbouring islands, and St Vincent suffers from high unemployment and a low standard of living. Two identifiable indigenous groups are to be found in St Vincent, numbering approximately 3,000 people and situated at the extreme northeast tip of the island. Some of these people are regarded as 'pure' or 'yellow' Caribs, while others are considered to be 'black Caribs', descendants of the island's indigenous population and of Africans brought to St Vincent as slaves. The majority of black Caribs were deported by the British colonial authorities in 1797 to Roatán Island, Honduras, after a series of revolts and confrontations, but a few communities are believed to have remained and survive to the present day.

Historically marginalized and denigrated by the dominant colonial culture, many people of Carib descent sought to reject their ancestry. Distinctions between Caribs, 'black Caribs' and the island's majority black population are not clear, and there is some disagreement as to whether the 'pure Caribs' can be considered the direct descendants of St Vincent's indigenous population since there has been considerable intermarriage with the majority black population.[1] The communities are geographically isolated from the rest of St Vincent. Their villages are among the poorest in St Vincent, and until recently they provided cheap labour for the island's sugar industry. In recent years, however, members of the Carib community have taken part in regional conferences on the theme of indigenous revival.[2] In 1995 a Garífuna council was formed in the Carib villages, while 14 August is now celebrated as Indigenous People's Day.

Minority-based and advocacy organizations

Committee for the Development of the Carib Community, Kingstown, St Vincent.

St Vincent and the Grenadines Human Rights Association, PO Box 614, Grenville Street, Kingstown, St Vincent; tel. 1 809 456 2656.

Suriname

Land area:	163,265 sq km
Population:	437,000 (1992)
Main languages:	Dutch, Hindustani, Javanese, Sranan Tongo ('Negro English'), Chinese, English, French, Spanish, indigenous languages
Main religions:	Christianity, Hinduism, Islam, indigenous and African-derived religions
Main minority groups:	East Indians 147,000 (33.6%), Javanese 65,000 (est., 15%), Maroons 40,000 (9.2%), indigenous (Arawaks and Caribs) 14,600 (3.3%), ethnic Chinese and Europeans
Real per capita GDP:	$3,670
UNDP HDI/rank:	0.737 (75)

The Dutch acquired present-day Suriname from the English in 1667, gradually gaining control of the coast, driving the indigenous population into the interior and importing over 300,000 slaves. Until the introduction of universal adult suffrage in 1949, Suriname was ruled by a small group of wealthy Europeans and Creoles. Internal autonomy came in 1954 with an Electoral Act based on racially demarcated constituencies. Economic, cultural and linguistic factors already divided the ethnic groups; this act encouraged ethnic divisions to continue in political organization.

Suriname has a small indigenous population, as well as ethnic Chinese and Europeans. A Creole population largely of African descent constitutes about one third of the population, as do East Indians, known locally as Hindustanis. Indonesian-descended Javanese make up about 15 per cent and another Creole group, the Maroons or 'Bush Negroes', 9.2 per cent.

In 1986 the Surinamese Liberation Army (SLA), a group of Maroons who claimed that government resettlement policies threatened the autonomy of their tribal society, began guerrilla activities against military posts on Suriname's eastern frontier. Civilians were killed in the escalating violence and 4,500 refugees fled to French Guiana. Peace negotiations with the SLA started in 1988, but in 1989 further guerrilla activity by the indigenous Tucayana Amazonica, demanding restoration of the Bureau of Amerindian Affairs, broke out in the west. Agreement was eventually reached between the government and guerrilla movements in May 1992. Guerrillas were included in the amnesty previously extended to the military and the government promised that the interior would receive priority in its programmes for economic development and social welfare.[1]

East Indians

Indians first came to Suriname in 1863. The Dutch had established control over the coastal areas in the years after 1667 and attempted to establish a plantation economy by the importation of African slaves. After slavery was abolished there was an agreement between Britain and the Netherlands for the importation of subcontinental Indians as contract labourers; 34,300 came in the years between 1873 and 1916. Many subsequently became small independent rice farmers, traders and business people. Many others emigrated to the Netherlands during the years of high unemployment prior to independence. While political power initially remained in the hands of Creoles, since 1987 when an East Indian was elected President of the National Assembly, East Indians have been taking on roles in public administration and politics.[3]

Maroons

The Dutch-speaking Maroons, descendants of African slaves who fled slavery to found a society in the interior jungles, have retained the distinctive identity based on their West African origins. They are organized in six main groups, one of which, the Aluku or Boni, also lives in French Guiana. Recently Maroons have moved to Paramaribo to work as labourers or in the bauxite settlements. Since independence Maroons have resented domination by Creoles, and particularly the military, who would like to remove them to urban settlements. Traditional treaty rights allowing for political, cultural and religious freedom have been ignored. Maroons are among the poorest sectors of Suriname society and were the chief victims of the violence of the mid-1980s.[2]

Other minorities

Legislation regarding indigenous peoples is still lacking. Some villages have titles to land but all ownership rights belong to the government. During the guerrilla warfare of the second half of the 1980s Arawaks, Caribs and Wayanas were relocated by government and guerrilla forces.

Around 35,000 Javanese from the Dutch East Indies were imported as contract labour slightly later than the East Indians. Many remained, and like the East Indians became small farmers. In 1987, the Front for Democracy and Development, which represents Javanese interests, won the elections. There are small ethnic Chinese and European communities in the towns.

Conclusions and future prospects

In April 1990 France and Suriname agreed terms providing for the repatriation of an estimated 10,000 Surinamese refugees from French Guiana. After alleged attempts at forcible repatriation by the French government, some 6,000 refugees were offered voluntary repatriation. The situation remains unstable and a new insurgent group, the Suriname Liberation Front, emerged in 1994.

Further reading

Colchester, M., *Forest Politics in Suriname*, Utrecht, International Books, 1995.

'Maroons of Suriname' and 'East Indians of the Caribbean', in MRG (ed.), *World Directory of Minorities*, 1st edn, London, Longman, 1990.

Trinidad and Tobago

Land area:	5,128 sq km
Population:	1.2 million (1993)
Main languages:	English (official), Hindi
Main religions:	Christianity, Hinduism, Islam
Main minority groups:	East Indians 500,000 (40%)
Real per capita GDP:	$8,670
UNDP HDI/rank:	0.872 (38)

The two-island state of Trinidad and Tobago lies at the bottom of the Antillean chain, with Trinidad only 10 kilometres away from the Venezuelan coast. Since the discovery of oil in 1902, Trinidad's economy has been dominated by petroleum. There are two dominant ethnic groups in Trinidad (Tobago's population is almost entirely African in origin), with Afro-Trinidadians representing approximately 39 per cent and East Indians about 40 per cent of the population. Although numerically the largest group, until recently Trinidad's East Indians could be seen as a minority in terms of their political and social status. Among the East Indian population there are Hindus (mostly small farmers), Muslims (mainly merchants and urban workers) and some predominantly middle-class Christians.

East Indians

East Indians – so-called to avoid confusion with Trinidad's long-disappeared indigenous population – first arrived as indentured labourers from India in the second half of the nineteenth century after the abolition of slavery. Most originated from the northern province of Uttar Pradesh. Working for low wages on the sugar plantations, they earned the enmity of the free black workforce who perceived them as 'cheap labour'. Most remained in the country after their five-year indentureship. Separated from the black population by language and religion, they remained culturally distinct. With the growth of the oil economy and modernization, Afro-Trinidadians tended to work in the petroleum sector and in urban, public-sector employment. East Indians, however, stayed predominantly in rural areas and in agricultural jobs; this pattern remains more or less the same today, with East Indians dominant in the countryside and black people a majority in urban centres.

Since independence in 1962, Trinidadian politics has been largely dominated by the People's National Movement (PNM). The PNM has always been associated with the interests of the Afro-Trinidadian community. Attempts to set up East Indian opposition parties were until comparatively recently largely unsuccessful. However, in 1986 the PNM recorded its first ever election defeat, when the National Alliance for Reconstruction (NAR), a coalition of four parties including the largely East Indian United Labour Front (ULF), won overwhelmingly. By 1989, however, the NAR had split, with Deputy Prime Minister Basdeo Panday and three other East Indian ministers leaving to form the opposition United National Congress (UNC). In 1991 the PNM regained power, with the UNC the main opposition party. In the election campaign Panday had argued that there was systematic discrimination against East Indians in the public sector and promised an Equal Employment Opportunities Commission.

In November 1995, fresh elections brought Panday and his UNC to power in coalition with NAR. This was the first time that an East Indian had become Prime Minister and marked a turning point in that community's political development. Prime Minister Panday named many East Indians to his Cabinet, while also maintaining an Afro-Trinidadian presence in government. Tensions between the Afro-Trinidadian and Indo-Trinidadian communities surface only sporadically and are usually related to adverse economic conditions. In the 1980s, when oil prices dropped steeply after the boom years of the 1970s, approximately 75,000 East Indians are estimated to have migrated to Canada.[1] In 1990 an abortive coup by an extreme Muslim group led to widespread looting in Port of Spain; many of the shops and businesses looted belonged to East Indians.

Conclusions and future prospects

Long-standing stereotypes and prejudices persist in Trinidad. In 1994 Panday remarked that the country 'reeks of racism, reeks with division'.[2] Conversely, some Afro-Trinidadians accuse East Indians of dominating the economy and owing their loyalty not to Trinidad but to India. It remains to be seen whether an East Indian-led government will succeed in changing such attitudes.

Further reading

Cross, M., *The East Indians of Guyana and Trinidad*, London, MRG report, 1987.

Minority-based and advocacy organizations

Trinidad and Tobago Bureau on Human Rights, Dalton House, 9 Harris Street, San Fernando, Trinidad and Tobago; tel. 1 809 652 4504.

Turks and Caicos Islands

Land area:	430 sq km
Population:	14,000 (1993)
Main languages:	English, Creole
Main religions:	Christianity
Main minority groups:	Haitians 6,000 (est., 46%)
Real per capita GDP:	—
UNDP HDI/rank:	—

Made up of more than thirty islands, the Turks and Caicos lie 800 kilometres south-east of Miami at the end of the Bahamas chain and are a British Dependent Territory. With the decline of the traditional salt industry, the Turks and Caicos have diversified into tourism and offshore financial services. Recent economic growth and employment possibilities have reversed years of outward migration, and the Turks and Caicos are estimated to have received 11,000 Haitian migrants in recent years. Of these 6,000 have legal documentation, while the others are deemed illegal immigrants. In April 1995 the islands' governor announced that a British ship would assist US coastguard vessels in preventing Haitians from landing there. This move followed the forcible repatriation of several hundred Haitians earlier in the year. No further minority rights issues have been identified.

Uruguay

Land area:	176,215 sq km
Population:	3.1 million (est.1993)
Main languages:	Spanish, indigenous languages
Main religions:	Christianity (majority Roman Catholic), Judaism, indigenous religions
Main minority groups:	Afro-Uruguayans 38,000 (est., 1.2%), Jews 23,800 (0.75%), indigenous Guaraní Mbyá
Real per capita GDP:	$6,550
UNDP HDI/rank:	0.883 (32)

The 1970s were marked in Uruguay by continual human rights violations by the armed forces and military government. Investigation of these violations became a political issue in 1986 when the government proposed an amnesty for those involved; a referendum held in 1989 upheld the amnesty by a narrow majority. Since the return to democracy in 1985 government has been hampered by industrial unrest and a series of major strikes. Little ethnic mixing took place between Uruguay's indigenous population and early Spanish colonists. Until recently, as a result of the deliberate genocide practised on the indigenous population in the nineteenth century, Uruguay had no indigenous minorities. A small number of Guaraní Mbyá have now returned; there are significant Afro-Uruguayan and Jewish populations.

Afro-Uruguayans

Integrated into the Viceroyalty of the River Plate in the colonial era, Uruguay had no large rural establishments which permitted the cultivation of cotton, coffee or sugar-cane and African slaves were employed as domestic servants. Slavery was abolished gradually between 1842 and 1852. Despite their positions of trust, Africans were marginalized and came to accept the negative stereotypes of the dominant culture. During the 1930s Afro-Uruguayans became politicized, but after 1945 Uruguay, like Brazil, followed a policy of *blanqueamiento* (whitening). Many of the earlier ethnic associations disappeared, and most Afro-Uruguayans are reported as largely uninterested in their African heritage. Economically they remain among the poorest sectors of Uruguayan society. In recent years Afro-Uruguayans have again formed their own organizations, such as Mundo Afro, which in 1994 hosted a regional conference on xenophobia and racism in Montevideo.[1]

Other minorities

The indigenous inhabitants of Uruguay were deliberately exterminated after having played a valuable part in the Army of Independence. As a result Uruguay has not had an indigenous population, but since the beginning of the 1980s several nuclear families of Guaraní Mbyá hunter gatherers, whose ancestral lands extend from the Paraguayan jungle to the Atlantic coast, have begun to settle in various parts of Uruguay, notably in the estuaries of the Plate and Uruguay rivers.

Uruguay's Jewish population resides almost exclusively in Montevideo.The country has no tradition of official anti-Semitism although there have been isolated incidents where Jews were attacked and killed or marked with swastikas.[2]

Conclusions and future prospects

As a result of the return of the Guaraní Mbya, the Indigenist Association of Uruguay has been created. The Mbya will need support in a country which believes in reinforcing a homogeneous Latin American identity rather than that of indigenous or other ethnic minorities.[3] While Mundo Afro and other groups face a difficult task in raising Afro-Uruguayan levels of political consciousness, hosting the 1994 conference provided not only the encouragement of solidarity but also a network of contacts with similar groups which was hitherto lacking.

Further reading

Luz, A. da, 'Uruguay', in MRG (ed.), *No Longer Invisible: Afro-Latin Americans Today*, London, Minority Rights Publications, 1995.

Minority-based and advocacy organizations

Amnesty International, Tristan Narvaja 1642, Apdo 2, CP11200, Montevideo, Uruguay; tel. 598 2 428848, fax 598 2 428849.

Organizaciones Mundo Afro, Zelmar Michelini 1244, Piso 2, Montevideo, Uruguay; tel./fax 598 2 916156, fax 598 2 901135.

US Virgin Islands

Land area:	354.8 sq km
Population:	102,000 (1990)
Main languages:	English, Spanish, Creole
Main religions:	Christianity (Protestant)
Main minority group:	—
Real per capita GDP:	—
UNDP HDI/rank:	—

The US Virgin Islands, comprising sixty-eight mostly uninhabited islands, are a US external territory and are heavily dependent on links with the US mainland and Puerto Rico (accounting for 90 per cent of trade). During the tourism boom years of the 1950s and 1960s, thousands of migrants from other Caribbean territories settled, but from the 1980s onwards immigration controls have been tightened up and many 'aliens' deported. No specific minority rights issues have been identified.

Venezuela

Land area:	882,050 sq km
Population:	20.7 million (est. 1993)
Main languages:	Spanish, indigenous languages
Main religions:	Christianity (majority Roman Catholic), African-derived and indigenous religions
Main minority groups:	Afro-Venezuelans 1.9–14 million (9–67%), indigenous peoples including Yanomami, Piaroa, Barí, Yukpa, Yabarana, Warao, Yekuana and Pemón 316,000 (1.5%)
Real per Capita GDP:	$8,360
UNDP HDI/ rank:	0.859 (44)

An attempted military coup in 1992 and a series of general strikes, due to discontent with economic and agricultural policies, have threatened Venezuela's democratic government. Although Colombia's claims to territorial rights in the Gulf of Venezuela have been settled, Venezuelan troops on the Colombian border have been reinforced to combat the growing traffic in drugs and arms carried out by Colombian guerrillas; relations between the two countries remain tense. Venezuela's dispute with Guyana concerning land west of the Essequibo River continues.

Venezuela's twenty-eight indigenous peoples, including Yanomami, Piaroa, Barí, Yukpa, Yabarana, Yekuana, Warao and Pemón, inhabit the lowland forests of the Orinoco Delta. There is also a sizeable Afro-Venezuelan population. During the Spanish colonial regime the indigenous population retained their *resguardos*, communally held reserved land, but these were largely destroyed after independence. In 1915 the Catholic Church was given responsibility for the conversion and integration of indigenous peoples. Since the 1950s Venezuela has had a National Indigenist Commission and a Central Office of Indigenous Affairs. The Agrarian Reform Law of 1960, administered by the National Institute of Agronomy, recognized certain indigenous rights to land, and in the 1970s and 1980s the institute granted land titles to about 100 communities, but 72 per cent of Venezuela's indigenous peoples still lack land titles.[1]

In March 1992 Congress considered reform of the 1961 constitution and in August leaders of three indigenous organizations, including the Consejo Nacional Indio de Venezuela, (Venezuelan National Indigenous Council, CONIVE), submitted proposals for inclusion. These covered official recognition of indigenous languages, prohibition of missionary activity, the right to communal ownership of territory, intercultural bilingual education, and legislation regarding territorial administration and preservation of the environment on the Brazilian frontier. The subsequent state of emergency and suspension of the constitution have delayed reform, although reinforcements were deployed along the country's border with Brazil following the 1993 massacre of sixteen Yanomami in Venezuelan territory by Brazilian gold miners.[2]

Afro-Venezuelans

Only a small number of slaves were transported to Venezuela in the sixteenth and seventeenth centuries but more arrived in the early eighteenth century to work on the numerous cocoa plantations. Many were brought from the British colonies in the Caribbean. These slaves were skilled labourers; their owners did not enforce rigid control and their administration was often undertaken by the church. Slaves settled on rural estates rather than in urban centres; they had their own plots and lived a communal life which differed little from that of free labourers. In the second half of the twentieth century migration to the cities increased substantially. Miscegenation has resulted in a wide variety of racial mixing with a correspondingly wide variety of terms to describe ethnic identity and skin colour. Afro-Venezuelan religion is a syncretic product with African, Spanish Catholic and indigenous components. African cultural elements persist but there is indigenous influence in social organization. Afro-Venezuelans came from the English-speaking Caribbean islands in the 1930s to work in the gold mines and oil industry; this group reflect English traditions and see their past as Caribbean rather than African.

Although there is little formal racism there is a wide spectrum of stereotypes and social prejudices. Most Afro-Venezuelans who work the land do not refer to themselves as black. They reject suggestions of African ancestry and see themselves as Creoles. Those living in the cities refer to themselves as 'the poor' or 'the working class', and see their position among the poorer social sectors not as the result of racial discrimination but of the social system.[3]

Yabarana

Yabarana have occupied lands along the Paracuito River in southern Venezuela since the eighteenth century when their numbers were decimated by the poor conditions under which they worked for rubber tappers. Now Yabarana are threatened by cattle ranching and tourism. Their gardens are invaded by cattle and they have been forbidden to hunt in land which 'must be preserved for tourists'. Tourism also threatens Yabarana water supplies. To gain legal title to their lands Yabarana have established the Yabarana Organization of the River Paracuito. They hope to unite with neighbouring Panaré hunter gatherers and 200 nomadic Hoti who have had only sporadic contact with the exterior.[4]

Barí and Yukpa

Barí and Yukpa are hunter-gatherers living in the forested mountain range on the border with Colombia. Barí now number only around 1,000. Lack of official land titles makes them vulnerable to usurpation by state-controlled coal and oil companies as well as landowners and logging concerns. Open cast mining, which is in contravention of national law, causes widespread pollution and devastation. Barí leaders attempting to set up blockades were threatened with arrest. Human rights groups fear that the 1994 change of government will lead to the renewed granting of previously frozen mining concessions.[5]

Warao and Kariña

Oil companies are working on lands around the Orinoco Delta occupied by the Warao and Kariña. Kariña villages have been wrecked, and imported diseases such as cholera have caused 500 deaths. Warao leaders have drawn attention to the pollution caused by the oil industry and to the displacement of communities caused by the construction of the Caroni dam. This dam is likely to become inoperative within 50 years due to the sedimentation resulting from extensive destruction of the forest by timber companies.[6]

Yanomami

The Venezuelan Yanomami are threatened by tourism (see also **Brazil**). The EU-funded biosphere reserve incorporates Yanomami land but does recognize their title. Expelled from Brazilian reservation lands, gold miners are crossing the border to work in Venezuelan Yanomami territory. In 1993 they were responsible for the massacre of 16 Yanomami at Haximú and the burning of their communal house.

Pemón

Since 1991 several groups of Pemón have been negatively affected by mining.In 1993 CONIVE protested against the signing of a contract for the development of Pemón land by the Ministry of Energy and Mines which would mean blasting part of the rock in Roraima National Park. Besides being in violation of Pemón religious beliefs, it brings into question the government's environmental policy. Pemón are also protesting against a plan for logging operations in the Imataca forest reserve, which disregards the land rights of Pemón, Kariña and other peoples.[7] Roraima forest peoples have requested the annulment of mining and logging concessions and, through CONIVE, conservationist NGOs are being asked for support.

Yekuana and Piaroa

Yekuana were invaded by colonists in the 1960s and 1970s resulting in internal fragementation of their political structure; this was further aggravated by the activities of rival religious institutions. Yekuana and Piaroa are threatened by proposed hydroelectric projects which would change the course of their rivers. Piaroa and Akawayo are also affected by bauxite mining.[8] Besides the continuing activities of logging companies, Piaroa are now being adversely affected by the large number of tourists visiting their territories, particularly those of the Guanay Valley. As a people they have formed a democratically elected parliament to proclaim their right to self-determination, and to understand and be understood in the political affairs of Venezuela.

Conclusions and future prospects

Venezuela's indigenous peoples continue to suffer severe neglect in health, education and territorial rights. They would benefit from the appointment of an international commission to review government policy regarding indigenous minorities. Afro-Venezuelans generally are reported as having little awareness of ethnic identity. Efforts are being made to preserve Afro-Venezuelan culture but survival is seen to depend on job opportunities rather than tradition and defenders of the culture are likely to remain limited to a middle-class elite.

Further reading

Bermudez, E. and Suarez, M.M., 'Venezuela', in MRG (ed.), *No Longer Invisible: Afro-Latin Americans Today*, London, Minority Rights Publications, 1995.

Colchester, M. with Watson, F., *Venezuela: Violations of Indigenous Rights*, report to the International Labour Office on the observation of ILO Convention 107, London, Survival International and World Rainforest Movement, 1995.

Minority-based and advocacy organizations

Amnesty International, Apdo Postal 5110, Carmelitas, 1010-A, Caracas, Venezuela; tel 58 2 576 5344, fax 582 572 9410.

Consejo Nacional Indio de Venezuela (CONIVE), Apdo 5156, Caracas 1010-A, Venezuela; tel. 58 2 541 1754/595 1754, fax 582 541 7717.

Organización Regional de Pueblos Indígenas de Amazonas, Avenida Orinoco, Urbanización Los Lirios, Mercado Amazonas, Estado Amazonas, Venezuela.

Notes

Introduction

Contributions to this regional section are as follows. Patrick Costello: Central America (regional introduction and country entries); Lindsey Crickmay: South America (regional introduction and country entries); James Ferguson: the Caribbean (regional introduction and country entries).

1 *Fourth World Bulletin*, Fall 1994/Winter 1995.

2 Gray, A., *Amerindians of South America*, London, MRG report, 1987.

3 Ibid.

4 Statistics for indigenous minorities in South American countries are quoted from those assembled by José Matos Mar for his article 'Grupos étnicos de América', *América Indígena*, 4, 1993, pp. 155–234.

Argentina

1 Gray, A., *Amerindians of South America*, London, MRG report, 1987.

2 Survival International *Newsletter* 33, 1994, pp. 8–10.

3 IWGIA *Bulletin*, no. 4, 1993, quoted in *América Indígena,* vol. 4, 1993, pp. 243–4.

4 Gray, op. cit.

5 *América Indígena*, vols. 1–2, 1993, pp. 338–9.

6 'Welsh of Patagonia', in MRG (ed.), *World Directory of Minorities*, 1st edn., London, Longman, 1990.

7 'Argentina', *Anti-Semitism World Report, 1995*, London, Institute of Jewish Affairs, and New York, American Jewish Committee, 1995.

8 Tigner, J.L., 'Japanese immigration into Latin America: a survey', *Journal of Interamerican Studies and World Affairs*, vol. 23, no. 4, 1981, 457–82.

Bahamas

1 *Caribbean Week*, Barbados, 16–29 April 1994.

2 *Caribbean Insight*, London, June 1994.

Barbados

1 Sheppard, J., *The 'Redlegs' of Barbados: Their Origins and History*, New York, KTO Press, 1977.

Bolivia

1 Plant, R., *Land Rights and Minorities*, London, MRG report, 1994.

2 Information on the growth of Katarismo is drawn from Albó, X., 'From MNRistas to Kataristas to Katari' in S. Stern (ed.), *Resistance, Rebellion and Consciousness in the Andean Peasant World: 18th to 20th Centuries*, Madison, University of Wisconsin Press, 1987, pp. 379–419.

3 Gill, L., '"Proper women" and city pleasures: gender, class and contested meanings in La Paz', *American Ethnologist*, 20 (1), 1993, pp. 72–88.

4 Leons, M.B., 'Risk and opportunity in the coca/cocaine economy of the Bolivian Yungas', *Journal of Latin American Studies*, 25, 1993, pp. 121–57.

5 Rivera Cusicanqui, S., 'Aymara past, Aymara future', in NACLA *Report on the Americas*, vol. 25, no. 3, December 1991.

6 *Debate*, octubre/diciembre 1993, Buenos Aires, reprinted in *América Indígena*, vol. 4, 1993, pp. 249–50.

7 Spedding, A., 'Bolivia', in MRG (ed.), *No Longer Invisible: Afro-Latin Americans Today*, London, Minority Rights Publications, 1995.

8 *Amigos de los Indios*, Madrid, quoted in *América Indígena*, vols. 1–2, 1993, pp. 348–9.

9 Tigner, J. L., 'Japanese immigration into Latin America: a survey', *Journal of Interamerican Studies and World Affairs*, vol. 23, no. 4, 1981, pp. 457–82.

10 *The Economist*, 30 September 1995.

Brazil

1 Gray, A., *Amerindians of South America*, London, MRG report, 1987; Plant, R., *Land Rights and Minorities*, London, MRG report, 1994.

2 This account of indigenous and tribal peoples draws extensively on Survival International newsletters and bulletins 1990–5, on the Survival International book *Yanomami* (London, 1990) and on articles included in *América Indígena* 'Noticias indígenistas' section for 1993 and 1994.

3 Davis, D.J. (ed.), *Slavery and Beyond: The African Impact on Latin America and the Caribbean*, Wilmington, DE, Scholarly Resources, Jaguar Books, 1995; Vieira, R.M., 'Brazil', in MRG (ed.), *No Longer Invisible: Afro-Latin Americans Today*, London, Minority Rights Publications, 1995.

4 Tigner, J.L., 'Japanese immigration into Latin America: a survey', *Journal of Interamerican Studies and World Affairs*, col. 23, no. 4, 1981, pp. 457–82.

5 'Brazil' in *Anti-Semitism World Report 1995*, London, Institute of Jewish Affairs, and New York, American Jewish Committee, 1995.

Chile

1 *América Indígena*, vol. 4, 1992, p. 201.

2 *World Rivers Review*, vol. 8, no. 4, 1993, quoted in *América Indígena*, vol. 4, 1993, pp. 276–7.

3 'Rapa Nui (Easter Island)', in MRG (ed.), *World Directory of Minorities*, 1st edn., London, Longman, 1990.

4 *Anti-Semitism World Report 1995,* London, Institute of Jewish Affairs, and New York, American Jewish Committee, 1995.

5 Tigner, J.L., 'Japanese Immigration into Latin America: a survey', *Journal of Interamerican Studies and World Affairs*, vol. 23, no. 4, 1981, pp. 457–82.

Colombia

1 Rappaport, J., 'Reinvented traditions: the heraldry of ethnic militancy in the Colombian Andes', in R.V.H. Dover, K.E. Siebold and J.H. McDowell (eds), *Andean Cosmologies through Time: Persistence and Emergence*, Bloomington, I.N., Indiana University Press, 1992, pp. 202–28; Plant, R., *Land Rights and Minorities*, MRG report, 1994.

2 De Friedman, N.S. and Arocha, J., 'Colombia', in MRG (ed.), *No Longer Invisible: Afro-Latin Americans Today,* London, Minority Rights Publications, 1995; Wade, P., 'The Afro- Colombians of Colombia', MRG *Outsider*, no. 39, 1994.

3 Rappaport, J., *op. cit*; *América Indígena*, vols. 1–2, p. 368. Considerable information on indigenous groups throughout Colombia is drawn from Survival International Urgent Action Bulletins for May 1991, January 1992, April 1994, and from *Indians of the Americas*, London, Survival International, 1992.

4 *América Indígena*, vol. 3–4, 1993; Gray, A., *Amerindians of South America*, MRG report, 1987.

5 'Colombia', *Anti-Semitism World Report 1995*, London, Institute of Jewish Affairs, and New York, American Jewish Committee, 1995.

Costa Rica

1 This section is largely based on Sawyers Royal, K. and Perry, F., 'Costa Rica' in MRG (ed.), *No Longer Invisible: Afro-Latin Americans Today*, op. cit.

Cuba

1 MRG (ed.), *World Directory of Minorities*, op. cit., p. 44.

2 NACLA, *Report on the Americas*, 'The Black Americas', New York, February 1992.

3 McGarrity, G. and Cardenas, O., 'Cuba', in MRG (ed.), *No Longer Invisible: Afro-Latin Americans Today*, op. cit., p. 86.

4 Ibid., p. 96.

5 Ibid., p. 101.

Dominica

1 MRG (ed.), *World Directory of Minorities*, op. cit., p. 51.

2 *Caribbean Insight*, London, January 1992.

Dominican Republic

1 Lemoine, M., *Bitter Sugar*, Zed Books, London, 1985, p. 135.

2 Anti-Slavery International, *The Price of Sugar: Haitian Forced Labour in the Dominican Republic*, London, 1994, p. 6.

3 Comité de Coordinación de las Instituciones Haitianas, *Le Cas des Refugiés Haitiens en République Dominicaine*, Santo Domingo, 1994.

Ecuador

1 Material for this section is drawn from Field, L., 'Ecuador's pan-Indian uprising', NACLA *Report on the Americas*, vol. 25, no. 3, December 1991, pp. 39–44; Corkhill, D. and Cubitt, D., *Ecuador: Fragile Democracy*, London, Latin America Bureau, 1988.

2 Information regarding Texaco and Maxus is drawn from Switkes, G., 'Ecuador: the people vs Texaco', NACLA *Report on the Americas*, vol. 28, no. 2, September/October 1994; *Fourth World Bulletin*, Fall 1994/Winter 1995.

3 Survival International *Urgent Action Bulletin*, September 1990, reproduced in *América Indígena,* vol. 1–2, 1993, pp. 380–2.

4 *América Indígena*, op. cit., *Fourth World Bulletin*, op. cit.

5 *Voz de CONFENIAE*, reproduced in *América Indígena*, vol. 3, 1993.

6 NACLA *Report on the Americas*, vol. 25, op. cit.

7 Whitten, N.E. and Quiroga, D., 'Ecuador', in MRG (ed.), *No Longer Invisible: Afro-Latin Americans Today*, London, Minority Rights Publications, 1995.

8 NACLA *Report on the Americas*, vol. 28, no. 2, op. cit.

El Salvador

1 US Department of State, *Country Reports on Human Rights Practices for 1994, El Salvador*, Washington DC, US Government Printing Office, 1995.

2 Dunbar Ortiz, R., *Indians of the Americas: Human Rights and Self-Determination*, London, Zed Books, 1984, p. 198.

Guatemala

1 Wearne, P., *The Maya of Guatemala*, London, MRG report, 1994, pp. 13, 17.

2 Ibid.

3 United Nations Commission on Human Rights, *Report by the Independent Expert, Mrs. Monica Pinto, on the Situation of Human Rights in Guatemala*, (E/CN.4/1995/15), Geneva, 1995, para. 74.

Guyana

1 Material on the history and politics of Guyana is taken from 'East Indians of the Caribbean', in MRG (ed.), *World Directory of Minorities*, 1st edn., London, Longman, 1990, and *The Europa World Year Book, 1995*, London, Europa, 1995.

2 Survival International press release, August 1995.

Jamaica

1 See Cardenas, O., 'The Maroons of Jamaica', MRG, *Outsider*, no. 40, October 1994, pp. 4–5.

2 Patterson, O., 'Ras Tafari: the cult of outcasts', *New Society*, London, vol. 4, no. 3, 1964.

3 Cashmore, E.E., *The Rastafarians*, MRG report, London, 1992, p. 9.

Nicaragua

1 Herrera, quoted in Dunbar Ortiz, R., *Indians of the Americas: Human Rights and Self-Determination*, London, Zed Books, 1984, p. 201.

2 Archer, D. and Costello, P., *Literacy and Power: The Latin American Battleground*, London, Earthscan, 1990, p. 183.

3 This section, and that on the Garífuna, is largely based on Freeland, J., 'Nicaragua' in MRG (ed.), *No Longer Invisible: Afro-Latin Americans Today*, London, Minority Rights Publications, 1995.

4 Ibid., p. 198.

Panama

1 Figures from Davis, D.J., 'Panama' in MRG (ed.), *No Longer Invisible: Afro-Latin Americans Today*, London, Minority Rights Publications, 1995, p. 207.

Paraguay

1 Gray, A., *Amerindians of South America*, London, MRG report, 1987.

2 *América Indígena*, vols. 1–2, 1993, pp. 446–7.

3 Discussion of Enxet is taken from Kidd, S., 'Land, politics and benevolent shamanism: the Enxet in a democratic Paraguay', *Journal of Latin American Studies*, vol. 17, part 1, 1995, pp. 43–6.

4 Gray, A., op. cit., p. 18.

5 Survival International *Urgent Action Bulletin*, September 1994.

6 Survival International *Urgent Action Bulletin*, March 1995; IWGIA Bulletin, 1993, quoted in *América Indígena*, vol. 4, 1993, pp. 319–22.

7 Discussion of Mennonites drawn largely from Kidd, op. cit., p. 53.

8 Tigner, J.L., 'Japanese immigration into Latin America: a survey', *Journal of Interamerican Studies and World Affairs*, vol. 23, no. 4, 1981, pp. 457–82.

Peru

1 Gray, A., Amerindians of South America, London, MRG report, 1987.

2 'Peru after Guzman', NACLA *Report on the Americas*, vol. 28, no. 3, November/December 1994.

3 Material concerning Sendero Luminoso is drawn from Starn, O., 'Missing the revolution: anthropologists and the war in Peru', *Cultural Anthropology*, vol. 6, no. 1, 1991; and from Amnesty International, *Human Rights in a Climate of Terror*, London, 1994.

4 *Fourth World Bulletin*, December 1993, July 1994; Survival International *Urgent Action Bulletin*, September 1993.

5 Luciano, J. and Rodriguez Pastor, H., 'Peru', in MRG (ed.), *No Longer Invisible: Afro-Latin Americans Today*, London, Minority Rights Publications, 1995.

6 Tigner, J.L., 'Japanese immigration into Latin America: a survey', *Journal of Interamerican Studies and World Affairs*, vol. 23, no. 4, 1981, pp. 457–82.

Puerto Rico

1 Whitten, Jr., N.E. and Torres, A., 'Blackness in the Americas', NACLA *Report on the Americas, The Black Americas 1492–1992*, New York, 1992, p. 21.

2 Santiago-Valles, K.A., 'Puerto Rico' in MRG (ed.), *No Longer Invisible: Afro-Latin Americans Today*, op. cit., p. 153.

3 Rey, C.A., 'Identitad y marginalidad: los dominicanos en Puerto Rico', mimeo, Puerto Rico, 1994, p. 9.

4 Rey, C.A. and Duany, J., 'La emigración dominicana a Puerto Rico', *Homines*, Puerto Rico, vol. 13, no. 2, p. 197.

St Vincent and the Grenadines

1 Information provided by Dr Adrian Fraser, School of Continuing Studies, University of the West Indies, St Vincent.

2 Mondesire, A. and Robinson, N. (eds), *Report on Conference of Indigenous Peoples: Caribbean Indigenous Revival*, Kingstown, St Vincent, 1987.

Suriname

1 Information on the recent political situation in Suriname is taken from *The Europa World Year Book 1995*, London, Europa, 1995.

2 'Maroons of Suriname', in MRG (ed.), *World Directory of Minorities*, 1st edn, London, Longman, 1990.

3 'East Indians of the Caribbean', ibid.

Trinidad and Tobago

1 Henry, A.V., 'Talking race in Trinidad and Tobago: a practical framework', in *Caribbean Affairs*, Port of Spain, April-June 1993.

2 *Caribbean Insight*, London, September 1994.

Uruguay

1 Luz, A. da, 'Uruguay', and Davis, D., 'Postscript', in MRG (ed.), *No Longer Invisible: Afro-Latin Americans Today*, London, Minority Rights Publications, 1995.

2 'Uruguay', in *Anti-Semitism World Report, 1995*, London, Institute of Jewish Affairs, and New York, American Jewish Committee, 1995.

3 IWGIA *Bulletin*, quoted in *América Indígena*, vol. 3, 1994, pp. 282–3.

Venezuela

1 Quoted from Gray, A., *Amerindians of South America*, London, MRG report, 1987.

2 Publication of CONIVE, reproduced in *América Indígena*, vol. 3, 1992.

3 Bermudez, E. and Suarez, M.M., 'Venezuela', in MRG (ed.), *No Longer Invisible: Afro- Latin Americans Today*, London, Minority Rights Publications, 1995.

4 Survival International *Newsletter*, no. 33, 1994; Survival International *Urgent Action Bulletin*, April 1994.

5 Survival International *Newsletter*, 1994, Survival International *Urgent Action Bulletin*, May 1993.

6 *América Indígena*, vols. 1–3, 1993.

7 Ibid.

8 CMPI Bulletin, quoted in *América Indígena*, vols. 1–2, 1993, pp. 464–5.

WESTERN EUROPE

Bridget Anderson

The minorities of Western Europe can be considered as comprising three broad categories. Indigenous peoples, such as Sami, who have inhabited the territory since time immemorial and maintained a close and sustaining relationship with the land and natural resources, constitute the smallest group of minorities. A second and far larger group consists of those 'historic' minorities that have been settled for a considerable time – in some cases since before the formation of the state – and preserve cultural, linguistic, religious or other characteristics that differ from those of the dominant population, for example Alsatians, Scots and Sorbs. Among such long-settled minorities are many small linguistic and cultural groups that have demanded recognition on the part of states, often successfully. A third category consists of 'new minorities': populations that were encouraged to come to Western Europe from former colonies to ease the labour shortage following the Second World War, as well as refugees of recent times and non-colonial guestworkers; this group includes communities of Middle Eastern, African, Caribbean and South Asian origin.

Both contrasts and similarities occur between the experience of minorities of different origin, and in some circumstances the distinction between categories is blurred. The Croatian presence in Burgenland in Austria, for example, began in the sixteenth century with the arrival of refugees from the Ottoman Empire but has been supplemented by a later wave of refugees from the conflict in former Yugoslavia. However, the former are protected by the Austrian State Treaty, while the latter are not. Differences also frequently arise from citizenship rights within the broad 'new minorities' grouping: for example, between immigrants and their children who do not have the right to citizenship, or between Southern European migrants now protected by European citizenship and 'third country nationals' from outside the European Union.

States and citizenship

Current Western European borders and many of the region's nation states are relatively recent constructions. The First World War brought about the dissolution of four multinational empires. Groups then emerged that could not assume the nationality of the successor state and became refugees or 'national minorities' within the successor state's borders. Thus the Lausanne Convention of 1923 provided for the compulsory exchange of nationals between the new Turkish Republic and Greece, resulting in the forced transfer of 1.5 million people, and also the mutual official recognition by the two states of their remaining Greek and Turkish minorities. The First World War also saw significant border changes, often at the expense of the defeated powers, with major implications for their populations. South Tyrol, for example, was declared part of Italy, while Alsace was integrated with France. Two tendencies were therefore at work in Western Europe during the 1920s. On the one hand, the mono-ethnic nation state was promoted as a source of stability and common interest. Minorities were feared; some were viewed as potential fifth columns for the irredentist ambitions of neighbouring states; others challenged the integrity of the state through demands for self-determination or calls for unity with another state. On the other hand, the presence of ethnic minorities within redrawn boundaries was an acknowledged reality. The League of Nations attempted to reconcile these realities by regulating the treatment of minorities, and adherence to principles of equality and protection as laid out in the minorities treaties was a condition of membership of the League. The League differentiated between citizens and non-citizens, guaranteeing the latter life, liberty and the free exercise of religion, but not equality of rights in civil and political matters.[1]

The consequences of discrimination between citizens and non-citizens were revealed in the Second World War, when non-ethnic Germans such as Roma/Gypsies and Jews were stripped of citizenship, and the automatic right to citizenship of all born on German territory was limited to a right of

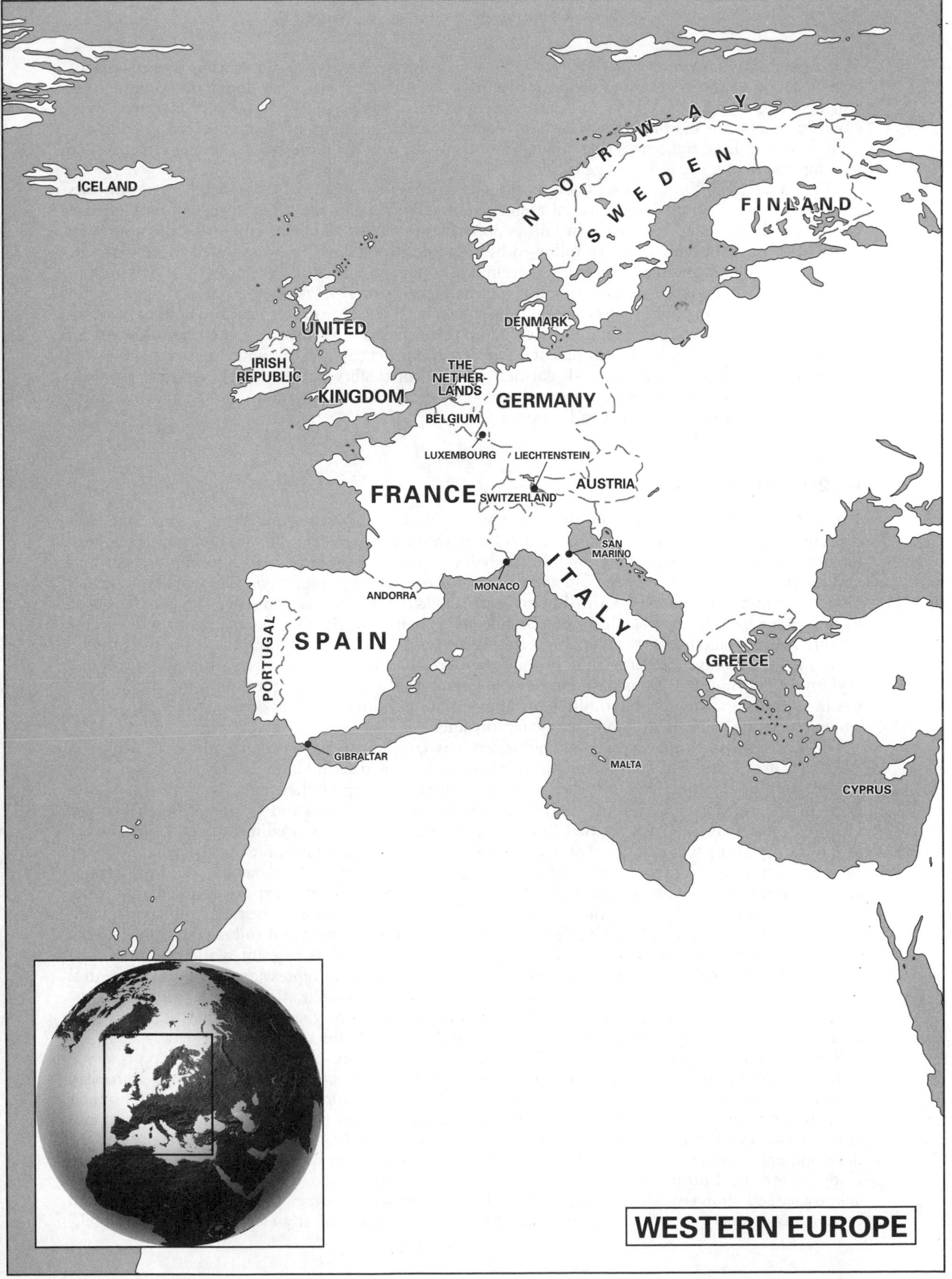
ICELAND
NORWAY
SWEDEN
FINLAND
DENMARK
UNITED KINGDOM
IRISH REPUBLIC
THE NETHERLANDS
GERMANY
BELGIUM
LUXEMBOURG
LIECHTENSTEIN
AUSTRIA
FRANCE
SWITZERLAND
SAN MARINO
ITALY
MONACO
ANDORRA
PORTUGAL
SPAIN
GREECE
GIBRALTAR
MALTA
CYPRUS
WESTERN EUROPE

descendants. *Ius sanguinis* (citizenship by descent), as opposed to *ius solis* (citizenship by birthplace), now operates in most Western European countries with little protest from dominant communities. During the Second World War millions of people were displaced. Hitler initially favoured mass emigration as a means of ridding Germany of its minority populations. But as receiving countries such as Switzerland tightened their immigration controls, this 'solution' was no longer effective and was superseded by the policy of genocide.

There were 14 million displaced people at the end of the war, many of them members of minority groups, including South Tyroleans, Alsatians, Roma/Gypsies and Jews. Fourteen million Germans would also be expelled from Eastern Europe, providing a major source of labour for the new West German state. Economic recovery followed by rapid economic growth necessitated more workers, and so began the immigration of workers from developing countries and the growth of new minority communities. Economic recession following the oil crisis of 1973 is often given as the reason for the anti-immigration policies introduced during the early 1970s. However, social and political reasons were equally important, as indicated by contemporary research published by the Organization for Economic Cooperation and Development.[2] The demand for cheap, flexible and exploitable labour in Western Europe, global economic disparities, political instability and extremely restrictive border controls mean that undocumented migration is on the increase. Immigration and citizenship status are key issues for new minorities in Europe.

Regional trends

The end of the Cold War has seen the reopening of ethnic antagonisms and the rise of the far right throughout Western Europe. This has coincided with the development of closer Western European integration and an upsurge of regionalism. Such developments have implications for minority groups and for the relationships between old and new minorities. Some groups have been working together to face common difficulties: the Anti-Racist Centre in Oslo, for example, campaigns on behalf of both Sami and asylum seekers. Similarly, the Basque struggle has sought to include all who work in the Basque country, including members of new minorities; and Plaid Cymru and the Scottish National Party in the UK have challenged the prevailing political consensus on matters of immigration and asylum. Other minority groups contain elements that adopt an anti-immigrant line, and the far right has in some cases attempted to infiltrate or appropriate minority struggles or targeted them as challenging a strong, centralized mono-ethnic nation state.

The position of Roma/Gypsies highlights what is common between many minority groups in Western Europe, old and new, including social and economic discrimination and assimilation, if not forced, then by default. They are recognized as a minority group by the United Nations, by institutions of the European Union and by the Organization for Security and Cooperation in Europe. However, many of the problems that Roma/Gypsies experience are shared most particularly by the new minority groups: difficulties of moving across borders, deportations by European Union countries such as Germany and France, racist attacks and police harassment. Many members of both groups are not citizens of the states in which they live. In Italy and Spain, Roma/Gypsies and new minorities have begun to work together to face these common problems. Because of their economic marginalization and poverty some Roma/Gypsies have taken up travelling again and still need to move across borders, as they have done for centuries, and are now categorized as migrant workers. Those who have fled from 'ethnic cleansing' in the former Yugoslavia, or from repression elsewhere in Central and Eastern Europe, are subject to Europe's stringent asylum policies. Current debate within the Roma/Gypsy movement is between calling for Roma/Gypsies to be given exceptional status in relation to these procedures, or advocating solidarity and universal human rights.[3]

Regionalism has come to the fore in Western Europe. More than 100 regions are now represented in Brussels, often bypassing the central government to have a direct relationship with the European Union. In the case of the UK, for example, Scotland, Wales and Northern Ireland are setting up their own missions in Brussels. This regionalism is in part a rejection of the perceived corruption and anti-democracy of some of Europe's nation states. It is also a celebration of cultural diversity and the development of a new sense of what it means to be 'European'. At the Conference for Security and Cooperation in Europe (CSCE) expert meeting on minorities in 1991 member governments acknowledged that issues concerning national minorities 'are matters of legitimate international concern and consequently do not constitute exclusively an internal affair of the respective state'.[4]

Means to implement and monitor previous commitments were affirmed, including elected bodies and assemblies of national minority affairs, the provision of mother-tongue education, and local and autonomous administration, or self-administration. The extent to which these measures, which apply to old but not to new minorities, have been adopted varies from state to state.

The CSCE meeting also reaffirmed the desirability of transfrontier contact between people who share a common ethnic or national origin, and undertook to encourage transfrontier cooperation. This kind of cross-border cooperation has been emerging for some time, particularly at a regional level. Groups such as the Arge-Alp (founded 1972), Arge-Alp Adria (1975) and Arge Pyrénées (1983) have developed common transfrontier policies on matters such as tourism, environment and transport and have become possible models for a new, decentralized and democratically accountable 'Europe of the regions'. The Committee of the Regions, established in 1994, is the only major European Union (EU) body after the European Parliament with democratic credentials – though it is still struggling over its own structure and its relationship with other EU institutions.

The potential of regionalism has been most developed in the predominantly German-speaking Tyrol, divided since the First World War between Italy and Austria. Demands for reunification, autonomy and self-determination could be met by the proposed creation of an Autonomous European Region Tyrol (AERT). This could be established through an Austro-Italian treaty transferring all powers to the region with the exception of defence, foreign policy, justice and monetary policy. Such developments offer new potential and challenges but have their critics. The AERT project is likely to have increased support as a result of Austria's joining the European Union in 1995.

The signing of the Schengen Agreement in 1985 by Germany, France and the Benelux countries (since joined by many other signatories, but not by the UK) committed the participants to abolish common border controls more fully and faster than within the European Union as a whole. This was of advantage to some minority groups related to populations across borders. Ease of cross-border movement for Alsatians, for example, means that many can commute daily from France to Germany for employment that is not available in recession-stricken Alsace. However, the new arrangements have also meant increased control of external borders and strong internal controls in the form of identity checks and surveillance. This arguably has civil liberties implications, particularly for members of black and other visible ethnic-minority groups if police increasingly rely on skin colour as the emblem of citizenship.

The 1990 text of the Schengen Convention contains only two articles which give guarantees to people in transit, and the remaining 140 are almost all devoted to tightening external border controls or internal surveillance. There is no accountability to judicial or parliamentary bodies, and freedom of movement does not apply to 'third country nationals'. Schengen has been criticized by the Dutch-based Standing Committee of Experts on International Immigration, Refugee and Criminal Law, which concluded that 'the cumulative effect of all the Schengen provisions is to increase the collective power of the governments and their law-enforcement agencies, while denying the individual any corresponding benefit except the notional freedom to cross an internal border without showing a passport'.[5] The Schengen Implementing Convention is not yet enforced because of technical and legal problems associated with the setting up of the computerized Schengen Information System.

Two particular areas of future concern may be identified. First, the increasingly heavy policing of Western Europe's external borders, and the separation of immigration and asylum policies from mainstream EU decision-making – and therefore from democratic accountability to the European Parliament and the national parliaments of member states – runs counter to demands for greater democracy made by the advocates of a 'Europe of the regions'. Second, the survival of many Western European minorities remains precarious; although assimilation no longer generally persists as official policy, and there is wide recognition of the multi-ethnic principle, assimilation appears likely to undermine the preservation of language and culture by smaller minorities in the region.

Note on statistics and methodology

In the following country descriptions, minority population statistics should be treated with caution. Definitions as to who does or does not belong to a minority group are frequently imposed from outside, and the way a minority is defined determines their numbers. Does the category Catalans, for example, consist of all residents of Cataluña, all Catálan-speakers, all fluent Catálan-speakers or all those of 'Catalan culture'?[6] Population statistics in relation to new minorities are notoriously inaccurate, with definitions varying from state to state and from year to year. Moreover, categories are not discrete: the giving of separate figures does not mean that members of new minorities are not also Corsican, Scots, and so on. Nor is minority identity immutable. For reasons of space, it has not been possible to present a full account of each minority group for each country in which that group is significant. Wherever possible, as in the case of the Basques of France, a cross-reference is provided to the country entry where the minority in question receives more detailed coverage, in this case Spain. Discussion of historic minorities usually precedes that of new minorities in the country entries in this part of the *Directory*.

Further reading

Benda-Beckman, K. van and Verkuyten, M., *Nationalism, Ethnicity and Cultural Identity in Europe,* Utrecht, European Research Centre on Migration and Ethnic Relations, 1995.

Bunyan, T., *Statewatching the New Europe*, London, Unison, 1993.

Collinson, S., *Europe and International Migration,* London, Royal Institute of International Affairs, 1994.

D'Souza, F. and Crisp, J., *The Refugee Dilemma*, London, MRG report, 1985.

Fawcett, J., *The International Protection of Minorities*, London, MRG report, 1979.

Joly, D., Nettleton, C. and Poulton, H., *Refugees: Asylum in Europe*, London, Minority Rights Publications, 1992.

Joly, D. with Nettleton, C. and Kelly, L., *Refugees in Europe*, London, MRG report, 1990, 1997.

Jones, B. and Keating, M. (eds), *The European Union and the Regions*, Oxford, Clarendon Press, 1995.

Liégeois, J-P. and Gheorghe, N., *Roma/Gypsies: A European Minority*, London, MRG report, 1995.

Palley, C. et al., *Minorities and Autonomy in Western Europe*, London, MRG report, 1991.

Robertson, A. and Merrills, J., *Human Rights in Europe: A Study of the European Convention on Human Rights*, 3rd edn, Manchester University Press, 1993.

Andorra

Land area:	468 sq km
Population:	64,300 (1994)
Main languages:	Andorran, Spanish
Main religions:	Roman Catholicism
Main minority groups:	Andorrans 11,860 (18.4%), Portuguese 7,035 (10.9%), French 4,685 (7.3%)
Real per capita GDP:	$19,988
UNDP HDI/rank:	—

The Principality of Andorra is a tiny state located in the eastern Pyrenees between France and Spain. From 1278 to 1993 it was a co-principality, its joint sovereigns being the French President and the bishop of the nearby Spanish town of Seu d'Urgell. Andorra's new constitution of 1993 gave it independence but allowed the co-princes a veto over treaties affecting borders and security. Nearly half of the total population are Spanish citizens. It is extremely difficult to gain Andorran citizenship, and foreigners cannot vote, own businesses or join unions or political parties.

Most Spanish and French in Andorra are wealthy tax exiles. Approximately 13 per cent of the population are migrant workers from Portugal, Morocco, Italy, India and the Philippines. The Andorran language is related to Catalan. Despite the existence of a government linguistic advice service, both language and tradition are being eroded by new forms of leisure and an annual 12 million tourists. No specific minority rights issues have been identified.

Austria

Land area:	83,859 sq km.
Population:	7.9 million (1994)
Main languages:	German
Main religions:	Roman Catholicism, Protestantism
Main minority groups:	former Yugoslavs, 197,886 (2.5%), other Central and Eastern Europeans 45,000 (0.6%), Turks 70,000 (0.9%), Roma/Gypsies 20,000–25,000 (0.15–0.30%), Burgenland Croats 19,109 (0.24%), Carinthian Slovenes 14,850 (0.19%), Styrian Slovenes 1,695 (0.02%), Burgenland Hungarians 10,000 (0.13%), Jews 8,000 (0.1%), Czechs 8,000 (0.1%)
Real per capital GDP:	$19,115
UNDP HDI/rank:	0.928 (13)

The Republic of Austria was occupied by French, British, US and Soviet troops after the Second World War. The Austrian State Treaty of 1955 restored sovereignty and included stipulations on the rights of the Croat and Slovene minorities. In 1976 the Austrian Parliament passed the Status of Ethnic Groups in Austria Act, extending the definition of ethnic groups, and one year later Ethnic Advisory Councils were set up to assist the federal government in all matters concerning Austria's Croat, Slovene, Hungarian and Czech minorities. This legislation was reviewed in 1989. The review report found that there was a problem of implementation of the State Treaty and other legislation, and that the survival of the ethnic groups was under threat.[1] A negative attitude towards minority languages was reported, and education in Slovene and Croat – theoretically guaranteed by the State Treaty – was not forthcoming.

Croats of Burgenland

Croats came to Burgenland between 1530 and 1584, fleeing the Ottoman Empire and enticed by Hungarian and Austrian landowners to repopulate their estates. They settled in territory that now falls between the states of Austria, Hungary and the Czech Republic. Burgenland Croatian, incorporating Hungarian and German elements, emerged as a written regional language during the Counter-Reformation, but assimilation tendencies began from the eighteenth century onwards. In the 1950s and 1960s the Croats' traditional agricultural way of life was undermined by mechanization and a general decline of agriculture. Increasing numbers commuted to Vienna on a daily or weekly basis or emigrated to the USA (both tendencies had begun during the interwar years).

Burgenland Croats are equal in their quality of life to the German-speakers of Burgenland and they are represented in politics, administration, education and the church. However, the continued erosion of traditional ways of life and cultural communities, and a lack of specifically Croatian economic institutions, means that they are in danger of losing their separate identity. The Croatian language is losing ground; although the law provides for bilingual schools at primary level, in most Croatian villages the language is used only for peripheral educational activities. In secondary schools, Croat may be studied as a subject but is not a language of instruction. The outcome of efforts to improve the status of Croat, and of increased subsidies for Croatian associations, remains uncertain.

Slovenes of Carinthia

The independent principality of Carantani was founded by the Slovenes in the seventh century and at its height extended to Salzburg, South Tyrol and Styria. By the Reformation the Slovene-speaking area had retreated roughly to a line across the centre of what is now the province of Carinthia. When the Kingdom of the Serbs, Croats and Slovenes (SHS), later renamed Yugoslavia, was founded in 1918 it claimed and occupied southern Carinthia. This led to a plebiscite in 1920, called to determine the territorial affiliation of the area; 59 per cent were in favour of remaining part of Austria, 41 per cent for joining the SHS. There followed intense activity to Germanize the region, reaching its peak under the Anschluss, when all Slovene teachers were removed and lands were taken from Slovene farmers and distributed to German settlers. Slovene wording was even removed from gravestones. Carinthia was the only area of Austria with strong, organized resistance to the Nazi occupation. Yugoslavia's territorial claims, which had some support among the Slovene population, were settled under the 1955 State Treaty.

Both streams of Carinthian Slovene political thought – the Zentralverband, which strongly supported a Yugoslav presence in Carinthia, and the Rat, which favoured upholding ties with Austria – have criticized postwar Austrian policy for giving in to German nationalistic forces in Carinthia. The Minority Schools Act of 1988, for example, is cited for allegedly reinforcing segregationist tendencies. The Zentralverband and Rat also came together under the Carinthian Unity List to contest elections to the Carinthian legislature, and the first Carinthian Slovene was elected to the Austrian Parliament in 1986.

Slovenes, like Burgenland Croats, were traditionally agricultural and badly affected by the postwar decline in agriculture. However, there are examples of specifically Slovene enterprises in a variety of sectors, mainly timber processing, but also clothing, and often in collaboration with counterparts over the border in Slovenia. There are a few bilingual kindergartens, and bilingual education is provided for the first three years of primary school. Secondary-school pupils can register for Slovene language instruction for four lessons a week, and for Slovene as a subject.

A small group of Styrian Slovenes live in the so-called 'Corner of Radkersburg'. Their rights are specifically mentioned in the Austrian State Treaty but have been largely ignored. They have set up a cultural association as their voice in discussions with the government and other minorities.

Burgenland Hungarians

Hungarians of Burgenland are the descendants of frontier guards sent during the eleventh century to protect the Magyar kingdom. Few in number, they nevertheless maintained a clear and complete social structure until divided from the Hungarian cultural heartland by the Iron Curtain. The reopening of Hungary has enabled relations to be resumed at all levels, with frequent business, cultural and sporting exchanges.

New minorities

Austria's position on the edge of Western Europe has made it a natural destination for refugees from Eastern and Central Europe. In 1991 these numbered more than 240,000 people, many of them settled in Burgenland. To constitute an ethnic group under Austrian law, members of a minority must be Austrian citizens. Austria's new minorities, which include Roma/Gypsies, recent Croatian migrants and Hungarians, cannot be so considered because, as in Germany, citizenship is by descent. Members of Austria's historic Roma/Gypsy minority (see **Germany**, **Spain**), in many cases settled permanently in Burgenland and, earning a living as blacksmiths and brickmakers, have been joined by many of their kin from former Yugoslavia and have since become a target of racist violence.

Austria has long had a shifting population. Immigration began after the first Turkish siege of Vienna in 1529. In 1910 the majority of Vienna's inhabitants were not born there, while the rural areas saw massive emigration to the USA. Many immigrant Czechs and Slovaks provided cheap labour for Austria's industrialization. Discrimination and the requirement of those who would settle to swear to uphold vigorously 'the German character of Vienna' resulted in most of them being assimilated within one generation. In the 1960s Austria, like Germany, invited *Gastarbeiter* (guestworkers), principally from Turkey and Poland; as in Germany too, neither they nor their children have residency rights. The 1993 Residency Act introduced strict income and accommodation criteria for foreigners, and the children of *Gastarbeiter* became liable to the same entry requirements as first-time entrants to Austria. Newly unemployed non-nationals are liable to deportation. Austria's tough policy on asylum seekers has been criticized.[2]

The policies of Austria's third largest political party, the pan-Germanic Freiheitliche Partei Osterreichs (FPO), are hostile to both old and new minorities. In 1992 it launched the Austria First Petition, calling for identity cards for foreigners and quotas on the number of foreign children in classrooms which attracted 417,000 signatures. In the 1994 elections it increased its share of the vote to 23 per cent.[3]

Conclusions and future prospects

The 1991 census showed that for the first time a halt had been called to the assimilation trend. This was borne out by the Austrian Ethnic Groups Centre, an organization founded in 1983 with government support to promote the interests of Croats, Hungarians, Slovenes, Roma/Gypsies, Czechs and Slovaks. Despite the finding that 'progress has been made in improving the climate of nascent dialogue between minorities and the majority',[4] the Ethnic Groups Centre does not consider this enough to guarantee their continued existence. It advocates a minority-focused programme that includes special economic investment and the recognition of Roma/Gypsies and Styrian Slovenes as ethnic groups. The growth of the FPO threatens both old and new minorities, as does the reported increase in racist violence.

Further reading

'Austria ethnica, state and perspectives', *Austrian Handbooks on Ethnic Groups*, vol. 7, Vienna, Austrian Ethnic Groups Centre, 1994.

Wischenbart, R., 'National identity and immigration in Austria', in Baldwin-Edwards, M. and Schain, M. (eds), *The Politics of Immigration*, London, Frank Cass, 1994.

Minority-based and advocacy organizations

Amnesty International, Apostelgasse 25–27, A-1030, Vienna, Austria; tel. 43 1 718 7777, fax 43 1 718 7778.

Austrian Ethnic Groups Centre, Teinfaltstrasse 4, 1010 Vienna, Austria; tel. 43 1 222 533 1504, fax 43 1 222 535 5887.

Burgenland-Hungarian Cultural Association, Schulgasse 3/1, 7400 Oberwart/Felsoor, Austria.

Central Association of Slovene Organizations, Traviser Strasse 16, 9020 Klagenfurt/Celovec, Austria; tel. 43 463 514300.

Council of Carinthian Slovenes, 10 Oktober Strasse 25/IV, 9020 Klagenfurt/Celovec, Austria; tel. 43 463 512 5280.

Croatian Cultural Association, Dr Lorenz-Karall Strasse 23, 7000 Zeljezno/Eisenstadt, Austria; tel. 43 2682 62936.

Croatian-Burgenland Cultural Association in Vienna, Schwindgasse 14, 1040 Vienna/Beci, Austria; tel. 43 1 222 504 6152.

International Helsinki Federation for Human Rights and Austrian Helsinki Committee, Rummelhardtgasse 2/18, 1090 Vienna, Austria; tel. 43 1 402 7387/408 8822, fax 43 1 408 7444, e-mail: helsinki@ping.at

Minority Council of the Czech and Slovak Ethnic Group in Austria, Margarethenplatz 7, 1050 Viden/Vienna, Austria; tel. 43 1 222 597 8308.

Refugees Aid Poysdorf, 2170 Poysdorf, Brunngasse 47, Austria; tel. 43 02552 2189, fax 02552 766.

Roma Centro, Vienna, Austria; fax 43 1 749 6336.

Belgium

Land area:	30,518 sq km
Population:	9.9 million (1992)
Main languages:	Dutch, French, German
Main religions:	Roman Catholicism
Main minority groups:	Flemings 5.5 million (55%), Walloons 3.2 million (32%), Italians 241,006 (2.4%), Moroccans 135,464 (1.4%), Germans 100,000 (1%), French 91,444 (0.9%), Turks 79,460 (0.8%), Jews 35,000–40,000 (0.3–0.4%), Luxembourgers 24,000–39,000 (0.2–0.4%), Roma/Gypsies 10,000–15,000 (0.1–0.15%), other new minorities 230,000 (2.3%)
Real per capita GDP:	$19,540
UNDP HDI/rank:	0.929 (12)

The constitution of the new state of Belgium was endorsed in 1831. Although the original constitution conceived Belgium as a 'unitary decentralized state' it did not achieve a sense of national unity because from the early Middle Ages there had been a linguistic and cultural divide between the German-dominated north and French-dominated south. Through a series of four constitutional revisions (1970, 1980, 1988 and 1993) Belgium moved to becoming as federal state made up of three Communities (French-, Flemish- and German-speaking) and three Regions (Walloon, Flemish and Brussels).[1] Communities and Regions each have distinct legal personalities and powers and separate executive organs. Although the original constitution made no specific commitment to the French language, French was the language of law, politics, the administration and the army. Only in 1967 was an authentic Dutch version of the constitution published. Legislative attempts to redress the linguistic balance were first made in 1898. The 1930s saw a body of legislation aimed at recognizing Dutch, and a unilingual system of Dutch in Flanders and French in Wallonia was implemented. In 1962 the previously flexible language boundary was permanently fixed.

Flemings (see also **France**)

The term Flemish described several Dutch-related dialects until it was standardized as Dutch in 1896. Flemish is spoken by some 5.8 million Flemings in the north of Belgium, in the provinces of East and West Flanders, Antwerp, Limburg and Flemish Brabant. Fifteen per cent of the Brussels population is Dutch-speaking. During the early years of Belgium's existence, Flanders, the agricultural north, was deeply impoverished, and Flemings were isolated from the systems of government and administration. Grievances were exploited by the Germans during their First World War occupation, resulting in Flemish nationalist collaboration. This pattern was repeated in the Second World War, when the Vlaams National Verbond collaborated with the Germans. Flemish nationalists were subdued for some time after the war, but the movement survived.

Massive postwar foreign investment facilitated industrial expansion in Flanders, which has since become a 'shop window' for new technology. Not only are Flemings numerically in the majority nationally, but their part of Belgium is now the more prosperous, and their influence predominates in the national government. In 1979 the aggressively nationalist and anti-immigrant Flemish Vlaams Blok ('Our Own People First') was founded, and the party has gained in popularity. Since the elections of October 1994 it has been represented on eighty-two municipal councils, and it won nearly a third of the vote in Antwerp in October 1994.

Walloons

There are 3.2 million French-speakers known as Walloons in southern Belgium, in the provinces of Walloon Brabant, Hainaut, Liège, Namur and Luxembourg. At the foundation of the Belgian state this area was prosperous, and the exploitation of its coal reserves supported the early development of heavy industry. The first Walloon organizations were established in Flanders in the last quarter of the nineteenth century. The political demands of these groups were imprecise, but they emphasized the importance of French remaining the principal language of Belgium. By the turn of the century Walloon nationalism was closely identified with socialism, and a division was becoming apparent between those who called for union with France and the federalists. Walloon nationalism was heightened after the Second World War as a response to Flemish collaboration, the sense that the relative numbers of Walloons were declining and anti-monarchist feeling. From the late 1950s Walloon nationalism was encouraged by the region's economic decline. Linguistic legislation in the 1960s led to accusations that the French language was being discriminated against, and French-speakers tended to support regionalist and Francophone parties. This support declined during the 1980s, and Walloons now generally support the Socialist Party.

A variety of regional languages are spoken on an occasional and informal basis in the French Community of Belgium.[2] Walloon is spoken by an estimated 600,000 people in the provinces of Liège, Namur and Hainaut. Picard is spoken by approximately 200,000 in Hainaut, and Lorrain by an estimated 20,000 in Luxembourg province. Champenois is spoken in some villages in Namur and Luxembourg. In 1990 the Council of the French Community of Belgium passed a decree concerning the protection and promotion of these regional languages, particularly through the education system, and a Council of Regional Languages was established. The languages are taught in some secondary schools but are not languages of instruction. There are some regional-language radio and television broadcasts. Luxembourgish is spoken in the region of Arlon/Arel, bordering Luxembourg. It is covered by the regional language decree, and there is increasing demand for Luxembourgish in schools despite a lack of qualified teachers.

Germans

One hundred thousand German-speakers live in the eastern cantons of Eupen, Malmedy and St Vith. Although under the new Belgian constitution Germans constitute a Community, they fall within the Region of Wallonia. German-speakers elect one out of 21 Community senators. In principle they have equal cultural and linguistic rights, as well as access to German publications and media from over the border.

New minorities[3]

The rights enshrined in the current Belgian constitution are for Belgian citizens rather than for those on Belgian soil. Approximately 9 per cent of Belgium's population are considered to be of 'foreign origin', including many born in Belgium, and they cannot attain citizenship. Large numbers of Jews and anti-Fascists fled to Belgium from Nazi Germany. In the late 1930s work permits, the concept of 'illegal immigration' and deportation centres for Jews were introduced. This prewar legislation for the control of refugees became the core of legislation for controlling postwar migrants. Primary immigration had virtually ceased by 1974, and recent legislation has concentrated on asylum seekers. The 1993 'Tobback' law allows for the summary rejection of asylum claims and for the detention without trial of asylum seekers and other foreigners deemed dangerous to national security. The Belgian state has been found guilty by administrative courts of subjecting asylum seekers to inhuman and degrading treatment and violating their legal rights.

There are some 870,000 members of new minorities in Belgium, including Italians, Turks, Moroccans, Zaireans, Tunisians and Algerians. The Italian community, situated mainly in Wallonia, now numbers 241,000 and has its roots in a treaty signed between Italy and Belgium after the Second World War when Belgium needed labour to work its coal mines. Some 70,000 Italians came in under the work permit system; they were mainly men but were later joined by Italian women.

The Moroccan minority, settled mainly in Flanders and Brussels, numbers approximately 135,000. These people were recruited directly from the Moroccan countryside in campaigns sponsored by the Belgian government. They came, together with Turks (now totalling almost 80,000) who had been similarly recruited, to work in processing and manufacturing industries in Flanders. Third-country nationals do not have the vote in Belgium and are barred from public service and government employment. Most Moroccans and Turks are confined to low-paid, low-status jobs, poor housing and poor education. Many experience difficulties in access to social benefits.

Conclusions and future prospects

In 1994 the President of Belgium's Christian Democrats, the party with largest support in Flanders, called for the creation of a loose confederation of two independent states. This was backed by other Flemish political parties. Indications are, therefore, that the recurrent constitutional crises of the Belgian state are not yet resolved. Far-right nationalist parties of both Flanders and Wallonia have experienced a growth of support. Along with a reported rise in racist murders of, and attacks against, members of the new minorities, this must be a matter for concern.

Further reading

Alen, A. and Ergec, R., *Federal Belgium after the Fourth State Reform of 1993*, Brussels, Ministry of Foreign Affairs, 1994.

Irving, R.E., *The Flemings and the Walloons of Belgium*, London, MRG report, 1980.

MRG (ed.), *Minorities and Autonomy in Western Europe*, London, MRG report, 1991.

Minority-based and advocacy organizations

Amnesty International, (Flemish) AI Vlaanderen, Karkstraat 156, 2060 Antwerp, Belgium; tel. 32 3 271 1616, fax 32 2 235 7812; (French) Rue Berckmans 9, 1060 Brussels, Belgium; tel. 32 2 538 8177, fax 32 2 537 3729.

Centre Culturel du Brabant Wallon, 3 Rue Belotte, 1490 Court St Etienne, Belgium; tel. 32 10 615777.

CBW Marokkaanse en Turkse Raad, Van Daelsstraat 41, 2140 Bougerhout, Belgium.

European Bureau for Lesser Used Languages, Sint-Jooststraat 49, B1210 Brussels, Belgium; tel. 32 2 218 2590, fax 32 2 218 1974.

European Migrants' Forum, Rue du Commerce 70/72, B1040 Brussels, Belgium; tel. 32 2 502 4949, fax 32 2 502 7876, e-mail: 101335.773@compuserve.com.

Information Diffusion Immigrés, Rue du Méridien 15, 1030 Brussels, Belgium; tel. 32 2 217 9782, fax 32 2 223 2485.

Mouvement contre le Racisme, l'Antisémitisme et la Xénophobie, Rue de la Poste 37, 1210 Brussels, Belgium; tel. 32 2 218 2371.

Vlaams Centrum voor Integratie van Migranten, Gaucheretstraat 164, 1210 Brussels, Belgium; tel. 32 2 201 0300, fax 32 2 201 0339.

Cyprus

Land area:	9,251 sq km
Population:	756,000 (1994)
Main languages:	Greek, Turkish
Main religions:	Greek Orthodox Christianity, Islam, Roman Catholicism
Main minority groups:	Turkish Cypriots 136,000 (18%), Maronites 11,000 (1.4%), Armenians, Latin-Cypriots and British combined 18,900 (2.5%), Roma 500–1,000 (0.07–0.13%)
Real per capita GDP:	$14060
UNDP HDI/rank:	0.909 (23)

Turkish and Greek Cypriots have lived together on Cyprus for more than four centuries. Although the majority population of the island has long been Greek-speaking, it was ruled by the Ottoman Empire until 1878, when Britain received Cyprus in return for providing protection against tsarist Russia. Movements against the British and favouring *enosis* (union with Greece) were spearheaded after the Second World War by the Orthodox Church and EOKA (the National Organization of Cyprus Fighters), whose guerrilla wing carried out attacks on British soldiers and establishments. The Turkish community preferred partition of the island to union with Greece. In 1959 representatives of the Greek and Turkish communities and of the British government approved a plan whereby

Cyprus was to become an independent republic with constitutional guarantees for the Turkish minority and British sovereignty over the island's military bases. Independence was proclaimed on 16 August 1960, and Archbishop Vaneziz Makarios, a veteran of the anti-colonial movement, took office as President.

Tensions between Greece and Turkey were reflected in deteriorating relations between the Greek and Turkish communities of Cyprus. EOKA-B continued the terrorist activities of EOKA and demands for *enosis*. The conflict came to a head on 15 July 1974, when the Cypriot National Guard under the command of Greek army officers ousted Makarios and installed pro-*enosis* Nikos Sampson. Five days later, a force of 6,000 Turkish troops plus tanks landed on the north coast of Cyprus. Heavy fighting occurred between the Turkish army and the Cypriot National Guard, and intercommunal conflict was reported from many parts of the island. Each community accused the other of atrocities. On 23 July the Greek government junta of colonels in Athens who had been behind the ousting of Makarios stepped down; and on the same day Sampson was relieved of his post by the National Guard. A ceasefire agreement was concluded on 16 August, by which time Turkish forces had occupied 39 per cent of the island to the north. Prisoners of war were exchanged, but each side continues to maintain that many people are unaccounted for: 2,700 Greek Cypriots and 240 Turkish Cypriots.

Cyprus is now divided into the Republic of Cyprus, inhabited by Greek Cypriots, and the Turkish Republic of Northern Cyprus, inhabited by Turkish Cypriots and Turks. In 1974 the Turkish sector contained most of the country's cargo-holding capacity in the port of Famagusta, most of the tourist industry and half of the island's agricultural and industrial production. Yet following the crisis Cyprus enjoyed a period of economic prosperity brought by tourism, foreign aid and international businesses that made the island a financial centre, replacing the city of Beirut whose money markets had been paralyzed by the Lebanese civil war. Today the Greek Cypriot Republic includes among its population more than 180,000 refugees from the north, the great majority of whom have been rehoused on new estates, although they still hope to return eventually to their homes in the north. Besides the two main ethnic groups, the island also has a small Maronite community and smaller Armenian, Latin-Cypriot and British communities.

Turkish Cypriots

A Turkish-Cypriot federal state was proclaimed in northern Cyprus in February 1975 with Rauf Denktash as its President. Denktash had previously headed the unrecognized 'transitional administration', established after independence in 1960 to govern the Turkish Cypriot community until constitutional provisions protecting them were fully effective. During his talks with Makarios at that time, four basic conditions were set for a negotiated settlement: the establishment of a bicommunal, non-aligned, independent and federal republic; an exact delimitation of the territories that each community would administer; internal restrictions on travel and ownership rights within the framework of a federal system, with equal rights for both communities; and sufficient federal power to ensure unity. Little progress was made in these negotiations.

On 15 November 1983 the Turkish Republic of Northern Cyprus was proclaimed with the imaginary 'green line' cutting through the capital, Nicosia, and dividing north from south. Turkey has been the only country to recognize this 'state'. The fighting had caused some 11,000 Turkish Cypriots from the south of the island to take refuge in the north; only about 130 remain in the south. Immigration from the Turkish mainland has been encouraged, and there are now about 40,000 Turkish farmers settled in northern Cyprus. With 35,000 Turkish troops on the island at any one time, the resulting demography currently produces one continental Turk on the island for each Turkish Cypriot. Living standards in the north, where fewer than 1,000 Greek-speakers remain, have plummeted, as a result partly of the lack of international recognition and partly of Greek Cypriot trade sanctions. The economy is now heavily dependent on aid from Turkey, and many Turkish Cypriots have emigrated (see **United Kingdom**).

Maronites

There has been a Maronite community in Cyprus since at least the twelfth century.[1] 'Eastern Catholics', followers of St Maron, a monk of the fourth and fifth centuries, Maronites established themselves first in Lesser Syria and Lebanon. In Cyprus they are a distinct community with a specific religious rite and affiliation, and a language unique in Europe: Cypriot Arabic. They look to Lebanon as their spiritual home but closely identify with Cyprus. The total Maronite population in Cyprus is approximately 6,000. Their numbers have long been in decline, and the process has recently been accompanied by displacement from the north of Cyprus. Whereas in the thirteenth century there were some 60 Maronite villages in Cyprus, now only four villages count a traditional Maronite population. Before the Turkish invasion of 1974 some 2,444 Maronites lived in the traditional areas; that number has now contracted to about 200 people.

In the settlement of Cyprus, the constitutional structures effectively ignored any separate claims of Maronites, who were required to opt for either the Greek or the Turkish community. Maronites opted for the Greek community. But their participation in the Republic of Cyprus is limited to a combination of representation and consultation that approaches but does not exhaust the substance of the right to participate set out in the UN Declaration on Minorities and other international instruments.

Maronites in the north of Cyprus, together with some 500 Greek Cypriots, are referred to in UN documents as 'enclaved groups'. The concept of an 'enclave' is regarded as antithetical to international standards of human rights but appears to exist as a reality in Cyprus in the sense of a territorially defined area of human rights deprivation. Remaining Maronite villages in the north are effectively under close Turkish occupation. Their population is elderly, and if present trends continue there will soon be no Maronite community in the north. According to a recent UN report, both the Greek Cypriot and Maronite communities in northern Cyprus were subject to 'very severe restrictions, which curtail the exercise of many basic freedoms and have the effect of ensuring that, inexorably with the passage of time, those communities will cease to exist'.[2]

Maronites have made claims concerning freedom of movement between north and south Cyprus, rights to property, health and education, and basic subsistence rights. They maintain that churches and monasteries in the north are in danger of destruction due to a lack of maintenance and, in some cases, alleged conversion into mosques. UN surveys support the impression of the northern community's precarious situation.[3] Threats to the continuation of a distinct Maronite identity in the south are different, arising because of intermarriage with Greek Cypriots and the increasing secularization of Cypriot society.

Conclusions and future prospects

The most promising chance of a workable settlement in Cyprus arose in 1985 when Denktash made significant concessions, offering to reduce the Turkish-held area from 39 per cent to 30 per cent and to accept a Greek President and a Turkish Vice-President (rather than a rotating presidency) and a 70:30 ratio of Greeks to Turks in the federal cabinet and lower house of parliament. However, talks collapsed amid recriminations on both sides, and the impasse remains. The Greek community, confident in its numerical superiority and economic prosperity, seeks the unification of Cyprus guaranteed by the United Nations. Turkish Cypriots, on the other hand, basing their position on the status quo and the superiority of the Turkish army, demand a binational federation under Ankara's protection.

The survival of the Maronites depends on the community itself and the efforts and perceptions of the world outside. The Cyprus question has been constantly under review. The process of setting up a customs union between Turkey and the European Union revitalized debates, and the possibility of the accession of Cyprus to the EU – as well as renewed US interest in the question – ensures that debates will continue. Maronites hope to conserve their presence and strive to ensure that the international community is aware of its symbolic and practical importance for the coexistence of Orthodox, Catholic and Muslim traditions. The loss of their language would represent a cultural blow to Europe.

Further reading

Kyle, K., *Cyprus*, London, MRG report, 1984.

Moosa, M., *The Maronites in History*, New York, Syracuse University Press, 1986.

Question of Human Rights in Cyprus, Report of the Secretary-General, etc., UN Doc E/CN.4/1996/54.

Minority-based and advocacy organizations

Committee for the Restoration of Human Rights, PO Box 4666, Limassol, Cyprus.

Denmark

Land area:	43,070 sq km
Population:	5.2 million (1993)
Main languages:	Danish, Greenlandic, Faroese
Main religions:	Lutheran Christianity, Islam
Main minority groups:	Faroese 48,000 (0.9%), Inuit (Greenlanders) 45,000 (0.9%), Asians 38,000 (0.7%), Turks 30,000 (0.6%), Germans of South Jutland 5,000–20,000 (0.1–0.4%), Jews 7,000 (0.1%), Roma/Gypsies 1,500–2,000 (less than 0.1%), other new minorities 70,000 (1.3%)
Real per capita GDP:	$20,200
UNDP HDI/rank:	0.924 (17)

The Kingdom of Denmark consists of the mainland of the Jutland Peninsula and the islands which constitute one-third of its territory. Its only land frontier is with Germany, to the south. The two Danish external territories are Greenland and the Faroe Islands. Denmark's parliamentary democracy was established by the 1849 constitution.

Faroese

The Faroe Islands are eighteen islands in the North Atlantic between Iceland and Scotland, totalling an area of 1,399 square kilometres. Predominantly Lutheran, their population speaks a language related to West Norwegian and Icelandic. The islands were first inhabited by Irish monks in about CE 650 and then by settlers from Norway and the British Isles some 200 hundred years later. They came under Danish rule after the Union of Kalmar. The ancient Parliament or Logting was abolished in 1816 and replaced by Danish judgeship, resulting in growing Danization and the decline of the Faroese language. The 1849 Danish constitution was held to apply to the Faroes.

In the 1890s, following the islands' fishing boom, demands were first voiced for home rule. Autonomists established the Self-Rule Party, which was opposed by the Faroese elite in the Unionist Party. A major step towards self-government was taken during the Second World War, when the islands were politically separated from Denmark and became prosperous through the export of fish. The population did not want to relinquish self-rule, and on 23 March 1948 the Danish Parliament passed the Faroese Home Rule Act. This granted limited self-rule, distinguishing between 'special affairs', which may be taken over and financed by home rule legislators, and 'affairs of state', which cannot. Thereafter Faroese was legalized as the principal language of the islands, although in public affairs Danish retains the same status as Faroese and is the language of the courts. Faroese is the language of instruction. The laws of the Logting are published in Danish parallel text. Danish involvement in Faroe Islands economic policy-making following the 1991 collapse of the fishing industry has increased Danish–Faroese tension and led to renewed calls for independence. Economic decline brought about a 14 per cent drop in the islands' population between 1989 and 1994, from 48,000 to 43,000, mainly as a result of the emigration of young people. There are now 10,000 Faroese living in Copenhagen, 5,000 more than in Torshavn, the Faroes' capital.

Inuit (Greenlanders)

Three-quarters of the immense land surface of Greenland is covered by permanent ice and unsuitable for permanent settlement. The majority of the island's 55,000 population are Inuit, comprising three linguistic groups: Kalaallit along the west coast; Inughuit in the north (the world's most northerly indigenous inhabitants); and Iit on the east coast. Greenland Inuit generally call themselves collectively Kalaallit and know their land as Kalaallit Nunaat (Greenlanders' Land). The first groups of nomadic migrants came to Greenland about 4,500 years ago; early settlers were mainly hunters of land mammals, but later migrants also harvested sea resources.

European settlement began in about CE 985. In the eighteenth century small trading stations were established along the west coast, and in

1776 the Danish government formed the Royal Greenland Trade Company, which had a monopoly on Greenland trade until 1950. The Inuit population was converted to Lutheran Christianity in the eighteenth century, but records remain of Inuit cosmology and moral codes. A complex series of taboos ensured regulation of human activity in relation to the environment. The early Danish colonizers were paternalistic and protective towards their Inuit subjects, enabling most Inuit to retain their small-scale subsistence economy. Economic modernization partly began as a result of climate warming during the early nineteenth century, which made a transition from hunting to commercial fishing possible.

In 1953 Greenland's colonial status was abolished, and it became an integral part of the Kingdom of Denmark. A large-scale development programme began. Inuit were encouraged to migrate from 'unprofitable' settlements in the outlying areas to west coast towns. Rapid urbanization resulted in the break-up of Inuit kinship and other customary networks, as well as in increasing immigration of Danes and growing Inuit politicization and demands for home rule.

The Greenland Home Rule Act was passed in 1978 and implemented in 1979. The right of the Danish Parliament to decide Greenland affairs was transferred to the Greenland Landsting, an elected legislative authority composed almost entirely of resident Greenlanders. Administrative functions are delegated to the Landsstyre, the government body. Home-rule government areas of responsibility include economic affairs, trade and industry, education, health, social affairs and the environment. The Danish government maintains control of defence, foreign affairs, policing and the administration of justice. In 1994 the Greenland Home Rule Administration set up the Greenlandic Legal Commission to review and recommend revision for the territory's justice system. The Greenland authorities aspire to greater independence from Denmark generally.

The official language of the territory is West Greenlandic, an Inuit language. It is taught in schools and used in broadcasting, administration, church services, literature and newspapers. Both Danish and West Greenlandic are official languages of instruction, and Greenlandic is not in danger of disappearing. Radio Greenland, run by the Inuit, broadcasts in Greenlandic.

As a result of the achievement of home rule, a national Inuit identity has emerged. Yet Inuit face a range of economic, social, health and environmental problems. While they enjoy constitutionally protected rights, their traditional way of life is threatened by both economic modernization and international campaigns led by animal rights activists against their traditional forms of subsistence hunting, which remain crucial in the north and east. Greenland's real per capita GDP is roughly half that of Denmark, and many Inuit are unemployed. In the mid-1980s overfishing caused serious problems for the economy. Danish subsidies are needed to buy Danish commodities and to pay the Danes who do the skilled work. Inuit also suffer from high rates of suicide and psychological disorder, and have an infant mortality rate five times higher than in Denmark. Changing dietary habits may account for many of their health problems. Substance abuse is common, especially among younger people, as is alcoholism, and the spread of AIDS and other sexually transmitted diseases is a matter of increasing concern.

Germans of South Jutland

The southern Danish border was first defined in the early eighth century and did not include Holstein. During the medieval period, the Holstein nobility came into possession of estates in South Jutland, and the Duchy of Schleswig was regarded as theirs. In 1460 they supported the Danish King and gave him power over Holstein on condition that it was not to be separated from Schleswig. This arrangement endured for 400 years. In 1864 both provinces were incorporated into the Prussian and later the German Empire, resulting in tens of thousands of Danes emigrating to Denmark and other European states. The end of the First World War saw the possibility of a border revision, and in 1920 a plebiscite was held in Schleswig. The north voted by 74 per cent to rejoin Denmark, while the middle voted by 80 per cent to remain with Germany. The total province-wide vote was 53 per cent in favour of rejoining Denmark. That same year the border was drawn between north and south Schleswig and it has remained unchanged despite pressures following the Second World War.

German minority collaboration with Nazi occupation resulted in the temporary loss of rights previously secured in Denmark. However, the German minority population now enjoy their full rights to equality and non-discrimination secured by the 1955 Bonn-Copenhagen Declarations. These were two parallel, unilateral declarations on the positions of the German minority in Denmark and the Danish minority in Germany (see **Germany**). The Copenhagen Declaration guaranteed the German minority equality and recognized its citizenship and concomitant rights, including the right to use the German language and to German schools, and its special interest in cultivating relations with Germany.[1]

New minorities

Denmark's history of third-country immigration is similar to that of Germany. Between 1960 and 1972 it recruited industrial guestworkers, mainly from Turkey, Yugoslavia and Pakistan. There are some 132,000 members of new minorities in Denmark. Denmark now operates restrictive asylum laws (in cooperation with Germany), carrier sanctions, fingerprinting and the safe-third-country principle. In early 1993 a relaxation of asylum procedures was promised following revelations that some relatives of Tamil refugees were assassinated in Sri Lanka after a delay in processing their papers. However, visa restrictions on citizens of Bosnia-Herzegovina imposed later that year caused asylum applications to fall significantly.

Conclusions and future prospects

The vulnerable economic situation of the Faroese and the Greenland Inuit has increased their dependency on Denmark. There currently seems little prospect of the Faroese achieving complete independence, particularly since they are losing their young people. Some population projections suggest that there will be only 400 women aged between 15 and 19 in the Faroes by the end of the century. In 1994 British environmentalists organized a fish boycott in protest at the traditional whale hunt which the Faroese claim to be part of local tradition and especially necessary in times of economic hardship. The social, cultural and economic survival of the Inuit is similarly under threat, ironically at a time when Inuit are mustering their indigenous knowledge to safeguard resources from the pollution generated by industrial centres to the south. Participation in the pan-Arctic Inuit Circumpolar Conference offers the Inuit some prospect of achieving recognition for their traditions and values. However, the weakness of Greenland's economy makes further resource exploitation, with its potential problems, equally likely. Meanwhile, Denmark's southern land frontier has come to prominence as the only immediate EU Schengen/non-Schengen border; increased policing along the border and German legislation have accelerated Danish consideration of Schengen membership.

Further reading

Johansen, T. and Olafsson, A. (eds), *The Faroe Islands' Culture*, Copenhagen, Faroese Government Office, 1989.

MRG (ed.), *Minorities and Autonomy in Western Europe*, London, MRG report, 1991.

Nuttall, M., 'Greenland', in MRG (ed.), *Polar Peoples*, London, Minority Rights Publications, 1994.

Minority-based and advocacy organizations

Amnesty International, Dyrkøb 3, 1166 Copenhagen K, Denmark; tel. 45 33 11 75 41, fax 45 33 93 37 46; and PO Box 1075, 110 Torshavn, Faroe Islands; tel. 298 15816, fax 298 16816.

Danish Helsinki Committee, Gothersgade 89, 1123 Copenhagen K, Denmark; tel. 45 33 91 81 18, fax 45 33 33 80 22, e-mail: dk-h-com@login.dknet.dk.

Danish Refugee Council, Kronprinsessegade 4, 1306 Copenhagen K, Denmark.

Faroes Tinganes, PO Box 64, 110 Torshavn, Faroe Islands; tel. 298 11080.

Federation of Ethnic Minority Organizations in Denmark, Blegdamsvcj 4 St, 2200 Copenhagen N, Denmark; tel. 45 31 39 21 43.

Grønlands Hjemmestyre, PO Box 1015, 3900 Nuuk/Godthåb, Greenland; tel. 299 23000.

League of North Schleswig Germans, Vestergade 30, 6200 Apenrade, Denmark; tel. 45 74 62 38 33.

Minority Rights Group Denmark, Department of Minority Studies, University of Copenhagen, Njalsgade 80, 2300 Copenhagen S, Denmark; tel. 45 31 54 22 11, fax 45 32 96 47 13.

Finland

Land area:	338,130 sq km
Population:	5.1 million (1996)
Main languages:	Finnish, Swedish
Main religions:	Evangelical Lutheran Christianity, Finnish Orthodox
Main minority groups:	Swedish-speakers 295,000 (5.8%), including 25,000 Åland Islanders (0.5%), Russian-speakers 15,000–20,000 (0.3–0.4%), Sami 6,400–7,000 (0.1%), Roma/Gypsies 6,000 (0.1%), others including Jews, Tatars and Old Russians
Real per capita GDP:	$16,320
UNDP HDI/rank:	0.935 (6)

What is now Finland belonged to the Kingdom of Sweden from the twelfth century to 1809, when the area, including the Åland Islands, was ceded to Russia. Finland declared independence in 1917, and its 1919 constitution gave it a parliamentary system with a strong presidency. Finnish and Swedish – but not Sami – were both designated national languages. The Soviet Union was one of the first states to recognize Finland, and the two maintained good relations; the former was the market for 25 per cent of Finland's exports in the 1980s. Finland joined the European Union in 1995.

Swedish-speakers

Swedish-speakers form some 5.8 per cent of the Finnish population. They live mostly in the coastal regions of Österbotten, Nyland and Åboland, and on the Åland Islands, areas inhabited by Swedish-speakers since before the twelfth century. Their social structures resemble those of the majority population. The official bilingual status of the country has given rise to special laws and decrees, notably the Language Act 1992. Sweden is, after Germany, Finland's largest trading partner, and this has tended to increase demand for Swedish-speakers in business circles, as has the large number of Swedish visitors who help bolster Finland's growing tourist industry. There are 15 Swedish-language newspapers, as well as Swedish-language theatres and Swedish-language broadcasts on Finnish radio and television. Throughout the education system, from primary schools to the Åbo Akademi University and bilingual universities, there is Swedish-language provision. Of the 200 members of the Finnish Parliament, 17 are native Swedish-speakers. Eleven of these are from the Swedish People's Party, which receives about 75 per cent of the Swedish-speakers' vote. The Swedish Assembly of Finland, a semi-official representative body set up in 1919, serves as an additional forum for political discussion and as a pressure group for matters of Swedish-speakers' interest.

Finland's 25,202 Swedish-speaking Åland Islanders constitute the vast majority of the population of the 6,500-plus Åland Islands. Ninety per cent of the population live on Fasta Åland, the largest island, and 40 per cent in Mariehamn, the only town. The Åland Islands have long been Swedish-speaking, and when Finland declared independence the islanders wanted reunion with Sweden. The question was referred to the League of Nations. In 1921 it was decided that Finland should retain sovereignty over the islands, and Finland in return agreed to respect and preserve the islands' Swedish language and culture. The 1920 Autonomy Act soon proved inadequate and was replaced in 1951. This Act too became outdated, and the present Act on the Autonomy of Åland came into force in 1993.

The Åland legislative assembly, the Lagting, has the right to pass laws in matters such as education, health and medical services, radio and television, the police, local administration and the promotion of industry. The authorities in Finland exercise competence over such areas as foreign affairs, customs and courts of justice. The Finnish state collects taxes, but the Lagting adopts the Åland budget and is also given a set percentage of the Finnish state budget to finance autonomy provisions. The Lagting appoints the Landskapsstyrelse, an executive council of between five and seven members. There is also an Ålandic Delegation, half of whom are appointed by the Finnish government and half by the Lagting. The President of Finland may impose a veto on laws passed by the Lagting if the latter has exceeded its competence or if any law affects Finnish security. The President's decision is based on advice from the Åland Delegation.

The Åland Islanders' long-standing basic industries of shipping, agriculture and fishing are declining, but tourism has been increasing. Combined with emigration to Sweden, this has helped keep unemployment low.

Sami

There are between 6,400 and 7,000 Sami in Finland, the country's only indigenous minority (see **Norway** for main discussion). Most of them live in northernmost Lapland, in an area known as the 'Sami Homeland'. They belong to three groups: Northern Sami (the majority), Greek Orthodox Skolt Sami (about 900), and Inari Sami (about 500). In early 1996 the Sami Assembly (Samedikki in Sami, Saamelaiskäräjät in Finnish) was constituted as a representative body for Sami and as the successor body to the Sami Parliament. The Sami Assembly is entrusted with limited decision-making power, relating to the distribution of money set aside in the state budget for Sami, and may also take initiatives in matters concerning Sami languages, culture and indigenous status. As a result of the legislative reform of 1995 the Finnish authorities now have an obligation to negotiate with the Sami Assembly in all important matters which may affect the status of Sami as an indigenous people.

The issue of Sami rights to the lands of northern Lapland is still unresolved. The Finnish government declared that it could not ratify ILO Convention 169 of 1989 Concerning Indigenous and Tribal Peoples in Independent Countries as long as Finnish legislation did not fully recognize, *inter alia*, 'the rights of ownership and possession over the lands which they traditionally occupy'. However, official government policy is still to ratify ILO Convention 169 and to change domestic legislation accordingly.

Roma/Gypsies

Roma/Gypsies of Finland belong to the eastern Kale group and settled at the end of the sixteenth century. Numbering about 6,000, they live mostly in urban areas. Since the 1960s Roma/Gypsies have campaigned for better housing and for instruction in the Romani language. The Finnish Gypsy (since 1990 'Romani') Association was founded in 1967, and an Advisory Board on Gypsy (since 1990 'Romani') Affairs has operated since 1956 in conjunction with the Ministry of Social Affairs and Health. In 1992 the Unit for the Development of Romani Education and Culture was set up by the Finnish National Board of Education to promote Romani language and culture. Although some of Finland's Roma/Gypsies still speak their Kale dialect, most speak Finnish. Since December 1992 Romani-language teaching at secondary level has been provided for every group of five or more Romani-speaking children. Since August 1995 Roma/Gypsies have had a constitutional right to protect and promote their language.

Other minorities

Russians who settled in Finland from the eighteenth century to the aftermath of the First World War are often referred to as Old Russians. The first group of Russians settled in the eastern province of Karelia. Old Russian communities in and around Helsinki, Turku and Tampere are mostly the descendants of civil servants, officers and merchants who settled during the nineteenth century. They may also be descendants of people who fled from the Russian Revolution. The most recent group of Russians in Finland (so-called New Russians) immigrated from the 1960s onwards. Russian-speakers are thus partly a historical minority and partly new immigrants, as well as partly people with Finnish citizenship and partly non-citizens. The number of Old Russians has been estimated to lie between 2,500 and 5,000. Due to recent immigration from the then Soviet Union and the Commonwealth of Independent States (CIS), the number of Russian-speakers in Finland is now close to 20,000. Russian-speakers have recently sought the status of a nationally recognized minority. In 1994 they set up an umbrella organization called the Forum of Russian-Speakers in Finland.

Jews first arrived in Sweden-Finland during the seventeenth and eighteenth centuries. Present-day Finnish Jews, numbering approximately 1,500, descend mainly from later arrivals of Russian origin. In 1918, after Finland gained independence, Jews were granted full rights as citizens. The Jews moving to Finland in the eighteenth century spoke Russian and Yiddish and upon settling in Finland chose Swedish as their first language. In 1932 it was decided that the language of instruction at the Jewish school in Helsinki should be Finnish instead of Swedish. Jews are basically bilingual, though the younger ones tend to be increasingly unilingual Finnish-speaking.

Islamic Tatars came to Finland from the Sergatch region on the Volga from the 1880s to the 1920s. They were merchants and settled mainly in the Helsinki area. In 1925 they founded the first Finnish Islamic congregation. Tatars number about 900, although the total number of Muslims in Finland, many of them recent immigrants from various countries in the Islamic world, is 10,000. Tatars have kept their Turkic language alive, using it mainly in family and private life. Their religious organization arranges the regular teaching of Turkic to children, and there are summer camp courses in Turkic.

Conclusions and future prospects

The Swedish language remains protected under the provisions of the Finnish constitution and the language legislation as an official language alongside Finnish. Swedish schools and institutes of higher education continue to ensure the future of Swedish language and culture. However, emigration to Sweden and the low birth rate among Swedish Finns mean that the proportion of younger age groups is decreasing, leading to a population decline. Prospects for Finnish Sami, as for all Sami, involve the struggle to maintain their culture as their traditional northern reindeer grazing lands are increasingly exploited by modern industry. Their main priority remains to protect their wildlife resources for sustainable use.

Further reading

Aikio, S., Aikio-Puoskari, U. and Helander, J., *The Sami Culture in Finland*, Helsinki, Lapin Sivistysseura, 1994.

Åland Islands, Mariehamn, Ålands Landskapsstyrelse, 1994.

Beach, H., *The Sami of Lapland*, London, MRG report, 1988.

Beach, H., 'The Sami of Lapland', in MRG (ed.), *Polar Peoples: Self-Determination and Development*, London, Minority Rights Publications, 1994.

MRG (ed.), *Minorities and Autonomy in Western Europe*, London, MRG report, 1991.

Pentikäinen, J. and Hiltunen, M. (eds), *Cultural Minorities in Finland*, Helsinki, Finnish National Commission for UNESCO, 1995.

Svenska Finlands Folkting (Swedish Assembly), *Swedish Finland*, Helsingfors, 1994.

Minority-based and advocacy organizations

Ålands Lagting (Ålandic Parliament), PB 69, 22101 Mariehamn, Finland; tel. 358 28 25 000, fax 358 28 13 302.

Amnesty International, Ruoholahdenkatu, 24D, 00180 Helsinki, Finland; tel 358 0 693 1488, fax 358 0 693 1975.

Finnish Helsinki Committee, Mariankatu 28, 00170 Helsinki, Finland; tel. 358 0 135 1470, fax. 358 0 135 1101.

Finnish Islamic Congregation [Tatar], Fredrikinkatu 33 A, 00120 Helsinki, Finland.

Forum of Russian-Speakers in Finland, Jaakonkatu 5 B, 00100 Helsinki, Finland; tel. 358 0 685 3055, fax 358 0 685 3066.

Institute for Human Rights, Åbo Academy University, Gezeliusgatan 2, 20500 Turku/Åbo, Finland; tel. 358 21 265 4325, fax 358 21 265 4699.

Jewish Community of Helsinki, Malminkatu 26, 00100 Helsinki/Helsingfors, Finland; tel. 358 0 694 1302, fax 358 0 694 8916.

Northern Institute for Environmental and Minority Law/Minority Rights Group Finland, University of Lappland, Box 122, 96101 Rovaniemi, Finland; tel. 358 60 324 591, fax 358 60 324 590.

Romani Educational and Cultural Development Unit, Hakaniemenkatu 2, 00530 Helsinki, Finland; tel. 358 0 7747 7308, fax 358 0 7747 7865.

Samedikki/Saamelaiskäräjät (Sami Assembly), PO Box 38, 99871 Inari, Finland; tel. 358 697 51181, fax 358 697 51323.

Samiraddi/Saamelaisneuvosto (Sami Council), 99980 Utsjoki, Finland; tel.358 9697 677351, fax 358 9697 677353.

Svenska Finlands Folkting (Swedish Assembly), Unionsgatan 45H 110, 00170 Helsingfors, Finland; tel. 358 0 135 1355, fax 358 0 135 1443.

France

Land area:	551,500 sq km
Population:	57.4 million (1994)
Main languages:	French, Breton, Corsican, Catalan, Basque, German, Occitan, Flemish, Arabic, Berbère
Main religions:	Roman Catholicism, Islam, Protestantism, Judaism
Main minority groups:	Occitan-speakers 2 million (3.5%), Alsatians 1.5–2 million (2.6–3.5%), Bretons 700,000 (1.2%), Portuguese 650,000 (1.1%), Algerians 614,000 (1.1%), Moroccans 572,000 (1%), Jews 500,000–700,000 (0.9–1.2%), Roma/Gypsies 280,000–340,000 (0.5–0.6%), Italians 252,000 (0.4%), Asians 227,000 (0.4%), Spanish 216,000 (0.4%), Tunisians 208,000 (0.4%), Catalans 200,000 (0.35%), Turks 198,000 (0.34%), Corsicans 170,000 (0.3%), Basques 80,000 (0.14%), Flemings 80,000 (0.14%), former Yugoslavs 52,000 (less than 0.1%), Germans 51,000 (less than 0.1%), Poles 40,000 (less than 0.1%), Luxembourgers 40,000 (less than 0.1%), others including sub-Saharan Africans 200,000 (est., 0.35%)
Real per capita GDP:	$19,510
UNDP HDI/rank:	0.930 (8)

Before the 1789 French Revolution nearly one-third of the population of France spoke one of the various regional languages. The revolution had a strongly centralizing effect: provincial traditions were eroded, and attempts to defend local languages and cultures were considered reactionary. The French language was promoted as a means of inculcating nation-state consciousness. Centralization was intensified under Napoleon. France remains one of the most centralized of European states, despite the establishment in 1981–4 of twenty-two regional councils with limited briefs covering regional development, training schemes and arts funding. The following discussion focuses mainly on France's larger historic and new minorities. Because of space limitations, it excludes coverage of the large Roma/Gypsy minority and of the estimated 200,000 Catalans of the Pyrénées-Orientales region and 80,000 Basques of the Pyrénées-Atlantiques; for a discussion of these three groups see **Spain**.

Occitan-speakers

Occitan is spoken in a large region of southern France, including the provinces of Languedoc, Provence, Limousin, Auvergne and Gascony. Occitan dialects are a result of the Latin influence on the language of the southern Gauls, whereas French has stronger Frankish influences. Of the 13 million inhabitants of the Occitan region, it is estimated that 48 per cent understand Occitan, 28 per cent can speak it, 13 per cent can read it and 6 per cent write the language.[1] Occitan has no public or official status but is used as a medium of instruction in some primary schools. The 1990s have seen a partial reassertion of Occitan identity among the young, and there is renewed interest in learning the language. Enthusiasts have been active in protests against restrictive immigration laws, and the movement is inclusive of North African, Senegalese and other immigrants.

Alsatians

Alsace, bordering Germany and Switzerland, existed for centuries with no direct relationship with a French central government. When annexed by France under the Treaty of Westphalia, the region maintained strong links with Germany until the 1789 Revolution, when the French language was imposed. The area was annexed by Bismarck in 1871 and incorporated into the German state structure, whereupon some of the population left for the French interior. The area was reclaimed by France under the Treaty of Versailles, a move generally welcomed by Alsatians. However, the strong centralization of France and the forbidding of the teaching of German led to the appearance of autonomous political parties. During the Second World War the Nazi regime banned the use of French in Alsace and confiscated French-speakers' land and property. The wartime collaboration of some leaders of the autonomy movement lost it most of its support after the war.

There are two forms of Alsatian dialect, or Elsasserditsch. In addition, in Thionese Lorraine, Lothringer Platt is spoken, another dialectical variant which is understood in the north of Alsace. The written form of these dialects is High German. By 1964, 80 per cent of Alsatians could not read or write German. However, by 1970 calls for autonomy were again increasing. The René Schickele Kreiss, an association in favour of decentralization and the protection of the region's cultural and economic life, was founded in 1969. The numbers of people speaking the region's dialects has continued to decrease, and the population has been affected by the decline of the region's coal and steel industries. Many Alsatians commute daily to work in Germany. There is significant support among Alsatians for the Front National (FN).

Bretons

Bretons came to north-west France from Britain as Celtic refugees fleeing the invasions of Angles and Saxons. Their language, which is closely related to Welsh, declined after the French Revolution, although in the nineteenth century there was some growth in cultural and regionalist organizations. Breton nationalism experienced an upsurge after the First World War, and during the Second World War some Breton nationalist leaders were approached by the Nazis. (The Vichy regime gave the Breton language and culture some recognition.) As a result of the wartime collaboration, Brittany suffered ferocious and indiscriminate repression in postwar France, although many nationalists had actively opposed the Vichy regime and the Nazis.

Brittany did not generally share in the postwar economic boom, and many young Bretons have emigrated. Children are educated in French, although there has been some revival in the Breton language, and some groups have organised teaching through Breton in primary and secondary schools. An estimated 700,000 people understand Breton and 400,000 speak it. The leading Breton nationalist organization is the Union Démocratique Bretonne (UDB), founded in 1964. While rejecting separation, the UDB seeks a popularly elected Breton Assembly and cooperates with the French parties on the left. Terrorist activity in support of the Breton cause has subsided.

Jews

Jews first settled in the area that is now France in Roman times.[2] They have experienced persecution and expulsions since the Crusades. In the sixteenth century many Marranos (covert Jews) fled persecution in Spain and Portugal to settle in France, where their descendants came to enjoy a high level of wealth and culture. However, most French Jews, living in the east of the country, particularly Alsace and Lorraine, were poor and subjected to widespread anti-Semitism. By the end of the nineteenth century, European Jews enjoyed the most successful period of their modern history, but a new and virulent form of anti-Semitism (a word coined in 1879) was coming to the fore. In France, the Third Republic was rocked by the Dreyfus affair. Captain Dreyfus, an Alsatian Jew and an intensely patriotic Frenchman who was the first Jewish officer in the French General Staff, was accused of selling military secrets to Germany and convicted by court martial. In 1906 the French government admitted that he had been framed and falsely convicted, yet for several decades anti-Semitism was a characteristic of the ultra-conservative right. The French army confirmed Dreyfus's innocence only in 1995.

The wartime Vichy government introduced anti-Jewish legislation, and 74,000 Jews were deported from France to die in concentration camps. In July 1994 President Mitterrand inaugurated an official monument in memory of the 13,152 Jews rounded up by French police in 1942, the first official acknowledgement of French complicity in the Holocaust. However, that same year Mitterrand was criticized by Jewish leaders for saying that it was too late to try Nazi war criminals. In 1995 President Chirac recognized the active participation of Vichy France in the Holocaust, but this appears to have had almost no impact on mainstream opinion. The rise of the FN, founded in 1972 and led by Jean-Marie Le Pen, has caused some concern to the Jewish community. Le Pen claims that Hitler's gas chambers were a mere detail of the Second World War. Sections of the press that support the FN have called for the repeal of laws against racism and Holocaust-denial. Overtly anti-Semitic groups, most notably the l'Ouvre Française, have increased their activities, and there has been an increase in anti-Semitic incidents, including desecrations of Jewish cemeteries.

Corsicans

Corsica, an island in the western Mediterranean, has been ruled by France since it was sold by Genoa in 1768. The island has experienced massive economic decline since the end of the nineteenth century. There is a large Corsican diaspora working principally in mainland France, although also in the USA and former French colonies. Emigration has left many villages empty or populated solely by older people; pensions now account for over half of Corsica's income. Approximately 70 per cent of the total population are of Corsican origin. Of these, some 86 per cent regularly use the language Corsu, native to the island. Corsu has no official status, although a campaign by the Conseil de la Culture of the Corsican Assembly has brought about an increase in road signs in the language.

Corsicans have a significantly lower standard of living than the mainland French. As a result of substantial immigration, much of the farm labouring work on the island is performed by Algerians and Moroccans. In 1962 some 18,000 *pieds noirs* (French former settlers from Algeria) were resettled in Corsica.[3] Many of them became wine growers, and they now control the crucial viticulture industry. The other principal industry on the island is tourism, dominated by large companies. The Corsican autonomist movement, beginning in the 1960s, has become increasingly militant. In 1981 Corsica was given an elected regional assembly with substantially wider powers than those granted to other French regional assemblies, including control of land transactions, employment and broadcasting. However, the long-standing domination of the electoral system by clans has caused problems in its operation. Clan domination also makes it difficult to assess support for autonomy among Corsicans.

In 1976 the various armed groups fighting for Corsican autonomy amalgamated to become the Front de Libération Nationale de la Corse (FLNC). This organization, which took both its name and its programme from the Algerian independence movement, the FLN, demanded independence and the expulsion of the *pieds noirs*. Since 1982 the FLNC has targeted the *continentaux* – people born in mainland France and living or working in Corsica – claiming responsibility for the destruction of large numbers of holiday homes. In 1994 French police reported the arrest of fourteen heavily armed Corsican separatists, allegedly as they prepared to set off bombs at Speronem, and the situation worsened further in 1995 and 1996.

New minorities

The first immigration to be regularized by the French state was organised between France and Poland in 1908 for agricultural and mining workers. In 1946 the government established the National Office of Immigration (ONI) to organize immigration, but employers continued to recruit 'clandestine' labour since it was cheaper and more easily laid off. By the 1960s only 23 per cent of immigrants came through ONI, while 77 per cent were 'clandestines'. In the 1970s immigration was restricted; 'clandestines' were deported; and for a while there was an unsuccessful policy of induced repatriation. In January 1994 the Central Directorate for Immigration Control was set up to control immigration and the employment of immigrants.

Altogether there are currently an estimated 3.5 million members of new minorities in France. A degree of intolerance of other cultures has continued to mark French official policy towards them. On the one hand, members of new minorities are encouraged to abandon their languages and cultures and to integrate and assimilate with France; on the other, they are treated as outsiders and, for example, subject to mass identity card checks. Police brutality against people of non-European origin has been documented, including eleven shootings in 1993 and 1994. In 1993 the right to French citizenship for all those born on French soil was withdrawn. Since then, French-born children of non-citizens have had to apply for citizenship between the ages of 16 and 21, and the application may be refused. In 1994 only 20,000 such applications were made, although the government estimated that 50,000 were eligible. The recent adoption of a new penal code means that these young adults may also be subject to deportation.

Throughout the 1980s significant segments of French popular opinion have moved to support the anti-immigrant right. The FN gained 12.5 per cent of the vote in the March 1993 general election. Anti-Arab as well as anti-Semitic, the FN calls for forced repatriations and an end to the 'Islamification' of France. In the first round of the 1995 presidential elections, Le Pen won 4.5 million votes (15 per cent) and he promised 1,200 expulsions a day to total 3 million in the course of his presidency. In the municipal elections of June 1995 the FN won three mayoral posts in south-east France, advocating a policy of overt preference to French nationals in jobs and housing.

Algerians and other North Africans

There are currently some 614,000 Algerians, 572,000 Moroccans and 208,000 Tunisians in France. Algeria had been conquered by France in 1830 and gained independence in 1962; Morocco was a French protectorate from 1912 (Treaty of Fez) until it achieved independence in 1956; Tunisia, a French protectorate from 1883, also became independent in 1956. In 1873 the French government began to expropriate Algerian land for French settlers, known as *pieds noirs,* who came to monopolize the fertile land. This caused great resentment among Algerians, and in 1945 the celebration of victory over Nazism turned into a popular rebellion. This triggered a massacre in which, according to French records, 45,000 Algerians and 108 Europeans died. Pressure for independence grew, and war broke out in Algeria in 1954. Algeria won its independence late, in 1962, partly because of the presence of 900,000 French nationals who exacted a promise from the French army not to leave the country.

Algerians began emigrating to France in large numbers during the First World War. Algeria was also a primary source of French labour after the Second World War. In 1947 France redefined Algeria's status with the Statut Organique de l'Algérie, conferring French citizenship on all Algerians and confirming freedom of movement between Algeria and France. By 1949, 265,000 Algerians had migrated to France. Algerian workers in France were subject to violent attacks during Algeria's independence struggle. After 1962 the French government restricted immigration. Some 500,000 Algerians returned to Algeria, while more than one million *pieds noirs* left, to be resettled with handsome grants in France. Between 80,000 and 100,000 'Harkis' – Algerians who had fought on the side of the colonists – also came to France, many of them settling in the south. Despised by both the host population and their fellow Algerians, they were held in special camps for their own protection. There is still animosity between Harkis and other Algerians.

Unemployment levels among Algerians are as high as 40 per cent for some age groups, and Algerians are subjected to racist and police violence.[4] In mid-1994 the entire Paris police force was mobilized to carry out mass identity checks in immigrant areas, following the killing of two French people in Algeria. Thirty thousand North Africans were stopped and searched in less than two weeks in August in what the Interior Minister later acknowledged was a 'fishing expedition' with no direct link to Algerian violence. Twenty-five Arabs were interned and twenty Algerians were subsequently deported. The deportations were later declared unlawful by French judges. Despite international criticism of the Algerian government and popular unrest in Algeria, there has been growing collaboration between the French and the Algerian governments. This has resulted in a low rate of acceptance of Algerian asylum seekers in France.

The experience of Moroccans and Tunisians in France has been broadly similar to that of Algerians, particularly with regard to police checks and far-right violence.

Other minorities

In Westhoek, in the north-eastern corner of France, bordering Belgium, there are pockets of Flemish-speakers (see **Belgium**). This minority is not united into a homogeneous society and is currently struggling to preserve its culture and language. At one time there were calls for reunification with Flanders, but Fleming collaboration with the Nazis under the occupation undermined the movement, which has not recovered.

Citizens of France's Overseas Territories and Dominions – that is, Antillean, Réunion and Maillote residents – are French by nationality and not considered immigrants, and they enjoy citizenship rights. However, they are vulnerable to every resurgence of racism in France.

Conclusions and future prospects

The outlook for France's historic minorities remains uncertain. For many years the home regions of Alsatians, Bretons and Corsicans lagged behind the national economy as a whole, encouraging outmigration, although Alsace and Brittany have recently gained ground in this respect. Regionalism is experiencing a growth in popularity and is having to adopt a position on the situation of Jews (considered in France a religious group, not a minority as such) and new minorities in France. Among a number of regional minorities – Alsatians, Bretons, Catalans, Corsicans, Lorrains and Occitanians – there is a determination to preserve language and culture. The rise of the far right and the credibility lent its agenda by official anti-immigration policies suggest a vulnerable future for new minorities.

Further reading

Giordan, H. (ed.), *Les Minorités en Europe*, Paris, Kimé, 1992.

Loughlin, J., 'Regionalism and ethnic nationalism in France', in Merry and Wright (eds), *Centre–Periphery Relations in Western Europe*, London, Allen & Unwin, 1985.

Stephens, M., *Linguistic Minorities in Western Europe*, Llandysul, Gomer, 1976.

Minority-based and advocacy organizations

Amnesty International, 4 Rue de la Pierre Levée, 75553 Paris, Cedex 11, France; tel 33 1 49 23 11 11, fax 33 1 43 38 26 15.

Biarritz Culture, Javalquinto, 64200 Biarritz, France; tel. 33 5 59 222021.

Centre de Recherches Tsiganes (Roma/Gypsy Research Centre), Université René Descartes, 106 Quai de Clichy, 92110 Clichy, France; fax 33 1 47 312923.

Cercle René Schickele, 31 Rue Oberlin, 67000 Strasbourg, France; tel. 33 3 88 364830.

Conseil Culturel de Bretagne/Kuzel Sevenadurel Breizh, Pt Jean-Louis Latour, 7 Rue Général Guillaudot, 3166 Rennes, France.

Conseil Régional d'Alsace, 35 Avenue de la Paix, 67070 Strasbourg Cedex, France; tel. 33 3 88 256867.

Écoles Arres [Catalan], Avenue Desnoyés, 66000 Perpignan, France.

Fondation France-Libertés, 1 Place du Trocadéro, 7116 Paris, France; tel. 33 1 47 44 81 81, fax 33 1 47 55 81 88.

Fondation du Judaïsme Français, Pte Nelly Hansson, 32 Place St Georges, 75442 Paris, France.

French Helsinki Committee, 4 Place Denfert-Rochereau, 75014 Paris, France; tel. 33 1 40 640025, fax. 33 1 42 798414.

Groupment pour les Droits des Minorités/ Minority Rights Group France, 212 Rue St Martin, 75003 Paris, France; tel. 33 1 45 750137, fax 33 1 45 798046.

Institut Culturel de Bretagne, 74F Rue de Paris, BP 3166, 35031 Rennes Cedex, France; tel. 33 2 99 875800, fax 33 2 99 385032.

Institut d'Études Occitanes, 1 Rue Jacques Darre, 31000 Toulouse, France.

Institut Kurde, Rue Lafayette 106, 75010 Paris, France; tel. 33 1 48 24 64 64, fax 33 1 47 70 99 04.

Maison des Travailleurs de Turquie, 20 Rue de la Pierre Levée, 75011 Paris, France; tel. 33 1 43 577628, fax 33 1 43 380132.

Mouvement contre le Racisme et pour l'Amitié entre les Peuples (MRAP), 89 Rue Oberkampf, 75543 Paris, France; tel. 33 1 43 14 83 53, fax 33 1 43 14 83 50.

SEASKA, Écoles en Basque, 8 Rue Thiers Karrika, 64100 Bayonne, France.

SOS Racisme, 1 Rue Cail, 75010 Paris, France; tel. 33 1 42 05 44 44, fax 33 1 42 05 69 69.

Tiddukla, Association de Culture Berbère, 37 bis, Rue des Maronites, 75020 Paris, France.

Union du Peuple Corse, Pt Max Simeoni, Bastia, Corsica, France.

Germany

Land area:	356,910 sq km
Population:	81.1 million (1994)
Main languages:	German
Main religions:	Lutheran Christianity, Roman Catholicism, Islam
Main minority groups:	Turks and Kurds 1.6 million (2%), former Yugoslavs 956,000 (1.2%), Italians 568,000 (0.7%), Greeks 324,000 (0.4%), Poles 324,000 (0.4%), Roma/Gypsies/Sinti 110,000–130,000 (0.1–0.2%), others including Jews (60,000–70,000), Danes (50,000–60,000), Frisians (52,000), Sorbs (40,000–45,000), Vietnamese (40,000), Spanish, Tunisians, Portuguese and Mozambicans totalling 2 million (2.5%)
Real per capita GDP:	$18,840
UNDP HDI/rank:	0.920 (18)

The Federal Republic of Germany took its present form in October 1990, with the unification of the former Federal Republic (West Germany) with the German Democratic Republic (East Germany). Disagreements over the form of postwar government for Germany had resulted in the creation of the two Germanys in 1949. Both states had historic minorities: Danes and Frisians in West Germany, and Sorbs in East Germany. West Germany, which was to become the economic powerhouse of Western Europe, needed to attract labour. The first phase of postwar immigration to the Federal Republic comprised 'ethnic Germans' expelled from Poland or fleeing from East Germany. This migration averaged 200,000 people a year, and had reached 9 million by 1961, when the Berlin Wall went up, forcing West Germany to turn to other sources of labour. So began the second phase of immigration, the recruitment of *Gastarbeiter* (guestworkers) from Yugoslavia, Italy, Greece, Spain, Portugal, Tunisia and, in greatest numbers, Turkey. Immigration continued until the oil crisis of 1973. East Germany, meanwhile, recruited foreign workers from Vietnam, Mozambique, Angola and Cuba.

Germany was unified in October 1990 under the West German federal system. The eleven *Länder* (states) expanded to become sixteen, and the population increased by 16 million. Initial euphoria at unification has dissipated, and there is now some hostility among former West Germans towards former East Germans. The economic strains of unification pushed the eastern part of the country into recession and caused widespread unemployment. These effects have combined with political and social factors to facilitate the rise of the far right across Germany, while also increasing support in eastern Germany for the Party of Democratic Socialism, the recast Communist Party.

Danes and Frisians

The constitution of the *Land* of Schleswig-Holstein safeguards the rights of the Danish and Frisian communities, and both groups have German citizenship.[1] Germany's Danish minority is concentrated in Schleswig-Holstein, in territory disputed with Denmark until 1920 (see **Denmark**). The Second World War reduced the Danish population, because many crossed the border into Denmark; and after the war one million German refugees entered the province. Danish is spoken by some 7.7 per cent of the region's population, and all of those speaking are bilingual Danish/German.

The Kiel Declaration of 1949 gave Danish schools government funding and established a committee to deal with Danish grievances. The Bonn Declaration of 1955 is parallel to the Copenhagen Declaration of the same year and protects the use of the Danish language in Germany as German is protected in Denmark. There are several Danish-language nursery and primary schools, and there is one Danish-medium secondary school. The Dansk Skoleforening for Sydslevig (Association of Danish Schools in Southern Schleswig) is responsible for the organization of Danish-medium education in the region. It receives 85 per cent of its funds from the Schleswig-Holstein authorities and 15 per cent from the Danish government. Although there is no broadcasting in Danish, it is possible to receive programmes from stations in Denmark.

Frisian is a Germanic language with three main variants, Northern, East and West. West Frisian is spoken in the Netherlands. North Frisians live in the part of Schleswig-Holstein known as the Kreis of Nord-Friesland. Of Nord-Friesland's total population of approximately 151,000, about 50,000 consider themselves Frisians. North Frisian (Friisk), which has nine dialects and is spoken by 8,000–10,000 people, is not an official language but is sometimes used in local council meetings. Some villages have Frisian road signs. There are no newspapers in North Frisian, although the language can be heard for five minutes each week on the regional station of the public national radio. It is taught for one or two hours a week in most schools in Nord-Friesland, where it is not compulsory but integrated into the official education programme. East Frisian is spoken in Niedersachsen by about 2,000 people. There is little contact between these and the other Frisian groups, since the East Frisians are regarded as having collaborated with the Nazis during the war. East Frisian receives little protection, and the number of speakers has declined. Few children learn the language, and it has no public presence.

Sorbs

In the early days of the Holy Roman Empire, Lusatia was inhabited by speakers of Sorb, an Indo-European Slavic language. The territory was later to come under German feudal lords, then under Bohemia, and in 1815 it was divided between Saxony and Prussia. From then on the Sorb language area decreased, while assimilation into Germany increased. Attempts were made to organize a nation state. In 1912 Domowina, a nationalist organization, was founded, and after the First World War there were calls for an independent Lusatia, or for the territory to be incorporated into Czechoslovakia. Germanization became overt repression under the Nazis, who refused to recognize Sorbs as anything but Slavic-speaking Germans. This led to fresh moves for separation after the Second World War, but these were resisted by the local German population, causing some resentment among Sorbs. Many Germans expelled from formerly annexed territories were resettled in Sorb lands in Brandenburg and Saxony, and the proportion of Sorbs on the territory consequently decreased. There are now only a few villages with a Sorb majority.

East Germany officially supported Sorb development and established national and cultural institutions. The East German Law for the Protection of the Rights of the Sorb People guaranteed equality and cultural rights in the Saxon part of Lusatia. Domowina was officially recognized, although no other Sorb groups were. The government also put up bilingual signs and financed Sorb-medium schools. However, resettlement and the destruction of rural communities meant that there continued to be a decrease in the number of Sorb-speakers. The German Unification Treaty of 1990 gave some protection to Sorbs and upheld their right to speak their language in court. However, legislative texts and legal documents are not published in Sorb. Moreover there has been a visible decline in bilingual public signposting. The Education Act of the Free State of Saxony guarantees the possibility of learning the language as a subject, and makes provision for the use of Sorb as a teaching medium in certain subjects in some schools. The University of Leipzig has an Institute of Sorbian Studies and a degree course in Sorb.

Rising unemployment in eastern Germany has caused many Sorbs to leave their homeland to seek work. There have been attempts to counter this with the Foundation for the Lusatian Sorb Nation, set up in 1991 with the support of the federal and *Länder* governments. Departments of Sorb Affairs have been established in Saxony and Brandenburg. Saxony has twenty hours of Sorb radio broadcasting a week, Brandenburg seven. There is a daily and a weekly Sorb newspaper. In the authorities and administrations of the Sorb areas, Sorb is permitted alongside German, but the staff of these authorities frequently do not know the language. Current estimates put the number of people who identify with the Sorb ethnic group and can speak Sorb at 40,000–45,000.

New minorities

There are some 5.8 million 'foreigners' in Germany, many of whom were born and educated in Germany. Turks and Kurds constitute the largest group, and there are also large numbers of former Yugoslavs, Poles, Tunisians, Mozambicans, Italians, Spanish, Portuguese and Greeks. Although the last four groups entered Germany as *Gastarbeiter*, as citizens of EU countries they have more rights than the others, and the following information on residence and work permits does not apply to them. Until recently, the 1965 *Ausländergesetz*, derived from legislation of 1939, regulated the presence of foreigners exclusively in the interests of the state.[2] This was amended in 1990, after which the issuing of work permits became subject to the discretion of the minister for internal affairs. A residence permit may be refused if not accompanied by a work permit, or if the family cannot provide for the applicant.

Although *Gastarbeiter* were originally supposed to be temporary and not to bring in their families, employers preferred to keep an already trained workforce and save further recruitment costs. When primary immigration was halted in 1973, family reunification increased as workers anticipated further restrictions, and a settled community of non-citizens was established in Germany. German citizenship is based on principles established by the law of citizenship of 1913. Before 1934 citizenship of the *Länder* had priority over federal citizenship. The Nazis abolished *Länder* citizenship and defined citizenship in terms of 'blood' (*ius sanguinis*, although there were elements of *ius soli*); this was used to legitimize depriving Jews and Roma/Gypsies of citizenship. Today, third-generation 'foreigners' may be deported to their grandparents' country of origin. By contrast, ethnic Germans from Eastern Europe and the former Soviet Union have a right to citizenship if they can prove their descent and that they have preserved the German culture (unless they were persecuted for doing so).

Members of new minorities, as well as Jews and Roma/Gypsies, have faced considerable racist violence in Germany in recent years.[3] Victims of such attacks who are citizens of EU countries have a right to state compensation, but the majority who are third-country nationals do not. The collaboration of German citizens and police with far-right violence was revealed in the parliamentary investigative committee established to examine the Rostock incident of August 1992, only one of dozens of attacks on refugee hostels.[4]

Germany has implemented a progressive tightening of asylum legislation, and its approach has proved influential in the development of European Union policy towards asylum seekers, one of whose main planks is the Dublin Convention by which asylum seekers may be returned to the first European Union country in which they arrived. Germany has made bilateral agreements with Central and Eastern European countries, enabling it to return asylum seekers in exchange for preferential trade terms. The creation of these buffer zones has a knock-on effect on asylum policies in Central and Eastern Europe. The European Parliament has condemned this 'refugee trading' and singled out for criticism a 1992 agreement between Germany and Romania. Germany was one of the first European Union countries to introduce the 'safe third country' principle, under which asylum seekers may be returned to lodge their claim in any 'safe' country through which they have passed. Its 'safe country of origin list' defines safe countries as ones that by definition cannot produce genuine refugees.

Turks and Kurds

German official statistics do not usually differentiate between Turks and Kurds, even though hostilities in Kurdistan/Turkey are reflected in relations between the two communities in Germany. Many of the problems both groups face, in terms of immigration status, racist attacks and discrimination, are shared. Turks and Kurds represent the largest group of 'foreigners' in Germany, numbering approximately 1.6 million. Some 70 per cent of these people were born in Germany, the children of immigrants who arrived between 1961 and 1973. More recent arrivals have entered the country under family reunification and asylum legislation. In fact, many early immigrants, entering Germany as part of the labour force, were political activists. Approximately one-third were qualified workers, mainly men from urban areas of more developed parts of Turkey with high levels of education and professional skills. They worked in iron and steel processing, plastics, rubber, asbestos processing and other manufacturing sectors. The majority of Turk and Kurd women came as 'wives', although many found work illegally. More than 75 per cent of the women work as unskilled labour, particularly in the textile, electronics and food industries.

In September 1993, Turkey's Prime Minister, on a visit to Germany, made a joint announcement with Chancellor Kohl concerning cooperation on the 'social integration' of Turkish people. Investigations were promised into the Kurdistan Workers' Party (PKK) which estimates it has 400,000 supporters among Kurds in Germany, comprising the majority of the Kurdish population in the country. One month later the German state banned the PKK and closed down Kurdish cultural organizations and the Kurdish press-agency.

Vietnamese

The majority of the estimated 40,000 Vietnamese in Germany are asylum seekers and former East German contract workers. In 1989 there were some 60,000 Vietnamese working in East Germany under contracts, half of them women.[5] In 1994 the German government revoked the residence permits of all former Vietnamese contract workers, transforming the entire group into 'illegal immigrants'. In January 1995 a government delegation to Vietnam signed a joint declaration with the Vietnamese government, under which Vietnam would take back 20,000 of its citizens within the next four years, and the remainder by the year 2000. The agreement explicitly recognizes that repatriation may be forcible. In return for accepting this repatriation programme the Vietnamese government will receive DM20 million in 'immediate aid'. Despite being condemned by the European Parliament, the agreement was confirmed by the Federal Interior Ministry in June 1995.

Roma/Gypsies/Sinti

Germany has an estimated 110,000–130,000 Roma/Gypsies (see **Spain**) and Sinti. The German government is the only Western European government not to have ratified UN Resolution 62 on the protection of Roma/Gypsies. Roma/Gypsies usually do not have citizenship, and an increasing number have entered Germany as asylum seekers as a result of the war in the former Yugoslavia and persecution in Central and Eastern Europe. Violent attacks on Roma/Gypsies in Germany have been reported, and the Roma National Congress claims that these are sometimes instigated by the police. In 1994 Roma/Gypsies were continuing to be deported to the former Yugoslavia, despite a case pending in the European Parliament to prevent these deportations.

Conclusions and future prospects

It seems likely that Sorbs and Frisians will continue to be subject to the process of assimilation, particularly in the current social and economic climate. Danes are maintaining their separate identity, though there are also assimilation processes at work. Of most concern in Germany is the alienation of millions of inhabitants without citizenship and full rights, and the widespread incidence of racist violence. The tightening of immigration and asylum laws has arguably done little to improve matters, and there is an urgent need for action to deal with the root causes.

Further reading

MRG (ed.), *Minorities and Autonomy in Western Europe*, London, MRG report, 1991.

MRG (ed.), *Minorities in Central and Eastern Europe*, London, MRG report, 1993.

Minority-based and advocacy organizations

Amnesty International, Heerstrasse 178, D-53108, Bonn, Germany; tel. 49 228 983 730, fax 49 228 630036.

Bundesamt für die Anerkennung ausländischer Flüchtlinge, Zollhausstr. 95, 90469, Nuremberg, Germany; tel. 49 911 943 5001, fax 49 911 943 4000.

Domowina-Verlag GMBH, Tuchmacherstrasse, Sukelnska 27, 02625 Bautzen, Germany.

Federal Union of European Nationalities (FUEN), Schiffbrucke 41, 24939 Flensburg, Germany; tel. 49 461 12855, fax 49 461 180709.

German Helsinki Committee for Human Rights, Security and Cooperation in Europe, c/o Bundestag, Bundeshaus, 53090 Bonn 1, Germany; tel. 49 228 168 5094, fax. 49 228 168 6498.

Immigrantenpolitisches Forum, Oranienstrasse 159, 10969 Berlin, Germany; tel. 49 30 614 5098.

International Romani Union, Berlin, Germany; tel./fax 49 30 854 8075.

KOMKAR, Hansaring 28–30, 50670 Cologne, Germany.

Nordfriesischer Verein, Andersen Haus Klockries 64, 25920 Risum-Lindholm, Germany; tel. 49 4661 5873, fax 49 4661 6334.

Roma National Congress, Simon von Utrecht Str. 85, 20359 Hamburg D, Germany.

Seelter Buund [East Frisians], Scharrellerdamm 3, 26169 Friesoythe, Germany.

Sorbische Kulturinformation, Kurt-Pchalekstrasse 26, 02625 Bautzen, Germany.

Sorbisches National-Ensemble, Aussere Lauenstrasse 2, 02625 Bautzen, Germany; tel. 49 30 3591 3580, fax 49 30 3591 43096.

Treff und Infoor fuer Frauen aus der Turkei EV, Manteuffelstrasse 19, 10997 Berlin, Germany; tel. 49 30 612 2050.

UGRAK Treffpunkt fur Frauen aus der Turkei, Weisestrasse 36, 12049 Berlin, Germany; tel. 49 30 621 1037.

Zentralrat Deutscher Sinti und Roma, Zwingerstrasse 18, 69115 Heidelberg, Germany.

Gibraltar

Land area:	6.5 sq km
Population:	32,000 (1994)
Main languages:	English, Spanish, Llanito, Arabic
Main religions:	Roman Catholicism, Islam
Main minority groups:	Moroccans 3,000 (9.4%)
Real per capita GDP:	—
UNDP HDI/rank:	—

Gibraltar consists of a narrow peninsula linked to the south-west coast of Spain by an isthmus. It was occupied by England in 1704 and ceded by Spain in 1714. Since 1964 Spain has tried to retrieve political control of Gibraltar. In 1967 a plebiscite opted overwhelmingly for continued dependency on the United Kingdom. Most Gibraltarians speak and read both English and Spanish and are British citizens by registration since 1981. There is also a local dialect, Llanito. In 1969 Spain closed its border with Gibraltar (reopening it in 1985), effectively withdrawing a large part of the labour force, who lived in Spain. British employers recruited replacement workers from Morocco, and there are now an estimated 3,000 Moroccans in Gibraltar, many of them working in the public sector and unskilled employment. There are also a few hundred people of Indian descent. Moroccans pay tax but are not entitled to benefit. Immigration legislation prevents their permanent residence or family reunification. Gibraltar-born Moroccan children have no right to stay, and Moroccans are subject to deportation if they become unemployed, however long they have lived in Gibraltar.

Gibraltarians of all origins have called for full residence rights to be granted to all third-country nationals who have completed a preliminary period of employment. However, Moroccans are gradually emigrating, often in poor health after many years of physically testing work.

Further reading

Joint Council for the Welfare of Immigrants, *Between a Rock and a Hard Place*, London, 1992.

Minority-based and advocacy organization(s)

Moroccan Workers' Association, Gibraltar; tel. 350 74185.

Greece

Land area:	131,990 sq km
Population:	10.5 million (1994)
Main languages:	Greek
Main religions:	Greek Orthodox Christianity, Islam, Roman Catholicism
Main minority groups:	Albanians 200,000–300,000 (1.9–2.9%), Vlachs 200,000 (1.9%), Arvanites 200,000 (1.9%), (Slavo-)Macedonians 200,000 (1.9%), Roma/Gypsies 160,000–200,000 (1.5–1.9%), Turks 50,000 (0.5%), Pomaks 30,000 (0.3%), other new minorities 200,000–300,000 (1.9–2.9%)
Real per capita GDP:	$8,950
UNDP HDI/rank:	0.909 (21)

When the Greek state was founded in 1830 it comprised one-third of the territory it rules today. As different 'nations' received their independence from the decaying Ottoman Empire, they entered into long and bloody conflicts, justified by historical revisionism and alleged ethnic ties, over territory which had not yet attained 'statehood'. Because of competing claims and allegiances there were frequent attempts to enforce homogeneity through expulsions and assimilation once areas of mixed populations became incorporated into a state. When the Balkan Wars came to an end in 1913, the Treaty of Bucharest delimited frontiers, and many members of ethnic groups migrated, voluntarily or not, to nations more favourably disposed to their presence. Not all ethnic groups had states to go to. Since the Second World War the Greek government has denied the existence of any non-Greek minority within its borders apart from the 'Islamic Greeks' recognized by the Treaty of Lausanne in 1923. All those who use Greek in everyday language are considered Greek, even if Greek is not their mother-tongue. This non-recognition of minorities is bolstered by a rigid notion of Greek national identity, closely identified with membership of the Greek Orthodox Church.

Distrust of minority groups was further compounded in Greece by the civil war of 1944–9. Towards the end of the civil war, up to 40 per cent of the Communist forces comprised (Slavo-)Macedonians, and the Communists declared an Independent United Macedonia. The military dictatorship of 1967–74 saw a worsening of the situation for minority groups. While repression eased with the restoration of democracy, minority groups continue to complain of discrimination. Greece is party to the CSCE agreements but refuses to recognize the existence of minorities within its borders. In 1993 the Greek Parliament overwhelmingly supported the obligatory listing of religion on national identity cards.

Vlachs

Vlachs, or Vlachophone Greeks, are traditionally mountain pastoralists. There are two Vlach languages in Greece: Megleno-Romanian, spoken by a population calling itself 'Vlasi', and Arumanian, spoken by people calling themselves Armin. Arumanian has many dialects, one of which is a neo-Latin language, Aromani, related to Romanian. In the early Middle Ages the Vlachs had powerful independent kingdoms. There are Vlachs in Albania, Macedonia, Serbia and Bulgaria, and in Greece they are scattered in the mountainous region of the Hellenic peninsula. The only area of concentrated Vlach population in Greece is Aminciu (Metsova) and surrounding villages.

Under the Ottoman Empire, Vlachs supported Greek political and cultural causes, and they played a leading part in Greek independence. However, some Vlachs, particularly in Macedonia, were attracted to Romania, and Romania established schools in Macedonia when it was under Ottoman rule. The 1913 treaty allowed for these schools to continue in the Greek state. During the Second World War an army of Vlach fascists was set up – 'The Roman Legion' – and an autonomous 'Principality of Pindus' was formed. The postwar Romanian state discontinued its support of Vlach schools and churches. There is currently no separatist feeling among Vlachs in Greece. Vlach cultural societies are permitted, and there is a Panhellenic Union of Vlach Cultural Associations. Vlachs are more tolerated than other minority groups by the Greek state. However, the official view is that Vlachs are Greeks who speak an unusual dialect, and there is popular hostility to the use of the Aromanian language, which has been internalized by many Vlachs themselves. This, combined with urbanization and other social, political and economic factors, has resulted in the language's decline.

Arvanites

Christian Albanian migration to Greece between the eleventh and eighteenth centuries ensured that large communities of Arvanites inhabited the territory before the Greek state was formed. The Arvanites consider themselves not Albanians but Greeks, and some have argued that they are descended from early inhabitants of Greece. The language, related to Albanian, is in decline because of non-recognition by Greece, economic reasons and the prevalent belief that it is 'backward'. There have, however, been efforts to preserve Arvanite culture through associations. Serious attacks have taken place on recent Albanian migrants in Arvanite areas of central and southern Greece.

(Slavo-)Macedonians[1]

The geographical term 'Macedonia' is a sensitive issue for Greece. Its 'appropriation' by Marshal Tito to describe the southern territory of Yugoslavia was regarded as a denial of Greek cultural heritage and a harbinger of long-term irredentism. When the former Yugoslav Republic of Macedonia declared its independence in January 1991, the Macedonian question became even more sensitive.

The area inhabited by (Slavo-)Macedonians (also known as Slavomacedonians or Macedonians) constitutes the former Yugoslav Republic of Macedonia and the borders of Bulgaria and Greece. In 1872 Macedonia was divided between Patriarchate Greeks and Exarchate Bulgarians, and at the turn of the century the region was populated by members of many ethnic groups speaking a common language closely related to Bulgarian. In 1903 the Internal Macedonian Revolutionary Organization (IMRO, founded in 1893) proclaimed independent administrations in two areas of Macedonia, expecting to receive support from the European powers for an independent Macedonia. This was not forthcoming, and IMRO was crushed, leaving Greece, Bulgaria and Serbia to struggle for the territory. When Macedonia was divided in 1913, the majority of the population were Bulgarophiles; yet Greece acquired most of the territory, Serbia one-third and Bulgaria only one-tenth. Some 15,000 (Slavo-)Macedonians left Greece, and harsh assimilation policies were established in all three states. In 1924 Greece and Bulgaria signed the Kalfov–Politis Agreement, placing the 'Bulgarian' minority in Greece under the protection of the League of Nations. In 1925 Greece reneged on the protocol and from then on considered the minority to be Greeks.

Greece's northern and eastern border is today approximately as it was fixed in 1913, but the demography has changed markedly. After the First World War between 52,000 and 72,000 Slavs left Greece for Bulgaria, and 25,000 Greek-speakers came to Greece from Bulgaria. They were resettled in Greek Macedonia and given land often formerly cultivated by the local peasants. They were joined by hundreds of thousands of refugees from Turkey after 1922. Following the civil war 35,000 Communist (Slavo-) Macedonians went into exile and were stripped of citizenship; land was distributed to 'nationally minded' Greeks who were resettled in Macedonia. Those who continue to assert (Slavo-)Macedonian nationality still cannot return. These rapid demographic changes were complemented by compulsory assimilation, including name changes, school closure and the prohibition of the Macedonian language in public and in the home. Greek control of education and job discrimination in particular have encouraged assimilation, making the (Slavo-)Macedonian minority increasingly difficult to define.

The independence of the former Yugoslav Republic of Macedonia has helped fuel Greek nationalism, and there has been a simultaneous resurgence in (Slavo-)Macedonian minority activism, demanding recognition, although not autonomy or secession. The Macedonian Movement for Balkan Prosperity filed candidates in the 1994 elections. Activists are subjected to harassment.

Turks and Pomaks

There are some 90,000 Muslims in Greece, most living in Western Thrace, the province bordering Turkey. Most (50,000) identify themselves as Turks, although they are of different origins, including Pomaks or Muslim Slavs (30,000) and Muslim Roma/Gypsies. When the Greek government recognized 'Islamic Greeks' in the Treaty of Lausanne, the population of Western Thrace was predominantly Muslim. In the 1920 population exchanges, however – and in contravention of the Treaty of Lausanne – some 60,000 Greek-speaking refugees from Asia Minor were resettled in Western Thrace; and under the 1967–74 dictatorship Greeks were given financial inducements to move there to land reallocated from Muslims, who were given inferior land in exchange. At the same time, subjected to economic, social and political pressures, Turks emigrated, mainly to Turkey, but also to other areas of Greece and to Germany, a pattern that continues today.

The Treaty of Lausanne gave the Muslim minorities the right to religious freedom and to education in their own language. The language used is Turkish rather than Pomak, which does not have a written form. This has encouraged Pomaks to identify with Turks, an identification which the Greek state attempts to discourage. However, Pomaks and Turks now share many problems, particularly since hostility between Turkey and Greece means that much of Western Thrace is militarized and movement is severely restricted. Turks and Pomaks have not been adequately compensated for land expropriated from them for public use. Turkish minority community boards, established by government decree in 1920, were abolished under the dictatorship and have never been reinstituted. Enforced name changes and even the prohibition of the adjective 'Turkish' in association names continue to be enforced, while education has become increasingly Hellenicized. Foreign nationals cannot buy land near border areas, and Turks and Pomaks claim that this is applied to them despite their Greek citizenship. 'Muslim-origin Greek citizens' can be, and are, deprived of citizenship under Article 19 of the Greek Nationality Law, and the Greek government annually reports this figure to the USA.

Community polarization in Western Thrace is increasing. In 1989 Dr Sadik Ahmet won a seat in Parliament as an independent Turkish candidate. In 1990 he was found guilty of provoking discord by claiming the existence of a Turkish minority in Greece. In the 1993 elections the Greek Parliament introduced a 3 per cent nationwide threshold to eliminate the possibility of such candidates winning seats; Ahmet was consequently not re-elected. (He died in a car accident in July 1995.)

New minorities

Greece has been a destination for significant numbers of non-EU migrants since the 1980s.[2] There are now an estimated half a million such people, approximately half of them Albanians and the rest exceedingly diverse, including Poles, Eritreans, Egyptians, Ethiopians, Iraqis, Iranians and Indians. Greek jurisprudence implicitly recognizes as of non-Greek origin 'all those who do not have a national consciousness, established on the basis of common racial origin, often but not always common language or religion, and especially common history and ideals'. Such people may be deprived of citizenship through Article 19 of the citizenship code. Greek citizenship is granted to people of non-Greek parentage after ten years' legal residency, preferably after they have converted to Greek Orthodoxy. Legal requirements make the former almost impossible for a non-EU citizen, particularly since 1992 when people from Africa, Asia and Latin America were declared ineligible for work permits. Members of new minorities complain of their lack of legal status, which bars them from access to health care, education and other public services. They claim discrimination in housing and employment, physical and verbal abuse on the streets, and police harassment.

Albanians

There are 200,000–300,000 recent Albanian migrants to Greece. Little is known of their situation, since most of them work illegally in construction and farming and as domestic workers. Conflict between Greece and Albania, particularly over the Greek minority in Albania, has led to this group being subject to reprisals by the Greek government and to increasing popular hostility, fuelled by media stereotypes of Albanians as predatory criminals. In 1993, 20,000 Albanians were deported in one week in retaliation for Albania's deportation of a Greek Orthodox priest. The Albanian authorities complained that those expelled were badly beaten and that their belongings were destroyed. In 1994, a further 115,000 Albanians were deported over a six month period in response to the trial in Albania of members of the Greek minority organization Omonia. Greek landlords and employers were encouraged to report Albanians to the police. An attempt to reduce this tension was made in April 1995, when the Greek government agreed to legalize Albanian migrants with identity documents.

Conclusions and future prospects

Resurgent Greek nationalism has been accompanied by a generalized intolerance towards non-Orthodox people, including Catholics, Protestants, Jews and Jehovah's Witnesses, as well as non-Greek-speakers. The situation of all minorities in Greece is weak. Some, such as

Vlachs, Arvanites and some groups of (Slavo-) Macedonians, are rapidly assimilating. The future of others depends on such external factors as Greece's relationship with its old ally, Serbia, developments in the former Yugoslav Republic of Macedonia, and Greco-Turkish relations. For new minorities, the outlook hinges on Greece's balancing of the demands of the European Union for tighter border controls with its own continued use of cheap migrant labour.

Further reading

Greek Monitor of Human and Minority Rights (Kifisia, MRG Greece), 1994.

MRG Greece, *The Arvanites of Greece* and *The Vlachs of Greece*, information sheets, Kifisia, n.d.

MRG Greece, Pettifer, J. and Poulton, H., *The Southern Balkans*, London, MRG report, 1994.

Poulton, H., *The Balkans*, London, Minority Rights Publications, 1994.

Minority-based and advocacy organizations

Amnesty International, 30 Sina Street, 10672 Athens, Greece; tel. 30 1 360 0628, fax 30 1 363 8016.

Greek Council for Refugees, 39 Arahovis Street, Exarhia, 10681 Athens, Greece.

Minority Rights Group Greece/Greek Helsinki Monitor, PO Box 51393, 14510 Kifisia, Greece; tel. 30 1 620 0120, fax 30 1 807 5767, e-mail: helsinki@compulink.gr

KASAPI Hellas, Methonis 54–56, Exarchia, 10681 Athens, Greece.

Macedonian Human Rights Movement, Filipou 11, 53200 Amyndeo, Greece.

Macedonian Movement for Balkan Prosperity (MAKIVE), Kolokotroni 7, 58400 Aridaia, Greece.

Movement for Human Rights of Macedonians in Greece, Amindeo-Florina, Filipon II 332, Greece.

Iceland

Land area:	103,000 sq km
Population:	260,000 (1992)
Main languages:	Icelandic
Main religions:	Evangelical Lutheran Christianity
Main minority groups:	—
Real per capita GDP:	$18,640
UNDP HDI/rank:	0.934 (8)

The Republic of Iceland was uninhabited until the ninth century CE, when Irish hermits settled there. The first Norwegian settlement dates from CE 874. In 1264 the independent republic of Iceland became part of the Kingdom of Norway. In 1381 Iceland and Norway were conquered by Denmark. When Norway separated from the Danish Crown in 1814, Iceland remained under Denmark's protection. In 1918 Iceland became an associated state of Denmark until it recovered its independence in 1944. The people of Iceland are an extremely homogeneous population, all descended from Northern European immigrants. There are no minority groups.

Irish Republic

Land area:	70,280 sq km
Population:	3.5 million (1994)
Main languages:	English, Irish
Main religions:	Roman Catholicism, Protestantism
Main minority groups:	Protestants 115,404 (3.3%), Travellers 22,000–28,000 (0.6–0.8%)
Real per capita GDP:	$15,120
UNDP HDI/rank:	0.919 (19)

The Republic of Ireland comprises 26 of the 32 counties of the island of Ireland. The other six counties, Northern Ireland, are part of the United Kingdom. England's conquest and colonization of Ireland began in the twelfth century. In the sixteenth century the Gaelic nobility were made vassals of the English Crown, and by 1603 England controlled all of Ireland. Full-scale rebellion broke out in 1641, lasting until Cromwell brought the English army to Ireland in 1649. Nearly all land that had belonged to Catholic landowners was given to soldiers for arrears of pay and to adventurers who had loaned the government money. A Protestant English upper class was created. By the mid-eighteenth century Catholics owned only 7 per cent of the land. Following a further rebellion in 1798, Ireland was made part of Great Britain by the Act of Union 1800. Restriction of trade and commerce made the country almost entirely dependent on agriculture. In 1845 a potato disease blighted the crop, and this combined with high rents and evictions to result in six years of famine in which an estimated one million people died, and between 1845 and 1855 some 2 million Irish, one-quarter of the population, emigrated (see **United Kingdom**).

Protestants were among the earliest people who articulated Irish nationalism.[1] Among them was Wolfe Tone, whose organization, the United Irishmen, was the first to call for a united Ireland, and whose membership included many Protestants. It was followed by the Catholic Association campaigning for Catholic emancipation, using the Catholic Church to organize the peasantry. In 1829, after a series of huge meetings, and amid widespread rural unrest, Catholic emancipation was passed at Westminster. The Catholic Association turned its attention to the repeal of the Union. When its leadership refused to use illegal means to achieve demands, the more militant group Young Ireland came to the fore, demanding independence or insurrection. The movement petered out, although many members would later join the Irish Republican Brotherhood, established in 1858.

In 1879 the Land League was established to organize the tenantry to protect itself against rack-renting and eviction. In some areas it virtually superseded English rule. To stave off demands for Home Rule, the Liberal government passed a series of land reforms, returning to the Irish most of the land seized by the English in the sixteenth and seventeenth centuries. Irish nationalism and self-confidence grew. The Gaelic League was formed in 1893 to promote the use of Irish and the publication of Gaelic literature. By 1906 it had a membership of 100,000. With it came a revival of Irish sports. The league improved the position of Gaelic, which had been in serious decline since the 1800, in both intermediate and primary schools; but the dream of a Gaelic-speaking Ireland could only be built on the economic and social rehabilitation of Gaelic-speaking areas, and this required political organization and agitation. In 1905 Sinn Fein was founded, aiming to re-establish independence by a withdrawal from Westminster and the setting up of an independent Irish Parliament in Dublin. Padraig Pearse read the Declaration of Independence from the steps of the Dublin Post Office during the 1916 Easter Rising.

In the elections of 1918 Sinn Fein swept the board. It boycotted Parliament at Westminster and set up an Irish Parliament, the Dail Eireann. The alternative government organized an army to support its claims for self-rule, the Irish Republican Army (IRA). By 1920 the IRA was an extremely effective guerrilla force against which, it was clear, full victory was impossible. In 1921 a truce was signed, and discussions commenced between De Valera and Lloyd George. The two major stumbling blocks were Ulster separatism and the position of Ireland inside the British Empire. The Irish negotiators finally capitulated on both points, against the wishes of many of the population, and in 1922 civil war broke out in the south between the Free State Party, which accepted the treaty, and those who opposed it. This civil war prevented Republicans from intervening in the north on behalf of a united Ireland. The Free State Party won, but partition was maintained, and in 1949 the Irish Free State became the Irish Republic, formally breaking its last links with the British Commonwealth.

With the establishment of the Free State in 1919 the restoration of the language was among the first priorities of the government.[2] The first session of the Dail was held largely in Irish. According to Article 8 of the constitution, 'the Irish language as the national language is the first official language'. Since 1946 there has been a remarkable increase in the numbers able to speak the language; the current figure is some 31 per cent of the population, or more than one million people. An estimated 4–5 per cent of people use the language regularly, most of them in the Gaeltacht, the sparsely populated western seaboard. The language is extensively taught in the education system, and teachers must be competent in both Irish and English. There is a network of Irish-medium primary schools; at secondary level Irish is mainly taught as a second language. Several hours of Irish public television broadcasting take place each week, and one national radio station has seventy-four hours of Irish broadcasting a week.

Protestants

The Protestants of the Irish Republic are concentrated in the counties immediately bordering Northern Ireland: Donegal, Cavan, Monaghan and Leitrim, the first three once part of Ulster. Protestants also form 9 per cent of the population of Dublin, with pockets scattered elsewhere in the republic, notably in Cork. They form a disproportionate number of large landowners and hold a disproportionate number of high-status jobs. This affluence and social status of Protestants has tempered many apparent restrictions. Article 44 of the Irish constitution, the most obviously discriminatory against Protestants – declaring that 'the State recognizes the special position of the Catholic Church as the guardian of the faith professed by the great majority of the citizens' – was repealed in 1972 after a referendum in which 88 per cent of the poll voted to abolish it. However, the real problems of discrimination come from the practices of the community and in particular intermarriage, since the Catholic Church extracts an undertaking that the children of the union will be raised in the Catholic faith, an undertaking enforceable in law.

Travellers

Travellers are indigenous to Ireland. There are two theories as to their historical genesis. The first considers them descendants of itinerant tradespeople from pre-Celtic times; the second, descendants of people driven to the roads during times of economic and political turbulence in the seventeenth and nineteenth centuries. Their origin is therefore different from that of Roma/Gypsies (see **Spain**), although they have been influenced by Roma/Gypsy cultures. In 1834 there were more than 2 million people on the roads of Ireland, among whom Travellers formed a distinct and recognizable group with a common language, Shelta or Gammon, deriving from the ancient secret languages of Ireland. The Travellers' way of life underwent dramatic changes from the 1950s as mechanization, the introduction of plastics, rural depopulation and the increased mobility of the remaining rural community meant that there was less demand for their craft skills and services. Only a minority of Travellers retain economic independence in an urban economy. Infant mortality among them is three times as high as that of the settled population; undernourishment is common, and their life expectancy is half the national average.[3]

Conclusions and future prospects

The 1937 Irish constitution considers Ireland to be a single country in which all inhabitants, north and south, have citizenship rights, and it formally claims Northern Ireland in Articles 2 and 3. But the Irish government has indicated that it would be prepared to change its constitution to achieve lasting peace in Northern Ireland. The outcome of any such peace process is unclear, as are its consequences for the Protestant community of the republic, which despite its continuing major economic influence is undergoing steady numerical decline.

Further reading

Darby, J., *Northern Ireland: Managing Difference*, London, MRG report, 1995.

Dublin Travellers' Education and Development Group, *Travellers Getting Involved*, Dublin, 1987.

Jackson, H. and McHardy, A., *Two Irelands: The Problem of the Double Minority*, London, MRG report, 1984.

Lyons, F.S.L., *Ireland since the Famine*, London, Fontana, 1973.

Noonan, P., *Travelling People in West Belfast*, London, Save the Children, 1994.

Minority-based and advocacy organizations

Amnesty International, 48 Fleet Street, Dublin 2, Ireland; tel. 353 1 6776 361, fax 353 1 6776 392.

European Bureau for Lesser Used Languages, 10 Sraid Haiste Iocht, Baile Atha Cliath, Irish Republic; tel. 353 1 6612205, fax: 353 1 6766840.

Institute Teangeolaichta Erin, 31 Plas Mhic Liam, Baile Atha Cliath, Irish Republic; tel. 353 1 6765489, fax 353 1 6610004.

Italy

Land area:	301,270 sq km
Population:	58.5 million (1996)
Main languages:	Italian, German, French, Greek, Albanian, Slovene, Sardinian, Friulian, Occitan
Main religions:	Roman Catholicism, Protestantism
Main minority groups:	Sardinians 1.6 million (2.7%), Friulians 600,000 (1%), South Tyrolese German-speakers 303,000 (0.5%), Roma/Gypsies 90,000–110,000 (0.15–0.17%), Slovenes 100,000 (0.17%), Moroccans 100,000 (0.17%), Albanians 100,000 (0.17%), Franco-Provençal-speaking Aostans 75,000 (0.13%), Occitans 50,000 (less than 0.1%), Tunisians 46,575 (less than 0.1%), Filipinos 40,292 (less than 0.1%), Jews 32,000 (less than 0.1%), Ladins 30,000 (less than 0.1%), Greek-speakers 10,000–12,000 (less than 0.1%), small numbers of French-speaking Aostans and Croatians, other new minorities including Cape Verdeans, Eritreans, Somalians and Ethiopians totalling 600,000 (1%)
Real per capita GDP:	$18,160
UNDP HDI/rank:	0.914 (20)

Italy was first unified under Cavour, the Prime Minister of Piedmont, between 1860 and 1866. This merger worked to the disadvantage of the impoverished south; and in the early days of unification southern autonomist and separatist sentiment revived periodically, to be forcibly suppressed. The southern Mafia presented itself as the protector of the southern people against the depredations of 'foreigners'. The new republic's constitution demanded it be '*una et indivisibile*'. Constitution, laws and institutions were simply expanded from Piedmont, which had followed heavily centralized French models, throughout the Italian peninsula.

The Italian postwar constitution provided for parliamentary government with two houses elected by proportional representation. It institutionalized regions as a means of decentralizing power and ensuring against totalitarian rule. The five 'special regions' are Sardinia, Valle d'Aosta, Trentino-Sudtirol, Sicily and Friuli-Venezia Giulia, with special status given to South Tyrol within Trentino-Sudtirol. There are also fifteen ordinary regions, put in place in 1970. Each region has an authorizing statute that functions as a constitution, a popularly elected unicameral regional council, an executive committee and a president, and special regions have powers to make laws and raise taxes. Ordinary regions are weak, a mirror of national-level politics rather than dealing with specific regional issues. However, with the resurgence of ethnic and cultural regionalism in the 1980s and 1990s, the regions began to call for more power and came increasingly into conflict with central government. The regions were excluded from the 1992 parliamentary commission to consider constitutional reform.

There have been fifty-three Italian governments since 1948. As traditional political parties have disintegrated into scandal and corruption, regional parties have assumed a new importance. In 1994 the Northern League was the most serious contender for partnership in Silvio Berlusconi's new government. However, opposition to its calls for a new federalist constitution meant that the National Alliance (AN), a coalition with fascist sympathies traditionally opposed to the encouragement of regional diversity, joined the government.

Sardinians

Sardinia, close to Corsica (see **France**), was administered by Spain from 1479 to the eighteenth century. Sardinians are the island's indigenous inhabitants. The Castilian language was used by officials and educators up to 1764, and Catalan (see **Spain**) is spoken in the town of Alghero. Several varieties of the Sardinian language are spoken, including Campidanese in the south and Logudorese in the north.[1] Sardinian is widely spoken among the island's population. Like the south of Italy, Sardinia has suffered from inappropriate policies dictated by northern industry, and emigration is high. The separatist Partidu Sardu Indipendentista had strong links with Corsicans and Basques. After the Second World War it was assumed that Sardinian autonomism would be a powerful force, and Sardinia was one of the first regions to be granted 'special status'. This has, however, done little to stop Sardinia's economic and cultural decline. Although Article 6 of the Autonomy Statute recognizes Sardinian as the second official language of the island, nothing has been done to secure its status, and the situation is complicated by the absence of a unified Sardinian language. Sardinian has recently been introduced as a subject in primary and secondary schools; and some Sardinian-language newspapers are published. In the early 1990s the more radical *Sardigna Natzione* was launched.

Friulians

There are an estimated 600,000 Friulian-speakers living in the provinces of Udine and Pordenone and in parts of Gorizia and Venice. The region of Friuli-Venezia Giulia, bordering Slovenia and Austria, has a total of 1,230,000 inhabitants. Although it was given autonomous status in 1947, it was not fully established until 1963. The decision to make Trieste the capital of the region met with resistance because Trieste is not a Friuli-speaking area and is regarded by the central government as a symbol of the achievements of the republic. The suggestion that Friuli should be made an administrative unit autonomous of Trieste and Venezia-Giulia has not so far been taken up.

Friulian, also known as Eastern Ladin, is a member of the Rhaeto-Romance language family and was used in government and law from the fourteenth century. Article 3 of the 1947 Regional Statute provides for instruction in local languages, but Friulian has been introduced only recently into state nursery schools. A 1993 regional act gave financial support to Friulian in primary schools, and it is taught as a separate subject in some secondary schools. Links have developed between Friulians and other Rhaeto-Romance language communities in South Tyrol and Switzerland.

South Tyrolese German-speakers

For fourteen centuries the inhabitants of South Tyrol, now on Italy's border with Austria, belonged to the German-speaking world. South Tyrol was ceded by Austria to Italy at the end of the First World War, together with predominantly Italian Trento. At that time the population of South Tyrol was 85 per cent German-speaking, and the annexation and consequent division of the Tyrol was widely resented. Mussolini vowed to achieve the complete Italianization of the region, and South Tyrolese experienced serious repression between the wars; speaking the German language in public was forbidden, German political parties and unions were liquidated, and schools and personal names were 'Italianized'. South Tyrolese were forbidden to participate in the industrialization of the province and barred from employment in factories; some also had land expropriated for industrial development. By the eve of the Second World War 25 per cent of the population was Italian, and South Tyrolese Germans were confined to the underdeveloped Alpine agricultural regions. In 1939 under an agreement between the Italian government and

Nazi Germany they were given the choice of maintaining their ethnic identity, by leaving their homes and transferring to Germany, or remaining in their homes and accepting full assimilation. Pressure was put on them to vote for Germany, and over 80 per cent did so; but by 1943 only 75,000 had left, and one-third of these returned after the war.

After the war many South Tyrolese Germans were anxious to have South Tyrol returned to Austria. However, with Austria occupied by Allied forces, the situation was uncertain. The Italian and Austrian governments signed the De Gasperi–Gruber Agreement of 1946, guaranteeing German-speaking inhabitants of Bolzano and Trento complete equality of rights with Italians and safeguards for their ethnic, cultural and economic development. German would be taught in schools, and German surnames were permitted once more. But the Austrians and South Tyrolese were disappointed and continued to insist on the possibility of eventual unification with Austria or self-determination. The Italian central government, wishing to forestall attempts to break away and to protect the Italian population in the region, granted very limited autonomy to the Province of Bolzano. On the regional level the province was twinned with Trento, a larger, wealthier and almost entirely Italian province. In the newly formed Trentino-Alto Adige region South Tyrolese were in the minority. Although the Autonomy Statute provided that the region 'normally' delegate its executive functions to the provinces, this was not the practice with Bolzano, and its practice was upheld by the constitutional court. The vast majority of South Tyrolese Germans supported the Sudtiroler Volkspartei (SVP), represented in the government of the province, but the cultural, economic and social development of South Tyrol remained in Italian hands in the region and in Rome. Increasing Italian immigration to the area created fears of Italianization. All this roused growing popular demands to make South Tyrol a region in its own right, and elements of the South Tyrolese resorted to terrorist attacks.

Internal and international pressures resulted in the improved autonomy package of 1972. While the newly named region of Trentino-South Tyrol still existed, many of its powers were transferred to the 'Autonomous Provinces' of Bolzano and Trento, including the remit for agriculture and tourism, which led to an economic boom in the area. Beneficial arrangements were made for financing the province. German was given full official-language status, equal with Italian, and all official announcements, documents and signs had to be in both languages. Education in the mother tongue, from nursery to tertiary levels, was guaranteed. Tourism has brought considerable wealth to the province, which is now almost wholly Germanic in language, culture and appearance, with a high standard of living and the best infrastructure and standard of public services in Italy. Such was the improvement in the situation of German-speakers that the problem has shifted to the decline of the Italian group in terms of numbers and morale – to the extent that some Italians declare themselves or their children 'Germans'.

While the majority of the South Tyrolese support the SVP, which won three seats in the 1994 elections, Italian-speakers in the region have given their vote to the neo-fascist AN, whose policies include the abolition of the Autonomy Statute. The notion of an Autonomous European Region of the Tyrol is attracting some interest. In principle this would allow for reunification of the Tyrol within Europe and leave central government with power only in matters of defence, justice, and foreign and monetary policy.

Slovenes

The majority of Slovenes live in 36 border municipalities in the Trieste, Gorizia and Udine districts of north-eastern Italy (see also **Austria**). Slovene-speakers number between 50,000–100,000 out of a regional population of 632,000. Trieste, the capital of Friuli-Venezia Giulia on the Istrian peninsula, was incorporated into Italy in 1919 but was claimed by Yugoslavia after the Second World War. The border between Italy and Yugoslavia (now Slovenia) was settled only in 1954 and confirmed in 1975 by the Osimo Treaty. In 1994 it was again in dispute as the National Alliance, coalition partners in the Italian government, claimed that the Osimo Treaty was no longer valid, having been drawn up with Yugoslavia, a state that in effect no longer exists. Italy based a territorial claim to the Istrian peninsula, now held by Slovenia and Croatia, on the rule of the Venetian republic from medieval times to the eighteenth century.

Berlusconi's government did not endorse these territorial claims but supported calls for compensation for Italian-speakers who had fled the Istrian region during and after the Second World War, and threatened to block Slovenia's application for membership of the European Union until this was forthcoming. This dispute has aroused fears of discrimination against the Slovene minority, exacerbated in 1994 when the National Alliance leader, then one of the parties of government, gave a speech demanding that the Slovenes 'kneel down before the Italian people'. However, Italian threats against Slovenia were lifted when the European Union supported a plan for Trieste to become a tax haven for Eastern Europe, a move which it is widely believed will bring prosperity to the region.

The Slovene minority in Trieste is protected by laws based on the London Memorandum of 1954 and reaffirmed in 1975. Slovenes are guaranteed equality with other Italian citizens and respect for their ethnic identity, most importantly in the provision of Slovene-language education from elementary up to further education in Trieste and Gorizia. However, in Udine Slovenes do not have clearly defined linguistic rights; nor do they have any right to use Slovene in dealing with the administration or legal system. The London Memorandum confirmed the latter right for the Slovene minority in Trieste, but it is realized in only four communities of the province. A 1975 Act making provision for television broadcasting in Slovene has never been put into practice, although there are radio services and some print media in Slovene.

Albanians, Greek-speakers and Croatians

Albanian-speakers (see **Greece**) in Italy number an estimated 100,000. Albanian has no legal language status. The language is taught in a small number of primary and secondary schools as an extra-curricular subject, and there are some bilingual road signs. The number of people learning to write Albanian is increasing, and the language's survival is bolstered by the Institute of Albanian Studies in Palermo. Greek is spoken in Puglia and Calabria by between 10,000–12,000 people. In Puglia, Greek is not used in nursery schools, although in two towns it is taught at elementary level. In Calabria it is taught at both elementary level and, in some schools, secondary level. Two Greek-language newspapers are published in Calabria. Croatian is spoken by some 2,000 people in three communities in the Molise region. It is not taught in schools and has no public presence, apart from some bilingual road signs.

Aostans and Occitans

The Valle d'Aosta borders Switzerland and France. The area was part of Savoy until 1860, when Savoy was joined to France, and Valle d'Aosta was joined to Italy. There was continuous emigration to France from the region until the Second World War. The French language was banned from schools in 1879 and from law courts in 1880. In 1919 Aostans sent a delegation to Bern to ask to be accepted into the Swiss Confederation, but they were refused. Italian slowly gained ground in the region, and this process accelerated between 1923 and 1934, when French was banned from all sectors of public life. Aostans were active in the wartime resistance and formed the Union Valdotaine (UV) after the war, demanding federal status within a French or Swiss state and representing some 80 per cent of the population. French troops entered the area in 1945 but withdrew under pressure when the Italian government set up an autonomous regime. The UV attempted to persuade the Western Allies to include bilateral guarantees for the region in the peace treaty with Italy, as had happened in the treaty between Austria and Italy over South Tyrol. This move failed. From 1948 to 1970 the Valle d'Aosta was governed by the 1945 statute and was an officially recognized region, with school lessons in both French and Italian and administrative posts filled by bilingual people. Other than this, however, the level of autonomy was more apparent than real.

The total population of the Valle d'Aosta is 115,000. Franco-Provençal is spoken by 75,000, while French-speakers comprise 5–7 per cent of the population. The 1984 Statute of Regional Autonomy gave French and Italian equal validity, but not Franco-Provençal. French may be used in court; place names are exclusively French; and recruitment for regional bodies is conditional on French proficiency. The statute stipulated that schools must devote the same time to teaching French as Italian; but again no provision was made for Franco-Provençal. In 1991 the regional council took a federalist stance, together with Trentino and Friuli.

South of the Valle d'Aosta, in the border area of Piedmont, close to France, there are an estimated 50,000 Occitan-speakers (see **France**). The Occitan language has no official status and is chiefly confined to the home. The region of Piedmont has, however, passed two laws promoting and protecting cultural resources and the area's linguistic and cultural heritage.

Ladins

Central Ladin, a neo-Latin language related to Romansh, is spoken by some 30,000 people (out of a total population of 35,000) in valleys in the Dolomites and Cortina d'Ampezzo. It has been officially recognized since 1948 in the province of Bolzano/Bozen, and since 1989 in Trento and Belluno. Ladin is afforded full legal and administrative protection in the former province, where some knowledge of Ladin is necessary to be eligible for employment in the local administration. Ladin is taught as a subject in Bolzano schools, but in Trento it is taught for one hour a week only in primary schools. Ladin television broadcasts have been transmitted by the regional station in Bolzano since 1988.

New minorities

In the nineteenth and first half of the twentieth centuries Italy was a country of emigration. Immigration, resulting from the workings of the free market in a country with a large informal sector, began in the 1970s, and the number of non-EU nationals in Italy is estimated at between 800,000 and 1 million. The first immigrants were women from the Philippines and Cape Verde, who came to work as domestic workers in private households. There were also male immigrants from Italy's former colonies of Ethiopia, Eritrea and Somalia who came to work as traders in agriculture and construction. The 1990 Martelli Law put an end to immigration and attempted to regularize foreign workers' status, but it was largely unsuccessful because of the demand for unregularized labour. Racist attacks on members of new minorities increased significantly in 1994 and 1995.

Conclusions and future prospects

Conflict between regions and central government is a major feature of Italian political developments. Regions refused to join the Conferenza Permanente Stato-Regioni, the consultative body linking regions and central government, because of disagreements over finance and reform. Loss of interest in traditional political parties, devastated by corruption allegations, and the crisis in the traditional political structure have resulted in the fostering of regional identities. However, regional reforms are exacerbating rather than mitigating the disparities between the north and south; northern regions, with their stronger civic traditions, are better placed to take advantage of regionalism and are strengthening their links with the European Union. Indeed, the new regionalism in Italy, although apparently an appeal to tradition, is a turning towards the European Union in protest at the ineffectiveness of central government. On the other hand, anti-European coalitions and parties that favour a strong central state and Italian nationalism have also gained ground. These developments have had a strong impact on minorities. Roma, southerners and 'immigrants' are scapegoated by northern regionalist parties. The UN Committee against Torture has highlighted a tendency towards racism on the part of law-enforcement officers in Italy. The UN Human Rights Committee also shares its concern that the majority of victims of ill-treatment in Italy are non-nationals or belong to minorities.

Further reading

Alcock, A., 'Trentino and Tyrol – from Austrian crownland to European region', in Dunn S. and Fraser, T. (eds), *Europe and Ethnicity*, London, Routledge, 1996.

Desideri, C., 'Italian regions in the EC', in Jones B. and Keating M. (eds), *The European Union and the Regions*, Oxford, Clarendon Press, 1995.

Keating, M., *State and Regional Nationalism*, Hertfordshire, Harvester Wheatsheaf, 1988.

MRG and TWEEC (eds), *Minorities in Central and Eastern Europe*, London, MRG report, 1993.

MRG (ed.), *Minorities and Autonomy in Western Europe*, London, MRG report, 1991.

Minority-based and advocacy organizations

Amnesty International, Viale Mazzini 146, 00195 Rome, Italy; tel. 39 6 3751 4860, fax 39 6 3751 5406.

Associazione Donne Arabe e Straniere in Emilia Romagna (ADASER), Via Ripa Inferiore 14, 41013 Castel Franco Emilia, Italy.

Associazione Internazionale per la Difesa delle Lingue e delle Culture Minacciate (International Association for Threatened Languages and Cultures), Via Firenze 24, 13053 Chiavazza, Italy; tel. 39 15 22744.

Associazione per i Popoli Minacciati (Society for Threatened Peoples), PO Box 6282, 50127 Florence, Italy; tel./fax 39 55 488600.

CONFEMILI (National Committee for Linguistic Minorities), Via P. Bonfante 52, 00175 Rome, Italy; tel./fax 39 6 7158 3488.

Federazione delle Organizzazioni delle Comunità Straniere in Italia, Via dei Salentini 3, 00185 Rome, Italy.

Frontiere magazine, Piazza Carducci 3/2, 40125 Bologna, Italy; tel. 39 51 349149, fax 39 51 6142684.

Italian Helsinki Committee, Corso Duco di Genova 92, 00121 Rome, Italy; tel. 39 6 56 46 313, fax 39 6 56 46 314, e-mail: a.stango@agora.stm.it

Liechtenstein

Land area:	160 sq km
Population:	30,000 (1994)
Main languages:	German
Main religions:	Roman Catholicism
Main minority groups:	Swiss 4,500 (15%), Walsers 2,500 (8.3%), Austrians 2,100 (7%), Germans 1,200 (4%)
Real per capita GDP:	—
UNDP HDI/rank:	—

Liechtenstein is a tiny European principality located between Switzerland and Austria. Its official language is German. The country is a constitutional monarchy divided into eleven *Gemeinden* (communes) governed autonomously but under central government supervision. Women received the vote only in 1984. Liechtenstein's Walsers are descendants of immigrants from the Swiss canton of Valais who settled in the mountain commune of Triesenberg at the end of the thirteenth century and continue to speak a distinctive form of German. (Other Walsers are settled in Italy, Austria and Switzerland.) Sixty per cent of the labour force are migrant workers.

Minority-based and advocacy organization(s)

Verkenhrsburo, Dorfzentrum Janaboda, 9597 Treisenberg, Liechtenstein; tel. 41 75 262 1926.

Luxembourg

Land area:	2,586 sq km
Population:	395,000 (1993)
Main languages:	Letzeburgish, French, German
Main religions:	Roman Catholicism
Main minority groups:	Portuguese 42,650 (10.8%), Italians 19,850 (0.5%), also French, Belgians, Germans and Roma/Gypsies
Real per capita GDP:	$25,390
UNDP HDI/rank:	0.895 (27)

More than 30 per cent of the population of the Grand Duchy of Luxembourg are non-citizens. Portuguese represent some 35 per cent of Luxembourg's minority populations, followed by Italians (18 per cent). Other significant communities of foreign nationals are French, Belgian and German. Citizenship is open only by birth in Luxembourg to a parent born in Luxembourg. The local population of some 270,000 speak Letzeburgish, a member of the Germanic language group, as the everyday, informal medium of oral communication, although it cannot be written with accuracy, and few Luxembourgers can read it easily. Luxembourgers also speak French and German and use both for written communication. Education is generally in German in the early years and later in French. French is the language of the courts and, in the main, of parliamentary documentation. Since the mid-1980s Letzeburgish has gained ground, and it is now recognized as a national language of Luxembourgers and permitted to be used in administrative and judicial matters.

Minority-based and advocacy organizations

Actioun Letzebuergesch – Eis Sprooch, 21 Breede Wee, L1917 Luxembourg; tel. 353 470 612.

Malta

Land area:	316 sq km
Population:	359,000 (1994)
Main languages:	Malti, English
Main religions:	Roman Catholicism
Main minority groups:	—
Real per capita GDP:	$11,570
UNDP HDI/rank:	0.886 (28)

The islands of Malta (Malta, Gozo and Comino) in the central Mediterranean have been settled since the third century BCE. By the Norman invasion of CE 1090 the islands had been ruled by the Carthaginians, the pagan Roman Empire, the Christian Roman Empire and the Arabs. The islands were then governed by feudal lords until 1530 when they were ceded to the Hospitaller Knights of St John of Jerusalem. By the 1814 Treaty of Paris the Maltese became subjects of Great Britain on condition that the Roman Catholic Church was maintained and the Maltese Declaration of Rights was honoured. Malta attained independence in 1964. About 95 per cent of the islanders are Maltese-born; the remaining inhabitants are mostly of English or Italian descent. The Maltese language, Malti, is the medium of everyday conversation. There are no minority groups.

Monaco

Land area:	1.5 sq km
Population:	30,000 (1994)
Main languages:	French, Italian, English, Monégasque
Main religions:	Roman Catholicism
Main minority groups:	Monégasque 4,600 (15.3%), Italians 4,600 (15.3%)
Real per capita GDP:	—
UNDP HDI/rank:	—

Situated on the Mediterranean coast of France, close to the Italian border, Monaco is the world's smallest state after the Vatican City. It has been independent since 1861. The majority of the population are French. Monaco's Monégasque and Italian-speaking communities number some 4,600 people each, and there are about 1,300 British inhabitants. The official language is French, and education is in French. Monégasque, a mixture of French Provençal and Italian Ligurian, has been introduced into the school curriculum and may be continued to *baccalauréat* level. There is an increasing awareness of the importance of maintaining Monégasque traditions and culture.

The Netherlands

Land area:	41,526 sq km
Population:	15.2 million (1994)
Main languages:	Dutch, Frisian
Main religions:	Protestantism (mainly Dutch Reformed Church), Roman Catholicism
Main minority groups:	Frisians 700,000 (4.6%), Indonesians 240,000–295,000 (1.6–1.9%), Turks 203,000 (1.3%), Surinamese 200,000 (1.3%), Moroccans 157,000 (1%), Moluccans 40,000 (0.3%), Roma/Gypsies/Sinti 35,000–40,000 (0.2–0.3%), Jews 25,000 (0.16%), Chinese 20,900 (0.14%)
Real per capita GDP:	$17,740
UNDP HDI/rank:	0.938 (4)

The United Kingdom of the Netherlands was dissolved in 1830 following the Belgian revolt, and the Netherlands was confined approximately to its present borders. Since the early nineteenth century the Netherlands has been characterized by political consensus and 'pillarization', whereby Catholics, Protestants and Socialists/Liberals each had their own political parties, trade unions, newspapers, broadcasting organizations, welfare associations and even football teams. This system has decreased in importance since the 1960s but is still influential.

Frisians

Frisians inhabited the land north of the Rhine and remained independent until the seventh century (see also **Germany**). From the eleventh century onwards Frisians developed a seawater drainage system which reclaimed for agriculture a vast peat bog. This led to an increase in population and brought about growth in industry and commerce as well as agriculture, helping to develop towns into centres independent of external authority. In 1648 Friesland joined the United Republic of the Netherlands. While this hastened the decline of the Frisian language, which was already under pressure from German and Dutch, it also marked the beginnings of the modern Frisian movement and its promotion of Frisian language and literature. The Frisian movement is principally a linguistic one.[1]

Unlike Frisians of Germany, Frisians of the Netherlands have had some political recognition. Their language enjoys official status and is promoted through the Ried fan de Fryske Biweging (Council of the Frisian Movement). The language is most widely spoken, by an estimated 400,000 people, in West Friesland. Emigration from Friesland to other provinces of the Netherlands has resulted in a diaspora of some 300,000 Frisian speakers outside Friesland.[2] In 1955 Frisian was recognised as a medium for instruction in the first two years at primary level and as a subject in later years, and in 1975 the Dutch government agreed to the introduction of Frisian as a teaching medium in all classes at primary level and as a compulsory subject. Frisian is not, however, represented at secondary level.

Indonesians, Moluccans and other new minorities

The immigration of Indonesians and Moluccans to the Netherlands began after the Second World War and the decolonization of Indonesia. From the late 1950s through the 1960s thousands of guestworkers were recruited first from Spain and Italy, and later from Turkey and Morocco. Initial government policy was based on the assumption that these workers were temporary. A policy shift occurred in the 1970s to 'integration with preservation of cultural identity'; this approach was at first intended for only the Moluccan community but later applied as a model for minority policies in general. After 1973 migration consisted mainly of family reunification.

Unemployment among the new minorities is high, and they are concentrated in poor urban housing. Since 1994 a policy of domestic surveillance of migrants has been formulated. Citizenship is acquired by birth in Netherlands to a

Netherlands-born parent, or by naturalization which requires 'integration into society'.

Moluccans were members of the Dutch colonial army fighting in Indonesia.[3] In 1949, when Indonesia won independence, the Dutch government undertook to negotiate with its former colony so that the Moluccans could return to an independent republic of South Molucca. In the meantime they would remain in camps – many of them dating from the German wartime occupation – in the Netherlands countryside. When it became clear that an independent South Molucca would not come into being, unrest arose among the Moluccan community. An agreement was reached whereby the Netherlands was released from its commitment to negotiate for an independent South Molucca, in exchange for Moluccan integration into the Dutch labour market. Affirmative action would be used to bring 1,000 Moluccans into government service. Some Moluccans moved into specially built neighbourhoods in the early 1970s; only very recently did the last of them move out of the camps.

Suriname provided the Netherlands with guestworkers in the 1950s and 1960s. A second migration came after 1975, when Suriname proclaimed independence, and middle-income Surinamese took advantage of their Dutch citizenship to emigrate. Nearly a third of the population left. Most of the migrants were of Asian Indian origin. By the 1990s approximately half of the Surinamese population lived in the Netherlands.

Conclusions and future prospects

Friesland has no regional organization directly responsible for its economic life, and the agrarian Frisian population has been hard hit by the mechanization of agriculture and by outmigration. The stresses this places on the language are increased by the region's growing role as a tourist centre. In 1992 and 1993 neo-Nazis attempted to take over the annual celebration on 26 September of the 1345 victory of a Frisian peasant army over a Dutch invading force. In 1994 the organizers decided to make anti-fascism the central theme of the event, an important development linking old and new minorities. With the 'minority debate' of 1992–3 the emphasis of national policy shifted from mechanisms excluding new minorities from participation in Dutch society to the responsibility of minorities for their own position; minority communities have since been blamed for their own marginalization. Amid a rise in racist attacks, the UN Committee on the Elimination of All Forms of Discrimination has condemned the Netherlands for not enforcing its criminal laws against racism.

Further reading

Hira, S., 'Holland: the bare facts', *Race and Class*, vol. 32, no. 3, Jan.-Mar. 1992.

MRG (ed.), *Minorities in Western Europe*, London, MRG report, 1993.

Minority-based and advocacy organizations

Amnesty International, Keizersgracht 620, 1017 ER Amsterdam, Netherlands; tel. 31 20 626 4436, fax 31 20 624 0889.

Fryske Akademy, Doelestrjitte 8, 8911 DX Ljouwert/Leeuwarden, Netherlands; tel. 31 58 131 414, fax 31 58 131409.

Gabungan Jajasan Maluku [Moluccan], Achter St Pieter 160, 3512 Utrecht, Netherlands; tel. 31 30 231 880.

Holanda Turkish Women's Association, Mauritskade 22d, 1091 GC Amsterdam, Netherlands.

Landelijke Organisatie Surinamese Vrouwen, Postbus 4062, 3502 HB Utrecht, Netherlands; tel. 030 541887.

Landelijke Sinti Organisatie, Best, Netherlands; fax 31 49 837 2915.

Marokaanse Vrouwenvereniging in Nederland, Hemonystraat 14, 1074 BP Amsterdam, Netherlands; tel 020 6647954.

National Federation of Welfare Organizations for Surinamese People, Oudegracht 312, 3500 Utrecht, Netherlands; tel. 31302 302 240.

Netherlands Helsinki Committee, Jansveld 44, 3512 BH Utrecht, Netherlands; tel. 31 30 302 535, fax 31 30 302 524.

Samenwerkingsvervand van Marokkanen en Tunesiers [Moroccan and Tunisian organization], Keistraat 4, 3512 HV Utrecht, Netherlands.

UNITED for Intercultural Action, Postbus 413, 1000 AK Amsterdam, Netherlands; tel. 31 20 683 4778, fax 31 20 683 4582, e-mail: united@antenna.nl

Norway

Land area:	323,900 sq km
Population:	4.3 million (1994)
Main languages:	Norwegian (two official forms: Bokmaal and Nynorsk), Sami
Main religions:	Lutheran Christianity
Main minority groups:	Sami 60,000–100,000 (1.4–2.3%), new minorities 100,000 (2.3%), small Roma/Gypsy and Jewish populations
Real per capita GDP:	$20,370
UNDP HDI/rank:	0.937 (5)

From 1814 to 1905 Norway was united with Sweden but retained its own parliament. Concern for Norway's northern border with Finland and Russia resulted in a concerted 'Norwegianization' policy from the 1860s onwards. There was a substantial Finnish-speaking community called the Kvens in that area, many of them intermarried with Sami, and the ill-conceived policy aimed to 'civilize' both groups. The Kvens were last registered as a separate group in the 1930 census; it is widely believed that the group has completely disappeared through assimilation. Norway has two standard forms of the same language: Bokmaal ('Book language', or Dano-Norwegian) and Nynorsk ('New Norwegian'); they have equal official and educational status.

Sami

Sami (previously known as Lapps, a name they consider derogatory) are the indigenous inhabitants of northern Norway, Sweden and Finland, and the far north-west and north-east of Russia.[1] In Norway they are concentrated mainly in Finnmark County, where there are some 25,000 out of an estimated 60,000–100,000 Norwegian Sami. The Norwegian Sami Act 1987 defined a Sami as someone who has Sami as a first language, or whose father or mother or one of whose grandparents has or had Sami as a first language, and who considers themselves a Sami. Within the prevailing unity of Sami ethnic identity exist linguistic, economic and cultural group distinctions.

Part of the Sami Act concerns the status of the Sami language. An estimated 20,000 people in Norway speak one of its three Finno-Ugric dialects. Sami is in everyday use in its northern core area and is now an official language in five municipalities in Finnmark County and one municipality in Troms County; it is therefore also an official language in the courts. In coastal and other areas, however, the language is losing ground to Norwegian.

Sami have lived in Samiland since time immemorial. Significant colonization of their areas by southern farmers began in the fifteenth and sixteenth centuries. The Norwegian government later encouraged this process as part of its Norwegianization policy. At the same time among Sami there occurred a gradual transition from the hunting of wild reindeer to the practice of herding, with the result that Sami became a nomadic people. The drawing of national borders, for example the 1751 division between Norway and Sweden, made their movement across traditional grazing lands more difficult. Many Swedish northern Sami were forcibly displaced from summer lands in Norway to southern areas of Sweden, and southern Sami were forced to accept them on their territory.

Today few Sami are nomads, and in Norway less than 10 per cent are now reindeer herders. Major elements of the Sami cultural tradition are the *yoik* (music consisting of rhythmic poems or poetic songs), the use of reindeer sleds for transport, crafts and a knowledge of ecology. Central to Sami culture, among both herders and non-herders, is the reindeer, and the continuation of herding is regarded as essential to the survival of Sami culture and identity. While the modernization of reindeer herding may offer new opportunities to Sami, the shrinking of their herding lands, coupled with environmental damage, threatens the continuation of this way of life.

Sami organizations have won significant concessions from the Norwegian state. In 1980 the Sami Rights Commission was established to deal with political and economic issues. Although this body has failed to address key legal questions of landownership and resource rights, it paved the way for the establishment of the Norwegian Sami

Assembly, the Sameting, which was inaugurated in 1989. The Sameting has the power to take initiatives in Sami concerns and to ensure that Norway fulfils its international obligations. In 1988 an addendum to the Norwegian Constitution declared it 'the responsibility of the authorities of the state to create conditions enabling the Sami people to preserve and develop its language, culture and way of life'.

Norway ratified ILO Convention 169 of 1989 on the rights of indigenous and tribal peoples in 1990 (although it claims that strongly protected rights of usage are sufficient to fulfil the criteria for admission of landownership rights). The same year the government submitted new legislation to give the Sami language equal legal status with Norwegian and to increase the possibilities for using Sami in an official context. Such moves are not entirely popular, however; in 1994 the leader of the far-right Progress Party called a fellow member of parliament an extremist after she made part of her speech in the Norwegian Parliament in Sami, and he asked whether MPs would be forced to listen to debates spoken in Sami, Urdu or any other 'language incomprehensible to most Norwegians'.[2]

There are also Swedish and Finnish Sametings (Assemblies) (see **Finland, Sweden**). Nordic cooperation among Sami was initiated in 1953, and in 1956 it was decided to establish the Nordic Sami Council. The Nordic Sami political programme, adopted in Tromso in 1980, sets out certain principles: Sami are one people and should not be divided by national boundaries; they have their own history, traditions, culture and language and an inherited right to territories, water and economic activities; they have a right to self-development; and they will safeguard their territories, natural resources and national heritage for future generations.

The Nordic Sami Council has been known as the Sami Council since 1992, when representatives of Russian Sami joined it. Through the Sami Council Sami participate on the World Council of Indigenous Peoples, and since 1989 the Sami Council has had consultative status with the Economic and Social Council of the United Nations.

New minorities

After the Second World War, Norway began to experience the immigration of foreign workers, a trend that accelerated with the development of North Sea oil in the late 1960s. In 1993 there were some 147,800 foreign workers in Norway, 3.4 per cent of the population. Many of these people were from elsewhere in north-west Europe, including 17,000 from Denmark, 12,000 from the UK and 12,000 from Sweden, but southern Europeans, Turks and refugees from former Yugoslavia are also present.[3] The proliferation of violent far-right groups is a problem in Norway, legitimized by the success of the anti-immigrant Progress Party. In 1993 the Department of Justice ruled that Turkish families had no right to give their children Turkish names, because this could 'cause serious social problems for the child' and create difficulties for schools and authorities.

Conclusions and future prospects

Norwegian Sami face problems of resource rights and imposed and non-sustainable development that are common to many indigenous peoples today. Their grazing lands are increasingly exploited by industry and tourism, and only a small minority are now directly involved in reindeer herding. Towns and municipalities that are majority Sami experience emigration to urbanized areas in other regions. It remains to be seen whether the Sami diaspora will participate in the Norwegian Sameting. Also of concern is the rise of the Progress Party, which doubled its support in local elections in September 1995 despite the acknowledged attendance of its immigration spokesperson at a meeting of racist fringe groups.

Further reading

Beach, H., *The Sami of Lapland*, London, MRG report, 1988.

Beach, H., 'The Sami of Lapland', in MRG (ed.), *Polar Peoples: Self-Determination and Development*, London, Minority Rights Publications, 1994.

Minority-based and advocacy organizations

Amnesty International, PO Box 702, Sentrum, 0106 Oslo, Norway; tel. 47 22 429460, fax 47 22 429470.

Norwegian Anti-Racist Center, Postbox 44, Sentrum, 0103 Oslo, Norway; tel. 47 22 171750, fax 47 22 170561.

Norwegian Helsinki Committee, Urtegaten 50, 0187 Oslo, Norway; tel. 47 22 570070, fax 47 22 570088.

Norwegian Institute of Human Rights, Grensen 18, N0159 Oslo, Norway; tel. 47 22 421360, fax 47 22 422542.

Norwegian Organization for Asylum Seekers, PO Box 8893, Youngstorget, 0028 Oslo, Norway; tel. 47 22 208440, fax 47 22 332748.

Norwegian People's Aid, PO Box 8844, Youngstorget, 0028 Oslo, Norway; tel. 47 22 037700, fax 47 22 200870.

Norwegian Sameting/Sami Assembly, Box 144, 9730 Karasjohka, Norway.

Portugal

Land area:	92,390 sq km
Population:	9.8 million (1994)
Main languages:	Portuguese
Main religions:	Roman Catholicism
Main minority groups:	Azoreans 350,000 (3.6%), Madeirans 300,000 (3%), Africans 45,000 (0.5%), Roma/Gypsies 40,000–50,000 (0.4–0.5%), Brazilians 11,000 (0.1%), Asians 4,000 (less than 0.1%)
Real per capita GDP:	$10,720
UNDP HDI/rank:	0.878 (35)

The Portuguese Republic consists of the south-western Iberian peninsula and the island possessions of Madeira and the Azores. Portugal's borders were fixed before those of the other current nation states of Europe and have remained unchanged since the fall of the old Muslim 'Kingdom of the West' in the Algarve. In the fifteenth century the nobility's imperial expansions took them to North and West Africa in search of gold and slave labour to work the Algarve estates. For the next two centuries the Portuguese Empire expanded to include Brazil, Macao and other territories in Africa. The African colonies won independence after the overthrow of Portugal's four-decades-old fascist regime in 1974.

Azoreans and Madeirans

Madeira and the Azores were settled in 1419 and 1427 respectively to supply corn and wheat to the mainland. The 1976 post-revolutionary constitution granted some autonomy to the islands, but both continue to press for greater autonomy and are critical of rule from Lisbon. Most Azoreans are peasant farmers employed by large landowners. Significant numbers of both Azoreans and Madeirans have emigrated in search of better opportunities – the former to North America, the latter to Venezuela. Remittances from the USA are a major source of income in the Azores. Madeirans, who are Portuguese citizens with full rights of entry and settlement in Portugal, have enjoyed improved standards of living in recent decades; infant mortality has fallen, educational provision has improved and emigration has slowed.

New minorities

In the 1970s considerable numbers of migrants came to Portugal from its former African colonies: Angola, Cape Verde, Guinea-Bissau and Mozambique. They lived in shanties on the outskirts of Lisbon or in ghettos in the old city and worked as casual labourers and domestics, replacing Portuguese who had migrated to work in northern Europe. Until 1992 any citizen of the former African colonies could come to Portugal, but restrictions were imposed following the ratification of the Schengen Convention in 1990. At the same time an increase has been reported in the number of Brazilians excluded, and Brazilian nationals have allegedly been mistreated by police at Lisbon Airport.

Conclusions and future prospects

Emigration from poorer areas of Portugal continues. Azoreans, whose islands are poor and have little tourism potential, appear unlikely to reverse patterns of emigration and remittance dependency. For Madeirans, with improving social and economic conditions, an economy based on tourism and agriculture, and prospects of economic diversification, the outlook is more hopeful. 'Portugal Day', 10 June, has been marked by far-right activity during the 1990s, and a recent increase in racist attacks is cause for concern.

Minority-based and advocacy organizations

Amnesty International, Rua Fialho de Almeida, No. 13, 1o, 1070 Lisboa, Portugal; tel. 351 1 386 1664, fax 351 1 386 1782.

OIKOS/Cooperação e Desenvolvimento, 35 Avenida Visconde Valmor, 1000 Lisboa, Portugal; tel. 351 1 764719.

Portuguese Committee for Aid to Refugees, Avenida Duarte Pacheco, Tôrre 2–5–2, 1000, Lisboa, Portugal; tel. 351 1 651327.

San Marino

Land area:	61 sq km
Population:	23,000 (1994)
Main languages:	Italian, Sanmarinesi
Main religions:	Roman Catholicism
Main minority groups:	—
Real per capita GDP:	—
UNDP HDI/rank:	—

The Republic of San Marino is surrounded on all sides by Italy and traces its origins to the early fourth century. During the nineteenth-century movement for Italian unification, San Marino offered asylum to revolutionaries, among them Garibaldi. Its independence has remained unthreatened ever since, save for when Italian troops massed on the border in 1957 to bring down the republic's communist government. This so-called 'bloodless revolution' led to rule by a centre-left coalition which continued until the 1990s, when a new Social Democrat–Christian Democrat coalition was formed. A sizeable element of San Marino's population now consists of non-San Marino citizens, mainly Italians. Sanmarinesi is a widely spoken dialect of Italian. No minority rights issues have been identified.

Spain

Land area:	504,780 sq km
Population:	39.1 million (1994)
Main languages:	Castilian Spanish, Catalán, Valenciano, Basque, Gallego (Galician)
Main religions:	Roman Catholicism
Main minority groups:	Catalans 6.25 million (16%), Galicians 3.1 million (7.9%), Basques 780,000 (2%), Roma/Gypsies 650,000–800,000 (1.7–2%), South and Central Americans 167,500 (0.4%), Moroccans 58,000 (0.1%), Asians 36,000 (less than 0.1%), Jews 20,000 (less than 0.1%)
Real per capita GDP:	$13,660
UNDP HDI/rank:	0.933 (10)

The Kingdom of Spain occupies most of the Iberian peninsula and also includes the Balearic Islands, the Canary Islands and small enclaves in Morocco. The North African Moors ruled most of the Iberian peninsula from the eighth to the fifteenth centuries. Outside their area of rule, in the far north, there arose powerful Christian local magnates with strong family alliances. From the eleventh century, during the period known as the Reconquista, the chief families gradually united against the Moors. In 1492 Ferdinand of Aragon and Isabella of Castile, rulers of the two most powerful kingdoms, ended the Muslim presence in Spain. The expulsion of an estimated 800,000 Jews and 3 million Muslims, and the persecution of Roma/Gypsies, enforced national unification through religious belief and orthodoxy, but local institutions survived. Spain embarked on three centuries of conquest in the Americas, during which time the separatist claims of the northern regions – each economically linked to different colonial possessions – grew. Under Bourbon rule in the eighteenth and nineteenth centuries the Spanish state was centralized, a tendency countered by the First Republic of 1873 with a disastrous attempt at federation. At the turn of the twentieth century, with the loss of its last American colonies, Spain plunged into crisis.

In 1936 the Popular Front gained a narrow electoral victory. Among its innovations was the granting of autonomy to the regions. Fear of political fragmentation was one of the rallying cries of the right under General Franco during the Civil War of 1936–9. Following the Nationalist victory, Franco's centralized state banned every language and dialect other than Castilian, and Spanish national unity was celebrated in education and the media. This fuelled a backlash, and regionalism and demands for autonomy grew. In 1975, following the death of Franco, the nature of relations between Spain's regions and the centre was the major constitutional question.[1] The 1978 constitution proclaimed 'the indissoluble unity of the Spanish Nation', while recognizing and guaranteeing 'the right to autonomy of the nationalities and the regions'. The 'nationalities' are Catalonia, Euskadi (the Basque Country) and Galicia, all of which had majority votes for autonomy under the 1931 constitution. Together with Andalusía, they have achieved autonomy under Article 151 of the 1978 constitution. Other regions negotiated autonomy statutes under Article 143, which gave reduced powers in comparison with Article 151. The constitutional court plays a crucial role in resolving disputes and in shaping the nature of the relationship between the seventeen autonomous regions and central government. Some nationalist aspirations will be satisfied only by complete independence. The aspirations of some autonomous regions, particularly the Basque Country, are viewed by the Spanish state as a threat.

Catalans

Catalonia, in north-east Spain, was a former principality and in medieval times the centre of a large trading empire. The language of the region, Catalán, is closer to Provençal than to Spanish, and its variants are spoken throughout the north-east, on the Balearic Islands (conquered by Catalans in the twelfth century), and in Andorra, France and Sardinia. Catalans have a tradition of strongly held regionalism. On 11 September every year they commemorate the 1714 siege of Barcelona by the Bourbon monarchy, which led to the loss of Catalan self-rule. A nationalist movement arose in the nineteenth century as Catalonia became increasingly industrialized and prosperous. It remains today one of Spain's wealthier regions.

During the Civil War, Catalans supported the Republicans and fiercely opposed the centralizing nationalism represented by Franco. With defeat in 1939 Catalans experienced severe repression at the hands of the Nationalists. Their autonomous government was abolished and its leader was shot; regionally based political parties were outlawed; economic sanctions were applied; and public use of the Catalán language, and expressions of Catalan culture, were banned. Official policy was partially relaxed during the 1950s, and Catalans came to the fore in resistance to Franco's dictatorship, although generally rejecting the violence of the Basque struggle. Catalans entered the post-Franco era with widespread strikes in support of their demands for regional autonomy. The 1978 Statute of Autonomy created the Generalitat de Cataluña with wide powers of local government. This has been dominated by the CiU (Convergence and Union), a centre-right coalition. Following the 1993 elections, the Partido Socialista Obreros Españoles (PSOE) government was reliant on the support of the CiU's 17 MPs to remain in power. It withdrew support in September 1995, causing a crisis in central government. The 1993 elections also saw the Esquerra Republicana de Cataluña winning 200,000 votes; the ERC calls for a 'greater Catalonia' encompassing Catalán-speakers of south-west France.

According to the 1986 census, 90 per cent of the population of Catalonia understand Catalán, and 64 per cent speak it. Under the Statute of Autonomy, Catalán is, together with Castilian, an official language, and in 1983 the Linguistic Normalization Act was passed, with the aim of encouraging the use of Catalán in all areas of life, including public administration and education. By 1990 approximately 30 per cent of children in Catalonia were being educated entirely in Catalán. Some channels of the public television network broadcast only in Catalán, and books and other cultural productions are often in Catalán.

Valencianos

There are an estimated 1.9 million Valenciano-speakers. Valencia's economy owes much of its prosperity to agricultural techniques introduced by the Moors. Valencian nationalists are marked by differences in attitudes to Catalonia. Some regard Valencia as part of a common political project for all Catalán-speaking territories, while others seek an independent relationship with Madrid. This is reflected in the political debate over Valenciano; although linguists agree that it is a variety of Catalán, the 100,000 supporters of the regionalist Unión Valenciana consider it a separate language. Valenciano is spoken by half the region's total population of 3.8 million. The inhabitants of the western strip of Valencia speak Castilian. Under Valencia's 1981 Statute of Autonomy, Valenciano and Castilian are official languages. Valenciano has some public presence and is used in signposts and information notices. Administrative procedures are carried out in both Castilian and Valenciano. In 1983 the Use and Teaching of Valenciano Act was passed, and Valenciano is now a compulsory subject at all educational levels.

Galicians

Galician, in the far north-west of Spain, is a region that withstood both Roman conquest and Moorish domination. One of the major languages of the Reconquista, Gallego (Galician) advanced through Galicia to Portugal, where it has since become the language of state. Galician culture shares roots with Celtic culture and includes the playing of bagpipes and a tradition of lyric poetry. In the wars against the Bourbons, Galicia acted as a separate kingdom, but only in the early twentieth century was an explicitly nationalist group founded, Solidaridad Gallega. Long one of Spain's poorest regions, the landowning patterns prevalent in Galicia have resulted in a highly dispersed and impoverished rural population without the economic or political strength to challenge Madrid. On the eve of the Civil War, however, four-fifths of Galicians voted for autonomy, and currently more than 90 per cent of the population of 2.8 million understand Gallego. In 1982 Galicia won its Statute of Autonomy, but it continues to be a poor rural area, with a high proportion of emigrants, both to other areas of Spain and abroad. There are currently disputes over whether Gallego, which is an official language, should be codified as it is spoken in Portugal or in Galicia.

Basques

Basques are the long-established inhabitants of the region on either side of the western Pyrenees;

the vast majority live in Spain rather than on the French side. Their language differs markedly from other Indo-European languages, and this distinctiveness indicates origins unlike those of their Western European neighbours. For Basque nationalists Euskadi, the Basque Country, takes in the four Spanish provinces of Álava, Guipúzcoa, Navarra and Vizcaya, and the French *pays* of Labourd, Soule and Lower Navarra. Situated between the mutually antagonistic powers of France and Spain, the region was divided in 1512 by a Franco-Spanish border treaty. While the Spanish provinces came under the rule of the Catholic kings, they were granted *fueros*, legal and financial arrangements which brought a measure of independence. Conquest in the Americas and the development of ethnography gave Basque intellectuals a new-found interest in their people.

Basque nationalism became significant in the nineteenth century, when the Basque country was industrialized. As the region's prosperity grew, its mining and shipbuilding industries brought large-scale immigration from poorer areas of Spain. This led to the alienation of rural Basques. Sabina Arana-Goiti, the first Basque ideologue, defined Basques anthropologically and linguistically, forbade 'intermarriage' and opposed Spanish immigration and immigrants. In 1895 he founded the Basque Nationalist Party (Partido Nacionalista Vasco, or PNV). In October 1936, on the eve of the Civil War, the Second Republic approved the Basque autonomy statute. Basques supported and fought with the Republicans in the Civil War, and their region suffered viciously at the hands of the Nationalists, whose German allies bombed Guernica, the ancient Basque capital. Franco's victory and the Republicans' defeat unleashed a tide of revenge against Basques. Some 21,000 Basques died in the aftermath of the war; thousands more went into exile or were imprisoned. Under the Franco regime all traces of self-government were lost; the Basque language was banned; and teachers unable to demonstrate 'political reliability' were removed from Basque schools. The PNV formed a government in exile in France.

In 1954 Basque Homeland and Freedom (Euskad Ta Azkatasurra, or ETA) was formed. Separatist and revolutionary-socialist, unlike the PNV it advocated class struggle, the overthrow of the dictatorship and solidarity with Spanish immigrants. According to ETA, anyone who sold their labour in the Basque Country was entitled to be considered Basque. ETA's war against the Spanish state – involving bank robberies, kidnappings and assassinations – had a huge impact. The government replied with repressive police tactics, including illegal detention and mistreatment of prisoners. In 1968 the government declared a state of emergency. ETA was in forefront of the struggle against Franco, and in 1973 it assassinated the Prime Minister and Franco's self-appointed heir, Admiral Carrero Blanco.

With Franco's death in 1975 Basque nationalists demanded full independence. Rejecting the 1978 Spanish constitution, they called for sovereignty, self-determination and measures to improve the working and living conditions of the working class. The regional autonomy statute agreed in 1979 left sections of Basque opinion unsatisfied. The PNV continued its commitment to greater autonomy (avoiding the word 'independence'). ETA proceeded with its bombing campaigns, experiencing a rise in popularity during the next decade. A new Basque left-wing alliance, Herri Batasuna (United People), which rejected working within the Spanish state system, also gained support. Also during the 1980s, according to recent allegations, government-financed units waged a 'dirty war' on ETA in which more than two dozen Basques were killed.

During the first half of the 1990s support for both the ruling Socialists (voted out of national office early in 1996) and for ETA – which has been accused of perpetrating indiscriminate violence – declined among Basques. In January 1995, 150,000 people took part in a silent march against terrorism in Bilbao. But Basque nationalism remains vibrant. With strong roots in popular culture, exemplified by the slogan '*martxa eta borroka*' ('liveliness and struggle'), it welcomes all those who 'feel Basque' to take part in the political struggle. It also continues to challenge the government.

The Basque language has official status in Basque-speaking and mixed areas, delimited by a 1986 Language Act. Basque is an official language in Euskadi, where all schools teach the language as a subject or have it as a medium of instruction. It is not the usual language of the regional administration, however. In Navarra, which borders the Basque Country (as defined by the Spanish state), Basque was once spoken almost universally. By the thirteenth century the language was in decline, and today approximately 50,000 people in northern Navarra speak Basque. Predominantly agricultural, Navarra did not experience the rapid industrialization of the other Basque provinces, and by the late 1980s less than 15 per cent of its population considered themselves Basque.

Roma/Gypsies

Of the estimated 10 million Roma/Gypsies throughout the world, between 7 million and 8.5 million live in Europe, and between 650,000 and 800,000 live in Spain.[2] After Spain, the largest Western European Roma/Gypsy populations are in France (280,000–340,000), Greece (160,000–200,000), Germany (110,000–130,000), the United Kingdom (90,000–120,000) and Italy (90,000–110,000). Also known variously by such names as Gating (in Spain), Romany, Rom, Sinti and Zingari, the first Roma/Gypsies left north-west India between the ninth and the fourteenth centuries. They are recorded in Europe as early as the fourteenth century in Serbia, and from there they appear to have spread through Greece, Bohemia, France and then Spain, where their earliest presence is noted from 1425. Throughout these travels some Roma/Gypsies attached themselves to a given territory, while others continued to migrate. They often encountered and mixed with indigenous European traveller groups, such as the Quinquis of Castile.

Those Roma/Gypsies who stopped or limited their travelling within a region mixed with the local sedentary population. Thus in Andalusía the local culture, particularly the music and style of dress, is profoundly influenced by Roma/Gypsy traditions. This is not to say that Roma/Gypsies were welcomed, however. The first anti-Roma/Gypsy laws in Spain were established in 1499, under Ferdinand and Isabella, when they were given sixty days to find themselves a trade and a master, and forbidden to travel in groups. In 1560 'the habit and the costume' of Roma/Gypsies were prohibited, while in 1611 they were compelled to take up farming on land left fallow by the Moors. Repressive anti-Roma/Gypsy legislation was enacted throughout Europe, and Spain was unusual among European countries of the Middle Ages in adopting a policy of enforced integration rather than exclusion. Whereas in Switzerland, Italy and France the stateless were condemned to torture or penal servitude – in 1727 any Roma/Gypsy over fifteen found in the jurisdiction of Berne was to have an ear cut off, for example, and if caught a second time was to be killed – in Spain Roma/Gypsies were ordered to integrate, on pain of death. Yet this did not protect them from the power of the state. In 1749 a round-up of thousands of Roma/Gypsies was carried out; those who had settled were easiest to locate and incarcerate. For centuries Roma/Gypsies have experienced deportations and extradition; their migrations to Africa and the Americas, for example, were mainly the result of deportations by the Portuguese and the Spanish in the seventeenth century, followed by similar measures taken by Britain and France. During the Second World War, hundreds of thousands of Europe's Roma/Gypsies died at the hands of the Nazis.

As their history in Spain and elsewhere makes clear, not all Roma/Gypsies are nomadic, and many have been sedentary for a long time. In Spain, partly because of centuries of enforced integration, urbanization and sedentarization, it is estimated that only 5 per cent are itinerant. In Europe as a whole, only an estimated 20 per cent, at most, of Roma/Gypsies and Travellers live in mobile accommodation and are regularly on the move, while semi-nomads travelling only part of the year constitute another 20 per cent of this population, and those who never travel (although many of them live in very precarious conditions) make up the remaining 60 per cent. Today, as in the past, sedentary Roma/Gypsies, like their itinerant counterparts, experience inequality, racism and persecution. In Spain their unhealthy living conditions and susceptibility to infectious diseases have resulted in low life expectancy – only 5 per cent of Roma/Gypsies are aged over 55 – and high infant mortality (eleven per thousand). With high birth rates, more than half the Roma/Gypsies of Spain are aged under fifteen; up to 75 per cent per cent are illiterate; more than half lack formal employment; and most of those employed earn less than the minimum wage. Racist attacks on Roma/Gypsies have taken place in Spain, as well as outbreaks of police violence towards them.

Some improvements have occurred. In Spain, local authorities have provided some housing. A Roma/Gypsy member of the Spanish Cortes (Parliament) achieved the repeal of discriminatory legislation dating from the Franco dictatorship, and the government has established reception classes for Roma/Gypsy children, although many remain entirely without formal education. Roma/Gypsies share many of the problems of the new minorities in Western Europe, partly because many members of both groups lack citizenship rights. Laws restricting freedom of movement within the European Union have impacted negatively on them.

Ceuta and Melilla

Ceuta is a Spanish enclave in Morocco, first occupied by Portugal in 1415, transferred to Spain in 1688 and retained after Moroccan independence. Melilla, a small peninsula on the Mediterranean coast of Morocco, has been occupied by Spain since 1495. Two-thirds of the territory of Ceuta, and more than half of Melilla, are retained by the Spanish state for military use. The Moroccan government was infuriated when, in September 1994, Spain approved autonomy statutes for Ceuta and Melilla, bringing them under the administration of Andalusia. Spain has been criticized for its treatment of new minorities in these territories. In 1992 the delegate of the Spanish government in Melilla ordered riot police to break up a meeting of one hundred Africans and put them into the inter-frontier zone between Melilla and Morocco, where they had to live for almost two months without aid in the desert. By 1995 in Ceuta some 300 refugees had been living for more than four years in a former discotheque with no electricity, running water, sanitation, or medical or legal help.[3]

New minorities

There are officially some 361,000 non-citizens in Spain, although these figures are almost certainly a major underestimate. It has been suggested that undocumented migrants number 170,000–260,000, or as many as half the total number of legally resident foreigners. Many of Spain's legal foreign residents are retired citizens from other EU countries. Central and South America have been the other main source of immigrants, while significant numbers have also come from North Africa, the Philippines, Guinea and Central Africa. Many of these migrant labourers work in mines and textile factories and on flower farms, and as construction labourers, vendors and domestic workers. Among Latin Americans, those from South America are often political exiles and well educated, while those from Central America and the Spanish-speaking Caribbean tend to be poorly educated and work mainly in domestic service.[4] Increasing numbers have come from the Dominican Republic, Argentina and Peru. Spanish citizenship is granted only by birth in Spain to a Spanish-born parent, thus giving rise to significant numbers of children deprived of legal rights. The 1986 Ley de Estrangeros made it almost impossible to enter Spain legally, and Spain has entered into agreements to control immigration with France, Turkey and Morocco.

Police violence against members of new minorities, as well as Roma/Gypsies, is widely documented. Harassment, beatings and murders by ordinary Spanish citizens have increased. In 1993 an opinion poll of young Spanish people found that 31 per cent supported the expulsion of all Roma/Gypsies, and 26 per cent the expulsion of North Africans and Arabs. There have been recent attempts to unify far-right groups under the racist and anti-Semitic Movimiento Social Español, which also calls for the Catalan and Basque nationalist movements to be outlawed.

Conclusions and future prospects

In 1994 the Spanish government agreed to consider reform of the Senate to increase regional representation, provided a consensus was retained on the constitutional process. This was in the face of increasing demands from the regions and popular disillusion with central government; the outcome remains to be seen. The authorities have also promised to clamp down on organized racist attacks, which increased in terms of the number of recorded incidents from 3 in 1991 to 250 in 1994; again, the results are still unclear. The current main concern within the Roma/Gypsy movement is whether, in the light of current European Union immigration and asylum policy, to take the path of a general and universalizing invocation of human and minority rights, or to emphasize Roma/Gypsy specificity and exceptionality within migratory populations.

Further reading

Abellan, A.C., *Marginalidad de la población gitana española,* Murcia, Universidad de Murcia, 1992.

Collins, R., *The Basques*, Oxford, Blackwell, 1986.

Forsyth, M., *Federalism and Nationalism*, Leicester, Leicester University Press, 1989.

Gunter, R. (ed.), *Politics, Society and Democracy: The Case of Spain,* Oxford, Westview Press, 1993.

Liégeois, J-P. and Gheorghe, N., *Roma/Gypsies: A European Minority*, London, MRG report, 1995.

Medhurst, K., *The Basques and Catalans*, London, MRG report, 1987.

Minority-based and advocacy organizations

Acción Cultural Pais Valencia, 46002 Valencia, Spain; tel. 34 6 6 351 1727.

Amnesty International, PO Box 50318, 28080 Madrid, Spain; tel. 34 1 531 2509, fax 34 1 531 7114.

Asociación de Enseñantes con Gitanos, Lele del Pozo 20, 28028 Madrid, Spain.

Asociación de Solidaridad con los Trabajadores Inmigrantes, Cava Alta 25, 28005 Madrid, Spain; tel. 34 1 265 6448.

Colectivo IoE, Calle Luna 11, 1 derecha, 28004 Madrid, Spain; tel. 34 1 531 0123, fax 34 1 532 9662.

Federación de Organizaciones de Refugiados y Asilados en España (FEDORA), Arlaban 7, Oficina 46, 28014 Madrid, Spain; tel. 34 1 523 1618/523 3491, fax 34 1 523 3491.

HOEGOA [Basque], Centro de Documentación e Investigación, Facultad de Económica de la UPV, 48015 Bilbao, Spain; tel. 9 4 447 3512, fax 9 4 476 2653.

Presencia Gitana, Valderrodrigo, 76 y 78 Bajos, 28039 Madrid, Spain.

Spanish Helsinki Committee, Monika zu Lowenstein, Donosco Cortes 8, E28015 Madrid, Spain.

Sweden

Land area:	449,960 sq km
Population:	8.7 million (1994)
Main languages:	Swedish, Finnish
Main religions:	Evangelical Lutheran Church of Sweden
Main minority groups:	Finns 260,000 (3%), citizens of other Nordic countries 90,100 (1%), former Yugoslavs 75,500 (0.9%), Iranians 51,000 (0.6%), Turks and Kurds 35,900 (0.4%), Roma/Gypsies 15,000–20,000 (0.2%), Jews 16,000 (0.2%), Sami 15,000 (0.2%)
Real per capita GDP:	$17,900
UNDP HDI/rank:	0.933 (9)

Sweden, which occupies about two-thirds of the Scandinavian peninsula, has been a constitutional monarchy since the early nineteenth century. Norway, its western neighbour, was united with Sweden until it became independent in 1905. When still a predominantly agricultural country in the nineteenth century, Sweden experienced massive emigration; one-fifth of its population left, mainly to find arable land and work in the USA. Sweden's long tradition of abstention from wars and military alliances, its almost unbroken period of government by the Social Democratic Labour Party between 1932 and 1976, and its apparently successful combination of industrial capitalism with a strong welfare state made it for many years a European model of social and political stability. In the 1990s, however, economic problems have led to cutbacks in welfare services, and for the first time since the 1930s large-scale unemployment has become a problem. Children of minority groups in Sweden have a right to teaching in their mother tongue; Finns of Tornedalen, Sami and Roma/Gypsies have special rights in this respect.

Finns

There are two Finnish-speaking groups in Sweden. Finnish-speakers have lived in the north of Sweden since before the Swedish state existed. In Tornedalen (Torne Valley) live approximately 25,000 speakers of Tornedal-Finnish, a variant of standard Finnish, and more Tornedal-Finnish-speakers live in other northern areas. At the turn of the century there was an intense 'Swedification' policy, but this had abated by the 1930s. In 1937 the Swedish and Finnish foreign ministries agreed on the principle of bilingualism for Tornedalen. There are also large numbers of more recent Finnish immigrants to Sweden.

Sami

Sami are indigenous to Scandinavia (see also **Finland, Norway**). Approximately 15,000 of them live in Sweden. The Swedish state gives resource privileges to Sami to maintain their unique culture, which is officially interpreted as 'reindeer herding'. Because of concerns about damage caused by Sami reindeer to settlers' property, herding and farming have been kept largely apart, with a significant area of territory officially designated as herding land, although much of this is unusable as pasture. Between 300 and 500 reindeer are permitted per family. Should a herder come to depend more upon non-herding sources of income, their membership in the herding collective with accompanying resource rights can be questioned. The herding unit, the *sameby*, can engage in no economic activity other than reindeer herding. In principle, the Swedish Supreme Court acknowledges Sami immemorial land rights, but these rights and Sami landownership are disregarded in practice. As elsewhere in Scandinavia, the rise of extractive industries and tourism poses a threat to herding and the traditional Sami way of life.

The Swedish Sami face serious language loss; 40 per cent of the non-herding population cannot speak the language, and 85 per cent cannot write it. However, as they have become better organized they have won increased support for the maintenance of their language, including the right to mother-tongue teaching in Swedish schools. There are six Sami schools in Sweden where children receive instruction in Sami at elementary level. Sami children are allowed four weeks a year out of school to participate in reindeer herding. Among the principal Swedish Sami organizations are the Sami National Union, founded in 1950, the Sami-Atnam, which is mainly a cultural organization, and the Confederation of Swedish Sami, which is composed chiefly of non-herding Sami. In 1992 the Swedish Parliament passed Proposition 1992–93:32 establishing a national Swedish Sami Assembly or Sameting, but this has only advisory status.

New minorities

Sweden recruited foreign workers from 1947 onwards to work in the expanding industrial sector.[1] Migrant workers came mainly from Finland, Yugoslavia, Turkey and, particularly following the 1967 coup, Greece. Except for Nordic citizens and family reunion, worker immigration was regulated in 1967 and stopped in 1972. After 1970 Sweden began to receive refugees from, first, Latin America and, later, the Middle East. More than 50 per cent of the immigrant population are naturalized Swedes. The Swedish constitution makes provision for the promotion of opportunities 'for ethnic, linguistic and religious minorities to preserve and develop a cultural and social life of their own'; and it states that 'a foreigner within the Realm shall be equated with a Swedish citizen in respect of protection against discrimination on grounds of race, skin colour, ethnic origin, or sex'.[2] These ideals have not always translated into reality. The unemployment rate among Sweden's new minorities is well above the national average; and despite having a higher-than-average degree of education, non-nationals work disproportionately in monotonous and physically strenuous jobs and for low earnings.

Conclusions and future prospects

Sweden's refusal to recognize Sami legal and resource rights has made Sami culture and identity vulnerable. Recent legislation limiting traditional hunting and fishing rights has caused huge protests. Swedish Sami have increasingly resorted to legal action to defend themselves and their rights, taking cases to the UN Human Rights Commission and the European Court of Human Rights, as well as the national courts. The Swedish government was in early 1996 considering accession to the European Charter for Regional or Minority Languages. With regard to its new minorities, although Sweden has accepted refugees openly since the Second World War it has recently tightened its definition of refugees to exclude so-called 'economic refugees'. The everyday racism and xenophobia experienced by members of new minorities are a matter of serious concern.

Further reading

Alund, A. and Schierup, C-U., *Paradoxes of Multiculturalism: Essays on Swedish Society*, Aldershot, Avebury, 1991.

Beach, H., *The Sami of Lapland*, London, MRG report, 1988.

Beach, H., 'The Sami of Lapland', in MRG (ed.), *Polar Peoples: Self-Determination and Development*, London, Minority Rights Publications, 1994.

Tagil, S. (ed.), *Ethnicity and Nation Building in the Nordic World*, London, Hurst, 1995.

Minority-based and advocacy organizations

Amnesty International, PO Box 23400, 10435 Stockholm, Sweden; tel. 468 729 0200, fax 468 34 1608.

Centre for Research in International Migration and Ethnic Relations, 10691 Stockholm, Sweden.

Life and Peace Institute, Sysslomansgatan 7, 75170 Uppsala, Sweden.

Minority Rights Group Sweden, Flogstavagen 47 A, 75263 Uppsala, Sweden; tel. 46 18 464046, fax 46 66 04586.

National Finnish Federation of Sweden, Box 3081, 10361 Stockholm, Sweden.

Raoul Wallenberg Institute, Sankt Annegatan 4, 22350 Lund, Sweden; tel. 46 46 107000, fax 46 46 104445.

Svenska Tornedalingars Riksförbund/Swedish Association of Tornedal-Finns, Aapua 6, 95794 Matarenki-Övertorneå, Sweden; tel. 46 927 24074, fax 46 927 24085.

Sverigefinska Riksförbundet Ruotsinsuomalainen Keskusliitto/Swedish Association of Finnish-Speakers, Bellmansg. 15 nb, 11847 Stockholm, Sweden; tel. 468 615 8343.

Swedish Helsinki Committee, Kammakargatan 9B III, 11140 Stockholm Sweden; tel. 46 8 791 8445, fax 46 8 791 8448.

Swedish Sameting/Sami Assembly, Geologgatan 4, 98131 Kiruna, Sweden; tel. 46 980 82702, fax 46 980 83541.

Switzerland

Land area:	41,290 sq km
Population:	7 million (1994)
Main languages:	Swiss-German/Schwyzerdutsch, French, Italian, Romansh
Main religions:	Roman Catholicism, Protestantism
Main minority groups:	French-speakers (including Jurassiens, c.67,000) 1.3 million (18%), Italian-speakers 500,000 (7%), former Yugoslavs 200,000 (2.8%), Portuguese 150,000 (2.1%), Spanish 120,000 (1.7%), Rhaetians/Romansh-speakers 50,000 (0.7%), Roma/Gypsies 30,000–35,000 (0.4–0.5%), Jews 18,300 (0.3%)
Real per capita GDP:	$22,720
UNDP HDI/rank:	0.926 (15)

Switzerland is a landlocked country at the crossroads of northern and southern Europe, bordering France, Italy, Germany, Austria and Liechtenstein. Sixty-five per cent of its population are Swiss-German-speakers, as is most of its business and financial community. The Swiss alliance dates from 1291, when the three states (cantons) of Uri, Schwyz and Unterwalden united against their oppressors to form the 'Everlasting League'. During the Reformation, Switzerland became increasingly polarized between the German-speaking Protestant cities and the French-speaking Roman Catholic countryside. Despite this, the unity of the federation held. During the European conflicts of the seventeenth and eighteenth centuries Switzerland remained neutral. Its policy of armed neutrality still obtains today.

Provision for French- and Italian-speaking minorities

Although Swiss-German-speakers constitute a numerical majority of the Swiss population, their language, Schwyzerdutsch, is a minority one among German-speakers generally.[1] Swiss-German-speakers are also a far from homogeneous group, comprising Protestants and Catholics, urban and rural dwellers, upland and lowland communities, and speakers of a range of local dialects and variants. Hence the belief widely held among Swiss that all Swiss are members of minority groups.

There are three levels of authority within the Swiss federal state structure, the lowest being the 3,000 communities.[2] Communities' rights and duties are set down by the cantonal laws and so depend on the canton where they are situated. The community legislative body may either be a communal assembly, in which all adult citizens participate, or, in larger groups, a communal parliament. Communities have taxation powers and may deal with matters such as schools, sport, traffic and refuse collection. The 26 cantons are the next level of authority, sovereign in all matters not specifically covered in the constitution, and sharing some responsibilities, such as education and culture, with the confederation. The legislative authority of the canton is a one-chamber parliament, and there is also a popularly elected cantonal executive. Cantons may tax their residents and have sole responsibility for care of the poor and police affairs. The confederation is ruled by the Federal Assembly, which comprises the 200-member National Council – the direct representatives of the people – and the Council of States. All legislation can be altered either by referendum or by initiative – that is, by formal procedures in which the citizen replaces the lawmaker. Thus the diversity and freedom of each canton are respected, and citizens are united in a way that transcends differences of language.

The Swiss system has been advocated as a constitutional model for the respect and management of diversity. Swiss cantons often have within them enclaves of other cantons, and language and political borders often cross each other, with the result that the Swiss appear at ease with 'political maps that look like patchwork quilts'.[3] Of the four Swiss official languages – German, French, Italian and Romansh – the first three must appear on state documents and federal regulations, for example, and do generally appear in such other contexts as journals and advertisements. Airline and railway announcers use whatever language is most useful in the specific situation. Italian-speaking deputies have the right to use Italian in parliament, although German and French are always used at committee stage. Despite these provisions, French- and Italian-speaking Swiss share a sense of belonging to minority communities, especially in the face of Swiss-German economic dominance.

Rhaetians/Romansh-speakers

Romansh, a Rhaeto-Romance language of Latin origins, is Switzerland's fourth national language. It is spoken by about 50,000 people. All Romansh-speakers live in the trilingual canton of Graubunden/Grisons (Grischun in Romansh) in eastern Switzerland. There is a chair of Romansh Literature at the University of Zurich. In June 1983 the Federal Parliament passed the Federal Law Concerning Contributions to Cantons Graubunden and Ticino for the Promotion of their Cultures and Languages. This stipulated that funds were to be set aside to encourage the Rhaeto-Romance language and culture, and it gave the Lia Rumanscha, the official representative of Romansh culture, the obligation to report through the cantonal government to the federal Department of the Interior. More effective laws were approved in early 1996.

Despite this, Romansh has continued its long decline, mainly for economic reasons, since Romansh-speakers are poor peasants in the high valleys of the upper Rhine. Many have now emigrated to lowland regions for work, and the tourist industry has brought large numbers of Swiss-German-speaking workers to the Romansh heartland. Now less than 50 per cent of the population in the canton speak the language. Unlike Italian and French, Romansh has no external support and cannot rely on media broadcasts and publications from countries where it is a widely spoken language.

Ticino and Jura: minority enclaves

Also protected in the Federal Law of June 1983 are the language and culture of the residents of the canton of Ticino, located in the south of Switzerland and surrounded on two sides by a border with Italy. Italian is the main language of Ticino and has been since the fifteenth century. Migration of Italian workers to Ticino has been significant since the end of the Second World War and currently accounts for about 40 per cent of the canton's population.

The Jura region, French-speaking for nine centuries, was joined to the predominantly German-speaking canton of Berne as a result of the Congress of Vienna in 1815. Although French remained the language of local administration and education, during the 1960s and 1970s Roman Catholic Jurassians formed a militant separatist movement, the Rassemblement Jurassien. This popular movement was frustrated for many years by the Swiss-German-speaking Protestant bureaucracy and resorted to arms to achieve its aim. This was achieved on 1 January 1979, when after a referendum the new canton of Jura, with a population of 67,000, became part of the Swiss federation. The Jura region was split in two, because Protestant villages had voted to remain in the Bern canton. There have been occasional outbreaks of violence on the part of those Jurassians who believe the split is a betrayal of nine centuries of history.

New minorities

Switzerland has a high proportion of non-citizens in its population, about 1.2 million out of a 7 million total. Perhaps a third of these non-citizens are Italian, and another third are non-European Union and non-European Free Trade Area (EFTA) nationals. Swiss nationality is by descent. Naturalization must be based on at least 12 years' residence, and integration and can be too expensive for workers' families to afford. In June 1994 voters rejected proposals to make it easier for young foreigners to obtain Swiss citizenship. Immigration is now limited to temporary, seasonal and border workers; the latter cross the frontier daily but reside in neighbouring European countries. Workers with seasonal or annual permits numbered 268,904 in 1990, many of them young men from impoverished areas of Portugal. Switzerland has historically not welcomed refugees.

Conclusions and future prospects

Switzerland has long been regarded as a model in dealing with minority communities by having a truly participative democracy beginning at the village level. This democratic structure satisfies the needs of its historic minorities, each of which has the right to defend its cultural identity, and has enabled the Swiss to avoid intercommunal strife. However, Switzerland gives little protection to its new minorities and may be viewed as a case study in difficulties arising from exclusive communities. Non-citizens are excluded from democratic participation, and Swiss communities rarely accept immigrants to their citizenship registers. In 1995 the Swiss people voted for the police sweeping new powers to imprison foreign workers. With Swiss territories linked with Italian, German and French territories through membership in the Arges (see **regional introduction**), questions of citizenship and territoriality are likely to remain on the Swiss agenda throughout the 1990s.

Further reading

MRG (ed.), *Minorities and Autonomy in Western Europe*, London, MRG report, 1991.

Minority-based and advocacy organizations

Amnesty International, PO Box, 3001 Bern, Switzerland; tel. 41 31 307 2222, fax 41 31 307 2233.

Fundaziun Retromana, Francetg Friber, Casa Cardun, 7163 Danis, Switzerland; fax 41 81 941 2419.

Groupement pour les Droits de Minorités/ Minority Rights Group Switzerland, CP 33, 1211 Geneva 16, Switzerland; tel. 41 22 733 7762, fax 41 22 734 4712.

Lia Rumantscha, Via de la Plessur 47, 7001 Coira/Chur, Switzerland.

Romani Union, Via Scazziga 10, Locarno-Muralto, Switzerland.

Soros Roma Foundation, Zurich, Switzerland; fax 41 13 836 302.

Swiss Helsinki Committee, Postfach 6363, Spitalgasse 34, 3001 Bern, Switzerland; tel. 41 31 311 0432, fax 41 31 312 5363.

United Kingdom

Land area:	243,368 sq km
Population:	57.8 million (1994)
Main languages:	English, Welsh, Gaelic, Bengali, Chinese, Gujarati, Urdu, Punjabi
Main religions:	Church of England, Roman Catholicism, Presbyterianism, Methodism, Baptism, Hinduism, Islam
Main minority groups:[1]	Scots 5.1 million (8.8%), Welsh 2 million (3.5%), Northern Irish 1.5 million (2.6%) (including Catholics 700,000, 1.2%), Indians 840,800 (1.5%), Afro-Caribbeans 499,100 (0.9%), Pakistanis 475,800 (0.8%), Jews 300,000 (0.5%), Black Africans 207,500 (0.4%), Bangladeshis 160,300 (0.3%), Chinese 157,500 (0.3%), Roma/Gypsies 90,000–120,000 (0.16–0.2%), also Manx-speakers, Irish, Cypriots and Vietnamese
Real per capita GDP:	$17,230
UNDP HDI/rank:	0.924 (16)

The United Kingdom of Great Britain was established in 1707 when the parliaments of Scotland and England joined together. The United Kingdom of Great Britain and Ireland was created in 1801 with the dissolution of the Irish parliament. The UK was weakened by the First World War and the following deep recession. In 1931 the British Community of Nations (Commonwealth) was established under the Statute of Westminster, which formally recognized the independence of Canada, Australia, New Zealand and South Africa. By the end of the Second World War, the power of the British Empire was eclipsed by the United States. India and Pakistan became independent in 1947, and most of Britain's colonies won independence during the following two decades.

Scots

The original Scots, who gave their name to Scotland, the northern part of the island of Great Britain, were Gaelic-speakers from Ireland who settled in the west of Scotland in the fifth century.[2] The territory had long been inhabited by Picts, and after centuries of war the Scots and Pict crowns were unified in 843. The use of the Gaelic language spread, even south of the border. Gaelic was never predominant in the Lothians, however, where following the invasions of Angles and Saxons people spoke Lallands, a dialect of Anglo-Saxon. This later accrued elements of Latin, French, Icelandic and Gaelic and developed into a language in its own right, Scots.

Following the eleventh-century Norman invasion, many English-speakers fled to Scotland, and in the following centuries English was also used as a language of trade by merchants from the European mainland who traded in Scotland. At the beginning of the fourteenth century Edward I of England was determined to incorporate Scotland into his kingdom. There followed long and destructive wars for 300 years. Southern parts of the land were occupied by English forces, and areas were planted by English settlers. Scotland had been converted to Christianity by the Celts, but there was no Gaelic or Scots Bible; English gained prestige as the language of the church. The Reformation divided lowlanders, who became Protestant, from Gaels, who remained Catholic. James VI of Scotland viewed Gaelic citizens as savages and settled the more 'civilized' lowlanders in the Highlands. This disrupted Gaelic contacts with Ireland, which had helped keep Gaelic culture alive. It also entrenched animosity between Gaelic- and Scots-speakers and dislocated Gaelic from Scottish nationality.

James VI acceded to the English throne in 1603, uniting the two crowns and ensuring the departure of the Scottish court to England. The Act of Union 1707 united the two parliaments and made English the language of legislation for all the countries of Great Britain. Scotland retained its independent institutional framework in law, local administration, education and religion.

By 1714, when a non-Scottish dynasty came to the throne, Scots Highlanders were on the defensive. After the Battle of Culloden in 1745 the clan system was dismantled; a monetary economy was introduced; and the Highlands were opened to 'development'. The Highland Clearances, when crofters were forced off the land they had farmed for centuries to make way for sheep, devastated the environment and forced many to emigrate. Emigrés established Gaelic-speaking communities in Canada, some of which survive. There are, for example, about 1,000 speakers of Scots Gaelic in Cape Breton Island, Nova Scotia, descendants of the eighteenth-century emigrants.

The Education Act (Scotland) 1872 enforced 'universal' education but contained no provisions for the teaching of Scots or Gaelic, accelerating linguistic assimilation. This Act introduced new forms of knowledge that had no relation to Scots and particularly Gaelic culture, and laid the basis for a system which identified able children and took them away from home. The quality of Scots so deteriorated that by the end of the First World War it was no longer in use as a communal language, despite the efforts of the poet Hugh MacDiarmid. Gaelic fared slightly better, due to the continuing support of emigrants and the founding of An Comunn Gaidhealach (the Highland Association) in 1891, with its annual Gaelic cultural festival, which developed into an education pressure group. The largest concentrations of Gaelic-speakers today are in the Western Isles (almost 80 per cent Gaelic-speaking in 1981) and Skye and Lochalsh (almost 54 per cent); there are other concentrations in Sutherland and Argyll, and small pockets of Gaelic-speakers in many Scots towns and cities. In 1958 Gaelic became the medium of instruction in primary schools in the Highlands, and since 1959 there has been Gaelic radio and television broadcasting. Scotland has its own legal and education systems, which differ at all levels from the English systems. However, the lack of education in the history and literature of Scotland, and the little use made of Gaelic by public bodies and the law courts, have been criticized.

Scots continue to fight for political independence. Between 1889 and 1927, 21 legislative attempts were made to regain Scottish independence. In 1928 an assortment of organizations campaigning for Home Rule and self-determination came together to form the National Party of Scotland, and in 1932 this merged with the Scottish Party to become the Scottish National Party (SNP). In 1978 the Devolution (Scotland) Act was passed, but it was not put into effect because of a requirement that it attract 60 per cent support in the ensuing referendum. The SNP is now the second party of Scotland after the Labour Party. Lack of support for the governing party of Westminster, the Conservative Party, whose share of the vote in Scotland had fallen to about 12 per cent by the mid-1990s, has increased Scots disillusion with current political structures. Scots nationalists are divided over plans for devolution; some regard it as a step in the right direction, others as a sop.

Welsh

Speakers of Welsh, a Celtic language related to Cornish and Breton, inhabited large areas of Britain under the Roman Empire. A sense of Welsh unity in the face of the Anglo-Saxon invasions seems to have emerged by the middle of the sixth century, when the inhabitants of the western peninsula of Britain called themselves Cymry ('fellow countrymen') and their territory Cymru. Anglo-Saxons called them Wealas ('foreigners'), from which derives 'Welsh'. The peninsula was regularly attacked, not just from the east but from the sea by the Norse. It had close contacts with Ireland and Cornwall, and for some time Welsh culture flourished. Until the Norman Conquest, Wales was ruled essentially as a number of dynastic principalities with shifting alliances; but by 1100 the Normans had overrun large areas of the east and south. In 1282 the last prince of Gwynedd died, and Edward I completed the English conquest. Owain Glyn Dwr's uprising of 1400 failed, and thenceforward Wales became more and more integrated into English political, territorial and economic life. Henry Tudor's winning of the Battle of Bosworth in 1485 hastened Welsh decline, precisely because he was of Welsh origins. The Welsh nobility rapidly became anglicized and remote from the people they ruled. King Henry VIII's Statute of Wales of 1536 and 1542 held that Wales had always been part of England and was henceforth to be administered in English, the intention being 'utterly to extirpe alle and singular the sinister usages and customs of Wales'.

This latter aim was not simple to achieve. The Bible was translated into Welsh, and Welsh was recognized as the official language of worship in the Established Church. Thus the language had a common literary standard and cohesion that helped maintain it, even in the face of the massive English immigration occasioned by later industrialization. In 1901 just over half the population of Wales were Welsh-speakers. However, Welsh was prohibited in schools, and discrimination against the Welsh language and people was a constant cause for protest. Michael D. Jones (1822–98) founded Y Wladfa, a colony in Patagonia, South America, where Welsh was to be the sole official language, and where people still speak Welsh today. In 1886 Cymru Fydd (Young Wales) was founded on the model of Young Ireland. The independence of Ireland served as a spur for the establishment of Plaid Cymru, the Welsh nationalist party, in 1925, which aimed to establish a Welsh parliament and to win recognition of Welsh as the official language of Wales.

A number of young people, frustrated at Plaid's commitment to constitutional measures, founded Cymdeithas yr Iaith Gymraeg (the Welsh Language Society). This organization has used civil disobedience, and violence against property – but not against people – to demand changes in the status of Welsh. It led the campaign for the first Welsh Language Act of 1967, which permitted the use of Welsh in courts and made Welsh-language contracts equally enforceable as those made in English. In 1992 a further act was passed giving people in Wales the right to deal in Welsh with public bodies when it was reasonable to do so, although without defining this condition. Welsh has not, therefore, declined as sharply as might have been feared earlier in the century. Since 1927 there have been Welsh primary schools in Welsh-speaking areas, and they also exist increasingly in predominantly English-speaking areas. The 1988 Education Reform Act stipulated that Welsh be taught in almost all Welsh schools, while there has been a significant increase in the number of schools using the medium of Welsh, at both primary and secondary level. There is also an increased use of Welsh by central and local government, and Welsh has more visible public presence in official documentation, on road signs and public notices, in chequebooks and advertisements, and so on. The annual eisteddfod, celebrating traditional Welsh culture, has done much to foster a sense of the Welsh-speaking community. Radio Cymru has broadcast in Welsh since 1978, and there is a Welsh-language regional television channel.

Despite such advances, however, Welsh continues to be under pressure. It is now spoken mainly in west and north-west Wales, though there are significant numbers of Welsh-speakers in the cities of the south. The census figure of just over 500,000 Welsh-speakers is probably an underestimate, because Welsh-speakers with no formal knowledge of the language do not usually consider themselves to be speakers. Plaid Cymru has four MPs at Westminster and is campaigning for an independent Wales by the year 2003. This would be a member of the European Union, and would allow for some reserved matters, notably defence, international relations and social security, to remain the responsibility of Westminster. A Constituent Assembly of Wales would draw up a constitution for an independent state. Labour Party proposals to create a Welsh parliament without full legislative powers are regarded by many Welsh nationalists with scepticism.

Northern Ireland

When Ulster, the historic nine counties in the north-east of Ireland, fell in 1603, its Gaelic nobility went into voluntary exile, leaving the English with no class to enforce their rule (see **Irish Republic**).[3] The solution was the Plantation: the confiscation of Irish land and its redistribution to colonists from Great Britain. The long tradition of Gaelic Ireland was overlaid by Anglo-Scottish settlers. Cut off by natural terrain, Ulster had always had a distinct character from the rest of Ireland, and this difference became more marked after the Plantation and with the development of the North in the Industrial Revolution. Trade policies that suppressed the economy of Southern Ireland encouraged the industrial growth of Belfast, with its close links to Glasgow and Liverpool. Protestants and Catholics flocked to the city, each to their own areas. In November 1885, the first election with adult male suffrage, two Irelands were revealed: the Loyalist minority in the north-east half of Ulster returned Unionists, while every other seat returned a Home Rule candidate.

The 1920 Government of Ireland Act proposed two Home Rule Parliaments, one for the counties of the South meeting in Dublin and one for the six counties of the North in Belfast, reduced from nine to ensure a Protestant majority. There was to be a Council of Ireland, with representatives from North and South to provide the basis for the reunification of Ireland. In the South, where the Dail Eireann (Irish Parliament) did not accept the authority of Westminster to legislate for Ireland, the Home Rule Parliament remained a dead-letter, but the North accepted the Act grudgingly. The six counties of Fermanagh, Tyrone, Armagh, Londonderry, Antrim and Down were politically separated from Southern Ireland in 1921. Following partition there were fears that the civil war of the Irish Free State might spread to Northern Ireland, and in 1922 the Special Powers Act was passed, giving the Home Office Minister power 'to take all such steps and issue all such orders as may be necessary for preserving peace and maintaining order'. This act was repeatedly invoked until 1972.

The Catholic population generally abstained from participation in the northern state in its early years, both because of disappointment at the failure to secure a united Ireland and under pressure and intimidation from the IRA and the South. Many other factors – including the formal claim to the North made in the Irish Republic's 1937 constitution – drove a wedge between Protestant Unionists and their Catholic Nationalist neighbours. Discrimination in jobs and housing occurred, as well as gerrymandering of local council wards (many Unionists held power by manipulating the electoral boundaries of Catholic-majority areas), as a reaction to the Catholic minority's rejection of the state and perceived threats from Dublin and the IRA.

Complaints of discrimination by the Catholic minority resulted in the forming in 1964 of the Northern Ireland Civil Rights Association, a broad-based non-sectarian group. Its demands included the outlawing of discrimination, the repeal of the Special Powers Act and the removal of gerrymandered boundaries. Civil rights marches were obstructed by Unionists, most notably the 1969 People's Democracy march, which was attacked by the Royal Ulster Constabulary (RUC), the Ulster police force. Trouble flared throughout Northern Ireland, and rioting continued through 1969, culminating in the 'Battle of the Bogside', when the RUC laid siege to the Bogside in Londonderry and residents fought back with stones and petrol bombs. In Belfast at the end of two days of rioting ten people were killed, 145 were injured and nearly 200 houses, mostly Catholic, were burnt out. British troops were now deployed in Northern Ireland. At first welcomed by the Catholics, they were soon regarded as an occupying force to keep the Unionist establishment in power. The Provisional IRA launched a bombing campaign against commercial targets. In 1971 all marches and parades in Northern Ireland were banned, and internment – indefinite imprisonment without trial – was introduced. In respect of internment, which was used exclusively against the Catholic community, the UK was taken to the European Court of Human Rights in Strasbourg and found guilty of 'inhuman and degrading treatment'. On 24 March 1972 the UK government prorogued Stormont, the Northern Ireland devolved government, and announced Direct Rule from Westminster. Constitutionally the province of Northern Ireland ceased to exist. Between 1969 and the IRA's ceasefire declaration of 1994, the Troubles had directly caused 3,173 deaths.

Catholics continue to experience higher levels of disadvantage than Protestants in Northern Ireland. The unemployment rate is 18 per cent for Catholics and 8 per cent for Protestants, with the discrepancy even greater between men: 23 per cent for Catholics and 9 per cent for Protestants. Catholics are significantly less likely than Protestants to hold professional and managerial positions and more likely to be represented in unskilled manual work. Nearly 12 per cent of Catholics leave school with no formal qualification, compared with 8.4 per cent of Protestants. Catholics are more likely to be disabled or to suffer from ill-health. Some discriminatory practices have been addressed, in particular by the 1976 and 1989 Fair Employment Acts, and by the Northern Ireland Housing Executive. Yet serious problems remain – including the small proportion of Catholics in the police and the judiciary.

The Northern Ireland (Emergency Provisions) Act of 1973, extending the army's right to stop and detain suspects, and the Prevention of Terrorism Act have been consistently renewed at Westminster with little debate. The PTA allows for a person to be detained for up to seven days without being brought before a court and can exclude a Northern Ireland resident from Great Britain for a minimum of three years by decision of the Home Secretary. No evidence to support such actions need be produced. According to the Repeal of the PTA Campaign, between 1986 and 1990 approximately 86,000 people, predominantly Irish, were detained for up to an hour under the act. The 'right to silence' was removed in 1988, despite the advice of the Standing Advisory Commission on Human Rights, and this was extended to the mainland in the Criminal Justice Act 1994. These measures have generally affected Catholics rather than Protestants, because it is Catholics who have challenged the constitution and the rights of the state. The principle of equality before the law is still frustrated by the Diplock court system, which distinguishes between security-related murders and 'ordinary' murders. A succession of successful appeals by Irish people overturning previous convictions in British courts has called into question the impartiality of police and judicial procedures in other parts of the UK.

There are an estimated 11,000 members of new minorities and Travellers in Northern Ireland (8,000 Chinese, 1,200 Travellers, 1,000 Indians and 700 Pakistanis), where there is no Race Relations Act. However, the UK government took the first step towards introducing legislation with the publication of a consultative document in December

1992. This document accepted the need to classify Irish Travellers as an ethnic group.

Manx

From early times the Gaelic-speaking Isle of Man was linguistically and culturally linked with Ireland and Scotland.[4] It was used by the Vikings as a base for coastal raids, and its traditions and culture have been heavily influenced by its Norse history. The annual open-air assembly held by the Norse to resolve disputes and make announcements survives as the Tynwald, the Manx legislature, which announces new legislation every 5 July. The Norse period came to an end in 1266 when a treaty between Norway and Scotland handed the island to the King of Scotland, but Scots rule was never consolidated. In 1346 the island came under English jurisdiction, and between 1405 and 1765 it was ruled by the Stanleys, English nobles, and largely cut off from the outside world. Manx Gaelic began to diverge from other Gaelic dialects and borrowed heavily from English. The Manx people were already deeply impoverished and subjected to harsh laws when the 1765 Revesting Act, whereby the island was returned to the British Crown, worsened their situation. There was massive emigration to escape poverty and disease.

Reforms of 1866 went some way to alleviate the situation of the Manx, establishing the present system of government. The island is not part of the UK but a Crown dependency. It is fiscally autonomous and enjoys a different tax structure to the UK. Its lower income tax and higher personal allowances, and the absence of capital gains tax, make Man a suitable 'offshore financial centre'. Thousands of wealthy immigrants have come to the island since 1958, causing housing problems for the indigenous population. In 1964 Mec Vannin, the Manx nationalist movement, was established, to revive and foster Manx culture and work for a fully autonomous and independent Manx state.

The Manx language continued to be the language of the majority of the people of Man until the 1765 Revesting Act; but by the 1840s William Kennish was writing an elegy for the language ('Lament for the Mother Tongue of the Isle of Man'). Like other nationalities Manx suffered from lack of provision under the Education Act 1870. In 1874 there were 12,000 Manx-speakers, but in 1901 only 4,419. The 1949 Manx Education Act paid little attention to the Manx language; and although Manx has validity in courts of law and business, it has no role in government or administration. The last native Manx-speaker, Ned Maddrell, died in 1974. The language is not dead, however. The 1991 census recorded 643 adults claiming fluency, 479 able to read the language and 343 able to write. Yn Cheshaght Chailckagh, the Manx Language Society, was founded in 1899 to maintain and revive the language, and has held night classes and published materials. In the 1950s a group had sought out the remaining native speakers and from them had learnt the language. In 1992 the Manx Language Project introduced classes to teach Manx Gaelic in all the island's primary and secondary schools. Inclusion in the scheme was voluntary, and take-up was a surprisingly high 20 per cent, 1,500 children. The scheme has the support of many of the island's immigrants, and the future of the language may lie in their hands as much as in the hands of native Manx.

Other historic linguistic minorities

Cornwall is unique in the UK in having claims to a separate identity and language but no constitutional status. The last mother-tongue Cornish-speaker, Dolly Pentreath, died in about 1780, although there may have been other bilingual speakers of the language until the end of the nineteenth century. Cornish is no longer a living language, but there are an estimated 200 fluent speakers of a revived form of Cornish. The Channel Islands, comprising Jersey, Guernsey, Alderney and some smaller islands, belong to the Crown although they do not form part of the United Kingdom. Most Channel Islanders speak English, but dialects of Norman French are still spoken in some parts, particularly on Jersey (where the dialect is known as *le jerriais*) and Guernsey (*le dgernesias*). There is no desire among Channel Islanders to change current political structures.

New minorities

Black people have lived in Great Britain since they were brought by the slave trade in the seventeenth century. The black population increased after the Second World War, when a shortage of labour was met mostly by immigrants from former colonies in the New Commonwealth – the Caribbean, Guyana, India, Pakistan and former East Pakistan, now Bangladesh – who had become British subjects by the Nationality Act of 1948.[5] Large numbers of Irish workers also came at this time. Concerns about the social and political costs of 'coloured' immigration resulted in immigration controls being legislated comparatively early in comparison with other European countries. In 1962 the Commonwealth Immigrants Act brought citizens from the Commonwealth under full immigration control, and they could come and settle only if they had a work permit or if they were dependants of people already settled in the UK. The 1971 Immigration Act permitted 'patrials' – Commonwealth citizens with a British-born grandfather (mainly white people from Canada, Australia and New Zealand) – to settle in the UK but abolished primary settlement from 'non-patrials', thereby limiting New Commonwealth immigration to family reunification. Thereafter the emphasis was to switch to questions of citizenship, and the British Nationality Act 1981 removed the automatic right to UK citizenship from those settled in Britain before 1973 and from those born in the UK. The 1988 Immigration Act introduced the 'primary purpose' condition, under which a couple must prove that none of their primary purposes of marrying was to gain access to the UK.

Race Relations Acts were passed in 1965, 1968 and 1976. However, racism continues to be a matter of major concern. According to the Commission for Racial Equality racism is endemic in all sectors of employment. There has been found to be unequal access to housing. The ascendancy of an exclusively defined British culture and language has been enshrined in educational legislation. Racist policing is seen by black, Asian and Irish communities as a serious problem, while racial violence is also widespread. The Home Office has estimated that more than 140,000 incidents of racial harassment take place each year. In 1992 ten people died in racially motivated incidents. Black people have died in police custody, and the increasing use of private security firms for deportations and associated security work has also aroused anxiety.

The new minorities have brought more than their skills and labour power to the UK. Their languages, religious festivals, music, dance, literature and food have enriched British life. Relative to many other European countries the UK is fortunate in having a range of anti-racist approaches and policies in education and more widely in local government, and in having the Race Relations Act, won largely thanks to the efforts of the new minorities themselves.

South Asians

South Asian servants, seamen and theatrical performers lived in Great Britain from the seventeenth century onwards. The first significant numbers of Asian migrants were men who came alone in 1955 and subsequently, generally finding work in factories, foundries and textile mills. Most were rural and had been cut adrift from their homes and jobs when India and Pakistan were partitioned in 1947. Imperial rule had left many deeply impoverished, and this provided a strong incentive to settle in the UK. There were often localized factors too, and regional origin was of great importance among South Asian migrants. As with Afro-Caribbeans, contact with British society has been responsible for bringing South Asians together in common perception as a single 'ethnic category'. Most early South Asian migrants knew little or no English and gradually found their social life in temples, mosques and cultural associations.

The UK still suffered from the postwar housing crisis even in the late 1950s. Asians, like Afro-Caribbeans, had restricted housing options and usually occupied lodgings in the private rented sector. This became a problem with family reunification in the 1970s and 1980s, whereupon many South Asian households became owner-occupiers, frequently of low-cost and poor-quality housing. Significant differences occur with regard to housing between the various South Asian groups. More than 80 per cent of Indians own their own home, for example, while just 44 per cent of Bangladeshis do. (Home ownership among the white population is 66.6 per cent.) This difference mirrors others among South Asians. Pakistanis and Bangladeshis have the largest proportion of young people with no formal qualifications and suffer the highest rate of unemployment of all ethnic groups in the UK (30.9 per cent for men and 34.5 per cent for women). Unemployment rates are far lower in the Indian community: 13.4 per cent for men and 12.7 per cent for women. Employment patterns also differ; 50 per cent of Bangladeshi men work in hotels and catering, particularly restaurants, for example, while 32 per cent of Pakistani men work in the manufacturing sector, especially textiles.[6]

With the passage of time new patterns have emerged among South Asians, such as their notable success, attributable to hard work and long hours, as neighbourhood shopkeepers and in other small businesses. At the same time, South Asians have built up a thriving community life. Although some Bangladeshis, in particular, still suffer considerable economic and social disadvantage, the achievements of the UK's South Asian communities in establishing themselves individually and collectively should be acknowledged.

Problems remain, however. Lack of access to childcare facilities, lack of alternative employment, language difficulties and the stratified local labour market push many South Asian women into homeworking, providing a cheap and flexible labour force for employers – a trend that has increased during in the 1990s. South Asians have also been affected disproportionately by the 'primary purpose' rule, introduced under the 1988 Immigration Act; in 1990 the refusal rate on grounds of primary purpose was estimated at 60 per cent of Bangladeshi spouses. The Joint Council for the Welfare of Immigrants alleges that this is because of prejudice on the part of immigration officials, who may ask 90 questions around this point of a South Asian man, while not directing any such questions at all towards Australian spouses, for example. Fear of racial violence remains another significant concern for many South Asians.

East African Asians

East African Asians are a special case. British rule in East Africa enhanced the position of Gujarati entrepreneurs who had operated there for centuries, and also introduced a large, though mainly temporary, population of Punjabi labourers. Following independence Kenya and Uganda introduced 'Africanization' policies that impacted badly on their Asian populations. During the 1960s the wealthiest Asian families of East Africa began to migrate to Britain, which led in 1968 to the second Commonwealth Immigrants Act. In 1972 General Amin ordered all Asians out of Uganda, and some 28,600 came to Britain, drawn from a variety of social classes and age groups. Many were highly successful business people and brought with them qualifications and capital that enabled them to succeed despite the constraints of racism and discrimination. Among East African Asians both men and women are concentrated in the retail distribution sector and have unemployment levels close to those of the white population.

Afro-Caribbeans

Immigration from the Caribbean to the UK is commonly dated from 22 June 1948, when 492 Jamaicans came ashore at Tilbury from the *Empire Windrush*. Ten years later there were some 125,000 Afro-Caribbean migrants in the UK, most of them having entered between 1954 and 1958. These people were usually described as West Indian, although this was not a term they used much themselves; they tended to describe themselves by the island they came from. It was arguably the experience of racism and discrimination in the 'mother country' that led to the development of a 'West Indian' identity.

In the British West Indies the cost of living had nearly doubled during the war. Unemployment, social dislocation and poverty were widespread. Migration to the UK, where there were employment opportunities that failed to attract British-born workers, was a strategy imposed largely by necessity. Most of those who came were young women and men in their early twenties, and almost all found work for which they were overqualified. The men worked in the metal goods, engineering and vehicles industries, and in transport and communications, while the women were concentrated in such occupations as nursing and catering. Some industries actively recruited workers in their home countries. In 1956 London Transport began recruiting staff in Barbados, for example, and by 1966 it had expanded to recruit in Trinidad and Jamaica.

By 1984 the Afro-Caribbean population in the UK no longer consisted predominantly of immigrants but was mainly UK-born. According to the 1991 census there are now some 500,000 people of Afro-Caribbean origin in the UK, 0.9 per cent of the total population. Four-fifths of the minority live in the metropolitan counties (compared with just 30 per cent of whites), and 58 per cent in Greater London. Afro-Caribbeans are still more likely than members of other ethnic groups to work in the transport and communications sectors and in the health service, and they are concentrated in poorly paid work. Unemployment is a particular problem for Afro-Caribbeans, especially the men, nearly 24 per cent of whom were unemployed in 1991 compared with 10.7 per cent of white men (and also compared with figures of 16.6 per cent for Afro-Caribbean women as opposed to 6.3 per cent for white women). Such discrepancies suggest discrimination in the labour market and the vulnerability of people in low-status jobs. High unemployment, heavy-handed policing and racism experienced in everyday life have caused a serious problem of alienation among second-generation Afro-Caribbeans, as manifested in urban riots during the 1980s.

Chinese

Chinese seamen were employed on British ships from the 1800s onwards.[7] The demand for seamen in the Second World War increased the Chinese population, but most were subsequently repatriated. The first permanent large-scale settlement of Chinese occurred in the 1950s when Britain's economic boom increased demand for restaurants. The population rose from 5,000 in 1951 to close to 50,000 by the mid-1950s, widely distributed across the country. Family reunification, settlement and the birth of children in the UK had increased the Chinese population to 157,000 by 1991. Eighty per cent of the community are from a small number of villages in the New Territories north of Kowloon. There are three main linguistic groups: Cantonese (75 per cent), Hakka (20 per cent) and Mandarin (5 per cent). Three-quarters of UK Chinese in employment work in hotels and catering, while related sectors such as wholesaling and importing account for another 10 per cent. The majority of first-generation immigrants thus do not speak English because it is not necessary in their work; yet this also contributes to their lack of access to welfare rights. Spatial dispersion of the Chinese community throughout the UK also means that they are often 'invisible', and this is exacerbated by the long and unsocial hours of the catering trade. There has recently been greater community organization and mobilization among Chinese people, particularly among younger Chinese.

Roma/Gypsies

There are 90,000–120,000 Travellers and Roma/Gypsies in the UK. They have experienced the imposition of policies of exclusion, containment and assimilation in the same way as their counterparts have throughout Europe (see **Germany, Irish Republic, Spain**), in addition to problems connected with their traditional economic activities, racism, poor living conditions and ill-health. Most recently Travellers in the UK have been detrimentally affected by the 1994 Criminal Justice and Public Order Act, which attempted to lump them together with 'New Age Travellers'. The Act's provisions on trespass and the extension of police and local authority powers to impound vehicles and evict, together with the removal of county councils' obligations to provide sites, threaten to criminalize Roma/Gypsies and Travellers wholesale.

Other new minorities

Large-scale Irish migration to Great Britain began during the mid-nineteenth-century potato famine. The migrants were unskilled labourers and domestic servants, mainly from western Ireland. Since then there has been a steady flow of Irish labour, particularly after the introduction of immigration quotas by the USA in the 1930s. The incoming Irish continued to be mainly poorer Catholics, although Protestants, landowners and professionals also migrated. Traditionally Irish people have settled in the major industrial cities of the UK, especially London, Liverpool and Glasgow, and have moved to areas of expanding economies, particularly because of the importance of the construction industry to Irish employment. Besides construction, dockwork, coal-mining and iron and steel have been major employers. The Second World War increased mobility for the Irish, and they began to work in skilled and white-collar occupations. As the newly arrived New Commonwealth immigrants took over unskilled and heavy labouring work, Irish people moved into manufacturing, and a number set up as contractors and subcontractors in the construction industry. The settlement and employment patterns of people of Irish descent in the UK are not clear, because official records count as Irish only those born in Ireland.

Substantial numbers of Greek and Turkish Cypriots came to Britain between 1955 and 1962. At the time of its independence in 1960 most of the population of Cyprus was rural, and few employment opportunities existed outside farming. Those who emigrated were white-collar and service workers from rural areas. Rather than acting as a replacement labour force for jobs vacated by the indigenous population in the UK, Cypriots have tended to move into occupations vacated by other minorities, such as Jews in the clothing industry and Italians in catering. Cypriot women have replaced indigenous women in unskilled and manual work, often in small clothing factories managed by Cypriot men. In general Greek Cypriot women and men have found it easier to move out of this ethnic economy than their Turkish Cypriot counterparts.

Until 1978 very few Vietnamese lived in the UK.[8] There are now some 20,000, mainly refugees accepted through an internationally organized quota system. Most UK Vietnamese are ethnically Chinese and originate from the northern part of the country, having fled to Hong Kong when China invaded Vietnam in early 1979. The majority are young, and almost 80 per cent of them were manual workers in Vietnam. The UK was unusual in not insisting on occupational skills as a qualification for entry, and perhaps largely for this reason only 12 per cent of those who settled in the UK had actually chosen to live there, the remainder having been allocated because no other country would take them. The UK government's resettlement policy involved dispersal in clusters of four to ten families to areas abandoned by the local population because of lack of opportunities. With few transferable skills and no English, the Vietnamese were left isolated and frustrated, and many have moved to cities, and to substandard accommodation.

Conclusions and future prospects

Relations between Scotland, Wales, Northern Ireland and central government, with all their implications for the main historic minorities of the UK, are one of the principal issues of UK politics in the 1990s. Proposals by the opposition Labour and Liberal Democrat parties for elected Scottish and Welsh authorities are an important policy difference between them and the Conservative government. In contrast, the Labour Party has supported the Conservative approach to the Northern Ireland peace process, resulting in the resignation of the former Northern Ireland shadow minister. There has also been a party-political consensus around immigration and asylum policies; but opposition to these policies and the organizing of black and South Asian communities, anti-racists and refugee support workers has also been notable.

More than 70,000 people in the 1991 census described themselves as 'Black British', suggesting the development of a new understanding of 'identity' and 'minority' among ethnic minorities in the UK. Many young people are working to foster alliances between ethnic minority groups in the UK and to highlight similarities between immigrants and their descendants of whatever origin, giving credence to the emergence of a new Black British identity.

Further reading

Cashmore, E.E., *The Rastafarians*, London, MRG report, 1984.

Claiborne, L. et al., *Race and Law in Britain and the United States*, London, MRG report, 1983.

Commission for Racial Equality, *Roots of the Future: Ethnic Diversity in the Making of Britain*, London, CRE, 1996.

Darby, J., *Northern Ireland: Managing Difference*, London, MRG report, 1995.

D'Souza, F. and Crisp, J., *The Refugee Dilemma*, London, MRG report, 1985.

European Bureau for Lesser Used Languages, *Mini-Guide to the Lesser Used Languages of the EC*, Baile Atha Cliath, Irish Republic, 1993.

Fryer, P., *Staying Power: The History of Black People in Britain*, London, Pluto Press, 1987.

Jones, T., *Britain's Ethnic Minorities*, London, Policy Studies Institute, 1993.

Runnymede Trust, *Multi-Ethnic Britain – Facts and Trends*, London, 1994.

Sivanandan, A., *A Different Hunger*, London, Pluto Press, 1982.

Stephens, M., *Linguistic Minorities in Western Europe*, Llandysul, Gomer, 1976.

The Troubles: The Background to the Question of Northern Ireland, London, Thames Futura, 1980.

Visram, R., *Ayahs, Lascars and Princes: The Story of Indians in Britain, 1700–1947*, London, Pluto Press, 1986.

Minority-based and advocacy organizations

Akina Mama wa Africa, Wesley House, 4 Wild Court, London WC2B 5AV, UK; tel. 44 171 405 6878.

Amnesty International, 99–119 Rosebery Avenue, London, EC1R 4RE, UK; tel. 44 171 814 6200, fax 44 171 833 1510.

An Comun Gaidhealach/Highland Association, 109 Sraid na h-Ealgaise, Inbhir Nis, Alba, Scotland, UK; tel. 44 1463 231226, fax 44 1463 715557.

British Helsinki Subcommittee of the Parliamentarian Human Rights Group, House of Lords, Westminster, London SW1, UK; tel. 44 171 793 0005, fax 44 171 738 7964.

Commission for Racial Equality, Elliot House, 10–12 Allington Street, London SW1E 5EH, UK; tel. 44 171 828 7022, fax 44 171 630 7605.

Cymdeithas yr Iaith Gymraeg/Welsh Language Society, Pen Roc, Ffordd y Mor, Aberystwyth, Dyfed SY23 2AZ, Cymru/Wales, UK; tel. 44 1970 624501.

Initiative on Conflict Resolution and Ethnicity (INCORE), Aberfoyle House, Northland Road, Derry BT48 7JA, Northern Ireland; tel. 44 1504 375500, fax 44 1504 375510, e-mail: incore@incore.ulst.ac.uk

Institute for Jewish Policy Research (formerly Institute of Jewish Affairs), 79 Wimpole Street, London W1M 7DD, UK; tel. 44 171 935 8266, fax 44 171 935 3252, e-mail: jpr@ort.org

Institute of Race Relations, 2–6 Leeke Street, London WC1X 9HS, UK; fax 44 171 278 0623.

Joint Council for the Welfare of Immigrants, 115 Old Street, London CE1V 9JR, UK; tel. 44 171 251 8706, fax 44 171 251 5110.

Justice, 59 Carter Lane, London EC4V 5AQ, UK; tel. 44 171 329 5100, fax 44 171 329 5055.

Minority Rights Group International, 379 Brixton Road, London SW9 7DE, UK; tel. 44 171 978 9498, fax 44 171 738 6265, e-mail: minority rights@mrg.sprint.com

Northern Ireland Council for Travelling People, 30 University Street, Belfast BT7 1FZ, Northern Ireland, UK; tel. 01232 237372.

Runnymede Trust, 11 Princelet Street, London E1 6QH, UK; tel. 44171 375 1496, fax 44 171 247 7695.

Scots Language Society, 16 Kinnoull Street, Perth, PH1 5ET, Scotland, UK.

Society of Black Lawyers, Unit 149, 444 Brixton Road, London SW9 8EJ, UK.

Southall Black Sisters, 52 Norwood Road, Southall, Middlesex UB2 4DW, UK; tel 44 181 571 9595, fax 44 181 544 6781.

Statewatch, PO Box 1516, London N16 OEW, UK; tel. 44 181 802 1882, fax 44 181 802 1727.

Yr Cheshaght Ghailckagh/Manx Language Society, Thie ny Gaelgey, St Judes, Ramsey, Isle of Man.

Notes

Introduction

1 See Fawcett, J., *The International Protection of Minorities*, London, MRG report, 1979.

2 OECD, SOPEMI, Paris, 1975 and 1976.

3 See Liegeois, J-P., and Gheorghe, N., *Roma/Gypsies: A European Minority*, London, MRG report, 1995.

4 MRG (ed.), *Minorities and Autonomy in Western Europe*, London, MRG report, 1991.

5 Quoted in Spencer, M., *States of Injustice*, London, Pluto Press, 1995.

6 A useful analysis of sources used by governments in their compilation of statistics on new minorities can be found in Salt, J., Singleton, A. and Hogarth, J., *Europe's International Migrants*, London, HMSO, 1994.

Austria

1 *Federal Government General Report on the Situation of Ethnic Groups in Austria*, Vienna, Federal Press Service, 1989.

2 Amnesty International, *Austria: The Alleged Ill-treatment of Foreigners – A Summary of Concerns*, London, AI, 1994.

3 Institute for Race Relations, *European Race Audit*, London, IRR, 1993–5, charts the rise of racism and the far right in Austria.

4 'Austria Ethnica, state and perspectives', *Austrian Handbooks on Ethnic Groups*, vol. 7, Vienna, Austrian Ethnic Groups Centre, 1994.

Belgium

1 Alen, A. and Ergec, R., *Federal Belgium after the Fourth State Reform of 1993*, Brussels, Ministry of Foreign Affairs, 1994.

2 Data on regional languages spoken by Walloons are from European Bureau for Lesser Used Languages, *Mini-Guide to the Lesser Used Languages of the EC*, Baile Atha Cliath, Irish Republic, 1993.

3 Information in this section is taken largely from Merkx, F. and Fekete, L., 'Belgium: the racist cocktail', *Race and Class*, vol. 32, no. 3, 1991; statistics from European Women's Lobby, *Confronting the Fortress*, Brussels, 1995.

Cyprus

1 Account of the Maronites based on information provided by Patrick Thornberry.

2 *Report of the Secretary General submitted pursuant to Commission on Human Rights Decision 1995/113*, UN Doc. E/CN.4/1996/54, para. 14.

3 The UNFICYP Humanitarian Review made a number of recommendations to the Turkish authorities in the northern part of Cyprus. These concern very basic but pressing questions including freedom of movement, the establishment of a village medical centre, connecting Maronites' houses with private telephones, improved water supply, access to Maronite holy places in order to restore them, etc., *Report of the Secretary-General*, para. 16.

Denmark

1 Text of the 1955 Copenhagen Declaration is given in MRG (ed.), *Minorities and Autonomy in Western Europe*, London, MRG report, 1991.

France

1 European Bureau for Lesser Used Languages, *Mini-Guide to the Lesser Used Languages of the EC*, Baile Atha Cliath, Irish Republic, 1993.

2 This section is based on information contained in Institute for Jewish Affairs, *Anti-Semitism World Report 1994*, London, IJA, 1994.

3 See McKechnic, R., 'Becoming Celtic in Corsica', in McDonald, S. (ed.), *Inside European Identities*, Oxford, Berg, 1993.

4 Amnesty International, *France: Shootings, Killings and Alleged Ill-Treatment by Law-Enforcement Officers*, London, AI, 1994.

Germany

1 This section is based on information from the European Bureau for Lesser Used Languages, *Mini-Guide to the Lesser Used Languages of the EC*, Baile Atha Cliath, Irish Republic, 1993.

2 Rathzel, N., 'Germany: one race, one nation?', *Race and Class*, vol. 32, no. 3, 1991.

3 See *European Race Audit*, London, Institute of Race Relations.

4 Reports of police beating and killing of non-German citizens are documented in Amnesty International, *Federal Republic of Germany: Failed by the System: Police Ill-Treatment of Foreigners*, London, AI, 1995.

5 Black and Migrant Women's Project Team (eds), *Confronting the Fortress*, Brussels, European Women's Lobby, 1995.

Greece

1 Information on (Slavo-)Macedonians is based on MRG Greece, Pettifer, J. and Poulton, H., *The Southern Balkans*, London, MRG report, 1994.

2 Information on new minorities gathered during field research by B. Anderson, funded by the Equal Opportunities Unit of the European Commission and Leicester University, to be published.

Ireland

1 Information on Irish nationalism is based on *The Troubles: The Background to the Question of Northern Ireland,* London, Thames Futura, 1980.

2 Information on language use is from European Bureau for Lesser Used Languages, *Mini-Guide to the Lesser Used Languages of the EC*, Baile Atha Cliath, Irish Republic, 1993.

3 Puxon, G., *Roma: Europe's Gypsies*, London, MRG report, 1987.

Italy

1 Information on the minority languages in Italy is based on European Bureau for Lesser Used Languages, *Mini-Guide to the Lesser Used Languages of the EC*, Baile Atha Cliath, Irish Republic, 1993.

The Netherlands

1 See Stephens, M., *Linguistic Minorities in Western Europe*, Llandysul, Gomer, 1976.

2 Figures and details of linguistic policy from European Bureau for Lesser Used Languages, *Mini- Guide to the Lesser Used Languages of the EC*, Baile Athe Cliath, Irish Republic, 1993.

3 Information on Moluccans and Surinamese based on *Third World Guide 1993–4*, Montevideo, Instituto del Tercer Mundo, 1994.

Norway

1 This section is based on information in Beach H., *The Sami of Lapland*, London, MRG report, 1988; and Beach, H., 'The Sami of Lapland', in MRG (ed.), *Polar Peoples: Self-Determination and Development*, London, Minority Rights Publications, 1994.

2 Reported in Institute of Race Relations, *European Race Audit*, London, IRR, 1994.

3 Figures from Salt, J., Singleton, A. and Howarth, J., *International Trends in Migration and Western Europe*, London, HMSO, 1994.

Spain

1 See Forsyth, M., *Federalism and Nationalism*, Leicester, Leicester University Press, 1989.

2 Based on information drawn from Liégeois, J-P. and Gheorghe, N., *Roma/Gypsies: A European Minority*, London, MRG report, 1995.

3 Institute of Race Relations, *European Race Audit*, London, 1994.

4 Office for Official Publications of the EC, *Immigration of Citizens from Third Countries into the Southern Member States of the EC: A Comparative Survey of the Situation in Greece, Italy, Spain and Portugal*, Luxembourg, 1991.

Sweden

1 This account is based on information provided by Wuockko Knocke, Swedish Institute for Work Life Research, Stockholm.

2 Quoted and discussed in Swedish report in *Minutes and Conference Papers from the ECRE Biannual General Meeting, Florence*, May 1995, London, European Council on Refugees and Exiles, 1995.

Switzerland

1 Discussion of historic minorities in this entry is based on Steinberg, J., 'Switzerland', in *Minorities and Autonomy in Western Europe*, London, MRG report, 1991.

2 An updated unofficial English translation of the Swiss federal constitution was published in 1991 and is available from the Swiss Federal Department of Foreign Affairs; the Swiss state structure is described in detail in the information sheet 'Federal Department of Foreign Affairs', *Switzerland – State and Politics*, Bern, 1993.

3 Steinberg, op. cit., p. 24.

United Kingdom

1 Minority populations from the 1991 census; percentages calculated using the 1991 census figure for the total UK population of 54.9 million.

2 Information on historic minorities drawn largely from Stephens, M., *Linguistic Minorities in Western Europe*, Llandysul, Gomer, 1976.

3 This account is based on *The Troubles: The Background to the Question of Northern Ireland*, London, Thames Futura, 1980.

4 Based on 'Mending up the rags: the return of Manx Gaelic in the Isle of Man', *Planet*, no. 101 1993.

5 For a simple history of UK immigration law see Joint Council for the Welfare of Immigrants, *Immigration Law Handbook*, London, 1995.

6 Statistics on new minorities mainly from Owen, D., *1991 Census Statistical Papers*, University of Warwick, Centre for Research in Ethnic Relations, 1992–3.

7 See Peach, C. *et al.*, 'Immigration and ethnicity', in Halsey, A. (ed.), *British Social Trends*, Basingstoke, Macmillan Press, 1988.

8 Ibid.

CENTRAL AND EASTERN EUROPE

Martyn Rady and Bogdan Szajkowski

Ethnographic maps published in the middle of the nineteenth century suggest that Western Europe contained at that time almost as linguistically diverse a population as Central and Eastern Europe. During the course of the nineteenth and early twentieth centuries, however, the strong national states carved out in Western Europe in the wake of the French Revolution succeeded in assimilating most of the smaller linguistic nations within their borders. Through compulsory education in the official language, service in the armed forces, bureaucracy and professions, and mass migration into the industrial cities, the scarcely developed ethnic consciousness of Cornish-speakers, Occitans and patois-speaking peasants was rapidly obliterated and replaced by a new collective consciousness of English or of French identity. Much the same process may be discerned in Italy, Germany and Scandinavia.

In Western Europe it was primarily the state which defined nations and impressed identities upon them. In Central and Eastern Europe, by contrast, nations acquired their self-consciousness before the arrival of modern states in the region. The romantic nationalism of the late eighteenth and nineteenth centuries created nations in Central and Eastern Europe which were built not by state jurisdictions and institutions but upon mythologies of a shared language, history and destiny. The legacy of the Habsburg, Ottoman, German and Russian empires was a proliferation of small nations, each of which was conscious of its own unique identity and desirous of its own separate statehood.

After the First World War, some attempt was made to create national states in Central and Eastern Europe. By this time, however, the consciousness of the small nations was sufficiently established to prevent their easy assimilation into the majority national communities. Croats and Slovenes rarely developed a sense of Yugoslav identity, nor Slovaks or Sudeten Germans of Czechoslovak identity. In the interwar period, at least 25 per cent of the region's population comprised ethnic minorities. The failure to create identities corresponding to state frontiers, together with the limitations of the international minorities protection regime instituted by the League of Nations, provided the entry point of Nazi foreign policy and contributed to the origins of the Second World War.

At the end of the Second World War, the solution to the incongruence between states and nations in Central and Eastern Europe was thought to lie in 'ethnic cleansing'. Already during the war itself, most of the historic Jewish population of Central and Eastern Europe had been either murdered or forced to flee. Now, after 1945, Germans were evicted from Poland, Czechoslovakia and Yugoslavia, while a part of the German population of Romania was conscripted into the Soviet labour force. Population transfers reduced the size of the Hungarian and Slovak minorities in Czechoslovakia and Hungary respectively, while Turks were driven out of Bulgaria, Macedonians out of Greece, and Ukrainians out of Poland.

The policy of eliminating rather than of accommodating minorities was maintained under the communist governments which took control of the region between 1944 and 1948. The closure of minority-language facilities in education, culture and the media, population transfer, and such devices as name-changing and forced internal migration reflected the overall interest of the communist authorities in assimilating minorities. The strong powers retained by the communists over the bureaucracy, judiciary and police meant that their assimilationist policies were frequently accompanied by gross violations of basic human rights. Nevertheless, communist abuses did not succeed in forging homogeneous national states any more than they managed to create a new 'socialist man'. According to the most recent census returns, 11 per cent of the population of Central and Eastern Europe do not regard themselves as members of majority nations. Since for fear of social stigma many members of minorities (especially Roma)[1] prefer not to register their true identity, and

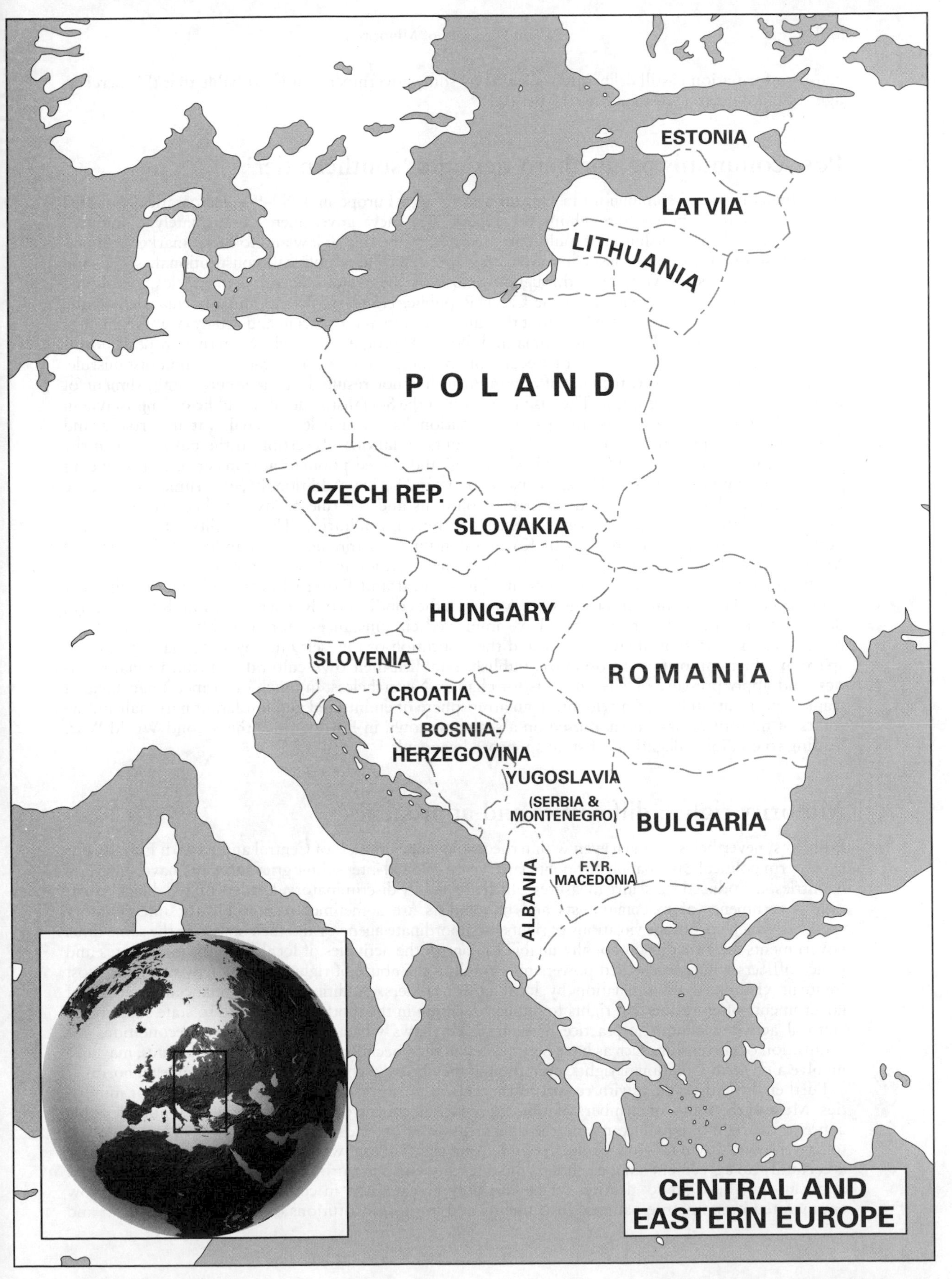
ESTONIA
LATVIA
LITHUANIA
POLAND
CZECH REP.
SLOVAKIA
HUNGARY
SLOVENIA
ROMANIA
CROATIA
BOSNIA-HERZEGOVINA
YUGOSLAVIA (SERBIA & MONTENEGRO)
BULGARIA
ALBANIA
F.Y.R. MACEDONIA
CENTRAL AND EASTERN EUROPE

census information is still deliberately skewed by some governments, it is probable that this percentage should be increased to at least 15 per cent.[2]

Post-communism: 'northern tier' and 'southern tier'

After the collapse of communism in Central and Eastern Europe in 1989–90, democratically elected governments took power throughout the region. The new governments immediately committed themselves to the establishment of multi-party politics, to the rule of law and to social market economics. Transition from communism involved, therefore, enormous political, constitutional, social and economic changes. Nevertheless, throughout most of the region, liberal democracies established themselves speedily and securely. In the Czech Republic, Hungary, Poland and Slovenia, democratic institutions have now taken such firm root that any return to authoritarian and arbitrary government is almost unthinkable. In Bulgaria, Romania and Slovakia, progress towards Western European norms continues, despite a condition of relative economic weakness and the long legacy of communist misrule.

Farther south, however, the end of communism has not resulted in the secure establishment of liberal, democratic government. The disintegration of the Socialist Federal Republic of Yugoslavia in 1991–92 was accompanied by an upsurge of nationalism which led to civil war in Croatia and Bosnia-Herzegovina, and to enormous human rights violations. Reverting to the pattern set in the wake of the Second World War, 'ethnic cleansing' and forced population transfer have become an instrument of policy in Bosnia-Herzegovina, Croatia and Serbia. Additionally, governments in a large part of the Balkans have adopted repressive solutions and the rule of law has been suspended in favour of discretionary justice, often meted out by paramilitaries. The inability of the Serbian authorities to resolve the problem of Kosovo continues to threaten the stability of Albania and Macedonia and hinders a complete democratic transformation in these countries.

The present condition of ethnic minorities in Central and Eastern Europe reflects the different experiences of post-communist transition. Although the condition of Roma gives grounds for concern, democratization and the rule of law have improved circumstances immeasurably in much of the region. The restoration of civil society and the institution of the 'self-limiting state' have permitted space in which minorities can organize, publish, establish their own cultural and educational facilities, and apply pressure on governments for change. Nevertheless, in much of former Yugoslavia, a tragic deterioration has been evident. In an atmosphere of embittered and intolerant nationalism, the rights of minorities have been abused on a scale unknown in Europe since the Second World War, leading to credible allegations of state-sponsored genocide.

Minority rights: difficulties and approaches

Problems, nevertheless, remain even within the stable 'northern tier' of Central and Eastern Europe. For short-term political gain, nationalist politicians have exploited inter-ethnic grievances and have, in several countries, introduced legislative measures which are plainly discriminatory. Leaders of 'red–black' coalition governments of ex-communists and nationalists are sometimes responsible for inflammatory speeches which encourage violations of rights by subordinate agencies and their staffs. At the same time, governments are often institutionally unable to control the activities of local officials, magistrates and police officers whose unchecked powers may result in the abuse of rights. Roma/Gypsies are the most frequent victims of discrimination by local power-holders. Additionally, the financial exigency of governments often means that rights to public education in the mother tongue and to state support for cultural activities cannot in practice be guaranteed. Laws which impose onerous preconditions for acquisition of citizenship, such as have been passed in the Czech Republic and the Baltic states, may also involve a *de facto* violation of rights, even though they broadly conform to international legal norms.

Further difficulties exist with regard to theoretical positions touching upon the rights of minorities. Most of the rights of members of minorities may be conceived within an individual human rights context: the right to equal treatment; the right to association; the right to use one's own language and to practise one's own religion. Collective and group rights are, however, more controversial and there is certainly no agreement among scholars or states anywhere in Europe as to their meaning, scope and application. The right to identity, which can only be exercised in community with others, is now enumerated in many international instruments and in the constitutions of a number of Central and

East European states. Does this right, however, oblige states to take active and expensive measures with regard to the provision of education in the mother tongue and to the erection of bilingual signposts, both of which might be considered important ways of preserving and reinforcing group identities? And if a minority on account of historic disabilities is disadvantaged, should it be entitled to group-based affirmative action policies, the purpose of which is to enable individual members of the minority to function more fully as equal citizens within the state? Even more problematically, are minorities entitled to functional or even, in the case of compacted communities, territorial autonomy? And if so, do they constitute discrete subjects of right interposed between the traditional right holders in the liberal polity, namely the individual and the state? Finally, just what constitutes a minority? Legislation in several Central and East European states, most notably Hungary and Slovenia, makes historic settlement a necessary qualification for the legal status of a minority. Such historically rooted definitions deny specific protection to new migrants, even when, as in the case of Croats and Serbs in Slovenia, there is a long historic connection between these minorities and the host state. The exclusion of non-historic minorities from legal protection may soon be tested in several countries as a consequence of the increased flow of migrants from the Balkans and the former Soviet Union.

Governments in Central and Eastern Europe generally subscribe to the liberal, centralist tradition which affirms the importance of individual rights of common citizenship while denying the relevance of group rights, particularly those which involve an apparent derogation of state sovereignty. As the Romanian representative at the 1990 Conference on Security and Cooperation in Europe (CSCE; after 1994 Organization for Security and Cooperation in Europe, OSCE) Copenhagen meeting put it:

'It is wrong to speak of minority rights or majority rights. Rights are best thought of as inherent in each human being, irrespective of what kind of ethnic, national, religious or cultural grouping he or she may belong to . . . The fact that certain rights, given their nature, are exercised collectively or jointly with other members of the group does not make them collective rights.'[3]

Territorial autonomy for compacted minorities has, therefore, been almost universally ruled out in Central and Eastern Europe and not just in Romania. It exists, on paper only, in the 1992 Croatian minorities law and in the texts of the various internationally brokered agreements for Bosnia-Herzegovina. Even the Hungarian government, the standard-setter for minorities protection in Central and Eastern Europe, has not extended rights of local autonomy to compacted ethnic minorities.

Nevertheless, Central and East European states have in many instances proved alert and responsive to the need to preserve and foster group identities. Most maintain a highly developed school system of mother-tongue education for historic minorities. Romania and Yugoslavia (Serbia and Montenegro) probably have the most extensive in Europe. Additionally, all Central and East European states provide facilities, often including state subsidies, for media broadcasts and publications in minority languages. Few constraints are applied on the activities of organizations representing the interests of minorities, although in Albania and Bulgaria political parties representing a specific ethnic constituency are prohibited. In Romania and Slovenia, deputies appointed by minority organizations are automatically represented in the legislature, while in Macedonia an informal consociational arrangement ensures that several ministerial portfolios are retained by political leaders of the Albanian minority.

International and regional instruments

In formal institutional terms, Central and Eastern Europe may now have overtaken Western Europe as the pace-setter for minorities protection on the continent. This development owes much, however, to the pressure exerted on states by international organizations. In order to hasten their integration in Europe and their membership of the European Union, states in Central and Eastern Europe have had to make commitments with regard to minorities protection which often involve more extensive obligations than those entered into by many Western European states. The leading role in this development was played after 1989 by the CSCE (now OSCE).

Until 1989, most international organizations had been satisfied with enumerating the 'negative rights' of members of minorities: freedom from discrimination, from arbitrary arrest, from imprisonment, and so on. In 1989, however, the concluding document of the Vienna meeting of the CSCE established the principle that protection should be considered not just in negative terms but as involving positive rights to identity. The 1990 CSCE Copenhagen Document developed this principle and enumerated the rights of minorities to association, to mother-tongue education, to participation in government and policy-making and (although these are laid with important qualifications) to functional or territorial autonomy and to affirmative-action policies. The subsequent CSCE meetings of experts held in Geneva and Oslo in 1991 resulted in the compilation of 'shopping lists' of recommendations for enhancing minority protection and the right to identity and to political participation.

Part of the concern of the CSCE was that minority problems, if left unresolved, might create instabilities and threaten regional security. In 1992, the office of CSCE High Commissioner on National Minorities was established, the purpose of which was to provide 'early warning' with regard to the 'nature of tensions' and 'the potential consequences for peace and stability within the CSCE area'. Although international bodies have long claimed a *droit de régard* in respect of human rights, the institution of the High Commissioner represents a new level of intrusion in the domestic affairs of states. The office of the High Commissioner has been active since its establishment in investigating, reporting and making recommendations upon the conditions affecting minorities in a number of CSCE/OSCE states, including Albania and Slovakia.

Other international organizations have joined the CSCE/OSCE in the task of standard-setting and monitoring. In 1993, the Parliamentary Assembly of the Council of Europe adopted Recommendation 1201, which elaborated rights to public information and education in the mother tongue and, although this is guardedly put, to autonomous self-government. The terms of Recommendation 1201 have recently been built into the text of the 1995 interstate treaty between Hungary and Slovakia. Two additional Council of Europe documents, the European Charter for Regional or Minority Languages, and the Framework Convention for the Protection of National Minorities, have recently been opened to signature by member states. In 1993–4, the Council of Europe sent missions to the Baltic states and Romania to investigate and report on state compliance with European standards for minority protection. In 1993, the Central European Initiative, a regional grouping established in 1989 and now having fifteen members (Albania, Austria, Belarus, Bosnia-Herzegovina, Bulgaria, Croatia, Czech Republic, Hungary, Italy, Macedonia, Poland, Romania, Slovakia, Slovenia and Ukraine) agreed in principle special measures for the protection of minorities, including self-government, and subsequently opened to signature an Instrument on the Protection of Minority Rights.

The United Nations and the European Union have additionally set international standards in respect of conditions affecting minorities. In line with the new international approach, visible after 1989, the first article of the 1992 UN Declaration on the Rights of Persons belonging to National or Ethnic, Religious and Linguistic Minorities obliges states not only to protect but also to promote identities of minorities. The European Union Guidelines on the Recognition of New States, published in 1991, also included clauses regarding the safeguarding of the rights of minorities in accordance with CSCE/OSCE standards. In the case of the successor states of former Yugoslavia, the guidelines made explicit reference to documents which contained clauses permitting minorities in the Yugoslav republics very substantial rights of self-government. These clauses were subsequently used to oblige Croatia to institute a law for the protection of its predominantly Serb minorities.

Weaknesses of the transnational regime

Since 1989, a transnational regime of protection for minorities in Central and Eastern Europe has been developed. It is underpinned by CSCE/OSCE commitments and reinforced by obligations contained in instruments of the Council of Europe, European Union and United Nations. Nevertheless, no adequate mechanism for enforcing compliance with these standards has been established, with the consequence that basic rights of members of minorities may still be violated with impunity.

In March 1995, fifty-two nations met in Paris to sign the European Stability Pact, promoted by the French Prime Minister, Edouard Balladur. The pact established the inviolability of borders and contained various clauses (of a rather weak nature) protecting the rights of minorities. Signature of the pact was accompanied by a hundred regional and bilateral agreements, including the Hungarian–Slovakian interstate treaty. The states belonging to the European 'southern tier' were, however, conspicuous by their absence. Several months later, the Croatian government initiated policies of 'ethnic cleansing' in Serb-populated regions of Croatia in defiance of the very minorities-protection law it had instituted in 1992 at the instigation of the European Union.

The failure of the European Stability Pact to draw in the Balkans and put an end to rights violations of the type perpetrated by the Croatian government indicates the limits of the present transnational regime. International standards of minorities protection are enforced by national governments. Where national governments are not prepared to adhere to these standards, the international community can do very little except monitor violations. Although much has been achieved since 1989 with regard to the protection of minorities in Central and Eastern Europe, the continued disregard of basic freedoms in parts of the Balkans sets both a limit and a challenge to the effectiveness of international human rights organizations.

Note on population data

Estimation of the size of minority populations is frequently a controversial matter in Central and Eastern Europe, as it can be elsewhere. In most cases in this part of the *Directory*, minority population data included in the statistical summaries at the start of each country entry are drawn from the last official census (frequently, if not always, based on voluntary self-identification). In addition, in a number of cases, additional estimates drawn from other sources are shown; although the accuracy of such further estimates is impossible to confirm, they may be considered broadly realistic.

Further reading

Brunner, G., *Nationality Problems and Minority Conflicts in Eastern Europe*, Gütersloh, Bertelsmann, 1996.

Joly, D., Nettleton, C. and Poulton, H., *Refugees: Asylum in Europe*, London, Minority Rights Publications, 1992.

Liégeois, J.-P. and Gheorghe, N., *Roma/Gypsies: A European Minority*, London, MRG report, 1995.

Minority Rights Group (ed.), *Minorities in Central and Eastern Europe*, London, MRG report, 1993.

Poulton, H., *The Balkans: Minorities and States in Conflict*, 2nd edn, London, Minority Rights Publications, 1993.

Szajkowski, B., *Encyclopaedia of Conflicts, Disputes and Flashpoints in Eastern Europe, Russia and the Successor States*, Harlow, Longman, 1993.

Albania

Land area:	29,000 sq km
Population:	3.4 million (1992)
Main languages:	Albanian, Greek, Romani, Aromanian
Main religions:	Islam (mainly Sunni), Eastern Orthodox Christianity, Roman Catholicism
Main minority groups:	*1989 census:* Greeks 59,000 (1.8%), Macedonians 4,700 (0.19%); *other estimates:* Greeks 150,000 (4.4%), Roma up to 100,000 (2.9%), Macedonians 40,000 (1.2%), Vlachs 35,000–50,000 (1–1.5%), 'South Slavs' up to 40,000 (1.2%)
Real per capita GDP:	$2,200
UNDP HDI/rank:	0.633 (104)

Albania is situated in the western Balkans. It is bordered by Greece to the south, Macedonia to the east and Serbia and Montenegro to the north. To the west, there is a 420 kilometre coastline with the Adriatic Sea. More than three-quarters of Albania is mountainous and almost a half is wooded. The Albanians are most probably the descendants of the ancient Illyrians who were colonized after the seventh century BCE by the Greeks and subsequently by the Romans. During the Middle Ages, modern-day Albania formed successively parts of the Byzantine, Bulgarian, Serbian and Angevin-Norman empires. The Albanian lands lay at the meeting point of Catholic and Eastern Orthodox Christianity. Following the schism between the two churches, the northern population generally adhered to Catholicism and the southern to Eastern Orthodoxy. In the fourteenth and fifteenth centuries, the Albanian lands were overrun by the Ottoman Turks. Most Albanians subsequently embraced Islam.

Under circumstances which are disputed, the Albanians spread eastwards into what is now southern Serbia (Kosovo province), western Macedonia and Greece. The Albanian national movement which developed in the late nineteenth century sought to unite Albanians in a single state. The independent Albania established on the eve of the First World War did not, however, include Kosovo and western Macedonia, which then had a combined population of about 800,000 Albanians. Aspirations for a state which united the Albanian people were briefly realized under the aegis of the Italians and Germans during the Second World War. After 1945, however, Albania returned to its former borders. It is presently estimated that two-thirds as many Albanians live in neighbouring states as in Albania itself. Besides the Albanian diaspora in the Balkans, there is the small Arboresh community in southern Italy, the origins of which go back to the fourteenth century.

In 1944, the communists led by Enver Hoxha imposed a strict Stalinist regime on Albania. In 1967, Albania was proclaimed 'the first atheist state' and all religious practices were banned. Churches and mosques were demolished or converted to secular use and in the mid-1970s personal names of a Christian religious character were prohibited. Hoxha died in 1985 and a moderate reform programme was introduced which accelerated with the collapse of communism in Central and Eastern Europe in 1989. In 1990, the ban on religious practice was lifted and the establishment of political parties was permitted. Multi-party elections held in March 1991 resulted in a victory for the communists, who subsequently renamed themselves the Socialist Party of Albania. New elections held in the spring of 1992 led to the formation of a coalition government headed by the opposition Democratic Party. In 1996 the Democratic Party recorded a landslide victory in a general election which was widely reported as unfair.

Population censuses indicate Albania to be one of the most ethnically homogeneous states in Central and Eastern Europe. In 1930, 7.5 per cent of the population belonged to ethnic minorities. According to the 1989 census this proportion had declined to 2 per cent (a figure which is contested), mainly on account of strong demographic growth among the ethnic Albanian majority. The relative weighting of the majority to the minority population has recently been affected by emigration. It is estimated that over 300,000 Albanians have left the country during the past five years, mainly to seek work abroad. Among the emigrants are thought to be a large number of ethnic Greeks.

The Albanian constitution of 1976 was suspended in 1991. A draft constitution was subsequently rejected by the electorate in a referendum, mainly because of the strong powers vested in the President. Article 44 of the draft stated:

'Members of a national minority have the right to exercise the basic human rights and freedoms in full equality before the law. They have the right to express and develop freely their ethnic, cultural, religious and linguistic identity, to learn and to be taught in their mother tongue as well as to join organizations and associations that defend their interest and identity.'

After the defeat of the draft, a commission, which included one representative of the Greek minority, was appointed to devise a second constitution. A charter of rights passed by the Albanian legislature in 1993 assures 'individuals belonging to minorities' full protection and equality before the law and makes provision for education in the mother tongue.

Greeks

Greeks make up the largest ethnic minority in Albania. According to the 1989 census, there were 58,758 Greeks. Although some émigré sources have put the number of the Greek population at 400,000, a more probable figure is 150,000.[1] The size of the Greek minority is especially contentious on account of the history of claims to southern Albania made by the Greek government in Athens, and of the substantial support within Greece and among Greeks in Albania, for the establishment of an autonomous district of 'Northern Epirus'. The Greek population is likely, however, to be in numerical decline as a consequence of emigration to Greece. Many Greek villages in southern Albania are reported to have already lost most of the active adult workforce.

The origin of the Greek minority is disputed. Many Greeks claim descent from the Greek population which settled in the Albanian lands during the pre-Christian period. Other sources indicate that Greeks moved into the region only much later, mainly as indentured labour during the Turkish period, or that many Greeks are really 'hellenized Albanians'. It is impossible to evaluate the accuracy of these divergent accounts, although it may be that all contain elements of truth. Certainly, there appears to be a continuous history of Greek settlement in several of the Albanian coastal cities. The majority of the present Greek population is, however, concentrated inland, south of a line running roughly from Vlora to Korca.

Assimilationist policies practised by the interwar governments led to the closure of Greek schools and to discriminatory measures against Greek Orthodox monasteries. After the communist take-over, a number of Greeks were appointed to high positions. Bilingual education in the first four grades of elementary schools was introduced for Greek children and one Greek-language newspaper was published. In general, the communists were less interested in discriminating on grounds of ethnicity as of religion. In this respect, the campaign against the churches hit the Greek minority disproportionately, since affiliation to the Eastern Orthodox rite has traditionally been a strong component of Greek identity.

After the reforms of 1990, Greek churches were reopened. The pressure group, and subsequent political party for the promotion of Greek human rights, OMONIA (Sociopolitical Organization – Democratic Union of the Greek Minority), founded in January 1991, took an active role in securing the return of ecclesiastical properties. A particular difficulty was, however, the absence of a trained clergy, which has led to a strong reliance upon priests coming from Greece. Greek language education was additionally expanded, and bilingual education was permitted in the first eight grades of elementary school. Although education in Greek and the establishment of new Greek schools were impeded by a government instruction in 1993, facilities have since been restored in designated 'minority zones'. The Conference on Security and Cooperation in Europe (CSCE) mission to Albania in October 1994 subsequently reported:

'That, in principle . . . the requirements regarding educational rights of persons belonging to national minorities laid down in the 1990 CSCE Copenhagen Document and other international standards have been met. Persons belonging to the Greek ethnic minority have been given adequate opportunity for instruction of their mother tongue . . . In this way, assimilation is actively prevented and pluralism is protected.'[2]

Nevertheless, tensions remain which are caused principally by fears of Greek irredentism. Having won five seats in the parliamentary election of March 1991, OMONIA was banned since it violated Law 7501 (1991) which forbade 'formation of parties on a religious, ethnic and regional basis'. On behalf of OMONIA, the Unity Party for Human Rights contested the 1992 elections. Following a border incident in 1994, provoked by Greek nationalists from Greece, six leaders of OMONIA were convicted of illegal arms possession, and of spying for Greece. Their trial was widely regarded as unfair and the six were subsequently released. In a separate incident in 1993, a Greek archimandrite, Chrysostomos Maidonis, was expelled on grounds of expressing 'openly territorial claims' and engaging in 'the distribution of maps, leaflets and brochures that present and demand the hellenization and annexation of southern Albania to Greece'. Demonstrations in support of the archimandrite were violently suppressed by the Albanian police. The Greek government responded to the expulsion of the archimandrite and to the OMONIA trial by deporting in 1994 about 100,000 Albanians working illegally in Greece.[3]

One particular fear is that these incidents may lead to a deterioration of relations on a local level. Already some observers have noted an increased purchase of small arms by Greeks and Albanians and increased surveillance activity by the Albanian secret police.[4] Additionally, the moderate position of the Greek minority organizations may in the event of a new crisis be jeopardized by extremists advocating a revision of the Greek–Albanian border.

Macedonians

According to the 1989 census there were 4,697 Macedonians in Albania, living mainly in the area of Prespa and of Lake Ochrid. At a party congress in 1976, Enver Hoxha referred to the Macedonian minority as no more than 'a question of some agricultural cooperative'. Nevertheless, the Belgrade daily, *Politika*, put their number in 1989 at 40,000 to 45,000, while several Macedonian publications have suggested figures as high as 100,000 or more.[5] At the end of the Second World War there were 13 Macedonian schools in Albania, using teachers and textbooks imported from Yugoslavia. The break with Tito in 1948 largely put an end to Macedonian-language education. In 1992, however, Tirana and Skopje came to an agreement whereby the Macedonian government would fund Macedonian minority schools in Albania. At present, no such schools are known to be operating. It is sometimes claimed that besides Orthodox Macedonians, there is a population in Albania of up to 100,000 Muslim Macedonians, known variously as Pomaks or Torbeshi. There appears to be little evidence to support these figures.[6]

Vlachs

Vlachs or Aromanians do not appear in the 1989 census. In 1916, their population was reckoned at 100,000. More recent estimates put their number at variously between 35,000 and 50,000. The Vlachs are mainly Eastern Orthodox in religion and have traditionally been either merchants or pastoralists. They are alternatively known in Albanian as cobane or shepherds, and they mainly live in the Prespa Lake region and areas of south-eastern Albania. The majority speak a Romance language akin to Romanian. Until the Second World War, Vlachs practised transhumance. With the communist take-over, strong attempts were made to force the Vlachs to settle. The Association of Aromanians in Albania, founded in 1991, has demanded that the government actively promote Aromanian education and publications and support the Vlach cultural 'renaissance' currently in progress.

Other minorities

During the seventeenth and eighteenth centuries, an unusually intense campaign of conversion was undertaken among Albanians, with the consequence that the majority embraced Islam. A large number of Albanian Muslims followed the Bektashi dervish religion, however. Albania remains confessionally divided with Bektashi, Eastern Orthodox and Catholic minorities. According to Italian sources compiled in 1942, 69.1 per cent of the population was Muslim, including 15 to 20 per cent Bektashi; 20.6 per cent Orthodox; and 10.3 per cent Catholic. More recent statistics are not available. The majority of Catholics live in the north, while the Orthodox population is centred mainly upon the southern towns of Gjirokaster, Saranda, Korca, Vlora and Berat. Albanian national identity is not defined by religion and there appears little discrimination on religious grounds. Yugoslav sources contend that administrative measures disadvantage the Goranci, Muslims of Slavonic origin who still keep certain Orthodox practices. Further information on this unusual ethnic and religious minority is not available.[7]

Albania's Roma minority was estimated at 10,000 in 1930, with quarters in the cities of Elbasan and Shkoder. Estimates of the current number of Roma vary between 5,000 and 100,000, although within this range a higher figure would seem more plausible. Albania has always had a minority of Jews, the number of which was augmented in the sixteenth century by an influx of Sephardic Jews from Spain. A steady decline in the Jewish population may be detected over the course of the century, from several thousand in 1910 to just 200 in the 1930 census. In 1990–1, the remnants of the Jewish minority, numbering about 300 people, migrated *en masse* to Israel at the invitation of the Israeli government. The 1989 census noted the presence of 100 Serbs, although official Yugoslav sources estimate that 40,000 'South Slavs', including Montenegrins, live in Albania.[8] There are also a few hundred Armenians mainly in Tirana and Vlora, and a small Italian community.

Conclusions and future prospects

There is no reason why Albania should not count as a Balkan 'success story' with regard to minority rights and protection. Notwithstanding the lack of firm legal and constitutional foundations, the rights of minorities appear relatively assured. A CSCE mission to Albania, undertaken in October 1994, headed by High Commissioner Max van der Stoel, reported favourably on the progress made by the Albanian government in implementing international standards for minority protection.[9] The principal danger at present is that interstate rivalries may spill over and begin to affect inter-ethnic relationships within Albania, particularly concerning the Greek minority. Greek politicians should, in particular, be wary of extracting gains from any confusion sown among Albanians in the Balkans by deteriorating conditions in Kosovo. At the same time, there is clear need for accurate and up-to-date information on the ethnic, religious and linguistic composition of the population of Albania. This is only likely to be obtained through an internationally supervised census.

Further reading

MRG Greece, Pettifer, J. and Poulton, H., *The Southern Balkans*, London, MRG report, 1994.

Norris, H.T., *Islam in the Balkans*, London, Hurst, 1993.

Pettifer, J., 'Ethnic minorities in Albania', *Blue Guide to Albania*, London, A & C Black, 1994, pp. 72–4.

Poulton, H., *The Balkans: Minorities and States in Conflict*, London, Minority Rights Publications, 1993, pp. 193–204.

Vickers, M., *The Albanians: A Modern History*, London, Tauris, 1995.

Minority-based and advocacy organizations

Albanian Helsinki Committee, Qendra Nderkombetare e Kultures, Bulevardi Deshmoret e Kombit, Dhoma 35, Tirana, Albania; tel./fax 355 42 33671.

Association of Aromanians, Roga Gjollesha, Palati 7, Shk 3, Apt 19, Tirana, Albania.

Open Society Foundation for Albania, R. Labinoti No. 125, Tirana, Albania.

Rromani Baxt, Tirana, Albania; fax 355 42 35197.

Bosnia-Herzegovina

Land area:	51,130 sq km
Population:	4.38 million (mid-1992)
Main languages:	Serbo-Croat (including Bosnian, Croatian and Serbian)
Main religions:	Islam (mainly Sunni), Eastern Orthodox Christianity, Roman Catholicism
Main minority groups:	*1991 census:* Muslims 1.9 million (43.7%), Serbs 1.4 million (31.4%), Croats 756,000 (17.3%), 'Yugoslavs' 240,000 (5.5%), others 93,500 (2.1%); *other estimates (pre-1992):* Roma 100,000 (2.3%)
Real per capita GDP:	—
UNDP HDI/rank:	—

Bosnia-Herzegovina (officially, Bosnia and Herzegovina) is triangular in shape. To the west and north the country juts into Croatia, while the eastern border adjoins Serbia and Montenegro. Bosnia-Herzegovina has a short maritime coastline of about 20 kilometres which is of little commercial or military significance. Much of the terrain is mountainous. The population of Bosnia-Herzegovina is the most mixed of all the republics of former Yugoslavia. None of the major ethnic groups – Muslims, Serbs and Croats – constitutes an absolute majority. Although there have been recent attempts to construct separate Bosnian and Croatian languages, all three groups speak the same *ijekavski* dialect of Serbo-Croat, and identities are constructed almost entirely on the basis of religious affiliation. Since the outbreak of hostilities in April 1992, there has been substantial voluntary and involuntary population movement and widespread slaughter of both military and civilian populations. In 1996 it was estimated that over 2 million people had been displaced, of whom more than 1 million had fled as refugees to neighbouring states. No data are available for the number of people killed, although unofficial figures suggest that more than 150,000 had died as a result of the conflict by 1993.[1]

The population of Bosnia comprises mainly Slavs who entered the region in the sixth and seventh centuries. The Slavs of Bosnia, which became a kingdom in the mid-fourteenth century, subsequently converted to Catholicism, although some embraced Eastern Orthodox Christianity and the Bogomil dualist religion. In the fifteenth century, Bosnia and the neighbouring duchy of Herzegovina were incorporated in the Ottoman empire. During the period of Turkish occupation, a part of the population adopted Islam. In 1878, following a rising, led in the main by Orthodox Christians, the Ottoman administrative districts of Bosna and Herceg were placed under Austrian Habsburg administration and they were later annexed by the Habsburg empire. After the First World War, Bosnia-Herzegovina formed a part of the Kingdom of Serbs, Croats and Slovenes (after 1929, Yugoslavia), and during the Second World War it was absorbed within the Croatian Ustasa state. After 1945, Bosnia-Herzegovina was established as a republic within federal Yugoslavia, although its borders were marginally adjusted allegedly to the detriment of the Serb population.

Interpretations of ethnic relations in Bosnia-Herzegovina differ. On the one hand, it is claimed that Bosnia-Herzegovina has for long represented an example of successful multiculturalism and that inter-ethnic conflict has been largely manipulated by external forces. This contention is supported by reference to the high incidence of cross-confessional marriage, particularly in the capital, Sarajevo. On the other hand, it is alleged that relations between the ethnic groups in Bosnia-Herzegovina were only superficially harmonious and that, in the countryside in particular, Bosnian society was deeply segmented. There can, however, be little doubt that the communists not only exploited but exacerbated ethnic differences. Communist policy supported the creation of a separate Muslim identity, whereas previously many Muslims had regarded themselves as either Serbs, Croats or 'undetermined'. The party-run system of appointments to office was characteristically based upon proportionality, according to which jobs were allocated on the basis of ethnicity.

Multi-party elections held in Bosnia-Herzegovina in 1990 indicate the strong influence of ethnicity on political affiliation. Each ethnic group formed its own political party: the Muslim-led Party of Democratic Action (PDA), the Serbian Democratic Party (SDP) and the Croatian Democratic Union (CDU). The votes received by the three ethnic parties corresponded closely to the ethnic division of the population, and pro-Yugoslav parties performed badly. A coalition government was subsequently established under Alija Izetbegovic, a long-standing anti-communist and Muslim activist.

As Yugoslavia began to dissolve in 1991, arguments intensified within the country over the sovereign status of Bosnia-Herzegovina. While the CDU, supported later by the PDA, pushed for complete independence for Bosnia-Herzegovina, the SDP demanded Bosnia-Herzegovina's continued association with Yugoslavia. During 1991, the SDP consolidated its power on a local level, taking over administrative control of the mainly Serb-populated municipalities. The declaration of Bosnian independence in April 1992 was followed immediately by the assertion of sovereignty by the self-declared 'Serbian Republic of Bosnia and Herzegovina' and by the start of civil war. In July 1992, the CDU declared the autonomy of 'Herceg-Bosna' in the mainly Croat-populated western Herzegovina and central Bosnia. Since the outbreak of hostilities in April 1992, there has been a massive movement of civilians fleeing the zones under the control of forces belonging to other ethnic groups. The flight of non-combatants has often been as a consequence of deliberate policies of 'ethnic cleansing' practised by parties to the conflict. Peace terms agreed in November 1995 at US-brokered talks held in Dayton, Ohio, put a halt to hostilities. The prospects for the reintegration of Bosnia-Herzegovina on the basis of new elections, as envisaged in the Dayton agreement, remain at the time of writing uncertain.

Muslims

Muslims of Bosnia-Herzegovina are descended from Christian (mainly Orthodox) Slavs who converted to Islam during the period of Ottoman occupation. Historically, Muslims formed a large proportion of the urban administrative and merchant class. Until the communist period, most Muslims did not regard themselves as constituting a specific ethnic group, but as either Serbs or Croats of Muslim religion or as 'undetermined'. In 1961, however, Muslims were given the right to declare themselves as such on censuses, and in 1971 Muslims were advanced to the status of one of Yugoslavia's constituent nations.

According to the 1991 census, there were in Bosnia-Herzegovina 1,905,829 Muslims, making up altogether 43.7 per cent of the population. The Muslim population of Bosnia- Herzegovina was widely distributed throughout the republic, although there were heavy concentrations in the cities. Muslims formed an absolute or relative majority in 52 of the 109 municipalities into which Bosnia-Herzegovina was divided in 1991. The present status of Muslims differs from place to place in Bosnia-Herzegovina. Although they may be considered the dominant ethnic group in those areas controlled by the Bosnian government in Sarajevo, in the 'Serbian Republic' and 'Herceg-Bosna' they constitute a small and vulnerable minority.

The constitution of the 'Serbian Republic' guarantees the protection of all minorities living within its boundaries. Many Muslims have, nevertheless, been coerced into departure. The ejection of Muslims has been accompanied by reliable reports of widespread killings, torture and, possibly also, systematically organized rape of Muslim women. Those Muslims who remain are often without employment, denied medical facilities, placed under curfew, targeted for involuntary population exchange, and subjected to routine detention and harassment. Marriages between Muslims and Serbs have been prohibited by local regulations in a number of municipalities. As part of a pattern of obliteration, Muslim cultural monuments have been destroyed. Of the 202 mosques in Serb-held Bosnia at the start of the war, only two remained in mid-1994.[2] The capture in the summer of 1995 of the government-administered enclaves of Srebrenica and Zepa in eastern Bosnia by Serbian forces is believed to have been followed by the murder of at least several thousand Muslims.

Muslims have, likewise, been 'ethnically cleansed' from the Croat-controlled areas of Bosnia-Herzegovina, which include 12 municipalities where Muslims previously formed a majority. There are reliable reports of atrocities practised against Muslims by Croat troops and paramilitaries during 1993 in Vitez and Ahmici, along the Lasva valley, and in the western part of the city of Mostar. The deliberate destruction of mosques has also been recorded in Croat-controlled areas.[3]

A growth of Islamic 'fundamentalism' among Muslims has been alleged, including attacks on women who are considered improperly dressed. Early reports suggest that these outrages may have been committed by foreign irregulars attached to the government forces.

Serbs

The 1991 census indicated 1,369,258 Serbs in Bosnia-Herzegovina, making up 31.4 per cent of the population and concentrated mainly in the east and north of the republic. The majority have historically been peasant farmers, as a consequence of which Serbs in pre-war Bosnia-Herzegovina owned approximately 60 per cent of the land. Although Serbs represent an overwhelming majority in those areas under the control of the 'Serbian Republic', they constitute minorities in those parts of Bosnia-Herzegovina administered by the Croatian and mainly Muslim government authorities. The Bosnian government has operated since 1991 without a constitution and with no legislative guarantees of minority rights. Nevertheless, it has always expressed a wish to found a multi-ethnic society where citizenship is not predicated upon ethnic or religious affiliation. In practice, however, substantial violations of the rights of Serb population have been recorded, although it is not possible to establish at what level these abuses were authorized.

The Bosnian Serb authorities published in January 1993 a list of 55 centres where Serb civilians were illegally detained by government and Croat forces. Emigré Serb sources have also published extensive documentation alleging the systematic rape and torture of Serb civilians.[4] United Nations documents record the substantial devastation of Serb villages along the Drina valley during the government offensive of 1992–3 and have listed allegations of massacres and of the discovery of mass graves, some of which may be independently confirmed by reference to autopsy reports held in Belgrade Military Hospital. Many Serb villages around Gorazde and Srebrenica are reliably reported to have been devastated. There is additional information that Serbs who have refused conscription into the government forces have been either imprisoned or, in some cases, forced to undertake dangerous front-line work. Serbs have, likewise, been refused permission to leave government-controlled cities and towns.[5] Reports that cross-confessional marriages have been forbidden in Sarajevo have not been verified. Severe violations of the Serb population at the hands of Croat forces have also been reported, particularly in the Mostar region, where many Serbs have been either murdered or evicted from their homes as part of 'ethnic cleansing'.

Croats

According to the 1991 census, there were 755,892 Croats in Bosnia-Herzegovina, making up 17.3 per cent of the total population and concentrated mainly in the western part of the republic neighbouring the border with Croatia. Since 1992, most Croats have lived in Croatian-administered 'Herceg-Bosna', although there are small Croat minorities in government-run areas and in the 'Serbian Republic'. Croats in Serb-run Bosnia have been subject to widespread intimidation, particularly in the four municipalities where before 1991 they formed a majority. Violations of basic human rights endured by Croats are similar in nature to those practised against Muslims in the territory of the 'Serbian Republic'. With the capture in 1995 of the Krajina in Croatia by Croatian government troops and the subsequent flight of the region's Serbs, Croats remaining in Banja Luka are alleged to have been expelled and their homes given to Serb refugees.

There are reliable reports also of the 'ethnic cleansing' of Croat civilians from areas under the control of Bosnian government forces. In mid-1993, government forces are known to have murdered Croats in the villages of Trusine, Miletici, Maljime, Doljane, Kriz, Uzdol and Kopijari and in the Vitez region. Eyewitnesses report that some of these atrocities were committed by foreign irregulars affiliated to the Bosnian government's Seventh Brigade. In several towns, notably Bugojno and Zenica, Croat civilians have been forbidden to leave voluntarily and have been used instead for exchanges. During fighting between Croat and government forces in 1993, Croat civilians were expelled from the eastern part of the city of Mostar, and their homes were occupied by Muslim refugees.[6]

Other minorities

According to the 1991 census, other minorities (excluding 'Yugoslavs') amounted to only 2 per cent of the population of Bosnia-Herzegovina. However, other sources indicate a sizeable Roma minority before the 1992–5 Bosnian war. Isolated cases of attacks on Muslim Roma communities were reported before the war; and during the war many Roma became refugees in Croatia, Germany and elsewhere, although some remained. At the end of 1996 an estimated 50,000 or more Bosnian Roma were still housed in refugee camps around Berlin, despite the German government's plans to repatriate them. Little information is available on the fate of the small Bosnian Vlach community, which appears to have experienced considerable assimilation over recent decades. The number of self-declared 'Yugoslavs' fell between the 1981 and 1991 censuses from 326,280 to 239,845, reflecting the larger ethnicization of Bosnian politics.

Conclusions and future prospects

The recent war in Bosnia-Herzegovina has witnessed the very substantial abuse of basic human rights. Local minorities have been the principal target of these violations, which include murder, rape, beatings, illegal detention, sequestration of property and forced population transfer. In view of these atrocities, it would seem unlikely that Bosnia-Herzegovina will be able to return in the near future to the condition of relative inter-ethnic peace which prevailed before 1991. Notwithstanding the terms of the 1995 Dayton agreement, the eventual partition of Bosnia-Herzegovina along ethnic lines, therefore, seems probable and, in the guises of territorialization or cantonization, has provided the basis for all internationally brokered negotiations since 1992. Whatever solution is eventually achieved, some minority populations are bound to survive within the regions of otherwise 'pure' ethnic settlement. The securing of the rights of these minorities after years of violent inter-ethnic strife will be particularly difficult and yet uniquely necessary. In addition, the fighting in Bosnia-Herzegovina has prompted a refugee crisis which requires the urgent attention both of neighbouring states and of international organizations.

Further reading

Amnesty International, *Bosnia-Herzegovina: Gross Abuses of Basic Human Rights*, London, October 1992.

Amnesty International, *Bosnia-Herzegovina: Rape and Sexual Abuse by Armed Forces*, London, January 1993.

Malcolm, N., *Bosnia: A Short History*, London, Macmillan, 1994.

Mojzes, P., *Yugoslavian Inferno: Ethnoreligious Warfare in the Balkans*, New York, Continuum, 1994.

Minority-based and advocacy organizations

Croatian Democratic Union of Bosnia-Herzegovina, 88000 Mostar, Dure Pucara, Bosnia-Herzegovina.

Party of Democratic Action, 71000 Sarajevo, Dure Pucara, Bosnia-Herzegovina.

Bulgaria

Land area:	111,000 sq km
Population:	8.49 million (1992)
Main languages:	Bulgarian, Turkish, Macedonian
Main religions:	Eastern Orthodox, Islam (mainly Sunni)
Main minority groups:	*1992 census:* Turks 800,000 (9.4%) Roma 313,000 (3.7%), others including Russians, Armenians and Macedonians 102,600 (1.2%); *other estimates:* Slav-speaking Muslims 250,000 (2.9%), Macedonians 250,000 (2.9%)
Real per capita GDP:	$4,250
UNDP HDI/rank:	0.796 (65)

Bulgaria is in south-eastern Europe and lies on the eastern side of the Balkan peninsula. It is bounded by Romania to the north, Serbia and Macedonia to the west, and Greece and Turkey to the south. The coastline of the Black Sea marks Bulgaria's eastern boundary. The Stara Planina or Balkan Mountains cross Bulgaria from west to east. The Rhodope Mountains lie to the south-west of the country near the frontier with Macedonia and Greece. The Bulgarians, who are a Slavonic people, established an empire in the Balkans in the ninth and tenth centuries, during which time they were converted to Eastern Orthodox Christianity. The Bulgarian state was overrun by the Turks at the end of the fourteenth century and remained a part of the Ottoman Empire until 1878, when it was recognized as an autonomous principality. In 1908 Bulgaria achieved full independence as a sovereign kingdom. After the Second World War, Bulgaria was taken over by the communists, who maintained a monopoly of power until 1989. Since the 'gentle revolution' of that year, Bulgaria has moved towards political pluralism, liberal democracy and a market economy. General elections held in 1990, 1991 and 1994 are acknowledged to have been reasonably fair.

During the five centuries of direct Ottoman rule, the population of Bulgaria became increasingly heterogeneous, acquiring in particular large Turkish and Slav-speaking Muslim minorities. Although many Turks and Muslims left the country after 1878, the population of Bulgaria has retained its ethnic, religious and linguistic diversity. The most recent (1992) census records a minority population of just under 15 per cent. The exclusion of certain categories from the census form and the reluctance of Roma to record themselves as such may mean that the real percentage is higher than the official figure given.[1]

During the late nineteenth and early twentieth centuries, the Bulgarian government made several attempts to convert the non-Christian population. In the 'Christianization' campaign begun at the time of the Balkan Wars of 1912–13, many Slav-speaking Muslims were forced to adopt Bulgarian names.[2] Throughout the interwar period, the government pursued a policy of neglect towards minorities, although Turkish and other minority schools were allowed to function.

Initially, the communist government adopted a reasonably tolerant attitude towards minorities. The constitution of 1947, while making the Bulgarian language obligatory in schools, affirmed that 'National minorities have a right to be educated in the vernacular . . . and to develop their national culture' (article 71). Attempts at assimilation began to be pursued with increasing vigour after 1948. Minority educational and cultural facilities were cut back, religious practices were circumscribed, and fresh attempts were made to have members of minorities adopt Bulgarian names. All references to minorities were removed from the 1971 constitution and facilities were, in practice, only permitted to Armenians and Jews.[3] The assimilationist policy practised by the communist authorities resulted in several waves of emigration and culminated in 1989 with the exodus of 350,000 Turks.

The restoration of the rights of minorities began with the collapse of the communist government in November 1989. Legislation was passed to restore the property of those who had fled the country and to permit the use of Muslim and Arabic names. After November 1989, minority-language publications and cultural groups were refounded. The Law on Public Education passed in October 1991 allows teaching in minority languages in schools, although its implementation has been uneven. A new constitution was approved by the Bulgarian National Assembly in July 1991. Bulgarian is retained as the official language (article 3) but the right is permitted to 'citizens whose national tongue is not Bulgarian . . . to study and use their own languages' (article 36). Although Eastern Orthodox Christianity is described as 'the traditional religion' of Bulgaria, religious freedom is affirmed (articles 12, 37). Controversially, article 11 of the constitution lays down that 'political parties may not be founded on ethnic, racial or religious bases'. Enforcement of this provision, which may violate international conventions, has led to the disqualification of several minority parties from participation in the electoral process.

Turks

Some scholars have sought to show that the Turks of modern Bulgaria are descended from Christian Bulgarians who, during the period of Ottoman rule, forsook both their religion and their language. Others assert that Bulgarian Turks are the descendants either of ethnic Turks who moved into the territory after the fourteenth century or of Turkic tribes which settled in Bulgaria during an even earlier period. Turks live in compact communities in the south of the country in the Arda basin, and in the north-east Dobrudja region. There are also Turkish villages scattered along the central and eastern Stara Planina. According to the 1992 census, there were 800,052 Turks in Bulgaria, constituting 9.43 per cent of the total population, most of whom lived in villages in the countryside.

Prior to the communist take-over, Turks were permitted their own Turkish-language schools, both religious and secular, which followed a separate curriculum. They had their own religious administration and ecclesiastical courts. Cultural segmentation led to most Turks being unable to function in the Bulgarian language. A survey conducted in 1946 revealed that about a half of the Turkish population did not understand Bulgarian.[4]

Communist policy initially respected Turkish-language culture and education while endeavouring to make Turkish students fluent in Bulgarian. Assimilation policy began seriously to affect Turks in 1958, when Turkish-language schools began to be merged with Bulgarian-language ones. By 1975, the teaching of Turkish had been eliminated from the curriculum altogether, and after 1984, newspapers and magazines, intended for Turks, appeared only in the Bulgarian language. In 1984–5 the government embarked upon a policy of forcing Turks to adopt Bulgarian names. Simultaneously, bans were imposed on Muslim religious practices and fines were also imposed for the speaking of Turkish in public places. Resistance to the name-changing campaign led to dismissal from employment, arrests and killings. Throughout the campaign, the government claimed that the name-changing was both voluntary and an aspect of the forging of a 'unified socialist state'.[5]

Mass protests and hunger strikes among Turks began in 1989 and were countered by violent police actions and by the expulsion of Turkish leaders to Turkey. Their departure was followed by a mass emigration of Turks which began in June 1989. Although many Turks were intimidated into leaving, the majority appear to have left voluntarily. By the end of August 1989, about 350,000 Turks had left Bulgaria. The majority of the emigrants were unable to leave with many possessions and were forced to sell their homes or to cancel rental agreements on disadvantageous terms. Many Turks spent only a brief period in Turkey, and by January 1990 about 130,000 had returned.

In December 1989, the Social Council of Citizens, appointed by the new government, recommended that Turks be given the right 'to choose their own names, practise Islam, observe traditional customs and speak Turkish in everyday life'.[6] In March 1990, the Names of Bulgarian Citizens Act was passed by the National Assembly, reinstating the right of all Muslims, including Turks, to choose their own names. Legislation passed between 1990 and 1992 facilitated the return of property to Turks who had left the country in 1989 and allowed the teaching of the Turkish language in schools as an extra-curricular subject. At present, about 920 mosques and *mechets* (religious schools) are active in Bulgaria; copies of the Koran are freely available; and religious instruction has recommenced in mosques. Turkish-language newspapers and magazines have resumed publication while local and national radio broadcast daily programmes in Turkish. The Movement for Rights and Freedoms (MRF), which represents the interest of the Turkish community, was in 1995 the fourth largest political party in Bulgaria.

The decline of the tobacco industry has affected the Turkish community disproportionately. At present, more than 25 per cent of Turks are unemployed, as opposed to 14.4 per cent of ethnic Bulgarians. Economic disadvantage has prompted the continued emigration of ethnic

Turks to Turkey. According to figures released by the Turkish government in October 1992, 160,000 Bulgarian Turks had entered Turkey in the preceding nine months.[7]

Slav-speaking Muslims

Slav-speaking Muslims are most probably descendants of Bulgarian Christians who converted to Islam during the period of Ottoman rule, while retaining the Bulgarian language as well as certain Orthodox practices. They are commonly known as Pomaks or Achrjani; the etymology of these two terms is uncertain, but both may be pejorative in origin. Although precise figures are not available in census data, the minority is estimated at about 250,000 people, dwelling mainly in the Rhodope Mountains.[8]

Slav-speaking Muslims were subjected to forcible conversion in 1912–13 and were the victims of government-led name-changing in the early 1940s. In 1948, the communist authorities initiated programmes aimed at their assimilation, including population transfer to areas of ethnic Bulgarian settlement. Between 1970 and 1973, vigorous attempts were made to oblige Slav-speaking Muslims to abandon their Muslim and Arabic names and adopt Bulgarian ones. These measures were accompanied by violence and led to many deaths. In the late 1980s Slav-speaking Muslims participated in the mass protests at the name-changing campaign of the communist government. Unlike ethnic Turks, Slav-speaking Muslims were refused permission by the authorities to emigrate to Turkey.

Identity among Slav-speaking Muslims is presently unstable and many are redefining themselves as Bulgarians. Some, mainly in the eastern Rhodope mountains, are converting to Christianity, mainly by joining the Uniate and Protestant churches. In the 1992 census, 27,000 Slav-speaking Muslims are believed to have identified themselves as Turks, while a further 35,000 are thought to have declared their mother tongue to be Turkish, even though they could not speak the language.[9] Economic disadvantage among Slav-speaking Muslims may be facilitating Turkicization, since emigration to Turkey is perceived as one way of overcoming employment difficulties. The MRF is presently wooing Slav-speaking Muslims, partly to make up for the decline of its own ethnic constituency on account of emigration.

Roma

Roma are first mentioned in Bulgaria in the fourteenth century but may have entered the country much earlier. Most Roma embraced Islam; presently about a half are Muslim. The 1992 census recorded 313,400 Roma in Bulgaria, although the real number may be twice this figure. The Roma community is deeply segmented and divided by religion, clan affiliation, language and traditional occupation.[11] The Roma were an early target of communist assimilation policy, which included name-changing and forcible settlement in fixed communities. After 1989, several Roma political organizations were established, most notably the Roma Democratic Union and the United Roma Organization. Since 1989 Roma newspapers have resumed publication and cultural activities have recommenced. From 1992, Roma children have been able to study the Roma language and culture in schools, although it has proved hard to find qualified teachers.

Roma continue to suffer severe economic and social disadvantages. Only 7 or 8 per cent of Roma attend secondary schools compared with 54 per cent of ethnic Bulgarians. The literacy rate for the community as a whole may stand as low as 16 per cent. The unemployment rate for Roma is about 60 per cent and Roma villages and quarters in towns frequently lack adequate sanitation and housing. A high incidence of crime is recorded among the Roma population. According to the Ministry of the Interior, 37 per cent of crime is committed by Roma. In 1990, 80 per cent of the prison population was reportedly Roma.[12]

Macedonians

The issue of whether a separate Macedonian language is spoken in Bulgaria and, if so, by how many people is highly controversial. Bulgaria has traditionally claimed that there are no such people as Macedonians since they are in reality ethnic Bulgarians. The 1992 census indicated 10,830 Macedonians. Some unofficial sources have claimed a population of up to 250,000, but this figure is strongly contended. The majority of Macedonians live in the Pirin region, in the south-west of Bulgaria, although there are reportedly Macedonian communities in Plovdiv, Burgas, Varna, Ruse, Pernik and Kyustendil.

Immediately after the Second World War, the Bulgarian Communist Party recognized a separate Macedonian identity, even to the extent of obliging ethnic Bulgarians in the Pirin region to define themselves as Macedonians on their identity cards. In 1947, Macedonian language and history were made compulsory in schools in the Pirin region. The deterioration of relations between Bulgaria and Yugoslavia in 1948 led to the abandonment of the policy of recognition. Macedonian-language education was halted and in the early 1960s identity cards which gave the bearer's nationality as Macedonian were reissued with the inscription of Bulgarian. Macedonian activists were prosecuted and some Macedonians compulsorily resettled. In order to defuse irredentist sentiments, the authorities invested heavily in the Pirin region.

At the end of 1989, several Macedonian political parties were established, most notably the United Macedonian Organization-Ilinden (UMO-Ilinden), which takes its name from the St Elijah's Day or Ilinden (20 July) rising against Ottoman rule in 1903. Its activities have, however, been circumscribed by the authorities on the grounds that the party contravenes article 11 of the 1991 constitution. The principal goal of UMO-Ilinden is to secure the recognition of the Macedonians as a minority in Bulgaria entitled to their own cultural and educational facilities.[10] Extremists within UMO-Ilinden and its rival party, Internal Macedonian Revolutionary Organization – Union of Macedonian Organizations, have advocated respectively the annexation of the Pirin region by Macedonia and the annexation of Macedonia by Bulgaria.

Other minorities

Bulgaria's other minorities also suffered as a consequence of communist assimilation policy. The Armenian community had 13,677 members, according to the 1992 census, the overwhelming majority of whom were town-dwellers. Armenian schools were closed down in the 1960s, although Armenian-language classes continued in several schools. Severe restrictions were also imposed on Armenian religious life. Presently, Armenian is taught for four hours a week in schools in Sofia, Plovdiv, Varna, Ruse and Haskovo. Several Armenian-language magazines and weeklies have resumed publication.

The majority of Bulgarian Jews are Hispanic-Ladino speakers and are the descendants of Sephardic Jews who fled from Spain to the Ottoman empire during the sixteenth and seventeenth centuries. About 40,000 Jews were recorded in Bulgaria during the interwar period, most of whom emigrated to Israel after 1945. The 1992 census records a Jewish population of 3,461. Although the Jewish minority was recognized by the communist authorities, most of the country's synagogues were closed. Ladino-language education has recently resumed in several schools.

The Russian minority numbered 17,139 people according to the 1992 census. Most of these are descendants of White Russians who emigrated to Bulgaria in the 1920s. In Kazachko in the Varna region and in the Tataritsa neighbourhood of Aidemir in the Silistra region are several communities of Russian-speaking Old Believers (Nekrasovtsi), numbering about 1,000 individuals. The Old Believers fled from religious persecution in Russia in the eighteenth century. They preserve strong communal customs including a rejection of tea, coffee, tobacco and modern technology, and maintain their own separate and disputatious church hierarchies. The custom of men to retain long beards continues to conflict with military regulations for conscripts.

Pastoral nomads include Romance-speaking Vlachs and the Greek-speaking Karakachans (also called Sarkatsans), each group numbering about 5,000 people according to the 1992 census.[13] Vlachs and Karakachans were forced to settle in fixed communities during the communist period. The yet smaller communities of Albanians and Muslim Tatars were obliged during the communist period to adopt Bulgarian names. Muslim Cherkez (Circassians), who were settled in Bulgaria in the nineteenth century by the Ottoman authorities, appear to have been entirely assimilated within the Turkish community. The 1992 census also records tiny minorities of Romanians, Ukrainians, Gagauz Turks and Germans. As many as 40,000 guestworkers were employed in Bulgaria during the communist period, the majority being Vietnamese. These appear to have now returned to their former homes.

Conclusions and future prospects

Conditions for minorities in Bulgaria have improved since 1989. Nevertheless, improvements have been secured principally in the field of individual rather than collective rights. Education in the mother tongue has not been established for Turks, except as an extracurricular activity amounting to four hours' tuition a week. The prohibition on ethnic parties is a cause of friction and is perceived by minorities as unjust, while reasoned discussion of the possible linguistic and cultural rights attaching to Macedonians appears to be impossible. Some minorities endure strong economic disadvantages, which may hasten their voluntary assimilation. The influential role paid by the Movement for Rights and Freedoms within Bulgarian domestic politics should, however, ensure that minority issues, especially those affecting the Turkish community, receive due notice and remedy by the authorities.

Further reading

Crampton, R.J., *A Short History of Modern Bulgaria*, Cambridge, Cambridge University Press, 1987.

Ilchev, I. and Perry, D.M., 'Bulgarian ethnic groups: politics and perceptions', *Radio Free Europe/Radio Liberty Research Report*, vol. 2, no. 12, 19 March 1993, pp. 35–41.

Liégeois, J-P. and Gheorghe, N., *Roma/Gypsies: A European Minority*, London, MRG report, 1995.

Poulton, H., *The Balkans: Minorities and States in Conflict*, 2nd edn, London, Minority Rights Publication, 1993.

Minority-based and advocacy organizations

Balkan Foundation for Cross-Cultural Education and Understanding Diversity, 3 Loznitsa Str., 9200 Provadia, Bulgaria, tel./fax: 359 518 3987.

Bulgarian Helsinki Committee, 6 Gurguliat Str., 1000 Sofia, Bulgaria; tel./fax 359 2 81 84 80.

Centre for the Study of Democracy, 1 Lazar Staner Str., 1113 Sofia, Bulgaria; fax 359 2 72 05 09.

Democratic Union of Roma in Bulgaria, Lyulin BL 208 VK II, et 2 Apt 68, 1343 Sofia, Bulgaria.

Helsinki Citizens' Assembly, ul Odrin 29, Block 14, en. G. Apt 34, Sofia 1301, Bulgaria.

Human Rights Project, 55-A Neophit Rilski Str., 1st Floor, Apt 3, 1000 Sofia, Bulgaria; tel./fax 359 2 88 26 16.

Inter-Ethnic Initiative for Human Rights/ Minority Rights Group Bulgaria, 17 Graf Ignatiev Str., 4th Floor, 1000 Sofia, Bulgaria; tel. 359 2 89 19 17, fax 359 2 87 29 65.

International Institute of Human Rights, Mladost 4, Block 435–2 Apt 33, 1115 Sofia, Bulgaria.

International Institute for Macedonia, PO Box 990, 1000 Sofia, Bulgaria; tel./fax 359 2 350 2449.

Movement for Rights and Freedoms, Ivan Vazov ul. Petor Topalor Schmid Bl 50, sh B Apt 55, 1408 Sofia, Bulgaria; fax 359 2 519 822.

Open Society Fund Sofia, 1 Bulgaria Square, NDK Office Building, 11th Floor, 1463 Sofia, PO Box 114, Bulgaria; tel. 359 2 65 81 77, fax 359 2 65 82 76.

Croatia

Land area:	56,540 sq km
Population:	4.79 million (1992)
Main languages:	Croatian, Serbian, Hungarian
Main religions:	Roman Catholicism, Eastern Orthodox Christianity, Islam (Sunni)
Main minority groups:	*1991 census:* Serbs 581,000 (12%), 'Yugoslavs' 104,700 (2.2%), Muslims 48,000 (1%), Hungarians 24,000 (0.5%), Slovenes 24,000 (0.5%), Italians 19,000 (0.4%), others 223,738 (4.7%)
Real per capita GDP:	—
UNDP HDI/rank:	—

Croatia lies in the north-western Balkans and extends in the shape of an inverted 'L' from Slovenia and Hungary in the north to Montenegro in the south. The independent state of Croatia was established in 1991, although until 1995 approximately one-third of its territory was administered by the self-declared 'Serbian Republic of Krajina'. The Croats are a Slavonic people who speak a language virtually identical to Serbian. A current process of linguistic reform is, however, reviving older idioms and making Croatian more distinct as a language. The Croats entered the

Balkans in the sixth and seventh centuries and established a kingdom which in 1102 was incorporated within Hungary. During the Middle Ages, the Croats were converted to Catholicism; adherence to the Catholic faith remains an important aspect of Croat identity. In the sixteenth century, a part of Croatia was overrun by the Turks and the rest fell under the control of the Austrian Habsburgs. On the border with the Ottoman empire, the Habsburgs established the Military Frontier (Vojna Krajina). The frontier was populated largely by peasant soldiers, many of whom were Serbs.

Civil Croatia remained a partially self-governing unit within the Habsburg empire until 1918, when it entered the Kingdom of the Serbs, Croats and Slovenes (after 1929, Yugoslavia). In 1941, Nazi Germany invaded Yugoslavia and established a puppet Croatian or 'Ustasa' state. After the Second World War, Croatia was incorporated within the reorganized federal state of Yugoslavia. During the 1980s, there was increased nationalist agitation in Croatia. Multiparty elections held in 1990 resulted in a decisive victory for the nationalist Croatian Democratic Union (CDU), which in June 1991 proclaimed Croatia a sovereign state.

At the beginning of 1991, Serb secessionists proclaimed their own independent 'Serbian Republic of Krajina' (SRK), including one-third of Croatian territory. The establishment of Serb Krajina, which was violently resisted by the Croatian army, was accompanied by severe human rights abuses, including the mass murder of civilians, illegal detention and forcible population transfer. Following a ceasefire in January 1992, Krajina Serbs retained possession of part of northern Dalmatia around Knin and Glina, western Slavonia centred upon the town of Okucani, and eastern Slavonia including Vukovar. Between 1991 and 1995, most of the 100,000 Croats living in the territory of the SRK were forced to leave. In summer 1995, the Croatian army retook the Krajina with the exception of east Slavonia.

In 1990, a new Croatian constitution was promulgated by the parliament in Zagreb. The constitution, which affirmed Croatia as the 'national state of the Croatian nation', included only vague guarantees of minority rights. The Charter on the Rights of Serbs and Other Nationalities, passed by the parliament in June 1991, affirmed the right of minorities 'to preservation and to cultural autonomy' and 'the right to participate proportionally' in local and central governments. Under EC pressure, the Croatian parliament passed in May 1992 the Constitutional Law of Human Rights and Freedoms, and the Rights of National and Ethnic Communities. The 1992 law gives extensive rights to minorities, including the right to education in the mother tongue, proportional representation in government, local administration and the judiciary, and substantial rights of self-government in areas of compacted minority settlement. The military reconquest of the SRK and the flight of its Serbs make implementation of the 1992 law unlikely.

The Croatian Citizenship Law, adopted in 1991, contains requirements which may be harmful to members of ethnic minorities, who as a consequence of the recent upheavals are denied residence papers (*domovnica*). Naturalization requires, *inter alia*, attachment to the 'legal system and customs' of Croatia and acceptance of 'the Croatian culture'. This subjective evaluation has allegedly been used to disadvantage members of minorities.[1]

The war in former Yugoslavia has led to a severe refugee crisis in Croatia. By the end of 1992, there were in the government-administered areas 264,000 refugees from the Krajina and 334,000 refugees from Bosnia-Herzegovina. During 1992, the Croatian government imposed a ban on refugees attempting to enter Croatia without letters of invitation. Croat refugees were in 1995 moved into properties in the Krajina from which their previous Serb inhabitants had fled; others remained temporarily housed in hotels along the Dalmatian coast.

Serbs

A total of 531,502 Serbs were recorded in the 1981 census and 580,762 in the 1991 census, making up 11.5 per cent and 12.2 per cent of the total population in Croatia respectively. The growth of the Serb minority is partly explained by the decline in the number of people declaring themselves as 'Yugoslavs', from 379,058 in 1981 to 104,728 in 1991. Before the war, Serbs constituted an absolute or relative majority in 11 municipalities running along the border with Bosnia-Herzegovina.[2] Although approximately 40 per cent of Serbs lived in the region subsequently incorporated within the SRK, the remainder were spread around the rest of Croatia, with a heavy concentration in Zagreb.

Serbs originally moved into the territory of modern-day Croatia as border guards and during the period of Habsburg rule, they were settled in the Military Frontier (Vojna Krajina). After the final abolition of the frontier in the late nineteenth century, Serbs were placed under the authority of the civilian government of Croatia, which until 1918 remained part of the Habsburg empire. During the Second World War, Serbs were the targets of violence and genocide practised by the fascist Ustasa government of Croatia. Memory of the terror practised by the Croatian war-time government has left its mark on Serb consciousness and has contributed to Serbs' reluctance to be governed again by Zagreb.

Relations between Serbs and Croats deteriorated rapidly in 1991. The establishment of independent Croatia was combined with a purge of Serbs from the bureaucracy and police force. The removal of signs in Cyrillic script and the adoption of nationalist insignia which recalled Ustasa emblems created further tensions. Serb fears for their future in an independent Croatian state were exploited by the nationalist leadership in Belgrade and hastened the process of territorial secession and of civil war.

During the fighting in the autumn and winter of 1991, Serb communities in Croatia suffered substantial violation of basic human rights. European Community Monitor Mission reports indicate the widespread destruction of Serb villages and churches in Slavonia (eastern Croatia).[3] There are additionally well substantiated cases of the mass murder of Serbs.[4] During 1991–2, Croat regular and paramilitary forces conducted a campaign of 'ethnic cleansing', forcing Serbs to flee their villages by methods of intimidation and violence.

Abuses were reported after the January 1992 ceasefire. In September 1993, Croatian armed forces 'ethnically cleansed' three villages and 11 hamlets in the Medak pocket in northern Dalmatia of their Serb inhabitants. Sixty-seven corpses were subsequently recovered. Croatian government sources attest to the continued destruction of Serb-owned property in many parts of the country, including the capital. During 1992, 7,489 buildings belonging to Serbs were damaged or destroyed and from January to March 1993 a total of 220. Other violations include the eviction of Serbs from their homes, often on the grounds that they were guilty of 'enemy activity against the State of Croatia', a verdict arrived at after only summary decisions of the Housing Commission.[5] Unconfirmed reports suggest that up to 14,000 such evictions had taken place by 1995.[6]

In May 1995, Croatian government forces reoccupied western Slavonia. Of the 70,000 Serbs in western Slavonia in 1991, only several thousand remained after the 1995 offensive.[7] In August 1995, the entirety of the SRK in northern Dalmatia was overrun by the Croatian army. Most Serbs left the region, fleeing into Bosnia and Serbia. The exodus of refugees, whose numbers are estimated as being in excess of 150,000 people, was facilitated by the Croatian army. UN spokespeople subsequently reported that Croatian army units engaged in the murder and robbery of Serb civilians.[8]

Muslims

In 1991, there were 47,603 Muslims in Croatia, making up 1 per cent of the population. They were principally concentrated in Zagreb, Rijeka and Dubrovnik. The majority of these are recent arrivals, since there is no historic Islamic community in Croatia. The number of Muslims has been swollen since 1991 by an estimated 200,000 because of the influx of refugees from Bosnia-Herzegovina. With the outbreak of fighting between Croat and Muslim forces in Bosnia-Herzegovina in April 1993, relations in Croatia deteriorated. There are reports of the intimidation of Muslim clergy and other leaders by local police and authorities, and of the destruction of Muslim-owned property in Dubrovnik, Split and Zagreb. It is further alleged that Muslims have been discriminated against in applications for citizenship. There are substantiated reports that Muslims have been expelled from Croatia and have been used in exchanges for Croat prisoners held by government forces in Bosnia-Herzegovina.[9]

Other minorities

The 1991 census recorded 23,802 Hungarians in Croatia, most of whom lived in Baranja in eastern Slavonia around the confluence of the Danube and Drava rivers. The Hungarian population has been in steady decline since the First World War, when 120,000 Hungarians were recorded in Croatia. Since then they have been permitted their own educational facilities. There is evidence that the Hungarian minority presently living under SRK rule in eastern Slavonia has suffered discrimination and violence. According to United Nations data, more than 40 per cent of the Hungarian population has left eastern Slavonia since the outbreak of hostilities in 1991.[10] Many of these, however, are likely to include young men avoiding conscription and economic migrants.

The 1991 census recorded 19,041 Italians, mostly living in Istria and along the Dalmatian coast. The census did not distinguish between the descendants of Italians who had migrated to the area when it was under Venetian rule or when

Istria formed a part of Italy, and speakers of Istro-Romanian and Istro-Romance, which are autochthonous Romance idioms. The number of Italians is likely to have increased over the past few years on account of the readiness of the Italian government to sell passports to Croats.[11]

According to the 1991 census, there were in Croatia 24,000 Slovenes, 14,000 Czechs, 14,000 Albanians, and 9,500 Montenegrins. There are additionally thought to be as many as 18,000 Roma and 3,000 Jews. In 1991, a bomb blew up the Jewish cemetery in Zagreb, but otherwise little anti-Semitism is reported. In Zadar, there are several hundred Arbanassians, who speak a variety of Albanian, but who, as Catholics, define themselves as Croats. Yugoslav nationality, claimed by 104,728 people in 1991, is presently in decline (down by 70 per cent since 1981).

There are, in addition, strong regionalist sentiments. In the 1991 census, 47,603 people defined themselves by a regional label, mainly as Istrians or Dalmatians. This figure contrasts strongly with the 1981 figure of only 8,657 'regionalists'. In elections held in 1993, the Istrian Democratic Alliance, which seeks autonomy within Croatia, took control of the local Istrian administration.[12]

Conclusions and future prospects

The nationalist direction of Croatian politics, which has led to the violation of rights of Serbs and Muslims, is likely to persist while severe tensions remain with neighbouring states. There is substantial evidence of the violation of basic human rights of Serbs and Muslims by civil and military authorities in Croatia, including murder, destruction of property and forcible population transfer. Croatia has, on paper, one of the most advanced laws on minority protection in Europe. Its implementation is now unlikely on account of the mass flight of Serbs from Croatian territory in the wake of the military victories of 1995. A new minorities law, which takes account of demographic changes in the period 1991–5 and establishes a firm framework for protection, is required, particularly since European Union recognition of Croatia was made conditional upon such legislation. Reports of violence and murder of civilians during the military campaigns of 1995 indicate the importance of unimpeded international monitoring of activities at the front-line and in recently occupied zones.

Further reading

Anti-Semitism World Report 1994, London, Institute of Jewish Affairs, 1994, pp. 156–7.

Dominis, I. and Bicanic, I., 'Refugees and displaced persons in the former Yugoslavia', *Radio Free Europe/Radio Liberty Research Report*, 15 January, 1993, pp. 2–3.

Singleton, F., *A Short History of the Yugoslav Peoples*, Cambridge, Cambridge University Press, 1985.

Minority-based and advocacy organizations

Croatian Helsinki Committee, Trg Bana J. Jelacica 3/11, 41000 Zagreb, Croatia; tel. 385 41 274 715, 432 754, fax 385 41 424 592, e-mail: hho.zg@zamirzg.ztn.zer.de.

Dalmatian Action, Kruziceva 2/11, 58000 Split, Croatia.

Istrian Democratic Assembly, Flanaticka 29/1, 52000 Pula, Croatia.

Serbian People's Party, Trg Mazuranica 3, 41000 Zagreb, Croatia.

Czech Republic

Land area:	79,000 sq km
Population:	10.3 million (1992)
Main languages:	Czech, Slovak, Polish, German
Main religions:	Roman Catholicism, Protestantism (mainly Lutheran)
Main minority groups:	*1991 census:* Moravians 1.36 million (13%), Slovaks 309,000 (3%), Poles 60,000 (0.6%), Germans 50,000 (0.6%), Silesians 44,000 (0.4%), Roma 33,500 (0.3%), others 137,000 (1.3%); *other estimates:* Roma up to 300,000 (2.9%)
Real per capita GDP:	$7,690
UNDP HDI/rank:	0.872 (38)

The Czech Republic lies in the heart of Central Europe, occupying a plateau which is surrounded by low mountain ranges. For most of the twentieth century, the lands constituting the present Czech Republic formed a part of Czechoslovakia. Czechoslovakia was disassembled in 1938–9, reestablished in 1945 and divided once again into the Czech Republic and Slovakia at midnight on 31 December 1992. The modern Czech Republic largely coincides in extent with the historic provinces of Bohemia, Moravia and 'Austrian' Silesia. In the Middle Ages, Bohemia and Moravia constituted an independent kingdom. After 1526, Bohemia and Moravia were incorporated along with Silesia in the Austrian Habsburg empire. Bohemia, Moravia and Silesia retained rights of self-government throughout the four centuries under which they lay under Habsburg rule, although most of Silesia was lost to Prussia in 1740. Strong regional sentiments persist in the modern Czech Republic. The 1991 census thus records Moravians as the largest minority.

For most of its history, the territory of the modern-day Czech Republic was ethnically diverse. Interwar censuses record that almost a quarter of the population of Czechoslovakia were ethnic Germans, most of whom lived in Bohemia, Moravia and Silesia. There is also a long tradition of Polish, Jewish and Roma settlement. During the Second World War, the Jewish and Roma minorities were almost entirely eliminated. After the war, about 3 million Germans were forced to emigrate. As a consequence, the population of the modern Czech Republic demonstrates considerable ethnic homogeneity.

In 1989, the communist regime which had ruled Czechoslovakia since 1948 was overthrown. Elections held in 1992, which demonstrated sharp divisions between Czechs and Slovaks over economic issues, led to Czechoslovakia's division into two independent states. In advance of the separation, a new constitution was promulgated by the Czech parliament which came into force on 1 January 1993. The constitution affirmed the Charter of Fundamental Rights and Freedoms, passed by the Czechoslovak federal assembly in 1991, which forbids discrimination on grounds of race, religion and ethnicity, and makes provision for minority-language education. The 1992 constitution, however, deals only briefly with the rights of minorities, permitting their right to identity and to use of their own language in public affairs, and to their protection from the will of the majority (article 25). In 1990, an official Nationalities Council was instituted to provide a forum for consultation between the government and representatives of minorities. In 1992, a new law on citizenship was passed, which contains provisions that may be considered discriminatory.

Slovaks

According to the 1991 census, Slovaks made up the second largest minority in the Czech Republic, accounting for 308,962 people or 3 per cent of the overall population. The majority of Slovaks are migrants or their descendants who entered the territory of the Czech Republic when it was still a part of Czechoslovakia. By 1991, about 150,000 Slovaks had already acquired Czech nationality which permitted them to assume citizenship almost automatically after the separation. Most of the remaining self-declared Slovaks are believed to have taken Czech citizenship during 1992 and 1993. In July 1994, an amendment passed to the citizenship law made it harder for Slovaks to obtain this status. Although they have their own cultural organizations, the Slovaks of the Czech Republic are likely to be speedily assimilated over the next few years. Only one Slovak elementary school, serving 98 pupils, was operating in 1993.

Poles

In the 1991 census, 58,573 people declared themselves as Poles, the majority of whom lived in Silesia. Poles represent a historic minority in the Czech Republic, and their principal area of settlement, the Tesin region, has for centuries been an area with a heavily mixed population. Although Polish cultural organizations have received state funding, the leading Polish minority organization, the Polish Council, has complained of deliberate delays in compensating Poles who were dispossessed of property under the communists. In 1993, there were 29 elementary schools providing Polish and Czech bilingual education in the Czech Republic, although most of these were reported to be short of funds and in serious disrepair.[1] The proximity of Silesia to the Polish border will probably ensure that a distinct sense of Polish identity persists in the region.

Germans

Until 1945, there was a substantial German population in the Czech lands, comprising mainly the descendants of German peasants and town dwellers, who migrated to the region during the Middle Ages, and of Austrian-German administrators and merchants. The majority of Germans lived in the Sudetenland adjoining the border with Germany. Of the 3 million Germans in interwar Czechoslovakia, only 165,000 remained in 1950, as a consequence of their mass expulsion after the Second World War. Voluntary German emigration continued for much of the postwar period. According to the 1991 census, the German population of the Czech Republic accounted for 50,000 people. Most Germans live in scattered communities across north-western Bohemia, mainly constituting only a small part of the local population. Although a recent revival of interest in their historical culture has been reported among Germans, their eventual assimilation is likely in the long term. There are no publicly funded schools in which German is a language of instruction (although some private schools have been set up), nor are there radio broadcasts in German. Several German language newspapers are published, but the language is reported to be in decline among ethnic Germans.

Roma

The 1991 census recorded 33,489 Roma in the Czech Republic. Since a social stigma attaches to Roma identity, it is probable that the number of Roma is far greater than the official statistic and may be as high as 300,000. The Roma community in the Czech Republic mainly comprises Slovak and Hungarian Roma who entered the territory after the Second World War. Nomadic Czech and Moravian Roma were almost entirely destroyed during the Nazi occupation.

Although recognized as a national minority in interwar Czechoslovakia, Roma were obliged to carry 'Gypsy Personal Identity Cards' and nomads had to register with the local authorities every time that they moved. Under the communists, attempts at forcible assimilation were introduced, which included a ban on nomadism and a policy of sterilization. During the 1970s and 1980s, assimilation gave way to segregation and to the construction of housing estates reserved for Roma. On the basis of flawed psychological tests, Roma children were often sent to schools for the handicapped where they were taught manual activities.

Some improvement in conditions followed the 1989 revolution. Cultural associations were founded and magazines in the Roma language began publication. In 1995, 15 such publications appeared regularly, although some newsagents are reported to have refused to stock them. Roma representatives participated in the Nationalities Council and a Roma museum was established in Brno. Nevertheless, Roma continue to face discrimination in employment, and in some parts of northern Bohemia 80 per cent of Roma are unemployed. Extremes of poverty combined with social marginalization have contributed to a high incidence of criminality. Although some standardization of the language has begun around the Romani *cib* dialect, there are as yet no bilingual schools for Roma children to assist their integration. Roma have also been subjected to violence on the part of members of extremist organizations, and to some alleged police harassment. Between 1990 and 1993, 16 Roma were murdered in racial attacks.[2] Throughout 1995–6 there were repeated allegations that local officials had forbidden Roma access to public baths.

Approximately one-third (100,000) of Roma in the Czech Republic are Slovak citizens. The Czech citizenship law, which came into force on 1 January 1993, makes citizenship conditional upon a prior two-year residency and five years without a criminal conviction. An amendment passed in June 1993 requires evidence of economic means and of stable accommodation. Although these measures are not in violation of international law, they have been criticized as discriminatory by the 1994 Conference on Security and Cooperation in Europe meeting on Romany Issues. Roma without Czech citizenship are not entitled to free medical care or education, nor may they participate in the privatization process. They may also be deported at will by the authorities.[3]

Migrants

The Czech Republic has attracted a substantial migrant community, partly because of its burgeoning economy and partly because it is a convenient transit point between Western and Eastern Europe. In 1993, it was calculated that there were in the Czech Republic 90,000 migrants working legally and 75,000 illegally. The latter figure may, however, be an underestimate; in 1993, Czech frontier police reported more than 43,000 illegal border crossings. The largest migrant community consists of US Americans, of whom there were 30,000 in Prague alone in 1993. Many of these work illegally, having entered the country on tourist visas, and may thus be vulnerable to exploitation. Of the 47,000 migrants with official residence permits, the largest share (27 per cent) were Poles, followed by Ukrainians (16 per cent), Vietnamese (12 per cent) and former Yugoslavs (9 per cent). Up to two-thirds of these migrants are male. Many live in barrack accommodation and work for half the wages of Czechs. Ukrainians are mostly active in construction; Yugoslavs in street vending.[4]

Other minorities

The 1991 census recorded 20,143 Hungarians, 1,711 Ruthenes and 6,807 Ukrainians. Most of these are migrants or their descendants from Slovakia, who entered the Czech Republic when it was still part of Czechoslovakia. The strength of regional identity led 1,356,267 Czechs to describe themselves as Moravians and a further 44,025 as Silesians in the census. The Movement for the Self-Governing Democracy of Moravia and Silesia, which has campaigned for regional devolution, won 14 out of 200 seats in the 1992 elections to the Czech parliament. Moravians and Silesians may not, however, constitute minorities by the accepted definition of the term. The Jewish community, which numbered over 180,000 people before the holocaust, is variously estimated at between 3,000 and 8,000. No information is currently available on the tiny Croat minority which has been resident in the territory of the Czech Republic since the eighteenth century.

Conclusions and future prospects

The principal legislative acts of the Czech Republic provide for the protection of minorities and for the preservation of their identity. Nevertheless, the policies pursued by the Czech government indicate a strategy of benign neglect which is likely to lead to the gradual assimilation of minorities. Insufficient funds are currently allocated towards the preservation, in particular, of Slovak, German and Roma identity, while neither legislation nor resources appear to be directed to the protection of new migrants. The impact of the 1992 citizenship law on the Roma community is potentially adverse and its full implementation can only serve to increase their social marginalization.

Further reading

Keersmaeker, G. de, 'Citizenship law in the Czech Republic', *Helsinki Citizens Assembly Quarterly*, no. 10, Summer 1994, pp. 19–20.

Krejci, J., *Czechoslovakia at the Crossroads of European History*, London, Tauris, 1990.

Liégeois, J.-P. and Gheorghe, N., *Roma/Gypsies: A European Minority*, London, MRG report, 1995.

MRG (ed.), *Minorities in Central and Eastern Europe*, London, MRG report, 1993.

Tritt, R., *Struggling for Ethnic Identity: Czechoslovakia's Endangered Gypsies*, New York, Human Rights Watch, 1992.

Minority-based and advocacy organizations

Association of Germans in Bohemia, Moravia and Czech Silesia, Doudlebská 8, 14000 Prague 4, Czech Republic.

Citizens' Solidarity and Tolerance Movement (HOST), PO Box 13, 12800 Prague 2, Czech Republic; tel. 42 2 2491 1338.

Czech Helsinki Committee, PO Box 4, 11900 Prague 12, Czech Republic; tel. 42 2 3337 2334, fax 42 2 3337 2335.

Decade of Human Rights Education, Polska 26, 120000 Prague 2, Czech Republic.

Foundation for the Renewal and Development of Traditional Romany Values, Malá Stepánská 6, 12000 Prague 2, Czech Republic; tel./fax 42 2 2421 0309.

Helsinki Citizens' Assembly, Milady Horakove 103, 16000 Prague 6, Czech Republic.

Moravian National Party, PO Box 394, Krenova, 61 Brno, Czech Republic.

Movement for the Self-Governing Democracy of Moravia and Silesia, Frantizkanska 1–3, Brno, Czech Republic.

Tolerance Foundation, Senovazne nam. 24, 11000 Prague 1, Czech Republic; tel. 42 2 2410 2314.

Estonia

Land area:	45,215 sq km
Population:	1,625,399 (1995)
Main languages:	Estonian (official), Russian
Main religions:	Lutheran Church, Baptist Church, Russian Orthodox
Main minority groups:[1]	Russians 474,834 (30.3%), Ukrainians 48,271 (3.1%), Belarusians 27,711 (1.8%), Finns 16,622 (1.1%), also smaller populations of Jews, Tatars, Germans, Latvians, Poles, Lithuanians and others
Real per capita GDP:	$6,690
UNDP HDI/rank:	0.862 (43)

The Republic of Estonia lies on the eastern coast of the Baltic Sea. To the west it borders the Baltic, to the north the Gulf of Finland, to the east the Russian Federation and to the south the Republic of Latvia. Its territory includes 1,521 islands in the Baltic Sea. Estonia also claims more than 2,000 sq km of territory currently in the Russian Federation, in the Narva and Pechora regions, based on boundaries established in 1920. Dominated since the thirteenth century by Danes, Germans, Poles, Swedes and Russians, Estonia was established as a modern nation-state in 1918. However, from the very beginning, Estonians had to fight for independence against the imperialist ambitions of Germany and Bolshevik Russia. The war of independence ended with the signing of the Tartu Peace Treaty in 1920. In this treaty Soviet Russia renounced all claims on the sovereign rights of Estonia. The country's first constitution was proclaimed in June 1920, and Estonia became a member of the League of Nations in 1921.

Estonia, together with Latvia and Lithuania, was occupied by the Red Army as a result of the Molotov–Ribbentrop Pact and the country was incorporated into the Soviet Union in August 1940, whereupon thousands of Estonians were arrested and killed and tens of thousands deported. The entire Estonian political and social infrastructure was destroyed and replaced with Soviet institutions. After Hitler's Germany attacked the Soviet Union, Estonia was occupied by Nazi forces from 1941 to 1944, when the Soviets again took over. As a result of deportations, war, mobilization and mass emigration, the population of Estonia decreased from 1,136,000 in October 1939 to 854,000 in January 1945. In 1945, Estonians formed about 90 per cent of the population. Subsequently, the ethnic composition of Estonia was substantially altered. Heavy industry introduced by the central Soviet authorities required a new workforce and hundreds of thousands of people were brought into the country from central Russia, the Ukraine and Belarus. During the whole period of Soviet occupation after the war, half a million more people came to Estonia than left. The percentage of Estonians in the population, according to the 1989 census, dropped to 61.5 per cent.

Mikhail Gorbachev's policies of *glasnost* and *perestroika* offered an opportunity for democratic forces to begin voicing protests against environmental damage, forced industrialization, Russification and the repression of Estonian national culture. The Estonian Supreme Soviet declared sovereignty (precedence of Estonian legislation over Soviet legal acts) in November 1988. Estonia issued a declaration in August 1991 on the re-establishment of independence. After protracted negotiations the armed forces of the Russian Federation withdrew from Estonia in August 1994, although a number of demobilized Russian officers remain in the country.

According to the 1989 Soviet census, 121 nationalities lived in Estonia. Of the total population of 1,565,662, Estonians constituted 61.53 per cent. Besides the ten largest minorities – in descending order, Russians, Ukrainians, Belarusians, Finns, Jews, Tatars, Germans, Latvians, Poles and Lithuanians – 110 other nationalities comprised 14,095 people or 0.9 per cent of the population. Some forty-eight nationalities were represented by fewer than ten individuals each. The non-Estonian population lives predominantly in the main industrial towns in the north-east of the country and in the capital, Tallinn.

The Estonian constitution of 1992 prohibits discrimination based on race, sex, religion or political or other beliefs. It guarantees the same fundamental rights to Estonian citizens and non-citizens alike (article 9). It provides for the right to assemble freely but prohibits non-citizens from joining political parties, although they may form social groups. The Law on Local Elections adopted in 1993 permits resident non-citizens to vote but not to run for office. Estonian law makes no distinction on the basis of lack of citizenship or other such grounds regarding business or property ownership (other than land). All residents of Estonia may participate equally in the privatization of state-owned housing.

As in the other Baltic states, one of the most important inter-ethnic issues in Estonia centres on the large number of non-citizens in the country. In January 1995, the Riigikogu (Estonian parliament) passed a new law on citizenship, which brings all the citizenship related regulations into one document. Estonian citizenship can be acquired by birth (if at least one of the child's parents is an Estonian citizen) or by naturalization. An Estonian citizen may not simultaneously be a citizen of another country (article 1). Citizens of foreign states who wish to become naturalized must be at least 18 years old and must have lived permanently in Estonia for at least five years before applying. According to article 9, an applicant must have knowledge of Estonia's state system and the Estonian constitution, and speak Estonian (language knowledge requirements are established by a separate law). In addition, an applicant must take an oath of loyalty to the Republic of Estonia and its constitution (article 6). Article 16 of the Citizenship Law Implementation Act bars the naturalization of:

'Foreign military personnel in active service; persons who have been in the employment of the security and intelligence organizations of the Union of Soviet Socialist Republics; persons who have been convicted of serious criminal offences against people or who have a criminal record of repeated convictions for felonies; and persons lacking a legal steady income.'

The Russian authorities, concerned with the plight of ethnic Russians in the former Soviet republics, have pushed for Estonia's adoption of a dual citizenship policy. The Estonian authorities argue that dual citizenship would raise serious questions for individuals in terms of where their loyalty lies and that the granting of automatic citizenship to all permanent residents in Estonia cannot guarantee loyalty to the continued existence of Estonia.

In response to criticism about the treatment of ethnic minorities, in 1992 the Estonian President established a Human Rights Institute to monitor human rights in Estonia, investigate reports of violations and provide information concerning ethnic and nationality issues.

Since 1993, all those employed in government offices and in the service sector are required to acquire appropriate Estonian-language competence within four years. In districts where the language of more than one-half of the population is a language other than Estonian, the inhabitants are entitled to receive official information in that language, and the local government may conduct business in that language. Western monitors have reported that the language office liberally grants extensions to people who can explain their failure to meet their requisite competence level in the permitted time. Estonian-language training is available, but some claim it is too costly. Representatives of ethnic Russians have commented that the language requirements are too difficult.

Russians

Various Russian communities have lived in Estonia over the past 1,000 years. Earlier communities consisted of traders, religious and political dissidents and settlers. Until the 1940s, these communities remained small, comprising some 8.2 per cent of the population. Since Estonia's incorporation into the USSR, large number of ethnic Russians were encouraged to migrate to

Estonia, to work as factory workers, state and communist party administrators, military and police personnel. By 1989, they comprised almost one-third of the total population. Ethnic Russians are mostly in the main industrial towns in the north-east of the country bordering the Russian Federation. They also constitute the majority of the non-citizen residents of Estonia. Treatment of ethnic Russian non-citizens continues to be a major issue domestically and bilaterally with the Russian Federation. Non-Estonians, especially Russians, allege occupational, salary and housing discrimination because of Estonian language requirements. Those who desire language instruction confront problems stemming from an insufficient number of qualified teachers, lack of funds, poor educational infrastructure and an examination process which some allege is arbitrary. Three Russian-language daily newspapers are published in Estonia. Several Russian-language programmes, funded by the Estonian authorities, are broadcast over state and private television channels. There is also an extensive Russian-language network of schools. However, state support for these institutions will be withdrawn in the year 2000.

Ukrainians and Belarusians

Ukrainians and Belarusians constitute the second and third largest ethnic minorities in Estonia. The 1989 Soviet census registered 48,271 Ukrainians and 27,711 Belarusians. The overwhelming majority of these minorities arrived in Estonia from the 1940s onwards. Both groups have found it difficult to accommodate themselves to the post-1991 situation. Many ethnic Ukrainians and Belarusians occupy prominent posts in industry, education, medicine and white-collar occupations which they feel are now being threatened because of Estonian-language requirements.

Other minorities

According to the 1989 census, Finns, whose language is fairly close to Estonian, numbered 16,622 (1.06 per cent), Jews 4,381 (0.4 per cent), Tatars 4,058 (0.25 per cent), Germans 3,466 (0.22 per cent), Latvians 3,135 (0.20 per cent), Poles 3,008 (0.19 per cent), and Lithuanians 2,568 (0.16 per cent). Other smaller minorities include Armenians, Azeris, Moldovans, Chuvash, Kraelians and Roma. Jews, whose first congregation was founded in Tallinn in 1830, have suffered perhaps the greatest decline in numbers. Several hundred Jews were deported in June 1941 and later that year, during the German occupation, some 1,000 who had failed to flee were murdered. The Estonian Jewish community today consists of about 1,000 people, more than half of whom are pensioners.

Conclusions and future prospects

As in Latvia and Lithuania the critical issue for minorities in Estonia is the naturalization of the large number – some 384,000 – of resident non-citizens. The new citizenship law can, in the long run, allow for naturalization, provided, as suggested by the Council of Europe Parliamentary Assembly in February 1996, the language test is simplified. There appears to be no prospect that the Estonian authorities will allow for dual citizenship as advocated by the Russian government. By mid-1995 more than 82 per cent of non-Estonian resident members of minority ethnic groups had applied for residence and work permits, thus indicating that they wish to remain in the country. In the long term, successful naturalization of the ethnic minority population may enable it to participate fully in the political life of Estonia, and this in turn offers the prospect of much reduced ethnic tensions, particularly between Russians and native Estonians.

Further reading

Baltic Observer.

Dahlgren, T. (ed.), *Human Rights in the Baltic States*, Helsinki, Advisory Board for International Human Rights Affairs, Finnish Helsinki Committee, 1993.

Hiden, J. and Salmon, P., *The Baltic Nations and Europe: Estonia, Latvia and Lithuania in the Twentieth Century,* London, Longman, 1994.

Rauch, G.V., *The Baltic States: The Years of Independence: Estonia, Latvia, Lithuania, 1917–1940,* New York, St Martin's Press, 1995.

Taagepera, R., *Estonia: Return to Independence.* Boulder, CO, and Oxford, Westview Press, 1993.

Minority-based and advocacy organizations

Estonian Union for Illegally Repressed People (Memento), PO Box 3410, Peapostkontor, 0090 Tallinn, Estonia; tel. 372 2 45 09 74.

Estonian Union of National Minorities, PO Box 3476, Peapostkontor, 0090 Tallinn, Estonia; tel. 372 2 31 64 42.

Jaan Tönisson Institute, 1 Nafta Street, 0001 Tallinn, Estonia; tel. 372 2 42 23 97, fax 372 2 42 43 61, e-mail: jti@jti.ee.

Jewish Congregation in Estonia, PO Box 3576, Peapostkontor, 0090 Tallinn, Estonia; tel. 372 2 43 85 66.

Legal Information Centre for Human Rights, Kanepi 4–53, 0003 Tallinn, Estonia; tel. 372 2 49 66 49, fax 372 655 2647, e-mail: lara@teleport.ee.

Hungary

Land area:	92,000 sq km
Population:	10.3 million (1992)
Main languages:	Hungarian, Romani, German, Slovak, Serbo-Croat
Main religions:	Roman Catholicism, Protestantism (Lutheran and Calvinist), Eastern Orthodox Christianity
Main minority groups:	*1990 census:* Roma 143,000 (1.3%), Germans 31,000 (0.3%), Croats 13,700 (0.1%), Slovaks 10,500 (0.1%), others 33,300 (0.3%); *other estimates:* Roma 250,000–800,000 (2.4–7.8%), Slovaks 120,000 (1.2%), Jews 100,000 (1%)
Real per capita GDP:	$6,580
UNDP HDI:	0.855 (50)

Hungary is bordered by Slovakia to the north, Romania and Ukraine to the east, Austria and Slovenia to the west, and Croatia and Serbia to the south. The eastern part of Hungary consists mainly of open plain; west of the Danube the countryside is more hilly. The Hungarians (Magyars), who speak a Finno-Ugrian language, entered the territory of present-day Hungary in the late ninth century. During the Middle Ages, the Hungarians established a kingdom which included substantial parts of present-day Romania and Yugoslavia and the whole of Slovakia. After 1526, Hungary was incorporated within the Habsburg empire of which it remained a part until 1918. The historic Hungarian state had a strongly multi-ethnic character. Only about a half of its population were ethnic Hungarians, the remainder being principally Germans, Slovaks, South Slavs and Romanians.

With the Treaty of Trianon (1920), two-thirds of Hungary was apportioned to neighbouring states, leaving Hungary with a largely homogeneous ethnic population. During the interwar period, Hungary practised a policy of assimilation with regard to its remaining minorities. Most official documents and signposts were written only in Hungarian and the Hungarian language constituted the sole vehicle of education in state schools. In the Second World War, about 600,000 Jews were deported and murdered. Thousands more emigrated after the war to Israel and the United States. Between 1945 and 1948, forcible resettlement and population exchange resulted in the expulsion of about 70,000 Slovaks and 200,000 Germans. For those members of minorities who remained, the Hungarian government instituted education in the mother tongue and authorized the introduction of bilingual signposts in areas of minority settlement. During the 1950s, however, the policy reversed as minority organizations were considered 'atoms of pluralism'. The teaching of Hungarian was increased in minority schools, cultural groups went into sharp decline, and no opportunity was permitted for dealing with the authorities in any language other than Hungarian. The policy of assimilation persisted until the 1970s when minority language education, at both elementary and secondary level, was promoted.

During the late 1980s, there was a marked increase in the number of minority organizations and a Secretariat (after 1990, Office) of National and Ethnic Minorities was established within the Ministerial Council to coordinate and oversee policy. Free elections, held in Hungary in 1990, led to the formation of a conservative coalition government. The new government was much concerned with the plight of Hungarian minorities abroad, principally in Romania. As part of its attempt to secure enhanced international standards of rights protection for minorities, the government actively championed the rights of minorities within Hungary itself.

Hungary retains the communist constitution promulgated in 1949, but it has been so heavily amended that it bears little relationship to the original text. Article 68 of the constitution, amended in 1989–90, declares:

'National and ethnic minorities are state-forming elements. The Republic of Hungary protects the minorities living on its territory and secures their collective participation in public matters, the fostering of their culture, the use of their native language, their native-language education, and the right to use their names according to their own language.'

Bilateral treaties concluded with Ukraine, Slovenia, Croatia and Germany in 1992, with Slovenia in 1994 and with Slovakia in 1995 reinforced these rights in respect of co-nationals of the signatories. In September 1992, the representation of minorities in the parliament by non-voting deputies received legislative approval, although this measure was subsequently withdrawn by parliamentary amendment in 1994. In June 1995, a parliamentary commissioner for minority rights was appointed, who was charged with ensuring the implementation of legislation affecting minorities.

Law on the rights of national and ethnic minorities (1993)

The corner-stone of minorities protection in Hungary is the 1993 Law on the Rights of National and Ethnic Minorities. The Act, which includes prohibitions against assimilation, discrimination and harassment, makes the provision of minority-language classes compulsory when demanded by more than eight children. The state is obliged to support cultural activities of minorities, and local bodies are instructed to make official documents and street names bilingual in areas of minority settlement. Most of the 1993 law, however, concerns the operation of minority self-government. Directly elected minority local governments are to be consulted by the local authorities in all matters pertaining to the minority, and they are given budgets with which to promote cultural activities, including local broadcasting and publishing. A national minority self-government, elected by representatives of local minority institutions, safeguards minority interests at state level. In accordance with the 1993 law, elections to minority local self-governments took place in 654 communities in December 1994. The right to participate in minority self-government elections is open to all citizens and does not depend upon public profession of membership of a minority.

Criticisms of the 1993 act include its vague wording in several places, particularly concerning the use of minority languages in national television and radio, and its refusal to permit a full devolution of state functions by grant of territorial autonomy. One unexpected difficulty may be the clause that in settlements where a minority constitutes a majority, the minority self-government may appropriate the powers of the local authorities. The Act makes no allowance, however, for the rights of local Hungarian minorities-within-a-minority created by this provision. It is additionally claimed that the minority self-governments lack sufficient resources of their own to be effective.

The 1993 act recognizes the existence of thirteen minorities: Armenians, Bulgarians, Croats, Germans, Greeks, Poles, Roma, Romanians, Ruthenes, Serbs, Slovaks, Slovenes and Ukrainians. All are entitled to establish minority self-government, even though, as with the thirty-seven self-declared Armenians in the 1990 census, their numbers may be very small.

Roma

The 1990 census recorded 142,683 Roma, although unofficial estimates variously put their number at between 250,000 and 800,000. Official sources privately concede a figure of 500,000. Hungarian Roma are divided between Lovari and speakers of the Bea dialects (although Romani is only spoken by about 40,000 Roma) and by strong clan allegiances. During the 1970s and 1980s, the communist authorities in Hungary embarked upon a policy of supporting Roma activities and culture which was quite exceptional at the time in Central and Eastern Europe.[1] Several hundred Roma organizations now compete for the allegiance of the minority and for state funds. Competition within the Roma community has meant that Roma political parties have been unable to establish successful coalitions with which to contest elections. In 1994, a Roma secondary school was opened in Pecs with the aim of educating a future Roma elite. Roma organizations report, however, continued discrimination in employment, racial attacks and police harassment.

Germans

Germans constitute the second largest minority in Hungary, numbering 30,824 people according to the 1990 census. German estimates that their number is in reality 200,000 are inflated. Germans are widely dispersed throughout the country and constitute a majority in only a few villages. In the late 1980s, there were three bilingual elementary schools and three secondary schools, in Budapest, Baja and Pecs. The number of schools providing German-language instruction may be on the increase. In one famous case, Slovaks reascribed to German identity in order to obtain German teaching in their school since this was considered a 'more useful' language. Although there has been a recent revival of interest in their history and culture, the German minority faces strong assimilationist pressures, and the German language has already allegedly become 'a grandmother language, spoken only by elderly people'.[2] Since 1987, the German federal government has provided roughly DM 2 million a year to support the Hungarian German community.

Other minorities

The 1990 census records 10,740 Romanians, concentrated mainly in the eastern part of the country. Although some Romanian-language schools remain, Romanians are slowly assimilating and about a half of all marriages involving Romanians are exogamous. The 1990 census also recorded 10,459 Slovaks living in the north of the country and near the Serbian border, but official sources privately suggest a figure of 120,000. Slovak spokespeople have referred to the rapid assimilation of the Slovak minority, and have demanded special measures to arrest this process. There were additionally 13,750 Croats and 2,905 Serbs, most of whom are settled in the south. Their numbers are believed to have increased substantially on account of emigration from former Yugoslavia. Unofficial estimates put the number of Jews at 100,000 living mainly in Budapest.

Although interwar Hungary acquired a reputation for anti-Semitism, recent anti-Semitic incidents have been rare. There are additionally very few Armenians, Bulgarians, Greeks, Poles, Ruthenes, Slovenes and Ukrainians, all of which groups are formally recognized as minorities and entitled as such to form minority self-governments. A growing migrant population, including up to 10,000 Chinese, has been reported. Migrants and members of minorities who do not have a history of settlement lasting over a century are specifically excluded from the terms of Hungarian minorities law.

Conclusions and future prospects

Hungary is a path-setter in Central and Eastern Europe with regard to minorities protection. Despite its deficiencies, the 1993 law may provide a model of good practice for other states in the region to follow. Nevertheless, Hungary has several obvious advantages, not least its relative prosperity and the very small size of its minority population. The condition of Roma may require a larger degree of affirmative action in employment, education and housing than the electorate is prepared to tolerate. While conforming to international norms, both the exclusion of migrants from the terms of the 1993 law and the 'century of settlement' criterion for minority status may be considered unduly harsh and are likely to be tested in the future.

Further reading

Anti-Semitism World Report 1995, London, Institute of Jewish Affairs, 1995.

Barany, Z., 'Roma: grim realities in Eastern Europe', *Transition*, 29 March 1995, pp. 3–11.

Hoensch, J.K., *A History of Modern Hungary 1867–1986*, London, Longman, 1988.

Liégeois, J-P. and Gheorghe, N., *Roma/Gypsies: A European Minority*, London, MRG report, 1995.

MRG (ed.), *Minorities in Central and Eastern Europe*, London, MRG report, 1993.

Patterson, G.J., 'Hungary's disappearing Romanian minority', *East European Quarterly*, 25, no. 1, 1991, pp. 117–23.

Minority-based and advocacy organizations

Amaro Drom [Roma], Tavaszmezo u. 6, 1084 Budapest, Hungary.

Association Lingo Drom [Roma], Budapest, Hungary; fax. 36 1 176 7435.

European Roma Rights Center, Nador u. 11, 4th Floor, 1051 Budapest, Hungary; tel. 36 1 327 3118 fax 36 1 327 3103.

Federation of Germans in Hungary, Nagymezö u. 49, 1396 Budapest, Hungary.

Hungarian Centre for Human Rights, Orszaghaz u. 30, PF25 Budapest, Hungary.

Hungarian Gypsies Peace Party, Dembinszky u. 2, VII Budapest, Hungary.

Hungarian Helsinki Committee, Jozsef Krt. 34.1.5, 1085 Budapest, Hungary; tel. 36 1 114 0885, 134 4575, fax 36 1 114 0885.

Office for National and Ethnic Minorities, Kossuth L. ter. 4, 1055 Budapest, Hungary; tel. 36 1 268 3800, fax 36 1 268 3802.

Roma Parliament Electoral Alliance, Tavaszmezo u. 6, VIII Budapest, Hungary.

Roma Press Center, Alada'r Horvátn, Ferenc Körút 22, II emelet 3, 1092 Budapest, Hungary; tel./fax 36 1 218 6476.

Romani Union, Fust Milauv w. 22 II, 1039 Budapest, Hungary.

Latvia

Land area:	64,600 sq km
Population:	2,565,854 (1994)
Main languages:	Latvian (official), Russian
Main religions:	Lutheran Church, Roman Catholicism, Russian Orthodox Christianity, Old Believers, Baptist Church, Judaism
Main minority groups:	Russians 849,300 (33.1%), Belarusians 105,100 (4.1%), Ukrainians 78,200 (3%), Poles 57,200 (2.2%), Lithuanians 33,200 (1.3%), Jews 13,284 (0.5%), also smaller populations of Armenians, Azeris, Bulgarians, Estonians, Georgians, Germans, Livs, Roma, Tatars, Uzbeks and Yakuts
Real per capita GDP:	$6,060
UNDP HDI/rank:	0.857 (48)

The Republic of Latvia lies on the eastern coast of the Baltic Sea. To the north it borders Estonia, to the south and south-west Lithuania, to the east the Russian Federation, and to the south-east Belarus. The origins of the Latvian state go back to the thirteenth century when a political union of several Baltic tribes was established under the Livonian Order of Knights on the territory of present-day Latvia and Estonia. This union included the Finno-Ugrians (Estonians and Livs). The Livonian War in the sixteenth century, which began as a Russian attempt to conquer Livonia, led to the division of the state between Sweden and the Polish–Lithuanian Commonwealth. A new wave of Russian expansion led in 1795 to the complete incorporation of the lands on the eastern shore of the Baltic Sea into the Russian empire. Latvians began to consider themselves a separate nation in the first part of the nineteenth century, when the first Latvian-language newspapers were published. Latvia remained part of the Tsarist empire until the end of the First World War. It declared independence in November 1918, although this was not recognized by Soviet Russia until the signing of the Peace Treaty of Riga in August 1920. The republic's first constitution was proclaimed two years later.

Like the other two Baltic states, Latvia was occupied by the Red Army as a result of the Molotov–Ribbentrop Pact and was incorporated into the Soviet Union in August 1940. Soviet legislation and judiciary were introduced with retroactive effect, resulting in the deportation of tens of thousands of individuals. A resistance movement against Soviet control continued for several years after the Second World War. By

1953, about 120,000 people had been killed, imprisoned or deported to labour camps in Siberia. The policy of intensive industrialization, combined with deliberate Russification, resulted in the influx of some 750,000 eastern Slav immigrants into Latvia. The proportion of indigenous Latvians in the country declined from 77 per cent in 1935 to 52 per cent in 1989.

The implementation of Mikhail Gorbachev's policies of *glasnost* and *perestroika* allowed Latvia to declare its sovereignty (priority of local legislation over all-Union legislation) in July 1989. Thereafter, despite objections from the Soviet authorities, Latvia declared the renewal of its independence in May 1990 and embarked on a period of transition, completed in August 1991 with a declaration of the full restoration of Latvian state authority. Both the 1990 declaration of restored Latvian independence and the declaration of *de facto* independence proclaimed the authority of the 1922 constitution, thus stressing the continuity of independence. Virtually all forces stationed by the Soviet Union in Latvia, with the exception of some 600 personnel operating the Skrunda naval nuclear station in western Latvia, had left the country by 31 August 1994. However, several thousand demobilized Red Army officers and soldiers are thought to have remained illegally.

Latvian government population statistics for 1994 show the presence of 120 ethnic groups. Of the total population of 2,565,854, Latvians constituted 54.2 per cent. Besides the eleven largest minorities – in descending order, Russians, Belarusians, Ukrainians, Poles, Lithuanians, Jews, Roma, Germans, Tatars, Estonians and Armenians, other ethnic groups, including Moldovans, Azeris, Chuvash and Georgians, numbered fewer than 1,000 people each; a further 84 ethnic groups, including Livs, numbered fewer than 200 individuals each. Latvia has a high rate of ethnic intermarriage: nearly one-third of marriages in general and one-fifth of all marriages involving an ethnic Latvian.

One of Latvia's most important future domestic policy tasks centres on issues related to the large number of non-citizens in the country – 740,231 people or about 29 per cent of the population, the overwhelming majority of whom are members of ethnic minorities. The Constitutional Law provides that only citizens may occupy state positions, establish political parties, own land or 'choose a place of abode on Latvian territory'. Under the constitution, all residents of Latvia enjoy equal rights under the law, but the majority of non-ethnic Latvians who are not citizens of Latvia cannot fully participate in the civic life of the country.

In October 1991, citizenship was restored to those who were citizens of prewar Latvia and their direct descendants. According to a new law on citizenship adopted by the Latvian parliament (the Saeima) in July 1994, a large portion of the remaining inhabitants of Latvia may qualify for citizenship through naturalization between 1996 and 2003. The main requirements are five years of permanent residence, command of the Latvian language, knowledge of Latvian history and constitution, legal source of income, renunciation of previous citizenship and a pledge of loyalty to Latvia. Citizenship shall not be granted to individuals decreed by the court to have acted anti-constitutionally against the republic after May 1990, or to have propagated fascist, chauvinist, national-socialist, communist or totalitarian ideas, or to have stirred up ethnic or racial hatred, or to those who are officials of a foreign government, have served in the armed forces or security services of a foreign state or have been convicted of a crime with a sentence of one year or longer. Latvia does not allow for dual citizenship in a naturalization process. Some non-citizens, particularly ethnic Russians, have criticized the law. The Council of Europe, the OSCE and the United Nations worked hard to secure modifications of the drafts of this legislation to improve consistency with international human rights standards. Latvia, like Estonia in the same situation, made some modifications, but the law remains an imperfect compromise.

The Latvian language law requires employees of the state and of all 'institutions, enterprises, and institutes' to know sufficient Latvian to carry out their profession. Some non-Latvians believe that they have been disenfranchized and that the language law discriminates against them, although there have been no reports of widespread dismissals of non-Latvian-speakers.

Russians

The first larger groups of ethnic Russians arrived in Latvia in the eighteenth century after the reform of the Orthdox Church. These people settled mostly in eastern present-day Latvia, which at the time was considered part of Poland. With the gradual annexation of Latvia's regions into Tsarist Russia, the Russian population increased; though up until the end of the nineteenth century it did not exceed 200,000. Postwar migration policy had increased the ethnic Russian population in Latvia to 905,000 by 1989. In 1995 Russians constituted by far Latvia's largest ethnic minority group – 849,300 people (33.1 per cent) living predominantly in urban areas. However, only 289,106 ethnic Russians have been able to acquire Latvian citizenship, leaving more than half a million people stateless. Although application of the new naturalization law will reduce the number of stateless persons, the law is unlikely to apply to an estimated 200,000 retired Soviet army officers, former KGB and Soviet Communist Party officials and their families. The number of ethnic Russians decreased between 1990 and 1994 by some 53,000 as a result of emigration. The highest rate of emigration has been registered in districts and cities with high concentrations of former Soviet army personnel.

Belarusians and Ukrainians

A small number of Belarusians have lived in Latvia near the border with Belarus for a long time, and about 100,000 Belarusians migrated to Latvia in the postwar period. In 1995, Belarusians constituted the third largest ethnic group in Latvia, numbering 105,100 (4.1 per cent of the population). Their number has decreased significantly since 1991, with some 16,000 emigrating. There were fewer than 2,000 Ukrainians in Latvia before 1939. A large number entered the country after 1945. In 1995, ethnic Ukrainians numbered 78,200 (3 per cent of the population). Like other Slavic groups they also began leaving Latvia in large numbers. Since 1991 about 14,000 have emigrated.

Other minorities

Poles have been present on Latvia's territory since the Middle Ages when eastern Latvia was under the influence of Poland. This encouraged the immigration of Poles as well as the 'Polification' of Latvian farmers in south-east Latvia. Many Polish farmworkers came to live in Latvia in the 1930s. In 1995, Poles numbered 57,200 (2.2 per cent). Lithuanians, who in 1995 numbered 32,200 (1.3 per cent) are, like the Poles, one of several historic minorities in Latvia. Other historic minorities include Jews. Less than one-third of the prewar Jewish population survived the Nazi genocide. In 1995, some 13,280 Jews, (0.53 per cent of the population) remained in Latvia. Jews have registered the highest rate of emigration since 1989; about 8,000, or one-third of the 1989 number have left Latvia, and the Jewish population has declined by a further 2 per cent a year since 1989 as a result of intermarriage and assimilation. Livs (also referred to as Livonians), alongside Latvians, are considered an indigenous people of Latvia. In 1995 they numbered just 207. During the Soviet era a ban on access and fishing in coastal areas accelerated the assimilation of Livs. In their ethnic territory on the Baltic shores of the Talsi and Ventspils districts (an area with a Liv majority before the Second World War), there are now only about 60 Livs, constituting about 3 per cent of the local population. The Latvian authorities have designated part of this area *Livöd Randa* (Liv Coast), hoping to renew and develop the traditional Liv way of life. Only a small number of Livs, almost all elderly, still know their native language. Baltic Germans have played an important role within Latvia's territory, both politically and economically, since the thirteenth century. In the 1930s Germans were the fourth largest ethnic group, but most left the country during the Second World War. In 1995 only about 2,100 (0.1 per cent) remained.

Conclusions and future prospects

Critical issues for minorities in Latvia are the refusal of the authorities to allow for dual citizenship and what many consider to be coercive linguistic policies. There appears to be little prospect of Latvia allowing dual citizenship in the foreseeable future. The government's citizenship and linguistic policies, while aimed at integration, can be viewed as assimilatory in intent and discriminatory in practice, since they do not facilitate the preservation of minority identities. The promotion of integration, and the provision of opportunities to participate fully in the political, social and economic life in the country, could arguably be better achieved by the authorities' acceptance of Russian as one of Latvia's official languages. At the same time, the progressive acquisition of Latvian-language skills by members of minority groups may help to lessen Latvian insecurities about the survival of the Latvian language and culture.

Further reading

Lejins, A. (ed.) *Latvia Today*, Riga, Latvian Institute of International Affairs, 1995.

Dahlgren, T. (ed.), *Human Rights in the Baltic States*, Helsinki, Finnish Helsinki Committee, Advisory Board for International Human Rights Affairs, 1993.

Hiden, J. and Salmon, P., *The Baltic Nations and Europe: Estonia, Latvia and Lithuania in the Twentieth Century*, London, Longman, 1994.

Misiunas, R.J. and Taagepera, R., *The Baltic States: Years of Dependence, 1940–1990*, London, Hurst, 1993.

Rauch, G.V., *The Baltic States: The Years of Independence: Estonia, Latvia, Lithuania, 1917–1940*, New York, St Martin's Press, 1995.

Minority-based and advocacy organizations

Armenian Society of Latvia, Ita Kozakiewicz Latvian Association of National Cultural Societies, Slokas iela 37, 1007 Riga, Latvia; tel. 371 7 614221.

Azerbaijani Society in Latvia 'Azeri', Ita Kozakiewicz Latvian Association of National Cultural Societies, Slokas iela 37, 1007 Riga, Latvia; tel. 371 7 613658.

Belarusian Culture Society of Latvia 'Svitanak', Ita Kozakiewicz Latvian Association of National Cultural Societies, Slokas iela 37, 1007 Riga, Latvia; tel. 371 7 612639.

Estonian National Cultural Society, Nometnu iela 62, 1002 Riga, Latvia; tel. 371 2 601282.

Georgian Culture Society in Latvia 'Samshoblo', Ita Kozakiewicz Latvian Association of National Cultural Societies, Slokas iela 37, 1007 Riga, Latvia; tel. 371 7 613788.

German Culture Society of Riga, Ita Kozakiewicz Latvian Association of National Cultural Societies, Slokas iela 37, 1007 Riga, Latvia; tel. 371 7 613638.

Latvia Union of Poles, Ita Kozakiewicz Latvian Association of National Cultural Societies, Slokas iela 37, 1007 Riga, Latvia; tel. 371 7 614034.

Latvian Russian Community (ROL), Palasta iela 9, 1050 Riga, Latvia; tel 371 7 215274.

Moldavian-Romanian Society of Latvia 'Dachija', Ita Kozakiewicz Latvian Association of National Cultural Societies, Slokas iela 37, 1007 Riga, Latvia; tel. 371 7 614221.

Riga Jewish Community, Skolas 6, 1050, Riga, Latvia; tel. 371 2 289 580.

Russian Cultural Society, Jurmalas gatve 32a, 1083 Riga, Latvia; tel 371 2 403613.

Tatar Society of Latvia 'Idel", Ita Kozakiewicz Latvian Association of National Cultural Societies, Slokas iela 37, 1007 Riga, Latvia; tel. 371 7 613638.

Ukrainian Culture Enlightening Society in Latvia 'Dnipro', Ita Kozakiewicz Latvian Association of National Cultural Societies, Slokas iela 37, 1007 Riga, Latvia; tel. 371 7 612801.

Yakutian Society of Latvia 'Choron', Ita Kozakiewicz Latvian Association of National Cultural Societies, Slokas iela 37, 1007 Riga, Latvia; tel. 371 7 613658.

Lithuania

Land area:	65,200 sq km
Population:	3,739,000 (1994)
Main languages:	Lithuanian (official), Polish, Russian
Main religions:	Roman Catholicism, Russian Orthodox Christianity, Old Believers
Main minority groups:	Russians 318,000 (8.5%), Poles 261,000 (7.0%), Belarusians 56,000 (1.5%), Ukrainians 38,000 (1.0%), Jews 7,500 (0.2%), also smaller populations of Armenians, Azeris, Germans, Karaini, Latvians, Moldovans, Roma, Tatars and Uzbeks
Real per capita GDP:	$3,700
UNDP HDI/rank:	0.769 (71)

The Republic of Lithuania lies on the eastern coast of the Baltic Sea. To the north it borders Latvia, to the east and south Belarus and to the south-west Poland and the Kaliningrad region of the Russian Federation. The first Lithuanian state was established in the thirteenth century. Under the Grand Duke Vytautas the Great, who ruled the country in the fifteenth century, Lithuania extended from the Baltic almost to the Black Sea. In 1569, the Kingdom of Poland and the Grand

Duchy of Lithuania were united into the Commonwealth of Poland and Lithuania. The Commonwealth came under threat from Prussia, Austria and Russia at the end of the eighteenth century. In 1795, with the partition of the Commonwealth by Russia, Prussia and Austria-Hungary, Lithuania was annexed by Russia. The new rulers tried to Russify the country, closing Vilnius University and banning the publication of Lithuanian books in the Latin alphabet. In the late 1800s, brutal persecution and economic necessity forced thousands of Lithuanians to emigrate.

The Lithuanian state was reestablished in 1918. One year later, following heavy fighting between Poland, Russia and Lithuania, Poland began to annex Vilnius, forcing Lithuania to transfer its capital to Kaunas. Like Estonia and Latvia, Lithuania was occupied by the Red Army as a result of the Molotov–Ribbentrop Pact and incorporated into the Soviet Union in August 1940. Soviet legislation and judiciary were introduced with retroactive effect, resulting in the deportation of tens of thousands of individuals. Armed resistance against Soviet control continued for about ten years after the Second World War. Political changes in the Soviet Union under the leadership of Mikhail Gorbachev allowed Lithuania to declare sovereignty (priority of local legislation over all-Union legislation) in May 1989. Thereafter, despite objections from the Soviet authorities, Lithuania reestablished its independence in March 1990. Subsequently, the country's independence was recognized by the Russian Federation, and Lithuania won international recognition and was admitted to the United Nations in September 1991. All forces stationed by Russia in Lithuania were withdrawn by the end of 1993.

Ethnic minorities make up a fifth of the population. Among them several – Poles, Jews, Tatars, Belarusians, Latvians, Germans, Karaini and groups of Russians – have lived in Lithuania since ancient times and are considered original inhabitants. Under Soviet occupation most nationalities, except Russians, were subjected to assimilation, as minority schools, churches, houses of worship, newspapers, museums and cultural centres were closed by the Soviet regime. According to the 1989 Soviet census 109 nationalities lived in Lithuania. Of the then total population of 3,674,802, Lithuanians constituted just under 80 per cent. The largest minorities were, in descending order, Russians, Poles, Belarusians, Ukrainians, Jews, Tatars, Latvians, Roma, Germans, Armenians, Uzbeks, Moldovans, and Azerbaijanis. The other 95 nationalities numbered less than 0.01 per cent of the population each and among this group 74 nationalities were represented by fewer than 100 individuals. No national census has been carried out in Lithuania since the re-establishment of independence, but in 1994 the government announced that the republic's population was 3,739,000, of whom 2.6 million (95 per cent of adults) were Lithuanian citizens. Since 1989, some 107,000 people had emigrated and 50,000 had immigrated, and the proportion of ethnic Lithuanians had increased from 79.6 per cent (1989) to 81.1 per cent (1994). The proportions of Russians, Belarusians, Ukrainians, Jews and other nationalities all declined after 1989, while the proportion of Poles remained stable.

In Lithuania the critical issue for ethnic minorities has been their rights as citizens of the new state. The Lithuanian constitution, adopted by referendum in October 1992, accords ethnic communities the right to administer their affairs, including cultural, educational and charitable organizations and mutual assistance. It promises state support for ethnic communities and gives the right to citizens who belong to ethnic communities to foster their language, culture and customs.

Specific minority rights are governed by the Citizenship Law, adopted in November 1989, before the renewal of independence. This law gives most people in the republic the right to choose if they wish to become a Lithuanian citizen. The right to citizenship extends to three categories of people: (1) those who had Lithuanian citizenship before 15 July 1940 and their children or grandchildren (if they were at any subsequent time permanent residents of Lithuania); (2) those who had a permanent residence in Lithuania as of 3 November 1989, provided they were born in Lithuania, or that at least one of their parents or grandparents was born in Lithuania, and provided they are not citizens of another state; and (3) those who were permanent residents of Lithuania as of 3 November 1989 and have permanent place of employment in the republic.

The 1989 Citizenship Law applies most directly to people who settled in Lithuania while it was annexed by the Soviet Union. The law originally gave them two years to choose between Lithuanian and Russian citizenship. It was revised in December 1991, when the two-year option period was replaced by naturalization procedures. Qualification for naturalization requires ten-year residency, permanent employment or other legal source of income, passing examination in the fundamentals of the Lithuanian constitution, renunciation of any other citizenship, proficiency in the Lithuanian language and taking an oath of allegiance to

Lithuania. More than 90 per cent of ethnic Poles, Russians, Belarusians and Ukrainians residing in Lithuania in 1991 renounced their previous citizenship and were granted Lithuanian citizenship. Non-Lithuanians, especially Poles, have expressed concerns about the possibility of job discrimination arising from implementation of the language requirement provision. Many public sector employees have been required to attain a functional knowledge of Lithuanian within several years, although the authorities have granted liberal extensions of the time frame in which this is to be achieved. There appears to be no evidence of dismissals based on application of this law.

The Citizenship Law was further amended in 1993 by the Seimas (Lithuanian parliament) to permit people who had served in the Soviet armed forces to apply for citizenship, provided they had ended their military service before 1 March 1992 and had obtained the initial citizenship 'certificates' before 4 November 1991. However, in April 1994 the Constitutional Court ruled that this amendment violates the constitution. The court also ruled that dual citizenship is possible only in exceptional cases and that service personnel who were Soviet citizens at the time of their military service had received citizenship 'certificates' unlawfully. The ruling has affected about 800 former Soviet service personnel.

Russians

The Russian minority, numbering some 318,000 (8.5 per cent of the population) can be divided into three main groups: (1) those whose ancestors settled in Lithuania between the sixteenth and early twentieth centuries; (2) those who settled in Lithuania between the two world wars as immigrants from the Soviet Union; and (3) those who moved to Lithuania after the Second World War as civilians or members of the Soviet military and/or police apparatus. Ethnic Russians live mainly in the urban areas and provide the main labour force in the industrial sector, especially in energy, transport and heavy industry. Initially tense relations between the Lithuanian authorities and the Russian minority have improved considerably since 1991 when the Seimas suspended the county council in Ignalina (formerly Snieckus) on the grounds of its support for Soviet rule during Lithuania's independence struggle and the August 1991 coup attempt. The Russian minority have ready access to primary, secondary and tertiary education in the Russian language. State radio and television broadcast a fair selection of programmes in Russian, and Lithuanian television regularly rebroadcasts programmes from two television stations in Russia. More than a dozen periodicals are published in Russian.

Poles

The Polish minority, settled mainly around Vilnius and in Salcininkai region in the south-east numbers about 261,000 (7.0 per cent of the population). Initially tense relations between Poles and the authorities have improved considerably after the election in February 1993 of two district councils that had been suspended immediately after the August 1991 coup attempt. Members of the councils, which represent predominantly Polish constituencies, had been charged with supporting Soviet rule during Lithuania's independence struggle and supporting the Moscow putsch. In the first local elections since independence, in March 1995, candidates of Polish Electoral Action (AWPnL) won in almost all the districts where they stood, and gained an absolute majority in Polish-majority regions. In Vilnius, the AWPnL increased its vote from three to 20 per cent. The key success of the AWPnL appears to be its advocacy of minority grievances, demands for increased cultural autonomy, recognition of a Polish university, and its voicing of concerns about possible job discrimination arising from the implementation of the language law. There is a danger, however, that its platform and success may generate nationalist Lithuanian reaction. Poles have ready access to primary, secondary and higher education in the Polish language. Lithuanian state radio and television broadcasts include programmes in Polish, and one of the private radio stations also broadcasts in Polish. Lithuanian television also rebroadcasts one television channel from Poland. Numerous periodicals are readily available in Polish, some backed by state subsidies.

Belarusians and Ukrainians

Belarusians and Ukrainians number 56,000 and 38,000 (1.5 per cent and 1.0 per cent of the population) respectively. They have access to education in their native languages at Sunday schools or at state schools as a supplementary subject.

Jews

Lithuania has a small Jewish community of 7,500 people (0.2 per cent of the population), mainly in the larger cities. Before the Second World War there was a vibrant Jewish life in Lithuania. Some 220,000 Lithuanian Jews were brutally murdered during the war. In September 1994, the Lithuanian Prime Minister publicly deplored these killings, apologized to the Jewish people for the fact that 10,000 Lithuanians had actively assisted the Nazis in carrying out this genocide, and pledged to prosecute suspected war criminals who are deported back to Lithuania. Today, the government gives financial support for the maintenance of several Jewish schools, a cultural centre and a museum in Vilnius. During 1994, Jewish leaders became apprehensive as a result of the publication of anti-Semitic articles in a leading independent newspaper. They also called on officials to provide better police protection for Jewish cemeteries in Kaunas, Vilnius, and Kalvaria, which have been subject to increasing vandalism and pilfering. The city government of Kaunas established an ad hoc committee, including police officials and Jewish community representatives, to look for ways to improve security at Jewish cemeteries.

Tatars

Tatars were brought to Lithuania from the Crimea by Grand Duke Vytautas in the fourteenth century. Before the Second World War they had a rich library, a Muslim religious centre, mosques in Vilnius and Kaunas and in several villages near Vilnius, as well as journals dealing with Tatar issues. Only three small village communities near the ancient Lithuanian capital Trakai have survived the Soviet period.

Conclusions and future prospects

By adopting the so-called zero option, which gives all people residing in the republic the right to choose, if they wish, to become a Lithuanian citizen, Lithuania has virtually eliminated the critical issue of citizenship that dominates inter-ethnic relations in the other Baltic countries. Nevertheless, the two large ethnic minority groups – Russians and Poles – have at times complained of discrimination in housing, employment and schooling. These problems appear to be more social than political in nature. The full opening of civic and political processes to ethnic minorities has clearly helped ease tensions.

Further reading

Dahlgren, T. (ed.), *Human Rights in the Baltic States,* Helsinki, Finnish Helsinki Committee, Advisory Board for International Human Rights Affairs, 1993.

Rauch, G.V., *The Baltic States: TheYears of Independence: Estonia, Latvia, Lithuania, 1917–1940,* New York, St. Martin's Press, 1995.

Smith, G. (ed.), *The Baltic States: The National Self-determination of Estonia, Latvia and Lithuania,* Basingstoke, Macmillan, 1994.

Minority-based and advocacy organizations

Armenian Cultural Society, Seskines 79, 2010 Vilnius, Lithuania.

Belarusian Cultural Society, Zygimantu 12, 2001 Vilnius, Lithuania.

Centre for Mutual Understanding, Iszaganitojo 2/4, 2001 Vilnius, Lithuania.

Lithuanian Human Rights Association, Laisves Pr. 60, 2019 Vilnius, Lithuania; tel. 370 2 42 90 36, fax 370 2 42 90 33.

Lithuanian Jews Cultural Society, Jasinskio 9, 2001 Vilnius, Lithuania.

Lithuanian Polish Union, Didzioji g. 40, 2002 Vilnius, Lithuania.

Lithuanian Tatar Cultural Society, A Vivulskio 3, 2009 Vilnius, Lithuania .

Russian Cultural Centre, Isganytojo g. 2/4, 2002 Vilnius, Lithuania.

Macedonia

Land area:	25,710 sq km
Population:	1,937,000 (1994)
Main languages:	Macedonian, Albanian, Turkish
Main religions:	Eastern Orthodox Christianity, Islam (mainly Sunni)
Main minority groups:	*1994 census:* Albanians 443,000 (23%), Turks 77,000 (4%), Roma 44,000 (2.3%), Serbs 39,000 (2%), others 46,000 (2.4%); *other estimates:* Roma 200,000 (10.3%)
Real per capita GNP:	$820 (1993 World Bank estimate)
UNDP HDI/rank:	—

As a geographic term, Macedonia refers to a territory in central south-eastern Europe bounded in the north by the Skopska Crna Gora and Stara Planina mountains, in the west by Lakes Prespa and Ochrid, in the east by the Rila and Rhodope mountains, and in the south by the Aegean coast and Thessaloniki. Of this geographic area, which extends approximately 67,000 sq km, 26,000 sq km belong to the (Former Yugoslav) Republic of Macedonia. The remainder is shared between Bulgaria (Pirin Macedonia) and Greece (Aegean Macedonia). The part of geographic Macedonia lying within the Republic of Macedonia is commonly referred to as Vardar Macedonia. The origin of the Macedonian people is debated. Some Macedonian historians claim that a Macedonian nation has existed since the Slavic invasion of the southern Balkans in the seventh and eighth centuries. Others insist that Macedonian identity is of recent origin, and may indeed be largely a product of Yugoslav nationalities policy since the Second World War. Irrespective of the origins of the Macedonians, Macedonian nationality must now be acknowledged as an established fact.

In the Middle Ages, geographic Macedonia formed successively a part of the Bulgarian and Serbian empires, and its Slav-speaking population was converted to Eastern Orthodoxy. At the end of the fourteenth century, the region was overrun by the Turks and it remained a part of the Ottoman empire until the eve of the First World War. Some Eastern Orthodox Slavs converted under Ottoman rule to Islam. Under circumstances which are still disputed, there was during the period of Ottoman rule a substantial influx of Albanian-speakers. The majority of Albanians embraced Islam and, among these, some follow the Bektashi dervish religion.

After the Balkan Wars of 1912–13, northern and central Macedonia were assigned to Serbia, southern Macedonia was apportioned to Greece, and the easternmost part of the region was given to Bulgaria. After the First World War, Bulgaria ceded an additional sliver of territory to the newly formed Kingdom of Serbs, Croats and Slovenes (after 1929, Yugoslavia). During the interwar period, the Yugoslav authorities denied the existence of a Macedonian identity and embarked upon a policy of assimilation. In 1943, however, the communist partisans, led by Tito, affirmed the existence of a Macedonian nation and, at the end of the war, the Socialist Republic of Macedonia was established along its prewar borders within the Yugoslav federation. After 1945, a Macedonian alphabet, orthography and grammar of the language were devised. The new republican authorities used their control of the bureaucracy and education to instil among Macedonian Slavs a sense of Macedonian ethnic identity and pride.[1] An autocephalous Macedonian Orthodox Church was established in 1967. Although denied recognition both by the Serbian Patriarch and by the wider Orthodox community, the Macedonian Church enjoys substantial support within Macedonia itself.

Although human rights were regularly abused in communist Yugoslavia, the authorities introduced a comprehensive system of collective rights for minorities, particularly in respect of educational provision. Minority cultural associations were also permitted, as well as publications and media in minority languages. Nevertheless, the minorities policy pursued in communist Yugoslavia proved insufficient to curb Albanian demands within Macedonia. Protests escalated in the 1980s, prompting in 1989 a change in the constitution of the republic.[2] In place of the clause defining Macedonia as 'the state of the Macedonian people and the Albanian and Turkish minorities', it was now affirmed that Macedonia was the 'national state of the Macedonian nation'.

In 1991, the Macedonian legislature adopted a declaration of sovereignty, which subsequently received almost 70 per cent support in a referendum. Since independence, Macedonia has been led by a coalition government dominated by the ex-communist Social Democratic Alliance. After 1992, the government included representatives drawn from the party representing the Albanian minority, the Party of Democratic Prosperity (PDP), and one minister of ethnic Turkish origin. A multi-ethnic coalition continued to rule after the general elections of October 1994.

In November 1991, a new constitution was promulgated. The preamble to the constitution states:

'Macedonia is established as a national state of the Macedonian people in which full equality as citizens and permanent coexistence with the Macedonian people is provided for Albanians, Turks, Vlachs, Roma and other nationalities living in the Republic of Macedonia.'

The constitution permits the official use of other languages and alphabets in areas where minority populations are concentrated (article 7). The constitution additionally provides minorities with the right to 'free expression of national identity' (article 8), and 'to instruction in their language in primary and secondary education' (article 48). There have, however, been substantial complaints at the slow pace at which minority-language facilities have been instituted. The Council on Inter-Ethnic Relations, established in accordance with article 78 of the constitution, has also been criticized as under-representing the Albanian minority and as being essentially powerless to influence government policy.[3]

Albanians

Albanians are the largest minority in Macedonia. According to the 1994 census there were 442,914 Albanians out of a total population in Macedonia of 1,936,877, constituting 22.9 per cent of the whole. Although some Albanians boycotted the census, it is unlikely that Albanians constitute 40 per cent of the population as is sometimes maintained by their spokespeople. Albanians are concentrated in compact settlements in the west of Macedonia, bordering Albania, in the north-west adjoining Kosovo, and in Skopje where they comprise at least 14 per cent of the population. The majority of Albanians are Muslims, and a large number are followers of the Bektashi dervish religion. There are a few Albanian Eastern Orthodox villages around Lake Ochrid and a small number of Albanian Catholics in Skopje. Albanians have been less affected than Slav Macedonians by the process of urbanization and most Albanians live in villages in the countryside. There is little intermarriage between the Albanian and Macedonian Slav communities.

The Albanian minority in Macedonia has recently grown on account of the arrival of refugees from Kosovo and of Albanians previously employed in other parts of former Yugoslavia. A new citizenship law passed in October 1992 required as a qualification either one's own or both parents' birth in the republic, or marriage to a citizen of Macedonia, or continuous residence in Macedonia for 15 years. It is claimed that these conditions are designed to make it harder for returning or refugee Albanians to become citizens. Possibly as many as 100,000 immigrant Albanians have been refused citizenship on technical grounds, although this number has been subsequently reduced by negotiation.[4]

Although Albanians suffered discrimination in the interwar period, they generally benefited from collective educational and cultural rights under communist rule. During the late 1980s, however, Albanian protests grew in Macedonia in response to the worsening conditions in neighbouring Kosovo. The reaction of the republican authorities was to clamp down on Albanian educational facilities and other alleged vehicles of Albanian nationalism, including personal names 'which stimulated nationalist sentiment and adherence to the People's Socialist Republic of Albania'.[5] Albanian civil servants and teachers were dismissed and a number of Albanian-language schools closed. The walls traditionally built around Albanian homes were razed on the grounds that they had become fortifications. These measures were countered by a school boycott in several areas and by increasingly violent demonstrations.

Albanian dissatisfaction with the terms of the 1991 constitution, which failed to define Albanians as a constitutive nation, led to confrontation with the new democratically elected government. In January 1992, an unofficial referendum among Albanians showed 95 per cent of voters favoured political and cultural autonomy in Albanian areas in western Macedonia. Several months later, activists declared an independent 'Republic of Ilirida'. Later in the year, clashes were reported in Skopje, during the course of which three Albanians and one Macedonian Slav were killed. In 1993, nine Albanians including a deputy minister were arrested on charges of gun-running and of fomenting insurrection and were sentenced to terms of imprisonment. Independent observers gave unfavourable assessments of the trial.

During 1994–5, tension gathered around the issue of the Albanian university in Tetovo. Previously, Albanians from Macedonia had attended the University of Pristina, but after 1990, their participation declined on account of the deteriorating conditions in Kosovo. No alternative facilities were arranged in Macedonia, where higher education continued almost exclusively in the Macedonian language. In 1991–2, only 386 of 22,994 students in higher education in Macedonia were Albanians. An attempt to establish a private Albanian-language university in Tetovo was blocked by the authorities. In response to these pressures, an Albanian-language department of teacher training was opened in the University of Skopje and a 10 per cent quota system for Albanians instituted throughout the university as a whole.

The PDP which represents the interests of the Albanian minority in Macedonia is divided between those who favour closer links with Albania, those supportive of autonomy, and those who would prefer the establishment of a 'civic' Macedonian state. In 1992, the coalition government included five Albanian ministers drawn from the PDP. After the elections of 1994, the PDP continued to hold four (subsequently three) ministries. The PDP has pressed for increased Albanian representation in the bureaucracy and police force, for improved educational opportunities including the university in Tetovo, and for a measure of home rule in Albanian-populated districts.

Albanian-language media operate daily television transmissions from Skopje. The proliferation of small radio stations broadcasting in Albanian has recently been arrested because of new government regulations. An Albanian newspaper has been published daily since May 1994. Allegations of discrimination in employment have resulted in inconclusive talks at governmental level concerning affirmative action policies and in the introduction of a quota system for recruitment in the Ministry of the Interior.

Turks

During the Ottoman period, a large body of Turkish administrators and of indentured rural labourers settled in the country. Their numbers were augmented by Turkish-speaking Muslims who fled from the Caucasus region in the nineteenth century. During the late 1940s and 1950s, the number of Turks in the Republic of Macedonia fell substantially because of emigration to Turkey and, possibly also, of assimilation into the Albanian community. According to the 1994 census, there were 77,000 Turks in Macedonia, who were dispersed throughout the country. Turks were recognized in the former Yugoslavia as a nationality and were allowed educational and cultural rights. The Democratic Party of Turks, established in 1992, alleges discrimination against Turks and has called for an increase in educational facilities and for proportional representation of Turks in government service.

Roma

The 1994 census listed 44,000 Roma. This represents a substantial decline from the 56,000 recorded in the 1991 census, and may reflect a growing tendency among Roma to identify with other national groups, particularly the Albanian. Unofficial estimates put the real number of Roma at 200,000 with 40,000 in Skopje alone. It is thought that 80 per cent of Roma have a Romani dialect as their mother tongue, although many also speak Albanian. The majority of Roma are Muslims. From 1983, the Roma language has been taught in some state schools. In 1980, a publishing house in Skopje brought out the first Romani grammar, written entirely in Romani script and orthography, and since then there have been a number of publications in the Romani language. Romani television and radio broadcast currently for half an hour a week.

Since at least the 1930s, a number of Roma in Struga and the Lake Ochrid region have repudiated Roma identity and redefined themselves as 'Egyptians'.[6] The Egyptian Association of Citizens founded in 1990, claims 30,000 'descendants of the Pharaohs' in Macedonia. The Party for Complete Emancipation of Roma and the Democratic Progressive Party of Roma in Macedonia, the two leading Roma political organizations, have both supported the establishment of a separate Roma state, Romanistan, in the Balkans which would include parts of Macedonia.[7]

Serbs

The 1994 census recorded 39,000 Serbs in Macedonia, most of whom live in villages in the north of the country in the Kumanovo valley and Skopska Crna Gora. The Serbs are not specifically recognized as a national minority in the 1991 constitution, and as a consequence, they have been denied the right to separate language instruction and to their own television and radio media. Some Serbs have shown support for Vojislav Seselj's Serbian Radical Party which has called for the annexation or partition of Macedonia by Serbia. Concern at a possible intervention by Serbian paramilitary or regular units in Macedonia prompted the deployment of a 1,000-strong United Nations observer force on the border in 1993.

Muslim Macedonians

The Muslim Macedonian minority, variously known as Torbeshi, Pomaks and Poturs, comprises Macedonian-speakers who embraced Islam during the period of Turkish rule. Their number has, according to censuses, fluctuated widely, ranging from 1,248 in the 1971 census, to 39,513 in the 1981 census, and to 31,356 in the 1991 census (the 1994 census figure is unavailable). The Muslim population is thought to have been swollen by the arrival of between 30,000 and 50,000 Muslim refugees from Bosnia-Herzegovina and the Sanjak in Serbia. Leaders of the Muslim Macedonian community have claimed that the minority is subject to deliberate attempts at Turkicization and Albanianization.

Other minorities

Recent censuses indicate approximately 8,000 Vlachs in Macedonia, living mainly in and around Bitola, Resen and Krusevo. Vlachs are historically Romance-speaking shepherds and merchants. Their numbers are in decline, mainly because of assimilation into the Macedonian Slav population. The process of assimilation was hastened by postwar Yugoslav legislation aimed against the private ownership of large flocks of sheep and cattle. Recently, a small Vlach renaissance has been evident, led by the League of Vlachs. The league has undertaken steps to complete a Vlach-language grammar book and to republish the Vlach-language journal *Feniks*. The 1991 census also recorded 1,762 Bulgarians.

Conclusions and future prospects

According to most theories on inter-ethnic conflict, Macedonia should have already fallen apart as a consequence of tension between the Macedonian Slav and Albanian populations. So far, however, Macedonia has defied predictions of its imminent demise. Nevertheless, any rapid deterioration of conditions in Kosovo may undermine Macedonia's stability by deepening cleavages between the Albanian and Macedonian Slav communities. Government policy in Macedonia has already moved cautiously in the direction of consociationalism at cabinet level and of proportional representation in the administration. As one recent article concludes: 'Given a renewed international commitment to Macedonia's future, this new state can survive, continue to surprise its detractors, and keep alive the possibility of multi-ethnic civil states in the Balkans.'[8]

Further reading

Mickey, R.W. and Albion, A.S., 'Success in the Balkans? A case study of ethnic relations in the Republic of Macedonia', in I.M. Cuthbertson and J. Leibowitz (eds), *Minorities: The New Europe's Old Issue*, Prague, Budapest, Warsaw, New York, Institute for EastWest Studies, distributed by Westview Press, Boulder, CO, 1993.

Poulton, H., *Who Are the Macedonians?*, London, Hurst, 1995.

Poulton, H., *The Balkans: Minorities and States in Conflict*, 2nd edn, London, Minority Rights Publications, 1993.

Liégeois, J-P. and Gheorghe, N., *Roma/Gypsies: A European Minority*, London, MRG report, 1995.

MRG Greece, Pettifer, J. and Poulton, H., *The Southern Balkans*, London, MRG report, 1994.

Minority-based and advocacy organizations

Democratic Party of Serbs, Partizanski Odredi 20, 91000 Skopje, Macedonia.

Helsinki Citizens' Assembly, St. 117, Nb. 2, 91220 Tetovo, Macedonia.

Helsinki Committee for Human Rights of the Republic of Macedonia, P Zografski 51, 91000 Skopje, Macedonia; tel. 389 91 118 553, fax 389 91 228 608.

Macedonian Information and Liaison Service, 8 Udarna Brigada 20-B, 91000 Skopje, Macedonia.

Party for Complete Emancipation of Roma, Orizari, 91000 Skopje, Macedonia; tel. 389 91 612 726.

World Macedonian Congress, Orce Nikolov 28, 91000 Skopje, Macedonia.

Poland

Land area:	312,680 sq km
Population:	38,654,561 (1994)
Main languages:	Polish
Main religions:	Roman Catholicism, Eastern Orthodox Church, Protestantism
Main minority groups:	Germans 750,000–1,100,000 (est., 1.9–2.8%), Ukrainians 350,000–500,000 (est., 0.90–1.3%), Belarusians 200,000–300,000 (est., 0.51–0.8%), Roma 15,000 (est., less than 0.1%), Lithuanians 10,000–30,000 (est., less than 0.1 %), Slovaks 10,000–20,000 (est., less than 0.1%), Czechs 5,000 (est., less than 0.1%), Greeks and Macedonians 2,000 (est., less than 0.1%), also smaller populations of Kashubs, Lemko Ruthenians, Tatars
Real per capita GDP:	$4,830
UNDP HDI/rank:	0.855 (51)

The Republic of Poland is bounded to the north by the Baltic Sea and the enclave of Kaliningrad (Russian Federation), to the north-east by Lithuania, to the east by Belarus, to the south-east by Ukraine, to the west by Germany and to the south by Slovakia and the Czech Republic. The creation of a unified Polish state was consolidated in CE 966 by the acceptance of Christianity by the Piast dynasty. With the demise of the Piast dynasty in the fourteenth century, the Polish throne passed to the Duke of Lithuania, Wladyslaw Jagiello. The rule of the Jagiellonian dynasty, considered the 'golden age' of Poland, lasted until the end of the sixteenth century. The Union of Lublin in 1569 united the Grand Duchy of Lithuania and the Kingdom of Poland into the Polish–Lithuanian Commonwealth. After the death of the last Jagiellonian king in 1572 no dynasty maintained itself for long. The participation of the entire nobility in royal elections frequently led to contested elections and civil wars.

Three successive partitions of Poland (1772, 1793, 1795) by Prussia, Russia and Austria-Hungary resulted in its disappearance from the map of Europe. During this period the occupying powers subjected the population to intense processes of Russification and Germanization. Poland regained independence in 1918. At that time ethnic minorities constituted some 34.5 per cent of the country's population. Estimates suggest that within its borders lived some 5,000,000 Ukrainians (16 per cent), 3,000,000 Jews (9 per cent), 2,000,000 Belarusians (6 per cent) and 800,000 Germans (2.5 per cent). Russians, Lithuanians, Czechs, Roma and other minority groups constituted about 300,000 (1 per cent).

On 1 September 1939, Germany invaded Poland and thus precipitated the Second World War. The German invasion was followed on 17 September by a Soviet invasion of eastern Poland under previously agreed terms of the Soviet–German Friendship Treaty. This fourth partition of Poland lasted until June 1941 when Germany attacked the Soviet Union and German troops overran the entire territory of Poland. During their occupation of Poland, the Nazis methodically exterminated a large part of the population by massacres and starvation and in the extermination camps such as Auschwitz (Oswiecim) and Majdanek. The worst fate was reserved for Polish Jews – about 3 million perished in concentration camps. Only an estimated 100,000 Polish Jews survived the Holocaust.

At the end of the Second World War in 1945, the borders of Poland were moved some 500 kilometres westwards. As a result of the loss of substantial territories in the east, 489,000 of the 600,000 Ukrainians on Polish soil were moved by the new Polish authorities to the Soviet Union between 1945 and 1946, along with an estimated 36,000 Belarusians. The extension of Polish territory to the west resulted in the expulsion of about 3,200,000 Germans between 1945 and 1949. Poland thus became one of the most ethnically and religiously homogeneous countries in Europe, with 97 per cent of its population being Poles and 95 per cent belonging to the Roman Catholic Church. Today, there are no accurate statistics concerning ethnic minorities in Poland.

Estimates suggest that the number of people belonging to minority groups ranges between 1,350,000 (3.5 per cent) of the country's population and 1,900,000 (4.9 per cent).

Germans

On the eve of the Second World War borders of Poland contained about 1 million ethnic Germans, who made up 3.5 per cent of the country's population. The German territories, east of the Oder and Neisse rivers, over which Poland gained control after the war, had been inhabited before 1939, by some 10 million people. There is no agreement on the number of Germans who were left in Poland after the end of the mass transfer of the German population in 1945–49. During the 1950s, the Polish authorities maintained that no more that 250,000 ethnic Germans remained in Poland, while West German sources put the size of the minority at 1.7 million people. This discrepancy is partly explained by the fact that many ethnic Germans were viewed by the Polish authorities as 'autochthones' – original inhabitants of the region whose equivocal ethnicity qualified them as prospective Poles. Bilingualism and mixed family background had always been common in the borderlands.[1]

Some 290,000 people were allowed to resettle in Germany between 1956 and 1959 under a family reunion scheme. These transfers were used by the Polish authorities as a justification for the closure of all German-language schools, church services, newspapers and radio broadcasts. From about 1960, Poland denied the continued existence of a German minority on its soil. From the normalization of relations between Poland and West Germany in 1970 to 1990, about 970,000 people were allowed to leave Poland. Since 1989, the reassertion of German ethnic identity has taken place in a new political climate.

The Polish–German Treaty of Good Neighbourhood and Cooperation, signed in July 1991 *inter alia* secures the right for ethnic Germans 'freely to express, preserve and develop their ethnic, cultural, linguistic and religious identity, both individually and collectively'. There is no agreement on size of the ethnic German minority in Poland today. Polish sources estimate the number at 750,000 (1.9 per cent) of the population, while German sources quote the figure of 1,100,000 (2.8 per cent). Both figures include ethnic Germans, many of whom are only now able to claim their ethnic identity, and being 'autochthonous'. The main German organization, the Federation of German Socio-Cultural Associations, has member associations in 16 of the 49 provinces. In the 1991 parliamentary elections, the German minority secured seven seats in the Sejm, the lower house of parliament, and one in the Senate.

Ukrainians

There is no agreement on the size of the Ukrainian minority in Poland today. Polish sources estimate the number at 350,000 (0.9 per cent of the country's population), while Ukrainian sources quote the figure of 500,000 (1.93 per cent). Some 70 per cent of ethnic Ukrainians belong to the Ukrainian Catholic Church (Uniate), 30 per cent to the Russian Orthodox Church. Their main organization, the Union of Ukrainians (formerly the Ukrainian Socio-Cultural Association) has 182 branches in 11 of the 49 provinces and publishes a weekly periodical, *Nasze Slovo* (*Our Word*). As in the case of the German minority, the rights of ethnic Ukrainians in Poland are guaranteed by a Treaty of Good Neighbourhood and Cooperation, in this case signed by Poland and Ukraine in May 1992.

Belarusians

Estimates of the size of the Belarusian minority in Poland for 1994 vary between 200,000 (0.5 per cent of the population) and 300,000 (0.8 per cent) individuals. The vast majority of Belarusians in Poland belong to the Orthodox Church and live in the north-eastern provinces adjacent to the country's borders with Belarus. The reassertion of Belarusian ethnic identity since 1989 has reinvigorated the Belarusian Socio-Cultural Organization (formed in 1956) and led to the formation of two political organizations – the Belarusian Democratic Union (the first ethnic minority party established in Poland), and the Union of Belarusian Students – and the creation of the Association of Belarusian Journalists. Besides the well-established weekly *Niva*, three new publications in Belarusian have appeared since 1989: a quarterly, *Fos*, published by the Brotherhood of Orthodox Youth; a monthly, *Czasopis*, published by the Association of Belarusian Journalists; and the *Belarusian Historical Records*, an academic journal. As in the cases of the Germans and Ukrainian minorities, the rights of Belarusians in Poland are guaranteed by a Treaty of Good Neighbourhood and Cooperation, in this case signed by Poland and Belarus in June 1992.

Roma

In the absence of reliable census data, estimates of the number of Roma in Poland vary greatly. Various Polish sources, including the Committee on Ethnic Minorities of the Polish parliament, give a figure of between 10,000 and 15,000. Some Western sources quote a figure of 50,000–60,000.[2] During the communist period, Roma were viewed as social misfits and, because of their lifestyle, politically difficult to control, and thus subjected to coercive integration. According to figures issued by the communist authorities, 25 per cent of them responded to offers of housing and employment by becoming sedentary. Attempts were made to set up cooperative workshops based on such traditional skills as coppersmithing. During the 1980s hundreds of Roma were deprived of Polish citizenship and expelled to Sweden and Denmark. Since 1989, like other minorities in Poland, Roma have begun to reassert their identity. Four Roma organizations have been founded in Tarnów, Olsztyn, Andrychów and Zyrardów provinces, along with the nationwide Association of Roma in Poland. In 1990 and 1991, anti-Roma disturbances took place in Kielce and Mtawa, towns with significant Roma populations. Subsequent heavy prison sentences and fines imposed on the rioters gave the local Roma population some reassurance. Also, during 1991, an extreme neo-fascist organization, the Polish National Front, distributed posters in several cities inciting acts of violence against Roma and demanding their expulsion from the country. These relatively isolated incidents, although condemned by the authorities, indicate the persistence of negative attitudes towards Roma and have added to their sense of insecurity.

Other minorities

Lithuanians, whose numbers were estimated in 1994 at between 10,000 and 30,000, live in a large concentration in the Punsk rural commune and in Sejny, in the north-eastern province of Suwalki. The number of Slovaks and Czechs was estimated in 1994 at 10,000 to 20,000 and 5,000 respectively. They are settled mostly in the southern province of Nowy Sacz. A community of some 2,000 Greeks and Macedonians consists of political refugees from the Greek civil war and their descendants, settled in the Wroctaw, Watbrzych and Jelenia Góra provinces. Smaller minorities such as Kashubs and Lemko Ruthenians have benefited from the post-1989 climate of tolerance and have experienced a revival.

Conclusions and future prospects

The small size of Poland's minority populations has made it possible for the authorities to improve their position considerably. The new post-1989 political climate allowed non-Poles to claim wider access to minority language education, mass media and publications, all of which were either curtailed or denied by the communist regime. The principal legislative acts of the Polish Republic provide ample protection for minorities and for the preservation of their identity. However, the process of reassertion of ethnic minority rights has not been without problems, particularly at grass-roots level. There have been reports of attacks against members of the German minority by skinheads, and some representatives of minorities complain of obstruction and intolerance on the part of local administrative bodies and individuals.

Further reading

Kolarska-Bobinska, L., *Aspirations, Values and Interest: Poland 1989–94*, Warsaw, IFiS, 1994.

Millard, F., *The Anatomy of the New Poland: Post-Communist Politics in Its First Phase*, Aldershot, Edward Elgar, 1994.

MRG (ed.), *Minorities in Central and Eastern Europe*, London, MRG report, 1993.

Mniejszosci Narodowe (*National Minorities*), Bulletin no. 4, European Centre of the University of Warsaw, Documentation and Information Unit of the Council of Europe, 1995.

Minority-based and advocacy organizations

Association of the Lemko, ul. Roosevelta 1, 59–200 Legnica, Poland.

Association of Roma in Poland, ul. Dabrowskiego 3, 32–600 Oswiecim, Poland; tel./fax 48 381 26989.

Belarusian Democratic Union [and related Belarusian organizations], ul. Suraska 1, 15–950 Bialystok, Poland; tel. 48 85 21033.

Belarusian Socio-Cultural Association, ul. Warszawska 11, 15–062 Bialystok, Poland; tel. 48 85 435118.

European Centre for Regional and Ethnic Studies, ul M. Sklogowskiej – Curie 11a, 85094 Bydoszcz, Poland.

Helsinki Foundation for Human Rights, Bracka 18 Apt 62, 00–028 Warsaw, Poland; tel./fax 48 22 828 69 96.

Lithuanian Association, ul. Pilsudskiego 7, 16–600 Sejny, Poland.

Organization of Ukrainian Youth 'Plast', ul. Koscieliska 7, 03–614 Warsaw, Poland.

Polish Union of Jewish Students, ul. Twarda 6, 00–950 Warsaw, Poland; tel. 48 22 200556. Poland.

Romani Advisory Council, ul. Armii Krajowej, 30–150 Krakow, Poland; tel./fax 48 12 366932.

Socio-Cultural Association of Czechs and Slovaks, ul. Sw. Filipa 7/4, 31–150 Krakow, Poland; tel./fax 48 12 341127.

Socio-Cultural Association of Jews in Poland, P1. Grzybowski 12/16, 00–104 Warsaw, Poland; tel. 48 22 200554.

Union of Associations of German Population in Former East Prussia, ul. Kosciuszki 13, 10–501 Olsztyn, Poland.

Union of Belarusian Journalists, and Union of Belorusian Youth, ul. Warszawska 11, 15–062 Bialystok, Poland; tel. 48 85 21033.

Union of Lithuanians in Poland, ul. Wiejska 16/16, 00–480 Warszawa-Srodmiescie, Poland; tel. 48 22 216951.

Union of Socio-Cultural Associations of Germans in Poland, ul. 1 Maja 61, 15–100 Opole, Poland; tel. 48 77 38507.

Union of Tatars in the Polish Republic, Rynek Kosciuszki 26/2, 15–062 Bialystok, Poland; tel. 48 85 322075/414970.

Union of Ukrainians in Poland, ul. Koscieliska 7, 03–614 Warsaw, Poland; tel. 48 22 679 9547/9695.

Romania

Land area:	230,000 sq km
Population:	22.7 million (1992)
Main languages:	Romanian, Hungarian, German, Romani, Ukrainian/Ruthene, Lipovan (Russian)
Main religions:	Eastern Orthodox Christianity, Roman Catholicism, Protestantism (Lutheran, Calvinist and Unitarian), Greek Catholicism (Uniate)
Main minority groups:	*1992 census:* Hungarians 1,620,000 (7.1%), Roma 409,700 (1.8%), Germans 120,000 (0.5%), others 258,000 (1%); *other estimates:* Roma up to 1.8 million (7.9%)
Real per capita GDP:	$2,840
UNDP HDI/rank:	0.703 (98)

Romania is bordered by Hungary and Serbia to the west, Ukraine and Moldova to the north, Bulgaria to the south and the coastline of the Black Sea to the east. The western portion of Romania, the area known as Transylvania, forms a part of the Carpathians and consists largely of a plateau ringed by mountains. Both Wallachia in the south and Moldavia in the north-east comprise fertile plains. Romanians claim descent from the indigenous population of the Carpathian region who were Romanized during the classical period. In the thirteenth century, independent Romanian principalities were founded in Wallachia and Moldavia which followed the Eastern Orthodox rite. These subsequently became vassal states of the Ottoman empire. During the nineteenth century, Wallachia and Moldavia were united in a common Romanian state which in 1878 was internationally recognized as a sovereign principality (later kingdom). Transylvania, which had previously been a part of the Habsburg empire, was joined to Romania after the First World War. Bessarabia, formerly a part of Russia, was awarded to Romania after 1918 but was taken by the Soviet Union in 1940. Bessarabia has since 1991 been a part of the sovereign state of Moldova.

With the acquisition of Transylvania in 1918, Romania inherited an ethnically diverse territory, containing substantial Hungarian, German and other minorities. Although at the time of Transylvania's incorporation into Romania in 1918, self-government was promised for the region's minorities, no such concession was forthcoming. During the interwar period, the Romanian government pursued a policy of neglect towards the minorities.

Communist rule in Romania was among the harshest in Central and Eastern Europe and resulted in widespread repression of the whole population. In the 1950s, the communists provided an extensive network of minority-language schools, publications and cultural organizations. Between 1952 and 1968, a Hungarian Autonomous Province functioned in the most compacted area of Hungarian settlement in Transylvania, although its powers of self-rule were only nominal. After 1968, communist policy moved by degrees towards assimilation. Minority-language schools were merged with Romanian ones and reduced to the status of 'sections' within predominantly Romanian-language schools. The number of subjects which might be taught in minority languages was also reduced and cultural organizations declined. Nevertheless, even in the late 1980s, Romanian television and radio continued daily transmissions in Hungarian and German.

The communist government was overthrown in 1989 and a democratic state proclaimed. In December 1991, a new constitution was approved in a referendum. The constitution defines Romania as 'a nation state, sovereign, unitary and indivisible' (article 1). It guarantees minorities the right 'to the preservation, development and expression' of identity, including education in the mother tongue, and affirms the equality of rights and freedom from discrimination (articles 6 and 16). The constitution additionally provides for deputies appointed by national minorities to be represented in the parliament.

Since 1990, conditions for minorities have improved immeasurably. After the publication of government regulation no. 521 in May 1990, there has been a substantial expansion of minority-language education: approximately twice as many children were educated in Hungarian in 1992–3 as in the 1985–6 school year. Minority cultural facilities and publications operate freely, and minority-language television and radio broadcasts have been extended. Political organizations representing minority interests do not encounter any overt harassment. In 1993, the government set up a Council for National Minorities to monitor and advise on minority affairs. The council submitted at the end of 1993 a draft National Minorities Law which provides for full mother-tongue education in schools, government assistance for cultural activities, provision for officials to speak the relevant languages in areas of minority settlement, and bilingual signposts in municipalities where a minority makes up more than 30 per cent of the local population. This figure may be considered unreasonably high by international standards.

Nevertheless, the regulation of minority rights and the implementation of the principles laid down in the constitution have been criticized, particularly on account of the discretionary powers assumed by local officials, police officers and judges, some of whom discriminate with impunity against members of minorities.[1] There is also evidence that the Romanian parliament has recently qualified its commitment to minority protection, partly as a consequence of pressure applied on the government party by its extreme right-wing coalition allies. The new penal code, approved by the parliament in 1995, imposes up to one year's imprisonment for 'the displaying of the flag or insignia or the playing of the national anthem of other states', which has been interpreted as a measure aimed against Hungarians. Additionally, a new draft law on education restricts mother tongue teaching in vocational institutions and prohibits the use of public funds for minority-language universities and denominational schools. Since 1993, broadcasting in minority languages has been reduced and subsidies for minority-language publications cut back. These restrictions have prompted allegations that government policy is 'window-dressing', intended to confuse international organizations monitoring Romanian compliance with European standards of minority protection.[2] It is additionally alleged that the government and local authorities have impeded the return of properties belonging to churches and other minority institutions which were seized during the communist period.

Hungarians

Hungarians are the most numerous minority in Romania and are overwhelmingly settled in Transylvania. According to the 1992 census, there were 1,620,199 Hungarians, making up 7.12 per cent of the total population. Hungarian sources claim, however, that the true number of Hungarians is closer to 2 million. The most compact area of Hungarian population is eastern Transylvania, which has historically been the home of Seklers. Seklers, who entered Transylvania at the end of the first millennium, hold a special (and recent) place in Hungarian national mythology. They are regarded as speaking the purest form of the Hungarian language and as embodying such national virtues as orderliness, resilience and reliability. Most Seklers describe themselves, however, on official documents as Hungarians. An additional subgroup within the Hungarian ethnic community are Csangos of Moldavia, who live in scattered rural communities near the Transylvanian border. Hungarians are either Catholics, Calvinists or Unitarians and are thus confessionally different from ethnic Romanians, most of whom are Eastern Orthodox or Greek Catholic (Uniate).

Hungarians have historically been the dominant social group in Transylvania. After Transylvania's incorporation in Romania, Hungarians were deprived of influence and, under the communists, they experienced a decline in educational and cultural opportunities. After the revolution of 1989, Hungarians rapidly asserted their rights and aroused Romanian animosities. In March 1990, inter-ethnic fighting broke out in the Transylvanian city of Targu Mures which left at least six people dead. Since then, however, relations between majority and minority communities in Transylvania have been peaceful. Extremist statements and provocations from right-wing Romanian parties, including the threatened demolition of Hungarian cultural monuments and the publication of racist literature and speeches, have not had the consequence of arousing inter-ethnic tension.

According to government statistics released in 1994, Hungarian-language education was available in 329 elementary schools, 241 middle schools and 33 secondary schools. In a further 78 elementary schools, 455 middle schools and 118 secondary schools, Hungarian children shared facilities with Romanians, while having part of the curriculum delivered in the mother tongue. According to the same source, about 80 per cent of Hungarian children receive some mother-tongue instruction in schools.[3] A particular complaint of Hungarians is that the further one progresses educationally, the less the opportunity is given for mother-tongue instruction and that, despite the provision of Hungarian-language education, Hungarian children tend to leave school earlier than their Romanian counterparts.

Although government statistics show state support for minority cultural and publishing activity, there are complaints that these subsidies are small, delivered late, and more than offset by inflationary costs. Additionally, since 1993, the amount of time devoted on television and radio to Hungarian-language transmissions has been reduced and their content restricted to cultural and ethnographic affairs.[4] Nevertheless, one national daily newspaper is published in Hungarian and there are additionally eight regional papers reporting in the same language.

The political organization representing Hungarians in Romania is the Democratic Alliance of Hungarians in Romania (DAHR), which claims half a million members. The DAHR began promoting the rights of minorities within the educational and cultural sphere, but after 1992, adopted a programme advocating the establishment of an 'auto-administrative' Hungarian region in Transylvania. The draft bill on national minorities submitted by the DAHR to the Romanian parliament in November 1993 envisages the establishment of autonomous communities and special status districts in areas of majority Hungarian settlement. There appears little likelihood at present that Hungarian demands for self-government will be met. The DAHR has also published extensive documentation alleging the judicial and police harassment of Hungarians. For their part, semi-official Romanian sources claim the 'ethnic cleansing' of Romanians in regions of majority Hungarian settlement.

Roma

The 1992 census recorded 409,723 Roma, although the real figure may be much higher. Classified material from the Romanian Interior Ministry, obtained clandestinely by a German Roma/Gypsy organization, suggests a population of 1.8 million.[5] Sixty per cent of Roma speak Romani or Romanian, the remainder Hungarian, German, Turkish or Bulgarian. Shortly after their arrival in Romania during the Middle Ages, most Roma were enslaved, and the institution of Roma slavery was abolished only in the nineteenth century. Throughout the twentieth century, Roma continued to be the target of discrimination. In the interwar years, however, the General Association of Roma in Romania published several journals, and in 1933, hosted the Gypsy World Congress. During the Second World War about 25,000 Roma were dumped in Transnistria by the pro-fascist authorities. Altogether, an estimated 40,000 Roma were killed during the period 1940–44.

Roma continue to suffer strong disabilities. According to Roma sources, a half of the active adult Roma population is unemployed; 27 per cent of children below the age of 14 are illiterate; and as much as 40 per cent fail to attend the first years of school. Roma sources indicate continued violence against Roma and allege more than one hundred attacks on settlements, including arson, in the period 1990–94. According to one opinion poll commissioned in 1991, almost 70 per cent of Romanians registered strong antipathy towards Roma. There is reliable evidence that some police harass Roma and fail to respond promptly to Roma calls for assistance.[6]

Currently, few facilities are available for Roma mother-tongue instruction and in 1994 only 55 children were reported as attending Roma-language classes. Government sources claim, however, that interest among Roma for mother-tongue education is negligible. A large number of Roma political organizations have been established, including the Democratic and Free Union of Roma of Romania, the Fiddlers' and Woodcarvers' Party, the Christian Democratic Party of Roma and the Tinsmith Roma Progressive Party. Leadership of the Roma community is contested between self-appointed emperors and kings. Divisions among Roma have prevented the formulation of a clear programme of action. To distinguish between 'Roma' and 'Romanian' the government has recently urged adoption of the new term 'Rroma'. This orthographic reform appears to have the support of Roma organizations.

Germans

The 1992 census recorded 119,436 Germans in Romania, the majority in Transylvania where they comprise three separate groups. 'Saxons' are the descendants of Germans who entered Transylvania in the twelfth and thirteenth centuries. 'Swabians' are descended from southern Germans who settled mainly in the Banat in south-west Transylvania during the eighteenth century. The small group of 'Landler' are descended from Protestants who took refuge in northern Transylvania in the eighteenth century. The number of Germans has been in steady decline since the interwar period when they were recorded as 761,000-strong (1930 census). At the end of the Second World War, German properties were seized and 75,000 Germans were transported to the Soviet Union as forced labour. Many more were permitted under the communists to emigrate to the Federal Republic of Germany in exchange for hard currency remittances.

After 1989, more than 100,000 Germans migrated to Germany, with the consequence that a large number of Saxon and Swabian villages are now deserted. In 1994, three German-language primary schools and five secondary schools were reported; the majority of German pupils were taught in sections in bilingual schools. A lack of teachers and of adequate accommodation is, however, reported. There are daily German-language broadcasts on radio and twice weekly on television, and several German-language publications. The social and cultural interests of the German minority are represented by the Democratic Forum of Germans in Romania, which was founded in 1990.

Other minorities

The 1992 census recorded 66,833 Ukrainians/Ruthenes, the majority of whom live in northern Transylvania in Maramures county, where there are also two Ukrainian/Ruthene-language secondary schools. Lipovans (Russians) accounted for 38,688 people according to the same census. Lipovans have several monthly Russian-language periodicals and weekly local radio broadcasts. Education in Lipovan has recently started. Serbs, Poles, Czechs and Slovaks live mainly in the Banat near the border with Yugoslavia, although many Serbs were forcibly resettled after 1948 in Wallachia. They have their own publications, language sections in schools (including one Serbian-language secondary school in Timisoara), and political organizations. The 1992 census additionally noted 30,000 Turks, 25,000 Tatars and 10,000 Bulgarians, who live mainly in the Dobrudja near the Danube estuary, and 4,000 Greeks. A tiny Armenian community remains in Transylvania, although it has been almost entirely assimilated into the larger Hungarian minority. In Moldavia and Wallachia 5,000 Armenians are reported. In the 1990s, mother-tongue education was commenced for Armenians as well as for the very few Italians who live mostly on the Black Sea coast. The number of Jews, 9,000, according to the 1992 census, has fallen considerably over the past 60 years as a result of the Nazi genocide and of state-sponsored immigration to Israel during the communist period. Jewish organizations indicate a recrudescence of anti-Semitism, an insufficiency of legal constraints on racist literature, and the occasional desecration of religious and cultural sites.[7]

Conclusions and future prospects

Romania has probably the most extensive network of minority-language education in Central and

Eastern Europe, as well as a substantial number of political and cultural organizations representing the interests of minorities. These facilities should be sufficient to preserve the identities of minorities and prevent their assimilation. Despite provocations, relations between majority and minority communities in Romania are not tense and the inter-ethnic violence of 1990 has not been repeated. Two difficulties remain. First, since the rule of law is not yet fully established in Romania, substantial discretionary rights still attach to local officials who may abuse their powers against members of minorities. In this respect, the long delay in establishing the office of ombudsman (or people's advocate) is to be regretted. Second, the government party depends on right-wing organizations for suport in the parliament. As a consequence, it is not always able to enforce legal provisions for minority protection and is obliged for short-term political advantage to support the passage of discriminatory legislation. The impression that both government and local authorities are neglectful of the basic rights of minorities encourages minority demands for protection through institutions of self-government.

As Romania moves towards European norms with regard to human rights protection, so it is likely that the discrimination still endured by members of minorities will lessen and demands for territorial autonomy become less insistent. The establishment of police complaints boards and the appointment of commissioners charged with protecting the interests of minorities, particularly Roma, might hasten development towards the rule of law and serve to protect members of minorities from abuses committed by local agencies.

Further reading

Anti-Semitism World Report 1994, London, Institute of Jewish Affairs, 1994, pp. 114–32.

Gallagher, T., *Romania after Ceausescu: The Politics of Intolerance*, Edinburgh, Edinburgh University Press, 1995.

Liégeois, J.-P. and Gheorghe, N., *Roma/Gypsies: A European Minority*, London, MRG report, 1995.

Rady, M., *Romania in Turmoil: A Contemporary History*, London, Tauris, 1992.

Schopflin, G. and Poulton, H., *Romania's Ethnic Hungarians*, London, MRG report, 1990.

Minority-based and advocacy organizations

Association for Hungarian–Romanian Friendship, Str. Iasilor 14, 3400 Cluj, CP 273, Romania; tel./fax 40 64 136 530.

Aven Amenza Cultural Foundation for the Emancipation of Roma, CP 22–165, Bucharest 70100, Romania, fax 40 1 222 3333.

Democratic Alliance of Hungarians in Romania, Herastrau 13, PO Box 63/27, Bucharest 71297, Romania; fax 40 1 212 1675.

Democratic and Free Union of Roma of Romania, Str. Tipografiei 28, 3400 Cluj, Romania.

Democratic Forum of Germans in Romania, Sibiu, Romania.

Democratic Union of Hungarians, Str. Pavlov 21, 3400 Cluj, Romania.

Heltai Gaspar Library Foundation, Clinicilor nr. 18, 3400 Cluj, Romania; tel. 40 64 190 096, fax 40 64 193 463.

Liga Pro Europa, P-ta Trandafirilor, PO Box 1–154, 4300 Tirgu-Mures, Romania; tel./fax 40 65 168 549.

Muslim Turkish Tatars Democratic Union of Romania, Str. Revolutiei din Decembrie 1989 6, Constanta, Romania; tel. 40 41 616 643.

Romani CRISS Center for Social Intervention and Studies, PO Box 2268, Bucharest 70100, Romania; tel./fax 40 1 211 7868, e-mail: romani@criss.sfos.ro.

Romania Helsinki Committee, Calea Victoriei 129, Bucharest, Romania; tel./fax 40 1 312 4528.

Romanian Institute for Human Rights, Piata Aviatorilor 3, Bucharest, Romania.

Russian Lipovans Community of Romania, Str Lipscani 18, er 1, cam. 13, 70421 Bucharest, Romania.

Serbian and Carasovens Democratic Union of Romania, Soseaua Victor Babes 18, Timisoara, Romania.

Union of Armenians of Romania, Str Armeneasca 13, sector 2, 70334 Bucharest, Romania; tel. 40 1 613 8459.

Slovakia

Land area:	49,000 sq km
Population:	5.3 million (1992)
Main languages:	Slovak, Hungarian, Romani, German, Ruthene/Ukrainian
Main religions:	Roman Catholicism, Protestantism (mainly Calvinist), Greek Catholicism, Eastern Orthodox Christianity
Main minority groups:	*1991 census:* Hungarians 567,000 (10.8%), Roma 80,600 (1.5%), others 110,000 (2%); *other estimates:* Roma up to 350,000 (6.6%)
Real per capita GDP:	$6,690
UNDP HDI/rank:	0.872 (40)

Slovakia is bordered by Poland to the north, Hungary to the south, Austria and the Czech Republic to the west, and Ukraine to the east. Most of Slovakia is mountainous, being crossed by the western arc of the Carpathians. For most of the twentieth century, Slovakia was a part of Czechoslovakia, although a separate Slovak state was briefly established as a satellite of Nazi Germany. On 31 December 1992, the union between the Czech lands and Slovakia formally dissolved and Slovakia became an independent state.

Slovaks speak a language closely related to Czech and other West Slav languages. They settled in the Carpathian region during the seventh century but were subsequently conquered by the Hungarians. From the tenth to the early twentieth centuries, Slovakia formed a part of the Kingdom of Hungary. In 1918, Slovakia was joined with Bohemia, Moravia, Austrian Silesia and Ruthenia in the state of Czechoslovakia. Slovak resentment of the centralizing policies pursued by the government in Prague facilitated the disintegration of Czechoslovakia in 1939. After 1939, the southern portions of Slovakia together with Ruthenia were occupied by Hungary. At the end of the Second World War, southern Slovakia was reincorporated in the restored Czechoslovak state, and Ruthenia was ceded to Ukraine, which was then a part of the Soviet Union.

Although minorities living in Slovakia alleged discrimination against them during the period of the first Czechoslovak Republic (1918–38), the most flagrant violation of their rights occurred during and after the Second World War. Almost all the Jewish population of Slovakia, which numbered approximately 70,000 in 1939, was deported and murdered. Today, only 3,000–6,000 Jews remain. Most of the 150,000-strong German population living in Slovakia and a part of the Hungarian minority fled or were expelled after 1945.

During the 1950s and 1960s, the communist government of Czechoslovakia practised a policy of assimilation. Nevertheless, following the 'Prague Spring' of 1968, Hungarians, Poles and Ukrainians were accorded the legal status of minorities and their rights to education in the mother tongue and to representation in state and local bodies were legally guaranteed. In practice, however, these rights were ignored. No education was provided in the Romani, Ruthene/Ukrainian or German languages, and between 1970 and 1989 the number of Hungarian children receiving mother-tongue instruction fell by almost a half.

The collapse of communist rule in 1989 promised a rapid improvement of the rights of minorities in Slovakia. The Charter of Fundamental Rights and Freedoms, adopted by the Czechoslovak federal assembly in January 1991, prohibited all forms of discrimination and reaffirmed the right to education in the mother tongue. For its part, the 1992 Slovak constitution gave minorities the right to develop their culture, to deal in their own language with state officials, and to be educated both in Slovak and in the mother tongue. Nevertheless, disquiet was registered since both these instruments seemed implicitly to deny minorities any 'state-forming' role within the new political structure. The retention after 1992 of a nationalist government aroused fears for the interests of minorities, while the more general weakness of democratic institutions in Slovakia provoked criticism from the United States and from European foreign ministers in October 1995.

Additional misgivings were aroused by specific legislative measures. In 1990, a new Slovak

Language Law confined official use of a minority language to administrative areas where the relevant minority constituted 20 per cent of the local population. The Surname Law of 1993 made compulsory the registration of names according to Slovak linguistic norms, although concessions to minority-language usages were made in 1994. Most notoriously, the 1993 'Vertical Road Signs' decree prohibited bilingual signposts. This enactment was, however, overturned by new legislation permitting bilingual signposts in communities where the minority population exceeds 20 per cent (currently 587 towns and villages). The right of minorities to use their own language may be further circumscribed by the 1995 Act on the State Language, which affirms the state language as Slovak and imposes harsh financial penalties for its misuse or misspelling. The use of minority languages is to be the subject of future legislation, although this had not reached draft stage by 1996. Proposals for new internal administrative boundaries seemed additionally intended to ensure that Hungarians would be unable to maintain a majority in any one district.

The Slovak government is aware that its minorities policy will influence the speed of Slovakia's accession to the European Union. Official Slovak sources indicate the very substantial disbursements made to minority cultural foundations and publishers,[1] but this information is outdated on account of severe cutbacks in funding during 1995. Although statistics affirming this trend are incomplete, the number of minority educational facilities appears to be increasing. Domestic legislation is, furthermore, being brought into line with European standards and the 1995 State Treaty between Hungary and Slovakia affirmed Slovakia's commitment to the provisions of the CSCE Copenhagen Document, the UN Declaration on Minorities, and Recommendation 1201 of the Parliamentary Assembly of the Council of Europe. Although a Minorities Council advises the government, Slovakia still lacks a dedicated law for the protection of minorities.

Hungarians

The 1991 census indicated a Hungarian population of 566,741 people, living almost entirely in the southern part of the country in the regions adjoining the Danube river and the border with Hungary, but some Hungarian sources put the true number of Hungarians closer to 700,000. Within the former Czechoslovakia, Hungarians constituted only about 3 per cent of the overall population. The dissolution of Czechoslovakia had the immediate consequence, therefore, of making Hungarians far more visible as a minority. More than 40 per cent of Hungarian marriages are exogamous, suggesting that the minority may in time become assimilated.[2]

After the Second World War, Hungarians experienced substantial discrimination at the hands of the Czechoslovak, Slovak and occupation authorities. Their properties were confiscated, between 70,000 and 90,000 were expelled to Hungary, and a further 44,000 were resettled in Bohemia and Moravia. Along with Roma, Hungarians continued to bear the brunt of communist assimilation policy between 1948 and 1989. Although conditions for Hungarians have improved immeasurably since 1989, they are still a frequent target of abuse for nationalist politicians and parties.

Hungarians allege that a lack of educational facilities has resulted in low attainment in qualifications and poor employment opportunities. Few Hungarians progress to secondary education and only about 6 per cent of Hungarian students gain entry to higher education. As of 1994, about 70,000 Hungarian children were receiving instruction in the mother tongue, amounting to 70 per cent of the relevant Hungarian age cohort.[3] Except in teacher-training, however, little progress has been made towards establishing bilingual facilities in higher education, and requests for a Hungarian-language university at Komarno have not been met. In 1994, Slovak television broadcast 30 minutes a week in Hungarian and there were in total 36 hours a week of Hungarian-language radio transmissions.

Roma

The 1991 census recorded 80,627 Roma, but the minority may in reality number more than 300,000 people. Although Roma suffered severe discrimination in Slovakia during the Second World War, most (unlike those in the Nazi Protectorate of Bohemia and Moravia) avoided extermination. After the war, many Slovak Roma settled in the Czech lands. Under the communists, Roma were forbidden to travel, and most were settled in dispersed accommodation blocks. Even in the late 1980s, however, one-third of Slovak Roma continued to live in shanty villages. Although a gradual improvement in employment opportunities was recorded (by 1981, 75 per cent of the active adult Roma population was employed), Roma were officially held responsible for 50 per cent of robberies and 60 per cent of petty thefts. On the basis of intelligence testing, Roma children were frequently educated in separate 'special schools'. From the 1970s, Roma women were encouraged to volunteer for sterilization.

Although flagrant human rights violations largely ceased after 1989, Roma still endure considerable discrimination in employment, accommodation and access to services. An attempt to alleviate the housing crisis among Roma had to be abandoned in 1992 because of financial constraints. Segregation is, additionally, reported in classrooms and maternity wards, while Roma have been the targets of violence from right-wing thugs and of constitutionally illegal measures introduced by several local authorities. No special Roma-language schools have yet been established, allegedly because no Roma have requested them. Nevertheless, government funds have been allocated to support Roma publications and cultural activities, and a Romani language centre has been established at the University of Nitra.

Other minorities

The 1991 census distinguished 16,937 Ruthenes (Rusyns) and 13,847 Ukrainians, whom many would consider as belonging to the same ethnic group. Ruthene/Ukrainian identity is weak and the minority is susceptible to assimilationist trends. Television and radio respectively broadcast ten minutes and seven hours a week in Ruthene/Ukrainian; and there is a small network of Ruthenian/Ukrainian-language schools. Ruthenes and Ukrainians often belong to the Greek Uniate and Eastern Orthodox churches, which jointly claim 200,000 adherents. There were in 1991, 5,629 Germans, most of whom lived in Bratislava and in the Kosice region. Some German communities in the Carpathians are reported still to use a form of High German. Since 1990, there have been radio transmissions in German, but no state-funded educational institutions teaching in German have been set up. The 1991 census additionally recorded 3,888 Moravians, 1,198 Silesians, 2,969 Poles and 1,624 Russians. Most of the 53,422 Czechs recorded in the 1991 census are believed to have either returned to the Czech Republic or to have assumed Slovak citizenship.

Conclusions and future prospects

The condition of Slovakia's Hungarian minority has been steadily improving since 1990, partly as a result of the pressure exerted by the government of Hungary through international institutions. Despite Slovakia's confirmation of the applicability of Recommendation 1201, the nationalist undercurrent in Slovak politics makes it unlikely that this improvement will be accompanied by a grant of territorial autonomy. The condition of the Roma community, allegedly 'the poorest and most profoundly affected in Eastern Europe',[4] gives cause for concern, but any amelioration depends upon the improvements in the overall economy. Slovakia has, nevertheless, confounded its critics. Relations between the national groups are good and, apart from incidents involving Roma, little conflict has been reported. Attempts to rally support around extreme nationalist positions have found little popular support. Nevertheless, the immaturity of Slovakia's new democratic institutions and recent legislation affecting the use of minority languages may have the consequence of engendering inter-ethnic tension in the future.

Further reading

Janics, K., *Czechoslovak Policy and the Hungarian Minority 1945–8*, New York, East European Monographs, 1982.

Krejci, J., *Czechoslovakia at the Crossroads of European History*, London, Tauris, 1990.

Liégeois, J-P. and Gheorghe, N., *Roma/Gypsies: A European Minority*, London, MRG report, 1995.

MRG (ed.), *Minorities in Central and Eastern Europe*, London, MRG report, 1993.

Tritt, R., *Struggling for Ethnic Identity: Czechoslovakia's Endangered Gypsies*, New York, Human Rights Watch, 1992.

Minority-based and advocacy organizations

Coexistence [Hungarians], Prazska 7, PO Box 44, 81499 Bratislava, Slovakia.

Charter 77 Foundation, Staromestska 6, 81336 Bratislava, Slovakia.

InfoRoma, Bajkalská 25, 82718 Bratislava, Slovakia; tel. 42 7 52 33303, fax 42 7 52 33478.

Minority Rights Group Slovakia, Bajkalská 25, 82708 Bratislava, Slovakia; tel. 42 7 523 3164, fax 42 7 521 4534.

Patrin [Roma], Presov, Slovakia; fax 42 9 173 902.

Slovak Centre for Conflict Prevention, Comenius University, Topolcianska 25, 85101 Bratislava, Slovakia.

Slovak Helsinki Committee, Zabotova 2, 81104 Bratislava, Slovakia.

Slovenia

Land area:	20,000 sq km
Population:	2 million (1992)
Main languages:	Slovene, Serbo-Croat, Hungarian, Italian
Main religions:	Roman Catholicism, Eastern Orthodox Christianity, Islam
Main minority groups:	*1991 census:* Croats 54,000 (2.7%), Serbs 47,000 (2.4%), Muslims 26,700 (1.4%), others including Hungarians 8,500 (0.4%), Italians 3,000 (0.1%) and 'unknown' and 'undeclared' 117,000 (6%)
Real per capita GDP:	$6,490 (1993 World Bank estimate)
UNDP HDI/rank:	—

Slovenia lies in the north-western part of south-eastern Europe. It is bordered by Austria to the north, Hungary to the east, Croatia to the south and Italy to the west. At its westernmost point, Slovenia has a short coastline on the Adriatic Sea. Slovenia is a mountainous country and is, after Montenegro, the smallest of the republics previously forming the Socialist Federation of Yugoslavia. Slovenes are a Slavonic people who speak a language related to Serbo-Croat. Slovenes entered the territory of present-day Slovenia during the fifth and sixth centuries but rapidly fell under Frankish and Catholic influence. From the fourteenth century, the Slovene lands became hereditary possessions of the Austrian Habsburgs and they remained a part of the Habsburg empire until 1918. After the First World War, most of the Slovene lands were incorporated in the Kingdom of Serbs, Croats and Slovenes (after 1929, Yugoslavia), although small areas of Slovene settlement remained within neighbouring Italy, Hungary and Austria. During the Second World War, Slovenia was partitioned between its neighbours, who adopted a harsh policy of assimilation towards Slovenes. After 1945, Slovenia was restored as a republic within federal Yugoslavia. Disputes over the frontier with Italy were not formally resolved until the 1970s.

The policy towards minorities was guided during the communist period by a collectivist approach which permitted the establishment of schools teaching in the language of Slovenia's historic Italian and Hungarian minorities. Until the early 1960s, however, these proved unattractive to parents, since they taught exclusively in the mother tongue and were thought damaging to children's educational and employment prospects.[1] Thereafter, minority-language schools were replaced by bilingual ones. Slovene children attending such schools were after 1980 obliged to learn the language of the minority, 'thus acquiring the foundations for bilingual communication and understanding of the cultural and other values of both nationalities as well as deepening bilateral coexistence'. By the terms of a law passed in 1980, street signs in areas of Hungarian and Italian settlement are to be written both in Slovene and in the minority language.

Resentment at the net outflow of resources from Slovenia to the rest of the Yugoslav federation propelled to power a pro-independence coalition in multi-party elections held in Slovenia in 1990. After a referendum, Slovenia formally declared itself an independent state in June 1991. An attempt by the federal army to prevent Slovenia's dissociation was defeated in the same month.

The Slovene constitution adopted in June 1991 ensures basic human rights 'irrespective of national origin, race, sex, language, religion'. It further permits individuals to communicate with state bodies in their own language (articles 14, 61). The constitution, however, grants collective minority and language rights only to Hungarians and Italians, who are recognized as belonging to 'autochthonous ethnic communities'. Likewise, only Hungarians and Italians have the right to education in their own language and to establish institutions and to engage in activities which 'preserve their national identity' (article 64). Hungarians and Italians are additionally permitted to elect one deputy each to the Slovene parliament, the National Assembly. The constitution additionally gives Hungarians and Italians the right as 'self-governing communities' to set up their own autonomous organizations (article 64).

A law on Self-Managing Ethnic Communities was passed by the Slovene parliament in October

1994 which amplifies article 64 of the constitution. The law permits the establishment of directly elected councils for the Hungarian and Italian minorities charged with preserving the interests and identities of their members. The councils may submit recommendations to relevant government bodies and participate in decision-making with regard to education. Below the Councils of the Self-Managing Ethnic Communities stand 'self-managing local communities' which make recommendations to local government bodies. The national and local ethnic community organizations are funded out of the national and municipal budgets respectively.

Croats, Serbs, Muslims, Macedonians, Montenegrins, 'Yugoslavs'

The circumstances in contemporary Slovenia of the Croat, Serb, Muslim, Macedonian, Montenegrin, and 'Yugoslav' minorities are broadly similar. During the 1970s and 1980s, the expansion of the Slovene economy attracted substantial migration of people from other parts of former Yugoslavia. Between 1953 and 1991, the number of Croats as a proportion of the overall population more than doubled, and the number of Serbs tripled. No special educational or linguistic facilities were, however, established to accommodate this influx. Although the migrants received some protection from federal legislation (as for instance with regard to the provision of interpreters in courts of law), they were largely excluded from Slovenia's minority-protection legislation.

According to the 1991 census, there were in Slovenia 53,688 Croats, 47,097 Serbs, 26,725 Muslims, 12,237 'Yugoslavs', 4,412 Macedonians and 4,233 Montenegrins. Collectively, these minorities amounted to 7.5 per cent of the overall population. The number of migrants from other parts of former Yugoslavia has increased substantially since the 1991 census, mainly on account of flight from civil war and from economic hardship. It is estimated that there were in 1994 at least 50,000 refugees in Slovenia from the former Yugoslavia.[2] Many of these suffer substantial social and economic disadvantages. Collective minority rights, including public education in the mother tongue, remain confined, however, to Hungarians and Italians. An amendment to the citizenship law, passed in April 1993, seems designed to arrest the influx of migrants to Slovenia. Official bodies acknowledge that the present policy of excluding migrants from the collective rights regime, although in accordance with international practice, may be unsustainable.[3]

Hungarians

According to the 1991 census there were 8,503 Hungarians in Slovenia, most of whom are descended from Hungarians who settled across the frontier, mainly during the nineteenth century. Hungarians are concentrated in the municipalities of Lendva and Murska Sobota in the north-western Prekmurje region (Mura-videk). Since 1959, Hungarian children have attended bilingual schools; previously they were educated solely in the mother tongue. Hungarian radio broadcasts began in the 1950s and, in the early 1990s, the Hungarian-language Pomurski Madzarski Radio commenced daily transmissions of eight hours. There is currently one Hungarian-language television programme a week, broadcast on the state channel, and one Hungarian weekly newspaper. The legal protection of the Hungarian minority has been further ensured through a bilateral treaty on the rights of minorities signed in April 1994, by the Slovene and Hungarian governments.[4]

Italians

The 1991 census records 3,064 Italians, living mainly in the three coastal municipalities of Izola, Koper and Piran. Italian children have since the 1960s been educated in bilingual schools. After the communist take-over, many Italians left Slovenia. The Italian government has recently reopened the issue of their compensation and restoration of properties. In 1994, Italy sought to block Slovenia's application for associate EU membership because of these outstanding claims. Relations with Italy have also been soured by Italy's allegedly poor treatment of its own Slovene minority.[5]

Other minorities

According to the 1991 census, there were 2,293 Roma in Slovenia, although unofficial estimates put their number at 7,000. The constitution recognizes Roma as autochthonous. Owing to an alleged lack of organization among Roma, it has so far proved impossible to establish a self-managing Roma ethnic community. The census additionally indicated 3,558 Albanians. Seventy thousand people were listed in 1991 in the census categories 'unknown' and 'undeclared'. Many of these are believed to be migrants from other parts of former Yugoslavia (principally Bosnia-Herzegovina) who settled over a period of years in Slovenia in contravention of the republican regulations on residence which were then in force.

Conclusions and future prospects

Slovenia has established a secure collective rights policy in the cultural and educational spheres for its historic Italian and Hungarian communities. Slovenia's interest in extending minority rights flows from traditions of self-management inherited from the communist period and from concern over the fate of the Slovene minorities in neighbouring states. Nevertheless, the scheme of ethnic self-management put forward in the 1994 law does not include territorial autonomy, which might be considered an aspect of the right of self-determination, particularly in the case of compacted communities. The exclusion of migrant minorities from any collective rights may prove hard to maintain, especially in view of the recent immigration to Slovenia of refugees and others from former Yugoslavia.

Further reading

Ethnic Minorities in Slovenia, Ljubljana, Institute for Ethnic Studies and Information Bureau of Government of Slovenia, 1994.

MRG (ed.), *Minorities in Central and Eastern Europe*, London, MRG report, 1993.

Zagar, M., 'Nationality, protection of ethnic minorities and transition to democracy: the case of Slovenia – II', *Teorija in Praksa*, vol. 32, no. 3–4, 1995, pp. 243–54.

Zagar, M., 'Position and protection of ethnic minorities in the constitution of the Republic of Slovenia', *Treatises and Documents*, 26–7, Ljubljana, 1992, pp. 5–20.

Minority-based and advocacy organizations

Amnesty International, Komenskega 7, 1000 Ljubljana, Slovenia; tel. 386 61 131 9134, fax 386 61 131 9134.

Helsinki Committee of Slovenia, Cigaletova 5, Ljubljana, 61101, Slovenia.

Institute for Ethnic Studies, Erjavceva 26, 61000 Ljubljana, Slovenia, fax 386 61 210 964.

Yugoslavia (Serbia and Montenegro)

Land area:	102,170 sq km
Population:	10,597,000 (mid-1992)
Main languages:	Serbian, Albanian, Hungarian
Main religions:	Eastern Orthodox Christianity, Islam (mainly Sunni), Roman Catholicism, Protestantism
Main minority groups:	*1991 census:* Albanians 1,727,500 (16.6%), Montenegrins 520,500 (5%), Hungarians 345,400 (3.3%), 'Yugoslavs' 344,000 (3.3%), Muslims 327,500 (3.1%), Montenegrins 140,024 (1.3%), Roma 137,265 (1.3%), Croats 109,214 (1%), others 270,497 (2.6%); *other estimates:* Albanians more than 2 million (19%), Roma 500,000 (est. 4.8%)
Real per capita GDP:	—
UNDP HDI/rank:	—

The present Federal Republic of Yugoslavia was proclaimed in May 1992 and consists of the republics of Serbia and Montenegro.[1] Serbia occupies the landlocked central portion of south-eastern Europe. The republic of Montenegro, which adjoins Serbia in the south, lies between Bosnia-Herzegovina and Albania, and the Adriatic coast forms Montenegro's western border. Except for the Vojvodina in the north of the country, Serbia has a rugged terrain, while Montenegro is almost entirely mountainous. Serbia and Montenegro are ethnically diverse. According to the 1991 census, Serbs constitute less than two-thirds of the population of Serbia, and Montenegrins just over 60 per cent of the population of Montenegro. Since 1991, however, the ethnic composition of Yugoslavia has been altered by flight or departure in parts of the Sanjak of Novi Pazar and the Vojvodina, and by an influx of mainly Serb refugees from Croatia and Bosnia-Herzegovina. The present number of refugees and displaced persons in Yugoslavia exceeds 500,000.

Serbs entered the Balkans in the sixth and seventh centuries. After several centuries of Byzantine and Bulgarian rule, during which time they were converted to Eastern Orthodox Christianity, Serbian princes established an empire which extended over a large part of the Balkan peninsula. In the late fourteenth century, the Serbian lands were incorporated within the Ottoman empire. During the early nineteenth century, Serbia gained autonomy and in 1878 it was recognized as a sovereign state. At this time, however, the Serbian state did not include a large proportion of the Serb people, who variously remained within the Ottoman empire, Habsburg-occupied Bosnia-Herzegovina, Hungary and Croatia (then also part of the Habsburg empire). During the late nineteenth and early twentieth centuries, Serbia endeavoured to bring these areas of Serb settlement under the rule of Belgrade.

After the First World War, Serbia formed a part of the Kingdom of Serbs, Croats and Slovenes (after 1929, Yugoslavia). The new state also included Montenegro, which had previously been an independent principality and had never been fully incorporated within the Ottoman empire. Despite the different historical, cultural and linguistic traditions of its constituent parts, the new Yugoslav kingdom was administered as a centralized state governed from Belgrade. Resentment of Serbian rule facilitated the disintegration of the Yugoslav kingdom during the Second World War.

After the communist take-over in 1944–5, Yugoslavia was established as a federal republic. Whereas Serbs had come to believe during the interwar period that they were the masters of Yugoslavia, under the communists, Serbs became increasingly convinced that they were being marginalized. The 1974 constitution, which gave substantial rights of self-government to Kosovo and the Vojvodina, was considered particularly damaging to Serb national interests. Serbs were also fearful of the rapid demographic growth of the Albanian minority in Kosovo and southern Serbia.

After the death of Tito in 1980 and the collapse of the Yugoslav economy, Yugoslav politics became increasingly ethnicized. In the late 1980s, President Slobodan Milosevic of Serbia mobilized Serb discontent by championing the cause of the Serb 'minority-within-a-minority' in Kosovo and by complaining of the bureaucratic devices used to reduce Serb influence within Yugoslavia. In 1989, the Serbian parliament revoked the right of self-government in Kosovo and the Vojvodina, and shortly afterwards Milosevic's supporters took control of the republican government of Montenegro. These measures gave additional incentive to nationalist forces elsewhere in Yugoslavia to establish their own independent national states. The dissolution of Yugoslavia in 1991–2 was followed by the establishment of a new federation, comprising solely Serbia and Montenegro. The new Yugoslavia is not, however, internationally recognized as legal successor to the former federation of the same name.

The constitution of Yugoslavia was promulgated in 1992 and gives substantial protection to minorities. Minorities are entitled 'to the preservation, development and expression of their ethnic, cultural, linguistic and other specificities as well as to the use of their national symbols' (article 11). Members of national minorities are additionally entitled to have their alphabets and languages 'in official use' in the areas which they inhabit, and to education in the mother tongue (articles 15 and 46). They may found institutions and plead in court in their own languages (articles 47 and 49). These rights may be found also in the 1990 constitution of Serbia and are elaborated in considerable detail in the 1992 constitution of Montenegro.

There is, however, substantial evidence that the rights entrusted to minorities in the federal and republican constitutions are frequently violated. These abuses should be viewed in the context of a general absence of the rule of law in contemporary Yugoslavia and of the current political impasse with regard to the Albanian minority in Kosovo. A distinction should also be made between Serbia and Montenegro. In the latter, there is a greater tradition of inter-ethnic cooperation. In 1993, the Montenegrin parliament established a Council for the Protection of the Rights of Members of National and Ethnic Groups, which has apparently won the confidence of the Montenegrin Albanian community.

Albanians

The 1991 census recorded 1,686,661 Albanians in Serbia, of whom 1,607,000 lived in Kosovo (official name, Kosovo and Metohija; in Albanian, Kosova). The remainder were concentrated in districts adjoining Kosovo's frontier with the rest of Serbia. Since many Albanians boycotted the 1991 census, the official figure for the Albanian population had to be arrived at by statistical projection. The Albanian population may in reality be as many as 2 million in Kosovo alone. In Montenegro, 40,880 Albanians were recorded in 1991. Most Albanians are Muslim, but there are a large number of Eastern Orthodox and Catholics, including 50,000 Catholics in Kosovo. Some Muslim Albanians belong to the Bektashi dervish sect.

Serbian sources frequently allege that most of Kosovo's Albanians are newcomers who emigrated from Albania after 1941. It is probable that Albanians have a long historic connection with Kosovo, and that they entered the region in waves from the fifteenth century onwards. In the decades following Serbia's acquisition of Kosovo in 1912, Serb families were moved into the region, and possibly as many as half a million Albanians were evicted to Turkey and Albania. Land reforms resulted in the dispossession of properties belonging to wealthy Albanians, while a policy of assimilation was practised in education, according to which all instruction was in Serbo-Croat.[2]

After the communist take-over, Albanians were recognized as a national minority and were permitted collective rights with regard to education in the mother tongue and the establishment of cultural institutions. In 1968, Kosovo was given a substantial element of home rule and, following the 1974 constitution, was granted full autonomy within Serbia. Nevertheless, these concessions proved insufficient to satisfy Albanian nationalist demands for complete republican status and for eventual unification with Albania. After riots in 1981, Albanian nationalist activity was suppressed. At this time, however, the relevant organs of the communist party and of law enforcement in Kosovo were overwhelmingly staffed by Albanians, and Albanians were still permitted extensive educational, linguistic and cultural rights. The oppression of the early 1980s should not, therefore, be viewed as one practised by a majority people against a minority.

During the 1980s, it was repeatedly claimed by Serbs that they were discriminated against in Kosovo, and that attacks on the Serb population were not remedied by the Albanian-dominated authorities.[3] Serbs viewed the 'Albanianization' of Kosovo with particular alarm since the region was home to many of the most important Orthodox monasteries and shrines. Responding to these fears, in 1989 the Serbian parliament stripped Kosovo of autonomy. The next year, the Kosovo Assembly (regional parliament) was closed down after it had issued a unilateral declaration of sovereignty. In 1991, the Kosovo presidency was abolished, thus completing Kosovo's institutional integration into Serbia. Between 1989 and 1991, the Albanian political leadership and bureaucracy were purged and military units were sent into the region. There were widespread reports of the shooting of demonstrators, arbitrary arrests and beatings, judicial partiality in the conviction of activists, and dismissals from employment on political grounds. Several instances of murder by the Serbian police have been reported. After 1989, publicly funded Albanian-language newspapers and media were either withdrawn or closed down, although privately funded publications continue to appear.

In 1990, a new curriculum was published for Albanian schools in Kosovo, the purpose of which was to bring Albanian teaching into line with the rest of Serbia. Although education at elementary school level continued in Albanian, after 1992 most secondary schools became Serbian-language only. At the same time, Albanian-language instruction in Pristina University was severely cut back and the proportion of Serb students studying there was deliberately increased. Thousands of Albanian teachers and professors lost their jobs in the course of the implementation of this programme. A school boycott was followed by the establishment of a 'parallel education system', whereby pupils and students were taught in private homes or in parts of existing school buildings. According to Kosovo Albanian sources, in the 1992–3 academic year, 274,000 Albanian children attended parallel primary education classes, and there were 63,000 pupils in secondary classes.[4] The 'parallel' schooling system lacks resources, particularly for scientific and medical training, and is unlikely, therefore, to arrest the educational disadvantage traditionally experienced by Albanians.

In September 1990, the Democratic League of Kosovo (DLK) was founded to promote the rights of Albanians in Kosovo. The DLK organized a referendum on independence for Kosovo which won overwhelming approval from the Albanian electorate. In October 1991, the DLK declared Kosovo's independence and the next year organized elections to a self-styled 'Kosovo Assembly'. The DLK remains firmly committed to secession from Serbia, although it is divided on unification with Albania.

The DLK-led government asserts sovereign jurisdiction in Kosovo, and claims to have its own police force and foreign representation. It supports its activities by levying 'taxes' on the Albanian population. Nevertheless, the Serbian police and army maintain a highly visible presence in Kosovo. The DLK is publicly committed to the peaceful attainment of independence, but more militant organizations have called for an armed struggle. During 1996, the moderate leadership of the DLK was reported to have lost ground to radical elements advocating a policy of insurrection. An increase in guerrilla activity was detected by several well placed sources, including, in May 1996, an attack by gunmen on police in Desani, which led to several deaths. Serbian sources allege arms shipments entering Kosovo, which are paid for through the international sale of narcotics.[5] There is no evidence of a spread of Muslim fundamentalism among Albanians.

Kosovo remains the poorest part of Serbia, despite substantial previous investment in the region. Presently, only 100,000 of the active adult population of 900,000 are registered as employed. Those without employment survive mainly from remittances paid by family members working abroad. During the autumn of 1995, possibly as many as 20,000 Serb refugees from Croatia were compulsorily relocated in Kosovo, thus exacerbating already tense inter-ethnic relations. Official spokespeople claim a substantial influx into Kosovo of migrants from Albania.

Most of Montenegrin Albanians are concentrated in the south, near the border with Albania. At least 80 per cent of the southern city of Ulcinj is Albanian. There are also concentrations of Albanians in Bar, Ostrog and Tuzi. Relations between Montenegrins and Albanians are not hostile, although mixed communities bear strong signs of social segmentation. The principal Albanian party is the Democratic Alliance of Montenegro, which has campaigned for autonomy for Albanian communities in Montenegro.

Montenegrins

According to the 1991 census, there were 380,484 Montenegrins in Montenegro, where they constitute 61.8 per cent of the population, and 140,024 Montenegrins in Serbia. Although there is a republic in Yugoslavia called Montenegro, the strong political and economic control exercised over its government by the Serb-controlled federal authorities may mean that the Montenegrins qualify as a non-dominant minority within Yugoslavia. Most Montenegrins and Serbs would, however, dispute the description of Montenegrins as a minority.

Montenegrins have historically been divided between those who, because they are Orthodox Christians and speak Serbian, consider themselves Serbs (the 'Whites') and those who see themselves as belonging to a separate ethnic group (the 'Greens'). There is little history of animosity between Montenegrins and Albanians; resentment is instead reserved for those Montenegrin families who converted to Islam.

Since 1989, the government of Montenegro has been led by the Democratic Party of Socialists, an ally of the Socialist Party of Serbia. Between 1991 and 1993, the Montenegrin government sought to distance itself from Belgrade and followed a moderate policy towards the war in Bosnia-Herzegovina. The authorities in Podgorica (formerly Titograd) have, furthermore, given shelter to Muslim refugees. The principal opposition party in Montenegro is the Liberal Alliance, which has adopted a 'Green' policy of Montenegrin independence. Recently, there have been attempts to recreate the historic Montenegrin language.

Hungarians

The 1991 census recorded 345,376 Hungarians, most of whom lived in the Vojvodina in northern Serbia. Before 1918, the Vojvodina was a part of the kingdom of Hungary and had a majority Hungarian population. Hungarians in the Vojvodina are mainly Roman Catholic, but there are communities of Calvinists, Methodists and Unitarians. Hungarians suffered discrimination after the First World War, when many of their properties were seized under the guise of land reform. Hungarian atrocities against Serbs in the Second World War were avenged by the murder of possibly as many as 30,000 Hungarians after 1945.

By the terms of the 1974 constitution, the Vojvodina acquired rights of autonomy analogous to those given to Kosovo. Under the communist regime, Hungarians had substantial collective rights, including more than 200 Hungarian-language elementary and secondary schools, a daily newspaper, and regular radio and television transmissions broadcast from Novi Sad. After the abolition of the Vojvodina autonomy in 1989, several attempts were made to bring editorial policy in Hungarian-language media under stronger supervision from Belgrade. In 1992, a new education law was passed by the Serbian parliament restricting teaching in Hungarian.

With the outbreak of war in Yugoslavia, a large number of refugees entered the Vojvodina, thus affecting the ethnic composition of many communities. By April 1992, there were already 62,000 refugees in the Vojvodina; more recent reports suggest an influx of up to 150,000 Serbs.[6] Hungarian political leaders have claimed that refugees have been compulsorily billeted in Hungarian villages as part of a deliberate attempt to change their ethnic balance. It is also alleged that a disproportionate number of Hungarians were conscripted after 1991 into the federal army. Although at least 50,000 Hungarians emigrated to Hungary after the outbreak of war, there is little evidence of a sustained campaign of intimidation against the Hungarian minority.

The principal Hungarian minority organization is the Democratic Community of Hungarians of the Vojvodina, which has published several ambitious plans for Hungarian territorial autonomy in the region.

Muslims

According to the 1991 census, there were 89,932 Muslims in Montenegro and 237,538 Muslims in Serbia, making up respectively 14.6 per cent and 2.4 per cent of the total Montenegrin and Serbian populations. Approximately 235,000 Muslims were in 1991 concentrated in the Sanjak of Novi Pazar (official name Raska), which straddles the Serbian-Montenegrin border. Muslims are descended from Serbs and Montenegrins who converted to Islam during the period of Ottoman occupation. The Muslims of the Sanjak are represented by the Party of Democratic Action (PDA) and the Muslim National Council of the Sanjak, which have campaigned since 1991 for territorial autonomy. A referendum organized by the PDA in October 1991 demonstrated overwhelming support for self-government for the Sanjak. In 1993, political leaders of the PDA indicated strong approval for the idea of fusing the Sanjak with Bosnia-Herzegovina.

In 1992–3, Yugoslav army and paramilitary units, with support from units of the Bosnian Serb Army, encircled Muslim towns in the Sanjak and intimidated the population. Communities along the border with Bosnia-Herzegovina were at this time reportedly 'cleansed' of Muslims, although the government strongly repudiates this allegation. During this period, approximately 75,000 Muslims fled the Sanjak. Since mid-1993, however, paramilitaries have been removed from the Sanjak and the Yugoslav Army has largely abandoned its harassment of the population.

Other minorities

According to the 1991 census, there were in Serbia 140,024 Montenegrins, 137,265 Roma, 109,214 Croats, 67,235 Slovaks, 47,577 Macedonians, 42,386 Romanians, 25,214 Bulgarians, 18,339 Ruthenes/Ukrainians, 17,557 Vlachs, 11,501 Turks, and 8,340 Slovenes. The majority of Croats (97,644), Slovaks (63,941), Romanians (38,831), and Ruthenes/Ukrainians (17,887) live in the Vojvodina. In 1985, 38 Romanian schools and 28 Slovak schools were listed as operating in the Vojvodina. There is evidence that Croats in the Vojvodina and, to a lesser extent, Ruthenes/Ukrainians and Slovaks have recently been the victims of severe harassment by the security and paramilitary forces. Between 1991 and 1993, 35,000 Croats are reported to have been 'cleansed' from the Vojvodina; a further wave of 'cleansing' is said to have taken place in the summer of 1995. The majority of Roma live in the larger cities, most notably in Belgrade and Nis. The Roma are linked in Serbia by 60 local associations of the Drustva Rom (founded in 1930) which together constitute the Romani Union. There are isolated examples of attacks on Roma, although it is not possible to establish whether these are racially motivated. The 1991 census also recorded 21,662 Bunjevci or Catholic Serbs.

In Montenegro, 57,176 people recorded themselves as Serbs in 1991. There is in Kotor a Catholic minority, about 12,000-strong and partly of Italian origin, which currently describes itself as Croat by nationality. In the coastal town of Ulcinj, a very few Negroes or Berbers remain, who are reputed to be the descendants of slaves and pirates. The Negroes are variously Albanian- and Montenegrin-speaking. They do not regard themselves, and nor indeed are they regarded, as constituting a separate ethnic group. About 2,000–3,000 Jews live in Yugoslavia, mostly in Belgrade. Despite the recent upsurge in nationalism and xenophobia, little anti-Semitism has been reported.

Conclusions and future prospects

The Federal Republic of Yugoslavia (Serbia and Montenegro) is a multi-ethnic state and is likely to remain so. Relations between the national groups have not deteriorated drastically since the outbreak of war in former Yugoslavia. It may be hoped that with the eventual restoration of peaceful conditions in the Balkans, the relative harmony which characterized inter-ethnic relations during the communist period will return.

Kosovo remains an intractable problem. It has been suggested that the solution to Kosovo might be the status quo for an indefinite period;[7] perversely, this may be correct. The present impasse at least allows Albanians collective cultural and educational opportunities, albeit obtained through underground and parallel institutions, while simultaneously preserving the semblance of Serbian sovereignty through the heavy Serbian security presence. The danger remains that precipitate military action by either side in Kosovo could provoke a wider political and refugee crisis which would draw Macedonia and Albania into conflict with Serbia and destabilize the 'southern tier' of the Balkans. Equally dangerous would be any attempt to change the ethnic balance in Kosovo by settling large numbers of Serb refugees in the province.

In the long run, it may be possible to reconstruct Yugoslavia as a state of 'perforated sovereignty', in which substantial devolved powers and degrees of special status are permitted to Kosovo, the Sanjak, the southern portion of Montenegro and parts or all of the Vojvodina. This would, however, probably require not only a change in the political leadership of Yugoslavia but also a readiness on all sides for compromise and concession.

Further reading

Kandic, N. (ed.), *Spotlight on Human Rights Violations in Times of Armed Conflict*, Belgrade, Humanitarian Law Center, 1995.

Kosovo: Oppression of Ethnic Albanians, London, MRG Urgent Issues Paper, November 1992.

MRG (ed.), *Minorities in Central and Eastern Europe*, London, MRG report, 1993.

Poulton, H., *The Balkans: Minorities and States in Conflict*, 2nd edn, London, Minority Rights Publications, 1993.

Singleton, F., *A Short History of the Yugoslav Peoples*, Cambridge, Cambridge University Press, 1985.

Woodward, S.L., *Balkan Inferno: Chaos and Dissolution After the Cold War*, Washington, DC, Brookings Institute, 1995.

Minority-based and advocacy organizations

Belgrade Helsinki Committee, Borka Pavicvic, Mladena Stojanovica 4, 11000 Belgrade, Yugoslavia.

Democratic Alliance of Croats of the Vojvodina, Trg Lazara, Nesica 1/X, 24000 Subotica, Yugoslavia.

Democratic Community of Hungarians of the Vojvodina, Trg Oslobodenja 11, 21000 Ada, Yugoslavia.

Democratic League of Kosova, Beogradska, 38000 Pristina, Yugoslavia.

Forum for Ethnic Relations, Narodnog Fronta 45, 11000 Belgrade, Yugoslavia; fax 381 11 643 525.

Helsinki Committee for Human Rights in Serbia, Obilicev venac 27/IV, 11000 Belgrade, Yugoslavia; tel. 381 11 624 969, fax 381 11 620 882, e-mail: h.odbor.bg@zamir-bg.ztn.zer.de

Helsinki Committee of Montenegro, Kristofora Ivanovica 3, 86000 Budva, Yugoslavia; tel. 381 86 44 225, fax 381 86 52 852, fax 381 11 645 589

Humanitarian Law Center, Terazije 14, Belgrade, Yugoslavia; fax 381 11 645 589, e-mail: hlc.bg@zamir-bg.ztn.apc.org

Kosova Helsinki Committee, Taslixhe 1 36a, 38000 Prishtina, Kosovo, Yugoslavia; tel. 381 38 34 786, fax 381 38 30 538, e-mail: khc.pr@zana-pr.ztn.apc.org

Romani Union, Romaniska 11/1, 18000 Nis, Yugoslavia.

Notes

Contributions to this regional section are as follows. Martyn Rady: regional introduction and entries on Albania, Bosnia-Herzegovina, Bulgaria, Croatia, Czech Republic, Hungary, Macedonia, Romania, Slovakia, Slovenia and Yugoslavia (Serbia and Montenegro); Bogdan Szajkowski: entries on Estonia, Latvia, Lithuania and Poland.

Introduction

1 Unlike the Roma/Gypsies of Western Europe, the Roma of Central and Eastern Europe reject the name 'Gypsy' because, in their view, it has acquired pejorative associations.

2 On census information more generally, see Liebich, A., 'Minorities in Eastern Europe: obstacles to a reliable count', *Radio Free Europe/Radio Liberty, Research Report*, vol. 1, no. 20, 15 May 1992, pp. 32–9.

3 Cited in Mastny, V., *The Helsinki Process and the Reintegration of Europe 1986–1992*, London, Pinter Publishers, 1992, pp. 238–9.

Albania

1 *Greek Monitor of Human and Minority Rights*, vol. 1, no. 5, September-October 1994, p. 12.

2 Letter of Max van der Stoel, CSCE High Commissioner on National Minorities, to Arian Starova, Acting Minister for Foreign Affairs of the Republic of Albania, 2 November 1994.

3 Robert Austin, 'Albanian–Greek relations: the confrontation continues', *Radio Free Europe/Radio Liberty Research Report*, vol. 2, no. 33, 20 August 1993, pp. 30–5; Fabian Schmidt, 'Albania: between political strife and a developing economy', *Transition*, vol. 1, no. 1, 30 January 1995.

4 MRG Greece, Pettifer, J. and Poulton, H., *The Southern Balkans*, London, MRG report, 1994, p. 34.

5 Karl-Josef Schukalla, 'Nationale Minderheiten in Albanien und Albaner in Ausland', in Grothusen, K-D.(ed.), *Sudosteuropa-Handbuch VII. Albanien*, Gottingen, Vandenhoeck u. Ruprecht, 1993, pp. 509–10.

6 Poulton, H., *Who Are The Macedonians?*, London, Hurst, 1995, pp. 144–5.

7 *Note verbale dated 14 December 1993 from the Permanent Representative of the Federal Republic of Yugoslavia*, UN document E/CN.4/1994/92, 22 December 1993.

8 Ibid. *Note verbale dated 9 June 1995, from the Permanent Mission of the Federal Republic of Yugoslavia*, UN document E/CN.4/Sub.2/1995/40.

9 Max van der Stoel to Arian Starova, loc. cit.

Bosnia-Herzegovina

1 *Situation of Human Rights in the Territory of the Former Yugoslavia*, Fifth Periodic Report, November 1993, UN document E/CN.4/1994/47, p. 4.

2 *Banja Luka and Bijeljina: Ethnic-Cleansing in Serb-held Bosnia*, Spotlight Report no. 14, August 1994, Humanitarian Law Center, Belgrade.

3 *Situation of Human Rights in the Territory of the Former Yugoslavia,* Fifth Periodic Report, op. cit. p. 10; *Situation of Human Rights in the Territory of the Former Yugoslavia,* Second Periodic Report, May 1993, UN document E/CN.4/1994/4, pp. 3–9, *Situation of Human Rights in the Territory of the Former Yugoslavia,* Fourth Periodic Report, September 1993. UN document E/CN.4/1994/8, pp. 2–5.

4 Information supplied by government of 'Serbian Republic'; additional documentation given in *The Case of 158 Serbs Imprisoned in the Muslim-held Silo Camp in Tarcin, Bosnia and Hercegovina 1995*, American Serbian Women's Caucus, 1995.

5 *Situation of Human Rights in the Territory of the Former Yugoslavia,* Fifth Periodic Report, op. cit. pp. 6–8; *Situation of Human Rights in the Territory of the Former Yugoslavia,* Periodic Report (unnumbered), May 1993, UN document E/CN.4/1994/3, pp. 10–12.

6 *Situation of Human Rights in the Territory of the Former Yugoslavia,* Fifth Periodic Report, op. cit. pp. 6–7; *Situation of Human Rights in the Territory of the Former Yugoslavia,* Second Periodic Report, op. cit. p. 8; *Situation of Human Rights in the Territory of the Former Yugoslavia,* Fourth Periodic Report, op. cit. p. 4.

Bulgaria

1 Aukerman, M. (Stiftung Wissenschaft und Politik, *Minderheiten im ostlichen Mitteleuropa: Deutsche und Europaische Optionen*, Bonn/ Ebenhausen, May 1994, p. 134) gives a figure of 20–25 per cent.

2 Hopken, W., 'Turken und Pomaken in Bulgarien', in G. Brunner and H. Lemberg (eds), *Volksgruppen in Ostmittel-und Sudosteuropa*, (Sudosteuropa Studien no. 52) Baden Baden and Munich, Nomos Verlagsgesellschaft, 1994, pp. 223–34.

3 Poulton, H., *The Balkans: Minorities and States in Conflict*, 2nd edn, London, Minority Rights Publications, 1993, p. 119.

4 *Minority Groups in Bulgaria in a Human Rights Context*, Sofia, Committee for the Defence of Minority Rights, 1994, p. 15.

5 Poulton, op. cit., 1993, p. 121; full details of the assimilation campaign are given in Poulton, op. cit., 1993, pp. 129–63, and in H. Poulton and Minnesota Lawyers International Human Rights Committee, *Minorities in the Balkans*, London, MRG report, 1989, pp. 8–22.

6 Nedeva, I., 'Democracy-building in ethnically diverse societies: the cases of Bulgaria and Romania', in I.M. Cuthbertson and J. Leibowitz (eds), *Minorities: The New Europe's Old Issue*, Prague, Budapest, Warsaw, New York, Institute for East-West Studies, distributed by Westview Press, Boulder, CO, 1993, p. 125.

7 Ibid., p. 139.

8 Committee for the Defence of Minority Rights, op. cit., p. 30.

9 Ibid.

10 Bugajski, J., *Ethnic Politics in Eastern Europe: A Guide to Nationality Policies, Organizations, and Parties*, Armonk, NY, and London, M.E. Sharpe, 1994, pp. 243, 252–4; Committee for the Defence of Minority Rights, op. cit., p. 43.

11 Committee for the Defence of Minority Rights, op. cit., p. 20.

12 Ibid., p. 23; Poulton, op. cit., 1993, p. 116.

13 Poulton (op. cit., 1993, p. 117) identifies the Karakachans as Romance-speaking.

Croatia

1 *Situation of Human Rights in the Territory of Former Yugoslavia*, Fifth Periodic Report, submitted by Mr Tadeusz Mazowiecki, UN document E/CN.4/1994/47, pp. 16–8.

2 Bugajski, J., *Ethnic Politics in Eastern Europe: A Guide to Nationality Policies, Organizations, and Parties*, Armonk, NY, and London, M.E. Sharpe, 1994, p. 41.

3 Letters dated 27 August 1992 and 7 November 1992, published by UN Commission on Human Rights, UN document E/CN.4/1994/113.

4 A summary of autopsy reports relating to some of these murders is published by Zoran Stankovic, 'Forensic-medical expertise of twenty four murdered citizens from Gospic and its surroundings', *Vojnosanitetski pregled*, vol. 49, no 2, 1992, pp. 143–70.

5 *Situation of Human Rights in the Territory of Former Yugoslavia*, op. cit., pp. 14–5, 18–9.

6 *Balkan War Report*, March 1995, p. 35.

7 Ibid., May 1995, p. 5.

8 *Guardian*, 9 September 1995.

9 *Situation of Human Rights in the Territory of Former Yugoslavia*, op. cit., pp. 19–20.

10 Ibid., p. 22.

11 Szajkowski, B., *Encyclopaedia of Conflicts, Disputes and Flashpoints in Eastern Europe, Russia and the Successor States*, London, Longman, 1993, p.159.

12 Markotich, S., 'Istrians seeking autonomy', *Radio Free Europe/Radio Liberty Research Report*, 10 September, 1993, pp. 22–6.

Czech Republic

1 Stiftung Wissenschaft und Politik, *Minderheiten im ostlichen Mitteleuropa: Deutsche und Europaische Optionen*, Bonn/Ebenhausen, May 1994, p. 88.

2 *Prognosis*, 29 September-5 October 1994.

3 Beck, J., *Citizens and Criminals: Notions of Citizenship in the Czech State in Transition*, unpublished MA dissertation, Dept of Sociology, Central European University Prague College, October 1994.

4 International Organization for Migration, *Transit Migration in the Czech Republic*, May 1994.

Estonia

1 Minority populations and percentages are taken from the 1989 USSR census.

Hungary

1 Puxon, G., *Roma: Europe's Gypsies*, London, MRG report, 1987, p. 10.

2 Geza Hambuch, of the Association of Germans in Hungary, quoted in J. Bugajski, *Ethnic Politics in Eastern Europe: A Guide to Nationality Policies, Organizations, and Parties*, Armonk, NY, and London, M.E. Sharpe, 1994, p. 420. Population figures published by Bugajski for Hungary are unofficial and disputed.

Macedonia

1 Poulton, H., *Who Are the Macedonians?*, London, Hurst, 1995, pp. 116–7.

2 Poulton, H., *The Balkans: Minorities and States in Conflict*, 2nd edn, London, Minority Rights Publications, 1993, pp. 76–84.

3 Bugajski, J., *Ethnic Politics in Eastern Europe: A Guide to Nationality Policies, Organizations, and Parties*, Armonk, NY, and London, M.E. Sharpe, 1994, pp. 107–08.

4 *Balkan War Report*, October-November 1994, p. 8.

5 Poulton, *The Balkans*, op. cit., pp. 79–80.

6 Duijzings, G., 'The making of Egyptians in Kosovo and Macedonia', unpublished conference paper.

7 Poulton, *Who Are the Macedonians?*, op. cit., pp. 139–42, 191–5.

8 Mickey, R.W. and Albion, A.S. 'Success in the Balkans? A case study of ethnic relations in the Republic of Macedonia', in I.M. Cuthbertson and J. Leibowitz (eds), *Minorities: The New Europe's*

Old Issue, Prague, Budapest, Warsaw, New York, Institute for EastWest Studies, distributed by Westview Press, Boulder, CO, 1993, p. 86.

Poland

1 MRG (ed.), *Minorities in Central and Eastern Europe,* London, MRG report, 1993, p. 37.

2 Liégeois, J-P. and Gheorghe N., *Roma/Gypsies: A European Minority,* London, MRG report, 1995, p. 7.

Romania

1 Committee on Foreign Relations, *US Senate, Country Reports on Human Rights Practices for 1994*, Washington, DC, 1995, pp. 929, 932; Amnesty International, *Romania: Broken Commitments to Human Rights*, London, AI, May 1995; additional documentation provided by Hungarian Democratic Union of Romania, Bucharest, and Hungarian Human Rights Foundation, New York.

2 Biro, A-M., 'What others can do', *World Policy Journal*, vol. 12, no. 1, 1995, p. 98.

3 Calculation based on statistics given in *The Legislative and Institutional Framework for the National Minorities of Romania*, Bucharest, Government of Romania, Council for National Minorities, 1994; other official sources give a figure of 75 per cent.

4 Szabo, Z.T., 'Romania: Hungarian media struggles', *Balkan War Report*, October/November 1994, p. 32; G. Kolumban, 'Romania: the Hungaromanian paradox', ibid, pp 26–7.

5 Noszkai, G., 'Romak delkelet-Europaban: Romania', *Amaro Drom*, March 1995, p. 12; Romanian official sources deny the existence of any such documentation.

6 Ibid; thus also, Amnesty International, op. cit., pp. 25–39.

7 Institute of Jewish Affairs, *Anti-Semitism World Report 1994*, London, 1994, pp. 114–32; S.J. Roth, *The Legal Fight Against Anti-Semitism: Survey of Developments in 1993*, Supplement to *Israel Yearbook on Human Rights*, vol. 25 (1995), pp. 95–6.

Slovakia

1 *An analysis of the allocation and disbursement of state budget funds to cater for the needs of national minorities and ethnic groups 1991–3*, Press and Information Department, Bratislava (undated).

2 Ocovsky, S., 'Interpretation of statistical data on nationalities', in J. Plichtova (ed.), *Minorities in Politics: Cultural and Languages Rights*, Bratislava, 1992, pp. 94–100.

3 Information supplied by Ministry of Foreign Affairs of the Slovak Republic, 6 January 1994.

4 Barany, S., 'Roma: grim realities in Eastern Europe', *Transition*, vol. 1, 29 March 1995, p. 8.

Slovenia

1 Szabo, I., 'Ketnyelvuseg es nyelvhasznalat a Muravideki magyarok koreben', *Regio Kisebbsegi Szemle*, 4, 1993, p. 56.

2 *Ethnic Minorities in Slovenia*, Ljubljana, Institute for Ethnic Studies and Information Bureau, Government of Slovenia, 1994, p. 22.

3 Ibid.

4 Eory, S., 'Slovenia: towards tolerance', *Balkan War Report*, October–November 1994, p. 38.

5 Pucer, E., 'Hardly a few houses', ibid., December 1994–January 1995, pp. 27–8.

Yugoslavia (Serbia and Montenegro)

1 The name 'Federal Republic of Yugoslavia' was used in reference to 'Serbia and Montenegro', in the wording of the General Framework Agreement for Peace in Bosnia and Herzegovina, signed in Dayton, Ohio, on 14 December 1995.

2 Islami, H., 'Kosova's demographic ethnic reality and the targets of Serbian hegemony', *Kosova Historical/Political Review*, no. 1, 1993, pp. 29–32.

3 *Kosovo: Oppression of Ethnic Albanians*, London, MRG Urgent Issues Paper, November 1992, p. 2.

4 *Note verbale dated 10 February 1994, from Permanent Mission of the Federal Republic of Yugoslavia to the Chairman of the Commission on Human Rights,* UN document E/CN.4/ 1994/ 119, February 1994.

5 *Kosovo Albanians I: Repression and Discrimination*, Belgrade, Humanitarian Law Center, Spotlight Report, no. 6, August 1993.

6 *Situation of Human Rights in the Territory of the Former Yugoslavia*, Fifth Periodic Report, November 1993, UN document E/CN.4/1994/47, p. 31.

7 Federal Minister for Minorities, Margit Savovic, to Martyn Rady, January 1995.

THE COMMONWEALTH OF INDEPENDENT STATES

Anna Matveeva, Neil Melvin and Suzanne Pattle

The demise of the Soviet Union at the end of 1991 and the creation of sovereign states in place of the Soviet Socialist Republics involved more than simply the end of the communist order. Independence marked the reversal of several hundred years of Russian imperial expansion and its accompanying trends of Russification. Such basic change has evoked considerable tension and has involved important shifts in the position of minority communities; indeed, changes in definitions of who constitutes a minority.

From Russian Empire to Soviet collapse

From the sixteenth century, imperial expansion brought a steady succession of non-Russian communities scattered across a vast geographical territory under Russian control. By the end of the nineteenth century, the Russian Empire consisted of a diversity of religious, cultural and ethnic communities variously arranged around the Russian core. Sizeable populations of Slavs, Muslims and Shamanists, as well as non-Slavic Christians, had been subordinated to Russian control.

Following Russian conquest, Russian settlers, language, culture and institutions were extended steadily into the non-Russian communities, inducing Russification and, on occasion, bloody resistance. The pattern of colonial domination was, however, far from homogeneous and, at one time or another, most groups experienced repression, tolerance and even coexistence. In the latter years of the Russian Empire many minority groups, including Muslim ones, came to enjoy full legal rights. As well as subordination to the tsarist order, the experience of imperial incorporation also exposed minority communities to the processes of modernization (industrial development, urbanization and rising levels of education) and to ideas of nationalism and national liberation. It was colonial rule that prepared the way for the range of nationalist movements that appeared amongst the minority populations in the late nineteenth century.

Following the Russian Revolution of 1917, the Soviet authorities drew upon elements of the Russian imperial order to help control minority communities (the use of Russian and Russified communities within non-Russian territories to ensure loyalty to Moscow was continued), but former policies were also supplemented with innovation. In the tsarist regime, ethnic identity had only been of second order significance; the Soviets placed the ethnic principle at the heart of the new administrative order. The disintegration of the Russian Empire provided a catalyst for the rapid development of nationalist movements within many minority populations. In the civil war that followed the Russian Revolution, the Bolsheviks were able to construct a powerful political and military coalition by virtue of a willingness to recognize the national aspirations of the minority populations in return for their support.

With the establishment of the Soviet Union in 1922, the principle of national territorial recognition of 'leading' non-Russian groups became a basic tenet of the Soviet administrative system. A significant number of peoples were granted their own Union republics. Russia itself became a federation with a range of minority groups granted territorial autonomy. The adoption of such an arrangement established a theoretical and practical contradiction at the heart of the Soviet system. A socialist state founded on the primacy of class-based identities over national ones, and which in practice

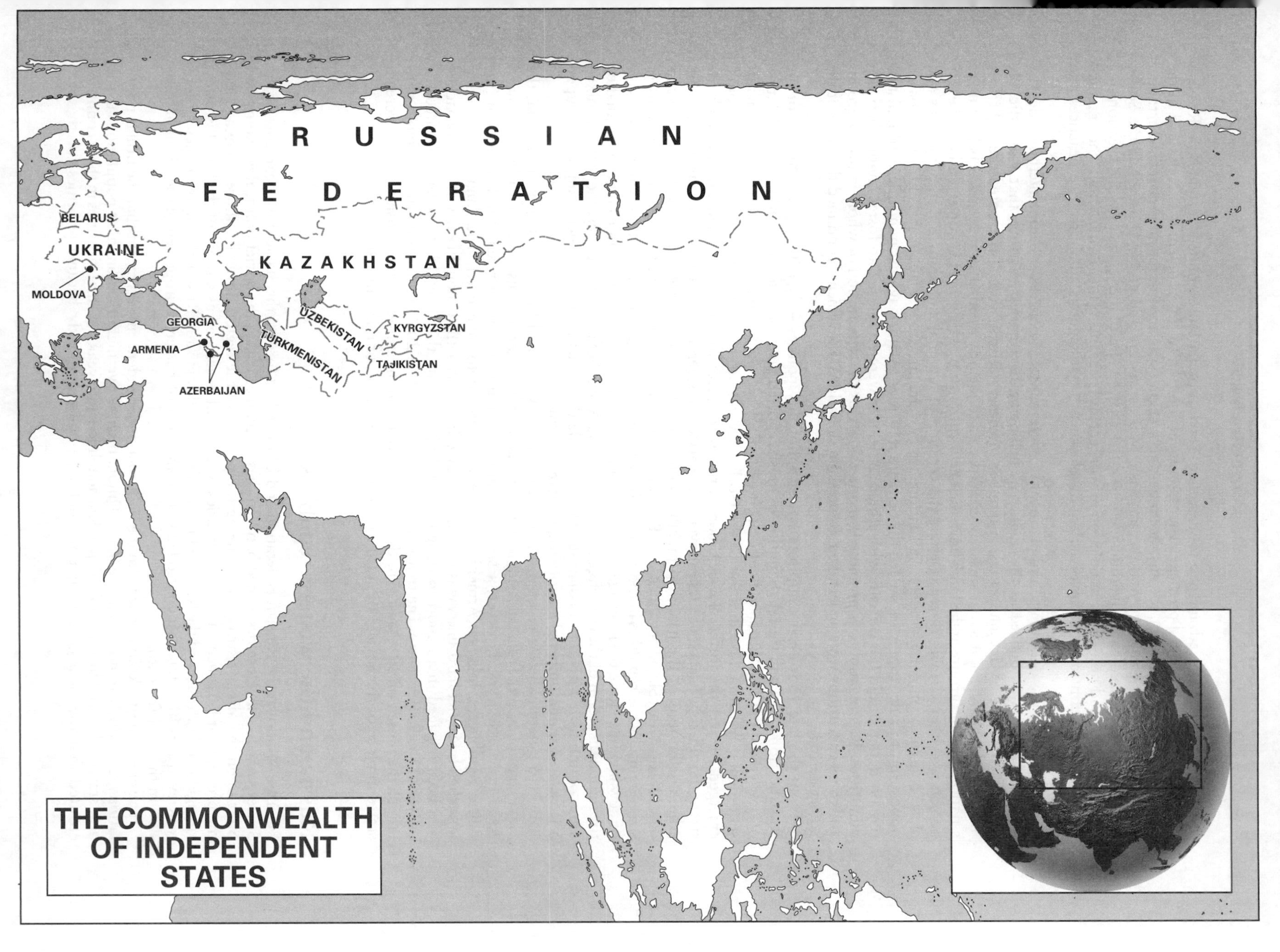
RUSSIAN FEDERATION
BELARUS
UKRAINE
MOLDOVA
KAZAKHSTAN
GEORGIA
ARMENIA
AZERBAIJAN
UZBEKISTAN
TURKMENISTAN
KYRGYZSTAN
TAJIKISTAN
THE COMMONWEALTH OF INDEPENDENT STATES

awarded considerable advantages to Russified Slavic populations, granted certain non-Russian minorities institutionalized privilege. The theoretical solution to this problem was contained in the formula 'nationalist in form, socialist in content'. Namely, it was argued, the administrative arrangement of the Soviet Union did not alter its basic Marxist nature and goals. Thus, while the Soviet authorities recognized national/ethnic identities, the avowed aim of the regime was the creation of a denationalized and non-ethnic population of workers and peasants (*Homo sovieticus*). The practical solution to the contradiction involved the development of ambiguous administrative practices and coercion.

In Soviet terms, citizenship and nationality were separate concepts. National/ethnic identity (*nasional'nost'*) was defined as the quality of belonging to a nation (*natsiya*) that was officially recognized by the Soviet authorities. A number of these 'nations' were also granted the right to a 'homeland'. Members of Soviet society were expected to identify themselves in terms of belonging to a national/ethnic group; at the same time, they held citizenship of their host Union republic and every person was also a Soviet citizen. Despite the creation of nominal autonomy for ethnic groups and close control of minority leaders and nationalist movements, anxiety about possible ethnic-based opposition to rule from Moscow led the Soviet authorities to move against minorities. Administrative borders that did not coincide with ethnic settlement were established to foster conflict between minorities, Russification was promoted, and in the 1930s the deportation of whole minority groups and mass executions were undertaken. Repression of national movements continued throughout the Soviet period.

From the late 1950s a relaxation in Soviet nationality policies – signalled by a softening of the Russification drive and the rehabilitation of most deported peoples – and the gradual consolidation of new ethnic-based political and cultural elites in many regions led to a steady growth of nationalist sentiments. With the liberalization of the Gorbachev period, national movements (popular fronts) emerged all over the former Soviet Union as the main forces to challenge Soviet rule, although the strength and significance of these movements varied considerably. Often the movements drew on ethnic definitions of the nation to mobilize political opposition to Moscow. Powerful movements developed in the Slavic republics, the Russian Federation, Armenia and Georgia. Declarations of sovereignty by the republics in the early 1990s (later in Central Asia than elsewhere) and the passage of new laws elevating the languages of the titular populations to the status of state languages signalled the nationalist form of the challenge to Soviet control. A number of the nationalist movements mixed anti-communism with anti-Russian sentiments, while the Soviet authorities increasingly drew upon a Russian national/imperial identity to preserve the Union.

By 1991 nationalist-based opposition to the Soviet system had become extensive in Russia, the Slavic republics and Transcaucasia, and weaker nationalist organizations were appearing in Central Asia. In March 1991, however, a sizeable majority voted in favour of retention of the Union (the Baltic republics, Moldova, Armenia and Georgia refused to take part). The August 1991 coup launched by Soviet hard-liners was in large part an effort to save the Union. In early 1991, Gorbachev had been engaged in an effort to design a new Union Treaty that would have severely limited the power of the Soviet centre. The treaty was due to be signed on 20 August, prompting the plotters to launch the putsch on 19 August. The defeat of the coup and the subsequent establishment of sovereign states in place of the Soviet Union led to a new configuration of minority issues.

Russia and the western republics

Belarus, Moldova, the Russian Federation and Ukraine had formed the Slavic–European core of the Soviet system. The close ties forged between these republics within the Soviet political economy had built upon the already strong links among the peoples of the region through culture, language and the presence of Russified settler communities, which had developed as a result of the long historical engagement in the area of the Russian Empire. Belarus, Ukraine and Russia also all trace their origins to Kievan Rus, the state that controlled significant parts of Eastern Europe before the Mongol invasion in the twelfth century.

The creation of Ukraine, Belarus and Moldova as independent entities meant that the titular populations, previously minorities in the Soviet Union, became overnight the dominant populations in the new states. The brief histories of independent statehood and weak national identities in these countries ensured that the twin goals of nation- and state-building quickly became priorities for the new governments. These goals were frequently pursued through policies of nativization (*korenizatsiya*) which aimed to sweep aside previous, often ethnically constituted, networks of power. The forces of ethno-nationalism that had helped drive the independence movements in Moldova and Ukraine appeared to threaten many of the minorities. This was especially the case for Russians and members of the heavily Russified communities, who had occupied leading positions in the Soviet order and suddenly found themselves to be ethnic and linguistic minorities.

Within Russia the issues of nation- and state-building have been complicated by the long history of Russian colonial settlement across the Eurasian continent. The civic notion of nationhood that had dominated the anti-Soviet movement has been challenged by ethnic nationalism from Russians, while rising national consciousness among some minority groups, notably Tatars and Chechens, has led to calls for autonomy and even independence from Moscow. As a result, in contrast to the other republics, notions of nation and state have been closely tied to a debate about the federal structure of Russia.

The new correlation of ethnic and political forces that came into existence following the collapse of the Soviet Union presented the new states with a set of similar minority problems. At the heart of these are two interrelated issues: first, what place should ethnicity occupy in the national identities of these new countries; and, second, how should each country confront the Russian/Soviet colonial past, especially the legacy of Russification (prominence of Russian language, culture and presence of Russian settlers)? These issues have been as pertinent in Russia, with its large numbers of minorities, its history of domestic colonial conquest and ethno-territorial administrative structure, as in the three non-Russian western republics.

Although subject to similar challenges, minorities in the states of the region have faced very different experiences since independence. In Moldova, for example, the drive to break free from Moscow produced fighting in 1992, which divided the country and left a legacy of separatism based upon ethno-regionalism. By contrast, in Belarus strong support for closer links to Russia has contributed to inter-ethnic harmony.

The various approaches adopted to the challenge of independence in the region have been codified in a variety of basic legislative acts: declarations of sovereignty and new constitutions have identified the source of state power (the right of an ethnic or civic nation to self-determination); legislation on citizenship has laid down the criteria for membership of each national political community; and language laws have established the central cultural identity of each country. Minority rights legislation has subsequently been developed to conform to these basic documents.

The question of the rights and obligations of states in respect to diaspora communities situated in neighbouring states has also been a subject of contention. Very large numbers of Russians (25 million), Ukrainians (12 million) and Belarusians (1.4 million) are currently resident outside their 'homelands'. The problems associated with diasporas, especially Russians, have promoted proposals to enhance the minority rights regime of the Commonwealth of Independent States (CIS) and led the Russian Federation to promote the idea of establishing legislation on dual citizenship, a move strongly opposed by Moldova and Ukraine. While Belarus, Moldova, the Russian Federation and Ukraine have sought to structure relations with and between minority communities through legislation and negotiation, migration and conflict have also played a leading role in shaping the post-Soviet minority situation in the region. Since 1990, tens of thousands of people have migrated in response to real or perceived discrimination, war or a deteriorating socioeconomic situation.

The Transcaucasus

The Transcaucasus, comprising the countries of Armenia, Azerbaijan and Georgia, has always been seen as the literal and symbolic border of Europe and Asia, Christianity and Islam. It is an area of great ethnic, cultural and religious diversity.

Following the collapse of the Soviet Union in 1991, these countries have had the difficult task of re-establishing their independence and coming to terms with their new identities, identities which had been undermined for years not only by Soviet dominance but also by competing imperial Russian, Persian and Ottoman influences. The new leaderships of these countries, struggling with the Soviet legacy of political and economic turmoil in the aftermath of independence, have in some cases used the rallying point of nationalism in an effort to build up a fragile national unity. This has had serious consequences, notably in Georgia and Azerbaijan, while in Armenia there has been growing intolerance towards religious minorities in particular. The emergence of nationalism has meant that in many cases what were predominantly political conflicts, about future constitutional and autonomous arrangements surrounding the status of particular regions with significant minority populations, rapidly degenerated into open warfare with an ethnic dimension. This has been particularly true in the cases of South Ossetia and Abkhazia (see **Georgia**). In other areas, the legacy of the Soviet period and the inability of the Soviet leadership in its final years to come to grips with problems associated with the defence and guarantee of minority rights, particularly in the case of the disputed enclave of Nagorno-Karabagh (see **Azerbaijan**), have left these countries with deeply entrenched problems.

Minority groups in areas other than the more obvious flashpoints have also experienced problems. In Georgia, all groups suffered as a result of President Gamsakhurdia's nationalist policies in 1990–1, where the declared policy of 'Georgia for the Georgians' implied that the loyalty of minority groups was questionable, even if they had been resident in Georgia for centuries. Each of the majority groups in the newly independent republics, paradoxically, has found that their position has changed, as a result of independence, from a minority status to that of a majority. For decades of Soviet rule they had been seeking to defend their culture, language and traditions, while at the same time the structures put in place by that very same Soviet system also played their part in 'nation-building'. As a result the dominant nationalities were left with a legacy of insecurity and of the means to assert their nationhood.

The Transcaucasus continues to be an area of competing influences, with each country suspicious of the Russian role in the region. Russia retains its strategic interests and has sought to maintain its influence through a variety of means, from playing an active 'peacekeeping' role in the areas of conflict, to exerting political and economic pressure with regard to the stationing of Russian troops and maintaining military bases. Although there is much economic potential in the region, such as oil resources in the Caspian Sea, which may play a part in the process of political stabilization, the potential for struggle between competing influences remains.

In some cases, the linkage between minority rights and the 'Russian factor' has been strong, obscuring legitimate grievances. This is perhaps most true in the case of Georgia. There is evidence that while ostensibly playing the role of honest broker in attempts at mediating in Georgia's internal conflicts, Russia was conducting a multiple track approach, aimed above all at securing its foreign policy interests in the 'near abroad'. To many Georgians, fears about their territorial integrity being undermined by separatist movements allegedly receiving covert support from Russian forces had the desired result: thus the sudden change in the fortunes of Georgian government forces in crushing the Zviadist rebellion in October 1993, following Eduard Shevardnadze's decision to join the Commonwealth of Independent States.

While the immediate crisis of the post-independence years may have eased in relation to the situation of minority groups, there are still outstanding issues of concern. Firm political agreements have yet to be reached over the status of Abkhazia, South Ossetia and Nagorno-Karabagh, while the human rights consequences in terms of loss of life and property, displacement of people and the general trauma of conflict remain. Azerbaijan and Georgia are in the process of formulating new constitutions which aim to provide guarantees of human and minority rights in line with international standards. Concern has been expressed that the new Armenian constitution, approved in July 1995, grants too many presidential powers at the expense of the parliament. The political situation in each of these countries remains volatile, which calls into question how much genuine political debate can take place. Concern has been expressed in each of these countries regarding the political representation of minority groups, which is by no means guaranteed. As elsewhere, the question is not only of the establishment of international legal norms regarding human and minority rights, but of the interpretation and implementation of these rights. In countries which have undergone considerable upheaval in political and economic terms, questions remain regarding the provision of adequate resources to safeguard linguistic, cultural and education rights for minorities, as well as education and training in minority issues for society as a whole.

Central Asia

With the break-up of the Soviet Union, independence was forced on the Central Asian states – Kazakhstan, Kyrgyzstan, Tajikistan, Turkmenistan and Uzbekistan – rather than won. Political elites lacked the benefit of political legitimacy that they might have gained from a struggle for independence. Central Asian leaderships were faced with new dilemmas involving fear of exclusion from the Commonwealth of Independent States (originally envisaged as a union of Slavic republics) and challenges of state-building and economic transition. Developments in Tajikistan soon after independence, resulting in a civil war, had a major impact on politicians elsewhere in the region. With the exception of Kyrgyzstan, lessons drawn from the Tajikistan experience were that a degree of authoritarianism would help suppress social divisions and maintain political order. Turkmenistan, Uzbekistan and Kazakhstan extended the offices of their presidents into the twenty-first century by means of referendums. With Tajikistan caught up in the civil strife, only Kyrgyzstan has tended towards a more pluralistic and less authoritarian political regime.

None of the Central Asian states is mono-ethnic, and nowhere does the titular nationality constitute an overwhelming majority. Each state incorporates distinct minority groups: European (predominantly Slavic) settlers, diaspora minorities indigenous to the region (other Central Asians) and peoples forcibly deported to the area. These groups are confronted with a choice between accommodation to the host society, assimilation or emigration. Emigration is a viable option only for minorities with relatively prosperous kin states outside the CIS, and emigration of Germans, Jews, Greeks and Turks looks likely to result in the disappearance of such Central Asian communities within a decade. Assimilation would be difficult because of the large numbers involved, their geographic concentration and most such minorities' sense of cultural superiority. Accommodation does not appear to be a credible solution because, in an era of nation-building, titular nationalities frequently regard minorities with suspicion. Minority loyalty to the newly established state might be doubted, and attempts have been made to deprive members of minority groups of positions of power.

Major divisions persist within the titular nationalities themselves, and regional and clan identities remain strong. Sometimes regionalism crosses ethnic lines. In many instances, the removal of the Soviet state's protective role created a vacuum into which these affiliations moved. Although such networks were in evidence during the Soviet period, now they frequently serve as the main social support system and as the basis for political mobilization.

The social and cultural environment of the Central Asian states appears increasingly Asian rather than European. Islam, suppressed during the Soviet era, is undergoing a revival. Such developments intensify the European consciousness among the non-indigenous population and create a wide grouping of 'Russian-speakers', including Russians, Ukrainians, Belarusians, Germans, Poles, Jews, Greeks and Koreans, who feel alienated in the growing Muslim, predominantly Turkic, surroundings. Russian-speakers tend to support conservative leaders in Central Asia, who, in their opinion, are more capable of maintaining inter-ethnic peace.

More than 10 million ethnic Russians live in the five Central Asian republics, with more than 6 million in Kazakhstan alone. A majority were born in Central Asia. Some Russians who migrated to the Russian Federation soon after independence returned after being disappointed with their reception there. While Russians living in Kazakhstan hold the view that this territory is also their historic homeland, in other Central Asian states they see themselves as immigrants. Since independence, they have had to adjust to the new official status of the languages of the titular nationalities, marking the end of the former dominance of Russian language and culture.

Russian-speakers' access to education is being reduced, as are their chances for promotion to senior posts. While they still hold strong positions in their traditional skilled and professional areas of employment, opportunities outside these sectors are increasingly problematic. Recognizing the skills of Russian-speakers, local leaderships implement policies aimed at inducing them to stay. However, in the long run the republics seek to replace Russian-speakers with local personnel. These factors, coupled with popular expressions of nationalism, make Russian-speakers feel increasingly insecure, and their emigration from Central Asia is gaining momentum.

Relations with the Russian Federation are of crucial importance for the Central Asian states. Cooperation with Russia is required by security and economic considerations and by the presence of the large Russian diaspora. Yet Moscow's 'stick-and-carrot' policy often produces an alienating effect. Russia's concern over the fate of ethnic Russians is expressed more through rhetoric than through practical policy. Moscow has pressed Central Asian leaders hard to allow dual citizenship for ethnic Russians in their republics but has achieved success only in the cases of Turkmenistan and Tajikistan.

Indigenous Central Asian peoples are majorities in their own republics, with the exception of Kazakhstan, but also constitute minorities in other Central Asian states. In the era of independence and growing national assertiveness indigenous minorities feel their position threatened. The presence of indigenous minorities across the border gives opportunities for kin states to interfere in the affairs of their neighbours. Because most of the border areas are populated by minorities, the possibility of border changes or disputes stemming from minorities' treatment is likely. Attention paid to Central Asian minorities living outside the CIS has also increased, leading to contacts over minority issues with China, Afghanistan and Iran.

Major changes have affected the position of the deported peoples. Formal rehabilitation has been gained, and legal restrictions on resettlement in their homelands have been abolished. However, with the disappearance of the central authority in Moscow, there is no authority to which such peoples can appeal in seeking to exercise their right to return. These small communities have resorted to struggling on their own against the bureaucracies in the newly independent states for their political and economic freedoms. Prospects for their successful reintegration into the states which have emerged in their historic homelands are often limited.

Among other issues affecting the position of minorities in the region, popular attitudes in the Central Asian republics follow the broader pattern of hostility towards Caucasian nationalities widespread in post-Soviet territories. Starting with anti-Armenian and anti-Azer sentiments, these attitudes now apply to people of Caucasian origin in general. Central Asia also suffers from severe environmental problems inherited from the Soviet past. A number of areas, notably the Aral Sea and Semipalatinsk, may be identified as ecological disaster zones. This situation affects mainly minorities indigenous to the region, as well as members of titular nationalities residing there. With the resurrection of Islam, women from European minorities are experiencing pressure on their lifestyle and job opportunities.

Further reading

Akiner, S., *Central Asia*, London, MRG report, 1996.

Azrael, J., *Soviet Nationality Policies and Practices*, New York, 1978.

Connor, W., *The National Question in Marxist-Leninist Theory and Strategy*, Princeton, NJ, Princeton University Press, 1984.

Hyman, A., *Political Change in Post-Soviet Central Asia*, London, Royal Institute of International Affairs, 1994.

Kolstoe, P., *Russians in the Former Soviet Republics*, London, Hurst, 1995.

Krag, H. and Funch, L., *The North Caucasus: Minorities at a Crossroads*, London, MRG report, 1994.

Lapidus, G.W., Zaslavsky, V. with Goldman, P. (eds), *From Union to Commonwealth: Nationalism and Separatism in the Soviet Republics*, Cambridge, Cambridge University Press, 1992.

Melvin, N., *Russians beyond Russia*, London, Pinter, 1995.

Naumkin, V. (ed.), *Central Asia and Transcaucasia: Ethnicity and Conflict*, Westport, CT, Greenwood, 1994.

Rashid, A., *The Resurgence of Central Asia*, London, Zed, 1994.

Russell, J., *Soviet Minorities*, London, MRG update pack, 1991.

Szajkowski, B., *Encyclopaedia of Conflicts, Disputes and Flashpoints in Eastern Europe, Russia and the Successor States*, London, Longman, 1993.

Armenia

Land area:	29,800 sq. km
Population:	3.4 million (1992)
Main languages:	Armenian
Main religions:	Armenian Apostolic Christianity
Main minority groups:	Kurds 60,000 (1.7%), Russians 15,000–20,000 (0.4–0.6%)
Real per capita GDP:	$2,040
UNDP HDI/rank:	0.680 (93)

The Republic of Armenia, formerly the Soviet Socialist Republic of Armenia, is situated in south-west Transcaucasia on the north-eastern border of Turkey. It borders Iran to the south, Azerbaijan to the east and Georgia to the north. Nakhichevan, situated between Armenia and Turkey, is an Autonomous Republic under the jurisdiction of Azerbaijan.

More than 95 per cent of the 3.4 million population are Armenian. Minority groups in the republic include Kurds (mainly Yezidis), Russians and small numbers of Assyrians, Greeks and other nationalities.[1] There is a large Armenian diaspora in the USA, and there are also significant communities in Canada, France, the Middle East, Russia, Georgia and Azerbaijan (in Nagorno-Karabagh).

Until 1994, the political situation in Armenia was relatively stable under the moderate leadership of President Ter-Petrossian, elected on 17 October 1991 following Armenia's declaration of independence. However, the country has experienced upheavals as a result of the Nagorno-Karabagh conflict and the aftermath of a devastating earthquake which destroyed Leninakan and Spitak on 7 December 1988. This left an estimated 25,000 dead and 500,000 homeless, sparking off a worldwide relief effort coordinated by diaspora Armenians.

The situation in Armenia was further complicated by the effects of the war over Nagorno-Karabagh, due to the imposition of an Azeri and Turkish economic blockade. Since Armenia was largely dependent on Azerbaijan for energy supplies this caused severe economic disruption. In addition, the disruption of supply routes through Georgia because of civil unrest led to the declaration of an economic state of emergency in early 1992.

Until 1994, Armenia had a comparatively better human rights record than neighbouring Georgia and Azerbaijan. However, the banning of the main opposition party, the Armenian Revolutionary Federation (Dashnaks), and the shutting down of media outlets with links to this party at the end of 1994, have raised serious questions about the extent of freedom of political association and freedom of expression in Armenia. It was widely believed that the ban, imposed on the pretext that the party was sheltering a terrorist organization which presented a threat to state security, was inspired by the fear that the ruling Armenian National Movement would lose in the July 1995 parlimentary elections. The victory of President Ter-Pretrossian in the September 1996 presidential elections was questioned by the opposition and international observers and was followed by disturbances in Yerevan.

Much political debate during 1995 centred around the promulgation of the new Armenian constitution, which was finally approved in July 1995. Concern has been expressed that it confers too much power to the President at the expense of Parliament and the judiciary. Minority groups have been concerned about the lack of representation afforded them under the new electoral law. There has also been a tangible growth in religious intolerance in a country where at least 80 per cent of the population, nominally at least, adhere to the Armenian Apostolic Church.

Nagorno-Karabagh: conflict with Azerbaijan

The conflict over the mainly Armenian enclave of Nagorno-Karabagh (see **Azerbaijan**) has had a serious effect both on the Armenian economy and on the population as a whole. Since 1989, Armenia has been subjected to an economic blockade imposed first by Azerbaijan and then by Turkey at the end of 1992, further exacerbating the economic situation in Armenia. Following pogroms against Armenians in Sumgait and other Azeri cities in 1988, some 167,000 Azeris were expelled from Armenia.[2] By the end of 1990, virtually all of the Azeri community in Armenia had left for Azerbaijan. There has been a corresponding inflow of Armenian refugees from Azerbaijan proper as well as the enclave of Nagorno-Karabagh, totalling some 400,000. There have been periodic allegations that ethnic Azeri hostages from the war in Nagorno-Karabagh are being held in Armenia. Similarly, Armenia has come under international criticism for the suspicious circumstances surrounding the deaths of nine Azeri prisoners of war while in custody in Yerevan.

Kurds (Kurdmanzh)

There are an estimated 60,000 Kurds in Armenia, almost all of them Yezidis, a culturally distinct group who practise their own religion. Many Sunni Muslim Kurds fell victim to mass expulsions along with the Azeris. Around 20,000 Kurds live in Yerevan, with the remainder living in a dozen or so compact settlements in the mountains.

Since 1987, there has been some recognition of Kurdish cultural needs, with the establishment of Kurdish language broadcasting and a twice-weekly Kurdish language newspaper. The Institute of Oriental Studies has a Department of Kurdish Studies. However, Kurdish representatives have expressed concern about the preservation of their language and culture. Most Kurds study in Armenian and are taught Kurdish language and literature in supplementary classes.

The Kurdish community has found itself to be an unwilling participant in the Nagorno-Karabagh conflict, since both Azeris and Armenians have sought to strike political bargains which might have some impact over control of territory, in particular the land corridor linking Nagorno-Karabagh with Armenia.

Concern has also been expressed that there is inadequate representation of the Kurdish minority at national and local levels. Even in areas of compact Kurdish settlement, local government representatives tend not to be Kurdish. In 1995, Kurdish representatives protested that the electoral system makes no special provision for minority representation, with seats in parliament being awarded strictly according to the territorial principle.

Russians

There are an estimated 15,000–20,000 Russians in Armenia. Increasing numbers of Russians have migrated from Armenia chiefly for economic reasons. The main concern of this minority centres on the language issue. With the introduction of an Armenian-only system and the closure of Russian schools, Russians and Russian-speakers are concerned that they will become disadvantaged in terms of education and employment.

Religious minorities

There has been increasing concern over the treatment of religious minorities in Armenia in the light of the political and religious dominance of the Armenian Apostolic Church and the Law on Religious Freedom and Religious Organizations, which places restrictions on those religions or sects 'whose doctrine is not based on Holy Scripture'. Concern has also been expressed about the role of the Armenian church in political life in the light of President Ter-Petrossian's expression of preference for one candidate over another in the recent election of a new Catholicos.

There are a number of religious minority groups in Armenia, including evangelical churches, Seventh Day Adventists, Hare Krishna sects, the Baha'i faith, Mormons and Jews. Many of these have been banned from proselytizing and in the worst instances have been subjected to violent attacks and disruption of religious rites and ceremonies. There have been cases of arrests of Hare Krishna devotees as well as of evangelical ministers. Concern has been expressed by religious and human rights groups over the increasing instances of harassment and attacks on minority religious groups in 1995.

The small Jewish community in Armenia has not suffered similar harassment and is able freely to practise its faith and pursue its culture. Many Jews emigrated to Israel during the Soviet era; those who remain tend to feel a strong attachment to Armenia.

Conclusions and future prospects

The July 1995 elections resulted in a victory by the ruling Armenian National Movement, although a number of groups expressed concern regarding the fairness of the elections in the light of the continuing ban on the Dashnak party. The disputed presidential election in September 1996 underlined these feelings. The new constitution has been vehemently criticized by opposition groups who fear that it grants too much power to the President. Minority groups continue to be marginalized from the political process, partly because of special measures to ensure minority representation in Parliament. While it is unlikely that serious unrest on the grounds of minority rights issues will occur, the political situation in Armenia will remain volatile.

Further reading

Bremmer, I. and Taras, R. (eds), *Nations and Politics in the Soviet Successor States*, Cambridge, Cambridge University Press, 1993.

Lang, D.M. and Walker, C.J., *The Armenians*, London, MRG report, 1987.

Walker, C.J. (ed.). *Armenia and Karabagh: The Struggle for Unity*, London, Minority Rights Publications, 1991.

Minority-based and advocacy organizations

Armenian Centre for National and International Studies, 5th Floor, 4 Khorhrdarani Street, 375001 Yerevan, Armenia; tel. 7 8852 528780, fax 7 8852 534846.

Centre for Democracy and Human Rights, 14 Karl Libnekht Street, Yerevan, Armenia; tel. 7 8852 537643, fax 7 8852 151450, e-mail: unhcr@arminco.com

Human Rights Centre, NGO Consortium, Yerevan, Armenia; e-mail: lucig@arminco.com

Azerbaijan

Land area:	86,600 sq km
Population:	7.3 million (1994)
Main languages:	Azeri, Russian
Main religions:	Islam (majority Shi'ite, minority Sunni)
Main minority groups:	Russians 440,000 (est. 1989, 6%), 300,000 Talysh (est. 4.2%), Lezgins 290,000 (est., 4%), Kurds 200,000 (est., 2.8%), Armenians 100,000 (est., 1.4%)[1]
Real per capita GDP:	$2,190
UNDP HDI/rank:	0.665 (96)

The Republic of Azerbaijan, formerly the Soviet Socialist Republic of Azerbaijan, is situated in eastern Transcaucasia on the western coast of the Caspian Sea. It borders Iran[2] to the south, Armenia to the west, Georgia to the north-west and the Republic of Dagestan in the Russian Federation to the north across the Caucasus mountain range. The Nakhichevan Autonomous Republic, bordering Armenia, Iran and Turkey, is also part of Azerbaijan. Nagorno-Karabagh, an autonomous region, lies in south-west Azerbaijan; populated largely by Armenians, it has been the focus of conflict since 1988.

Since Azerbaijan's declaration of independence on 30 August 1991 the country has suffered much political and economic instability, largely influenced by the shifting fortunes of Azeri forces in the conflict over Nagorno-Karabagh, the effects of the war in both human and economic terms, the collapse of the Soviet system, and the absence of strong democratic institutions. *Perestroika* and *glasnost* burst onto the Azerbaijani scene at the end of 1988 when the Nagorno-Karabagh issue rapidly become a rallying-point for Azeri nationalism: it has since become a barometer of Azeri political life. Military reversals and economic problems have been instrumental in the downfall of four successive presidencies in the last six years.

Continuing political instability and upheavals have had a damaging effect both on the progress of democratic reforms and on the human rights situation in the republic. The imposition of emergency rule from October 1994 to June 1995 led to harassment of opposition parties, and restrictions on freedom of association and freedom of the press. Violations of human rights have occurred on both sides of the Nagorno-Karabagh conflict.

According to figures from 1994, 71 per cent of

the population of Azerbaijan are Azeri. The largest minority groups according to the 1989 census were Armenians and Russians; however almost all Armenians outside Nagorno-Karabagh and many Russians have left Azerbaijan. The largest minority is now probably the Talysh (estimates of their numbers vary), followed by Russians, Lezgins, Kurds, Armenians, Avars and other Dagestani ethnic groups. Minorities in Azerbaijan, in the absence of a specific law guaranteeing their rights, are protected by a Presidential Decree of November 1992.

The foremost human rights problem currently faced by Azerbaijan is the situation of refugees and internally displaced persons, mainly as a result of the Nagorno-Karabagh conflict. Azerbaijan also received over 50,000 Meskhetian Turks fleeing inter-ethnic disturbances in Uzbekistan in 1989. United Nations High Commission for Refugees (UNHCR) figures estimate a total of 238,000 refugees and 668,000 internally displaced persons, mainly from Nagorno-Karabagh and the surrounding districts now occupied by Karabagh Armenian forces, as well as some 185,000 ethnic Azeris who fled Armenia following the eruption of the conflict in 1988–9. This has put a great strain on the infrastructure, particularly on the provision of social security, housing and sanitation, with many of these services disrupted as a result of conflict.

Russians

Russians represented 6 per cent of the population in 1989. However, it is not known how many Russians, particularly from the younger educated strata, have emigrated from Azerbaijan as a result of political instability and economic hardship. Russians are not widely discriminated against in Azerbaijan, although some concern was expressed following the introduction of an Azeri language programme promoting wider use of the Azeri language in 1989–90. Russians and Russian speakers feared that they would become increasingly disadvantaged in terms of education and employment opportunities. The status of Russians and Russian-speakers has been improved since moves to ban the tuition of Russian in schools were overturned. Russian Orthodox believers enjoy freedom of worship in Azerbaijan.

Talysh (Tolish, Talush)

Talysh are a predominantly rural people who speak a north-west Iranian language. They are culturally close to the Azeris. Unofficial estimates put their number at between 200,000 and 300,000, while some researchers in Azerbaijan itself have stated rather surprisingly that they make up 11 per cent of the total population (around 800,000). The Talysh have suffered as a result of the long-term deprivation of cultural and education rights and from the effects of economic neglect of their region, situated in south-east Azerbaijan and bordering Iran and the Caspian Sea. Azeri fears of the emergence of pro-Iranian separatist sentiments led to the formation of the Azerbaijan Talysh National Party in 1992. In June 1993, as part of the general political unrest resulting from the campaign against the then President, Elchibey, Ali Akhram Hummatov declared the formation of the Talysh Mugansk Republic. This was short-lived, however, although it is demonstrative of the potential for the exploitation of legitimate minority grievances in order to destabilize the government in Baku.

Lezgins (Lezgi, Kyurin)

Lezgins are a Caucasian mountain people related to smaller groups including Aguls, Rutuls and Tabasarans. Their language belongs to the north-east Caucasian language group. Current figures state that Lezgins constitute 4 per cent of the population (290,000). However, some estimates claim that their number is approaching 1 million. In general, Lezgins enjoyed better rights in the Autonomous Republic of Dagestan under the jurisdiction of the Russian Federation than in Azerbaijan itself, where they were subjected to assimilation policies. This partly explains the small number who actually declared themselves to be Lezgin in the census.

The area known as 'Lezgistan' was divided between the tsarist districts of Derbent and Baku in 1860, a division which has continued to this day. Lezgin demands were influential in the formation of a Consultative Council of Small Nations which reports directly to the President on the resolution of Lezgin and other issues. In 1992 the organization Sadual was estimated to promote Lezgin rights. Lezgins have traditionally suffered from unemployment and a shortage of land. Resentments were fuelled in 1992 by the resettlement of 105,000 Azeri refugees from the Karabagh conflict on Lezgin lands and by the forced conscription of Lezgins to fight in the conflict. This has contributed to an increase in tensions between the Lezgin community and the Azeri government over issues of land, employment, language and the absence of internal autonomy. A major consequence of the outbreak of the war in Chechnia in 1994 has been the closure of the border between Russia and Azerbaijan: as a result the Lezgins have for the first time in their history been separated by an international border restricting their movement.

Kurds (Kurdmanzh)

Recent estimates suggest that the Kurdish population may be as high as 200,000. The majority of Kurds were situated in the Lachin area of Azerbaijan, where from 1923 until its abolition in 1930 they enjoyed the status of having an autonomous area. The Kurds have been caught up in the Nagorno-Karabagh conflict with some allegations that the Armenians are attempting to exploit any separatist aspirations in order to weaken Azeri influence in the area. A campaign was begun by the Kurdish populations in Lachin, Kubatly and Kelbajar in 1992 for the restoration of the Kurdish Autonomous Area, receiving support from militant activists from Yerevan. In 1993 the Kurdish population of the Kelbajar region were forced to flee as a result of a military offensive by the Karabagh Armenians and it is therefore difficult at this time to establish their exact number in Azerbaijan. Kurdish resentment against Azerbaijan has also been fuelled as a result of forced conscription of Kurds into the Azerbaijani army.

Armenians

In 1989 there were around 400,000 Armenians in Azerbaijan. Around one-third of the Armenian population was resident in the enclave of Nagorno-Karabagh, and there were also significant Armenian communities in industrial centres such as Baku and Sumgait. Following the escalation of tensions over the Nagorno-Karabagh issue and pogroms against Armenians in Baku and Sumgait, an estimated 300,000 Armenians left the country. It is estimated that only around 18,000 Armenians remain in Azerbaijan proper, while there are no accurate figures for the current Armenian population of Nagorno-Karabagh.

The conflict over Nagorno-Karabagh first surfaced in 1988 following a campaign by Nagorno-Karabagh Armenians for reunification with Armenia. The area had originally been designated as Armenian by the Bolsherik Caucasus Bureau in 1921; however, days later this decision was revoked by Stalin in his capacity as Commissar for Nationalities and the area was handed over to Azerbaijan. Both Armenians and Azeris claim a historic right to the territory.

By 1988 the territory, an autonomous oblast under the jurisdiction of the Soviet Socialist Republic of Azerbaijan, was 75 per cent Armenian. The campaign for secession from Azerbaijan and the formation of the Karabagh Committee sparked demonstrations in Yerevan in support of the campaign. Karabagh Armenians had long-held grievances against the Azeri administration over the lack of education and cultural rights, as well as the neglect of ancient Armenian monuments (these grievances were disputed by the Baku authorities). It was also alleged by Armenians that the area had suffered deliberate economic neglect, although Azeris maintain that the general standard of living in Nagorno-Karabagh was better than in Azerbaijan as a whole, albeit lower than in Armenia itself. Tensions escalated. As the violence increased direct rule was imposed by Moscow but attempts to calm the situation failed and the region was returned to Azerbaijani rule in November 1989. Armenia responded with a Supreme Soviet declaration that Nagorno-Karabagh should belong to Armenia, a declaration declared null and void by the Soviet authorities. Following the declaration of a state of emergency in mid-1991, Soviet troops were deployed in the region, with little success other than to fuel the resentments of Karabagh Armenians. Strikes and violent protests continued in the enclave.

With the dissolution of the Soviet Union at the end of 1991, Armenia and Azerbaijan found themselves as independent states facing an increasingly intractable conflict. Nagorno-Karabagh declared its secession from Azerbaijan on 2 September 1991, as a republic, according to the then still valid Soviet Union Law on Secession, although it stopped short of an outright declaration of independence. By December 1991, a referendum on independence was held and confirmed on 6 January 1992 by the newly elected Nagorno-Karabagh legislature; 1992 witnessed a transition from sporadic outbreaks of violence to outright war.

Attempts at mediation were made by a number of parties, including CIS countries, notably Russia and Kazakhstan, the Conference on Security and Co-operation in Europe (CSCE), Turkey and Iran. Since mid-1992 mediation efforts have been undertaken by the CSCE Minsk Group of 11 countries. By the beginning of 1994 Nagorno-Karabagh was in the hands of Karabagh Armenian forces, as was the Lachin corridor linking it to Armenia, and the surrounding territory, representing around 15 per cent of Azerbaijani territory. Human rights violations were committed by both parties, including indiscriminate shelling, the taking of hostages, summary executions and the large-scale displacement of civilians.[3] A cease-fire negotiated in May 1994 has held till the present, despite sporadic instances of violence. The Karabagh Armenians have established self-rule, electing a President and holding parliamentary elections in May 1995.

Negotiations under the auspices of the renamed Organization on Security and Co-operation in Europe have continued on a regular basis, with the Budapest Review Conference, held in December 1994, pledging to dispatch an international peace-keeping force of 3,000 to the area following the conclusion of a major political agreement, which has yet to be reached. Azerbaijan has refused to recognize the Karabagh Armenians as a separate party to the conflict, insisting on the inclusion of ethnic Azeris formerly resident in the enclave in any negotiations. It will not countenance a political settlement until areas occupied by Karabagh Armenian forces outside the enclave are vacated. Karabagh Armenian forces maintain that the occupation of these areas, the Lachin corridor in particular, is essential for the security of Nagorno-Karabagh. Azeri proposals to strengthen regional autonomy are rejected by the Karabagh Armenians, who now insist upon full independence. The future status of Lachin and Shusha is seen as a major difficulty in the negotiation process, with the issues of the return of refugees to the region presenting further obstacles.

Conclusions and future prospects

In terms of minority rights, the most pressing need in Azerbaijan is to resolve the conflict over the status of Nagorno-Karabagh now that negotiations are under way. In general, minority rights need to be safeguarded both in terms of constitutional guarantees and through specific legislation. However, prospects for the general development of democracy do not currently look favourable, given the prevailing political instability, although the state of emergency imposed in October 1994 was lifted during 1995. Impediments to open elections remained and several political parties were unable to register for the parliamentary elections in November 1995 which were criticized by foreign observers. Progress on drafting a new constitution has been slow, and the economy, with oil profits still far away, appears unable to support the programmes to which minority groups are entitled.

Further reading

Fuller, E., *Azerbaijan at the Crossroads*, London, Royal Institute of International Affairs and RFE/RL Research Institute, 1994.

Human Rights Watch/Helsinki, *Azerbaijan: Seven Years of Conflict in Nagorno-Karabagh*, New York, 1994.

Krag, H. and Funch, L., *The North Caucasus: Minorities at a Crossroads*, London, MRG report, 1994.

Walker, C.J. (ed.), *Armenia and Karabagh: The Struggle for Unity*, London, Minority Rights Publications, 1991.

Minority-based and advocacy organizations

Human Rights Centre, Baku, Azerbaijan; tel 994 12 947550, fax 994 12 987555, e-mail: eldar@hrcenter.baku.az

Belarus

Land area:	207,600 sq km
Population:	10.15 million (1989; 10.2 million est. 1992)
Main languages:	Belarusian, Russian
Main religions:	Christianity (Eastern Orthodox, Roman Catholic and Uniate)
Main minority groups:	Russians 1,342,100 (13.2%), Poles 417,700 (4.1%), Ukrainians 291,000 (2.9%), Jews 111,900 (1.1%), others 84,000 (0.8%)[1]
Real per capita GDP:	$4,244
UNDP HDI/rank:	0.787 (61)

The Republic of Belarus, formerly the Belorussian Soviet Socialist Republic (BSSR), is situated between Ukraine, to the south, the Russian Federation to the east, Poland to the west, and Lithuania and Latvia to the north. Belarusians, like Russians and Ukrainians, trace their ancestry to Kievan Rus. Later, Belarusian territories were dominated by Lithuania and Poland. With the Polish partitions between 1772 and 1795 much of contemporary Belarus was incorporated into the Russian Empire. Following the collapse of the empire, an independent Belarus was established (1918), only to be abolished by the Soviets (1919). Under the Treaty of Riga (1921) Western Belarus was ceded to Poland (reclaimed 1939), and in 1922 the remaining lands joined the Soviet Union as the BSSR.

The cultural affinity between Belarusians and Russians, the large numbers of Russians in Belarus and policies of Russification have led to an extensive linguistic assimilation of Belarusians to Russian. In 1989, 20 per cent of Belarusians spoke Russian as their first language. Many others were bilingual. This fact, together with the absence of a significant indigenous intelligentsia, and consequent lack of a strong Belarusian culture, has discouraged the emergence of ethnolinguistic nationalism.

During *perestroika* the Belarusian Popular Front adopted an inclusive, civic definition of Belarusian nationhood. Citizenship was granted to all permanent residents, irrespective of ethnicity. The Declaration of Sovereignty (July 1990) states that the citizens of Belarus constitute the Belarusian people. The new Belarusian passport, unlike its Soviet predecessor, has no place for ethnic identification. The Law on Languages (January 1990) established Belarusian as the official state language, but allowed a transition period for its introduction of ten years.

A powerful movement to reunite Belarus with the Russian Federation has emerged, led by President Alyaksandr Lukashenka. On the initiative of the Russian-speaking Lukashenka, a referendum on integration with Russia was held in May 1995. Of those participating, 83.3 per cent voted in favour of closer ties with Russia and for a proposal to make Russian the state language. On April 1996 Belarus and Russia concluded a treaty designed to bring about the integration of the two countries. Even before it was signed the agreement gave rise to mass demonstrations, both in support and in opposition to it. While opposition to the agreement was led by a revived Belarusian nationalist movement, demonstrations were not directed against Russians or other minorities living within Belarus, rather against the increasingly authoritarian President Lukashenka and the threat of a loss of independence.

Russians

The large number of Russians in Belarus and the prominent place accorded to the Russian language (Russian dominates official business) means that minority status holds few problems for Russians. The leading position of Russians in Belarus is reinforced by a prevailing view of history among Russians that identifies Belarusians as a subdivision of the Russian people. Russian organizations in Belarus have therefore emphasized the 'unity of the East Slav peoples'. The pro-Russian Slavic Assembly has been criticized by Belarusian nationalist groups for denying the existence of a distinct Belarusian nation. Given the aim of integration with the Russian Federation, the Belarusian government has been extremely sensitive to the situation of Russians. The only issue to stir up tension in the republic was that of the status of the Russian language. The May 1995 referendum and April 1996 treaty on integration with Russia calmed anxiety on this issue.

Poles

The Polish presence in Belarus is the product of a centuries-long struggle for dominance of East-Central Europe between Poland and Russia. There has been a significant Polish influence in the area since the mid-sixteenth century. Poland brought much of the Belarusian Orthodox hierarchy under the authority of the Vatican. The Uniate Church, created in 1596, retained the Eastern rite while simultaneously embracing a number of Roman Catholic practices.

Russian policy in the lands 'rejoined' to Russia following the Polish partitions promoted Russification and conversion from the Uniate to the Orthodox faith. Following uprisings against tsarist rule (1831 and 1863) tens of thousands of Poles were exiled to Siberia. Measures to eradicate Polish influence were introduced. Russian replaced Polish as the language of government and education. In 1839, the Uniate Church, to which most Belarusians belonged, was abolished.

Under Soviet rule, pressure on the Polish community intensified. In the 1930s Polish autonomous areas in Belarus were dissolved. Between 1936 and 1938 thousands of Poles were deported. Today, the Polish community is concentrated in a strip of territory 120 kilometres wide and some 300 kilometres in length, stretching from the Polish border in the north-west along the border with the Baltic states. Only 13 per cent of the Poles speak Polish as their native language; 64 per cent claim Belarusian.

During *perestroika* there was a revival of Polish culture. In 1990 the Belarusian Union of Poles was founded and there has been an increase in Polish language publications. The Roman Catholic Church has also revived with the assistance of Polish priests. A treaty of friendship between Poland and Belarus (23 June 1992) recognized the Polish–Belarus border as inviolable, rejected any mutual territorial claims and required that both sides fully observe minority rights.

Ukrainians

Large numbers of Ukrainians speak Russian as their first language (49 per cent) and many, especially in urban areas, have been assimilated by the Russian community. Rural Ukrainians retain their language and a separate identity. A number of Ukrainian organizations have been created but cultural and linguistic revival is modest.

Jews

Although Jews once formed a large community in Belarus (Belarus was part of the Pale Settlement between 1815 and 1917), Nazi genocide, war and emigration have depleted the population. In the late 1980s the population was further reduced by a new wave of emigration. In 1989 99 per cent of Jews were Russian-speakers. There has, nevertheless, been a revival of the Jewish culture and religion. There is no official anti-Semitism and Belarusian nationalists have not sought to exploit the issue.

Conclusions and future prospects

Belarus has relatively few minority problems. The weakly developed sense of a separate Belarusian identity has ensured that ethno-nationalism has played little part in Belarusian politics. As a result, a politically rather than an ethnically defined state has been established. The government's desire to remain on good terms with Belarus's neighbours, especially Poland and Russia, has encouraged the development of a liberal minorities regime. While full integration with Russia might prompt an upsurge in Belarus ethno-nationalism or alarm among the Polish community, Russian resistance to the costs of unification makes such a radical change unlikely.

Further reading

MRG (ed.), *Minorities in Central and Eastern Europe*, London, MRG report, 1993.

Solchanyk, R., 'Ukraine, Belorussia, and Moldovia: imperial integration, Russification, and the struggle for national survival', in L. Hajda and M. Beissinger (eds.), *The Nationalities Factor in Soviet Politics and Society*, Boulder, CO, Westview, 1990.

Urban, M. and Zaprudnik, J., 'Belarus: a long road to nationhood', in I. Bremmer and R. Taras (eds), *Nations and Politics in the Soviet Successor States*, Cambridge, Cambridge University Press, 1993.

Zaprudnik, J., *Belarus: At a Crossroads in History*, Boulder, CO, Westview, 1993.

Minority-based and advocacy organizations

Belarusian Association of Political Repression Victims, Ul. Skoriny 1, Rm 308, 22072 Minsk, Belarus; tel. 7 172 394 893/609 333.

Belarusian League for Human Rights, Prosp. Skoriny 4, 220010 Minsk, Belarus; tel. 7 172 265 897, fax 7 172 248 061.

Human Rights Committee, Shevchenko Blvrd 3, Apt 22, 224030 Brest, Belarus; tel. 7 162 254 028.

Georgia

Land area:	69,700 sq km
Population:	5.6 million (1995)
Main languages:	Georgian, Mingrelian, Svan, Armenian, Russian
Main religions:	Georgian Orthodox Christianity, Islam
Main minority groups:	Armenians 500,000 (9%), Russians 300,000 (5.4%), Azeris 300,000 (5.4%), Ajarians 200,000–300,000 (3.6–5.4%), Ossetians 160,000 (2.9%), Abkhaz 95,000 (1.7%)[1]
Real per capita GDP:	$1,750
UNDP HDI/rank:	0.645 (101)

The Republic of Georgia, formerly the Soviet Socialist Republic of Georgia until independence in 1991, is situated in west/central Transcaucasia at the southern foothills of the Greater Caucasian mountain range. It borders on the North Caucasian republics of the Russian Federation (Daghestan, Chechnya, Ingushetia, North Ossetia, Kabardino-Balkaria and Karachay-Cherkessia) to the north, Azerbaijan to the south-east, and Turkey and Armenia to the south, and it has a western coastline on the Black Sea.

Georgia's human rights record in recent years has been marred by the outbreak of conflict in South Ossetia and Abkhazia and by civil strife resulting from the ousting of President Gamsakhurdia in December 1991. Recent reports have criticized the Georgian authorities for arbitrary arrest, ill-treatment of prisoners and the denial of a right to a free trial.

Georgians have long held the reputation of being fiercely proud of their nation. The strength of nationalist sentiment even before the Gorbachev era had led to some feelings of unease among other ethnic groups in Georgia. The particularities of Georgians as an ethnic group have, according to some, played a role in the development of civil conflict in the republic. Georgians tend to refer to themselves as Kartveli, and the Kartli dialect spoken around the capital, Tbilisi, became the foundation for the modern literary language. At the same time, the Mingrelians in western Georgia and the Svans in the Caucasus mountains speak related languages using Georgian as their literary language and lingua franca. The Laz, the bulk of whom live in Turkey, speak another related language. According to some analysts, the various regions of Georgia have not been fully integrated into a Georgian nation.

Georgia declared its independence on 9 April 1991, and former dissident and leader of the Georgia Round Table Coalition Zviad Gamsakhurdia was elected President in May 1991 by an overwhelming majority. However, his policies were increasingly authoritarian, undermining the coalition of disparate political forces which originally supported him, leading ultimately to civil strife and outright conflict in December 1991. President Gamsakhurdia was ousted in January 1992. Some perceived the conflict which erupted in Georgia between supporters of the deposed President and the new leadership under Eduard Shevardnadze as having an ethnic dimension. In the civil war which ensued, many of Gamsakhurdia's supporters were concentrated in areas of central and western Georgia (Mingrelia). Shevardnadze, the former Soviet Foreign Minister, returned to Georgia at the invitation of the forces that had ousted President Gamsakhurdia in March 1992 and was elected Chairman of Parliament in the autumn 1992 elections.

President Gamsakhurdia's authoritarianism and increasing Georgian nationalism, in particular the policy of 'Georgia for the Georgians', had led to an intensification of inter-ethnic tensions. Minority groups experienced a greater degree of insecurity in the light of policies on language, electoral laws and citizenship which threatened to exclude them from national and political life. Debates regarding the future political status of the autonomous regions soon became overlaid with ethnic issues.

Armenians

Armenians, who number half a million, are the largest minority group in Georgia. Many Armenians reside in Tbilisi, with rural Armenian settlements concentrated in the South Georgian districts of Akhaltsikhe and Alkhalkalaki and Ninotsminda near the Georgian–Armenian border. There are also significant Armenian communities in Abkhazia and Ajaria. Some claim that the number of Armenians in Georgia is actually far higher since Georgia took in many refugees from the Armenian earthquake, with 800,000 in Georgia and 300,000 living in Tbilisi alone.

An estimated 50 per cent of Armenians in Tbilisi speak Russian rather than Armenian, while in the more compact rural settlements the Armenian community feels a much stronger attachment to Armenia. Some have expressed a desire to emigrate in recent years due to the political tensions in Georgia: however, Armenia has not encouraged this due to the problems it is experiencing housing refugees from Azerbaijan connected with the Nagorno-Karabagh conflict. The Armenian government has not made any territorial claims on Georgia, but some Armenian political groups in southern Armenia (supported by some Armenian political parties) support the idea of secession. There have been fears that the Nagorno-Karabagh conflict would spill over into areas of Armenian and Azeri settlement in Georgia, with some incidents such as the sabotage of supply routes to Armenia being reported. However, the situation in Georgia has not degenerated into outright conflict between the two communities.

The Armenian community in Georgia are quite well organized and have reasonably good access to education in their own language. There are over 100 Armenian libraries in Georgia, a daily newspaper is produced and there are Armenian radio and theatre. Some difficulties were experienced in 1990–1 over land rights: some nationalist Georgian societies were accused of buying up land in areas of Armenian settlement with a view to encouraging more Georgian settlement and changing the local population balance.

Russians

There were approximately 300,000 Russians in Georgia in 1989, concentrated mainly in urban areas and including 75,000 in Abkhazia and 30,000 in Ajaria (Batumi). Their numbers in Georgia have declined steadily since the Soviet era. They do not form a compact ethnic or territorial group. In general, anti-Russian sentiment in Georgia is quite strong, with Russians often being perceived as representatives of a colonial imperialistic power. This attitude is particularly marked towards Russian troops who have been stationed in Georgia.

Russians have access to mother-tongue education as well as media and, until independence, Russian was the main language taught to other minority groups in Georgia, apart from those who had their own schools and who were therefore taught Russian alongside the minority language.

The war in Abkhazia led to significant numbers of Russians leaving Georgia and in general the level of migration of Russians is on the increase for reasons of political instability and the pursuit of better economic opportunities elsewhere.

Azeris

An estimated 300,000 Azeris live in Georgia. They tend to live in Rustavi and areas of compact settlement in south-east Georgia bordering Azerbaijan. There are 20,000 Azeris living in the capital, Tbilisi. In some areas they form a numerical majority, but they are under-represented in local administrations. The Azeri community have made demands for enhanced cultural autonomy since 1989.

Most Azeris tend to speak only their own language, although there is a growing realization of the need to master Georgian if they are not to become entirely marginalized. They are badly represented at the national level, and some instances of discrimination by the local authorities have been cited in recent years. They have a cultural society and two Azeri language weekly newspapers, as well as some degree of access to mother-tongue education at primary level.

Ajarians

A large proportion of Ajaria is inhabited by Muslim Georgians who speak a dialect of Georgian heavily influenced by Turkish. Numbering approximately 200,000 to 300,000, they adhere to the Hanaifi rite of the Sunni branch of Islam. The Ajarians were accorded separate status as an Autonomous Soviet Socialist Republic in 1922. Rebellion against anti-religious campaigns and collectivization in the late 1920s led to punitary measures, and large numbers of Ajarians were deported to Central Asia. Recognition of Ajarians as a separate ethnic group was withdrawn and they have been considered a Georgian subgroup ever since. However, in deference to the religious differences between Ajarians and Georgians, the status of autonomous republic has been retained to this day.

There has been no significant unrest in the Ajarian autonomous republic, although disquiet was expressed by Ajarians at attempts at Christianization under the Gamsakhurdia regime in 1991 and a movement to preserve Ajaria's autonomy was formed in response to the threat of its removal by President Gamsakhurdia. The current leader of the republic, Aislan Abashidze, has attempted to steer a delicate path in relations with the central authorities, seeking to maintain a large degree of political and economic autonomy. He has resorted to increasingly authoritarian methods to stay in power. During the Georgian parliamentary and presidential elections in September 1995 numerous election irregularities were reported in Ajaria by international observers. As with the other regions of Georgia, the future of Ajaria rests on Georgia's ability to agree on a proper constitutional framework for a federal agreement between the centre and the regions.

Ossetians

Ossetians speak a language of the North Iranian language group and are, according to some historians, descendants of Iranian tribes, the Alans, who came into the Caucasus region in the fourth century. They enjoyed a brief period of unity in 1905 when they were grouped together in one national district; however, since then, like other groups in the Caucasus, they have been subjected to numerous border changes and were divided by Stalin into the North Ossetian Autonomous Republic in the Russian Federation and the South Ossetian Autonomous Region in the Soviet Socialist Republic of Georgia. Approximately 70,000 Ossetians lived in South Ossetia in 1989, with a further 100,000 living elsewhere in Georgia before the outbreak of conflict. A further 300,000 Ossetians live in the Republic of North Ossetia-Alonia (under the jurisdiction of the Russian Federation).

As in Abkhazia, there were tensions between the South Ossetian political leadership and the central authorities in Tbilisi over fears of discrimination against the Ossetian language and culture by the late 1980s. Following promulgation of legislation strengthening the status of the Georgian language in South Ossetia in August 1989 tensions escalated, with the South Ossetian Popular Front (Adaemon Nykhas) protesting against perceived discrimination against Ossetians and campaigning for an enhanced republican status. These demands soon turned into requests for reunification with North Ossetia. The local Georgian population protested, which lead to clashes in December 1989 and the despatch of Soviet Interior Ministry Troops in January 1990. As the year progressed, the South Ossetians, like other minority groups, felt increasingly marginalised from the political debate, a feeling which was confirmed by the restrictions imposed by the Supreme Soviet on participation by regionally or ethnically based parties in the autumn elections.

The South Ossetian declaration of sovereignty in September 1990 was met by firm resistance by the central authorities, culminating in the abolition of South Ossetia's autonomous status at the end of the year and the deployment of the Georgian National Guard in the capital Tskhinvali. The imposition of National Guard rule over the territory led to widespread human rights abuses. Following the South Ossetian declaration of independence in December 1991 the intensity of the conflict increased, leading to the displacement of thousands of people. The outflow of refugees into North Ossetia (in the Russian Federation) had an impact on the development of the conflict between North Ossetia and Ingushetia (see **Russian Federation**). Georgian attempts to reassert control over the territory were hampered both by the political turmoil in the country as a whole and by the fact that South Ossetia received support from North Ossetia and other areas of the northern Caucasus, as well as covert support from Russia. A cease-fire agreement was reached in Sochi between Georgia and Russia on 24 June 1992, providing for a peacekeeping force, the setting up of a control commission and joint Ossetian-Georgian patrols, observed by the Organization for Security and Co-operation in Europe (OSCE) in Tbilisi.

Some progress has been made since then in

negotiations, with South Ossetia suffering from the results of war and economic crisis. It is estimated that more than 100,000 Ossetians fled from Georgia and South Ossetia to North Ossetia as a result of the fighting. Most ethnic Georgians formerly resident in the region have also fled to Georgia proper. Little attention has been focused on the outcome of the South Ossetian conflict since the cessation of hostilities, but South Ossetian leaders are awaiting the outcome of negotiations between Abkhaz and Georgians. The OSCE and Russia have played an active role in these negotiations. Some progress has been made with the implementation of confidence-building measures in the region. In November 1996 Liudvig Chibirov was elected President.

Abkhaz (Apswa)

Abkhaz (Apswa) speak a distinct north-west Caucasian language related to Circassian. Numbering only 94,706, they are concentrated in the Republic of Abkhazia, where they form only 17 per cent of the population, with Georgians (largely Mingrelians) the single largest group, with 45 per cent, in 1989.

During the Soviet era there were periodic demands from the Abkhaz for secession from Georgia and transfer to Russia, a campaign which gathered momentum during the 1970s and ultimately becoming a demand for a return to full republican status from 1988. Demonstrations in Tbilisi on 9 April 1989 in which nineteen Georgian demonstrators were killed by Soviet troops, were partly fuelled by hostility towards earlier Abkhaz demands for sovereignty and the whole issue became enmeshed in Georgian demands for independence from the Soviet Union.

During the 1920s the Abkhaz had enjoyed republican status with treaty ties to Georgia: this was however reduced to that of an autonomous republic within Georgia in 1931. Large numbers of western Georgians were settled in the region during the 1930s allegedly in order to shift the demographic balance in favour of ethnic Georgians. In the 1950s policies were introduced which aimed to grant enhanced rights to the Abkhaz. An Abkhaz university was established at Sukhumi, provision of education in the Abkhaz language was improved and Abkhaz enjoyed favourable recruitment policies, including a guarantee of quotas for administrative and party positions and thus a high proportion of ethnic Abkhaz occupied top republican and administrative posts. This led to increased resentment among the Georgian/Mingrelian population, who felt that they were being systematically disadvantaged in an area where they were in a majority. Abkhaz fears of a resurgence of Georgian nationalism and the Georgian independence movement led to outbreaks of hostility between ethnic Georgians and Abkhaz in the republic in the late 1980s. Tensions were fuelled by the attempt to establish a Georgian section of Tbilisi University in Sukhumi: this was perceived by the Abkhaz to be the beginning of a concerted campaign to Georgianize the republic.

An Abkhaz declaration of sovereignty on 25 August 1990 led to further protests by Georgians in the republic and was declared invalid by the central Georgian authorities. The situation worsened as a result of the political instability in Georgia as a whole. The Georgian decision to send troops into Sukhumi in August 1992, following the Abkhaz reinstatement of their 1925 constitution in July, was justified by the need to combat an insurgency by supporters of deposed President Gamsakhurdia in Mingrelia which was able to use Abkhazia as a refuge. The Abkhaz authorities viewed the arrival of Georgian troops as an invasion. This led to full-scale war in August, in which the Abkhaz were joined by volunteers from the North Caucasus and received substantial support from Russia. The conflict lasted until the Abkhaz finally defeated Georgian forces in October 1993. The war resulted in serious human rights violations on both sides, with instances of 'ethnic cleansing', harassment of Abkhazians, Georgians and representatives of other ethnic groups resident at that time in Abkhazia, hostage-taking and indiscriminate shelling on civilian populations[2]. After the defeat of Georgian forces the majority of the Georgian/Mingrelian population of Abkhazia fled to Georgia proper.

Negotiations have since taken place under UN auspices, while CIS (Russian) peacekeeping troops, mandated originally by the Sochi Agreement brokered by the Russian Federation in July 1993, continue to be stationed in Abkhazia. The negotiations have been fraught with difficulty in particular over reaching an agreement over the political status of Abkhazia and the return of mainly ethnic Georgian/Mingrelian internally displaced persons (IDPs) to the Gali region. Progress was made with the signature of an agreement to consider the political status of Abkhazia in April 1994 which included the return of IDPs. Little progress has been made with the repatriation of refugees. The Abkhazians say they are reluctant to accept them back before a political settlement has been reached, while many observers believe that the Abkhazians are hoping for a permanent shift in the ethno-demographic balance in their favour. Negotiations have reached a stalemate, with the Abkhazians demanding equal status with Georgia in a future confederation, while the Georgians have only been willing to offer a federation.

Other minorities

Georgia also has small Greek, Ukrainian, Kurdish, Chechen, Jewish and Bats minorities. For many the primary concern is for the preservation of culture and language, and the ability to form links with their compatriots abroad. For Meskhetians, the main issues are centred around the desire for repatriation to Georgia. An ethnically mixed Turkish/Kurdish and Islamized Georgian Armenian group, they were deported from their homeland in South Georgia in 1944 and settled in Central Asia, where they suffered violent attacks in 1989, causing most to flee. One group of Meskhetians has campaigned vigorously for the right to return to their homeland, whilst another wants to migrate to Turkey. Georgia remains resistant to their return for reasons of land, economy and political instability, arguing that their real homeland is Turkey. Their compact area of residence is now occupied by Armenians in Georgia, and the authorities are reluctant to resettle them for fear of aggravating tensions among the Armenian population.

Conclusion and future prospects

Georgia has undergone considerable political turmoil and economic upheaval in recent years. The development of political conflict into perceived 'ethnic wars' was largely a result of the nationalist policies pursued by President Gamsakhurdia in the years up to and immediately following independence, the general lawlessness and proliferation of rival militias and the lack of strong political institutions. There was also strong Georgian suspicion of Russia and a belief that the 'Russian factor' was present in minority demands for enhancement of rights. These demands were perceived to present an implicit threat to the future territorial integrity of Georgia.

The constitution which was adopted in October 1995 envisages a federal structure but has left the precise division of powers open until agreement has been reached with the former autonomies. However, it is doubtful that the Abkhaz in particular will be prepared to accept an autonomous area within Georgia since they still strive for independence. Another issue which needs to be resolved is the question of the political representation of minority groups. Laws on human rights and minority rights are currently being drafted and minority representatives have been included in the consultative process. Much depends on whether mutually acceptable agreements can be reached with the former autonomous entities.

Further reading

Krag H. and Funch, L., *North Caucasus: Minorities at a Crossroads*, London, MRG report, 1994.

Suny, R.G., *The Making of the Georgian Nation*, 2nd edn, Bloomington and Indianapolis, Indiana University Press, 1994.

Wesselink, E., *Minorities in the Republic of Georgia*, Utrecht Pax Christi Netherlands, September 1992.

Minority-based and advocacy organizations

Armenian Cultural Charitable Society of Georgia, 8 Ketevan Tsamebuli Street, Tbilisi, Georgia; tel. 995 8832 741 656/625 783.

Caucasian Institute for Peace, Democracy and Development, 6th Floor, 89/24 David Agmashenebeli Avenue, Tbilisi 380008, Georgia; tel. 995 8832 954 723, fax 995 8832 954 497, e-mail: ghian@cippd.ge

Centre for Cultural Relations, 20 Galaktioni Str., Tbilisi 380007, Georgia.

Cultural Centre of Kurds, Tbilisi, Georgia; tel./fax 995 8832 931 893.

Forum of Youth Organizations of Different Nations of Georgia, c/o Young Citizens' Union of Georgia, Tbilisi, Georgia; fax 995 8832 959 146.

Helsinki Citizens' Assembly, Georgian National Committee, Cinamdzgvrishvili 31, Tbilisi 380002, Georgia; tel. 995 8832 351 914, fax 995 8832 351 674.

Imedi, Tbilisi, Georgia; tel. 995 8832 936 035/128 254.

International Centre for Conflict and Negotiation, 16 Chavchavadze Avenue, Tbilisi 380079, Georgia; tel. 995 8832 223 618.

Jewish Youth Centre, 25 G. Chubinashvili Street, Tbilisi, Georgia; tel. 995 8832 237 037, fax 995 8832 998 992.

Kurdish Youth Unity, 5 Pushkin Street, Tbilisi, Georgia; tel./fax 995 8832 931 983.

Vsmaroni (Brotherhood), 29 Lado Asatiani Street, Tbilisi, Georgia; tel. 995 8832 983 679.

Kazakhstan

Land area:	2,717,300 sq km
Population:	16.9 million (est. 1994)
Main languages:	Kazakh, Russian, Uzbek
Main religions:	Sunni Islam, Orthodox Christianity
Main minority groups:	Russians 5,769,000 (34%), Ukrainians 820,000 (4.8%), Germans 575,000 (3.4%), Uzbeks 372,400 (2.2%), also Tatars, Belarusians, Uighurs, Koreans, Poles, Jews, Greeks, Meskhetian Turks and others
Real per capita GDP:	$3,710
UNDP HDI/rank:	0.740 (72)

The Republic of Kazakhstan is the second largest state of the former Soviet Union. It borders the Russian Federation to the north, Turkmenistan, Uzbekistan and Kyrgyzstan to the south and the People's Republic of China to the east, and it shares the Aral Sea with Uzbekistan. Kazakhs constitute a numerical minority in their own country (46 per cent of the population) among a total of 106 nationalities. They are a Turkic people, descendants of nomadic tribes who came under Russian domination in the eighteenth century. Islam was introduced in most of their area relatively late, also in the eighteenth century.

The traditionally nomadic Kazakh lifestyle survived until the forced collectivization of the 1930s, although the society was already changing. Kazakhs are divided between three hordes (*zhusii*), each with different territorial allegiances. The hordes consist of clans. These allegiances are far from clear, and the divisions are complex. Horde affiliation plays a role in appointment to socially prestigious positions but has little bearing in everyday social and economic life. There are no major cultural or linguistic differences.

Social differences between Kazakhs are greater than among any of the non-Kazakh minorities. The main division is between rural-traditional groups and Russified urban groups, and this distinction has had a pronounced impact on political and social life. Numerous Kazakhs hold high positions in state administration and management, banking, education and state-controlled enterprises. High ranking positions are now often occupied by first-generation city dwellers who retain a traditional rural outlook. Since independence, the cities, which used to contain large European populations, have experienced an influx of Kazakhs from the countryside. Thus European urban populations increasingly feel alienated. Because Kazakhs do not constitute a majority in Kazakhstan, and the country was heavily Russified during the Soviet period, they have an acute fear of losing their culture and traditions, and are highly sensitive in relation to national pride.

Slavic settlers came to Kazakhstan from the late eighteenth century onwards. Later, during Soviet times, they came to participate in various development undertakings, beside those resettled from labour camps. So-called 'punished peoples' were deported to Kazakhstan before and during the Second World War. These groups include Volga Germans, Crimean Tatars, Koreans, Poles, Greeks, Chechens, Ingush and others believed at the time to be unreliable or accused of collaboration with the enemy. Some, such as Chechens and Ingush, returned in large numbers to their homelands at the earliest opportunity, in the late 1950s. Others, such as Germans and Koreans, settled in Kazakhstan and were gradually accepted in Kazakh society.

The emigration of non-indigenous minorities increased during *perestroika* and has continued to do so. By 1994, 957,000 had left Kazakhstan – mainly Russians, Ukrainians, Belarusians, Germans, Poles and Jews returning to their historic homelands. The main reasons for this exodus are probably the deteriorating economic situation and the infringement of minority rights. Public policies limit access to political offices: only a few members of ethnic minorities are in elective office, the civil service and other high ranking positions, and access to higher education is limited.

As a result of this emigration, as well as the immigration of ethnic Kazakhs from abroad and their much higher birth rate, Kazakhs increased as a proportion of the republic's population by about 17 per cent between 1989 and 1994. Regions of the country with the highest proportion of ethnic Kazakhs are Kzyl-Orda (92 per cent) and Atyrau (83 per cent). In addition, 1.8 million Kazakhs live in the other CIS states, mainly in Central Asia, and 1.5 million in the rest of the world, including more than 1 million in China. Kazakh government policy has been to promote opportunities for ethnic Kazakhs to return to their homeland, which many fled in the 1930s as a result of the impact of the Soviet policy of collectivization. These groups are granted special privileges, and by 1994 immigration exceeded 507,000.

During *perestroika*, violence erupted in Kazakhstan as an expression of Kazakh anger at Moscow's interference in their internal affairs and as the first demonstration of force by regional elites. Riots occurred in Almaty in December 1986 when first secretary of the Kazakhstan Communist Party D. Kunayev was replaced by an ethnic Russian, G. Kolbin, drafted in from Moscow. Kazakh nationalist feelings were aroused, mainly among students. During the same period, inter-ethnic conflict took place in the town of Noviy Uzen, involving various Caucasian groups.

Kazakhstan came into being as an independent state in December 1991. Its political regime might be interpreted as authoritarian democracy. The authorities allow opposition groups to function, but their members cannot occupy positions of influence or bid for power. President Nazarbayev is committed to preserve ethnic peace as a pragmatic precondition for economic revival, and remains wary of nationalism. However, the jailing of ethnic minority leaders on flimsy pretexts, and the manipulation of election rules to exclude nationalist parties, have occurred. Outbreaks of mass xenophobia have also taken place.

President Nazarbayev was elected in 1991 for a five-year term. He has enjoyed the confidence of the major ethnic minority groups in Kazakhstan, which regarded him as a guarantor of inter-ethnic peace. The first Kazakh Parliament was elected in 1990 and dissolved itself on presidential initiative in December 1993. A new Parliament was elected in March 1994, in which minorities were under-represented, only to be dissolved by the President in March 1995 on the grounds of a ruling by the Constitutional Court. In April 1995 Nazarbayev's presidency was extended to December 2000 by referendum. In August 1995 a new constitution was adopted by means of a referendum, introducing strong presidential rule and a *defacto* unitary state. Elections for a two-chamber Parliament took place in January 1996, resulting in a Kazakh majority. These developments indicate moves towards a more authoritarian style of rule and have alarmed minorities. Division of society along ethnic lines and mutual suspicion among ethnic groups appear to be increasing.

Russians, Ukrainians, Belarusians

Russians in Kazakhstan fall into two broad categories. First, Cossacks ('free men') are descendants of Russian peasant fugitives who settled along the southern and eastern perimeter of Russia and fulfilled the function of border protection, entering the Kazakh steppes mainly in the nineteenth century. Second, Russians, Ukrainians and Belarusians have come in several later waves: drafted in according to the Soviet strategy of 'compulsory engagement' in the 1930s to take part in the industrialization programme; arriving in the 1950s as a result of the Virgin Lands project; or settling after their release from labour camps in the post-Stalin era.

Russian-speakers remain a majority in Kazakhstan's northern and eastern oblasts. This led the Russian writer Alexandr Solzhenitsyn, among others, to suggest that northern Kazakhstan be annexed to Russia, with the rest left to the Kazakhs. Northern Kazakhstan is reportedly referred to as 'South Siberia' in the jargon of Russian nationalists, who argue that the Russian regions of Astrakhan and Urals ceded territory to Kazakhstan in 1936, and that there is a good case for taking back some of the lands. This suggestion of partition is immensely provocative to Kazakhs, who can claim that the whole of this steppe region was nomadic Kazakh land long before Russian expansion. Nationalistically minded Kazakhs perceive Russians as conquerors, who repressed their national language, culture and religion, and they blame Russians for environmental damage caused by nuclear testing in the Semipalatinsk region. Russians, for their part, consider they have made a positive contribution to the economy and culture of Kazakhstan and feel discriminated against.

Three Cossack communities – the Ural, Orenburg and Siberian Cossacks – are historically located partly on Russian and partly on Kazakhstani territory. The Semirech'e Cossacks are entirely Kazakhstani based. Since 1992 new Cossack movements have demanded recognition of the repression endured during Soviet times; official second-language status for Russian, the return of historical names for Cossack settlements, recognition as a population indigenous to Kazakhstan and implementation of traditional forms of Cossack self-rule have also been sought. Cossack associations are active in areas of traditional Cossack settlement. The movement is regarded with suspicion by the authorities. Some Cossack communities are not allowed official registration; their meetings have been banned and atamans (leaders) have been arrested. Relations between Kazakh nationalists, who enjoy limited support from the government, and Cossacks, especially in heavily Russian Petropavlovsk and Ust-Kamenogorsk regions, are tense and have led to sporadic violence.

Russian-speakers have several significant cultural and political organizations. The most prominent organization representing the Slavic community in general is the Republican Slavic Movement (known by the abbreviation LAD). Its stated goals are the preservation of Slavic identity, equal rights for all to a share of national property and participation in the state administration. The organization appeals to Russians not to leave the republic. It seeks state language status for Russian and the legalization of dual citizenship, while also campaigning for better job opportunities for Russian- speakers, and generally seeking to awaken Russian national consciousness, which it considers dormant. Certainly, many Russians have no clearly defined objective or positive programme for action, because their identity is state rather than ethnic-related and their outlook is based on the Soviet past.

Some Russian cultural centres that operate freely are actively engaged in right-wing politics and have established stable relations with the nationalist parties in Russia proper. Debates within the Russian community also revolve around approaches towards establishing a national-cultural autonomous region within Kazakhstan with strong local self-government and control of education and language.

According to the 1989 language law and previous (1993) constitution, Kazakh was the state language while Russian was declared a language of inter-ethnic communication. According to the new (1995) constitution, which contains more assertive nationalist rhetoric, Russian is an 'official language', while Kazakh is the only state language. The outcome of this change of terminology remains unclear. Only 2 per cent of Russians in Kazakhstan claimed fluency in Kazakh in 1992. The law also provided that in regions where a certain national group lives in compact communities, the language of that group can be elevated to the status of a local official language. The decision was adopted to switch to a fully bilingual administration by 2000, a goal now considered unrealistic due to the lack of interest in learning Kazakh among minorities and to a shortage of Kazakh teachers and textbooks. Moderate Slavic activists complain about violations of the law on the part of administrative bodies, rather than about the law itself, especially in regions where Russians constitute a minority, thus reducing job opportunities. In December 1992, 15,000 demonstrators in northern Kazakhstan demanded that Russian should be recognized as a second state language. For two years the Kazakh parliament refused to discuss the issue.

President Nazarbayev rejected dual citizenship on the grounds that it would divide loyalty by creating groups with different rights, and could lead to fragmentation of the state, bringing the heavily Russian oblasts in the north closer to unification with Russia. Dual citizenship for ethnic Kazakhs living abroad is abolished in the new constitution. However, Nazarbayev signed a package of agreements with Russia in March 1994, including a number of palliative solutions whereby Russia and Kazakhstan consented to leave their borders open and no visa regime is required. People who migrate both ways would acquire citizenship in their country of choice without difficulties, and should be able to sell their homes and take property with them. An agreement on citizenship was signed in early 1995 which facilitates Russians' and Kazakhs' swapping citizenship when they change countries. However, this disappointed the hopes of many Russians who had expected dual citizenship to be granted.

Despite President Nazarbayev's initial policy of

inclusive state-building, many Russians suspect that the balance is altering in favour of a more nationalistic and exclusive variant. Their fears are nurtured by the campaign to rename Kazakhstani towns, regions and streets, changing not only names reflecting the legacy of communism, but also traditional Russian place-names in compactly Slavic regions. The authorities are also encouraging ethnic Kazakhs to move to the north where Slavs predominate and to settle in borderlands to boost the Kazakh population there. Many contend that the proposed transfer of the capital from Almaty to Akmola, set for about 2000, is to enable the Kazakhstani government to control Russian communities in the north.

The top echelons of power in northern Kazakhstan have become increasingly Kazakh. Russians perceive that they are being pushed out of the country in order to provide space for repatriated Kazakhs, who are resettled in traditionally well-kept former German villages and receive cash subsidies and interest-free loans from the government. Meanwhile many Russian-speakers employed in industrial jobs do not receive salaries for months and are sent on unpaid leave because factory production is depressed due to the disruption of economic ties with Russian suppliers.

Government relations with the Russian political community have deteriorated. In April 1995, prior to the presidential referendum, the Kazakh prosecutor general closed down the journal *Kazakhstanskaya pravda*, the voice of the ethnic Russian movement in Kazakhstan, charging that it was fomenting ethnic hatred. The same fate befell *Russkii vestnik* (Russian Messenger). Political opponents, especially among the Russian community, increasingly use Russian Federation newspapers to circulate their views. Before the presidential referendum the Republican Slavic Movement (LAD) encouraged people to vote 'no' to extending the President's term.

Russian emigration is gaining momentum, especially among younger and more educated members of the community. The experience of Belarusians and Ukrainians has been broadly similar.

Germans

Germans were deported from European Russia, mainly from the Volga German Autonomous Soviet Socialist Republic (ASSR) to Kazakhstan, in 1941–2 as a precautionary measure against advancing German troops. The Volga Germans were politically rehabilitated in 1964, but the Volga German ASSR was not re-established. By the 1970s the number of Germans in Kazakhstan had risen to 839,000. The majority remained in Karaganda and the northern regions, but their numbers had been growing proportionately much faster in the south-east.

After the dissolution of the Soviet Union the majority of Germans shared the negative attitudes of the local Slavs towards independence and assertiveness on the part of Asian Muslims. They too feared educational and language discrimination, deterioration of the economic situation and the possibility of some future major destabilization. In addition, the older generation experienced too much suffering in the Soviet Union to believe in a future in former Soviet Central Asia. Almost 200,000 ethnic Germans left the former Soviet Union for Germany in 1992, most of them from Kazakhstan, and large-scale emigration has continued, some Germans moving to Russia and Ukraine. The quota for German emigration from Kazakhstan is 200,000 a year, and it is being fulfilled, with a long waiting list.

The Kazakh authorities, encouraged by financial support from the German government, have made some efforts to persuade Germans to stay, but there is pessimism about the success of such a policy. However welcome Germany's subsidies are in Almaty, the government cannot for political reasons permit these benefits to go exclusively to the German population. The German government is keen for Germans to stay where they are, at least for the present, and tries to promote German culture in Kazakhstan and the economic well-being of the German minority, providing funding for German-language radio broadcasts and for computers for German-medium schools. Such measures are unlikely to stem the exodus of Germans, and for those who stay there may be little alternative but cultural assimilation into the much larger Slavic community. Local Germans have made solidarity with other Russian-speakers in protests against ethnically discriminatory policies. In 1994 they took part in meetings organised by Russian communities in Petropavlovsk after the German Wiedergeburt (Revival) society was denied official registration following its refusal to accept the definition 'Kazakh Germans'.

Uzbeks

Uzbeks live mainly in the Chimkent oblast, which is contiguous to Uzbekistan. Areas of traditional Uzbek settlement used to change hands between Uzbek and Kazakh rulers, and this pattern continued into Soviet times. Historically the key division lay between nomadic Kazakh and sedentary Uzbek lifestyles. In 1993 Uzbeks made up 2.2 per cent of the population and they have the highest natural increase rate. Most Kazakhs were traditionally xenophobic about the Uzbek sedentaries who were gradually encroaching on Kazakh territory. Anti-Uzbek feelings have grown since independence, largely because Uzbeks, with their strong tradition as traders among other Central Asian nationalities, have prospered with the market economy. There is anecdotal evidence that Uzbeks control most of the trade in the south of the republic.

Volga Tatars

Volga Tatars in Kazakhstan live mainly in the north of the country, in the Petropavlovsk and Kokchetau *oblasts*, and in Almaty. Tatars have penetrated the area since the nineteenth century, entering the region as traders offering manufactured goods to nomadic Kazakhs. They were also Islamic missionaries, and Tatar settlers were the conduit of Islam into the region. The Tatar lifestyle traditionally represented standards to which the local population aspired. Women play a dominant role in Tatar families. Tatars are well assimilated in Kazakh society, and mixed marriages are widespread. This assimilation was facilitated by language and cultural closeness and by a shared sense of belonging to the Turkic world. However, the Tatars' situation has deteriorated since independence, as loyalty to the new Kazakh state is increasingly determined by ethnicity. Russian and not Kazakh as a second language is widespread in Tatar families, and they have experienced the same language disadvantages as Russian-speakers. During the Soviet period many Tatars occupied positions in the medium-level administration and they comprised a significant part of the Kazakhstani intelligentsia. Today they are politically rather inactive, although each Kazakhstan oblast has its own Tatar-Bashkir cultural centre, dedicated to preserve ethnic identity. Of the large minorities of Kazakhstan, the Tatars occupy the third place (after Germans and Russians) in their pace of emigration.

Uighurs

Uighurs, a Turkic ethnic group, number more than 7 million, the majority residing in the Xinjiang region of the People's Republic of China. Kazakhstan historically contained an Uighur population, and the Uighur Raion exists in the Almaty *Oblast*. In 1962 between 60,000 and 120,000 Uighurs and Kazakhs fled into Kazakhstan to avoid repression in China. The situation has since changed; while Xinjiang is still one of the poorest Chinese provinces, many Uighurs and Kazakhs there seem aware that their kin across the border are materially worse off. They currently number about 200,000 in Kazakhstan.

The Soviet authorities allowed Uighurs a considerable degree of cultural self-expression, perhaps partly to destabilize the political and social situation in neighbouring China during the Sino-Soviet rift. Uighurs were permitted Uighur-language newspapers, television, radio and theatre. In June 1992 advocates of an independent Uighurstan convened their first congress in Almaty. This resulted in the creation of the East Turkestan Committee and the Uighurstan Organization of Freedom. Registration of the former by the Kazakh authorities prompted a Chinese protest. Uighur Kurultai (Congress) in Almaty has campaigned for increased autonomy in Xinjiang, greater civil and religious freedoms there, and more freedom to travel to and from the region. The Chinese authorities have protested against meetings organized by groups calling for an independent Uighurstan, but the Kazakh government has tolerated them. During the visit of Li Peng in April 1994, the Kazakh government restricted travel in several border regions and in the Uighur Raion to avoid public protests against China's policies in Xinjiang.

Koreans

Koreans, one of the 'punished peoples', were deported from Maritime Province in the Far East to Kazakhstan during the height of Soviet–Japanese tension over Manchuria in 1937. That year *Pravda* published an article accusing Koreans in the Soviet Far East of collaborating with the Japanese. After deportation, Koreans took root in their new area of residence; most lost their language, except for the older generation, and were Russified, becoming well integrated into Soviet society via education. Their orientation was almost completely Soviet rather than Korean, except in the traditional ethnic sense. Significant numbers of Koreans were visible in Soviet Kazakhstan as high officials in ministries and industrial enterprises, while others were engaged in agriculture, mainly in onion cultivation, where they remain active. There are approximately 140,000 Koreans in Kazakhstan, and their main area of compact settlement remains Uzun Agach.

Since independence, Koreans have played a

positive role in the new market economy, and they are clearly the minority which gained most out of the economic transition. Kazakhs, with no tradition as traders, are overshadowed by more commercially minded Koreans, who have been quick to establish themselves in private business. The position of the local Korean population has been enhanced through strong contacts with South Korea, whose corporations have taken an interest in the opportunities offered.

Other minorities

The first 500,000 Poles were deported to Kazakhstan in 1939–41, mainly because of Stalin's fear of their opposition to the Soviet take-over of eastern Poland. The second wave of deportation started in 1944 and finished with Stalin's death. Poles deported at that time were suspected of participating in the anti-communist Polish resistance. Their ethnic identity was nationalistic and Roman Catholic, which made them unreliable in the eyes of the Soviet authorities. Initially persecution made Poles more nationalistic and more religious, but they gradually became integrated into the broader Slavic community in Kazakhstan. Generally they face the same problems as other Slavs and act in solidarity with them in campaigns to improve minority rights, while also sharing their inclinations to emigrate, although discouraged by Poland.

It is difficult to estimate the size of the Jewish community in Kazakhstan. Ethnic Jews and people of mixed-Jewish descent often have a different nationality in their passport. Jewish emigration to Israel and the USA continues but is poorly documented. Jews were relatively well represented in the previous Kazakh parliament compared to other minorities. Anti-Semitic sentiments were expressed by the nationalist *Kazakhskaya pravda*, published during 1994–5, which called for the expulsion of all foreigners from Kazakhstan. The newspaper was forced to close in April 1995 after calling for the 'cleansing' of the Kazakh homeland of the 'aliens from the Middle East'.

The campaign against Greeks in the Soviet Union began in 1937–9, and Pontic (or Black Sea) Greeks were deported to Kazakhstan from border zones in Georgia and Ukraine. A second wave of deportations came in 1944, after the liberation of Crimea from Nazi occupation, when the entire Crimean Greek population was transferred to Kazakhstan. In 1949 Greeks from Ukraine, southern Russia and the Caucasus were sent to Central Asia and Siberia as a part of Stalin's anti-Tito drive. Later that year about 10,000 members of the Democratic Army of Greece, the Greek Communist Party and their supporters became political refugees in the Soviet Union. They were initially settled in Odessa but soon were sent to Central Asia. Since 1956 Greeks who wished to return to the Black Sea coast, with the exception of Crimean Greeks, were allowed to do so. The right to return was later granted to Crimean Greeks. After 1956 Greeks were allowed to emigrate to Greece in limited numbers, especially political refugees and their families. The desire to return to Greece is widespread among the civil war refugees and their descendants. Greece recognizes the right of all people of Greek descent to return.

Meskhetian Turks underwent a deportation from Uzbekistan in June 1989, when they became the victims of pogroms in the Fergana valley (see **Uzbekistan**). Up to 6,000 were resettled in Kazakhstan, where they were unwelcome. Many Meskhetians seek to emigrate to Georgia and Turkey.

Conclusions and future prospects

Relations with Russia and Russian internal developments will play a crucial role for the future of Kazakhstan, both because of the large Russian-speaking population and because of the long border with the Russian Federation and the potential for border disputes. In the long term, the prospects of stability in Kazakhstan appear fragile. National interests of Russians and the indigenous population seem more at odds here than anywhere else in Central Asia, precisely because the numerically large non-Kazakh population has such economic and cultural influence, which it is reluctant to relinquish. Similarly, Kazakhs face significant constraints in imposing their wishes for the future on the rest of the population – a situation likely to exacerbate their sense of frustrated nationalism. With the highest percentage of minority-dominated *oblasts* (regions) located along the Russian border, Kazakhstan has had to deal with the question of potential breakaway regions. If not resolved, irredentism may lead to serious inter-ethnic conflict. In the event of a major aggravation of Kazakh–Russian relations, Russian-speakers are more likely to fight for their rights or insist on partition of the country than to emigrate to Russia, and it is in any case unlikely that Russia would absorb a massive influx. Any disruption of ethnic relations between the two major communities in Kazakhstan could therefore lead to grave consequences. However, if the status quo prevails, small-scale Russian emigration is likely to continue.

The scale and pace of emigration of other minorities (notably Germans, Jews and Greeks) suggest that these communities will gradually disappear. In the short run, ethnic tensions may emerge with regard to those minorities that gain economic benefits in the changing market conditions, namely Uzbeks, Koreans and Jews. Another group of minorities that may attract indigenous hostility is Caucasians (Armenians, Chechens, Ingush and Azeris), matching a general racist tendency against Caucasians – who are popularly associated with criminality – experienced by all former Soviet Union states. Caucasians' enterprising skills and community bonds provoke some resentment among both Kazakhs and Slavs. As for Uighurs, cross-border trade between entrepreneurs in Kazakhstan and Xinjiang will continue to develop, although almost certainly without significant political consequences.

Further reading

Akiner, S., *Central Asia*, London, MRG report, 1997.

Blandy, C.W., *Instabilities in Post-Communist Europe: Central Asia*, Sandhurst, Conflict Studies Research Centre, January 1994.

Dixon, A., *Kazakhstan: Political Reform and Economic Development*, London, Royal Institute of International Affairs, 1994.

International Helsinki Federation for Human Rights, *Human Rights in Kazakhstan: The Almaty Helsinki Committee Annual Report*, Almaty, 1994.

Kolstoe, P., *Russians in the Former Soviet Republics*, London, Hurst, 1995.

Sheehy, A. and Nahaylo, B., *The Crimean Tatars, Volga Germans and Meskhetians: Soviet Treatment of Some National Minorities*, London, MRG report, 1980.

Minority-based and advocacy organizations

Almaty Helsinki Committee, Koktem-1 26, Apt 43, Almaty 480070, Kazkhstan.

Association of Germans, 9/3 Samal Mikroraion, Almaty, Kazakhstan; tel. 7 3272 248 537.

Association of Korean Cultural Centres, 61–7 Panfilova Street, Almaty 480004, Kazakhstan; tel. 7 3272 324 034.

International Turkic Centre, 111/113 Pushkin Street, Almaty 480100, Kazakhstan; tel. 7 3272 617 364/618 862.

Kazakh International Foundation of Indigenous Peoples and Ethnic Minorities, 67 Oktyabrskaya Street, Altmaty, Kazakhstan; tel. 7 3272 629 740.

Regional Foundation for Promotion of Korean Culture, 70 8th March Street, Almaty, Kazakhstan.

Russian Community, 6/72 Kosmonavtov Street, Almaty 480072, Kazakhstan; tel. 7 3272 605 489.

Russian Union, 109/401 Vinogradova Street, Almaty, Kazakhstan; tel. 7 3272 631 629.

Society of Assistance to the Cossacks of Semirech'ie, 26 Ushtobinskaya, Almaty, Kazakhstan; tel. 7 3272 296 723.

Uighur Interrepublican Association, Room 101, 111/113 Pushkin Street, Almaty 480100, Kazakhstan; tel. 7 3272 614 391.

Vatan Meskhetian Turks Society, 8 Pavlova Street, Kaskelen, Almaty City Area, Kazakhstan; tel. 7 3272 390 677.

Kyrgyzstan

Land area:	198,500 sq km
Population:	4.43 million (est. 1994)
Main languages:	Kyrgyz (official since 1989), Russian, Uzbek
Main religions:	Sunni Islam, Orthodox Christianity
Main minority groups:	Russians 757,500 (17.1%), Uzbeks 612,000 (13.8%), Ukrainians 80,000 (1.8%), Tatars 60,000 (1.3%), Kazakhs 41,500 (0.9%), Uighurs 40,000 (0.9%), Germans 35,000 (0.8%), also Dungans, Tajiks, Jews
Real per capita GDP:	$2,320
UNDP HDI/rank:	0.663 (99)

The Kyrgyz Republic is a landlocked state bordering Kazakhstan to the north, Uzbekistan to the west, Tajikistan to the south-west and the People's Republic of China to the south-east. Kyrgyz make up about 58.6 per cent of the population. There are 375,000 Kyrgyz in the Xinjiang Region of the People's Republic of China. Kyrgyzstan declared independence in August 1991. President Akayev, who enjoyed widespread support, embarked on a process of political reform and economic restructuring. His economic policy and legislative initiatives have since been often criticized. The compromise Akayev achieved with Kyrgyz nationalist forces is reflected in the constitution adopted in May 1993 and in the renaming of the Republic of Kyrgyzstan as the less ethnically neutral 'Kyrgyz Republic' at the same time. The constitution's bias towards an ethnic concept of the state is a matter of concern to minorities.

While official policies demonstrate commitment to minority protection, the situation of minorities is affected by a worsening economic situation and rising crime levels. These factors have contributed to an increase in emigration. Clan politics based on north–south rivalry also make the country less governable. Minorities fared badly in the 1995 parliamentary elections. Only five minority groups – Russians, Uzbeks, Germans, Dungans and Karachai – have representatives in Parliament. In 1995 over 1 million signatures were collected in support of calls for a referendum to extend the President's term of office till the year 2001. The legislative assembly voted against such a referendum. In the presidential elections of December 1995, President Akayev was re-elected for a second term. In February 1996 a referendum resulted in the President's gaining more delegated power over foreign and domestic affairs.

Russians and Ukrainians

Slavs – mainly Russians but also Ukrainians – constitute the largest minority in Kyrgyzstan. Unlike in other Central Asian states, a significant proportion of Slavs are rural dwellers. European farmers have long cultivated the fertile Chu Valley. There is now a tendency for Slavs to emigrate. Russians declined in number between 1989 and 1994 from 21.5 to 17.1 per cent of the population, Ukrainians from 2.5 to 1.8 per cent. In response to the constitutional preamble which emphasizes the special place of the titular nationality in Kyrgyzstan, Slavs have demanded proportional ethnic representation in the organs of state power. A related issue is dual citizenship, rejected in the new constitution. In February 1994 President Akayev opened a discussion on this subject but was opposed by Kyrgyz nationalist parties.

In Soviet times Kyrgyz elites adopted the Russian language as their preferred medium of expression, leaving Kyrgyz underdeveloped in technical areas. Since independence, steps have been taken to promote Kyrgyz. Higher education and official correspondence are set to switch to Kyrgyz by 2000, although this is an unrealistic goal. The constitution identifies Kyrgyz as the state language but includes a clause disallowing language discrimination. A presidential decree of June 1994 stipulates that Russian should be considered the official language in territories and workplaces where Russian-speakers predominate. Russian remains widespread. To assuage Russian-speakers' fears of reduced educational opportunities, the Russian-Kyrgyz (Slavonic) University was opened under the joint auspices of the Kyrgyz and Russian governments in 1993.

Uzbeks

Forming 13.8 per cent (612,000) of the population, Uzbeks are concentrated mainly in the Fergana valley. In June 1990 clashes between Uzbeks and Kyrgyz in the city of Osh, arising from disputes over the award of building plots, claimed at least 48 dead and 300 injured. In April 1991 an agreement was signed between local Uzbek and Kyrgyz leaders to give Uzbeks a share of the administration, and Uzbek schools were opened. However, the two communities remain polarized. Uzbek minority leaders claim that the Osh city borders were redrawn to include Kyrgyz villages and exclude Uzbek districts. The state of emergency in the Osh Oblast was lifted in September 1995 prior to the presidential elections. In the Djalal-Abad Oblast relations are similarly strained. There are three main Uzbek cultural centres in Kyrgyzstan, in Bishkek, Osh and Djalal-Abad.

Uighurs

The Kyrgyz government discourages Uighur migration from China but wishes to avoid antagonizing Uighurs living in Kyrgyzstan. Uighur shepherds sometimes cross from Xinjiang into Kyrgyzstan. There are two democratically elected and officially recognized Uighur organizations: the Uighur Freedom Organization and the Ittipak cultural centre. Both have close relations with the Uighur diaspora in Xinjiang and with the Tibet Liberation Movement, and are active in protests against Chinese nuclear testing. Because of Chinese official sensitivities, the Kyrgyz government has warned these organizations against continuing such activities. A new group of Uighurs loyal to the government, consisting mainly of business people, now has official support. An Uighur department exists at the national university. One newspaper and a small number of books and educational texts are published in the Uighur language. The illegal entry of Uighurs who are Chinese nationals, and ethnic Chinese, especially in and around the free-trade zone established in the city of Naryn in 1993, represents a new problem for the government.

Other minorities

Two German districts dissolved by Stalin in 1942 were re-established in 1992 by presidential decree. The majority of Germans were unwilling to invest energy in this project, which was obstructed by local officials. Emigration of Germans continues, making them the country's fastest disappearing minority. Jews, once numerous in the capital and respected for their contribution to health care, engineering and culture, are another rapidly disappearing group. The majority emigrate to Israel, others to the USA and Germany.

Conclusions and future prospects

Out migration presents a serious challenge for Kyrgyzstan. It causes a drain of skilled workers, adversely affects the economy and impairs the establishment of stable public institutions which need non-Kyrgyz staff. It can also result in the remaining members of minorities becoming more vulnerable to xenophobia. The government seeks to guarantee minority rights protection and to create a more inclusive civil society, although deteriorating economic conditions and widespread intolerance make this difficult. The tendency of European minorities to emigrate looks set to continue. Russians and Ukrainians are likely to view positively their prospects in their respective homelands, which currently appear more attractive than remaining in Kyrgyzstan, especially for younger generations. However, Slavic communities are still receptive to efforts to secure their future in Kyrgyzstan. Uzbeks potentially constitute a greater problem. If tensions arise again in the Fergana valley, they could demand a redesignation of borders to enable them to join Uzbekistan. The situation of Tajiks is also problematic, because the Tajik–Kyrgyz border is not yet well defined. Unregulated migrations of Uighurs, Xinjiang Kyrgyz and Han Chinese across the Chinese border could result in an aggravation of relations with China.

Further reading

Akiner, S., *Central Asia*, London, MRG report, 1997.

Kangas, R., 'The state and civil society in Central Asia: the role of ethnic minorities', paper presented at the International Studies Association Conference, Chicago, IL, February 1995.

Rashid, A., *The Resurgence of Central Asia*, London, Zed, 1994.

Szajkowski, B., *Encyclopaedia of Conflicts, Disputes and Flashpoints in Eastern Europe, Russia and the Successor States*, London, Longman, 1993.

Minority-based and advocacy organizations

Human Rights Movement, 2nd Floor, Room 31, 205 Abdymomunova Street, Bishkek 720000, Kyrgyzstan; tel. 7 3312 222 486.

Kyrgyz-American Bureau on Human Rights and Rule of Law, 175 Sovetskaya Street, Bishkek 720011, Kyrgyzstan; tel. 7 3312 265 754, fax 7 3312 263 865.

Slavic Diaspora, 57 Babkina Street, Jalal-Abad 715600, Kyrgyzstan; tel. 7 3312 233 292.

Slavic Foundation, 78 Pushkin Street, Bishkek 720040, Kyrgyzstan; tel. 7 3312 264 312/228 377.

Moldova

Land area:	33,700 sq km
Population:	4.3 million (1989; 4.4 million est. 1992)
Main languages:	Moldovan/Romanian, Russian
Main religions:	Eastern Orthodox Christianity
Main minority groups:	Ukrainians 600,000 (13.9%), Russians 562,000 (13.0%), Gagauz 153,000 (3.5%), Bulgarians 88,000 (2.0%), Jews 66,000 (1.5%), others 71,000 (1.6%)[1]
Real per capita GDP:	$2,370
UNDP HDI/rank:	0.663 (98)

The Republic of Moldova, formerly the Moldavian Soviet Socialist Republic (MSSR), is situated between Ukraine to the north, east and south, and Romania to the west. At the heart of contemporary minority problems are the different relationships that developed between Moldova's ethnic groups under the various empires that have controlled the region – the Ottoman Empire, the Russian Empire and the Soviet Union. The legacy of external control for Moldova is a society arranged around a complex series of loosely interconnected socioeconomic, political and ethno-territorial subsystems often organized on the basis of divergent sets of interests. Of central importance is the different imperial history experienced by the peoples living in the Moldovan territories east of the Dniester river and those to the west.

Prior to the collapse of the Soviet Union, the left bank of the Dniester river had enjoyed almost uninterrupted links to Moscow for nearly 200 years and the region had only intermittently experienced Romanian rule. In 1791 (Treaty of Jassy), the eastern lands were absorbed into the Russian Empire. After a brief period of autonomy following the Russian Revolution, the left bank territories were joined to the Soviet Union in 1922, and on 12 October 1924 the Ukrainian government established the Moldavian Autonomous Soviet Socialist Republic (MASSR) in the area between the left bank of the river Dniester and the southern Bug river, known as the Transdniester region. Tiraspol became the capital of this new political entity, which then formed the border between the Soviet Union and Romania.

The western lands of Moldova have enjoyed a very different relationship to Moscow. Only in 1812 was Bessarabia – the historical territory located between the rivers Dniester, Prut and Danube – annexed to Russia. The absorption of Bessarabia led to a flood of Slavic migrants to the region, as well as Romanian-speakers from beyond the Prut, Gagauz and Bulgarians. The region remained part of the Russian Empire for over 100 years but after 1918 Bessarabia was joined to Romania and remained under Bucharest's rule until 1940.

In the summer of 1940, the Soviet Union annexed Bessarabia. Subsequently overrun by Axis forces, in 1944 the area was reconquered by the Red Army. The bulk of Bessarabia was united with the territories of the MASSR (the Bukovina region in the north and Budjak in the south were given to Ukraine) to form the MSSR. Chisinau (Kishinev in Russian) became the capital. The lack of indigenous communists in Bessarabia, especially in rural areas, meant that the extension of Soviet power in the region had to rely upon personnel from the former MASSR. Thus, the postwar order in Moldavia was constructed on a system of institutionalized advantage for the Moscow-oriented east bank territories.

In the 1950s and 1960s, rapid industrialization brought a steady flow of Sovietized Slavs to the region. The new settlers were concentrated in the industrial centres, particularly the Transdniester region. By 1989, ethnic Russians constituted 27 per cent of the republic's urban population and only 4 per cent of rural dwellers.

During the Soviet period, strenuous efforts were made to foster a local identity, separate from a Romanian one, among the Bessarabians. The indigenous population was required to identify itself as Moldavian and a Cyrillic script was introduced in 1940 to distinguish the Moldavian language from Romanian. The issue of Romanian/Moldovan identity, especially the language question, became the initial focus of protest groups in the late 1980s.

The perestroika period

The Popular Front of Moldova (PFM) campaigned for independence and a shift to the promotion of Romanian/Moldovan culture and language. As the drive for independence accelerated, a radical pan-Romanian movement of largely ethnically Moldovan organizations took control of the PFM. Its aim was the 'restitution of the unitary Romanian state'. Unification with Romania rapidly became the leitmotif of the Popular Front.

Moves to raise the numbers of ethnic Moldovans in the state apparatus and expand the use of the Romanian/Moldovan language intensified. The new language law (31 August 1989) downgraded Russian to 'the language of inter-ethnic communication' and Moldovan became the state language. At the same time, plans were announced to replace the Cyrillic script with a Latin one. The position of the radicals was strengthened by success in the February-March 1990 parliamentary elections.

These changes, particularly those involving language, caused alarm among Russian-speakers, especially those in the Transdniester region. The language law provided the catalyst for the creation of opposition organizations among the non-Moldovans, of which the leading ones were: the Unity Internationalist Movement in Defence of *Perestroika* (Interfront) in Chisinau, the United Council of Work Collectives (OSTK) in towns in eastern Moldova, and the Gagauz Halki in Gagauzia.

Independence and civil war

After independence (27 August 1991), the Moldovan Communist Party was banned, permitting radical elements in the PFM to dominate republican politics. Efforts at Romanianization and the campaign for unification with Romania were intensified. Following Chisinau's declaration of independence, the authorities in Tiraspol announced independence for the east bank region of the Dniester (originally termed the Transdniester Moldovan Soviet Socialist Republic, and since October 1991 the Transdniester Moldovan Republic or PMR), and the Gagauz authorities also established their own republic.

Skirmishes between paramilitary groups from these two regions and Moldovan security forces escalated in 1992 and eventually led to conflict in the summer between the forces loyal to Chisinau and to Tiraspol. Several hundred people were killed. Fighting halted with the intervention of the Russian Fourteenth Army, which was permanently based in the region. The ceasefire negotiated in August 1992 established Russian peacekeeping forces in the region.

A new national identity

The fighting in 1992 led to important political changes in Moldova. The coalition government that assumed power in July 1992 presented itself as a government of national consensus. It pledged to act on behalf of all of the population and to observe the civil/political rights of all persons regardless of nationality. The drive for unification with Romania was halted and efforts to Romanianize society slowed. The triumph of the Agrarian Democratic Party (ADP) in the parliamentary elections of early 1994 reinforced the movement to develop a Moldova separate from Romania. The new constitution (1994) implicitly defined Moldovans as a people distinct from Romanians and Moldova as a multi-ethnic society.

The new correlation of political forces within Moldova following the fighting in 1992 allowed the ethno-political problems of the Gagauz region and the PMR to be addressed. Talks on autonomy for the Gagauz gathered pace from 1994 and led to the creation of a self-governing Gagauz region in early 1995. The complex ethnic mix of the PMR prevented a similar ethno-territorially defined autonomy being offered to the area, although various forms of regional autonomy were put forward by the Moldovan authorities. The continuing presence of the Russian army in the region provided a barrier to reintegrating the PMR into Moldova.

Ukrainians

Although Ukrainian settlement of Moldova predates that by Russians, and Ukrainians outnumber Russians, Moldovan Ukrainians have been heavily Russified, especially in urban areas. Many speak Russian as their first language (37 per cent). Most Ukrainians have lined up with the Russians to oppose changes in language and unification with Romania. The Moldovan government has made some efforts to encourage Ukrainian culture, schools and clubs, measures in part designed to split the 'Russian' bloc. The Ukrainian government has sought to promote cultural and language activities among Ukrainians in Moldova.

Almost half of the Ukrainians in Moldova live within the area of the PMR. The large number of rural Ukrainians in the region who speak Ukrainian as their first language has meant that, unlike the right bank, a Ukrainian identity separate from that of the Russian-speakers in Tiraspol has been preserved. However, even here 37 per cent of Ukrainians speak Russian as their native language (1979) and 80 per cent as their second language.

Russians and Russian-speakers

The development of sizeable Russian settlement in the region dates from Russia's annexation of Bessarabia at the beginning of the nineteenth century. The rapid urbanization and industrialization of Moldova from the 1950s to the 1980s marked the most significant period for Russian migration to Moldova. Between 1959 and 1989 Russians increased from 292,000 (10.2 per cent of the population) to 562,000 (13 per cent). By the 1990s, nearly two-thirds of the Russian population in Moldova consisted of recent migrants or their children. The Russians were concentrated in urban areas, particularly the capital and Tiraspol, and enjoyed disproportionately high levels of education.

The relatively small percentage of Russians in Moldova belies the influence of Russian language and culture, which for almost two centuries played a leading role in Bessarabia and the Transdniester region, especially following Soviet annexation. A Cyrillic script was introduced for the Moldovan language and Russian was taught in all schools. In the postwar period, knowledge of Russian was a necessity for almost all of the adult population. The influx of Russian-speaking settlers further strengthened the position of Russian in the republic.

The centrality accorded to Russian ensured that a reactive ethno-linguistic nationalism developed among Russian-speakers – a sociological category embracing Russians, Ukrainians, as well as the Gagauz and Bulgarians, for whom Russian was important as a second language, and Russian-speaking Moldovans, especially in the Transdniester region – in response to efforts to promote Romanian/Moldovan. These groups share a set of common interests – primarily employment in the state sector and education opportunities – built around their knowledge of Russian and threatened by the new language law.

As fears of Romanianization grew, the Interfront emerged as the leading political organization of the Russian-speakers. In the parliamentary elections of 1994, the Interfront (renamed Unity and in alliance with the Socialist Party) was second only to the ADP and formed an informal coalition with the Agrarians to support legislation that promoted a multi-ethnic Moldovan national identity. Unlike the main political organizations representing the Russian-speakers, which were built on Soviet or pro-Soviet institutions, the cultural organizations that have emerged in Moldova have sought to promote new identities, either an ethnic one (the Russian Cultural Centre) or a Slavic one (the Society of Slavic Letters).

Transdniester

On 2 September 1990 the authorities in Tiraspol announced the creation of the PMR based on the left bank of the Dniester river and the city of Bendery, located on the right bank. Ethnic Russians form the fourth largest ethnic group in the PMR (population 601,660 of which 39 per cent are Moldovans, 26 per cent Ukrainians and 24 per cent Russians). Nevertheless, Russian-speakers dominate the area and 41 per cent of Tiraspol's population are ethnic Russians.

In 1992 fighting between PMR and Moldovan forces erupted as a result of fears about the prospects for the Russian language in a Moldova that appeared to be moving towards unification with Romania. Language rather than ethnicity became the defining element in this struggle and Russian-speaking ethnic Moldovans found leading positions in the PMR government. Since 1992, the use of Romanian/ Moldovan has been severely curtailed in the PMR.

The Tiraspol authorities demanded that the

PMR be granted the status of a state within a Moldovan confederation. In response, Chisinau proposed regional autonomy for the PMR with power distributed along similar lines to the Gagauz agreement. Tiraspol's negotiating position was enhanced by the presence of the Russian Fourteenth Army in the region. The agreement to withdraw the army (signed October 1994) caused considerable alarm in the PMR. A referendum on the future of the army organized by the Tiraspol authorities (26 March 1995) found over 90 per cent of those who voted were against withdrawal.

Gagauz

The Gagauz are either Christianized and Bulgarianized Turks or linguistically Turkicized Christian Bulgarians; they speak the north-western dialect of Turkish with many Slavic, particularly Bulgarian and lately Russian, additions. The Gagauz claim that they migrated to Bessarabia in the late eighteenth and early nineteenth century. Only a handful now remain in their original area of settlement, the western shores of the Black Sea (Romania and Bulgaria). With the annexation of Bessarabia to Russia, the Gagauz settled in southern Bessarabia as privileged colonists.

Following the Soviet annexation of Bessarabia in 1940, the Gagauz populated areas were divided between the Moldavian and the Ukrainian SSRs. The Gagauz populate some of the poorest areas of Moldova. Under Soviet rule, the Gagauz were subject to Russification with the Cyrillic script introduced in 1957 and Russian taught in schools from the late 1950s. Some 73 per cent of Gagauz consider Russian to be their second language, and most of the political elite are Russian-speakers.

Within the Soviet Union, the Gagauz was the largest Turkic population not to have its own territorial formation. Throughout the Soviet period, ethnic awareness remained weakly developed among the Gagauz. This situation changed rapidly in the late 1980s as fear of Romanianization spread. Although the 1989 language law permitted the use of Gagauz, strikes against the elevation of Moldovan to the status of state language took place in Gagauz areas. In response to the Moldovan declaration of sovereignty, the authorities in Komrat, the administrative centre of the Gagauz region, announced the creation of the Gagauz Soviet Socialist Republic.

Gagauz actions led to a period of dual power in the region. During 1992–3, Gagauz paramilitary units intermittently clashed with Moldovan local authorities, but the Gagauz stayed out of the Dniester conflict. Nevertheless, Komrat worked in tandem with Tiraspol to promote the idea of developing Moldova as a confederation of three states. As 70 per cent of the world's Gagauz live in Moldova, the Gagauz do not consider themselves a national minority but rather a people with a right to a national territory. The Turkish mission in Moldova has supported the more moderate idea of autonomy for the Gagauz within the context of a united Moldova.

In February 1994, the Gagauz agreed to abandon their aim of confederation and to participate in parliamentary elections in return for support for Gagauz demands for autonomy. The Gagauz areas cast their vote for the Unity-Socialist alliance – the Russian-speakers' bloc. In July 1994, a new Moldovan constitution was approved with an article guaranteeing autonomy for the Gagauz-inhabited districts.

In December 1994 the law 'On The Special Legal Status of *Gagauz Yeri* (land)/Gagauzia' was passed. The preamble of the law recognizes the Gagauz as a 'people' – not an ethnic group or ethnic population, as Soviet theory had indicated – and recognizes their right to self-determination within Moldova. The initiative combines two principles: it links nationality as a corporate body to a specific territory and a notion of constitutional guarantees, devolution of powers, representative institutions, checks and balances. The law also allows Gagauz self-determination if Moldova should change its status as an independent state.

Under the terms of the law, the Gagauz autonomous region is to have its own legislature – the *Halk Toplusu*, elected for four years – and executive authorities – a chief executive (*Baskan*), to hold the *ex officio* position of a deputy prime minister of Moldova – both exercising substantial devolved powers; and three official languages – Gagauz, Moldovan, and Russian. Gagauzia is to have its own judicial, police and security bodies under shared regional and central jurisdiction. The central authorities retain sovereignty over citizenship, finance, defence and foreign policy.

On 5 March 1995 a referendum to determine the boundaries of the *Gagauz Yeri*/Gagauzia was conducted. On 28 May 1995 an election for the Gagauz *Baskan*, and the Popular Assembly and a referendum to determine the administrative centre of the region (Komrat) were held.

Bulgarians

Bulgarians live in the rural south of Moldova. Like the Gagauz, they arrived in Bessarabia in the eighteenth and early nineteenth centuries seeking refuge from Ottoman persecution. Subsequently, many assimilated to Russian culture and the remainder are highly Russified; although 79 per cent of Moldovan Bulgarians claim Bulgarian as their first language, 68 per cent identify Russian as their second language. Since 1991, Bulgarian has become a language of instruction in schools situated in areas of compact Bulgarian settlement. From the late 1980s, Moldovan Bulgarians have established links to Bulgaria.

Jews

Within the Russian Empire, Chisinau and the surrounding area were designated part of the Pale of Settlement and had a thriving Yiddish-speaking community. In 1897 Jews made up 12 per cent of Bessarabia's population. Nazi genocide, war and emigration had reduced numbers to 65,700 (1.5 per cent) by 1989. Since the late 1980s, sizeable numbers of Jews have emigrated. Most Jews are native Russian-speakers (73 per cent), living in urban areas. Within the Russian-speaking community, anti-Semitism has appeared among more extreme Russian nationalists. At the same time, there has been a religious revival and a chief rabbi has been appointed to Chisinau.

Conclusions and future prospects

Since the conflict of 1992, the Moldovan government has sought to ensure the well-being of minorities. Even before the fighting, Moldova had adopted a liberal Citizenship Law (5 June 1991) granting automatic citizenship to those who had held it before 28 June 1940 and to all residents registered before 23 June 1990. Following the fighting of 1992, the Chisinau authorities developed the twin-track strategy of granting cultural autonomy to all minorities (a law on minorities was passed in 1994) and offering territorial autonomy to special-status regions. Underlying these policies is the belief that accommodation can win the loyalty of non-ethnic Moldovan citizens and thereby reinforce the state's territorial integrity. The central puzzle remains the status of Transdniester, a question that can only be solved in the broader context of relations with Russia.

Although powerful political forces have emerged since 1992 in support of the development of an ethnically inclusive non-Romanian identity, the nature of the Moldovan nation remains contested and subject to political manipulation. In March 1995, large student demonstrations occurred following a decision to teach 'Moldovan' rather than 'Romanian' national history and to call for the state language to be renamed Romanian instead of Moldovan. In summer 1995, President Snegur repudiated many elements of the distinct Moldovan identity and sought to reintroduce a Romanian definition of Moldova's language and people. Prior to the presidential elections of November 1996, the question of Moldovan identity became an important issue in the political campaign. The Moldovan parliament has, however, resisted President Snegur's attempts to reopen the debate about the relationship between Moldova and Romania. The bitter experience of fighting in 1992 suggests that politicians will exercise caution in regard to minority questions in the future.

Further reading

Chinn, J. and Roper, S.D., 'Ethnic mobilization and reactive nationalism: the case of Moldova', *Nationalities Papers*, vol. 23, no. 2, 1995, pp. 291–325.

Dailey, E., *Human Rights in Moldova: The Turbulent Dniester*, New York, Human Rights Watch, 1993.

Fane, D., 'Moldova: breaking loose from Moscow', in I. Bremmer and R. Taras (eds), *Nations and Politics in the Soviet Successor States*, Cambridge, Cambridge University Press, 1993, pp. 121–53.

King, C., 'Moldovan identity and the politics of pan-Romanianism', *Slavic Review*, vol. 53, no. 2, 1994, pp. 345–68.

Minority-based and advocacy organizations

Chisinau Human Rights and Historical Society 'Memorial', Taylor Street 4, Chisinau 277043, Moldova; tel. 373 0422 227 010, fax 373 0422 232 830.

Helsinki Citizens' Assembly in Moldova, Taylor Street 4, Chisinau 277043, Moldova; tel. 373 0422 227 010, fax 373 0422 232 830.

Joint Committee for Conciliation and Democratization, Botanica Veche Street 6, Apt 103, Chisinau 277062, Moldova; tel./fax 373 0422 540 751.

Russian Federation

Land area:	17,100,000 sq km
Population:	148.5 million (1989; 148.1 million est. 1992)
Main languages:	Russian
Main religions:	Eastern Orthodox Christianity, Islam, Buddhism, Shamanism
Main minority groups:	Tatars 5,522,000 (3.7%), Ukrainians 4,363,000 (2.9%), Chuvash 1,774,000 (1.2%), Bashkirs 1,345,000 (0.9%), Belarusians 1,206,000 (0.8%), Mordovans 1,073,000 (0.7%), Chechens 899,000 (0.6%), Germans 842,000 (0.6%), others 7,762,000 (5.2%)
Real per capita GDP:	$4,760
UNDP HDI/rank:	0.804 (57)

The Russian Federation, formerly the Russian Soviet Federated Socialist Republic (RSFSR), stretches from Ukraine, Belarus and the Baltic states in the west, to the Pacific coast in the east and from Finland and the Arctic Sea in the north to the Caucasus, Central Asia and China in the south. The disintegration of the Soviet order, coupled with the radical political, economic and social reforms instituted in Russia since the late 1980s, has exacerbated inter-ethnic tensions and highlighted the complex ethno-political inheritance from the Russo-Soviet imperial order. The principal legacy of this earlier period is an intricately interwoven set of ethno-territorial units, sizeable minorities outside or lacking their own 'homeland' and significant populations opposed to rule from Moscow. Since independence, minority communities have had simultaneously to redefine their relationship with Moscow and begin to come to terms with the Russian colonial past. Negotiating the process of building a new multi-ethnic, multicultural Russia has generated a wide variety of problems and, on occasion, violence.

Russia before Peter the Great was constituted by a core of several medieval principalities united under Moscow's control. The majority of the population in this early Russia was ethnically homogeneous, being primarily Slavs. However, as the borders of the Russian Empire were pushed ever wider, the ethnic balance was disturbed. In the sixteenth and seventeenth centuries the conquest of Siberia brought new communities under Russian control. The conquest of the Caucasus region in the nineteenth century, accompanied by the incorporation of a variety of Central Asian populations, further shifted the ethnic composition of the empire. By the end of the nineteenth century, the expansion of the Russian Empire had brought several hundred different ethnic communities and a variety of religious minorities under Russian control.

Although annexation to Russia marked the end of independence for the conquered peoples, initially little was done to extinguish their separate identity. Indeed, provided these groups were prepared to accept a degree of assimilation to Russian values, representatives of the minority communities could advance to high positions within the imperial order. From the middle of the nineteenth century, however, the processes of urbanization, industrialization and the migration of Russians to the new 'Russian lands' gathered pace. For the first time, local identities and ways of life faced a serious challenge.

In the 1830s, the Russian authorities began to promote Russification and conversion to Orthodoxy, especially among Muslim Tatars. This initial drive led to civil unrest and the policy was moderated. Towards the end of the nineteenth century, however, Russification was again pursued, although, at this stage, the idea of creating a specifically ethnically Russian order was balanced by the aim of building a powerful imperial state.

Growing national sentiment among many of the minority populations in the Russian Empire was accelerated by the collapse of the tsarist order in 1917. In the civil war that followed, the Bolsheviks developed a pact with leading ethnic groups that offered these groups territorial advantages in return for their allegiance. With the eventual triumph of the Soviet forces, the practice of granting ethno-territorial autonomy to leading ethnic groups was institutionalized as an organizing principle of the Soviet state.

In 1918, the predominantly ethnic Russian core territories of the Russian Empire were reconstituted as the Russian Soviet Federated Socialist Republic. Within the RSFSR a wide variety of groups were awarded some level of territorial autonomy, marking an important distinction from the imperial administrative structure. In place of the pre-revolutionary arrangement of provinces (*guberniya*), the Soviets introduced an administrative system built around a structural asymmetry based on ethnicity. Although this system underwent a prolonged evolution, ethnicity remained a central principle at the heart of the Russian administrative order. By the 1980s, the RSFSR was organized into 88 administrative components (subjects) of higher than city and district level. These subjects were divided into two categories.

First, ethno-territorial units: 16 autonomous Soviet socialist republics (ASSRs) – based around sizeable non-Russian ethnic groups and considered the embodiment of the national statehood of their titular populations; 5 autonomous *oblasts* (regions) (AOs) – smaller ethnic-based units; 10 autonomous *okrugs* (districts) (AOks) – the lowest level ethnic units, situated within an *oblast* or *krai* (province). Second, the remaining areas of the RSFSR, comprising most of its constituent members and accounting for about 70 per cent of its territory and more than 80 per cent of the population, was divided into territorial formations: 6 *krais* (mostly large and lightly populated areas), and 49 *oblasts* – largely ethnically homogeneous, Russian-populated districts. In addition, Moscow and Leningrad (now St Petersburg) were given a status broadly equivalent to that of an *oblast*.

Despite the fact that the Soviet constitution accorded Russia the status of a federation, the federal structure of the RSFSR was largely a fiction. Regional and minority interests were subordinated to the security, economic and diplomatic concerns of the Soviet government. Steps were taken to ensure that the ethno-territorial units did not develop as centres for nationalism.

A wide variety of minority populations were subject to deportations – notably peoples of the North Caucasus and Volga Germans – and to forced assimilation to the prevailing Russo-Soviet culture. From the 1930s, teaching of Russian became compulsory and many native languages disappeared from schools. The migration of Russian-speaking Slavs to the previously non-Russified regions reinforced the process of Russification.

Despite these measures, from the 1960s a growing ethnic and then national awareness came to characterize many of the minorities in the RSFSR. The emergence of indigenous political and cultural elites within many of the minority territories during Leonid Brezhnev's tenure as General Secretary of the Communist Party further accelerated these developments. In the 1980s, the combination of growing nationalist sentiment, the emergence of a reformist General Secretary (Mikhail Gorbachev), and the ethno-territorial arrangement of the Russian Federation provided the conditions for minority issues to assume central significance in the RSFSR.

The perestroika period

Under Gorbachev, rising ethnic tension on the periphery of the Soviet Union was accompanied by increasing tension in the RSFSR itself. In the latter years of *perestroika*, the nominally federal structure of the RSFSR assumed a real significance for the conduct of domestic politics. Following the elections for the Russian Supreme Soviet in 1990, a strong movement for increased regional powers, built on an alliance between regional economic interests and local nationalist groups, developed in the ethnic territories, especially the ASSRs.

Emboldened by the new freedoms of the period, this movement was further encouraged by the struggle for power between Gorbachev and Boris Yeltsin. Russian democrats saw the haemorrhage of power to the regions as a means to undermine further Gorbachev's position. As a result, substantial autonomy was granted to the republics by Yeltsin and the Russian Parliament. In a speech in Kazan, the capital of Tatarstan, in September 1990 Yeltsin called on the republics to 'take as much independence as you can handle'.

Gorbachev, too, sought to use the republics, but his plan was to enlist them against the Russian democrats and thereby prevent the disintegration of the Union. In the All-Union Law on the Delimitation of Powers between the Soviet Union and the Subjects of the Federation (26 April 1990) the ASSRs, like the Union republics, were described as 'subjects of the federation'. The first draft of the Union treaty (November 1990) put the ASSRs on a par with the Union republics – both were described as republics and as sovereign states.

The opportunity for increased autonomy created by the political struggle at the centre accelerated moves to assert local control. The drive for greater autonomy was led by the ethnic republics, particularly Tatarstan, with Bashkortostan and Sakha-Yakutia close behind. In summer/autumn 1990, following the Russian Declaration of

Sovereignty, a number of the ethnic republics adopted declarations of sovereignty. The extent of powers claimed in these declarations varied considerably, with Karelia acknowledging that some powers would be delegated to the RSFSR and to the Soviet Union and Tatarstan adopting a declaration that failed to mention the RSFSR at all.

Russian independence

The collapse of the Soviet Union at the end of 1991 marked a new phase in the development of the minorities issue in Russia. The final demise of the Soviet system led to the creation of a new Russia but this was not a nation state, rather a multi-ethnic, multi-religious and multicultural state. Since independence, Russians and minority populations have faced two principal and inter-related challenges.

First, the position of ethnic Russians, Russian culture and history, and the Russian language in the new Russia must be determined. In the late 1980s, while powerful ethno-national popular fronts emerged in the Union republics, the multi-ethnic nature of Russia militated against this in the RSFSR. Instead, a Russian democratic movement was formed around a civic notion of Russia. After independence, growing ethno-nationalism induced the disintegration of the democratic movement. Determining the nature of Russian national identity – whether it is to be centred on ethnic Russians or incorporate the diversity of peoples and cultures of the Russian Federation (RF) – has become one of the central issues in Russian politics.

Second, due to the link between territory and political/economic rights that developed in the late 1980s, the administrative arrangement of the RF has become extremely important. The contradiction between the Kremlin's desire to maintain dominance over the regions and the wish of many of the minorities for autonomy or even independence has fostered a power struggle heavily informed by ethnicity between federal and regional authorities. The issue of who has a right to an ethnic territory and the rights and obligations of these regions has become a dominant theme in Russia.

In response to these challenges, a formal constitutional process has developed to try to remake Russia and to define the position of the minority populations. This process has involved changes in the rights of some ethnic territories and peoples, the negotiation of a federation treaty, the April 1993 referendum and December 1993 parliamentary elections and a new constitution, and the negotiation of a series of bilateral agreements between Moscow and the republics. Change has also involved large-scale migration and bloody conflict.

Forging a new Russia

Since independence the central authorities have been committed to the idea of moving the foundation of the federation onto a territorial, rather than ethno-territorial, basis. However, the conflict between the executive and the legislature in Moscow from early in 1992 initially encouraged a further disintegration of the federation. Both branches of central government offered increased rights to the regions in return for their support.

The first autonomous republic to challenge Moscow was Chechen-Ingushetia. In November 1991, the leadership of the republic declared independence from Russia and immediately set about consolidating its independence and securing international economic and political support.

As the drive for autonomy gathered pace in the RF, the fight for ethnic territories became more intense, particularly in the North Caucasus. In early 1992, following failure over Chechnia, which had separated from Ingushetia, and as other republics pushed for increased rights *vis-à-vis* the centre, Moscow began to campaign for the implementation of a new federation treaty. In negotiations, the ethnic republics proved the most intransigent and the central authorities eventually gave in to a number of their demands; in particular, in the treaty the republics were described as 'sovereign' republics within the Russian Federation.

In its final form, the federation treaty consisted of three sets of agreements reflecting the unequal distribution of power between levels of administrative units. Each agreement outlined a different distribution of power between Moscow and the regions, with the ethnic republics receiving the greatest autonomy. At the end of March 1992, the treaty was signed by all the subjects of the Russian Federation, except Chechnia, Ingushetia and Tatarstan.

Overall, the new federation treaty did little to clarify the division of powers between the centre and the regions. The delegations from the republics of Bashkortostan, Karelia and Sakha only agreed to the treaty when President Yeltsin and Ruslan Khasbulatov, Speaker of the Supreme Soviet, signed bilateral addenda granting them additional rights.

By January 1993, the politics of ethno-regionalism had produced a situation in which the Russian central authorities had recognized the special nature of most ethnic-based administrative units within the RF and had given some of the AOs the status of republics. Republican status had been reached by 21 units, leaving 6 *krais*, 49 *oblasts*, 1 autonomous *oblast* and 10 autonomous *okrugs*. Of the 21 republics, 17 had formerly been ASSRs (Chechen-Ingushetia was divided) and 4 were former AOs once attached to *krais* (Altai from Altai *Krai*, Karachai-Cherkess from Stavropol *Krai*, Khakassia from Krasnoiarsk *Krai* and Adygei from Krasnodar *Krai*) which had been elevated to republic status.

Prior to 1993, Yeltsin and his team had, at best, a poorly developed nationalities/regional policy for Russia. Following fighting between North Ossetians and Ingush (November 1992), the first signs of a change at the centre began to emerge. Sergei Shakhrai, a specialist on ethnic issues, was placed in charge of regional and nationalities policy and a more directed and coordinated policy began to develop. In April 1994, a decree established the Ministry of Nationalities and Regional Policy. The foundation of this new approach was to be a new Russian constitution. In early 1993, when a Constitutional Assembly convened to work out the final draft of the new constitution, one of the central issues was the distribution of powers between the centre and the regions.

President Yeltsin's decision to abolish the Russian Supreme Soviet in October 1993 halted, at least temporarily, regional challenges to central authority. Following the use of force against the White House, Yeltsin moved against the regions, disbanding the local soviets and transferring power to the head of the local administration. The system of executive power was then used to generate support for the new Russian constitution, which was meant to institutionalize a shift in power from the regions back to the centre.

The constitution, which was adopted in December 1993, contained important changes from the draft produced by the Constitutional Assembly in the summer. The principle of equality for all regions, which aimed to stem the disproportionate drift of power to the ethnic republics, was established. At the same time, the non-ethnic Russian character of the federation was acknowledged (sovereignty was located in the 'multinational people of the RF'). The constitution also guaranteed the language rights of the non-Russian populations, thereby reinforcing the Declaration on the Languages of the Peoples of Russia (25 October 1991), which granted all peoples the choice for their language of education and upbringing. However, the previously guaranteed position of minority representatives in the legislature was ended when the Council of Nationalities was replaced by an upper chamber with each subject of the federation electing two representatives. (See Figure 1, p. 298.)

In fact, the new constitution failed to clarify the precise division of powers between the federal centre and the provinces. Despite the equality among the subjects of the federation institutionalized in the constitution and the apparently clear delimitation of authority, relations between the centre and the regions continued to be characterized by a struggle for power. This situation led Moscow and some of the republics to conclude bilateral treaties. The first treaty to delineate responsibilities and powers between the federal and republican authorities was signed with Tatarstan in 1994 and has been followed by treaties with other republics. Following treaties with the republics, Moscow has concluded bilateral agreements with many of the *oblasts*.

While the struggle for power between the ethnic republics and Moscow has been taking place, there has also been a general revival of the linguistic, cultural and ethnic practices of minority populations in the RF. Religious organizations from all of the main minority groups have also emerged. A relationship of 'confessional coexistence' has developed between the Russian Orthodox Church and many of the other faiths of the RF. Some sections of the Orthodox movement have, however, called for the prohibition of 'non-traditional religions' such as Mormons, Hare Krishna and Protestant groups and have promoted anti-Semitism.

The ambiguous, and often contradictory, rights allocated to the ethnic republics in the main agreements regulating centre–regional relations have further reinforced the pyramid of inequality which has developed among the minorities in the RF. Those minorities with their own officially recognized territory ('homeland') usually enjoy considerable advantages over the other minority populations in the RF. However, the titular groups of autonomous areas with high concentrations of Slavic settlers have often faced problems similar to those of minorities lacking a formal homeland.

MINORITIES WITH AN OFFICIAL RECOGNIZED HOMELAND

Minorities that have been granted territorial recognition can be broadly divided into two

Figure 1: The New Political System of the Russian Federation

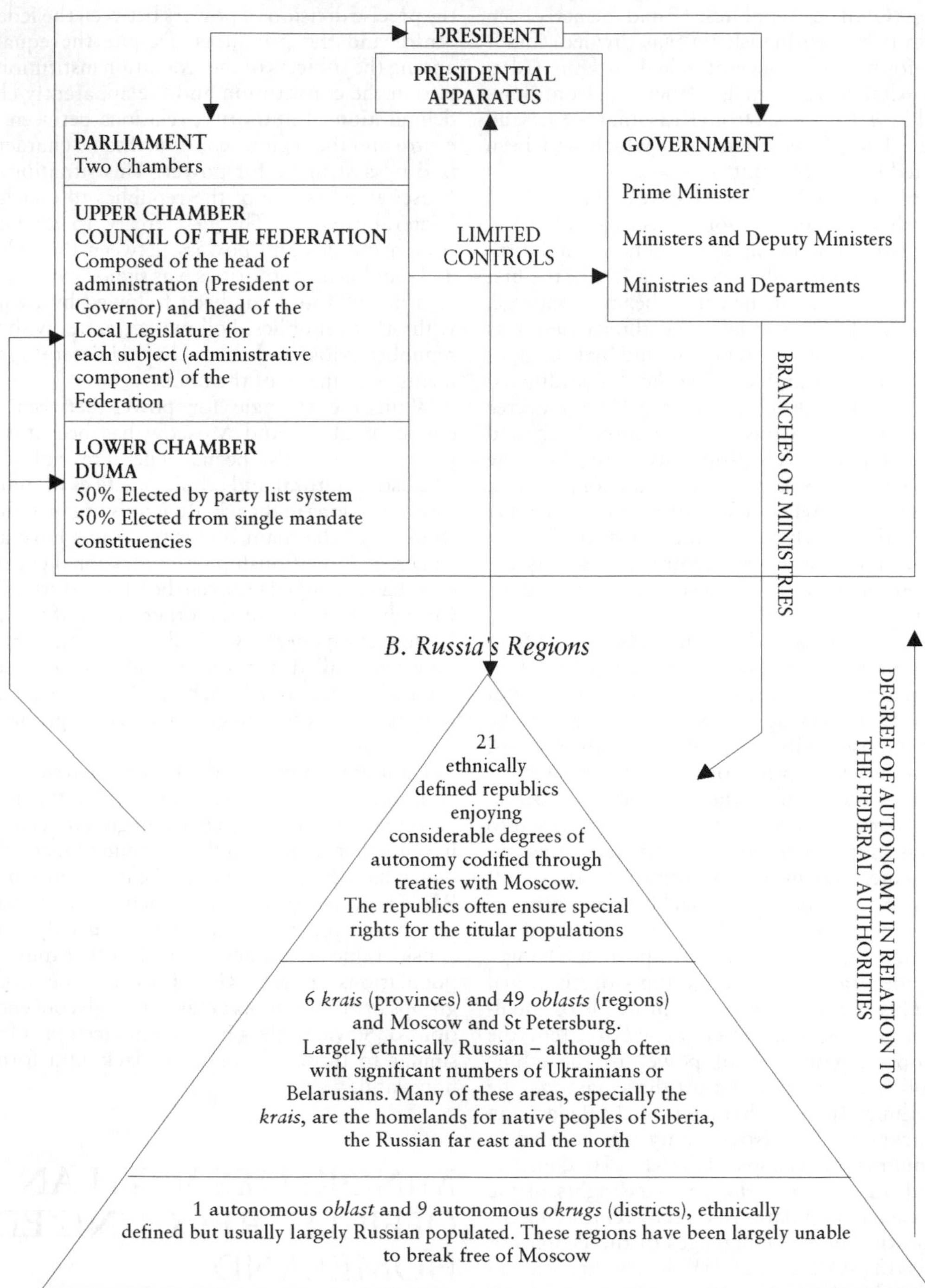
A. Political Centre
PRESIDENT
PRESIDENTIAL APPARATUS
PARLIAMENT
Two Chambers
UPPER CHAMBER
COUNCIL OF THE FEDERATION
Composed of the head of administration (President or Governor) and head of the Local Legislature for each subject (administrative component) of the Federation
LOWER CHAMBER
DUMA
50% Elected by party list system
50% Elected from single mandate constituencies
LIMITED CONTROLS
GOVERNMENT
Prime Minister
Ministers and Deputy Ministers
Ministries and Departments
BRANCHES OF MINISTRIES
B. Russia's Regions
21 ethnically defined republics enjoying considerable degrees of autonomy codified through treaties with Moscow. The republics often ensure special rights for the titular populations
6 krais (provinces) and 49 oblasts (regions) and Moscow and St Petersburg. Largely ethnically Russian – although often with significant numbers of Ukrainians or Belarusians. Many of these areas, especially the krais, are the homelands for native peoples of Siberia, the Russian far east and the north
1 autonomous oblast and 9 autonomous okrugs (districts), ethnically defined but usually largely Russian populated. These regions have been largely unable to break free of Moscow
DEGREE OF AUTONOMY IN RELATION TO THE FEDERAL AUTHORITIES

categories: religious and linguistic minorities. This distinction does not reflect any official division between groups based on religion or language, but rather the primary element around which group self-identity is formed in each case.

RELIGIOUSLY DEFINED GROUPS

Religiously defined groups form the largest set of minorities.

Buddhists: *Buriats, Kalmyks, Tuvans*

The RF contains a number of Buddhist groups, mostly of the Lamaist faith. Since the late 1980s, there has been a strong revival of Buddhism.

Buriats

Along with the Kalmyks, the Buriats (417,000) speak a Mongolic language. The Buriats are concentrated in the Buriat Republic (pop. 1,038,252: Buriats 25 per cent, Russians 70 per cent, Ukrainians 2 per cent, others 3 per cent) as well as Irkutsk *Oblast*, northern Mongolia and north-west China. The Buriat Lamaist church is part of a Buddhist sect which spread from Tibet to Mongolia in the seventeenth and eighteenth centuries. Some Buriats have adopted Eastern Orthodoxy. Although Russians penetrated the Buriat homelands as early as the seventeenth century, contacts between the two peoples remained limited until large-scale Russian migration in the eighteenth century. A Buriat nationalist movement developed at the turn of the century in response to the growing Russian presence. In 1921, a Buriat-Mongol AO was established in the Far Eastern Republic; in May 1923 a Buriat-Mongol Autonomous Republic was created. In May 1923 they were merged to form the Buriat-Mongol ASSR.

In 1937, the Buriat-Mongol ASSR was divided into three units. Territory west of Lake Baikal (12 per cent of the territory) went to Irkutsk *Oblast*, establishing a Buriat enclave (the Ust-Ordynsk AOk); the eastern steppe (12 per cent) was incorporated into Chita *Oblast*, where another enclave (Aginsk AOk) was created. This division of the Buriat lands caused resentment. In 1958, in an attempt to eliminate any link with Mongolia, the word Mongol was dropped from the region's title leaving the Buriat ASSR. Mongolian cultural influence, however, remained powerful and led, at the end of the 1980s, to a revival of Buddhism and Lamaism in the region. A movement for closer links with Mongolia emerged. Together these elements laid the foundations for the declaration of sovereignty for Buriatia. Since the late 1980s, Buriatia has become a centre for Buddhists in the RF with the Central Theological Department of Russian Buddhists located in Ulan-Ude. The Buddhist revival has brought the region into close contact with Mongolia, Tibet and Kalmykia.

A session of the Buriat Parliament in June 1992 declared that the 1937 division of the republic was unconstitutional. The main nationalist organization in the republic, the Buriat-Mongolian Peoples' Party has demanded reunification of all Buriat-Mongolian lands on both sides of the Russian–Mongolian border. Although Buriats are outnumbered by Russians in Ust-Ordynsk AOk (Buriats 36 per cent, Russians 57 per cent) and form only a small majority in Aginsk AOk (Buriats 55 per cent), both regions remain subjects of contention.

Kalmyks

Kalmyks (166,000) are primarily settled in the Kalmyk-Khalmg Tangch Republic, formerly the Kalmyk ASSR (pop. 322,579: Kalmyks 45 per cent, Russians 38 per cent, others 17 per cent), with settlements in the Astrakhan, Rostov and Volgograd *oblasts* and Stavropol *Krai*. Kalmyks lived as nomadic herders in western Mongolia until the early seventeenth century, when they migrated to the northern shores of the Caspian Sea. In 1771, most of the population decided to return to Mongolia. The majority was killed *en route*. One community did not undertake the trek and became part of the Don Cossacks. Kalmyks practise a variety of Tibetan Buddhism strongly influenced by Shamanism and speak a Mongolic language.

In November 1920 the Kalmyk AO was created in the lower Volga region of the RF. In October 1935 the *oblast* was upgraded to the status of an ASSR. In the 1920s and 1930s Buddhist temples and monasteries were destroyed and almost all of the spiritual leaders were arrested. In 1938 the Kalmyk literary language was changed into the Cyrillic script. In 1943 the whole people was deported to Siberia for alleged collaboration. A fifth of the population is thought to have perished during and immediately after deportation. The Kalmyk ASSR was abolished in December 1943. Following Khrushchev's 'secret speech' in 1956, Kalmyks were allowed to return to their homelands. On 9 January 1957, the Presidium of the Soviet Union Supreme Soviet issued a decree re-establishing the Kalmyk AO, which on 29 July regained its former status as an ASSR. Population numbers did not recover to the levels that existed prior to deportation until 1970.

Perestroika led to the emergence of a variety of different political movements in the republic. The Popular Front of Kalmykia was created in 1990. In 1990 the Republic of Kalmykia adopted a Declaration of Sovereignty. There has been no serious inter-ethnic tension registered in Kalmykia. Independence has brought a revival in the study of the Kalmyk language and, with the help of Buddhist monks from abroad, of religious practices. Buddhism and Christianity have been given the status of state religions. The local Supreme Soviet decided in 1992 to change the name of the republic to Khalmg Tangch. In June 1993, the Kalmyk authorities laid claim to the 3,900 square kilometres of the Volga delta that were not returned to Kalmyks when the Kalmyk ASSR was recreated in 1957. The Kalmyk authorities claimed that under the terms of the 1991 Law on the Rehabilitation of Repressed Peoples, the lands, currently in the Astrakhan *Oblast* and Dagestan, would formally belong to Kalmykia with effect from 1 July 1993.

Tuvans

Tuvans (206,000) live primarily in the Tuvan Republic (pop. 308,557: Tuvans 64 per cent, Russians 32 per cent and others 4 per cent) and are primarily pastoralists. Most belong to the Buddhist Lamaist faith. Tuvans are mainly descendants of nomadic groups of Turkified Mongols and speak a Turkic language. Their literary language was converted to a Cyrillic script in 1943. The area was conquered by Russians in the early nineteenth century. Although it retained some degree of autonomy for 23 years after the civil war (as the Tuvan People's Republic), it was effectively a client-state of the Soviet Union from 1921. In October 1944, the area was joined to the Soviet Union. Initially it became the Tuvan *Oblast* but was subsequently upgraded to an ASSR in October 1961. After incorporation into the Soviet Union, Tuva experienced a large influx of Russian settlers, although Tuvans remain in the majority.

Nationalist aspirations were first openly voiced in the area in 1989 when the Tuvan Popular Front was set up and demanded secession from the RF. Other pro-independence parties, including the Peoples' Party of Sovereign Tuva (1992), have been established. In 1993 Tuva's Parliament adopted the right of secession from the RF. However, the republic remains very poor with most of its finance coming from Moscow. After 1990 Tuva became the site for a number of inter-ethnic conflicts related to the higher standard of living enjoyed by Russians living in the republic compared to the Tuvans. Significant numbers of Russians have left the republic in recent years as a result of these conflicts.

Muslims: *Middle Volga and North Caucasus*

The RF contains sizeable Muslim populations, and since the collapse of the Soviet Union there has been a revival of Islam and Muslim culture. Most Muslims are of the Sunni branch of Islam. A number of Muslim political parties have been formed. The territorially based Muslims can be subdivided into two main geographical groups: Tatars and Bashkirs of the Middle Volga, and peoples of the North Caucasus.

Middle Volga Tatars and Bashkirs

Tatars

Tatars (5.5 million) are by far the largest minority in the Russian Federation. The greatest concentration of Tatars is found in Tatarstan (pop. 3,641,742: Tatars 49 per cent, Russians 43 per cent, others 8 per cent) and Bashkortostan (Tatars 1,120,702). The Tatar language belongs to the Turkic branch of the Uralo-Altaic language family. Tatars in the RF are descendants of the Golden Horde, the Turkic tribes led by the Mongols that subjugated Russia from 1237. The end of Tatar-Mongol rule in 1480 and the fall of the two Tatar khanates of Kazan (1552) and Astrakhan (1556) to Ivan IV marked a shift in power to the Russians and away from their former rulers. From this point, the various Tatar areas in the Russian Empire – Crimea, Siberia, and Lithuania – developed separately. Today, these communities retain only the most tenuous links.

In the Russian Empire, the Volga Tatar elite became the leaders of Russian Islam and were used to help incorporate other Muslim areas into the empire. This situation led to the emergence of a prosperous Tatar merchant class, high rates of urbanization, literacy and assimilation, and a mobilized diaspora throughout the empire. Harsh measures were employed against the mass of the Tatar population. Efforts to convert Tatars forcibly from Islam to Christianity were undertaken. Tatars were involved in a number of revolts against Russian domination. Following the Bolshevik Revolution, the Tatars were promised their own republic but the consolidation of Soviet power in the region after fierce fighting led only to the establishment of the Tatar ASSR in May 1920. The borders of the Bashkir and Tatar republics were drawn so that 75 per cent of the Tatar population were left outside the Tatar republic. The fact that Volga Tatars were not granted Union republic status caused resentment among them. During the Soviet years, fear of a 'Tatarization' of neighbouring peoples prompted official support for the languages and cultures of Bashkirs, Chuvash, Komis, Komi-Permiaks, Mordovans, Maris, and Udmurts.

Perestroika helped in the rebirth of Tatar nationalism, which had first flourished during the October Revolution. From the late 1980s, Tatarstan was at the forefront of the movement for regional autonomy. Tatarstan declared sovereignty on 30 August 1990. A referendum held on 21 March 1992 on the transformation of Tatarstan into an independent republic won wide support. The Tatarstan authorities refused to sign the Federation Treaty (March 1992). Particular efforts have been made to build links with the Tatar diaspora. The constitution of 1992 allowed for dual citizenship and for two state languages. In 1992–3 a number of organizations, including the Tatar Public Opinion Centre, demanded outright independence for the republic. The main nationalist drive has not, however, been for full independence but rather for associative membership of the RF. The wide dispersal of Tatars – in 1989 only 32 per cent of Russia's 5.5 million Tatars lived in Tatarstan – prevented Kazan's campaign for power from turning into a struggle for ethnonational liberation. The Tatarstan authorities signed a historic power-sharing agreement with Moscow (15 February 1994) that grants the republic important rights.

Bashkirs

Bashkirs (1.3 million) are the product of an intermingling of Finno-Ugric and Turkic tribes. The majority of Bashkirs live in Bashkortostan (pop. 3,943,113: Bashkirs 22 per cent, Russians 39 per cent, Tatars 28 per cent, others 11 per cent) and they are also found in Cheliabinsk *Oblast* (161,169) and Orenburg *Oblast* (53,339). The Bashkir language is part of the Turkic branch of the Uralo-Altaic language family. The Tatar and the Bashkir peoples are closely related, their languages being similar, but relations between them are often tense. Tatars have traditionally been better educated. With the fall of Kazan in the sixteenth century, Bashkirs also fell under Russian control. Like Tatars, Bashkirs were involved in revolts against Russian rule.

At the time of the Russian Revolution there was a strong Muslim-led nationalist movement among Bashkirs. On 23 March 1918, a Tatar-Bashkir SSR was declared but Bashkirs pressed for their own republic. The Bashkir ASSR was established on 23 March 1919. During the Soviet period, Bashkortostan (then Bashkiria) was industrialized but remained closely ruled by Moscow. In the late 1980s fear of assimilation by Tatars – up to a third of Bashkirs speak Tatar as their native language – helped generate a Bashkir national movement (1988). The first all-Union congress of the Bashkir people was convened in December 1989. However, overall political and economic issues rather than ethno-nationalism have driven politics in the region. The Bashkir authorities declared sovereignty on 11 October 1990 and changed the name from the Russified Bashkiria to Bashkortostan on 25 February 1992.

Tension over the issue of the numerical dominance of Tatars has continued to influence Bashkir demands. A significant number of Bashkirs remain outside the borders of Bashkortostan and Bashkirs make up only the third largest group in the republic. In June 1992, the Tatar National Movement of Bashkortostan demanded that the Tatar language should be given official status, like Bashkir and Russian. The Bashkortostan constitution does not, however, include the right to Tatar, although there are Tatar-language schools in Bashkortostan. Fear of the growing anti-Tatar sentiment among Bashkirs led to calls for the Tatar-populated areas to secede if Bashkortostan became independent. In December 1993 the republic's parliament adopted a constitution that declared the republic a 'sovereign state' and all of its natural resources the property of the multi-ethnic people of Bashkortostan. Bashkortostan signed the Union treaty and in August 1994 negotiated a bilateral treaty with Moscow that gave the republic even more powers than Tatarstan had obtained in its agreement.

Peoples of the North Caucasus

The North Caucasus was annexed by tsarist Russia in the early nineteenth century but not fully pacified until the 1860s. In the twentieth century the region has been subject to a range of turbulent developments ranging from the civil war to deportations (1940s). Since the demise of the Soviet system, the North Caucasus has emerged as the most ethnically volatile region in the RF. The area is riven with territorial and border disputes involving many of the more than 60 distinct national, ethnic and religious groups (Christian and Muslim) in the region. In response to the new challenges that have faced the peoples of the region, a number of initiatives to create organizations to challenge Moscow's control of the region have been launched.

The First Congress of Mountain Peoples of the Caucasus met in August 1989 with the Abkhazia region in Georgia playing a leading role. The aim of the congress was to work towards the creation of a Caucasian Federal Republic. The emergence of this organization was a sign of the growing discontent of the local leaders with the RF and a response to the emergence of Cossacks as an organized force. At the end of its Third Congress in November 1991, the congress became the Confederation of the Mountain Peoples of the Caucasus, incorporating 16 nations. In October 1992 it became the Confederation of Peoples of the Caucasus. The Congress created a Confederation of Caucasian Republics – continuing the tradition of the Union of Mountain Peoples created in 1917. Despite efforts to present a unified political front, it has proved difficult to establish a common agenda and internal rivalries over territory and relative influence in the region remain intense.

Beyond the Caucasus area, people from the region have faced popular prejudice and harassment by the Russian authorities, in part because of the conflicts in the Caucasus and in part reflecting the widespread perception that people from the region are involved in criminal activities.

Chechens

Chechens (899,000) are indigenous to the North Caucasus and are ethnically close to the Ingush. The majority of Chechens live in Chechnia (pop. 1,270,429: Chechens 57 per cent, Ingush 13 per cent, Russians 23 per cent, others 7 per cent) and some in adjacent Dagestan. Chechens are Sunni Muslims. The dominant form of social organization among the Chechens is the clan. Chechen is one of the Caucasian family of languages. Prior to deportation, Chechens lived primarily in the mountain areas of Chechnia; they resettled on the plains. Chechnia was incorporated into the tsarist empire after a prolonged war in the nineteenth century. Following the Bolshevik Revolution, Soviet rule met considerable opposition in the region. Some areas were not subordinated until the 1920s. In 1922, the Chechens were granted their own AO. In December 1934 this was merged with the Ingush autonomous area to form the Chechen-Ingush AO, which became the Chechen-Ingush ASSR in December 1936. In the 1920s and 1930s Russians began to flood into the area. Immigration produced a strengthening of clan and religious brotherhoods in the region.

In 1944 Chechens and Ingush suffered mass deportation on Stalin's orders. Some 459,486 were sent to Central Asia. The territory of the Chechen-Ingush ASSR was partitioned. In the 1950s, Chechens and Ingush were gradually rehabilitated and allowed to return to their former lands, which had by then been populated by Russian settlers. From the 1970s, the area experienced a growth in ethnic sentiment and a rise in demands for autonomy. With the collapse of the Soviet Union, tension between Ingush and Chechens mounted. Chechens demanded complete independence from Russia, while Ingush wished to stay within the Federation in order to regain land that had been placed under the jurisdiction of North Ossetia.

From late 1990 the Chechen self-determination movement was led by Dzhokhar Dudayev, a former Soviet Air Force General. In November 1991 Dudayev became President of Chechnia. Chechnia declared independence and Russian troops were sent to restore control. The Russian Parliament refused to support the move and the troops were withdrawn. Moscow introduced an economic blockade of the republic. The Chechen authorities sought to consolidate their new-won statehood. On 17 March 1992, a new Chechen constitution was adopted. Chechen and Russian became the state languages and the Latin script was introduced instead of Cyrillic. Russians began to leave the area. Relations deteriorated between Ingush and Chechens and on 4 June 1992 the Russian Parliament passed legislation to create a separate Ingush republic.

In Chechnia a struggle developed between the President and Parliament. Moscow sought to influence events by offering covert support for opposition forces. Internal opposition to President Dudayev was steadily eradicated in 1992–3. In the autumn of 1994 a civil war broke out in

Chechnia when opposition factions challenged Dudayev. The failure of this action led to growing tension between Russian and Chechnia. At the end of 1994, Russia mounted a full-scale invasion of the republic. Tens of thousands of lives were lost in the war that followed. Despite the high casualties on both sides, Moscow has continued to pursue a military solution to the Chechen issue while Chechens have remained committed to the idea of independence. The war has spilled over into neighbouring areas and has frequently threatened the stability of the whole Caucasus region.

Ingush

In 1989 the total population of Ingush in the RF was 215,000. The majority (163,762) lived within the western part of the Chechen-Ingush republic, which now forms the Ingush Republic, and prior to fighting in 1992 many (32–60,000) lived in North Ossetia. Since Russian conquest, the fate of the Ingush has been closely linked to that of the Chechens. The formal division of Chechens and Ingush dates from the 1880s when the western clans of the Chechens did not take part in the war with Russia and were subsequently termed by Russians Ingush. Ingush is a language very close to Chechen and a part of the Caucasian language family. A Cyrillic script was introduced in 1938. Ingush were among the last of the peoples of the North Caucasus to convert to Islam (1860s).

Under Soviet rule Ingush were initially part of the Autonomous Mountain SSR created in 1920. The republic ceased to exist in July 1924 and Ingush were given their own autonomous *oblast*. In January 1934, Ingush and Chechens were merged into a single AO. In December 1936 the *oblast* became an ASSR. Deported with Chechens in 1944, Ingush began to return to the region following rehabilitation (1956–7).

Frictions between Chechens and Ingush developed from 1989 and especially after the declaration of independence in November 1991. Ingush constituted only 12.9 per cent of the 1.2 million population of the Chechen-Ingush ASSR. With apparent Russian support (in order to weaken the Chechens), Ingush began to advocate the creation of a separate Ingush republic which was created on 4 June 1992. The borders with Chechnia were provisionally agreed to be those that had existed pre-1934. The borders remain contested, however, especially with respect to North Ossetia, where fighting broke out in 1992.

Karachai and Cherkess

Karachai (150,000) are ethnically Turkic and share a literary language with the Balkars (Karachai-Balkar). The language is from the Turkic branch of the Uralo-Altaic language family. Cherkess (51,000) were part of the Circassian people until this group was divided in the 1920s and 1930s into Kabards, Adygei and Cherkess. Cherkess speak the same language as Kabards (Kabardino-Cherkess), which is close to Adygei, and belongs to the Caucasian language family. The majority of Karachai and Cherkess live in the Karachai-Cherkess Republic, formerly the Karachai-Cherkess AO in Stavropol *Krai* (pop. 414,970: Karachai 31 per cent, Cherkess 10 per cent, Russians 42 per cent, others 17 per cent) and in Stavropol *Krai*.

In January 1922 the Soviet authorities established the Karachai-Cherkess AO. In 1944, Karachai were deported to Central Asia, where they remained until 1958–9. Roughly half of the Karachai died in the first year of deportation. The AO was dissolved and most of the territory was transferred to Georgia. The region was reconstituted as the Karachai-Cherkess AO in the 1950s.

On 17 November 1990 the region's Soviet of People's Deputies proclaimed the area a republic. The main Karachai organization, the Islamic Rebirth Party, has called for the full rehabilitation of the Karachai and the restoration of their statehood within former borders. Leaders of the Cherkess have been active in movements to reunite the Circassian people. Disputes over land have led to tension with local Cossack groups.

Kabards and Balkars

As early as 1557 Kabards (386,000) formed part of the Terek Cossack district. They were among the last of the North Caucasian people to be converted to Islam. In the pre-Soviet period, along with Cherkess and Adygei, Kabards were considered part of the Circassian people. In the 1930s, Kabards were given the status of a distinct ethnic group. They share a language with Cherkess. Balkars (78,000) formed following the merging of tribes from the Northern Caucasus with Iranian and Turkic-speaking peoples. Balkars are ethnically, linguistically and culturally close to Karachai. Kabards and Balkars live in the Kabardino-Balkar Republic (pop. 753,531: Kabards 48 per cent, Balkars 9 per cent, Russians 32 per cent, others 11 per cent).

The Kabardin AO was created in September 1921 and amalgamated with Balkaria to form the

Kabardino-Balkar AO in January 1922. In December 1936, the AO became the Kabardino-Balkar ASSR. Balkars were forcibly deported to Central Asia and Siberia in 1944. Balkar territories were transferred to the Kabard ASSR. Balkars were permitted to return to the reconstituted Kabardino-Balkar ASSR after 1956. They were not allowed to resettle in their former lands and were instead dispersed throughout Kabardino-Balkaria. In November 1991, Kabardino-Balkaria declared its sovereignty.

Since independence, there has been some tension between Kabards and Balkars. The main problem has been the issue of the full rehabilitation of the Balkars. In November 1990, the Kabardino-Balkaria Supreme Soviet established a commission to study the restoration of the 'historically Balkar regions'. In a referendum held in December 1991, Balkars voted to create a separate Balkar republic. The Congress of Balkars has demanded restoration of the Balkar homeland and a return to Balkars of their pre-1944 territories. These claims on former lands have worried Kabards. In April 1993, the Congress of the Kabard People requested the Supreme Soviet of the Russian Federation to refrain from passing a resolution 'On the Rehabilitation of the Repressed Balkar People'. There have also been calls for the republic and the neighbouring region of Karachai-Cherkess to be broken up into separate Karachai-Balkar and Kabardino-Cherkess regions.

Adygei

Adygei (123,000) were part of the Circassian people until the 1920s, when they were divided from Cherkess and Kabards. The majority of Adygei live in the Adygei Republic, formerly the Adygei AO in Krasnodar *Krai*, (pop. 432,046: Adygei 22 per cent, Russian 68 per cent, others 10 per cent) and in Krasnodar *Krai*. There is also a large expatriate Adygei community in Turkey. Adygei areas became an AO in July 1922. Leading members of the Adygei resented the fact that they were not given republican status. Of all of the territories of the North Caucasus, the Adygei region has the highest concentration of Russians. In August 1991 Adygei created a special commission to oversee the return of expatriates, primarily the large communities in Turkey. The first All-Adygei Congress was held on 28 March 1992. Large numbers of Russians in the Adygei regions have identified themselves as Kuban Cossacks. They have demanded their own Cossack region in Krasnodar *Krai* but have also supported the Adygei. Some Adygei have participated in the movement to unite Circassian peoples.

Peoples of Dagestan

Dagestan is one of the most ethnically complex areas of the former Soviet Union. The republic has no titular population (pop. 1,802,188: Avars 28 per cent, Dargins 16 per cent, Kumyks 13 per cent, Lezgins 11 per cent, Russians 9 per cent, Nogai 2 per cent, others 21 per cent). Except for Russians, the largest groups – Avars, Dargins, Kumyks, Lezgins – are all Sunni Muslim. The Dagestan ASSR was established in January 1921. The republic declared its sovereignty in May 1991. The complexity of minority issues in Dagestan – there are at least 32 separate ethnic groups within its borders – and the close identity between many of these groups and certain territory has led to calls for the republic to become a federation. Establishing a balance of ethnic groups in the republic has proved to be a particularly difficult and delicate task. Dagestan is the centre of Islam in the North Caucasus.

Avars (544,000) are a mountain people and are numerically the largest group in Dagestan. Traditionally they have controlled the political system in the republic, although the introduction of free elections has challenged this position. The Avar people was constituted from a variety of local groups in the 1930s. Literary Avar belongs to the Caucasian language family. In May 1993 clashes over disputed territory in the mountains broke out between Avars, Laks, and Chechens.

Dargins (353,000) are the second largest group in Dagestan. They live primarily in south-central Dagestan and are Sunni Muslim, although there is a small Shi'i minority. Their language belongs to the Caucasian family of languages.

Kumyks (227,000) live in the plains and the foothills of Dagestan. Well into the twentieth century, Kumyks were assimilating other Dagestani peoples (notably Dargins and Avars) and many other groups have shifted over to speak Kumyk. Part of the Turkic branch of the Uralo-Altaic language family, Kumyk emerged as a *lingua franca* for the North Caucasians. Although numerically small, the cultural, linguistic, economic and political influence of Kumyks on the region has been great. Kumyks are mainly Sunni Muslim. Since the collapse of the Soviet Union, leaders of the Kumyk nationalist movement *Tenglik* ('Equality') have demanded the creation of a separate Kumyk republic within Dagestan. Clashes have taken place between Dargins and Kumyks.

Lezgins (257,000) are the fourth largest ethnic group in Dagestan and the fourth largest group in Azerbaijan (171,395 or 3 per cent of the population). They live in south-western parts of Dagestan and adjacent areas in Azerbaijan. Lezgin belongs to the Caucasian family of languages. The Lezgin Democratic Movement *Sadval* ('Unity') was created in 1990. Its leadership has called for the unification of all Lezgins. In December 1991, the All-National Congress of Lezgins established the Lezgin National Council. The Council has called on Russia, Azerbaijan and Dagestan to redraw present borders to unite the Lezgins in the region. The introduction of a border regime between Dagestan and Azerbaijan produced strong protests from Lezgins.

The majority of Nogai (74,000) live in the Nogai steppe of northern Dagestan and in the Chechen, Ingush, and Karachai-Cherkess Republics and in Stavropol Krai. The Nogai nationalist movement *Birlik* ('Unity') has called for the creation of a Nogai state separate from Dagestan but still within the RF. The lack of compact settlement among Nogai has, however, weakened their case.

Christians: *Chuvash and Ossetians*

Chuvash

Chuvash (1.8 million) are descended from Volga Bolgars who assimilated local Finnic and Turkic peoples. Chuvash live, primarily, in the Chuvash Republic (pop. 1,338,023: Chuvash 68 per cent, Russians 27 per cent, others 5 per cent) as well as in Tatarstan (134,221) and Bashkortostan (118,509). The Chuvash language is from the Turkic branch of the Uralo-Altaic language family. Chuvash are Eastern Orthodox in religion. The Chuvash AO was established in June 1920 and became an ASSR on 25 April 1925. The republic has the lowest concentration of Russians in the region.

Ossetians

The majority of Ossetians (402,000) are Eastern Orthodox, although one group converted to Islam during the seventeenth and eighteenth centuries. Most Ossetians in the RF live in the North Ossetian Republic (pop. 632,428: Ossetians 53 per cent, Russians 30 per cent, others 17 per cent). The language generally spoken by Ossetians has used, with only minor interruption, a Cyrillic script since the middle of the nineteenth century. The Ossetian region became part of Russia in 1774. In July 1924 the Ossetian AO was created and in December 1936 it became the North Ossetian ASSR. Ossetian Muslims, the Digor, were deported in 1944 along with other Muslim peoples of the North Caucasus. Some of the survivors were allowed to return in the 1950s. The mass deportation of Ingush was followed by the abolition of the Ingush region and North Ossetia took control of the frontier districts of Ingushetia (Prigorodnyi district) and parts of the city of Vladikavkaz. After 1944 this area was populated by Ossetians. Despite the rehabilitation of Ingush and the restoration of their autonomy, these territories remained under North Ossetian control.

Growing tension with Ingush over the status of the land they had lost in 1944 led the Supreme Soviet of North Ossetia to suspend the citizenship rights of Ingush in September 1990. The introduction in 1991 of the Union-level 'Law on the Rehabilitation of Repressed Peoples' intensified the tension between Ingush and Ossetians. In 1992 fighting flared up over disputed territory and President Yeltsin introduced a state of emergency in North Ossetia and the Ingush Republic (2 November 1992), and sent in thousands of troops. In 1993, conflict over the Prigorodnyi district continued. Over 30,000 Ingush refugees fled the area. The area remains disputed. North Ossetia has sent aid to its ethnic kin in South Ossetia to support their struggle with Georgia. There have also been calls for the unification of the two regions, although mainly from South Ossetia.

Shamanist: *Altai, Khakass, Yakuts, northern native peoples*

Altai

Altai (69,000) consist of a variety of tribes. The Altai language is from the Turkic branch of the Uralo-Altaic language family. Altai live, primarily, in the Altai Republic, formerly Gorno-Altai AO in Altai *Krai* (pop. 190,831: Altai 31 per cent, Russians 60 per cent, Kazaks 6 per cent, others 3 per cent). The Altai religion is a mixture of Shamanist and Eastern Orthodox beliefs. Russians conquered the region from the Chinese in the middle of the nineteenth century. Russians soon began to migrate to the area. After the Bolshevik Revolution, the Oirot AO was created (1922), and this became the Gorno-Altai AO in 1948 to counter potential aspirations for reintegration with Mongolia. The region declared its sovereignty in 1990 and became a full republic in May 1992. In spring 1992, conflict broke out between Altai and the richer Russians. Many Russians have left the region.

Khakass

Khakass ethnicity is derived from a mixture of Uigur Turkic, Tuvan and other groups. The dominant language among Khakass (Khaas) (79,000) belongs to the Turkic branch of the Uralo-Altaic language family. The majority of Khakass live in the Khakass AO (pop. 566,861: Khakass 11.0 per cent, Russians 80 per cent, others 9 per cent) and adjacent areas in southern Siberia. The Khakass religion is a mixture of Shamanist-animist and Eastern Orthodox beliefs. The groups that came to form the Khakass fell under Russian domination in the seventeenth century. Prior to the Bolshevik Revolution, these groups did not identify themselves by a single name. In the early twentieth century, a nationalist movement sprang up among Khakass as a reaction to Russian immigration. After the Bolshevik Revolution, in response to Khakass nationalist demands, the Soviet regime established an AOk in 1925 and this became an AO in 1930. The traditionally close ties to Tuvans and Altai have led nationalists to demand the restoration of the 'historical unity' of Khakassia, Altai and Tuva.

Yakuts

Yakuts (380,000) have developed from a Turkic speaking people once resident around Lake Baikal. Their language belongs to the Uralo-Altaic language family. The majority of Yakuts live in the Republic of Yakutia-Sakha, formerly the Yakut ASSR (pop. 1,094,065: Yakuts 33.4 per cent, Russians 50 per cent, others 17 per cent) as well as Magadan, Sakhalin and Amur *oblasts*. The Yakut religion is a mixture of shamanist-animist and Eastern Orthodox beliefs. Russian penetration of the region began in the seventeenth century and a major revolt against Russian occupation occurred in 1642. In the early twentieth century a nationalist movement emerged in the area (the Yakut Union). In April 1922, the Bolshevik regime established the Yakut ASSR. In 1924, the discovery of gold in the south led to large scale Russian migration to the region. In 1926, Yakuts comprised 81.6 per cent of Yakutia's population, by 1989 this had fallen to 33.4 per cent.

Russian migration produced an intensification of inter-ethnic tension and led to clashes and mass demonstrations in the 1980s. In the autumn of 1990, the Yakutia Supreme Soviet renamed the republic Sakha-Yakutia. Sakha-Yakutia has been at the forefront of the movement demanding increased control over local resources. A new constitution for the republic has established Sakha-Yakut citizenship. In April 1995 the republican authorities concluded a bilateral treaty with Moscow. Given the small numbers of Yakuts and their weak position, little of the region's wealth is likely to reach them.

Native peoples of the north, Siberia and far east

The native peoples of the north, Siberia and the Russian far east have been under a variety of economic, linguistic and cultural pressures since Russian expansion into their homelands in the twelfth century. Their shamanist practices have been repeatedly attacked. Under the Russian and Soviet empires, the image of these regions as frontier zones and state subsidies encouraged in-migration by Slavs. Within the Soviet Union, native peoples were gradually pushed towards extinction by policies promoting modernization, forced settlement and Russification. Since the collapse of the Soviet Union, these peoples have been able to organize themselves more effectively and Russian migration and industrial exploitation have slowed. However, native peoples have also had to face a new set of challenges, the most important of which, land privatization, threatens the security of their land rights and their aim of creating 'reserved territories'. The growing demands for access to the resource-rich areas of the north by domestic and international mineral extraction companies has raised the issue of what rights the native peoples should have in the future economic exploitation of their homelands.

The centre-piece of the Russian government policy has been the Council of Ministers decree (11 March 1991) 'On the State Programme for the Development of Economy and Culture of the Minority Peoples of the North 1991–5'. The Committee for the North and Minority Peoples was created in the Council of the Federation in April 1994. The Russian Parliament passed a law 'On the Foundations of the Legal Status of the Indigenous Peoples of the Russian North', although President Yeltsin vetoed it in the summer of 1995 under pressure from the oil and gas lobby.

Native peoples have been active in their own defence, establishing organizations to campaign on their behalf. The First Congress of the Northern Minorities took place in March 1990. It called for a return of historic lands and the creation of traditional tribal councils. Russia recognizes only a limited number of native peoples, leaving more than 20 unrecognized. Some of those who are recognized have their own autonomous areas, but even here they are usually heavily outnumbered by Slavic settlers.

Nenets and Dolgan

Nenets (34,000) are the most numerous of the Samoyedic peoples and speak a language of the Uralian division of the Uralo-Altaic language family. The Nenets literary language was created in 1932 using the Cyrillic script. Nenets are mainly shamanist. They live in the Yamalo-Nenets AOk (pop. 494,844: Nenets 4 per cent, Russians 59 per cent, Ukrainians 17 per cent, others 20 per cent), the Nenets AOk (pop. 53,912: Nenets 12 per cent, Russians 66 per cent, Komi 10 per cent, Ukrainians 7 per cent, others 5 per cent) and the Taimyr (Dolgano-Nenets) AOk (pop. 55,803: Nenets 4 per cent, Dolgans 9 per cent, Russians 67 per cent, others 20 per cent). In March 1993, encouraged by the secession of the Chukchi AOk from Magadan *Oblast* and by the prospect of controlling the oil resources of the area, Yamalo-Nenets and Khanti-Mansi, also within Tiumen *Oblast*, decided to press for the status of separate republics.

Dolgan (6,600) are a Yakut-speaking people of Tungusic origin. They are being assimilated by the Yakuts but still retain a separate identity. They live in the Taimyr (Dolgano-Nenets) AOk. There are some Christian additions to their shamanist-animist religion.

Evenk

Evenk (30,000) are composed of a number of groups that cover a vast area (approximately a quarter of Siberia). They were, however, awarded an AOk in Krasnoyarsk Krai (pop. 24,769: Evenk 14 per cent, Russians 68 per cent, others 18 per cent) on 10 December 1930.

Chukchi

Chukchi (15,000) are ethnically close to Koriak and speak one of the Chukotic languages. The Chukchi literary language was created in 1931 using the Cyrillic script. Chukchki live primarily in the Chukchi Republic, formerly the Chukchi AOk (pop. 163,934: Chukchi 7 per cent, Russians 66 per cent, Ukrainians 17 per cent, others 10 per cent) in the north-eastern part of Magadan *Oblast* and in adjacent areas and in the Koriak AOk (1,460). In September 1990, the Chukchi AOk Soviet proclaimed autonomy and in March 1991 decided to separate from Magadan *Oblast*. In May 1993, the Russian Constitutional Court supported the right to secede.

Koriaks

Koriaks (8,900) are ethnically and linguistically close to Chukchi. Koriak was established as a literary language in 1932 using a Latin script and in 1937 converted to Cyrillic. Koriaks mainly live in the Koriak AOk (pop. 39,940: Koriaks 16 per cent, Russians 62 per cent, Ukrainians 7 per cent, others 15 per cent). In December 1990, the *okrug* soviet sought to convert the Koriak AOk to a republic as an indication of the rights of the peoples of the Russian Far East to assert their indigenous rights, especially over the area's rich gold deposits.

LINGUISTICALLY DEFINED GROUPS

Linguistically defined groups form the second main category of minorities.

Finno-Ugrian peoples

There are 16 Finno-Ugric ethnic groups within the former Soviet Union. In November 1992 the First World Congress of Finno-Ugrian peoples took place in the Komi Republic. Delegates called for self-determination for all indigenous peoples and national minorities and condemned 'Russian imperialism'. Although there are nearly 16 million Finno-Ugrians in the former Soviet Union, they are only in the majority in Komi-Permiak. The Second Congress of Finno-Ugric Peoples was held in July 1995 to demand new rights, including property rights in their traditional areas of settlement and language privileges.

Karelians

Karelians (125,000) are Finns who adopted Eastern Orthodoxy. The Karelian language is primarily a Russified form of Finnish. The majority of Karelians live in the Karelian Republic (pop. 790,150: Karelians 10 per cent, Russians 74 per cent, others 16 per cent). The Karelian population in Russia has been steadily declining since the turn of the century due to assimilation by Russians and migration to Finland. The area has had a variety of administrative designations and has been the subject of a dispute between the Soviet Union and Finland since it was created. The Karelian Labour Commune was established in June 1920 and became the Karelian ASSR in July 1923. In March 1940 the status of Karelia was upgraded to that of the Karelo-Finnish SSR in connection with Soviet plans to incorporate Finland into the Soviet Union. The region's status was reduced in July 1956. Karelia was the first ASSR to declare sovereignty in 1990. Although Finland renounced any claims to the territory of Karelia in December 1991, the Karelian Association in Karelia continues to campaign for unification with Finland.

Mari

Mari (644,000) are distinct from other Finnic peoples of the Middle Volga area because they never fully converted to Christianity, and retain their shamanist-animist beliefs. The Mari literary language was formed using the Cyrillic script by the Eastern Orthodox church in the early to mid-nineteenth century in an unsuccessful attempt to convert the population to Christianity. The majority live in the Mari-El Republic, formerly the Mari ASSR (pop. 749,332: Maris 43 per cent, Russians 48 per cent, others 9 per cent). Mari nationalism since the nineteenth century has been directed towards preserving their religion. The region was established as an AO in November 1920 and became the Mari ASSR in December 1936. From the late 1950s to the early 1970s, Mari lost nearly all of their ethnic privileges; in the 1960s language teaching was banned. Sovereignty was declared on 22 October 1990 and the name of the republic was changed to Mari-El.

Udmurts

Udmurts (715,000) are linguistically and culturally close to Komi and Komi-Permiaks and share similar shamanist-animist beliefs with Maris. Their language belongs to the Permian branch of the Finno-Ugric language family. Most Udmurts live in the Udmurt Republic (pop. 1,605,663: Udmurts 31 per cent, Russians 59 per cent, Tatars 7 per cent; others 3 per cent) and Tatarstan, Mari-El, Bashkortostan, Kirov and Perm *oblasts*. Originally established as an AO (Votsk) in November 1920, Udmurtia became an ASSR in December 1934. It declared sovereignty on 19 September 1990. The nationalist Demen Society of Udmurt Culture has pressed for the establishment of Udmurt as the official language. Russian is spoken by a sizeable percentage of the population. In 1992 the Supreme Soviet of the republic failed to elect a president because none of the candidates spoke Udmurt fluently.

Mordovans

Mordovans (1.1 million) are divided into two main groups: Erzya (two-thirds) and Moshka (the remaining third). Their languages are mutually unintelligible. The population is scattered in the Middle Volga with the largest concentration in the Mordovan Republic (pop. 963,504: Mordovan 33 per cent, Russians 61 per cent, others 6 per cent). Initially constituted as an AO in January 1930, Mordova became an ASSR in 1934. Over three-quarters of all Mordovans live outside the republic. Particular concern has been expressed by Estonia about the extensive assimilation of this population by Russians. More than 70 per cent of Mordovans are bilingual (Mordovan/Russian).

Komi

Komi (336,000) are closely related to Komi-Permiaks and Udmurts of the Middle Volga and they share a common religion, Eastern Orthodox Christianity. They live in the Komi Republic (pop. 1,250,847: Komi 23 per cent, Russians 57 per cent, Ukrainians 8 per cent, others 12 per cent). The area became a principality of Moscow in the fourteenth century. In August 1921, the region was constituted as the Komi (Zyrian) AO. In December 1936 it became an ASSR within the RSFSR. The Komi People's Congress, which is 'dedicated to the defence of the cultural and ethnic rights of all Komi people', has advocated the retention of all Komi natural resources in order to bargain with Moscow over independence and unification with the Komi-Permiak national area.

Komi-Permiaks

Komi-Permiaks (147,000) are ethnically close to Komi and share a common language, Komi. They are shamanist-animist in religious belief. Most Komi-Permiak live in the Komi-Permiak AOk (pop. 158,526: Komi-Permiak 60 per cent, Russians 36 per cent, others 4 per cent) in the Perm *Oblast*. The Komi-Permiak AOk was formed in February 1925. Since the late 1980s a local movement has advocated the unification of the AOk with the Komi republic.

Khants and Mansi

Khants (22,000) are culturally and linguistically close to the Mansi (8,300). Khants and Mansi together make up the Ob-Ugrian branch of the Ugrian division of the Uralo-Altaic language family. They are mainly shamanist-animists. The literary language of Khants was established in 1930 and that of Mansi in 1932. Both converted to a Cyrillic script in 1939–40. Khants and Mansi live mainly in the Khanty-Mansi AOk (pop. 1,282,396: Khants 9 per cent, Mansi 5 per cent, Russians 66 per cent, Ukrainians 11 per cent, others 9 per cent) in Tiumen *Oblast*. The Khanty-Mansi AOk was established in December 1930. In March 1993 the *okrug* authorities decided to press for the status of a separate republic. Similar demands were also made in Yamalo-Nenets.

LEADING MINORITIES LACKING AN OFFICIALLY RECOGNIZED HOMELAND

Although Moscow has taken some important steps to create an environment supportive to the development of minority groups, those groups that lack their own homeland face particular problems. Many of these groups do not have compact forms of settlement and therefore face the prospect of assimilation.

Jews

The vast majority of Jews (537,000) came to Russia following the incorporation of Polish and Lithuanian territories into the Russian Empire in the eighteenth century. During the nineteenth century Jews faced repression and were not allowed to integrate into Russian society. The establishment of the Pale of Settlement restricted Jews to the western borders of the empire and in the late nineteenth century there were officially organized pogroms against Jews. There are two main groups of Jews in Russia: the Ashkenazi (originally Yiddish-speaking or East European) and a small community (18,513) of Mountain Jews who live primarily in Dagestan and Kabardino-Balkaria (speaking the Persian-based language Tati). Most Jews today speak Russian as their first language (86.6 per cent). Jews are scattered across the RF with most living in urban areas, especially Moscow and St. Petersburg.

Jews were never formally recognized as a nation because they lacked compact settlement, although Stalin accorded them the status of a nationality (*natsional'nost'*). In 1928 the Soviet authorities set aside a territory in the Russian Far East for Jews. On 7 May 1934 this became the Jewish AO in Khabarovsk *Krai*. Only a small percentage of Jews settled in the region. In 1989 Jews numbered only 8,887 of the 214,085 population of the *oblast*. In the period following the Second World War, there have been successive waves of Jewish emigration, primarily to the USA and Israel. During the years of Gorbachev's stewardship the numbers of emigrants increased dramatically. Since Russian independence this movement has continued, although it has slowed in recent years. Anti-Semitism is not in evidence at an official level, although it is an important theme in some Russian nationalist organizations. There has been a strong cultural and religious revival among Jews remaining in the RF.

Ukrainians, Belarusians and Kazakhs

The collapse of the Soviet Union has presented a number of groups in the RF with a particular dilemma. The large Ukrainian (4.4 million), Belarusian (1.2 million) and Kazakh (636,000) communities in the RF now have independent 'homelands' outside Russia. The Russian government has given little support to the revival of indigenous language and cultures among these diaspora populations. Instead, each community is expected to fund its own development. A Congress of Russian Ukrainians has been formed.

Russian or Volga Germans

Large-scale German settlement in Russia first occurred in the sixteenth century following Catherine the Great's decree of 1763 granting steppe land along the Volga River to Germans. Volga Germans (842,000) were primarily Lutheran and Mennonite in religion. In 1924 the Soviet regime created the Volga German ASSR with German as its official language. The republic was disbanded during the war and its German population (895,637) deported to Siberia and Central Asia. The Germans were not allowed to resettle in the region despite being rehabilitated in 1965.

Since the late 1980s, a number of German organizations have been established: Revival (*Wiedergeburt*, *Vozrozhdenie*); Freedom (*Freiheit*, *Svoboda*); and the Interstate Organization of Russian Germans (*Zwischenstaathischer Verein der Russlanddeutschen*). These organizations have campaigned for the restoration of their homeland but have faced strong opposition from the local populations of the Saratov and Volgograd *oblasts*. The German government has allocated significant funds for the creation of German cultural centres and schools in Central Asia and Russia. This has not, however, deterred hundreds of thousands of Germans from emigrating to Germany.

Meskhetians or Meskhetian Turks

Meskhetians (est. 30,000) are Turkicified Georgians. Until 1944 they lived in Meskhetia and Dzhavakhetia along the Georgian–Turkish border. For many years they were classified as Turks. In 1944, the Meskhetians were deported to Central Asia. Rehabilitated in 1968, they were not allowed to return to Georgia despite several attempts in the 1970s. Meskhetians are Shi'i Muslims. In June 1989 Meskhetians living in the Ferghana valley in Uzbekistan were attacked by Uzbeks and more than 100 were killed. Most Meskhetians fled to the Caucasus with more than 11,000 moving to the Krymski district in Krasnodar *Krai*. Georgia has refused to resettle Meskhetians and they have faced strong opposition to their presence in Russia, especially from Kuban Cossacks. Most have moved to Azerbaijan. Two organizations were formed by Meskhetians in 1991, *Vatan* ('Homeland') and Salvation. Meskhetians are seeking to emigrate to Turkey.

Roma

Roma (153,000) in the RF are part of a much larger international Roma community. They migrated to Russia in three main waves beginning at the end of the fifteenth century. Roma in Russia can be divided into several groups differentiated by language, culture, kinship ties, dialect, and occupation. There is often strong rivalry between these groups and each has developed different relationships with Russian state and society. The leading group has achieved success in the performance arts. In the mid-1920s Roma were classified as a national minority of Indian origin and policies were developed to assimilate them. In the 1930s many were deported to Siberia. In 1956 Khrushchev decreed that Roma must be settled. Today the majority of Roma are sedentary. There was a cultural revival in the last decades of the Soviet Union when the Moscow Romani theatre was established.

In popular perception Roma are linked to begging, crime and music. In the past their movement has been regulated; from 1759 to 1917 they were banned from entering St. Petersburg. Today they are restricted in the work they can get by prejudice and strong desires to preserve their autonomy. Since the demise of the Soviet Union, discrimination has become more visible. Although they are not the subject of nationalist hatred, there have been some violent clashes involving Roma. Roma lack representatives in positions of authority and their political concerns have remained unheard since the break-up of the Soviet Union. As a diaspora community without a recognized claim to a homeland their efforts for linguistic self-determination have also failed. UNESCO has funded a school for Roma in Moscow. The official census data are believed to underestimate significantly the number of Roma in the RF.

Cossacks

Cossacks (est. 80,000) were a social group that had begun to develop some ethnic characteristics prior to the Russian Revolution. Cossack communities (hosts) were formed in the sixteenth to eighteenth centuries by runaway serfs. Traditionally Cossacks guarded the frontiers of the Russian Empire and in return were granted land privileges. Cossacks were also used to repress uprisings against the Russian state. By the end of the nineteenth century, Cossack settlement stretched from southern Russia to the Pacific. Under the Soviets, Cossacks were deported and repressed. The Communist regime never recognized Cossacks as a national or ethnic group and they were listed as Russians or Ukrainians. In the late 1980s, Cossack groups began to revive and the Association of Cossacks was formed (July 1990). Cossacks have presented themselves as guardians of Russia's frontiers, especially in the North Caucasus. Cossacks fought with the separatist forces in the Transdniester conflict in Moldova in 1992 (see **Moldova**). In June 1991 President

Yeltsin issued a decree marking the political rehabilitation of Cossacks, and on 11 March 1993 Yeltsin signed a further decree granting them state support. In August 1995, Yeltsin announced that Cossack units would be formed in the Border Guards of the Russian Army. The Cossacks have strong aspirations for local self-government and have also sought national autonomy. The Don Cossack Grand Council has led these demands. The Terek Cossacks, whose lands encompassed the territories of North Ossetia, Dagestan, Chechnia and Ingushetia, have aggressively pursued land claims, bringing them into conflict with North Caucasian peoples.

Native peoples of the north, Siberia and far east

Certain of the more numerous native peoples have been granted territorial recognition. Most of the smaller groups (Nanai, Nivkhi, Selkup, Ulchi, Itelmen, Udegei, Sami (Lapp), Inuit, Chuvan, Nganasan, Yukagir, Ket, Oroch, Tofalar, Aleut, Negidal, Ent, Orok) have not. While the larger sedentary groups have often assimilated to Russian life, this is not the case with the less numerous peoples. Their small numbers, however, suggest they have a precarious future. Scattered across the north, Siberia and the Russian far east, the largest group without an official ethnic homeland, the Nanai, has a population of 12,021, while the smallest, the Orok, number just 190.

Conclusions and future prospects

Since the early 1990s, the struggle for power between the federal authorities and the ethno-territorial units has gradually transformed the RF from a unitary empire into something that resembles a federation. However, although the struggle for a genuine federation has fostered a transfer of powers to the ethnic republics, it has also reinforced the link between control of territory and the power and rights that minorities can enjoy. In this way it has accelerated the competition between ethnic groups to claim their own 'homeland'. Faced with these problems, the federal authorities have repeatedly stressed the need to move the basis of the federation away from the ethnic principle and on to an arrangement in which all subjects would have equal status. Such a change would, however, require minority groups to abandon their aspirations for nationhood.

The ethnic republics have fiercely resisted any moves to undermine their position. The conclusion of a series of bilateral treaties with the republics indicates that federal authorities have accepted that these areas cannot be forced to participate in the federation. The continuing struggle between Moscow and the ethnic republics, especially the decision to invade Chechnia in 1994, suggests, however, that basic problems remain.

Minority issues cannot be tackled effectively until the distribution of basic powers is resolved and, in particular, the issue of the relationship between rights and territory is decided. Most politicians concede that, at minimum, borders will have to be redrawn, especially in the North Caucasus. Moreover, until the ethno-territorial principle is reconciled with individual rights, the RF will continue to be characterized by a two-tier system of minority rights.

Determining the federal structure of the RF will not, however, solve the basic question about the dominance of Russians in the RF. The 'race for sovereignty' in the early 1990s helped provide many of the leading minority groups with a guaranteed legal status and, in principle, republican-level support for the development of indigenous cultures and languages. In many of these regions, however, the numerical dominance of ethnic Russians and other Slavs ensures that ethnic autonomy is largely a fiction. For those without an officially recognized homeland, the pressures to assimilate are even greater.

Further reading

Akiner, S., *Islamic Peoples of the Soviet Union*, London, Kegan Paul, 1986.

Krag, H. and Funch, L., *The North Caucasus: Minorities at a Crossroads*, London, MRG report 1994.

Sheehy, A. and Nahaylo, B., *Crimean Tatars, Volga Germans and Meskhetians*, London, MRG report, 1980.

Smith, G. (ed.), *The Nationalities Question in the Post-Soviet States*, London, Longman, 1996.

Vakhtin, N., *Native Peoples of the Russian Far North*, London, MRG report, 1992; and in MRG (ed.), *Polar Peoples: Self-Determination and Development*, London, Minority Rights Publications, 1994.

Wixman, R., *The Peoples of the Soviet Union*, Armonk, NY, Macmillan, 1984.

Minority-based and advocacy organizations

Amnesty International, PO Box 212, Moscow 12019, Russia; tel. 7 095 291 2904.

Association of Indigenous Peoples of the North, Nab. T. Chevtschenko, 3/3/119, Moscow 121248, Russia.

Human Rights Commission under the President of the Russian Federation, 4/10 Ipatievsky Pereulok, Moscow 103132, Russia; tel. 7 095 206 3439, fax 7 095 206 0069.

Institute of Ethnography of the Russian Academy of Sciences, Moscow, Russia; tel. 7 095 937 1779/095 7 938 0043.

Memorial, Malyi Karetnyi pereulok 12, Moscow 103051 , Russia; tel. 7 095 200 6506/7 095 299 1180, fax 7 095 973 2094.

Moscow Helsinki Group, Luchnikov pereulok. d. 24, pod. 3, kv.5, Moscow 103982, Russia; tel. 7 095 206 0923/0924, fax 7 095 116 7682, e-mail: hrcenter@glas.apc.org

Moscow Research Center for Human Rights, 4 Luochnikov Lane, Suite 5, Moscow 103982, Russia; tel. 7 095 206 0923, fax 7 095 206 8853.

Non-Violence International, Profsoyuznaia Str. 98/10, Apt 55, Moscow, Russia; tel. 7 095 336 7771, fax 7 095 336 5323.

Peace and Human Rights Organization OMEGA, Samarkandskii Boulv. 15/5, Apt. 30, Moscow 109507, Russia; tel. 7 095 206 8618, fax 7 095 206 8853.

Right to Life and Human Dignity, Luochnikov Pereulok, Room 19, Moscow 103982, Russia; tel. 7 095 206 8589, fax 7 095 963 9929.

Romani Union, Kalinina 42–249, Lubercy 2, Moscow, Russia.

Society of Russian-Armenian Friendship, Simferopolskaia Str. 18, Apt 413, Krasnodar 350080, Russia; tel./fax 7 8612 335374.

Tajikistan

Land area:	143,100 sq km
Population:	5.99 million (est. 1994)
Main languages:	Tajik, Russian, Uzbek, Yagnobi, Pamiri languages
Main religions:	Islam (Sunni, Ismai'li), Orthodox Christianity
Main minority groups:	Uzbeks 1.5 million (25%), Pamiri Tajiks 185,000 (est., 3%), Russians fewer than 100,000 (1.7%), and declining, Tatars 84,000 (1.4%), Kyrgyz 63,800 (1%), Ukrainians 41,400 (0.7%), Germans 32,700 (0.5%), Turkmen 20,500 (0.3%), Koreans 13,400 (0.2%)[1]
Real per capita GDP:	$1,380
UNDP HDI/index:	0.616 (105)

The Republic of Tajikistan is a landlocked republic in south-east Central Asia. The terrain is mountainous, with the northern part of the country (Khujand) cut off from the rest of the republic. Historical affiliations reflect this geographical divide: while Khujand was formerly a part of the Kokand Khanate, territories to the south belonged to the Bukharan emirate. Tajikistan borders Uzbekistan to the north and west, Kyrgyzstan to the north-east, the People's Republic of China to the east and Afghanistan to the south. Its territory includes the autonomous region of Gorno-Badakhshan in the Pamiri Mountains. The Tajiks are an Iranian people, making up 65 per cent of the population of Tajikistan and constituting minorities in other Central Asian countries, notably Uzbekistan and Afghanistan. Tajikistan is a home to over eighty ethnic groups, most notably Uzbeks, Russians, Tatars, Kyrgyz and Ukrainians. Pamiri Tajiks arguably also constitute a minority group. A small minority in the southern province of Kurgan Tyube consider themselves Arab by descent, although they speak Tajik.

Tajikistan declared independence in September 1991 and established a presidential republic. Rahmon Nabiyev, a former first secretary of the Tajikistan Communist Party, was elected President obtaining 57 per cent of the vote. His main rival, Davlat Khudonazarov, representing various democratic and Islamic parties, obtained 30 per cent. The important factor in Nabiyev's victory was the backing by the Khujand clans and the Uzbek and Russian minorities, who feared that the country might be transformed into a Tajik ethnic and Muslim state.

Aggravation of the economic situation and Nabiyev's unwillingness to enter a meaningful power-sharing arrangement with the opposition, as well as the latter's inability to accept defeat, led to political deadlock. Riots started in April–May 1992 and resulted in armed clashes in Dushanbe, the capital. The civil war, which erupted in summer and autumn 1992, claimed up to 100,000 dead and 1 million refugees. The civil war saw mobilization of supporters along regional and clan lines in the struggle to resolve the ideological conflict between Islam and secularism and the political question of who would rule the country. Tajiks have always been region- rather than ethnic-oriented people, and the war led to the fragmentation of the country. Three regions – Khujand, Kulob and West Gharm – supported the government, while the opposition was supported by the Kurghan-Teppe, East Gharm, Ramit Valley and Gorno-Badakhshan regions.

President Nabiyev was forced to resign on 7 September 1992, but this failed to stop the war in the south. Neither side was strong enough to win a decisive victory. The governmental forces had the backing of neighbouring Uzbekistan, while the opposition was aided by the Afghan *mojahedin* across the border. Events in Tajikistan alarmed other Central Asian leaders, notably President Islam Karimov of Uzbekistan, who appealed to the UN for assistance and then urged Russia to intervene. In November 1992 the Tajikistan Parliament accepted Nabiyev's resignation, abolished the presidency and elected Imomali Rahmonov as parliamentary chairman, the highest executive post. CIS peacekeeping forces for Tajikistan were created. In December the 'opposition-led' government fell, and Rahmonov took office. Uzbek and Russian military support ensured that the new government stayed in power. These developments finalized the first round of power redistribution in Tajikistan, when a Khujand–Kulob alliance was installed in power again, with Kulobis on top.

A viable state failed to emerge. Ethnic and social fragmentation increased, but Tajikistan was transformed into a presidential republic once again in 1994. To improve the legitimacy of the regime, presidential elections took place in November 1994, were won by Rahmonov, and the new constitution was adopted. These elections and the simultaneous constitutional referendum were severely criticized by opposition leaders and by international organizations[2] as unfair and undemocratic. Parliamentary elections took place in February 1995 following the same pattern.

The mandate of the CIS peacekeeping troops was extended into 1996. Following important military gains by the opposition, a UN-brokered peace agreement was signed by Tajik President Emomali Rakhmonov and Islamic opposition leader Sayed Abdullo Nouri in December 1996. As well as an end to fighting, the agreement called for a general amnesty, a prisoner exchange and the repatriation of refugees. The December agreement was designed to become the cornerstone for the creation of a national reconciliation commission in 1997. The peace process, however, remained extremely fragile.

Uzbeks

The proportion of ethnic Uzbeks in Tajikistan increased from 23.5 to 25 per cent of the population as a result of the changed demographic balance since 1992 as many ethnic Tajiks sought refuge in Afghanistan. Uzbeks are indigenous to the area. Regions with a heavily Uzbek population include Khujand, Hissar and Kurgan Tyube. Before the war ethnic Tajiks in these areas were heavily Turkicized, and bilingualism and intermarriage were widespread. Uzbeks were allied to the ruling groups in Tajikistan, and were therefore suspected by the opposition to be supporters of Nabiyev. Tajiks who supported the opposition believed Uzbeks of Kulob to be guilty of 'ethnic cleansing'.[3]

Because of Tajik emigration, in some areas bordering Uzbekistan there are virtually no Tajiks left. However, Uzbeks perceive the share of power they obtained as a result of the postwar settlement as small compared to their expected reward for supporting the current regime, and are increasingly dissatisfied with Kulobi domination. Relations are especially strained in the Vakhsh valley, where Uzbeks and Tajiks from different areas were resettled because of the hydroelectric power project development. Tensions arise when

Uzbeks intimidate Tajik returnees and are themselves intimidated by ruling Kulobis.[4] A disarmament campaign launched by the government in 1994 officially relates to all citizens but in reality is directed mainly against Uzbeks. Relations between Presidents Rahmonov and Karimov of Uzbekistan, who originally backed the authorities in Dushanbe, have deteriorated over the issue of ethnic Uzbeks in Tajikistan and Rahmonov's unwillingness to negotiate a compromise with the political opposition. These tensions resulted in an attempted coup led by two former pro-regime warlords, ethnic Uzbeks, in January 1996. Ibodullo Boimatov, the former mayor of Tursunzade, and Major-General Mahmud Hudoberdiev from Kurgan-Tyube demanded changes in central and local government, rebelling against the predominance of Rahmonov's clan.

Pamiri Tajiks

Pamiris were always considered 'Tajik' by the authorities in Dushanbe, although it is claimed in many ethnographic and linguistic publications that they constitute a separate ethnic group, differing from Tajiks in terms of linguistic and confessional affiliations, as well as culturally.[5] Pamiris live mainly in the autonomous *oblast* of Gorno-Badakhshan (185,000) and are divided into several groups: Shughnanis and Wakhi in the western and central parts of the province, and Darwazi and Yazgulami in the north. Discussions continue around the issue of whether to include Pamiris in the Tajik nation, since they speak distinct languages of the Iranian language group, adhere to the Ismai'li branch of Shi'ism and are less Turkicized than lowland Tajiks. During the late 1980s a separatist movement emerged that allied itself with the Islamic and democratic opposition, but Badakhshan remained relatively calm during the fighting in 1992. Nevertheless, the central authorities regard Badakhshan with suspicion because lowland Pamiri Tajiks fought on the opposition side and were associated with atrocities committed during the civil war; and because the Tajik-Afghan border in Badakhshan is difficult to control and serves as the main access for opposition fighters to enter Tajikistan. In 1993 the government introduced certain reconciliatory policies, having signed an agreement with the Gorno-Badakhshani authorities. Nevertheless, the government afterwards imposed an economic blockade on Badakhshan and carried out punitive expeditions and detentions of local leaders. In response, 'self-defence' paramilitary units, linked to the local authorities and the opposition across the border, began to emerge. Gorno-Badakhshan was the main scene of military operations in 1994 and 1995, with opposition attacks provoked by the increasing government military presence in Tawildara. Since 1993, although officially a part of Tajikistan, Badakhshan has become a *de facto* self-ruled breakaway area. The main source of external support comes to Pamiris from the Aga Khan Foundation. The Aga Khan, the spiritual leader of the Ismai'li Muslims, visited Tajikistan in May 1995.

Russians and Ukrainians[6]

Russian (388,000 people according to the 1989 census) and Ukrainian (41,000 in 1989) communities have rapidly declined since Tajikistan's independence, mainly as a result of migration following the start of the civil war. Fewer than 100,000 Russians now remain in the country, mainly in Khujand. Their further emigration is restricted mainly by financial constraints. In September 1995 Tajikistan signed an agreement with Russia on dual citizenship.

Russian emigration started during *perestroika*. The first wave followed the proclamation of the Tajik language law in 1989 which made Tajik the sole state language, followed by a new wave after violence directed against Armenians broke out in February 1990, leaving 50 people dead. During the civil war Russian-speakers' sympathies were with the Nabiyev side, yet even with the victory of the latter Russian-speakers fear further destabilization. The effects of the Russian exodus are felt in a number of key occupational sectors.

Russian-speakers' organizations include *Migratsiya* (Migration), which tries to give practical assistance to those who have decided to leave. Another organization, *Russkaya Obshchina* (Russian Community), unites those who refuse to be uprooted unless the lives of their families are directly threatened. These activists believe that drastic measures will be necessary to induce Russians to stay. They claim that Russia should provide Russians in Tajikistan with financial support and the military capability to defend themselves. The Russian Orthodox Church in Tajikistan encourages Russians to stay.

Conclusions and future prospects

Russian policy is crucial for conflict resolution in Tajikistan. Russia maintains the biggest military presence outside its borders in Tajikistan and subsidizes the Tajik economy. However, Russian influence on internal developments in Tajikistan is limited, as is its capacity to make the government reach a meaningful agreement with the opposition. Until the political will on both sides towards peace emerges, peace remains fragile. The next few years are likely to witness an exodus of the remaining Russians, Ukrainians, Germans, Tatars and Koreans, with the pace of German emigration prevailing over the others. Pamiri Tajiks in Gorno-Badakhshan are in a severely disadvantageous position, so any peace settlement would improve their access to educational, economic and administrative opportunities. In the event of major destabilization the autonomous region might attempt to declare sovereignty and cut itself off from the rest of the country. The Uzbek community might face problems in the case of an increase in government of anti-Uzbek sentiment. Potentially the Uzbek community presents the main danger in case of further destabilization, as the heavily Uzbek regions might attempt to secede from Tajikistan and join with Uzbekistan. After any peace settlement will arise the problem of the return of refugees who fled the fighting in 1992. Most of the refugees who fled to former Soviet Union countries have yet to return. Their return and subsequent attempts to claim back their property are likely to increase tensions between ethnic and regional groups.

Further reading

Akiner, S., *Central Asia*, London, MRG report, 1997.

Atkin, M., 'Tajikistan: ancient heritage, new politics', in I. Bremmer and R. Taras (eds), *Nations and Politics in the Soviet Successor States*, Cambridge, Cambridge University Press, 1993, pp. 361–84.

Jawad, N. and Tadjbakhsh, S., *Tajikistan: A Forgotten Civil War*, London, MRG report, 1995.

Makhamov, M., 'Islam and the political development of Tajikistan after 1985', in H. Malik (ed.), *Central Asia: Strategic Importance and Future Prospects*, Basingstoke, Macmillan, 1994.

Rubin, B., 'The fragmentation of Tajikistan', *Survival*, vol. 35, no. 4, 1993–4, pp. 71–91.

Rubin, B., 'Tajikistan: from Soviet Republic to Russian-Uzbek protectorate', in M. Mandelbaum (ed.), *Central Asia and the World*, New York, Council on Foreign Relations Press, 1994, pp. 207–25.

Turkmenistan

Land area:	488,100 sq km
Population:	4,254,000 (est. 1993)
Main languages:	Turkmen (official since 1990), Russian, Uzbek
Main religions:	Sunni Islam, with elements of Sufi mysticism, Orthodox Christianity
Main minority groups:	Russians 404,100 (9.5%), Uzbeks 382,900 (9%), Kazakhs 106,350 (2.5%), Volga Tatars 39,250 (0.9%), Ukrainians 35,600 (0.8%), Azeris 35,000 (est., 0.8%), Armenians 31,800 (0.7%), Baluchis 28,300 (0.7%), Kurds
Real per capita GDP:	$3,128
UNDP HDI/rank:	0.695 (90)

The Republic of Turkmenistan is situated in south-west Central Asia. It borders Uzbekistan to the north, Kazakhstan to the north-west, Iran to the south and Afghanistan to the south-east. The Caspian Sea lies to the west. The Kara-Kum Desert covers over 80 per cent of the country, occupying the entire central region. Turkmen are a Turkic people of the Oghuz southern Turkic language group. A strong sense of tribal loyalty, reinforced by dialect, is preserved among Turkmen, who define themselves by tribe and clan. Major tribes include Tekke in central Turkmenistan, Ersary in the south-east and Yomud in the west. Almost 1 million Turkmen live in Iran, and an estimated 350,000 in Afghanistan. Turkmen were converted to Islam earlier than other nomadic Central Asian groups (in the twelfth century), and have had relatively little to do with their neighbours. Turkmenistan is the most ethnically homogeneous state of Central Asia, with Turkmen making up 73.3 per cent of the population. Most non-Turkmen live in urban areas.

Saparmurat Niyazov, the former first secretary of the Communist Party of Turkmenistan, was elected President in October 1990. Turkmenistan declared independence in October 1991. In June 1992 Niyazov was re-elected unopposed, receiving 99.5 per cent of the votes. In January 1994 a referendum was held to exempt Niyazov from having to seek re-election in 1997 to allow him time to complete his programme of economic reform, and extended the term of his office to 2002. His style of leadership is authoritarian, and his popularity is gained by such concessions as free electricity, gas and water supplies for all citizens since January 1993, although these supplies are scarce and available mainly in urban areas. The country's relative prosperity is based on substantial natural gas and petroleum reserves.

The Turkmen government does not pretend to appear democratic. Niyazov claimed that premature political pluralism would threaten national stability and has declared himself 'Turkmenbashi' (head of Turkmen). There is no independent press. Opposition political activity is severely restricted. Agzybirlik, the only remaining opposition group, cannot function openly. However, in the capital, Ashgabat, in July 1995 peaceful demonstrations were held, mainly by Turkmen, demanding democratic rights. The monitoring of human rights in the country is problematic because of the government's policy of isolation.

Russians and Ukrainians

Many local Russians identify themselves with the republic. The majority are the descendants of those who arrived in the 1930s and are now second- or third-generation Turkmenistanis. They are mainly employed as engineers in oil and gas production and other extraction industries. Prospects for economic recovery seem greater than in other Central Asian states, although in Soviet times Turkmenistan had one of the lowest standards of living. The relative stability and absence of ethnic conflict also seem attractive to Russians. The government understands that the good performance of Turkmen industry depends on retaining Russians, and Ukrainians, in technical professions. In December 1993 Presidents Niyazov and Yeltsin signed an accord granting dual Russian and Turkmen citizenship to ethnic Russians in Turkmenistan. Nevertheless, Russians are leaving Turkmenistan. In 1994, 20,300 migrated to the Russian Federation. The Turkmenization of official life and the influence of Islam become more apparent as time passes, and the media publish articles whose interpretation of history is not favourable towards Russians and other Slavs. In May 1992 an attempt on the part of Russians to found a community organization was banned by the authorities as unconstitutional.

Uzbeks

Uzbeks, a minority indigenous to the region, account for 9 per cent of the population and are concentrated mainly in Tashauyz *Oblast*. Uzbeks are a matter of concern for the government. Clashes between the then nomadic Turkmen and sedentary Uzbeks had a long history up to the nineteenth century. Although there have been no reports concerning Turkmen–Uzbek friction in the republic, the government remains on the alert.

Kurds

Kurds are indigenous to Turkmenistan, although historically they mainly resided in the Transcaucasus. Kurds were the first to suffer deportation to Central Asia to prevent irredentist aspirations following the abolition of 'Red Kurdistan' in 1930.[1] In Turkmenistan Kurds have campaigned for the creation of a Kurdish autonomous territory, as territories on the Turkmen–Iranian border were the areas of traditional Kurdish settlement. No population statistics are available for Turkmenistan's Kurdish minority.

Conclusions and future prospects

Relative economic stability and the authoritarian leadership of President Niyazov provide basic 'law and order' for the majority of the population, among whom political activity appears dormant. Hidden tensions within the Turkmen nation itself, such as the relationship between tribes, are perhaps the most significant potential problem. Despite the law on dual citizenship, Turkmenistan is likely to witness a continuous out-migration of Russian-speakers in the long run. Uzbeks may advance a claim for transfer of the Tashauyz oasis and the middle Amu Darya oasis to Uzbekistan in the event of significant deterioration in Turkmen–Uzbek relations.

Further reading

Akiner, S., *Central Asia*, London, MRG report, 1997.

Blandy, C.W., *Instabilities in Post-Communist Europe: Central Asia*, Sandhurst, Conflict Studies Research Centre, 1994.

Bushev, A., 'Turkmenistan: a kind of prosperity', *Bulletin of the Atomic Scientists*, January/February 1994.

Shashenkov, M., *Security Issues of Post-Soviet Central Asia*, London, Brassey's, 1992.

CSCE, *Report of the CSCE Rapporteur Mission to Turkmenistan, Uzbekistan and Tajikistan*, 1993.

Ukraine

Land area:	603,700 sq km
Population:	51.4 million (1989; 51.6 million est. 1992)
Main languages:	Ukrainian, Russian
Main religions:	Christianity (Orthodox and Uniate Catholic)
Main minority groups:	Russians 11,356,000 (22%), Jews 486,000 (0.9%), Belarusians 440,000 (0.9%), Romanians/Moldovans 325,000 (0.6%), Bulgarians 234,000 (0.5%), Crimean Tatars 47,000 (0.1%)[1]
Real per capita GDP:	$3,250
UNDP HDI/rank:	0.719 (80)

The Republic of Ukraine, formerly called the Ukrainian Soviet Socialist Republic (UkSSR), is situated between the Russian Federation to the east, Belarus to the north, Poland, Slovakia, Hungary, Romania and Moldova to the west, and the Black Sea to the south. Ethnic divisions in Ukraine are, to a large extent, a legacy of imperial political geography and different conceptions of history held by the peoples of the region. Since the thirteenth century, Ukrainian lands have been at the intersection of shifting empires – the Grand Duchy of Lithuania, the Ottoman Empire, the Polish–Lithuanian Commonwealth, the Crimean Tatar Khanate, Austro-Hungary and Russia. The prolonged experience of borderland status – Ukraina means borderland – has produced a society consisting of a variety of religions, cultures, ethnic groups and languages but little in the way of common institutions to mediate these diverse interests. With the collapse of the Soviet Union, the Soviet system, which had ensured the primacy of Russians and Russified regions over other ethnic groups and regions, was challenged by new political forces, primarily Ukrainian nationalists. The struggle for power that developed from the late 1980s fostered the emergence of a complex series of interlinked regional and minority problems.

At the heart of contemporary ethnic relations in Ukraine are the competing historical interpretations of the region held by different ethnolinguistic groups. The prevailing Ukrainian historiography, supported particularly by western Ukrainians and the Ukrainian intelligentsia, identifies the emergence of a Ukrainian people separate from the Russians. It is claimed that this identity manifested itself on three occasions when something resembling an independent Ukraine was established: first, the state of Kyivan Rus, which existed from the ninth to the twelfth centuries and collapsed due to internal unrest and Mongol-Tatar invasion – Kyiv was sacked in 1240; second, from the sixteenth to the eighteenth centuries, Zaporozhian Cossacks established a number of autonomous territories within central and eastern Ukraine; finally, in the period 1917–18 a number of 'Ukraines' came briefly into existence before being crushed by external forces. By the early 1920s, the territories that constitute modern Ukraine were divided between Romania, Poland, the Soviet Union and Czechoslovakia.

For Russians, in contrast, Ukraine, in terms of both territory and people, is seen to have been historically an organic part of Russia. Most Russian historians take Kyivan Rus to be the forerunner of the modern Russian state. Kyiv occupies a central place in Russia's political mythology and reclaiming 'Russian' territory lost with the Mongol invasion has been an important justification for Russian expansion to the west. The territorial vision of the region has been reinforced by an ethno-cultural theory that links Ukrainians, Russians and Belarusians ('three brotherly peoples') who together constitute 'the Russian people'.

In the past, the Russian interpretation of history has been used to justify the introduction of Russian institutions into Ukraine, as well as language, culture and Russian settlers. In imperial Russia, the southern Ukrainian lands were known as Malorossiya (Little Russia) or New Russia, which with Russia and the lands of Belarus constituted the 'natural' territory of the Russian state. At the same time, Moscow-inspired policies of modernization fostered a progressive integration of the Ukrainian borderlands into the political and economic core of the Russian Empire.

In Tsarist Russia Ukrainian was viewed not as a separate language but as a dialect of Russian and its use as a means of public communication was restricted. The local intelligentsia was also drawn into the Russian cultural orbit. The Ukrainian Autocephalous Orthodox Church was absorbed into the Russian Orthodox Church in the late seventeenth century. Although it was briefly revived in the 1920s and 1940s, it was not to re-emerge fully until 1990. The western territories also contained significant numbers of Ukrainians from the Uniate Church.

The Soviet period

While Ukrainian lands remained subordinated to Moscow following the 1917 revolution, Bolshevik rule did lead to an important change in the relationship between Russia and Ukraine. For the first time, the view that Ukrainians, Belarusians and Russians constituted a single people was officially repudiated in Moscow. In the years after the civil war, three separate Slavic republics were established. However, as power was centralized in the Soviet state, pro-Ukrainian policies were reversed. Russian language became compulsory in all secondary schools throughout the republic and it became difficult to publish material in Ukrainian.

Along with the establishment of Ukraine as a separate political unit, the most significant change that took place under Soviet rule was the three-stage territorial annexation along Ukraine's western border. In 1939, the Red Army occupied the predominately Ukrainian territories of Poland; in 1940, Soviet Ukraine was extended to include northern Bukovyna and Bessarabia (from Romania). Finally, in 1945 union with Transcarpathia was effected. In 1954, Nikita Khrushchev transferred Crimea from the jurisdiction of the Russian Federation to Ukraine.

Perestroika

The political liberalization that accompanied Mikhail Gorbachev's reforms led to the emergence of a variety of nationalist groups. The activity of these groups reinforced the patchwork of ethnic and linguistic identities that have developed in the region over the past 200 years. Ethno-regionalism quickly became the primary fault line in Ukrainian society. However, the leading pro-independence organization was the moderate Rukh. The dominance of Rukh, coupled with the conversion of much of the Ukrainian communist leadership to the cause of Ukrainian nationhood, undermined the position of the ethno-nationalists and allowed for a civic definition of an independent Ukraine. The largely non-ethnic notion of Ukraine was codified in a series of legislative acts.

The Law on Languages (October 1989) provides for 'the free use of Russian as a language of inter-ethnic discourse', although Russian was not granted the status of a state language. The law also stipulates a gradual transition to Ukrainian. The Declaration of Ukrainian State Sovereignty (July 1990) guarantees 'all nationalities that reside on the territory of the republic the right to national-cultural development'. The Law on Citizenship (October 1991) utilized the 'zero' citizenship principle: granting citizenship to everyone resident in Ukraine prior to independence irrespective of ethnicity. The Declaration of the Rights of Nationalities (November 1991) established a broad range of minority rights, while the Law on National Minorities (June 1992) provided state support for the development of minorities. A Ministry of Nationalities and Migration was set up in spring 1993.

On 28 June 1996 Ukraine's parliament adopted a new constitution. Ukrainian is designated the offical language of the state, but the constitution also allows for the free development of other ethnic languages used by Ukrainian citizens. Only a single citizenship is recognized, a blow for many among the Russian community who had sought a dual citizenship regime. Although the constitution stipulates that Ukraine is a unitary state, special provisions are made for the Autonomous Republic of Crimea.

Russians and Russian-speakers

Significant Russian settlement in the region occurred towards the end of the eighteenth century when the northern Black Sea littoral region was officially opened up to Russian settlement. The Russian conquest of Crimea from the Ottomans in 1783 brought new opportunities for Russian settlement in southern lands. With rapid industrialization in the late nineteenth and early twentieth centuries, significant numbers of Russians moved to urban centres in Ukraine. Between 1890 and 1930, 2 million Russians settled in Ukraine, primarily in the east. In the 1930s, a further million Russians moved to Ukraine. The Russian community also absorbed other national groups and minorities, notably Serbs, Greeks and Jews.

Following the Second World War, significant numbers of Russians settled in connection with postwar reconstruction, especially in the eastern industrial regions. In the 1960s there was a surge in Russian immigration. Between 1959 and 1989, the number of Russians as a percentage of the Ukrainian population rose from 16.9 per cent to 22.1 per cent (7.1 million to 11.36 million). In this period, the largest numbers of Russians went to Crimea.

As a result of these migrations, Russians reinforced their traditional dominance of industry, administration and education in the urban areas of the east and south. By 1989, although Russians were only in the majority in Crimea, they formed sizeable minorities in many of the other regions – Donets'k (43.6 per cent), Luhans'k (44.8 per cent), Kharkiv (33.2 per cent), Dnipropetrovs'k (24.2 per cent), Zaporozhia (32 per cent) and Odesa (27.4 per cent). The numerical strength of the Russians is reinforced by the importance of the Russian language in the republic. The 1989 Soviet census indicated that almost 4.6m (11 per cent) ethnic Ukrainians considered Russian their first language. There continues to be extensive bilingualism in Ukraine and many of those who identified themselves as Ukrainian-speakers also know Russian very well.

Following independence, fears of separatist activity by Russians caused considerable alarm in Kyiv. The geographical proximity of the heavily Russified east and Crimea to the Russian Federation has prompted fears of a possible unification of these areas with Russia. Growing divisions in Ukrainian society were clearly apparent when, in June 1992, the formation of the Ukrainian Orthodox Church divided the orthodox religious community, with many remaining loyal to the Moscow Patriarchate.

In general, however, with the exception of Crimea, the main thrust of Russian/Russian-speakers' demands has been towards increased autonomy and protection of the Russian language rather than secession from Ukraine. In a referendum in December 1991, large numbers of Russians voted for independence. The electoral success of representatives from the east and south of Ukraine – including President Kuchma – in 1994 also helped to weaken demands for secession or unification with Russia. However, important divisions remain in Ukrainian society; the most explosive issue is that of Crimea.

Crimea

In 1989 the total population of the Crimean peninsula (area 27,000 sq km) stood at 2,430,495, of whom 1,629,542 (67 per cent) were Russians, 625,919 (25.8 per cent) Ukrainians, of whom 47 per cent were Russian-speakers, 38,365 (1.6 per cent) were Crimean Tatars, and 136,669 (5.6 per cent) other nationalities.

In 1944, following liberation from Nazi occupation, the peninsula's populations of Tatars, Bulgarians, Armenians and Greeks were deported after being accused of collaboration with the Nazis. In June 1945, the peninsula lost its autonomous status and became part of the Russian Federation. In 1954, Nikita Khrushchev transferred Crimea to the jurisdiction of Ukraine as a symbol of the friendship between Ukrainians and Russians.

With large numbers of Russians living on the peninsula, the majority of whom are recent migrants, following independence Crimea became the centre for pro-Russian and secessionist sentiments in Ukraine. Tension in the area stems from a mixture of fear of Ukrainianization and Crimea's difficult socio-economic position. The region is one of the poorest in Ukraine and is overpopulated. The increased pressure on resources brought about by the return of the Tatars from Central Asia has helped to channel social and economic competition into ethno-political confrontation. Russians, Tatars and Ukrainians, who are largely settled in the north of the peninsula, have all sought to establish their own ethnically exclusive organisations.

In 20 January 1991, the Crimean Communist Party organized a referendum on the question of reviving the Crimea's status as an autonomous region within the UkSSR. Of those who voted, 93.26 per cent supported a change of status. In July 1991, Russian became the official language of the peninsula. In August the Republican

Movement of Crimea (RDK), a Russian nationalist organization led by Yurii Meshkov, was formed. On 4 September 1991, the Crimean Supreme Soviet voted to declare sovereignty over Crimea. In December 1991, only 54 per cent of the population of Crimea voted for Ukrainian independence. The RDK reached the height of its influence in mid-1992. On 5 May 1992, the Crimean Soviet declared independence (although this was subsequently suspended). By early December 1993, the movement had split into various factions. Unity was temporarily restored to the nationalists in December 1993 with the establishment of the 'Russia' bloc to promote Meshkov's presidential campaign.

The election of Meshkov as President of Crimea in January 1994, gaining 70 per cent of the vote, led to a significant rise in tensions between Kyiv and Simferopol as Crimea seemed to be moving towards independence. On 27 March, a majority voted in support of the 'consultative' questions that Meshkov had placed on the ballot for national elections (the creation of dual citizenship provisions on the peninsula and for relations with Ukraine to be conducted on the basis of bilateral agreements). The Russia bloc also won a large majority (54 of 94 seats) in the Crimean Parliament.

While these results appeared to set the stage for a major confrontation between Kyiv and Simferopol, in fact they were the prelude to a dramatic disintegration of the Russian nationalist movement on the peninsula. Underlying this political collapse was an increasing dispute about economic reform and, in particular, a fight to control privatization. In autumn 1994, the growing dispute about the direction of economic reform came to a head in a bitter confrontation between the Parliament and the President. The pro-Russia political elite in Crimea gradually disintegrated. On 21 March 1995, President Kuchma issued a decree placing the Crimean government directly under Kyiv's control. Friction between Kyiv and the Crimean parliament continues to cause instability amongst the Crimean political elite. In early summer 1995 Yevhen Suprunik, a less confrontational figure, was elected leader of the Crimean parliament. Suprunik was himself replaced as Crimean parliamentary speaker in the autumn of 1996 by Vasyl Kyselyov. At the end of February 1996 a new Crimean Prime Minister, Arkadii Demydenko, was appointed in place of Anatolii Franchuk, who was dismissed in December 1995 because of his alleged support for Kyiv's politics towards the penisula.

Despite the collapse of the Russian nationalist movement, minority questions remain acute in Crimea. The presence of the Russian military in Sevastopol offers hope to Russian nationalists that the peninsula may eventually be unified with Russia. The dominance of the Russian language in the region has meant that local Ukrainians have found it extremely difficult to organize the teaching of Ukrainian in schools.

The return of Crimean Tatars continues to cause friction. Although supported by the authorities in Kyiv, not least because they opposed the Russian nationalists on the peninsula, Tatars have received insufficient financial assistance to support their repatriation programme. Unemployment among Tatars is extremely high. The intense competition for land means that Tatars have been forced to settle in the least fertile parts of Crimea. In summer 1995, frustration at the economic situation led to confrontation with an allegedly criminal group that developed into a major confrontation with the police. A number of Tatars were killed.

Despite the difficulties, the numbers of Tatars in Crimea are estimated to have risen from 38,000 in 1989 to more than 250,000 in 1994. Tatars have also achieved important political successes with Tatar representatives playing a prominent role in the regional parliament.

Russian–Ukrainian relations

Minority issues have been at the heart of relations between Moscow and Kyiv since 1991. A variety of radical nationalist groups in Russian sought to provoke conflict over the question of Russian-speakers in Ukraine. With the destruction of the Russian Supreme Soviet, a centre for these groups, in October 1993, such activity diminished considerably. The Russian government has, however, promoted its own minority-based agenda at interstate negotiations. Since early 1994, Russia has sought dual citizenship for Russians living in Ukraine, a move fiercely resisted by Kyiv.

The question of Sevastopol and the Black Sea Fleet, which is largely staffed by ethnic Russians, has also been important. Sevastopol is seen as a symbol of the Russian identity of Crimea. A decision to examine the status of the city was taken at the Seventh Congress of People's Deputies. In 1995, members of the Russian Duma again sought to raise the question of Sevastopol through the Russian Supreme Court. In June 1993, Russia and Ukraine agreed to divide the fleet, causing a rise of tension in the region. Subsequently, however, the agreement was not implemented and disagreement about ownership of the fleet and where it should be based, along with the question of dual citizenship, became the main stumbling blocks to the conclusion of a treaty of friendship between Kyiv and Moscow.

Other minorities

Since the 1989 census a sizeable emigration has severely depleted the Jewish population. At the same time, a lively Jewish cultural and religious life has developed in many parts of Ukraine. Jews have also organized a Jewish Congress. Jews are largely settled in Russified urban areas and the majority of them are Russian-speakers (91 per cent). The Ukrainian government has made significant efforts to foster good relations with the Jewish community and has also sought close contacts with Israel. There are, however, numerous anti-Semitic groups active in Ukraine.

There are 135,000 Romanians and 325,000 Moldovans in Ukraine. Some 184,500 Romanians and Moldovans live in Chernivtsi and 144,500 live in the Odessa region. Determining the exact number of each group is controversial because of uncertainty about the nature of Moldovan identity (see **Moldova**). Northern Bukovyna (Chernivtsi) and southern Bessarabia (parts of the Odessa *Oblast*) were transferred from Romania to the UkSSR under the terms of the Molotov–Ribbentrop Pact (23 August 1939). The Romanian/Moldovan population of Chernivsti has been active since independence demanding cultural and political concessions from the Ukrainian government, particularly special language rights in areas of compact settlement. In December 1991, some Romanians/Moldovans in Chernivsti are reported to have boycotted the referendum on Ukrainian independence. The Romanian government declared the referendum void in the area and has sought to raise the issue of the 1939 territorial transfer in negotiations with Ukraine. The Ukrainian government has refused to discuss the territorial question or to repudiate the Molotov–Ribbentrop agreement.

Ethnic Bulgarians are concentrated in the Odessa region, around the town of Bolhrad and on the Zaporizhian coast. As with the Bulgarians in Moldova, the Bulgarian government has sought to build ties to the Bulgarian minority in Ukraine

In 1941, 350,000 Germans were exiled from Ukraine. In 1992 Germany and Ukraine agreed that Ukraine would resettle up to 400,000 Germans from Russia/Kazakhstan in the southern districts of Ukraine. Settlement has been limited, with most Germans preferring to relocate to Germany itself. Those Germans who have moved to Ukraine have received some assistance from the German government.

Conclusions and future prospects

The long history of settlement by different peoples in Ukraine has created a set of overlapping and competitive identities among the population. With the territory of contemporary Ukraine only unified in the last fifty years and an independent Ukraine an even more recent development, uniting these diverse peoples within a single state has proved difficult. Following the disintegration of the Soviet Union, forging a national identity capable of uniting the various regions and peoples of Ukraine became one of the central tasks facing the Ukrainian leadership. The range of identities that have emerged in Ukraine over the centuries have since independence manifested themselves in the form of ethno-regionalist movements. Ukraine's relationship to Russia has been especially difficult because of the large number of Russians in Ukraine and the shared history, as well as the close cultural and linguistic ties between Ukrainians and Russians.

In response to these challenges, the Ukrainian political elite has, with important exceptions, sought to foster a multi-ethnic and territorial sense of nationhood among the population. Ukrainianization has been pursued in a perfunctory fashion and has been largely abandoned in heavily Russified regions. The liberal legislation on minority issues and the moderate reaction of the Ukrainian government to ethnic questions, notably the secessionist movement in Crimea, indicate that the majority of politicians view Ukraine in terms of a melting pot for different peoples and cultures rather than as an ethnically defined state. These developments suggest that unless ethnic tensions are aggravated by external forces, notably Russian nationalists, minority relations are likely to develop in a peaceful direction.

Further reading

Motyl, A.J., *Dilemmas of Independence: Ukraine After Totalitarianism*, New York, Council of Foreign Relations, 1993.

Sheehy, A. and Nahaylo, B., *Crimean Tatars, Volga Germans and Meskhetians*, London, MRG report, 1980.

Subtelny, O., *Ukraine: a History*, 2nd edn, London, Macmillan, 1994.

Wilson, A., *The Crimean Tatars*, London, International Alert, 1994.

Minority-based and advocacy organizations

Crimean Tatar Medzhils, Samokisha 8, Simferopol 333270, Crimea, Ukraine; tel. 7 0652 273167.

Jewish Council of Ukraine, Bul. Nimans'ka 7, Kiev 103, Ukraine; tel. 7 044 244 3006.

LITA, Prosp. Gagarina 72, Apt 357, Kharkov, Ukraine; tel./fax 7 0572 278087.

Ukrainian-American Bureau for Protection of Human Rights, PO Box 336/3, Kiev 254210, Ukraine; tel. 7 044 410 4160/3739, fax 7 044 410 3739.

Ukrainian Legal Foundation and Centre for Human Rights, 64 Chervonoarmiyska Street, Kiev 252005, Ukraine; tel. 7 044 227 2124/220 4740, fax 7 044 227 2398/2220.

Uzbekistan

Land area:	447,400 sq km
Population:	21.6 million (est. 1994)
Main languages:	Uzbek, Russian, Tajik, Kazakh, Tatar
Main religions:	Sunni Islam, Orthodox Christianity, Judaism
Main minority groups:	Russians 1,792,000 (8.3%), Tajiks 1,015,000 (4.7%), Kazakhs 885,000 (4.1%), Volga Tatars 518,000 (2.4%), Karakalpaks 453,000 (2.1%), other smaller minorities including Koreans, Crimean Tatars, Meskhetian Turks, Jews
Real per capita GDP:	$2,510
UNDP HDI/rank:	0.679 (94)

The Central Asian Republic of Uzbekistan borders Kyrgyzstan and Tajikistan to the south-east, Turkmenistan to the south-west and Afghanistan to the south. North-western Uzbekistan consists of the Karakalpak Autonomous Republic (165,600 square kilometres), which includes part of the Aral Sea. Uzbekistan borders Kazakhstan to the north and west. The Uzbeks are descendants of nomadic Turkic tribes who mixed with the sedentary inhabitants of Central Asia of Turkic origin. In the eighteenth and nineteenth centuries the most prominent political formations were the khanates of Bukhara, Khiva and Kokand. Uzbeks now constitute the most numerous Central Asian nation, and an estimated 2.5 million of them live in Afghanistan. Uzbeks, like Tajiks (see **Tajikistan**), have tended historically to be strongly region-oriented people, with three regions playing a major role in the dynamics of Uzbek politics: Tashkent, Bukhara/Samarkand and Fergana. The Uzbek leader Islam Karimov is a Samarkandi, although during his presidency the importance of regional affiliation for political promotion has diminished. The Fergana valley, shared by Uzbekistan with Kyrgyzstan and Tajikistan, is one of the main strongholds of Islam in Central Asia; its growing unemployment and impoverishment, and high rate of population increase, makes it a location of potential future conflict.

Relations between Moscow and Tashkent soured considerably as *perestroika* proceeded. Allegations that Uzbekistan had been sacrificed as a cotton colony for Soviet needs were widespread. Over-planting of cotton, urged by the Soviet (identified as Russian) central authorities, had led to inadequate food supplies, water pollution, and severe environmental and health problems, including the decline of the Aral Sea, which remains a major threat to the survival of the Karakalpak people. Relations were strained from 1984 when large-scale falsification of data on cotton production and processing was revealed. Investigations into the matter undertaken under Mikhail Gorbachev were perceived by Uzbeks as a punishment inflicted by Russians against the whole nation, and aggravated Russian–Uzbek relations.

During *perestroika*, Uzbekistan was a scene of serious inter-ethnic violence. In 1989 bloody clashes occurred between Uzbeks and Meskhetian Turks in the Fergana valley, and further inter-ethnic tensions arose when fighting broke out between Kyrgyz and Uzbek populations of the Osh *Oblast* (Kyrgyzstan) in 1990. Border crossings were sealed to prevent up to 15,000 armed Uzbeks joining their co-nationals in Kyrgyzstan to retaliate. A state of emergency was declared in the Andijan *oblast*, bordering Osh in Kyrgyzstan.

Uzbekistan declared independence on 31 August 1991. Islam Karimov, a former first secretary of the Uzbekistan Communist Party, was elected President. Russian-speaking minorities supported Karimov, seeing him as capable of restraining the nationalist opposition. During 1992 Karimov's rule became increasingly authoritarian. Opposition movements and Muslim groups were suppressed and dissidents prosecuted. In December 1994 elections were held for a new parliament. Karimov's People's Democratic Party (former Communist) won 231 of the 250 seats, with the remainder going to close allies in the Party of National Progress. In March 1995 a referendum extended the mandate of President Karimov until the year 2000. Uzbekistan has made little movement towards Western-style democracy but has avoided overt expressions of political, social and ethnic tension.

In autumn 1992 Uzbekistan intervened in the conflict in Tajikistan and it has participated ever since in the CIS joint peacekeeping forces for Tajikistan.

Poor environmental conditions remain a major problem. The excessive use of chemical fertilizers and irrigation water on the cotton fields has caused soil salinization and the desiccation of the Aral Sea. In January 1994 the five Central Asian states established a joint fund and permanent committee to save the Aral Sea and improve the health of populations living in its basin.

Russians and Ukrainians[1]

According to the census held in 1989, 1,653,475 Russians and 153,197 Ukrainians lived in Uzbekistan. The Slavic minorities are almost exclusively urban, 45 per cent of them residing in the Tashkent *Oblast*. Many Russians date from the pre-Soviet period, when peasant settlers entered the region. Blue-collar workers and intellectuals arrived during the first two five-year plans. During the Second World War the evacuation of plants and research institutions from European Russia brought a scientific and technical intelligentsia to the republic. The last wave of Slavs arrived after the earthquake in Tashkent in 1966 to help with reconstruction of the city. Although Slavs are a significant presence among industrial workers and in technical professions, Uzbeks represent about 70 per cent of all heads of industrial enterprises.[2]

Russians and Uzbeks have remained largely separate communities. Despite growing fears of unemployment, Uzbeks and other Central Asians are in no position to take over Russian jobs. Recognizing the need for Russian specialists, the government offers them incentives to retain their services. Yet some Russians are leaving the country, and several large industrial enterprises have begun to experience a lack of technical expertise. In the long run, nationalist policies are likely to prevail, and Uzbekistan may experience a significant decline in the number of Russian-speakers.

The Uzbekistan constitution adopted in December 1992 does not envisage any preferential treatment for Uzbeks, but members of the Russophone community point out that in terms of practical policy Uzbeks are in a better position. The composition of the government and state apparatus is becoming more mono-ethnic. Russian organizations are relatively weak. In May 1992 a National Association of Russian Culture obtained official recognition. Its stated aim is to advance the culture of Russians and other Slavic peoples.

The law declaring Uzbek the state language was adopted in October 1989. Command of the titular language among Russians is more advanced than in the other Central Asian countries, but only a small proportion are fluent in it. The language law is liberal in its requirements and stipulates an eight-year transition period. However, the information media are already switching over to a predominantly Uzbek language format.

Russian emigration remains relatively high. The switch to a national currency in Uzbekistan in November 1993 caused a wave of emigration. A further current factor appears to be incidents of inter-ethnic violence and increasing tension on the popular level, directed against Russian-speakers.[3] The much higher birth rate among Uzbeks has tipped the ethnic balance in the cities. In the deteriorating economic situation Russian-speakers feel vulnerable, lacking any social-security 'safety net'. Uzbeks and other Central Asians, with their tight community structures, are in this regard in a more secure position than Slavs, who have nothing similar and must rely on the state, which is increasingly felt not to be working for them. Threats perceived by Slavs in Uzbekistan include fear of renewed inter-ethnic violence, and decreased job and education opportunities. Many Russians are afraid that if they do not emigrate now they may never have another chance. Emigration is officially permitted but in practice difficult, with the authorities sometimes causing delays to reduce the economic impact of this loss of highly skilled workers.

Tajiks

Some Tajiks in Uzbekistan are rural-dwellers; others inhabit the ancient cities of Bukhara and Samarkand, historic centres of Tajik civilization. They have a long tradition of friction with Uzbeks. Uzbeks nevertheless point out that despite linguistic differences they have more in common culturally with Tajiks than with other Central Asian peoples. Tajiks and Uzbeks together once comprised the great urban civilization of the region, as distinct from the more nomadic Kyrgyz, Kazakhs and Turkmen. However, today language and ethnicity take precedence over religion and culture. The number of Tajiks in the country is difficult to estimate, since as a result of forced 'Uzbekization' many Tajiks were registered as Uzbeks, spoke Uzbek in their workplace and had to conceal their true identity. Tajiks in Uzbekistan have never engaged in secessionist activity, but the Uzbek government, concerned about possible Tajik national assertiveness, discourages the affirmation of their rights. The Tajik Department of Samarkand University has had many difficulties, especially during the early days of independence. The Tajik cultural and social organization, the Samarkand National Cultural Centre, is constantly harassed.[4] This organization campaigned for the right for ethnic Tajiks registered as Uzbeks to change their nationality in their passport, and sought to promote the use of the Tajik language in areas densely populated by Tajiks. In March 1991 an open letter with 10,000 signatures was addressed to President Karimov by the National Cultural Centre of the Tajik-speaking peoples, asking for the upgrading of the Tajik language and the renewal of the historic Turkic-Uzbek and Farsi-Tajik dual-language character of the region. The head of the Samarkand National Cultural Centre, Utkam Betmykhamedov, was imprisoned for undisclosed reasons in 1992. The organization's activists are forbidden official contacts with their co-nationals across the border.

Volga Tatars and Crimean Tatars

Volga Tatars mostly entered the region before and soon after the 1917 October Revolution as merchants and teachers. They remain predominantly urban dwellers. In 1989, 10 per cent of the 6.6 million Tatars in the Soviet Union lived in Uzbekistan, almost 130,000 of them in Tashkent.

Crimean Tatars were deported from Crimea for their alleged collaboration with Nazi Germany. They lost not only their homeland but their separate national identity. During the postwar period, they were included with Volga Tatars under the general label 'Tatars'. The number claiming to be Crimean Tatars stood at 272,000 in 1989, most of them living in Uzbekistan (189,000), particularly in large towns such as Tashkent (132,000). Many Crimean Tatars possessed a high degree of national consciousness and the vast majority claimed Crimean Tatar as their native tongue.[5] They began to campaign for the restoration of their rights in 1956, and in November 1989 the Soviet Union Supreme Soviet formally condemned the 1944 deportation and conceded significant Tatar demands, including the right of organized return. However, before financial aid was disbursed, the Soviet Union had collapsed and the Tatars were left to their own fate. Since 1989 Tatars have started to return to Crimea in large numbers, strongly attracted by their ancestral homeland (see **Ukraine**). The community in Uzbekistan is disappearing. The Organization of the Crimean Tatar National Movement was formed in May 1989 in Uzbekistan and currently operates in Crimea.

Karakalpaks[6]

Karakalpaks are a Turkic-speaking people, ethnically and culturally closely allied to Kazakhs and living alongside the Aral Sea. Regional or tribal identification is one of the strongest social bonds, and concealed competition takes place among kin groups. Despite reciprocal assimilation, major groups such as the Mangit, Kipchak and Ktai retain territories where they are the predominant inhabitants and where most people consciously identify with the tribe. The Karakalpak ASSR was transferred to the Uzbek SSR in 1936. Karakalpaks are the titular nationality and number about half a million. In 1993 the Supreme Soviet of the autonomous republic of Karakalpakia approved a new constitution, according to which it was transformed into a sovereign parliamentary republic renamed Karakalpakstan, within the Uzbekistan state. Constitutionally, Karakalpakstan can function apart from the national Uzbek government, as long as it complies with Uzbekistan laws. More nationalistic Karakalpaks demanded that the republic be given full independence, but such demands have been restrained by the fact that Uzbeks control the flow of water to Karakalpakstan. The local population is gravely affected by the Aral Sea disaster, which has resulted in the contamination of water, soil and air and the loss of 2 million hectares of land for farming. It has been predicted that by 2015 the sea may disappear. The Aral crisis has brought about unemployment, a deterioration of public health, and emigration from the region. About half the residents of the city of Muinak have emigrated. The economy of the city was based on fishing and navigation, but the coast is now 120 kilometres away from the port, and ship repairing and fish canning have been phased out. Health issues are at stake in Karakalpakstan; as a result of environmental damage, infant mortality has increased alarmingly.

Koreans

Koreans (see **Kazakhstan**) were deported from the Maritime Province in the Far East in 1937. Out of all deported peoples they adapted most successfully to their new area of settlement. Using their agricultural skills, Korean farmers began to grow rice and other crops, most notably cotton. Their collectives thrived and steadily produced a modern elite of agricultural technicians, agronomists, managerial workers, artists and intellectuals.[7] More than 320,000 Koreans lived in Central Asia in 1989. In Uzbekistan Koreans emerged as a new and powerful business class. Today they often act as go-betweens for South Korean–Uzbekistani business ventures. The South Korean government has expressed interest in encouraging Koreans to stay in Central Asia. In 1992, when the Uzbek government refused to consider the request for Korean territorial autonomy, an increasing number of Koreans began to leave for the Maritime Province in the Russian Federation from where they were originally deported. Korean returnees have been supported by the Association of Ethnic Koreans in the former Soviet Union and by South Korea, though they met with some hostility from local Russians.

Meskhetian Turks

Meskhetian Turks were deported from Georgia in November 1944 as a preventive measure 'for their own safety' – the accusation of 'collaboration with the enemy' never being advanced against them. They never acquired official permission to return to their homeland. In 1989, 208,000 Meskhetian Turks lived in the Soviet Union, the main settlements being in Uzbekistan (106,000) and Kyrgyzstan (21,000). Meskhetian Turks became victims of pogroms in the Fergana valley in June 1989; inflamed by economic competition, unemployment and population pressure, rioting continued for two weeks, leaving at least 100 Turks dead and more than 1,000 injured. The scale of violence required the intervention of Soviet troops and the urgent evacuation of 60,000 Meskhetians. In September 1989 Soviet military planes airlifted 500 more from Uzbekistan, as ethnic violence spread again. These Meskhetians were resettled in Azerbaijan, Kazakhstan, central Russia, Chechnia and Ingushetia, and Kabardino-Balkaria. Their native Georgia did not welcome their return. The Georgian government has long hindered their immigration, denying them residence permits and even using force against them in 1991. As a result, some Meskhetians have gone back to Uzbekistan.[8] The main goal of the majority of Meskhetians is emigration to Georgia and Turkey. The latter agreed in 1993 to accommodate some Meskhetian Turks.

Jews

It is estimated that some 65,000 European and 28,000 Central Asian Jews live in Uzbekistan. In 1989, 37,000 declared themselves Bukharan Jews. The official distinction was introduced for the first time, separating them from the European (Ashkenazi) Jews, who entered the area mainly during the Second World War as a result of the evacuation of industries from the western parts of the Soviet Union to Central Asia. Central Asian Jews are indigenous to the region, having preserved Judaism in spite of the Muslim conquests of the area. They are Sephardic (Eastern) rather than Ashkenazi Jews. Linguistic Russification is less widespread among Sephardi than among Ashkenazi Jews. After the Mongol invasion, Jewish families moved from Samarkand to Bukhara, where a special quarter was established in sixteenth century. After the October Revolution the Bukharan Jews were forced to make a choice between Zionism and communism, but Bukharan Jewish culture flourished until the Stalinist repressions.

Between 1936 and 1940 most of the elite was put into jail or murdered, as a result of which the intellectual stratum was lost and became mainly a community of traders and artisans. Under Brezhnev, the Bukharan Jews, like all Soviet Jews at that time, were given some limited religious freedom, but Judaism in Central Asia did not become a means of political expression. Members of the Bukharan community began to emigrate to Israel in the 1970s, mainly out of religious motives. Before *perestroika*, Bukharan Jewish emigration was proportionally one of the largest in the Soviet Union. A brief revival of Jewish culture and social organization took place during the Gorbachev period, leading to the establishment of a cultural centre in Samarkand and two different associations, one to help Jews to emigrate, the other to help them stay. In Tashkent and Samarkand Jewish restaurants serving kosher food were opened. Hebrew courses were established.[9]

The period of independence brought new uncertainties to the community, and emigration to Israel and the USA is on the rise. Almost half of the Bukharan Jewish community has emigrated since 1990, although financial penalties imposed on émigrés by the Uzbek government are making it much harder for the remaining population to leave. No anti-Semitic violence has occurred in Central Asia, but Jews in Uzbekistan fear that they may become a target of future xenophobia.

Conclusions and future prospects

The potential for ethnic tensions and conflict in Uzbekistan is great, as indicated by events during the *perestroika* period. The present ethnic stability is preserved rather artificially by the authoritarian style of President Karimov. The state-directed Assembly of Peoples of Uzbekistan has been created to help control ethnic minorities. The current policy of suppressing grievances is unlikely to be productive for conflict resolution in the long run. If the economic situation continues to deteriorate, an outbreak of ethnic conflict could take place. The majority of Slavs see no future for themselves, or their children, in an independent, assertive and nationalistic Uzbek state, which they believe is steadily emerging. Therefore emigration to Russia is an ultimate goal for many if not most of them. However, the pace of their exodus will depend on what opportunities await them in Russia, on financial constraints and on the respective policies of the Uzbek and Russian governments. In the event of major destabilization or serious economic deterioration, Russians and other non-indigenous minorities are more likely to leave quickly than to campaign for their rights.

Unlike immigrant populations in Uzbekistan, Tajiks are indigenous to the region and have nowhere else to go, given the current instability in Tajikistan. Their continuous disenfranchisement in Uzbekistan may lead to increased militancy among their community. The Uzbek population of Tajikistan, in their turn, might face reprisals for any mistreatment of Tajiks across the border.

Karakalpaks remain the most threatened minority in the country because of the ecological catastrophe. Their position will not improve without significant external intervention to tackle the problems of the Aral Sea, which are too great for the Central Asian governments to cope with alone. The UN-sponsored conference on the problems of the Aral Sea held in September 1995 attracted widespread attention and resources, but significant practical progress is yet to be made.

Such small ethnic minorities as Koreans, Turks, Jews and Armenians, who are doing relatively better in the market economy than the titular population, could experience future difficulties if the state relaxes its authority. However, despite a generally poor record on democracy and human rights, Uzbekistan has managed to maintain ethnic peace so far.

Further reading

Akiner, S., *Central Asia*, London, MRG report, 1997.

Blandy, C.W., *Instabilities in Post-Communist Europe: Central Asia*, Sandhurst, Conflict Studies Research Centre, 1994.

Craumer, P., *Agricultural and Rural Development in Uzbekistan*, London, Royal Institute of International Affairs, 1995.

Human Rights Watch/Helsinki, *Human Rights in Uzbekistan*, New York, 1993.

Sheehy, A. and Nahaylo, B., *The Crimean Tatars, Volga Germans and Meskhetians*, London, MRG report, 1980.

Notes

Contributions to this regional section are as follows. Anna Matveeva: Central Asian republics (regional introduction and country entries); Neil Melvin: Russia and the Western republics (regional introduction and country entries) and general regional introduction; Suzanne Pattle: the Transcaucasus (regional introduction and country entries).

Armenia

1 Network on Ethnological Monitoring and Early Warning of Conflict, *Bulletin*, June 1995, p.17.

2 Ibid. Azeris claim that the number of expulsions was far greater. The information given in the *Bulletin* comes from an Armenian source.

Azerbaijan

1 Network on Ethnological Monitoring and Early Warning of Conflict, *Bulletin*, June 1995, p.18. These statistics come from sources within Azerbaijan and should be treated with caution.

2 There are 15–18 million ethnic Azeris in northern Iran.

3 Human Rights Watch/Helsinki, *Azerbaijan: Seven Years of Conflict in Nagorno Karabagh*, New York, 1994.

Belarus

1 Minority population data drawn from the 1989 Soviet census.

Georgia

1 UN Centre for Human Rights, *Report of a Needs Assessment Mission to Georgia*, Geneva, January 1995.

2 UNPO *Report of an UNPO Co-ordinated Human Rights Mission to Abkhazia and Georgia*, July 1994.

Moldova

1 Minority population data drawn from the 1989 Soviet census.

Russian Federation

1 Minority population data drawn from the 1989 Soviet census.

Tajikistan

1 1994 minority population estimates from Open Society Institute's *Forced Migration Monitor*, no. 5, May 1995.

2 'Human rights in Tajikistan on the eve of presidential elections', *Human Rights Watch Helsinki*, vol. 6, no. 13, October 1994.

3 International Alert, reports from Oxfam operatives in refugee camps in northern Afghanistan, in *Tajikistan: Preliminary Briefing Report.*

4 'Return to Tajikistan: continued regional and ethnic tensions', *Human Rights Watch Helsinki*, vol. 7, no. 9, May 1995.

5 Bruk, S.I., *Encyclopaedia of the Peoples of Russia*, Moscow, 1994, pp. 28–9.

6 This account largely based on Kolstoe P., *Russians in the Former Soviet Republics*, London, Hurst, 1995, pp. 209–15.

Turkmenistan

1 Russell, J., 'The deported peoples', in *Soviet Minorities*, London, MRG update pack, 1991, p. 4.

Ukraine

1 Minority population data drawn from the 1989 Soviet census.

Uzbekistan

1 This account is based largely on Kolstoe, P., *Russians in the Former Soviet Union*, London, Hurst, 1995, pp. 218–30.

2 Ibid., p. 219.

3 See e.g. Mostovoi, A., 'Uzbekistan: the alien desert sun', *New Times*, December 1994, pp. 38–40.

4 Shashenkov, M., *Security Issues of Post-Soviet Central Asia*, London, Brassey's, 1992, p. 20.

5 Wilson, A., *The Crimean Tatars: A Situation Report*, London, International Alert, 1994, p. 11.

6 This account is largely based on Oreshkin, D., 'Ethnic dimensions of the Aral sea crisis', in M. Buttino (ed.), *In a Collapsing Empire: Underdevelopment, Ethnic Conflicts and Nationalisms in the Soviet Union*, Milan, 1993.

7 Huttenbach, H.R. 'The Soviet Koreans', *Central Asian Survey*, vol. 12, no. 1, 1993, p.66.

8 Claire Messina 'The Meskhetian Turks', 13 July 1994.

9 This account is largely based upon Poujol, C., 'The Central Asian Jews in the post-Soviet era: the beginning of the end?', in Buttino, op. cit., pp. 335–40.

THE MIDDLE EAST

David McDowall

Although minority rights are now a matter of universally applicable international law, in the Middle East context it is especially important to understand the broad factors that have determined both state and popular attitudes to the question of minorities and their place in society. In part, these attitudes have been formed by the culture usually described as Islamic which prevails in the region.[1] But they have also been formed by interaction with the West.

Minorities in the Middle East

The term 'minority' itself is a Western one, born in the context of nineteenth-century European nation states which were either already well established at the outset of, or came into being during the nineteenth century. The term became current in the region only with the establishment of the modern states system after 1918. One might infer from the term an oppositional relationship to a majority subscribing to some other identity, but such an assumption can be misleading. Most minority groups in the region share much in common with the 'majority'. Most Christian and Shi'i Arabs probably share a strong sense of common ethnic identity with other Arabs, for example, while devout Muslims are often willing to subordinate differing ethnicity to the religious identity they hold more dear.

Certainly, Middle Eastern minorities exist in the sense of groups of people with a clear sense of an identity which is in outright political or cultural opposition to a majority.[2] One might also speak of 'minorities' in the sense of certain groups denied the possibility of establishing a political entity of their own. The Palestinian and Kurdish peoples immediately spring to mind, the former because of the betrayal of their once internationally recognized rights, the latter because the sheer size of the community compels the idea of self-determination. It would be much harder to advance a case for small groups, like the Yoruk or Tahtaci in Turkey, if these ever asked for self-determination.

In most cases absolute terms of opposition are inappropriate or only relate to minority–state relations but not minority–majority relations. In several cases, where no tension exists, it might be better to talk of 'distinct traditions', a description preferred by many members of minority communities.

The term 'minority' also suggests a certain fixed neatness. Yet nations, ethnic communities and even religious sects have identities that may be far from static since they are to do with how people view themselves.[3] The terms 'Turk', 'Arab' and 'Kurd', for example, were essentially socio-economic rather than ethnic terms until the late nineteenth century. We cannot be sure precisely what meanings such terms may have in the future. Furthermore, it should be remembered that all people have a multiplicity of identities and use these selectively as most appropriate to given situations, and also that there are few minorities listed in this part of the *Directory* which cannot themselves be dissected into different sects, ethnicities, dialects, territorialisms or traditions.

Many categories today called minorities could hardly have been regarded as such a century ago. This is true of virtually all the ethnic groups, which, although they already existed, only really acquired a sense of community during the twentieth century. Two notable exceptions are the European Jews of Palestine and the Circassians, both of which arrived as migrants or refugees with their own languages in the nineteenth century.

Yet religious and ethnic pluralism has characterized Middle Eastern society since the beginning of history. Islam became the dominant religion of the region in the seventh century CE. It tolerated its three predecessor monotheistic religions, Judaism, Christianity and, with greater reluctance, Zoroastrianism, and accorded protected *(dhimmi)* status to their adherents. These communities were allowed to regulate their internal affairs under the overall sovereignty of the Islamic state. Technically, all other religious groups were obliged to convert to Islam on pain of death. In practice certain local religious beliefs survived.

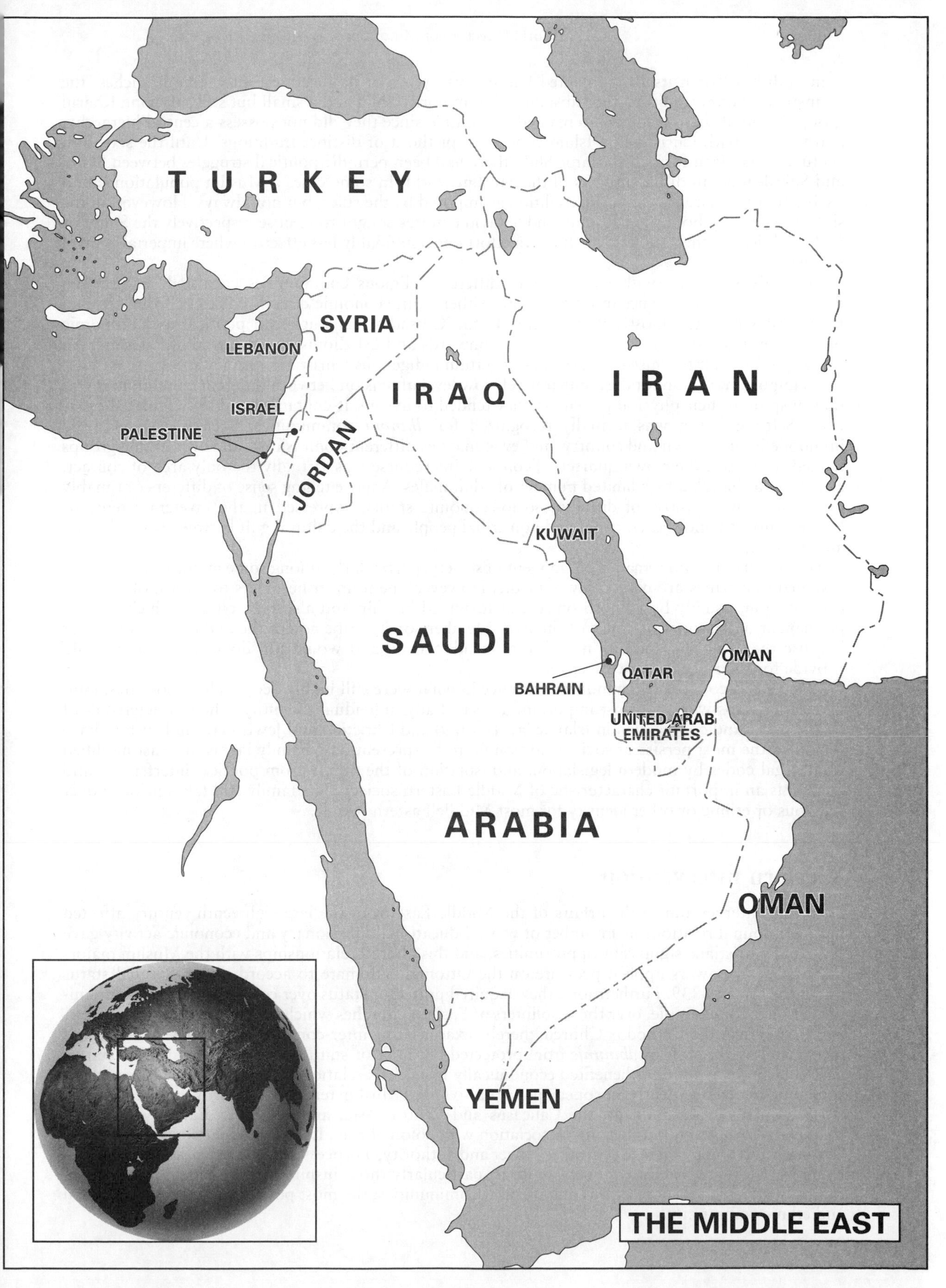
TURKEY
SYRIA
LEBANON
ISRAEL
PALESTINE
JORDAN
IRAQ
IRAN
KUWAIT
SAUDI
ARABIA
BAHRAIN
QATAR
OMAN
UNITED ARAB EMIRATES
OMAN
YEMEN
THE MIDDLE EAST

In addition, Islam itself fragmented within forty years of its inception into three branches, the mainstream Sunni tradition, the substantial but minority Shi'a and a small but still surviving Khariji group. None of these traditions remained monolithic since they did not possess a central hierarchy, and thus, as with Christianity, Islam contains a plethora of distinct traditions. Until the sixteenth century, when Iran formally became Shi'i, there had been periodic political struggles between Sunni and Shi'i leaders in different parts of the Muslim world. In some cases a Muslim population found itself under pressure to accept the tradition as imposed by the ruler, but not always. However, in the sixteenth century both the Ottoman and Safavid empires sought to impose respectively the Sunni or Shi'i tradition on their subject Muslims, an effort understandably less effective where imperial control was weaker.

Generally speaking, within each polity different religious communities coexisted successfully. Periodic tension or violence tended to result either from economic circumstances or from external factors of which the most notable were (1) the Crusades, (2) European political and economic penetration from the late eighteenth century onwards and (3) Zionist colonization of Palestine. All three episodes compromised the position of certain indigenous Christians and Jews.

An important reason for the comparatively low level of tension between different communities was that in spite of their physical proximity they tended to live a self-contained and self-regulated existence. Self-regulation was formally recognized for *dhimmi* communities. Society was relatively immobile in both town and country, and even in cities different confessional and even ethnic groups tended to inhabit their own quarters. Economic intercourse was virtually the only area of contact, and this was handled by a limited number of adult males. A more telling sense of difference arguably persisted between those of different socio-economic status, expressed in the inveterate tensions between nomad and settler, tribal and non-tribal people and the cultural gulf between town dweller and peasant.

Tribes still exist and remain a component of society, particularly among some minorities. It is often assumed that tribes are necessarily nomadic. However, the term 'tribe' refers to a form of political organization, usually based both on real or imagined kinship and also on territory, which may be permanent or seasonal or a mix of the two. Members of the tribe accept the authority of its leader because they need his mediation with the outside world, and would not do so if the state could provide for their needs more effectively.

Given a self-contained community existence in what were still highly decentralized societies, family relationships were the most important aspect of any individual's identity. The characteristics of family order and codification in Islamic law (*shari'a*) and Christian and Jewish law and custom have remained the most persistent social tradition up to the present day. Family law is the least modified of all legal codes by modern legislation, and isolation of the family from political interference and control is an important characteristic of Middle Eastern society. The family still takes priority over religious or ethnic or other identity for most Middle Eastern people.

Western intervention

European intervention in the affairs of the Middle East from the late eighteenth century affected inter-communal relations in a number of ways. Educational, missionary and economic activity gave Jews and Christians significant opportunities, and this altered relationships with the Muslim majority. European powers applied pressure on the Ottoman sultanate to accord *dhimmis* equal status under the law in 1839. Furthermore, they acquired protector status over certain Christian communities: France, for example, over those splinters of Eastern churches which became 'uniate' with Rome, and Russia over the Orthodox Church, thereby exacerbating inter-communal relations. Muslims felt threatened by the shift of *dhimmis* from protected but inferior status to protected and equal status, particularly since *dhimmis* benefited economically from their relationship with Europeans, and they sometimes reacted violently. European powers also seized Muslim territory militarily, France in North Africa, Russia in the Balkans, the Caucasus and Central Asia, and Britain in Egypt, where they frequently co-opted minorities into association with colonial rule. European technology enabled the Ottoman and Qajar states to centralize power and authority, a process started but far from completed by 1914. More importantly, European ideas, particularly those inspired by the French Revolution, radically affected self-perceptions among most communities, the most potent being ideas of national and ethnic community.

This process was accelerated by the defeat of the Ottoman Empire in 1918, accompanied by Allied utterances encouraging self-determination for the 'peoples' of the region, and by the drawing of new international borders that suited the imperial strategy of the Allies without regard for local communities. The modern state system replacing the old empires sought to impose and foster new national identities based upon the majority within each new territory. France and Britain exploited the communal fault lines in the territories they governed (see **Iraq, Lebanon, Palestine** and **Syria**) to weaken opposition to their rule. After 1948 Israel also adopted a policy of emphasizing communal differences in domestic and foreign policy to undermine feelings of Arab unity. One result is a deep rooted and understandable scepticism among dominant majorities, some intellectuals and governments in the Middle East regarding 'minority rights', which can easily be portrayed as a Trojan horse for continued foreign interference, or as a threat to territorial integrity.

There are other reasons for Westerners to tread with sensitivity regarding minorities in the region. Certain minorities coexist relatively successfully with majorities so long as they are not perceived as politically compromised by the West (or by Israel). This is true, for example, of some Christian communities and Jewish remnants in the Arab world. Such groups do not necessarily welcome interest or concern, unless it is expressed with great tact.

In applying the minority definition applicable for this *Directory*, certain exceptions have been included here, for example the Alawis in Syria (a currently dominant minority) and the Bidoun in Kuwait (defined merely by their absence of civic status). This has been done so because they are of legitimate interest, and many consulting this volume would be surprised by their omission.

Religious identities

Islam

The majority confession (probably about 70 per cent of the whole) in the region is Sunni Islam, and those Sunnis who also belong to the mainstream Turkish or Arab ethnic and linguistic groups might crudely be reckoned to be the 'dominant majorities' of the Middle East. Such a view, however, requires qualification, because Sunni Arabs, Turks and Shi'i Persians do not represent monolithic blocs. Sunni Islam is divided between four traditions of jurisprudence (governing family law, for example): the Hanafi, Hanbali, Maliki and Shafi'i schools (*madhhab*, pl. *madhahib*). Even where a majority of Sunnis within one country, for example Turkey, belong to one school, a substantial number may follow the teachings and practices of different religious brotherhoods (*tariqa*, pl. *turuq*), which are often locally based and may themselves have rival branches. The best known brotherhoods in the region are the Qadiriya and Naqshbandiya. The brotherhoods represent a powerful populist strain within the Islamic tradition, a strain traditionally in tension with formal Islam. Formal Islamic theology regards the Qur'an, supplemented by the traditions (*sunna*) of the Prophet, as the sole and sufficient repository of the faith. It rejects any priesthood as necessary to mediate the faith to believers or for an infallible interpretation of the scriptures. That infallibility, difficult to pinpoint in practice, belongs to the community as a whole, although the business of interpreting the Qur'an and *sunna* has been carried out over the centuries through a consensus of jurists and theologians. The Sunnis (followers of the *sunna*) consider community consensus based upon the Qur'an and traditions of the Prophet to be infallible and binding. Sunnis believe that following the Prophet's death in 632 CE, the responsibility of 'caretaker', or caliph, for the community passed to members of the Quraysh tribe, and thereafter to Quraysh descendants and the Umayyad (660–750) and Abbasid (750–1258) dynasties.

However, a fundamental schism in Islam occurred soon after the Prophet's death, because a party, or *shi'a*,[4] within the community claimed that the Prophet's cousin and son-in-law, Ali, should have been appointed caliph in 632 CE. Ali was only acknowledged caliph in 656, the fourth since the death of the Prophet, and was killed in 661 during the struggle for supremacy within the Muslim community. Although they lost the struggle, the Shi'i supporters of Ali clung to their cause with fervent devotion. In 680 Ali's younger son, Husayn, tried to contest Ummayad rule. He and his small party were surrounded and massacred close to Karbala in southern Iraq in 680. Husayn's death became a powerful symbol of martyrdom and suffering for the Shi'i community. The Shi'a articulated belief in a succession of imams, viewed as infallible in the interpretation of law and doctrine, whose essential qualification was descent from Ali and for whom Shi'ites have an almost mystical devotion. Some

Shi'ites, the Isma'ilis, broke away from the mainstream of Shi'ites after the death of the sixth imam, supporting descendants of his disinherited elder son, isma'il (see **Iran**). The majority of Shi'ites (Ithna'asharis), however, believe the twelfth was the last visible imam, in the ninth century CE. The Ithna'asharis believe their hidden imam will re-emerge to rule the world. Both Ithna'asharis and Isma'ilis themselves produced splinter groups, some of which moved to the very edges of recognizable Islam. Yet there has tended to be a reluctance within the Muslim community to denounce alien branches as heretical. In this sense Muslim doctrinal disagreements have not been as bitter as Christian ones.

The religious conflict between Sunni and Shi'i masked a socio-political one, between the ruling Arab tribal element in the nascent empire, and those who were conquered converts to Islam, for example in southern Mesopotamia and further east, and felt second class despite Islam's universe egalitarianism. Shi'ism, with its resonances of martyrdom, remained attractive to Muslim communities which felt excluded from power. Although the Sunni and Shi'i traditions formally accept each other as Muslim, at a popular level there is a deep animosity which periodically finds expression, particularly in the Shi'i community when it annually commemorates the martyrdom of Imam Husayn on 'Ashura', the tenth day of Muharram.

Another group also broke away from the Sunna and then from the Shi'a over the succession to the caliphate. These, the Kharijites (the 'Seceders'), believed that there was no need for the caliph to come from the Quaraysh tribes (the Sunnis) let alone from the Prophet's immediate family (the Shi'is). Anyone who led a blameless life, followed the true path and had the necessary qualities of leadership could be elected caliph. The Ibadis of Oman (see **Oman**) are the only surviving community of Khariji origin.

Christianity

Long before the Muslims conquered greater Syria and Mesopotamia, the Christian church had already split into a plethora of sects. The Ancient Church of the East, or 'Assyrian' Church, had already been expelled at the Council of Ephesus in 431, but three other 'Oriental' Orthodox churches were also expelled following the Council of Chalcedon, 451, all over issues concerning the precise nature of Christ: the Armenian Orthodox (or Apostolic), the Coptic Orthodox (Egypt) and the Syrian Orthodox.

The main Orthodox Church, which regarded itself as the guardian of the true faith, formally split in the eleventh century into the 'Greek' Orthodox (Constantinople) and 'Latin' Catholic Churches (Rome), although in practice they had parted company a good deal earlier. The Greek Orthodox predominated in the Middle East.

The Muslim authorities learnt to deal with each individual church, allowing each to regulate its own affairs. During the eighteenth and nineteenth centuries, virtually every eastern church was split as a result of European Catholic missionary endeavour. Thus, alongside the tension between Christian and Muslim caused by European involvement, bitter tensions were also created within the Christian community itself. Some of those tensions between the Orthodox and 'Uniate' churches (that is, the splinter churches that entered union with Rome) persist among the 4 million or so Christians in the region today.

The twentieth century

With the establishment of the modern states system after 1918, several factors radically changed the perception of minorities in the Middle East. The first of these was the ability of the new states to exercise an unprecedented degree of centralizing control over small and traditionally autonomous rural communities. This particularly affected socio-economic groups like nomadic peoples but also those of distinct ethnic or linguistic tradition.

Such groups were required to subordinate long-standing community identities to the official new 'national', in fact state, identity. The new state identity had little in common with the old, for it was grounded in an essentially Western notion of the ethnic basis of nations. Thus Turkish, Persian and Arab nationalists sought to forge new unitary nations in which everyone – whether they belonged to 'minorities' or not – was expected to subordinate long-established identities, usually of a religious kind, to the demands of the modern nation. This provoked some to retreat into their old identities, and others – most notably the Kurds – to acquire their own ethnic consciousness.

In addition the convulsions of war had already led to major population disintegration or movement. The most notorious case was that of the deportation of Armenians by Turkey in May 1915, an exercise which rapidly descended into the genocide of over one million people. But there were other population movements, primarily affecting other inhabitants of Anatolia, but also including Zionist settlement in Palestine, which disturbed the status quo and forced hitherto unselfconscious communities to re-examine their identities, sometimes in political terms.

This explosive new mix was heated by the idea of self-determination adumbrated by US President Woodrow Wilson in January 1918 in his Fourteen Points for World Peace. Since then the region has been in a state of ferment concerning the status and ambitions of various groups of people. The claims of ethnicity and nationalism, particularly pan-Arabism, which dominated political discourse in the middle years of the century gave some ground in the period 1955–85 to leftist ideologies, and more recently to political Islam.

Since 1945 other factors have come into play, most notably urbanization, economic transformation and state education. For a long time it was assumed that cities would be a melting pot in which a new national identity could be forged. But in Beirut, Istanbul and other large cities, recently rural people often reconstructed in more extreme form the religious or ethnic dimension of their pre-urban identity, a defence mechanism against the anonymity of city life. Economic transformation has introduced a new class dimension that has accelerated social change. It has fostered ethnic consciousness in some cases, but class or religious consciousness in others.

State education has been a powerful vehicle in social transformation. All too often though, it has sought to create a homogeneous community, frequently banishing any discussion of plurality within society and refusing to permit minority languages to be used or taught. But such denial can provoke strong reaction, exciting a passionate new political identity to compensate for cultural loss. In other cases, education is used to control or even co-opt minority groups, for example the Israeli Druzes, as servants of the state.

The idea that gender could be a minority issue was wholly alien to the Middle East until comparatively recently. Certain facts, however, suggest that it is a factor to bear in mind. Female babies have a generally higher mortality rate in this region indicating, in view of the greater natural rate of male infant mortality, that society is less assiduous in caring for girls. Female enrolment rates in education are lower, and the opportunities for higher or further education more limited. Except in limited cases, women are excluded from all formal areas of economic or political power as a result of long-standing social or religious custom. In most states, Islamic family law remains in force, denying women equal rights or power. Over the past fifty years there has been greater female participation in public life, but status varies according to country, community and decade. The rise of political Islam has undoubtedly threatened some of these advances because governments either feel obliged to pay lip service, or actually subscribe, to its values.

Another factor in society that impinges on the minority question is labour migration. It is as migrant workers, for example Kurds in Germany and Palestinians in the Gulf, that much national formation has taken place. Attitudes vary from state to state, but broadly speaking all the oil producing states have been willing to admit large numbers but careful to ensure they depart the moment their economic usefulness ceases, and to limit very strictly their civil rights. The proportions of migrant workers in 1983 were as follows: Bahrain 29 per cent, Kuwait 60 per cent, Oman 26 per cent, Qatar 66 per cent, Saudi Arabia 27 per cent, United Arab Emirates 70 per cent.

Finally, it should be borne in mind that virtually all communities in the Middle East feel they are a minority in terms of power when compared with the secular West. The vast majority of Arabs, Turks, Persians and Kurds, Muslims and Christians, resent what they perceive as the West's bullying interference in the political and economic spheres, its moral hectoring, which is seen as self-serving hypocrisy, and its ignorant prejudice concerning Islam, which tends to compromise inter-confessional understanding in the region.

Further reading

Ahmad, L., *Women and Gender in Islam*, London and New Haven, CT, Yale University Press, 1992.

Atiya, A., *A History of Eastern Christianity*, London, Methuen, 1968.

Connell, D., 'Middle East and North Africa', in M.S. Miller and Cultural Survival (eds), *State of the Peoples: A Global Human Rights Report on Societies in Danger*, Boston, MA, Beacon Press, 1993.

Dearden, A. (ed.), *Arab Women*, London, MRG report, 1983.

McLaurin, R. (ed.), *The Political Role of Minority Groups in the Middle East*, New York, Praeger, 1979.

MRG, *Minorities in the Middle East*, London, MRG update pack, 1992.

Nisan, M., *Minorities in the Middle East: A History of Struggle and Self-Expression*, Jefferson, NC, McFarland, 1991.

Owen, R., with update by van Hear, N., *Migrant Workers in the Gulf*, London, MRG report, 1992.

Schulze, K., Stokes, M. and Campbell, C. (eds), *Nationalism, Minorities and Diasporas: Identities and Rights in the Middle East*, London and New York, Tauris, 1996.

Tapper, R. (ed.), *Some Minorities in the Middle East,* London, School of Oriental and African Studies, 1992.

Zubaida, S., *Islam, the People and the State: Political Ideas and Movements in the Middle East*, London, IB Tauris, 1993.

Bahrain

Land area:	695 sq km
Population:	486,000 (1993)
Main languages:	Arabic, Persian
Main religions:	Sunni and Ithna'ashari Shi'i Islam, Christianity, Hinduism, other faiths among non-Bahrainis
Main minority groups:	Bahraini nationals: Sunnis 102,000 (35%), Ithna'asharis 190,000 (65%); *total population*: Christians 34,000 (7%), Hindus 15,000 (3%)
Real per capita GDP:	$14,590
UNDP HDI/rank:	0.862 (44)

Bahrain is an archipelago, consisting of Bahrain Island, about 48 kilometres in length, and some thirty smaller islands. Sixty per cent of the population is native born, the rest are Arab, Iranian, Pakistani and Indian migrant workers. Bahrain was internally controlled and loosely linked to Persia through protection agreements. It was captured by the Al Khalifa family from Zubara, north of Qatar, in 1783. This brought the island and the original Bahrani Shi'i population under Sunni control. Sunnis belong to three broad categories: those who arrived with the Al Khalifa; traders from Najd; and Arab traders who settle periodically on alternate coasts of the Gulf, known as Hawila. Bahrain came under British influence in 1820, formalized in protectorate status in 1880. The administrative measures introduced by Britain in the 1920s tended to strengthen the authority of the Al Khalifa, to the detriment of previously largely autonomous groups, and undermined the idea of consensus among the general public. Iran made periodic claims to sovereignty over Bahrain. In 1971 Bahrain became fully independent.

The Al Khalifa allowed a national assembly from 1973 to 1975 but suspended it, disliking any form of democratic voice. The 1973 constitution was likewise suspended. In 1974 an emergency law was introduced with powers to ban meetings and to detain people without trial for up to three years. Inevitably, the subordinate position of the Shi'a became inextricably linked with the denial of any popular representation. Petitions for restitution of the constitution and parliamentary elections signed by 300 leading Sunni and Shi'i citizens in 1992 and by 25,000 citizens in 1994 led to waves of arrests and the forcible exile of leading Shi'i clerics. In 1992, eleven Bahrainis were detained without trial, accused of belonging to the Islamic Opposition. Throughout the period detainees have complained of torture, others have been expelled to Iran in small boats. Bahrain has been of serious concern to the United Nations, Amnesty International and other human rights groups. The police are largely immigrant Pakistanis, Baluch and Indians, led by British senior officers.

The situation is exacerbated by economic recession. Thirty per cent Bahraini unemployment (1994), hitting Shi'is hardest, when there are 120,000 resident foreign workers (65 per cent of the total workforce) appears indefensible, but foreign workers are a cheaper option. Oil, the mainstay of the economy, is expected to run out within fifteen years.

Christians and Hindus are migrant workers and do not form coherent and cohesive minority communities.

Ithna'ashari Shi'is

Approximately 65 per cent of Bahrainis are Shi'i. Traditionally the Baharina (sing. Bahrani), the indigenous Shi'is, were engaged in date palm agriculture, and pearl diving, but since oil was first struck in 1931, many became oil field workers. About 5–10 per cent of Shi'is are of Iranian origin, some left over from Iranian rule in the eighteenth century or earlier, and others who arrived in the 1920s and 1930s to escape taxation.

The prime centres for Shi'i social and cultural activity are the *ma'atim*, religious associations which organize the annual Ashura commemoration, and which symbolize 'the rejection of worldly power and the forms of government associated with it'.[1]

Shi'is have always felt excluded from the political process. Popular tensions have exploded from time to time, with periodic serious affrays which started during Ashura in 1953, and lasted until 1956, in which some Shi'is were shot dead by police.

Inevitably the Iranian Revolution excited Shi'i expectations and in some cases attempts to undermine the state. In 1981, 73 Shi'is, mainly Bahrainis, were arrested in a supposed Iran-inspired coup plot. In 1984 a small arms cache was found in a Bahrani village. In 1988 three Shi'is were convicted of attempted sabotage of an oil refinery.

The Shi'is are increasingly unwilling to accept the political, economic and social exclusion practised by the Al Khalifa establishment. Throughout the 1980s and into the 1990s, Shi'is have been the prime, though not exclusive, target of state violence, torture and expulsion. Shi'i clerics who have dared criticize the government during their sermons have been routinely arrested, some spending years in jail without trial. In 1981, when Shi'is were expressing anti-government sentiment, the Bahraini Prime Minister was reported as saying 'I will bundle every Bahraini Shi'a in a sack and throw him into the sea'.[2] All forms of Shi'i expression became a target. Clerics were harassed, and in 1984 the Islamic Enlightenment Society, a Shi'i charity that had been operating since 1972 and which ran three girls schools, was closed down.

Conclusions and future prospects

Since 1993 democratic opposition forces have gained ground and support among increasingly frustrated Shi'is, with mass demonstrations, and police shootings, and assaults on people and mosques. Shi'i protest is essentially an integral part of the growing constitutional protest movement against authoritarian dynastic rule by the Al Khalifa.

Further reading

Amnesty International, *Bahrain: Violations of Human Rights*, London, 1991.

Amnesty International, *Banned from Bahrain: Forcible Exile of Bahraini Nationals*, London, 1993.

Article 19, *Bahrain: Time for Change*, London, December 1991.

Khouri, F., *Tribe and State in Bahrain: The Transformation of Social and Political Authority in an Arab State*, Chicago, IL, Chicago University Press, 1980

Minority-based and advocacy organizations

Committee for the Defence of Human Rights in Bahrain, PO Box 2945, Damascus, Syria.

Bahrain Freedom Movement [represents both Shi'is and Sunnis], BM Box 6135, London WC1N 3XX, UK; tel./fax 44 171 278 9089.

Iran

Land area:	1,648,000 sq km
Population:	60.8 million (1993)
Main Languages:	Persian, Azeri and other Turkish dialects, Arabic, Kurdish, Baluchi
Main religions:	Ithna'ashari, Sunni and Isma'ili Islam, also Ahl-i Haq, Mazda-yasnie (Zoroastrian) religion, Baha'i faith, Armenian and Assyrian Christianity, Judaism
Main minority groups:	*estimated*: Azaris 15 million (25%), Kurds 6 million (10%), Baluch 1.5 million (2.4%), Ahl-i Haqq 1 million (1.6%), Arabs 1 million (1.6%),Turkomans 900,000 (1.4%), Qashqa'i 800,000 (1.3%), Baha'is 300,000 (0.5%), Armenians 250,000 (0.4%), Assyrians 100,000 (0.15%), Mazda-yasnie (Zoroastrians) 45,000 (0.07%), Isma'ilis 30,000 (0.05%), Jews 25,000 (0.04%)
Real per capita GDP:	$5,420
UNDP HDI/rank:	0.770 (70)

Ever since the foundation of the Iranian state by the Achaemenids in the sixth century BCE Iran has experienced alternating phases of political coherence and regional disintegration. This is due in part to the size and ruggedness of the terrain – a vast and in parts desert plateau surrounded by some areas able to sustain agriculture and urban life and other areas only suitable for transhumance. The state had to handle its indigenous tribes and also absorb periodic waves of tribal invasion, mainly Turkic ones from the Central Asian steppes. This could only be done through a highly decentralized polity in which regions and tribal groups enjoyed a large measure of freedom.

At the beginning of the nineteenth century over one-third of the Iranian population was tribal. For the past 1,000 years, with only one notable exception, every ruling dynasty has been of tribal origin. Tribes only began to settle and some to lose their solidarity in the past century or so. Tribal identity has been based on political organization formed for socio-economic purposes rather than feelings of ethnic or kin identity, even if these elements are discernible.

In Iran as elsewhere although people have long been aware of ethnic differences these only began to acquire political importance during this century when the state had the means to enforce centralization. Reza Khan (from 1925 Reza Shah), who seized power in 1920, sought to forge the disparate peoples of Iran into a single nation. The state adopted Persian, spoken by 45 per cent of the population, as the official language and used it for all administration and education, banning publication in other languages. It also tried to inflict European-style dress on the population and to settle nomadic pastoralists, by force if need be. Such measures created a sharp sense of difference among those peoples which did not belong to the dominant Persian community and helped create a sense of ethnic distinctiveness.

Under his son, Muhammad Reza Pahlavi, the sense of difference between the dominant Persian heart of the country (which forms a broad arc from Mashhad through Tehran to Isfahan and Shiraz) and the predominantly non-Persian districts increased. Muhammad Reza Pahlavi's rush to industrialize and modernize was concentrated on the central and central northern areas of Iran. By 1976 the average level of urbanization in Iran was 46.8 per cent; the level in Kurdish and Baluchi regions, at opposite ends of the country, was less than 25 per cent, however, while that for the Persian-dominated Central Province was over 80 per cent. Other indices, for example literacy or electrification of homes, followed similar proportions. It was quite clear that the non-Persian periphery was subsidizing the industrialized core. Thus, community self-awareness on the periphery was also driven by economic discrimination.

Regarding religion, the Pahlavis liked to emphasize the ancient and pre-Islamic nature of the Iranian state. In fact Iran had a strong Shi'ite tradition going back to the initial schism with the Sunnis. In the sixteenth century the Safavid dynasty adopted Shi'i Islam and eliminated the

Sunni *ulama*' (religious clerics). Virtually all Iran became Shi'i with the exception of certain communities on the state peripheries. The Pahlavis underestimated the ability of the Shi'i *ulama*' to mobilize popular disapproval and dissatisfaction.

In the spring of 1979, following the Shah's overthrow, the Islamic Republic of Iran was proclaimed. All the ethnic minorities, except the Azaris, sought autonomy, hoping that Tehran would be unable to maintain its grip on the periphery. The new regime feared that conceding autonomy to one community would lead to the disintegration of the state. Ayatollah Khomeini also argued that ethnic autonomy violated the universalism implicit in Islam. Furthermore, regardless of the theological recognition of Sunnis as part of the *umma* (the universal Muslim community), Article 5 of the constitution defines Iran as a Shi'i Islamic republic, and Article 115 debars non-Shi'is from presidential office.

In accordance with traditional Islamic prescription, the new republic formally recognized the *dhimmi* communities, but was less tolerantly disposed towards small Protestant (and therefore Western-inspired) churches, and was vehemently hostile to the Baha'is.

RELIGIOUS MINORITIES

Sunnis

Most Kurds, Turkomans, Baluch and some Arabs are Sunni, and are discussed as ethnic communities since they do not form a cohesive coherent whole as Sunnis and tend to express their identity in ethnic terms. Altogether they probably represent almost 15 per cent of Iran's population.

Ahl-i Haqq

There are probably about a million Ahl-i Haqq in Iran, mainly located in Luristan and Gurani-speaking areas of southern Kurdistan. A few smaller groups exist further north, near Urumiya and Maku. Ahl-i Haqq religion started as a variant of Sufism in fifteenth century Kurdistan. It has an exaggerated veneration for Ali, lies on the periphery of Shi'ism, and seems to be a syncretic agglomeration of pagan, Christian and Muslim traditions. Its adherents are frequently called Ali Illahi (deifiers of Ali). They believe in a system of seven incarnations, and were almost certainly influenced by early Nusayri (see **Syria**) ideas in the lower Tigris valley. The community is split into several ethnic, tribal and religious groupings and has no unified organization or canonical scripture.

Coherent political leadership only emerged during this century specially among southern Kurdish tribes-people when the Haydari *sayyids* (those who claim descent from the sect's founder) displaced chiefs as community leaders during Reza Shah's drive against tribal chiefdoms. The 1979 revolution was a moment of potentially great peril, had the new regime decided to extirpate the Ahl-i Haqq. Sayyid Nasr al Din Haydari handled the situation with skill. As soon as war with Iraq broke out, he raised Ahl-i Haqq volunteer forces to defend the frontier. The large community around Sahna, east of Kirmanshah, has less cohesion.

A reformist wing developed from the 1960s and spread among urban educated Iranians, but increasing opposition from 'traditionalists' led to schism in 1992. The mainly rural and tribal traditionalists wish to retain their Ahl-i Haqq identity. The mainly urban reformists, known as Maktabi, seek to redefine their faith in line with *ithna'ashari* orthodoxy, and are gaining converts both inside Iran and among exiled communities.

Baha'is

There are an estimated 300,000 Baha'is in Iran out of an estimated 5 million world-wide. They have been persecuted intermittently since the foundation of the religion in the mid-nineteenth century. The Baha'i faith originated with the declaration of a Shirazi merchant that he was the Bab, or 'gateway' to the Twelfth Imam. 'Babism' had already attracted a large following, mainly among the Shaykhi revivalist strand of Shi'ism, by the time of his execution for heresy in 1850. Most Babis transferred their discipleship to Mirza Husain Ali, who styled himself Baha'ullah (the Glory of God) in 1848 and later settled in Haifa. Under his son and grandson the new religion rapidly attracted followers in the West.

The Baha'i religion is, briefly, that God is unknowable in human terms but has been made manifest in the prophets which include the leaders of most major religions. Baha'ullah is the most recent of these. Baha'is therefore accept the validity of other major religions. No one can be born a Baha'i, but must consciously embrace the faith. They believe in gender equality, universal education and world peace, and oppose all forms racial, class or ethnic discrimination. During the Pahlavi period, 1920–79, the Baha'is were generally able to prosper without undue harassment, although they remained unrecognized, and with no legal right to exist. With the 1979 revolution Shi'i clerics aroused anti-Baha'i fervour, not a difficult task since in Muslim eyes Baha'is were apostates, punishable under the *shari'a* by death. Furthermore, despite their political quietism, their belief in the monarchic principle exposed them to the charge that they were supporters of the Shah and agents of SAVAK, the feared Pahlavi secret police. The existence of a large Baha'i community in the United States also made Iranian Baha'is vulnerable.

The floodgates of persecution were now opened. In 1980 all 11 members of the National Spiritual Assembly were arrested and disappeared without trace, and the same fate befell their successors the following year. Scores of others were subsequently executed or arbitrarily imprisoned. Individually and collectively, the Baha'is have been the target of economic discrimination, losing welfare rights, public sector employment and frequently private businesses. Baha'i marriage is not recognized, and couples are therefore liable to punishment for immorality. They are not allowed to leave Iran. During the 1990s the level of persecution abated somewhat. However, Baha'i properties remain confiscated.

Armenians

There are approximately 250,000 Armenians in Iran, mainly in Tehran, Tabriz and Isfahan. A portion of Armenians have lived under Iranian rule since 387 CE when Rome and Iran partitioned Armenia. In the early seventeenth century Shah Abbas moved hundreds of thousands of artisan Armenians from the plain of Ararat to his capital of Isfahan. In 1827 Iran lost Armenia to Russia, but a considerable community remained in Isfahan, some moved to Tabriz as it became the economic capital in the nineteenth century, and others moved to Tehran as it acquired economic dominance in the mid-twentieth century. The smaller Armenian community in West Azerbaijan suffered massacre and depredation by Turks and Kurds in 1915, and was largely extinguished.

Armenians prospered commercially under the Pahlavi regime but have found life more unpredictable under the Islamic Republic. The community is formally *dhimmi,* and represented in parliament. But like the rest of the commercial sector, Armenians have been hard hit by the rigours of war with Iraq and international isolation. However, the community is able to publish several periodicals, including leftist ones banned before 1979, its schools and churches still function and it has re-opened a cultural and sporting club.

Assyrians

The Assyrian community, approximately 100,000 strong, is located in Urumiya and environs, in north-western Iran. It has probably been in the area since the fifth century. Unlike those in the Hakkari mountains in Turkey to the west, the Assyrians of Urumiya were largely non-tribal and faced intermittent difficulties as a Christian minority and also as peasantry under a system of tribal protection and extortion. In the late nineteenth century their position became increasingly compromised with the growth of Russian and British political influence and Orthodox, Catholic and Protestant missionary activity in the region, all of which heightened Muslim fears. With the outbreak of war in 1914, the Assyrians became victims of wholesale Turkish and Kurdish massacres around Urumiya (1915), and Russian and British encouragement to side with the Allies in early 1917. In view of their precarious situation, and of the Armenian genocide in 1915, the Assyrians threw in their lot with the Allies, only to find Russia withdrawing from the war in October 1917, and British forces too far away to help. Most Assyrians fled southwards from Urumiya and were given asylum in Iraq.

The Assyrian remnant fared relatively well under the secular Pahlavis. Life under the Islamic republic has been more difficult in spite of formal *dhimmi* status and representation in parliament. Assyrian traders in Urumiya have suffered from informal boycotts by militant Muslims. Although they do not feel persecuted, pressure to conform to the public precepts of the *shari'a* and the closure of Assyrian schools and publications has led to migration to the West.

Mazda-yasnie (Zoroastrians)

There are probably about 45,000 Zoroastrians living mainly in Yazd and Kirman, to which areas those who refused periodic pressure to convert had retreated, and also in Tehran in recent decades. The proper name for Zoroastrians is 'Mazda-yasnie', or worshipper of Ahura Mazda, who is God, literally the Great Wisdom Giver. Zoroaster, or more correctly, Zaruthustra, is the 'Righteous Man' of the faith. As the established monotheism, the Muslim conquerors accepted Zoroastrians as *dhimmis*.

Today most Zoroastrians are self-employed or are farmers working their ancestral land, to which they are strongly committed. In 1882 they were relieved of their *dhimmi* status, and enjoyed equal rights and responsibilities with other Iranians.

However, following the 1979 revolution, *dhimmi* status was reapplied and the *khums* (one-fifth) tax on land transactions reintroduced retrospectively, even though they were not exempted from military service as granted to *dhimmis* by the *shari'a*. In practice the state discriminates: it generally rejects Zoroastrian job applicants, particularly for teaching or military service, by introducing strict Islamic tests, but also occasionally uses them in appointments that require financial probity.

Isma'ilis

There are probably about 30,000 Isma'ilis in Iran today, half of whom live in Khurasan, while the remainder live in the towns of Kirman, Mahallat and Yazd, and their neighbouring villages.

The Isma'ili community acquired political prominence in the ninth and tenth centuries as a revolutionary movement spread by missionaries across the Muslim world. The community has experienced two schisms concerning the imamate succession. After the establishment of the Isma'ili Fatimid dynasty in Egypt, the Iranian and Syrian Isma'ilis broke away in the late eleventh century after Nizar was denied the succession and murdered. These 'Nizari' Isma'ilis established a formidable network of fortresses in the mountains of north-western Iran, of which the most famous was Alamut. In 1256 the Mongols destroyed their forts and attempted to extirpate the community in Iran. It survived only by dissimulation (*taqiyya*), and by moving to the desert fringes of central Iran. It re-emerged and grew during the Safavid period. In the early nineteenth century Isma'ili imams acquired public prominence, one of whom received the honorific title of Aga Khan from the Qajar Shah. Following his revolt in 1841, the Aga Khan fled to Afghanistan and then to India. A large number of Isma'ilis, especially community leaders, followed him. In the nineteenth century and in the Constitutional period, 1906–9, Isma'ili leaders and communities were sometimes harassed by Shi'i *ulama*' and urban mobs.

Since then, however, Isma'ilis have prospered. Sultan Muhammad Shah Aga Khan III (1877–1957) encouraged schools and agricultural projects in Khurasan, and many urban Isma'ilis became civil servants and teachers. In 1973 two committees were organized by the present Imam, Aga Khan IV, to regulate the Iranian community, one in Mashhad (for Khurasan) and the other in Tehran for Kirman, Yazd, Mahallat and Tehran itself. Good relations have been maintained with the Ithna'ashari majority.

Jews

Jews have dwelt in Iran since the sixth century BCE. Apart from a brief period of forcible conversion by Shah Abbas in the early seventeenth century, they generally enjoyed *dhimmi* protection and status under Islam. Most made their living as traders and artisans. The Pahlavis removed *dhimmi* restrictions in 1948, when 28,000 Jews out of almost 100,000 in Iran migrated to the new Israeli state. Those who remained prospered under Pahlavi rule.

Following the 1979 revolution the Jewish community was quick to seek the protection of the new Islamic republic. Like Christians and Zoroastrians, they were formally accorded *dhimmi* status and community representation in parliament. Many Jews, however, felt unsafe under so vehemently anti-Zionist a regime and up to 30,000 had left by 1984. A decade later the remaining community was estimated at only about 25,000.

Jews soon found a contrast between their formal acceptance and daily experience in the Islamic republic. The underlying tone of the regime, regardless of its formal utterances, seemed overtly hostile. The community leader, Habib Alqanian, was arrested and executed as 'an individual who wished to equate Jewry with Zionism'. What really worried Jews was that Iranians were encouraged to make no distinction between Jews and Zionists. During the US Embassy hostage crisis, 1979–80, Jews were widely harassed and some had their property confiscated by neighbouring *komitehs*.

ETHNIC OR SOCIO-ETHNIC COMMUNITIES

Azaris

There are probably 15 million Azaris in Iran, almost one-third of the total population. Descendants, like virtually all other Turkic groups in the Middle East, of the Oghuz branch of the Turkic people, they settled in north-western Iran from the eleventh century, mingling to some extent with Kurds and Persians. They are a border minority, cut off from their more numerous fellows in territory which was captured by Russia in the nineteenth century and is now the Republic of Azerbaijan. Having embraced Shi'i Islam, Azaris are closer to other Iranian Shi'is than to the (Sunni) Turks of Turkey, and predictably the Shi'i–Sunni divide is an intermittent source of friction with neighbouring Kurds. Until the present century the province of Azerbaijan, like the rest of Iran, was divided between its tribal, peasant and urban constituencies.

Although a distinctive Turkic group linguistically, Azaris have tended to identify with Iran, priding themselves on taking a political lead in national issues. They played an important role in events leading to the Constitutional Revolution of 1906, in the National Front of Mossadegh, 1950–3, and in the revolution of 1978–9.

There have been two short occasions of Azari ethno-political expression, but both were symptomatic of the power vacuum in 1918 and 1945. In 1920 Azadistan, or 'Land of the Free', lasted for a few months, but far from being separatist it remained committed to Iran's integrity. In 1945 a leftist and autonomous democratic government was formed with Soviet encouragement. It lasted barely a year. It was partly a response to Pahlavi attempts to suppress Azari language and culture. In 1946 Tehran restored its authority and executed those associated with the democratic government. Tabriz, the provincial capital, remained suspect of leftist rather than separatist dissent. In 1979 most Azaris campaigned against Tehran and Qum for a more secular and more decentralized form of Islamic republic, and most boycotted the constitutional referendum at the end of that year. Azari political dissent was crushed in 1980–1. Although there is a distinct Azari consciousness it is unlikely to find nationalist expression, and there is no sign of a desire to reunite with ex-Soviet Azerbaijan. Common Shi'i identity, involvement with the wider economy of Iran and the presence of many Azaris in Tehran all suggest that in the future Azaris are likely to be less interested in ethnic distinctiveness than in seeking to influence state politics, possibly to moderate the nature of the Islamic republic and allow for a more decentralized system of government.

Kurds

There are probably six million Kurds in Iran, mainly living along the borders with Iraq and Turkey, except for about 400,000 who were forcibly resettled in Khurasan in the early seventeenth century. Kurds do not form an ethnic whole in the sense of having a common ancestry, but are descended from waves of Indo-European tribes which entered the Zagros mountains from the east and from the north, over many centuries from the second millennium BCE, and from later Arab and Turkic elements absorbed into Kurdish tribal and linguistic culture. One indicator of varied origins is the substantial dialect differences between Kirmanji, spoken in the northern reaches of Iranian and most of Turkish Kurdistan, and Sorani, spoken in most of Iranian and Iraqi Kurdistan. In the southern reaches some Kurds speak Gurani, a distinct language related to Zaza (see **Turkey**) and suggesting a separate origin, and others around Kirmanshah, a dialect closer to Persian. In northern Luristan the Lak dialect tribes are also considered Kurds.

Until the Islamic conquest the term 'Kurd' seems to have meant nomad, with a geographic rather than specific ethnic connotation. Although there have always been peasant Kurds, the prevailing image has been of pastoralist tribesmen until the 1960s.

Reza Shah suppressed a major Kurdish tribal rising in 1922, and dealt ruthlessly with those that defied his will. After his abdication in 1941, a class of urban educated Kurds who had nothing in common with the tribal chiefs began to emerge in Iran. Based in Mahabad, they propagated the idea of Kurdish ethnic autonomy, an idea that spread quickly among non-tribal Kurds. The Soviets, who controlled much of north-western Iran, encouraged the leadership in Mahabad to declare their own republic in January 1946, but did little to ensure its survival. At the end of the year Iranian government forces recaptured Mahabad and hanged the leaders. Most Kurdish tribes sided with the government.

During the 1960s and 1970s the Kurdistan Democratic Party of Iran (KDPI) tried to revive the struggle. But most of their fighters were captured either by government troops or by the Iraqi Kurdish leader Mulla Mustafa Barzani who, depending on the Shah for help against Baghdad, handed over Iranian Kurdish fighters to Tehran.

It was the Shah's land reform in the 1960s and growing economic change that really created much greater support for the KDPI. With the Shah's destruction of the old tribal and landlord patronage systems, uneducated Kurds also began to think about their identity in ethnic terms. In 1979 they tried to establish autonomy and, following the failure of talks with Tehran, drove the armed forces out of the region. Iranian government forces recaptured the entire area in 1982–4; since then the KDPI has sustained a campaign of night guerrilla attacks from over the Iraqi border. The authorities carried out mass executions of Kurdish fighters and those suspected of supporting them. In 1989 the KDPI tried to enter into dialogue with the government but its leader, Abd al Rahman Qasimulu, was assassinated, as was his successor 18 months later. Kurds assumed that the government was responsible for these killings.

The Kurds did not act as a whole. The Kirmanji-speaking minority in the north had attacked the KDPI on behalf of the government in 1979–80. Meanwhile in the south that proportion – roughly 15 per cent – who were Shi'i, and some Ahl-i Haqq, declared for the government. Kurdish resistance was also dogged by dissension. The two nationalist parties, the KDPI and the Marxist-Leninist group Komala (supported mainly in the Sanandaj region), fought between themselves from 1984 for four years before lapsing into an informal truce. The KDPI was also victim to internal schism.

While the government appears now in firm control, two factors are likely to strengthen Kurdish ethnic solidarity. First, the majority of Shi'i Kurds in the south became disenchanted with Tehran and have become more sympathetic to Sunni Kurdish nationalists. Second, population growth and economic difficulties have driven an increasing number of Kurdish young men to seek work elsewhere, particularly in the oilfields of Khuzistan. The sense of alienation common among migrant workers is likely to strengthen ethnic identity, and also create circumstances in which Kurds may cooperate with other disenchanted communities to seek decentralization. However unlikely such circumstances may currently seem, the government may face popular protest as the economic situation, already serious, continues to deteriorate.

Few Kurds seek outright independence and the slogan of the KDPI is 'autonomy for the Kurds, democracy for Iran'. Yet the government remains firmly convinced that any form of autonomy will lead to the progressive break-up of Iran.

Baluch

There are between one and two million Baluch in south-eastern Iran, part of a larger community which extends into Pakistan as well as Afghanistan. They are located in the hill regions from Harhad to Makran. The Baluch have a strong nomadic and tribal culture and also Indo-European, Arab and Turkic origins, but form a coherent Indo-European linguistic group. Existing on the fringes of Iranian government control, the Baluch have retained their strong Sunni identity. A small minority of Baluch living in the approaches to Kirman, in the west, are Shi'i. Divided by rugged country, any sense of collective identity beyond tribalism and semi-caste relations is only now in the process of formation. While outsiders, especially British colonialists, were the first to imagine a Baluch community identity, until recently most Baluch identified themselves by tribe and kinship, not ethnicity.

The Pahlavis exempted the Baluch from the tribal suppression practised elsewhere. They successfully co-opted and rewarded many tribal chiefs and *hakom* rulers (quasi-feudal major landlords), while keeping the region generally undeveloped but well garrisoned. Without education or development to raise local consciousness, it was easy to stifle any Baluch expression and also to encourage Persian settlement in Zahidan and elsewhere. To a degree the Baluch were also divided administratively so that they no longer formed a coherent whole. Only two serious revolts took place, both limited tribal affairs, in 1957–9 and a more serious bushfire guerrilla war funded by Iraq, in 1968–73.

The Baluch were largely unprepared for the 1979 revolution. However, in response to the Shi'i character of the emergent republic, Sunni clerics displaced the discredited old chiefs as community leaders. As the Islamic Unity Party, they sought formal government recognition of their Sunni identity and the right to play a part in their own administration. When denied these concessions they orchestrated a mass Baluch boycott of the constitutional referendum in December 1979. Fighting subsequently broke out with the government *pasdaran*, (revolutionary guards) who were supported by the Shi'i Persian community in Zahidan and by Sistanis from further north. A smaller but more organized struggle was waged by left-wing intellectuals, who formed an umbrella organization, the Baluchistan People's Democratic Organization, which sought autonomy for Baluchistan and democracy for Iran, and cooperated with the main Marxist opposition parties in Iran. By the end of 1981 Tehran had reasserted its authority throughout Baluchistan, imprisoning or executing those leftist rebels which it caught and driving others into exile. Although Tehran's writ currently runs unchallenged, Shi'i rule since 1979 has accelerated Baluch community feeling. In the 1990s Sunni clerics trained in Pakistan and Saudi Arabia and inspired by the *Mojahedin* in Afghanistan have strengthened the Sunni dimension of Baluch identity, leading to serious demonstrations and clashes with government forces in early 1994. There is a considerable Baluch migrant population in some Gulf countries, notably Bahrain and Oman.

Arabs

There are probably one million Arabs, mainly Shi'i, living primarily along the Gulf littoral in the province of Khuzistan and more generally in the south. The Arabs of Khuzistan and of southern Iraq form a cultural unit. Many Arabs on the coastline are Sunni, originally from the Arabian Peninsula, and have a history since the sixteenth century of migrating between the east and west sides of the Gulf. They are thus thought of as neither wholly Iranian nor wholly Arab. As a group they are known as Hawila (sing. Huli(m) Huliya (f)). In spite of such factors Iraqi attempts to foment unrest for the Pahlavis and the Islamic republic have been largely unsuccessful. Arabs of Khuzistan demanded autonomy, like the Baluch, Kurds and Turkoman in 1979, but demonstrated their loyalty to the Islamic regime during the Iran-Iraq war 1980–8.

Turkoman

There are probably 900,000 Turkoman along the north-eastern border of Iran, from the Caspian shore to Sarakhs, where the border turns sharply southwards. They are a tribally organized nomadic people, part of a much more substantial community in the ex-Soviet Republic of Turkmenistan. They make their livelihood by stockrearing, agriculture, fishing and carpet weaving. They belong to three principal confederations, the Yomut, Gukalan and Takeh. Like the Baluch and the Kurds, the Turkoman are ethnically, linguistically and religiously different from the ruling Persian Shi'i centre.

From the early 1920s Reza Khan used draconian methods on the Turkoman, as on other tribal groups, to compel them to settle, and most fled to the Soviet side of the border in 1925. It was not long before they found Stalinist Turkmenistan to be worse, and returned to face cultural discrimination and virtual vassalage since most of the Turkoman lands became Reza Shah's personal estate, for which the tribes were compelled to pay rent. They were forbidden to migrate on their traditional routes or to construct permanent buildings. It was forbidden to teach or publish in Turkoman. They remained under tight political and military control during Muhammad Reza's reign. Although intended to turn them into dutiful Iranian citizens, this policy fostered Turkoman ethno-linguistic consciousness.

In 1979 the Turkoman sought autonomy but, like the Kurds and Baluch, were compelled by force to accept Shi'i centralization. Their best prospect of autonomy would be in the event of a collapse of central authority, and the combined effort of minority communities to create a new decentralized state.

Qashqa'i

The Qashqa'i tribal confederation is probably about 800,000 strong, primarily located in the southern Zagros Mountains. It was formed in the early eighteenth century and played a major part in local, provincial and national affairs during the nineteenth and twentieth centuries. Although ethno-linguistically diverse – including central Asian, Caucasian, Iranian and Turkish elements – Persian domination of the state this century drove the Qashqa'i to assert a Turkish identity. By 1950 Turkish was the first language of almost the whole confederation. To be Qashqa'i is to cleave to tribal identity and values, even in the case of the many permanently settled in villages and towns.

The Qashqa'i paramount chiefs were divested of power and the constituent tribes ruthlessly controlled during the Pahlavi years. The senior surviving stratum of chiefs derived new status as mediators with government bureaucracy and the army, which disarmed the Qashqa'i and rigidly supervised seasonal migration after the nationalization of pasturage in the early 1960s. They suffered with other tribal groups from the government's import of meat and dairy products while neglecting pastoralist produce.. With the 1979 revolution the old paramounts tried to resume their positions but they and those Qashqa'i who supported them were finally defeated in 1982. Although like other nomadic pastoralists the Qashqa'i have been encouraged to resume their traditional lifestyle, leadership is now in the hands of a council of younger men answerable to the government.

Conclusions and future prospects

As revolutionary fervour dissipates, there may be in practice, but probably not in theory, greater religious tolerance in Iran. Ethnic communities face a less promising future. Islamic Iran is marginally more tolerant than Pahlavi Iran, certainly regarding cultural expression, allowing publications in local languages, for example. It has also allowed a revival of nomadic pastoralism under strict controls, and this marks a significant improvement for tribal groups, notably the Bakhtiyari and Qashqa'i. Any real improvement for ethnic communities depends on greater decentralization. The only chance of this happening is remote: that increasing economic difficulty will lead to a serious popular challenge to the regime leading to a more decentralized administration.

Further reading

Aghajanian, A., 'Ethnic inequality in Iran: an overview', *International Journal of Middle East Studies*, 15:2, May 1983.

Bainbridge, M. (ed.), *The Turkic Peoples of the World*, London, Kegan Paul International, 1993.

Beck, L., *The Qashqa'i of Iran*, New Haven, CT, and London, Yale University Press, 1986.

Cooper, R., *The Baha'is of Iran*, London, MRG report, 1991.

Daftary, F., *The Isma'ilis: Their History and Doctrines*, Cambridge and New York, Cambridge University Press, 1990.

Harrison, S., *In Afghanistan's Shadow: Baluch Nationalism and Soviet Temptations*, New York and Washington, DC, Carnegie Endowment for International Peace, 1981.

Higgins, P., 'Minority–state relations in contemporary Iran', A. Banuazizi, and M. Weiner (eds), *The State, Religion and Ethnic Politics*, New York, Syracuse University Press, 1988.

McDowall, D., *The Kurds*, London, MRG report, 1991, 1996.

McDowall, D., *The Kurds: A Nation Denied*, London, Minority Rights Publications, 1992.

McDowall, D., *A Modern History of the Kurds*, London, Tauris, 1995.

MacEoin, D., *The Baha'i Community of Iran in the Twentieth Century*, London, School of Oriental and African Studies, 1988.

Mir-Hosseini, Z., 'Inner truth and outer history: the two worlds of the Ahl-i Haqq of Kurdistan', *International Journal of Middle East Studies*, no. 26, 1994.

Moosa, M., *Extreme Shi'ites: The Ghulat Sects*, New York, Syracuse University Press, 1987, pp. 185–254.

Waterfield, R., *Christians in Persia*, London, Allen & Unwin, 1973.

Wirsing, R., *The Baluchis and Pathans*, London, MRG report, 1987.

Minority-based and advocacy organizations

Assyrian Cultural and Advice Centre, 18 The Green, London W5 5DA, UK; tel. 44 181 579 0192, fax 44 181 566 3548.

Baha'i Community of the UK, 27 Rutland Gate, London SW7 1PD, UK; tel. 44 171 584 2566, fax 44 171 584 9402.

Baluch Research and Cultural Association, 20 Holmesdale House, Kilburn Vale, London NW6 4QU, UK; tel. 44 171 372 3400.

Centre for Armenian Information and Advice, Hayashen, 105a Mill Hill Road, London W3 8JF, UK; tel. 44 181 992 4621, fax 44 181 993 8953.

Institute for Isma'ili Studies, 30 Portland Place, London W1N 3DF, UK; tel. 44 171 436 1736.

Institut Kurde, 106 Rue La Fayette, 75010 Paris, France; tel. 33 1 48 24 64 64, fax 33 1 47 70 99 04.

Kurdish Human Rights Project, Suite 236, Linen Hall, 162–8 Regent Street, London W1R 5TB, UK; tel. 44 171 287 2772, fax 44 171 734 4927.

Iraq

Land area:	438, 317 sq km
Population:	19.3 million (1993)
Main languages:	Arabic, Surani and Kirmanji Kurdish, Turkish
Main religions:	Ithna'ashari Shi'i and Sunni Islam, Christianity (Eastern and Uniate Churches), Yazidi faith, Sabian faith, Judaism
Main minority groups:	*estimates:*, Ithna'ashari Shi'is 10.6 million (55%), Kurds 4.2 million (22%), Sunni Arabs 3.3 million (17%), Christian confessions 750,000 approx. (4%), Turkoman 700,000 (4%), Yazidis 150,000 (0.7%), extreme Shi'i groups 90,000 (0.4%), Sarliya-Kakaiya 30,000 (0.2%), Sabians 20,000 (0.1%)Shabak 20,000 (0.1%) (*percentages exceed 100 since most communities maximize their population, rendering internal consistency impossible*)
Real per capita GDP:	$3,413
UNDP HDI/rank:	0.617 (106)

Iraq is composed of several ethnic and religious groups. The state was formed out of the three Ottoman provinces of Basra, Baghdad and Mosul captured by Britain during 1916–18. In 1921 Britain made Iraq a monarchy under the Hashemite King Faisal, recently ousted from Syria. At the time the political separation of 'Southern Kurdistan' (that is, those Kurdish areas under British control) was still under consideration, but Faisal made its inclusion a vital condition of accepting the crown. His reason was simple: without the predominantly Sunni Kurds, Sunni Arabs would be seriously outnumbered by Shi'i Arabs. He and every successor regime ensured both Sunni and Arab control. The monarchy allowed more community representation than its successors, but remained dependent on co-opting notables and chiefs. The state failed to engage minorities sufficiently. Family, tribal, ethnic or confessional loyalties still have first call on the average Iraqi citizen, although the ordeal of the Iran–Iraq War, 1980–8, has done more to forge Iraqi national identity than any other event.

In 1958 the monarchy was overthrown. For a moment it seemed possible to build a republic based upon communal and individual egalitarian principles, but the coup leader, Brigadier Qasim, became increasingly distrustful of power residing anywhere except in his own hands. After his overthrow in 1963, Arab nationalists and Ba'athists (see **Syria** on Ba'ath origins) took over, but the latter were soon marginalized. In 1968, however, the Ba'athists ousted the Arab nationalists and established a one-party state.

The new vice-president, Saddam Hussein, emerged as the most powerful member of the regime. He established a regime of secret police and informers so extensive that ordinary Iraqis were fearful of making any political criticisms even in private. Having defeated the Kurds in 1975, Saddam Hussein sought to destroy the leadership of all other groupings which might pose a threat to the regime. All forms of social and economic association were penetrated in order to identify and eliminate all those who dissented from the totalitarian regime now being created. When Saddam assumed the presidency in 1979 he purged hundreds of senior members from the administration, narrowing the regime to a small coterie from his home town of Tikrit, family and trusted friends. The Ba'ath became largely irrelevant to the exercise of power.

In 1980 Saddam launched a full-scale war against Iran in the belief he could rapidly defeat it. But Iran soon pushed Iraqi forces back and only agreed to a cease-fire in 1988 when Western support for Iraq rendered an Iranian victory impossible. Two years later Saddam seized Kuwait. Iraq was put under an international trade boycott. Having failed to withdraw unconditionally, Iraqi forces were driven out of Kuwait by an international coalition force. In the mid-1990s Iraq was still under boycott because of its reluctance to implement fully UN Security Council resolutions regarding weapon stocks. As a consequence, the people of Iraq found themselves starved of food stocks and other essential commodities, and the country bankrupt.

RELIGIOUS MINORITIES

Ithna'ashari Shi'is

Ithna'ashari Shi'is probably number between 10 and 11 million and form about 55 per cent of the population, but they have been consistently denied power as a community. Yet it is a mistake to consider the Shi'is simply as alienated from the state or from the ruling Sunni community. On the contrary, the Shi'is want to play the full role within the state that they have so far been denied. Thus their aim is quite different from the Kurds who seek autonomy.

Shi'is have only became a majority in the past century, almost fortuitously. Although the birth of Shi'ism is associated with Najaf and Karbala, these two cities were of minor importance until Persian Shi'i clerics sought refuge there during the Afghan occupation of Persia, 1722–63. With Wahhabi attacks (see **Saudi Arabia**), these clerics consciously sought the conversion of the nominally Sunni nomadic tribes to Shi'ism. The growing economic importance of the two cities, the subsequent diversion of the Euphrates via the Hindiya canal, and Ottoman tribal policy all made agricultural settlement around the two cities attractive to many nomadic tribes. With settlement, tribes underwent structural change, chiefs depending increasingly on a new class of *sayyids*, men claiming descent from the Prophet, who acted as arbitrators and religious foci for tribal groups. By the beginning of this century virtually all settled tribes of central and southern Iraq had embraced Shi'ism. Culturally, their faith differed from that in Iran, since it retained a strong Arab dimension.

By the turn of the century the Shi'i clergy had emerged as a coherent political leadership, which raised volunteer forces to help resist the infidel (British) invasion of south Iraq and, once under British occupation, also organized the only widespread rebellion against it in 1920. In both cases this leadership acted in solidarity with Sunnis, not against them. It even welcomed the idea of a Hashemite (Sunni) ruler in 1919.

It was precisely the Shi'i leadership's ability to mobilize the masses which worried successive Sunni administrations in Baghdad. Both the British and the Hashemites deliberately sought to detach the Shi'i religious leadership from politics, encouraging landlords and tribal chiefs as an alternative leadership. Najaf and Karbala were deliberately neglected.

Following the 1958 revolution, other factors came into play. The new ruler, Qasim, upheld Iraqi as opposed to Arab nationalism. This suited some Shi'is, for the Shi'a were a slight majority in Iraq while barely 10 per cent of the Arab world. In addition, pan-Arab nationalism offended many of the more religiously observant Shi'is on account of its secularism. Pan-Arab nationalism also tended to feel Sunni in character to Shi'is, just as it tended to feel Islamic to Arab Christians.

Arab and Iraqi nationalism, however, both carried a strong whiff of secularism. In 1957 several clergy of Najaf founded a clandestine party, to become known as al Da'wa al Islamiya (The Call), primarily to warn Muslims of the growing secularist danger. From 1968 a clash was inevitable between a regime that identified with the secular left and an organization established to advance the Shi'i faith.

It was also inevitable that the Ba'ath should renew the efforts of previous regimes to neutralize any Shi'i religious intrusions into state politics. In 1974 the regime executed five leading clerics, as a warning. At Ashura, in 1977, major protests at government interference took place in Najaf and Karbala, and eight Shi'i leaders were executed and hundreds imprisoned as another warning.

Throughout the 1970s the government also expelled those 'of Iranian origin'. In the first census after 1918 the population had been required to state either Ottoman or Iranian origin. Fifty years later the Ba'ath traced approximately 200,000 Kurdish (Faili) and Arab Shi'i descendants and expelled them to Iran.

The Iranian Revolution in 1979 inevitably excited Shi'i expectations – not of Iranian triumph over Iraq but of Islam over the forces of tyrannical secularism. The Da'wa party openly hailed the revolution. As the war of words between Iran and Iraq grew in early 1980, Saddam sent another warning to the Shi'i community to stay out of politics: he executed the Da'wa party leader, Ayatollah Baqir al Sadr. Baqir al Sadr had been the only Arab among the eight senior clerics of Shi'i Islam. His execution was therefore also intended to undermine Najaf and Karbala as centres of Shi'i learning. Membership of Da'wa was made a capital offence, and suspects were executed or imprisoned. Yet, if anything demonstrated that the Shi'i community was first and foremost Arab, it was that it provided the majority of troops in the long and bloody war with Iran. It did not rebel.

Following Iraq's defeat in Kuwait in 1991, the Shi'a of south Iraq rose spontaneously, in the hope that the army was already so badly demoralized it would abandon Saddam. That they lacked organization and leadership was indicative of the way the regime had undermined and largely destroyed the traditional clerical leadership. Like the Kurds in the north, they were now defeated as Saddam's forces committed wholesale slaughter without regard to age or sex, and destroyed the shrines and libraries of Shi'ism in both Najaf and Karbala. This was not mindless violence. It was the deliberate destruction of Shi'i learning in Iraq, a logical conclusion to government policy since the 1920s. There had been 2,000 clerics and theological students in Najaf in 1958 (a paltry figure compared with the 180,000 in Iran on the eve of revolution in 1979), which had steadily diminished to only 800 by 1991. Most of the 800, many of them foreign students, now disappeared.

Shi'i resistance continued in the Marshes by Shi'i rebels, army deserters and the inhabitants, the Mada'in. The latter had always been held in low esteem by other Shi'is but now they became heroic martyrs in the struggle against a godless and anti-Shi'i regime. In order to defeat them Saddam dug a major canal to drain the marshes – in the words of the UN monitor; 'the environmental crime of the century'. Thus the wheel has come full circle. Just as the provision of water to Najaf proved a major factor in the growth of Shi'ism in south Iraq some 150 years ago, so now the destruction of the Marshes alongside the destruction of Najaf's libraries may signal an irreversible decline in Iraqi Shi'ism.

Assyrians

There are, conservatively estimated, about 250,000 members of the Assyrian 'Ancient Church of the East' (the Nestorians) in Iraq or, according to Assyrians, between 1 and 2 million. They form a distinct community, but with three origins: (1) those who inhabited Hakkari (in modern Turkey), who were predominantly tribal and whose leaders acknowledged the temporal as well as spiritual paramountcy of their patriarch, the Mar Shimun; (2) a peasant community in Urumiya (see **Iran**); and (3) a largely peasant community in Amadiya, Shaqlawa and Rawanduz in Iraqi Kurdistan. Because of its expulsion from the 'Orthodox' community at Ephesus in 431, the Assyrian Church operated entirely east (hence its title) of Byzantine Christendom, establishing communities over a wide area. But its heartlands were at the apex of the fertile crescent. The Mongol invasions, however, virtually wiped out the Assyrian Church except in the limited areas mentioned above.

On the whole the Assyrians co-existed successfully with the neighbouring Kurdish tribes. In Hakkari, Assyrian tribes held Kurdish as well as Assyrian peasantry in thrall, just as Kurdish tribes did, and rival Assyrian tribes would seek allies among neighbouring Kurdish tribes, and vice versa. Religious tensions only developed in the 1840s, partly a result of European penetration and interest in Christian communities, partly the product of local rivalries, and partly because of growing Sunni–Armenian tensions. Sunni persecution of the Assyrians was a regular feature by the beginning of the twentieth century. In 1915 the Hakkari Assyrians were encouraged to revolt against the Turks (who had started massacring Armenians) by Russian forces, which then proved unable to support them. The community fought its way to Urumiya but with the collapse of Russia in 1917 was compelled to march southwards to the British occupied zone. The survivors, 25,000 or so, were settled in Iraq.

After the war several factors led to tragedy: it proved impossible for Assyrians to return to Hakkari as they wished; they were denied the kind of autonomy they had enjoyed in Hakkari; and growing mistrust existed between the community and the Arab government, partly because the British used the Assyrians' formidable fighting qualities in a specially raised force to guard RAF installations. Assyrians viewed Iraqi independence in 1932 as a British betrayal. Growing tension led to a confrontation in 1933, followed by a series of massacres perpetrated by the Iraqi army, in which anything between 600 and 3,000 perished. Many Assyrians left for America, including the Mar Shimun, but the greater part remained and accommodated themselves within the Iraqi state. Many moved south to Baghdad.

Assyrians were unable to avoid the Kurdish conflict. As with the Kurds, some supported the government, others allied themselves with the Kurdish nationalist movement. In 1979 a number of smaller parties combined to form the Assyrian Democratic Movement (ADM), formally joining the Kurdish armed struggle in 1982. Assyrian villages and people were victims like the Kurds in the Anfal, 1987–8. ADM was part of the Kurdistan Front, and participated in the 1992 Kurdistan election, five seats being reserved for Assyrian representatives. ADM demands Assyrian recognition in the Iraqi constitution, full cultural rights and equal treatment. If the Kurds achieved a federal state, the Assyrians would demand autonomy within it, but there is a widespread desire to emigrate.

Rivalry over the Patriarchate led to a split in 1964, but in 1990 the two patriarchs met and agreed terms for a reunion.

Chaldeans

There are probably over 300,000 Chaldeans in Iraq, now mainly in Baghdad. They broke away from the Assyrian Ancient Church of the East as a result of long-running dynastic conflicts, to become fully uniate with Rome in 1778. Until the 1950s the Mosul plain had always been the centre of Chaldean life. Like the Assyrians, many moved southwards from 1933 onwards. Whereas in 1932 70 per cent of Iraqi Christians lived in and around Mosul, by 1957 only 47 per cent remained there. There was a further reduction following the Ba'ath coup of 1963, when many Christians who had supported Qasim or the Communist Party fled Ba'ath reprisals. By 1979 it was reckoned that half Iraq's Christians were in Baghdad, 14 per cent of the city's population.

While the Assyrians generally insist on their ethnic difference from Arabs, many Chaldeans have tended to assimilate into Arab identity. Their sectarian name and the title of their spiritual head, 'Patriarch of Babylon', hark back to pre-Islamic Iraq. Since 1972 the Ba'ath has recognized cultural rights for Iraqi Christians of the Syriac rite. Many Chaldeans, notably Tariz Aziz, have risen to high command within the Ba'ath and the army, while others serve in the presidential palace. The regime consciously exploits the Chaldean sense of vulnerability in order to co-opt many members into its support. Some Chaldeans in the north, however, have supported the Kurdish national movement.

Armenians

There is a community of about 25,000 Armenians, almost entirely in Baghdad. Most are descended from refugees of 1915–18, from Urumiya and eastern Anatolia. They seek to avoid notice.

Syrian Orthodox and Catholic

There are about 50,000 Syrian Orthodox and another 40,000 Catholics in Iraq. Many are descended from Anatolian refugees. Traditionally, the Syrian Orthodox heartlands lay at the apex of the fertile crescent, within the region bounded by Urfa and Diyarbakir (modern Turkey), Aleppo (Syria) and Mosul (Iraq). Within Iraq Mosul is the traditional centre, but many have moved south to Baghdad.

Yazidis

All Yazidis are ethnically and linguistically (Kirmanji) Kurdish. There are probably approximately 150,000 Yazidis left in the region, almost wholly now in Jabal Sinjar, 150 kilometres west of Mosul, with a smaller community in Shaikhan, the Kurdistan foothills east of Mosul, where their most holy shrine of Shaykh Adi is located. There are also some 10,000 in Syria (see **Syria**), while those in Diyarbakir province of Turkey have been virtually extinguished by Sunni oppression. There may be another 60,000 or so in the Republics of Armenia, Georgia and Azerbaijan, who fled Sunni persecution. It is unclear how many consider themselves still Yazidi, or merely Kurds.

The Yazidi religion seems to be a synthesis of pagan, Zoroastrian, Manichaean, Jewish, Nestorian Christian and Muslim elements. They are dualists, believing in a Creator God, now passive, and Malak Ta'us (Peacock Angel), executive organ of divine will. They believe they are descended from Adam but not Eve and are thereby different from the rest of humankind. Excommunication, therefore, has dire implications. Conversely, one cannot become a Yazidi. The name probably derives from the Persian *ized* (angel, deity).

Yazidis traditionally were tribally organized. Some tribes were willing to combine in confederation with Muslim and Christian tribes under an acknowledged paramount chief. Until the nineteenth century they were a formidable presence around Mosul, but endured devastating assaults from Sunni Kurdish tribes and Ottoman troops, partly because of the disorder created by Yazidi tribes but also because of growing religious antipathy, heightened by European interest in the Yazidis.

Following the formation of Iraq, the Yazidis proved resistant to both British and Iraqi efforts to extend direct administration to the region. Iraqi efforts to introduce conscription led to repeated risings, notably 1935–40, critically at a time when the Shammar bedouin were encroaching on traditional Yazidi pasturage. Conscription was closely associated with Ottoman rule, removed vital manpower, and exposed Yazidis to cohabitation in barracks with 'sons of Eve'.

The Yazidis have always remained on the fringes of Iraqi society, but because of the strategic position of Jabal Sinjar they have been exposed to the unwonted attentions of state security. Since the Ba'ath came to power, repeated efforts have been made to Arabize the area and also to persuade Yazidis they are really Arab. Reaction has been mixed, but some Yazidis support the Kurdish national movement. Yazidis reluctantly served in the army against Iran, and the community escaped the Anfal, the Kurdish genocide, 1987–8. The dynastic prince of the Shaikhan Yazidis, still mediates between government and the community, though in a modernizing economy this role must be in progressive decline.

Extreme Shi'i groups

The Bajwan, or Bajilan, are a small extreme Shi'i farming community living in the Khusar basin, tributary of the Tigris, north of Mosul, and an even smaller number in Zuhab and northern Luristan, Iran. Besides beliefs and practices peculiar to themselves, they also share many in common with the Shabak and Qizilbash Alevis (see **Turkey**). They are almost certainly related to the Kurdish Bajilan tribe which was moved by the Ottomans from Mosul district to Zuhab, and which is now Sunni but was once Ahl-i Haqq.

The Ibrahimiya are a very small extreme Shi'i community, inhabiting Tal Afar, north west of Mosul. They are ethnically and linguistically Turkoman with a strong affinity with Qizilbash Alevis. Like the Shabak (see **Turkey**), they believe in a trinity of Allah, Muhammad and Ali.

Sarliya-Kakaiya

These are two names for the same sub-sect, known as Sarliya around Mosul, and more commonly as Kakaiya around Kirkuk, the two cities between which the majority are to be found. The former may be of Turkoman origin, the latter being more probably Kurds. They probably came to the Mesopotamian plain from Iran, possibly fleeing Tamerlaine. They all use Gurani Kurdish as an in-group language. They are highly secretive about their religion, but their beliefs seems to be virtually identical with Ahl-i Haqq (see **Iran**). Like many Sufis they believe that the universe and all that is in it is God, and that every being in existence shall return to him. They also believe in metempsychosis, a belief of Buddhist origin imbibed by Sufis in Afghanistan in the ninth or tenth century. The Sarliya live on the banks of the Tigris, and are mainly farmers and fishermen. The Kakaiya are more urban and educated, some of them being doctors, lawyers or teachers. Their population is probably not more than about 30,000.

Shabak

The Shabak are a sect located in a handful of villages east of Mosul. Both religiously and ethnically they seem to be different from other Iraqis, speaking a language which is a confection of Turkish, Persian, Kurdish and Arabic. They are mainly farmers. They are extremely reticent concerning their beliefs, but are probably a residue of Qizilbash (Alevis, see **Turkey**) who fled from Ottoman territory at the time of the battle of Chaldiran, 1514, when northern Mesopotamia was still in Persian Safavid hands. Their beliefs indicate a close association with the Safavi Sufi order of that time. They probably number no more than 20,000.

Sabians

In 1947 Sabians, or Mandaeans, were reckoned to number about 7,000, and may have increased to about 20,000 since then. But they have been highly assimilated into nominally Muslim society since the 1930s. They are confined to lower Iraq, except for minuscule communities in Khorramshahr and Ahwaz, in south-western Iran, and a community of silversmiths and their families in Baghdad. They are primarily located in the Marshes or on the two rivers, at al Amara, Qal'at Salih, Nasiriya, Suq al Shuyukh and Qurna.

The religion is a form of Gnosticism, descended from ancient Mesopotamian worship, with rituals that resemble those of Zoroastrian and Nestorian worship. They practise immersion in flowing water, symbolic of the creative life force, as an act of ritual purity. They enjoy *dhimmi* status as 'people of the book', mentioned in the Qur'an.

The Sabians should not be confused either with the 'Sabians' of Harran, a pagan sect which deliberately adopted the name Sabian in order to avoid Muslim persecution, or with the Sabaeans, the inhabitants of ancient Sheba, in south Yemen.

The Sabians traditionally specialized in carpentry, boat building and silversmithing, pursuits still practised. They face extinction not only from the process of modernization but also from the drainage of the Marshes, which is destroying the locus of the community.

ETHNIC MINORITIES

Kurds

Kurds probably number 4.2 million, about 22 per cent of Iraq's population, and inhabit the mountains, foothills and parts of the plain from approximately Khaniqin in the south in an arc to

Zakhu in the north, and with the outpost of Jabal Sinjar to the north-west, where the Kurds are Yazidi. The Kurds do not form an homogenous whole (see **Iran**, **Turkey**). Those north of the Greater Zab river speak Kirmanji Kurdish, as do most Turkish Kurds, while those south of it speak Sorani and have greater affinity with Iranian Kurds. The majority are Shafi'i Sunni, but about 150,000 in Baghdad and the south-east were Shi'i (known locally as Faili), mostly of Luri (see **Iran**) origin. In Baghdad the Failis were important both as traders and porters in the main *suq*. Most were expelled by the government in the 1970s.

Kurdish society and politics were until recently dominated by tribalism. Urban or educated Kurds have only assumed political leadership in the last twenty years. There are two main political parties, the Kurdistan Democratic Party (KDP), led by Mas'ud Barzani, which is dominant north of the Greater Zab and upholds more traditional values, and Jalal Talabani's Patriotic Union of Kurdistan (PUK), which claims a 'progressive' ideology and is led by urban Kurds.

Kurdish nationalism was born during the 1930s, when young urban nationalists challenged tribalism within, and the Arab-dominated government outside, the community. It resented the way in which Kurdish political and cultural rights had been ignored by successive regimes. It acquired momentum during the 1960s, when it was still possible to resist army assaults. But until 1991 there have always been almost equal numbers of Kurds who have fought for the government, either willingly or under duress.

In 1970 Saddam offered the Kurds a formal autonomy agreement. It seemed an historic landmark until it became clear that Saddam intended to rob the term autonomy of its meaning. In 1975 he defeated the Kurdish forces. The Iran–Iraq War gave the Kurds another chance to force government troops out and demand autonomy. But as Iranian offensives began to lose momentum, Iraq used chemical warfare and genocide against Kurds. In March 1988 5,000 Kurds perished in a chemical attack on Halabja. During the same period the government embarked on genocide, the notorious 'Anfal', killing in the order of 180,000 men, women and children, and razing almost 4,000 out of 5,000 villages and hamlets in Kurdistan.

In March 1991 the Kurds followed the Shi'i example and rose against government forces, initially driving them out of Kurdistan. A counter offensive precipitated mass flight of about 1.5 million Kurds to the Turkish and Iranian borders. Only intervention by the international coalition to guarantee aerial protection north of latitude 36 created the conditions for Kurds to return and start rebuilding their lives. An attempted negotiation with Saddam collapsed.

In 1992 Kurds living in the *de facto* autonomous zone voted in a free election. The PUK and KDP won almost exactly equal shares of the vote, and so shared government. However, in 1994 fighting broke out between them, since each represented rival patronage networks. In August 1996 the partition between PUK and KDP zones broke down with open and mobile warfare between the two parties, the PUK backed by Iran and the KDP by Saddam Hussein. In the meantime, ordinary Kurds live in straitened circumstances, enduring the international blockade of Iraq and Saddam's blockade of Kurdistan. A modesty quantity of relief goods enters autonomous Kurdistan from Turkey.

The future is unclear and dangerous, more so on account of Kurdish political disunity. Saddam, or a successor in Baghdad, will do his best to exploit this division to achieve Kurdish obedience to Baghdad.

Turkoman

There are anything between 600,000 and 2 million Turkoman, the former figure being the conservative estimate of outside observers and the latter a Turkoman claim. They live in an arc of towns and villages stretching from Tel Afar, west of Mosul, through Mosul, Arbil, Altun Kopru, Kirkuk, Tuz Khurmatu, Kifri and Khaniqin. They are probably descended from Turkic garrisons or, in the Shi'i case, fugitives from early Ottoman control. Approximately 60 per cent are Sunni, while the balance are Ithna'ashari or extreme Shi'i. Shi'is tend to live at the southern end of Turkoman settlement, and also tend to be more rural. Tiny extreme Shi'i communities (for example, Sarliyya and Ibrahimiya) exist in Tuz Khurmatu, Ta'uq, Qara Tapa, Taza Khurmatu, Bashir and Tisin, and Tal Afar.

The Turkoman face multiple minority difficulties. They live under a chauvinist Arab regime which denies them cultural, linguistic or political rights, and which has deliberately replaced thousands of Turkoman (and Kurdish) inhabitants of Kirkuk and its environs with Arabs. No Turkoman has ever held ministerial office since the foundation of the state. They have been subject to purges, including the systematic removal of all Turkoman holding senior posts in the Kirkuk oil fields and in the army, and the assassination of many. They suffered particularly in Kirkuk and Tuz Khurmatu when the 1991 Kurdish uprising was crushed.

However, although the Iraqi National Turkoman Party (established in 1988) cooperates with the Kurdish authorities in the *de facto* autonomous area, Turkoman relations with the Kurds are uneasy. It was the burgeoning oil industry which drew thousands of Kurdish workers into Kirkuk at the same time that some Turkomans were moving to Baghdad, thereby ending historic Turkoman preponderance in the 1950s. A similar process happened in Arbil. In 1959 Kurds and communists rioted, killing Turkomans in Kirkuk, an event which left a permanent scepticism about Kurdish political intentions. It is only the fact that the regime in Baghdad is unquestionably worse that persuades Turkomans to cooperate with the Kurdish national movement. Many Sunni Turkomans look to Turkey for support and a few might welcome Turkish intervention. However, Shi'i Turkomans do not share such feelings, fearing Turkey's deep antipathy for Shi'ism, and many of them support the Iraqi Shi'i Da'wa Party.

Conclusions and future prospects

It is impossible to speculate whether or when there will be a successful coup, who might succeed Saddam, or whether a successor would be both able and willing to allow minority groups adequate self-expression and self-administration to satisfy their sense of particular identity. Like most of Middle Eastern society, the social structure of Iraq operates on patronage networks – either through extended families or through other solidarity groups. This makes the transition to an open, democratic and representative society a formidable task.

Further reading

Drower, E.S., *The Mandaeans of Iraq and Iran*, Leiden, E.J. Brill, 1962.

Guest, J., *Survival Among the Kurds: A History of the Yezidis*, London and New York, Kegan Paul International, 1993.

Joseph, J., *The Nestorians and Their Neighbours*, Princeton, NJ, Princeton University Press, 1961.

Lawless, R., 'The Turkic peoples of Iraq', in M. Bainbridge, *The Turkic Peoples of the Middle East*, London and New York, Kegan Paul International, 1993.

McDowall, D., *The Kurds*, London, MRG report, 1991, 1997.

McDowall, D., *The Kurds: A Nation Denied*, London, Minority Rights Publications, 1992.

McDowall, D., *A Modern History of the Kurds*, London and New York, IB Tauris, 1995.

Middle East Watch, *Endless Torment: the 1991 Uprising in Iraq and its Aftermath*, New York, Human Rights Watch, 1992.

Middle East Watch, *Genocide in Iraq*, New York and Washington, DC, Human Rights Watch, 1993.

MRG, *The Marsh Arabs of Iraq*, occasional paper, London, June 1993.

Moosa, M., *Extremist Shiites: The Ghulat Sects*, New York, Syracuse University Press, 1988, chs 1, 14, 15.

Nakash, Y., *The Shi'is of Iraq*, Princeton, NJ, Princeton University Press, 1994.

Minority-based and advocacy organizations

Al Khoei Foundation, Chevening Road, London NW6 6TN, UK; tel. 44 171 372 4049, fax 44 171 372 0694, e mail: nadeem@al-khoei.demon.co.uk.

Assyrian Culture and Advice Centre, 18 The Green, London W5 5DA, UK; tel. 44 181 579 0192, fax 44 181 566 3548.

Culture and Mutual Aid Association of Iraqi Turks, Zeynep Kamil Sok. No. 62/4, Laleli, Istanbul, Turkey; tel. 90 212 513 9065, fax 90 212 511 6840.

Institut Kurde, Rue Lafayette 106, 75010 Paris, France; tel. 33 1 48 24 64 64.

Kurdish Cultural Centre, 14 Stannary Street, London SE11 4AA, UK; tel. 44 171 735 0918.

Kurdish Human Rights Project, Suite 319, Linen Hall, 162–8 Regent Street, London W1R 5TB, UK; tel. 44 171 287 2772, fax 44 171 734 4927.

Israel

Land area:	21,946 sq km
Population:	5,451,000 (1993)
Main languages:	Hebrew, Arabic, Yiddish, Russian
Main religions:	Judaism, Sunni Islam, Christianity, Druze faith, Baha'i faith
Main minority groups:	Palestinians (excluding Druzes) 1 million (17.5%), Druze Palestinians 85,000 (1.5%), Karaite Jews 12,000 (0.2%), Circassians 5,000 (0.1%),
Real per capita GDP:	$14,700
UNDP HDI/rank:	0.907 (21)

The State of Israel was established in May 1948 following the UN partition of Palestine (see **Palestine**) and the successful war fought between March and September that year to establish a Jewish state in the greater part of Palestine. This was the culmination of Jewish settler strategy, first to gain ascendancy over the economy of Palestine and then physically to take possession. In the final stage, the Jewish *yishuv* (or settlement) was spurred on by the Holocaust in Europe, and by the sympathy and support it received internationally, 1945–8.

By the time the 1948 Arab–Israeli War was over, only 160,000 Palestinian Arabs remained, largely in the Galilee and a fraction of the bedouin native to the Negev.[1] This residue only inadvertently survived the policy of removing the Arab population. Today the Palestinian Arab minority has grown to 19 per cent of the total population (from the 11 per cent to which it had been reduced by the 1960s). Its position, unrecognized as a national minority and isolated from political or economic power, has remained marginalized, even since the Israeli–Palestine Liberation Organization (PLO) peace process began in 1993. Israel remains 'the State of the Jewish people', not the state of its citizens, and Palestinian Arabs thus remain second class citizens.

The Jewish population numbered approximately 500,000 at the end of 1947, but between 1948 and 1972 Israel was flooded with some 600,000 immigrants from Europe and 700,000 from Africa and Asia. Thus, Jewish Israel was composed of immigrants from more than 100 countries, with their own languages, ethnicity, social and cultural practices and religious rites. In that sense it is difficult to talk of Jewish 'minorities'. Powerful cohesive forces, namely Arab hostility, Jewish faith and nationality and an impressively revived language and literature, all militated to forge the new nation. Nevertheless, two broad issues affect Jewish society: cultural origin and religious adherence. Although it is difficult to describe either as a specific minority issue, a brief discussion may be helpful.

Jewish cultural origin

Almost half a century after the foundation of Israel, there is still a clear social division between Ashkenazi Jews of European or Western origin, who currently form 53 per cent of the Jewish community, and those from Africa and Asia, known as Sephardim but more properly as Oriental Jews or Mizrachim. (Sephardim, strictly speaking, are Jews of Spanish/Portuguese cultural and linguistic origin.) The division is not only cultural but also about power. As early as 1912 Yemeni Jews were introduced to Palestine to provide cheap enough labour to avoid employing indigenous Arabs. But the real influx occurred after 1948. As more Arab Jews arrived in Palestine with a significantly higher birth-rate and an Arab rather than European culture, the Ashkenazi community viewed Mizrachim as numerically threatening as well as culturally inferior, with attitudes that amounted in some cases to racism. Immigrant Mizrachim resented the discriminatory way they were settled in remote and inaccessible parts of Israel.

Although the tensions of the 1960s have abated, Mizrachim continue to occupy the lowest strata of Israeli Jewish society, in education, housing and employment, perpetuated in the second and third generations. Until or unless that power balance changes, the ethnic issue will continue to lurk beneath the surface.

Jewish religion

The State of Israel was declared without specifying an established religion. However, its Laws of Return and Citizenship, granting any Jew the automatic right of residence and citizenship, beg the question of who is a Jew. Can one be a Jew by ethnicity (despite the manifestly varied ethnicity of the Jewish people) or only by religion? This has caused considerable controversy ever since 1948. In pure terms a Jew is one who performs the Mitsvot, the 613 religious injunctions of Judaism, but in practice the religious authorities of Israel insist that only someone who conforms to the requirements of religious law (*halacha*), and who, in addition, 'is a person who is born of a Jewish mother, or one converted to Judaism by a recognized orthodox authority', can be recognized as a Jew. The first definition requires performance of religious rites, the second relies primarily on matriarchy, by implication ethnicity or at least descent. The debate is unlikely ever to be satisfactorily resolved.

Two important categories are not recognized as Jewish by the state, since they do not conform to Jewish orthodoxy: Conservative and Reform Judaism. Both are unacceptable because their conversion procedures do not satisfy Orthodox criteria, and Reform Judaism accepts as a Jew the child of a Jewish father and non-Jewish mother. In the early 1980s the Sephardic Chief Rabbi sought the symbolic conversion of Ethiopian Jewish refugees on their arrival in Israel because they were not deemed properly Orthodox. About 50,000 recent Russian immigrants are also not considered truly Jewish by the religious authorities since they were not born of a Jewish mother.

That aside, a proportion of religiously observant Jews saw a contradiction between the religious requirement to glorify only God while awaiting messianic fulfilment and the Zionist aim to create a Jewish state. Strictly religious Jews, the Haredim, cover the whole political spectrum from fervent Zionist to anti-Zionist. However, a substantial number of ultra-Orthodox Jews believe the state of exile persists even in the Land of Israel until the arrival of the Redeemer. Significantly, the vote share of Haredi political parties grew from 5 to 11 per cent in the 1980s, even though many ultra-Orthodox do not vote. Holding the balance of votes, Haredi parties have been essential to most administrations, their price being control of the religious (and if possible education) portfolios. Tension between secular and Haredi Jews has increased considerably, partly because of the latter's growing demands in national life but also because they avoid conscription and appear to carry none of the national burdens. Haredim have a significantly higher birth rate than secular Jews. They are concentrated in Jerusalem, where they outnumber secular Jews.

Palestinians (Christian and Muslim)

Including the Druzes, the Palestinians form 19 per cent of Israel's population, approximately one million. However, they form 25 per cent of those under twenty years old and will probably continue to grow proportionately. Within the community distinctions between Christians and Muslims are rarely made since they are common victims of discrimination and share the agenda of achieving communal and individual equality with the Jewish majority. Christians are in relative decline, from 21 per cent of Israeli Palestinians in 1949 to only 12.5 per cent today.

Following Israel's victory in 1948, Arabs were kept under military government until 1966, dependent on permits to leave their villages or obtain work outside them. In this way it was impossible to organize any protest or civil resistance. They were also co-opted to support the system by the offer of certain benefits, that is, employment or educational opportunities, in return for service to the state or a political party. Since Palestinians were overwhelmingly farmers, the state deliberately sequestrated over half their farmlands in order to destroy any independent economic viability, encourage emigration and concentrate food production in Jewish hands.

Military government was abandoned to allow free movement of labour in Israel's economic expansion, but Arabs have generally found it impossible to integrate into the mainstream, except as cheap labour. Land confiscations continue, building permits are withheld despite the population increase, Arab rental of accommodation in Jewish areas is resisted, and discriminatory underfunding of virtually all state services is exercised in the Arab sector. Many locations, particularly bedouin ones, remain 'unrecognized', even though most pre-date the establishment of Israel. Education is not only seriously underfunded compared with the Jewish sector, but designed to keep Palestinians subordinate and submissive.

The bedouin are a tribally organized society, once nomadic but largely settled pastoralists by the beginning of the twentieth century. Out of 92,000 bedouin in the Negev in 1947, only 11,000 remained after the foundation of Israel. The others were never fully accounted for. Survivors were given a particularly hard time, uprooted time and again and forced to live in reservations. In 1995 they numbered approximately 85,000 (about 8.5 per cent of Israeli Palestinians). Israel has emphasized their distinctiveness. In socio-economic terms there is no doubt they were in many respects different from the peasantry in 1947, but state transformation of both communities into a subordinate landless rural proletariat has erased such differences.

Politically, Palestinians have remained compromised, some feeling they should support Labour in the peace process. Their options are limited since it is illegal to form a party that challenges the Zionist nature of the state, even though this definition confers inferior status on non-Jews. For the first time, in May 1995 Palestinian Knesset members forced the government to abandon its policy of land seizures in Arab Jerusalem by threatening a vote of no confidence. Despite their size, or possibly because of it, the Palestinians remain unrecognized as a national minority.

Druze Palestinians (see also **Lebanon**, **Syria**)

There are about 85,000 Druzes, 8.5 per cent of the Palestinian population, located in eighteen villages, some exclusively Druze, others mixed, in the Galilee and Mt. Carmel (see **Syria** for Golan Druzes). Due to long-standing tensions with Sunni landlords, reluctance to be drawn into the Palestinian conflict with the Yishuv (Zionist settlement of Palestine) and skilful diplomacy by the Zionist leadership, the Druzes distanced themselves from the rest of the Palestinian community and cooperated with the Jewish state from 1948. They accepted conscription in 1956, and were allowed to establish Druze religious courts in 1961. In 1970, to separate them further, special government departments were established solely for Druzes. None of this protected them from the land confiscations and discriminatory budgets suffered by other Arabs, though not on quite the same scale. There have always been Druzes who repudiated the alliance their leadership made with the state, and a growing number are reassessing their cooperation with a state which still discriminates against them.

Circassians

There are about 5,000 Circassians, concentrated in two Galilee villages, Kufr Kana and Rihaniya. They arrived in Palestine in the nineteenth century (see **Syria**). Like the Druzes, they have been co-opted by the state and accept compulsory military service. Circassian is taught and used for broadcasting.

Other minorities

There are about 12,000 Karaites in or near Ramla in central Israel. This movement began among Jews in Iran in the eighth century CE, rejecting oral tradition (the Talmud) as a source of divine law, and cleaving only to the Torah.

About 200 Samaritans exist in Holon near Tel Aviv (see **Palestine**).

Conclusions and future prospects

Israel remains gripped by two ideological binds. In the religious sphere it has so far been unable to reconcile orthodox and secular views of who is a Jew, a fact of potential importance since, for example, civil marriages are not allowed. More importantly, since Israel remains 'the State of the Jewish people' rather than of its citizens, its growing Palestinian minority are bound to become increasingly frustrated with their exclusion from full participation in the state and with denial of their status as a national minority.

Further reading

Firro, K., *A History of the Druzes*, Leiden, New York and Cologne, E.J. Brill, 1992.

Friendly, A. and Silver, E., *Israel's Oriental Immigrants and Druzes*, London, MRG report, 1981.

Haj, M. et al., *Education, Empowerment and Control: The Case of the Arabs in Israel*, Ithaca, NY, State University of New York Press, 1995.

Kessler, D. and Parfitt, T., *The Falashas: The Jews of Ethiopia*, London, MRG report, 1985.

Kyle, K. and Peters, J., *Whither Israel? The Domestic Challenges*, London, Royal Institute for International Affairs and Tauris, 1993.

Lustick, I., *Arabs in the Jewish State: Israel's Control of a National Minority*, Austin, TX, University of Texas, 1980.

McDowall, D., *The Palestinians*, London, MRG report, 1987.

McDowall, D., *The Palestinians: The Road to Nationhood*, London, Minority Rights Publications, 1992.

Maddrell, P., *The Bedouin of the Negev*, London, MRG report, 1990.

Minns, A. and Hijab, N., *Citizens Apart: A*

Portrait of Palestinians in Israel, London, Tauris, 1990.

Orr, A., *The unJewish State: The Politics of Jewish Identity in Israel*, London and Ithaca, NY, State University of New York Press, 1983.

Swirsky, S., *Israel: The Oriental Majority*, London, Zed, 1989.

Minority-based and advocacy organizations

Al-Lajnat al-Mubadira al-Durziya (Druze Initiative Committee), PO Box 54, Yarka 24967, Israel; tel. 972 4 961 393, fax 972 4 968 841.

Amnesty International, PO Box 14179, Tel Aviv 61141, Israel; tel. 972 3 560 3357, fax 972 3 560 3391.

Arab Association for Human Rights, PO Box 215, Nazareth 16101, Israel; tel. 972 6 561 923, fax 972 6 564 934.

Association for the Defence of Bedouin Rights, PO Box 5212, Beersheba, Israel; tel. 972 7 31687.

Centre for the Defence of the Individual, 4 Abu Obeidah Street, Jerusalem 97200, Israel.

Palestinian Centre for Peace and Democracy, PO Box 25220, Shu'fat, Jerusalem, Israel; tel./fax 972 2 828 693.

Jordan

Land area:	89,206 sq km (excluding the Palestinian West Bank)
Population:	4.1 million (1993)
Main languages:	Arabic, Circassian, Armenian
Main religions:	Sunni Islam, Druze faith, Christianity
Main minority groups:	Palestinians 2.1 million (51%), Christians 400,000 (10%), Circassians and Chechens 35,000 (0.9%), Druzes 10,000 (0.2%)
Real per capita GDP:	$4,380
UNDP HDI/rank:	0.741 (70)

The Kingdom of Jordan was established in two phases. Britain awarded Transjordan (the area east of Palestine and the Jordan river) to the Hashemite Amir Abdallah in April 1921. Transjordan had a small settled population in the north-western part but was otherwise largely desert and marginal land inhabited by bedouin tribes. The Amir co-opted the tribes into his paternalist form of rule, and recruited a small armed force largely from the southern tribes.

In 1948 Transjordan fought Israel to retain the West Bank, part of the putative Palestinian Arab state (see **Palestine**), formally annexing it to create the Kingdom of Jordan in 1950. During the 1948 war the population tripled from about 430,000 to over 1.2 million with the addition of refugees and West Bank inhabitants. Even in the East Bank today, people of Palestinian origin probably outnumber East Bankers. Abdallah sought to expunge Palestinian identity, while giving Palestinians full citizenship of Jordan.

Palestinians

There are probably about 2.1 million Palestinians in Jordan, located overwhelmingly in the north-western part of the country, principally in the environs of Amman, Zarqa and Irbid. The vast majority are of 1948 refugee origin. Their attitude to Jordan was ambivalent from the outset, since although Jordan defended the West Bank, it had also already reached a secret understanding with the Zionists to incorporate this area.

Following the loss of the West Bank in 1967 (and the influx of another 300,000 displaced, most of whom were already refugees), Palestinians flocked to the guerrilla movement. In 1970, fearing the collapse of his authority, King Hussein sent his troops against strongholds of the guerrilla movement principally in Amman and Irbid, and the Palestinians were ruthlessly suppressed. It has left a permanent scar on relations.

In 1974 the Palestine Liberation Organization (PLO) was recognized as sole legitimate representative of the Palestinian people, and Hussein immediately reduced Palestinian participation in the administration of the state. Pressure on Palestinians to choose between two identities has always been a problem, but it intensified during the *intifada* (see **Palestine**) when Jordan relinquished its formal ties with the West Bank.

It is too early to say whether a resolution of the Palestine–Israel dispute will resolve Palestinian ambivalence within Jordan. Many Palestinians, particularly wealthier ones, settled down successfully and happily as Jordanians. It is in the camps and low-income areas that ambivalence and discontent are greatest.

Jordan was very dependent on remittances from (overwhelmingly Palestinian) migrants in the Gulf, until their 1991 expulsion from Kuwait and some other Gulf states. This lead to an influx of over 250,000 returnees and resulted in 30 per cent unemployment, factors which may destabilize relations in future.

Christians

There are a number of Christians, mostly Palestinians but also some long established East Bank families, in the north-west of the country. Altogether, they constitute nearly 10 per cent of the population. Most are Greek Orthodox but there are members of most other Orthodox and Uniate churches and a community of about 2,000 Armenians. Their economic influence far outweighs their numbers, since certain families control, or are highly influential in, the finance sector of the country.

Circassians and Chechens

There are about 30,000 Circassians and 4,000 Chechens who have retained their identity, located in Amman and six villages in northern Jordan. The Circassians (and a few Shi'i Chechens) were deliberately settled on the almost completely deserted East Bank by the Ottomans (see **Syria**), 1878–1909, to form a bulwark against predatory Bedouin and also to develop the region agriculturally. They created the first proper settlements at Amman, Zarqa and Jarash. On the creation of Transjordan, they numbered about 7,000 and formed an elite and loyal core retinue for Abdallah, well represented in the armed forces and administration. They largely abandoned agriculture in favour of business, the professions and government service and integrated into Arabic-speaking society.

A Circassian became Jordan's first prime minister in 1950, an indication of the influential position a number of Circassians had achieved under Abdallah. However, since the 1960s the Circassian community has lost its position of influence. Because they did not constitute a single corporate group, but many extended families, in 1979 some of the surviving leaders from the days of influence sought the formation of a Circassian/Chechen Council that could act in a similar way to the Arab tribes, providing patronage and mediation for the community as a whole in its dealings with others. It was a conscious decision taken by community elders, who do not want minority status since that might erode their own influential position within the community.

Many Circassians have emigrated to the USA. Those who remain are now an integral part of Jordanian society, while retaining community consciousness.

Druzes

There is a small community, perhaps 10,000, of Druzes from the Syrian border area around Umm al Jamal running south to the oasis of Azraq. These were cut off from the rest of Jabal Druze by the Syria-Transjordan border, formalized in 1931 (see **Syria**).

Conclusions and future prospects

Jordan has made greater strides towards a successful parliamentary democracy than almost any other Arab state. However, it remains highly vulnerable to the Palestine question until it is adequately resolved. Furthermore, the Jordanian population has a very high annual growth rate of 3.7 per cent, promising a volatile future unless gainful employment can be found for the majority of the young.

Further reading

Abu Jaber, K., *The Jordanians and the People of Jordan*, Amman, Jordan University Press, 1980.

Fathi, S., *Jordan – An Invented Nation?*, Hamburg, Deutsches Orient-Institut, 1994.

Rogan, E. and Tell, T., *Village, Steppe and State: The Social Origins of Modern Jordan*, London, British Academic Press, 1994.

Shami, S., *Ethnicity and Leadership: The Circassians in Jordan*, Berkeley, CA, University of California, 1984.

Minority-based and advocacy organizations

Al-Urdun Al-Jadid Research Center, PO Box 910289, Amman, Jordan; tel. 962 6 657 143, fax 962 6 657 132.

Kuwait

Land area:	17,818 sq km
Population:	1,505,000 (1995), of whom only 660,400 are nationals
Main languages:	Arabic, Persian, Urdu, Hindi
Main religions:	Sunni and Ithna'ashari Islam, also Christianity and Hinduism among migrant workers
Main minority groups:	Ithna'ashari Shi'is 180,000 (27% of Kuwait nationals), Bidoun 100,000 (7% of total population), Palestinians 25,000 (1.7% of total population)
Real per capita GDP:	$21,630
UNDP HDI/rank:	0.836 (51)

Kuwait is a primarily desert state, with only a few fertile areas. Virtually the entire population lives in Kuwait city, or one of the three or four other urban centres.

Kuwait emerged as an autonomous sheikhdom in the mid-eighteenth century, when a sheikh from the Al Sabah family was chosen as ruler by the six leading notable families. In 1899 Britain acquired control of Kuwait's external affairs. When Kuwait became independent in 1961, Iraq claimed it, but British deterrence and admission of Kuwait to the Arab League and United Nations brought Iraqi recognition.

Because of its oil wealth, heavily exploited since the 1950s, Kuwait welcomed a large community of migrant workers. Native Kuwaitis are just under half the total population. The largest worker contingent comes from the Arab world, followed by a number of Pakistanis and Indians, and a smaller number of Filipinos, Thais, Koreans and Sri Lankans. About 24,000 of these East Asians, mainly Filipino women, are engaged in domestic duties. Some of them have been subject to extreme forms of labour or sexual exploitation.

Unlike other Gulf states, Kuwait has a parliamentary tradition, organized opposition groups and a relatively free press. The main opposition groups reflect liberal, leftist, state nationalist, Arab nationalist and Sunni and Shi'i interests. However, the Al Sabah became increasingly unpopular during the 1980s, particularly after they suspended the constitution and dissolved the *majlis* in 1986.

Iraq's invasion and occupation of Kuwait, August 1990 to February 1991, were a major trauma. Apart from the loss of human life, plant was looted and immovable material destroyed. The cost of recovery was considerable. Kuwaitis acted with indiscriminate bitterness towards those non-Kuwaitis who remained in the city and were deemed to have cooperated with the Iraqis. The largest single contingent of migrant workers had been Palestinian, but other Arab workers were also either expelled or rendered unable to stay by the withdrawal of work permits.

Expectations of a more representative and participatory political system in Kuwait after the occupation have been only partially fulfilled. The Al Sabah 'returned to their autocratic and free-spending ways'.[1] In the 1992 *majlis al umma* election, a total of 80,000 males were entitled to vote, 15 per cent of the adult population. Thirty-three out of fifty seats were won by critics of the government. Various candidates represented religious ideological positions; fifteen Sunni revivalists won seats, and three Shi'is. The Amir accepted the result, promising not to dissolve this *majlis*, as had been done previously.

As in the rest of the Gulf, women are excluded from the exercise of full civil rights. Women constitute less than 48 per cent of the Kuwaiti population, about 3 per cent below the natural ratio.

Ithna'ashari Shi'is

About 27 per cent of the Kuwait population is Shi'i, of four different origins: Iran, al Hasa (Saudi Arabia), Bahrain and Iraq. They used to be mainly small shopkeepers and boat builders. Traditionally, the Shi'i community had been supportive of the Al Sabah (for example, supporting suppression of the first representative assembly in 1938), and this only changed with the Iranian Revolution of 1979. During the 1981–5 *majlis* session, Shi'is deputies ceased to be pro-government. The Iran– Iraq War and American anti-Islamic intervention in Lebanon heightened Sunni Shi'i tensions.

Since 1991, when Shi'i Kuwaitis proved that their commitment to Kuwait was no less than that of Sunnis, relations between the communities has much improved.

Bidoun

The term *bidoun jinsiyya* means 'without nationality', and refers to the large number of residents in Kuwait, many of them Shi'i, who for one reason or another are without nationality. Technically, they did not constitute a cohesive and coherent minority until the authorities began to coerce them to leave Kuwait. There were up to 300,000, but it is widely believed that this number has fallen to about 100,000 following the Gulf War, as a result of expulsions, mainly into Iraq. There are two categories of Bidoun: (1) those, and their descendants, who did not register for citizenship in 1959 on the eve of independence because they were illiterate or suspicious of registration and (2) those attracted to Kuwait from neighbouring countries to benefit from the oil boom, many of whom had no valid passport.

Until 1986 Kuwait treated the Bidouns as citizens, albeit ones living in abject poverty, but that year it tightened regulations and those Bidouns without ID cards found themselves unable to work officially, own a car, leave the country and return freely, obtain a marriage licence, obtain state education or health care. Some were summarily deported.

During the Iraqi occupation most Kuwaitis fled, but without travel documents the Bidouns were trapped. Bidouns were accused of assisting Iraqi forces, even though 82 out of the 320 killed resisting Iraqi forces were Bidouns. Like Palestinians, Bidouns were among those tortured, executed or 'disappeared' following the liberation of Kuwait. A number of Bidouns traditionally served in the Kuwaiti armed forces and police, and were normally able to escape the negative effects of their status through favours dispensed by the state via influential intermediaries. About 12,000 have been reinstated in these services since 1991. All other government-employed Bidouns were sacked.

Bidouns demand at least five years' residence in Kuwait, or leave to remain in Kuwait on probation for citizenship. The state seems determined to expel 95 per cent of Bidouns, including all those currently serving in the armed forces. Private schools have been instructed not to accept Bidoun children. A government committee is currently considering what to do with all categories of Bidoun. Ironically, virtually all Kuwaiti nationals originate from land that is outside Kuwait.

Palestinians

There are about 25,000 Palestinians left in Kuwait out of a total of over 400,000 prior to the Gulf War. They more than any other group had developed Kuwait since the 1950s. Few Palestinians sided with Iraq, but there was undoubtedly resentment against Kuwait, grounded in the state's denial of civic rights, or rights of domicile to people who had spent their lives serving the state and building the economy. The rule that all migrant workers and their dependants must leave Kuwait on cessation of employment was rigorously enforced. The power this system gave to employers was resented. Kuwait was an important centre for the growth of Palestinian nationalism during the 1950s and 1960s and, ironically, Kuwait was more supportive of the Palestinian cause than any other Gulf state. Bitterness understandably exists on both sides.

Conclusions and future prospects

Kuwait's oil is expected to last for well over another century, but wealth alone cannot guarantee internal and external stability for the Al Sabah. The cost of buying – in Western defence could prove heavy if Iraq repeatedly renews its claim. Meanwhile, a number of difficult civil rights matters lie ahead, particularly the enfranchisement of women and the question of citizenship (currently confined to males who had a male forebear resident in 1921). The Al Sabah also face the problem of introducing some form of taxation in return for which the population is bound to demand greater public accountability. The outcome of all these issues is certain to influence Kuwaiti policy on minority issues.

Further reading

Ghabra, S., 'Kuwait: elections and issues of democratization in a Middle Eastern state', *Digest of Middle Eastern Studies*, vol. 2, no. 1, winter 1993.

Hardy, R., *Arabia after the Storm: Internal Stability of the Gulf Arab States*, London, Royal Institute for International Affairs, 1992.

Human Rights Watch, *The Bidouns of Kuwait: Citizens without Citizenship*, New York and Washington, DC, 1995.

Lawyers' Committee for Human Rights, *Kuwait: Building the Rule of Law; Human Rights in Kuwait after Occupation*, New York, 1992.

Owen, R., *Migrant Workers in the Gulf*, London, MRG report, 1992.

Minority-based and advocacy organizations

Committee for Defending the Rights of the Kuwaiti Bidoons, PO Box 722, Harrow, Middlesex, HA2 0DR, UK.

Public Affairs Committee for Shi'a Muslims, Stone Hall, Chevening Road, London NW6 6TN, UK; fax 44 171 372 0694.

Lebanon

Land area:	10,452 sq km
Population:	2,900,000 (official est., 1993; the true figure is probably nearer 4 million)
Main languages:	Arabic, Armenian, Kurdish, French
Main religions:	Islam: Sunni, Ithna'ashari Shi'i, Alawi, Druze; Christianity: Maronite, Orthodox, Oriental Orthodox, Uniate, Armenian, Protestant denominations; Judaism
Main minority groups:	Ithna'ashari Shi'is 1.2 million (32%), Syrian nationals 750,000–1 million (20–27%), Sunni Muslims 700,000 (18%), Maronites 600,000 (16%), Palestinians 390,000 (10%), Druzes 260,000 (7%), Greek Orthodox 200,000 (5%), Greek Catholic 180,000 (5%), Armenians 125,000 (3%), , Alawis 100,000 (3%), Kurds 50,000 (1%) (*percentages based on the aggregate of estimated populations, not on the official country estimate*)
Real per capita GDP:	$2,500
UNDP HDI/rank:	0.675 (101)

Greater Lebanon was established by France in 1920 when it acquired the League of Nations mandate for Syria and Lebanon. The heart was the Mount Lebanon range, inhabited primarily by Maronites and Druzes, who had enjoyed special status within the Ottoman Empire on account of France's protective interest in the Maronites and other Catholics. France added surrounding parts of Syria, hoping to create a viable but predominantly Catholic and Francophile entity: (1) on the central coast, Beirut, Syria's most important port, which was predominantly Sunni; (2) in the north, Tripoli, Syria's second port, also mainly Sunni and its hinterland, the Akkar, peopled by Sunnis and Alawis, and the Kura, mainly Orthodox; (3) in the east, the rich Biqa'a valley, inhabited by various Christian and Muslim communities; and (4) in the south, the ports of Sidon (Sunni) and Tyre (Shi'i) and the latter's mainly Shi'i hinterland.

While Maronite Christians looked to France and the Mediterranean world, most Muslims and Orthodox Christians looked to the Arab hinterland as their political lodestar. Lebanon's informal political constitution was based on its unrepeated official census of 1932. Out of a then population of 785,543, Christians made up 52 per cent (Maronites 29 per cent, , Greek Orthodox 10 per cent, Greek Catholics 6 per cent, Armenians 4 per cent, Latins, Protestants and others 3 per cent). Muslims made up 48 per cent (Sunnis 22 per cent, Shi'is 19 per cent, Druzes 7 per cent).

On independence in 1943 a 'National Pact' confirmed existing practice that key posts be allocated on a confessional basis: the (executive) presidency, Maronite; the premiership, Sunni; and presidency of the Chamber of Deputies, Shi'i. The chamber itself was to be composed of deputies on a ratio of six Christians to five Muslims, thereby ensuring a slight Christian preponderance. It was a fragile basis for national consensus, even assuming that the birth rates of all communities would remain in parity.

Within the Muslim communities some desired to be more closely associated with the Arabism of Syria, but others accepted the idea of a multi-confessional Lebanese polity. Leading Sunni families tended to support the latter viewpoint and became part of a Maronite–Sunni establishment that dominated Lebanon. Within the Christian community, some viewed Lebanon as primarily a Christian homeland, for which continued French protection was crucial, while others sought a national Lebanese identity, to which all confessions could give assent.

The arrangement was unable to endure the internal and external stress to which Lebanon was exposed. During the 1950s and 1960s Lebanon's free trade economy developed rapidly, and the country was transformed into a city state as rural migrants flocked to Beirut, where the wealthy city centre contrasted with shanty areas populated by the new migrants. With different traditions juxtaposed in alien urban and highly cosmopolitan surroundings, confessional identities took on an adversarial potency they had lacked in the village. There was also growing resentment at the corrupt nature of an electoral system operated by patronage, run by cross-confessional alliances of powerful political families. By the end of the 1960s it was well known that the confessional ratio was changing rapidly in favour of Muslims in general and the Shi'a in particular.

Lebanon was also exposed to intense external pressure. In 1948 Palestine refugees arrived, amounting to 10 per cent of the country's population. Palestine was the central issue of Arab nationalism. Lebanon could not now escape this issue nor the way the Arab world split in the 1950s between the pro-Western and non-aligned Arab nationalist camps. In 1958 civil war was narrowly averted after brief fighting. The build-up of Palestine Liberation Organization (PLO) guerrilla operations from south Lebanon after 1967 brought Israeli reprisals, brought into question the sovereignty of the government and heightened the internal conflict between the mainly Maronite camp that wished to maintain the political status quo and avoid embroilment in the Palestine conflict, and the mainly Muslim camp that was interested in constitutional change, was sympathetic to the Palestinian cause, believed in Arab nationalism and felt Lebanon should not evade its 'Arab duty'.

In 1975 these tensions exploded in civil war between two broad camps, the mainly Christian 'rightist' Lebanese Front and the mainly Muslim and Arab nationalist 'leftist' National Movement, supported by Palestinian groups. The war was characterized by the kidnap, rape and massacre of those caught in the wrong place as each side eliminated 'enemy' enclaves – mainly Christian or Muslim low-income areas. With Syrian intervention the military situation was stabilized, but in 1978 Israel invaded the south to deal with the PLO. Under US pressure, and under United Nations Security Council Resolution 425, it was required to withdraw completely and unconditionally, but left advisers and a surrogate Maronite force in southern Lebanon. In 1982 Israel invaded again with the aim of destroying the PLO, which it besieged in West Beirut. It killed 19,000 people, of whom not more than 5,000 were combatants.

Israel was obliged to withdraw as a result of guerrilla attacks by Lebanese resistance forces, but hung on to a portion of southern Lebanon, assisted by its local surrogate, the South Lebanon Army. At each phase of withdrawal Israel achieved further social fragmentation. The Druzes drove the Maronites out of the Shuf mountains as soon as Israel withdrew in 1983, and from the villages near Sidon the following year. In both cases Israel had encouraged Maronite forces to provoke local Muslims.

Meanwhile, Syria drove the PLO from Lebanon,

while Druzes and Shi'is cooperated with Syrian policy: the Druzes drove Sunni fighters off the streets of Beirut, while Shi'i forces ruthlessly attacked the Palestinian camps to prevent PLO recovery. Both the Maronite and Shi'i communities also fell victim to internal power struggles.

Having defeated Israel in the competition to dominate Lebanon, Syria made repeated attempts to reconstitute the country politically, to achieve stability while bringing Lebanon more closely under its control. In 1989, under Syrian pressure, a quorum of Lebanese deputies met in Ta'if (Saudi Arabia) and accepted a new formula to replace the National Pact. The Charter of National Reconstruction proposed to reduce the Maronite presidency to essentially titular powers; vest the cabinet (which would be half Muslim, half Christian) and Prime Minister with executive power; enlarge the Chamber of Deputies and ensure 50:50 Christian/Muslim participation; and eventually abolish confessionalism in political life.

In 1990 Syrian forces defeated Christian opponents of Ta'if in a final round of fighting in Beirut. In the face of Syrian determination, the various militias stood down, allowing the Lebanese army to deploy throughout the country except for Hizballah-controlled areas and Israeli-occupied south Lebanon. It seemed the civil war might be over, at an estimated cost of 150,000 lives.

The Eastern Orthodox, Protestant and Jewish communities are so small that they have been omitted from the discussion below.

THE MAJOR CONFESSIONS

Ithna'ashari Shi'is

There are probably about 1.2 million Shi'is in Lebanon, in three principal concentrations: their two traditional heartlands in the northern half of the Biqa'a and Jabal Amil, the region east of Tyre; and in the southern suburbs of Beirut. The Shi'i heartlands were probably originally a refuge from the Sunni-dominated interior of Syria. Jabal Amil has been noted for centuries for the scholarship of its religious leaders.

The Shi'is were not as hostile as Sunnis to their inclusion in Lebanon in 1920. For them the pill was sweetened since France formally recognized the Shi'a as a distinct confession, something Sunni regimes had never done. However, the Shi'a remained on the political and economic periphery, except for a few wealthy landlord families representing the community in parliament. This began to change rapidly when the trickle of Shi'i migrants to Beirut turned into a flood in the 1960s. By 1975 40 per cent of the Shi'is of Jabal Amil had moved to Beirut, where they became acutely aware of their comparative poverty and state of neglect. The Biqa'a and Jabal Amil communities, which had never had much contact before, began to fuse in the slum quarters of Beirut, and became politicized.

Politically, migrant Shi'is began to challenge their old leaders and turned to leaders of the Lebanese and Palestinian left until two factors threw them back on their own resources. First, the Palestinian war against Israel launched from southern Lebanon brought savage reprisals which drove a wedge between the two peoples. Second, a politically articulate clerical leadership emerged, principally in the person of the charismatic Imam Musa Sadr. Although many Shi'is died during the civil war, they only became major participants after the Israeli invasion. They humiliated the rightist Maronite regime installed by Israel and attacked Israeli forces, which had turned from 'liberator' (from the PLO) to occupier of their heartland.

Amal, the main Shi'i militia, took a pragmatic view of Lebanese politics. It worked in cooperation with Syria to prevent any armed Palestinian recovery, dominating Beirut's southern suburbs. But in the south a more visionary movement emerged, Hizballah (Party of God), which drew inspiration from the revolution in Iran and advocated an Islamic republic. While Amal soft-pedalled its war against Israel, Hizballah undertook a bitter struggle, vowing 'to liberate Jerusalem'. Amal and Hizballah fought inconclusively for undisputed leadership of the Shi'a in the mid-1980s. In practice both contain a spectrum of outlook, from the pragmatic to the more visionary. Hizballah knows that whatever its rhetoric concerning the establishment of an Islamic republic in Lebanon, in practice it cannot impose a formula unacceptable to the other confessions, which collectively still easily outnumber the Shi'a.

Sunnis

There are probably about 700,000 Sunnis in Lebanon, approximately 18 per cent of the total population, concentrated in Beirut, Tripoli, Sidon and in the countryside of the Akkar and the central Biqa'a. Unlike the Druzes and Maronites, with their distinctive identity and solidarity, the Sunnis felt part of a larger and more amorphous community. They were more loosely organized, through trade guilds, mosques and charitable institutions. There was no Sunni leadership in 1920 when they were reluctantly coerced into the new republic. They wanted to retain their vital ties with the Syrian interior. The National Pact of 1943 assigned to the Sunnis a position only slightly subordinate to the Maronites. In reality it was the merchant families of Beirut who supported the National Pact since they could share the Christian vision of a liberal merchant republic. In Tripoli and among lower class urban and rural Sunnis, there was little support.

The political leadership that emerged operated largely on patronage networks, but by 1960 these networks were decaying. While the masses responded to the appeal of Nasserism, Ba'athism and other currents of Arab nationalism, Sunni leaders seemed allied with the Maronite power brokers in spite of their Arab nationalist rhetoric. Many Sunnis began to look to Kemal Junblat, leader of Druzes as their natural leader.

The Sunni elite was swept aside in the civil war, as local militias emerged, led by army officers and men of the artisan class. Lack of community cohesion meant that they proved weaker than other contestants. In Beirut they fought alongside the Palestinians, but were removed from the streets by the Druzes in 1984. In Tripoli a Sunni revivalist movement, al Tawhid, challenged the Syrians and their local protégés the Alawis, 1983–5, before they were also crushed.

At face value the Sunnis seem to have lost as much as the Maronites from the civil war. There is no indication, despite their numerical importance, that they will cohere in the way other major contestants have done, and unless this changes they are likely to remain largely acquiescent in future developments.

Maronites

Of an estimated 2.2 million Maronites worldwide, about 600,000 are in Lebanon, home of the Maronite Church. This Syriac church traces its origins to Mar Marun, a fourth century hermit. Byzantine persecution on doctrinal grounds and conflict between Muslim and Byzantine forces drove the Maronites from the Syrian plain to the safety of the Qadisha Gorge of northern Lebanon.

The Maronite Church was the only Eastern Church fully to cooperate with the Latin Crusaders, seeking union with Rome in 1182. Union was formalized circa 1584, when a Maronite college was established in Rome, the result of increasing contact between the two churches in the intervening period. Rome recognized the Patriarch of the Maronite Church, the Patriarch recognized papal supremacy.

The Maronites traditionally inhabited the northern reaches of Mount Lebanon and also the south, from Jezzine down to the present Israeli border, but began to spread into Druze areas, providing their services to Druze landlords in the Matn and Shuf. During the nineteenth century, they eclipsed the Druzes economically and then politically, the middle years punctuated by major confrontations culminating in Druze massacres of Christians in 1860. Thereafter, France oversaw the protected status of Mount Lebanon (until 1943) in close consultation with the Maronite Patriarch, who remained a key determinant of political authority until the civil war in 1975.

When it was clear that the demographic balance was changing in the early 1970s, the Maronite leadership opposed constitutional compromise and tried to preserve its effective hegemony over a pro-Western republic. The civil war was catastrophic for the community, which shrank from an estimated 800,000 in 1975 to 600,000 or so by 1990. In 1982 the Maronite-led Lebanese Forces and Kata'ib party militia openly cooperated with Israel against the Palestinians and Syria. When Israel could no longer afford to occupy half Lebanon, these forces refused to come to terms with Syria (the other external contender) until the latter had smashed Maronite military independence. By 1984 the Maronite paramilitary leadership had fallen victim to internecine strife and personal ambition.

Although a Maronite still holds the presidency, the community cannot recover its former power. The future of the Maronite community depends on an ability to re-invent its role and relationships in Lebanon, just as the Druze community was obliged to do a century earlier.

Druzes

There are probably about 260,000 Druzes in Lebanon, located mainly in the Matn, Gharb and Shuf, and smaller communities in Wadi al Taym in southern Lebanon and in Beirut. The Druze faith emerged from the *batini* or esoteric tradition of the Isma'ili faith in the early eleventh century, when a small group of Isma'ilis hailed the Fatimid Caliph, al Hakim (996–1021), as the *mahdi* (or Guided One) and manifestation of God in his unity; hence they call themselves *al muwahhidun* (Unitarians).

Persecuted in Egypt, they gained footholds in

the Shuf and Wadi al Taym. The sect soon became a closed and secret one to preserve itself in a hostile environment. The majority of Druzes remain ignorant concerning the tenets of belief, while a minority (including women) become initiate in the secrets of the faith.

Politically, Druzes enjoyed supremacy in the Gharb and neighbouring areas from the twelfth to the sixteenth centuries, when certain Druze clans gained ascendancy in Mount Lebanon and the Ma'an dynasty was acknowledged by the Ottomans as the family through which to control an unruly region.

Druze hegemony over Mount Lebanon declined in the eighteenth and disintegrated in the nineteenth century, the result of internal conflict between ascriptive kinship groups, later exploited by external rulers, who sought to introduce taxation. Decline also reflected progressive demographic and economic ascendancy by the Maronite and Greek Catholic communities, mainly from inland Syria, and the failure of the religious leadership to provide cohesive direction to the community. Many Druzes left Mount Lebanon for the Hawran (see **Syria**) in the nineteenth century.

Druzes resented the French creation of Greater Lebanon in 1920, with its institutionalized Catholic ascendancy and the formal political separation of Lebanese and Syrian Druzes. Several leading Druzes had strongly supported the short-lived kingdom of Syria. However, they accepted the inevitable, playing a fuller part in Lebanese political life than their community size might have suggested.

Under Kemal Junblat, the Druze community espoused Arab nationalism and the Palestinian cause in the 1960s, though they were careful not to allow Palestinians a foothold in the Druze Shuf. Junblat's Druze-dominated Progressive Socialist Party advocated the deconfessionalization of Lebanese political life, since he could thereby acquire greater influence for himself and the community. Given the socio-economic pressures in Lebanon and the psychology these engendered, Junblat's vision remained an ideal for which the leftists fought with declining credibility during the civil war. Druzes supported Junblat's non-confessional ideas, primarily because he was their leader, and acted with greater communal solidarity than any other group. After his assassination by Syria, his son Walid succeeded as community leader. Until 1982 the Druzes managed to keep the civil war almost entirely outside the Shuf, but that year the Israeli invaders introduced the Maronite Lebanese Forces militia into the area. The moment Israel withdrew, the Druzes rose and expelled not only the Lebanese Forces but also the Christian inhabitants of the Shuf. During the 1980s they created a virtually independent state in the Gharb, Shuf and southern Matn. They also displaced the Sunni militia in West Beirut. They reluctantly accepted Ta'if and encouraged the return of expelled Christians, but on the strict understanding of Druze hegemony in the Shuf. They dislike the Syrian presence and have quietly buried their enthusiasm for Arab nationalism. They remain the only confession which has retained relatively undivided internal political solidarity.

Greek Orthodox Christians

There are probably about 200,000 Greek Orthodox Christians in Lebanon. From the seventh century the Greek Orthodox with the Sunnis formed the core population of coastal towns and plain, with Orthodox concentrations in Kura, south of Tripoli, and in several mixed villages of the Gharb and Shuf (the mountains immediately east and south of Beirut). Like Greek Catholics, the Orthodox were noted merchants and bankers, prominent in the marketing of manufactured goods. Until 1917 they enjoyed the 'protection' of Tsarist Russia, and discreet ties with Russia survived through the Soviet period. Tension between Orthodox and Catholic in Lebanon, based on different doctrine, politics and culture, also reflected Franco-Russian rivalry for pre-eminence in Greater Syria.

From the late nineteenth century the Orthodox played a major role in the Arab nationalist, literary and cultural revival. Because of the sizeable community inland, many Orthodox supported Syrian Arab nationalism. The idea of Greater Syria appealed as a multi-confessional world in which the Orthodox could play a significant role, hopefully dominated neither by the Francophile Catholic dimension of Lebanon, nor by the Islamic tendency of the wider Arab world. The political vehicle of Syrian nationalism, the Syrian Social Nationalist Party, became closely identified with the community in Lebanon, though some Orthodox joined secular leftist parties. Most responded to the Arab dimension of the Palestine question. Unlike Greek Catholics, few sided with the Christian right in the civil war. The Orthodox are probably the keenest Christians to see Ta'if succeed and the least alarmed by Syria's dominant role in Lebanon.

Greek Catholics

There are probably about 180,000 Greek Catholics and they are the most successful businessmen of

Lebanon. They left the Orthodox Church to acknowledge the supremacy of Rome in 1683 (formalized in 1724 when the Patriarchate of Antioch fell vacant and they elected their own patriarch). While this departure resulted from French missionary influence, it also reflected resentment of Greek management of an essentially Arab church. Many Greek Catholics left inland Syria for Lebanon to avoid Orthodox harassment and benefit from trade prospects. During the nineteenth century they became concentrated in, and outnumbered the Druzes of, Zahleh in the Biqa'a. Zahleh was the scene of fierce conflict between Catholics and Druzes in 1860. Smaller communities exist in Sidon and Tyre.

In 1920, like the Maronites, the Greek Catholics tended to favour French tutelage, on account of their special connection. During the mandate period the small but powerful merchant community grew in Beirut. As Lebanon polarized in the early 1970s, the majority of Greek Catholics aligned with the major Maronite militias. However, as with the Maronite Church, by the end of the 1970s the Patriarchate was increasingly uneasy with the Maronite political leadership's adventurist alliances with Israel and the USA. As a minor political player, the community remains focused more on economic recovery than on hankering after the idealized visions of Lebanon so alluring to Maronites.

Armenians

There are probably about 125,000 Armenians in Lebanon, concentrated mainly in north Beirut, Tripoli and at Anjar in the Biqa'a. The first to arrive in Lebanon were Cilician Catholics in the eighteenth century, escaping the harassment of the Armenian Orthodox Church from which they had split. Much more substantial waves arrived fleeing massacre by the Turks in 1895–6 and the greater genocide of 1915. More came when France failed to establish an Armenian entity in Cilicia in 1920–1, and the final influx arrived from Alexandretta when France handed this to Turkey in 1939. The Armenians were welcomed by the Maronite leadership to enlarge the Christian population and were offered Lebanese citizenship. Lebanon became the principal focus of the Armenian diaspora, and Beirut or its environs became the seat of the Orthodox Catholics, the Catholic patriarch, and also the Armenian Evangelical Church.

The community was cautious in political life, tending to support candidates already endorsed by other communities. It was a modest force for political stability and, apart from some individuals, the community generally avoided being drawn into the civil war. It has suffered particularly heavy emigration as a result of that war, because virtually every family has relatives well placed in more stable and prosperous countries.

Alawis

There are probably about 100,000 Alawis in Tripoli and the Akkar. Some are indigenous to the region, but possibly half have entered the country since the Syrian intervention in 1976 (see Syria, and Syrians, below).

IMMIGRANT COMMUNITIES

Syrians

An unknown number of, but possibly a million, Syrian migrants have established themselves in Lebanon under the protection of Syria's informal tutelage of Lebanon since 1976. Most of these are petty traders or casual labourers, who have squeezed out low-income Lebanese and Palestinians. Because they enjoy informal protection, these immigrants cannot be challenged. If their presence becomes permanent, it is likely to affect political developments.

Palestinians

There are about 390,000 Palestinians, mainly in Beirut and the outskirts of Sidon, Tyre and Tripoli. About 110,000 refugees arrived in Lebanon in 1948, from Jaffa, Haifa, Acre and Galilee. They were settled in official camps, though many moved into neighbouring low-income areas. No new camp sites have been established, despite the fourfold increase in population, and the total destruction of four camps during the 1970s and the almost total destruction of Shatila camp in 1985–6.

A few middle class and mainly Christian Palestinians obtained Lebanese citizenship, but the vast majority were given the status of foreigners, requiring work permits. They thus formed pools of cheap and casual labour located almost solely in predominantly Muslim areas. During the 1960s, the heyday of revolutionary nationalism in the region, from which the Lebanese state tried to protect itself, the camps were kept under tight surveillance and control by the Deuxième Bureau. In 1969, with the growth of Palestinian national feeling, the camps ejected the Bureau and its many agents, and established Palestinian control of the camps.

With the transfer of the PLO from Amman to Beirut in 1971, the Palestinians effectively took control of much of southern Lebanon and parts of Beirut and Sidon, and launched raids into Israel. Their alliance with the Shi'a, was destroyed by punitive Israeli raids on Lebanese as well as Palestinian targets, and by high-handed behaviour towards the indigenous population that was expected to subordinate its own concerns to the guerrilla war.

After its short-lived invasion of 1978, Israel invaded again in 1982, determined to destroy the PLO and install a right-wing regime in Beirut. Israel failed in these objectives, although the removal of PLO forces from Beirut and the south left the refugee population vulnerable to the contesting forces, demonstrated in the massacre of over 1,000 inhabitants of Shatila camp in 1982 by the Lebanese forces acting under Israeli auspices, and the bloody sieges of Shatila by (Shi'i) Amal forces with Syria's blessing, 1985–7.

Since Ta'if (1989), the Gulf War (1991) and the PLO-Israeli Declaration of Principles (DoP, 1993), the Palestinian predicament in Lebanon has seriously deteriorated. The community faces the loss of remittances following eviction from Kuwait and other Gulf states, the collapse of political and financial support for the PLO, a high level of unemployment in Lebanon and widespread eviction of war-displaced people from unauthorized accommodation. Perhaps most seriously, Palestinians see the DoP as almost certainly liquidating the refugee question. Refugees in Lebanon are in a more serious dilemma than in Syria or Jordan. The government has stated that 'under no circumstances will Lebanon agree to give Palestinians citizenship',[1] and spoken of a 'redistribution' of refugees, a euphemism for the expulsion of a substantial proportion of refugees. They thus seem destined to remain without civic rights. Refugees share with Lebanon a commitment to the right of return, but both parties know that Israel is unlikely to honour this humanitarian obligation even in part.

Kurds

Kurdish workers arrived in Lebanon from Syria in the 1950s and 1960s. There are probably about 50,000, mainly in Beirut. During the civil war they tended to identify with the left, in particular the Druze-led Progressive Socialist Party. Like Palestinians they do not have civic rights.

Conclusions and future prospects

By 1996 Lebanon seemed to be slowly recovering, with freedom of movement established except in the Israeli-occupied south. However, power resides primarily with Syria and with similar power brokers and militia leaders to those of 1975. Moreover, everyone has become more acutely aware of their confessional identities, which in many cases have been sharply redefined in the trauma of civil war. Confessional separation has taken place in many parts of Lebanon where Muslims and Christians had previously coexisted. In particular, the Christian presence was, by 1988, heavily concentrated in the Matn, Kisrawan and Jbail (the mountains and coast immediately north of Beirut) and, compared with 1975, had dropped from 53 to 31 per cent in northern Lebanon, and from 76 to 21 per cent in the Biqa'a. Muslims, on the other hand, had been reduced to 1 per cent in these Maronite heartlands.

Interest in wider political currents in the Arab world has declined. The Lebanese population itself has fallen by about 15 per cent since 1975. It is far from clear whether Lebanon's fundamental political and confessional problems are in the process of resolution.

Further reading

Abu-Izzeddin, N., *The Druzes*, Leiden, E.J. Brill, 1984.

Ajami, F., *The Vanished Imam: Musa Sadr and the Shia of Lebanon*, London, Tauris, 1986.

Firro, K., *A History of the Druzes*, Leiden, E.J. Brill, 1992.

Hourani, A., *Political Society in Lebanon: A Historical Introduction*, Oxford, Centre for Lebanese Studies, n.d.

McDowall, D., *Lebanon: A Conflict of Minorities*, London, MRG report, 1986, 1996.

Mallat, C., *Shi'i Thought from the South of Lebanon*, Oxford, Centre for Lebanese Studies, 1988.

Messara, A., *Prospects for Lebanon: The Challenge to Co-existence*, Oxford, Centre for Lebanese Studies, 1988.

Moosa, M., *The Maronites in History*, New York, Syracuse University Press, 1986.

Salame, G., *Lebanon's Injured Identities: Who Represents Whom During a Civil War?*, Oxford, Centre for Lebanese Studies, 1986.

Salibi, K., *A House of Many Mansions: The History of Lebanon Reconsidered*, London, Tauris, 1988.

Sayigh, R., *Too Many Enemies: The Palestinian Experience in Lebanon*, London, Zed, 1994.

Minority-based and advocacy organizations

Association Libanaise des Droits de l'Homme, PO Box 166742, Beirut, Lebanon.

Centre for Lebanese Studies [multiconfessional and committed to pluralism], 59 Observatory Street, Oxford OX2 6EP, UK; tel. 44 1865 58465.

Committee for Human Rights in Lebanon, PO Box 135485, Shouran, Beirut, Lebanon.

Middle East Council of Churches, PO Box 5376, Beirut, Lebanon; tel. 961 1 861 670, fax 961 9 515 621.

Oman

Land area:	212,457 sq km
Population:	2 million (1993)
Main languages:	Arabic, Gujarati, Baluchi
Main religions:	Ibadi, Sunni and Isma'ili Islam, Hinduism
Main minority groups:	Sunnis 400,000 (33% of nationals)
Real per capita GDP:	$10,420
UNDP HDI/rank:	0.715 (91)

The Sultanate of Oman is predominantly Ibadi, including the ruling dynasty. The Ibadiya broke away from the Khariji movement of early Islam (see regional introduction). Disagreement with Sunnis hinged only on the question of succession to the imamate/caliphate, Ibadis insisting that anyone, not merely members of the family of the Prophet, could be elected to this office.

The Ibadis established themselves in the mountains of central Oman following their expulsion from Basra in the 720s. They were led by a succession of imams, frequently elected on a kinship basis among the dominant tribes of the region. The greater the relations, hostile or friendly, with the outside world the more the imamate acquired a temporal character. It was in reaction to the centralizing tendency of the imamate that resentful tribes on the periphery of authority, particularly in the northern and south-eastern parts of Oman, embraced Shafi'i Sunni Islam. It lent doctrinal difference to what was essentially a political conflict.

Another major divide is between the interior, Oman proper, and Muscat, the coastal region. The latter area depended on international trade, particularly with India and Africa, and was therefore more tolerant than the interior regarding religious practice.

The spiritual and temporal leadership of the Ibadiya divided in the mid-eighteenth century, the former remaining in the interior, the latter moving to Muscat. It was only in the 1970s that the Sultan was able to exercise his undisputed authority throughout Oman (as internationally defined) without the overt assistance of external (British) forces.

Minority groups

There are about 400,000 Sunnis belonging to mainly to the Shafi'i school, but also some Malikis. Sunnis are found mainly in the north, south-east, and some in Muscat and other ports.

There are probably about 1,000 Hindus in Oman, concentrated in Muscat and other ports. There have been Indian traders since the early Islamic period and possibly earlier.

Information on the size of Oman's Khoja population is unavailable. Originally they were Lohana caste Indians from Sindh, Kutch and Gujarat who converted to Nizari Isma'ilism in the fourteenth century. They practised *taqiyya* (dissimulation) extensively to avoid persecution, and many became so accustomed to their adoptive sect – usually Sunni or Ithna'ashari Islam – that they lost their Isma'ili beliefs. They are part of a highly successful merchant network with other Khojas in East Africa and India.

Information on Oman's Baluchi population is unavailable. Baluchis are concentrated on the coastal region.

Conclusions and future prospects

There is no reason to suppose that the current amicable relations between Oman's communities are likely to change.

Further reading

Kelly, J., *Sultanate and Imamate of Oman*, Oxford, Royal Institute for International Affairs and Oxford University Press, 1959.

Owen, R., *Migrant Workers in the Gulf*, London, MRG report, 1992.

Shorter Encyclopaedia of Islam, Leiden and London, E.J. Brill and Luzac, 1961.

Wilkinson, J., *The Imamate Tradition of Oman*, Cambridge, Cambridge University Press, 1987.

Palestine

Definition:	Although all Israel and the Occupied Territories form geographical Palestine, the definition here refers to all those areas of Palestine captured by Israel in 1967, namely the West Bank (including East Jerusalem) and the Gaza Strip.
Land area:	6,163 sq km
Population:	2.3 million (excluding Jewish settlers; total approx. 7 million if all refugees are included; 1996)
Main languages:	Arabic, Hebrew
Main religions:	Islam, Christianity, Judaism
Main minority groups:	indigenous Palestinians 2.3 million (89%), Jewish settlers 280,000 (11%)
Real per capita GDP:	—
UNDP HDI/rank:	—

Indigenous Palestinians

The indigenous people were rendered a minority in Palestine and large refugee communities created in neighbouring countries as a result of the implementation of the Jewish nationalist ideology, Zionism, which claimed Palestine for the Jewish people. Zionism began in Europe, as a solution to pogroms in the east and assimilation in the west. Its intention was to achieve control of the economy of Palestine and to achieve a numerical majority. Alongside settlement, the idea of removing the indigenous population became a recurring theme among Zionist leaders.[1] By 1910 Zionism was the most important political issue in Palestine. When Britain captured Palestine from the Ottomans in 1917, the Foreign Secretary, Balfour, made a declaration promising to facilitate the establishment of a Jewish national home in Palestine. This undertaking was enshrined in the League of Nations Mandate for Palestine, which ascribed to the Jewish Agency (pledged to employ only Jewish labour) the task of developing Palestine economically.

Palestine was a highly decentralized village society composed mainly of Sunni Muslims, but with about 10 per cent Christians. Fear of progressive dispossession began to create a sense of national identity among the politically aware. But Palestinian society could not compete with highly organized and capitalized European settlers.

The Holocaust transformed international attitudes to Palestine. When Britain could no longer handle the conflict it had helped produced, the United Nations decided in November 1947 to partition Palestine, awarding the Jews, then only one third of the population, over half the territory. The Arabs rejected the plan, and fighting between the two communities commenced almost immediately. Jewish forces were better organized and experienced and rapidly defeated local Arab forces, driving out the civilian population.

Expulsion of the Palestinian population was a premeditated strategy.[2] When Britain withdrew on 15 May 1948, over 200,000 Arabs had already been compelled to abandon their homes. Neighbouring Arab states now entered Palestine but were defeated by the new Jewish state. By the end of hostilities Israel controlled 72 per cent of Palestine, and 750,000 out of approximately 1 million Palestinians were made refugees. Israel claimed that the refugees had abandoned their homes 'voluntarily', refused to allow them back and razed most of their villages. From 1948 refugee camps and communities became a permanent feature of the Arab-held portion of Palestine and neighbouring countries. Egypt administered the Gaza Strip and Jordan annexed the West Bank. The Palestine question destabilized the region. In 1967 Israel again defeated its neighbours, capturing the West Bank and Gaza Strip and forcing another 300,000 into exile.

The Palestinians formed their own resistance movement, despairing of deliverance by the Arab states. The Palestine Liberation Organization (PLO) conducted a guerrilla war and committed attacks on civilian targets. Civil conflict in Jordan and Lebanon became a by-product of its guerrilla war. In 1982 Israel tried to extirpate the PLO in Lebanon, killing 19,000 people, mainly civilians, in the process.

Israel decided on permanent control of the Occupied Territories, though it never declared this formally. It progressively expropriated (by 1995) 60 per cent of the West Bank and 40 per cent of the Gaza Strip. It carried out a major settlement programme throughout the territories, designed to retain strategic control and to ring Palestinian population areas. It also illegally annexed East Jerusalem, took total control of all water resources and changed the demographic balance by building massive settlements around the Old City. It changed the body of law regarding the Occupied Territories with well over 1,000 of its own administrative orders. By stifling economic development in the Occupied Territories and dumping excess produce on a captive market Israel made its military occupation profitable. Civil as well as armed resistance was crushed with collective punishments, curfews, home demolitions and indefinite detention without charge or trial. All these measures violated the Fourth Geneva Convention of 1949. Israel denied it was bound by this convention. Between 1987 and 1991 an *intifada* or uprising took place against the occupation. While it made occupation costly it failed to force Israel out of the territories. The PLO formally recognized the Israeli state in November 1988, hoping it would no longer be treated as an international pariah. It was disappointed. International action to uphold Palestinian rights or secure a just solution remained frustrated by the USA which supported Israel, routinely vetoing UN resolutions that attempted to uphold international law and norms.

Palestinians today

In 1996 the Palestinian people were estimated to be scattered in the following manner:

West Bank	1,250,000
Gaza Strip	880,000
Israel	810,000
Jordan	2,170,000
Lebanon	395,000
Syria	360,000
Other Arab states	517,000
Rest of world	500,000
Total	6,882,000

In August 1993 Israel finally recognized the PLO and agreed an outline plan, the Declaration of Principles, whereby administrative responsibility for an unspecified proportion of the Occupied Territories would be handed to the PLO, and from which Israeli forces would be withdrawn. Certain contentious issues were deliberately postponed for a final settlement: the status of Jerusalem, the Jewish settlements, the refugees, water resources. By 1996 Israel had handed over 60 per cent of the Gaza Strip and 5 per cent of the West Bank to the Palestine National Authority (PNA). But these populated areas under Palestinian control are ringed by Israeli-occupied zones, thus fragmenting Palestinian areas into a captive mosaic. The PNA is held responsible for Palestinian 'good behaviour', and has frequently acted in an autocratic manner towards its subject population. The administration remains strapped for cash, and its people almost wholly dependent on Israel to provide employment and income.

Christian Palestinians

There are approximately 400,000 Christian Palestinians world-wide of whom only 51,000 live in the Palestinian Israeli-Occupied Territories (less than half the number in Israel), 2.9 per cent of the entire population of the territories. They are concentrated in central Palestine – Ramallah, Jerusalem and Bethlehem – and tend to be among the more highly educated cadres of the population. Among them are members of every Eastern denomination and most Western ones. They identify strongly with the rest of the Palestinian community against the Israeli occupation and dislike being treated as if they were a distinct minority. But their emigration level is more than twice the national average, with 35 per cent of the entire Christian community having left since 1967, leaving behind an ageing and preponderantly female population. They leave because of the negative effects of the Israeli occupation on education, employment, housing and daily life.

Jewish settlers

By 1995 there were approximately 3,500 Jewish settlers in the Gaza Strip, 170,000 in East Jerusalem and another 100,000 in the rest of the West Bank, totalling almost 280,000. Such settlements began straight after the 1967 war. The presence of Jewish settlers violates the requirements of the Fourth Geneva Convention regarding protection of civilian populations under occupation. Settlers are subject to Israeli law, not to the laws applying to the Occupied Territories. Settlers are armed and may shoot unarmed Palestinians when they believe the circumstances justify this. In February 1994 a settler shot dead 29 worshippers in the Mosque of Abraham, Hebron.

Settlers belong to two broad categories: those who have settled for ideological reasons, often in the least hospitable areas, for example the Gaza Strip; and a larger number of those who settled in the metropolitan commuter areas of Jerusalem and Tel Aviv because of the opportunity to inhabit good housing much more cheaply than inside Israel. There is a broad overlap between the two categories, with a general attitude that Arabs may stay only if they 'behave'. The international community has taken no effective steps to persuade Israel to terminate settler violation of the Geneva Convention.

Samaritans

About 250 Samaritans live in Nablus; they claim descent from Israelites from before the Assyrian exile of 722 BCE. Their sole norm of religious observance is the Pentateuch. They live in semi-isolation, only marrying within the community.

Conclusions and future prospects

The prospects for the Palestinian people continue to deteriorate. Israel seems determined to retain absolute control of Jerusalem and continues its demographic strategy of settling more Jews in the Arab sector and denying Palestinians from outside the Jerusalem area access to the city. It also seems determined to retain control of the territories through maintaining its settlements and creating a new settler road network. The USA backs Israel as strongly as ever, with military and economic aid. Palestine remains economically dependent on Israel. The authoritarian nature of the PNA bodes ill for Palestinian democracy and human rights, and threatens to undo the long-standing work of local non-governmental organizations to foster grass roots democracy under occupation. It remains to be seen whether an electoral process can change this or whether, in a situation of scarce resources, reliance on patronage systems will perpetuate authoritarian rule under Israeli direction. Much will depend on whether the Israeli government and electorate begin to view the process as leading to a genuine resolution of the conflict and whether, as a result, they recognize that Israel's own future will be improved by Palestinian stability and prosperity.

Further reading

Brand, L., *Palestinians in the Arab World*, New York, Columbia University Press, 1988.

Hilterman, J., *Behind the Intifada*, Princeton, NJ, Princeton University Press, 1991.

McDowall, D., *The Palestinians*, London, MRG report, 1987.

McDowall, D., *The Palestinians: The Road to Nationhood*, London, Minority Rights Publications, 1994.

Masalha, N., *The Expulsion of the Palestinians: The Concept of 'Transfer' in Zionist Political Thought, 1882–1948*, Washington, DC, Institute of Palestine Studies, 1992.

Prior, M. and Taylor, W., *Christians in the Holy Land*, London, World of Islam Festival Trust, 1994.

Sayigh, R., *Palestinians: From Peasants to Revolutionaries*, London, Zed, 1979.

Shehadeh, R., *Occupier's Law: Israel and the West Bank*, Washington, DC,Institute of Palestine Studies, 1985.

Minority-based and advocacy organizations

Al Haq, 31 Main Street, PO Box 1413, Ramallah, West Bank, Palestine, via Israel; tel. 972 2 995 6421, fax 972 2 995 4903.

Gaza Centre for Rights and Law [closed during 1995 by PNA], PO Box 1274, Gaza, Palestine, via Israel; tel./fax 972 7 866287.

Palestine Human Rights Information Center, 4201 Connecticut Ave NW, Suite 500, Washington, DC 20008, USA; tel. 1 202 686 5116, fax 1 202 686 5140.

Institute for Palestine Studies, 3501 M Street, NW, Washington, DC 20007, USA; tel. 1 202 342 3990, fax. 1 202 342 3927, e mail: ips.dc@cais.com.

Qatar

Land area:	11,437 sq km
Population:	521,000 (1993) (of whom less than 30% are Qatari nationals)
Main languages:	Arabic, Indian and Pakistani languages, Persian
Main religions:	Strict Wahhabi Sunnism, and Ithna'ashari Islam
Major minority groups:	Ithna'ashari Shi'is 21,000 (14% of Qatari nationals)
Real per capita GDP:	$22,380
UNDP HDI/rank:	0.838 (56)

Qatar became politically independent of the British in 1971. Before 1949 Qataris were among the poorest people in the world. However, following the commencement of oil production that year, Qataris became progressively wealthier, enjoying one of the world's highest per capita incomes by the 1970s. Qatar has a strong Wahhabi (see **Saudi Arabia**) tradition.

As elsewhere in the Gulf, rapid economic expansion was accompanied by a vast influx of migrant labour, outnumbering Qataris by more than three to one. The majority of migrant workers are from Pakistan, but there are also a large number of Iranians, accounting for three-quarters of the 10 to 18 per cent of the population that is Ithna'ashari Shi'i, the other Shi'is coming largely from al Hasa (see **Saudi Arabia**). They do not seem to form a coherent or cohesive minority group.

There is so far little sign of a challenge to the way Qatar is governed. In 1991 a petition for fundamental political reform signed by fifty young liberals of leading families was successfully ignored.

Further reading

Crystal, J., *Oil and Politics in the Gulf: Rulers and Merchants in Kuwait and Qatar*, Cambridge, Cambridge University Press, 1990.

Zahlan, R., *The Creation of Qatar*, London, Croom Helm, 1981.

Zahlan, R., *The Making of the Modern Gulf States: Kuwait, Bahrain, Qatar, the United Arab Emirates and Oman*, London, Unwin Hyman, 1989.

Saudi Arabia

Land area:	2,240,000 sq km
Population:	17.4 million (1993)
Main languages:	Arabic
Main religions:	Sunni, Ithna'ashari, Zaydi and Isma'ili Islam, Christianity among migrant workers
Main minority groups:	Ithna'ashari Shi'is 2.3 million (14%), Isma'ilis 250,000 (1.4%), Zaydis 200,000 (1.2%)
Real per capita GDP:	$12,600
UNDP HDI/rank:	0.771 (63)

The Kingdom of Saudi Arabia is the product of two forms of organization in tandem, one religious and the other secular. The religious impulse derives from the eighteenth century Wahhabi reformist and fundamentalist movement, which was harnessed to the fortunes of the Najdi tribal dynasty of Ibn Saud. Wahhabis, who themselves upheld a stringent form of the purist Hanbali school (see regional introduction), considered all who failed to agree with their particular brand of revivalism to be infidel. The Wahhabi–Ibn Saud domain reached its apogee in the early nineteenth century before being crushed by Egyptian forces in 1818.

In 1901 a young adventurer, Abd al Aziz Ibn Saud, began to recover the Saudi domain, gaining control of central Arabia with his Ikhwan (Brotherhood) bedouin fighters of Wahhabi persuasion, who had abandoned their tribal nomadism in favour of agricultural camps. Ibn Saud progressively conquered most of the peninsula, taking the Hijaz (Mecca, Medina and Jedda) in 1925.

Saudi Arabia, as the monarchy was known from 1932, never threw off its religious connotation. Wahhabism, the dominant religious culture of the Najd, remained a strong and institutionalized ideological feature of the Saudi kingdom. Acquisition of the holy cities of Mecca and Medina conferred the sacred responsibility of custodianship, which has both brought criticism and proved a liability.

Religion remains the single most potent domestic issue in the kingdom. The reformist movement, which is natural heir to Wahhabism, is critical of Saudi laxity and seeks to apply its own rigorous standards throughout the kingdom. However, the Hijazis are either Shafi'i or Hanafi, both traditions more tolerant in outlook than the Hanbali school. Consequently, there is tension within the Sunni community, between the Wahhabi reformists and the Shafi'is and Hanafis.

The second pressure upon a family-controlled monarchy comes from the growing liberal and educated constituency. Although weaker than the Islamic reformists, liberals demand political, civil and human rights. Liberals are able to embarrass the House of Saud internationally. As more Saudis become educated, they will inevitably demand a say in how the state is run.

The third pressure is over political alignment. Saudi Arabia forged a special relationship with the USA from the 1930s. Given the latter's open espousal of Israel since 1964, this friendship is controversial, particularly since Saudi Arabia has proved unable to moderate the USA's pro-Israel policy in the region.

Finally, the House of Saud is vulnerable economically. This is not only a matter of dependence on oil revenues, but one of general economic transformation and the ability to keep the population quiescent under an unaccountable monarchy. Saudi Arabia will eventually have to introduce taxation, and those who pay it will then begin to demand accountability and subsequently participation in government.

These issues became evident in the Gulf crisis of 1990–1. Saudi Arabia's need to call in Western forces to protect it and regain Kuwait demonstrated its dependence on the West against another Arab state. The presence of 'infidel' forces on Saudi soil offended the reformists. Western intervention likewise inspired 'liberals' to agitate for greater popular participation in running the kingdom. Finally, the cost of Western intervention was borne to a great extent by Saudi Arabia when it was experiencing for the first time serious budget difficulties.

Saudi Arabia's migrant workers enjoy little protection. When Yemen sounded sympathetic to Iraq's invasion of Kuwait, Saudi promptly expelled 800,000 Yemeni workers. Since the Gulf War, Christian workers, who do not form a coherent minority community, have been the target of Sunni harassment, most notably those from Third World countries. There are about 250,000 Filipino workers, many of them in domestic service. Some migrant workers endure slave-like treatment, especially those in domestic service, captive to employers who hold their passports.

Saudi women are among the most restricted in the region, forbidden to drive cars and subject to harassment from the *mutawwa* (religious police) if they fail to dress or behave correctly in public. The enforcement of prayer-time observance in the public domain creates a climate of enforced hypocrisy in daily life.

Ithna'ashari Shi'is

About 14 per cent of Saudis are Shi'i, mainly in the Eastern Province, but with a substantial community in Medina, and some in Mecca. Relations with the Wahhabi movement, and thus with the House of Saud, have been tense ever since the rise of Wahhabism. In 1801 Saudi-led Wahhabi forces had sacked the Shi'i shrine of Karbala in Iraq. A Shi'i took revenge by assassinating the head of the Saudi House.

After Ibn Saud and his Ikhwan recaptured the Shi'i oases of Qatif, Seihat and al Hasa in 1913–14, Saudi governors had to prevent Wahhabi hatred of the Shi'is from violent expression. It was harder to contain Wahhabi utterances. In 1927, for example, the *ulama'* (religious leadership) issued a *fatwa* (binding religious opinion): 'As to the Shi'a, we have told the Imam [Ibn Saud] that our ruling is that they must be asked to surrender to true Moslems. Shi'as must be forced to study Sheikh Ibn Abdul Wahhab's Three Principles. Any places specially erected for the practice of their rites must be destroyed and these practices forbidden in mosques or anywhere else. Any Shi'a who refuses to keep to these rules must be exiled from Moslem territory.'[1]

Shi'is were forbidden to mark the Ashura commemoration publicly and to construct *husayniyas* (religious and cultural centres), and were excluded from advancement in government service. It was only under the then US company Aramco that Shi'is enjoyed high employment levels in the Eastern Province. During the 1970s conditions improved for Shi'is, with a Shi'i appointed head of the Jubail Industrial Project, a major industrial venture in al Hasa.

Saudi's Shi'is have always looked to clerics in the Shi'i cities of Karbala, Najaf (Iraq) or Qum (Iran) for moral and spiritual support. The Iranian Revolution of 1979 gave the Saudi Shi'a renewed self-confidence. In November 1979 Ashura was performed publicly as Shi'i leaders had announced, but this led to clashes with Saudi security forces, rioting and the loss of seventeen lives. It was a defining moment. More bloodshed occurred in 1980.

The state and Sunni majority reacted negatively to the Shi'i revival. There was particular sensitivity because the Shi'a happened to live in the Saudi oilfields. Aramco, having come under Saudi ownership in 1978, began to remove Shi'is from responsible positions in the company. The state executed four Shi'is for acts of sabotage in 1988 and sixteen for bombings during the 1989 *hajj* (pilgrimage).

Since the Gulf War there has been greater Sunni activism and harassment of Shi'is. Shortly after the war, a senior member of the Sunni *ulama'*, Sheikh Abd Allah Ibn Jibrin, issued a new *fatwa* which denounced Shi'is as heretics worthy of death, and forbade marriage or social intercourse between Shi'is and Sunnis, indicating a revival of Wahhabi intolerance. Indeed, in 1992 a devout Shi'i was publicly executed in Qatif, charged with blasphemy. Other Shi'is have been detained without trial and tortured. In 1991 the Shi'a petitioned the king for financial assistance in building Shi'i mosques and *husayniyas* (since Sunnis receive similar state help), the reinstatement of those dismissed from Aramco, and equal opportunities to enter university and the army. Given the strength of Wahhabi feeling, the government did nothing. The appointment of only one Shi'i to the *majlis al shura* (Consultative Council) indicates Saudi caution.

There are also 28,000 Iraqi Shi'i refugees confined to a major camp complex at Rafha, subject to 'treatment unacceptable by any international standards',[2] including torture, degrading treatment, and deliberate attempts to convert refugees from Shi'i to Sunni Islam.

One might conclude that relations between Shi'is and Sunnis are not improving, but in 1993 the government struck a deal with the Shi'i Reform Movement, which had successfully propagated embarrassing information internationally concerning Saudi Arabia's human rights record with the Shi'a. The Reform Movement agreed to suspend its information network in return for allowing exiles to return home, the release of Shi'i prisoners and the easing of conditions for Shi'is. However, the public exercise of Shi'i practices remains circumscribed, surveillance continues and foreign travel remains restricted for Shi'is.

Other minorities

There are approximately 250,000 Isma'ilis in the region of Najran, including the religious leadership (see **Yemen**).

There are up to 200,000 Zaydis in the country, some being the northern reaches of Zaydi communities in Yemen, others being long-standing immigrants now with Saudi nationality (see **Yemen**).

Conclusions and future prospects

In 1993 King Fahd finally nominated sixty appointees to a *majlis al shura* (Consultative Council), originally promised in 1932, but this hardly implied more representative government. In the end Saudi Arabia must reconcile the contradictions implicit in the pressures mentioned above, or be engulfed by them. The prospects for minority groups remain precarious. The most powerful challenge to the Saudi monarchy comes from Islamic reformist hardliners, and the monarchy is reluctant openly to defy them.

Further reading

Amnesty International, *Religious intolerance: the arrest, detention and torture of Christian worshippers and Shi'a Muslims*, London, September 1993 and *Unwelcome guests: the plight of Iraqi refugees*, London, May 1994.

Hardy, R., *Arabia after the Storm: Internal Stability of the Gulf Arab States*, London, Royal Institute for International Affairs, 1992.

Middle East Watch, *Empty Reforms: Saudi Arabia's New Basic Laws*, New York, May 1992.

Minnesota Lawyers International Human Rights Committee, *Shame in the House of Saud: Contempt for Human Rights in the Kingdom of Saudi Arabia*, Minneapolis, 1992.

Minority-based and advocacy organizations

Public Affairs Committee for Shi'a Muslims, Stone Hall, Chevening Road, London NW6 6TN, UK; fax 44 171 372 0694.

Syria

Land area:	184,050 sq km
Population:	13.4 million (1993)
Main languages:	Arabic, Kirmanji, Turkish
Main religions:	Sunni, Alawi, Druze, Isma'ili and Ithna'ashari, Islam; Greek Orthodox, Syrian Orthodox, Maronite, Armenian, Syrian Catholic, Greek Catholic and Roman Catholic Christianity; Judaism
Main minority groups:	Alawis 1.4 million (11%), Kurds 1 million (8%), Greek Orthodox and Catholics 450,000 (4.3%), Druzes 400,000 (3%), Palestinians 360,000 (2.7%), Armenians 200,000 (1.5%), Isma'ilis 200,000 (1.5%), Syrian Orthodox and Catholics 120,000 (0.9%), Turkomans 80,000 (0.7%), Circassians 50,000 (0.4%), , Ithna'asharis 50,000 (0.4%)
Real per capita GDP:	$4,960
UNDP HDI/rank:	0.761 (78)

Syria owes its configuration to the Allied partition of the Arab Near East after 1918, and in particular to French administration, 1920–46. Under the Ottomans the geographical, economic and cultural concept of Syria embraced all of modern Israel/Palestine and Lebanon as well as modern Syria.

Many of the minority groups of Syria are also found in neighbouring countries. Physical and human geography have been major determining factors in today's social fabric: city, desert, mountain and sea. Until the present century social divides between town dweller, peasant and bedouin, and the conflict between the latter two, were quite as important as religious differences.

In the mountain ranges stretching along the littoral, and across to Mount Hermon and the Jabal Druze in south Syria, religiously dissident communities were able to hold their own against Muslim or Christian orthodoxy. On the coastline a more cosmopolitan Mediterranean trading culture existed which had as much in common with other seafaring cultures of the Mediterranean as it had with its hinterland.

With the defeat of the Ottomans, a congress of representatives from Greater Syria met in Damascus in 1919 and affirmed its intention to found 'a constitutional monarchy based upon principles of democratic and broadly decentralized rule which shall safeguard the rights of minorities'. This intention was thwarted by French military intervention in 1920 when Feisal, King of Syria, was driven into exile. Within a month France allocated the ports of Tripoli, Sidon and Tyre, and their respective hinterlands, and the Biqa'a valley, to its creation of Greater Lebanon, and in 1939 surrendered the Sanjaq of Alexandretta (subsequently, the Hatay) to Turkey (in violation of its mandate obligations).

France played upon minority differences and ignored a more fundamental underlying common identity to fragment the rest of Syria into four territories, for the Alawis in the north-western Nusayri mountains, for the Druzes in Jabal Druze, while Damascus and Aleppo were formed into two separate entities. It was only in 1936 that these parts were reunited as a result of Arab nationalist pressure. Among the minorities, notably the Alawis and Druzes, there was division between those who wished to foster minority separatism, frequently the dominant chiefs for whom this guaranteed and enhanced their authority, and newly educated people of lowlier birth, who saw their future in a wider nationalist context.

France recruited minority groups – Alawis, Druzes, Isma'ilis, Christians, Kurds and Circassians – into its local force, Les Troupes Speciales du Levant, a policy which not only caused tension with the Sunni Arab majority but also paved the way for later minority control of Syria. Military service offered the opportunity for betterment for low-born but ambitious, often nationalist, recruits. Syria became independent in 1946 and three years later a coup installed the first of a succession of Kurdo-Arab officers in power, each of whom relied on minority or localist support.

In the meantime the Ba'ath (Renaissance) Party, founded in 1940 with a socialist Arab nationalist ideology, made progress in the poorer parts of Syria, particularly the Alawi and Druze areas, and within the military. Part of its appeal to confessional minorities was its secular emphasis on the equality of all Arabs, irrespective of religion, and its view of Islam as a cultural rather than religious component of Arab national identity. In 1963 the Ba'ath seized power, purging the army of 'disloyal elements' and replacing them with officers drawn disproportionately from the Alawi and Druze communities. By 1966 many Sunnis had been removed from positions of responsibility. In 1966 a Druze attempt to displace Alawi ascendancy in the Ba'ath failed, and many Druzes were purged from the security forces. Although power was already concentrated in the hands of a largely Alawi leadership, Isma'ilis were the next to be purged from the armed forces. In 1970 Hafiz al Asad won the struggle within the Alawi community. Although many posts in the armed forces and security apparatus were held by Sunnis, Alawis from al Asad's own family, tribe or village neighbourhood held the essential keys to control of the state.

From 1979 the regime began to face a serious Sunni revivalist challenge, as civil disobedience spread from one city to another. In 1982 an uprising in the city of Hama was only suppressed with the reported deaths of up to 20,000 and mass destruction. Since then the Muslim Brotherhood seems to have been largely subdued.

The regime has maintained its position by tight security control, which has led to widespread human rights abuses. Generally speaking, these are applied at an individual level, and no minority is the specific target of persecution. Technically it is an offence to 'incite strife among the various sects or elements of the nation' (Press Code of 1948) or to carry out 'sectarian activities' (Law of Associations 1958). However, there can be little doubt that the present government has continued the policy of its predecessors in using one group against another or applying pressure to any minority which demonstrates political cohesion. The regime has ensured that no community in Syria has the ability to displace the Alawis. Crudely speaking, the heart of the regime lies in the overlap area between three concentric 'circles of power': the army, the Ba'ath and the Alawi community.

Women have enjoyed a measure of emancipation under Ba'athi rule, some elected to Parliament, others appointed to senior professional positions. Yet social attitudes are extremely varied, especially in the countryside.[1] Emancipation has a long way to go.

Syria has an idiosyncratic position regarding Islam. Its constitution includes the requirement that 'Islam shall be the religion of the head of state', included at popular insistence. Along with Lebanon, Syria is unique in the Arab world in not enshrining Islam as the religion of the state itself.

RELIGIOUS COMMUNITIES

Alawis

Alawis number about 1.4 million and comprise approximately 11 per cent of the population. Their ancestral heartlands are in the agriculturally poor Nusayri Mountain range in the coastal part of north-west Syria, but with sizeable communities on the inland plains of Homs and Hama, in the Hatay of Turkey (see **Turkey**) and the Akkar of north Lebanon (see **Lebanon**). There are negligible small communities in Iraq and Palestine.

Until this century Alawis were generally known as Nusayris, after their ninth-century founder Muhammad Ibn Nusayr. Alawis adopted the name partly to indicate that through their devotion to Ali they belonged within the Shi'a. Alawis subscribe to the idea of a Divine Triad, expressed in seven emanations of the Godhead, each embodied in three persons. Although Ibn Nusayr seems to have been an Ithna'ashari, religiously there seems to be much in common with the Isma'ilis, particularly the idea of exoteric and esoteric beliefs. The Alawis disregard the basic Muslim ritual duties.

The Nusayris were well established in the tenth century and only fled to the mountains to escape persecution in the eleventh. Since then they have had deep and bitter conflict with the dominant Sunni culture on the plain. After attempts to unite with the Isma'ili sect in 900 and 1291 failed, there has been a history of conflict between these two sects also.

Social stratification among the Alawis is both religious and secular. Both initiates and religious sheikhs stand above the community in moral terms. In the secular field most Alawis were tribal, only achieving social solidarity in the twentieth century. Until then the four confederations, or constituent tribes, had little hesitation in fighting each other. Large numbers of peasant Alawis joined Les Troupes Speciales. In the 1940s many also joined the Syrian Social National Party but then moved *en masse* to the Ba'ath, which seemed strategically better placed to gain power. Both parties stressed a secular identity in which religious nonconformity would not count against them. Unlike the old notable and sheikhly class, which begged the French to keep them as a separate political entity, the young upwardly mobile members of the military and the Ba'ath saw that the best opportunity for the community lay in secular Arab nationalism.

The broad process whereby the Alawis removed their rivals is described in the country introduction. Since 1950 the rapid growth of an Alawi middle and professional class, where none existed before, has transformed the community into a coherent and economically powerful group and arguably the best educated. Family and tribe, however, still count in patronage networks. Both the Sunni and Shi'i *ulama'* (religious leadership) have been persuaded formally to recognize Alawis as Shi'i Muslims, an intended safeguard against any religious backlash.

Greek Orthodox and Catholics

There are probably about 350,000 members of the Antiochene Patriarchate of the Orthodox Church (Greek or Byzantine Orthodox Church) in Syria. They are concentrated in and around Damascus and also in Latakiya and the neighbouring coastal region. Orthodox Christians never identified with the Christian West (which sacked the Orthodox capital Constantinople in 1204). They feel comfortable as Christians within an Islamic culture and some view the Prophet Muhammad as founder of a united Arab nation. Orthodox Christians took a lead in nationalist thinking during the twentieth century. The appointment of an Arab, rather than Greek, Patriarch of Antioch in 1898 was the first overt expression of Arab nationalism. Since then, Orthodox Christians have played an active part in the short-lived Kingdom of Syria, in Syrian nationalist movements and in Arab nationalism. Orthodox Christians continue to prosper in Syria and do not suffer erosion by emigration to the same extent as other Christian communities.

The Melkite (Imperial) Church (Greek Catholic Church) split from the Orthodox Patriarchate of Antioch to enter union with Rome in 1724. It immediately appointed an Arab rather than Greek Patriarch. Out of 1.2 million members world-wide, about 100,000 live in Syria. President Asad has tended to foster close relations with the churches of Syria and Lebanon, particularly the Melkite Church.

Druzes

The Druzes number about 400,000, approximately 3 per cent of the Syrian population, located primarily in Jabal Druze (also known as

Jabal al Arab or Jabal Hawran) on the southern border abutting Jordan, but with significant communities on the Golan (Jawlan), seventeen villages in Jabal al A'la, roughly midway between Aleppo and Antioch in the north-west, and four villages just south of Damascus. (For the Druze faith, see **Lebanon**.)

The first Druze settlers probably arrived in the Jabal Druze from Mount Lebanon and Aleppo at the end of the seventeenth century. Their chief concerns were to establish communities where they would not be molested by Ottoman authorities or the Sunni population, and that were defensible against bedouin raids. Jabal Druze was ideal. As a result of the events of 1860 in Mount Lebanon, the Jabal experienced a massive influx of Druze migrants from Lebanon and the population rocketed, as the south and eastern slopes of the Jabal were colonized. Throughout the nineteenth century the Ottomans unsuccessfully attempted to subdue the Druzes into submission to taxation and conscription like the rest of the province of Syria. They only succeeded in 1910.

Alongside a religious leadership based on heredity within three clans, the real leaders of the Jabal were the various clan leaders who mediated the outside world for their followers, who were composed both of kin and dependent families who settled in the clan's villages.

The Druze responded ambivalently to the short-lived Arab kingdom of 1919–20, and welcomed the establishment of an independent Druze territory by France. But certain leaders were profoundly suspicious of French intentions and in 1925 a major revolt, in unison with Arab nationalists in Damascus, nearly ejected France from the country. After the revolt's suppression in 1927, two trends were discernible in Druze society. The old established notable class clung to separate status, trusting to France to uphold it, while the younger generation and those of lower status favoured Arab nationalism. Many of these joined the army and in due course the Ba'ath party, and helped defeat the separatists.

During the 1960s the Druzes were purged from power within the army, the Ba'ath and security services after an unsuccessful coup attempt by a Druze officer. Nevertheless, the Druzes, like other communities, share in government but the reins of real power remain in Alawi hands. Like the Alawis, the Druzes have supported secular nationalism but remain anxious to be considered within the fold of Islam, even if some feel their beliefs barely merit it, and fear being disavowed by the Sunni majority, especially at a time of Sunni revivalism.

About 15,000 Druzes have lived under Israeli military occupation on the Golan since 1967. The Druzes have resisted attempts to seduce them into Israeli citizenship. As one Golani Druze remarked, 'Israel may be a Jewish democracy and Syria a dictatorship, but I shall always be part of the body politic in Arab Syria, something I can never be in Jewish Israel.'

Isma'ili Shi'is

There are about 200,000 Isma'ilis living mainly in Salamiya, east of Hama, with a rump in Masyaf and Qadmus in the southern part of the coastal mountain range. (For Isma'ili origins, see **Regional Introduction** and **Iran**.)

The Syrian Isma'ilis established themselves in the coastal mountain range south of the main Alawi areas under direction from Alamut (see **Iran**). In the twelfth century they acquired the major fortress of Banyas, and also Qadmus and Masyaf, from where they inspired fear in both Muslim and crusader rulers. They became divided into two main groups, the Hajjawis and Suwaydanis, following a leadership succession dispute.

In the first half of the nineteenth century, the community was decimated by conflict with Alawi tribes, with which there was long-standing rivalry, and by government punitive expeditions. Thereafter, substantial numbers moved to the marginal zone on the desert frontier around Salamiya.

Like the Alawis and Druzes, individual Isma'ilis eagerly enrolled in Les Troupes Speciales, and later in the Ba'ath. Although a number of Isma'ilis continue to enjoy senior posts in government, they have been carefully excluded from substantive power. Isma'ilis in Salamiya have advanced economically much faster than those in Masyaf.

Armenians

There are about 200,000 Armenians in Syria, mainly in Aleppo, but also in Damascus and the Jazira. Some are descended from those who left Anatolian Armenia in the eleventh century and Cilicia a century later. The majority, however, are descended from the 100,000 or so survivors of the genocide in Anatolia during the First World War. Most, 150,000, belong to the Armenian Apostolic or Orthodox Church (Gregorian), but about 40,000 belong to the schismatic Armenian Catholic Church, and 3,500 to the Evangelical Church. They tend to avoid politics and public life.

Syrian Orthodox and Catholics

There are probably about 80,000 Suryanis, or members of the Syrian Orthodox Church, located mainly in the Jazira, Homs, Aleppo and Damascus. Having rejected the verdict of Chalcedon, 451, the Suryani were virtually eradicated by Roman imperial forces. Muslim Arab conquest was a relief from persecution and their numbers grew. They were numerically preponderant in the Syrian countryside until virtually exterminated by Tamarlaine's forces in the late fourteenth century. Some of the Suryani today are survivors from the massacres carried out around Mardin by Turkey in 1915. They dislike being described as Jacobite (after Jacob Baradeus, who led the community after expulsion at Chalcedon, 451). They still use the Aramaic – or Western Syriac – liturgy (the language spoken by Jesus), and may freely teach it and their cultural traditions to children of the community.

The uniate Syrian Catholic Church, established in 1781 by schismatics from the Syrian Orthodox Church, has about 40,000 adherents in Syria, in small communities mainly in Aleppo, Hasaka and Damascus.

Other religious minorities

There are possibly up to 50,000 Ithna'ashari Shi'is living in a handful of communities near Homs and to the west and north of Aleppo.

Maronites

There is a community of about 20,000 Maronites mainly in the Aleppo region, a surviving remnant from before the majority sought safety in Mount Lebanon in the sixth century (see **Lebanon**).

Assyrians

About 9,000 Assyrians moved from Iraq to Syria following the Iraqi massacre of 1933. They were settled in the Khabur valley in the Jazira (north-east Syria), where they established sixteen farming villages. Most of today's 25,000 Assyrians in Syria belong to the Assyrian Ancient Church of the East (see **Iraq**), but approximately 8,000 belong to the Chaldean Catholic Church (see **Iraq**). The community is in decline as members of both churches decide to emigrate. Assyrians are represented in Parliament by an Assyrian member of the Ba'ath.

Yazidis

Yazidis are ethnically Kurds (for their religion see **Iraq**). Because of assimilation into Islam, there are probably less than 10,000 in Syria, located in two principal areas. One community is in Jabal Sim'an and the Afrin valley in north-west Syria, and dates back at least to the twelfth century. A larger group, composed of refugees mainly from southern Turkey but later also some from Iraq during the 1920s and 1930s, is located mainly around Hasaka in the Jazira, north-east Syria.

Jews

Until 1948 there was a population of 40,000 or so Arabic-speaking Jews, mainly in the cities of Damascus and Aleppo. Although few were Zionist, many moved to Palestine for economic reasons in the 1930s. Syrian Jews were fatally compromised by events in Palestine, which left them exposed to Zionist efforts to make them migrate and Arab nationalist demands of loyalty to the state. Two major mob attacks occurred on Jewish life and property in Aleppo in 1945 and 1947, both inspired by events in Palestine. Many left covertly, forbidden to leave Syria for fear they would go to Israel. In 1992 travel restrictions were lifted and only 400 or so are left.

ETHNIC COMMUNITIES

Kurds

There are probably just over one million Kurds in Syria, found in two main areas: Kurd Dagh, north-west of Aleppo; and along the Turkish border in northern Jazira – from Jarablus to Qamishli. The inhabitants of Kurd Dagh and some in Jarablus have been living there for centuries. Even if they still speak Kurdish, they also belong to the local Arab culture.

The larger community in Jazira is largely composed of those who fled the Turkish republic during the repression there in the 1920s. It is among these Kurds that national awareness and tension with the Arab majority is most felt. The French policy of encouraging minority separatism fostered intercommunal tensions, for example with the Assyrian and Armenian communities in the Khabur valley. Kurds were recruited into Les Troupes Speciales and encouraged to found Khoybun, a Kurdish nationalist party of the 1920s and 1930s, which made Arab nationalists uneasy.

The first three coups following Syrian independence were carried out by officers of part-Kurdish background, each relying on officers of similar background. Following the overthrow of the last of them, Kurds were purged from senior army ranks. During the heyday of Arab nationalism, 1958–76, Kurds came under increasing repression, partly because of their close identity with the Syrian Communist Party. Many Kurds were arrested, imprisoned and tortured. In 1961 a census in Jazira discounted 120,000 Kurds as foreigners. In 1962 a major population transfer was announced, intended to settle Arabs all along the Turkish border. Although never fully implemented, 60,000 Kurds left the area for Damascus. Ba'ath repression lessened under Hafiz al Asad.

It is probably because of Syria's support for the Kurdish movement in Turkey and Iraq that in 1990 politically active and nationalist Kurds were elected to the Syrian Parliament. This does not imply either that they will be able to mobilize Kurdish sentiment regarding Syria's internal affairs nor that Kurds will enjoy full civil and cultural rights. Kurds still suffer inferior status with many still denied citizenship, an ID card or a passport. Kurdish language and cultural expression continue to be suppressed, with Kurdish place names replaced with Arab ones. Ethnic discrimination, although greatly lessened, still continues.

Turkomans

There are reportedly 80,000 Turkomans, all of whom are Sunni, and some of whom still speak Turkish. Further information is unavailable.

Circassians

There are probably about 50,000 Circassians in Syria, descended from refugees of 1877 who were settled mainly in the Jawlan (Golan). Here they came into conflict with the Druzes. They were mobilized as auxiliary forces against the Druzes in 1896 and 1910 and by the French in 1925. In 1967 over half the Circassian community lost their homes when Israel captured the area. Most still live in Damascus in theory waiting to return, but some migrated to the USA. They retain their distinct identity.

RECENT IMMIGRANT COMMUNITIES

Palestinians

There are about 360,000 Palestine refugees in Syria, a fourfold increase on those arriving in 1948. At first Syria toyed with resettling them in a depopulated part of the Jazira. The refugees themselves refused any solution short of returning to Palestine. Syria did not grant them citizenship but placed them on a virtually equal footing with Syrians in employment, commercial activity and education. Consequently, they have successfully integrated into society and the economy.

As with Syrians, membership of the Ba'ath (or the Palestinian military wing, al Sa'iqa) is essential for advancement. Damascus is home for the 'rejectionist' parts of the Palestinian movement, notably the Popular Front for the Liberation of Palestine (PFLP) and Democratic Front for the Liberation of Palestine (DFLP), and consequently suppresses expressions of support for Arafat. From 1983, when Asad expelled Arafat's forces from Lebanon, severe restrictions were applied on travel and public expression, and many Palestinians arrested. In the words of Middle East Watch: 'Of all the people from all groups tortured to death in Syria during this period (1983–6) at least half have been Palestinians . . . As of summer 1990 Syria held 2,500 Palestinians as political prisoners, including about 2,000 within Syrian territory (the balance presumably in Lebanon).[2] Like all large migrant communities, the Palestinians are vulnerable to popular hostility if a major downturn in the economy leads to unemployment.

Jewish settlers in the Golan

Israel captured the Golan (Jawlan) in 1967 and subsequently expelled almost 100,000 civilians. Approximately 15,000 Druzes remain. In the rest of the Golan, Israel settled 13,000 Jews in thirty-two settlements and annexed the area in 1981, both violations of the Fourth Geneva Convention.

Conclusions and future prospects

The future stability and confessional balance of power in Syria must remain an open question. Any regime will wish to downplay a minority predominance and emphasize 'the Syrian nation', regardless of the realities. But in a society dependent politically and economically on patronage systems, the emergence of a state in which confessional, family or regional identity plays little or no part is difficult to imagine.

Further reading

Dam, N. van, *The Struggle for Power in Syria: Sectariansim, Regionalism and Tribalism in*

Politics, 1961–78, London, Croom Helm, 1979.

Firro, K., *A History of the Druzes*, Leiden, E.J. Brill, 1992.

Gibb, H.A.R. and Kramer, J.E. (eds), *Shorter Encyclopaedia of Islam*, Leiden and London, E.J. Brill and Luzac, 1961.

Gubser, P. 'Minorities in power: the Alawites of Syria' and 'Minorities in isolation: the Druzes of Lebanon and Syria', in R.D. McLaurin (ed.), *The Political Role of Minority Groups in the Middle East*, New York, Praeger, 1979.

Lescot, R., *Enquete sur les Yezidis de Syrie et du Djebel Sindjar*, Damascus, Institut Français, 1938, reprinted Beirut, Libraire du Liban, 1975.

Lewis, N., *Nomads and Settlers in Syria and Jordan, 1800–1980*, Cambridge, Cambridge University Press, 1987.

Marsden, P., *The Crossing Place: A Journey among the Armenians*, London, Harper Collins, 1993.

McDowall, D., *The Kurds*, London, MRG report, 1991, 1997.

Middle East Watch, *Syria Unmasked: The Suppression of Human Rights by the Asad Regime*, New Haven and London, Yale University Press, 1993.

Musa, M., *Extremist Shiites: The Ghulat Sects*, New York, Syracuse University Press, 1987, chs 22–36.

Vanly, I., 'The Kurds in Syria and Lebanon', in P. Kreyenbroeck and S. Sperl (eds), *The Kurds: A Contemporary Overview*, London, Routledge, 1992.

Minority-based and advocacy organizations

Centre for Armenian Information and Advice, Hayashen, 105a Mill Hill Road, London W3 8JF, UK; tel. 44 181 992 4621, fax 44 181 993 8953.

Institute of Isma'ili Studies, 30 Portland Place, London W1N 3DF, UK; tel. 44 171 436 1736.

Kurdish Human Rights Project, Suite 319, Linen Hall, 162–8 Regent Street, London, W1R 5TB, UK; tel. 44 171 287 2772, fax 44 171 734 4927.

Hevgirtin/Kawa [Syrian Kurds], Jindrisska 14, Box 537, 11121 Prague 1, Czech Republic.

Turkey

Land area:	779,452 sq km
Population:	59.8 million (1993)
Main languages:	Turkish (only official language), Kirmanji and Zaza Kurdish, Laz, Arabic
Main religions:	Sunni Islam, Alevism (not officially recognized), Greek, Armenian and Suryani Christianity, Judaism
Main minority groups:	Kurds 13 million (22%), Alevis 10 million (17%), Zaza language group 3 million (5%), Balkan origin 2 million (3.3%), Circassian and other Caucasus groups 1.3 million (2.2%), Arabs 1.2 million (2%), Turkoman groups 500,000 (0.8%) (*some of these identities overlap*)
Real per capita GDP:	$4,210
UNDP HDI/rank:	0.711 (84)

Turkey within its present border was established in 1923, following the Ottoman defeat in 1918 and bitter wars against mainly Greek, French and Armenian attempts to implement Allied plans to dismember Anatolia from 1919 until 1922. Nationalist Turks successfully appealed to Kurds to assist them in the name of the Muslim fatherland, a cause which had great appeal in view of the Armenian Christian threat in eastern Anatolia. The Treaty of Sèvres, 1920, which the

Allies had failed to impose on Turkey, had allowed for the creation of a Kurdish state, but at a time when Muslim Anatolia was under threat few Kurds were interested in independence under Allied (Christian) auspices.

However, in 1923 Turkey began to formulate its position on minorities. It agreed a population exchange whereby almost all Orthodox Christians in Turkey were transferred to Greece in return for Greece's (non-Albanian) Muslims, about 400,000 in all. Only a small number escaped this transfer, but the Greek Orthodox Patriarchate of Constantinople remained in the city. Turkey also negotiated the Treaty of Lausanne, 1923, with the Allies from a position of strength. The Allies pressed for the inclusion of all minorities, for example Kurds, Circassians and Arabs, in the treaty terms, but Turkey refused any distinct status for non-Turkish Muslims. Only Greek and Armenian Christians and Jews were formally acknowledged as minorities. However, it agreed that 'No restrictions shall be imposed on the free use by any Turkish national of any language in private intercourse, in commerce, religion, in the press, or in publications of any kind or at public meetings' (Article 39) or orally in court. Turkey failed to honour this commitment with regard to Kurdish, Arabic and other minority languages. It also drove the small Assyrian and Chaldean Christian communities across the border into Iraq, 1924–5. In 1926 it adopted the Swiss civil code, and renounced the minority rights secured for the Jewish, Armenian and Greek communities. Under pressure, all three formally agreed to this renunciation and were assured that the new code would apply to all citizens without distinction of race, nationality or religion.

Turkey evolved a new state ideology to create a modern state on European lines, based on a single secular national identity. It abolished the sultanate (1922) and the caliphate (1924), thereby removing the Islamic basis on which Kurds had helped defeat the Christian threat. It insisted that all Muslims in the republic were Turkish regardless of ethnic origin. Its concept of Turkishness was based on social and cultural conditioning not ethnicity. Anyone could rise to the highest positions of state so long as they identified themselves as Turkish.

During the nineteenth century the Ottoman Empire had already absorbed large numbers of Muslims from the Balkans and Caucasus as it lost control of these regions to Christian powers. On the whole, Turkey took the view that such people became Turks on settling in Turkey, though a few on the far right believe in ethnic purity and pan-Turanic solidarity, that is, among all Turkic peoples from Turkey through Turkic-speaking communities as far as China.

The state, under its founder, Mustafa Kemal (Ataturk), brooked no opposition, allowing only one political party. In its drive to modernize, it enfranchised women and encouraged them to play a full part in the life of the state. As in Europe, this has only partially been fulfilled. Among conservative citizens of the republic, the status of women is still determined by traditional social values. The state also made items of Western dress compulsory and replaced Ottoman Arabic with a variant of Latin script for written Turkish.

The state saw religious sentiment as one of the greatest threats to its aims. It therefore took direct control of formal Islamic institutions and also proscribed the populist Sufi brotherhood (*turuq*) networks, executing religious leaders who defied state will, but were unable to destroy the *turuq* once they had gone underground.

Yet it has also remained implicit that those who are not Sunni Muslim are somehow less Turkish than those who are, because in the logic of Ziya Gokalp, the founding father of Turkish state ideology, religious identity is a key element in nation building even in a secular republic.

RELIGIOUS COMMUNITIES

Alevis

There are at least 10 million Alevis, of whom perhaps 3 million are Kurdish. Some claim there could be as many as 20 million, but it is impossible to have any accurate estimate because Alevi (follower of Ali) is a generic term used for virtually all non-Sunni Muslims. However, the vast majority of Alevis are probably of Qizilbash or Bektashi origin, two groups subscribing to virtually the same system of beliefs but separately organized. The Alevis (Qizilbash) are traditionally predominantly rural and acquire identity by parentage. Bektashis, however, are predominantly urban, and formally claim that membership is open to any Muslim. Alevi and Bektashi beliefs are presumed to have their origins in Central Asian Turkoman culture. However, they are likely to have absorbed Christian beliefs when Byzantine peasantry moved into the Alevi faith during the Turkic conquest of Anatolia during the tenth and eleventh centuries, and Iranian pre-Islamic ideas, since Qizilbash beliefs derived from the founders of the Iranian Safavid dynasty. Turkish Alevis are found in central, western and northern Anatolia, especially around Sivas, Tokat, Yozgat, Nevsehir, Corum, Amasya and Erzincan. Kurdish Alevis are widespread in Bingol, Maras, Malatya, Erzincan and Tunceli provinces. A large number of Kurdish Alevis speak Zaza, rather than Turkish or Kirmanji.

Alevis share a way of truth unavailable to the uninitiated, and like Sufis claim that the Qu'ran has both an open and a hidden meaning. There are progressive levels of divine understanding from obedience to *shari'a* Islam through *tariqa* (brotherhood) to *ma'rifa* (mystical understanding of God) and ultimately to *haqqiqa* (immanent experience of divine reality). Their profession of faith includes Ali along with God and the Prophet Muhammad. Alevis differ outwardly from Sunni Muslims in the following ways: they do not fast in Ramadan but do during the Ten Days of Muharram (the Shi'i commemoration of Imam Husayn's martyrdom); they do not prostrate themselves during prayer; they do not have mosques; and do not have obligatory formal almsgiving, although they have a strong principle of mutual assistance.

Isolated within what became Sunni Ottoman territory, Alevis have always been reviled as non-Muslims of dubious loyalty, victims of scurrilous libels. To avoid persecution, Alevis practice dissimulation, *taqiyya*. Many Alevis celebrate the life of the sixteenth-century saint, Pir Sultan Abdal, a symbol for community cooperation and opposition to injustice.

Until the present century Alevis survived by living in remote areas. Hopes of faring better under a secular republic failed to take account of popular prejudice. With conscription and the drift to towns in search of work, Alevis, especially Kurds, have increasingly been exposed to Sunni prejudice and animosity.

However, there has also been a change in what Alevism signifies. Traditional Alevism, based upon village and rural life, broke down in the context of urbanization. In its place Alevism strongly identified with the political left. The Sunni Islamic revival of the 1980s has provoked a reaction among Alevis. The revivalist process has been an ethno-political movement rather than a strictly religious one, with a spate of publications in Turkey concerning Alevi religion and history. Initiation into the esoteric aspects of the religion is dying out, but an Alevi cultural renaissance is undoubtedly taking place.

Tension between the Sunni rightists and Alevi leftists has grown over the past two decades. At a local level the state connives with this harassment, frequently to the point of persecution. Alevis harassed by Sunnis seldom seek redress either from the police or the law courts since they believe the latter to be deeply prejudiced against them. In 1978 well over 100 Alevis were massacred in Maras by members of the extreme right National Action Party. In July 1993, 67 Alevis were killed in Sivas at the climax to the eight – hour siege of a hotel by Sunnis, while the police stood by. In March 1995 more than 20 Alevis were killed by vigilantes and police in Istanbul. Alevis remain economically underprivileged.

In part it is the migrant drift of Alevis from mountainous or unproductive land to seek work in predominantly Sunni towns which has been a major catalyst in Sunni – Alevi tensions.

Politically, Kurdish Alevis face a dilemma. Should their prior loyalty be to their ethnic or religious community? Some care more about religious solidarity with Turkish Alevis than ethnic solidarity with Kurds, particularly since many Sunni Kurds deplore them. Some fear such tensions may lead to new ethno-religious conflict.

Armenians

There are about 30,000 Armenians, primarily in Istanbul. They are the residue in Turkey of Ottoman pogroms against the Armenians in 1894–5 and the genocide of 1915. Although the state respects their minority status, they are regarded as foreigners by most Turks even though they have inhabited the land of modern Turkey for well over 2,000 years, substantially longer than the Turks. Armenians still find it hard to register their children as Armenian. However, the community successfully operates its own schools, old peoples homes and its own press. In the east, ancient Armenian churches are allowed to fall into ruin, regardless of their spiritual and architectural significance, and the Armenian origin of Saljuq architecture remains unacknowledged.

Jews

There are an estimated 25,000 Jews in Turkey, 18,000 of them in Istanbul, 1,600 in Izmir and others in Ankara, Bursa and other places. Many speak Ladino, the main Sephardic language. Jews of Kurdish or Arab culture in eastern Anatolia tended to leave for Israel in the 1950s. As a designated minority, Jews lost official positions to Muslims after 1923. They diminish progressively, and young Jews tend to marry other non-Muslims.

Syrian (Suryani) Orthodox Church

There may still be up to 4,000 Suryanis left in Turkey in the province of Mardin, largely in the area of Tur Abdin, and also a few in Diyarbakir, part of the ancient community more strongly represented in Syria. Always denied any form of recognition by the republic, it is a community in steep decline, under pressure from Islamic revivalists, Sunni Kurdish landlords who seek to acquire their lands, and local security forces which consider Christians 'un-Turkish' and therefore turn a blind eye to local harassment. Many have migrated to Germany or Sweden. The community is rapidly losing its viability.

Greek Christians

There are probably barely 3,000 ageing Greek Christians, mainly in Istanbul, the residue of 80,000 still there in 1963. Formal expulsions, police harassment and a climate of fear and popular animosity have since then reduced the community to its present number. Greek Christians have no control over the Greek schools (permitted by the Treaty of Lausanne); their press is subject to stringent censorship; the Orthodox Church faces official manipulation and Islamic revivalist hostility; and while their religious identity is acknowledged, their ethnic identity is denied.

PREDOMINANTLY ETHNIC COMMUNITIES

Kurds

Kurds probably number about 13 million, over 20 per cent of the population. They inhabited the south-east of modern Turkey before the arrival of the first Turkic tribes in the tenth century CE. Most Kurds in Turkey speak Kirmanji, but many Alevis and some Sunnis north and north-west of Diyarbakir speak Zaza (see below). Kurdish tribes enjoyed virtual autonomy until the last years of the Ottoman Empire. Fearful of the Armenian threat during the First World War, they cooperated in Turkey's genocide of one million Armenians, only to find themselves the target of forcible assimilation themselves in the 1920s and 1930s. Repeated Kurdish rebellions were suppressed with ruthlessness, bordering on genocide. All Kurdish expression was outlawed. A few Kurds began to call for recognition in the 1960s, and a growing number identified with the Turkish left in the 1970s. In 1984 Kurdish nationalism found violent expression in the PKK (Kurdistan Workers Party), which embarked on a guerrilla war against the state, which by 1996 accounted for 20,000 deaths. In tandem with state brutality, the PKK also succeeded in mobilizing much of the Kurdish civilian population. The struggle has been partly a class one. With incomes in Kurdistan less than half Turkey's national average, Kurdish identity was infused with a sense of economic as well as political deprivation. The PKK deliberately targeted certain members of the Kurdish landlord class as accomplices with the system of oppression (though some landlords identified with the PKK, often for reasons of local rivalry). By 1996 the state only retained control of south-east Turkey through the forced evacuation of over 3,000 Kurdish villages, the consequent destitution of 3 million people, and widespread and routine arrests and arbitrary torture. At least 6 million Kurds live in Istanbul, Ankara, Izmir and other industrial centres outside Kurdistan.

Kurds are technically allowed to publish in Kurdish, but face police harassment and death squads if they do so, however moderate these may be politically. Kurdish remains absolutely forbidden in education. Moderate or non-violent Kurdish groups are routinely closed down.

The Kurdish struggle for cultural and political rights is complicated by social and religious factors. Many rural Kurds are primarily motivated by clan or tribal loyalty, with long-standing local conflicts reflected in support for rival political parties at national level. Inter-tribal politics can determine whether support will be given to the PKK or government forces. Loyalties are also determined by religious sentiment. Possibly up to 25 per cent of Kurds in the south-east are still primarily motivated by religious affiliation. Many still accept *tariqa* guidance when it comes to voting. This has benefited parties of the right and the religious Refah Partisi (the Welfare Party). There is barely 50 per cent literacy in Kurdistan compared with a Turkish national average of over 75 per cent. Until education is improved, Kurds will remain susceptible to such factors, and be unable to play a mature part in the democratic process. The Kurdish birth rate in the south-east is almost twice as high as the Turkish birth rate in western Anatolia.

Balkan immigrants

An estimated 750,000 Balkan Muslims sought refuge in Ottoman Turkey in the period 1876–96. Since then at least another one million have migrated from the Balkans, mainly Yugoslavia, partly as a result of the Balkan War 1912–13. Others came later as fugitives from communism. They are mainly Sunni or Alevi. More recent arrivals have still not fully integrated.

Circassians

There are probably about 1 million people of Circassians or Abkha descent in Sakariya, Bolu, Bursa, Eskisehir, Sinop, Samsum, Tokat and Kayseri who were expelled from the Caucasus during the Russian capture of that region, 600,000 coming in the period 1856–64, and more in 1877–8. As Hanafi Muslims they share the same religious identity as indigenous Turks. They are increasingly integrated into the Turkish population.

Arabs

Sunni Arabs

There are probably about one million Arabs in the provinces of Urfa, Mardin, Siirt and Hatay (Alexandretta). Unlike the Turkish Sunni majority, Sunni Arabs belong to the Shafi'i tradition (which they share in common with most Sunni Kurds). They are denied the opportunity to use their language except in private, and the use of Arabic is forbidden in schools.

Alawi Arabs

About 200,000 Alawi, or Nusayri, Arabs live in the Hatay, the northern-most settlements of the larger Alawite community in Syria (see **Syria**). They are a distinct religious community from Alevis, but have in common reverence for Ali, the Prophet's son-in-law, as an emanation of the Divinity. Alawites have an uneasy relationship with Sunnis, but are more comfortable with Christians.

Christian Arabs

There are still about 10,000 Orthodox and Melkite (uniate with Rome) Christians (or, as they call themselves, Nasrani) in the Hatay. About 250,000 left in 1939 when France transferred the Hatay from Syrian to Turkish sovereignty. They feel under pressure, like other Arabs, to 'Turkicize'.

Bulgarian Muslims

Numbering well over 150,000, Bulgarian Muslims arrived mainly during the mass expulsion 1950–1. They were deliberately scattered over western and central Turkey to integrate them into the Turkish population but they are still readily identifiable. Another estimated 300,000 arrived in 1989, escaping Bulgarian persecution. They are mainly Sunni but some are Alevi. Many have been settled in abandoned Christian settlements in eastern Thrace, and others on the Aegean coast and erstwhile Greek islands, and are consequently sometimes called Adali (Islanders).

Georgians

There are about 80,000 Sunni Georgians, Hanafis like Sunni Turks. They are located mainly in Artvin province in the north-east. Their principal moment of migration was during the Turco–Russian war of 1877–8, to avoid Russian rule. Georgians are generally bilingual and intermarry with Turks. Another 10,000 or so are Orthodox Christians.

Azeri Turks

There are probably about 75,000 Azeri Turks living in the north-east border area around Kars, Ardahan and Artvin. Many came following the Treaty of Leninakan, 1920, to avoid Bolshevik rule. Although Turkish, they are Ithna'ashari Shi'i and live in tension with neighbouring Sunni Kurds. A few belong to the Karapapakh and Terekeme tribal confederations, some are Alevi or Ahl-i Haqq (see **Iran**). Others are Sunni, of the Hanbali school.

LINGUISTIC COMMUNITIES

Zaza

The Zaza are a linguistic group, possibly numbering 3 million, mainly in the Tunceli area and north of Diyarbakir. Most Zaza speakers are Alevi, but a minority are Sunni. Zaza's closest linguistic relative is Gurani, spoken by Kurds in the southern part of the Zagros range. The languages probably share a distant common root in a Caspian dialect of Persian about 2,500 years ago. Some Zaza speakers aspire to forming a solidarity group, and describe their linguistic region as 'Zazaistan'.

Laz

Laz is a south Caucasian language related to Georgian, and there are 150,000 Laz-speakers in Turkey, all Hanafi Sunnis. There is a very imprecise idea of what Laz (or being Laz) means in Turkey. Some Laz are bilingual, but the Laz language does not have a written form and is in decline.

SOCIO-ECONOMIC/ ETHNIC COMMUNITIES

Turkomans

At the end of the last century there were probably about 300,000 Turkomans, that is, Turkic tribal peoples who were still nomadic. This may seem a surprisingly small number, but Ottoman Turkey consistently sought to settle migrant Turkic tribes from the sixteenth century onwards. Few escaped this process, unlike the Kurds, who were able to retain their pastoralist lifestyle largely on account of their remoteness from government. Alevi Turks may be erstwhile Turkomans. Very few Turkomans are still unassimilated, except the Yoruk and Tahtaci.

Yoruk

The Yoruk are a Turkoman group, numbering 70,000 in the Taurus Mountains. Once nomadic, they are now largely settled, some are Alevi. Economic antagonism with the neighbouring settled population is a factor in their distinct identity.

Tahtaci

These possibly number as many as 100,000, living in the forested part of the Taurus. They are Alevi and consider themselves Turkoman. Traditionally, they are lumbermen and sawyers. They are stigmatized more than other Alevis.

Roma

There are probably 50,000 Roma, or Gypsies, mainly Romani speaking. They arrived from north-west India sometime between 800 and 1300 CE. Many have lived in Balat in Istanbul since the Turkish conquest in 1453. Some are sedentary but most are nomadic. Some of the nomads travel with the Yoruk (see below). They are nominally Muslim and a very few Christian. They are widely stigmatized and excluded from mainstream Turkish society.

Conclusions and future prospects

Turkey has discovered the limit to its ambitions to remodel itself along prescribed lines. In 1945 internal disputes forced the government to abandon its one party system. Opposition parties soon attracted the support of those who had suffered under the Kemalist regime, notably the religious. Since then formal and populist Islamic expression has regained a strong position in national life and by 1990 was a major electoral issue. Relations between Islam and the state remain unresolved. After nearly seventy years of denial, Turkey has also been forced openly to recognize the existence of large Kurdish and Alevi communities, even if it has not yet made any substantive concessions to either. In other words, the pluralism it sought to eliminate in the 1920s has proved stronger than state ideology. The state has pursued its aims since 1923 at the price of widespread human rights abuse. It now faces an impasse: it still does not dare allow free political expression or assembly, or to abandon the widespread use of torture and imprisonment, but pays a growing price in terms of its political and economic relations with the West, and in terms of growing internal dissent.

Further reading

Amnesty International, *Turkey: Escalation in human rights abuses against Kurdish villagers, London*, July 1993.

Amnesty International, *Turkey: Disappearances and political killings: human rights crisis of the 1990s*, London, September 1993.

Amnesty International, *Turkey: time for action*, London, February 1994.

Amnesty International, *Turkey: a policy of denial*, London, February 1995.

Andrews, P.A. (ed.), *Ethnic Groups in the Republic of Turkey*, Weisbaden, Ludwig Reichert Verlag, 1989.

Bozarslan, H., 'Political aspects of the Kurdish problem', in P.G. Kreyenbroeck and S. Sperl (eds), *The Kurds: A Contemporary Overview*, London and New York, Routledge, 1992.

Bozarslan, H. (ed.), 'Les Kurdes et les états', *Peuples Méditerranéens*, nos 68–9, July-December 1994.

Helsinki Watch, *Denying Human Rights and Ethnic Identity: The Greeks of Turkey*, New York, Human Rights Watch, 1992.

McDowall, D., *The Kurds*, London, MRG report, 1991, 1997.

McDowall, D., *A Modern History of the Kurds*, London, Tauris, 1995.

Moosa, M., *Extremist Shiites: The Ghulat Sects*, New York, Syracuse University Press, 1987, chs 2–4, 10, 38.

Yalcin-Heckmann, L., *Tribe and Kinship among the Kurds*, Frankfurt/Main, P. Lang, 1991.

Minority-based and advocacy organizations

Cultural and Cooperation Association of Iraqi Turks, Balipasa Cad. Soyak Apt. No. 42, Kat. 3 Daire. 4, Fatih, Istanbul, Turkey; tel. 90 216 532 5455.

Human Rights Foundation of Turkey, Menekse 2 Sk. No. 16/6, Kizelay, Ankara 06440, Turkey.

Institut Kurde, Rue Lafayette 106, 75010 Paris, France.

International Association for Human Rights in Kurdistan, POB 10 45 51, W-2800 Bremen 1, Germany; tel. 49 421 703932, fax 49 421 703885.

Kurdish Human Rights Project, Suite 319, Linen Hall, 162–8 Regent Street, London W1R 5TB, UK; tel. 44 171 287 2772, fax 44 171 734 4927.

Kurdish Information Centre, 10 Glass House Yard, London EC1A 4JN, UK; tel. 44 171 250 1315, fax 44 171 250 1317.

London Alevi-Bektashi Meeting and Cultural House, 86 Balls Pond Road, London N1 4AJ, UK; tel. 44 171 254 0387.

Tur Abdin Solidarity Group [Surgani], Bethlehemstrasse 20, A-4020 Linz, Austria; fax 43 732 7735 78.

Turkish Human Rights Association, Tunali Hilmi Caddesi, 104/4 Kavaklidere, Ankara, Turkey; tel. 90 312 432 0957, fax 90 312 425 9547.

Turkish League for Human Rights, M. Kemal Pasa Caddesi, Yildirim Palas No. 17/10, Aksaray-IST, Turkey.

United Arab Emirates

Land area:	77,700 sq km
Population:	2 million (1993) (of whom approximately 33% are UAE nationals)
Main languages:	Arabic, Indian and Pakistani languages, Persian
Main religions:	Sunni and Ithna'ashari Shi'i Islam, Christianity
Main minority groups:	—
Real per capita GDP:	$20,940
UNDP HDI/rank:	0.864 (42)

The United Arab Emirates were formed in 1971, when Britain completed its political withdrawal from what were known as the Trucial Oman States. The following sheikhdoms form the UAE: Abu Dhabi, Dubai, Sharjah, Ajman, Umm al Qaiwain, Ras al Khaimah and Fujairah. Until the early 1960s these were relatively poor settlements on the coastline, ruled by the leading families, with a largely bedouin or settled tribal population, the latter being usually involved in Indian Ocean trade. Dubai was easily the most prosperous of these sheikhdoms. In 1958, however, oil was struck in Abu Dhabi and thereafter the area was rapidly transformed with oil installations, high-rise and other modern buildings. The population rocketed from 180,000 in 1968 to a million by 1982 and 2 million by 1993.

There had always been a cosmopolitan atmosphere in Dubai and other Gulf ports, particularly with Iranians and Indians, but from 1960 onwards the area was flooded mainly with Arabs, but also with Pakistanis, Indians and Iranians. All these and other noticeable groups, like Filipinos, came to join the work force. Although all these immigrant groups tend to socialize with their own kind, they have not formed coherent or cohesive ethnic or religious associations. Migrant workers lack full civic rights and are expected to leave once their employment is terminated. Any migrant worker trying to form a cohesive group could expect to be expelled.

Even with so large an expatriate presence, well over 90 per cent of the population is Muslim, albeit one-fifth of these are probably Ithna'ashari. About 4 per cent of expatriates are Christian. These religious groupings do not form cohesive minorities either.

Further reading

Peck, M., *The United Arab Emirates: A Venture in Unity*, Boulder, CO, Westview Press, 1986.

Zahlan, R., *The Origins of the United Arab Emirates: A Political and Social History of the Trucial States*, London, Macmillan, 1978.

Zahlan, R., *The Making of the Modern Gulf States: Kuwait, Bahrain, Qatar, the United Arab Emirates and Oman*, London, Unwin Hyman, 1989.

Yemen

Land area:	536,869 sq km
Population:	12.5 million (1993)
Main languages:	Arabic and South Arabian (Mahri, Shahri, etc.)
Main religions:	Sunni, Zaydi and Isma'ili Islam, Judaism
Main minority groups:	Zaydis 5 million (40%), Isma'ilis 100,000 (0.8%)
Real per capita GDP:	$2,410
UNDP HDI/rank:	0.424 (137)

The Republic of Yemen was formed in May 1990 by the union of the Yemen Arab Republic (northern Yemen) and the Peoples' Democratic Republic of Yemen (southern Yemen). Yemen can be very crudely divided between its mountainous interior, its western coastal plain of Tihama, and the Hadramawt region in the south-east. Yemen was at first only superficially Islamicized. However, in the late ninth century, most of mountainous Yemen became dominated by Zaydi Shi'i imams, who achieved a symbiotic relationship with the mountain tribes. From about the twelfth century the coastal areas and south came to be dominated by the Shafi'i school of Sunni Islam, the Sunni school most tolerant towards Shi'i practice.

Britain's occupation of Aden in 1839 resulted in *de facto* partition of Yemen. The Aden Protectorate ended with the establishment of a Marxist-Leninist state in southern Yemen in 1966. In the north, rule by the Zaydi imams, which had intermittently been interrupted by Ottoman rule, came to an end in 1962, when a republic was declared.

Zaydi Shi'ism

About 40 per cent of the Yemeni population is Zaydi, mainly from Dhamar northwards. Zaydism is traced from Zayd b. Ali, a grandson of the Imam Ali, martyred outside Kufa in 740. Zaydism recognizes as imams those of the Prophet's house who strove to assert the authority of the imamate, if necessary through armed struggle. Apart from a small state on the southern Caspian shore that was expunged by the Safavids, Yemen was the sole region of Zaydi success. A succession of imams established themselves from the late ninth century in the mountainous northern part of Yemen, acting as arbitrators between tribes and thereby acquiring both a religious following and secular ascendancy. The imamate itself was overthrown in 1962, and subsequently died out, although Zaydism still predominates in the mountains. Zaydi relations with Shafi'i Sunnis have tended to be free of difficulty.

Isma'ilis

There are probably fewer than 100,000 Isma'ilis in Yemen. They are Musta'lis, following the line of al Musta'li in the succession dispute with his brother Nizar in Fatimid Cairo in 1094. They are mainly concentrated in Jabal Haraz, near Manakha, west of Sana'a, but a few live on the Saudi border at Najran oasis, with a larger number inside Saudi Arabia. Most belong to the Sulaymani sub-branch, following another succession dispute in 1591; a few others adhere to the Bombay-based Daudi sub-branch. Their current status is unknown but one must suspect that like the Zaydis they may become a target for Sunni reformist denunciation.

Jews

There are only about 800 Jews left in Yemen. Yemen was a Jewish kingdom in the fifth century CE, which succumbed to Ethiopian and Byzantine assault in 525. Jews remained subject to *dhimmi* status throughout the Islamic period and endured persecution in the nineteenth century. Some moved to Palestine from 1874 onwards, drawn by economic opportunity rather than interest in Zionism. In 1948 almost all remaining Jews were brought to Israel. From 1962 Jews were forbidden to leave until 1992, when 250 migrated to Israel. Remaining Jews are caught between Zionists urging migration and Hasidic Satmar Jews urging them to stay and avoid 'contamination' in Israel. Emigration has halted because of adverse reports of returnees who found Israel culturally alien.

Conclusions and future prospects

Over the past decade there has been a rising tide of Sunni reformist (see **Saudi Arabia**) propaganda against Zaydism and religious 'laxity'. Reformists condemn Zaydis as *rafidin* (religious renegades). It is widely feared that these reformists may prove a growing threat to Zaydis, Isma'ilis and the more tolerant tradition of Shafi'i Sunnism.

Further reading

Dresch, P., *Tribes, Government and History in Yemen*, Oxford, Oxford University Press, 1989.

Gochenour, D., 'Towards a sociology of the Islamization of Yemen', in B. Pridham (ed.), *Contemporary Yemen: Politics and Historical Background*, London, Croom Helm, 1984.

Nyrop, R., (ed.), *The Yemens: Country Studies*, Washington, DC, The American University, 1986.

Wenner, M., *Modern Yemen, 1918–66*, Baltimore, MD, Johns Hopkins University Press, 1967.

Minority-based and advocacy organizations

Organization for the Defence of Human Rights and Democratic Freedoms, PO Box 4116, Crater, Aden, Republic of Yemen; tel. 967 2 23 3777, fax 967 2 23 1066.

Notes

Introduction

1 See Mayer, A., *Islam and Human Rights: Tradition and Politics*, Boulder, CO, San Francisco, CA, and London, Westview and Pinter, 1991.

2 The clearest example is the case of Israeli Palestinians. It is no accident that Jewish Israelis are themselves recent settlers introducing an alien political culture into the area. Another case might be that of the Baha'is in Iran who are a religious anathema to the Islamic Republic, itself an innovation in Iranian political life.

3 Their identity – even within an apparently static religious group – mutates as historical or mythic memory is revised or traditions invented, something particularly true of nation states in which

governments consciously foster a sense of identity to displace other loyalties; see Anderson, B., *Imagined Communities: Reflections on the Origin and Spread of Nationalism*, London and New York, Verso and New Left Books, 1983; and Smith, A., *National Identity*, London, Penguin, 1991.

4 Shi'a has two meanings: the party of Ali, and a collective meaning of the community of Shi'ites either globally or the community in a particular country. 'Shi'i' also has two meanings: it means a member of the Shi'a, and is also in the same way an adjective.

Bahrain

1 Khouri, F., *Tribe and State in Bahrain: The Transformation of Social and Political Authority in an Arab State*, Chicago, Chicago University Press, 1980, p. 156.

2 'The outrage of the dispossessed', *Voice of Bahrain*, no. 32, August 1994.

Israel

1 The term 'bedouin' comes from the Arabic *badwiyyun*, meaning inhabitants of the desert. The term is officially capitalized as 'Bedouin' in Israel because the government uses it as one among several classifications of the Arab population.

Kuwait

1 Hardy, R., *Arabia After the Storm: Internal Stability of the Gulf States*, London, Royal Institute for International Affairs, 1992.

Lebanon

1 *Middle East International*, no. 475, 13 May 1994.

Palestine

1 For a scholarly but compelling analysis, see Masalha, N., *The Expulsion of the Palestinians: The Concept of 'Transfer' in Zionist Political Thought, 1882–1948*, Washington, DC, Institute of Palestine Studies, 1992.

2 See Masalha, op. cit.; 'Yosef Weitz and the transfer committees, 1948–9', in Morris, B., *1948 and After: Israel and the Palestinians*, Oxford, Clarendon Press, 1990; Pappe, I., *The Making of the Arab-Israeli Conflict, 1947–51*, London, IB Tauris, 1992.

Saudi Arabia

1 Wahba, H., *Arabian Days*, London, Arthur Barker, 1964, p. 135.

2 Amnesty International, *Unwelcome Guests: The Plight of Iraqi Refugees*, London, May 1994.

Syria

1 In the Ghab valley, where Alawis cultivate the west side and Sunnis the east, school enrolment rates for girls on the Alawi side in the 1980s were in the order of 35 per cent but on the Sunni side only 8 per cent.

2 Middle East Watch, *Syria Unmasked*, New York, 1993, pp. 107–9.

NORTH, WEST AND THE HORN OF AFRICA

Julia Maxted and Abebe Zegeye

The relative underdevelopment of states, as well as the socio-economic systems anchored on those exploitative relations, in North, West and the Horn of Africa has created fertile ground for struggles over control of economic and political power to be framed in ethnic terms. Ethnic identities, while having a 'beneficial' spillover for many members of the ethnic group or groups in power, are primarily utilized to consolidate and serve the interests of the ruling classes of the dominant ethnic groups. The contemporary destruction of the legitimacy and accountability of many of the states in this region results in part from their territorial awkwardness. Formed by the colonial partition and 'transferred' to African hands, overlapping ethnicity is often more a source of suspicion than of unity between states. In the past two decades hundreds of thousands of people have been victims of violent conflicts and dictatorship in the region. Many have fled, highlighting their alienation from the state, as they become part of Africa's disheartening refugee problem.

States of North, West and the Horn of Africa are undermined by acute environmental degradation. A fragile ecological inheritance of cyclical drought and commercial devastation has been exacerbated by armed conflicts. Pastoralists and other hinterland populations have been among the primary victims. Desertification, drought, environmental degradation and resource scarcity have displaced large numbers of people across national borders, either as migrants or as environmental refugees. In addition to the pressures which such groups put on state boundaries, their arrival sometimes engenders feelings of insecurity or intolerance among local populations, who suddenly find themselves competing for limited resources. The threats experienced are specific and measurable and include deforestation and soil erosion in the Sahelian zone, as well as widespread water shortages in highly populated places such as the Nile Delta.

The economic sovereignty of African states is being undermined by pressure to join regional blocs at the same time as banditry and unofficial cross-border trading networks are growing. A further threat to state autonomy and civilian populations arises from the growing militarization of conflicts. As the stability of states is undermined, low-level warfare, famine, deprivation and political crisis overlap. Those nominally in control of the state cannot provide security for their citizens, cannot lay the basis for economic improvements, are not in full control of its territory and are unable either to co-opt or to defeat their opponents. Economic pauperization and an ideological vacuum arising from the uglier side of nationalism – its capacity to erode basic human freedoms – are fuelling a contemporary upsurge in religious cults and extremism. Where the state and societal fabric disintegrates, it is the most historically vulnerable groups – women, children and minorities – who often bear the brunt of the crisis. The phenomena outlined above are forcing a redefinition of social cohesion and civil space, and amid this insecurity the implications for minorities throughout the region are a major cause for concern.

Democratization and the mobilization of ethnic identity

Since 1989 many countries in North, West and the Horn of Africa have experienced unprecedented waves of demands for democracy, which have succeeded in bringing about the downfall of several authoritarian regimes and forced others to accept multi-party elections. It remains to be seen if events turn out in democracy's favour. Authoritarian regimes have retained control over security forces, economic resources and the funding and support of Western powers and multilateral institutions such as the World Bank. Despite waving the flag of democracy and human rights, these institutions

MOROCCO
TUNISIA
ALGERIA
LIBYA
EGYPT
MAURITANIA
CAPE VERDE
MALI
NIGER
SENEGAL
GAMBIA
GUINEA-BISSAU
GUINEA
BURKINA FASO
BENIN
TOGO
GHANA
NIGERIA
SIERRA LEONE
LIBERIA
CÔTE D'IVOIRE
SUDAN
ERITREA
DJIBOUTI
ETHIOPIA
SOMALIA
NORTH, WEST AND THE HORN OF AFRICA

have not yet dared pursue such sentiments to their logical conclusion. Economic austerity programmes have been used to advantage by the ruling class. The dismantling of the public sector which donors demand without creating a true market has recentralized power in many cases. The politics of structural adjustment are thus not so very far from those of nationalization pursued over the previous two decades.[1]

A precarious balance is maintained in many countries – between the authority of a state increasingly compromised politically and economically, and a political periphery formed from an alliance of marginalized groups as yet unable to compel the formation of new governance structures to reflect their needs. The change in climate has, however, emboldened opposition organizations, journalists, human rights activists and others to challenge existing authorities. Such activism has often resulted in heightened social tensions, articulated through the proliferation of ethnically or regionally based parties. In itself ethnicity cannot provide the basic reference point for the post-colonial political arena. Even as a schema of identification it is contextual and does not exclude other lines of identification – family, age, gender and religious and economic affiliations.[2] Ethnic identity cannot be divorced from the social matrix of which it is a part, or from the changes of this century – urbanization, the construction of new communications networks, the introduction of new relations of production and the increase in migratory and commercial movements.

Most situations where the structuring of the contemporary political arena seems to be expressed in terms of ethnicity relate to identities which did not exist a century ago, or were not then so clearly defined. Since the notion of ethnic group or tribe was one of the ideological premises of the colonial administration, it became the means of affirming one's own existence, developing into a language of relationship between subject peoples. Increasingly ethnic representation became crucial in the flow of goods and services established by the functionaries of the colonial bureaucracy.[3] As the possibility of independence loomed, the colonial powers turned to building nation-states. This crystallized the division of Africa's many hundreds of peoples and cultures into a few dozen states, each claiming sovereignty against each other. Striving to transform colonial territories into national territories, it proved difficult to fit such diversity into their schemas. This ideology was appallingly reductive, as though the wealth of cultures was really an impoverishment.[4]

The contemporary force of ethnic consciousness comes more, however, from the struggle of different communities to receive an adequate proportion of the state resources. This reflects the fact that certain groups remain outside national government concerns. Ethnicity is almost never absent from politics, yet at the same time it does not provide its basic fabric. Manifestation of ethnicity inevitably involves other social dimensions, and in the context of the contemporary state ethnicity exists mainly as an agent of accumulation of wealth and political power. 'Tribalism' is thus perceived less as a political force in itself than as a channel through which competition for the acquisition of wealth, status or power is expressed.[5] The post-colonial state functions as a taproot of personal networks and assures the centralization of power through the agencies of family allegiance and friendship. The political use of kinship acts as compensation against the weakness or the incapacity of state institutions to protect citizens and advance their interests. What often ensues is a socially stratified system whereby those who belong to dominant networks receive a disproportionate share of the country's resources and prospects.

State disintegration

The state is under increasing pressure in Africa, a phenomenon which is having continued repercussions on the conditions of minorities throughout the North, West and Horn. Internal social tensions are co-joining with external pressure for larger groupings more able to respond to the global economy. Technological innovations, which helped make nation-states possible, are now helping to undermine national borders as capital and information flows show little respect for national boundaries. Supranational groups such as the Economic Community of West African States are encroaching upon national sovereignty from above, while the failure to resolve internal tensions is weakening government from within.

However diverse the origins of social conflict – some pre-date colonization, while others derive from colonial manipulation – it is increasingly difficult to contain them with present state frameworks. The cases of state failure in Somalia and Liberia illustrate that the monopoly of power by one group backed by foreign sponsors may lead to government failure and civil war. Increasingly too differences between war and crime are being eroded. For many of the poverty-stricken followers of African warlords, membership of rag-tag armies is a step up, not down.[6] Facing such armed bandits, Africa's professional armies are often found wanting. Their budgets are smaller, their equipment more dilapidated, their salaries late or unpaid, and morale is sinking. War's advantage over mere delinquency is that it legitimizes in the name of 'justice' or the 'revolution' the use of arms and violence in order to gain access to the resources of the state. What is striking is the ease with which regular armies and regimes of increasing numbers of African states have been defeated and replaced by insurgent guerrilla forces organized from among their own citizens. One major problem for these new regimes is how to disarm and demobilize the plethora of ethnically based guerrillas even as they embark on forming new armies. Another challenge relates to the training, recruitment and organization of new armies in these recently emerged political orders, many of which remain ethnically polarized. Further, the colonial practice of recruiting from and promoting smaller, often less politically powerful ethnic groups in the army has created one of the major sources of instability that beset army/state relations in post-colonial Africa. The structure of military and state relations has become unhinged, such that the geo-ethnic make-up of the group which wields military power need not reflect or articulate the outlook or position of the group whose members claim the mandate to rule. This process is open to manipulation of old prejudices by elites on all sides of the political conflict.

These processes outline the instability of the post-colonial state in the region, lending some weight to the proposition that state boundaries as recognized by the Organization of African Unity (OAU) may be altered in the future. The list of provinces which have detached themselves from central authority grows inexorably, and alternatives ranging from federalism to territorial secession persist as political options. To date, secession has been the exception, with Eritrea being the most relevant case. More generally, minority communities who have suffered at the hands of dominant groups holding the reins of political and/or military power are claiming that their rights as groups be recognized and that actions be taken to satisfy their demands. Seemingly less sustainable has been the approach adopted by various religious-based groups whereby they ignore rather than contest the state, for example by avoiding the payment of taxes.

Towards greater justice for minorities

The contemporary situation in the region reveals a crisis of the institutions with which Africans have had to live since decolonization.[7] Frequently the argument over institutions has been debased to the level of what is said to be 'democracy' vis-à-vis what is said to be 'tribalism'. Yet contemporary 'tribalism' has little to do with a healthy and thriving civil society. Rather it flourishes in disorder and flouts the rule of law such that banditry has become one of its principal modes of action. The question is less whether the nation state can be rescued than how long and painful will be the inevitable transition to new forms of governance. This is not to say that the state system in Africa is on the brink of collapse. Indeed, the most viable states will be shored up and strengthened to provide a bridge to more effective regional arrangements. But it is also clear that the territorial division of Africa into nation states based on colonial partition, with boundaries sanctified by the OAU as inviolable, is under the greatest pressure since independence. From this time African states have placed great emphasis on the principle of territorial integrity, in part to counter their weakness and artificiality. The demise of the one-party state in many countries, together with the ending of much foreign sponsorship, is exposing the worst ethnic dictatorships in the region to new political forces. It is becoming an increasingly recognized principle that consideration must be given to the long-term needs of communities who wish to practise a way of life different from that of the dominant culture.

For the most part African nationalism has been official rather than popular, political rather than cultural. The largely urban, Westernized elites who formed the first political parties and campaigned for independence had little difficulty in forging inter-ethnic alliances so long as the object was to get rid of the colonial powers. Once independent, they faced a crisis of legitimacy: by what rights did they rule? The answer came with the OAU settlement of 1963. This document reflected agreement to reinforce the conventional interpretation of national self-determination. Its charter, like that of the United Nations, is based on the twin principles of territorial integrity and non-interference in the domestic affairs of states. In the OAU's case, these principles were strengthened in 1964 by the adoption in Cairo of a resolution binding African states to recognize the 'tangible' reality of the borders they inherited at independence. Taken together, the charter and the Cairo resolution provide a powerful basis for the territorial status quo.

A variety of different arrangements have been suggested which might serve to further the cause of social justice as well as minorities. For example, it has been proposed that failed states should be put under regional trusteeship. This type of 'benign' recolonization would critically depend on the cooperation of regionally powerful states. Yet it is not enough to deal with the supranational issues alone. Addressing the need for effective devolved government and finding new institutional arrangements to contain regional, ethnic and class loyalties will be as exacting as establishing new regional institutions. While most African constitutions guarantee equal enjoyment of human rights, some specifically provide that these rights should be enjoyed by all without reference to ethnic origin. There is however no reference to minorities in the African Charter of Human and Peoples Rights (the Banjul Charter) of 1986. Here 'people' refers to the people of the state as a whole, and not to minority communities. Many constitutions have adopted the Universal Declaration of Human Rights, but the formal inclusion of human rights provisions is not enough to ensure that they are recognized or fulfilled in practice.

Further claims for self-determination are likely to continue as long as basic human rights and collective rights are not effectively guaranteed and protected. What originated as the right of nations to independence has been transformed into a concept with variable and varying content. The right is slowly being extended to peoples as well as nations, whether colonized or forming part of an independent state. While African governments are in principle opposed to the dismemberment of states emanating from colonial territorial demarcation, that process can only be arrested if certain social groups are made to feel and believe that they are part of the instruments and machineries by which decisions affecting them are made. This process and its monitoring by international human rights bodies can only be hampered by the dearth of material on minorities in Africa. The information available, including that presented in this part of the *Directory*, is limited by three factors: language, access, and an uneven spread of information. Where extensive research exists it is often highly selective. In addition, population statistics in many instances can only be estimates and should not be taken as definitive; in some countries census results have been suppressed because information on population figures is politically sensitive. Until reliable data exists it is extremely difficult to describe with any certainty the current position of minorities in many countries of North, West and the Horn of Africa.

Further reading

Asante, S.K., *The Political Economy of Regionalism in West Africa*, New York, Praeger, 1986.

Bayart, J.F., *The State in Africa: The Politics of the Belly*, London, Longman, 1993.

Davidson, B., *The Black Man's Burden*, London, James Currey, 1992.

Gellner, E. and Michaud, C. (eds), *Arabs and Berbers: From Tribe to Nation in North Africa*, Lexington, MA, Heath, 1972.

Human Rights Watch/Africa, *Human Rights in Africa and US Policy*, New York, 1994.

International Work Group for Indigenous Affairs, *The Indigenous World 1995–96*, Copenhagen, IWGIA,1996.

Plant, R., *Land Rights and Minorities*, London, MRG report, 1994.

Yansane, A.Y., *Decolonization in West African States*, Cambridge, MA, Schenkman, 1984.

Algeria

Land area:	2,381,741 sq km
Population:	26.1 million (1992)
Main languages:	Arabic (official), Berber, French
Main religions:	Islam
Main minority groups:	Berbers 7 million (27%) (including Kabyles, Shawiya, Mozabites and Tuareg), Saharawi 120,000 (0.5%)
Real per capita GDP:	$5,570
UNDP HDI/rank:	0.746 (69)

Africa's second largest nation after Sudan, Algeria borders Tunisia, Libya, Niger, Mali, Mauritania, Morocco and the Western Sahara, and stretches from its 1,104 kilometre Mediterranean coastline south through a varied topography to the Sahara Desert. Algerians are primarily of Arab and Berber descent. The French population, approximately 10 per cent of the total in colonial times, has fallen to about 1 per cent today. Many other Europeans and almost all of the 150,000 Jews in Algeria also left the country after independence. More than 1 million Algerians live abroad, chiefly in France. Arabic, the national language, is spoken by about 82 per cent of the population. Berber dialects are spoken, especially in Kabylia where government efforts to reinforce national identity through an 'Arabization' programme have provoked outrage. The Shawiya of the Aures, the Mozabites centred in the city of Ghardaia, and the nomadic Tuareg speak their own dialects. The emergence of a politicized Islamist movement whose vision is of a society strictly governed by the laws of Islam demanding a greater role for religion in this secular state has created disturbances since the 1980s. This entry focuses mainly on the Berbers, Algeria's only numerically significant minority. (For an account of the Saharawi see **Morocco**.)

Berbers

Berbers call themselves Imazighen, meaning noble or free born. The term 'Berber' derives from the Greek *barbario* and the Latin *barbari* from which Arabs derived the term *barbariy*, meaning primitive or foreign. The Berber-speaking population of Algeria comprises a little over one quarter of the population of 26 million and is concentrated in the mainly mountainous areas of Kabylia, Chaouia, the Mzab and the Sahara. Berbers are the indigenous inhabitants of the North African littoral, isolated from the rest of Africa by the Sahara Desert. From the mid-seventh century, waves of Arab migration into the region brought cultural changes and introduced Islam, which the Berbers accepted. Although rural Berber life remained largely unchanged, those living in the cities found their language, tribal law and oral literary traditions being replaced by Arabic traditions. From the eleventh to the fifhteenth centuries, forced back into the mountain regions by the city-based sultanates, the Berbers refused to recognize central authority or to pay taxes.

Several distinctive Berber subcultures exist in Algeria and have relatively little in common other than the common root of their spoken dialects. About half of the Berber-speaking population comes from the mountainous areas east of Algiers – Kabylia – and this area and its language have played the most important Berber role in modern Algeria. The Kabyles have moved in large numbers to the cities of both Algeria and France in search of employment. The second largest Berber group, the Shawiya, inhabit the rugged mountains of eastern Algeria. Two smaller Berber communities are the Mozabites of the area around Ghardaia and the Tuareg nomads of the south. Geographical dispersion of Berber-speakers has hindered the emergence of a common identity. Kabyles are the most cosmopolitan and are more likely to speak French than other groups. All Berbers, except Mozabites, are Sunni Muslims.

At independence Arabic became the sole national language of Algeria. Linguistic and cultural expressions of Berber were forbidden, and this created resentment among Berber-speakers, as did attempts to increase the numbers of Arabic-speakers in the administration. In 1963, Hocine Ait Ahmad, a Kabyle leader of the anti-French resistance, led a revolt against the government. The revolt was crushed, and Ait was arrested and sentenced to death; he later fled to France, where he formed the Front des Forces Socialistes (FLS). Ahmed Ben Bella, independent Algeria's first leader, linked the Arabization of the state to the success of socialism. Government policy aimed at centralization. The government's authority and its claim to legitimacy was based upon its leadership in the struggle for independence, yet Berbers had played a full part in that struggle. The 1990 Arabization Law projected the complete Arabization of official activities during 1992 and of higher education by 1997. Although the government feared Berber separatism there appears to be little support for separatism. There is support, however, for a greater recognition of Berber identity and rights for Berber-speakers within a more democratic and pluralist Algerian state. The most enduring form of Berber opposition has come from broader based cultural movements.

The Kabyle capital, Tizi-Ouzou, is the bastion of opposition to Arabization. Throughout the 1970s Berber musicians and poets used a modernized form of traditional Berber music to implicitly criticize the Algerian regime. Although popular demand eventually forced the government to allow such music to be broadcast, singers and groups were not allowed to perform in the Kabyle region. In 1980, when the government banned a lecture on ancient Kabyle poetry at Tizi-Ouzou University, demonstrations and strikes took place throughout Kabyle and other Berber areas, and in Algiers. These were met with violence by government troops; over 30 people died and several hundred were injured and arrested. The Berber Cultural Movement and other Berber organizations have generally supported the idea of Algeria as a bilingual state, with recognition given to the Berber language and to colloquial Arabic, which, rather than literary Arabic, is the language of the majority of the population. They also stress the fusion of Berber and Arabic. As a result they have often allied themselves to non-Berbers who wish to achieve a more democratic and pluralist government.

In 1985 there were further arrests and imprisonment of Berber activists. The spontaneous nationwide protests of October 1988 in which Berbers participated in Algiers and in Kabyle forced the Algerian government to support constitutional change including ending the one-party system. In July 1989 a new political parties law was passed by the national assembly which allowed for groups independent of the Front de Liberation Nationale (FLN) to apply for registration and to compete in national elections. Among those parties that applied were the FLS and the Rally for Culture and Democracy, a Berber organization. The new law however prohibits groups based 'exclusively on a particular religion, language, region, sex or race' and states that parties must use only the Arabic languages in their official *communiqués*.

The 12,000 Tuareg, who are nomadic Berbers, live almost exclusively among the mountainous massifs of Ajjer and Ahaggar in southern Algeria. Raiding and the control of caravan routes were the traditional mainstays of Tuareg economic organization in pre-colonial times, but increasing French control limited raiding and necessitated the development of salt caravans to Niger. Independence brought the almost total disruption of Tuareg society with its large class of slaves, *iklan*, brought from Sudan, and former slaves, *haratin*. Socialist ideology and nationalism committed Algeria to the assimilation of minority groups and the welding of the north and south into a unified state. Freed slaves, *haratin*, began to rise against the Tuareg and refuse to pay their contract dues for cultivating land. Violent skirmishes resulted in the imprisonment of some Tuareg and a policy of promoting sedentarization through the construction of cooperatives. By the end of the 1960s the Tuareg had little choice but to assimilate into the Algerian system.

Other minorities

The Jews of Algeria (see also **Egypt, Morocco, Tunisia**) pre-date the Arab and Muslim conquest. Jewish communities played a prominent political and commercial role throughout the country's history. When persecution in Spain intensified in the late fourteenth and fifteenth centuries many Jews migrated to Algeria. Later, the Turks discriminated against Jews, who were targeted with special taxes. At the time of French colonization there were 30,000 Jews in Algeria. The FLN urged Jews to support independence and promised tolerance. Jews were sympathetic to the nationalists but many identified culturally with France. Attacks on Jews and the desecration of Jewish holy places in the late 1950s and 1960s led to large-scale emigration to France and Israel. The situation deteriorated further under Houari Boumedienne, an Arab nationalist and supporter of the Palestine Liberation Organization (PLO). By 1970 there were fewer than 1,000 Jews left, and today only about 400, mostly elderly, remain.

Conclusion and future prospects

High unemployment, inflation and corruption sparked massive popular unrest in Algeria in the late 1980s. In December 1991 Algeria, then a pluralistic nation with virtually no political violence, held the first round of what were probably the freest parliamentary elections the Arab world had ever seen. The Islamic Salvation Front, a coalition of non-violent Islamic groups, won a plurality. Three weeks later the military staged a coup, arguing that if the Islamic Front had been allowed to take power those elections would be Algeria's last. The military dissolved parliament and suspended the constitution. In March 1992 it outlawed the Islamic Front and imprisoned thousands of its members. This strengthened the radicals, who argued that violence was now their only option and formed the Group Islamique Armée (GIA). Defence Minister Liamine Zeroual was appointed President in 1994 and in 1995 elected to office with vague promises to end the war. Many Algerians assumed this meant talking to the non-violent opposition, many of whom remain in detention. He has not done so.

Since 1992 an estimated 50,000 Algerians have been killed in the conflict. Although much of the killing has been blamed on the radical Islamist groups, government forces have been equally murderous. The GIA and the Armée Islamique du Salut now control tracts of the high plateaus which lie behind the coastal strip and terror-ridden urban neighbourhoods. Women comprise 52 per cent of the Algerian population, but only 10 per cent of the workforce. The growth of the Islamist movement demanding a greater role for religion in Algerian society and an increase in persecution and harassment of women, with the intention of excluding women from public life, is causing grave concern. Women played important roles in the War of Independence and traditionally in Berber society, but a Family Code passed in 1984 places them under the guardianship of men.

In December 1996 the government claimed that a constitutional referendum outlawing Islamic parties, stripping power from the parliament and allowing the President to rule by decree was approved by 86 per cent of Algerians. No independent verification of the vote was allowed. People have long lost confidence in the military-backed government. In the climate of fear and violence, moderates of all persuasions have been pushed to the margins of public life, and there has been an infringement of liberty for all.

Further reading

Bennoune, M., *The Making of Contemporary Algeria, 1830–1987*, Cambridge, Cambridge University Press, 1988.

Entells, J.F. and Naylor, P.C. (eds), *State and Society in Algeria*, Boulder, CO, Westview, 1992.

Keenan, J., *The Tuareg: People of Ahaggar*, New York, St Martins, 1977.

Roberts, H., *Revolution and Resistance: Algerian Politics and the Kabyle Question*, London, Tauris, 1989.

Minority-based and advocacy organizations

Algerian League for Human Rights, 19 Rue Abane Ramdane, Algiers, Algeria.

Amnesty International, BP 377, Algiers, RP 16004, Algeria; tel. 213 2 732 797, fax 213 2 738 797.

Benin

Land area:	112,622 sq km
Population:	5.2 million (1993)
Main languages:	French (official), Fon, Yoruba, Bariba, Fulani
Main religions:	traditional beliefs, Christianity, Islam
Main minority groups:	Bariba 220,000 (4.2 %), Fulani 100,000 (1.9%), Somba 95,000 (1.8%), Dendi 40,000 (0.8%)
Real per capita GDP:	$1,650
UNDP HDI/rank:	0.327 (154)

Benin is located on the Bight of Benin in the Gulf of Guinea and is bordered by Nigeria, Niger, Burkina Faso and Togo. Formerly a French colony, Benin was known from 1960 to 1975 as the Republic of Dahomey. Fon are the largest and dominant ethnic group. Constituting 39.2 per cent of the total population they predominate in the south. Other southern ethnic groups include Adja, Ewe, Aizo and Yoruba. In the north the principal ethnic groups are Bariba, Fulani (traditionally nomadic herders) and Somba. Benin's population is unevenly distributed; more than two-thirds of the people live in the south; the northern savanna grasslands, although half of the country in terms of area, are only sparsely settled.

Independent Dahomey was established in August 1960 with a weak economy and a poorly integrated society rife with ethnic and regional cleavages. Society rapidly polarized into three ethnic/regionally-based movements. A rotating presidency among Fon, Yoruba and Bariba, formed in 1970, was overthrown in 1972 in a military coup led by General Mathieu Kérékou, who formed the Military Council of the Revolution (CNR) to govern the country and adopted Marxism-Leninism as the national ideology. The country was renamed Benin in 1975. By the mid-1980s the military regime was financially and morally bankrupt. Economic crisis and popular protest led to the abandonment of Marxism in December 1989. Kérékou was defeated in elections in 1990. The government remains dominated by the Fon ethnic group. Northerners are poorly represented.

The intense regionalism that has characterized Beninois politics has been the result of the interaction between historical conflict and animosity between certain groups and towns, and the geographic and socio-economic neglect of certain groups such as Somba and Bariba. The uneven spread of education, politicization and economic development in southern Benin to the detriment of the northern regions has likewise driven a wedge between the various ethnic groups. All of these were exploited by Benin's early political elite, especially under the triumvirate, in its quest for political power. In the process no single 'national' candidate emerged but rather regional politicians with electoral fiefdoms in their respective national strongholds.

Bariba

Historically an important ethnic group, Bariba live in northern Benin, especially in the Borgou, a region artificially bisected by the Benin-Niger border. This area was contested by the French and British, with the latter incorporating part of Bougou into its Nigerian colony, splitting the Bariba into two administrations. Bariba, who are of Sudanese origin, call themselves Batoma, 'the people'. Their society is stratified and traditionally held slaves. They are mainly cattle herders who delegate herding either to ex-slaves or to Fulani in exchange for protection and permission to graze on Bariba lands. With large clan cavalries, Bariba were feared as far as the Togo borders as slave raiders. Largely isolated from European or other influences from the south, once the Bariba regions were integrated into the colony of Dahomey they collapsed economically. Towns which in the nineteenth century had boomed with activity and sustained populations of over 20,000 declined to villages. The abolition of slave raiding and domestic slavery eliminated the source of livelihood and triggered a massive outflow of ex-slaves and manual labour from Bariba villages to new 'freedom villages'. The region fell into decay, lagging in social, economic and political development.

This represented a major obstacle to nation

building after independence. Regional frustrations were exploited by modern political elites, and distrust of the Yoruba catapulted regional leaders to prominence and intensified the north–south cleavage. Bariba mistrust of southerners is matched by a continued feeling of superiority over other groups in the north, traditionally raided for slaves, such as the Somba. This complicated the efforts of Kérékou, a Somba, to secure a political base in the north between 1972 and 1990, especially since he was rejected in the south as a northerner.

Other minorities

Fulani are Muslims, although the Islamic faith in Benin is strongly influenced by contact with surrounding animist populations. Fulani are pastoralists and live with the Bariba, whose cattle they tend in exchange for protection. They comprise 22 per cent of the population in the Bourgou region. Fulani have often formed alliances with Dendi. Dendi are a non-indigenous minority primarily involved in trade and dispersed throughout urban areas of northern Benin. Although they are Muslim and speak their own language, many have intermarried with the local population. Gando constitute one of the largest social strata in traditional Bariba society, and have a similar geographical distribution. They are of various ethnic origins; many were Yoruba in origin, some were the slaves of Fulani and Bariba. Mahi are an ethnic group, living north of Abomey who were a prime target in pre-colonial raids for slaves by Fon, to whom they are closely related. 'Brazilians' are Beninois of mixed Euro-African parentage, descended from exiles and deported Africans from the time of the Dahomey dynastic wars, and from slaves or descendants of slaves taken to Brazil and returning to Dahomey in the nineteenth century. Mostly Roman Catholic and well-educated, they lived in the coastal areas as traders and played a dominant role in the early days of French colonial rule. With independence their political significance declined. Devoid of ethnic networks, they lack the building blocks for political power in Benin, and after the change of government in 1972 many emigrated to France.

Conclusions and future prospects

A general atmosphere of protest has pervaded Benin since the late 1980s as student unrest has increased and civil service strikes over pay issues and structural adjustment programmes have grown. Since 1990 the government of President Christophe Soglo has broken with Kerekou's autocratic methods, and human rights reforms are reported.

Further reading

Allen, C. and Radu, M.S., *Benin, the Congo and Burkino Faso: Economy, Politics and Society*, New York, Pinter, 1989.

Decalo, S., *Historical Dictionary of Benin*, Metuchen, NJ, Scarecrow Press, 1995.

Minority and advocacy-based organizations

Amnesty International, BP 01 3536, Cotonou, Benin; tel/fax. 229 32 36 90.

Study and Research Group on Democracy and Economic and Social Development, BP 1258, Cotonou, Benin.

Burkina Faso

Land area:	274,000 sq km
Population:	9.7 million (1992)
Main languages:	French (official), More, Dioula, Gourmantche
Main religions:	traditional beliefs, Islam, Christianity
Main minority groups:	Peul, Tamajek and Bellah pastoralists 1.8 million (19%), Gurunsi 900,000 (9.3%), Mandé-speakers (Senoufo, Dioula) 200,000 (2.1%), Bobo 105,000 (1.1%)
Real per capita GDP:	$780
UNDP HDI/rank:	0.225 (170)

Burkina Faso, formerly Upper Volta, is bordered by Niger, Mali, Benin, Togo, Ghana and Côte d'Ivoire. The poor semi-arid soil supports few crops, produces low yields and loses its fertility rapidly. Extreme variations in rainfall have led to severe droughts in 1969–74 and 1981–3, with large loss of life and livestock. There is a great linguistic and ethnic diversity among the inhabitants (known as Burkinabe). The Voltaic linguistic group includes Mossi, Gurunsi, Bobo and Lobi. Mande-speakers include Senoufo, Dioula and Busani. Other groups include Peul and Hausa. Most Burkinabe adhere to traditional beliefs. About one-fifth are Muslim, a faith that was historically resisted. Roman Catholics form a tiny but influential educated minority.

Mossi arrived in the area in the eleventh to thirteenth centuries and established a powerful kingdom, a centre of contact with trans-Saharan traders and the forest kingdom to the south. France asserted control over the area in the 1890s, first dividing it among other colonies but then reconstituting it within its present borders from 1919 to 1932, and again from 1947. A Mossi-dominated political party led Upper Volta to independence in 1960. Political life has since been dominated by the small educated elite, military officers and labour unions. A civilian government elected in 1978 was overthrown in a military coup in November 1980 and a series of military governments followed, with a radical left-wing regime coming to power in 1983. Captain Thomas Sankara and a group of radical young officers strove to revolutionize society; people were encouraged to create Committees for the Defence of the Revolution (CDRs) in cities and villages in order to build schools and clinics, run cooperatives and exercise local power. The government sought to divert funds from costly urban civil services to rural development, and Sankara came to symbolize popular democracy. With the assassination of Sankara by his deputy, Marxism-Leninism was abandoned in 1987. Military rule ended in 1991 with the installation of a transitional government and the adoption of a new constitution which allowed for multi-party politics.

Peul, Tamajek and Bellah

Peul (Fula) herders and Tamajek (Tuareg) clans with their vassals, Bellah, are all pastoralists, and are predominantly Muslim. They constitute almost 20 per cent of the population and inhabit the northern Sahelian region and the border areas with Mali. These groups have been severely affected by environmental degradation. Running along the border between Mali and Burkina Faso is the Beli river, which has its source in Mali. Uncertainty about land and water rights has been a constant source of friction between the two countries; and on either side of the border families are arbitrarily separated by the frontier. The main economic and culturally valued activity of these semi-nomadic groups remains herding of camels, goats, oxen and sheep and their continual wandering for water and fodder leads them to cross the border, which has always been irrelevant to them. Tension mounted after alleged cattle raids by Malians brought in its wake an influx of weapons. In 1974, during the Sahelian drought, Upper Volta declared it had a right to deny Malian herders access to water resources in the disputed Agacher strip, and Malian troops and tanks subsequently moved in to occupy part of the area. As drought returned in the early 1980s Mali again launched a military attack on Burkina Faso. The remaining population in the Agacher strip was displaced, losing grain and animals to occupying soldiers. International arbitration has since determined that the frontier should run along the river.

Other minorities

Christianized Gurunsi and Bobo live along the border with Ghana in south and south-east Burkina Faso. The Gurunsi are an independent group of cultivators; highly individualistic, they have never organized to protect themselves and have often been raided by their more powerful neighbours.

Of Burkina Faso's Mandé-speakers, Dioula are an indigenous Muslim minority, whose language is the country's commercial *lingua franca* (see **Côte d'Ivoire**). Most refused to send their children to French schools in the colonial era and so few Dioula attained posts in the emerging bureaucracy. However commercial expansion has loosened lineage solidarities and pitted men against women in the economic sphere. Senoufo, a small segment of a larger Muslim Côte d'Ivoire and Malian ethnic group, live in the extreme south-west along the frontier. Far from central control, they have often viewed the government with mistrust.

Originally from north-west Ghana, Lobi migrated into contemporary Burkina Faso at the end of the eighteenth century, settling along the sparsely populated border with Côte d'Ivoire. Lobi live in extended families with no larger political structure. Social order is assured by the head of the extended family and by a series of cultural interdictions. Despite foreign influence, Lobi have retained their cultural identity and have displayed strong resistance to colonial rule, Islam, Christianity and modernity. Their strong individualism has given their society great staying power and strength.

Conclusions and future prospects

Burkina Faso's first legislative election in fourteen years was held in May 1992. Blaise Compaoré, the country's present leader, has eradicated the power of traditional chiefs in this predominantly rural-dwelling country. Many of those imprisoned after Compaoré's 1987 coup remain in prison, and only among civil servants and trade unionists is there any opportunity for political involvement. Drought and population pressure in the south have increased the flight from the land, accelerating the trend of emigration of young Burkinabe to Ghana and Côte d'Ivoire. Poverty and a lack of access to health give the country one of the lowest life expectancy rates and highest infant mortality rates.

Further reading

Benoit, M., *Introduction to the Geography of the Sudanese Pastoral Areas of Upper Volta*, Paris, ORSTOM, 1977.

Duval, M., *Un totalitarisme sans État; politique a Partir d'un village Burkinabe,* Paris, Harmattan, 1985.

Goody, J., *The Social Organisation of the Lo Willi*, London, Oxford University Press, 1967.

Pere, M., *Les Lobis: tradition et changement*, Laval, Siloe, 1988.

Quimby, L., 'Islam, sex roles and modernization in Bobo-Dioulasso', in Jules-Rosette, B. (ed), *The New Religions of Africa*, Norwood, Ablex Publishers, 1979.

Tarrab, G. and Coenne, C., *Femmes et pouvoir en Burkina Faso*, Paris, Harmattan, 1989.

Minority-based and advocacy organizations

Burkinabe Movement for Human and Peoples' Rights, BP 2055, Ouagadougou 01, Burkina Faso.

Cape Verde

Land area:	4,033 sq km
Population:	400,000 (1992)
Main languages:	Portuguese (official), Crioulo
Main religion:	Roman Catholicism
Main minority groups:	Badiu (no data)
Real per capita GDP:	$1,820
UNDP HDI/rank:	0.539 (122)

The Republic of Cape Verde consists of ten main islands and five islets located in the Atlantic Ocean some 600 kilometres off the western tip of Africa. Cape Verde has an arid climate and is subject to cyclical drought. The islands gained independence in July 1975. After the abolition of slavery the sparse Portuguese population intermarried with the African majority, brought mainly from the area known as the 'Guinea Rivers' from Cap Vert in Senegal to Sierre Leone, to produce a distinctive Crioulo culture. Cape Verde society had a complex racial structure cut across by higher levels of wealth, power and education which 'lightened' one's appearance. The legal status of *assimilado* – open to anybody of European ancestry – incorporated and perpetuated negative colonial images of Africanness. Repressive prison camps and strict ideological control, exerted through schools and churches, supported colonialism.

Until the end of the colonial period 90 per cent of the population laboured in an agricultural system dominated by sharecropping and absentee landlords. Under a 1930 act, the vast majority of the African population were made wards of state and denied their civil rights, including the right to vote. They were also subject to a head tax, restricted movement and to severe and arbitrary punishment. The few known instances of slave and peasant rebellions were among the Badiu population of the São Tiago interior, who preserved their Africanness. Many Badiu were transferred to the cocoa plantations of São Tomé and Príncipe; the group's survival is undocumented. The population of Cape Verde today is 71 per cent Creole, 28 per cent African and 1 per cent European.

Further reading

Meintel, D., *Race, Culture and Portuguese Colonialism in Cabo Verde*, Syracuse, NY, Syracuse University Press, 1984.

Cote d'Ivoire

Land area:	322,463 sq km
Population:	13.8 million (1994)
Main languages:	French, Baule, Dioula
Main religions:	Islam
Main minority groups:	Manding (Mandé; incl. Malinké) 2.2 million (16%), Voltaic (incl. Senoufo, Lobi) 1.5 million (11%), Kru 1.3 million (9.4%), Lagoon (Ebrié) 600,000 (4.4%), Dan 375,000 (2.7%), Gagu 320,000 (2.3%), Kweni (Guro) 180,000 (1.3%), Kwa (no data), Fulani (no data), Lebanese 100,000 (0.7%), migrants from Burkina Faso, Ghana and Mali
Real per capita GDP:	$1,620
UNDP HDI/rank:	0.357 (147)

Côte d'Ivoire (Ivory Coast) is a West African nation located in the Gulf of Guinea. It is bordered by Ghana, Burkina Faso, Mali, Guinea and Liberia. Formerly a territory within French West Africa, it achieved independence in 1960. The country has over sixty ethnic groups, whose linguistic and cultural identities and interrelationships are diverse and complex. The four main cultural clusters are: the dominant Akan-speakers, mainly in the south-east; Manding (Mandé), mainly in the north; Voltaic peoples (including Senuofo in the north, and Lobi in the central region); and Kru in the south-west. The Baule, an Akan subgroup comprising appoximately 12 per cent of the population, are the largest single ethnic group. Thirty per cent of the population of Côte d'Ivoire consists of migrants from Burkina Faso, Mali and Ghana. There is also a non-African population of 100,000 Lebanese and 60,000 French. The population is one-quarter Muslim, one-eighth Christian; the remainder follow traditional beliefs.

Until 1990, the only legal political party was the Parti Democratique de Côte d'Ivoire (PDCI), dominated by the Akan ethnic group, in particular by Baule from the south. Akan comprise two-fifths of the population yet over half of the country's political leaders. Dominant among these was Félix Houphouët-Boigny, who died in 1993 and whose shadow continues to fall over the polity. He virtually suspended public politics in Côte d'Ivoire and subjected what remained to his stern and unrelenting control. He was disdainful of the Organization of African Unity (OAU) and its African Commission on Human and Peoples Rights. Northerners as a whole have been underrepresented in national politics. The PDCI has raised the spectre of religious extremism and conflict if Muslims take power. West African Islam is orthodox Sunni but generally retains local tradition and is generally tolerant of diversity. Islam has recently been making many converts, especially in urban areas.

Manding (Mandé)

The northern Manding or Mandé grouping – after Akan-speakers the country's second largest cultural cluster – includes Malinké (Maninka), Dioula and Bambara. Malinké (Maninka), one of the most important subgroups of this grouping are mostly Muslim and located in both north-west and southern Côte d'Ivoire. According to tradition they are the descendants of the people who founded the Mali empire. In the north-west theirs is the dominant culture; they moved into southern Côte d'Ivoire in the sixteenth to eighteenth centuries.

Dioula, a large Muslim minority living in the north had commercial networks in pre-colonial times, that stretched from Senegal to Nigeria and from Timbuktu to northern Côte d'Ivoire. With colonization these expanded into the new towns of the coastal areas. *Dioula* is a contextually defined term, meaning itinerant trader, but 'Dioula' has come to be applied to all Muslim merchants from the north, of whatever ethnic or cultural background including Malinké. The true Dioula – those for whom this is primarily a cultural rather than an occupational designation – are from the region of Kong, once an important trans-Saharan trading centre but then devastated in the early 1890s by drought and the interruption of trade caused by the capture of the cities of

Djenne, Mopti and Bandigara in Sudan by the French.

Dioula are underrepresented in the structure of power. Most support the opposition Rassemblement des Republicains (RDR). The worsening economic climate is heightening ethnic tensions, and the commercial predominance of the Dioula provokes envy. The ruling PDCI is trying to capitalize on such resentment and to sabotage the RDR's alliance with the Front Populaire Ivorien (FPI), which draws support from the south and west, particularly among urban populations hard hit by currency devaluation in 1994. The PDCI exploited anti-Islamic sentiment in the run-up to the elections of October 1995, claiming that a vote for the RDR would be a vote for Islamist revolution. The removal of senior Muslims from the civil service and the prosecution for sedition of two Muslim journalists has put the Muslims further on the defensive.

Voltaic peoples

Senoufo, at 1.3 million people the largest Voltic ethnic group, are people of Bambara origin who live in north-central Côte d'Ivoire, Mali and Burkina Faso. Senoufo villages are completely independent of one another. A Senoufo secret society plays a major role in three periods of the first thirty years of man's life. After this, men are no longer obliged to perform agricultural work. Each Senoufo village has a sacred forest in which ritual activities are carried out. Islamization of Senoufo began before the colonial period and spread rapidly among the chiefs; groups of Dioula live in enclaves in many Senoufo villages.

Lobi, who number about 100,000 are a Voltaic group without village organization or chiefs, based on matrilineal lineage. Towards the end of the eighteenth century Lobi moved north-west and east because of population pressure and incursions. The consequence was a massive emigration and the non-violent occupation of new land. The immigrants mixed with present occupants, and Lobi – traditional hunters and warriors – were welcomed by the kingdom of Bouna. They remained isolated from Dioula and were never conquered by Manding, or British or French colonization, although they were nominally 'pacified' by 1901. Lobi migration continued in the colonial period from Upper Volta and Ghana to the sparsely populated Kulango areas and extreme north-east around Bouna. They are among the poorest populations in Côte d'Ivoire.

Kru

A language cluster encompassing ethnic groups in south-west Côte d'Ivoire and southern Liberia (see **Liberia**), Kru are organized in segmentary lineages. Once inhabiting large areas to the north and east, about 200 years ago they were pushed to the sea by Manding and Akan movements south and west. More generally Kru is a term applied by Europeans to the coast between Monrovia and Grand Lahou and the coast population who have served for many generations as sailors on European ships. The development of the port of San Pedro is bringing economic modernization to their region, but Kru have until now lagged behind other groups in political and economic participation.

Part of the Kru language group, Bété number approximately 750,000. They are concentrated in some 800 villages in the triangle among the cities of Daloa, Soubre and Gagnoa. Bété did not enter into regional commercial exchange until the end of the nineteenth century, their last resistance against colonial rule taking place in 1906. During the colonial period the Bété hunting and martial activities were replaced by coffee and cocoa farming. This in turn brought substantial immigration of 'Dioulas', Voltaics and Baules that has continued up to the present. At the same time many Bété moved to the coast, especially to Abidjan. Thus the population of the traditional Bété region is now composed of equal numbers of Bété and migrants.

An ethnic movement started in the 1930s among the Bété in an attempt to represent the interests of a region and a people who felt a special discrimination under the colonial system. The period since independence has heightened Bété self-awareness. This name was not used before the colonial era but originated as a designation for those people working on the plantations of south-east Côte d'Ivoire. Since the colonial era, outsiders – both European and African – have held pejorative stereotypes of the Bété. Bété identity is now influenced by these indigenous/outsider, rural/urban contrasts rather than by pre-colonial factors.

The Bété home region has been the site of periodic upheavals, including a harshly suppressed rebellion in 1970 in Gagnoa. Kragbe Ngragbe, a Bété student who attempted to found an opposition party, the PANA, in 1967, tried to mobilize resistance to participation in one-party elections. Ngragbe led a march of several hundred from different Bété villages to Gagnoa where they pronounced the republic of 'Eburnea' which was meant to group the various Kru ethnic peoples in the west. The gendarmerie and army were sent in from village to village making hundreds of arrests. Those arrested were held until 1976 when most were set free. Ngragbe was mortally wounded by soldiers.

Dida (330,000) are a people of the Kru ethnic cluster, concentrated in south-central Côte d'Ivoire, self-identified by an exclusive network of political and economic relations. Traditionally Dida society is very decentralized, although each village recognizes one lineage as proprietor of village lands. Culturally they are influenced by Baule to the north. Dida resisted colonial rule during 1909–18 and did not engage in cash crop production until after the Second World War. Dida currently constitute a third of the population of Divo department.

Guere (250,000) are Kru people traditionally residing in west-central Côte d'Ivoire. Guere is a designation developed by a colonial administrator for the people living south of the Dan. Female initiation societies have been maintained, and age grades of both sexes are still prominent. A cultural trait is the presence of women chiefs. Guere society is characterized by weak political authority beyond the lineage or village, with spiritual leadership having a separate role. Until recently Guere were exclusively subsistence farmers; cash cropping has brought rapid social and economic changes and many Guere have migrated.

Lagoon

The Lagoon, a further ethnic cluster, is the designation of the Ebrié (Kyama), an extremely complex grouping of people along the south-east coast and the lagoons. Numbering about 600,000, they have largely shifted from traditional occupations to cash crop farming and speak a Kru language. Lagoon people have attracted many migrant labourers to their farms, especially Mossi from Burkina Faso. Baule and Diola have also moved in and assumed political and economic prominence to the concern of the original inhabitants. Ebrié originally came further inland around 1750. Ebrié never organized into central states; their most inclusive political unit has been the village. Age grades are an important part of social cohesion. Ebrié occupy the area around Abidjan, Bingerville and Dabu and were the indigenous people of the site of the city of Abidjan. Although numerically overwhelmed by immigrants, they have managed to preserve their identity and some aspects of traditional culture which was oriented towards the waters of the sea and the lagoons. They are however becoming increasingly attracted to Christianity and integrated into the wider economy and society.

Other minorities

Dan (375,000) are an ethnic group classified as peripheral Mandé, sharing the cultural patterns but not the language of the Kru. Dan live in the extreme west of Côte d'Ivoire and into Liberia. Self-awareness as a distinct culture emerged only as recently as the eighteenth and nineteenth centuries. Dan were pushed into their present mountainous and forest location by Manding expansion. At a high altitude they cultivate rice and trade kola nuts for dried fish from the Niger River through Dioula traders. Dan resisted Islam even though living on its southern frontier. Armed resistance against colonial rule was put down in 1905–8. Young men traditionally migrate to the coast to work on ships and in ports.

Gagu people of south-central Côte d'Ivoire are thought to be the oldest residents of the country. Gagu (320,000) practise hunting and gathering as a supplement to agriculture and use bark as a material for clothing and bedding. They assimilated into Kweni (Guro) culture, and the first language of most Gagu is Guro.

Kweni – often known by the Baule term Guro and numbering about 180,000 – are of Manding origin and are located between Bété to the west and Baule to the east in west-central Côte d'Ivoire. They entered the forest under pressure from Malinké migration; however, their movement east was halted by Baule. The last Kweni resistance to French colonial rule was in 1907. Over 50 territorial groupings formerly had an economic and military function, but intermarriage has brought cultural assimilation with Bété, Gagu and others. Kweni have no hereditary chiefs. They had no sense of communal identity before the French colonial era. Traditionally they grew plantain, manioc, yam and taro and more recently have moved into coffee, cocoa and cotton production. The migration of Kweni to work on southern palm oil plantations has disrupted marriage and family stability.

Because of the Sahelian drought in the 1970s large numbers of Fulani began to move south with their herds into Côte d'Ivoire. Although welcomed by the government because of their contribution to beef production, they soon came into conflict with Senoufo farmers of the northern region whose fields were damaged by their herds.

Lebanese in Côte d'Ivoire numbered 100,000 in 1990. This represents the largest Lebanese community outside Lebanon. Concentrated in distribution and retail sales, Lebanese occupy a marginal social position. They supported the PDCI at independence and maintain close ties to the regime. With the liberalization of economic policies in the late 1980s Lebanese firms have become dominant over European concerns in the import and distribution of consumer goods.

Conclusions and future prospects

Until relatively recently Côte d'Ivoire was seen as an 'oasis of African economic development'. However, in mid-1987, payments on foreign debt were suspended as a depressed world market for cocoa and coffee, the country's leading exports, dealt a major blow to hopes for national development. New economic austerity measures, the continued repression of trade union activity and the threat of mass redundancies have increased the political tension. Once welcomed, now the country's 4 million foreign residents are blamed for rising crime and unemployment. All of these issues have fuelled political tensions along polarized ethnic and religious lines.

Further reading

Handloff, R.E., *Côte d'Ivoire: A Country Study*, Washington, DC, US GPO, 1991.

Zartman, W.I. and Delgado, C.C. (eds), *The Political Economy of the Ivory Coast*, New York, Praeger, 1984.

Minority-based and advocacy organizations

Amnesty International, 04 BP 895, Abidjan 04, Côte d'Ivoire; tel/fax. 225 248 006.

Djibouti

Land area:	23,200 sq km
Population:	391,000 (1992)
Main languages:	French (official)
Main religions:	Islam, Christianity
Main minority groups:	Afar 175,000 (44.7%), non-Issa Somalis (Issak and Gadabourse) 95,000 (24.3%)
Real per capita GDP:	$775
UNDP HDI/rank:	0.287 (164)

Djibouti is a small republic situated just north of the Horn of Africa on the strait of Bab el-Mandeb, the gateway to the Red Sea. Bordered by Ethiopia, Somalia and Eritrea, Djibouti has been adversely affected by regional tensions. It owes its *raison d'être* to foreign interests and its continued existence to foreign aid. The population is mainly divided between two groups, Afar of the north and dominant Issas and other Somali-speakers in the south and the capital. Both are Muslim and were traditionally pastoral nomads who roamed across large areas without regard for political boundaries. Djibouti has experienced large influxes of refugees from Ethiopia and Somalia over the last twenty years. Formerly known as French Somaliland, Djibouti gained independence in 1977. In 1981 a one-party system was introduced. The government under Hassan Gouled – head of state since independence – tends to represent the slightly larger Issa population, who, together with other related Somali tribes, are in the majority.

Afar

Afar belong to the same ethnic group as the neighbouring Ethiopian Danakil. Before independence the Afar community had a greater share of political influence, but afterwards the reverse has been true. Gouled forced many Afar out of the government, administration and army in the 1970s. There are, for example, only two Afar permanent secretaries but 17 from the Mamassen clan of the Issas (the presidential family clan). In 1981 the government banned the opposition Parti Populaire, which it falsely claimed was an Afar ethnic pressure group. An Afar-based armed rebellion that called for a more equitable distribution of resources began in the north in late 1991 and soon gained control of much of the country. In 1992 Gouled introduced a multi-party constitution and in 1993 he won a fourth term in Djibouti's first multi-party presidential election, although the election was boycotted by much of the opposition.

Civil strife continues. Dozens of villagers were reportedly killed in 1993 as civilians became the main targets of the army in its war against the Afar armed movement, the Front pour la Restauration de l'Unité et de la Democratie (FRUD). This followed the failure of a government offensive seeking to dislodge FRUD guerrillas from the Mabla Mountains. The Afar rebels operate from bases in the mountains around Tadjoura and Obock. Although Prime Minister Barkot Goured is an Afar he and two other Afar ministers have been powerless to prevent extrajudicial killings, the rape of Afar women, torture and the internment of civilians. Traditional Afar leaders have spoken out for the first time and protested.

Divisions between Issas and Afars remain deep. Intensification of the conflict would have repercussions in Eritrea and Ethiopia, which also have Afar populations. The Ethiopian-backed Afar Liberation Front (Front Afar) has been monitoring the treatment of Ethiopian Afar refugees in Djibouti and claims that indiscriminate arrests and imprisonment without trial are common.

Non-Issa Somalis

Issaks, with an estimated population of 40,000, and Gadabourse, numbering about 45,000, resent the Issa, especially the Mamassen clan who wield most power. In May and June 1988 the government detained some 800 Issaks who were demonstrating in favour of the Somali National Movement (SNM).

Conclusions and future prospects

By initially refusing to enter talks with FRUD the Djibouti government lost financial aid from France and the political support of neighbouring countries. Economically pressed, a peace accord was signed in December 1994. Djibouti has declined economically since the reopening of the port of Massawa in Eritrea.

Further reading

Amnesty International, *Djibouti: Torture and Political Imprisonment*, London, Amnesty International, 1992.

Egypt

Land area:	1,001,449 sq km
Population:	59 million (1993)
Main languages:	Arabic (official)
Main religions:	Islam, Coptic Christianity
Main minority groups:	Copts 5.5–8 million (est., 9.3–13.6%), Nubians 100,000 (0.2 %)
Real per capita GDP:	$3,800
UNDP HDI/rank:	0.611 (106)

Egypt occupies the north-eastern corner of Africa, the Sinai Peninsula and several islands in the Gulf of Suez and the Red Sea. It is bounded by the Mediterranean Sea, Sudan, the Red Sea, Israel and Libya. Many Egyptians are descended from the successive Arab settlers who followed the Muslim conquest in the seventh century. Nubians living south of Aswan have been Arabized in religion and culture although they still speak the Nubian language. Nomads who live in the semi-desert comprise an Arab–Berber mixture.

Egyptian civilization was established in the fourth millennium BCE. Conquered by the Arabs in the seventh century, Egypt was part of the

Ottoman Empire from 1517 to 1798 and held by the British from 1882 to 1922. It then became an independent monarchy until the monarchy was abolished after a military coup in 1952. In 1954 Colonel Gamal Abdel Nasser became President, shaping Egypt into a socialist republic. From 1974 President Anwar Sadat followed opposing policies to those of Nasser by promoting peace with Israel, economic liberalization and Egyptian nationalism. In 1981 Sadat was killed by Muslim fundamentalists. Sadat had favoured accommodation with the Muslim Brotherhood while cracking down on more radical armed Islamic groups. His successor, Hosni Mubarak, however, outlawed the Muslim Brotherhood, as a 'terrorist organization' linked to the militant El Gammaa el Islamiya. Gammaa's low level guerrilla war has undergone a resurgence since August 1994, with attacks on Egyptian Copts, prominent secularists and tourists. The government has used incommunicado detention, torture and severe force to contain Islamic militants, and several hundred people have been killed, mainly police and militants. Gammaa's political manifesto remains vague, but grievances include government corruption and incompetence, especially in the neglected south of the country. Political apathy is demonstrated by low turn-outs in the 1990 and 1995 multi-party elections, and the government has been accused of using the crackdown on militants to stifle wider opposition.

Copts

Egyptian Copts are the biggest Christian community in the Arab world. Estimates of their numbers in Egypt vary between 5.5 million and 8 million. They are most numerous in Upper Egypt. Most Copts are working class peasants and labourers, although there is a Coptic business upper class and a middle class of urban professionals and small landowners. Copts are present in all institutions of the state, and there are Coptic members of all political parties.

Egypt became part of the Byzantine Empire in 395 CE, and the Egyptian Church was separated from the Christian community in 451. From the ninth century onwards the Copts were persecuted by their Muslim rulers, in turn Arab, Circassian and Ottoman. Churches were destroyed, books burnt and elders imprisoned. By the time the British had taken Egypt in 1882, Copts had been reduced to one-tenth of the population, mainly as a result of centuries of conversion to Islam. Arab Muslims governed Christians and Jews by the rules of the Islamic *sharia*. By Islamic law, as *zemmi* people, they had to wear different colours and clothes from Muslims, could not build new places of worship or repair old ones without permission, or construct them in such a way as to overshadow those of Muslims. They were subject to a heavy poll tax. With the Arabization of governmental positions, Coptic clerks sought to study Arabic and teach it to their children, given the tradition of inheriting jobs. There was a gradual change to the use of Arabic, with the Coptic language being abandoned, and many Copts converted to Islam.

In the mid-nineteenth century, Mohammed Ali Pasha, Viceroy of Egypt under the Ottomans, who became hereditary ruler of Egypt in 1841 when he defeated the Sultan, reconstructed the administration, modernizing industry and creating a modern education system. Copts were employed in financial and accounting positions and were appointed rulers in a number of local governates. They had rights of land ownership, and a large financial and commercial bourgeoisie developed. There was a clear separation between church and lay life. Under the Hamayouni Decree of 1856, a lay council was created to represent the Coptic community. Religious freedom and equality in employment were guaranteed. The peak of Coptic integration was in the liberal period from the 1919 'revolution' to 1952. Christians united with Muslims in their fight for independence against the British colonialists. There were two Coptic prime ministers during this period and widespread political participation as MPs and in the media. The British tried to separate Copts and Muslims, attempting to isolate Copts from the nationalist movement by inciting sectarian strife. Copts opposed British intervention in the Egyptian constitution and did not call for rights for religious minorities in the 1923 constitution.

The revolution in 1952 brought in nationalization and agricultural reform. Middle and lower class Copts benefited, as did their Muslim counterparts. However, the Coptic elite lost 75 per cent of their property through nationalization; hitherto they had controlled a major share of transportation, industry, banking and agricultural land. Nasser also issued two decrees which had implications for Copts: one enforcing religion as a basic subject in the curricula rather than complementary to it, and a second in which Al Azhar University was confined to Muslim students. Copts sided with Arabs in the conflict with Israel in the 1940s, but when Arabs demonstrated violently against Jewish settlement in Palestine, Copts were often victims of political abuse and physical assault. The dissolution of predominantly Coptic political parties such as the Wafd Party, the seizure of Coptic endowments in 1957 and the limitation of Copt landholding to 200 acres, created an atmosphere of tension and led to increased emigration of Copts.

At the onset of the Sadat era in 1971 the dissolution of economic centralization benefited upper class Copts. However, as social frustrations mounted in the 1970s with the rise of Islamic radical movements, strikes and protests, Sadat initially flirted with the Islamicists, politicizing religion and using Muslims as new allies in confrontation with the left. Old scapegoats were sought out. In 1972 Coptic churches, houses and shops were burnt. Islamic groups became increasingly organized and violent, until the government began to confront the militants, arresting thousands. Copts demanded the cancelling of discriminatory laws and protested at the use of *sharia* as the source of legislation. Numerous confrontations took place in 1978 and 1979 between Muslims and Copts in Upper Egypt. In 1980 Sadat tried to implicate Pope Shenouda III in a plan to undermine state security; the Pope was stripped of authority and exiled to a desert monastery; 125 Coptic clergy and lay activists were arrested, Coptic associations were banned and all Coptic publishing concerns were closed down. The Pope was kept under house arrest for four years until his re-appointment in 1985.

Sadat's assassination in 1981 left behind a divided nation. As economic recession deepened, violence against Copts again erupted in the second half of the 1980s, continuing up to the present. Other Coptic concerns include restrictions on the building and repair of churches – which limit their freedom of worship and often cause sectarian confrontation – and the educational curriculum, which distinguishes between Copts and Muslims and ignores Coptic culture in general. Furthermore, the mass media frequently promotes hatred and division. In addition, Egyptian military and police colleges restrict Christian admission, and there is a reluctance to admit Copts to some faculties and universities. The number of Copts appointed in the People's Assembly has decreased in 1990s to half the number of the 1960s.

Nubians

Nubians live in the Upper Nile region. Although Egypt remained the stronger power for most of its dynastic period, it did not destroy its southern neighbour, Nubia; nor did Nubia, in spite of its adoption of Egyptian gods and ideas of kingship, completely succumb to its neighbour's ways. From 1720–1550 BCE Nubians took control of Egypt and stabilized the kingdom. The Nubian city of Meroe was sited on the banks of the Nile about 200 kilometres north of present-day Khartoum, growing rich from control of trade on the Nile until the fourth century CE. Its wealth gave rise to elite patronage of art work such as pottery and shield rings, worn on the forehead, a practice that Nubians continue today. The incorporation of Egypt into the Byzantine Empire brought Christianity to the Nile region. Coptic Christianity spread to Nubia, where a Christian kingdom existed from the sixth to the fourteenth centuries.

When the Condominium Agreement of 1899 fixed the boundary between Egypt and Sudan, Lower Nubians found themselves under direct Egyptian rule and politically separated from their kin to the south. This arbitrary frontier divides the Mahasi-speaking group more or less equally between Egypt and Sudan. Close ties of culture, language and family continue to unite the people north and south of the border, and until the evacuation of 1964 that accompanied the building of the Aswan High Dam there was continual visiting back and forth between them. Egyptian Nubia is part of the Governate of Aswan which also includes a populous area whose inhabitants are not Nubian. As a result, Nubians have found themselves a minority within their native province.

Rural Nubians have been neglected and exploited for much of the twentieth century. From about 1910 until their final destruction in the 1960s, the villages of Egyptian Nubia were populated chiefly by women, children and older people; most able-bodied men were forced to migrate to find work. For the sake of increased agricultural production downstream, their land has been destroyed piecemeal by the building of successive dams at Aswan without any effort to gain their consent. Over a period of 70 years about 60 per cent of Egyptian Nubia territory has been destroyed or rendered unfit for habitation, and roughly half the surviving Nubian-speaking people have been obliged to find new homes. Some attempt has been made to compensate Nubians for the loss of their farms and date groves and create new livelihoods for them, but development south of Aswan has failed to keep pace with the rest of the country. For thousands of years 'Nubian' and 'slave' were virtually synonymous in the Egyptian mind; although this prejudice has lessened in the modern era, Nubians are still largely excluded from Egyptian national life.

Other minorities

By the twelfth century there were up to 20,000 Jews in Egypt. Under Ottoman rule their position deteriorated, but during the nineteenth century their lot improved, and they achieved prominence in commerce and industry. By the 1940s, 65,000–70,000 Jews lived in Cairo, Alexandria and other urban communities. The 1948 Arab–Israeli war saw hundreds of Jews arrested, their property and businesses confiscated; bombings in Jewish areas killed and maimed hundreds. Some 25,000 Jews left Egypt between 1948 and 1950, many going to Israel. In 1952 anti-British sentiment led to attacks on Jewish establishments, and after the 1956 war, 3,000 Jews were interned and thousands of others were given a few days to leave the country, while their property was confiscated by the state. By 1957 only 8,000 Jews were left. Hundreds of Jews were arrested and tortured after the 1967 war, and those still in public employment were dismissed. As a result of further emigration, by 1970 there were only 1,000 Jews in Egypt, and today there are fewer than 250, most of them elderly.

Conclusions and future prospects

Egypt's emergency laws introduced after the 1981 assassination of Sadat remain in force. The authorities can arrest and question people without charge for an unlimited time. Significant numbers of Islamic militants are reportedly summarily executed through a shoot-to-kill policy. In November 1995 a military court convicted fifty-four senior members of the Muslim Brotherhood, a move widely seen as the climax of a campaign to ensure another overwhelming majority for the ruling National Democratic Party in the country's elections. The trial was denounced by most Egyptian political parties, including secular ones. The Brotherhood rejects violence and insists on its belief in parliamentary democracy. Yet the government's current approach tends to reinforce extremist positions by suggesting that democracy in Egypt is a mockery and that the resort to violence is the only means available to those concerned about corruption, mismanagement and poverty. Like other moderates in the country, Copts consider that the solution to their current concerns lies in social and economic reform, and in the consolidation of a democracy based on pluralism and equality between all segments of society. They stress the importance of civil society and its institution in combating injustice and curtailing prejudice, hatred and extremism.

Further reading

Ibrahim, S.E. *The Copts*, Cairo, Ibn Khaldun Center for Development Studies, 1995.

Ibrahim, S.E. et al., *The Copts of Egypt*, London, MRG report, 1996.

Minority-based and advocacy organizations

Afro-Asian Peoples' Solidarity Organization, 89 Abdel Aziz Al Saoud Street, Manial El-Roda, Cairo, Egypt.

Arab Lawyers' Union, 13 Ittehad El-Mouhameen El-Arab Street (Ex Toulombat), Garden City 11451, Cairo, Egypt.

Arab Women Solidarity Association, 4A Dareeh Saad Street, off Kasr El Eini Street, Cairo, Egypt.

Cairo Institute for Human Rights Studies, 9 Rustom Street, Garden City, Cairo, Egypt; tel. 20 2 354 3715, fax 20 2 355 4200.

Egyptian Organization for Human Rights, 17 Midan Aswan el Hohandessin, Giza, Egypt.

Egyptian Society for Human Rights, c/o Faculty of Law, Assuit University, Ali Basha Elal No. 19, Elmatria, Cairo, Egypt.

Ibn Khaldoun Center for Development Studies, 17 Street 12, Mokattam, PO Box 13, Cairo, Egypt; tel. 20 2 506 1617/0662, fax 20 2 506 1030.

Eritrea

Land area:	93,679 sq km
Population:	3.3 million (1992)
Main languages:	Tigrinya, Afar, Beni Amer, Tegre, Saho, Arabic
Main religions:	Ethiopian Orthodox Christianity, Islam
Main minority groups:	Tegre 1 million (30%), Afar 110,000 (4%), Saho 90,000 (3%), Beni Amer 90,000 (3%), Bilen 30,000 (1%), Kunama 15,000 (0.5 %), Baria 9,500 (0.3%)
Real per capita GDP:	—
UNDP HDI/rank:	—

Eritrea is divided between a mountainous central plateau, where the capital Asmara is situated, and the lowlands in the north, west and along the Red Sea Coast. The Eritrean Plateau joins the Ethiopian highlands and is similar in vegetation, climate and rainfall. Its inhabitants are very close to their Ethiopian neighbours in Tigray in language, traditions, social structure and culture. Most belong to the Ethiopian Orthodox religion and their language Tigrinya is descended from Ge'ez (ancient Ethiopic), as is Amharic. The lowland Eritreans are largely Muslim, speaking local languages such as Danakil and Saho as well as Arabic. Peoples of the far west originally descended from northern Sudan.

The unification of Eritrea and the demarcation of its present boundaries were achieved only in 1890 by the Italians. Until then, the highlands had been part of the Christian province of Tigray and the lowlands had been penetrated successively by Turks, Egyptians and Mahdi forces from Sudan. In 1893 the colonial authorities began a policy of expropriation of land, sparking anti-colonial peasant uprisings. As the cities underwent rapid growth, Eritreans of diverse social and ethnic backgrounds were drawn to urban centres in search of work. By the end of the colonial period Eritreans – especially Muslims, who had gained most from the expansion of health, education and other modern services – had begun to see their territory as distinct from Ethiopia. However, given the diversity of groups, it took more than half a century of collective oppression under colonial rule to produce a unified nationalist tradition.

In 1941 Eritrea came under British military occupation. In the post-war period it was ravaged by unemployment and inflation. Christian highlanders suffered most; those who migrated to cities for jobs found none, while those who stayed in the plateau watched as land was taken arbitrarily from them. Urban and rural Muslims were only mildly affected by the new regime. Indeed those in towns prospered to become the creditors of the Christian highlanders, creating disparities in their political evolution. One response saw the creation of a Christian separatist movement which aimed for the restoration of the ancient Tigray province, with its ancient capital Aksum. Muslim landlords from the northern highlands, to where Muslim nationalism can be traced, joined the unionist cause in search of allies to restore privileges. In 1942 the serfs rose against the landlords and refused to pay their annual tributes. Their demands were championed by merchant groups in Keren and Agrodat which traced ties to the various serf clans. This group led by Ibrahim Sultan Ali formed the Muslim League of Eritrea in 1946 and opposed union with Ethiopia.

The Unionist Party, supported largely by Christians, was the dominant party in the plateau and its urban centres. The Muslim League, concentrated in the lowlands and the northern highlands, sought to create an independent Eritrea stressing the need to defend Muslim rights. A 1948 referendum was polarized along these lines. In 1950 the UN General Assembly passed a resolution calling for Eritrean autonomy and legislative, executive and judicial authority over its own domestic affairs with all other matters falling under federal, Ethiopian jurisdiction. In September 1952, after a two-year interim period, Eritrea became a semi-autonomous self-governing territory in federation with Ethiopia.

Eritrea was to have its own government, Parliament, Prime Minister, national flag, police force and two official languages, Arabic and Tigrinya. The British had allowed political parties, a free press and trade unions. This stood in contrast to Ethiopia, where there were no political parties nor institutionalized representation of popular interests. Between 1952 and 1962 Addis Ababa gradually encroached on Eritrean rights, suspending the constitution, imposing Amharic as the language of government, education and business, outlawing political parties, packing the assembly with pliant supporters of the central government and finally incorporating Eritrea into its empire as a province like any other. Open rebellion by Muslim separatists broke out in western Eritrea in 1961. The systematic corrosion of Eritrean autonomy added fuel to the separatist movement. Eritrean politicians insisted that Eritrea presented a colonial not a secessionist problem. The demand for independence was on the grounds that Eritrea was a colony of Italy, transferred to British administration and illegally annexed by Ethiopia. The nationalist movement however exhibited the disunity of Eritrean people who had more in common with their neighbours than with each other. The religious and ethnic diversity of Eritrea led some of the nationalist forces to identify with the Arab and Muslim world.

The Eritrean Liberation Front (ELF), formed in 1960, drew its leadership from the Tegre- and Arabic-speaking Muslim clans of the coastal plain and its cities. Its main external source of support was the Ba'athist Syrian regime. During the 1960s Ethiopian military repression and enforced Amharization radicalized much of the politically aware Tigrinya-speaking youth. Having failed to obtain easy access to the ELF, some of them established the Eritrean People's Liberation Front (EPLF) in 1969. The immediate cause of the split was the ELF's portrayal of the Eritrean struggle in Islamic terms in order to secure assistance from the Arab world, thus effectively ostracizing the Christian populations of the highlands. The EPLF attempted to break down national divisions and include both Muslims and Christians by opting for a secular and Marxist-Leninist ideology. It began attracting the support of young Christians from urban centres and successfully challenged the older organization in a conflict which lasted from 1969 to 1974.

For a time after the revolution in Ethiopia in 1974 it seemed that the military government might be prepared to make concessions on Eritrean issues. The new Prime Minister (not a member of the Dergue, the ruling military council), General Aman Andom, was an Eritrean and favoured regional autonomy for Eritrea within the Ethiopian state. Just when the Ethiopian government was politically in a most favourable position to resolve the conflict, parochial elements within the Provisional Military Administrative Council (PMAC) launched a military offensive in February 1975. The brutality and indiscriminate anti-Eritrean terror campaigns in urban areas of Ethiopia and Eritrea threw tens of thousands of Eritrean youth into the folds of the two fronts. In 1981, the EPLF, supported by its Tigrayan ally, the Tigrayan People's Liberation Front (TPLF), drove the ELF out of Eritrea, with many members fleeing to refugee camps along the Sudanese border. Harassment and killings of ELF members in Sudan and Ethiopia have continued until the present.

In 1989 a shift occurred in the power balance due to the EPLF's defeat of the Dergue army at Afabet, the TPLF's capture of Mekelle, low morale of a largely conscript and increasingly teenage Ethiopian army, and an abortive military coup. Within two years the EPLF took control of Eritrea and the Ethiopian People's Revolutionary Democratic Front (EPRDF) entered Addis Ababa one day after Asmara fell to the EPLF. The EPLF formed a provisional administration and vowed to hold a referendum on Eritrea's future within two years, because of the problem of international recognition. Although Eritrea had fought militarily for its independence, recognition was bolstered by a referendum which received UN and international support. The Republic of Eritrea was declared on May 1993 following a 99.8 per cent vote in favour in the referendum.

Tegre

To the north and west of the Eritrean Plateau the land gradually diminishes into the broken hill region, known as the Rora. In this hot and arid region, Tegre peoples, who represent one-third of the country's population, are dominant. Culturally and ethnically, they are related to the Beja of Sudan. Claiming Arab origin, their language, Tegre, is Semitic. Mostly Muslim, their primary occupation is cattle herding. Most are nomadic, however, some have settled by rivers such as the Barka and on state cotton plantations.

Tegre is used to describe the people who speak Tegre and the language itself. It shared origins with Tigrinya but is now very different. Its use is declining under the impact of Tigrinya in Eritrea. Tegre means 'serf'. They were originally Muslim vassals of the Christian Bet Asgede. During the nineteenth century the Muslim rulers adopted the language of their subjects as well as their religion but kept them serfs. Tegre are made up of three groups, Habab, Ad Teklei and Ad Temaryam. They are all nomadic herdspeople except for Ad

Teklei who have settled in Keren. Other Tegre-speakers live between Mensa and Bilen (Bogos) on the Dahlak Islands and among the Beni Amer.

Afar (Danakils)

The highland mass narrows and falls abruptly into desert on its eastern and south-western sides. In the east, the depression is known as the coastal lowland, a northward extension of the Rift Valley. These lowlands are blisteringly hot, support no plant life and are inhabited by Afar. These Hamitic people are Muslim. They speak Afar and Arabic and are pastoral nomads. In the early 1970s these nomads suffered greatly from famine. In this arid semi-wilderness they had to use pasture over a wide area in order to support their herds. In previous times of drought, they had to move to other areas, which included the traditional regions of the Tcheffa Valley, and pastures along the inland delta of the Awash River. But during the 1960s the Tcheffa Valley became the location of commercial sorghum farms, and large cotton plantations were developed along the Awash. Not only were 20,000 Afar pastoralists displaced by irrigated land, but when drought hit they were unable to move to their traditional grazing lands. Their mobility has been restricted by the flow of weaponry to their nomadic competitors the Issas (ethnic Somalis) and clashes over wells. Afar leaders are highly critical of the EPLF, although they were in favour of the freedom enjoyed by Danakalia's Afar regional assembly, and Eritrea's promise to provide humanitarian and medical support to the Afar Front pour la Restauration de l'Unité et la Democratie (FRUD) in Djibouti. There are also fears that inter-ethnic conflict in Ethiopia could spread to Afar in south Eritrea as well as Djibouti.

Saho

Sandwiched between Afar and Tegre are Saho nomads and semi-nomads. Mostly Muslim, they have imported many social and cultural values from the plateau. Saho speak local languages but have also used Arabic in commercial dealings and have long been exposed to foreign influence in the form of trade with expanding empires. Much of the land taken for resettlement of the 500,000 refugees in Sudan is likely to be that used by these nomads.

Beni Amer

The western lowlands are strikingly similar to western Sudan. The northern part of the plains are hot and arid, with no vegetation, except along river banks. The southern part, known as the Gash-Setit Basin, supports a dense equatorial vegetation, rich soils and monsoon rains. The northern lowlands are inhabited by the Beni Amer branch of the Tegre tribes, who, like their cousins in the Rora, are related to the Beja of Sudan. They are Muslim and nomadic pastoralists. Prior to the introduction of mechanized farming, only Beni Amer and Sudanese pastoralists used the grazing land of the area between the Setit and Gash. From the 1950s, however, many new groups and their herds started to appear as their own traditional grazing lands disappeared. At present there are three nomadic, two semi-nomadic and four semi-sedentary groups using these resources for all or part of the year, especially during the dry season. Between 2–3,000 nomads, mostly Beni Amer from Northern Eritrea, bring 40–80,000 cattle annually into the area. Other cattle are brought by local elders and semi-sedentary groups, and wealthy farmers hire Beni Amer to look after them. It has become increasingly difficult for Beni Amer to find grazing because the area is now farmed and used by other herders. Beni Amer are also numerous among the 500,000 refugees awaiting return from Sudan.

Bilen

Both a region and an ethnic group, Bilen inhabit the most northerly district of Tigray, Bogos, divided from the rest of that province by the Mereb River. In earlier times Bilen were prey to slave and cattle raiders from Egyptian Sudan. Keren, their capital, was occupied by the Egyptians in 1872. The return of Bogos was guaranteed by the Adwa Treaty in 1884 but the Italians annexed it and retained control until after World War Two. The mostly agricultural people comprise two main tribes of about 15,000 each: Bet Teqwe and Gebre Terqe. They became Christians but adopted clothing in colours worn by Muslims as a form of defence and so not to be easily recognized. The Gebre Terqe were slower to become Islamicized because of efforts of Roman Catholic and Swedish evangelical missionaries. About a quarter of the Bilen population is Roman Catholic today.

Kunama and Baria

The southern part of the western lowlands, the Berentu area, is the dwelling place of the Kunama and Baria tribes which are of Nilotic origin like the inhabitants of western Ethiopia and southern

Sudan. The Baria were forcibly Islamicized, depriving them of the equality that had existed between the sexes. The Kunama remain matrilineal and approximately one-third are Christian. Tropical diseases and periodic slave raids from Sudan and Ethiopia have diminished the number and significance of this agricultural society of Baria and Kunama peoples. Baria is a derogatory word for people with 'Negroid' characteristics.

Conclusions and future prospects

The EPLF espoused a multi-party system with restrictions on religious- and ethnically-based organizations. These restrictions have already posed a problem in relation to Afar nationality. Initially provincial administrations were set up encouraging people to identify with their own regions and Afar, Kunama and Saho indicated strong support for this. However, in hindsight the government thought this likely to escalate ethnic tensions. The problem of building a functioning state from a guerrilla movement with little financial backing is severely testing President Aferwork Issayas's political skills. The main difficulty remains in feeding the population. Despite the mobilization of the military and peasantry, only 317,000 tonnes of food were produced in 1995 where an estimated 650,000 tonnes were needed. The land issue remains controversial. Eritrea had two land use systems, communal *diesa* in which land use rotates among villages, and the *tselmi* system of individual ownership with land divided among descendants and land owned by the government. New laws vest ownership of land in the government but grant usufructory rights, allowing the distribution of 'unowned' or state land. The return of refugees is critical. Eritrea would like their return, although concern exists over where and how they should be repatriated.

Further reading

Legum, C. and Firebrace, J., *Eritrea and Tigray*, London, MRG report, 1983.

Ehrlich, Haggai, *The Struggle Over Eritrea*, CA, Hoover Institution Press, 1983.

Minority-based and advocacy organizations

Regional Centre for Human Rights and Development, PO Box 222, Asmara, Eritrea; tel. 291 4 111 761, fax 291 4 111 221.

Ethiopia

Land area:	1,221,900 sq km
Population:	50.3 million (1992)
Main languages:	Amharic, Tigrinya, Oromigna
Main religions:	Ethiopian Orthodox Christianity, Islam, animism
Main minority groups:	Oromo 23 million (43%), Sidama 4.5 million (8%), Somalis 3.2 million (6%), Berta 3 million (6%), Afar 2.2 million (4%), Gurage 1.1 million (2%), Anuak 530,000 (1%), also Adare 30,000, Beta Israel 4,000
Real per capita GDP:	$420
UNDP HDI/rank:	0.237 (168)

Ethiopia is located in the north-eastern extension of Africa known as the Horn. It is bordered by Eritrea, Somalia, Djibouti, Kenya and Sudan. More than eighty languages are spoken with the greatest diversity found in the south-west. Amharic (a Semitic language), Oromo, Tigrinya and Somali are spoken by two-thirds of the population. Ethiopian Orthodox Christianity and Islam are each adhered to by about 40 per cent of the population. The remainder are Protestant, Roman Catholic or followers of traditional religions. A small group, Beta Israel, are Jewish. Historically the Semitic, Amhara and Tigray peoples of the northern highlands have dominated political life in the region.

From 1941 to 1974, Emperor Haile Selassie strove to erase the identities of non-Amhara nations and nationalities in the name of Ethiopian unity. Amharic and Amhara culture became the essential attributes of being Ethiopian. As a result, peoples of the south in particular suffered comprehensive domination – economically, politically and culturally. The military dictatorship from 1974–91 sought to maintain the imperial state and to modernize and secularize the country by first breaking down the social and economic power of the church and landed aristocracy. But the breakdown of authority and erosion of the social institutions on which it had rested encouraged the proliferation of regional nationalism directed against the central government in Addis Ababa. The Dergue sought to purge all members suspected of harbouring ethnic loyalties, mainly Eritreans. It recognized the right of all nationalities to a form of self-determination, defined not as a right to secession but as regional autonomy. The Somali invasion put an end to this tendency. However, after the Ogaden War in 1978, Colonel Mengistu, leader of the Dergue, exploited clan differences between the two largest dissident pastoral communities, Somalis and Afars. A third, smaller group, the Boran in Sidamo, were driven into the arms of the Dergue by opposition to Somali expansion. The largest ethnic group, the Oromo, also failed to create an effective national movement despite a history of ethnically-based rebellion and the existence of the Oromo Liberation Front (OLF). Other local peoples of the south such as Gurage and Sidama, also want to create separate states, but the complicated patterns of residence would make the drawing of boundaries an insoluble problem.

Oromo

Oromo are the largest ethnic minority group in Ethiopia, and are speakers of Oromo languages (Oromigna, Oromiffa, 'Galla'). They are predominant in southern, south-eastern and south-western Ethiopia but also live in the highland areas. There are also Oromo refugees in Djibouti, Kenya, Somalia and Sudan. Historically, Oromo are the group which has most reason to view the Amhara as arrogant and exploitative colonial conquerors. This is due in part to the fact that Oromo are the most numerous group in Ethiopia and live in every region except Gondar. They are diverse in terms of their culture, social organization and religion, although most retain some features of their unique and complex generation-grading system, *gada*. In some areas they are too assimilated with the Amhara to be easily organized into a disciplined national opposition. From the nineteenth century until the 1987 Ethiopian constitution, it was clear that Oromo would continue to be entirely subordinated to central control and direction. Besides, the Ethiopian Orthodox Church also received land grants to encourage proselytization of the largely pagan and Muslim population. Between the mid-nineteenth and early twentieth centuries Oromo lost between two-thirds and three-quarters of their land.

After Haile Selassie was restored by the British in 1941, tenancy was reintroduced and continued up to 1974, despite periodic protests from Oromo. In 1973 this discontent resulted in the formation of the OLF. Many Oromo suffered greatly in the famine of 1973–4, especially in Wollo province, along with Tigrayans and Afars. One quarter of a million people died before the government acknowledged the disastrous situation. The new regime under the Dergue ended the tenancy system but enforced collectivization and resettlement came in its wake. In Oromo lands, 95 per cent of ex-landlords were Amhara. They also controlled the police force and bureaucracy. Between March 1975 and April 1976 violent clashes took place as they took revenge on Oromo peasants for the loss of their land under tenure reorganization. By 1978 the OLF reported that 80,000 Oromo peasants had been killed by armed Amhara in Haraghe. The Dergue's policy of villagization began in the province of Haraghe where there was much OLF activity and Oromo were charged with collaboration with the Somali Liberation Front in the Ogaden War. By February 1986, 3 million people had been moved into centralized villages, facilitating political control over the region. Oromo faced heavy taxation, forced labour on state farms and abduction into the armed services. They were discriminated against in education and only small numbers held skilled or professional jobs. Civilians were also subjected to armed aggression. The effects of the famine in 1984 were exacerbated by military conscription of males and because little aid reached the eastern Oromo region.

Historically Oromo have never formed a single state but were organized in small societies of clans and villages. There are four main groups: western Oromo, mainly in 'Wollegha', many of whom have been Christianized by missionary churches; northern Oromo, of Mecha-Tulam, modern Shoa and the area to the south, who are more integrated into Amhara culture than other Oromo groups, are mostly Christians of the Ethiopian Orthodox Church and speak Amharic; southern Oromo, who often have semi-nomadic lifestyles and are not incorporated into any larger regional or religious unit; and Borana, believed by some to be the seminal branch of the Oromo because of their rigid observance of the *gada* social system, and who live in an arid area of Ethiopia along the border with Kenya. Eastern Oromo of Haraghe include the Muslim population of Harar and Dire Dawa, among others. This group has strong links to the Arab world and its local leaders have a strong Muslim orientation. The term Oromia, signifying an independent Oromo state, is important to the Oromo and the OLF, allowing them to consolidate their various regional and related groups into one Oromo nation.

In the second half of the 1980s, the TPLF's new leadership tried to widen support for its organization by recruiting members from among the different peoples of Ethiopia. The Ethiopian People's Revolutionary Democratic Front (EPRDF) was formed in January 1989 and an Oromo journal claims it set out to gain new recruits from captured Oromo conscripts who had been forced into the Dergue's army, to create the Oromo People's Democratic Organization(OPDO). Most of the Oromo abroad and the intellectual leadership were pro-OLF. The extension of EPRDF control over Oromo territory during operations against the Ethiopian army in spring 1991 induced a negative response from the OLF who feared a new colonization of Oromo land. Oromo continue to feel insecure in Ethiopia, a political state torn between ethnically-based protective responses and the ideology of collective nation-building.

Sidama

There are eight distinct groups of Sidama people living in parts of Shoa and Sidamo-Borana provinces. They speak Cushitic and have an *ensete* (false banana) planting culture. Before Oromo migration, Sidama inhabited almost the whole of southern Ethiopia. Oromo used the term, *sidama*, meaning 'foreigner', and one of the eight groups retains that name. An interchange of Sidama and Oromo institutions took place during the seventeenth and eighteenth centuries. Consequently, some are animist, others Christian or Muslim. By 1891 Sidama people had been incorporated into the empire.

Somalis

Somali populate the Ogaden area. The Somali irridentist movement in Ogaden peaked during the 1970s and declined after the defeat of Somali incursions. Disintegration of the state in Somalia in the late 1980s and early 1990s led to the few remaining Somali organizations in Ogaden rejecting irredentism and reorienting themselves towards Ethiopian political life. However, Somali and other Muslim organizations have limited influence and the Ogaden National Liberation Front is pushing for rights of self-determination and possible secession.

Berta ('Shankella', Beni Shangul)

Berta regard themselves as descended from a single family whom they trace back to 1720. Islam was established among them by 1855. They were conquered in 1897–8 by imperial forces while their leader, Shaikh Khojali, preserved their autonomy by regular tribute of alluvial gold. Emperor Menelik II granted a gold mining concession in 1899 to an English company but stipulated they were not to interfere with local gold working. They and other Nilotic peoples have been labelled perjoratively as 'Shankella', although this was officially discouraged by Haile Selassie. Many Berta were brought to the capital as slaves. Slave trading was a business which the Shaikh Khojali family conducted with Sudan-based traders as well as Ethiopians. Berta were much desired as slaves by raiders on both sides of the Sudan–Ethiopian border.

Afar (see **Djibouti, Eritrea**)

Afar have been most affected by the creation of an independent Eritrea. At the time of its inception, the Afar Liberation Front (ALF) leader, Ali Mirah Anfere, declared that the ALF's goal would be to establish an independent Islamic state for Afars. Its boundaries were to be decided on the basis of Afar ethnic habitation, including the Awash River Basin and neighbouring territories and the southern part of Eritrea. Mengistu's creation of an autonomous province of Assab did nothing to settle the Afar issue, since the most fertile land in the Awash Valley remained in Amhara control. The ALF has an uneasy relationship with the EPRDF. The latter organized a seminar of the Afar Democratic Union in 1990 suggesting it was trying to build an alternative to the ALF. A substantial part of Afar reluctance to accept an independent Eritrea is a result of their unwillingness to see their people divided by state boundaries.

Gurage

There are 14 to 16 groups in the Gurage cluster. The western group formed a political federation in the mid-nineteenth century consisting of seven clans inhabiting an area around Lake Zway in Shoa. They are *ensete* cultivators like their neighbours in Sidamo. Some claim descent from a Tigrayan noble who came to conquer them in the fourteenth century. Eastern Gurage (Soddo) trace their origins to the Harar area from which they fled during the sixteenth century invasion of Ahmad ibn Ibrahim. An attempt at unifying the western Gurage under one leader was allegedly made by a Christian commander who came to relieve them of Oromo raids. Emperor Menelik II incorporated both eastern and western Gurage into the empire by 1889. Gurage men weave and market cloth. Certain subcastes tan hides or smelt iron. Pottery is the woman's craft. Gurage women continue to be excluded from land ownership. The Soddo Gurage reportedly follow the Christian custom of circumcising both boys and girls in infancy, while the western group are said to circumcise both boys and girls (clitoridectomy) at age of eight and ten respectively. Christian, Muslim and traditional Gurage belief in the god Waq, coexist to varying degreees depending on the area. In the country and in cities Gurage are adept at forming self-help societies and are active traders.

Anuak

Associated with Sudanic penetration of a vaguely defined 'Ethiopia', these people date from the first millennium BCE with a culture preoccupied with cattle raiding and millet growing. Anuak are hunters, agriculturists and fishers living in the fertile Gambela forest region of south-western Ethiopia. At the end of 1979 their land was seized by the government and there were attempts to draft them into the army and into forced labour on collective farms. Many Anuak fled into the bush in an attempt to reach Sudan and were shot and imprisoned. Their numbers have halved from a generation ago and they have been displaced from their traditional lands as northerners resettled in the area.

Adare (Harar)

The Oromo and Amhara residents of greater Harar call the inner-city residents Adare. There are about 30,000 in the old city, with a distinct language and culture. Adare are distinguished for being the only people in Ethiopia to have developed a tradition centring on a single large urban centre. In their own language the term for Adare is Gefu, literally, person of the city. Adare is also the language spoken in Harar and is written in Arabic characters. Harar is the premier Muslim city of Ethiopia. An overlapping social network is divided into kinship networks, groups and neighbours. The latter concerns itself with the expenses of weddings and funerals in a cooperative way. A school was established in 1972 to counter the central government effort to spread the Amharic language and restrict Islamic religious instruction. In 1975 the Dergue imposed a *kebelle* system of local government, as the neighbourhood groups refused to be politicized.

Beta Israel

Also known as Ethiopian Jews, and until recently by the derogatory name Falasha (meaning stranger or exile in Ge'ez), at their peak in the seventeenth century there were over 1 million Beta Israel. Before mass migration to Israel in the 1980s they numbered approximately 30,000 and lived in Gondar province and the Simien Mountains in northern Ethiopia.

The Beta Israel perceive themselves to be Jewish, living a traditional form of life evolving from at least the fourteenth century, although some suggest that their origins are more ancient. Their ancestors were deprived of the right to hold land as a result of the north-west expansion of the core Abyssinian state. Beta Israel consider contact with Christians to be ritually impure, and this reinforced the self identity of Beta Israel and allowed them to continue their religious and social life in the face of pressure to convert, while being excluded from positions of authority within the state. Their basic tenets are those of Judaism.

Most Ethiopian Jews lived in small rural communities in Gondar and Tigre provinces, where they suffered from prejudice at the hands of neighbouring peoples. The Ethiopian Orthodox Church opposed the development of Jewish schools. After World War Two, they continued to face discrimination and suffer evictions, extortionate taxes and rents, and attacks on cemeteries. After the revolution of 1974, in theory the position of Beta Israel was improving because of the land reform. But Jews were often given inferior land and their freedom to travel was restricted. Beta Israel had much to gain from the land reforms and were made the target of the counter-revolutionary Ethiopian Democratic Union, composed of the old nobility and landlords in Gondar. During 1977–9 they were forced to flee remote villages and move to areas of greater concentration. They were also attacked by the Ethiopian Peoples Revolutionary Party for alleged Zionist tendencies. Substantial numbers of Jews were among the thousands tortured, imprisoned, and massacred in the 1978 'Red Terror' campaigns waged by the Dergue. In March 1984, at the height of the famine in northern Ethiopia, thousands of Beta Israel began to move to Sudan by foot. Several thousand lost their lives in transit, children were orphaned and separated from their parents, and disease and malnutrition were rife in the refugee camps. At the end of 1984 Operation Moses brought many more to Israel, and others left in 1991 in Operation Solomon.

Conclusions and future prospects

The government of Ethiopia faces twin problems of ethnic identity and state control. After 1991, EPRDF government forces took control in all the rural areas, with few exceptions, putting EPRDF parties in positions of administrative power. Initially offering cooperation with the other liberation movements, the issues of nationality and landownership remain contested and gradually groups other than the TPLF were eased out of the transitional government. There is considerable opposition to EPRDF policies. The government has used administrative techniques as a weapon of regulation and discipline. In the 1992 elections the EPRDF controlled the electoral commission and allegedly prevented the registration of opposition candidates.

Ethnic tensions have been heightened by government restrictions on political competition. Multiparty elections were held in 1995 under a new constitution which permits the secession of ethnically-based regions from the federation in theory, but fails to protect minorities and ethnic groups dwelling outside of their own administrative regions. After the elections of May 1995 the EPRDF controlled 548 seats in the Council of Representatives and seven regional state councils either directly or through EPRDF-sponsored parties. In three out of ten regions where a genuinely ethnically-based opposition exists, elections were postponed for security reasons. The constitution is based on the notion that Ethiopia can be divided into nine regions and nationalities, each with its own region and each (except multi-ethnic Addis Ababa) sending representatives to the federal council whose main function is to oversee 'equality' in these regions. Yet the new regions do not correspond to territory inhabited by distinct ethnic groups. Moreover, the government is generally seen as being run by Tigrayans. The security forces remain predominantly Tigrayan and a prohibition on the dissemination of 'false information' is used to detain journalists and publishers.

Afar, Oromo, Sidama and Somalis support secessionism, while the All Amhara People's Organization and other groups are against the break-up of the nation state. Many Ethiopians dislike the idea of splitting the country along ethnic lines. Political apathy pervades and in such a vacuum the country is witnessing a revival of religion and intense rivalry between the Ethiopian Orthodox and the Pentecostal churches. Mass migration is swelling the numbers of urban unemployed and poor. In the climate of economic insecurity the government has disabled the trade union movement. Structural adjustment policies demanded by Western financiers are contributing to rising prices and rents and are allegedly being used to remove opposition. There has been a rapid proliferation of private companies in transportation, distribution and construction with close links to the EPRDF. With the lifting of taxes between Tigray and Eritrea it is alleged that Tigrayan merchants are obtaining goods tax free and are pushing traditional merchant groups out of business. There is increasing concern over human rights violations. The government has been detaining and jailing activists from both pro- and anti-secessionist movements and the army is still seen as an occupying force in many areas. When the EPRDF entered Addis Ababa in 1991, 3,000 party members and higher officials were detained. They are to be tried by a special prosecutor under a legal process based on the Nuremberg trials.

Further reading

Prout, C. and Rosenfeld E., *Historical Dictionary of Ethiopia and Eritrea*, Metuchen, NJ, Scarecrow Press, 1994.

Lefort, R., *Ethiopia: An Heretical Revolution?*, London, Zed Press, 1983.

Amnesty International, *Ethiopia: End of an Era of Brutal Depression and a New Chance for Human Rights*, London, 1992.

Kessler, D. and Parfitt, T., *The Falashas*, MRG report, London, 1985.

Quirin, J., *The Evolution of the Ethiopian Jews*, Philadelphia, University of Pennsylvania Press, 1992.

Minority-based and advocacy organizations

African Commission of Human and Peoples' Rights, c/o Organization of African Unity, PO Box 3243, Addis Ababa, Ethiopia; tel. 251 1 517 700.

Ethiopian Human Rights Council, PO Box 2432, Addis Ababa, Ethiopia; tel. 251 1 514 489, fax 251 1 514 539.

Institute of Development Research, University of Addis Ababa, PO Box 1176, Addis Ababa, Ethiopia; tel. 251 1 123 230, fax 251 1 551 333.

Inter-Africa Group, PO Box 1631, Addis Ababa, Ethiopia; tel. 251 1 518 790, fax 251 1 517 554.

Gambia

Land area:	11,295 sq km
Population:	1.2 million (1992)
Main languages:	English (official), Manding (Malinké) and other indigenous languages
Main religions:	Islam, Christianity
Main minority groups:	Fula (Fulani, Fulbe, Peul) 153,000 (13%), Wolof 138,000 (12%), Dioula (Jola) 80,000 (7%), Serahuli 75,000 (6%), Aku 40,000 (3.5%)
Real per capita GDP:	$1,190
UNDP HDI/rank:	0.292 (162)

The Republic of Gambia is situated in the far west of the African continent, bordered by Senegal on three sides. The country extends roughly 10 kilometres on each bank of the Gambia River. The boundaries of Gambia are artificial, they result only from a long history of conflict among European colonial powers which almost ended with its disappearance. These boundaries prevent Gambia from having free access to its hinterland and separate the Gambian Wolof, Jola, Mandinka, and Fula people from their kin in Senegal. The peoples of Gambia comprise two major linguistic groups. Dominant Mandinka agriculturists and Seranuleh traders speak West Atlantic languages. Manding-speakers include the pastoralist Fula as well as Wolof and Dioula cultivators. Although each people has its own language, Mandinka serves as a *lingua franca*, while English is the official language. Gambia became an independent state within the Commonwealth in 1965 and a republic in 1970. Mandinka have dominated the People's Progressive Party and Gambian electoral politics since the election prior to independence. However, the recent census suggests that Gambian minorities have begun to weaken the Mandinka's hegemony.

Fula (Fulani, Fulbe, Peul)

A pastoral people from the Upper Senegal River region, Fula speak a variant of the Niger-Kordofanian language family. They were the dominant group in the ancient kingdom of Tekrur until its overthrow in the eleventh century. Fula then created a series of smaller states from the western segment of that kingdom where they continued to rule until the Tuculour majority seized power and established a strict Muslim rule. Between the thirteenth and eighteenth centuries a large number of Fula were involved in a series of long and complicated migrations. They were present in large numbers in the Upper Gambia region in the nineteenth century and took part in several rebellions against Mandinka overlords.

Wolof

Wolof in Gambia mainly inhabit upper and lower Saloum districts, Banjul, and the northern sections of Niani, Sami, Niumi and Jokadu. The Wolof language is part of the northern subgroup of the Niger-Kordofanian family and is a commercial language spoken beyond the boundaries of Senegal and Gambia. Wolof social organization is extremely complex based upon a tripartite division of society into freeborn, low-caste people and slaves. Although many contemporary Wolof are involved in trading and urban life, the majority are agriculturists and live in villages. Historically Wolof in the area of the Gambia Protectorate had not established strong central polities before the Soninke–Marabout wars of the nineteenth century and were politically subordinate to Mandinka or Serer overlords.

Dioula

While Dioula comprise only 7 per cent of Gambia's population, they are very close to the more numerous Dioula of Senegal's Casamance region. Casamance was historically part of the Gambia River complex before being arbitrarily separated from Gambia in 1889. Today, a majority reside in the Foni areas south of Bintang Bolon. It is likely that Dioula are among the longest-residing people in the Gambia region. Their political and social organization has traditionally been village-oriented. It was reported in the eighteenth century that although Dioula paid tribute to Mandinka, they had not been completely subjugated and continued to exercise great freedom. It is possible that the Dioula of Gambia support the Dioula-led separatist movement of the Casamance region of Senegal.

Serahuli

Serahuli form the largest group in the extreme Upper River region of Gambia, inhabiting part of the area which once was the ancient kingdom of Wuli. They are a mixture of Mandinka, Berber and Fula. Primarily farmers, they are hampered by the poor soil in the area. Until the end of the 1950s Serahuli experienced seasonal shortfalls in food.

Aku

Aku are the descendants of Africans (mainly Yoruba) in transit as slaves to the Americas who were liberated, mostly by warships or the British West Africa Patrol. They were called 'recaptives' because they were taken twice. In the 1820s and 1830s they found their way to Gambia and became a nucleus of a Westernized population in Banjul. In the late nineteenth and early twentieth centuries Aku came to exercise an influence in Gambia disproportionate to their number. Adopting Western lifestyles, they accepted Christianity and educated their children in Sierra Leone and the UK. Aku became successful traders, entered the civil service and in the period between 1945 and independence came to dominate many important government positions in Gambia.

Conclusions and future prospects

In 1994 a military coup overthrew Sir Dawda Jawara who had been in power for 29 of Gambia's 30 years of independence. The Armed Forces Provisional Ruling Council (AFPRC) took power, led by Yahya Jammeh, a Dioula. In the aftermath of the coup, several governments, including Britain, issued warnings for tourists to stay away from Gambia. Since between 50 and 60 per cent of tourists were British, hotel closures were inevitable. Within weeks, the economy was in such a precarious position that in December 1994 the military government revised the 1994–5 budget downwards by 23 per cent, leaving much less to spend on health, education and other government business. An estimated 20 per cent of the paid labour force was made redundant. Civilian governments in the region (all Francophone, except for Ghana, whose government has strong military roots) fear a spillover due to what they see as a chain of unstable Anglophile military governments in Liberia, Nigeria, Sierra Leone and now Gambia, along the West African coast.

Further reading

Gailey, H.A., *Historical Dictionary of the Gambia*, Metuchen, NJ, Scarecrow Press, 1987.

Bowman, J., *Ominous Transition: Commerce and Colonial Expansion in the Senegambia and Guinea, 1857–1919*, Aldershot, Avebury, 1996.

Minority-based and advocacy organizations

African Centre for Democracy and Human Rights, Kairaba Avenue, Komo Street, Mary Division, Banjul, Gambia; tel. 220 394 525.

African Commission on Human Rights and Peoples' Rights, Kairaba Avenue, PO Box 673, Banjul, Gambia; tel. 220 392 962, fax. 220 390 764.

Ghana

Land area:	228,533 sq km
Population:	16 million (1992)
Main languages:	English (official), Akan and other indigenous languages
Main religions:	Christianity, animism, Islam
Main minority groups:	Ewe 1 million (6%), Konkomba 250,000 (1.5%)
Real per capita GDP:	$2,000
UNDP HDI/rank:	0.467 (129)

Migrants from the ancient kingdom of Ghana to the north-west may have settled in present-day Ghana although the two should not be confused. Between 1500 and 1870 an estimated 10 million slaves left Africa, about 19 per cent of them from the Gold Coast. The British, who from 1660 were the chief competitors of the Dutch, greatly increased their involvement in the Gold Coast between 1850 and 1874, by which time they had practically broken the authority of the traditional African rulers.

Ghana is located on the Gulf of Guinea in West Africa and is bordered by three Francophone nations: Côte d'Ivoire, Burkina Faso and Togo. Its population is composed of over fifty distinct groups. While most are from Akan, Ewe, Ga and Mole-Dagbai backgrounds, Ghana has attracted migrants from all of West Africa such that almost every West African group is present in its heterogeneous population including Fula, Hausa, Igbo, Mande, Mossi, Songhai and Yoruba. About 21 per cent of the population maintains traditional animistic beliefs. Christianity is the religion of about half of the population. About 16 per cent of Ghanaians are Muslim.

Ghana became independent within the Commonwealth in 1957. It was created from the British Gold Coast Colony, Asante, the Northern Territories Protectorate and the UN Trust Territory of Togo. Since the overthrow of the country's first President, Kwame Nkrumah, in 1966, Ghana has experienced long periods of military rule interspersed with short-lived civilian governments. The Ashanti, part of the majority Akan tribe, wanted to carve up the country into a federation which would enable them to regain control over cocoa, timber and gold from the coastal Ewe, Fanti and Ga politicians who controlled much of the economy.

Ghana has recently experienced an upsurge of regionalist, ethnic and other exclusivist sentiments which have accompanied a restructuring of local government into 110 district assemblies. These have become the focus of ethnic power struggles, especially over the issue of paramount chiefs. Towns have competed to be the headquarters of these new assemblies and the Provisional National Defence Council (PNDC) has upgraded a significant number of chieftains in the new districts to the status of paramount chiefs. Chieftancy power was traditionally chauvinist, rooted in ethnic particularity and is strongly patriarchal. The government has interfered in chieftancy matters in a *rapprochement* with those groups and institutions whose power it had previously threatened. Chiefs now enjoy an influence unrivalled since the colonial era. However some groups, such as the Konkomba, have been traditionally excluded from the paramount chieftancy system and land ownership, and their petitioning for the elevation of some of their chiefs to paramount status has been seen by other ethnic groups as a back-door move towards land ownership.There is currently fighting between areas that have chieftancy and those that do not.

Ewe

Eweland is an area between the Mon river in Togo and the Otla, Eastern Volta region in Ghana. From 1885 to 1914 it was divided between British and German rule. During World War One, most Ewe were under British rule in the form of a League of Nations mandate. In the aftermath, the eastern region of Eweland became part of French-ruled Togo, while the rest was administered by Britain either as a mandate or as part of the Gold Coast. In a 1956 plebiscite undertaken in the British mandate territory, the majority cast in favour of joining Ghana. At the same time, many Ewe still desire to form a union with the Ewe in Togo as a separate nation. Periodic efforts have been made by the Ewe towards self-determination in some instances pushing for secession.

Ewe are also found in Benin and southern Togo as well as in south-west Ghana. They speak various dialects of Ewe which belong to the Kwa family of Niger-Congo dialects. Traditionally their government was a configuration of many small kingdoms governed by a council of chiefs and was less complex and powerful than that of the Fon to whom the Ewe are related. Ewe are subsistence farmers, craftspeople and traders. Fishing in coastal waters is important. Descent is patrilineal, and the largest kinship unit is the patrilineage. Displacement of Ewe who straddle the Togo–Ghana border in 1991–92 as the result of conflict with Kabrye in Togo led to an influx of refugees in Ghana. At the same time large numbers of refugees from the Liberian civil war were also entering Ghana. Though a minority in terms of numbers, Ewe are well represented in positions of power in Ghana.

Konkomba

Kokomba have been marginalized in Ghana by virtue of not having paramount chieftancy (*nas*) but religious leaders (*tendamas*). The *tendamas* have no formal political power or land rights. However, Dagomba, Gonja and Nanumba have their own long established chieftancy system and claim suzerainty over the Konkomba. Fundamental disagreement over issues of land and political representation have led to bloody clashes between Konkomba, Nanumba and their Dagomba allies. Gonja support Namumba and Dagomba, while neighbouring groups with a similar religious-based organization such as Basare, Nawuri and Nchumuru, side with Konkomba. Nanumba, Dagomba and Gonja claim Konkomba as their subjects, that is, strangers who settled in their land and have paid tribute such as brides, free labour, crops and livestock for centuries. Konkomba say they were regarded as 'subjects' only because Dagomba and their allies occupied ancestral Konkomba land. Konkomba claim to be indigenous to north-east Ghana and north-west Togo, a claim supported by historians and anthropologists. Dagomba royal history says Yendi, the seat of the Ya-Na (president of Dagomba Traditional Council) was a Konkomba town when they captured it. When tracing their ancestry, Konkomba invariably say they came from a hole in the ground while the Nanumba, Dagomba and Gonja find their forebears among the cavalry-led groups who plundered their way south from what is now northern Burkina Faso.

Having no paramount chiefs means Konkomba have limited political power and land rights. They are not represented in the Northern Region House of Chiefs which is a major political institution taking key decisions in development and distribution of government largesse. National institutions recruit from the chiefs and northern government members are from Nanumba, Dagomba and Mamprosi. Konkomba, however, feel that they are being unjustly excluded from having a chieftancy title. They felt aggrieved that the National Democratic Congress (NDC), which they had backed in 1992, failed to respond favourably to their request. The last few years have seen a severe rise in the number of casualties suffered as a result of violent conflict between Konkomba, Nanumba and Dagomba. The Konkomba Youth Association has asked the UN to intervene over the question of paramount chieftancy, which they believe would significantly enfranchize the population.

Conclusions and future prospects

The political climate under the regime of Jerry Rawlings since 1992 is one of insecurity and economic uncertainty. As the promise of austerity measures remains unfulfilled, various groups throughout the country continue to hope for just resource redistribution. Some remain faithful to Rawlings, while others seek alternatives. Rawlings won 90 per cent of the vote in the Volta region; his opponent won 70 per cent in Ashanti. Ashantis believe the current regime to be controlled by Rawlings's minority, the Ewe, who hold key military posts. Exhibiting this frustration, the biggest anti-government protest since independence was held in Accra on 11 May 1995.

Further reading

Amnesty International, *Ghana: Political Imprisonment and the Death Penalty*, London, 1992.

Sarris, A., *Ghana under Structural Adjustment*, New York, New York University Press, 1991.

Tait, D., *The Konkombas of Northern Ghana*, Oxford, Oxford University Press, 1961.

Minority-based and advocacy organizations

African Bar Association, PO Box 3451, 29 La Tebu Street, East Cantonments, Accra, Ghana.

Amnesty International, PO Box 1173, Koforidua ER, Ghana; tel. 233 81 22685, fax 233 81 22685.

Christian Council of Ghana, PO Box 919, Accra, Ghana.

Guinea

Land area:	245,957 sq km
Population:	7.3 million (1993)
Main languages:	French (official), Fulani and other indigenous languages
Main religions:	Islam
Main minority groups:	Kissi 400,000 (5.5%), Kpelle 370,000 (5%), Bassari 130,000 (1.8%), Badiaranke 75,000 (1%), Loma 70,000 (1%), Diakhanke 68,000 (1%), Conagui 40,000 (0.5%)
Real per capita GDP:	$1,800
UNDP HDI/rank:	0.306 (160)

Guinea is a small state on the Atlantic Coast of West Africa bordered by Sierra Leone, Liberia, Senegal, Guinea-Bissau and Mali. The name Guinea possibly originates from a Portuguese corruption of the Berber, Akal n Iguinawen 'land of the black people'. As present boundaries were determined by colonial powers with little regard to existing ethnic or linguistic groups, the people of the region are often divided by state boundaries. As to the country itself, its four major geographical regions largely correspond to four major ethno-linguistic groups. In the Fouta-Djallon Mountain Plateau live Fula cattle herders who constitute 35 per cent of the population. There is some tension between them and smaller groups like Bassari, Badiaranke, Conagui, Diakhanke and Susu, who were historically oppressed by the Fula. Susu (20 per cent of the population) live along the coast near Conackry and on the nearby plain. Malinké of the Niger plains constitute about 30 per cent of the population. Smaller groups like Kissi, Kpelle and Loma live mostly in the forested Guinea highlands.

A powerful Fula Muslim state dominated the region before being dislodged by French rule. After much local resistance, the area of Guinea was incorporated into French West Africa in 1895. Under the leadership of Sékou Touré, a trade union leader and ardent nationalist, Guinea became the only West African state to reject colonial association with France in a 1958 referendum. Initially isolated by a vengeful France, Guinea pressed for the independence of all African states and for radical socioeconomic change in Guinea. Many of the earliest political groups in Guinea were ethnically- or regionally-based. Touré, a Malinké, succeeded in overcoming the dominance of this trend, creating a strong sense of Guinean. Under Touré, one party domination quickly became one-man rule, as an oligarchy of the political elite struggled for power within the confines of an increasingly autocratic state.

Over the course of the Touré period, various ethnic groups were targeted by the government, for anti-social and related activities.

When Touré died in 1984 the Guinean military seized power. It released political prisoners and reopened Guinea to private trade and capital. Yet continued inter-ethnic conflict among the leadership, particularly in the military, has destabilized the country. Opponents of the current regime have been executed following secret trials. After popular protest, political parties have been legal since 1992 in the slow process back to constitutional rule. The country is now in an ambiguous state as the recently elected former military President Lansoma Conte has rejected opposition demands for pluralism after winning a disputed multi-party election in 1993.

Since the death of Touré, formerly displaced and migrant populations have returned to Guinea from neighbouring states in significant numbers.

Smaller minorities

Kissi are a rice growing ethnic group in the Guekedou and Kissidougou areas of the Forest region. Other Kissi live just inside the borders of Sierra Leone and Liberia. Culturally and linguistically, Kissi are unrelated to the dominant Mande-speaking population in the north, and have therefore been neglected in the political and economic life of present-day Guinea.

Kpelle is the term used by the ethnic group of the Forest region to designate themselves. In French, they are referred to as Guerze. In Guinea this group is mainly concentrated in the Nzerekore administrative district. They are linguistically most closely related to the Mende of Sierra Leone and thus represent an ancient intrusion of more northern people into the rainforest area of the south-west.

Bassari are one of the least Europeanized or Islamicized ethnic groups in Guinea (see **Senegal**). Historically among the oldest inhabitants of Guinea, Bassari preserve their matrilineal organization, religion and way of life in the rugged areas of the Futa Djallon close to the Guinea-Bissau and Senegal borders.

Badiaranke are an ethnic group closely related to the Conaigui and Bassari living on the Senegal–Guinea border. Beekeepers and farmers, they were once also renowned for cotton weaving. Only assimilated into national life relatively recently, they have maintained a larger degree of cultural and religious autonomy than most of Guinea's ethnic groups.

Loma are concentrated to the east of the Kissi in the Macenta administrative region. Unrelated to their Kissi neighbours, they represent an early incursion of savanna peoples into the forest zone about 500 years ago. In Guinea, they are gradually being assimilated into the larger Malinké populations.

The Diakhanke Mande population of the south and central part of the Futa Djallon inhabited the Futa before the Fula state was established in the eighteenth century. Some accepted Islam and stayed on as allies of the Fula while others fled to the south and east.

Conagui share the area around Koundara in the northern part of Middle Guinea and over into Guinea-Bissau with a host of other small ethnic groups. Together with Bassari they were once fairly widespread. Having been subject to slave raids by the dominant Malinké and Fula, they took refuge in the hills of north-central Guinea as their numbers dwindled.

Conclusions and future prospects

Rising tensions have been hard to contain in Guinea. Constitutional restrictions on civil and political rights have been used by the government in view of the national 'crisis'. Malinké are concerned that a national inquest into the Touré years would be used as an ethnic witch hunt. Under Conte (a Susu), Malinké officers have been rounded up and executed but most Fula and Susu officers were released unharmed.

Guinea is marked by high levels of political conflict fuelled by ethnic and regional diversity. Opposition forces have been nurtured by the deterioration of living conditions partly due to International Monetary Fund conditionalities. Guinea is also going through a period of tremendous social change which continues to affect the lifestyles of various groups throughout the country. For a predominantly Muslim country, the condition of women is relatively emancipated. Internal forces in Guinea have also been magnified by external factors. The Liberian and Sierra Leonean civil wars have increased the migration of poor populations towards the forest region while other towns have growing shanties of rural and urban migrants. Potentially one of the richest countries in the subregion, its agricultural and mineral resources make it a valuable target for an ambitious rebel movement from Liberia. Charles Taylor's National Patriotic Front of Liberia has been deriving an income from Migergui iron ore mine on the Guinea–Liberian border in the Nimba Mountains.

Guinea-Bissau

Land area:	36,000 sq km
Population:	1 million (1992)
Main languages:	Portuguese (official), Crioulu
Main religions:	animism, Islam
Main minority groups:	Fula 250,000 (24%), Mandyako 151,000 (14.5%), Malinké 135,000 (13%), Papel 100,000 (10%), Dioula 53,000 (5%), Susu 50,000 (5%), Felupe 32,000 (3%), Cape Verdean 10,000 (1%)
Real per capita GDP:	$860
UNDP HDI/rank:	0.297 (161)

Guinea-Bissau is a small West African country which includes numerous tiny offshore islands located off the Atlantic Coast between Senegal and Guinea. One of the world's poorest countries, it waged a long war against Portuguese colonialism that contributed to the fall of the Portuguese African empire. Major groups of the predominant black African community include Balante, Fula, Malinké, Mandyako and Papel. Although small in numbers, Creole (people of mixed African–European decent) from nearby Cape Verde are among the most educated of the country and hold many senior government posts. Cape Verdeans organized a nationalist movement to struggle against the colonial power. While the Portuguese received Fula and Malinké support, the movement also drew support from assimilated black Africans and from many Balanté. Tension continues between Cape Verdeans and black Africans based on historical roles and the relative socio-economic advantages enjoyed by Cape Verdeans. The official language is Portuguese. Crioulu, a Creole dialect of Portuguese, is spoken by most people.

Guinea-Bissau was a major centre of the slave trade. Until 1879, the region was controlled from Cape Verde, 900 kilometres away, a quasi-extension of Portuguese rule. Unable to control the interior until well into the twentieth century, Portuguese colonial rule provided little in terms of education and development for the colonized.

Amílcar Cabral organized the African Party for the Independence of Guinea and Cape Verde (PAIGC) in 1956, launching an armed struggle against the Portuguese in 1962. The PAIGC formed a government and declared independence on 24 September 1973, before fighting had ended. Cabral was assassinated in 1973, and his brother Luis became the first President of the country, whose independence was recognized on 10 September 1974. In 1984 an elected National People's Assembly was introduced but economic crisis and alleged discrimination against the Balante sparked a major coup attempt in 1986. Under pressure from international donors, Guinea-Bissau's first democratic multi-party elections were held in mid-1994. They were said to be free and fair by all observers including, after some disagreement, members of the opposition. Yet ethnic factionalism continues to beset the country, preventing the formation of truly representative government.

Papel (Papel, Papeis)

Concentrated on Bissau Island and related estuaries on the Geba, Papel also live north of the River Mansoa. Petty chiefs have held limited authority over these non-Islamic rice cultivators. Partly because of their coastal location, Papel suffered the most direct colonial repression of any group in Guinea-Bissau. On the other hand, some were involved in the slave trade in Bissau. Papel have frequently risen in the face of oppression.

Dioula

Dioula are related to the Senegalese Serer. They are rice cultivators and live in Casamance and the north-west and coastal portions of Guinea-Bissau. They were frequent targets of Manding slave raiders who sold their captives to the Portuguese. An economically important ethnic group of Manding derivation, mainly from the Soninke branch with some Fula ancestry, the Dioula are mainly Muslim. Functioning as a specialized class of itinerant traders, they integrated Portuguese economic concerns with those of the people of the interior until the colonial era. Dioula stimulated local production of gold and kola nuts, and exchanged slaves for imported goods such as salt, textiles and firearms in the pre-colonial era, often working in close association with the Mali and Manding kingdoms. As the Portuguese penetrated the interior they broke up Dioula commerce which hastened the Dioula 'revolutions' from 1835 to the 1880s during which time they tried to re-establish their commercial authority.

Other minorities

Susu live in the extreme south of Guinea-Bissau's coastal areas and in adjacent Guinea, playing an important role in commerce. They are related to Dioula and Soninke, who were the chief founders of the Empire of Ghana. Many had fled to the coast from the Futa Djallon as Fula *jihads* in the late eighteenth century reduced them to slaves. Susu are now one of the three major ethnic groups in Guinea (Conakry) (see **Guinea**).

A numerically small Senegambian group closely related to Balante and Baiote, Felupe are famed rice cultivators, using flood irrigation techniques. They are mainly located in the north-west corner of Guinea-Bissau especially south of the Casamance, north of the Cacheu River and towards the coast. Felupe are currently involved in the Casamance separatist movement.

Conclusions and future prospects

Although Guinea-Bissau prides itself on the good relations between its more than thirty ethnic groups, divisions along ethnic lines began to surface in the army in 1986 soon after Brigadier-General João Bernado Vieira ordered the execution of some soldiers for a coup attempt. One executed Balante soldier, Correia, was prominent in the struggle for independence, as was Paulo Vieira, himself from the Papel group. Relations with neighbouring Senegal have been strained by Senegalese rebel activity in the border area. Operations aimed at insurgents in the Casamance region of Senegal have resulted in a number of injuries and loss of life in Guinea-Bissau particularly when the Senegalese army has chased these rebels over the border. Guinea-Bissau is seen as a tacit supporter of the Casamance movement. The fighting in Casamance has forced thousands of Senegalese to flee into Guinea-Bissau, a burden the country can ill afford, joining refugees from Sierra Leone and Liberia. The refugees are without work or shelter and unprecedented crime rates are increasingly being attributed to refugees. A joint commission has been reactivated to find ways to improve this situation.

Further reading

Amnesty International, *Guinea-Bissau: Human Rights Guarantees in the New Constitution*, London, July 1992.

Forrest, J.B., *Guinea-Bissau*, Boulder, CO, Westview, 1991.

Lopes, C., *Guinea-Bissau: From Liberation Struggle to Independent Statehood*, Boulder, CO, Westview, 1987.

Minority-based and advocacy organizations

INEP, Caixa Postal 112, Bissau, Guinea Bissau.

Liberia

Land area:	97,000 sq km
Population:	2.8 million (1992)
Main languages:	English (official), Gola, Kpelle, Kru
Main religions:	traditional religions, Christianity, Islam
Main minority groups:	Kpelle 550,000 (18.3%), Bassa 400,000 (13.3%), Dan (Gio) 250,000 (8.3.%), Kru 230,000 (7.7%), Grebo 225,000 (7.5%), Ma 215,000 (7.2%), Loma 180,000 (6%), Krahn (Wee) 140,00 (4.7%), Americo-Liberians 125,000 (4.2%), Gola 120,000 (4%), Manding 120,000 (4%), Kissi 100,000 (3.3%), Vai 90,000 (3%), Gbandi 80,000 (2.7%), Kuwaa 15,000 (0.5%), Mende 15,000 (0.5%), Dei 11,000 (0.4%)
Real per capita GDP:	$843
UNDP HDI/rank:	0.311 (158)

The Republic of Liberia is located on the Atlantic Coast of West Africa and is bordered by Sierra Leone, Guinea and Côte d'Ivoire. An independent nation since 1847, Liberia is the only nation in black Africa never to have been under colonial rule. Liberia has a 560 kilometre coastline and mountains in the north and east. The country contains vast timber reserves, including over ninety commercially exploitable species. Mineral resources include substantial deposits of iron ore, diamonds and gold.

Liberia is located in the geographical area called the forest belt covering major portions of Sierra Leone, Liberia, Côte d'Ivoire, Ghana and Nigeria. The forest belt has always been populated by a large number of ethnic groups. In Liberia there are sixteen ethnic groups, each belonging to one of three major language groupings. The south-eastern Kru linguistic group comprises Bassa, Kru, Grebo, Krahn and Dei. The second largest group, the Mandé, is subdivided into the Mandé-Ta (Manding and Vai) and the Mandé-Fu (Kpelle, Dan, Ma, Loma, Gbandi and Mende). Most of these people were once migrants who chose to settle in the forest belt. The Gola and Kissi, who scholars say are the only groups in Liberia today descended from Liberia's original inhabitants, belong to a third linguistic group known as the West Atlantic.

Most of Liberia's ethnic groups came to the forest belt in southward waves of migration, creating a number of different population layers. Some came to uninhabited areas; others imposed themselves upon groups already in the area. By the time black immigrants began arriving from the Americas 250 years had passed since the major migration movements, which had consolidated into a relatively stable pattern of alliances and rivalries. English-speaking Americo-Liberians, descendants of people who came from the New World, mostly from the USA, between 1820 and 1865, dominated Liberian society through the True Whig Party from 1878 until the military coup of 1980.

In 1816 the American Colonization Society was founded in the USA to resettle former slaves in Africa. A few years later, black settlers arrived and their settlement was named Monrovia after US President James Monroe. More settlers gradually arrived and established separate colonies. In 1847 the colonies united, and Liberia became the first independent nation in black Africa. The new nation faced a variety of problems, including resistance to the government by the local population, a decline in demand for Liberian exports, and territorial encroachment by British, French and Germans. Liberia was able to maintain its independence only with US support, eventually receiving the largest amount of US aid *per capita* in sub-Saharan Africa between 1980 and 1987.

Many actions of the central government served to strengthen and crystallize ethnic self-identification. Prior to colonization people were not necessarily born into a particularistic exclusive body known as an ethnic group inhabiting a well-marked geographical space and adhering to never changing customs.

The indigenous population were not given citizenship until 1904 and were not granted the right to vote until 1944. This right was then restricted to property owners or those who paid a 'hut tax'. Non-Americo-Liberian peoples generally received little economic benefit from developments such as agricultural improvement and foreign investments. The remote hinterland home of Gio (Dan), Mano, Loma, and Krahn was not penetrated by road or rail until after the Second World War. Through sheer weight of numbers, the indigenous population dominates the armed forces. However, any hint of unrest was severely punished and Americo-Liberians pursued a policy of divide and rule in maintaining control over the army through ethnic stereotyping.

The ruling True Whig Party maintained a kind of feudal oligarchy until well into the third quarter of the twentieth century, monopolizing political power and subjugating the largely peasant population with the help of the Liberian Frontier Force (LFF), an army of non-Americo-Liberians deployed to collect taxes and forcibly recruit labourers for public works projects. While the settlers along the coast developed an elaborate lifestyle reminiscent of the ante-bellum Southern USA, the original population endured poverty and neglect in the hinterland. Repression and corruption were especially acute during the prolonged regime of President V.S. Tubman (1944–71). Tubman attempted reform but heightened expectations that could not be satisfied within the existing political structures. This hastened his undoing as the country began to experience more frequent labour disputes and political unrest. Sergeant Samuel Doe's 1980 coup was initially greeted with enthusiasm. Doe had promised to liberate the masses from the corrupt and oppressive domination of the few and pledged a more equitable distribution of wealth. However, this did not happen. Soldiers of the Armed Forces of Liberia (AFL) proved a law unto themselves, and there were persistent reports of looting, arson, floggings, arbitrary arrests, rape, summary executions and brutality. In 1984 voters approved a new US-style constitution. Doe remained head of the civilian government following elections in 1985, from which the main opposition parties were barred.

South-eastern Kru linguistic group

Bassa

Bassa speak Kruan and live in Grand Bassa country in southern Liberia. Together with Dei they settled early on in Monrovia and became assimilated into the settler economy as artisans, clerks and domestic servants.

Kru

Kru live along the southern coast bordering Côte d'Ivoire. According to Kru stories their people migrated to the coast of West Africa in the sixteenth century and became sailors and fishers. By the eighteenth century the generally short and stocky Kru seamen were a common sight on European sailing ships that trafficked in slaves. According to oral tradition Kru escaped slavery themselves by making a bargain with Europeans; slaves could be transported across their territory to the coast without interference if Kru themselves would not be taken into captivity. Therefore Kru wore a tattoo – a vertical line down the centre of their forehead – so they would be identified. Kru received slaves from inland societies and transferred them to Europeans. Kru traditionally lived in permanent settlements along the coast and lacked strong political structures. In 1915 they revolted, largely because of a tax imposed by the government, which they viewed as the latest of a series of injustices at the hands of merchants who neglected to pay wages and continually raised the prices of goods sold to local people. In 1930 another uprising was unsuccessful, and taxation was imposed. This led to an outmigration of Kru primarily to Monrovia.

Grebo

Grebo live along the coast on both sides of the Cavall river, which serves as a border between Liberia and Côte d'Ivoire. They divided into coastal dwellers, Grebo, and forest dwellers, Half Grebo. They migrated in to Liberia during the sixteenth century. They lacked strong central structures; village ties were primary rather than clan affiliation. They were subject to a twenty-year campaign of subjugation by the Americo-Liberian-dominated government. Episcopalian missionaries introduced Western-style education and Christianity.

Krahn (Wee)

This group is commonly known as Krahn in Liberia, but Wee is used for similar peoples in Côte d'Ivoire. Living in Nimba, Grand Gedeh and Sinoe countries this small group have historically been disparaged as 'uncivilized' by both the ruling Americo-Liberians and members of the larger indigenous ethnic groups. When Doe took power in 1980 Krahn, in particular those from Doe's own village, became dominant in power. Krahn

(Wee) from Côte d'Ivoire made up the Executive Mansion Guard. In 1990, during the civil war, Charles Taylor's National Patriotic Front of Liberia (NPFL) attacked Krahn civilians in Nimba county and elsewhere as they moved through the country, especially in Grand Geddeh country, and many fled to Côte d' Ivoire.

Dei

A Kruan-speaking people who live in Bomi county surrounded by the Atlantic Ocean and Vai, Gola and Americo-Liberians, Dei were among the first to come into contact with the settler immigrants, settling in Monrovia early on and becoming assimilated like the Bassa.

Kuwaa

A Kruan-speaking people who live in Lofa county, Kuwaa have been referred to by the Liberian government as Belle, a name that has disparaging connotations.

Mandé linguistic group

Mandé-Ta (Manding and Vai)

The Manding population immigrated into Liberia from Guinea over the past 200 to 300 years and are now widely scattered, though concentrated in upper Lofa county. Their trade routes linked other Liberian populations with the savanna. Manding settled amongst Mano and Vai and became involved in agriculture and craft industries, including blacksmithing, leather and gold work. With the expansion of central government control Manding used the opportunity to diversify their economic activities. By the 1950s they owned a majority of transportation business and worked in commerce. Manding were seen as distinct because of their religion and they were viewed as outsiders by both the Americo-Liberian government and other groups, as a group whose main ties lay in Guinea. This supposed divided loyalty was used to exclude Manding until the belated attempt by President Tubman to integrate the original Liberian population into the economy and polity. For many groups the policy failed dismally, but for Manding it brought political and economic benefits. Manding were brought into government offices and given commercial contracts. Consequently Manding were resented by other groups for alleged government favouritism, and they became increasingly isolated after the 1980 coup. Doe played Manding off against other ethnic groups, and prominent Manding went on television to pledge support for Doe after an abortive coup in 1985. This caused many groups who hated Doe to intensely mistrust Manding. Manding were attacked in the civil war by Taylor's NPFL; thousands were killed, property was destroyed, and many fled into exile.

Vai live on both sides of the border between Liberia and Sierra Leone in an area extending 90 kilometres up the coast from the Vannje River in Sierra Leone to the Lofa River in Liberia, and into the hinterland. Vai were part of the large-scale migration in the sixteenth century. Before coming to the coast they probably inhabited the savanna region roughly 150 kilometres inland. Vai had a developed political structure, were engaged in trade and were mostly Muslim converted by itinerant Dioula traders. Their largest political unit was based on kinship ties, and Islam had no political function. Although individual Vai leaders formed coalitions with Americo-Liberians and established trade links with them, Vai resisted taxation until 1917.

Mandé-Fu (Kpelle, Dan, Ma, Loma, Gbande and Mende)

The largest single group in Liberia, Kpelle also live in Guinea, where they are known as Guerze. They inhabit the centre of Liberia around Bong county, having moved from Guinea into Liberia during the sixteenth century. Kpelle united and held out for many years against the imposition of Americo-Liberian rule.

Dan are more commonly known as Gio, which stems from the Bassa phrase meaning slave people, but the term Dan is preferred and used by the people themselves. Dan are a southern Mandé-speaking group and those living in Liberia live in Nimba county surrounded by the Côte d'Ivoire, Ma(no), Bassa and Krahn (Wee). Historically, Dan accepted the rule of the Americo-Liberians. Thomas Quiwonkpa, a Dan, was one of the 1980 coup leaders, along with Samuel Doe. In 1985 he led an abortive coup against Doe's ruthless concentration of power. Not only was he brutally killed, but Dan in Nimba county and the capital were subject to remorseless arrest, torture, raping and killings by the AFL. This brutality helped swell the numbers of supporters for Charles Taylor, and many Dan joined his NPFL.

The Ma are Mano, a name given to them by the Bassa and meaning literally 'Ma-people' in

Bassa. They reside in Nimba county surrounded by Kpelle, Bassa and Dan. Ma also live in Guinea. They suffered killings, imprisonment and torture in Nimba county and in the capital at the hands of the Doe government after the unsuccessful coup in 1985, and again at the hands of the AFL after Charles Taylor's forces entered Liberia in 1989. Many Ma have joined Taylor's NPFL.

Loma also live in Guinea where they are known as Toma. They are a south-west Mandé-speaking group who live in upper Lofa County, surrounded by the Republic of Guinea, Manding, Kuwaa and Kpelle populations.

Gbandi and Mende are both south-west Mandé-speaking peoples living in upper Lofa County. Their homeland is surrounded by Sierra Leone and Guinea and by Kissi and Gola. They formed part of the migration into Liberia from Guinea in the mid-sixteenth century as political refugees from Manding (Malinké) expansion in the north-west.

West Atlantic group (Gola and Kissi)

Gola live in a 6,000 square kilometre area in the western Liberian hinterland, along the St Paul river in Lofa and Grand Cape counties. Gola became apprentices to Americo-Liberians and formed a lower-middle-class group. Their neighbours on the coast include Vai and Dei; to the north and east are Kissi, Manding, Loma, Kpelle, Dan and Ma, to the south Bassa, Kru and Grebo. Gola used to live in the forested mountains of north-east Liberia and south-east Sierra Leone but migrated to the coast as traders. Gola had a tradition of accepting protected status through the exchange of women. They did not assimilate but instead succeeded in assimilating Dei and Vai people into their society. They then gained ascendancy over their former patrons as their numbers increased through migration. Many Gola fled to Sierra Leone especially from the northern region prior to 1918 as the government conducted a ruthless campaign against them.

Kissi live in mountainous parts of Liberia, surrounded by Guinea and Sierra Leone and by Manding groups. Other members of this group live in Sierra Leone and Guinea. Kissi and Gola are the only groups in Liberia who are descendants of Liberia's original peoples.

Conclusions and future prospects

Since the 1980 coup, relations between the country's distinct groups have been increasingly strained. Members of a clan within the Krahn community, many of them from Doe's home village, appeared to emerge with a disproportionate share of authority. The seeds of violent ethnic conflict were sown in the aftermath of an abortive coup against Doe in November 1985, followed by reprisal killings against Dan and Ma. At the time of the coup attempt, five of the sixteen government ministries, and the armed forces were headed by Krahns. Krahns historically were maligned by other, larger groups. Thomas Quiwonkpa, leader of the coup attempt, was a Dan (Gio) from Nimba county. After the 1985 coup failed, Grebo, Dan and Ma soldiers and civilians were herded into the grounds of the Executive Mansion, home of the head of state, and Barclay Training Center in Monrovia, where they were stripped and executed. Others were subject to arrest, beatings, extortion and killings carried out by Krahn soldiers and civilians, including high-school students wielding machetes and whips. Quiwonkpa was battered and dismembered. High-ranking government officials took the view that the government could not be held responsible for such abuses.

A constitution was set in place in 1986, but many of the decrees curtailing free speech and limited popular participation under martial law remained in effect. The government failed to end or acknowledge human rights abuses. On 24 December 1989, as political repression increased and the economy neared collapse, Charles Taylor's NPFL launched an incursion against Doe from Côte d'Ivoire. The AFL responded with a ruthless counter-insurgency campaign, and this brutality served to swell the ranks of NPFL recruits, many of whom were Dan (Gio) and Ma boys orphaned by the fighting. Within weeks, over 160,000 people had fled into neighbouring Guinea and Côte d'Ivoire, beginning a refugee exodus that escalated to about one-third of the total population by late 1990. By June 1990 the NPFL had reached Grand Gedeh county, largely populated by Krahn. NPFL fighters attacked civilians and devastated the area, prompting a huge number of Krahn to seek sanctuary in Côte d'Ivoire. Other groups threatened by the NPFL included those who were mistaken for Krahn, particularly Grebo and Vai, and anyone who had served or cooperated with the Doe government. Mandinka, for the most part traders and businesspeople, were considered by the rebels to have been collaborators.

In August 1990 a multinational West African force entered Liberia to try to end the civil war. Doe was killed on 9 September 1990, but the war continued. The multinational force installed an interim government headed by Dr Amos Sawyer and gradually established control in Monrovia. Taylor's forces controlled most of the countryside, while former members of Doe's army controlled the two western provinces.

The United Liberation Movement for Democracy in Liberia (ULIMO) was formed in 1991 by former AFL soldiers (predominantly Krahn and Manding) who had fled to Sierra Leone. One focus of concern about ULIMO, in addition to human rights abuses and the manipulation of humanitarian aid, is the use of child soldiers. The NPFL also operated a 'small boys unit' which became one of Taylor's most trusted divisions. Scores and perhaps hundreds of these boys died in the swamps surrounding Monrovia in 1992. Since NPFL fighters were not paid they were promised the loot of Monrovia. Many of the houses that were not destroyed were 'claimed' by NPFL who wrote their names and units on the walls, hoping to return to claim the homes after the fighting.

In 1992 the ethnic character of the killing was less apparent, as murder became incidental to robbery. The UN did not address the Liberian crisis in political terms until November 1992, almost three years after the crisis erupted. Responsibility was shifted to the Economic Community of the West African States (ECOWAS). By 1993 it was estimated that 150,000 had died in the civil war, many of them civilians. Half the population had fled the country or been internally displaced. In July 1993 the various factions signed a peace accord calling for a ceasefire, disarmament by a reconstructed West African peace-keeping force and the holding of elections in 1994. Elections were held in 1995, and transitional government was inaugurated on 1 September 1995. This included rebel leaders Charles (now Jhankay) Taylor, George Boley and Alhaji Kromah. Numerous violations of this ceasefire have been recorded, and the encouragement and strengthening of civil society throughout the country are an urgent priority.

Further reading

Africa Watch, *Liberia: Flight from Terror*, New York, 1990.

Lawyers' Committee for Human Rights, *Liberia: A Promise Betrayed*, New York, 1986.

Minority-based and advocacy organizations

Centre for Law and Human Rights Education, PO Box 2314, Monrovia, Liberia.

Libya

Land area:	1,759,540 sq km
Population:	4.5 million (1992)
Main languages:	Arabic, Berber
Main religions:	Islam
Main minority groups:	Berber 150,000 (4%), Haratin 120,000 (3%), Tebu and Tuareg 40,000 (1%)
Real per capita GDP:	$6,125
UNDP HDI/rank:	0.792 (59)

Libya, located in North Africa, is Africa's fourth largest country. After centuries of foreign rule by Ottoman Turks, Italy, France and Britain, Libya gained independence in 1951 as the United Kingdom of Libya. In 1969, Colonel Muammar al Qudhafi led a military coup that ended the monarchy and proclaimed the Libyan Arab Republic. In 1977 the country's official name changed to Popular Socialist Libyan Arab Jamahiriya (state of the masses). Since 1959 petroleum and gas have financed the transformation of Libya from a poor nation at the time of independence to a rich one with vast sums to spend on social, agricultural and military development.

Around 90 per cent of the population belong to the Arabic-speaking majority of mixed Arab–Berber ancestry. The Sunni branch of Islam is the official and nationally dominant political, cultural and legal force. The country is governed on the basis of the Qur'an and *sharia* law. Berbers who retain the Berber language and customs are the largest non-Arab minority. They form only 4 per cent of the population and are concentrated in small isolated villages in the west. Other minorities include the Arabic-speaking Haratin of West African ancestry who inhabit the southern oases, and the Berber-related Tuareg and Tebu in the south. There are also 30,000 Palestinian refugees in Libya. In 1995 Qudhafi expelled thousands of Palestinians to punish the Palestine Liberation Organization for engaging in the peace process with Israel.

Tebu and Tuareg

Centred in the Tibesti mountains and other parts of southern Libya, early Tebu economy was based on pastoralism with the margins of survival widened by caravanning, slavery and raiding. In the latter half of the nineteenth century Tebu mobility was curtailed by conquest and policing of the southern desert, first by colonial powers and later by the independent states of Libya and Chad. Since the second half of the twentieth century Tebu have been administered from centres such as Benghazi and Baida in Libya. Though converted to Islam by Sanussi missionaries in the nineteenth century, Tebu retain many of their earlier religious beliefs and practices. Their language is related to a Nigerian language.

Tuareg number a few thousand in Libya. Once traders on the north–south Sahara caravan route, the ending of this and the 'pacification' of the desert deprived Tuareg of their traditional way of life, reducing many to penury. Tuareg adhere to a form of Sunni Islam intermeshed with Sudanese and West African beliefs in sorcery and witchcraft. Marriages are monogamous and women have a high status in Tuareg society. Both men and women wear veils as a protection against dust storms.

Conclusions and future prospects

Qudhafi's popularity is declining as the result of economic mismanagement and the country's foreign policy. Widely spread throughout Libyan society, Islamic opposition is neither cohesive nor necessarily part of a wider movement with origins outside Libya itself.

Further reading

Wright, J., *Libya, A Modern History,* London, Croom Helm, 1982.

St John, R., *Historical Dictionary of Libya,* Metuchen, NJ, Scarecrow Press, n.d.

Mali

Land area:	1,240,192 sq km
Population:	9.8 million (1992)
Main languages:	French, Mandé (incl. Bambara), Berber
Main religions:	Islam, traditional religions
Main minority groups:	Peul (Fula) 800,000 (8%), Malinké 685,000 (7%), Soninke (Sarakole) 600,000 (6%), Senoufo and Minianka 600,000 (6%), Bobo 150,000 (1.5%), Diawara 90,000 (0.9%), Khassonke 80,000 (0.8%), Maure 60,000 (0.6%), Bozo/Somono 50,000 (0.5%), Tuareg 50,000 (0.5%), Songhai, Dogon
Real per capita GDP:	$530
UNDP HDI/rank:	0.223 (171)

The Republic of Mali is a landlocked state on the edge of the Sahara in West Africa, bordering Senegal, Mauritania, Algeria, Niger, Burkina Faso, Côte d'Ivoire and Guinea. Mali was a French colony until its independence in 1960. Mali is located in the transitional zone with the Sahara to the north and tropical Africa to the south. Mali's largest and dominant ethnic group, the Bambara, constituting 3 million, 30 per cent of the population, live in central and southern Mali along the middle Niger Valley. Of the other large ethnic groups, Malinké (685,000, 7 per cent of the population) live in the south-west and west; Peul (Fula) (800,000, 8 per cent) are concentrated in the inland delta of the Niger River; Soninke (600,000, 6 per cent) live in north-west Mali; Senoufo and Minianka (600,000, 6 per cent) live in south-eastern Mali. Bobo, Maure and Tuareg live in the Sahelian region; Diawara and Bozo/Somono fishers live by the Niger. In central, west and southern Mali, Bambara is the *lingua franca*; in the inland delta of the Niger River, Fulfulde, the Peul's language, is the *lingua franca*; in the north, Songhai is widely spoken.

Bambara and to a lesser extent Malinké have dominated the political life of Mali through their geographical proximity to the seat of national government – Bamako – and embracing Western education in the colonial period. Ethnic rivalries and ethnicity have not been a major feature of the Malian political scene to date. The various groups often compliment each other. Diverse farming groups such as Bambara, Malinké, Songhai and Dogon, do not compete for the same lands and do not produce sufficient surplus to become marketplace rivals. However, the pastoralists of the hinterland have suffered from neglect and the ravages of drought. The national political system has easily accommodated ethnic groups whose representatives have often looked after their constituents' interests. Urbanization is increasing and ethnic relations are breaking down; ethnic preferences have been detected in employment practices in some state-owned and private businesses and in the allocation of building lots in Bamako, administration and education. In the emerging urban cash economy, ethnic diversity may lead to conflict due to limited resources. Inter-ethnic marriage is frowned upon by most families. Within ethnic groups, marriage is restricted to members of one's own class. A unifying cultural element is Islam, which is embraced by 65 per cent of the population. Among professed Muslims many elements of indigenous religions are retained. The rest of the population adhere to traditional religions, and about 800,000 are Catholics and Protestants. Social and economic pressures often have forced Christian Malians to convert to Islam.

Few specific minority rights issues have been identified in connection with many of Mali's ethnic and linguistic groups.

Peul (Fula), Soninke (Sarakole), Senoufo and Minianka

Peul (Fula) live in the great inland delta of the Niger and in eastern Mali. Some are cattle raisers, others semi-sedentary farmers.

Soninke (Sarakole) inhabit north-west Mali and are descendants of the Ghana empire. They are Muslim and live throughout West Africa as merchants, migrating to the marketplaces of West and Central Africa as well as to Western Europe.

Senoufo are an important ethnic group in south-east Mali, who with the Minianka number 600,000. Many more Senoufo live in Côte d'Ivoire. They are divided into five factions of which Mininka is one. Mostly sedentary, both groups are subsistence farmers, although some cotton is grown as a cash crop. They are predominantly animist, having resisted the imposition of Islam. Senoufo call themselves Siena, and many of their number have migrated to France and Côte d'Ivoire.

Maure and Tuareg

Berber-speaking nomadic groups of stock breeders have dominated much of the semi-arid steppe area bordering the Sahara for some 800 years. Living in northern Mali, their herd numbers are normally limited by the extent of grazing areas. Famine and drought are recurring problems. Major drought throughout the Sahelian region between 1968 and 1973 produced a heavy death toll of up to 80 per cent among herds, with the effects borne largely by nomadic cattle raisers. Maure are a group of Berber nomads who number 60,000 and are more numerous in Mauritania. Herders of goats and sheep, and providers of camel and donkey transport, they were greatly affected by drought in the 1970s and 1980s.

In 1974, there were reports that the Malian government withheld food aid from Tuareg nomads in refugee camps. There have also been allegations that the military government misappropriated development funds supposedly allocated to reintegration programmes for Tuareg. Drought returned in 1984 and by mid-1985 aid workers stated that tens of thousands of Tuareg nomads were starving to death in the remote interior of Mali. Traditional structures broke down as men left to work in the cities while villages were populated by women, children and older people.

In the 1960s Tuareg living in Mali had attempted to ally themselves with Algeria but were brutally repressed by the regime of President Modibo Keita. In colonial times France's fleeting interest in the Saharan zone had raised the false expectation of an autonomous state, Azawad. Tuareg rebels have continued the armed struggle for autonomy. They feel alienated from the rest of the country as many Malians regard them as Arabs or Libyans. There have been attacks on Tuareg and Moorish-owned businesses, notably in Timbuktu.

By August 1995, there were signs that relative peace was returning to northern Mali. At the same time, fundamental questions related to Tuareg identity and belonging in Mali persist. Up to 160,000 Malian Tuareg refugees continue to be encamped in southern Algeria, Mauritania and Burkina Faso. In 1994, the government and the Movements et Front Unifié d'Azawad were divided by a deep disagreement over the number of Tuareg fighters who should be integrated into the national armed forces. Outbreaks of violence continued on all sides. Tuareg raiders attacked travellers and even settled villages along the northern bend of the Niger River. Songhai villagers in this area retaliated by forming their own self-defence militia, the Ganda Koy. Meanwhile there are also reports of army repression including attacks on civilian Tuareg encampments. In January 1995 talks began between Ganda Koy and Tuareg groups. Since November 1995 the process of integrating rebels into the national army has gained momentum. However, the army continues to attack militant Arab groups in the north, on the Algerian border.

Other minorities

Bobo live in the San and Tominian regions but are more numerous in Burkina Faso. Bobo farmers have retained traditional beliefs and customs to a remarkable degree although many have become Christians. They are descendants of the Soninke diaspora after the fall of the Ghana Empire. A Bobo revolt in 1916 against forced labour and conscription in the army in the San region was harshly put down and its leaders hanged.

Diawara are an ethnic group living in the Niora and Nara regions. They speak the Sarakole language of the more numerous groups who surround them but they are not a subgroup of the Sarakole.

Khassonke live in the western Mali. Their homeland is known as the Khasso, which formerly consisted of several small chiefdoms and kingdoms.

Bozo are fishers of the middle Niger, believed to be descendants of Soninke who left the Ghana empire after its fall and migrated south-east to Niger. Divided into clans, Bozo fishers now organize co-operatives to market their fish catch, which constitutes one of Mali's prime exports.

Songhai live in eastern Mali, alongside the Niger, as sedentary subsistence farmers. They are descendants of the fourteenth – and fifteenth – century Songhai empire of Gao, which was destroyed by the Moroccans in 1591. They were Islamicized in the thirteenth century.

Dogon are a relatively small ethnic group who live in cliff villages on the Bandiagara plateau and the sand dunes of Seno. The traditional way of life and art forms have survived. They speak a distinct language of which there are several dialects. They are gradually converting to Islam.

Conclusions and future prospects

On the surface Mali appears to represent an exemplary transition from military one-party authoritarian rule to civilian multi-party democracy. Mali's third republic was inaugurated amid considerable political optimism and expectation. However, the popular alliance of trade unionists, teachers and students who brought President Alphar Oumar Konaré to power is gradually eroding as a result of the impact of the structural adjustment policies that have worsened economic conditions. A dangerous state of semi-anarchy, with a breakdown of law and order, has set in. Environmental degradation is a major threat to the security of pastoral groups in the north, as the struggle over control of the country's limited natural resources continues.

Further reading

Cross, N., *The Sahel: A Peoples' Right to Development*, MRG report, London, 1990.

Minority-based and advocacy organizations

Association Malienne pour le Développement (AMADE), BP 2646, Bamako, Mali.

Mauritania

Land area:	1,030,700 sq km
Population:	2.1 million (1992)
Main languages:	Arabic, Wolof, Fulani, Tucouleur, Serer, French
Main religions:	Islam
Main minority groups:	black Africans (Fula, Soninke, Tucouleur, Wolof) 950,000 (45%), Haratin 850,000 (40%) (*census figures since 1965 have been suppressed*)
Real per capita GDP:	$1,610
UNDP HDI/rank:	0.353 (149)

Mauritania, located in north-west Africa, forms a bridge between Arab Africa to the north and sub-Saharan Africa to the south. Mauritania's neighbours include Senegal, Mali, Algeria, Morocco and the disputed territory of the Western Sahara. To the west, Mauritania has a 700 kilometre coastline on the Atlantic. The northern region covers two-thirds of the land and is part of the Sahara. The smaller southern region is composed of the Sahel and the northern portion of the Senegal River, known locally as the Chemama. Four-fifths of Mauritania's small population live in the Chemama and Sahel.

The Arab Berbers or Moors who make up 60 per cent of the population are divided into a dominant group, Beydan, and their former slaves, Haratin, who are black but of the same Arab–Berber culture as their former masters. Beydan control the instruments of state and foreign trade. Although slavery was abolished several times, most recently in 1980, measures to provide for their economic emancipation has never been enacted. Beydan and Haratin still retain a master–slave relationship in rural areas.

The country is undergoing severe social transformation, exemplified by the last twenty-five years which have seen a rapid decline in nomadism. In 1963, 83 per cent of the population was nomadic. In 1980, this figure had fallen to 25 per cent. Since the early 1970s, the Sahelian drought has increasingly forced nomadic Moors out of the desert and arid zones. They have migrated into urban areas and the fertile Senegal River Valley where the country's black population is concentrated. In the course of the struggle for access to limited agricultural land, black settlers have been dispossessed and often forced to flee the country. Arabization policies have alienated black people and caused ethnic unrest between Senegal and Mauritania. Internally, the policy has led to purges of black people from the administration, army and police. Detention and death penalties have been imposed on black people, who now have no legitimate political voice.

The original inhabitants of Mauritania are the Bafours, said to be related to contemporary Soninke. It is thought that Berbers conquered the Bafours. In the first millennium CE, Berber nomads controlled the area down to the Senegal River. Islam filtered southwards from North Africa from the seventh century CE. In the fourteenth century, Hassaniya Arabs began their invasion imposing Arabic language and culture on the Berbers, who were already Muslim. The French military conquest began in 1850. The black population, being sedentary and more accessible from the south, were exposed to mission education from the early twentieth century and became instrumental to the French administration. Cooperation and co-option were secured through sedentarization. Land titles and aid were distributed to the elite who used slave labour to set up oases, dams and cultivation plots in the south. Escaped slaves often became slaves of the southern land-owning elite (primarily Tucouleur). Partly to deal with struggles over slave ownership, the French allocated plots in groups to escaped slaves.

Mauritania became independent as the Islamic Republic of Mauritania in 1960 and was ruled by Moktar Ould Daddah until 1978. African Mauritanians resisted the attempt by Arab citizens to declare the country the 'Arab Islamic Republic of Mauritania'. When Spain withdrew from the Western Sahara in 1975, the territory was split between Mauritania and Morocco. From 1975 Mauritania was at war with the Saharawi, who are ethnically close to the Beydan. The war was unpopular in Mauritania and caused a severe drain on an ailing economy. Black people and Haratins were drafted into an army which expanded from 1,500 to 17,000 during the course of the war. The black population was against the expansion into Saharawi territory which would increase the Moor majority. Despite support from France and Morocco, Mauritanian forces could not accomplish their occupation. In August 1979 Mauritania renounced claims to Saharawi territory.

Black Africans

The south of the country is inhabited by black ethnic groups, principally Bambara, Fula, Soninke, Tucouleur and Wolof. Fula are by tradition nomadic, but this is now changing. Closely related to Fula in language and culture are Tucouleur who are mixed ethnically and culturally. Their mixed and complex oral tradition also link them to Soninke and Mandinka empires. In historical terms Arab-Berber, Wolof and Serer influence is evident. Soninke are currently concentrated in southern Mauritania and speak their own language which belongs to the Manding group. These groups have highly stratified social systems encompassing warrior, scholar, artisan and slave castes, and are all nominally Muslim. Ethnically, southern black Africans are closer to populations in Senegal and Mali than to other groups within their own national boundaries.

The most densely populated area in Mauritania is the fertile Chemama land on the Mauritanian bank of the Senegal River in the south-west where the black population is concentrated. However, the river has been at record low levels in recent years and riverine cultivation has therefore been reduced. Competition over these lands, brought about by the undermining of the nomadic economy during the long drought from the early 1970s into the 1980s, is one of the major factors underlying ethnic conflict in Mauritania today. Many black people claim to have been forcibly dispossessed of their land and assert that legislation has been enacted to this end as with the land reform of 1983.

Due to early French contact and education, a large number of southern black Africans, particularly Tucouleurs, work in the educational sector and the middle levels of civil administration. Since independence, Beydan have controlled the top level administrative and military positions. The mid-1960s saw ethnic violence in response to Arabization policies. In 1966, Arabic was made compulsory in secondary schools. Haratin were used by the Beydan to attack black people and crush a revolt of black students in Nouakchott. Several ministers and black civil servants were purged and discussion of ethnic problems was banned. A resurgence of ethnic unrest began in early 1979, again centring on the Arabization issue. The results of the 1977 census were suppressed and black students fared badly in exams which favoured Arabic-speakers. Teachers and students rebelled, supported by a black opposition movement, the Union Democratique Mauritienne (UDM), based in Senegal. Some minor concessions on the use of French were made but arrests of black people continued into 1980 and the government has pressed ahead with full implementation of *sharia* law.

In April 1986, the Dakar-based Forces de Liberation Africaine de Mauritienne (FLAM) published the *Oppressed Black Minorities* manifesto. Distribution of this document provoked the arrest of 30 prominent black Africans in September 1986; 20 were sentenced to prison. As a wave of civil disturbances swept across the country in October, the military regime responded with further arrests. In municipal elections in late 1986, lists of black candidates were by-passed in favour of government sponsored lists and black people were allegedly intimidated when trying to vote. After a failed coup attempt by black officers in 1987, 51 Tucouleur officers were arrested. Three were executed and riots followed in Nouakchott, Borghe and Kaedi. A state of emergency existed in Borghe for six months, while black people were purged from the police and army.

In 1991 Arabic became the sole official language. A national referendum in July 1991 provided for universal suffrage and elections for president, senate and prime minister. Political parties, banned since 1978, were authorized soon afterwards, but could not be racially- or regionally-based, nor could they be opposed to Islam. FLAM contested the result of the constitutional referendum, claiming it took place under police violence and intimidation of black Mauritanians.

On 3 May 1989, the Mauritanian government announced that it would begin repatriating Senegalese who had settled there since 1986. However, the expulsion of Senegalese also seemed to affect the Mauritanian black population. Of the estimated 80,000 who appeared to have fled or been forced to leave Mauritania by July 1989, at least 30,000 are thought to be Mauritanian, a minority of whom are middle-class black people and a few senior government officials. Many black people were rounded up in their villages, stripped of their possessions and identity cards, and shipped across the river to the Senegalese bank. More than 90 per cent of them were Fula agro-pastoralists and nomadic herders. Many were long term residents.

In August 1989, Senegal referred grievances over the crisis to the UN Security Council, demanding a settlement which would resolve border disputes and end the expulsion of black people. While 200,000 penniless Mauritanians returned from Senegal, others remained as refugees. The main road from St Louis to Bakel became the focus of refugee settlements. These refugees cut wood to make huts and gathered straw over a 20 kilometre area; camps of the refugees, who number between 50,000 and 100,000, stretch over several hundred kilometres from Dagana to Bakel. The availability of food aid has upset the local trade as refugees sell some of it, causing agricultural prices to fall. The environment has been degraded through deforestation and there is extreme pressure on water supplies. Tension over the Senegal River resources have coincided with a number of long-standing problems related to environmental degradation. The diminution of resources has its roots in the Mauritanian government's neglect of crucial questions on resources and as a consequence of intensive agriculture and population pressure on the Senegal River and its fertile banks. At the same time, developments in the Senegal River area have been dominated by Arabs. These have been supported by the World Bank, despite the country's politically enforced racial hierarchy.

Haratin

The black African origin of Haratin, black Moors, is beyond doubt, while their language, culture and identity are Arab, the product of centuries of enslavement to Beydan masters. Beydan are descended from Berber Arabs and black African groups from the Sahara. Moors, the largest ethnic group of Arab and Berber origin, speak dialects of Hassinya related to Bedouin Arabic. Moor society is traditionally divided on social and descent criteria. The slave community is divided into three levels: the total subject, the part slave, and the true Haratin. The government has long described all forms of slave as *haratine* or 'newly freed', thus implying the end of slavery. Yet, slavery is said to be particularly widespread in the eastern part of the country, where there are few black people other than slaves. As well as enslaving the black Moors, Beydan have dominated other groups including Imraguen fishers and the Aghazazir salt miners (mixed African/Berber) who labour under debt bondage in salt mine areas.

Urbanization and migration have broken down the slave system to some extent and certain districts of the capital Nouakchott have become a haven for escaped slaves. These escapees form the basis of the emancipation movement El Hor (the free), formed in 1974. El Hor argued that emancipation was impossible without practical measures to enforce anti-slavery laws and provide former slaves with the means to gain economic independence. To this end, it called for land reform and encouraged Haratin to set up agricultural co-operatives. El Hor's emphasis on social issues and its demand for redress and justice inevitably brought it into confrontation with the government. A substantial number of the movement's leaders were arrested, tortured and many of them exiled at the end of the 1970s. In January 1980, a military coup brought President Mohamad Khouna Duld Haidallah to power, whose government embarked on a policy of undermining the movement by appearing to satisfy its demands. The 1980 'abolition' of slavery which was accompanied by the co-option of some of El Hor's spokespeople was also prompted by the government's desire to forestall any possible political links between the opposition and black opposition groups. This divide and rule tactic has meant that El Hor, despite representing the largest population group, does not constitute a significant political force. Indeed many Haratin have been responsible for attacks and discrimination against black Africans. In 1981, Anti-Slavery Society (UK) estimated that there were around 100,000 people still enslaved, plus approximately 300,000 Haratin.

Conclusions and future prospects

Mauritania's political history is characterized by persistent tension between its communities. This situation has been complicated by the existence of slavery and the established practice of successive Beydan-dominated governments exacerbating black divisions by using Haratin and slaves whenever there are confrontations with black people from the south. There are other reasons for keeping the two black communities apart. It is difficult to state with any degree of precision what percentage of Mauritania's population Beydans constitute since governments have refused to make the information available. The result of 1977 and 1988 censuses remain a secret. Black people see this as confirmation of their belief that the result recorded a dramatic increase in their numbers, with Beydan comprising no more than 25–30 per cent, and slaves and Haratin estimated at up to 40 per cent. Making sure Mauritania's black population do not join forces, which would place them in a strong position to challenge Beydan monopoly of economic and political power, explains the need to ensure that slaves and Haratin identify with the Beydans. The repressive regime of President Moaouia Ould Sid Mohammed Taya remains a major obstacle to the weakened opposition movements. The International Monetary Fund (IMF) continues to demonstrate its support for the government's economic reforms by approving a series of loans, but structural adjustment policies have produced enormous consumer price increases. The army has been brought in to end violent protests as opposition leaders are periodically arrested and taken into indefinite 'preventive' detention.

Further reading

Africa Watch, *Mauritania: Slavery Alive and Well, 10 Years after It Was Last Abolished*, New York, 1990.

Human Rights Watch/Africa, *Mauritania: Campaign of Terror*, New York, n.d.

Mercer, J., *Slavery in Mauritania Today*, Anti-Slavery Society, London, 1981.

Minority-based and advocacy organizations

Mauritanian League of Human Rights, Nouakchott, Mauritania.

Morocco

Land area:	446,000 sq km
Population:	27.5 million (1994)
Main languages:	Arabic, Berber
Main religions:	Islam
Main minority groups:	Berbers 8 million (40%), Saharawis 150,000 (0.5%), Jews 30,000 (0.1%)
Real per capita GDP:	$3,270
UNDP HDI/rank:	0.534 (123)

The Kingdom of Morocco is located in north-west Africa. Bounded by water on two sides, it fronts the Atlantic Ocean, the Mediterranean Sea, Algeria and the Western Sahara. Morocco became Muslim in the seventh century, as the Arab conquests pushed the Berbers into the mountains. Between the eleventh and thirteenth centuries, a Moroccan dynasty ruled north-west Africa and Spain. It never came under the Ottoman Empire and was a French and Spanish protectorate between 1912 and 1956. The country regained independence on 2 March 1956 and restored a traditional monarchy. Morocco has the world's highest proportion of Berber-speakers. Black Africans also live in Morocco. They were originally introduced into the Maghreb as slaves and concubines. Arabs and Berbers seldom intermarried with black people.

Berber

The term 'Berber' derives from the Greek, *barbaroi* and the Latin *barbari*, and was used by the dominant Arabs to designate those who spoke a different language. In referring to themselves, Berber use tribal names. The many dialects of the Berber language, along with tribal forms of organization, prevented them from cooperating easily among themselves. Each group was fiercely independent and only emergencies led to ephemeral tribal confederations.

After independence Berbers were well represented in the Moroccan army and police force but much less so in government. They very often felt isolated from central government as their patrons, under the French, lost their influence and Berber tribal groups suffered accordingly. In the first three years of independence there were two major tribal uprisings and constant rural agitation against Istiqlal, the urban nationalist group which had led the independence struggle. The uprisings were crushed by the army and were used by the monarchy as an excuse to curb the political power of Istiqlal. Berber resentment was formalized, with encouragement from the monarchy, in the formation of an explicitly Berber-based political party in 1958. The main causes of Berber resentment include economic deprivation and a sense that the central government ignores their problems. Frustration is amplified as the Berber language is reduced in importance by constant migration to cities where Arabic is an essential means of communication and where Berber social structures are eroded.

Saharawis (see Algeria)

Since 1975, Saharawis have been fighting a bitter war against occupying Moroccan, and until 1978, Mauritanian forces. Saharawis are of mixed Berber, Arab and black African descent. They inhabit the harsh desert region stretching from southern Morocco to the valleys of the Niger and Senegal and traditionally lived a nomadic life as traders. The assembly (*djemaa*) established its own body of law, the *orf*, to complement the basic Islamic judicial code the *sharia*. Under harsh conditions and dispersal no single group has been able to draw on sufficient power or resources to establish even a semblance of supra-tribal government.

As nomads, Saharawis were distinct from Berber Tuareg nomads to their east, as well as from black African farmers to the south, and semi-nomadic or sedentary Berbers to their immediate north. Saharawi society is highly stratified along tribal, caste and gender lines. Politically each tribe and faction regulated its affairs through *djemaa* of the heads of its most distinguished families, men who enjoyed the greatest respect. The first European contact with Western Sahara was made by Portuguese traders in the fifteenth century and a lucrative trade in slaves and gold started. In the late nineteenth century Spain laid claim to the territories. In 1934 the French succeeded in gaining the border regions of north-western Sahara while the Spanish continued to govern the Spanish Sahara as an appendage of the protectorate in northern Morocco.

Until the late 1950s most Saharawis were still nomadic. Their lives began to change rapidly when the territory's rich mineral resources became known to the West. The Western Sahara has large oil reserves onshore, with rich iron ore and phosphate deposits offshore. It is also one of the best fishing zones in the world, unexploited by the Saharawis. The economic changes of the 1960s and early 1970s brought about the rapid modernization of Saharawi society; a majority of the population became sedentarized, while the urban population trebled in seven years. Inspired by Moroccan radicals who had brought about Moroccan independence in 1956, Saharawis rebelled against the French and Spanish in the region, but it was not until 1971–2 that the anti-colonial movement was effectively organized, largely by Saharawi living in Morocco and Mauritania. On 10 May 1973 the Polisario Front was formed, growing rapidly into a mass movement. In 1975 thousands of pro-Polisario demonstrators took to the streets to greet a UN mission of inquiry which found there to be an 'overwhelming consensus among (West) Saharans . . . in favour of independence'.

Since 1956 Morocco has laid claim to a vast portion of the Algerian Sahara, the whole of the Western Sahara and Mauritania and the north-west tip of Mali. The Mauritanian government however viewed any loss of Western Saharan territory as a grave security threat in view of the 1,570 kilometre border between the two countries. Almost half of this border is within 50 kilometres of the strategic iron ore railway upon which Mauritania depends for 85 per cent of its export earnings. In response to the series of UN resolutions on the holding of a referendum on the self-determination of Western Sahara, King Hassan II of Morocco was determined to thwart what was clearly a prelude to independence. Hoping to force Spain to cede the territory to Morocco, he launched a patriotic crusade to recover the 'Moroccan Sahara' and aroused enormous enthusiasm among Moroccans. He massed 20,000 troops near the Western Saharan border and forced a postponement of the referendum pending a decision on the dispute at the International Court of Justice (ICJ) in The Hague. The referendum was never held and in 1975 the ICJ found that neither Mauritania nor Morocco had ties of sovereignty with Western Sahara. Precluding the judgement, Morocco and Mauritania had reached agreement with Spain according to which Spain would cede the Western Sahara to both countries in return for fishing and other interests. On 14 April 1976 Western Sahara was formally partitioned with two-thirds of the territory going to Morocco. This division of Western Sahara was carried out without consideration of Saharawi determination to resist annexation. Polisario had consistently rejected any settlement which did not grant the territory full independence within its pre-1975 borders. Refugees began to leave the disputed area and within six months 50,000 people were living in camps on Algerian territory. These camps were soon populated almost entirely by women and children as men left to join Polisario's Saharawi Peoples Liberation Army (SPLA). An independent Western Saharan state, the Saharan Arab Democratic Republic (RASD) was proclaimed by Polisario on 27 February 1976.

The war was unpopular with most Mauritanians. Many were Moors, thus related to the Saharawis, while others, black Africans, saw it as an inter-Arab affair. In July 1978, following a military coup in Mauritania, a peace agreement was signed according to which Mauritania abandoned all claims to Western Saharan territory. Morocco, on the other hand, intensified the fighting, seizing Dahkla and naming Tiris el Gharbia a Moroccan province. In March 1980, Hassan began building a Great Wall of the Sahara from the Algerian border in the north-east to the Atlantic Coast. By 1988 the wall was 1,600 kilometres long and covered almost two-thirds of the territory. Morocco maintained 100,000–200,000 troops there and received military backing from France and the USA. The wall was highly fortified, constructed of sand banks, minefields and barbed wire with intermittent artillery placements and observation posts. It effectively pushed the guerrillas further into the desert. By the end of the 1980s Morocco was in undisputed control of 80 per cent of Western Sahara, but 140,000 troops were needed to maintain this elaborate system. Hopes for a peaceful, just settlement rose when former UN Secretary General Perez de Cuellar launched a peace plan in August 1988. In September 1991 the UN began developing a multinational force to supervise a ceasefire and organized a referendum.

King Hassan has continued to regard Moroccan withdrawal as unthinkable. It would offend nationalist sentiments shared by most major political parties and army officers, and risk his political survival. The UN meanwhile has been unwilling to risk destabilizing Morocco given the escalation of civil war in Algeria. Internationally, the Polisario Front's Saharan Arab Democratic Republic has won diplomatic recognition from 72 states whereas

Hassan has failed to secure recognition of Morocco's claim. While the UN has committed itself to sending military police and civilian units as part of the UN Mission for the Referendum in Western Sahara to oversee the partial withdrawal of the Moroccan forces, it has not pressured Rabat to carry out the referendum. There is some concern about whether a free and fair referendum can take place. Voter registration is not straightforward as Saharawis are traditionally nomadic, in addition to refugee and migrant flows resulting in the settlement of many people outside the territory's arbitrary colonial borders. A 1975 Spanish census counted only those physically within the border of Spanish Sahara, recording 73,497 people. In July 1991 the Moroccan government presented the UN with lists of 120,000 Moroccans who had settled there since 1975, threatening to swamp the core list. Although the UN is supposed to organize and conduct the referendum, its local administration continues to remain in the hands of Morocco. Finally, a referendum would cost an estimated $200–250 million.

Although King Hassan announced an amnesty for all Polisario fighters on 12 June 1991 and subsequently freed about 3,000 civilian Saharawi prisoners, Amnesty International state that as of 28 August 1991 hundreds of 'disappeared' Saharawis were unaccounted for, being either dead or still in secret detention. There are fears concerning the short- and long-term security of returning refugees, in addition to the inadequacy of funds available for their repatriation. Morocco is determined to avoid voting in areas beyond its control and the Forces Armées Royales (FAR) staged air strikes in August 1991 beyond the wall, bringing an end to the *de facto* ceasefire that had prevailed since early 1990. There have since been reports of people fleeing into the desert. Finally, Algeria's contemporary political instability has weakened Polisario's position there and raised serious concerns about the prospects for the remaining 100,000 Saharawi refugees in Algeria.

Jews

The most important influx of Jews to Morocco came in the wake of expulsions from Spain in 1516–17, when several thousands settled in the northern towns of Tangier, Fez and Rabat. Most were traders and skilled artisans, and some were highly educated. By 1948 there were some 270,000 Jews in Morocco. This number had fallen to 162,420 in 1960 and 53,000 in 1967, as many fled fearing the implications of independence. Today about 30,000 live in Casablanca, Fez, Marrakech, Meknes and Tangier. Accompanying the declaration of the state of Israel, numerous attacks took place on Jewish premises and individuals. After Moroccan independence their situation improved as Jews were granted full suffrage and near-complete freedom of movement. While Jewish emigration was made illegal, many continued to leave for Israel. Morocco is currently the only Arab country where Jews enjoy equal rights and privileges to the rest of the community.

Conclusions and future prospects

Although the war in Western Sahara is a dispute over sovereignty between indigenous Saharawis and Morocco, the war has ramifications beyond the border of Western Sahara. It has strained relations with Algeria while compounding Morocco's economic difficulties and so undermining the stability of King Hassan II's pro-Western monarchy. Many Saharawis have lost faith in diplomacy and in the UN. Morocco has thus far avoided an Islamist eruption but radical students are making their presence felt and an upsurge in Islamic sentiment is inflaming local politics. Police surveillance on the Islamist movement is intense. Hassan is determined not to lose control over the mosques of which he is the spiritual head. The traditionally nationalist Istiqlal Party has added Islamic appeal to its platform and charitable Islamist organizations have won support – especially among the growing young urban unemployed populations, particularly in Casablanca and Fez where divisions of wealth are widest.

Further reading

Amnesty International, *Morocco: Amnesty International Concerns*, London, 1991.

Amnesty International, *Morocco: A Pattern of Political Imprisonment, 'Disappearance' and Torture*, London, 1992.

Hodges, T., *The Western Saharans*, London, MRG report, 1984, 1991.

Minority-based and advocacy organizations

Association Berbère du Maroc, 23 Abdelkarim Elhahabi, Rabat, Morocco.

Moroccan Association for Human Rights, 5 Zankat Soussa, Rabat, Morocco.

Moroccan League for the Defence of Human Rights, Bad el Had, Rabat, Morocco.

Niger

Land area:	1,267,080 sq km
Population:	8.1 million (1993)
Main religions:	Islam, traditional religions
Main languages:	French (official), Arabic, Courtemanche, Djerma, Fulani, Hausa, Kanuri, Tamashek, Toubou
Main minority groups:	Songhai 1.7 million (22%) (incl. Kurtey 425,000), Tuareg 800,000 (10%), Fula (Fulani) 750,000 (9%), Kanuri 500,000 (5%), Teda and Daza (Toubou) 80,000 (1%), Manga 80,000 (1%)
Real per capita GDP:	$790
UNDP HDI/rank:	0.204 (174)

The Republic of Niger is a landlocked state on the southern edge of the Sahara in West Africa. Niger is bordered by Algeria, Libya, Chad, Nigeria, Benin, Burkina Faso and Mali. More than half the population are Hausa, settled agriculturists who live in the south. Second to them, comprising a fifth of the population, are Songhai cultivators whose homeland is located west of the Hausa territory. The arid north and centre are home to Tuareg camel and goat herders, who speak Tamashek, a language related to Berber. Other pastoralists are Fula (Fulani), a cattle herding group whose West African language indicates proximity to groups in Senegal. Teda and Daza (Toubou) live in the east and north-east, small groups of herders who speak Saharan languages. Related by language but not livelihood are Kanuri agriculturists of the south-east, many of whom are now urban dwellers.

During the Middle Ages the western part of present-day Niger was part of the Songhai empire established during the seventh century by the Berbers. Islam, the country's dominant religion, was introduced in the eleventh century. In the fourteenth century, Hausa city states were established in the south. These were conquered by Fula in the nineteenth century. Niger became a formal colony within French West Africa in 1922. In 1960 Hamani Diori, who led the independence movement, became the first President and governed until 1974. A military and civilian council ruled until 1989, when the first elections took place since 1960. Rising demands for political reform produced a national conference which stripped the new ruling President Ali Seybou of his position. A multi-party constitution was introduced in December 1992 and the former ruling party was defeated in the 1993 elections by a six-party reformist grouping. In January 1996 Niger's first democratically elected President was ousted in a military coup and an army colonel took over as head of state.

Songhai

Songhai are a broad constellation of ethnic clans including Songhai-Djerma and Dendi, and also often Gube, Kurtey, Sorko and Woga. Songhai are spread out from south-eastern Mali to south-west Niger and other areas of northern Benin. Djerma (Zerma) are found east of the River Niger between Niamey and the Hausa belt and along the River Niger from Mali to Niger and Benin. They are socio-economically assimilated with the Songhai. Djerma are believed to be descended from the Malinké and the Sarakole and to have migrated southward from Mali before the rise of the Songhai empire and to have adopted Islam in the tenth century. Dosso, their loose confederacy of small village states, became powerful in the nineteenth century, especially under colonial rule. Dendi, who live on the Niger–Benin border and in some areas north of Benin, are essentially descendants of Songhai who resisted the Moroccan conquest of central Songhai and Gao. Djerma have traditionally shunned manual labour. Historically a loose confederation of small clans and village states, Djerma developed a feeling of deeper affinity only after wars with the Fulani and pressure from the Tuareg.

Niger has a history of sedentary–nomadic clashes as Tuareg clans have been forced south by population pressure. Tuareg regarded the French as infidel conquerors to be expelled; the Franco-Tuareg wars greatly decimated the Tuareg and in particular whole warrior castes. To the Songhai, the French were sought-after allies who could assist them to stem the dual pressure from the north and south of Yuareg and Fulani respectively. Djerma in particular were avidly Francophile and joined in the French military pacification of the area. Hausa were alienated to some extent by France's refusal to assist them in regaining lost territories from the Fulani. The Parti Progressiste Nigérieri (PPN) is effectively controlled by Songhai, but traditional Hausa and Fulani leaders were placed in cabinet positions to prevent the growth of regional sentiment in the early 1970s. The civilian government collapsed under internal pressure from students, unions and the effects of drought and in 1974 was replaced by a military government which brought Djerma hegemony.

Other groups linked with the Songhai are Kurtey, who are descended from the intermarriage of Fula (Fulani) with Songhai. A Fula clan or Fula former slaves migrated as a result of an internal schism, coming to Niger in 1750 and settling on riverain lands around Niamey. As pastoralists they tended Songhai cattle and adopted the local language and customs, though maintaining some Fula traits. The Kurtey fell apart from the Songhai prior to the colonial era. They were regarded as overseers of the Niger River by some and river pirates by others as they would travel as far as 500 kilometres in slave raids. As much as 40 per cent of the population now migrates as seasonal labour to Ghana.

Tuareg (Kel Tamashek) (see also **Algeria, Libya, Mali**)

Tuareg pastoralists are indigenous to three African countries: Algeria on the northern side of the Sahara, north-eastern Mali and central and northern Niger. There are negative connotations associated with the term Tuareg, an Arabic word meaning 'the abandoned of God', and these people call themselves Kel Tamashek, the people who speak Tamashek. The greatest number of Tuareg live in Niger, mostly south and west of Air massif, with smaller populations in Algeria, Mali and Libya. Tuareg began a continuous migration south-west in the seventh century with the Arab conquest of the Maghreb, arriving in Niger from the eleventh century onward. As the result of intense population pressure from this continuous migration they pushed resident Hausa communities southward and overran more sedentary groups. Extremely independent, the Tuareg formed a number of sultanates and converted to Islam but retained pre-Islamic customs. In the eighteenth and nineteenth centuries the Tuareg extended control over desert trade and led resistance to French rule, and in the early twentieth century instigated a number of rebellions. Tuareg society is highly stratified and consist of several castes; nobles, *imajeren* 'the proud and free'; *imrad*, free but subordinate; *ineslemen*, the religious caste; *ikelan*, slaves who today live in neo-peonage, tending the palm groves and vegetable gardens of their masters. *Inadin* are an artisan caste of silversmiths living outside regular Tuareg society, which looks down upon their lifestyle. They wander from Tuareg encampment to encampment also serving as fortune tellers and medics. Tuareg language is Tamashek, a written script related to ancient Libyan.

At independence several top Tuareg chiefs in Niger and Mali attempted to form a federation to keep themselves outside the political control of the 'black south'. In Mali this was severely repressed. In Niger the sultan was deposed in favour of his son and exiled but in Niger, unlike Mali, the incident did not bring further agitation on the part of the Tuareg. In 1980 Libya tried to foment sub-nationalist feelings following a diplomatic break with Niamey, and a number of Tuareg civil servants were enticed to Tripoli. The drought a few years later hit the Tuareg of Air hardest of all as overseas aid was embezzled, and by 1985, 50,000 had been displaced. Tuareg lands in Niger are rich in uranium and minerals; Libya has actively pressed for an independent Sahel state for Tuareg.

Today Tuareg are struggling for survival. The droughts of 1970s and 1980s devastated the nomadic way of life. This was further destroyed by the Niger government's failure to provide assistance for recovery. Some Tuareg sought refuge in neighbouring countries; others abandoned nomadism altogether.

After the drought of 1984–5 several thousand Tuareg from Mali and Niger sought alternative pasture on the northern side of the Sahara in Algeria. Some went as far as Libya. The International Fund for Agricultural Development (IFAD) joined forces with the governments of Algeria, Mali and Niger to resettle the group back in Mali. Because this took three years to organize, Tuareg were directed to provisional camps around the town of Tchin Tabaraden. Anger over the inadequacy of this government response, and frustration due to Tuareg lack of political voice and power, turned to violence. The food aid they should have received through the Niger government had apparently not arrived. Three or four young Tuareg occupied the police post in Tchin

Tabaraden and then fled into the desert, taking a forestry guard as hostage. The government sent the army after them and the arrival of soldiers seems to have caused panic in the town. People ran away into the desert and into small villages around Tchin Tabaraden. It was the dry season in Niger, when pastoralists have to water their animals at least once every two days. Tuareg claim that the military occupied the water points in the area and shot at pastoralists as they approached. They claim that the military encircled camps, raped women, stripped elders and killed young people.

Events in Niger had an impact in Mali. The border between the two countries was created during colonial times. It has always been considered artificial by pastoralists as it runs through the centre of their traditional grazing areas. Malians and aid agency staff became the target of politically motivated violence. Rebel attacks continued throughout the north, spilling into the town of Gao. The Malian government responded by enforcing a crackdown on Tuareg and increasing the number of arrests.

One Tuareg objective is to achieve a Saharan state for pastoralist people stretching from the Atlantic coast to Chad. Tuareg felt disenfranchised, sentiments expressed by the Minister of Communication in Niger, Khamed Abdoulaye, the only Tuareg minister. He stressed that the pastoralist lifestyle meant that they had no effective participation in the decision-making processes of the country. Rare moments of contact were limited to tax collection or when pastoralists were brought out to welcome a figure of authority from the capital. Contact between pastoralist people at the grassroots and the administration is with the gendarme and Republican Guard who generally behave as though they are on conquered territory, thus symbolizing violence to the population.

Although the immediate response of the Malian and Niger governments was to use force to suppress Tuareg protests, it appears that the outbursts have encouraged a search for a longer term solution. April 1995 marked a critical breakthrough in the recent history of Niger – the initialling of a permanent peace accord between the government and the Tuareg rebels who had been intermittently fighting for autonomy since 1990. The deal marked the culmination of six months of mediation by France, Burkina Faso and Algeria. In February 1994 the Tuareg Coordination de la Résistance Armée (CRA) had set out ambitious terms for any settlement – it sought autonomy for more than 80 per cent of the national territory, mainly the desert of the north and centre where the nomads have traditionally lived. It also sought seven ministries, fifteen parliamentary seats and half the senior army posts. By late 1994, the two sides could agree on one fundamental principle, the decentralization of many responsibilities from central government in Niamey to authorities in the regions. It was this consensus over regional autonomy that formed the basis of the settlement.

Fula (Fulani)

Fula, also called Fulani, are chiefly Muslim and speak Fulfulde. A significant percentage are cattle herders. Their ancestors were known as Bororo, who form a subgroup today which is less Islamicized than sedentary Fula. The origin of the Fula is uncertain; it has been postulated that they may be of Ethiopian origin. Most migrated to Niger from northern Nigeria during the colonial era and are now principally sedentary. Fula were once prominent in northern Nigeria, having overrun several Hausa principalities. By 1910, four out of seven Hausa states had fallen to Fula armies. Today they live in a small concentration in central-south Niger.

Kanuri

Kanuri are known in Niger by their Hausa name, Beri Beri. They inhabit the area near Lake Chad, in eastern Niger from Zinder to Maine-Soroa and western Chad; and many live in Borno province in Nigeria. Kanuri settled in Niger during the expansion of the Kanen-Bornu empire; today, together with Toubou nomads, some Kanuri continue to exploit remote salt pans and desert oases of Kaouar. The Kanuri spread from bases further south.

Teda and Daza (Toubou)

Toubou are inhabitants of Tu, the local name for the Tibesti Mountains. Toubou resisted colonialism. They are nomadic, traditionally extracting a levy on all caravans and tribute from sedentary villages. In Niger, Toubou control the salt pans, acting as intermediaries between the Kanuri population of the oases and the Tuareg overlords. Toubon are comprised of Teda (Braouia) and Daza. Teda are a branch of the Toubou found mostly in northern Chad and in small numbers in eastern Niger. They call themselves Tedagada (those who speak Tegada) and are related to

Kanuri. In Niger they are found in Kaouar and Djado areas. Muslim and intensely anti-French and anti-infidel, Teda were driven out of Niger at the onset of the colonial era and in the 1920s. In Chad the Teda have been in rebellion against Njamena since 1966. Certain clans have been pushed into Niger by the rebellion and the Niger government has been very apprehensive about the possibility of rebellion spreading. Of approximately 200,000 Daza, 50 per cent are in northern Chad and 30 per cent are in Libya. There are very small numbers in north-eastern Niger, around Lake Chad. They call themselves Dazagada.

Manga

There are approximately 80,000 Manga living in central Niger. They speak Kanuri and live east of Zindar on the Niger–Chad border, in the vast expanses of Agadez department.

Conclusions and future prospects

The Tuareg crisis reflects to some degree the clash of interests between nomads mainly reliant on livestock herding, being driven south into areas traditionally occupied by arable farmers. There was also a conflict of interest between inhabitants of Niamey, largely Djerma and many employed in public services, and people in more rural areas. The thrust of economic reform begun in 1994 and 1995 (but not followed through) was to shift the balance of spending power away from the city and towards the countryside, to encourage farm output and to reduce the cost of the public sector. One factor that threatened to challenge the practical functioning of autonomy was a change of government. Elections held in January 1995 brought a decisive victory for the Mouvement National pour la Société du Développement (MNSD), which had ruled Niger in the one-party era and enjoyed strong support among the Djerma people of the Niger Valley around Niamey. This engendered fear that the southern-based MNSD might be less flexible in ensuring the smooth functioning of any new autonomy for Tuareg. There was also concern that new tension might arise between MNSD and Hausa, Niger's largest ethnic group and the bedrock of support for the defeated Convention Democratique et Sociale (CDS) of Mahamane Ousmane.

Further reading

Charlick, R., *Niger: Personal Rule and Survival in the Sahel*, Boulder, CO, Westview, 1991.

Cross, N., *The Sahel: The Peoples' Right to Development*, MRG report, London, 1990.

Keenan, J., *Tuareg: People of Ahaggar*, London, Allen Lane, 1977.

Marnham, P., *Nomads of the Sahel*, MRG report, London, 1979.

Norris, H.T., *The Tuaregs: Their Islamic Legacy and Diffusion in the Sahel*, Warminster, Aris & Phillips, 1975.

Panos Institute, *Green War*, London, Panos, 1991.

Nigeria

Land area:	923,768 sq km
Population:	119.3 million (1993)
Main languages:	English, Hausa, Yoruba, Ibo
Main religions:	Islam, Christianity, traditional religions
Main minority groups:	Ibo (Igbo) 24 million (20%), delta minority groups (Andoni, Brass, Dioubu, Etche, Ijaw, Kalibari, Nembe, Ogoni, Okrika) 6 million (5%), Tiv 4 million (3%), Ibibio-Efik 3.3 million (2.8%), Kanuri 3 million (2.5%), Edo (Bini) 500,000 (0.4%), Nupe 500,000 (0.4%), Jokun (no data)
Real per capita GDP:	$1,540
UNDP HDI/rank:	0.400 (137)

The Federal Republic of Nigeria, on the Atlantic Coast of West Africa, is bounded by Benin, Niger, Chad and Cameroon. It is Africa's most populous country, made up of some 250 different ethnic groups. Four of these groups – Fula (Fulani), Hausa, Yoruba and Ibo (Igbo) – account for 65 per cent of the total population. The south is divided into a western, Yoruba-speaking area and an eastern Ibo-speaking area, a mid-section of related but different groups and areas of Niger Delta peoples on the eastern and central coasts. The north is predominantly Hausa and pastoralist Fula (Fulani), but Kanuri dominate in the north-east with a belt of peoples between the two. The middle belt area, from the Cameroon highlands on the east to the Niger River valley on the west, includes some 50 to 100 linguistic and ethnic groups, ranging from larger Tiv and Nupe to much smaller language groups. Islam claims just under one-half of all Nigerians and is the dominant religion in the north. Christianity, claiming one-third of the population, is dominant in the south. The remaining population holds traditional religious beliefs.

The spread of Islam, predominantly in the north but later also in the south-west, began a millennium ago. The creation of the Sokoto caliphate in the *jihad* (holy war) of 1804–8 brought most of the north and adjacent parts of Niger and Cameroon under a single Islamic governance. The great extension of Islam within present-day Nigeria dates from the nineteenth century. This helps to account for the dichotomy between north and south and for divisions within the north that have been so strong during colonial and post-colonial eras.

The slave trade had a profound influence on virtually all of Nigeria. The trans-Atlantic trade accounted for the forced migration of perhaps 3.5 million people between 1650 and 1860, while a steady stream of slaves flowed north across the Sahara for a millennium. Within Nigeria slavery was widespread with social implications that are still evident. The Sokoto caliphate had more slaves than any other modern country except the USA in 1860. Slaves were numerous among the Ibo, Yoruba and many other ethnic groups. Many ethnic distinctions, especially in the middle belt between north and south, were reinforced because of slave raiding and defensive measures adopted against enslavement. Conversion to Islam and the spread of Christianity were intricately associated with issues relating to slavery and with efforts to promote political and cultural autonomy. The colonial era was relatively brief in Nigeria, but it unleashed rapid and lasting change. Expansion of agricultural production as the principal export earner and development of infrastructure resulted in a severely distorted economic growth that has subsequently collapsed. On the other hand, social dislocation associated with the decline of slavery and the internal movement of population necessitated the reassessment of ethnic loyalties which have been reflected in politics and religion. Colonial Nigeria was initially ruled as three distinct political units: the Northern Protectorate, the Southern Protectorate and Lagos Colony. In 1906 the Lagos Colony and Southern Protectorate were merged. In 1914 the three units were amalgamated into one nation. Partly in recognition of the major ethno-linguistic differences between Ibo and Yoruba in the south, the Southern Protectorate was split in 1939 into Eastern and Western Provinces. This was given constitutional backing when in 1947 Nigeria was divided into Northern, Eastern and Western regions, a move which gave prominence to the three dominant groups: Hausa-Fula in the north, Ibo in the east and Yoruba in the west. Each of the former three regions had minorities who formed themselves into movements agitating for constitutional safeguards against opposition from the larger ethnic group that dominated the affairs of the region. The minority 'problem' became a major political question when it became clear that Nigeria would adopt a federal system of government. Since each region was dominated politically by one ethnic group, minorities began to aspire to separate existence. This question was important in the 1954 federal and 1957 constitutional conferences. The north and east refused fragmentation while the west supported the creation of a midwestern state if others did the same. Palliative measures included setting up the Niger Delta Development Board and the inclusion of fundamental human rights in the federal constitution to protect minorities.

In 1963 Edo and Western Igbo were granted a separate midwestern region, reducing both Yoruba and Ibo dominance in this region. British protection of the Muslim north and British reliance on the authority of the traditional Muslim rulers, the emirs, created major problems after independence. Northern political power, a result of its large population, was combined with an underdeveloped economy and educational system. Friction increased between Hausa and Ibo in the north, where many Ibo had moved as traders and business people and lived in residential areas set aside for strangers and 'aliens'. In January 1966 Ibo carried out a military coup which brought reprisals against them in the north. As a result many Ibo fled to their traditional homeland in the south-east, and northerners were attacked in Port Harcourt. Six months later another coup placed General Yakubu Gowon, a non-Muslim northerner in command. Gowon replaced the four regions with twelve new states (increased to nineteen in 1976), attempting to lessen the power of the larger ethnic groups. In 1967, Ibo, under the leadership of Odumegwu Ojukwu, attempted to secede as the republic of Biafra, which led to a bloody civil war and the death of hundreds of thousands of Ibo.

Since independence in 1960 Nigeria has experienced a number of successful and attempted coups and a brutal civil war, let corrupt civilian governments siphon off the profits from the oil boom of the 1970s and faced economic collapse in the 1980s. When a pro-military candidate lost in the presidential elections of 1993 Army Chief of Staff General Ibrahim Babangida annulled the results and imprisoned the winner, Moshood Abiola. Defence Minister General Sami Abacha seized power on 17 November 1993, and the country returned once more to military rule.

Ibo (Igbo)

Ibo, also called Igbo, dominant in eastern Nigeria, are largely Christian, well educated and entrepreneurial. Over a period of many years, over 1 million have left their home areas to work in other parts of Nigeria. They have been deeply resented by northerners, especially Hausa who regarded them as infidels and segregated them in northern towns. Regional tension became acute after independence as politicians fought ruthlessly for the spoils of office. Easterners staged a bloody military coup in January 1966, regarded as an attempt by Ibo to take over the country, and six months later an even bloodier coup brought General Gowon to power. In September, Radio Cotonou in neighbouring Benin broadcast a rumour that some northerners were killed in the east. Northern mobs went on the rampage, brutally killing thousands of Ibo civilians, while Ibo soldiers were hacked to death in army barracks. Those who survived fled east, injured and often destitute, posing massive problems of relocation.

There followed a major exodus of skilled Ibo from other parts of Nigeria towards the east. The Nigerian government made little effort in public to heal the wounds or condemn the atrocities. The new division of Nigeria proposed by Gowon would have broken up the region and given control of its rich oil deposits to non-Ibo minorities. Easterners, exasperated beyond endurance but comforted too by the presence of oil, felt they had little choice but to break away from Nigeria and establish an independent state in the east – the Republic of Biafra. The federal government saw this as rebellion, and civil war followed from 1967 to 1970. Following their defeat, Ibo have been excluded from significant representation in higher echelons of military and government.

Delta minority groups

The Niger Delta, a lush region of mangrove swamps, rainforest and swampland, is home to 6 million people, including 500,000 Ogoni (also called Khana). It is the site of rich oil and natural gas reserves. Oil accounts for 90 per cent of Nigerian exports and 80 per cent of government revenue. Shell Nigeria produces 900,000 barrels a day, half of the country's total output. In the federal capital, Abuja, delegates from the delta argue that the local authority has a right to share in deciding how resources are used. Northern delegates, including nominees of the military government, insist that mineral resources are a federal responsibility. Delta minority groups, including Andoni, Brass, Dioubu, Etche, Ijaw, Kalibari, Nembe, Ogoni and Okrika, have joined forces against the northern-dominated military government, with the National Democratic Coalition backing the imprisoned winner of the 1993 presidential election, Moshood Abiola.

By 1990 communities which had remained in poverty for years had decided to take action against the pillage of their resources which has left a legacy of polluted soil and water, rusting pipelines criss-crossing farmland, oil spillages and continual gas flares. In that year Etche demonstrated peacefully against Shell in the village of Umuechen. Shell called for police protection in case of further action. The Mobile Police Force proceeded to massacre 80 people and destroy 495 homes. Although an inquiry blamed the police, local people held Shell responsible for not negotiating. Since then, protesters have met with similar and sometimes more severe brutality.

By this time Ogoni, who live in the north-eastern fringes of the delta, were also involved and began a campaign calling for the cleanup of environmental damage, greater revenue from oil production and political autonomy. Their Movement for the Survival of the Ogoni People (MOSOP) issued an Ogoni Bill of Rights, which demanded immediate compensation for ecological damage from Shell and self-determination for Ogoniland. Ogoni lands had been given limited autonomy in 1947 with the creation of the Ogoni Native Authority, and Ogoni had begun to enjoy some modernization of education and health care. The gradual transfer of power during the 1950s to the major ethnic groups inaugurated a period of exploitation and marginalization. During the 1967–70 Biafran War, Ogoniland was occupied first by rebel Ibo and then by federal troops. Although oil worth $30,000 million has been produced from Ogoniland, the area is one of the least developed areas of Nigeria, with poor roads, few clinics or schools and lacking piped water for the majority. Very few of Shell's 5,000 Nigerian employees were Ogoni.

MOSOP was originally an umbrella organization which united traditional chiefs and intellectuals, such as writer, entrepreneur and former cabinet minister of Rivers State Ken Saro-Wiwa. It came under severe pressure from the military government, and its leaders were detained and harassed. MOSOP's demands pitted it fully against the Nigerian government, which owns a 51 per cent share in Shell Nigeria, by threatening its huge oil revenues.

When elections were being discussed in May 1994 for representatives to a national constitutional conference, splits in the Ogoni community erupted. Four chiefs, including a former vice-president of MOSOP, were murdered. The military regime charged Saro-Wiwa with murder, although clear evidence indicates a solid alibi. The military claimed that he, along with eight other Ogoni activists, incited the killers. The authority which confirmed the conviction was the Provisional Ruling Council, in effect, the government. Nigeria received international condemnation following the execution of Saro-Wiwa and the other eight activists on 10 November 1995 after a show trial. Nigeria was suspended from the Commonwealth and given two years to restore democracy or face total expulsion.

Delta minority militants still sabotage oil installations, and in 1995 the military administrator of Rivers State set up an internal task force to quell what he called 'inter-communal' fighting. It has been blamed by human rights groups for encouraging violence.

Tiv

Tiv, the country's fifth largest ethnic group, live in the central-eastern state of Taraba and neighbouring states. Tiv are prosperous subsistence farmers and traders growing yams, millet and sorghum and raising small livestock and cattle. Their villages are comprised of compounds of sleeping huts, reception huts and granaries with a central marketplace. They speak Nyanza or Benue-Congo, part of the Niger-Congo language family, and traditionally formed a classic segmentary society in which strongly organized patrilineages linked large portions of the ethnic group into named non-local segments. Local organization, land tenure, inheritance, religious beliefs, law and allegiances were all related to this segmentary lineage. Tiv political organization and the possibility of conflict or alliance among territorial groups are traditionally based on the relative closeness of patrilineal descent members to a male ancestor. Nonetheless all Tiv have united against neighbouring enemies because of their common ancestors. They were never conquered by the Muslim *jihad*. Traditional lineage elders settled political disputes. Tiv had no paramount chiefs although one was established by the British in 1948. Violence between Tiv and Jokun broke out on the eve of independence in 1959, and again in 1990, over claims and counter-claims concerning the historical occupation of the town of Wukari. Under indirect rule Jokun, who constitute 25 per cent of the regional population, were given power over the Tiv majority, a domination which has continued to the present.

Wider administrative units were introduced under British rule, and mission-led education and conversion to Christianity helped create a sense of separateness from the Muslim north, based on educational disparity and religion. Tiv rioted in 1952 against the Hausa – Fulani rulers of northern Nigeria, who took harsh punitive action against them. In 1960 Tiv again became disaffected with the Native Authority System. Tiv were among members of the United Middle Belt Congress which opposed the rule of the Native Authority which supported the Northern People's Congress (NPC), the ruling party of the north. During the uprisings of 1960 and 1964 many people were killed. The Tiv attempt to create a separate region was blocked by northern Muslim-based political parties.

Ibibio-Efik

Ibibio-Efik are a group of six related peoples living in southern Nigeria. Most are subsistence farmers, but two subgroups are fishers. Ibibio-Efik had a long history of contact with Europeans, in particular slave traders. Market trading and handicrafts are well developed. The Ibibio language belongs to the Benue-Niger subfamily of the Niger-Congo languages. Ibibio have lived on their present lands east of the Niger River in the southern part of Cross Rivers State for a long time, Efik are ethnically related to Ibibio and form the second largest population in the former eastern region of Nigeria.

Traditionally Ibibio had no central government. The village was the most important political entity, and public order was maintained by powerful secret societies run by men. Today many Ibibio are Christianized. Together with Edo they proposed that the coast between the Niger Delta and Calabar become a new region in order to end Ibo domination in this area prior to 1963. However, only a new midwestern region was approved in 1963. Ibibio-Efik society has been deeply affected by the pull of migration to Lagos and Port Harcourt.

Kanuri

Kanuri, speakers of a Saharan group of Sudanic languages, inhabit most of Bornu Province in north-east Nigeria near Lake Chad. In addition to the more than 3 million Kanuri in Nigeria in the mid-1980s (there has not been an accepted census since 1963) an estimated 400,000 live in Niger and Chad, chiefly in urban areas. Kanuri entered Nigeria from the central Sahara as Muslim conquerors in the fifteenth century, setting up a capital and subduing and assimilating the local Chadic speakers. Strategically located along the trans-Saharan trade routes, they early developed a stratified organized empire, Bornu, that reached its peak of influence during the sixteenth century, covering large areas of the central Sahara and many of the Hausa city states. Traditionally Kanuri society included a hereditary nobility and socially mobile commoner and slave classes. Even though Kanuri language, culture and history are distinctive, other elements of their society are similar to Hausa. Kanuri live in u-shaped towns open to the west, with the town's poetical leader housed in the arms of the u.

The Kanuri subsistence economy is based on agriculture, with peanuts grown as a cash crop. Kanuri have long-standing trade networks with neighbouring Fula, Arabs and Berbers. There has been large-scale immigration of Hausa and Fula into Borno since it became part of a newly enlarged north-east state, which also included large sections of Hausa-Fula areas. This sudden incorporation, the introduction of mass communication and interstate commerce brought increased contact with Hausa culture. By the 1970s Kanuri-speakers were finding it better to get along by assimilating Hausa culture and language.

Edo

Edo, or Bini are a people of southern Nigeria who live in the vicinity of the city of Benin, capital of a once powerful empire founded in the twelfth century. Over several centuries Edo conquered and subjugated many other peoples. The *oba* or king was a sacred figure, kept a large harem and rarely left his palace; he was assisted by a large administrative hierarchy. Workers in the palace specialized in numerous crafts, especially metalwork. Edo speak a Kwa language of the Niger-Congo family and grow yams and other vegetables for subsistence and cacao, oil palms and rubber for cash crops. Trade is large scale and complex. Descent and inheritance are traced through the father's line and marriages are polygamous. Formerly the men in each village were divided into age grades – youth, warriors and elders – each group being assigned community duties.

Nupe

Numbering some 500,000 in the late 1980s, Nupe live in west central Nigeria. They speak a language of the Kwa subfamily and live in villages growing yams, cassava and maize and raising goats, sheep and chickens. Traditionally Nupe was a kingdom, reaching its peak from the sixteenth to the late eighteenth centuries. It was conquered and converted to Islam by Fula early in the nineteenth century. Bida, the Nupe capital, was the centre of highly specialized production and large-scale market exchange. Artisans worked in craft guilds at metalwork, glassmaking, beadwork, weaving, carpentry and building.

Conclusions and future prospects

The north of Nigeria remains more politically cohesive than the south. The prevalence of Islam and widespread usage of the Hausa language have been important unifying factors. Northern minorities are showing a new militancy against Hausa and Fula domination, motivated by increasingly strident Christian evangelism. After independence, Kano State was declared secular, and since then Christianity has been gaining in the north. The growth of Islamic radicalism and resentment at the north's relatively poor economic and educational performance are unsettling the political establishment. The faithful, angered by rising unemployment and poverty, view the traditional Muslim elite as a corrupt pawn of the military government. A radical group known as the Muslim Brothers is gaining ground among Hausa. Their message is that Christianity is being favoured by the military government and the emirs and traditional leaders have forfeited their role as champions of Islam. Observers from both sides of the religious divide have blamed Nigeria's military authorities for the worsening situation.

Nigeria is in the throes of an unprecedented political crisis with an intensely unpopular military regime, presiding over a ruptured economy and a disillusioned populace. An early warning of ethnic or religious strife might be found in the handling of divisions between northern and southern Nigeria caused by the military suppression of democracy advocates. Some Nigerian newspapers warn of the potential break-up of the federation, amid striking parallels between developments in 1962–6, immediately before the civil war, and those of 1992–6. A northern-dominated government has ensured that it has compliant allies in the south who can divide potential opposition. Powerful loyalties to local communities still militate against national political organization and allow central government to divide the opposition. Arguments about revenue sharing among different communities have sharpened, especially in oil-producing areas. As popular resentment against military rule intensifies, the government increasingly relies on coercion to settle political problems. The politicization of public institutions including the judiciary, civil service and army, splitting them on ethnic and regional lines, has left them severely weakened. There is a lack of national integration and increasing alienation of minorities from central government. The power of the centre is increasingly perceived as a threat to local interests.

Further reading

Diamond, L., *Class, Ethnicity and Democracy in Nigeria*, Basingstoke, Macmillan, 1988.

Human Rights Watch/Africa, *Nigeria: Dawn of the New Dark Age,* New York, 1995.

Human Rights Watch/Africa, *Nigeria: The Ogoni Crisis,* New York, 1995.

Nnoli, O., *Ethnicity and Development in Nigeria*, Aldershot, Avebury, 1996.

Suberu, R.T., 'The travails of federalism in Nigeria', in Diamond, L. and Plattner, M.F. (eds), *Nationalism, Ethnic Conflict and Democracy*, Baltimore, MD, Johns Hopkins University Press, 1994.

Minority-based and advocacy organizations

Amnesty International, PMB 59, Agodi Ibadan, Oyo State, Nigeria.

Civil Liberties Organization, 24 Mbonu Ojike Street, off Alhaji Masha Road, Surulere, Lagos, Nigeria; tel. 234 1 848 513, fax 234 1 584 0288.

Committee for the Defence of Human Rights, PO Box 7247, Lagos, Nigeria.

Constitutional Rights Project, 48 Falolu Road, PO Box 4447, Surulere, Lagos, Nigeria.

Ethnic Minority Rights Organization of Africa, 63 Tejuosho Street, Lagos, Nigeria.

Human Rights Africa, 34 Aje Street, PO Box 2959, Yaba, Lagos, Nigeria.

Movement for the Survival of the Ogoni People (MOSOP), 24 Aggrey Road, PO Box 193, Port Harcourt, Nigeria.

Nigerian Human Rights Association, Ozumba Mbadiwe Street, Victoria Island, PMB 12610, Lagos, Nigeria.

Women in Nigeria, PO Box 253, Smaru, Zaria, Nigeria.

Senegal

Land area:	196,192 sq km
Population:	7.7 million (1992)
Main languages:	French, Wolof, Serer, Fula
Main religions:	Islam, traditional religions, Roman Catholicism
Main minority groups:	Dioula 800,000 (10%), Lebanese 25,000 (0.3%), Bassari 12,000 (0.15%)
Real per capita GDP:	$1,710
UNDP HDI/rank:	0.331 (153)

Senegal, Africa's western-most country, has a 600 kilometre coastline on the Atlantic Ocean and shares a border with Guinea-Bissau, Guinea, Mali and Mauritania. Gambia nearly divides the country in half. The dominant ethnic group is Wolof, and their language is spoken by 70 per cent of the population. Dioula, Fula, Lebu, Malinké, Serer and Soninke are among the other main ethnic groups. Senegal was granted internal self-government by the French in 1956. In 1959 Senegal and French Soudan (Mali) joined in the Malian Federation, although Senegal would break up the federation soon after independence. Since then, Senegal has been a multi-party democracy. Periods of centralized presidential rule have alternated with others which saw the prime minister as head of government. From 1982–9 Senegal and Gambia coordinated defence, economic and foreign policy through the Confederation of Senegambia.

Senegal has had a high degree of political stability, a large bourgeoisie and a long tradition of representative politics. It has been politically dominated by the intellectual and poet Leopold Senghor, who retired as President in 1980. In most respects it has led other Francophone African states in a major commitment to human rights, although economic stagnation from the mid-1980s has threatened this record. In terms of the degree to which party political organization is practised, Senegal is unique in Africa. At the same time, political mobilization in rural areas depends largely on clientele networks controlled by local notables. Seventeen parties campaigned in the 1988 presidential and national assembly elections. In Senegal the dilemma for governing parties is how to balance the desire for a veneer of electoral openness with the need for a continued grip on power and national policy. They face three critical issues: economic survival, the potential for Islamic radicalization among a population that is almost entirely Muslim, and protest and separatist sentiment in the Casamance region.

Dioula

Dioula are predominant in the area around the mouth of the Senegal river in the south-west. Historically, most Dioula have been farmers, especially rice cultivators, and traders. During and since the colonial period, their traditional culture and beliefs have been eroded by Islam, Christianity and Western education. Recently there has been an increasing tendency for Dioula youth to migrate, at least seasonally, to urban centres. Dioula are at the forefront of recent

Casamance separatist movements. Casamance is a small area between Gambia and Guinea-Bissau. It comprises Ziguinchor and Kolda, two of the country's eight administrative regions, and is almost completely separated from the state by Gambia. Present day Casamance was historically part of the Gambia River complex and in 1889 was arbitrarily separated from Gambia. During the colonial and early independence period it was a distant and neglected region. Today, Casamance is the most productive area of Senegal, producing 75 per cent of the country's main staple, rice. Several movements for the independence of Casamance from Senegal developed in the late 1960s and 1970s. A few separatist groups emerged in the early 1980s. In December 1990 there was another serious uprising among the Dioula in Ziguinchor where the revolt was crushed. Because regional parties are banned, the separatists have overwhelmingly voted for the opposition Parti Democratique Senegalais.

Despite the ban, several movements from Attika, the armed wing of the Mouvement des Forces Democratiques de Casamance (MFDC), have been waging a guerrilla war. There have been attacks on airports and general harassment. Troops and civilians have been caught in ambushes by the Front Sud, primarily composed of Dioula youth. As a result of the conflict thousands of Senegalese refugees have crossed into Guinea-Bissau.

Lebanese

Migrants from Lebanon and Syria (both are called Lebanese locally) began arriving in Senegal during the 1890s. This flow grew rapidly between the two world wars when Lebanon was under French domination. As a minority in Senegal, Lebanese assumed key commercial roles during the colonial period. Lebanese remain prominent as middle level merchants, in real estate, transportation and light industry. Since 1975 their numbers have swelled, fed largely by the refugee flow from Lebanon's civil war. From the mid-1980s the Senegalese government has tried to limit the outward flow of money to Lebanon by enforcing export restrictions. Lebanese have generally preferred to export their earnings rather than invest in Senegal, causing friction between the government and the growing Lebanese community. There is also tension between Lebanese and African Senegalese, especially in Dakar. The clashes with Mauritania also fuelled resentment towards the Lebanese, who were perceived as being supportive of the Moors.

Bassari

A numerically small ethnic group concentrated in south-eastern Senegal and north-eastern Guinea, Bassari are more closely linked to groups in Guinea's rainforest than with Muslims of the savanna. They were primarily hunters and gatherers with only limited cultivation and no pastoralism. Due to the isolation of their villages, Bassari were generally afforded protection from slave raiders, mainly Fula. Until recently Bassari maintained their traditional religious and ancephalous political systems, with an isolationist attitude towards their stronger, centralized Muslim neighbours. Many Bassari have now migrated to towns such as Kedougou and Dakar to seek wage employment.

Conclusions and future prospects

Devaluation of the Communauté Financière Africaine franc has been followed by social unrest, mainly because of the decline in the consumer's purchasing power. Senegal has been hit particularly hard because of its heavy reliance on imported goods especially foodstuffs such as rice. The Islamic Brotherhood is a growing power in Senegal, having historically played a role in indirect rule, a rule 'softened' by their involvement. Increasingly, young people are joining the ranks of more radical religious groups like El Moustarchidine wal Moustrachidate. The earlier success of Senegal as a stable pro-Western democracy with multi-party politics now looks less secure.

Further reading

Amnesty International, *Senegal: An Escalation in Human Rights Violations in the Casamance Region*, London, 1992.

Minority-based and advocacy organizations

African Institute of Human Rights, BP 1921, 43 Blvd Pinet Laprade, Dakar, Senegal.

Amnesty International, 126 Rue Joseph Gomis, BP 3813, Dakar, Senegal.

Institute for Human Rights and Peace, Faculty des Sciences Juridiques et Economiques, Université de Dakar – FANN, Dakar, Senegal.

InterAfrican Union of Lawyers, Commission on Human Rights and the Rights of People, 56 Rue du Docteur Theze, BP 1732, Dakar, Senegal.

Senegalese League for Human Rights, 18 Blvd de la République, 17ème Etage, Dakar, Senegal.

Sierra Leone

Land area:	72,325 sq km
Population:	4.5 million (1993)
Main religions:	Islam, Christianity, animism
Main languages:	English, Krio, Limba, Mende, Temne
Main minority groups:	Temne 940,000 (21%), Limba 273,000 (6%), Kono 120,000 (2.6%), Kuranko 106,000 (2.3%), Sherbro 91,000 (2%), Fulani (Fula) 80,000 (1.7%), Loko (Lokko) 80,000 (1.7%), Susu 80,000 (1.7%), Mandinka (Manding) 61,000 (1.3%), Kissi 60,000 (1.3%), Krio (Creole) 48,000 (1.1%), Kru 8,000 (0.2%), Vai 8,000 (0.2%)
Real per capita GDP:	$860
UNDP HDI/rank:	0.219 (173)

Sierra Leone is a West African republic bounded by Guinea, Liberia and the Atlantic Ocean. Temne- and Mende-speakers are the country's numerically dominant ethnic groups. Temne probably inhabited present-day Sierra Leone by the twelfth century, and Mende moved in from the northern savanna in the fifteenth century. In 1787 British opponents of the slave trade founded a colony of freed slaves at the site of Freetown. Freetown became a Crown Colony in 1808 and the interior was declared a British Protectorate in 1896. Although they initially intermarried with the indigenous population, the former slaves gradually acquired British education and culture, setting themselves apart from the local majority. The British were careful not to let Krio (Creole) elites dominate colonial politics. The 1951 constitution established the framework for independence ten years later.

In 1965, following the death of the first Prime Minister, Milton Margai, his brother and successor as head of the Sierra Leone People's Party (SLPP), Albert Margai, began to replace Krio with Mende supporters from his own southern region. Krio shifted their support to Siaka Stevens's All People's Congress which narrowly won the 1967 election but was prevented from assuming power by a coup. Stevens's regime returned to power in another coup in 1969; it gained the support of the Krio elite and instituted a repressive one-party state. When Stevens resigned in 1985, he was succeeded by General Joseph Saidu Momoh, who continued the repressive policies of his predecessor. Momoh reluctantly acceded to domestic demands for political reform, but was ousted by dissident soldiers in 1992 led by Captain Valentine Strasser after suspending the 1991 constitution.

Since 1991 Captain Foday Sankoh's Revolutionary United Front (RUF) and Liberian mercenaries have occupied large areas of the east and south. There has been a general breakdown of central authority, with increasing lawlessness and looting along the borders with Guinea and Liberia. Ethnic resentments were partially at the root of the rebellions, with rebels claiming that the government was dominated by southerners – Krio and Mende. This came after years of northern-dominated government. Strasser, a Krio, was accused of allowing Mende and Krio peoples from the south-east to dominate the government while marginalizing those from the north. Krio never had a monopoly of power similar to that of the Americo-Liberian elite in Liberia. However, because they were well-educated professionals with a disproportionate degree of influence over the government and economy, Krio unwittingly caused animosity and resentment among other groups. The Krio community, amounting to only 5 per cent of the population, was dominant during the colonial era. Minorities living in the border regions have been particularly ravaged by the civil war.

Minority groups

The dominant Mende group, 30 per cent of the population, inhabit the south. Temne, over 20 per cent of the population, inhabit an area inland from the coast to an area north of Mendeland. Limba live in the north-west quadrant. Fifteen minority groups, including the Krio but primarily Muslim groups from the north, make up the remainder. Some ethnic groups on the basis of their proximity to Mende and Temne tend to identify with the two larger groups, so developing a north/south split. Historically the most conscious ethnic division has been between the Krio of the Sierra Leone peninsula and the groups of the hinterland.

Groups living in the eastern regions of Sierra Leone include the Kissi, Vai, Kono and Gola, all groups with larger numbers living in Liberia. Refugees have fled over the border into Guinea from these areas. Kenema, like many other south-eastern states, has been cut off from relief agencies for long periods by the fighting. Malnutrition and disease are rife among the remaining population. Vast areas of the countryside have been cut off and mounting atrocities are reported from around Bo and Kenema. Abduction of children is a severe problem, and both government and guerrillas use children as spies.

As a consequence of uneven regional development, Northern Province in Sierra Leone has lagged behind the rest of the country in economic development. In the 1950s Krio of Freetown and the Sierra Leone peninsula had the advantage over the provinces in roads, schools and hospitals. In the 1960s the distribution between the provinces became the dominant question; northerners believed the south and west had more than its fair share of Western-style education, transportation, communications and economic development. Temne, Limba, Susu and Kono occupy relatively deprived areas and have been pushed by poverty from the north. Northerners tended to migrate to more prosperous regions such as Freetown and the diamond fields of the Eastern Province.

Mende benefited from the relative prosperity of their southern homeland. Mende came to occupy the heavily forested southern half of Sierra Leone in migratory waves late in the eighteenth century and the regional economy has been based on forest goods and transportation. Whereas the SLPP was dominated by Mende, among the Susu, Limba and Kono a growing sense of identity vis-à-vis the rest of the country and the south led to the emergence of a distinct northern identity. The All People's Congress (APC) was born as a northern party amid this sense of regional deprivation.

Conclusions and future prospects

In April 1995, three years after coming to power in a military coup, the government of the National Provisional Ruling Council (NPRC) announced the lifting of the ban on politics. Head of State Captain Strasser announced a start to the process that would eventually see a civilian President sworn-in in February 1996. The military regime enlisted the help of South African mercenaries to protect commercial interests and prepare the country for presidential elections in February 1996. The handover of power to the civilian government of Al Hadjin Ahmed Tejam Kabbah, leader of the SLPP, took place at the end of March 1996. The government appears to be fighting a losing battle against the RUF. Huge portions of the country have become ungovernable. A peace agreement, brokered by Côte d'Ivoire, was signed in Abidjan on 1 December 1996, ending the five-year civil war in Sierra Leone.

Further reading

Alie, J., *A New History of Sierra Leone*, London, Macmillan, 1990.

Minority-based and advocacy organizations

Amnesty International, PMB 1021, Freetown, Sierra Leone; tel. 232 22 227 354, fax 232 22 224 439.

Council of the Churches of Sierra Leone, PO Box 404, Freetown, Sierra Leone.

Somalia

Land area:	637,657 sq km
Population:	9.3 million (1995)
Main languages:	Somali, Arabic, Gosha
Main religions:	Islam, local religions
Main minority groups:	'Bantu' (Gosha, Shabelle, Shidle, Boni) 190,000 (est., 2%), Ormo 120,000 (est., 1.3%), Gabooye caste groups (Tumal, Yibir, 'Migdan') 45,000 (est., 0.5%), Swahili-speakers (Benaadiri, Amarani, Bajuni) 45,000 (est., 0.5%), Ogadeni and other refugees from Ethiopia 480,000 (est., 5.2%)
Real per capita GDP:	$712
UNDP HDI/rank:	0.221 (172)

The Somali Republic is the eastern-most extension of the African continent, located in the Horn of Africa. It is bordered by Djibouti, Ethiopia, Kenya, the Gulf of Aden and the Indian Ocean. Sixty per cent of the population is nomadic and concentrated primarily in the north. The southern region between the Juba and Shebelle rivers is the main area of settled agriculture. However, as only 13 per cent of the land is arable, there is intense pressure on available pasture and water.

Somalia is widely considered to have an ethnic homogeneity unusual in Africa, with Somalis constituting 97 per cent of the country's population. Somalis are divided into three major clan families: Saab, Irir and Darood, each of which comprises numerous subfamilies and lineages. This intricate system is held together by a loosely accepted set of unwritten codes called *xeer*, and a collective blood paying process, the *diya*. While Irir and Darood are predominantly pastoralist, Saab who live in the south have long mixed herding with peasant farming. Pastoral producers faced grave problems as environmental degradation of the Somali graining lands, especially in the north, intensified during the 1980s.

European colonization resulted in the division of Somali territory into five different colonies. The question of reunification was to preoccupy successive elites at the cost of addressing more concrete issues. National issues remained undebated while the cultivation of clan and subclan interests accentuated the demise of kinship and the rise of clannism. Somalia became independent from Italian and British colonial rule in 1960. Traditional rivalries among various Somali clans, including Isaaq of the north, Ogadeni of the south and Hawiye of central Somalia, were exacerbated by the divide and rule policies of Mohammed Siad Barre, whose regime (1969–91) had one of the world's worst human rights records. As many as 500,000 Somalis starved to death as warring clans struggled for power.

The weakness of the military state became conspicuous with the disappearance of Soviet aid and technical assistance. The failing economy and political system reawakened long suppressed discontent over the regional neglect of the north, compounded by the fact that various clan groups in the north were not treated equally. The historically strong and wealthy Isaaq had been systematically undermined in military and civil service posts and through the unequal development of resources and the siting of development projects. Barre constructed the inner core of his government from representatives of three clans belonging to the Darood clan family. By mid-1988 Somalia was embroiled in one of the most brutal civil wars in Africa, involving the government and five armed opposition groups.

Clan divisions

While clan refers to the social organization, clannism is the politicization of the clan structure by elites, for personal gain. Clan is an important social organization in the Somali social structure. It impacts on politics, economics and social status. The beneficiaries of clan politics are frequently opportunistic individuals while the consequences are suffered by the entire members of the clan.

Isaaq

The Isaaq clan family occupy the north-western portion of the country, numbering (with Dir) between 1.5 million and 2 million and forming the largest clan family in former British Somaliland. When Somali refugees from Ethiopia (predominantly Ogadeni) were settled in northern Isaaq pastoral lands, increasing pressure on scarce resources, Isaaqs perceived this as a calculated policy to replace them. This suspicion was intensified when the government illegally recruited refugees into the army and created paramilitary groups among them. Military and party officials in the north were southerners with close family links to Barre. In 1981 the Somali National Movement (SNM) was formed in London with financial support from the Isaaq diaspora, and granted operational space by Ethiopia. Isaaq had two long-standing grievances: that Darood and Hawiye had dominated power and privilege in the country at the expense of Isaaq since independence, and that southern Somalia, being both more developed and denser in population, had tended to dominate the northern region. Before the summer of 1988 they had little power. However, the government tried to undermine support by gearing spending towards areas not sympathetic to the SNM or the Somali Salvation Democratic Front (SSDF) and unleashing a regime of terror and pillage in those areas viewed as sympathetic to rebel groups.

In the mid-1980s Somalia and Ethiopia had severe problems including continuing hostilities between the two states and growing insurgencies within each state. In 1987 Barre offered the Ethiopian government a peace treaty in which Somalia gave up its territorial claims on the Ogaden region in return for depriving the SNM of their Ethiopian bases. Ethiopia agreed and thus the SNM decided to attack in north-west Somalia and liberate their clan territory, the Hargeisa, Berbera and Burao triangle. The government responded by unleashing all military forces and reinforcements from the south. Tens of thousands of civilians were killed. Burao was razed to the ground, and under aerial bombardment and heavy artillery fire 70 per cent of Hargeisa was destroyed. In Berbera, Isaaq men were rounded up and murdered and hundreds of fleeing refugees were killed. With the destruction of Hargeisa, some 400,000 people fled into eastern Ethiopia, including urban-dwellers and nomads. In May 1991 the SNM declared unilateral independence in the north-west of what it calls the Republic of Somaliland, seeking, but not receiving, international recognition.

Majerteen

In the aftermath of defeat in the 1977 Ogaden war, a body of disgruntled army officers predominantly from the Majerteen clan, part of the Darood clan family, attempted to stage a coup in April 1978. When this failed, many were executed while others fled and founded the SSDF in Addis Ababa. The SSDF began to make forays along the Ethiopian–Somali border. During their pre-eminence in civilian regimes, the Majerteen had alienated other clans. Thus when Barre began to punish them collectively in a scorched earth policy in north-east and central Somalia little concern was exhibited from the rest of the country. Crack units, the dreaded 47 *Duub Cas* or Red Berets, were sent into Majerteen country in the Mudug region (central Somalia). In this semi-arid region, water was collected in reservoirs dug out of the ground during the short rainy season to be used during the dry season. Neutral eyewitness testimony states that the Red Berets destroyed the reservoirs. In May-June 1979, over 2,000 people died of thirst and the clan lost 50,000 head of cattle and 100,000 goats. In Gaalka'ayo, members of the Guulwadayaal or Victory Pioneers raped and kidnapped Majerteen women and girls.

Raxanwayn and Digil-Mirifle

The Saab clan families Raxanwayn (also called Rahanwayn) and Digil-Mirifle intermarried with 'Bantu 'and Oromo who occupied the fertile area between the Juba and Shebelle rivers before the Somalis came. Numbering some 1.5 million, they are regarded by Samaal clans (Darood, Dir, Hawiye and Isaaq) as less 'pure' racially, with a dialect being little more than a lower form of the Somali language. Their dominant occupation, agriculture, has long been seen as a menial occupation by the pastoral Samaal. Farmers of the Raxanwayn and Digil-Mirifle agricultural communities have been displaced from the Lower Shebelle and other areas by Habar Gedir, a subclan of the Hawiye clan who come from the Mudug region in north-central Somalia. Some have been allowed to return as labourers to work the land they used to own and on plantations owned by Habar Gedir. Raxanwayn are now dominated by other clans in the Juba River region of Gedo, such as Mareexan, despite their numerical majority. Using the labour of the former owners, Habar Gedir export bananas for multinationals. Finance for 'security operations' has been provided by these foreign fruit companies.

Hawiye

Occupying the south-central portions of the country, Hawiye (part of the Irir clan family) possess a numerical strength that is the largest or perhaps second largest after the Darood clans. Since independence they have occupied important administrative positions in the bureaucracy and the top ranks of the army. In the late 1980s their disaffection with Barre's regime grew. Hawiye exiles in Italy launched an opposition movement, the United Somali Congress (USC). In response, security forces persecuted and slaughtered hundreds of people from Hawiye subclans in 1989 and 1990. However, in January 1991 Mogadishu fell to Hawiye clanspeople under the banner of the USC. In April 1994 long-standing rivalry between the Hawaadle and Habar Gedir subclans led to an outbreak of fighting in south Mogadishu. After fierce clashes, all Hawaadle were expelled from the city, and summary executions took place.

The Abgal subclan of the Hawiye, who originate in northern Mogadishu and the middle Shebelle region, still dominate. Habar Gedir, under the command of General Aideed's son, Hussein, are now an occupying force in much of the region extending from Mogadishu to the Juba River ; northward, south-west and throughout the coastal area of the Lower Shebelle. Although the estimated 800,000 people of the Habar Gedir subclans were primarily concentrated in the region of central Somalia prior to the civil war, the taking of Mogadishu by military force in the overthrow of Barre, and the subsequent consolidation of control by Habar Gedir over southern Mogadishu, has led to a population movement of clan members into the city as well as into the rich agricultural areas of the adjacent region of the Lower Shebelle.

'Bantu'

The so-called 'Bantu' groups are thought to descend from African peoples brought from further south in the continent to Somalia in the eighteenth and nineteenth centuries. Some groups, such as Shebelle and Shidle, also descend, in part, from groups resident prior to the Somali invasion. Many are Muslim, speak Somali and have assimilated into local Somali clans or are linked to them as clients. All the same, they have retained a low status. Those Bantu groups collectively known as (Wa) Gosha (literally, 'people of the forest') live in the Lower Juba Valley and faced the most displacement during the civil war. Other Bantu communities are located in the Shebelle Valley.

Gosha are the principal non-Somali minority group in the country. They were the main victims in the civil war and famine and they remain particularly vulnerable. Gosha speak a Bantu language and are often referred to as, and call themselves, Bantu. They are predominantly peasant farmers and plantation workers in the agricultural region between and along the banks of the Juba and Shebelle rivers and many of the original settlements were havens for escaped slaves. The Italians categorized the ex-slave population from the 'pure' Somali population separately for the purpose of conscripting labourers.

The Gosha community historically has not been a politically unified force in Somalia. Any political action taken by Gosha above the village level was mediated through Somali clan affiliations. In the Shebelle region and the Hiran region north of Mogadishu, Gosha suffered displacement and starvation early on in the civil war. A scorched earth policy was in operation against Bantu and other agricultural communities in the region between the Juba and Shebelle rivers in 1991–2, removing their very means of survival. Communities were raided, stripped of their resources or expelled. Wells were destroyed, and seeds, stocks and livestock looted.

Displaced Gosha in camps have frequently been targeted for abuse. Those who have been able to return have been forced to work the land they used to own as contract farmers, providing labour to the dominant clans. In Hiran, Gosha lands have been taken by the Hawaadle and Habar Gedir, and throughout the Juba Valley they have been forced to pay protection money. There is evidence of measures to prevent them from organizing independent organizations. Falling outside the Somali clan structure their communities lack militias, and ethnic Somalis accord them low social status. They are also outside the traditional system of arbitration and compensation. Gosha women are particularly vulnerable. Members of the Bantu agricultural community of the Juba River area describe rape as a routine of the raiders who loot, intimidate and sometimes kill the rural population. Gosha have also been pushed from the west to the east bank of the Juba River, primarily by Ogadeni bandits looking to expand their territory.

Shabelle and Shidle own land along the Shebelle River and are descendants of both freed slaves and original inhabitants of Somalia who successfully defended their lands. Federated into villages, they have historically been aligned with the Mobilen clan of the Hawiye clan. Boni are hunters and gatherers who live in the southern coastal areas. They traditionally supplied Somalis with giraffe, antelope and rhino skins. They are descendants of pre-Cushitic inhabitants of Somalia.

Oromo

Oromo are a Hamitic people, descendants of pastoral Oromo who migrated from south-west Ethiopia in the late nineteenth century. Menelik II sought to extend his empire southwards, driven partly by famine in the Ethiopian Highlands and the need to provide for his soldiers. This culminated in the displacement of the indigenous non-Amhara population in order to settle Amharas from the north. Oromo pastoralists, especially women and children, were captured by Somalis during raids and wars. Captured Oromo women became wives, concubines and domestic slaves. In some cases, entire Oromo groups were absorbed as serfs or clients of Somali clans. More recently the resettlement policies of the Dergue, together with punitive taxation and military conscription, drove 60,000 new Oromo refugees into Somalia in 1984. Oromo comprise some 20 per cent of refugees from Ethiopia in Somalia, approximately 120,000 people. Together with the 'Bantu' minority population, Oromo suffered badly during the civil war.

Gabooye caste groups

Small groups of people known collectively as Gabooye live in Somalia, descendants of hunting peoples believed to have been in the Somali peninsula before the Somali penetration. Gabooye have traditionally been considered distinct and lower-caste groups. These groups usually held a client relationship with a patron group working as smiths, barbers and leather workers and as medicinal advisers and midwives. Tumal are blacksmiths; Yibir (Yahhar in the south) are traditional medicinists; 'Migdan' (the term is now prohibited) women and men performed infibulation and circumcision respectively.

Swahili-speakers

Benaadiri descend from a mixture of coastal Somalis and Arab and Persian migrant settlers who dominated the southern coast until the seventeenth century. They are an urban people, culturally closer to the Swahili of East Africa than to the Cushitic culture of Somalis. They live in Mogadishu, Merca and Baraawe (Brava) and had the misfortune of being located in zones hotly contested by the USC and Somali Patriotic Front during the post-1991 civil war. Benaadiri were also singled out for rape and abuse by Aideed's troops and for looting by the Darood militias. Like other coastal peoples, they were forced to flee.

Amarani live in Baraawe (Brava), Merca and Mogadishu. Merchants and sailors, they speak a Swahili dialect. In the port of Baraawe (Brava) they are also known as Bravanese. In Amarani oral tradition their ancestors are believed to have come from southern Arabia and some may have left Arabia during the expansion of Islam. Banjuni are a non-Somali ethnic group living on Banjuni Island, off the coast at Kismayo. They are fishers and sailors and speak a Swahili dialect. They are descended from an intermarriage of Arab and Persians with the local population, though there has been speculation about a possible Melanesian origin.

Conclusions and future prospects

Basic civil institutions disappeared during the last years of Barre's rule. By 1991 Somalia was a nation without a government or central security force, where a collection of armed clan militia fought over spoils, and in a combination of political and ethnic conflict, ravaged the land and systematically killed and displaced the civilian population. As many as 500,000 Somalis are estimated to have died and another 2 million fled their homes to become displaced persons within their own country or unwelcome refugees in Kenya, Ethiopia and Djibouti. By the time UN troops arrived in force two years after Barre's fall, the crisis was far advanced. These two years allowed warlords to fragment the country in an attempt to consolidate their force and to deny resources to civilian communities as the source of this power. The arrival of UNOSOM, with aid and resources, provided them with a new surge of strength.

Minority groups faced expulsion from their land as well as looting, which were the means by which armed militias of more powerful groups survived. The victimization of women, particularly the displaced, was widespread. Others under threat included community leaders seen to pose a threat to the coalition led by rival warlords. In the early 1990s the UN had little success in breaking the cycle of civil war, human rights abuse and famine, even though international standards had been grossly violated. With the last UN troops gone, as of March 1995, traditional clan leaders, not faction leaders, tried to meet to discuss free movement, grazing and water rights, and interclan family disputes. But within this process, clan identity of victim and accused often resulted in bias and impunity. With clans protecting rights and security, justice too often depended on kinship group and its relative power in the local community. Under this traditional system, members of minorities possessed few realizable rights, either as groups or as individuals.

Further reading

Africa Watch, *Somalia: A Government at War with its Own People*, New York, 1990.

Castagno, M., *An Historical Dictionary of Somalia*, Metuchen, NJ, Scarecrow Press 1975.

Human Rights Watch/Africa, *Somalia Faces the Future: Human Rights in a Fragmented Society*, New York, 1995.

Prendergast, J., *The Gun Talks Louder than the Voice: Somalia's Continuing Cycles of Violence*, Washington, DC, Center of Concern, 1994.

Samatar, S., *Somalia: A Nation in Turmoil*, MRG report, 1991, 1995.

Sudan

Land area:	2,505,065 sq km
Population:	27.4 million (1993)
Main languages:	Arabic (official)
Main religions:	Sunni Islam, traditional religions, Christianity
Main minority groups:	Dinka 3 million (11%), Nuba 2.5 million (9%), Nuer 1.5 million (6%), Fur 1.5 million (6%), Nubians 600,000 (2%), Beja 570,000 (2.3%), Copts 270,000 (1%)
Real per capita GDP:	$1,350
UNDP HDI/rank:	0.359 (146)

Sudan is the largest country in Africa. Located in the north-east of the continent, it is bordered by Egypt, the Red Sea, Eritrea, Ethiopia, Kenya, Uganda, Zaire, the Central African Republic, Chad and Libya. Away from the Nile River, most of Sudan is comprised of semi-arid plains. From 7000 BCE, farmers and herders lived along the Nile in what is now Sudan. Most settled in Nubia, known to the Egyptians as Cush. Nubian civilization reached its peak between 1750 and 1500 BCE and is thought to be the oldest civilization in sub-Saharan Africa. In the sixth century, northern Sudanese adopted Christianity. By the mid-seventh century, Arab Muslims had conquered Egypt and raided Nubia. In the early 1500s black African Muslims called Funji conquered Sudan. Meanwhile black Africans settled in central and southern Sudan, including Azande, Dinka, Nuer and Shilluk people. From the seventeenth to the nineteenth centuries the rulers of these increasingly Islamic Sudanese states adopted an Arab identity. When Egyptian forces later penetrated southern Sudan, they brought in their wake northern Sudanese and European merchants. The growth in the supply of slaves led to their being used increasingly as domestic servants in northern Sudan.

Western Nilotes – Anuak, Dinka, Nuer and Shilluk – were, and are, the largest Sudanese linguistic group. Predominantly pastoral, they traditionally lived in southern Sudan, occupying parts of Southern Kordofan and White Nile province. Further south in present-day Equatoria are Eastern Nilotes, including Azande, Latuka, Madi, Moru, Taposa and Turkana. Northern Sudanese generally regarded the south as part of a large labour reserve. Because southerners were needed for indentured labour this weighed against converting them to Islam, which would have ruled out their use as slaves. By the time of the Anglo-Egyptian Condominium, 1898–1955, the attitudes of the north towards the south had become entrenched. Regional underdevelopment increased, and educated southerners believed that self-government for Sudan would not necessarily result in self-government for the south. They tried to delay independence and later proposed a federation. When this was rebuffed in 1958, secession seemed the only alternative. A series of post-independence civilian and military regimes failed to reconcile deep-seated differences between the south and the north. General Nimeiri seized power in 1968, and in 1972 ended a seventeen-year civil war by granting the south regional government and local autonomy. The conflict resumed in 1983 when Nimeiri imposed Islamic law and ended regional self-government.

A civilian government assumed power in May 1986 although it failed to end the war in the south. Prime Minister Sadiq al Mahdi was overthrown on 30 June 1989 in an Islamist-inspired coup led by General Omar al Bashir. Government forces made gains in 1991 in the civil war when the southern rebels split over whether to seek a secular Sudan or full independence. In October 1993 the ruling military junta disbanded after appointing Bashir President, increasing the powers of Parliament and issuing a decree making Islamic law the basis of the Sudanese political system. Exceptionally harsh in its treatment of opponents, the government has manifested disregard for human rights on a massive scale in the relocation and 'cleansing' of minority populations in northern and southern Sudan. There has been a re-emergence of slave trading in southern and Nuba children in the south-west.

'Peace villages' and 'peace camps' are being established for displaced, marginal peoples. Parastatal Islamic endowment agencies under the Ministry of Social Planning are given exclusive permission to provide facilities for education and development. Peoples from so-called marginal areas are under intense pressure to adopt a Muslim identity merely to survive, or, if already Muslim, to adopt a narrower National Islamic Front (NIF) interpretation of Islam, and to aspire to Arab-Sudanese culture in denial of their own background. One group of the displaced especially targeted by the government are young boys. Hundreds of boys, mostly southerners, are rounded up in the markets and on the streets and dispatched to camps run by Islamicists. No attempts are made to contact their families. The boys are beaten for small breaches of discipline, given a religious (Islamic) education regardless of their or their families' beliefs and at the age of 15 incorporated into the government armed militia.

Failing conversion and assimilationist policies, Bashir's regime has sought military solutions, bringing the estimated death toll in southern Sudan to over 1.3 million by May 1993. Repeated upheavals of communities have been prompted by killings, rapes and the destruction of villages and crops. The government has increasingly used armed militias as a vanguard for the regular armed forces. The south has been devastated by famine and civil war in which food has been used as a weapon. The conflict has also spread north. The peoples of the Nuba Mountains of Southern Kordofan have been suffering the effects of conflicts between the army, government-sponsored militias and the Sudanese People's Liberation Army (SPLA). The once peaceful and prosperous Nuba Mountains have become a battlefield where villages are destroyed and people are driven from their land, herded into government camps or killed.

Dinka

Dinka are the largest single southern Nilotic group representing 10 per cent of the Sudanese population. They are transhumant cattle herders living in northern Bahr al Ghazal and areas south and west of the white Nile. Living on the frontier between Nilotic southern peoples and cattle herding Arabs has meant that the Dinka have been less isolated than other southern peoples and to a certain extent have played a brokerage role between them and the Arabs. However this proximity today has made the Dinka most vulnerable to raids from Arab militias who shoot the men and enslave the women and children. They are kept as personal property or marched north and sold. Many recent sources, ranging from UN documents to the *New York Times*, document the revival of slavery in Sudan.

They have experienced severe displacement as a result of SPLA operations and pro-government militia attacks aiming to depopulate Southern oil fields and expand large-scale mechanized agriculture, and resulting famine.

The first large exodus came in 1983, and the process reached a peak between 1986 and 1988. The displaced were not granted access to urban land. The only available sites were rubbish dumps and other wasteland. In 1991 when faced with those displaced by the war from southern Sudan, the Khartoum authorities relocated 150,000 displaced persons and squatters from Khartoum and housed them in a series of mud brick, government-controlled, transit camps too far from the city to commute to work.

The arming of the Rizeigat Arabs by the NIF government in the war against the SPLA has contributed to slavery and banditry. In March 1988, 1,000 Dinka men, women and children were massacred by the Rizeigat Arabs in western Sudan. Some parents, desperate to escape the civil war in the south, have handed over their children as slaves to pay for their own transport by truck to the north. War and famine have brought growing numbers of unaccompanied Dinka children from rural areas to the streets of northern Sudanese urban areas. They are open to many forms of abuse and are frequently taken to *inqaz* 'salvation camps' located far out in the desert, for 're-education' and training for militia forces.

Nuba

A group of fifty or more autonomous and ethnically diverse tribes, Nuba inhabit the mountainous Kordofan in central Sudan. They speak several mutually intelligible dialects of the Cushitic group of the Hamito-Semitic language. Some traditional religions survive but most Nuba have been converted to Islam or Christianity. Historically, Nuba migrated to the mountains for protection or improved water sources to cultivate beans, cotton, millet, and maize, and to raise cattle, goats and sheep. Their traditional rivals, the cattle herding Sudanese Arabs known as Baggara, who live in Southern Kordofan, have been allies of central power in Sudan since the nineteenth century, while Nuba have been peripheral to the main currents of Sudanese politics, neither aligned with the Arab-dominated North nor belonging to the South.

Baggara, and their militia the *murahaliin*, were armed by the transitional government in 1985–6 and then by the governing Umma Party from 1986–9 and thereafter by the government of the NIF. After the NIF took power, the Popular Defence Act of 1989 legitimized the *murahaliin* militia as part of the paramilitary Popular Defence Force (PDF) which stepped up its raids, now in conjunction with the army. While the SPLA raided villages for food and conscripted soldiers, violence by army and *murahaliin* escalated. In February 1990 some Baggara leaders negotiated a truce with the SPLA to gain access to traditional grazing lands in SPLA-controlled Dinka areas of the southern region of Bahr el Ghazal. In response, the central government intensified its efforts to inflame Baggara historical competition with the Nuba with the objective of ridding Nuba land of its Nuba inhabitants and replacing them with Baggara Arabs. The army arrested, tortured and executed Nuba leaders and confiscated their land, evicting entire communities. In January 1992 the Provincial Governor of Kordofan declared a *jihad* in the Nuba Mountains to rout the 'remnants' of the SPLA.

The situation of Christians in the Nuba Mountains remains particularly difficult. Churches have been destroyed and meetings prohibited even in their ashes. With the creation of Islamic schools, 'peace camps' are part of an Islamicization policy. Nuba children from the Kadugli/Tulisci areas have been rounded up by the PDF and sent to Libya and the Gulf countries. The Nuba Timu group that lived in the lower lands of the mountain ranges of Tulisci near Lagaw have been virtually eliminated, as all males down to the age of six or seven have been massacred. Nuba deportees are also forced to work in the large mechanized schemes in agricultural lands which originally belonged to them before their distribution by the government to Jellaba (a northern Muslim mercantile class operating in the south) and Baggara. These deportees are increasingly dependent on food charity given by Islamic relief organizations and are gradually being distanced from Nuba cultures.

The attempt to destroy the Nuba people and culture, and their forcible conversion to Islam, is not new. Some local authorities prohibited stick fighting which relates to Nuba cosmology and agricultural and religious practices. Prohibition of these rituals implies an indirect obstruction to the basic cultural traits and value systems which maintain and foster Nuba ethnic identity. The imposition of *sharia* law has reinforced discrimination. Like many non-Muslims in Sudan, Nuba fell prey to *sharia* law and suffered amputations for what would be considered minor offences under most secular laws. The government has embarked on the 'comprehensive call' campaign which aims at Islamicizing Nuba via the imposition of Islamic teaching, the intimidation of clergy, resettlement and torture.

Nuer

Nuer and associated subgroup, Atuot, are among the most numerous groups in southern Sudan, numbering some 700,000 to one million. A Nilotic people, they are seasonally migrating pastoralists. Cattle are a profound measure of wealth, status and personal influence and are used to pay debts, fines and bride prices, although this latter practice is in decline. Relatively homogeneous in language and culture but without political centralization or formal regional integration, Nuer are divided into a number of independent tribes organized into clans, lineages and age groups. Kin connections between these groups create alliances of approximately equal size that are the basis for support in disputes. Nuer have no central authority or hereditary rulers: order is maintained through consultation and mediation. The patrilineal system of descent, built around a segmentary lineage principle, allows a high degree of mobility and political autonomy for each segment. Nuer have a strong history of resistance to British control in the twentieth century.

Fur

Fur are a people of western Sudan province and the former Islamic Sultanate of Darfur. As sedentary farmers, Fur rely mainly on the cultivation of millet during the rainy seasons. They are Muslim and have adopted Arab names and dress. Fur communities are matrifocal, so Fur elders are surrounded by daughters and their daughters' husbands. Today the traditional hierarchy of the Fur chiefs is integrated into the Sudanese administrative system. The 3.5 million people living in Darfur region are geographically isolated and neglected by the Khartoum government. The relatively peaceful equilibrium between the region's ethnic groups has been destroyed by environmental degradation along with the divide and rule tactics of the central government, and the influx of modern weaponry. Earlier conflicts were predominantly clashes between nomadic groups over access to pasture and water or theft of animals. Since the 1980s attempts have been made by nomadic groups to occupy land in the central Jebel Marra with entire villages wiped out and thousands of lives lost on both sides. While drought-stricken livestock herders attempt to survive by encroaching on the fertile central zone, Fur struggle to retain what they perceive to be their land. Racial prejudice became entwined with the environmental roots of the conflict with the formation of an alliance of 27 Arab nomad groups and their declaration of war against the 'black' and non-Arab groups of Darfur. The response of the Fur was to form their own militias. By the time of the 1989 peace conference, 5,000 Fur and 400 Arabs had been killed, tens of thousands displaced and 40,000 homes destroyed.

Nubians (see **Egypt**)

Nubians have a very long history linked to the rise of agriculture, ancient states and urbanism which parallels their association with ancient Egypt. Nubia is sometimes defined as the region between the first cataract at Aswan to the third near Dongola, although this is disputed. Nubians are descendants of the Khartoum mesolithic, the hunter-gathering culture near the site of modern Khartoun, c. 4000 BCE, with some admixture from the Egyptian population to the north. Ancient Nubians began grain cultivation in Khartoum the Neolithic period. Their language is not linked to Afro-Asiatic or Semitic languages further north and east.

Nubia was a source of gold, slaves, cattle skins, ivory, ebony, ostrich feathers, gum and incense which played a very important role in the basic accumulation of Egyptian wealth and power. When the Nubian kingdom was defeated by the Axumite kingdom it reorganized as three Christian kingdoms. This delayed the arrival of Islam until the fourteenth and fifteenth centuries. Some Nubians fled to remote locations in Dafur and Kordofan; other groups stayed in Nubia, retaining a tradition of religious scholarship and teaching.

Beja

Beja of the deserts of eastern Sudan are among the country's longest established peoples, having been resident for over 4,000 years. They number approximately 570,000 and extend into Egypt and Eritrea. They inhabit large areas of Sudan between the Egyptian border, Eritrea and the River Setit, and from the Red Sea coast to the River Atbara and the Nile. Beja have traditionally followed a nomadic way of life, mostly as camel herders. Colonial economic ventures attracted various groups from outside the region when mechanized farming was introduced in the 1940s. Most significantly, as a result of the construction of the Aswan Dam from 1964–7, Nubian inhabitants of Wadi Haifa were resettled in the south-western part of Beja land, increasing population concentration and putting pressure on scarce land resources. The Aswan Dam inundated important pastures for the Bish, a subgroup of the Beja, causing massive impoverishment.

Beja were especially hit by drought in the 1970s and therefore shifted their livelihood from camel rearing to breeding smaller animals and working in Port Sudan. Further devastating droughts of the 1980s caused major depopulation of the Beja herds with losses estimated at 80 per cent of their animal wealth. The area available for Beja livestock was rapidly diminishing as the development of cotton plantation schemes robbed them of their grazing reserves. The expansion of mechanized farming further south has caused a gradual decrease in humidity which has affected the vegetation. The destruction of the animal wealth of the Beja has brought about increasing urbanization to which there now appears to be no alternative. The NIF coup in 1989 brought no positive changes; on the contrary, the NIF is alarmed by the Beja's pride in culture and traditions which the NIF considers incompatible with Arab-Islamic identity.

Copts (see **Egypt**)

Followers of the Egyptian Coptic Church live in such northern Sudanese towns as Al-Obeid, Atbara, Dongola, Khartoum, Omdurman, Port Sudan and Wad Medani. They number 200,000, with 23 churches and two bishops, and their presence dates back over 1,300 years. Because of the Copts' advanced education, their role in the life of the country has been more significant than their numbers suggest. Adoption of a passive, non-confrontational approach coupled with lightness of skin has helped them avoid the worst excesses of racial discrimination. However, in recent years, they have been harassed and intimidated on religious grounds by the NIF.

Copts began moving to Sudan in the sixth century CE to escape persecution in Egypt. Under Islamic rule which began in Egypt in the seventh century, they became subject to the code of *dhimma* which offered them protection while according them second class citizenship. Initially this was an improvement over their vulnerable status under previous rulers but as the Islamization process became consolidated, strict regulations were imposed on the building of churches. Emigration from Egypt peaked in the early nineteenth century and the generally tolerant reception they received in Sudan was interrupted by a decade of persecution under Mahdist rule at the end that century. Many were obliged to relinquish their faith and adopted Islam, intermarrying with Sudanese. The Anglo-Egyptian invasion in 1898 allowed Copts greater religious and economic freedom and they extended their original roles as artisans and merchants into trading, banking, engineering, medicine and the civil service. Proficiency in business and administration made them a privileged minority. The return of militant Islam in the mid 1960s and subsequent demands for an Islamic constitution prompted Copts to join in public opposition to religious rule.

General Nimeiri's introduction of *sharia* law in 1983 began a new phase of oppressive treatment of Copts, among other non-Muslims. Although Copts did not immediately suffer the extremes such as amputations, they felt sufficiently threatened to join the campaign against the new laws. This reduced Copts' status as court witnesses and the abolition of the legal sale of alcohol affected them as non-Muslim traders. A Christian alliance, including Copts, was formed to defend the rights of Christians of all denominations. After the overthrow of Nimeiri, Coptic leaders encouraged support for a secular candidate in the 1986 elections. When the NIF-backed military regime seized power in 1989 discrimination returned in earnest. Hundreds of Copts were dismissed from the civil service and judiciary.

Conclusions and future prospects

Non-Muslims in Sudan continue to hold a tenuous position under a regime that has declared its intention of building an Islamic state according to a version of Islam which discriminates against non-Muslims. Non-Muslims are theoretically excluded from high level government offices including the judiciary, the military and any position in which a non-Muslim would exercise authority over a Muslim. More restrictions and discrimination apply to believers in non-scriptural religions than to Christians and Jews but even the status of the latter groups is inconsistent with the requirements of international human rights law. The regime's practice is not fully consistent with its own declared ideological position and legal system in that a few non-Muslims have been appointed to high offices, and there are some instances of non-Muslim participation in public life. The vast majority of non-Muslim Sudanese, however, suffer discrimination and oppression.

The military coup which overthrew the elected civilian government in 1989 brought to power a military regime dominated by a minority party that achieved only 18.4 per cent of the popular vote in the 1986 elections. Elections were held in the north and only in parts of the south because of the civil war which started in 1983. Public dialogue in Sudan has been silenced. After political parties were banned in 1989, top ranking leaders of all opposition parties were arrested repeatedly. The efforts of the NIF have resulted in a series of laws which place women and non-Muslims in a legally inferior relationship to men and Muslims. While the government continues to violate the rights and freedoms of minorities on a major scale, the achievement of long-term stability will depend on an equitable resolution of the causes of the civil war, which have barely begun to be recognized by the political leadership of the country or the international community.

Further reading

Africa Watch, *Sudan Eradicating the Nuba*, New York, 1992.

Human Rights Watch/Africa, *The Copts*, New York, 1993.

Human Rights Watch/Africa, *Sudan in the Name of God: Repression Continues in Northern Sudan*, New York, 1994.

UN General Assemby, A/50/569, *Situation of Human Rights in Sudan*, interim report by UN Special Rapporteur of the Commission on Human Rights, 16 October 1995.

Verney, P. et al., *Sudan: Conflict and Minorities*, London, MRG report, 1995.

Minority-based and advocacy organizations

Gambella Relief Association, c/o RO-COIE, PO Box 3182, Khartoum, Sudan.

Sudan Council of Churches, PO Box 469, Khartoum, Sudan.

Togo

Land area:	56,785 sq km
Population:	4 million (1992)
Main languages:	French, Ewe, Kabye
Main religions:	traditional religions, Christianity, Islam
Main minority groups:	Ewe (Ewe, Ouatchi, Mina, Fon, Adja) 1.8 million (45%), Moba (Moba, Konkomba) 280,000 (7%), Kotokoli (Kotokoli, Bassari) 280,000 (7%), Hausa 20,000 (0.5%)
Real per capita GDP:	$1,020
UNDP HDI/rank:	0.385 (140)

The Republic of Togo, located on the Gulf of Guinea, is one of Africa's smallest countries and lies between Benin, Ghana and Burkina Faso. Present-day Togo originated as a German colony. The agreed boundary with the British Gold Coast to the west was fixed in 1904 and cut through the tribal territories of several large ethnic groups. In 1919 parts of northern Togo reverted to the Gold Coast and the rest was given trustee status under Britain and France. In 1957 the British trusteeship area was incorporated into newly independent Ghana, while in 1960 the French-administered area became Togo. There are eighteen or thirty different ethnic groups, depending on different classifications. The dominant Kabye ethnic group numbers about 560,000 or 14 per cent of the population, with related Losso (215,000) and Lamba (145,000) making up a further 9 per cent of the population.

Since independence, there has been a historical tension between the northern Kabye and southern Ewe. This has been translated into political violence. Many southerners were prejudiced against the north, regarding its inhabitants as savages. Sylvanus Olympio, the first President of independent Togo and a southern Ewe, was assassinated in 1963. His successor, Nicolas Grunitzy, fled after a coup in June 1967 and was replaced by General Gnassingbé Eyadéma, a northerner, as head of the armed forces. Eyadéma appointed a civilian cabinet and in 1969 made Togo a one-party state. Widespread protest in 1991 led Eyadéma ostensibly to surrender some of his authority. However, with military backing Eyadéma thereafter regained his lost power.

The Eyadéma government is based on an alliance between his own northern Kabye people and southern groups excluding Ewe. This alliance also excludes northern groups such as the Muslim Kotokoli and the Bassari. Ethnic tension has been heightened by Eyadéma's favouring of Kabye in government positions and in the army. Kabye now account for up to 90 per cent of the country's military and security forces. Ironically Eyadéma and his foreign backers justified his personal rule as a necessary burden to encourage national unity among Togo's ethnic groups. Regardless of the imbalance, increasing numbers of Kabye dislike Eyadéma's strong-arm government but have no clear political alternative. Eyadéma has remained in control of the state apparatus long after democracy was supposed to have arrived with the February 1994 elections. Widespread involvement of the security services in human rights abuses has been reported.

Ewe

Ewe are a group of Adja-speaking peoples living in south-east Ghana and south-west Benin as well as in Togo. They trace their origins to Oyo in Nigeria. Ewe were quick to profit from opportunities arising with the advent of colonial rule, especially education. Since the German occupation they were regarded as future administrators, and the French administration used skilled and educated Ewe in the colonial civil service in Togo and elsewhere. The civil service remains dominated by Ewe and Mina, and the gross disparity between all social indicators in the south and those in the north has contributed to inter-ethnic strife in Togo and grudges in the north against dominant southern elements. In the colonial period Outachi, Adja and other coastal groups attempted to bring about the unification of all Ewe under one administration, resulting in several pan-Ewe movements. The Ewe 'problem' is still not resolved; Ewe remain divided by the Ghana–Togo border. President Eyadéma has exploited this challenge to the Ghanaian government and has supported irredentist 'liberation' movements on both sides of the border.

Mina, coastal-dwellers who are prominent in Togo's commercial, intellectual and political life, and Ouatchi, a group of comparatively late migration, are related to the Ewe.

Moba

One of Togo's most homogeneous ethnic groups, Moba are also indigenous. They inhabit rich agricultural lands in north Dapaongarea and speak a dialect influenced by the More language of the Mossi of Burkina Faso.

Konkomba are an ancient ethnic group in northern Togo and Ghana, related to Moba. Konkomba in Togo live on the Oti River, a tributary of the Volta, north of Basseri. They live in clans with no central structure. Konkomba rose against the Germans and French and have never forgiven their Namumba neighbours in former British Togo for voting in a 1956 plebiscite for union with Ghana. Konkomba moved in large numbers across the border to join fighting in Ghana in 1981 when hundreds of Namumba were killed (see **Ghana**).

Bassari

Bassari, who belong to the Kotokoli ethnic cluster, live north-west of Sokode and in neighbouring Ghana. Inhabiting the area around Mount Bassari, they call themselves Bi-Tchambe, metalworkers, their pre-colonial occupation. Not to be confused with the Bassari along the Guinea-Senegal border, Bassari of Togo live among large numbers of non-Bassari. Historically they have suffered from Dagomba attacks in Ghana and escaped to areas of poor agricultural soil in Togo.

Hausa

Hausa number no more than 20,000 in Togo but form an important mercantile and religious group. Togo's Hausa have been the prime transmitters of Islam in Togo.

Conclusions and future prospects

Togo is unlikely to undergo democratization at this stage. Far too much brutality has been committed since 1990 to allow a smooth political transition into Ewe hands when it finally takes place. In May 1994 a journalist was sentenced to four years' imprisonment for questioning the probity of African leaders; this indicates how little has really changed in Togo.

Further reading

Delcalo, S., *Togo*, Santa Barbara, CA, Clio Press, 1995.

Froelich, J.C., Alexandre, P. and Cornevin R., *Les populations du nord Togo,* Paris, Presses Universitaires de France, 1963.

Gayibor, N., *En savoir plus sur – les peuples et royaummes du golfe du Benin*, Cotounou, University of Benin Press, 1986.

Toulabor, C.M., *Le Togo sous Eyadéma*, Paris, Karthala, 1986.

Welch, C., *Dream of Unity: Pan Africanism and Political Unification in West Africa,* Ithaca, NY, Cornell University Press, 1966.

Minority-based and advocacy organizations

Commission on Human Rights and the Status of Women, Soroptomist International Club of Lomé, BP 423, Lomé, Togo.

National Commission of Human Rights, BP 3222, Lomé, Togo.

Togolese League for Human Rights, 178 Blvd 13 du Janvier, BP 2302, Lomé, Togo.

Tunisia

Land area:	155,000 sq km
Population:	8.7 million (1994)
Main languages:	Arabic, French, Berber
Main religions:	Islam
Main minority groups:	Berbers 450,000 (5%), Jews 3,000 (est.)
Real per capita GDP:	$4,950
UNDP HDI/rank:	0.727 (78)

The Republic of Tunisia borders Algeria and Libya, and has a 1,300 kilometre Mediterranean coastline. It became independent in 1956 after more than seventy years as a French protectorate. Large numbers of Spanish Arabs settled in Tunisia in the sixteenth century, and Italian and French colonists arrived after 1850. Tunisia is the nearest continental African country to an East Asian economic tiger, with little real poverty and 4 per cent average annual growth. The broadly secularist, pro-Western, yet authoritarian government considers the pursuit of economic growth paramount, and it fears that tourism and its strategy of investment-led growth could collapse if the country's Islamic opposition were allowed to become militant. Islamist critics say the security clampdown, including widespread detentions, goes well beyond what is needed to counter the Islamist threat.

Berbers

The Berber-speaking minority in Tunisia is much smaller, in both absolute numbers and as a proportion of the population, than their counterparts in Morocco or Algeria. They live mainly in isolated pockets in southern Tunisia. The government claims that they have been integrated into Arab Muslim culture and do not constitute an autonomous localized minority of specific character. Because of this, it is difficult to evaluate the Berber situation, but they do not appear to have faced the same problems or developed the same opposition to government as in the other countries of North Africa (see **Algeria, Morocco**).

Jews

The Tunisian Jewish community was one of the oldest and most important in North Africa. In Muslim countries around the tenth century, they were regarded as 'People of the Book' and thus deserving of protection. In general, Jews were not forced to convert, although they suffered a host of restrictions. How seriously these rules were applied depended on local conditions.

Confronted by such adversity, Jewish communities were held together by the solidarity of the local group which revolved around a synagogue and by treatment received from the higher authorities. Jews continued to be present in the cities as merchants and artisans. As in other French colonies, Jews later fared well under colonial rule, but during the brief German occupation of Tunisia in World War Two, many were imprisoned in forced labour camps. Tunisia's Jewish population dwindled from 105,000 in 1948 to 12,000 after the 1967 Arab-Israeli war. There are now thought to be only about 3,000 Jews in Tunisia. There have been cases of attacks on Jews and Jewish property in the 1980s but the government has made efforts to reassure the Jewish community.

Conclusions and future prospects

In the 1994 multi-party elections the ruling Constitutional Democratic Group maintained a tight rein on power. The government has taken a tough line against Hizb Ennadha, the country's main Islamist movement, which has been driven underground. President Ben Ali has used the Islamist threat to stifle other opposition. With a weak and divided legal opposition, and the gap between rich and poor smaller than in any other Arab African country, Tunisia remains largely depoliticized.

Further reading

Parfitt, T., *The Jews of Africa and Asia*, London, MRG report, 1987.

Minority-based and advocacy organizations

Amnesty International, 40 bis Rue Ibn Khaldoun, Tunis 1001, Tunisia.

Arab Institute for Human Rights, 23 Avenue Moheddine Kilibi, El Manar III, Tunis 104, Tunisia.

Association for the Defence of Human Rights and Public Liberties, 27 Rue Hached, Les Hauts de Gammarth, La Marsa, Tunisia.

Tunisian League for Human Rights, 1 Rue du Canada, Tunis, Tunisia.

Notes

Introduction

1 Bayart, J.-F., *The State in Africa : The Politics of the Belly*, London, Longman, 1993, pp.xi, xii.

2 Ibid., p.50.

3 Ibid., p.52.

4 Davidson, B., *The Black Man's Burden*, London, James Currey, 1992, p.10.

5 Bayart, op. cit., p.56.

6 *Africa Confidential*, 6 January 1995.

7 Davidson, op. cit., p.10.

CENTRAL AND SOUTHERN AFRICA

Chris Dammers and David Sogge

The countries of Central and Southern Africa range from densely settled micro-states to huge but sparsely populated territories. Together they cover a vast area several times the size of Europe and larger than the United States and Mexico combined. In the mid-1990s they were home to 270 million people. Uneven distribution of rainfall and surface waters, soil quality, vegetation and mineral deposits results in extremely unequal resource endowments and varied patterns of settlement. Traditional livelihoods reflect this diversity. The majority of people have been settled farmers, working their grandmothers' fields. A minority have been pastoralists, nomadic where arid conditions demanded. A much smaller minority have lived by hunting and foraging in the forests or on the open plains.

Incorporation into the Western world system has compounded natural inequities and added new ones. The process dates back to the haemorrhage of enslaved people dragged to the Americas from the Congo river basin in the early sixteenth century; European settlement in the Cape and the Zambezi valley dates from the seventeenth. However, incorporation began to take its current form in the 1880s with the drawing of boundaries and imposition of rule by semi-private companies and colonial armed forces. Today Western power operates less directly, but the mere threat of action by banks, or soldiers, continues to give enormous leverage.

New social hierarchies emerged in the period of formal colonialism from the 1890s to the 1960s. Changes were profound: land was grabbed, labour marshalled and commercial monopolies established. Schooling and churchgoing established new cultural codes, and social mobility for some – those whose sons and grandsons make up much of the region's elite today. Though political activity was stifled, resistance to colonial authority was widespread and varied, ranging from insurrection to disengagement and retreat. Challenges to the authorities emerged from within the new, intermediate social strata. Religious groups often posed a threat: Christianity often took syncretic or messianic forms; Islam continued to adapt and spread. But the conflict was unequal: Africans had come to live in a framework moulded by Western intervention, changing not only how they lived but how they saw themselves and their compatriots. In pursuit of social control, colonial authorities granted powers to authorized traditional leaders; approved identities and loyalties were reinforced. The disruptions of the colonial economy, notably through urbanization and wage labour, brought different groups together. Divide and rule policies promoted ethnic identities that for Africans had been of only limited significance.

Today, as scrambles for survival intensify, calls for ethnic allegiance, especially from elites under threat or driven by frustrated ambitions, are widely heard. Many people are prepared to pick up a weapon when persuaded by demagogues that they will otherwise be doomed. Internal colonialism, resource wars, mass expulsions and even genocide can be the result. Non-dominant groupings, whether numerical minorities or not, become increasingly vulnerable.

Origins of 'minority' status

Minorities, as defined in this *Directory*, number hundreds if not thousands of groups in Central and Southern Africa. However, only some of these, mostly smaller groupings, conform to the paradigm of multiple marginalization, that is, of being deprived on several grounds at once – language, belief system, livelihood and ethnicity. Most hunter-gatherer and former hunter-gatherer communities fit this paradigm, as do nomadic pastoralist groups. Disadvantage or subordination in other cases may be less 'multidimensional' but affect much larger numbers of people, sometimes even the majority in a region or country. The causes are varied and complex.

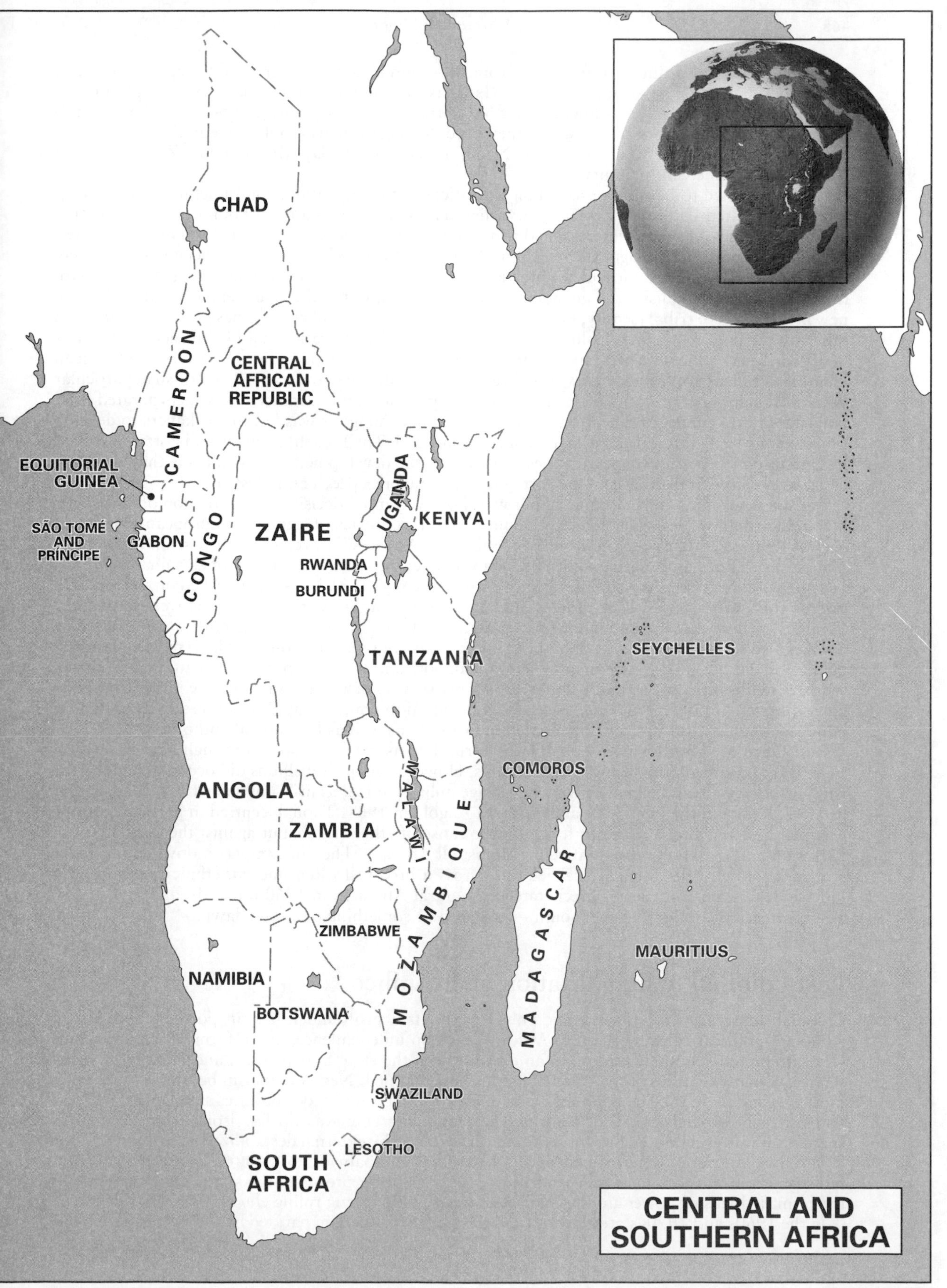

CHAD
CAMEROON
CENTRAL AFRICAN REPUBLIC
EQUITORIAL GUINEA
SÃO TOMÉ AND PRÍNCIPE
GABON
CONGO
ZAIRE
UGANDA
KENYA
RWANDA
BURUNDI
TANZANIA
SEYCHELLES
COMOROS
ANGOLA
MALAWI
ZAMBIA
MOZAMBIQUE
MADAGASCAR
ZIMBABWE
MAURITIUS
NAMIBIA
BOTSWANA
SWAZILAND
LESOTHO
SOUTH AFRICA
CENTRAL AND SOUTHERN AFRICA

One cause of subordinate status arises from pre-colonial social hierarchies. Categories of slave, commoner and noble arose in pre-colonial Madagascar, among Zulu people of Natal and in Cameroonian kingdoms, to name a few. In parts of Central Africa pastoralist groups established ascendancies over the cultivators among whom they lived. Subjugation also took shape in the aftermath of military campaigns, such as those of the Ngoni across present-day Mozambique, Zimbabwe and Malawi in the nineteenth century.

Colonialism led to new, more wide-ranging varieties of stratification, contradicting or reinforcing those that existed before, and creating new hierarchies. The new national boundaries followed the acquisitive logic of imperial interests and rivalries, scarcely coinciding with African political entities, still less with patterns of linguistic and cultural affinity. People whose points of social reference were limited to family and clan found themselves, particularly in urban environments, juxtaposed with those of differing linguistic and geographical backgrounds. Often they were encouraged to develop new perceptions of tribal identity, even to consider themselves members of tribes protected from each other by the colonial power. Colonial ideology, initially incorporating full-blown racialist theories and always persisting with half-baked anthropological ones, developed a European version of African identities – taller peoples as soldiers, aristocrats as administrators, and so on. The British in particular developed elaborate strategies of indirect rule through chiefs and headmen. They incorporated local languages into systems of education and evangelization, though it was left to Afrikaners to develop this ideology to its farcical and grim extreme in apartheid. The French, Belgians and Portuguese paid less attention to African ethnic identities and more to the development of a small elite that would be as far as possible French, Belgian or Portuguese in manners, speech and lifestyle.

The quest for land, minerals and labour was, however, more decisive in the creation of new social hierarchies than were the ideologies of domination. In countries of significant European settlement, such as Kenya, Zimbabwe, Angola and above all South Africa, Whites claimed the best land. Company plantations, mines and logging enterprises had parallel impacts. Huge tracts of savanna and forest became wildlife zones. As a result, in many parts of the region Africans were pushed on to land with poorer soils, worse rainfall or more mountainous topography. Often such areas were designated 'reserves', where those whose labour was not required could live at minimal cost to the state. Such policies also served to push men onto the labour market. Burdens on women, who typically remained behind on family plots, increased. Where job opportunities were limited or unattainable, casual workers with little or no land could be stigmatized as lazy and dissolute, with self-fulfilling consequences of poverty and exclusion. Such denigration could be applied wholesale to particular ethnic or linguistic groups, and be adopted by Africans as well as by colonial authorities.

Resistance to subordination, particularly in rural areas, was widespread though usually passive, more direct confrontation being too dangerous. However, major rebellions did occur: all among the rural dispossessed, and all put down with savage military force, as in Namibia in 1904, Madagascar in 1947, Kenya in the late 1950s and northern Angola in 1961. Though centred in particular ethnic groups, these rebellions were not fought in the cause of ethnic rights but against the dispossession, exclusion and racial oppression affecting almost all Africans. The same targets motivated the wider struggles for self-rule, generally carried out across a broad, if often uneven, ethnic spectrum. But independence, when it came – precipitately in Central Africa from 1960 onwards, and much later, after protracted conflicts, further south – proved to be something of a false dawn.

Post-colonial marginalization and conflict

Colonial autocracy and bureaucratic power have left a profound legacy in post-colonial Africa. Although political control passed to African hands on independence, and reforms of various kinds were attempted – notably leading to an expansion of the state bureaucracy, and initially of social services – many features of the colonial model were retained. Neo-colonialism became a fact of life, most pervasively in the Francophone ex-colonies. Where Eastern bloc countries supplanted the West and ostensibly socialist policies were pursued, the state elite was no less isolated and economic stagnation was even more acute, or rendered catastrophic by external destabilization. Although some White-owned estates were broken up in Kenya and Zimbabwe, no country has seen significant redistribution of assets since independence. Despite growing pressures the state apparatus remains the primary locus of power and the state class a self-perpetuating ruling elite.

In the 1960s and 1970s state activities and revenues expanded, in part fed by foreign aid and loans.

The gap between government insiders and the rest of the population was cushioned by increasing access to some of the benefits, such as educational and health services. However, dramatic declines in the value of exports, combined with the increasing costs of food and other imports, soon began to alter the equation. Declining revenues and mounting debt burdens, often combined with spiralling military expenditure, put state apparatuses under enormous pressure. Corruption on the part of government officials has been a further damaging factor.

In the 1980s new Western orthodoxies began reversing earlier notions favouring planning and rational state governance. The new aim has been to shrink the state apparatus, reduce collective sector consumption and make African economies even more externally oriented. All countries have been compelled to undergo 'structural adjustment' on pain of denial of life-saving loans. The immediate impact has been a reduction of social services, an expansion of poverty and an even greater vulnerability to market forces. Urban dwellers have been hit by falling wage rates and rising malnutrition. Ex-government employees have joined the ranks of the 'new poor'. Those in the mushrooming informal sector eke out meagre, desperate livelihoods in streets and markets. As the global economy depends less and less on low-skilled labour, African economies, unable to pay for education and training, cannot compete. Meanwhile in many areas pressure on the land has led to soil exhaustion, erosion, overgrazing and conflict over resources. Few societies can sustain such disintegration without political upheaval.

By the mid-1990s several states in Central and Southern Africa were in various stages of paralysis and collapse – some indeed had long been in this condition. In yet more countries reciprocity between governments and citizens has all but broken down. Under growing pressure, and lacking any constituency to provide legitimacy and support, ruling elites have built up patron–client relationships based on lineage and ethnic ties. Loyalties and resentments, 'insider' and 'outsider' status, increasingly correlate with ethnicity. For 'outsiders' the most accessible form of redress, if any, is to get one's own patron and group into power. Ethnically based warlords have emerged to challenge central governments, provoking bloody civil conflicts.

There is no lack of will to counter these trends. Millions of people are tapping reserves of patience and resourcefulness to oppose forces of exclusion and hatred. Nor is there a shortage of organizations and people – churches, trade unions, women's associations, community groups, legal and human rights activists, writers and journalists – prepared to fight for justice and tolerance and bring to bear what pressure they can on political elites and their external supporters. They are key to any reversal of the decline sketched above, but in most countries their power is all too limited.

Ethnicity and politics: minorities and minority rights

Questions of ethnicity and politics generate fierce debate in relation to Africa. At one extreme ethnicity is posed as the central determining factor in African politics. In the popular imagination of the West the continent's problems are often seen as the result of tribal conflicts fuelled by primordial (and incomprehensible) hatreds. Condescending media coverage often contributes to this conception, whose links with colonial ideology are clear. An alternative extreme argues that since tribal or ethnic identities are artificial constructs, their significance is limited. This viewpoint was widespread during the African nationalist heyday of the 1950s and 1960s, when both academics and politicians too readily assumed that in building new nation states such divisions would decline in significance or even disappear. Colonial enthusiasm for 'tribal divisions' only fuelled this reaction.

Neither view is sustainable. In the coverage of Central and Southern Africa we have tried to outline the significance as well the origins of ethnicity in the region, albeit in a necessarily generalized and schematic way. At the same time we have tried to point to the more fundamental political and economic factors that have led to the current crisis. Nevertheless, there is a danger that a focus on minorities and minority rights could create the impression that ethnicity is more central than it is. While ethnic hatreds undoubtedly exist in Africa, they are more symptom than cause of conflict. Ethnic sentiments generally represent an opportunity for unscrupulous politicians; they are only rarely a driving force in everyday relations. Locating the framework of ethnic discourse is as important as recognizing its destructive potential. Yet failing to recognize the potential for mobilization on communal lines can be as tragic a mistake as conflating African politics with tribalism. The genocide in Rwanda and the desperately precarious situation in Burundi provide graphic illustrations. Though seldom optimistic, most commentators underestimated the catastrophic potential for communal mobilization in these countries. Demythologizing the nature and origins of divisions between Hutus and Tutsis is important, but people's perceptions of themselves and each other, and the potential for these perceptions to be exploited, are yet more significant – no matter how complex, arbitrary or 'imaginary' such divisions may be, nor whether they should best be described as 'ethnic', 'communal' or 'caste-like'. Though Rwanda and Burundi are extreme cases, and here as elsewhere the causes of tragedy are many and complex, reluctance to recognize and respond to the dangers of ethnic domination – a danger only made greater by democracy and political pluralism – remains a feature of many countries in the region.

Neither 'minorities' nor 'minority rights' are common paradigms of discourse in sub-Saharan Africa. The concepts have more resonance where indigenous populations have been completely overwhelmed by settlers, as in Australia and throughout the Americas, or where smaller national groupings find themselves living in a country with a clearly identifiable dominant majority, as in China or Russia. Only in a few countries in Central and Southern Africa does one particular ethno-linguistic group form an overall majority of the population; consequently almost everybody in the region can be considered a member of a minority, though they may not immediately define themselves as such. An added complication is that the concept of 'minority rights' has been used in support of the maintenance of White domination and privilege in South Africa and elsewhere, giving the idea a distorted and negative connotation in the eyes of some. Additionally, where the lack of provision of basic needs comprises the greatest denial of human rights, linguistic, cultural and religious rights can be seen as secondary.

This by no means implies that conceptions of minority rights lack meaning or legitimacy in Africa. Large numbers of people suffer disadvantage or persecution as a result of their ethno-linguistic status, and indeed for religious or cultural reasons. The distinction between an ethno-linguistic group and a 'minority' is largely semantic. One consequence, however, is that minority rights considerations apply with equal force to members of large minorities, or to numerical majorities, who may not be multiply marginalized in line with the standard paradigm, but may still suffer greatly from repression or exclusion.

Forest dwellers, hunter-gatherers and 'indigenous people'

Three or four hundred thousand members or descendants of forest-dwelling and hunter-gatherer groups, most of them maintaining their traditional lifestyles only in part, conform more directly to the classic paradigm of the disadvantaged minority, typically suffering from a wide range of discrimination and stigmatization. Yet they have difficulty gaining recognition as distinct groups with distinct needs. In most cases such groups can legitimately claim to have lived where they are living for longer than their neighbours – in some case for very much longer. Yet claims advanced for a special status as 'indigenous people' have limited resonance when almost all Africans regard themselves as indigenous, contrasting their situation primarily with that of European and Asian settlers and immigrants.

However, such pan-African sentiment, even when combined with a principled desire to undermine the 'politics of ethnicity', can serve as an excuse for failing to recognize the specific and often acute disadvantages and needs of such minorities, in any case a much stronger basis for assessment of their claims than questions of historical precedence. Typically, government policies reflect beliefs that the sooner such people lose their distinctive identity the better. In most of Central Africa official policy is that 'Pygmy' groups should be sedentarized and assimilated rather than afforded particular support or consideration. Elsewhere the descendants of hunter-gatherers face indifference or hostility to their demands for special provisions to overcome disadvantages directly related to their distinctiveness as a group. For such groups much can be gained by learning from experiences in other parts of the world, by the development of autonomous institutions, and by active campaigning. All these remain at an early stage of development.

Gender

Though oppressed numerical majorities are considered, women are not viewed as a distinct 'minority' for the purposes of this *Directory*. However, their position as a disadvantaged group throughout the region deserves emphasis. Traditional divisions of labour, combined with patterns of male migration in search of work, mean that the burdens of impoverishment fall heavily and disproportionately on women, who head a third of rural households in the region and do the greater part of all agricultural and domestic work. Women are largely absent from the region's political elites. As usual, abuse of human rights, and of the rights of minorities, is predominantly a male preserve. Women's subordinate status is a central feature of the problems described here.

Selection criteria

We have faced a dilemma in deciding what, and whom, to include in this part of the *Directory*. A comprehensive survey of hundreds of ethno-linguistic groups – to say nothing of other paradigms for minority status – would have been impossible. Nor would it have been appropriate to focus only on multiply marginalized minorities with so many others facing disadvantage or persecution. Where we have been able to move beyond the briefest summary we have been motivated by the extent of disadvantage and denial of human rights, giving greater emphasis to the countries and regions where major conflicts have occurred, and devoting some space to the historical background essential to any understanding of them. Current or former forest dwellers, hunter-gatherers and nomadic pastoralists themselves comprise hundreds of groups if criteria of language and culture are strictly applied. With a few exceptions we have been able to consider only major groupings, rather than individual groups, in any detail. A focus on ethnicity, the dominant paradigm for minority status in the region, means that other paradigms, notably religious affiliation but also social class and occupational status (as well as gender), cannot receive the attention they would otherwise deserve. More generally, a human rights focus, combined with acute limitations of space, greatly reduces the scope for detailing cultural aspects, or more positive aspects of the region's cultural diversity.

Conclusions

The people of Central and Southern Africa have not been able to develop their own destinies on their own terms. Historical forces, originating largely outside the continent, have brought the region to its current position, widely marked by impoverishment, disintegration and conflict, often accompanied by the exploitation of ethnic identities by competing demagogic elites or outright warlords. The interplay of such manipulation with wider issues of control – of land, of labour, of the state – has been the theme of this introduction. Minority rights issues cannot be isolated from broader questions of human rights and economic justice – least of all in Central and Southern Africa. The need to transform political and economic relations is critical. A profound change of political will, inside and outside the continent, is needed if current trends towards disintegration are to be reversed.

Further reading

Adekanye, J., 'Structural adjustment, democratization and rising ethnic tensions in Africa', *Development and Change*, vol. 26, 1995, pp. 355–74.

Barker, J., *Rural Communities under Stress: Peasant Farmers and the State in Africa*, Cambridge, Cambridge University Press, 1989.

Charney, C., 'Political power and social class in the neo-colonial African state', *Review of African Political Economy*, no. 38, 1987, pp. 4865.

Ellis, S. (ed.), *Africa Now: People, Policies and Institutions,*The Hague, Netherlands Ministry of Foreign Affairs (DGIS), Portsmouth, NH, Heinemann, and London, James Currey, 1996.

Iliffe, J., *The African Poor: A History*, Cambridge, Cambridge University Press, 1987.

International Work Group for Indigenous Affairs, *The Indigenous World 1995–96,* Copenhagen, IWGIA, 1996.

Ivan-Smith, E., Tandon, N. and Connors, J., *Women in Sub-Saharan Africa*, London, MRG report, 1988.

Lemarchand, R., 'Political clientalism and ethnicity in tropical Africa: competing solidarities in nation-building', *American Political Science Review*, vol. 66, 1972.

Reyntjens, F., *Burundi: Breaking the Cycle of Violence*, London, MRG report, 1995, 1996.

Vail, L. (ed.), *The Creation of Tribalism in Southern Africa*, London, James Currey, 1989.

Watkins, K., *The Oxfam Poverty Report*, Oxford, Oxfam Publications, 1995.

Angola

Land area:	1.2 million sq km
Population:	10–11 million (est. 1994)
Main languages:	umBundu, kiMbundu, kiKongo, uChokwe, Portuguese (official)
Main religions:	indigenous beliefs, Christianity
Main minority groups:	Ovimbundu 4 million (est., 37%), Bakongo 1.5 million (est., 14%), pastoralists up to 800,000 (est., 7%), San and Kwisi up to 50,000 (est. 0.5%)
Real per capita GDP:	$674
UNDP HDI/rank:	0.283 (165)

Greed and violence, often inspired by outside interests, have driven the history of Angola for centuries. Slaves, land, oil and diamonds have generated streams of wealth, enriching foreign and domestic elites, and provoked bloody conflicts. The manipulation of racial and ethnic fears and resentments has helped to mobilize and direct the armed forces behind the violence. Portuguese rule ended officially in 1975, but outcomes of colonial policies live on in exclusion, cultural arrogance and humiliation based on social hierarchies. At the bottom were the *indígenas*, the officially undifferentiated mass of non-Westernized Africans. Above them, together with the White colonists, were thin strata of Europeanized *assimilados* (those Africans certified as Westernized) including *mestiços* (people of mixed race). Living mainly in cities, they fulfilled intermediate roles in an economy based largely on the cheap labour of a rural unskilled semi-proletariat.

These sub-elites provided leadership to Angola's nationalist movements. Broadly corresponding to the main ethno-linguistic clusters, these crystallized in the 1950s and 1960s in three blocs: the Movimento Popular de Libertação de Angola (MPLA) assembled under *mestiço* and *assimilado* leadership with a strong following among Mbundu people of the centre-north, but also embracing smaller ethnic groups in the east and south; the Frente Nacional de Libertação de Angola (FNLA), formed under traditional and *assimilado* leadership and rooted exclusively among Bakongo people in the north-west; and União para a Independencia Total de Angola (UNITA), formed under younger *assimilado* leadership and drawing its main following among Ovimbundu people, the pre-eminent ethnic group of the central highlands.

At the time of the Portuguese withdrawal a three-way tussle for power was in progress. Despite vigorous backing from the United States, abetted by Zaire and South Africa, the FNLA and UNITA lost out. The winner, the MPLA, took all. Its upper echelon – the *nomenklatura* – was composed disproportionately of *mestiços*, Whites, and much of the better-schooled Black African population. It became the party of a 'state class' reliant on multinational oil companies and Eastern bloc and Western suppliers of hardware and advice. Crucially, it chose not to revive the agrarian economy, and not to rely on the majority farming population, but rather to feed the cities and wage-earners largely with imported food.

A US-led project to 'roll back' communism largely propelled the ensuing war that began in earnest around 1980. The Soviet Union and Cuba pursued their brand of proxy warfare up to 1989 in backing the MPLA, whose vulnerabilities stemmed from its neglect of rural residents, compounded by long-standing ethnic and racial resentments. The MPLA government tried to curb centrifugal political tendencies by drawing discontented ethnic elites into well-oiled systems of clientalism, and by recruiting its armed forces from all ethnic groups. Radio and television broadcasts in national languages and programmes about local music and dance have drawn attention to local cultural expression. But this hardly adds up to 'due regard for the legitimate interests of persons belonging to minorities' (UN Declaration on Minorities, 1992, Article 5). The main 'minority' issues are deeply entangled with struggles among elites over state power and especially shares of state-controlled export revenues.

Ovimbundu

A largely rural people whose farming systems were once highly productive, Ovimbundu became migrant wage-earners in large numbers as Portuguese settlers began taking over their lands in the 1940s and 1950s. In urban settings they gained reputations for hard work, such as in the building trades. But urban classes in Luanda and elsewhere have treated them with condescension.

In the face of privilege, corruption and arrogance among the MPLA *nomeklatura*, UNITA's leadership, frustrated at being shut out of power, successfully played on feelings of humiliation and resentment among Ovimbundu and other minorities. As less than 2 per cent of the MPLA's members in 1980 were small farmers (a category comprising about three-quarters of Angola's population at the time) and as its policies neglected rural residents and enriched urban elites, there was ample basis for discontent. However, UNITA's leadership sought to channel this bitterness chiefly into anti-*mestiço* and anti-White feeling. Yet for the Ovimbundu the war brought suffering on a scale and depth felt by no other ethnic group.

National elections in 1992 revealed a strong but by no means universal Ovimbundu allegiance to UNITA; in the three Ovimbundu-dominated provinces it gained two-thirds of the parliamentary vote. The elections also revealed an even stronger fear among Angolans of UNITA's barbarism and ruthlessness; two-thirds of the national parliamentary vote went against it. UNITA's rejection of the election results and its return to war provoked countermeasures: waves of 'ethnic cleansing' of Ovimbundu (and Bakongo) broke out in several cities, and the MPLA itself returned to war, with terrible blood-letting on both sides.

Bakongo, including Cabindans

Spanning both sides of the Zaire river (see **Congo**, **Zaire**) Bakongo people predominate in Angola's impoverished but oil-rich north-west, including the Atlantic enclave of Cabinda. Bakongo are known as shrewd and energetic people, whether as organizers of businesses, syncretic churches, or political movements. In 1961 Bakongo coffee estate workers created the largest colonial uprising in any part of tropical Africa during the entire colonial period. In multi-ethnic Luanda, a place of 'savage capitalism', Bakongo men and especially women have been successful in trade, virtually all of which is unregulated, and hugely dependent on untaxed and pilfered merchandise. Other Angolans have resented this, and scapegoated Bakongo as 'Zairians', implying both illegitimate citizenship and unfairly gained wealth. In January 1993 armed civilians killed over sixty Bakongo in Luanda marketplaces. Police and judicial protection of Bakongo people has been at best half-hearted. A Bakongo-based movement, Mako, with an active armed wing, emerged in the early 1990s. It advocates an independent Bakongo federation including Cabinda.

Cabinda comprises only 0.5 per cent of Angola's territory and about 1.5 percent of its population, but it accounts for about 60 per cent of the country's oil output. Ordinary Cabindans have not benefited more from this wealth than other Angolans. Despite efforts by both the MPLA and UNITA to recruit them into privileged ranks, aspiring Cabindan politicians have set up various separatist movements down through the years, most with tacit backing from neighboring Congo and Zaire, and from French military and multinational oil interests. These groupings have tended to split up and regroup, some in alliances of convenience with either the MPLA or UNITA, neither of which wishes to see an independent Cabinda. Rather, plans for greater provincial autonomy, including limited redistribution of revenues, have been mooted.

Other minorities

In south-western provinces, semi-nomadic cattle-keeping peoples – mainly Ambo, Nyaneka-Nkumbi and Herero – have faced *de facto* denial of grazing rights, expropriation of land, unfair terms of trade and lack of respect for their traditions. Reciprocity between these minorities and the government has largely broken down. Although victimized by war, drought, and paternalistic aid-providers, these peoples have shown enormous resilience, relying on their own systems for survival. Scattered bands of San and Kwisi peoples, who live chiefly by hunting, gathering and petty trade, continue their nomadic existence in the southernmost provinces. No current information about them was available for this edition.

Conclusions and future prospects

The gravest problems affecting members of minorities in Angola stem less from their minority status than from the tensions ultimately traceable to Western dependency on cheap oil and to bullying driven mainly by imperial ideologies. Up to 1995 the war had cost the lives of more than a million people, and had totally transformed the society. Whereas in 1970 about 85 per cent of the population lived in rural areas, in the mid-1990s a mere 30 per cent lived there; lives of urban squalor are the lot of most Angolans. War has also planted seeds of further wretchedness, as about 9 million land-mines sit waiting to explode and thousands of weapons still circulate in the hands of jobless and uprooted youth. As of 1996, despite a peace deal and reconciliatory gestures, the war smouldered on among the ashes. Angolan elites are likely to continue to find it hard to make common cause against these miseries, and to refrain from further manipulation of minority fears and hatreds.

Further reading

Birmingham, D., *Frontline Nationalism in Angola and Mozambique,* London, James Currey, 1992.

Human Rights Watch/Africa, *Angola: Arms Trade and Violations of War since the 1992 Elections*, London, 1994.

Jamba, S., *Patriots*, London, Penguin, 1990.

Minter, W., *Apartheid's Contras: An Inquiry into the Roots of War in Angola and Mozambique*, London, Zed Press, 1994

Botswana

Land area:	570,000 sq km
Population:	1.5 million (est. 1995)
Main languages:	Setswana, English, minority languages
Main religions:	traditional religions, Christianity
Main minority groups:	Kalanga 110,000 (7%), Bakgalagadi (Kgalagari) 80,000 (5%), Basarwa (N/oakhwe, San, Bushman people) 50,000 (3%), Mbanderu (Herero), 40,000 (3%), Yeei (Koba, BaYeyi), 31,000 (2%), Mbukushu (Mpukushu) 18,000 (1%)
Real per capita GDP:	$5,220
UNDP HDI/rank:	0.741 (71)

Much of Botswana consists of the Kalahari (or Kgalagadi) Desert; the most fertile country comprises the eastern borderlands, a region long occupied by Tswana clans. The British Protectorate established in 1885 acted as a buffer against further encroachment from South Africa. Colonial rule was indirect and European settlement limited. Tswana society was (and remains) highly stratified, but traditional chiefly authorities were outmanoeuvred in the run-up to independence in 1966, resulting in a democratic and constitutional state, incorporating a Bill of Rights widely regarded as a model. Mineral and diamond deposits have sustained a comparatively buoyant economy.

The great majority of Botswana citizens are Tswana. Several ethnic minority groups, primarily living in the north and west of the country, experience varying degrees of exclusion, despite democratic structures and an official 'non-racial' ideology. Complaints concerning the refusal to allow school instruction in minority languages have been prominent, although only the most disadvantaged grouping is considered here. Small minority groups include Europeans, Asians, Pedi, Subiya, Damara, Nama, Balala, Ndebele and Teti.

Basarwa (N/oakhwe, San, Bushman people)[1]

About 50,000 Basarwa of the Naron, !Xo, G/wi, G//ana, Shua, Deti, /Auni, /Xam, //Xegwi, Kwe, Ju/'hoansi and //Khau-/eisi ethno-linguistic groupings live in Botswana. The Basarwa are traditionally hunter-gatherers, and their presence long predates that of the Bantu-speaking people of the region[2]. Basarwa people have, however, long depended on a mixed economy. None survive solely as hunter-gatherers and only a few thousand are significantly dependent on foraging. Over a long period competition with pastoralists, loss of hunting territory to ranches and game parks, declining game, and alternative economic opportunities (however limited) have all contributed to the demise of traditional lifestyles. The isolated Bushman, untouched by history, exists only in the mind of external myth-makers (see **Namibia**). Yet Basarwa languages and culture survive under pressure.

Most Basarwa work on farms, as small cattle farmers, or as labourers and casual workers on cattle posts or in towns, often supplementing their income by selling handicrafts, meat or foraged products such as thatching grass or firewood. A few hundred work in the tourist industry. Employment relationships are often highly exploitative, with wages systematically low. Unemployment and dependency are widespread. In many places apathy, demoralization and alcoholism are rife. Basarwa face considerable social discrimination. Many Basarwa live in Remote Area Dweller settlements, where tenure rights are uncertain. Such settlements are generally dominated by other groups even where Basarwa are the majority; despite their changing occupational status, Basarwa are often still regarded as foragers who do not need rights to land or grazing.

The Botswana government is reluctant to admit that rights and needs of the Basarwa relate in part to their situation as an ethnic grouping (albeit a very varied one) rather than simply to their poverty and economic marginalization. Official policies promote sedenterization, acculturation and assimilation, processes already far advanced. Remaining foraging areas, most notably in the Central Kalahari Game Reserve, are under renewed threat. Basarwa calls for rights to land in particular have been dismissed as unwarranted special pleading, as tribalist, or even as secessionist. Yet, in common with the experiences of people in similar situations elsewhere, unrelievedly assimilationist strategies, even if well meant, are only likely to perpetuate demoralization and inequity. Opportunities exist for trying to ensure that Basarwa receive equitable treatment under existing development schemes, especially in a country with a functioning legal system and reasonable human rights record, but parallel developments allowing a specific voice for Basarwa are also essential if deepening cycles of marginalization are to be reversed. Basarwa organizations, and indeed pan-Basarwa consciousness, are currently limited, but this is beginning to change.

Conclusions and future prospects

Comparative economic stability and well-established democratic institutions should insulate Botswana against the disintegrative pressures of many other countries in the region: the grievances of minority groups are unlikely to have a seriously destabilizing effect. For those most marginalized, notably the Basarwa, the resulting political and legal space should allow for the development of autonomous organizations and of more active campaigns on behalf of their needs and rights.

Further reading

Mogwe, A., *Who was (T)here First? An Assessment of the Human Rights Situation of Basarwa in Selected Communities in the Gantsi District, Botswana*, Gaborone, Botswana, Botswana Christian Council, 1992.

Saugestad, S., 'Botswana: the inconvenient indigenous peoples', *IWGIA Newsletter*, no. 2, Copenhagen, 1993.

Stephen, D., *The San of the Kalahari*, London, MRG report, 1982.

Wily, E.A., 'Hunter-gatherers and the land issue in Botswana', *Indigenous Affairs*, vol. 2, no. 94, 1994.

Minority-based and advocacy organizations

Ditshwanelo (Botswana Centre for Human Rights), Private Bag 00416, Gaborone, Botswana; tel. 267 306 998, fax 267 307 778.

Kgeikani Kweni (First People of the Kalahari), PO Box 173, Ghanzi, Botswana.

Kuru Development Trust, Box 219, Ghanzi, Botswana; tel. 267 596 102, fax 267 596 285.

Burundi

Land area:	28,000 sq km
Population:	6.2 million (1995)
Main languages:	Kirundi, French (administrative)
Main religions:	Christianity (mainly Roman Catholicism), traditional beliefs
Main minority groups:[1]	Hutus 5,000,000 (est., 80%), Tutsis 1,200,000 (est., 19%), Twa (less than 1%)
Real per capita GDP:	$670
UNDP HDI/rank:	0.282 (166)

Burundi is a small, impoverished, densely populated country bounded to the north by Rwanda, the west by Zaire and the east by Tanzania. In recent history Burundi has witnessed extremely high levels of violence, mostly perpetrated by the overwhelmingly Tutsi army against the (numerical) majority Hutu population.

The original inhabitants of Burundi are the forest-dwelling ancestors of the Twa, now a tiny minority. The origins and evolution of Burundi society are the subject of dispute; however, the popular conception of Tutsi pastoralists dominating Hutu agriculturalists does little justice to the complex and multi-faceted hierarchies of Burundi's pre-colonial kingdoms. Historically the potential for conflict between the two main groups was contained by the existence of a princely class, the *ganwa*, who provided an aristocracy for Tutsis and Hutus alike, and were originally seen as distinct from both. For most Hutus and Tutsis relations were comparatively equable and peaceful, with intermarriage common; language and culture are shared. Although in general Tutsis were in a dominant position, status, not ethnic identity, was the principal determinant of rank and privilege.

Burundi (together with Rwanda) was absorbed into German East Africa in 1899 and came under Belgian rule in 1916. Current conflicts are best understood in relation to developments since the late colonial period. Hutus and Tutsis are considered together since their situation and prospects are integrally linked.

Hutus and Tutsis

Political conflict in the period immediately preceding Burundi's independence in 1962 was not primarily along intercommunal lines but between the nationalist Union pour le Progrès National (UPRONA) and the more conservative and pro-Belgian Parti Démocrate Chrétien (PDC). Both parties were effectively controlled by small *ganwa* elites and their competition related to comparatively narrow rivalries as well as to ideology. The more radical UPRONA, led by Prince Rwagasore, the eldest son of the King, gained a massive victory in pre-independence elections in 1961, not least because its stance was seen as more sympathetic to Hutu interests. Two weeks later Rwagasore was assassinated following a PDC plot, and in the absence of his unifying influence politics became increasingly polarized along communal lines. In the early years of independence Burundi remained a monarchy, with the King attempting to assume some degree of ethnic balance in the administration. However, the assassination of the Hutu Prime Minister in 1965 led to a political crisis and a decisive Hutu victory in the resulting elections. The King then appointed a *ganwa* Prime Minister, precipitating an attempted coup by a faction of the Hutu-dominated gendarmerie which was repressed with great violence: virtually the entire Hutu political elite was massacred, along with thousands of their supporters. For over twenty years Hutu involvement in Burundi's political life was minimal.

In 1966 the King was deposed by his son who in turn was deposed in a military coup. Burundi was declared a republic; purges of Hutu army officers consolidated Tutsi supremacy. In 1972, following another abortive coup attempt, Hutus were brutally massacred on an enormous scale: between 100,000 and 200,000 were murdered, with educated Hutu systematically targeted. Some 300,000 fled to neighbouring countries. The failure of the international community to react to these atrocities compounded the outrage: the genocide proved a watershed for the whole region, compounding mutual fear and suspicion between Hutus and Tutsis, and generating a traumatic and long-lasting impact on Rwanda as well as Burundi. No one has ever been called to account or prosecuted for these crimes, reinforcing a culture of impunity which has continued ever since. The massacres, followed by pervasive discrimination against Hutus, most significantly in educational opportunities, consolidated wholesale Tutsi domination of economic and political life. Pressure on land, with many cases of expropriation by Tutsi elites, became a particular focus for Hutu resentment.

The pattern of Tutsi domination through military rule continued through the 1970s and 1980s. In the mid-1980s the Catholic church and some Protestant denominations came under government attack. Economic stagnation and growing impoverishment, exacerbated by falling coffee prices (often passed on to Hutu producers by Tutsi merchants) further aggravated tensions. In 1987 a further coup from within the army brought Pierre Buyoya to power. In 1988 conflict erupted in the northern provinces; in the resulting repression perhaps 15,000 people were killed, almost all by the army, and almost all Hutus. Around 60,000 fled to Rwanda. Buyoya eventually responded by opening a national debate on the need for unity, and a reforming programme of readmitting Hutus to positions of political responsibility. The civil service began to appoint Hutus in large numbers, and educational discrimination slowly began to decline. However, the overwhelmingly Tutsi army resisted change and elements within it became increasingly disaffected with the reforms, attempting coups in 1989 and 1992.

Under continuing pressure from donor countries Buyoya carried on with his reforms, leading to presidential elections in June 1993. Melchior Ndadaye, a Hutu, decisively beat Buyoya, and his party, the Front Démocratique de Burundi (FRODEBU), which broadly represented Hutu aspirations, won the subsequent parliamentary elections by a landslide. Sections of the unreconstructed Tutsi army remained violently opposed to these developments. President Ndadaye and several of his colleagues were killed in a military coup in October 1993, leading to Hutu uprisings and killings of Tutsis in many parts of the country, followed by massive army reprisals. Although the coup was officially crushed within days, and surviving members of the government reinstated, FRODEBU had lost much of its power and credibility and the reforms went into reverse. The replacement President, Cyprien Ntaviyamira, was killed along with his Rwandan counterpart when their plane was shot down over Kigali in April 1994, provoking another crisis which was prolonged by long delay in confirming the appointment of his successor Sylvestre Ntibantunganya (like both his predecessors a Hutu from FRODEBU).

The resulting war in Rwanda led to waves of refugees; first Rwandan Tutsis fleeing the massacres, later Rwandan Hutus fleeing the advance of the victorious Rwandan Patriotic Front. The refugees moved into a country starkly polarized first by the fighting following the October 1993 coup attempt and later by the Rwandan genocide itself – in which, for the first time, Tutsis in Burundi lost their lives in numbers comparable to the Hutu victims of the violence. In Burundi *de facto* segregation of Tutsis and Hutus had taken place, with Tutsis fleeing the countryside in search of military protection in towns, and Hutus fleeing from towns to countryside to escape the soldiers; in Bujumbura 'ethnic cleansing' of Hutus (and later of Zairois immigrants) was carried out in several quarters. The conflict continued throughout 1995, with an escalation in the activities of Hutu militias and an estimated 10,000 people killed. In July 1996, Pierre Buyoya, supported by the military, mounted a successful coup, leading to international protests and sanctions, the imprisonment, exile or death of many Hutu politicians, and growing support for the Hutu militias. Killings continued in the countryside and by the end of the year prospects for peace seemed ever more remote.

Other minorities

The Twa of Burundi are of 'Pygmy' origin, and traditionally work as potters or as musicians and entertainers. Traditionally despised by both Tutsi and Hutu, the historical links of some Twa with the Burundi court, and more significantly their recruitment by the army, link them with Tutsis in the eyes of many Hutus. In anti-Tutsi reprisals Twa have also been targeted.

Although most immigrants to Burundi, including long-standing Swahili-speaking communities in Bujumbura, have tried to avoid taking sides in the country's conflicts, they remain vulnerable to the suspicions of Tutsi extremists unwilling to trust any but fellow-Tutsis, a situation reinforced by the tendency of most 'outsiders' to show some sympathy for the plight of the Hutus. In 1995 immigrant communities were expelled from parts of Bujumbura as part of a process of making all but outlying areas of the city almost exclusively Tutsi.

Conclusions and future prospects

Few countries face prospects as bleak as Burundi in the mid-1990s. The 1994 genocide in Rwanda reinforced the belief of many Tutsis that only the army stands between them and a fate similar to that of the Tutsis of Rwanda. Yet Hutus are no less certain to continue to respond to the injustices and oppression they have suffered for so long. For many Hutus the massacres of 1965, 1972, 1988, 1991 and 1993 are perceived as part of a continuing genocidal plan by Tutsi extremists, and Buyoya has appeared unwilling or unable to embark on the reforms that marked the later stages of his earlier regime. Many Tutsis are no less genuine in their fear that retribution is at hand and that as a minority they are particularly vulnerable. The continuing violence of the military and the growing influence of Hutu militias may signify a drift to all-out civil war.

The reforms of the first Buyoya regime opened a national debate on the overwhelming need to overcome ethnic distrust – indeed, for the first time there was official recognition of the ethnic dimension to the conflict. The 1993 election and related developments improved the comparative position of the Hutu majority. Some hoped that a degree of equity in the 'balance of terror' might even result in a compromise settlement. However, the 1996 coup appeared to abolish any such prospect.

In his 1995 MRG report on Burundi, Filip Reyntjens highlighted the following key areas for action if Burundi was to escape the abyss. While stressing that only solutions promoted by Burundian actors and politicians have any hope of success, the international community should play a significant role in promoting: the organization of round-table negotiations between all political factions; the ending of impunity for serious crimes and outrages – this would require the incorporation of international investigators, prosecutors and judges into the Burundi judiciary; parallel to this, international human rights monitors should be deployed in Burundi on a large scale; promotion of the gendarmerie for internal peacekeeping, with a view to confining the army to barracks and its role to that of national defence; training of the army and gendarmerie should have a strong international dimension, where possible African; restriction of inflammatory press and radio outlets, and promotion of those seeking peace and reconciliation, again with appropriate international financial and training support; and reform and monitoring of the educational system at all levels. A year later the prospects for such developments looked remote, yet in the long term they remain among key conditions for any end to the conflict.

Further reading

de Carolis, A., 'Changements socio-économiques et dégradation culturelle chez les Pygmoides Ba-Twa du Burundi', *Africa* (Rome), June 1977.

Lemarchand, R., *Burundi: Ethnocide as Discourse and Practice*, Cambridge, Cambridge University Press, 1994.

Reyntjens, F., *Burundi: Breaking the Cycle of Violence*, London, MRG report, 1995, 1996.

Minority-based and advocacy organizations

Association pour la Promotion des Groupes Défavorisés (APGD), PO Box 6040, Bujumbura, Burundi.

Ligue Burundaise des Droits de l'Homme (ITEKA), BP 177, Bujumbura, Burundi; tel. 257 22 8636, fax 257 22 0004.

Cameroon

Land area:	469,440 sq km
Population:	13.1 million (est. 1994)
Main languages:	Bamiléké, Fang, Ewondo, Kirdi, Fulfulde, Pidgin English, French (official), English (official)
Main religions:	indigenous beliefs, Christianity, Islam
Main minority groups:	northerners 4 million (30%), Anglophone West Cameroonians 2.7 million (21%), Baka and other forest nomads 15,000 (0.1%)
Real per capita GDP:	$2,220
UNDP HDI/rank:	0.481 (127)

Struggles among elites for advantage, especially state power, have helped tease out antagonisms along ethnic and regional lines in Cameroon. Overlaid by diversity among agro-ecological zones and resulting livelihood patterns, differences verge on becoming social polarities. In this complexity, minority 'winners' and 'losers' have not always been the same peoples over time. European commercial and industrial interests have enjoyed rich pickings in the post-independence economic boom, augmented since the late 1970s by oil revenues. Cameroonian politicians have tried to meet their respective group interests through clientalist networks. Relative to poorer neighbours, Cameroon's system has shown some regard for the legitimate interests of some minorities.

An outcome of German, British and especially French imperial interests, Cameroon's frontiers include some 250 ethnic groups and sub-groups, many of which spread across neighbouring countries. Major clusters are the Fang- Pahouin conglomeration of the southern provinces, the largest of which are Ewondo and Beti. The apex of the political elite, including Cameroon's (in 1996) President Paul Biya, comes from the Bulu sub-group of the Beti cluster. In the northern three provinces are Fulbé and other Muslim and non-Muslim ethnic groups. In the centre-west and west are a range of ethnic groups, among them Bamiléké, noted and resented for their success in farming and commerce, and the Islamicized Bamoum, noted for their cultural resourcefulness. Ethnic identity has loomed large in post-colonial Cameroon politics, but not to the point of provoking acute instability. Under the twenty-four-year rule of the country's first President, Ahmadou Ahidjo (a Fulbé from the north), 'The ethnic arithmetic formula for distributing political power was in reality a sophisticated patronage system through which ethnic groups were transformed into pressure groups with the responsibility of articulating, aggregating, and resolving particularist interests and demands.'[1]

The two main schisms in Cameroon are, crudely stated, between northerners and southerners and between Anglophones and Francophones. Marginalization of nomadic forest peoples ('Pygmies') is not a major issue in national life.

Northerners

North of Cameroon's forest zone, people speaking Sudanic and Chadic languages comprise about 30 per cent of the country's population. Cotton, rice and livestock are main pivots of the commercial economy. The mainly Muslim Fulbé (Peulh, Fulani), whose elites had enjoyed certain privileges during the Ahidjo regime, are politically prominent. Outnumbering them three to one, yet with much less organized political strength are the Kirdi, a collective name for several non-Muslim peoples. Fulbé raiding in the nineteenth century forced many of them into refuge in highlands or outside Cameroon (see **Central African Republic**). Resentments toward Fulbé remain. By the mid-1990s, conflicts along the borders with Chad and Nigeria have involved Shua Arabs (or 'Black Arabs') against government forces as well as against rival Muslim Kotoko people. The conflicts resemble 'resource wars' just as those in Chad, led by warlords.

Opportunities for schooling and full participation in national economic life remain more limited in the north than elsewhere in Cameroon. In the mid-1990s, the main political party reflecting northern concerns met hostility and intimidation from central authorities. Under Ahidjo,

Muslim minority interests (schools, radio broadcasts) had gained respect and resources. Despite an obvious Muslim–non-Muslim dimension to the north–south divide, and notwithstanding steady growth in Muslim numbers, the religious factor has not been salient in political life.

Anglophones

Following the First World War, the German colony of Kamerun was partitioned into a small western portion (about 10 per cent of all territory) under a British mandate and the rest under a French mandate. Two colonial traditions, and subsequent reunification in 1961, laid the basis for Anglophone claims of discrimination. Francophones largely dictated the terms of reunification, forcing West Cameroonians (about one-fifth of the population) to adjust to their norms and structures, as well as language. Anglophone elites have had essentially three grounds of complaint. First, government favouritism towards Francophone zones (seen as especially unfair since the state derives revenues from oil pumped and refined in the Anglophone zone); second, the ascendancy of French language and educational systems has blocked social mobility for those trained in English; and third, the denial of Anglophone control over territory and resources, and under-representation in organs of state power and parastatal enterprises. These claims can be seen as overstated, or primarily raised by an Anglophone elite to advance narrow corporate interests. However, in the 1990s, in the face of increasing hostility and repression by central government, Anglophone pressure groups persisted in challenging their second-class status and calling for greater regional autonomy.

Baka, Gyeli, Tikar

Three erstwhile nomadic forest peoples, commonly referred to as 'Pygmies', eke out precarious livelihoods in shrinking forests of the south-west and south-east. Both the government and the Catholic Church have tried to sedentarize them in 'pilot villages' or forced settlement along roadways. Local farmers, logging companies and plantations pay them below legal minimum wages, and more importantly make inroads into their forest environment. In some cases the children of forest nomads have been denied access to local schools; formal schooling is rarely relevant to their culture and real economic prospects.

Conclusions and future prospects

Regional self-determination for Anglophones remains a major issue, particularly for Anglophone elites. Economic growth and careful ethnic balancing among elites have kept the problem, and north–south tensions, from spilling over into serious violence. But with the advent of economic decline, shrinking state services, renewed authoritarian rule, further accumulation of political and economic power in the hands of the current President's ethnic sub-group, and deteriorating reciprocity between citizens and government, it may become more difficult to contain such tensions.

Further reading

Bahuchet, S., 'Les Pygmées d'aujourd hui en Afrique centrale', *Journal des africanistes*, vol. 61, no. 1, 1991, pp. 5–35.

DeLancey, M.W., *Cameroon: Dependence and Independence*, Boulder, CO, Westview, 1989.

Geschiere, P., *Village Communities and the State: Changing Relations among the Maka of Southeastern Cameroon since the Colonial Conquest*, London, Kegan Paul, 1982.

Kofele-Kale, N., *Tribesmen and Patriots: Political Culture in a Poly-ethnic African State*, Washington, DC, University Press of America, 1981.

Kofele-Kale, N., 'Ethnicity, religionism and political power: a post-mortem of Ahidjo's Cameroon', in Schatzberg, M.G. and Zartman, I.W. (eds), *The Political Economy of Cameroon*, New York, Praeger, 1986.

Minority-based and advocacy organizations

Human Rights Defence Group, PO Box 359, Bamenda, Mezani, NW Province, Cameroon.

Central African Republic

Land area:	623,000 sq km
Population:	3.1 million (1992)
Main languages:	Sango (official and lingua franca), French (official)
Main religions:	indigenous beliefs, Christianity, Islam
Main minority groups:	Mboum 120,000 (est., 3.9%), Mbororo (Fulbé) 60,000 (est. 1.9%), Aka 40,000 (est., 1.3%), 'Hausa' 20,000 (est., 0.6%)
Real per capita GDP:	$1,050
UNDP HDI/rank :	0.355 (148)

A sparsely populated land, the Central African Republic contains peoples of great cultural diversity. Minorities face disadvantages, but their relations with others are not marked by the gross violence seen in neighbouring countries. More serious is the country's endemic material poverty and food insecurity; on several indices, it is among the poorest of Africa's poor countries. The history of the Central African Republic has been marked by long episodes of predation and conflict. The Atlantic slave trade gave rise to a network of riverine peoples in the south who raided peoples further north. Demand for slaves and ivory via Egypt and Sudan led merchants based in Muslim emirates of the savanna to carry out raids from the north. Besides helping to depopulate vast areas, these traumas left residues of hostility in the historical memory of several groups. France's armed conquest and colonial domination were a decisive factor. Missionaries and administrators sought to distinguish African ethnic groups, and then to arrange them in hierarchies. Further, local ecologies and coping strategies have served to set apart nomadic peoples of both the forests and the savannahs.

The minorities discussed below are best understood against a background of other, less marginalized groupings. The first policemen and clerks, and later the bureaucratic bourgeoisie, were recruited from among the riverine Ubangi-speaking people first exposed to French schools – Banziri, Sango, Yakoma and Mbaka (or Ngbaka), who together constitute about 5 per cent of the population. Three major linguistically related groups based in the middle and west of the country together make up the majority: Banda, Gbaya and Manja peoples. Linguistically distinct, but also Sahelian farmers, are Sara peoples, with about 10 per cent of the population; they live chiefly along the northern border with Chad (see **Chad**). Azande peoples, accounting for perhaps 1 per cent of the population, inhabit the far south-east.

Mboum

Now accounting for about 4 per cent of the population, many Mboum fled from highlands in Cameroon to escape Mboro (Fulbé) raids that had persisted into the twentieth century. Today they exist on the margins of society, being described as very poor refugees. Little information is available about this group.

Mbororo and 'Hausa' Muslims

Known also as Fulbé (also as Peul, Fula or Fulani – see also **NORTH, WEST AND THE HORN OF AFRICA**), Mbororo are semi-nomadic Islamic pastoralists. They are found throughout the western grasslands. From present-day Cameroon, Fulbé spearheaded slave raids among Gbaye and Mboum peoples in the nineteenth century. Resented for their relative wealth in cattle, they have been subject to harassment, bandit attacks and police shakedowns. The term 'Hausa' is popularly applied to Islamic African petty traders, said to account for three-quarters of all petty traders in the country, who probably number less than 1 per cent of the population. Muslim traders of Chadian origin were objects of rioting and looting in 1994. In 1993, six Muslims gained seats (out of eighty-five) in the national assembly, but there are few Muslims in senior government positions.

Aka

Also termed Ba'Aka or 'Pygmies', Aka people live largely nomadically in the forested areas of the south-west, gaining livelihoods through hunting and gathering; local residents and traders regularly buy meat and other produce from them. In some zones, Aka men sell their labour to local residents and to forest industries. Socially subordinated, they are paid less than others for the same work. Aka social bonds are disintegrating; health problems, including alcoholism and diseases of the respiratory tract, are increasing. Literacy levels, low throughout the country, are negligible. Formal schooling offers no means to learn their history and culture. Their cultural survival is severely threatened.

As with similar peoples elsewhere in Central Africa, outsiders have tried to turn Aka to settled farming. The government has left 'integration' efforts to Catholic missionaries, who have established 'pilot villages'. Other mission efforts, such as in schooling, have failed to retain pupils, as Aka families keep moving in the forests. For most, defence is a matter of always being able to move away from difficulties. Their future as a distinct cultural group depends greatly on the vulnerable forest ecology. Here as in Congo and Gabon, those forests are under great pressure from rapacious and mainly illegal logging. In deals made between the timber companies and government agents, Aka people have no voice.

Conclusions and future prospects

The interaction of Islamic groups, with their livelihoods in trade and livestock, and settled non-Muslim farmers, with their particular land-use interests and residual sense of past wrongs at the hands of Muslims, could lead to conflict, though the situation is difficult to predict. Other inter-ethnic tensions may sharpen as most citizens face deteriorating living standards in the face of continued conspicuous privilege for a Francophone elite, consisting of a relatively large, mainly French expatriate community (including some 1,500 military personnel) and a thin stratum of African politicians and officials whose resources to manage clientelist politics are shrinking.

Further reading

Kalck, P., *Central African Republic*, Oxford, Clio Press, World Bibliographical Series, no. 152, 1993.

O'Toole, T., *The Central African Republic: The Continent's Hidden Heart*, Boulder, CO, Westview Press, 1986.

Chad

Land area:	1,259,200 sq km
Population:	6.2 million (est. 1994)
Main languages:	Sara, Sango, Arabic (official from 1978), Chadic dialects, French (official)
Main religions:	Islam, indigenous beliefs, Christianity
Main minority groups:	southerners 2.8 million (45%)
Real per capita GDP:	$690
UNDP HDI/rank:	0.291 (163)

France established Chad's boundaries late in the imperial scramble for Africa, gaining control over the desert peoples of the northern tier only in 1914. French forces have been stationed in Chad ever since (about a thousand in the mid-1990s) partly on the pretext of defending Chadian sovereignty over Saharan territory.

Like other countries in Africa's Sudano-Sahelian zone, Chad comprises radically different cultures and livelihood systems polarized along a north–south axis. Uneven patterns of impoverishment, a deteriorating economy, crumbling state services marginally supported by foreign aid, ecological stress and military intervention by foreign powers have contributed to ethnic antagonisms. National policies and programmes have had scant regard for the legitimate interests of minorities. Rather, since the early 1960s a succession of authoritarian juntas and warlords have sought to advance interests of particular clans or ethnic groups through violence.

Ecology and ethnicity

Chad is divisible into three agro-climatic zones. First, the northern 'BET' (Bokou, Ennedi, Tibesti) area of the Sahara, accounting for over a third of Chad's territory, is home to only about 6 per cent of its population. Two nomadic peoples, collectively known as Toubou, make up virtually all its population; Teda people, concentrated near Tibesti in mountainous reaches of the far north; and Daza (in Arabic: Gorane) peoples, concentrated further south and east. The ethnic roots of Hissen Habré, Chad's ruthless strongman from 1979 to 1990, are in a small eastern Gorane sub-group. Second, the arid Sahelian scrublands of the middle belt account for over half of Chad's territory and somewhat less than half its population. They are home to nomadic and semi-nomadic peoples whose livelihoods depend largely on livestock, as well as sedentary peoples dependent on farming, fishing and trade. Like the peoples of the BET, virtually everyone in this zone is Muslim. In the Ouaddai prefecture bordering Sudan to the east, Zaghawa peoples (between 1 and 2 per cent of Chad's population) have been salient in recent history. Zaghawa make up much of the feared Republican Guard, an army unit answerable to the President, and responsible for much of the brutality and bloodshed of the 1990s. Chad's President since 1990, Idriss Déby, is of the Bidéyat people, who are closely allied with Zaghawa.

A significant proportion of Chad's population (25 to 30 per cent) adhere to Arab customs and, notwithstanding centuries of intermarriage with African peoples, consider themselves Arabs. About 13 per cent speak Arabic as a first language and 40 per cent as a second language; a majority of Chadians comprehend Arabic. In current Chadian politics, the Arabic language issue is a 'high tension line'.

The third zone is the south. Because southerners currently lack effective state power, and continue to bear the brunt of much, but by no means all, of the violence and intimidation by armed groups, they are treated together here in greater detail. Other minorities, in the central and northern zones of Chad, while also subject to abuse and predatory practices, are not considered here chiefly because their sufferings, while considerable, are relatively less serious.

Southerners

The five prefectures of the far south account for only about a tenth of Chad's territory but about 45 per cent of its population. Ethno-linguistic groupings here include: Sara, a cultural cluster of twelve major clans, constituting about 30 per cent of Chad's population; Toubouri and Massa (or Banana), with about 5 per cent; Mboum/Laka, with 3–4 per cent; and, Moundang, with 2–3 per cent. The last three groupings live in the westernmost prefectures of Mayo-Kebbi, Logone Orientale and Tandjile. Islam has never penetrated the southern prefectures, where centuries of slave-raiding from the Islamic emirates make it unwelcome. Christians are found virtually only in the south. Chad is a secular state, and although Muslim chauvinism is surfacing strongly, no regime has placed restrictions on religious freedoms. The Sara language is used as a medium of instruction in lower and upper primary school levels, as is Arabic and French. Primary school enrolment, although higher than in the north, is low, especially for girls. Most Chadian girls, both south and north, undergo genital mutilation. However, southern women – especially Roman Catholics – show considerably higher incidences of mutilation than Muslim (northern) women.

Southerners have traditionally been exploited for their labour. French interests from the 1930s on forced people to grow cotton under the exactions of French-appointed 'traditional' chiefs. Through missions, commoditization, and the growth of towns and state services, a thin stratum of clerks, policemen, teachers, soldiers and health workers emerged. During the Second World War, French recruitment of soldiers made Sara people 'the great military reservoir of French Equatorial Africa'.[1]

The post-colonial government recruited most of its administrators among southerners. In 1975, a little over a quarter of all southerners could read and write French, while only a small fraction of northerners could do so. Chad's first president was from the south, as were most members of his cabinet, army, and officialdom. Southerners' schooling credentials have put them at an advantage for waged employment, but they are not as prominent in commerce, where men from the middle Sahelian regions, and non-Chadians, excel.

Most southerners are settled farmers. Virtually all cultivable land, a mere 2 per cent of Chadian territory, is in the far south. Rising prices of inputs and unstable prices of produce (especially cotton), and elimination of many waged jobs have forced down living standards. Drought in Chad's central Sahelian rangelands have sent livestock herders further south in search of pasture, thus worsening competition for land, and probably fuelling inter-ethnic conflict.

Southerners' hegemony began to be challenged soon after independence in 1980, especially as the government began actively discriminating against Muslim northerners. Towards the end of the 1970s it suffered wholesale reversals. Although today they still retain posts in the civil service and the army, southerners have been effectively sidelined, commanding few streams of resources to manage clientalist politics. A consortium of US and French companies now plans to exploit oil in the southernmost prefecture of Logone Occidentale. People of that prefecture, and those of neighbouring Logone Orientale, are seen as particularly hostile to the northern-dominated central government. From around 1984 on, armed insurgency led by southern warlords has set in motion a violent spiral of reprisal and counter-reprisal. Major bloodshed began in 1979, when killings of southerners in the capital city N'Djamena led to reprisal killings of 5,000–10,000 mainly Muslim Arabs resident in the south. In all, some 40,000 people are said to have died during the Habré regime, while in the period under Déby from 1990 up to mid-1995 more than 2,000 were killed by government forces, who have also burned villages and otherwise terrorized civilians. Rebel forces have also been implicated in murder and intimidation, some of it deliberately aimed at Muslims from the north.

Violence has sent southerners streaming into neighbouring countries. By the mid-1990s about 43,000 were in Cameroon (refugees from the Hibré era) and about 21,000 in the Central African Republic. Chad's frontiers are porous, and rebel groups have made use of neighbouring countries as rear bases, adding to intergovernmental tensions. Central government and rebels have occasionally reached truces and temporary deals, thus short-circuiting moves – at times a demand of southern rebels – for decentralization of power and a federal system.

Conclusions and future prospects

Efforts by Chadians and outsiders to promote respect for human rights have not, as yet, brought about major improvements. In most of Chad, reciprocity between citizens and authorities scarcely exists. Yet the absence of any serious secessionist movements suggests that a break-up of Chad is not likely for the time being.

Further reading

Amnesty International, *Chad: Never Again? Killings Continue into the 1990s*, London, February 1993.

Amnesty International, *Tchad: de vaines promesses – les violations des droits de l'homme se poursuivent en toute impunité*, London, April 1995.

Buijtenhuijs, R., *La conférence nationale souveraine du Tchad*, Paris, Karthala, 1993

Comoros

Land area:	2,236 sq km (incl. Mayotte, 374 sq km)
Population:	624,000 (incl. 94,000 on Mayotte) (est. 1994)
Main languages:	Comorian, Arabic (official), French (official)
Main religions:	Islam, Christianity
Main minority groups:	—
Real per capita GDP:	$1,130
UNDP HDI/rank:	0.399 (139)

An archipelago of four spice-exporting islands between the northern coasts of Mozambique and Madagascar, the Comoros are divided. Three islands constitute a state with formal political independence; the fourth island, Mayotte (also called Mahoré), is ruled as an overseas territory of France. In a 1974 referendum, residents of Mayotte voted nearly two-to-one against independence from France, while on the other three islands some 96 per cent voted for independence. Peopled first by Melano-Polynesians and later by peoples from the African mainland, Madagascar and Arabia, Comorians represent an amalgam of cultures. They are today bound together by Islam. Literacy in the Comorian language is nearly universal, but Cormorian is spoken in ways distinctive to each island. Loyalties to an island's culture strongly influence affiliation to one or another political party, of which there are at least eighteen opposed to the ruling party. People of Mwali, the smallest and least populous island, with a mere 5–6 per cent of the archipelago's population, have voiced concern at under-representation in the Federal Parliament, and are bitter at their disproportionately small share in government budget allocations. Political demonstrations there have been put down with deadly force. Mayotte has attracted migrants from the Comoros Republic, giving rise to resentment towards non-Mayotte Comorians and a crackdown on immigration by the French authorities.

Further reading

Ottenheimer, M. and H., *Historical Dictionary of the Comoro Islands*, Metuchen, NJ, Scarecrow Press, 1994.

Congo

Land area:	341,500 sq km
Population:	2.4 million (est. 1994)
Main languages:	Lingala, Koutouba or Kikongo, Téké, French (official)
Main religions:	indigenous beliefs, syncretic Christianity, Islam
Main minority groups:	Bakongo 1.1 million (est., 46%), Batéké 500,000 (est., 21%), M'Boshi 330,000 (14 %)
Real per capita GDP:	$2,750
UNDP HDI/rank:	0.517 (125)

As in other oil-exporting poor countries, struggles over state power and revenues take on a particularly hard edge in the Congo. Ethnicity defines the chief ways elites pursue their rivalries and gain adherents. With the coming of multiparty competition in the 1990s, rivalry intensified. Ethnically based parties set up armed militias, and all groups resorted more frequently to lethal force. French concessionary companies set the pattern of coercive labour practices and ecological destruction at the outset of the colonial period. Replacing that private-sector-led approach in 1910, the French government continued many of those practices until the late 1950s. An urban bias set in early, as Brazzaville served as capital for French Equatorial Africa. More than half the Congolese population now lives in urban areas, a third in Brazzaville alone. The politics of ethnic exclusion have marked public life in the Congo, although official state socialist discourse, and rising public expenditure (as long as oil revenues were high), masked and deflected overt conflict until the 1990s. Ethnic and political divisions have strong regional dimensions.

Bakongo

The largest ethnic cluster is Bakongo, constituting 46 per cent of the population. Traditionally cassava farmers and fishing people, Bakongo women in particular are noted (sometimes with animosity) for their enterprise in cash-cropping and especially in trade. They have stood out as assiduous organizers, especially in religion and politics. Bakongo are also numerous in western Zaire and north-western Angola (see **Angola**). The Bakongo heartland in the Congo is the south, where they are divided into competing sub-groups, Lari and Vili.

Along the Congo river at Brazzaville/Pool, Lari are the most numerous Bakongo sub-group and the one historically most advantaged by schooling and commoditization. However, since 1963 there has been no Lari representative at the top of the state pyramid. In the 1990s, a political party with a strong Lari following emerged with particular strength in the Pool region around Brazzaville. In the Congo's second city Pointe Noire, on the coast, where the Congo's oil revenues are derived, Vili people are numerous. Political figures from among them have made alliances with politicians of Bembembe people, strongest in the 'Nibolek' (Niari, Bouenza, Lekoumo) upland area in the west. Emerging from this zone was a party led by Pascal Lissouba, who in 1992 became the first President to be elected through universal suffrage in twenty-seven years of one-party militarized rule.

Batéké

The second major ethnic cluster is Batéké, forming about 21 per cent of the population. Their home terrain is forested country to the north of Brazzaville, extending into southern Gabon. They are well represented in the Cuvette region in the middle-north. Colonial interests dispossessed most Batéké of land and marginalized them as labourers in the forest industries and towns.

M'Boshi

The third and smallest of the main ethnic clusters is Boulangui, found mainly in the north and in Brazzaville. M'Boshi, who account for about 14 per cent of the country's population, form its largest group. Among its sub-groups are Likoula and Kouyou people. M'Boshi-Kouyou leaders have compensated for their group's inferior numbers through their pre-eminence in the armed forces, especially the officer corps. The two Presidents in the period 1968 to 1979 were from the Kouyou sub-group, while the third and last, Denis Sassou-Nguesso (who gained a mere 17 per cent of the vote in the first open elections in 1992), was M'Boshi.

Other minorities

Non-Congolese Africans face denial of rights. In 1991 the government expelled some 30,000 to 40,000 Zairians, some of whom had lived in the Congo for decades. In 1993 and 1994 thousands of Kikongo-speaking people from the Angolan enclave of Cabinda streamed into the Congo to escape fighting between Cabindan separatists and Angolan government troops. By early 1995 some 13,500 Cabindans had registered as refugees (see **Angola**). A nomadic forest people, BaBongo or Akoa, also known as Babinga ('Pygmies'), number from 7,000 to 15,000. From the 1930s onward, public authorities and the Catholic Church have worked to sedentarize them. Historically able to evade forced labour in the past, some BaBongo were reported in the 1990s working in semislavery in northern forest enterprises.

Conclusions and future prospects

Political groupings overlap strongly with regional and ethnic clusters in the Congo. During the 1980s a northerner–southerner polarity prevailed. However, cross-cutting alliances with north–north and south–south dimensions have developed in the 1990s. Each major political/ethnic faction maintains its own armed militia in Brazzaville's *quartiers*, where fighting in 1993 and early 1994 cost hundreds of lives. As living standards remain under continual downward pressure and capital flight continues unchecked, the current truce appears fragile.

Further reading

Allen, C. et al., *Benin, The Congo, Burkina Faso: Economics, Politics and Society*, New York, Columbia University Press, 1989.

Fegley, R., *The Congo*, Oxford, Clio Press, World Bibliographic Series, no. 162, 1993.

Thompson, V. and Adloff, R., *Historical Dictionary of the People's Republic of the Congo*, Metuchen, NJ, Scarecrow Press, 1984.

Equatorial Guinea

Land area:	28,051 sq km (incl. Bioko Island, formerly Fernando Póo, 2,017 sq km)
Population:	410,000 (est. 1994)
Main languages:	Fang, Bubi, Ibo, Pidgin English, Spanish (official)
Main religions:	syncretic Christianity
Main minority groups:	Bubi 15,000 (est., 3.7%), Annobon Islanders 2,000 (est., 0.5%)
Real per capita GDP:	$1,800
UNDP HDI/rank:	0.461 (131)

Marked by 190 years of Spanish colonial rule, slave-trading and forced labour, since formal independence in 1968 Equatorial Guinea has seen no significant departures from an oppressive past. In the mid-1990s, despite non-violent citizen protest and rising pressures from abroad, the country remained notorious as a place ruled by 'tropical gangsters'.[1] Power has been in the hands of two dictators since the end of the colonial period. First, under Macías Nguema, a reign of terror saw hundreds die and up to a third of the citizenry flee abroad, together with tens of thousands of foreign workers. In 1979 his nephew Teodoro Obiang Nguema seized power, continuing an only somewhat less brutal despotism.

The Fang ethnic group (see **Cameroon, Gabon**) make up 80 to 90 per cent of the population of Equatorial Guinea, chiefly in the mainland province of Río Muni (Mbini). Eligibility for top positions depends on status in the Esangui clan of the Nguemas. With the exceptions of timber and oil concessions, most businesses are in the hands of senior government officials and their families, as are most opportunities to benefit from bribery and to allocate state revenues and aid funds. Important minorities include: Fang not belonging to the privileged clan; Ndowe, a small group based on the mainland coast where contact with foreign traders goes back a century or more; foreign Africans, holdovers from the tens of thousands (mainly Nigerian labourers) forced out in the 1970s; Fernandinos and land-owning and better-educated Creole people found mainly on the island of Bioko and targets of Nguema repression; and Bubi and Annobon peoples.

Bubi and Annobon Islanders

Bubi people, numbering perhaps 15,000, are indigenous to the island of Bioko, where they were once in the majority. Farmers and traders, their forebears resisted the grabbing of land and pressures to work on Spanish and Fernandino cocoa plantations. From the 1960s (with Spanish encouragement) some Bubi leaders sought separation of the island from mainland Equatorial Guinea. However, repression under the Nguema regimes led to the death and exile of many politically active Bubi, and for many more a period of forced labour on the island. By the 1980s Fang dominated the island numerically as well as politically. As prominent figures in a coalition of opposition parties, Bubi leaders called for a boycott of elections held in 1993 under unfree and unfair circumstances. Violent intimidation was the government's response. The approximately 2,000 people of the small island of Annobon, 670 kilometres south of Bioko, exist in great isolation, having no link with the outside world besides the twice-yearly visit of a supply vessel. Medical care is poor and schooling nonexistent. In 1993, security force violence against civilians, and the banning of aid flights, created extreme distress. An early 1994 report by a UN Special Rapporteur on Human Rights singled out Bubi and Annobon Islanders as victims of ethnic discrimination.

Conclusions and future prospects

By the mid-1990s, opposition groups were active abroad and on home ground in Equatorial Guinea, though within extremely narrow and life-threatening bounds. Their purposes are much broader than minority interests, being concerned with ending a dictatorship. Spain and France – after two decades of tacit complicity – are with some embarrassment withdrawing support from the regime. United Nations and US human rights reports are becoming more bluntly worded. The country remains subject to a UN Human Rights Rapporteur. However, the regime is gaining leverage against outside pressures as oil revenues come on stream; as is the case in other oil-producing countries, Western dependencies on cheap petroleum can weaken official commitments to human rights.

Further reading

Klitgaard, R., *Tropical Gangsters*, London, I.B. Tauris, 1990.

Sundiata, I.K., *Equatorial Guinea: Colonialism, State Terror, and the Search for Stability*, Boulder, CO, Westview Press, 1990.

United Nations, Commission on Human Rights, *Report on the Human Rights Situation in the Republic of Equatorial Guinea Prepared by Special Rapporteur of the Commission*, New York, 1 January 1994.

Gabon

Land area:	257,670 sq km
Population:	1.1 million (est. 1994)
Main languages:	Fang, Mbédé, BaPounou/Eshira, French (official)
Main religions:	Christianity, indigenous beliefs, Islam
Main minority groups:	Fang 370,000 (est., 34%), non-Gabonese Africans 200,000 (est., 18%, following 1995 expulsions)
Real per capita GDP:	$3,861
UNDP HDI/rank:	0.557 (120)

Since the mid-1960s Gabon's foreign earnings have boomed, chiefly in petrodollars. It is today one of the richest countries in Africa by conventional indices. Yet between 1965 and 1988, the proportion of the rural population below the poverty line rose from 25 to 41 per cent, representing an increase of 155,000 people. The ruling oligarchy is strongly tied to France. Social standing and life chances depend greatly on that leadership's choices of who is eligible for state largesse and who is not. Some ethnic elites are 'more equal than others', but careful balances struck among Gabonese groups, and ample petrodollars, have exempted any one Gabonese minority from wholesale marginalization. French military and economic power has guaranteed that the resident European minority remains large and suffers no privation. However, the non-Gabonese African minority has faced a very different fate.

The Gabonese population is culturally diverse, but with few of the major schisms by language family, form of livelihood, spatial isolation and differing ecologies that divide neighbouring countries. As the language of instruction is French, even in lower primary schools, no Gabonese ethnic group enjoys adequate possibilities to learn and value its mother tongue. Of nearly fifty ethno-lingusitic groups, Fang stand out as a minority under pressure. Among many minor ethnic groups are Batéké, from whom President Bongo comes. In 1995 the US State Department reported that '[t]here was evidence, especially within the armed forces, that members of the President's ethnic group occupied a disproportionate number both of senior positions and of jobs within the ranks.'[1]

Fang

Numerically the most important Gabonese ethnic group with about a third of the country's population, Fang immigrated from present-day Cameroon in the nineteenth century. They represent a southern branch of a people spread across southern Cameroon and all of Equatorial Guinea. Fang are active as accumulating entrepreneurs and farmers in the northern Woleu N'Tem area, where Protestant churches and schools are numerous, and some enjoy a small margin of economic autonomy from government. Under Fang leadership in 1981, a political grouping emerged, at first in exile in Paris, to challenge President Bongo's one-party rule. In the 1990s, a party derived from that group leads the principal opposition bloc, which is said to enjoy Catholic backing. There are credible claims of systematic discrimination against Fang in government appointments, and of intimidation by security forces.

Non-Gabonese Africans

Recruited to take up hard or dangerous work in mines, forests and plantations, or otherwise drawn by the petro-dollar boom, foreigners from elsewhere in Africa are Gabon's vulnerable underclass. They come chiefly from Cameroon, Congo, Equatorial Guinea and Benin. While a small number may have done well as traders, most work as farm hands and casual labourers, usually under poor and precarious conditions. According to the US State Department, in 1994:

'There were numerous reports of prisoners and detainees – principally foreigners – being forced to provide unpaid labour. Security forces routinely 'sweep' African neighbourhoods to check residence and identity documents, and at times they even detain without charge foreigners in possession of valid paperwork. Police or gendarmes often hold these persons in prison overnight and force them to work at government facilities, on public grounds, or even in the homes of ministers, military officers, or other members of the Government.'[2]

The same report cites claims that government officials privately use foreign child labour, chiefly as domestic or agricultural help, and that such children do not go to school, and are often victims of abuse. Gabon's leadership has led xenophobic campaigns against foreign Africans. Special targets were immigrants from Cameroon and Equatorial Guinea, mainly of the Fang ethnic group, a source of political opposition. Anti- (African) foreigner feeling reached a peak in early 1995, when the government tightened enforcement of resident permit requirements. By mid-February, following a major logistical effort, and against the protests of many African governments, some 55,000 had been forced to leave Gabon.

Other minorities

Several thousand nomadic Bongo ('Pygmies') pursue isolated and nomadic livelihoods in the forests, mainly in the north-east, where a major new wave of logging is putting them under enormous stress. In 1987 the government outlawed a number of small, mainly syncretic sects, which it suspected of serving as a cover for political opposition. Among them was the Jehovah's Witnesses; but the ban against their tiny fellowship has not been enforced. More serious was the outlawing of the Bwiti sect, a significant indigenous syncretic cult with strong traditions of mutual welfare.

Conclusions and future prospects

Gabon remains a French neo-colony, its leadership kept in power by the French military and security services. The 25,000–30,000 French and other Western residents hold positions of privilege and power. Opposition has been strongly polarized on ethnic lines. If demands for more transparent democratic practices (such as fair elections) are met, this polarity may diminish. However, key minority issues appear unlikely to be resolved in the near future as long as a large intermediate stratum of non-Gabonese Africans serves as a scapegoat, and the influence of a privileged European minority continues to prevail.

Further reading

Barnes, J.F., *Gabon: Beyond the Colonial Legacy*, Boulder, CO, Westview Press, 1992.

Kenya

Land area:	582,644 sq km
Population:	27.3 million (est. 1995)
Main languages:	Swahili, English, local languages
Main religions:	traditional religions, Christianity (mainly Roman Catholicism), Islam
Main minority groups:	estimates:[1]Muslims 6,100,000 (22%), Kikuyu 5,550,000 (20%), Luhya 3,400,000 (14%), Luo 3,150,000 (11%), Kamba 2,700,000 (10%), Kalenjin 2,700,000 (11%), Kisii 1,450,000 (5%), Meru 1,350,000 (5%), Somalis and nomadic minorities 700,000 (2.5%), Maasai 240,000 (1%), others (including Okiek and Aweer) 450,000 (1.5%)
Real per capita GDP:	$1,400
UNDP HDI/rank:	0.473 (128)

Kenya is a country of great ethnic, linguistic, religious and cultural diversity. Agriculturalists and pastoralists often have competing claims to land. Nomadic pastoralists are in ceaseless conflict with the authorities. Divisions between Christians and Muslims are of growing significance. In recent years political conflict on ethnic lines has increased dramatically, exacerbated by the combination of political pluralism and economic decline. Nevertheless, ethnic categorizations are complex and sometimes overlapping.

Colonial Kenya saw large-scale expropriation of agricultural land for European settlement in what is now the Rift Valley province – mostly land occupied at the time by pastoralists. Some of this land was subsequently settled by people from agriculturalist groups who had been recruited to work on the White farms, later acquiring some land themselves. Pastoralist groups played a less important role in the independence struggle and subsequent settlement, but their more recent political ascendancy has put them in a stronger position to reopen long-standing grievances. The legacy of other migrations to Kenya is also reflected in current tensions. Arab traders and slavers profoundly influenced East Africa, leading to the creation of comparatively well-educated Swahili-speaking communities in coastal regions as well as the conversion of a quarter of the population to Islam. Declining political influence, combined with the impact of Islamic politics elsewhere, has led to growing resentment among many Kenyan Muslims. Kenyans of South Asian origin have also attracted hostility as a result of their commercial dominance. Nomadic pastoralists in the north and north-east of the country have long been viewed with suspicion if not outright hostility by the authorities, compounded in the case of Somalis by long-standing disputes between Kenya and Somalia.

From 1969 to 1991 Kenya was effectively run as a one-party state. Growing international pressure for reform led to the reintroduction of multi-party politics, culminating in presidential and parliamentary elections in December 1992. Daniel arap Moi, President since 1978, won with 36 per cent of the vote over a divided opposition; his Kenya African National Union (KANU) party won a narrow majority of seats in Parliament. Irregularities were believed to be significant but not decisive. Multi-party politics increases opportunities for mobilization on ethnic (and religious) lines. The 'ethnic card' is then difficult to remove, but there can be changes in the fortunes of 'winners' and 'losers' – those who dominate today being subordinated tomorrow. Kenya has already seen one such reversal and may face more.

All Kenya's ethnic groupings are can be considered minorities, and almost all can be considered vulnerable. The conflicts of recent years involve some of the main ethnic groups in the country, who are considered together. Other vulnerable minorities are considered separately. In the case of smaller minorities it has only been possible to give selected examples.

Muslims

Kenya's Muslims are not a homogeneous group, as they comprise converts from different ethnic groupings (going back many centuries), Arabs and people of mixed Arab-African descent, Somalis and some other nomadic groups, and more recent migrants from South Asia. Most Muslims live in the Coastal province, where their sense of common identity is strongest. Unemployment and landlessness are exceptionally high in the province – one estimate puts the number of squatters there as more than a million, the majority of the population. Well-publicized land purchases by outsiders, notably Whites, Asians and cabinet ministers, particularly in tourist areas, have added to local grievances.

In the run-up to the 1992 elections a group of businessmen and intellectuals in Mombasa founded the Islamic Party of Kenya (IPK), which the government refused to register. The arrest on several occasions of a radical Muslim preacher, Sheikh Khalid Balala, increased sympathy and support for the IPK. The government responded by setting up a rival Muslim organization, and by trying to highlight differences between Muslims of Arab and of African descent. Levels of rhetoric in government–IPK conflict have been high, with death threats issued by both sides, and President Moi himself equating Islam with slavery. Kenyan Muslims cannot yet claim a systematic pattern of persecution or of denial of their religious and cultural rights, but this may change as the pattern of increasing political polarization on ethnic and religious lines continues, with the danger of the country's substantial Muslim minority being drawn into conflicts with religious demarcation lines.

Kikuyu, Luhya, Luo, Kalenjin and Maasai

As the largest and geographically most central group in Kenya, Kikuyu had a dominant role in pre- and post-independence politics. Luo politicians were also prominent. By contrast in the late colonial period many pastoralists (who include Kalenjin and Maasai) were allied to or co-opted by the British authorities in an attempt to counteract the radical nationalism represented by the Mau Mau insurgency. Jomo Kenyatta, the country's first President, consolidated the Kikuyu position while also maintaining an ethnic balance in his administration. However, politicians from pastoralist ethnic groups came to exert a significant, then a dominant, role within the ruling KANU, not least through the growing patronage wielded by Kenyatta's deputy and successor, Daniel arap Moi.

In the 1990s the most serious conflict in Kenya has focused on land disputes in western Kenya between settled agricultural communities of Kikuyu, Luhya and Luo people and pastoralist Kalenjin and Maasai. Many Kikuyu settled in these regions early in the century, acting as a labour reserve for White farms, though unable formally to own land until the immediate pre-independence period. Since 1992, according to most independent observers, over 200,000 people, the great majority Kikuyu, have been displaced from their homes in the Rift Valley province and other parts of western Kenya. As many as a thousand have been killed. Characteristically the perpetrators have been organized bands of Kalenjin or Maasai 'warriors' – young men armed with bows and arrows or machetes, often wearing improvised uniforms – whose activities have gone unhindered by the authorities. In most cases the authorities have also conspicuously failed to bring the aggressors to justice. There have also been reprisal attacks on Kalenjin and Maasai.

The violence began in the period preceding the 1992 election and escalated after it, as did the extent of patronage on ethnic lines. Moi's new twenty-five-member cabinet was dominated by members of his own Kalenjin tribal group, with only one Kikuyu and one Luo member. Moi had held the elections reluctantly, under pressure from donor countries. His stated view that tribal conflict is the inevitable consequence of multiparty politics may be the excuse for a return to more authoritarian political practices, and possibly for a form of ethnically based federalism favoured by many Kalenjin and Maasai politicians. A related motive may be to consolidate his stronghold in the Rift Valley, the heartland of Kenya's agricultural economy. Less elaborate explanations cite the punishment or intimidation of ethnic groups who have largely supported opposition politicians. Levels of conflict, antagonism, mistrust and hatred have reached high levels.

The primary victims of the conflict – Kikuyu, Luo and Luhya – are members of groups too large to be generally considered minorities. Indeed their size and former political position increase the prospects for retaliation and revenge. Kalenjin, Maasai and other pastoralist groups face not only retaliation now but the threat of more serious retribution if and when they lose their current political ascendancy. The ethnic politics currently being pursued by the Kenyan government risk precipitating conflict on an expanding scale.

Somali and other nomads

The two arid northern provinces of Kenya comprise half the land area of the country yet are home to less than 3 per cent of the population, mainly nomadic pastoralists of many ethnic identities and many more tribal and clan affiliations and rivalries. Principal groupings are Somalis (250,000), Turkana (250,000), Samburu (74,000), Boran (or Borana) (69,000), Gabbra (35,000), Orma (32,000), Rendille (26,000, of which Ariaal 7,000), and Sakuye (10,000). (The figures must be considered very approximate. The figure for Somalis includes both pastoralists and many long-standing residents of urban areas, but does not include refugees in recent years from Somalia itself.) Competition by nomadic groups over cattle and grazing combined with periods of drought have perpetuated a way of life close to subsistence and seldom far from conflict – though most efforts at economic improvement have failed by upsetting the precarious equilibrium between people and resources. Conflict in Somalia has caused further widespread disruption, and the great availability of firearms has exacerbated traditional and more recent enmities.

From colonial times the government has treated the northern parts of Kenya mainly as a security problem. Other interventions have primarily been to try to persuade nomads to settle. Emergency powers have enabled the authorities to bypass the judicial system. Although the situation is confused, with a variety of colonial and post-colonial legislation being enforced or ignored, draconian measures are widely available and often used. These include powers to arrest, move or detain people, confiscate or destroy livestock, prohibit gatherings, and impose a mandatory death penalty for illegal possession of firearms. The northern districts are Trust Lands with very limited defences against expropriation, an important factor in recent moves to privatize land, particularly for ranching.

Somali-speaking nomads have attracted the greatest government hostility. The eastern parts of northern Kenya are traditionally inhabited by Somalis of the Degodia, Ajuran and Ogaden clans. These areas have long been claimed by Somalia, with recent disavowals having limited impact on Kenyan suspicions. The inhabitants voted to secede from Kenya in a referendum held shortly before independence in 1963. The results were ignored by the incoming government, leading to a three-year secessionist war. A mixture of secessionist insurgency, inter-ethnic and clan warfare, and outright banditry has characterized the region ever since. The 1977–8 war between Ethiopia and Somalia, and the civil war in Somalia in the 1990s, which created over a quarter of a million refugees, have led to armed incursions from Somalia and exacerbated instability.

Hostility between Somalis and the authorities have led to continuous conflict over efforts to control movement, such as the impounding of cattle, resulting in extremely serious abuses, including massacres in Garissa in 1980 (300 people) and Wajir in 1984 (up to 2,000) and 1987 (300). The impact of such killings affects all Kenyan Somalis – including those long resident in urban areas – who feel themselves treated as second class citizens. A specific grievance has been the requirement since 1989 for Kenyan Somalis to carry a separate pink identity card, in addition to the national identity card carried by all Kenyans. This is ostensibly to distinguish them from Somali refugees, numbering about 220,000, who have also suffered abuse at the hands of the authorities, including alleged rape by soldiers. Identification of many urban Somalis with the Islamist currents described below is both symptom and cause of further disaffection.

Other groups have also faced harassment and persecution. Boran and Sakuye nomads have been subjected to wholesale confiscation of stock, disrupting social relations as well as economy. The creation of the Sibiloi Nature Reserve excluded Gabbra nomads from traditional summer grazing. Efforts have been made to break the age sets of Samburu.

Banditry and lawlessness combined with traditional ethnic and clan-based enmities among nomads comprise an unenviable problem for the authorities. Yet their extremely heavy-handed responses betray a hostility towards nomads and a contemptuous attitude towards the nomadic way of life, compounded by a more general disregard for human rights. Recommendations made by Survival Inter-national for ameliorating the situation include: restricted encroachment by farmers on nomads' land, and legal protection for communal land rights; international agreements for frontier crossing to benefit nomads; the development of meat markets and measures to ensure fair prices for nomads; a reduced focus on water-oriented development projects, with small wells favoured over deep boreholes; mobile rather than static health, veterinary and educational services; and respect and support for new and existing indigenous and nomad institutions. Such a programme would require major changes in government policies and attitudes.

Okiek and Aweer

Okiek comprise about two dozen ethno-linguistic groups, totalling about 40,000 people, living in or near the highland forests of central Kenya. Traditionally hunter-gatherers and still dependent on forest resources, most are now primarily involved in agriculture and/or pastoralism. Many Okiek have land rights on the fringes of forests, but government policies of converting communal land to individual ownership have led to much being sold off to others, jeopardizing the long-term position of Okiek. A programme in the Mau forest, the largest forest of indigenous trees in East Africa, aims to involve Okiek in forest protection and the development of sustainable forest resources such as honey, wax, fruits and traditional medicines, but it is too soon to say how much such initiatives can stem the trend towards marginalization.

Aweer are another traditional hunter-gatherer group, numbering about 2,000, living in the Lamu district of eastern Kenya and now largely dependent on shifting agriculture which is more destructive of wildlife and forest resources than the hunting which has been banned by the government in the name of conservation. Poor rainfall has resulted in chronic nutritional shortages; insecurity in this border region has grown even greater following the wars in Somalia, rendering government services almost non-existent. Most men have left the region in search of work. Unless plans permitting hunting and use of forest resources are introduced, the position of Aweer people is set to decline still further.

Conclusions and future prospects

In 1996 Kenya avoided the descent into ethnic fragmentation and civil war which had been predicted, but levels of tension along ethnic and religious fault lines remain. The government has given every impression of allowing or promoting such conflicts in the pursuit of narrow sectarian and political interests. Realization of this may encourage moves away from the brink, but the damage done will be difficult to reverse. Conflicts based on religious divisions may be particularly hard to defuse. While conflicts involving Kenya's nomadic minorities have less of a destabilizing impact, the continued abuse of their rights is likely to worsen in conditions of general political deterioration.

Further reading

African Rights, *The Nightmare Continues: Abuses against Somali Refugees in Kenya*, London, 1993.

Carver, R., 'Kenya: aftermath of the elections', *Refugee Survey Quarterly*, vol. 13, no. 1, Spring 1994, Geneva, Centre for Documentation on Refugees/UNHCR.

Cruise O'Brien, D., 'Coping with the Christians: the Muslim predicament in Kenya', in H. B. Hansen and M. Twaddle (eds.), *Religion and Politics in East Africa*, London, James Currey, 1995.

Human Rights Watch/Africa, *Divide and Rule: State-Sponsored Ethnic Violence in Kenya*, London, 1993.

Survival International, *Unquiet Pastures: The Nomadic Peoples of North East Kenya*, London, 1994.

Minority-based and advocacy organizations

All Africa Conference of Churches/World Council of Churches, PO Box 14205, Westlands, Nairobi, Kenya.

National Council of Women in Kenya, PO Box 43741, Nairobi, Kenya.

Lesotho

Land area:	30,355 sq km
Population:	2 million (est. 1995)
Main languages:	Sesotho, English
Main religions:	Christianity (primarily Roman Catholicism)
Main minority groups:	—
Real per capita GDP:	$980
UNDP HDI/rank:	0.464 (130)

The land comprising Lesotho was part of a powerful Sotho kingdom under attack from both Boers and Zulus when Britain offered protection, in return for loss of land, in 1868. Though entirely surrounded by South Africa, the territory remained under British rule until independence in 1966. The population is almost entirely Sesotho-speaking, with small European, Asian and Xhosa-speaking minorities. No minority rights issues have been identified.

Madagascar

Land area:	581,540 sq km
Population:	13.4 million (est. 1994)
Main languages:	Malagasy (official), French (official)
Main religions:	indigenous beliefs, Christianity, Islam
Main minority groups:	Comorans 20,000 (0.1%), Asians 20,000 (0.1%)
Real per capita GDP:	$700
UNDP HDI/rank:	0.349 (150)

With a single national language, strong traditions of self-organization, indigenous forms of conflict resolution, and no fixed overlap between ethnic group and political bloc, Madagascar's political order lacks strong majority–minority polarization. The economy pivots largely on farming, with no dominant mineral export to concentrate revenues in few hands. Thus there is somewhat greater reciprocity between state and citizen – including minority citizens – than in many countries in the region. However, Madagascar is not exempt from the marginalizing consequences of social hierarchies and economic deterioration. In the 1990s, austerity measures are provoking inter-group hatreds.

Competing hypotheses about the origins of the population concern when and how, some 1,500 to 2,000 years ago, Malay and Indonesian immigrants mixed with African immigrants, with some Arab and Indian admixtures. These hypotheses have gained and lost prominence depending on political circumstances. Hypotheses emphasizing the unity of the population have been salient for nationalist purposes, while those emphasizing diversity have been elaborated to suit specific group interests.

The Merina/côtier division

Census data divide the population into eighteen official ethnic groups. The largest, with about a quarter of the population, is Merina, descendants of people of somewhat more marked Indonesian origins, whose central plateau kingdom dominated much of the island in the nineteenth century. Groups on the periphery of the Merina, and in some cases dominated by them, are commonly termed *côtier* people, as some of them inhabited coastal zones. African origins are rather more marked among them. The distinction between Merina and *côtier* coincides to some extent with urban–rural distinctions, as Merina are disproportionately urbanized. However, with the urbanization and emergence of elites among *côtier* peoples on the basis of education, accumulation in trade, and position in the state apparatus, the distinction is losing its class content. Use of the Malagasy language, the standard medium of instruction in lower primary schools, and an emphasis on Malagasy culture since 1972, has helped transcend inter-ethnic divisions.

Ethnicity does not have the same salience in Madagascar as in some other African countries. Polarities are based more on social class, making educational and language policy explosive issues. Most groups, including Merina, were stratified by castes. Descendants of slaves are usually distinguished from 'freemen', who may be further divided (as with Merina) between descendants of nobles and commoners. These patterns have interacted with schooling and other stratifying institutions in complex ways. However, the distinction between slave and non-slave has carried over into socio-economic status today. Declining purchasing power and joblessness are reviving ethnic animosities, but more so animosity towards those identifiable as 'strangers'. Therefore, in this short overview, only key non-Malagasy minorities are highlighted for attention.

Comorans

Muslim people of the Comoros Islands were once the second largest non-Malagasy minority. Most lived in the Majunga region in the north-west, where their numbers (about 60,000 in 1970) formed half the population. Many were petty traders. In 1976 and 1977, however, at a time of national political change and the ending of special status for holders of French passports, anti-Comoran riots broke out, leaving over a thousand people dead. As most Comorans had opted not to become citizens of Madagascar at independence, many were forced to go to the Comoros. Today perhaps 20,000 remain, most in the capital city.

Other minorities

Immigrants in the twentieth century, people of both Indo-Pakistani origin (about 10,000) and Chinese origin (about 10,000), operate small shops and other businesses, both registered and 'parallel market'. Indo-Pakistanis especially have met popular animosity and have been targets of boycotts.

Conclusions and future prospects

Given the many indigenous and colonially imposed hierarchies in Madagascar's society, it is perhaps remarkable how much the forces of social exclusion and domination have been held in check. Today, however, the implosion of the state and imposition of free-market orthodoxies are putting intense downward pressure on living standards. Such trends have revived dormant animosities and provoked 'a prodigious explosion' of ethnic chauvinism, 'transformed into a true feeling of hatred and a total rejection of 'the other' through purely racist behaviour'.[1] The outlook for minority rights is now far from promising.

Further reading

Covell, M., *Madagascar: Politics, Economics and Society*, London, Frances Pinter, 1987.

Schlemmer, B., 'Crise et recomposition des identités à Madagascar', *Revue tiers monde*, vol. 36, no. 141, Jan.–Mar., 1995.

Malawi

Land area:	118,848 sq km
Population:	9.7 million (est. 1994)
Main languages:	Chi-Nyanja/Chi-Chewa (first language for 50%) (official), Lomwe, Yao, English (official)
Main religions:	Christianity, indigenous beliefs, Islam
Main minority groups:	southerners (mainly Nyanja, Lomwe and Yao) 4.8 million (50%), northerners (mainly Tumbuka) 1.1 million (11%),
Real per capita GDP:	$710
UNDP HDI/rank:	0.321 (157)

Malawi has a history of nineteenth-century armed conquest and twentieth-century manipulation of ethnic antagonisms, during which attempts have been made to create social hierarchies based on ethnicity. In 1994, however, an era of dictatorship ended, thus improving the chances for greater social justice. Imperial interests of Britain, in competition with those of Portugal, set the country's boundaries in about 1890. These drew diverse peoples into one artificial grid. Earlier, the settled farming populations had suffered invasion by Ngoni, a people originating in Natal and Swaziland and organized for combat. Their raids for cattle, slaves and other booty spread across present-day Mozambique, Zimbabwe and Zambia in the mid-nineteenth century. With their captives and cattle, Ngoni settled in central and northern Malawi.

Arab-Swahili slave-traders based in coastal enclaves were a further predatory factor. Their collaborators, Yao people of present-day Mozambique and Tanzania, began to settle in Malawi in the latter part of the century. Suppression of the slave trade was a major pretext for British claims to the territory. The most decisive wave of settlement began in the 1890s: missionaries (particularly from Scotland), administrators, labour recruiters for mines and farms elsewhere in Southern Africa, and traders of Indian origin. The first British Commissioner of the Central Africa Protectorate (1891–1907) in present-day Malawi wore a hatband of White, yellow and Black stripes as emblems of the social hierarchy to be created: Whites on top, Indian merchants in the middle and Black people at the bottom. Colonial policy aimed at both creating and manipulating ethnic identity. Loosely affiliated clans and speakers of similar dialects were grouped under appointed chiefs, and formally transformed into 'tribes'. These in turn were played off against one another, a practice continued in the post-colonial period. Creation of the Northern, Central and Southern regions further sharpened distinctions.

The post-colonial 1962–94 reign of the Malawi Congress Party (MCP), headed by Hastings Banda, a Chewa physician, saw the practice of 'racial discrimination as a matter of law and ethnic persecution as a matter of consistent policy'.[1] Promotion of Chewa hegemony was the regime's major project, including the projection of Chewa culture as that of the Malawian nation as a whole. Real or perceived challengers in the spheres of business, religion and especially political power were intimidated, often brutally; some were murdered. By the mid-1990s some legal scaffoldings of the old order had been dismantled. But much of what was built still stands, largely on regional lines. Victimized minorities no longer suffer active discrimination, but accumulated grievances remain. The situation of such minorities is highlighted below. Other minorities, such as Ngoni, have not been explicitly subject to discrimination in the past and are not treated in detail here. Intermarriage, compounded by dubious census methods in the colonial era and post-colonial ethnic re-labelling of people has put in question the validity of much ethno-linguistic categorization in Malawi. Ethnic self-identification has never taken deep root. Socio-political loyalties appear instead to correspond more consistently with regions, their political parties and leaders, although these overlap with ethnic clusters.

The Central Region

With about 38 per cent of the country's total population, the Central Region is home of the Congress Party and its Chewa ethnic base. The region is relatively homogeneous; Ngoni-speaking people constitute a minor part of its population. In the colonial era mission schools were fewer and attendance lower than in other regions; they were run by French-speaking Catholics and Afrikaans-speaking Protestant missionaries, who did not encourage the use of English. Few intellectuals or small business owners emerged as leaders here. Literacy and other skill levels tend to be lower than national averages, which are low in Southern African terms. Although many other Malawians were as poor or marginalized as the Central Region's Chi-Chewa, the Banda regime cited these shortcomings to justify its effort to favour people of this region with new infrastructural projects, farm loans and direct patronage. They also gained, where groups in the Northern and Southern regions lost, means to learn about and celebrate their culture, albeit in an often exaggerated and artificial form. In return the people of the Central Region have shown consistent loyalty to Banda's Congress Party. The women's branch of the party was given special prominence, with paradoxical tasks of promoting women's position (the Chewa trace descent through the mother's family) while mobilizing political support for a system dominated by men.

Southerners

About half Malawi's population lives in the Southern Region, whose economy pivots on urban commerce and services, and plantation agriculture with mixed small and medium-scale rural production. The principal southern minorities are considered below.

Nyanja-speaking peoples constitute the largest ethno-linguistic grouping in the south, and account for about a fifth of the country's total population. Although the Banda regime portrayed them as kindred to Chewa, and therefore bearers of 'true' Malawian culture, Chi-Nyanja-speaking elites found their ambitions for economic and political opportunity blocked. The winning party of the 1994 election, the United Democratic Front (UDF), includes many Nyanja.

The cluster of groups referred to collectively as Lomwe account for about a fifth of the country's total population. Their forebears entered Malawi from Mozambique (where they are culturally akin to Macua) as cheap labourers for European tea and tobacco planters in the densely settled south-eastern highlands of Mulanje and Thyolo districts. While never gaining social power and strong ethnic identity through schools and a local petit-bourgeois leadership, Lomwe-speakers nevertheless came to staff the Malawian army in disproportionate numbers during Banda's rule.

The third major ethno-linguistic group of the Southern Region, Yao people make up about 8 per cent of Malawi's total population. Most are Muslims. The British promoted their chiefs as indirect rulers over the Lomwe labouring peoples and as earners of export revenues through small-scale tobacco production. However, both Christian mission schooling and Muslim schools were discouraged; thus an important basis for broad ethnic identity and socio-political power never developed among Yao as it did for Tumbuka people (see below). Nevertheless, the Banda regime practised deliberate discrimination and subtle vilification of Yao people as accomplices in the slave trade. Yao could therefore not fully participate in economic and social life, nor enjoy full opportunities to gain knowledge of their traditions, language and culture. Financed from abroad, a programme of mosque-building gained momentum in the 1980s, somewhat compensating for anti-Muslim practices. In 1981 Banda expelled from his cabinet, following other expulsions of rivals, a popular Yao nationalist politician and Muslim businessman, Bakili Muluzi. In May 1994 Muluzi became Malawi's president, ending an era of anti-Yao machinations.

Northerners

The Northern Region is a remote and thinly populated region containing about 12 per cent of Malawi's population. It has long been a source of labour to other countries in Southern Africa as well as to the rest of Malawi. Migrant labourers from the north constitute a vulnerable part of this minority. Tumbuka-speakers are the most numerous northern ethnic group. In the 1994 elections, the northern-based Alliance for Democracy (AFORD) party, with a Tumbuka leadership, won all constituencies in the Northern Region.

The establishment of mission schools in the north of Malawi in the late nineteenth century helped put northerners on a faster track of social mobility. Northerners became clerks, skilled traders and wage-earners in relatively greater numbers than other Malawians. In the post-colonial period, northerners accounted for about half of university entrants and formed the backbone of the nation's educational staff and civil service. A number of Malawi's most active nationalist leaders at the time of political independence were from the region. It was this leadership that Banda, shortly after coming to power, began to expel from government, jail, force into exile, vilify, and even, it is alleged, murder.

For nearly thirty years it was the regime's policy to exclude northerners, especially Tumbuka-speaking people, from social and political achievement. In 1968 it made Chi-Chewa an official language of instruction, a compulsory subject of study in school, and medium for radio and the press. Speakers of Tumbuka, among others, lost means to enjoy and promote their language and culture. Over the years, the regime took other steps to frustrate the social mobility of northerners, especially through access to secondary and tertiary level schooling. In 1987 for example, it imposed a quota system governing university admissions so that Chi-Chewa-speakers, hitherto under-represented, would be guaranteed more places. Northerners in government positions were periodically purged in the 1980s. These measures, some of which were never fully applied, seem not to have decisively changed Chewa social standing; but they did serve further to polarize political life and to discredit the Banda regime. With the advent of the new government in 1994, a number of discriminatory measures were rescinded. National radio resumed broadcasting Tumbuka-language programmes after a hiatus of twenty-six years.

Other minorities

Three small but notable minorities reside mainly in urban areas of the Southern Region: 'Asians', numbering several thousand; 'coloureds' (people of mixed descent), numbering a few thousand at most; and 'Europeans', numbering perhaps five or six thousand, and holding privileged managerial, social service and technical occupations, as well as property ownership. Under the Banda regime, Asian traders were forced out of rural areas, their businesses restricted to major towns. Within months of coming to power in 1994, Malawi's new President appealed to Asians who had left Malawi in the 1980s to return. Although intended to win foreign investment, this gesture did not gain immediate popular support: two days after the appeal, African employees of Asian business-owners went on strike for higher pay. From about 1984 to 1992, over a million Mozambicans found sanctuary from war as refugees in Malawi. Relations between Malawians and these refugees, some of whom lived in marginally better conditions, were rarely harmonious. By 1996, almost all had returned home to Mozambique. The Jehovah's Witnesses sect was banned under the Banda regime from 1967 to 1993. No evidence was available for this edition suggesting that they have suffered discrimination since their subsequent legalization.

Conclusions and future prospects

To begin combating poverty, land reform in this wholly agrarian country is the biggest challenge. Until 1994, political advantages allowed a Chi-Chewa-speaking elite to accumulate property and social power. They struck deals with foreign companies and hired White farm managers from ex-Southern Rhodesia. More than 75 per cent of arable land came into the hands of companies and individuals who grew mostly export crops, such as coffee, tea, tobacco and sugar. In 1970, there were 229 commercial estates with about 79,000 hectares; in 1991, there were 23,000 estates occupying 1.14 million hectares. This process helped dispossess tens of thousands of African smallholders, 40 per cent of whom were left with 0.7 hectares or less – too little land to support a farming livelihood. In 1965, 85 per cent of Malawi's rural population lived below the poverty line; in 1988, the proportion had risen to 90 per cent – in absolute numbers, a rise of about 3 million people in poverty. The process was fully underwritten by Western aid agencies, which had a honeymoon with Malawi. In the balance is the question of Western willingness now to help redress a situation bearing comparison with Central America's gross disparities in land holdings.

Further reading

Palmer, R.H., 'Johnston and Jameson: a comparative study in the imposition of colonial rule', in B. Pachai (ed.), *The Early History of Malawi*, Evanston, IL., Northwestern University Press, 1972, pp. 293–322.

Vail, L. and White, L., 'Tribalism in the political history of Malawi', in L. Vail (ed.), *The Creation of Tribalism in Southern Africa*, London, James Currey, 1989, pp. 151–92.

Mauritius

Land area:	1,860 sq km
Population:	1.1 million (est. 1994)
Main languages:	Kreol (household language of at least 62%), Bhojpuri, French, English (official)
Main religions:	Hinduism, Christianity, Islam
Main minority groups:	Creoles 300,000 (27%), Ilois of Diego Garcia 2,000 (0.2%)
Real per capita GDP:	$12,510
UNDP HDI/rank:	0.825 (54)

Mauritius is at the head of the list of African countries in indices of general welfare, and with one of the non-Western world's lowest proportions of people living in absolute poverty, it has, like some other micro-states, managed to combine growth with equity despite great cultural diversity which may seem an unpromising basis for democracy and redistributive practice. India, Africa, Madagascar, France and China provided its peoples; 65 per cent are of Indian origin, while those of 'mixed' origins make up most of the rest. In Mauritian history, 'British colonization, carefully brought to life ethnic, religious, and racial particularisms in order to maintain its domination over the different communities of the island'.[1] Prosperity and social mobility, and the success of a political movement combining working class and intellectual leadership, have helped to build a sense of Mauritian identity that tolerates multiculturalism. There has been no serious inter-ethnic violence since 1969.

Creoles, including the Ilois of Diego Garcia, form a minority commonly relegated to the bottom of social hierarchies. Other minorities, such as lower castes (Rajput and Revi Ved), and non-Biharis in the Indo-Mauritian Hindu community, are not considered here.

Creoles

Mauritian Creoles, constituting about 27 per cent of the population, reflect mixtures of African, French and Indian origins across a broad range. Black Creoles especially have been subject to discrimination. Many neighbourhoods are ethnically segregated, with low-status Creoles invariably in the poorest housing. The Kreol language, a patois of French and Afro-Malagasy languages, is spoken by virtually all Mauritians and is the 'ancestral language' of 36 per cent of the population. It is considered socially inferior to English and French. Yet it gained status, and served as a rallying-point, through the coming to power of a left-of-centre government in 1982. Since the mid-1980s it has become a language of instruction for the first three grades of primary school.

Ilois of Diego Garcia

As a condition of Mauritian independence, the British government in the mid-1960s persuaded nationalist politicians to relinquish claims to the Chagos Archipelago, a group of islands including the coral atoll Diego Garcia (land area: 60 sq km), some 2,400 kilometres to the north-east of Mauritius. The aim was to provide a base for the US and British military. Britain then secretly removed the 2,000 mainly Creole residents – the Ilois – from Diego Garcia and eventually deposited about 1,200 of them in Mauritius, where for years most lived in slums. This 'act of mass kidnapping' was exposed in 1975. After a long fight for compensation, the Ilois got land for housing and cash grants from the British government – on condition that they would renounce rights to return home to the islands, since 1966 officially known as the British Indian Ocean Territory (BIOT). Many Ilois express the wish to return, even if only to visit family graves. The British and US governments have rejected virtually all efforts to gain recognition of Mauritian claims of sovereignty over the archipelago.

Conclusions and future prospects

In Mauritius, most employment chances no longer depend on ethnic favouritism, so mutual fears appear to be declining. Individualism and nationalism are replacing communalism and ethnicity. Yet the economic boom has not erased ethnic and caste inequality. Should that economic bubble – which provides jobs to all but 1.6 per cent of the Mauritian workforce – burst, minority tensions could resurface. The Ilois may yet win a day in court; adjudication about BIOT/Diego Garcia by the International Court of Justice has been mooted, though by then there will be a new generation of Ilois with roots in Mauritius.

Further reading

Bowman, L., *Mauritius: Democracy and Development in the Indian Ocean*, Boulder, CO, Westview Press, 1991.

Lehembre, B., *L'Ile Maurice*, Paris, Karthala, 1984.

Madley, J., *Diego Garcia: A Contrast to the Falklands*, London, MRG report, 1982, 1985.

Minority-based and advocacy organizations

Amnesty International, BP 69, Rose Hill, Mauritius; tel. 230 454 8238, fax 230 454 8238.

Centre for Documentation, Research and Training on the South West Indian Ocean, BP 91, Rose Hill, Mauritius.

Mozambique

Land area:	784,090 sq km
Population:	16.5 million (est. 1994)
Main languages:	Macua, Sena, Lómuè, Chona (Ndau), XiTsua, Chuabo, Tsonga (XiShangana), Ronga, Marendje, Nianja, Portuguese (official)
Main religions:	indigenous beliefs, Christianity, Islam
Main minority groups:	'northerners' 11 million (67%)
Real per capita GDP:	$640
UNDP HDI/rank:	0.261 (167)

Mozambique's land and labour have been at the disposal of outsiders for over a century. Until 1975, the country suffered repressive rule by a backward colonial power, Portugal, itself in the grip of fascism. Soon after political independence, a war began at the behest of White supremacists in neighbouring Southern Rhodesia (later Zimbabwe) and South Africa, emboldened by the US-led project to 'roll back' communism on the world's periphery. Over fifteen years, that war killed one in fifteen and displaced one in three Mozambicans. In a cumulative spiral of violence and impoverishment, it also teased out and inflamed regional and ethnic antagonisms. Minority issues are not sharply drawn in the usual sense in Mozambique. However, the effects of uneven colonial development and post-colonial policies led many northerners to resent a southern-dominated political class. For these reasons the issue of 'northerners' is treated below.

Portuguese colonial rulers paid little attention to ethnicity apart from limited categorization of some groups as 'loyal' and others as 'warriors'. Rather, the accent rested on ethno-cultural hierarchy, with Whites on top, *mestiços* (people of mixed race) and *assimilados* (Africans certified as Westernized) in subordinate positions, and the undifferentiated mass of the *indígenas* at the bottom – a system formally rejected by the post-colonial government of the Frente de Libertação de Moçambique (FRELIMO) when it set about building, from the top down, a modern, secular nation, attempting to promote national consciousness through such slogans as 'Only One People, Only One Nation'. Foreign-inspired aggression was the chief obstacle to this project. Compounding the difficulties were the sheer poverty of human and physical resources, state policies that disadvantaged most rural people, and a certain blindness towards local cultures on the part of the state/party elite. More perhaps through inadvertance than design, national policies and programmes had little regard for minority group interests. Despite a constitution attaching importance to local cultures, the post-colonial leadership in practice suppressed cultural difference in the name of modernization. Portuguese, for example, is the official language of instruction at all levels of schooling, although it is the mother tongue of less than 2 per cent of the population and is still unknown to most Mozambicans.

'Northerners'

About two-thirds of Mozambique's population inhabit the seven provinces north of the River Save. The country's largest ethno-linguistic clusters are here: Macua and related Lómuè (the foremost group in the northern provinces of Nampula, Zambezia, Cabo Delgado and Niassa), Sena (foremost in Sofala province), Chuabo and Marendje (important in Zambezia), Nyanja (foremost in Tete), and the Shona-speaking Ndau people (dominant in Manica and important in Sofala). Through uneven processes of underdevelopment, northerners have suffered greater disadvantage. More schools were established in the south, and systems of waged labour developed there from an earlier date. Nationalist leadership emerged in the 1950s in the south, mainly from Shangaan- (Tsonga-) speaking areas in Gaza province, as well from as urban *mestiço* and Asian (Goan) strata. New social strata developed and technological change spread faster and wider in the south than in central and northern Mozambique, where health and nutrition indices and public infrastructure remain poorer. Northerners are thus a numerical majority with the effective status of a minority.

Northern peoples have long been subject to coercion by powerful outsiders, though not without resistance. The mid-nineteenth-century history of violent conquest (by Ngoni armies based in southern Gaza) has served to intensify northern resentment towards the southern elites, especially in the central provinces of present-day Manica and Sofala (see **Malawi, Zimbabwe**). Assessing any post-independence governmental bias against northerners is made more difficult by wider biases against small rural producers and 'traditionalists' in all parts of the country. Moreover, the economic geography of much of the south provided alternative sources of livelihood; the more purely agrarian economy of the north did not. Thus the impact of those biases, and the manner of state intervention (villagization at the point of a gun) was harsher in the north, and the compensatory benefits fewer. Moreover the war cut off the government, and private economic actors, from large parts of central and northern regions.

An armed opposition was thus able to gain adherents by playing on anti-southern and anti-state resentment. Ethnic antagonism, if not the foremost factor, played a part in the Resistencia Nacional Moçambicana (RENAMO) army campaign against the southern-dominated state class of FRELIMO. Despite RENAMO's barbarities against people in central and northern zones, it gained substantial majorities in all but two of the northern provinces in the October 1994 elections. In the south RENAMO won hardly any seats, ending with 45 per cent of the overall national vote. The results reveal considerable alienation from the country's ruling party in the north and centre of Mozambique.

Conclusions and future prospects

In the mid-1990s Mozambicans were attempting to reconstruct a country ravaged by civil war, while wholly exposed to an unbridled capitalism and the attentions of the world aid industry. Structural adjustment policies imposed by donors on the country are supposed to redress rural–urban imbalances and thus favour the smallholder heartlands in the north and centre. But free-market orthodoxies have begun shifting assets – especially land – into the hands of private individuals and companies, worsening old disparities and creating new inequalities. Although more northerners now hold positions of influence than before, the outlook for Mozambique's rural majority everywhere holds little promise of inclusion and prosperity.

Further reading

Finnegan, W., *A Complicated War: The Harrowing of Mozambique*, Berkeley, CA, University of California Press, 1992.

Geffray, C., *La cause des armes: anthropologie de la guerre contemporaine au Mozambique*, Paris, Karthala, 1990.

Hanlon, J., *Mozambique: Who Calls the Shots?*, London, James Currey, 1991.

Hanlon, J., *Peace without Profit*, Oxford, James Currey, 1996.

Minter, W., *Apartheid's Contras: An Inquiry into the Roots of War in Angola and Mozambique*, London, Zed Press, 1994.

Minority-based and advocacy organizations

Liga Moçambicana dos Direitos Humanos, Ave. 24 de Julho 776, Maputo, Mozambique; tel. 258 1 423 185, fax 258 1 430 706.

Namibia

Land area:	824,292 sq km
Population:	1.6 million (est. 1995)
Main languages:	OshiWambo, OtjiHerero, Nama/Damara, Afrikaans, English (official)
Main religions:	Christianity (mainly Protestantism, some Roman Catholicism), traditional beliefs
Main minority groups:	Kavango 27,000 (8%), Damara 105,000 (6.6%), Herero 100,000 (6%), Whites 87,000 (5%), Nama 6,000 (4%), Coloureds 55,000 (3%), Caprivians 50,000 (3%), San/Bushman people[1] 38,000 (2%), Basters 34,000 (2%), Tswana 10,000 (0.6%), also Himba and Topnaars or !Gaonin
Real per capita GDP:	$3,710
UNDP HDI/rank:	0.573 (116)

San hunter-gatherers and Nama pastoralists have lived in Namibia since prehistoric times, joined at an early but unknown date by the Damara, also originally hunter-gatherers. All speak distinctive languages featuring click sounds. In the sixteenth and seventeenth centuries, or possibly earlier, Bantu-speaking Herero pastoralists moved into central and north-western Namibia, and Ovambo agriculturalists into the far north of the country. The Kavango region and the Caprivi Strip in the north-east of the country are also primarily inhabited by Bantu-speaking peoples.

In the early nineteenth century displaced Afrikaans-speaking communities trekked to Namibia from the Cape in search of land. The introduction of firearms exacerbated conflicts over land and livestock, notably between the Nama and Herero. German colonialism from the 1880s led in 1904 to Herero then Nama rebellions which were crushed with genocidal brutality. In central and southern Namibia an estimated 60 per cent of the African population were killed, including over three-quarters of all Hereros. Most of the land was allocated for European settlement. In 1915 German colonial forces surrendered to South African troops. South Africa ruled the territory until 1967, first under League of Nations mandate, then illegally until independence in 1990. The latter period saw a protracted war between the South African army and the guerrilla forces of the Southwest Africa People's Organization (SWAPO), the principal liberation movement, as well as South African imposition of a comprehensive version of apartheid, complete with 'homelands' for Namibia's different (African) ethno-linguistic groups.

As in South Africa, the legacy of apartheid has led to scepticism over notions of 'minorities' and 'minority rights'. For more than a century the principal political conflict was over White colonial domination, and, though unity against 'divide and rule' policies was often limited, there remains a strong official commitment against politics conducted along ethnic lines. However, historical and demographic factors make it difficult to outlaw ethnic politics. Ovambos comprise about half of the population; moreover, support for SWAPO, now in government, is traditionally highest among Ovambos, who bore the brunt of the liberation war. Fears of Ovambo domination remain significant despite government efforts at ethnic balance in the administration. Few groups can claim to suffer active discrimination on ethnic or linguistic grounds, those described here being the most significant exceptions. Consequently while nearly all groups in Namibia have some claim to be considered 'minorities' this entry will focus on those whose situation is distinctly marginalized.

Property rights in the constitution, the result of a compromise between the South African government and SWAPO, mean that much of the most productive land in Namibia remains in the hands of Whites. Communal land in the former 'homelands' (which comprised about 15 per cent of the land area of Namibia) is primarily vested in the state rather than the occupants, a carry-over from colonial legislation which has been the subject of legal challenge, still unresolved and particularly affecting some of the country's more marginalized people.

Namibia's Whites consider to themselves a

minority despite their privileged status. They are predominantly Afrikaans-speaking but include English-, Portuguese- and German-speakers, the last-named being the only significant such community in Africa and retaining a strong sense of identity. As in South Africa, Whites retain a highly privileged position following their loss of political power.

San (Bushman people)

About 38,000 people in Namibia, living mostly in the north and east of the country, are identified as San or Bushman people, of the Hei//om, Ju/'Hoansi, !Xu (or Vasekele), Kwe (or Khwe), //Khau-/eisi, Nharo, !Xo, /Auni and /Nu-//en ethno-linguistic groups. Few people have been subjected to such intensive myth-making as the San. Their status as the descendants of the original inhabitants of much of Southern and Eastern Africa serves to reinforce persistent ideas of their living isolated lives as hunter-gatherers unaltered since prehistory. In fact San people face a situation resulting from centuries, if not millennia, of interaction with their neighbours, a relationship which has generally been at best highly exploitative and at worst genocidal. Such interaction has all but overwhelmed traditional hunting and gathering culture. European myths of Bushmen leading blameless, idyllic lives untouched by history may be marginally preferable to earlier perspectives of Bushmen as less than human, but are an equally effective barrier to understanding.

Hunting and gathering San communities traditionally coexisted but also competed with pastoralists and sometimes cultivators. While this competition was often unequal, the expansion of settlers (and firearms) from the Cape was probably decisive in their dispossession. The influx of German colonists into north-east Namibia, particularly from 1907 following the suppression of the Herero and Nama rebellions, was especially devastating. Loss of land led to conflict which the German authorities pursued murderously against 'wild Bushmen' who raided livestock as an alternative to retreating to more arid regions or accepting a life of degradation and servitude on the farms. Settlers had virtual carte blanche to shoot any Bushman suspected of stock theft and often did so, a situation improving only slightly following the South African take-over in 1915. As Bushman people gradually became less of a threat to the settler economy the severity of their persecution declined, but they were still perceived by the authorities as people with even fewer rights and needs than other Africans.

To make way for settler farms Herero pastoralists had also been pushed eastwards off their land into traditional San territory, where Herero 'native reserves' were first declared in the 1920s. San were widely employed by Hereros, who often fostered San children, developing a relationship of authoritarian paternalism, by no means free of conflict, which continues today. Herero 'homelands' were expanded following the imposition of full-blown apartheid structures in 1964. In 1970 a largely waterless Bushman 'homeland' was delineated in north-east Namibia from what was left of traditional San territory. By this time a large proportion of San people were living on farms or in townships, working as labourers or craftsworkers or eking out a living from state pensions. Many others, along with San from Angola, had been recruited into the South African army whose Bushman bases dominated western Bushmanland and West Caprivi. In eastern Bushmanland some independent initiatives helped a few communities to restore an existence based on stock-rearing as well as foraging and small-scale agriculture. Conditions on the farms where most San lived generally fell somewhere between serfdom and slavery, a situation which has changed only slowly. In the townships conditions of degradation and dependency generated social problems, including alcoholism. Lack of access to education, in particular, has reinforced the position of San at the bottom of the social heirarchy.

Despite scepticism over 'group rights' the post-independence Namibian government has given a degree of recognition to the specific needs and status of San people. In 1991 land rights in the Otjozondjupa region (former Bushmanland) based on the *n!ore* (hunting territory) system were acknowledged, though inadequately defined, and government support was forthcoming in the subsequent peaceful persuasion of Herero pastoralists who had moved into the region to leave – though some subsequently returned. In West Caprivi Kwe and !Xu communities have been moving out of the former military bases and are attempting to establish new settlements. (Others were taken by the South African army to South Africa following Namibian independence – see **South Africa**). Hei//om groups have petitioned for land rights within the area occupied by the huge Etosha National Park. Communities with hopes of regaining or retaining access to land remain in any case a minority; problems faced by other Bushman people may be no less acute.

As in Botswana, advocacy for the rights of San/Bushman people has historically been largely the preserve of sympathetic outsiders. This is beginning to change, with more autonomous organizations emerging. As in Botswana too, Namibia's comparatively robust legal and constitutional framework provides considerable potential for advocacy and change.

Basters

The Basters, a mixed-race Afrikaans-speaking community, are descendants of groups which migrated from the Cape to settle at Rehoboth, south of Windhoek, in 1868, rapidly establishing their own institutions which continued in one form or another until independence. Though far less marginalized than other groups considered, many Basters have a strong sense of minority identity. Since independence Basters have challenged the state's claim to ownership of Baster communal lands. Rulings in favour of Baster claims in 1993, and in favour of the government in 1995, then went to further appeal, and have implications for communal land rights elsewhere in Namibia.

Himba

Himba are Herero-speaking semi-nomadic pastoralists living in north-western Namibia and south-western Angola. Currently numbering about 5,000 people, their comparative isolation and impoverishment in a harsh and arid region mean that they have retained traditional social and cultural patterns to a greater extent than Hereros elsewhere in Namibia. A catastrophic drought from 1979 to 1982 decimated herds and turned many Himba to wage-labour, foraging and relief handouts. At the same time the opening of a new front in the war between SWAPO and the South African army restricted mobility and caused many casualties from land-mines. More recently the planned construction of a dam at Epupa on the Cunene river has threatened dry season grazing land and sacred burial sites. Opponents argue that the dam is costly and unnecessary, as alternative sources of electricity (mainly from South Africa) are available and may be cheaper. In 1995, however, it appeared that the main threat to the scheme was availability of loan finance, with the status of Himba land rights remaining uncertain.

Topnaars or !Gaonin

The Topnaars are about 650 surviving members of the Nama-speaking Hurinin and !Naranin tribes who orginally inhabited parts of coastal Namibia but are now largely confined to a small portion of land in the Kuiseb river valley, for many decades part of a national park, placing traditional rights of access to land and natural resources under dispute. Depletion of underground water for industrial development on the coast has depleted riverine vegetation, notably the unique *!nara* plant on which the Topnaars are partly dependent for food. Campaigns for land rights and water resources have had little impact.

Conclusions and future prospects

Namibia has gained credit for the peace and stability that have followed its exceptionally long and bitter anti-colonial war, as well as for a democratic constitution that gives adequate weight to the protection of individual human rights. Whilst the future possibility of ethnicized politics can not be ruled out in a country of great diversity and substantial historical conflict, it can at least be hoped that the experience of apartheid will continue to deter politicians from pursuing such a route. For the San/Bushman people, who remain Namibia's most dispossessed and marginalized minority, social, economic and political rehabilitation will at best remain a long process, requiring the pursuit of policies that recognize their status as a disadvantaged group. Similar considerations apply to such groups as the Himba and Topnaars.

Further reading

Fraenkel, P. and Murray, R., *The Namibians*, London MRG report, 1985.

Gordon, R.J., *The Bushman Myth: The Making of a Namibian Underclass*, Boulder, CO, Westview Press, 1992.

Marshall, J. and Ritchie, C., *Where are the Ju-/wasi of Nyae Nyae ?*, Cape Town, University of Cape Town Africa Studies Programme, 1984.

Stephen, D., *The San of the Kalahari*, London, MRG report, 1982

Volkman, T.A., 'The hunter-gatherer myth in Southern Africa', *Cultural Survival Quarterly*. vol. 10, no.2, pp. 26–32, Cambridge, MA, 1986.

Minority-based and advocacy organizations

Human Rights and Documentation Centre, University of Namibia (New Campus), Private Bag 13301, Windhoek, Namibia; tel. 264 61 242 421, fax 264 61 242 421.

National Society for Human Rights, PO Box 23592, Windhoek, Namibia; tel. 264 61 236 183/235 447, fax 264 61 234 286.

Nyae Nyae Development Foundation of Namibia [San], PO Box 9026, Eros, Windhoek, Namibia; tel. 264 61 236 327, fax 264 61 225 997.

Working Group of Indigenous Minorities of Southern Africa [San], PO Box 11778, Windhoek, Namibia; tel./fax 264 61 229 865.

Rwanda

Land area:	26,338 sq km
Population:	(before 1994 war and genocide) 7.5 million
Main languages:	Kinyarwanda, French (administrative language)
Main religions:	Christianity (mostly Roman Catholicism), traditional beliefs, often combined with Christianity
Main minority groups:[1]	*(before 1994 war and genocide)* Hutus 6,750,000 (90%), Tutsis 675,000 (9%), Twa (Batwa) 30,000 (est., 0.4%)
Real per capita GDP:	$740
UNDP HDI/rank:	0.332 (152)

From April to June 1994 Rwanda witnessed the worst case of genocide the world had seen in fifty years. Most of the country's minority Tutsi population, as many as half a million people, were systematically massacred by compatriots loyal to the country's then ruling political party and other ostensibly more extreme Hutu groupings. The genocide was the appalling climax to long-standing political conflicts exacerbated by economic decline and pressure on the land. Since late colonial times such conflicts increasingly devolved along intercommunal lines, a process continually reinforced by injustices and atrocities, notably leading to waves of Tutsi refugees fleeing to neighbouring countries.

In 1990 the Rwandan Patriotic Front, a movement dominated by such refugees, invaded the country from Uganda, launching a war which culminated in the defeat of the Hutu-dominated government, though not in time to avert the genocide. During the war over 2 million refugees fled the country and many more were displaced internally. Although the new government has been able to impose a degree of comparative stability, the underlying political conflicts remain unresolved throughout the region and the country faces an extremely troubled future. All Rwandans are acutely affected by the instability in the country and region, whether as minorities or majorities, oppressors or oppressed. The destinies of Rwandans remain intertwined; for this reason the principal ethnic groupings are considered together.[2]

Hutus and Tutsis

The tragic conflict between Hutus and Tutsis in Rwanda arose despite a common heritage and a long history of at least comparatively peaceful coexistence, with intermarriage and mobility between the groups quite common. Hutus and Tutsis share a common language and to a considerable extent a common culture. The standard (if disputed) conception of pre-colonial Rwanda, in which Tutsi pastoralists moved from the north to rule over Hutu agriculturalists four hundred years ago, does little to illuminate the complex hierarchies and regional variations within traditional Rwandan society. Undoubtedly, however, Tutsis were in a dominant position, owning most of the land as well as cattle, and developing an ideology of supremacy which reinforced their position. The German and subsequently Belgian policy of indirect rule (from 1899 and 1916 respectively), with its corresponding belief in the natural superiority of the Tutsis, served to reinforce Tutsi domination, as well as provoking resistance when Hutu chiefs in the north-west of the country were replaced with Tutsis. Colonial education policy systematically favoured Tutsis, who increasingly came to dominate the civil service and the economy. Only the churches provided a significant outlet for Hutu aspirations.

In the 1950s, under pressure to move the country towards independence, the Belgians began to suspect that long-term minority rule might be unsustainable, and also to view with alarm radical pan-Africanist tendencies among Tutsi political elites. Unlike in Burundi, however, these elites were unable successfully to repress emerging Hutu aspirations. Local elections in 1960, won by the Party of the Movement for Hutu Emancipation (PARMEHUTU), were marred by violent conflict on inter-ethnic lines; hundreds were killed and over 200,000 internally displaced. Independence in 1962 was accompanied by continuing violence; by 1964 an estimated 150,000 people, virtually all Tutsis, had fled to surrounding countries. Throughout most of the 1960s Tutsi refugees launched attacks from abroad; in 1963 perhaps 15,000 Tutsis in Rwanda were massacred in retaliation by Hutu gangs.

In 1972 widespread killings of Tutsis followed the genocidal massacres of Hutus in Burundi. The following year Juvenal Habyarimana, the army Chief of Staff who was suspected of orchestrating the killings, mounted a successful coup. In 1975 Rwanda became a one-party state under the newly created National Revolutionary Movement for Development (MNRD). Habyarimana's movement represented a consolidation of Hutu domination and anti-Tutsi sentiment, as well as shift in power from the south to the north of the country.

Rwanda's monolithic political system coexisted with the promotion of a devolved cooperative sector with some impressive achievements. Most Rwandese live or lived as peasant farmers; principal exports are coffee and tea. The economy was badly hit by the collapse of coffee prices in 1987, precipitating a decline which further exacerbated political and intercommunal tensions. After the end of the Cold War donor pressure for democratic reform served further to open up the impending struggle for control of the state – a fundamentally political conflict of which intercommunal violence became the vehicle.

The (Tutsi) refugees' desire to return home was given considerable impetus by their persecution in Uganda in 1982 and 1983 as well as by subsequent recruitment into Yoweri Museveni's National Resistance Army (NRA) (see **Uganda**). In 1990 4,000 NRA deserters launched an attack on Rwanda; though initially repulsed, with the help of troops from France, Belgium and Zaire, the impact was enormous. Although the Rwandan Patriotic Front (RPF) invaders insisted they were not bent on restoring Tutsi hegemony, and managed to attract an element of Hutu support, Tutsis within the country were automatically suspected of sympathy or collaboration with the invaders, leading to growing abuses. An International Commission on Human Rights reported that the Rwandan government had killed about 2,000 people between October 1990 and January 1993, most of them Tutsis but including Hutus from opposition parties which had emerged following pressure from donor countries for a multiparty system. The government responded by establishing theoretically autonomous militias, which continued the violence whilst enabling the government to deny responsibility. Despite this, several governments, notably France (via Egypt) and South Africa, continued to arm the rapidly expanding government forces.

The civil war continued inconclusively for three years with the RPF controlling the north-east of the country. The Arusha Accords of August 1993 brokered a power-sharing agreement between the government and the RPF, to be overseen by a UN force of 1,260, but it soon became clear that forces within the government itself, as well as the overtly extremist militias it had spawned, were opposed to the compromise. The hands of Hutu extremists were strengthened by the October 1993 coup by Tutsi army officers in Burundi; the violence continued to escalate, turning by early 1994 into full-scale purges of opposition politicians and human rights activists, Hutus as well as Tutsis. Particularly significant was the anti-Tutsi propaganda disseminated in the media, notably by Radio/TV Libre Milles Collines, which was partly owned by members of the President's family.

On 6 April 1994 an aircraft bringing President Habyarimana (as well as President Ntariyamira of Burundi) back from Arusha was shot down as it approached Kigali airport, killing all on board. Within two days most leading opposition politicians (both Hutus and Tutsis, including many serving within the new coalition government) and hundreds of Tutsi civilians had been killed by

Hutu soldiers and militiamen. Within a week over ten thousand had been killed in Kigali alone.

The war resumed in earnest, with the RPF army advancing from the north on Kigali (where it already had a garrison as part of the political settlement). So did a well orchestrated campaign of genocide against Rwandan Tutsis, in which government officials throughout the country were directly involved. Defenceless men, women and children were killed with machetes, hoes and iron bars, or rounded up and shot. The perpetrators were mostly young Hutu men, though others were encouraged or forced to participate; their victims were often neighbours and sometimes friends. The great majority of Rwandan Tutsis – as many as half a million people – were killed. The killers were convinced that this was the only way to prevent Tutsis returning to reclaim their former powers and privileges – a conviction derived from propaganda orchestrated by the politicians and intellectuals who have a central responsibility for what took place.

After the plane crash the UN forces in Rwanda, which had reached 2,539 personnel, were sharply incapacitated by the abrupt withdrawal of the large Belgian contingent, following the deaths of ten soldiers and the implausible if revealing accusation from the new administration that Belgian troops had shot down the aircraft. On 21 April the Security Council cut the remaining force from 1,700 to 270 – a decision causing widespread condemnation, not least because 15,000 Tutsi civilians were already under UN protection in hotels and other refuges in Kigali. No doubt the UN was fearful of involvement, as elsewhere, in a war it could not control, but the majority of the genocidal killings were carried out by civilians without guns, against whom even lightly armed soldiers could have an enormous deterrent effect, and the decision appears to have been a result of the predominance of strategic over humanitarian priorities. The fact that the rump UN contingent (eventually 444 remained) succeeded in protecting its charges in Kigali illustrates what a larger commitment might have achieved elsewhere.

Attempts to negotiate cease-fires failed, the RPF claiming that only its own victory could end the massacres. The RPF advance precipitated some of the largest and fastest movements of refugees ever recorded. On 29 April an estimated 200,000 people crossed the Rusumo Falls bridge to Tanzania; in early July, towards the end of the war, a million refugees crossed to Zaire in a few days. Although RPF abuses bear no comparison with the genocide perpetrated by their opponents, very few Hutus believed RPF assurances that they were not bent on reasserting Tutsi control, nor on taking revenge for the genocide.

Ostensibly in response to UN inaction, France sent troops to south-western Rwanda in mid-June where they were belatedly able to have at least some impact on the carnage and to help to stem the huge flow of refugees to Zaire. An estimated 1.5 million Hutus sought refuge in this zone, which from August was administered by the UN, with RPF forces gradually assuming control over the zone only in October, eventually disbanding the refugee camps in Gikongoro prefecture. Many people were killed resisting their 'repatriation', notably in a massacre of several thousand displaced people in Kibeho.

Despite this the RPF government succeeded in imposing a measure of stability. However, it was unwilling or unable to contain extensive reprisals, especially in parts of the country away from journalists or international observers. Amnesty International reported 'hundreds, possibly thousands' of extra-judicial killings and executions between April and October 1994. Reports of these abuses had wide circulation in refugee camps; by August 1995 only a tiny proportion of more than 2 million refugees outside the country had been persuaded to return. At that time the Zaire authorities began the forcible repatriation of Rwandan refugees, tens of thousands of whom fled from the camps to avoid such a fate. The repatriation was called off, following international protests.

Two years after the genocide extremely little progress had been made in bringing those responsible to justice. Rwanda's judicial system remained in tatters. The United Nations Human Rights Commission had an inadequate mandate compounded by acute underfunding and mismanagement. The International Tribunal on war crimes has made painfully slow progress. The overwhelming impact of the genocide, as well as the continuation of intercommunal violence in Burundi and a stream of incidents in Rwanda itself, kept tensions between Hutus and Tutsis at a very high level.

In October 1996 Zairean Tutsi militias supported by Rwandan troops attacked the refugee camps in the Zairean province of North Kivu, proking the repatriation of several hundred thousand Hutu refugees, though leaving hundreds of thousands more in Zaire. By December 1996 the Tanzanian army was pressurizing Hutu refugees in Tanzania to return home as well; some were doing so, though others were trying to disperse elsewhere. All these returnees face an uncertain future back in Rwanda.

Twa

The Twa people (or Batwa) can be considered the forgotten victims of the Rwandan war and genocide; their suffering has gone largely unrecognised. Twa can claim to be the original inhabitants of Rwanda, being related to other 'Pygmy' peoples of Central Africa. In appearance, though generally short in stature, they are not, however, readily distinguishable from their compatriots, whose language and religious beliefs they also share. However, Twa maintain a rich and distinctive cultural tradition centred on songs, dance and music. Of the 29,000 Rwandan Twa recorded in the 1991 census only a small minority known as Impunyu – estimates of their numbers vary between 1,000 and 3,000 people – maintain a traditional forest-dwelling existence, almost entirely in the Nyungwe forest in the south-west of the country. Other Twa are dispersed throughout the country in small groups. Most work as potters, though others earn a living as day labourers or porters. Almost none own land or cattle.

Twa are widely stigmatized by both Hutus and Tutsis who consider them ignorant and uncivilized – the Impunyu above all. Taboos surround eating together or even using utensils used by Twa. Social and economic integration of Twa in Rwandan society is extremely limited; they can be characterized as a disadvantaged and marginalized caste. Before independence a small number of Twa obtained a privileged position at the Tutsi royal court as entertainers (and in a few cases as executioners). Despite the limited numbers involved, there is a widespread Hutu perception that Twa are sympathetic to Tutsis, reinforced by the involvement of some Twa in Burundi with the overwhelmingly Tutsi army.

Very many Twa were killed in the war and genocide. The Unrepresented Nations and Peoples Organization (UNPO) estimates that about 10,000 people, more than a third of the Twa population of Rwanda, were killed and that a similar number fled the country as refugees. The situation varied considerably from area to area. In some places Twa were killed as Tutsi sympathizers or allies; in others Twa participated in the massacres of Tutsis. UNPO reports discrimination against Twa in the distribution of food and other supplies in the refugee camps. Discrimination against Twa is certain to continue in Rwanda (and in Rwandese refugee communities); there are some signs that the new Rwandan Patriotic Front government is more sympathetic to the issue than its predecessor, but a prolonged programme of education and advocacy is needed to protect the rights of the Twa.

Minority religious sects

In the 1980s several sects – Jehovah's Witnesses, Temperates, Abantu Hima (Men of God Who Repent) and Abakore (the Elected) – were accused of not respecting the laws of Rwanda, provoking disobedience, and refusing to send children to school. Many of their leaders were sentenced to long prison terms in 1986. In Rwandan circumstances, however changed, it is reasonable to assume the appeal of such sects will continue, as well as their potential to aggravate the authorities.

Conclusions and future prospects

In the long term there is every danger of Rwanda facing further protracted violence. The RPF government gained credit for containing, to a degree, the overwhelming antagonisms generated by the genocide, but has also pursued an increasingly transparent policy of Tutsi domination which, even if unsurprising, provides little basis for a long-term solution. There has been little progress towards a viable political settlement, nor agreement about what that might comprise. Prospects for bringing judicial procedures to bear on all of the countless thousands who perpetrated the genocide are negligible, but the importance of bringing to justice at least the political leaders most directly responsible can hardly be overestimated. The impact of the International Tribunal for Rwanda is likely to be very limited. Although there were few reports of major abuses during the initial stages of the repatriation of hundreds of thousands of refugees from Zaire, in October 1996, and of smaller numbers from Tanzania in December, the prospects for the returnees are extremely uncertain. There are no precedents for people living peaceably together in the immediate aftermath of atrocities as extreme as those perpetrated in Rwanda, and the intimacy of the genocide, with neighbour killing neighbour, will make reconciliation and lasting peace very difficult to achieve. Averting further castrophes will require a huge effort of will not only among Rwandese but among the international community whose response to the crisis has been so consistently inadequate.

Further reading

African Rights, *Rwanda: Death, Despair and Defiance*, 2nd edn, London, 1995.

African Rights, *Rwanda: 'A Waste of Hope' – The United Nations Human Rights Field Operation*, London, 1995.

Amnesty International, *Persecution of Tutsi Minority and Repression of Government Critics 1990–92*, London, 1992.

Human Rights Watch/Africa, *Genocide in Rwanda, April-May 1994*, New York, Washington, DC, London, 1994.

Lemarchand, R., *Rwanda and Burundi*, London, Pall Mall, 1970.

Overeem, P., *Batwa*, draft final report, The Hague, Unrepresented Nations and People's Organization, 1995.

Vassall-Adams, G., *Rwanda: An Agenda for International Action*, Oxford, Oxfam Publications, 1994.

Waller, D., *Rwanda: Which Way Now?*, Oxford, Oxfam Publications, 1993.

Minority-based and advocacy organizations

Association for the Promotion of Batwa, BP 2472, Kigali, Rwanda; tel./fax 250 74671.

São Tomé and Príncipe

Land area:	964 sq km
Population:	130,000 (est. 1995), 96% on São Tomé
Main languages:	Lungwa san tomé (Creole dialect), Portuguese (official)
Main religions:	Christianity
Main minority groups:	—
Real per capita GDP:	$600
UNDP HDI/rank:	0.458 (132)

São Tomé and Príncipe, a two-island republic off the coast of Gabon, has been a slave entrepôt, a Portuguese penal colony from which few returned alive and a virtual forced labour camp dedicated to producing cacao for European chocolate makers and consumers. Traces of this history are still present in social hierarchies. Because the economy has always been outwardly oriented, internal social frictions often stem directly from the country's external vulnerabilities. Differing access to land has stratified society sharply. There are two types of landless people: the *forros* or *filhos da terra* (children of the land), and imported plantation labourers or *serviçais*. Unable to force the local islanders on to the plantations, the Portuguese imported workers from Angola, Mozambique and the Cape Verde Islands. The end of Portuguese rule, and departure of many plantation owners around 1975, led many thousands to quit plantation life and its second class status. Cacao cultivation remains the feeble mainspring of the economy, and working conditions are lamentable. Nearly 40 per cent of the workforce are unemployed, their ranks swelled by thousands of São Tomean migrants expelled from Gabon in 1995.

Seychelles

Land area:	455 sq km
Population:	72,000 (est. 1994)
Main languages:	Creole, English, French
Main religions:	Christianity
Main minority groups:	—
Real per capita GDP:	$4,960
UNDP HDI/rank:	0.792 (60)

An archipelago in the Indian Ocean, the Seychelles is a micro-state whose high income flows chiefly from tourism. This formal prosperity has yet to transform the living standards of all Seychellois on an equitable basis. White and Asian political commercial elites and their foreign associates have been the main beneficiaries of the islands' prosperity. The numerical majority Creoles – people of mixed African, Asian and European ancestry – have benefited only unevenly. Their material poverty and social exclusion have been addressed to some degree, especially since 1977 when a White politician, Albert René, seized power. Promotion of the Creole language (a patois of French), including its use in primary school, has probably boosted self-esteem, although the use of Creole rather than French or English is said to block social mobility. Other post-1977 policies, from housing and minimum wages to free public schooling, have also shown regard for the legitimate interests of the majority Creole people. In 1993 their votes confirmed René in office by a landslide. But power and wealth remain mainly in the hands of the non-Creole elite.

Further reading

Benedict, M., *Men, Women and Money in the Seychelles*, Berkeley, CA, University of California Press, 1982.

South Africa

Land area:	1,211,037 sq km
Population:	42 million (est. 1995)
Main languages:	English, Afrikaans, Zulu, Xhosa, Northern Sotho, Southern Sotho, Tswana, Shangaan, Ndebele, Swazi, Venda
Main religions:	Christianity, traditional beliefs, Hinduism, Islam, Judaism
Main groupings[1]:	Blacks 31 million (74%), Whites 6 million (14%), Coloureds 3.5 million (8%), Indians 1 million (2.4%),
Other 'minorities':	Zulus 6.3 million (15%), Afrikaners 3.3 million (8%), San 4,250 (0.01%), African immigrants 3 million (est., 7%)
Real per capita GDP:	$3,127
UNDP HDI/rank:	0.649 (100)

South African history embodies a supreme example of the manipulation of questions of 'race', ethnicity and culture for political ends. To perpetuate White domination, elaborate strategies were developed which culminated in the apartheid system, a unique form of coercion enforced by a powerful state, leading to a society with extreme inequalities of wealth and opportunity.

The progressive dispossession of the Black people of South Africa dates from the earliest years of European settlement in the seventeenth century, and had been achieved to a far greater extent than anywhere else on the continent long before the Union of South Africa was established in 1910. Legislation in 1913 and 1936 formally allocated 87 per cent of the land for settlement by Whites. Apartheid, progressively introduced following the National Party victory in the White elections of 1948, was the culmination of such policies. All South Africans were categorized according to 'race' and forced to live in their own 'group areas'. Additionally Black South Africans were categorized according to 'tribe' and huge numbers were uprooted to the corresponding 'bantustans' or 'homelands', which roughly coincided with the land already reserved for Black settlement. The bantustans were generally located away from the main centres of economic activity and functioned as labour reserves, and increasingly as dumping grounds for the homeless. Although economic requirements sometimes ran counter to the strict dictates of this ideology, and although apartheid was imposed on a country already heavily segregated on racial lines, over 3 million South Africans were forcibly removed from their homes in pursuit of these plans.

The 1994 elections which heralded the end of apartheid and the establishment of a Government of National Unity resulted from a compromise between the African National Congress (ANC) and the National Party, neither of which was prepared to countenance the mounting violence and disruption involved in perpetuating the struggle over apartheid. However, political and economic factors severely constrain the ability of the new interim Government of National Unity to counteract the extreme inequalities of wealth and opportunity which have developed on racial lines. The status of the disadvantaged and marginalized – predominantly the Black rural poor and urban unemployed, between them comprising a majority of the population – will not change very fast.

South Africa can be considered a country of minorities, yet questions of minority rights take a distinctive form, made more complex by the expropriation of the term to refer to the rights (legitimate or otherwise) of Whites. Pervasive opposition to the enforced racial and tribal classifications of apartheid has led to considerable scepticism over calls for any defence of rights on a group basis. The interim constitution – despite last-minute concessions made to White right-wingers and to the Zulu Inkatha, and substantial devolution of authority to provincial governments – puts a high premium on individual rights as opposed to those of any particular grouping.

Political conflict in South Africa has been primarily across the fault-line of White domination. Consequently the strenuous efforts of the apartheid regime to promote divisions among Blacks on tribal lines had limited success, even by comparison with the efforts of many colonial regimes in Africa. (The promotion of Inkatha was an exception to this.) The primary apartheid division into Whites, Coloureds, Indians and Blacks has left a more profound and immediate legacy. However, the demographic and institutional inheritance from apartheid could help facilitate such divisive 'tribal' politics in future.

In South Africa the numerical majority Black population continues to suffer acute disadvantages which correlate far more with the racial divisions enshrined by apartheid than with specific ethnolinguistic groupings.[2] The particular status of each of South Africa's Black linguistic groups, despite variations, is of lesser significance. Zulus, with their claims for distinctive political or cultural status, are an exception to this, as are the very small but highly marginalized San communities, and these groups are discussed separately below. The situation of White South Africans – and more specifically Afrikaners – is also briefly considered, in recognition of their recent (if partial) loss of political power.

South Africa has become almost synonymous with racialized politics. However, the dangers of reducing political analysis to questions of 'race' and ethnicity are no less marked than in other parts of the continent. Stratification along lines of social class and economic interest is far advanced – more so indeed than anywhere else in the region. To some degree such factors cut across racial divisions; certainly they promote the class-based politics of a partly industrialized and outstandingly inegalitarian society. Nevertheless, much of the text and particularly the subtext of South African politics will continue to link to racial fault lines for the foreseeable future. The more recent brand of 'ethnic' politics, as exemplified by Inkatha, is also set to continue.

Blacks

Black South Africans, defined as those whose mother tongue is an African language, comprise three-quarters of the population of the country and share the common experience of the gross disruptions and abuses of White domination and apartheid – notably their wholesale incorporation into a migrant labour system combined with banishment for most to overcrowded and unproductive 'homelands'. Linguistic and tribal divisions have been of less significance. There are certainly variations in the situations and prospects of different groups, correlating mainly with economic opportunities and access to resources which in turn relate to distance from metropolitan areas. The Shangaan and Venda in the northern and eastern Transvaal are disadvantaged in this way. Xhosa-speakers from the Eastern Cape, a traditional stronghold of the ANC, have a disproportionate political influence at a national level. The situation of Zulus is considered separately below.

Despite high expectations only slow progress can be expected in reducing the enormous disadvantages faced by most Black South Africans, except for the case of professional and political elites. Political and economic constraints, related to the compromise settlement between the Nationalist Party and the ANC, have limited the potential for fundamental change. The land question in particular is unresolved. Clauses protecting property rights in the interim constitution make the alienation of virtually all White-owned land impossible for the next five years and perhaps indefinitely; and although possibilities exist for the restitution of land alienated since 1913, owned by the state, or through commercial mechanisms, the scope is decidedly limited. Despite an increase in migration to metropolitan shanty towns, in pursuit of limited employment opportunities, the former homeland areas are likely to remain impoverished reserves unable to support their populations and subject to continuing environmental degradation. It will be difficult for very many Black South Africans to escape from the cycle of poverty and marginalization.

Whites

White South Africans are a notable example of how an 'imagined community' can be created, in pursuit of common political interests, from people of diverse ethnic, linguistic, religious, social and cultural backgrounds. The first settlers, from the mid-seventeenth century onwards, were primarily from Holland and France. British take-over of the Cape Colony in 1806 led to an influx of English-speaking colonists. European migration increased greatly following the discovery of diamonds (1867) and gold (1886), notably including Jews from Eastern Europe. While migration from Britain continued, the apartheid years saw increasing numbers from Southern and Eastern Europe, as well as from Angola, Mozambique and Zimbabwe. Increasingly, White South Africans saw themselves as distinct group, and very often as a 'threatened minority'.

Even the bitter Anglo Boer conflict of 1899–1902 was eventually subsumed under efforts to maintain domination supported by the overwhelming majority of Whites. The nineteenth-century wars of subjugation and the wholesale expropriation of Black land lent support to a pervasive mythology, actively promoted by successive minority regimes, that the only alternative to White domination would be Black retribution. The nature of the 1994 settlement means that Whites are well placed to maintain their privileged position, despite relinquishing political control and acquiescing in the advancement of a Black elite. However, reversing the polarization of South African society on racial lines is an overwhelming task. While White South Africans can expect a slow erosion of their privileges, notably in education and public sector employment (a process set to gather pace following the five-year transitional period from 1994) the subjugation or dispossession widely feared among Whites are unlikely to materialize, and indeed would only result from protracted destabilization and conflict.

Coloureds

South Africans of 'mixed race' were classified as Coloured under apartheid, a designation preceding and set to continue beyond the apartheid area. In fact under almost any definition many other South Africans are of 'mixed race'. The communities designated as Coloured are primarily descended from the Khoikhoi people who originally inhabited the western parts of South Africa, from Asian and African slaves brought to the Cape from the earliest years of the colony, from European settlers, and from other Africans. The long process of mixing and acculturation led to the extinction of the Khoi language; most Coloured people speak Afrikaans as a first language and most still live in the Western and Northern Cape provinces, where they comprise an overall majority of the population.

In many ways the exploitation of the Coloured community, living in longer and closer proximity to European settlers than most Black communities, has been the most intensive in South Africa. Traditional cultures were destroyed and replaced with almost universal conditions of servitude and subservience. Labour conditions on the farms of the Western Cape have been notorious. The forced removals of mixed-race communities from Cape Town in the 1950s and 1960s were among the most pitiless in the annals of apartheid; the new ghettos which resulted contain some of the worst crime and social problems in the country.

Coloured voting patterns in the 1994 election provide a striking example of the potential for the continuation of racial politics in democratic conditions. Although opposition to Coloured co-option into the apartheid system via the 'tricameral parliament' in 1983 had been widespread, a decade later most Coloured votes went to the National Party, the instrument of decades of racial oppression. The reasons are complex but a central core is lack of identification, for cultural and linguistic reasons, with the majority Black population.

The Coloured community, like other South African 'minority' groups, is likely to be well served by the legal and constitutional provisions of the transition and the future, as well as by the official 'non-racial' orthodoxy of post-apartheid South Africa. However, except among an educated elite their distinctiveness as a community is unlikely to change very quickly. The logic of pluralist politics in a racially conscious society points to an expansion of the tentative political alliance with Whites, particularly with Afrikaners, whose language, religion and culture they largely share. The long-term consequences of this are unpredictable, but in conditions of further instability the alliance of the non-White oppressed that was built up under apartheid may not survive.

Indians

Between 1860 and 1911 over 140,000 indentured labourers were brought from India to South Africa, predominantly to work in the sugar plantations of Natal in conditions that amounted to semi-slavery – an option more economical and manageable to White settlers than the recruitment of Africans engaged in varying forms of resistance to the expropriation of their land. Though initially mainly Hindi-speakers from north-eastern India, eventually over two-thirds were Tamil- and Telegu-speakers from the south. The great majority were Hindus. A much smaller number of merchants and traders, mostly Gujarati Muslims, also came to South Africa, forming the basis of an Indian commercial class. Their descendants comprise much the largest community of South Asian origin in Africa, numbering around 1 million people. For a long time the authorities considered their position in South Africa to be 'temporary', with numerous schemes for repatriation to India planned and to some degree implemented. (These policies were formally abandoned only in 1962.) Most were restricted from moving outside Natal and none was allowed to live in the Orange Free State. Campaigns against White domination, notably those led by Gandhi, focused mainly on such specific grievances; only much later, from the 1950s, did Indian political leaders generally make common cause with the African majority.

As labourers and increasingly as industrial workers Indians were often in direct competition with Africans, usually receiving comparatively favourable treatment in relation to wages and opportunities, and later benefiting from the right to form trade unions which was denied to Africans. In the prevailing circumstances of racialized politics and campaigns for Indian repatriation, tensions between Indians and Africans were often considerable. In 1949, 142 Indians lost their lives in riots in Durban. Under apartheid Indians suffered from the abuses and humiliations heaped upon most South Africans. Large numbers lost homes and businesses as a result of the Group Areas Act which hit small traders particularly hard and served further to increase inequalities among Indians as well as within the wider society. Many Indians came to identify with broader anti-apartheid and liberation politics, mounting substantial boycotts against the tricameral elections held in 1983 which aimed at the co-option of Indians and Coloureds into the ruling elite. Though this did a lot to promote solidarity and improve relations between Indians and Africans, some tensions remained, particularly in Natal, sometimes focused on disputes over land, and frequently exploited by Inkatha, whose anti-Indian bias results not only from Inkatha's own brand of ethnic politics but from the identification of many Indians with the Congress movement.

The political, religious, cultural and linguistic rights of South African Indians after apartheid will doubtless remain well protected legally and constitutionally, as well as by the official 'non-racial' ideology. However, if political instability in Natal continues their position could again be vulnerable.

Zulus

During the nineteenth century Zulu kingdoms established a pre-eminence which enabled them to expand their territorial control and mount Africa's most prolonged and successful military resistance to European colonization. This unique history has served to reinforce a strong sense of Zulu identity. In the twentieth century Zulus continued to play a prominent role in resistance to White domination, as well as in the ANC. In

1972 Chief Gatsha Buthelezi, a grandson of the last independent Zulu king, was appointed Chief Executive of the assembly of the KwaZulu 'homeland'. Buthelezi presented himself as an anti-apartheid nationalist as well as a Zulu royalist, using his position and considerable powers of patronage to build up Inkatha, a political movement (and later party) which came to oppose the ANC and its allies. Ostensibly the conflict was over questions of political violence and economic ideology, though also over Inkatha's promotion of a distinctive and autonomous Zulu political identity and increasingly over its growing collaboration with the minority government.

Support for the ANC among Zulus remained extensive, particularly in urban townships, with traditional Zulu loyalties to the monarchy stronger in rural areas and in northern Natal. Inkatha and the ANC have been involved in protracted violent conflict which claimed 10,000 lives between 1984 and 1995. Support for Inkatha from the White minority regime, anxious to divert support from the ANC, and police involvement in numerous atrocities, are now well documented. Inkatha also attracted external support, notably from Germany, because of its free-market ideology. Participants on both sides of the Inkatha/ANC conflict in Natal have been Zulus, though the extension of the conflict to the Gauteng region (metropolitan Johannesburg) has generally pitted Zulu hostel-dwellers against non-Zulus.

Inkatha narrowly won the provincial elections in KwaZulu/Natal in 1994, despite allegations of fraud, and has continued to call for a federal system. Buthelezi's position has been weakened following his open conflict with the Zulu monarch. State and other external support has eroded, but Inkatha shows every sign of being able to continue to mobilize support and to take advantage of new opportunities, in more democratic conditions, for citing or creating 'ethnic grievances'. The violence between supporters of Inkatha and ANC supporters continues at a high level. The long-term consequences are unpredictable and potentially alarming.

Afrikaners

In the seventeenth and eighteenth centuries European settlers in South Africa were predominantly Dutch-speaking. Afrikaners, defined as those considering themselves White and speaking Afrikaans, a derivative of Dutch, still comprise the majority of the White population. Conflicts between Afrikaner farmers who colonized the interior of South Africa, establishing the republics of the Transvaal and the Orange Free State, and British imperial interests, led to the Anglo-Boer Wars of 1899–1902 and a legacy of bitterness compounded by the comparative educational and economic disadvantages experienced by Afrikaners in relation to English-speaking Whites. The Afrikaner nationalist movement, culminating in the victory of the National Party which ruled the country from 1948 to 1994, mobilized Afrikaners against this imbalance as well as in support of White supremacy.

Despite the nationalist project of establishing a shared identity and common mythology, Afrikaner divisions have always been significant: landowners versus tenants, urban versus rural, Cape versus interior. In recent years the reformist policies of the National Party have been opposed, sometimes violently, by right-wingers opposed to the end of apartheid and/or demanding an Afrikaner state. The most militant groups have adopted a neo-Nazi ideology, and though small in numbers, their members have almost all had military training and are heavily armed. In the view of many observers their efforts to destabilize the 1994 elections were only narrowly averted by the success of ANC and National Party negotiations with less extreme right-wing groupings.

The desire to contain and defuse White right-wing sentiment, whose significance far outweighs its numerical support, is likely to remain a continuing feature of South African politics, though the much discussed 'Afrikaner homeland' is unlikely to materialize. Afrikaner linguistic and cultural rights are likely to be protected, though the prominence of Afrikaans will be eroded. More generally, prospects for Afrikaners are similar to those for other Whites.

San

In South Africa there are two main San communities, about 250 =Khomani San in the Northern Cape, and about 4,000 from the !Xu and Khwe groups brought to the country by the South African army from Namibia and southern Angola following Namibian independence in 1990. (For more background on the San or Bushman people, including the question of appropriate names, see **Namibia** and **Botswana**.) The =Khomani are descendants of people evicted from the Kalahari Gemsbok National Park on the borders of South Africa, Namibia and Botswana when it was established in 1931. Though now scattered and often living in conditions of poverty and servitude, and including some working as a tourist attraction on a private ranch, in 1995 they were fighting for restoration of land rights within the southern section of the park. San people from Namibia and Angola were still in 1995 living in extremely poor conditions in a tented army camp at Schmidtsdrift near Kimberley, being almost entirely dependent on army salaries still drawn by about 600 of them. After five years their resettlement claims were still under negotiation. The Namibian and Angolan governments were reportedly unenthusiastic about the professed desire of many to return home, particularly since they have accepted South African citizenship, and the South African national and provincial governments were also reported as regarding their plight with little sympathy.

African immigrants

Perhaps 3 million immigrants – estimates vary greatly – are currently living illegally in South Africa. The great majority are from other African countries, particularly Mozambique and Zimbabwe but increasingly from all parts of the continent. They have been subjected to growing harassment and resentment, principally on the grounds that as unregistered (as well as non-unionized) workers they are unfairly competing for jobs. Many have been resident for long periods, a significant number with South African spouses and children. Some 96,000 were deported in 1993, mostly to Mozambique, and deportations are continuing under the new government. Although there are discussions of an amnesty, prospects do not seem good. In view of the economic decline and disintegration elsewhere in the region, migration to South Africa is likely to continue to escalate, increasing the status of such immigrants as one of the country's largest and most marginalized groups.

Conclusions and future prospects

The task of predicting developments in South Africa is made difficult by the unique and contradictory nature of South African society. Apartheid consolidated extremely marked social stratification on racial as well as class lines, taking the process considerably further than colonial regimes elsewhere in Africa. The exploitation of ethnic division elsewhere has encouraged some to believe that South Africa, where the divisions are in many ways more acute, is unlikely to avoid a similar fate. Against this can be set the legacy of the long struggle against apartheid, which put great emphasis on anti-racist and anti-tribalist sentiment, leading to a substantial (if far from universal) commitment among politicians to avoid the temptations of ethnic politics, a perspective embodied in the inspirational figure of Nelson Mandela. Economic problems, though considerable, are less overwhelming than in much of Africa. Constitutional factors, too, should counteract destabilizing trends, supported by a reasonably functional and independent judicial system armed with a battery of anti-discriminatory legislation. An active and experienced human rights lobby should also play its part. However, whether such factors will be strong enough to overcome the profound bitterness generated by apartheid, and the continuing opportunities for the exploitation of South Africa's deep social divisions in a newly democratic environment, remains to be seen.

The long-term impact of the wider legacy of injustice and inequality may prove as significant as the racial and tribal divisions promoted so actively under apartheid. Expectations among South Africa's poverty-stricken majority are unlikely to be met. The land question is unresolved. The tremendous dislocations of the migrant labour system have generated great social instability, reflected in extremely high rates of violence and crime, notably against women. Though governmental and corporate resources that can be mobilized to try to meet these expectations are considerable, the difficulties of this taking place with sufficient effectiveness and speed, while at the same time retaining the confidence of local and international investors and power-brokers, cannot be underestimated. The threats from the White right wing and, still more, from Inkatha have not been defused, and the potential for new political formations to exert a destabilizing influence is considerable.

Further reading

Ginwala, F., *Indian South Africans*, London, MRG report, 1985.

Maré, G., *Ethnicity and Politics in South Africa*, London and New Jersey, Zed Books, 1993.

Manby, B., 'South Africa: minority conflict and the legacy of minority rule', *Fletcher Forum of World Affairs*, vol. 19, no. 1, pp. 27–52, 1995.

Marks, S., 'Patriotism, patriarchy and purity: Natal and the politics of Zulu ethnic consciousness', in L. Vail (ed.), *The Creation of Tribalism in Southern Africa*, London, James Currey, 1989.

Parfitt, T., *The Jews of Africa and Asia*, London, MRG report, 1987.

Minority-based and advocacy organizations

African Centre for the Constructive Resolution of Disputes (ACCORD), University of Durban-Westville, Private Bag X54001, Durban 4000, South Africa; tel. 27 31 820 2816, fax 27 31 820 2815, e-mail: info@accord.udw.ac.za.

!Xu and Khwe Trust, PO Box 1022, Stellenbosch 7599, South Africa; tel. 27 21 883 3189/8069, fax 27 21 883 8910.

Swaziland

Land area:	17,363 sq km
Population:	908,000 (est. 1995)
Main languages:	siSwati, English
Main religions:	Christianity, traditional beliefs
Main minority groups:	Zulus, Shangaan, Europeans, Asians
Real per capita GDP:	$2,940
UNDP HDI/rank:	0.586 (110)

The survival and current boundaries of the Swazi Kingdom were determined by nineteenth-century conflicts between Afrikaner, British and Zulu interests. Independence from Britain dates from 1968. Ninety per cent of the population is siSwati-speaking. No minority rights issues have been identified.

Tanzania

Land area:	945,087 sq km
Population:	27.9 million (est. 1995)
Main languages:	Swahili (official), English, 120 others
Main religions:	traditional beliefs, Islam, Christianity, Hinduism
Minority groups:	more than 100 ethno-linguistic groups including Barabaig 30,000 (0.19%) and Hadza
Real per capita GDP:	$630
UNDP HDI/rank:	0.364 (144)

Tanzania has largely avoided the severe internal conflicts of many of its neighbours, as well as the corresponding development of politics along ethnic lines. The country does not lack ethnic diversity – there are around 120 linguistic groups. Most Tanzanians are agriculturalists but there are several pastoralist groups (notably Maasai and Tatoga) as well as small numbers of hunter-gatherers. Tanganyika (mainland Tanzania) gained independence in 1961 and Zanzibar (the offshore islands) in 1963, the new government in Zanzibar being overthrown almost immediately in a revolutionary uprising. The countries merged to form Tanzania in 1964, while retaining separate administrations and separate versions of one-party rule. Differences exacerbated by despotic practices in Zanzibar were reduced when the parties were merged and a new constitution promulgated in 1977. However, the dual administration was largely retained. In 1992 opposition parties were permitted and elections were held in 1995.

The Arusha Declaration of 1967 proclaimed a socialist policy which notably included the establishment of *ujamaa* (communal) villages. 'Villagization' was forcibly implemented from 1974 with disastrous consequences for peasant economy and society. The policy also incorporated a system of pervasive political control which may have contributed to the stability of the country, though without significantly ameliorating economic problems and mounting indebtedness. A millennium of Arab and Shirazi (Iranian) settlement on the islands and the coast, as well as the ravages of the slave trade in which Zanzibar played a prominent role, have left a major fault line in Tanzanian society which may prove more serious in more democratic and pluralist conditions. Tensions between Christians and Muslims have also emerged in what has traditionally been a fairly tolerant and politically secular society. From 1986 the Tanzanian government adopted liberal economic policies proposed by the International Monetary Fund and World Bank, greatly increasing inequalities in Tanzanian society, as well as resentment against the rich, often identified with the country's 250,000-strong Asian community.

All ethno-linguistic groups in Tanzania could be considered 'minorities'. Though ethnic factors can play a role in political opportunities and resource allocation at a local level, only a few groups face acute or systematic disadvantage or discrimination. Often this is a reflection of prejudices against pastoralists and hunter-gatherers, as illustrated below by the cases of the Barabaig and Hadza.

About 750,000 Rwandan Hutu refugees fled from Rwanda in 1994 – a third of them reportedly entering the country across a single bridge in two days at the end of April. By December 1996 the Tanzanian army was pressurizing these refugees to return to Rwanda; some were doing so, though others were trying to disperse elsewhere.

Barabaig

In the early part of the nineteenth century Tatoga pastoralists migrated southwards from the Serengeti plains and Ngorongoro highlands under pressure from the more powerful Maasai. Dispersal and separation led to the creation of sub-tribes, among them the Barabaig, now numbering at least 30,000, who have occupied the plains around Mount Hanang in north-central Tanzania for the last 150 years. Since 1969 the Barabaig have been in dispute with the Tanzania Canada Wheat Project which has alienated over 400,000 hectares of the best grazing land in Hanang district. The dispute has been accompanied by numerous abuses against Barabaig, including assault, house burnings, shooting and confiscation of cattle, destruction of rights of way and desecration of sacred sites, including destruction of graves by ploughing.

Legal procedures for alienating the land to which Barabaig had customary rights were improperly applied. In the face of court applications raising these issues the government, in 1989, extinguished customary land rights in the areas under the occupancy of the para-statal National Agricultural and Food Corporation. The retroactive nature of this legislation violated basic principles of human rights law; it also enabled prosecutions to be brought against Barabaig for trespassing on land they considered their own. Since then a human rights commission and legal rulings have vindicated Barabaig claims, but compensation has been paltry.

Hadza

Hadza, numbering perhaps 1,000, are nomadic hunter-gatherers living in the rocky hills and arid valleys to the east and south-west of Lake Eyasi in northern Tanzania. They number about a thousand people and speak a language currently unrelatable to any other. They are acknowledged by neighbouring people to be the original inhabitants of the area. Hadza social structures are communal and egalitarian, with no system of chiefs and strong obligations to share resources, particularly food. Hadza reliance on hunting and gathering remains high. Adequate supplies of fruits, berries and tubers as well as abundant game make this way of life nutritionally adequate and ecologically sustainable. However, government policies reflect the widespread belief that hunting and gathering is unacceptable and degrading, and should be given up. In colonial times unsuccessful attempts were made to convert Hadza to peasant farmers, a policy intensified after independence though still with only limited success.

Hadza land has been treated as if it were unoccupied, and both agriculturalists and pastoralists have been encouraged to settle there, even though aridity makes it unsuitable for crops and tsetse fly make it unsuitable for cattle. However, in recent years Barabaig pastoralists displaced from their own land have taken over large areas of Hadza country. In the west of Hadza territory Sukuma farmers have also settled in large numbers. Following pressure from Hadza and from a Canadian volunteer organization, a limited amount of land was registered in 1994 in the core area of Hadza country. However, the government has retained rights over hunting, subsequently leasing them out to a commercial company. The political weakness of the Hadza makes it impossible for them to resist settlement even over the land where their rights are recognized.

A further threat to Hadza society comes from the nature of the education system. Although most Hadza want their children to attend school their only option is for children to board over nine months a year from the age of six, being taught only in Swahili from non-Hadza teachers – a process amounting to forced assimilation on lines which have failed elsewhere. It would be unrealistic to argue solely for the retention of traditional Hadza hunter-gatherer lifestyle and culture; the further development of external social and economic relationships is not only inevitable but can be beneficial. Yet without adequate support and protection (including improved land rights, control over hunting, and more appropriate education) the familiar paths of demoralization and disintegration, and the familiar options of landlessness, day-labour, beggary and prostitution, are all too likely to develop.

Conclusions and future prospects

The long-term impact of multi-party politics and the 1995 election is difficult to predict, though the traditions of comparative stability and tolerance between Tanzanian groups and factions must give some hope that the pitfalls of ethnicized politics can be avoided. Tensions between Zanzibar and the mainland are likely to resurface, however, and those between Christians and Muslims to increase. Anti-Asian sentiment will also probably grow. Inappropriate policies against pastoralists, and still more so against hunter-gatherers, often based on deep-seated prejudices, are likely to persist.

Further reading

Africa Watch, *Executive Order Denies Land Rights: Barabaig Suffer Beatings, Arson and Criminal Charges*, New York, London, Washington, DC, 1990.

Lane, C., *Alienation of Barabaig Pastureland: Policy Implications for Pastoral Development in Tanzania*, London, Pastoral Land Tenure monograph, International Institute for Environment and Development, 1991.

Minority-based and advocacy organizations

Amnesty International, PO Box 4331, Dar es Salaam, Tanzania; tel. 255 51 31708, fax 255 51 44192.

Bulgalda [Barabaig], PO Box 146, Kapesh, Arusha, Tanzania.

Ilaramatak Lolkonerie (Olkonerei Integrated Pastoralist Survival Programme), PO Box 12785 (Orkesumot), Arusha, Tanzania; tel. 255 57 859 318.

Mongo wae Mono [Hazda], c/o Community Development Office, Box 9, Mbulu, Tanzania.

Uganda

Land area:	236,860 sq km
Population:	18.8 million (est. 1995)
Main languages:	English (official), Swahili, numerous local languages
Main religions:	Christianity (Roman Catholics slightly outnumber Protestants), traditional beliefs, Islam
Main minority groups[1]:	several dozen ethno-linguistic groups, most included in four main groupings – see below (adequate statistics unavailable)
Real per capita GDP:	$910
UNDP HDI/rank:	0.326 (155)

Uganda is a country of very great ethnic, linguistic and religious diversity, whose roots lie in a complex early history of overlapping migrations and interactions. All its ethnic groups can be considered minorities, and most have faced persecution at one time or another. Gross abuses of human rights, with a considerable ethnic dimension, took place under the Amin, Obote and Okello regimes of the 1970s and 1980s. Although more recent years have seen a degree of comparative stability, the legacy of these conflicts remains a powerful mobilizing factor in Ugandan politics. Factors behind the conflicts have been complex and multi-faceted; economic, religious, ideological and regional aspects have all been significant. In addition to the unstable and overlapping nature of ethnic categories, conflicts have themselves featured a variety of complex alliances.

For the sake of simplicity, Uganda's major linguistic groupings may be summarized as follows.

(1) Speakers of Bantu languages, who are largely agriculturalists, living principally in the south and west of the country, comprise about two-thirds of the population. Historically they include centralized societies governed by royal families (Baganda, Banyankole, Banyoro, Batoro), as well as many others with less elaborate hierarchies. In western Uganda two pastoralist groups (Bahima and Batutsi) established ascendancy over the agriculturalist communities (Bairu and Bahutu) among whom they settled and whose languages they share.

(2) Speakers of Western Nilotic languages in northern Uganda, traditionally agriculturalists organized in chiefdoms, include the Acholi, Langi, Alur and Jonam tribal groups.

(3) Speakers of Eastern Nilotic languages, primarily in eastern Uganda, include Karamojong and Teso (as well as Kakwa in the north-west). Traditionally pastoralists, they have a social organization that is based on clans and age sets.

(4) Central Sudanic-speakers such as the Lugbara and Madi inhabit the far north-west of Uganda (as well as neighbouring regions of Sudan); traditionally they are agricultural peoples with a non-hierarchic social organization.

In the late nineteenth century Uganda was a powerful magnet for missionaries, traders and later colonial authorities, lured by the fertility of the country and stimulated by Anglo–French and Arab–European rivalry. Missionary competition, initially focused on the most powerful Ugandan institution, the Baganda court, left a legacy of division between Catholics and Protestants. In the south and west of Uganda the fertility of the land and the absence of wholesale expropriation for European settlement meant that the introduction of cash crops such as coffee and cotton, along with accompanying taxation and control, was less oppressive than in many parts of the continent. Economic development was heavily weighted towards the south, where missionary activity and educational opportunities were greater. The Baganda monarchy, despite its earlier resistance (followed by capitulation), was granted recognition and a degree of autonomy. The Baganda came to be widely seen as favoured by the British colonial authorities.

Northern and eastern regions remained comparatively isolated and disadvantaged throughout the colonial period. Southerners comprised the majority of the civil service and of the educated and commercial elite. Later, however, northerners came to be recruited to colonial military and police forces, to which they were drawn by economic necessity and for which imperial ideology deemed them suitable for being taller as well as more 'warlike'. This division into 'warrior' and 'educated' groups, reinforced by the policies of the later colonial period, increasingly became part of Ugandans' own perceptions.

Politics in the run-up to independence in 1962 were contested by three main parties. Within the Buganda heartland Protestants loyal to the monarchy were generally in opposition to the largely Catholic Democratic Party (DP). Elsewhere Milton Obote's United People's Congress (UPC) was generally dominant. Although initially combining against the DP, the monarchists and the UPC soon fell out violently over the status of Buganda and the other southern kingdoms. In 1966 government troops bombed and shelled the king's palace; hundreds were killed and the Kabaka fled into exile. Obote abolished the monarchy and later declared a one-party state, strongly repressing Bagandan monarchist and nationalist sentiment. Increasingly government came to be dominated by Obote's fellow Luo-speakers (Acholi and Langi) as well as Teso, whilst the army commander Idi Amin (a Kakwa-speaking Nubi Muslim) recruited soldiers from his home region in the north-west, and increasingly from across the Sudanese border. In 1971 Amin mounted a successful coup, supported initially by most southerners as well as by the British and Americans opposed to Obote's socialist policies.

In 1972 Amin's wholesale expulsion of Ugandan Asians, a community of around 75,000, was only a foretaste of his growing ruthlessness. Extensive purges of both government and army, especially of those suspected of loyalty to the exiled Obote, continued. During Amin's eight-year dictatorship between 100,000 and 500,000 Ugandans were killed. Economic collapse heaped further burdens on the country. The Tanzanian army, acting in support of the Ugandan National Liberation Front, deposed Amin in 1979. Obote's UPC and the DP were once again the major parties in the 1980 elections, retaining their traditional ethnic and religious support bases. The UPC victory was widely regarded a fraudulent. Several guerrilla armies began to operate against the government – notably the National Resistance Army of Yoweri Museveni in the west and south, as well as north-westerners loyal to Amin. Obote's UPC government was dependent on the army, itself dominated by Acholi and Langi.

Extension of army control to the far north-west was accompanied by widespread abuses as revenge was exacted on people considered sympathetic to Amin. Estimates of those killed range from 5,000 to 30,000, with over 200,000 refugees fleeing to Sudan and Zaire. In 1982 another wave of ethnic persecution began in the south-west, with around 100,000 Banyarwanda (Bahutu and Batutsi) as well as Bahima being forced out of their homes and fleeing to Rwanda or to refugee camps on the border. The operation was orchestrated by UPC activists and officials in co-ordination with the police. The causes are complex and relate not only to Banyarwanda support for the (essentially Catholic) Democratic Party but to competition for land and resentment against the traditionally dominant position of Batutsi and Bahima. Worse was to develop in the 'Luwero triangle', the rural heartland of southern Uganda where anti-Obote feeling was widespread and where Museveni's National Resistance Army (NRA) guerrillas initially operated. The army implemented a policy of starving out the guerrillas and punishing those held to sympathize with them with massive reprisals against the civilian population. Estimates of those killed range from 100,000 to 500,000.

Though belated international pressure and the growing success of Museveni's NRA played their part, Obote's regime eventually collapsed from feuding between Langi and Acholi factions in the military. Acholi troops overran Kampala in July 1985, looting the city and forcing Obote into exile. Tito Okello became head of state. Six months later the NRA took over the city, installing Museveni as President. NRA discipline, generally much better than its rivals, deteriorated as attempts were made to pacify the north of the country where remnants of the Amin and Obote armies continued to operate. In 1986 Alice Lakwena's charismatic Holy Spirit Movement mounted an insurgency in the Acholi region which has continued in various guises ever since. Attempts were made, with limited success, to pacify the traditionally rebellious and, since 1979, heavily armed Karamojong. Other rebellions took place among the Teso in the north-east (following which thousands of Bakenyi were expelled from the region by the NRA) and the Bakonjo in the north-west.

Nevertheless, security and human rights both improved by comparison with the preceding fifteen years. The 'resistance committee system', a 'non-party' regime controlled by the NRA but with an element of local democracy based on village councils, provided a degree of stability, if with considerable regional variation. Large numbers of refugees returned to the West Nile region from the Sudan, joined later by others fleeing the Sudanese war. By the 1990s the economy, badly hit by the collapse of coffee prices, was showing signs of recovery. The AIDS epidemic continued to ravage the country. The fortunes of Ugandans have depended on national and regional political and military circumstances, which have been extremely fluid and may become so again despite the comparative stability of recent years. In the longer term, all groups must be considered potentially vulnerable to abuses relating in part to ethnic and linguistic factors and as such deserve discussion, although space permits only brief accounts of prospects currently facing major groupings.

Baganda and other Bantu-speakers

Collectively Ugandan Bantu-speakers comprise the majority of the population. Under the northerner-dominated governments of 1962–86 they suffered varying hardships which during the second Obote regime culminated in the Loweru triangle massacres. Such circumstances could return only if Uganda were once again seriously destabilized and the current regime replaced. Despite its ideological opposition to ethnically based institutions, the government has permitted the re-establishment of the Baganda (1992), Batoro (1993) and Banyoro (1994) monarchies with largely symbolic status, a guarded attempt to accommodate ethnic sentiment.

Acholi, Langi and Teso

In its efforts to establish control over north-central Uganda from 1985 onwards the NRA gave priority to disarming former soldiers and others. One consequence was that people lacked the means to defend themselves against cattle raids by Karamojong, who had recently acquired automatic weapons in large quantities. Moreover, such raids were often viewed with indifference at best by NRA soldiers who had long been fighting armies dominated by northerners. The Teso and eastern Acholi regions were particularly affected. One manifestation of the resulting vulnerability and antagonism has been the continuation of armed opposition, notably in Acholi and notably under the aegis of the Sudanese-backed Lord's Resistance Army, a descendent of the Holy Spirit Movement of 1986, which continues to disrupt and destabilize the region. More generally the government has failed to gain the confidence of many people in northern Uganda, as well as failing to prevent persistent human rights abuses by the army.

North-westerners

Tensions have continued between the NRA and many inhabitants of the north-west of the country, particularly those suspected of loyalty to Amin, who are also often Muslims. Militias derived from the Amin-era army, such as those made up from the Oringa Lugbara and Nubi groups, have remained active (often in Sudan rather than Uganda), causing friction between members of the group and the authorities, persisting human rights abuses by the army, and a spirit of alienation similar to elsewhere in northern Uganda.

Bairu, Bahutu, Bakiga, Bahima and Batutsi

Although Bantu-speakers, Bairu and Bahutu have traditionally been in a position subordinate to the pastoralist groups who inhabit the same areas, the Bahima and Batutsi. Bakiga are in a similar situation to Bahutu, to whom they are closely related. Many Bairu were sympathetic to Obote and opposed to Museveni, a Muhima. Bahutu – those who did not leave for Rwanda in the early 1980s – are mistrusted by Batutsi following the Rwandan genocide and wary of the alliance between Uganda and the new Rwandan government. However, despite the earlier involvement of many Batutsi with the NRA, their position in Uganda remains somewhat precarious, the defection of Batutsi from the NRA to the Rwandan Patriotic Army (RPA) from 1990 greatly increasing this insecurity. Though many Batutsi have moved to Rwanda following the RPA victory, others have remained in Uganda. In view of the unresolved regional conflicts the position of all these groups must be considered vulnerable.

Karamojong and related groups

Karamojong pastoralists of north-east Uganda, numbering around 100,000 people, along with related groups, comprise the most significant marginalized minority in Uganda, isolated geographically, economically and politically, and widely despised by their compatriots as violent and underdeveloped. Related groups, whose differentiation from Karamojong as separate ethnic or tribal groups is a result of often arbitrary external ethnographic categorization, include Tepeth, Labwor, Dodoth, Napore, Teuso and Pokot. The ecological crisis in north-east Uganda dates primarily from water development and disease control programmes begun in 1938, which quickly led to overstocking, overgrazing and environmental degradation, exacerbating periodic drought-induced famines. Cultivation in the central belt also suffers from drought, which often causes complete crop failure.

Since colonial times governments have treated Karamojong primarily as a security problem, and since the widespread introduction of automatic weapons in the early 1980s the region has been a virtual no-go area, save primarily for military expeditions to punish cattle-raiding and the intermittent efforts of relief agencies to supply food during the frequent periods of drought and famine. Up-to-date information about the position of Karamojong and other groups in the region is hard to obtain, but the isolation and impoverishment combined with drought and unresolved political problems perpetuate a disadvantaged and marginalized existence.

Other minorities

In many parts of the country smaller ethnic groupings can be marginalized in the struggle for resources precisely because of their political insignificance – a situation different from groups associated with opposition to the government who need to be appeased. Groups cited in this context include the Madi in the far north-west, as well as the Gisu and other groups in the south-east. Among the most marginalized are the Batwa. Originally forest dwellers, the few thousand Batwa in Uganda have been almost entirely dispossessed of their land by the combined pressures of government departments responsible for conservation, and cultivators, notably Bakiga, claiming land. Despite the absence of detailed information on the situation of Batwa in Uganda, it is clear that conditions of exploitation and servitude are widespread, paralleling in an acute form the problems faced by (former) forest dweller populations elsewhere.

Ugandan Asians expelled by Amin in 1972 have been able in recent years to submit claims for the repossession of their confiscated property, a major incentive for their return, though only some are interested in doing so. Asians have benefited from the comparative stability, improved human rights, and official disavowal of ethnically based politics. But the unpopularity generated by their privileged economic position could easily make them vulnerable once again if instability returns. In 1995 Uganda was additionally host to an estimated 300,000 refugees from the war in Sudan, with limited prospects for return. The alliance between the Sudanese government and forces such as the West Nile Bank Front ultimately derived from Amin's army are a particular source of instability. Refugees from Zaire and Rwanda were also living in the country in 1995.

Conclusions and future prospects

Despite the comparative success of the Ugandan government in stabilizing the country and improving human rights, the outrages of the Amin and Obote years in particular have left a legacy of mistrust between many sections of Uganda's population, notably between many northerners and the present military authorities. The long-running debate over the new constitution and growing demands for greater democracy at a national level, as well as proposals for greater decentralization and local autonomy, will generate new dynamics whose outcome is difficult to predict. Additional pressures are generated by economic insecurity and above all by continuing conflict and instability in Sudan, Zaire, Rwanda and Burundi.

Further reading

Amnesty International reports, *Uganda: Deaths in the Countryside: Killings of Civilians by the Army in 1990*, 1990; *Uganda: Human Rights Violations by the National Resistance Army*, 1991; *Uganda: Detentions of Suspected Government Opponents without Charge or Trial in the North*, London, 1994.

Amnesty International, *Uganda: The Failure to Safeguard Human Rights*, London, 1992.

Hooper, E. and Pirouet, L., *Uganda*, London, MRG report, 1989.

Mutibwa, P., *Uganda since Independence: A Story of Unfulfilled Hopes*, London, Hurst, 1992.

Minority-based and advocacy organizations

Foundation for Human Rights Initiative (FHRI), PO Box 11027, Kampala, Uganda; tel. 256 41 53 0095, fax 256 41 54 0561.

Zaire

Land area:	2,344,855 sq km
Population:	42.5 million (est. 1995)
Main languages:	French (official), Lingala, Kikongo, Tshiluba, Swahili
Main religions:	Christianity (mainly Roman Catholicism), traditional beliefs
Main minority groups:	hundreds of ethno-linguistic groups including Kasaians, Banyarwanda, Hunde, Nyanga, Nande, Bangala, Batwa, Bambuti (adequate statistics unavailable)[1]
Real per capita GDP:	$300
UNDP HDI/rank:	0.371 (141)

Zaire is a vast country of great geographical diversity. From early times densely forested areas have been home to communally organized hunting and gathering bands of 'Pygmies'. On the forest fringes and rivers agricultural and fishing communities showed much greater social differentiation. By the fifteenth century powerful kingdoms had developed in the south and west of the country, although these were unable to prevent the depredations of Portuguese slavers. In the late nineteenth century King Leopold of Belgium organized a unique variety of colonialism in what is now Zaire, vesting himself with sole ownership of the entire territory and following such brutal and exploitative policies as to cause, even then, an international outcry. Repressive military campaigns were a notable feature. Later (from the 1920s on) resistance was primarily expressed through messianic movements, notably Kimbanguists and Jehovah's Witnesses, whose supporters have faced persecution before and after independence.[2] Belgian rule relied heavily on customary local authorities, though this often involved the disruption of pre-existing political relations, the creation and manipulation of chieftainships, and the entrenchment of ethnic divisions. This process was also reinforced by an educational system, implemented mainly by the Catholic Church and confined almost entirely to primary level, which favoured certain regions, additionally serving to formalize linguistic divisions.

Belgian opposition to the radical nationalism of Patrice Lumumba's Mouvement National Congolais encouraged the escalation of regional and ethnically based parties during the hectic transition to independence in 1960, and the secession of the southern province of Katanga (now Shaba) immediately afterwards. A prolonged period of chaos and civil war followed, in which regional and ethnic factors came to the fore. The eventual victor was General Joseph-Desiré Mobutu, who mounted his (second) coup in 1965, and has ruled the country ever since. Despite the continuation of insurrectionary movements in north-east Shaba and in Upper Zaire (Haut-Zaïre), Mobutu at first achieved comparative stability by the ruthless suppression of opposition and by increasing the concentration of power in presidential hands. However, the defeat of the Zairean army in Angola in 1975, combined with economic collapse, provoked a succession of army mutinies, as well as renewed rebellion in Shaba, suppressed with the help of Moroccan and later French and Belgian troops. Increasingly Mobutu moved members of his own Ngande group into positions of power, particularly within the elaborate security apparatus.

Instability, indebtedness and economic decline, combined with gross corruption and pervasive human rights violations, continued through the 1980s without threatening the support from Mobutu's external backers until the end of the decade, when external pressure led to the formal establishment of multi-party politics in 1990. Increasing popular discontent exploded into widespread rioting in many cities in 1991, following army massacres of students in Lubumbashi and of demonstrators in Kinshasa. In 1992 a long-postponed all-party Sovereign National Conference, with transition to democracy on its agenda, elected Etienne Tshisekedi as Prime Minister. This precipitated a crisis with the military and with Mobutu, who refused to ratify the appointment and the provisional constitution. In 1993 Zaire had rival governments and rival prime ministers. One response of pro-Mobutu factions was to play the 'ethnic card' with a vengeance, precipitating the anti-Kasaian riots and mass expulsions – apparently following a strategy equating democracy with instability and ethnic hatred, as a justification for blocking reform and maintaining Mobutu in power. Mobutu's control of the central bank and other sources of finance, combined with rivalries among Tshisekedi's supporters, enabled him to gain the upper hand in 1994. Developments in Rwanda and Kivu also enabled him to regain wavering international support, particularly from France. In October 1996 a revolt in eastern Zaire spearheaded by local Tutsi militias and backed by Rwanda and Uganda threatened to topple the regime and change the balance of power in the whole of Central Africa; by the end of the year the rebels were in control of much of the northeast of the country.

For a country variously assessed as having 200 ethnic groups and up to 700 languages and dialects, definitions of minorities are complex even by the standards of the region. Ethnicity, while a powerful mobilizing force in Zairean politics, has been a particularly fluid and changeable category, linguistic and regional agglomerations being overlaid with factors of religion, class and education. Nor are the most vulnerable minorities necessarily the smallest or most marginalized. This entry primarily considers ethnolinguistic groupings which are victims or potential victims of Zaire's current instability, regardless of their size or precise status. The Batwa and Bambuti 'Pygmy' groupings are also considered; though less directly involved in national conflicts, they are more systematically marginalized.

Kasaians (Luba, Lulua)

The Kasai region of south-central Zaire attracted Christian missionaries at least twenty years before the southern province of Shaba (formerly Katanga). When copper was discovered in Shaba in the late nineteenth century mineworkers were recruited from outside the region, particularly from areas such as Kasai where education and acculturation to colonial practices were more advanced. Economic opportunities continued to attract migrants from Kasai to Shaba even after the discovery of diamonds in Kasai; many Kasaians adopted local languages and many have lived in Shaba for several generations. Most are of Luba origin, from Kasai Oriental. Estimates of their numbers before the expulsions range from 500,000 to 1,000,000 people, comprising over a third of the population of mining towns such as Likasi and Kolwezi, as well as of the regional capital Lubumbashi. Kasaians attracted resentment from Shabans as a result of their educational and economic advantages, but coexistence had generally been peaceful.

Violence against Kasaians in Shaba began soon after the election of Etienne Tshisekedi, himself a Kasaian of Luba origin, as Prime Minister in 1992. Highly inflammatory speeches denigrating Kasaians were made by leading pro-Mobutu politicians, including the Governor of Shaba. In a prolonged campaign of harassment and violence around 6,000 people were killed and up to 400,000 have been forced to flee to Kasai, overcrowding its cities and often facing unemployment or destitution. Those remaining in Shaba continue to live in fear of further pogroms.

North Kivu: Banyarwanda, Hunde, Nyanga, Nande

When colonial boundaries were drawn in the late nineteenth century many Banyarwanda (Hutus, Tutsis and Twa, who all speak Kinyarwanda) found themselves on the Zaire side of the Rwandan border, in Kivu province. More Banyarwanda subsequently crossed from Rwanda to work on Belgian colonial farms. In the late 1950s (and subsequently) Tutsi refugees fleeing persecution in Rwanda also crossed to Zaire; Banyarwanda came to comprise around half the population of north Kivu, yet were widely viewed as 'foreigners' by other ethnic groups. The waves of immigration intensified competition over land. Hunde chiefs in particular, whose ownership of land bestowed a degree of political influence out of proportion to the size (and impoverishment) of their community, bitterly resented expropriation of land (often that traditionally used for hunting) by Banyarwanda settlers. Other groups, notably Nyanga and Nande, were also in competition for land.

Although at independence anyone who had lived in the country for ten years was entitled to citizenship, the law was amended in 1981: only those who could trace their ancestry within the country to 1885 were now eligible. The change was primarily aimed at Banyarwanda. From 1991 the nationality issue acquired much greater significance when registration began in anticipation of elections. Conflict escalated in 1992–3 into a virtual civil war, with raids and counter-raids between Banyarwanda and other groups, accompanied by widespread burning of villages and crops. Thousands were killed. Troops failed to intervene, and there were widespread reports of them participating in or profiting from the violence. An estimated 270,000 people, from all ethnic groups, were displaced.

Though church-led reconciliation initiatives had achieved a good deal, north Kivu was still in chaos when a million Rwandan Hutu refugees fleeing the Rwandan Patriotic Army arrived in 1994, following the genocide in which many of them were implicated. Three-quarters of these refugees crossed the border within a week in July, the largest refugee movement ever recorded. An estimated 70,000 died from cholera and related diseases. They were subject to control and intimidation from Rwandan soldiers loyal to the deposed regime, as well as looting and extortion from Zairean soldiers. In August 1995 the Zairean authorities began to repatriate refugees to Rwanda, but stopped after international protests. However, in October 1996 local Tutsi militias, supported by Rwandan troops, attacked the refugee camps, provoking the repatriation of most though by no means all of the Hutu refugees. Other refugees, including soldiers of the former Rwandan army, retreated west. At the time of writing the numbers and situation of these refugees were subject to much speculation and dispute, but in most cases their condition can be assumed to be desperate. Many Zairean communities, in Kivu and further west, appear to have been subject to serious depredations by retreating Zairean troops.[3]

Bangala

Bangala are less of a traditional ethnic group than people from the north-west of the country who are or have become predominantly Lingala-speaking. Their predominance in the Zairean army is symbolized by the widespread use of Lingala as a military language. They have become strongly identified with the unpopular Mobutu regime in the eyes of many Zaireans, many of whom also look down on such 'forest people'. Their dominant position depends on the survival of the regime, which at the time of writing looks uncertain. If the Mobutu regime collapses, Bangala-speakers, who are widely dispersed throughout the country, may themselves be vulnerable.

Batwa and Bambuti

The main 'Pygmy' groupings in Zaire are the Batwa (or BaTua), numbering up to 100,000 in the Lake Tumba region of north-west Zaire, as well as a few thousand in Kivu near the Uganda and Rwanda borders, and the Bambuti of the Ituri forest in north-east Zaire, numbering about 35,000. The term Batwa is used to cover a number of different cultural groups. Many Bambuti and Batwa depend in part on forest hunting and gathering, and both groups have symbiotic if often subservient relationships with neighbouring agriculturalists; but whilst many Bambuti retain traditional semi-nomadic residence patterns, most Batwa are sedentarized and very many are cultivators.

Bambuti provide a good illustration of the pressures on Pygmy populations, even among a group generally considered closest to traditional ways of living. Despite being viewed by cultivators as inferior and even not fully human, the Bambuti, like most Pygmy people, benefited from reciprocal relationships whereby game, skins and other forest products were exchanged for food, while allowing autonomous social and cultural traditions to be maintained. For most Bambuti such long-standing relationships substantially survived the depredations of the slaving and colonial eras. In the civil conflicts of the 1960s, however, many outsiders sought refuge in the forest, and stayed on as traders and gold prospectors. Increasingly the Bambuti were drawn into a monetarized economy, selling meat for cash and engaging in menial wage-labour, invariably for a fraction of normal rates. Large areas of the forest were reserved as national parks, from which hunting was banned. Women increasingly married outsiders, further disrupting the basis of Bambuti society. Traditional relationships have increasingly degenerated into those of exploitation and servitude, sometimes bordering on outright slavery, accompanied by social disintegration and loss of morale, and often by social problems such as alcoholism and prostitution.

Official government policy in Zaire is that Pygmies should be 'emancipated' and considered as being no different from other citizens – indeed the use of the term 'Pygmy' is officially banned. In practice this means promoting sedentarization and agriculture – a policy also pursued to some degree in colonial times and reflected in many missionary programmes. Many observers believe such policies to be misguided and destructive, inevitably leading to unequal competition and social disintegration. Efforts should instead be directed where possible to supporting Pygmy attempts to maintain traditional forest-based lifestyles. This first of all involves protecting the forest, whose destruction is less advanced in Zaire than in much of the region but is undoubtedly threatened. Hunting rights must also be protected; and there can be a coincidence between ecological concerns, which the government has at least recognized, and the interests of forest dwellers, which attract only indifference or hostility. The key is to give forest dwellers land rights and to revolutionize their own currently negligible involvement in discussions over their future.

Conclusions and future prospects

The people of Zaire have suffered greatly from the economic mismanagement, indebtedness and corruption, all condoned by Mobutu's external supporters, which have been both cause and consequence of the conflicts which have plagued the country. These conflicts have increasingly, though not exclusively, been conducted along lines of ethnic division, and it remains to be seen whether the rebellion of 1996 will avoid replicating this, since most militias as well as the Zairean army are organized on an ethnic basis. Access to land and resources will also remain a major source of conflict. The prospects for Zaire's different ethnic groupings depends on the shakeout of such wider conflicts as well as on the outcome of the 1996 revolt. Future victims of conflict, which is all too likely to continue, may not coincide with those of recent upheavals.

Prospects for Zaire's Pygmies, particularly for those still maintaining in whole or in part a forest-dwelling existence, also relate to developments at a national level. Zaire's forests represent a huge economic resource, whose survival has partly been a consequence of the political instability and economic chaos which has inhibited infrastructural development and the viability of commercial logging. If Zaire gained stability the forest, as elsewhere in the region, would be under greater threat, and the social and cultural disintegration of Pygmy society, already far advanced, would be likely to accelerate.

Further reading

Bahuchet, S., 'Les Pygmées d'aujourd'hui en Afrique centrale', *Journal des africanistes*, vol. 61, no. 1, 1991, pp. 5–35.

Beauclerk, J., *Hunters and Gatherers in Central Africa: On the Margins of Development*, Oxford, Oxfam Publications, 1993.

Human Rights Watch/Africa, *Zaire: Inciting Hatred: Violence against Kasaiens in Shaba*, New York, Washington, DC, London, 1993.

Lawyers' Committee for Human Rights, *Zaire: Repression as Policy: A Human Rights Report*, New York, 1990.

Roberts, R.G., *Inducing the Deluge: Zaire's Internally Displaced People*, Washington, DC, US Committee for Refugees, 1993.

Minority-based and advocacy organizations

Human Rights League, BP 5316, Kinshasa 10, Zaire.

Programme d'Intégration et de Développement du Peuple Pygmé au Kivu, Avenue Route d'Uvira, BP 1098, Bukavu, Zaire.

Pygasse – Assistance aux Pygmées et Environnement, BP 881, Goma, Nord Kivu, Zaire.

Zairian Assocation for the Defence of Human Rights, Avenue Mutombo Katisi No. 7/91, Kinsha Gombe, Kinshasa, Zaire.

Zambia

Land area:	740,720 sq km
Population:	9.2 million (est. 1994)
Main languages:	Bemba, Nyanja, Tonga, Lozi, Lunda, Luvale, Kaonde, English (official)
Main religions:	Christianity, indigenous beliefs, Islam
Main minority groups:	Lozi 300,000 (est., 3.3%), Lamba 200,000 (est., 2.2%), Asians 4,000 (est.)
Real per capita GDP:	$1,110
UNDP HDI/rank:	0.411 (136)

Zambia's extensive and convoluted boundaries betray its origins as an artefact of imperial competition, taking no real account of indigenous cultures and histories. Its vast territory is quite sparsely populated, its people settled mainly in river valleys and urban areas. The growth of cities and longstanding patterns of labour recruitment to mines and farms mean that the experiences of (semi-) proletarianization, urbanization and resulting contact among ethnic groups are widely shared. Although shifting and amalgamating throughout the twentieth century, at least seventy-three linguistically similar, yet culturally specific, indigenous African ethno-linguistic groups have been distinguished in Zambia. Bemba-speakers have held key positions in central government, but there is no one dominant ethno-linguistic group. English is used in upper levels of primary school and above and is the language of government. As such, it spans all ethnic groups; however, lack of mastery of English can entail social exclusion. Shona, Swahili and various Zairian languages may be heard among immigrants and traders.

Despite often strident political competition and a steep decline in living standards since the 1970s, post-colonial Zambian politics and society have seen few episodes of upheaval, nor serious and consistent violations of civil and political rights. According to a recent academic study, 'ethnic diversity in Zambia does not seem to be accompanied by high levels of antagonism along cultural, linguistic and regional lines; indeed the data reveal that Zambians report trusting ethnic strangers only slightly less than ethnic kin'. Referring to Zambia's post-independence administrations (1964–91), nineteen of them officially under a one-party system, the writers go on to observe: 'Perhaps the current reported levels of inter-ethnic trust are one positive outcome of [former President Kaunda's] accommodative style of centralized one-party rule.'[1]

Selecting only those which have suffered disadvantage through official acts of omission or commission, the following minorities merit attention here: Lozi, among whom there are stirrings of secession; Lamba, a case study in social exclusion; and Asians, who are subjected to continuing resentment.

Lozi

Termed Barotse under British colonial rule, Lozi people form one of Zambia's smaller but more distinctive ethno-linguistic groups. They make up rather more than 3 per cent of the population. Since the latter half of the seventeenth century, the Lozi kingdom has dominated the flood plain of the Zambezi river in western Zambia. Alliances between the Lozi elite and the British for mutual political advantage helped reinforce a sense of ethnic identity. Especially after the Second World War, the colonial government emphasized the 'special position' of Barotseland through modernization projects and privileges for the Lozi monarchy.

Around the time of Zambia's formal political independence in 1964, members of the Lozi elite made unsuccessful efforts to secede or at least gain special status for the Lozi nation within the new Zambian nation-state. Although resentful of White racism, they made overtures to White colonialists opposed to the Zambian nationalist mainstream. In the event, those leaders gained little popular support, as Lozis voted massively for the mainstream nationalist parties.

Stripped of powers to allocate land and other benefits, and unable to out-manoeuvre central government, Lozi elites failed to capitalize on popular resentments until the early 1990s. Those resentments arise from frustrations at declining living standards – the reduction in government services and worsening real returns to labour – that affect people all over Zambia. No laws or government measures explicitly disadvantage Lozi. Traditions and the language are consistently promoted. But it is not uncommon for Lozi traditional leaders to explain their circumstances as an outcome of active discrimination by central authorities. By the mid-1990s, a Lozi secessionist movement, backed by landed families, was active and acquiring weapons via traders linked with UNITA forces in Angola.

Lamba

Comprising slightly over 2 per cent of Zambia's population, Lamba people live in northern-central Zambia, along the Copperbelt; many others live across northern border, in Zaire's mining zone. As farmers with simple technologies in small, dispersed villages, they were prey to slave raiders in the nineteenth century. In the twentieth they were marginalized and stigmatized as a backward and timid 'bumpkins' who take part only unwillingly in urban industrial life. Few gained access to the better-paying waged work of the copper mines, to good education, or the benefits of patronage of the political classes. They were given jobs as unskilled labourers and domestic servants. Some made a livelihood from market gardening, to which Lamba women added beer-brewing and prostitution.

Much Lamba impoverishment stems from the loss of their lands, early in the century, to European mining and farming interests, and later to other immigrant farmers. They were thus among Zambia's first 'development refugees'. In 1928 the government began putting them in a 'native reserve' far from Copperbelt markets, thus obliging them to abandon their then promising business in market gardening. Schooling came relatively late and was of mediocre quality. Manipulated and denied access to ladders of social mobility, as yet unable to gain protection or assert their rights through self-organization, Lamba people are an African equivalent to a low-status caste.

Asians

People of Indo-Pakistani origin in Zambia today may number only a few thousand, down from 10,705 in 1970. Most work in commerce and transport, mainly in urban areas. Up to 1971, only 298 Asians had elected to take up Zambian citizenship following independence in 1964. In 1970 the government forced many noncitizens to abandon their businesses, especially in rural areas. In 1988, during a crackdown on the illegal parallel market, the government seized 203 shops suspected of illegal dealings. Most belonged to Zambian Asians. Many of the shops, assets and trading licences were soon returned, however, and compensation promised. Members of the Asian minority continue to voice concern at official hostility.

Other minorities

Some rural residents, especially of small and politically marginal ethnic groups, today appear vulnerable to loss of assets due to an influx of land speculators, especially White South Africans. With central government approval, rights to forest land traditionally used as 'commons' by Luvale and Lunda minority communities in western and north-western Zambia are being transferred to foreign business interests on easy terms, with little or no public consultation. These communities are fearful that such land alienation will grow, with major consequences for their future livelihoods. Jehovah's Witnesses have been subjected to hostility and violence in the past, and are formally prohibited from proselytizing. A point of political concern to colonial and post-colonial rulers, they are today, however, left to practise their passivist religion unmolested.

Conclusions and future prospects

Certain minorities in Zambia have occasionally faced stress and outright discrimination, but never on a scale and depth of brutality seen in neighbouring countries. Despite mounting material want, the chief preoccupation of most Zambians, national policies and programmes have gone some way towards taking legitimate interests of minorities into account. The mounting alienation of Zambian assets by foreigners could, however, lead to dangerously unstable polarization along racial lines.

Further reading

Bratton, M. and Liatto-Katundu, B., 'A focus group assessment of political attitudes in Zambia', *African Affairs*, no. 93, 1994.

Burdette, M., *Zambia: between Two Worlds*, Boulder, CO, Westview Press, 1988.

Caplan, G.L., *The Elites of Barotseland 1878–1969: A Political History of Zambia's Western Province*, London, Hurst, 1970.

Hodges, T., *Jehovah's Witnesses in Africa*, London, MRG report, 1985.

Siegel, B., 'The "wild" and "lazy" Lamba: ethnic stereotypes on the Central African copperbelt', in L. Vail (ed.), *The Creation of Tribalism in Southern Africa*, London, James Currey, 1989, pp. 350–71.

Minority-based and advocacy organizations

Afronet, PO Box 31145, Church House, Cairo Road, Lusaka, Zambia.

Catholic Commission for Justice and Peace, Unity House, Corner Freedom Way and Katunjila Road, PO Box 31965, Lusaka, Zambia.

Law Association of Zambia Human Rights Committee, c/o Ellis & Co., PO Box 71536, Ndola, Zambia; tel. 260 2 61 1041/1043, fax 260 2 61 3488.

Zimbabwe

Land area:	387,670 sq km
Population:	11 million (est. 1994)
Main langages:	Shona, SiNdebele, English
Main religions:	(syncretic) Christianity, indigenous beliefs, Islam
Main minority groups:	Ndebele and Kalanga 2 million (18%), Shangaan 93,000 (0.8%), Venda 70,000 (0.6%), Tonga 66,000 (0.6%)
Real per capita GDP:	$2,100
UNDP HDI/rank:	0.534 (124)

Beset by ethnic and racial tension for over a hundred years, Zimbabwe has seen minority/majority antagonisms spill over into armed conflict. The focal point has been state power, the main means of group advancement and protection. Those who have it commonly restrict access to benefits to those deemed eligible by virtue of their 'race' or ethnicity. An abiding theme of Zimbabwean history has been minority elite attempts to make good their claims to legitimacy while advancing their claims to material accumulation. Despite the transfer of formal political power from a junta representing the White numerical minority to a Black numerical majority government subject to the vote, this issue is still in the balance.

Control of land and bigger businesses by local Whites and by foreign interests remains a flashpoint in post-colonial Zimbabwe, especially for an aspiring Black African business elite. Since the transfer of formal power, political conflict has pivoted on relations between elites of the minority Ndebele and majority Shona peoples. In the country's first free elections of 1980, and those of 1985, a Shona-dominated party, the Zimbabwe African National Union (ZANU), overwhelmed the largely Ndebele Zimbabwe African People's Union (ZAPU), with voting largely following ethnic lines. That competition supposedly ended in 1987 with the absorption of ZAPU into an expanded version of the ruling ZANU party, making Zimbabwe *de facto* a one-party state.

The Shona-speaking people, who today form about 77 per cent of the population, did not originally see themselves as a 'tribe'. 'Scattered over a large area, in contrasting environments, and pulled in different directions by trading links and military alliances . . . these Shona-speakers were not conscious of a cultural identity, still less a political one.'[1] 'Shona-ness' is thus a creation of the past hundred years. Colonial missionaries and administrators set about categorizing Shona into clusters or sub-tribes on the basis of largely spurious inferences. These artificial constructs took on lives of their own, and sub-groupings and hierarchies emerged: Zezeru (central), Karanga (south-central) and Manyika (east) are the three largest blocs. Politicking among ZANU leaders has led to alienation of one of the smaller Shona blocs, Ndau, in the south-east, whose voters send to Parliament virtually the only representatives outside the ruling party.

Either because their members enjoyed privileged circumstances (Whites), or because in the mid-1990s they were not subject to active discrimination (Asians, Jehovah's Witnesses), or because their general situation is considered elsewhere (San), a number of minorities are not discussed here.

Ndebele (and Kalanga)

With about 14 per cent of the population (18 per cent if the affiliated Kalanga are included), Ndebele are Zimbabwe's largest minority. Their prominence also derives from their history of vigorous action and organization in a region poorly endowed for farming. A cattle-keeping people kindred to the Zulu, and part of a broad advance of Ngani peoples northwards in the nineteenth century, Ndebele invaded in the late 1830s, some fifty years before the main European advance. Settling in the south-western highveld around present-day Bulawayo, they established a formidable new nation with powers to extract tribute from neighbouring Shona and other peoples. Armed settlers smashed Ndebele power and grabbed their land and cattle, but cultural humiliation did not follow. For the White settlers, 'the Ndebele were regarded as courageous and stubborn fighters, they basked in the high esteem generally reserved for pastoralists, and were accorded something of the same mystique which Europeans in Kenya exhibited for the Masai, a mystique which betrays unmistakable signs of racialism.'[2] Mission schools and hiring patterns generated strata of White- and blue-collar workers from which nationalist leaders and cultural brokers were drawn.

Discord between the leadership of ZAPU and ZANU after 1980 deteriorated into a low-level but bitter civil war from 1983 to 1987, most of it played out in Matabeleland, with civilian Ndebele the main victims. The ZANU-controlled central government sent in army units to stamp out armed 'dissidents' linked with ZAPU. Government soldiers sometimes acted with extreme brutality. It is alleged that their slogan was, 'Mandevere muchakaura' (Ndebeles, you will suffer). Several thousand people are thought to have been killed or to have disappeared at this time. The ZANU-ZAPU merger ended the war and brought a number of ex-ZAPU Ndebele leaders into positions of power and political patronage. But empowerment of some Ndebele political figures has not meant improved living standards for ordinary citizens. The crux of current discontent is not about denial of rights to enjoy their culture, to receive instruction in the mother tongue or to form associations – all of which are afforded – but rather about denial of equal access to social and economic benefits.

Evidence of active discrimination against Ndebeles and Matabeleland is mixed. Placement of new health centres in the period 1980–85 seems to have favoured Matabeleland, bringing it up to par with the rest of Zimbabwe. Persistent allegations are made, however, that central government has favoured Matabeleland less than other regions, including the deliberate blocking of investment in water supply and the development of the regional capital Bulawayo.

Shangaan, Venda and Tonga

At the political and geographical margins outside the Shona–Ndebele polarity are three peoples together making up about 2 per cent of Zimbabwe's population. Shangaan and Venda people live mainly in the far south of Zimbabwe. In 1985–86 the government moved to introduce teaching of primary school classes 1 to 3 in these minorities' own languages. However, their cultural rights have been realized only partially, prompting leaders to press for respect of these rights. In 1995, Zimbabwe's national radio began broadcasting periodic programmes in these three minority languages. The situation of the Shangaan and Venda minorities is not as well known as that of the Tonga of Zimbabwe's north-west.

In 1957–58, some 57,000 Tonga people – about two-thirds of them on the northern (Zambian) and one-third on the southern (Zimbabwean) shores of the Zambezi river – became 'development refugees'. They were forced to abandon their ancestral homes as waters backed up behind the new World Bank-financed hydroelectric dam at Kariba. Central government investment, relief grain allocations, and cultural support such as primary school instruction in the Tonga language have, according to local Tonga leaders, been inadequate.

Conclusions and future prospects

The most serious challenges facing ordinary Zimbabweans today stem from their powerlessness to control economic changes forced upon them, especially structural adjustment based on free-market dogmas promoted by the International Monetary Fund and World Bank. Until the full force of these orthodoxies hit in the early 1990s, most indices of well-being for poorer Zimbabweans had been on an upward track. No longer: poverty is now spreading and showing no respect for ethnic differences. A reading of Zimbabwe's history suggests, however, that political elites will not deny themselves the use of the 'ethnic card' in deflecting the resulting discontent.

Further reading

Hitchens, C. et al., *Inequalities in Zimbabwe*, London, MRG report, 1981.

Palmer, R., 'Johnston and Jameson: a comparative study in the imposition of colonial rule', in B. Pachai (ed.), *The Early History of Malawi*, Evanston, IL, Northwestern University Press, 1972.

Palmer, R. and Birch, I., *Zimbabwe: A Land Divided*, Oxford, Oxfam Publications.

Ranger, T., 'Missionaries, migrants and the Manyika', in L. Vail (ed.), *The Creation of Tribalism in Southern Africa*, London, James Currey, 1989.

Watkins, K., *The Oxfam Poverty Report*, Oxford, Oxfam Publications, 1995.

Minority based and advocacy organizations

Catholic Commission for Justice and Peace, PO Box 8493, Causeway, Harare, Zimbabwe.

Centre for Inter-Racial Studies, Box MP, 167 Mount Pleasant, Harare, Zimbabwe.

Southern Africa Human Rights Foundation, PO Box 430, Kwekwe, Zimbabwe.

Notes

Contributions to this regional section are as follows. Chris Dammers: regional introduction and entries on Botswana, Burundi, Kenya, Lesotho, Namibia, Rwanda, South Africa, Swaziland, Tanzania, Uganda and Zaire; David Sogge: regional introduction and entries on Angola, Cameroon, Central African Republic, Chad, Comoros, Congo, Equatorial Guinea, Gabon, Madagascar, Malawi, Mauritius, Mozambique, Såo Tomé and Príncipe, Seychelles, Zambia and Zimbabwe.

Botswana

1 Basarwa is the Tswana term for people more widely known as 'San' or 'Bushman'. All three terms can have pejorative connotations, but there is no widely acceptable alternative. This is in part a reflection of the number and variety of Bushman languages from where an appropriate term might be expected to originate. In Botswana some Basarwa are adopting the term N/oakhwe ('first people' or 'red people'), and a few the term 'Khoe'. Some simply refer to themselves as 'the dispossessed'. However 'Basarwa' remains the majority usage in Botswana; unlike in Namibia there is little of the assertive revival of the term 'Bushman'. In Botswana Basarwa are often identified with the non-ethnic, government-favoured category of 'Remote Area Dwellers', who are defined on a geographical and socio-economic basis. About three-quarters of all Remote Area Dwellers are Basarwa. However, this term too (the Setswana equivalent is Batengnyanateng) is also unpopular among Basarwa themselves.

2 For more on the history of the Basarwa/San/Bushman people and the mythmaking which surrounds them, see the **Namibia** country entry, which complements this one.

Burundi

1 All groups in Burundi face potential oppression as a result of their status. Tutsis are essentially a dominant yet vulnerable minority. Hutus are essentially an oppressed majority. Population figures generally quoted are Hutu 85 per cent, Tutsi 14 per cent and Twa 1 per cent. However, these figures derive from surveys undertaken in the 1930s and take no account of subsequent migrations and massacres which have increased the proportion of Tutsis in Burundi. Nevertheless, the

figures given here must be considered extremely approximate. Debate also surrounds how best to describe the differences between Hutus and Tutsis – see **Central and Southern Africa: Introduction**. In this entry on Burundi both 'communal' and 'ethnic' are used to categorize the groups; it is recognized that almost any term is problematic.

Cameroon

1 Kofele-Kale, N., 'Ethnicity, regionalism and political power: A post-mortem of Ahidjo's Cameroon', in Schatzberg, M.G. and Zartman, I.W. (eds), *The Political Economy of Cameroon*, New York, Praeger, 1986, p. 77.

Chad

1 Whiteman, K., *Chad*, London, MRG report, 1988, p.5

Equatorial Guinea

1 See Klitgaard, R., *Tropical Gangsters*, London, I.B. Tauris, 1990

Gabon

1 US State Department, 'Gabon', in *Country Reports on Human Rights Practices: Report Submitted to the Committee on Foreign Relations, US Senate and the Committee on Foreign Affairs, US House of Representatives,* Washington, DC, 1995.

2 Ibid.

Kenya

1 Minority population figures are extrapolated from the last official government census in 1979 and must be considered approximate. The terms Luhya and Kalenjin were introduced in the colonial period, grouping together large numbers of smaller ethnic groups. Among smaller ethnic groups are the Teso (110,000), South Asians (50,000), Arabs (27,000) and Europeans (12,000).

Madagascar

1 Schlemmer, B., 'Crise et recompostion des identités à Madagascar', *Revue Tiers Monde*, vol. 36, no. 141, Jan.–Mar., 1995, p. 135.

Malawi

1 Africa Watch, *Where Silence Rules: The Suppression of Dissent in Malawi*, London, 1990, p.55

Mauritius

1 Lehembre, B., *L'Ile Maurice*, Paris, Karthala, 1984, p.237 (translation D.Sogge).

Namibia

1 Controversy surrounds the appropriate designation for these people, who lack a common language and so a common term for themselves. Terms from other languages, including the Nama. 'San', can have pejorative connotations, as well as having been applied at various times to various people. The term 'Bushman' has the added disadvantage of being gender-specific but is undergoing a comeback in Namibia, being endorsed at a San national conference in 1992. Both terms are used in this entry. Questions of how many Bushman people there are, and of who is or is not a Bushman, and of San ethnography in general, have given rise to protracted debate.

Rwanda

1 All groups in Rwanda face actual or potential oppression as a result of their status and so are considered in this entry. Tutsis are now in a dominant position yet are still potentially vulnerable. Hutus were the politically dominant majority before 1994 but are now seriously disadvantaged. The pre-1994 population figures almost universally quoted for both Rwanda and Burundi are Hutus 85 per cent, Tutsis 14 per cent and Twa 1 per cent. However, these figures derive from flawed surveys undertaken in the 1930s and take no account of subsequent migrations which undoubtedly decreased the proportion of Tutsis in Rwanda. Figures for the post-war period are even more difficult to establish, and continue to change. A majority of Tutsis in Rwanda were killed in the genocide. A high proportion of the Hutu population fled the country; many of the rest sought refuge in Rwanda's south-western corner. With as many as 2 million Hutu refugees outside the country the post-war proportion of Tutsis increased considerably, only to diminish as refugees returned towards the end of 1996. The government estimates that after the war 750,000 long-term (Tutsi) refugees returned, including many born outside Rwanda.

2 Controversy surrounds how best to describe the differences between Hutus and Tutsis – see **Introduction**. This entry on Rwanda uses both 'communal' and 'ethnic' to categorize the groups, while recognizing that almost any term is problematic.

South Africa

1 Questions of race, ethnicity and 'minority rights' reach levels of considerable complexity and

controversy in South Africa. While the positions of all principal 'population groups' in South Africa are considered here, as well as the other minorities mentioned, this does not of course imply any endorsement of the categorizations enforced under apartheid, though it reflects the extent to which apartheid and preceding formations succeeded in constructing social identities. In South Africa Black is usually used to refer to Black Africans, that is, those whose mother tongue is an African language, and this usage is followed here (along with 'African' when referring to earlier periods). Black can alternatively be used to refer to all South Africans not considered White. Local usage is also followed in calling South Africans of predominantly European origin White.

2 Acknowledging the significance of 'racial' divisions in South Africa does not imply that such divisions are other than fundamentally social and political constructions. Many South Africans, notably including most Afrikaners, have a very mixed genetic inheritance, and racial classification under apartheid reached heights of pernicious absurdity. Nevertheless, political constructs acquire a reality of their own and in South Africa some can only easily be described as 'racial' precisely because they can cut across ethnic, linguistic and cultural categories.

Uganda

1 Uganda's ethno-linguistic groups are 'strictly speaking' 'minorities', and all are actually or potentially vulnerable to discrimination based in part on their affiliation.

Zaire

1 Groups listed are those prioritized mainly on grounds of vulnerability.

2 During this period the Bakongo of western Zaire, who were prominent in commercial activities, suffered much persecution, with some parallels to the later situation of Kasaians (see **Angola**).

3 A similar if slightly less acute situation affected around 180,000 Hutu refugees from Burundi in south Kivu. Zaire in the mid 1990s was also host to long-standing refugee communities from Angola (220,000 in 1995) and Sudan (110,000 in 1995) both fleeing the protracted conflicts in those countries.

Zambia

1 Bratton, M. and Liatto-Katundu, B., 'A focus group assessment of political attitudes in Zambia', *African Affairs*, no. 93, 1994, p. 551. (Electoral outcomes in 1996 suggest that Bratton's conclusions are, however, rather optimistic.)

Zimbabwe

1 Ranger, T., 'Missionaries, migrants and the Manyika', in L. Vail (ed.), *The Creation of Tribalism in Southern Africa*, London, James Currey, 1989, p. 120.

2 Palmer, R., 'Johnston and Jameson: a comparative study in the imposition of colonial rule', in B. Pachai (ed.), *The Early History of Malawi*, Evanston, IL, Northwestern University Press, 1972, p. 297.

SOUTH ASIA

Javaid Rehman and Nikhil Roy

South Asia provides an instructive example of the difficulties involved in protecting the rights of minorities. The political geography of the states of the region reflects the mosaic and heterogeneous character of the elements of which they are formed. The region's religions splinter into denominations of creed and sects; its languages branch out into numerous dialects; and the ethnic picture reveals a multiplicity of peoples living in relative close proximity. Amid this richness of cultures, antiquity of civilizations and diversity of religions and beliefs, more languages are spoken than in the entire continent of Europe.

South Asia is beset with conflicts and civil wars involving minorities. These include disputes involving Kashmiris of India and Pakistan, Sikhs of the Indian Punjab, Tamils of Sri Lanka, Biharis and Adivasis of the Chittagong Hill Tracts of Bangladesh, and Muhajirs of urban Sindh in Pakistan. Consideration of all of these disputes forms an essential focus of this part of the *Directory*. However, any exercise analyzing conflicts between minority groups, on the one hand, and between a minority group or groups and the state, on the other, cannot be undertaken in isolation from the historical and political context. The history of South Asia is replete with political strife and intrigue, factionalism and internal feuds, while the excesses of the colonial period have left an enduring legacy.

Many indigenous peoples of the region, such as Veddhas (Wanniy-a-Laato, or forest dwellers) of Sri Lanka and Adivasis of India and Bangladesh, found themselves colonized long before the advance of the European imperialist powers. During the transformation of the colonial world to one of new nation states, the term 'indigenous' was equated with those wanting independence from Western rule or, as one author has put it, was interpreted in terms of 'pigmentational' or 'racial' sovereignty.[1] In the march towards independence, the replacement of European colonizers by a local, though equally oppressive, form of colonization has been particularly disillusioning to many indigenous peoples.[2]

Colonialism and post-colonialism

For the peoples of the colonial world generally, the most serious and enduring experiences were those of the period of colonialism. The colonial empires were built not on the concerns and needs of the indigenous communities but upon the interests of the colonizers, resulting in many instances of gross violations of the rights of these peoples. The arbitrary demarcation of boundaries such as the Durand line of 1893, on the Pakistan – Afghanistan border, separating peoples of the same ethnic origins and religion, the plantation of communities such as the 'Up Country' Tamils in what is now Sri Lanka, and the oft-quoted policy of 'divide and rule' as practised in India were to provide recipes for future disasters. Yet, if the excesses of colonialism are well documented, the destruction wreaked upon many groups as part of the progression towards decolonization, and also in the newly independent states, has been more painful to digest. The independence of British India in 1947 was a giant step towards the emancipation of colonial peoples. However, there was a marked inability or unwillingness to agree on a constitutional framework that would adequately cater for the rights of the Muslim minority; and as a consequence of the intransigence of the Muslim League and Congress leaders, India had to be partitioned. The incision was both arbitrary and 'unforeseen in magnitude, unordered in pattern, unreasoned in savagery . . . as many Indians would lose their lives in that swift splurge as Americans in four years of combat in World War II'.[3] Partition acted as a catalyst for a brutal and savage conflict, and gave rise to arguably the largest inter-country transfer of population of the twentieth century. Almost a million people were killed during this period; approximately 8 million people migrated from India to Pakistan, while there was a similar exodus of Hindus and Sikhs from Pakistan to India.

India and Pakistan led the way to further decolonization in the region. Ceylon (which adopted the

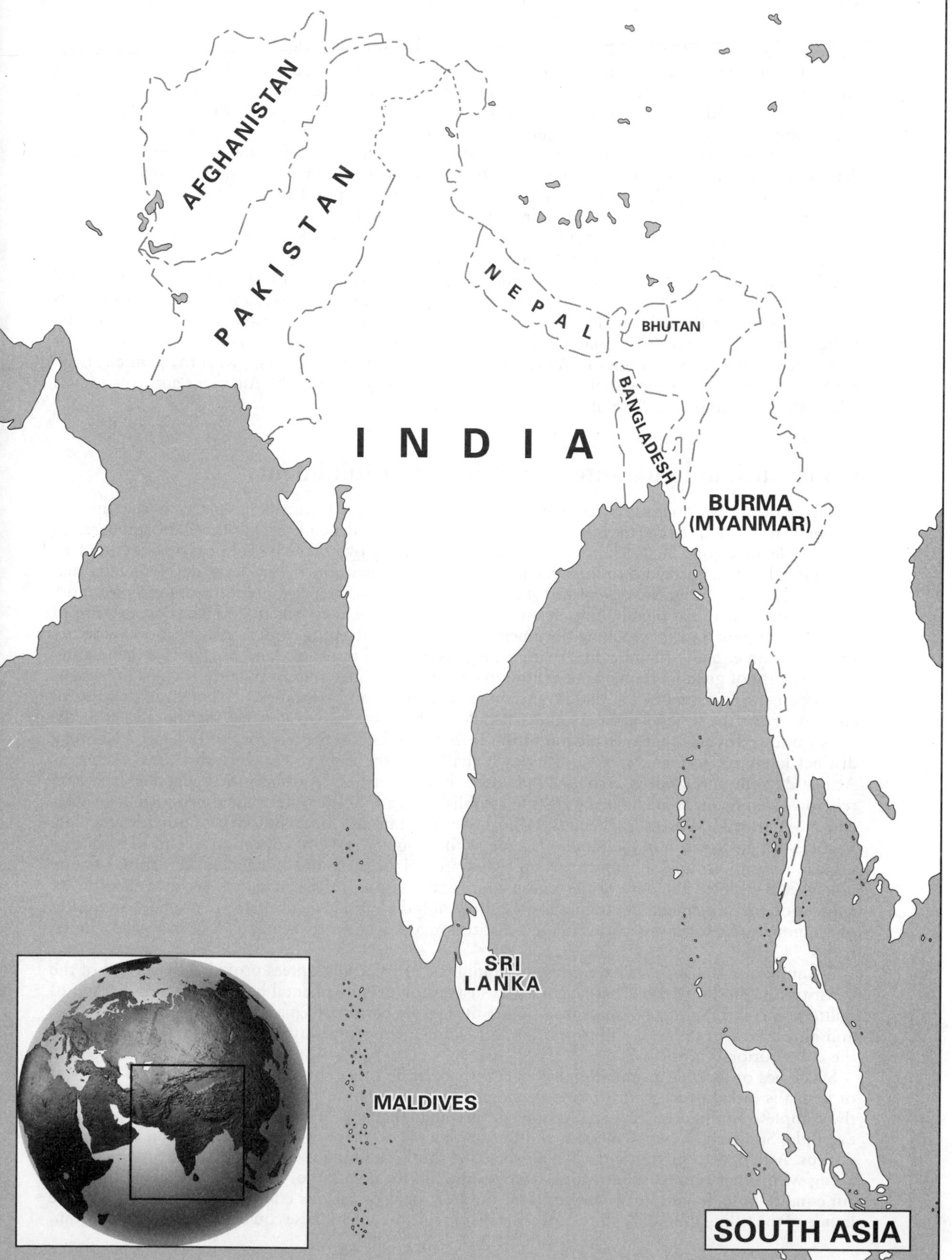
AFGHANISTAN
PAKISTAN
NEPAL
BHUTAN
BANGLADESH
INDIA
BURMA
(MYANMAR)
SRI
LANKA
MALDIVES
SOUTH ASIA

name Sri Lanka in 1972) and Burma gained independence in 1948, the Maldives in 1965. The new states that emerged, in common with those that had not been directly colonized, such as Afghanistan and Nepal, had to face serious challenges from their minorities, including their indigenous peoples. The arbitrary nature of the boundaries of many of the states in the region led to fears of secession and fragmentation. Insensitivity to minority aspirations and unwillingness to compromise, on the part of states, were reflexes in response to aspirations and demands for autonomy and self-determination. There was a determination to build nation-states comprising one dominant culture, language and religion. There was often a denial that a minority problem existed or, as in the case of Pakistan, that there were any ethnic minorities at all.[4] The hypothesis, in so far as Pakistan was concerned, proved wrong when East Pakistan seceded in 1971, in the first, and until recently the only, successful secessionist movement of the post-colonial era.

When confronted with the issue of indigenous rights, some states denied that the term 'indigenous' could legitimately be employed for their peoples. Bangladesh, for example, adopted this stance in its constitutional practices. A noted authority on the subject of indigenous peoples cites Bangladesh and India (as well as China, Indonesia and the former Soviet Union) as having maintained the view that there are no indigenous peoples in Asia, only minorities. This is in keeping with the former Soviet Ambassador Sofinsky's view that 'indigenous situations only arise in the Americas and Australasia where there are imported "populations" of Europeans'.[5]

Constitutional guarantees and their non-fulfilment

The constitutional safeguards to protect minority rights that were put in place at the time of colonialism's retreat from South Asia, and the emergence of independence in the region, appeared to have noble intentions. But such provisions were subsequently overtaken by political realities and lack of political will with regard to implementation, and by constitutional and legal developments that cancelled out the progressive elements of earlier versions, replacing them with legislation of a more Draconian nature. An illuminating example of this process can be taken from the constitution of India, a complex and far-reaching document at the time of drafting. India's constitution combines provisions on equality of individuals with principles designed to protect and consolidate the identity and integrity of groups. Elements of affirmative action or positive discrimination for certain groups are present, for instance: 'for the advancement of socially and educationally backward classes of citizens or for the scheduled castes and scheduled tribes'. For group identity, Article 29 (1) of the constitution provides that 'any section of the citizens residing in the territory of India and having a distinct language script or culture of its own shall have the right to conserve the same'. Whereas Article 29 refers to citizens, Article 30 (1) describes minorities: 'All minorities, whether based on religion or language, shall have the right to establish and administer educational institutions of their choice.' Article 350a provides that it is the goal of every state and local authority 'to provide adequate facilities for instruction in the mother tongue at the primary stage of education to children belonging to minority groups'. Linguistic group rights are balanced against the general direction of state policy; it is deemed the duty of the Union to promote Hindi 'so that it may serve as a medium of expression for all elements of the composite culture of India'. Broad guarantees are provided in respect of religion, and extensive sections in the constitution are devoted to scheduled castes and scheduled tribes.

A number of factors have led to the non-fulfilment of basic guarantees provided by several of the constitutions in the region. These include the suspension of fundamental human rights as a result of military and civilian dictatorships (as in India during the period of Emergency from 1975 to 1977), and also a lack of political will to substantially implement progressive legislation contained within the constitutional framework.

Strategies of forcible assimilation have been apparent in other countries of South Asia. Treatment of Bengalis in Pakistan (prior to the secession of East Pakistan in 1971) amounted to an attempt at the complete annihilation of a civilization, culture and language. Sri Lanka provides a contemporary example. Similarly in Nepal, Bhutan and Burma there is evidence of forced assimilation of minority groups. Attempts to subjugate the Nepali-speaking southern Bhutanese and to eradicate their culture, along with other repressive measures, have resulted in the creation of more than 100,000 refugees. An equally unfortunate story emerges from the treatment of various ethnic groups in Burma at the hands of the ruling junta. The impact of centralizing rule in each of these countries – as in Afghanistan, where the king was an important centralizing influence on political life until the invasion of the Soviet Union, and in the Maldives, where the office of the President is the strongest political entity with few real checks or balances – has been to alienate minority communities and peoples away from the political mainstream and towards more militant and secessionist politics. Pakistan and Bangladesh have had long periods of military dictatorship which prevented any autonomous development on the part of ethnic minorities and indigenous peoples; additionally, emphasis on an Islamic system of government, and its associated rhetoric, has been used to repress the rights of religious minorities.

Concluding observations

Consideration of the predicament of minorities in South Asia leads to some observations which may be of relevance to minorities generally. There is no universally accepted definition of what constitutes a minority, and this perhaps contributes to a significant weakness in the protection of minority groups at the international level. Certain states have not hesitated in exploiting this weakness to their fullest advantage in denying recognition. The case of indigenous peoples poses even greater problems, because the weakness of their position in many countries makes them especially vulnerable to modern political developments.

In this analysis of minority rights, one feature of prime importance is the value of the norms of democracy as a rightful expression of internal self-determination, and autonomy as a right of minorities. Despite the existence of considerable ambiguity as to the precise meaning of 'democracy', in practice democracy may not be too difficult to recognize, since it essentially entails

> minimum standards to be observed by those wielding authority . . . these standards relate to the structures of government, the restraints on government, and the objectives of government; and . . . those standards involve accountability of the institutions of government to those women and men whom they govern and the observance of accepted notions of justice.[6]

'Democracy is not everything.'[7] Unruly and uncaring democracies could probably pose greater threats to the existence of minorities than ineffectual or enlightened dictatorship and, indeed, the whole ideal of minority rights is engineered to protect minorities from dominant majorities. There is hence no guarantee that a democratic regime would be the ultimate panacea for the protection of individual or collective rights. Yet, as one noted authority put it, 'on the whole, democracy tends to march with respect for human rights, and respect for human rights tends to march with freedom under law'.[8] Genuine democracies, it is contended, would cater for the autonomous development of minority groups within the constitutional frameworks of existing states. The emergence of democratic institutions in the states of Pakistan, Bangladesh and Nepal in the 1990s must therefore be taken to be a positive step.

In considering the situation of minorities, practical realities must not be overlooked. The legacy of the colonial era in much of South Asia has made the integration of disparate groups into components of a nation state a hazardous undertaking. We should perhaps acknowledge the complexities involved in this process and not imprudently encourage the fragmentation of existing states. If the right to self-determination is not to exhaust itself or degenerate into perpetual anarchy, it must be regarded as a continuum of rights, forming a natural spectrum from individual human rights at one end to meaningful internal self-determination at the other, and catering adequately for all peoples to pursue their own forms of political, economic, social and cultural development.

Further reading

Barnes, R., Gray, A. and Kingsbury, B. (eds), *Indigenous Peoples of Asia*, Ann Arbor, MI, Association for Asian Studies, 1993.

Engineer, A.A. (ed.), *Ethnic Conflict in South Asia*, Delhi, Ajanta Publications, 1987.

Hannum, H., *Autonomy, Sovereignty and Self-Determination: The Accommodation of Conflicting Interests*, Philadelphia, PA, University of Pennsylvania, 1990.

Heinz, H., *Indigenous Populations, Ethnic Minorities and Human Rights*, Berlin, Quorum Verlag, 1988.

International Work Group for Indigenous Affairs, *The Indigenous World 1995–96*, Copenhagen, IWGIA, 1996.

Nissan, E., *Sri Lanka: A Bitter Harvest*, London, MRG report, 1996.

Rupesinghe, K. and Mumtaz, K. (eds), *Internal Conflicts in South Asia*, London, Sage, 1996.

Thornberry, P., *International Law and the Rights of Minorities*, Oxford, Clarendon Press, 1991.

Vajpeyi, D. and Malik, Y. (eds), *Religion and Ethnic Minority Politics in South Asia*, Glendale, CA, Riverdale, 1989.

Welch Jr, C. and Leary, V. (eds), *Asian Perspectives on Human Rights*, Boulder, CO, Westview Press, 1990.

Afghanistan

Land area:	650,000 sq km
Population:	19.2 million (1995)
Main languages:	Pashtu, Dari (a Farsi dialect) (both national languages)
Main religions:	Islam (majority Sunni, significant minority Shia), Sikhism, Hinduism, Judaism
Main minority groups:	Pashtuns 5,760,000 (30%), Tajiks 5,760,000 (30%), Hazaras 3,072,000 (16%), Uzbeks and Turkmens 2,496,000 (13%), Koochis 1 million–3 million (5–15%), Baluchis 384,000 (2%)
Real per capita GDP:	$800
UNDP HDI/rank:	0.229 (169)

Afghanistan is a landlocked country bordered by Iran to the west, Pakistan to the south and east, the People's Republic of China to the far north-east and the Central Asian republics of Turkmenistan, Uzbekistan and Tajikistan to the north. Its political life has always been dominated by Pashtuns, who make up approximately 30 per cent of the population. They are Sunni Muslims, and their language is Pashtu; about 12 million Pashtuns also live in Pakistan, where they are known as Pathans (see **Pakistan**). Other minorities who are included in this entry include Tajiks, Hazaras, Uzbeks and Turkmens, Koochis (nomads), Baluchis, Nuristanis, Panjsheris and Aimaq.

Afghanistan's modern history has been one of conflict and civil war. Afghanistan's first constitution was drafted in 1923. However, the constitutional monarchy that was introduced in 1964 came to an end with the overthrow of King Zahir Shah by the then Prime Minister (later President) Mohammad Daoud in a coup in 1973. President Daoud was himself overthrown by the People's Democratic Party of Afghanistan (PDPA), a small Marxist-Leninist party which took power in a coup in April 1978. This led to a civil war, which intensified after the entry of Soviet troops in December 1979. The Soviet invasion resulted in the establishment of a puppet communist regime in Kabul and ushered in years of further conflict which have persisted since the Soviet Union withdrew its troops from the country in 1989. During the Soviet occupation the United States maintained through military and financial support an Islamic and fundamentalist opposition against the Soviet and Afghan governmental forces. Regional powers including Pakistan, Iran and Saudi Arabia each supported their own factional groups. Fuelled by outside powers, the civil war has continued to the present. Afghans of all ethnic, religious and linguistic backgrounds are the primary victims of this war. It is estimated that by the end of 1995 more than a million Afghans had perished, while several millions fled to become refugees in neighbouring Pakistan and Iran.

Among those worst affected by the conflict

have been the women and children. Even in the absence of civil strife and political unrest, women have had a very subservient, underprivileged and burdened existence in Afghanistan. Strict purdah means that many spend most of their lives in seclusion, and cultural norms limit their access to health services, education and training. Nine out of ten Afghan women are illiterate; on average they bear seven live children; and their life expectancy, at 42 years, is lower than that of Afghan men. More than a quarter of a million Afghan women have been killed, 100,000 maimed and 300,000 widowed in the civil war. Some 80 per cent of the refugees are women and children, as are most of the internally displaced. With family structures broken, and menfolk killed or absent, Afghan women have taken on heavy additional burdens, often including sole responsibility for children and disabled relatives. Half a million Afghan children depend on widowed women.[1]

After the withdrawal of Soviet forces in February 1989, civil war continued between the Soviet-backed government of President Najibullah and the Afghan guerrilla groups known as the *mojahedin* (holy war fighters), who had fought against the Soviet troops until their withdrawal. *Mojahedin* groups also began to fight among themselves. The United Nations offered to mediate in this conflict between various factions of the *mojahedin*, proposing a peace plan, although this effort collapsed in April 1992. One result of the UN's efforts was the transfer of power to the *mojahedin* faction representing Tajiks from the north, led by Burhanuddin Rabbani, who became President in July 1992. President Rabbani's government was supported by Ahmad Shah Masoud, a former guerrilla commander and prominent Tajik representative. Strong opposition was led by Gulbuddin Hekmatyar, leader of the Hezb-e-Islami faction of the *mojahedin* which represents the Pashtun population.

Civil war between the various Afghan factions has created untold misery. While many people seek to rebuild their lives, the return of thousands of refugees from the borders has added to the problem. There have also been severe abuses of human rights. Between April 1992 and August 1994, according to the International Committee of the Red Cross, 13,500 people were killed and 80,000 wounded in Kabul alone. It has been estimated that more children under the age of five die of disease in Afghanistan than in any other country.[2]

Early 1995 saw the emergence of the Taliban, an army of Islamic jurists, mullahs and seminary students. The origins of this movement are not clear, but many Taliban members were enrolled in religious schools in northern Pakistan as young refugees. Many are ethnic Pashtuns from southern Afghanistan. The Taliban gained control of Kabul in September 1996 and took upon themselves to establish what they regard as an Islamic form of government. Their hard-core policies have adversely affected the rights of minorities and women.

Pashtuns

Pashtuns are seen as the historic founders of the Afghan kingdom and are Sunni Muslim by religious belief. Before 1978 Pashtuns made up about 40 per cent of the Afghan population, living mainly in the east and south of the country adjacent to Pakistan. After the Soviet invasion some 85 per cent of the more than 3 million Afghan refugees in Pakistan were Pashtuns. Pashtuns have always played a central role in Afghan politics, and their dominant position has been a major catalyst in triggering the current conflict. For example, conflict arose between partners in the coalition which fought the Soviet troops and opposed the regime of Najibullah – the regime of President Rabbani represents the Tajik minority, whereas opposition troops led by Gulbuddin Hekmatyar, and those of the Taliban, are mainly Pashtun.

The social structure of the Pashtuns is based on the Pashtunwali (or Pukhtunwali) code. This requires the speaking of Pashtu and adherence to established customs. Hospitality is an important principle, as are a reliance on the tribal council *jirga* for the enforcement of disputes and local decision-making, and the seclusion of women from all affairs outside the home. A major aspect of the Pashtunwali code emphasizes personal authority and freedom. Political leadership is based on personalities rather than on structures or ideologies. Economically, the majority of Pashtuns survive on agriculture and animal husbandry, with some involved in trade.

Despite the dominant position they have held, Pashtuns do not form a homogeneous group, and many have fallen victim to oppression at the hands of their own elites. The power and leadership of individuals are perhaps what divides Pashtuns, not only into different tribes but also into numerous sub-tribes, each isolated within its own borders. Interference in one another's affairs has caused conflicts among sub-tribes throughout their history. Yet, external interference, or interference by the central government, has usually resulted in a unified response.

Tajiks

Tajiks make up about 30 per cent of the Afghan population. Most are Sunni Muslims and speak a form of Farsi close to the national language of Iran. Tajiks are of Central Asian origin, and 4 million of this ethnic group live in the neighbouring Central Asian state of Tajikistan. Tajiks have significant political influence in Afghanistan because of their level of education and wealth. Unlike in the case of Pashtuns, there is no specific Tajik social structure. They are divided between the north, the west, and Kabul, and have adopted the social and cultural patterns of their neighbours.

Hazaras

Constituting about 10 per cent of the Afghan population before 1978, and 16 per cent today, Hazaras live mainly in the central highlands. They follow the minority Shi'a confession and speak Farsi. Hazaras settled in Afghanistan at least as far back as the thirteenth century. Economic pressures and social and political repression have resulted in Hazaras combining with other Shi'a minority groups during the 1960s and 1970s and playing a prominent role in the prolonged civil war for the past two decades.

Hazaras have always lived on the edge of economic survival. From the 1880s onwards and particularly during the reign of Amir Abdul Rahman (1880–1901), they suffered severe political, social and economic repression. As the Pashtun Amir started to extend by force his influence from Kabul to other parts of the country, the Hazaras were the first ethnic group to revolt against his expansionism. Pashtun tribes were sent to the central highlands to crush the revolt. As a result, thousands of Hazara men were killed, their women and children taken as slaves, and their land was occupied. To strengthen the forces against the Hazara rebellion that followed, the Amir played on Sunni religious sensibilities and even attracted Tajiks and Uzbeks (both Sunnis) to help the Pashtuns against the Shi'a Hazaras. Those who survived the initial period of the raids managed to escape to the north. A number fled to British India. Today, the Hazaras make up a significant and influential ethnic group in the Pakistani town of Quetta.

Having lost most of their fertile land to the Pashtuns during this period, and to the nomads in later stages, Hazaras were forced to occupy the dry mountains of the central highlands. Many Hazara males migrated to major Afghan cities and towns, particularly Kabul, and later to Iran and Pakistan. Many of those who migrated with their families to the capital saw their wives working as servants in the houses of middle class Kabulis for minimum wages. Their thrift and industry have enabled Hazaras to establish a strong position in the transport industry.

Uzbeks and Turkmens

Forming together about 13 per cent of the population in 1978 and possibly more today, Uzbeks and Turkmens are Sunni Muslims. They are ethnically and linguistically Turkic, closely related to the people of modern Turkey to the west, and identical to the majority Muslim population of Central Asia across the border to the north. They occupy the greatest share of Afghanistan's arable land in the north. In addition, the production of carpets by Uzbek and Turkmen women has brought considerable supplementary income. Cotton production has added significantly to the wealth of these two groups. Because of their relative prosperity, Uzbeks and Turkmens have not been dependent on the central government and have not attempted to gain political influence.

Koochis

The Koochis – whose name means 'nomad' – are not an ethnic group but a social one in Afghanistan. Nevertheless they have some of the characteristics of a distinct ethnic group. The issue of nomads has long been controversial, both among Afghan government officials and among foreign scholars. Numerous studies give wildly differing figures for the numbers of nomads. Estimates range from 1 million to 3 million. According to some studies in the 1960s and 1970s, each year roughly 2 million Koochi nomads crossed the frontier into Pakistan to reach their winter pastures and returned to Afghanistan for the summer.

Tribes are formed among the Koochis along patrilineal lines. A clan is composed of a core family, their offspring and their families. The leader of the tribe, the Khan, is responsible for the general well-being of the community, for governing the group and for representing it to visitors. Tribes live communally, and on becoming too large separate in order to manage more efficiently. Typically, there are three types of Koochi: pure nomads, semi-sedentary and nomadic traders. The majority are semi-sedentary, living in the same winter area year after year. Pure nomads have no fixed abode, and are dependent on animals for their livelihood; their movements are determined by the weather and the availability of good pasturage. Traders constitute the smallest percentage of Koochis; their main activity is the transport of goods. The semi-pastoral groups are increasingly evolving a sedentary way of life. The majority do so because they can no longer support themselves from their livestock. Life for Koochis is difficult, especially for women. Male and female roles, as in other segments of traditional Afghan society, are rigidly adhered to, men tending to livestock while women are responsible for food and water preparation and for sewing and weaving of clothes and tents. The major responsibility for child-rearing rests with the women.

The nomadic peoples as a whole are a silent minority in Afghanistan, with 10 per cent of the population living in urban areas, 70 per cent in small villages, and 20 per cent as nomads. Farmers receive minimal assistance and Koochis none. The future of Afghanistan's nomadic peoples is not bright. Each tribe is a self contained unit and there is little communication between groups. None of the clans, separately or as a united front, have had any political power or representation within the past national governments. In recent years, the collapse of the central authority and the increasing bitterness with which civil war has been fought have meant deteriorating circumstances for Koochis, threatening their nomadic way of life and providing no adequate substitute.

Baluchis

Baluchis number about 384,000 in Afghanistan, 2 per cent of the population. They live in the pastoral lands of the south-west and south and practise Sunni Islam. Their language is Baluchi, and their main economic activity is agriculture and animal husbandry. Divided between three countries – Pakistan, Iran and Afghanistan – they have a tradition of rebellion against their respective central governments to maintain their autonomy, and they have also had ambitions to create an independent state of Baluchistan. In the past, their demands have faded after they experienced political repression at the hands of all three countries. Unlike the Kurds', the Baluchis' struggle for independence has rarely attracted attention in the outside world.

Nuristanis

Nuristanis have a population of approximately 100,000 in Afghanistan. They reside mainly in the east – between the Pashtun tribes of Kunar, the Kalash in Pakistan's Chitral, and the Tajiks of Badakhshan in the north. Their scattered settlement is another result of Amir Abdul Rahman's late-nineteenth-century expansionism. During his rule, what was then called Kafiristan was converted to Nuristan ('land of light') by forced Islamization of the tribe. Even in recent times, many other ethnic groups were suspicious of them for still being 'kafirs' – a word which can be interpreted as 'infidel'. Nuristan is located in the middle of the Hindu Kush mountain range in four valleys, with each valley having its own distinct language/dialect: Kati, Waigali, Ashkun and Parsun. Nuristan has very little arable land, the vast majority of the territory being covered by forest. The main base of the economy is animal husbandry – mostly goat-herding. A little maize and barley are grown but the Nuristani people survive mainly on milk and milk products. Very few Nuristanis have had access to education. Yet, among those who have travelled to Kabul and been able to gain access to schools, some have gained prominence as well-known figures in the army and the government in Kabul.

Panjsheris

Although Panjsheris are not always classified as a separate group, they are Tajik and display some of the characteristics of a minority, and their important role as a resistance force during Soviet occupation has reinforced this status. Like Nuristanis, they comprise a population of approximately 100,000. They practise Sunni Islam and speak a language known as Panjsheri, a dialect of Dari. They live in the mountainous areas north of Kabul. Again, like Nuristanis, they live in high mountains with limited access to land, and traditionally derive their livelihood from animal husbandry. After Hazaras, Panjsheris form the second largest group of unskilled labourers in Kabul city. A significant number have traditionally worked in semi-skilled professions, as drivers and mechanics. Socially and politically, Panjsheris have been as insignificant as Hazaras and Nuristanis, with only a few people in high-ranking positions in the army and the government in Kabul. All three groups initially remained independent, without affiliation to any political party, during the war with the Soviet Union, but Panjsheris later achieved prominence under the command of Ahmad Shah Masoud, when their army came to control vast areas of northern Afghanistan.

Aimaq

There are estimated to be several hundred thousand Aimaq people living on the steppe land in the north-west. They are a subgroup of the Turkish population. Like Uzbeks and Turkmens, their main economic resource is carpet-weaving; however, they lack rich agricultural land.

Conclusions and future prospects

Afghanistan has a history of political strife and bitter internal feuds. The current situation of a country torn by civil war has resulted in grave violations of individual and collective rights. The role of the international community in efforts to bring peace to Afghanistan has been disappointing, especially when contrasted with the involvement of Pakistan, the United States and other countries during the period of Soviet occupation. With the end of the Cold War, and the Soviet withdrawal, international support and sympathy went into decline as dissensions among various factions within Afghanistan were translated into an open civil war. Prospects for peace are uncertain. Despite its limited role so far, the possibility remains that the UN will bring together Afghanistan's rival factions in an effort to resolve the dispute. The Taliban's forcible seizure of control of the government is another way that the civil war may come to an end. A possible way forward could begin with a future regime pursuing government through policies of reconciliation and bringing together the many ethnic and religious groups of the country. Future power-sharing agreements and forms of government need to take into account the great diversity within Afghanistan and should attempt to evolve a form of government which will address the needs of the various sectors of the community.

Further reading

Amnesty International, *Afghanistan: International Responsibility for Human Rights Disaster*, London, 1995.

Jawad, N., *Afghanistan: A Nation of Minorities*, London, MRG report, 1992.

Wirsing, R.G., *The Baluchis and Pathans*, London, MRG report, 1987.

Minority-based and advocacy organizations

Writers' Union of Free Afghanistan, PO Box 867, University of Peshawar, Pakistan.

Bangladesh

Land area:	143,998 sq km
Population:	128 million (1995)
Main languages:	Bangla (national language), English
Main religions:	Islam, Hinduism, Buddhism
Main minority groups:	Hindus 20,480,000 (16%), Adivasis 1,280,000 (1%), Biharis 250,000–300,000 (0.2%)
Real per capita GDP:	$1,290
UNDP HDI/rank:	0.365 (143)

Bangladesh is surrounded to the west, north-west and east by India, shares a south-eastern border with Burma and has the Bay of Bengal to the south. The People's Republic of Bangladesh emerged as an independent state on 16 December 1971 after a bitter civil war between the Bengalis and the West Pakistan army. Prior to independence, the Bengalis, who formed 54 per cent of the total population of Pakistan (98 per cent of the population of East Pakistan), had serious reason to believe that they were being discriminated against and deprived of their due share in government. Failure of the West Pakistan army and politicians to honour their promise to convene a national parliament after Pakistan's first democratically held elections in December 1970 resulted in the 1971 civil war. The civil war lasted for several months and culminated in the Indo-Pakistan War, the ultimate surrender of Pakistan forces and the creation of the state of Bangladesh.

The years following independence were difficult years for Bangladesh, with economic problems compounded by multiple natural disasters and repeated changes of government following the army take-over from, and assassination of, the founder of independent Bangladesh, Sheikh Mujibur Rahman. Two long periods of military rule were brought to an end by a remarkable movement of popular protest in late 1990, which resulted in general elections in February 1991. In March 1991, Begum Khalida Zia was sworn in as the country's first woman prime minister. The presidential system installed by the former military rulers was abolished in September 1991, and in the resulting constitutional amendments full powers were restored to Jatiya Sangsad, a unicameral legislature consisting of 330 members. The return to democracy alone could not resolve the myriad problems confronting Bangladesh, however. Faced with economic and political instability, the newly formed government became an easy target for the opposition and religious fundamental parties. Persistent political unrest forced Begum Zia to call fresh elections in February 1996. The ruling Bangladesh National Party (BNP) was re-elected to office. The result of the election was, however, suspect as a result of the boycott on the part of the main opposition parties. After a period of political turmoil, protests and unrest the BNP was forced to a second general election of the year in June 1996. In the re-election the Awami League won the largest number of seats and its leader Sheikh Hasina Wajid was sworn in as the country's new prime minister. After by-elections held for fifteen seats on September 1996, the Awami League had secured an absolute majority of 176 seats in the Jatiya Sangsad.

Minority groups making up Bangladesh's total population include several religious groups (Hindus represent the single largest religious minority group) and nearly 1 million Adivasis (indigenous peoples). Biharis form a small but significant minority ethnic group living in and around the capital city Dhaka.

Hindus

Hindus form the largest religious minority group in Bangladesh. Prior to the partition of India, Hindus formed a significant proportion of the population of Bengal. Immediately after the creation of Pakistan, many Hindu families migrated to urban pockets of West Bengal in Calcutta. A similar exodus took place at the time of the civil war in 1971. The 1981 census put the proportion of Hindus to the total population at 12.1 per cent (an absolute figure of approximately 12 million); the Hindu population has grown significantly since, through natural increase and migratory flows. Although Islam was made the state religion of Bangladesh under the Eighth Constitutional Amendment in 1988 (thereby overturning the 1971 constitution which declared Bangladesh to be a secular state), Article 41 of the constitution recognizes other religions and gives citizens the right to practise and promote their religious beliefs. Further provisions of Article 41 guarantee an individual's right to refuse to practise a religion, or to be compelled to be educated in a religion other than their own. Sections 295, 296, 297 and 298 of the Penal Code deal with offences against religious places or practices.

Despite these provisions and the constitutional principle of non-discrimination, Hindus and other observers have alleged that there is covert and overt discrimination against Hindus as well as direct persecution of them. The Eighth Constitutional Amendment was seen by many observers as a step leading towards the imposition of *shari'a* (Islamic law) in Bangladesh, along the same lines as in Pakistan. Fundamentalist agitation directed against Hindus and other religious minorities has increased during the late 1980s and 1990s. Among the most serious incidents were clashes in November 1990 when, against a backdrop of communal disturbances in neighbouring India around the controversy over the Babri mosque, in Ayodhya, India, mobs set fire to Hindu temples in Chittagong and Dhaka. The mobs were whipped up by religious zealots and local leaders using Islam as a pretext for violence against Hindus; according to independent witnesses, police stood in silence nearby. It appears that in many cases the real reason for violence against religious minorities is to pressure them to leave their lands in an attempt to take over these lands.

The most explicit and officially tolerated means of depriving Hindus of their lands has been the use of the Vested Property Act. The roots of the Vested Property Act can be traced to the Enemy Property Ordinance of 1965, promulgated as a consequence of the seventeen-day war between India and Pakistan. Companies, lands and buildings of Indian nationals and those residing in India fell under the control and management of the Pakistan government. Although they were to be returned to their rightful owners after the war ended, the state of war was never officially lifted right up to the time of Bangladesh's independence in 1971, and India, at least for the time being, was not the enemy.[1] However, instead of abrogating the Enemy Act, the newly formed Bangladesh government reinforced its provisions with the Vested and Non-Resident Property (Administration) Act of 1974. The Vested Property Act has been and continues to be applied indiscriminately not only against the Hindus but also against other religious and ethnic minorities.

Adivasis

The term Adivasis (see **India** for etymology), is not confined to any particular geographical or political boundaries but is generally used in the Indian subcontinent to denote indigenous peoples. Like India, Bangladesh has its Adivasis, though their proportion in the population is much smaller, perhaps 1 per cent. The Adivasis of Bangladesh, again like those of India, represent a broad category encapsulating at least twenty-seven different indigenous peoples. Despite their many differences, Bangladeshi Adivasis share major ethnic, cultural, religious and linguistic distinctions from the majority Bengalis. Adivasis inhabit the border areas of the north-west and north-east Chittagong Hill Tracts (CHT) of Bangladesh. Both prior to the creation of Bangladesh and afterwards, successive governments have been reluctant to take a census of the Adivasi population on the basis of language and religion. Government figures of 1981 put Adivasi numbers at 897,828, and the population is now thought to be well over a million. In 1981 43.7 per cent of Adivasis were estimated to be Buddhist, 24.1 per cent Hindus, 13.2 per cent Christian and 19 per cent as following other religions. It is widely believed that the Bangladesh government has deliberately undercounted the Adivasi population to emphasize its marginality. Lower numbers mean that their legitimate demands can be more easily dismissed or ignored by governments and thus excluded from relief aid or development programmes. Undercounting also allows Adivasi land claims to be seen as more tenuous and their traditional ways of life as mere fragments of the past rather than as a living culture.

Almost all Bengalis, including many Adivasis, speak Bangla; and indigenous languages have assimilated many Bangla words as their own. Adivasis who have been formally educated through the school system, mostly males, are more likely to speak Bangla than illiterates, especially illiterate females. By religion the CHT inhabitants are mainly Buddhist, while Khasi and Mandi are predominantly Christian. Other indigenous peoples have retained their original animism or have affiliated with Hinduism, especially the Hajong, while Rajbansi either are Hinduized or have become Sunni Muslims.

The most populous indigenous peoples in Bangladesh are the Santal (200,000), Chakma (195,000), Marma (66,000) and Mandi (60,000). Of these the first and last are considered plains-dwelling Adivasis, with the Mandi living in north-central Bangladesh and the Santal in the north-west. In comparison with Bengalis, Adivasis are generally regarded by Bengalis themselves as more open, friendly, generous and honest. They have a strong relationship with the land and there is a deep interrelationship between their religious beliefs (animism) and their social structure. Whereas communal land ownership represents a vital element of their life pattern, the major problem for all Adivasis is so-called 'land-grabbing' by Bengalis. Although all indigenous land is theoretically considered to be communal land, it was fortunate that plains Adivasis for the most part received individual title deeds to their land under British rule. Communal land claims have proved far more difficult to sustain in law. Yet individual landholdings are also threatened in many ways. These include seizure by trickery or force and, as in the case of Hindus, illegal application of the Vested Property Act. Adivasis generally have been discriminated against and persecuted, although the position of those of the CHT has aroused the greatest concern and gained the most international attention.

The CHT covers 10 per cent of the total area of Bangladesh and is home to twelve or thirteen different indigenous peoples of which Chakma, Marma and Tripura total approximately 90 per cent. Sometimes know collectively as Jumma, because of their traditional shifting – *jum* – method of cultivation, these groups belong to the Tibeto-Burmese language group. Chakma account for more than half the indigenous population of the CHT. They and the Marma are Buddhist, while Tripura are Hindus. Most of the CHT peoples migrated into the area from the south between the sixteenth and nineteenth centuries although the arrival of Bengali settlers forced many CHT peoples to retreat further into the hills. The British colonial period was a less disturbing time for the CHT indigenous peoples and saw the promulgation of laws granting a measure of autonomy, most prominently reflected by the promulgation of the Chittagong Hill Tracts Regulations of 1900. These measures confirmed that in internal matters the CHT was largely self-governing within the recognized structure; and they delineated categories of land, notably *khas* (government) land, specifically excluding non-indigenous peoples from settling in tribal areas.

At the time of the partition of India in 1947 the award of the CHT to East Bengal, despite the fact that it contained almost no Muslim population, raised considerable opposition among the peoples of the CHT. Soon after, the Pakistan government allowed Bengali Muslims to move into the CHT, causing resentment among the indigenous peoples. The pace of Bengali settlement increased once the special status of the CHT was abolished in 1964. The years 1979–83 witnessed large-scale government-sponsored programmes of Bengali settlement in the Hill Tracts.[2] Successive governments have actively pursued this policy, with the aim of forcibly assimilating the indigenous peoples of the CHT as well as depriving them of their lands.

Prior to the creation of Bangladesh, the Kaptai hydroelectric project had a devastating effect on many indigenous peoples. Built in the 1960s, the huge Kaptai dam flooded large tracts of cultivable land. More than 100,000 people – a quarter of the population of the CHT – were displaced. It is estimated that 40,000 environmental refugees fled to India, where many of them are currently living in the north-east state of Arunachal Pradesh, citizens neither of India, which has refused to grant them citizenship, nor of Bangladesh, and having no rights in either.

The civil war of the Bengali people against the West Pakistan military and politicians and its ultimate success, with the overt support of Indian forces, gave renewed hope to the hill peoples of a realization of their right to self-determination. A delegation representing Adivasis petitioned the new government for a restoration of autonomy for the CHT, but it received an unsympathetic response. The government of Sheikh Mujibur Rahman considered the request to be secessionist, and the government launched raids into the CHT in 1972. As a reaction to this the Jana Samhati Samiti (JSS) United People's Party, and its military wing, the Shanti Bahini (peace force), were formed to resist government forces. Numbering up to 15,000, the Shanti Bahini was staffed mainly by Chakma, but also contained Marma and Tripura, and it has since conducted a guerrilla war against the state, with brief interludes at the negotiating table.

During its discussions with the government between October 1987 and February 1988, the JSS put forward a number of demands, contending that this was the only way of protecting Adivasi interests. These demands included: withdrawal of Bengali settlers and the prohibition of future settlements by non-indigenous peoples; withdrawal of all Bangladesh military forces from the CHT; retention of the CHT Regulations of 1900; a specified degree of autonomy within the CHT; guarantees that these provisions could not be changed without a plebiscite within the CHT; economic development to benefit Adivasis; dismantling of the model villages and release of JSS prisoners; and the involvement of international agencies such as the United Nations High Commissioner for Refugees (UNHCR) or the International Committee of the Red Cross (ICRC) in the implementation of such an agreement. Successive governments have failed to accept such terms, particularly where the issue of autonomy is concerned.

Although an apparent cease-fire has been in operation and the government has been negotiating with the JSS since November 1992, massive human rights abuses continue to take place in the CHT. Various non-governmental organizations, including the Chittagong Hill Tracts Commission, Survival International and Anti-Slavery International, have gathered first-hand accounts of ill-treatment and torture, threats and killings, along with army destruction of houses and temples.[3] The attitude of Bengalis towards Adivasis in general is based on culturally inherited stereotypes of Adivasis as primitive or 'jungly' and uncivilized. Many instances of overt discrimination against Adivasis, both by the public as well as by governmental officials, have been recorded, and the most serious threat to the peoples of the CHT remains the policy of depriving them of their lands.

Biharis

The term 'Biharis' refers here to the 250,000 to 300,000 non-Bengali citizens of the former East Pakistan who remain stranded in camps in Bangladesh (many others have assimilated into the Bengali population). Most of these people originated from the north Indian state of Bihar. Today many Biharis also live in Pakistan and India. Like the majority of Bengalis, Biharis are generally Sunni Muslims. Some Biharis migrated to what is now Bangladesh during the period of British colonization of the subcontinent, primarily as skilled craftsworkers on the railways. After the partition in 1947 there was a mass movement of peoples between India and Pakistan. Although transfers of population took place largely across the Punjab, of the 1.3 million who moved to East Pakistan, 1 million were Muslims from Bihar. They came to be known collectively as Biharis.

On arrival in East Pakistan, Biharis found work as small traders, clerks, civil service officials, skilled railway and mill workers, and doctors. Many were appointed by Pakistani officials to replace educated Hindus in administrative jobs and in the mills. The Urdu-speaking Biharis became increasingly unpopular and were seen by Bengalis as symbols of West Pakistani domination, which created a climate of hostility against Biharis. In the December 1970 elections most Biharis supported the pro-Pakistan Muslim League rather than the Awami League, which was largely a Bengali nationalist movement. When the independent state of Bangladesh was formed in December 1971 several thousand Biharis were arrested as alleged collaborators, and there were many cases of retaliation against Biharis.

By mid-1972 the number of Biharis in Bangladesh was approximately 750,000. Some 278,000 were living in camps on the outskirts of Dhaka, another 250,000 were living around Saidpur in the north-west. Reconciliation programmes were initiated, and Urdu-speakers were taught Bengali in an effort to overcome the most obvious obstacle to their acceptance by Bengalis. However, there were, and remain, deep psychological barriers to overcome, and most Biharis feared further retaliation. The majority of Biharis in Bangladesh have consequently expressed a wish to be repatriated to Pakistan. The Pakistani government initially agreed to take 83,000 Biharis; the number was later increased. By 1974 108,000 had been transferred to Pakistan, and by 1981 163,000.

During the 1980s there were new initiatives to resettle Biharis in Pakistan but these have resulted in few concrete results. In July 1988, President Zia-ul-Haq, partly in the inertia of his rhetoric of Islamization and partly because of his own Mohajir background (see **Pakistan**) and genuine sympathy for the plight of Biharis, signed an agreement with the World Muslim League which provided for the resettlement of the Biharis. His assassination in August 1988 left the matter in limbo. The outcome of Pakistan's national elections in 1988 provided the Mohajir Quami Movement (MQM), which has been the most enthusiastic supporter of Bihari settlement in Pakistan, with an opportunity to extract concessions from the two main contenders for the government. A deal was struck with the Pakistan People's Party in which the PPP promised that 'all Pakistanis living abroad by choice or by compulsion had the same rights as citizens of Pakistan'.[4] The terms of the agreement were ambiguous, and its realization seemed impossible in so far as the Biharis were concerned. The first air flight of Biharis from Bangladesh to Pakistan was cancelled in January 1989 after protests by the Sindhi National Alliance and Punjabi-Pakhtun Itehad.[5] The Bihari issue contributed immensely to the straining of relations between the MQM and the PPP in Pakistan, ultimately leading to the breakdown of the coalition. A new agreement stated that 'all stranded Biharis in Bangladesh shall be issued Pakistan passports and in the meantime arrangements shall be made to repatriate them to Pakistan immediately'.[6]

Entering into such an ambitious programme of action was one thing, its implementation was quite another. Although settlement procedures for Biharis were initiated, with the first batch of 323 Biharis arriving in Lahore in January 1993 and being housed near Okara in Punjab, further settlements had to be stalled, due largely to opposition both from within the ranks of the governments and from the local population. The political, economic and cultural ramifications of a group of such numerical strength, as well as distinct ideological and political convictions, would, it is feared, generate tensions in Punjab while at the same time exacerbating already existing divisions in the urban Sindh.

The camps in Bangladesh still face difficulties and discrimination. Their past allegiance to the West Pakistan army has not been forgotten and has led to attempts to try some Biharis on charges of war crimes during the Bangladesh war of independence in 1971.[7] Biharis in Bangladesh generally describe themselves as 'stranded Pakistanis', and some have organized themselves into the Pakistani General Repatriation Committee, which advocates militant action to achieve repatriation. Camp conditions are in many cases appalling.[8] The Bihari community as a whole feels humiliated and betrayed by successive Pakistan governments. Yet, existing political divisions in Pakistan make the prospect of their resettlement a forlorn hope. The recently dismissed PPP government's determination to purge urban Sindh of illegal immigrants, and its assertion of complete unwillingness to accept any Biharis, led to a diplomatic row in December 1995, when 288 Bengali-speaking Muslims were deported from Pakistan.[9]

Conclusions and future prospects

After two and a half decades as an independent sovereign state, Bangladesh finds itself confronted with chronic political and economic instability.

An unprecedented rate of population growth, massive and rising unemployment and a high rate of inflation, along with frequent natural disasters such as the devastating cyclone in April 1991 followed by serious floods two months later, have not helped democracy establish its roots. So far as the protection of the rights of minorities is concerned, the rise of religious fundamentalism has been a source of serious concern. The treatment of the Hindu community in the aftermath of the razing of the Babri mosque and other incidents reflected the tenuous position of religious minorities. More significantly, the pressure on the government of Begum Zia to bring to trial the writer-activist Taslima Nasreen for alleged blasphemy, and widespread militant Islamic factionalism, reflects the rising surge of fundamentalism which cannot be a positive sign for an improvement of the position of religious minorities. The role of the government as well as the law enforcement agencies in violating the rights of Adivasis is a matter of further grave concern. Although the ending of military rule is a welcome sign, return to democracy alone cannot resolve the myriad problems of Bangladesh, particularly those facing minority peoples. The challenge for present and future governments of Bangladesh is to find a balance between dealing with the severe economic situation, on the one hand, and ensuring social justice and the protection of the rights of all its people, on the other.

Further reading

Amnesty International, *Unlawful Killings and Torture in the Chittagong Hill Tracts*, London, September 1986.

Chittagong Hill Tracts Commission (CHTC), *Life Is Not Ours: Land and Human Rights in the Chittagong Hill Tracts*, London, 1991.

Roy, R.D., 'The problem of dispossession of lands of indigenous peoples of the Chittagong Hill Tracts by government-sponsored migrants: in search of a solution', paper presented at an Open Dialogue and Seminar on the Chittagong Hill Tracts Problems and its Solution, organized by the National Committee for the Protection of Fundamental Rights in CHT, German Cultural Centre, Dhaka, Bangladesh, June 1995.

Timm, R.W., *The Adivasis of Bangladesh*, London, MRG report, 1991.

Minority-based and advocacy organizations

Ain O Salish Kendra, Human Rights and Legal Aid Centre, 26/3 Purana Paltan Lane, PO Box 3252, Dhaka 1000, Bangladesh; tel. 880 2 835 851, fax 880 2 833 966, e-mail: hameada.ask@driktap.tool.nl.

Amnesty International, 100 Kalabagan, 2nd Lane, Dhaka 1205, Bangladesh; tel./fax 880 2 818 938.

Association for Social Advancement, 5/12 Block B, Humayun Road, Mohammadpur, PO Box 2507, Dhaka 1207, Bangladesh.

Bangladesh Human Rights Commission, 77 Purana Paltan Lane, 1st Floor, Dhaka 1000, Bangladesh.

Bangladesh Indigenous and Hill Peoples' Association for Advancement, Plot No. 4, Mirpur 13, Dhaka 1221, Bangladesh; tel. 880 2 802 686/ 838 844, fax 880 2 804 803.

Chittagong Hill Tracts Women's Federation, Baikali-9, Road No. 7, Dhanmondi Dhaka, Bangladesh.

Commission for Justice and Peace, GPO Box 5, Dhaka 1000, Bangladesh; tel. 880 2 417 936, fax 880 2 834 993.

Coordinating Council for Human Rights in Bangladesh, 113 Siddesari Road, Dhaka 1217, Bangladesh.

Hill Watch Human Rights Forum, 470 October Smriti Bhavan, Jagannath Hall, Dhaka University, Dhaka, Bangladesh.

Institute for Law and Development, 369 Outer Circular Road, 1st Floor, Rajarbag, Dhaka, Bangladesh.

Institute of Democratic Rights, House No. 13, Road No. 7, Dhanmondi R/A, Dhaka 1205, Bangladesh.

Justice and Peace Commission, PO Box 5, Dhaka 1000, Bangladesh.

ODHIKAR, 3/6 Shegun Bagicha, Dhaka 1000, Bangladesh; tel. 880 2 813 014.

Society for Environment and Human Development, 44/8 North Dhanmondi, 2nd Floor, West Panthapath, Dhaka 1025, Bangladesh; fax 880 2 810 254.

Bhutan

Land area:	46,500 sq km
Population:	1.7 million (1995)
Main languages:	Dzongkha (national language)
Main religions:	Buddhism (state religion), Hinduism
Main minority groups:	Nepali-speakers 595,000 (35%), indigenous and others 170,000 (10%)
Real per capita GDP:	$790
UNDP HDI/rank:	0.307 (159)

Bhutan is a small mountainous Buddhist kingdom located in the southern slopes of the eastern Himalayas, squeezed between India and China. Bhutan borders the Indian states of Arunachal Pradesh to the east, Assam and West Bengal to the south, and Sikkim to the south-west. To the north, Bhutan borders Tibet, ruled by China. From the seventeenth century, when the foundation of present-day Bhutan was carved out of the smaller holdings of local religious and secular strongmen, to the beginning of the twentieth century, Bhutan was a theocracy ruled by the reincarnate *shabdrung*, a temporal and spiritual Buddhist leader, similar to Tibet's Dalai Lama.

Plagued by local feuds and instability, the *shabdrung*'s government was supplanted by the current hereditary monarchy of the Wangchuck dynasty in 1907. The present King, Jigme Singye, is the fourth of the Wangchuck line to occupy the throne. Bhutan is the stronghold of the *drukpa kargyud* school of Mahayana Buddhism, the state religion. The different peoples who follow the sect are collectively known as the *drukpa*, though this label is also used to refer to all of the people of Bhutan. The diverse ethnic groups who are *drukpa* Buddhists are a combination of the earliest inhabitants of the country and the immigrant Tibetan and Mongoloid peoples who settled in Bhutan as late as the tenth and eleventh centuries.

The Bhutanese population comprises many distinct peoples, but four ethnic groups – Ngalong, Sarchop, Kheng and Nepali-speakers – make up 98 per cent of the population. Ngalongs, Sarchops and Khengs comprise the *drukpa* group, although each has a distinct identity as well. Ngalongs are people of western Bhutan and of Tibetan origin; they form the ruling and social elite.

Dzongkha, Bhutan's national language, is derived from Ngalong speech and has been imposed on the entire country since 1988. Sarchops are possibly the earliest settlers of Bhutan and share the same religion as the Ngalong, but they have their ethnic roots in Arunachal Pradesh and are of Indo-Mongoloid rather than Tibetan descent. Khengs are inhabitants of central Bhutan and may be indigenous people of Bhutan. All three groups are culturally integrated to some extent.

Numerous other ethnic groups are present in Bhutan on a much smaller scale: Adivasi, Birmi, Brokpa, Doya, Lepcha, Tibetan and Toktop. These smaller groups, though adding great diversity to Bhutan's ethnic make-up, represent approximately 10 per cent of the total population. Nepali-speakers are a mostly Hindu ethnic group, predominantly based in the south of Bhutan and called *lhotshampa*, literally southern border people, by the *drukpa*.

Although no reliable figures are available, it is estimated that at least a third of the population of Bhutan comprises Nepali-speaking people, a proportion that has increased in recent decades. Despite their growing numbers, Nepali-speaking Bhutanese have been the victims of persecution in recent times and therefore form the focus of this entry.[1]

Nepali-speakers

The Nepali-speaking people of southern Bhutan live mainly in the southern belt and are relatively recent immigrants to the area.[2] They comprise a combination of caste and ethnic groups, including Bahun, Chhetri, Gurung, Limbu, Newar, Rai and Tamang. Effectively, however, they form a single community bound together by the common Nepali tongue and the Hindu religion. Nepali-speaking people began migrating into Bhutan in significant numbers in the mid-nineteenth century, eventually accounting for at least a third of the country's population. However, in early 1996 nearly 100,000 people from Bhutan, the large majority of them Nepali-speakers, were residing in refugee camps in Nepal as a result of a series of discriminatory measures pursued by the Bhutanese government beginning in the 1980s.[3]

Several factors have contributed to the present situation. A number of efforts, principally the 1958 and 1977 legislation to regularize citizenship, culminated in the 1985 Citizenship Act. The act contains provisions to the detriment of Nepali-speaking Bhutanese people and appears to have been applied in an arbitrary manner. The act can be used to exclude from citizenship many people who are not members of the dominant ethnic group, as well as those who oppose government policy by peaceful means.

A census operation to identify illegal immigrants and Bhutanese nationals, which started in 1988 and still reportedly continues, gave rise to fears that those not recognized as Bhutanese nationals would be forced to leave the country. These fears were borne out by the arbitrary fashion in which the census was conducted, and by the way opposition to government policy among sections of the southern Bhutanese population was suppressed by government forces. After 1988 a process of systematic discrimination was begun, with people being required to provide written proof of residency in Bhutan in 1958. In 1992 'illegal' families were forced to sign 'voluntary leaving certificates' and evicted from land with little or no compensation, while those identified as 'anti-nationals' and their families were harassed, imprisoned and tortured.

Forced eviction has been the main form of discrimination against, and repression and exclusion of, Nepali-speakers. Other more subtle mechanisms have also been adopted, for example the policy of national integration on the basis of northern Bhutanese traditions and culture, decreed by King Jigme Singye in January 1989. This policy has aroused fears that the government intends to erase Nepali culture in Bhutan by requiring the whole population to adopt distinctive northern Bhutanese practices.

The cultural code imposed a form of dress – the traditional *gho* (for males) and *kira* (for women) – that was to be worn during such activities as schooling and visiting government and local administrative offices and monasteries. The integration policy also involves a code of conduct stipulating how people should behave on certain occasions. Failure to comply with the code has been declared punishable with imprisonment or a fine. The royal decree also included a halt to the teaching of the Nepali language.

As a result of the discriminatory stance of the government, the arbitrary implementation of the citizenship legislation, and the intimidation and harassment of Nepali-speakers, a large outflow of refugees to Nepal began in mid-1991. Previously, only about 10,000 people had left Bhutan, but in June 1991 a campaign of forced eviction began. By December 1991 a mass exodus had built up, continuing until late 1992. Although the flow of refugees diminished thereafter, Nepali-speaking Bhutanese refugees in Nepal numbered at least 85,000 by mid-1993. Health-related problems have emerged in the refugee camps, stemming from malnutrition, poor sanitation and disease.

Conclusions and future prospects

Talks began on the refugee question in November 1992 between the governments of Bhutan and Nepal, but the negotiations made little headway. The Bhutanese government refused to recognize Nepali-speakers as citizens, asserting that only a small number could be legitimately resettled in Bhutan. Further attempts were made to resolve the crisis through mediation and deliberation. King Jigme Singye of Bhutan and the Prime Minister of Nepal discussed the matter in Dhaka in April 1993, and further talks in July 1993 led to the establishment of a joint ministerial committee with the mandate to (1) determine the different categories of people claiming to have come from Bhutan in the refugee camps in eastern Nepal; (2) specify the position of the two governments on each of these categories; and (3) arrive at a mutually acceptable agreement on each of these categories as a basis for the resolution of the problem.

The joint committee had its first sitting in 1993 in Kathmandu and agreed to categorize the refugee population into four groups: (1) bonafide Bhutanese forcibly evicted; (2) Bhutanese who emigrated; (3) non-Bhutanese; and (4) Bhutanese who have committed criminal acts. No agreement was reached about the criteria or the mechanism to be used to decide which categories people would be placed in. Despite continuation of the talks (the last session being held in April 1996) no concrete steps have been taken towards repatriation of the refugees.

Nepal has shown concern for the plight of Nepali-speaking Bhutanese, but is not in a position to keep the refugees indefinitely in its territory. Despite Nepal's requests to India to exert diplomatic pressure on the government of Bhutan to facilitate the return of the refugees, India has refrained from becoming directly involved in the matter. One hundred and fifty Bhutanese refugees were arrested by West Bengal police in January 1996 when they attempted to cross from Nepal into India.

It may take years to repatriate all the refugees. The United Nations High Commissioner for Refugees considers that realistically they will not go home until the turn of the century. Repatriation remains the only permanent solution to the problem, but the refugees need reassurances regarding their democratic rights in Bhutan.

Further reading

Amnesty International, *Bhutan: Forcible Exile*, London, August 1994.

Amnesty International, *Bhutan: Human Rights Violations against the Nepali-speaking Population in the South*, London, December 1992.

Dhakal, D.N.S. and Strawn, C., *Bhutan: A Movement in Exile*, New Delhi, Nirala Publications, 1994.

Minority-based and advocacy organizations

People's Forum for Human Rights Bhutan, EPC 5028, GPO 8975, Kathmandu, Nepal.

Burma

Land area:	676,552 sq km
Population:	43.7 million (1995)
Main languages:	Burmese (national language)
Main religions:	Buddhism, Christianity, Islam
Main minority groups:[1]	Karen 4 million (9.1%), Shan 1.6–2.5 million (3.7–5.7%), Mon 1.2–3.5 million (2.7–8%), Chin 1–1.5 million (2.3–3.4%), Kachin 1–1.5 million (2.3–3.4%), Arakanese Muslims, 690,000 (1.6%), Karenni 250,000 (0.6%)
Real per capita GDP:	$650
UNDP HDI/rank:	0.451 (133)

Burma – renamed Myanmar by its rulers in 1989 (the new name is not fully recognized internationally) – is located to the east of India and Bangladesh and to the south-west of the People's Republic of China. It is a country of enormous ethnic diversity, containing approximately 135 major ethnic groups and seven ethnic minority states, in addition to seven divisions, populated mainly by the Burman majority. Burma's geographic position has resulted in the country attracting settlers from many different backgrounds throughout its long history.

Today, minority ethnic groups are estimated to make up at least one third of the country's total population and to inhabit half the land area. An acknowledgement of this existence of a multitude of ethnically diverse groups is even made by the State Law and Order Restoration Council (SLORC), which has ruled Burma with an iron fist since 1988. While conceding that Burma consists of as many as '135 national races' the SLORC nonetheless has not come up with any reliable data on ethnic numbers.

Burma gained independence from the British in 1948, and was ruled by the civilian U Nu until 1962. That year, after a military coup, General Ne Win took over, ruling until 1988. During General Ne Win's regime, the 1947 constitution, which had outlined an essentially federal structure for independent Burma, including guarantees of secession for certain ethnic minority states, was replaced in 1974 by a new constitution which created a more centralized state and withdrew many of the provisions guaranteeing rights of ethnic minority groups agreed in 1947.

The repressive regime of General Ne Win was eventually challenged by the people of Burma in 1988, when riots swept through the capital,

Rangoon, and for a period it looked as though the people's will would prevail and democracy would be established. However, the army regained control in September 1988 and cracked down on the democratic movement, putting hundreds of people in jail and ushering in the SLORC era. The SLORC began by promising elections. But when the election results of 1990 showed a landslide victory for the opposition National League for Democracy (NLD), led by Aung San Suu Kyi (daughter of the founder of independent Burma, Aung San), the government was quick to declare the elections null and void and to impose complete dictatorial control over the country.

The period since 1990 has seen severe repression against the many ethnic minority groups of Burma, many of which are living in exile on the borders with Thailand and have taken recourse to armed struggle to oppose the repressive policies of the SLORC. There has also been an exodus from Burma of several groups, most notably by the Rohingya Muslim population who fled to neighbouring Bangladesh to escape oppression at the hands of the SLORC regime.

Ethnic-minority resistance and international pressure to call the Burmese government to account have resulted in some changes in the situation. Aung San Suu Kyi was released in 1995 after a long period of house arrest. Cease-fires have been agreed with fourteen armed groups representing ethnic minorities. International observers have been allowed to visit Burma, and discussions on the new constitution have slowly moved forward. All these developments have given the SLORC regime surface respectability, enabling a certain amount of international trade and business to be carried out with the government, and the prospects of Burma re-entering the international political and diplomatic arena after many years of isolation.

The main ethnic groups living in the seven ethnic minority states of Burma are the Karen, Shan, Mon, Chin, Kachin, Arakanese and Karenni; each of these is described below. Other main groups include the Nagas, who live in north Burma and are estimated to number about 100,000, constituting another complex family of Tibeto-Burmese subgroups. The great majority of Nagas, more than million, live in India (see **India**), and the possibility of a Naga self-administered zone is being considered under the SLORC's new constitution.

Karen[2]

Karen are a little-documented community but, together with related subgroups in Burma, make up the second largest ethnic group in the country. The actual population figures remain in dispute, with the Karen National Union (KNU) claiming more than 7 million. The SLORC say the figure is approximately 2.5 million, and anthropologists put the figure at 4 million, with another 200,000 currently residing in Thailand.

Karen live throughout much of lower Burma but do not occupy a single geographical region. There are a large number of subgroups (over twenty), but more than 70 per cent come from two subgroups, the Sgaw and Pwo. The main political representation is through the KNU, which was formed in 1947 and is militantly nationalist. The majority of Karen are Buddhists, although large numbers converted to Christianity during British rule.

Karen experienced a sense of liberation, and release from oppression by Burman kings, under British rule, and this led in turn to ethnic polarization which continues today. The Karen also have a legitimate concern in that they have become a minority in their own Karen state with less than 25 per cent of the Karen population of Burma. It is thus not surprising to note a pervading sense of underrepresentation with the conviction that a future settlement would require a fair and equitable political demarcation. Karen have probably seen the most severe reversals of fortune since independence, with few Karen in any prominent national positions. The entire Karen region has collapsed, quashing dreams at independence of a prosperous free state of Kawthoolei – declared in 1949 by the KNU, but ruthlessly dealt with by the Ne Win regime, including the forced relocation of entire communities. Following the formation of the National Democratic Front (NDF), which aims at federation within Burma and which the KNU played a leading role in establishing, KNU demands for secession have been largely ignored.

Shan

The Shan state stretches over a vast highland plateau, measuring 155,801 square kilometres. Claims have been made by Shan nationalists that ethnic Shans comprise more than half of the state's estimated 6 million inhabitants. However, the SLORC puts the figure at just 1.64 million out of a total of 4.25 million. Other ethnic groups with significant numbers include Paaung, Wa, Kachin, Danu, Lahu, Akha, Pao, Kokang Chinese and possibly Kayan, each with a distinct language, tradition and background. The Shan state was given the right of secession after a ten-year trial period, but this was rejected after the coming to power of the Ne Win regime. Recent cease-fire arrangements give a surface appearance of peace; however, while political conditions remain fluid, the very existence of the Shan people is precarious. The SLORC continues to use its growing military presence to divide and rule. Only four of the elected nationalist parties – Shan, Pao, Kokang and Lahu – were accepted as legal and allowed to attend the SLORC's National Convention. After decades of bitter internal conflict the need for a humanitarian operation among the Shan is greater than ever before. Reports from various internal agencies reveal a consistent pattern of gross violation of human rights by the military authorities. Enslavement and torture are manifested in several forms. While male children are conscripted into militia, female children and young women escaping these cruelties are often forced to flee across the border and enter into prostitution.

Mon

Tracing their ancestry to the large Mon-Khmer dynasty, Mon have claims to an ancient civilization with a rich culture and literature. In contemporary terms, however, four decades of conflict have left Mon people devastated and displaced, with threats to their lands, language and culture. Mon nationalists contend that Mon number about 4 million. The SLORC puts the figure at just over a million. The official figure of Mon refugees in Thailand is about 10,000, although in reality their numbers could be closer to 100,000. There is a ban on Mon language after primary level in state schools, and there is considerable evidence of discrimination and persecution of Mon intellectuals and political activists. In recent years the Burmese army has conducted persistent raids in Mon villages, allegedly causing severe human rights violations, including enforced labour, displacement, rape and murder. As a result, there has been a mass exodus of Mon to Thailand.

After independence, Mon political demands were largely ignored, with no explicit recognition of Mon territorial claims. Following the lead of Karen insurrection, Mon also raised an insurgency. Under a ceasefire agreement it was subsequently decided to create a Mon state, although it took another sixteen years before the 1974 constitution accorded formal recognition to the Mon state. Mon nationalism continued after the 1962 coup when the present-day New Mon State Party (NMSP) took up arms. The NMSP has supported the continued revival of a Mon cultural movement. The Mon National Democratic Front won five seats in the 1990 elections, but was then deregistered by the SLORC. With little international support for the cause of the Mon people, in early 1994 the NMSP entered a cease-fire agreement and started negotiating with the SLORC. The relatively weak position of the Mon at the negotiating table does little to suggest a favourable outcome to these talks.

Chin

Chin are people of Tibeto-Burmese origin, inhabiting a vast mountain chain covering western Burma through to Mizoram in north-east India. More than forty different subgroups have been identified among the estimated 11.5 million Chin in Burma. The 1974 constitution finally established the Chin state, improving the previous administrative demarcation of the Chin special division. The practical impact of this administrative change was, however, minimal, as the Chin continue to suffer from neglect and marginalization. With the Chin firmly at the bottom of Burma's educational league table, and with only one major road crossing their territory, development prospects for them look bleak. Chin leaders are wary of proposals for development initiated by the SLORC regime, fearing that these are intended to change the ethnic balance in the local population.

The return of seven nationalists and five National League for Democracy candidates in the 1990 elections reflected the Chin people's clear preference for autonomy and the restoration of democratic institutions. In response, the SLORC ordered the arrest of two MPs and declared all Chin political parties illegal. Forced relocations of Chin took place, and thousands of dissidents went into exile. The accounts of refugees arriving in India indicate that many casualties have resulted from ill-treatment and lack of food during population transfers. Many Chin youth have opted to join the Burmese army as a means of escaping from poverty. This has resulted in Chin being held up as an example of successful cooperative development with their Burman cousins. Although the Chin have not been prominent in insurrections when compared with other ethnic groups, nationalist feelings run high among them, and attempts by the regime to bring them into the mainstream of Burma's development remain unpredictable in outcome.

Kachin

Among the many ethnic groups inhabiting north-east Burma, the Kachin deserve a special mention, for they have been most vociferous and determined in their demands for the establishment of a federal or independent nation state. The nationalist movement has led to the creation of a strong political identity among the estimated 1–1.5 million Kachin (more than two-thirds of whom are Christians), made up of different subgroups, including Jinghpaw, Maru, Lashu, Atsi, Nung-Rawang and Lisu, all of them enmeshed in a set-up of clans and tribes. The Kachin state, comprising an area of 89,042 square kilometres, was created under the 1947 constitution. In the 1960s the Kachin armed nationalist movement gathered momentum with the formation of the Kachin Independence Organization (KIO). The movement has suffered heavily during the SLORC era, and against this background of conflict, poverty has continued to increase. A cease-fire agreement was formally signed on 2 February 1994 between the KIO and SLORC. Although grave political and human rights problems remain, for the first time in three decades co-development and economic projects are under discussion.

Arakanese Muslims

The territory of Arakan is home to the Arakanese people, divided between the majority Rakhine people (who are Buddhists) and the minority Rohingya Muslims. Despite formal recognition of the 36,778 square kilometre Arakan state and its official name of Rakhine under the 1974 constitution, tensions between the state and the Burmese government, as well as among the peoples of the state themselves, have continued for a number of years. The most serious problem has been violations of the rights of the Muslim population, including a 1978 census operation to check identity cards that was targeted against the Muslim population. More than 200,000 Muslims fled into neighbouring Bangladesh at this time, amid reports of killings and torture. The situation further declined after the assumption of power by the SLORC regime. By July 1992 more than 260,000 Arakanese Muslims had fled into Bangladesh, and several international agencies produced reports documenting the human rights violations perpetrated against their community. There has been widespread international pressure on the Burmese government to stop military action and begin a process to enable the Muslim population to return home. By early 1995, 155,000 had reportedly been repatriated. However, it appears that in most cases repatriation was not voluntary. According to a report published by the US Committee for Refugees:

'Throughout their stay in Bangladesh, the safety and welfare of the refugees have been issues of concern. Reports by USCR, Refugees International, Amnesty International and Human Rights Watch (Asia) documented severe and systematic abuses of the refugees by camp officials, the police, and the local populace. Beatings, torture, and the deprivation of food and shelter have been at the forefront of these concerns.'[3]

Karenni

Karenni constitute an estimated 250,000 inhabitants of present-day Kayah state. More than a dozen ethnic groups live in this mountain region of 11,730 square kilometres, and most are related to the Karen, such as Kayan, Kayow and Paku. In addition, there is a small Shan minority, and recent years have also seen an influx of Burman immigrants. The constitution of 1947 had accorded the Karenni state the right to secede following a trial period of ten years. However, in 1948 the Karenni leader U Bee Htu Re was assassinated. His assassination led to an insurgency which has continued to this day. As a reaction to the nationalist movements, successive governments have tried to repress any demands for Karenni independence, and the constitutional right to secede on the part of Karenni was eventually abolished by the 1974 constitution. Lack of development has left Kayah state very poor, and some Karenni leaders still look forward to secession as the ultimate solution. In January 1994, ceasefires between the Karenni National Progressive Party and the rival left-wing Karenni Nationalities People's Liberation Front brought the prospects of peace a little nearer. There continue to be reports of serious violations of individual and collective human rights. Added to this, and as a consequence of these violations, several thousand Karenni remain as refugees in Thailand.

Conclusions and future prospects

Ever since its independence in 1948, Burma has been torn between political strife and ethnic unrest. An imposing military presence has for years suppressed the democratic aspirations of the peoples of Burma, and in the process, ethnic minorities have been particularly targeted and victimized. Since

1988, when the SLORC assumed power, several hundred thousand people have been forced to become refugees. Many small minority groups such as the Karen have as many as 20 per cent of their population either displaced within Burma or taking refuge in neighbouring Thailand. Prospects of peace for Burma's ethnic minority groups depend on the possibility of constitutional reforms and autonomy for minorities. Thus, while future constitutional talks hold an important key to the way in which Burmese politics will evolve, changes in the human rights situation and commitments to economic development and social justice, under whatever form of government the country adopts in the coming years, will be equally crucial for Burma's minority populations.

Further reading

Smith, M., *Burma: Insurgency and the Politics of Ethnicity,* London, Zed Books, 1991.

Smith, M., *Ethnic Groups in Burma,* London, Anti-Slavery International, 1994.

Minority-based and advocacy organizations

All Burma Students' Democratic Front (ABSDF), PO Box 1352, GPO, Bangkok 10501, Thailand; tel./fax 66 2 300 0613.

India

Land area:	3,287,263 sq km
Population:	953 million (1996)
Main languages:	Hindi (official), English, Urdu
Main religions:	Hinduism, Islam, Sikhism, Christianity, Janism, Buddhism, Judaism
Main minority groups:	Dalits (scheduled castes) 145,360,000 (15.8%), Muslims 104,880,000 (11.4%), Adivasis (scheduled tribes) 69,000,000 (7.5%) including Nagas 700,000 (0.1%); also Christians 22,080,000 (2.4%), Sikhs 13 million (1.4%), Kashmiris 8.6 million (est., 0.9%) Buddhists 6,440,000 (0.7%), Jews, Anglo-Indians, Andaman Islanders
Real per capita GDP:	US $1,240
UNDP HDI/rank:	0.436 (135)

The Republic of India is one of the largest countries in the world, sharing a northern frontier with Tibet in the People's Republic of China, and with Nepal and Bhutan. To the north-west it borders Pakistan, to the north-east Burma and to the east Bangladesh. India's great southern peninsula stretches far down into the tropical waters of the Indian Ocean, where its territorial boundaries extend to the Andaman and Nicobar Islands in the Bay of Bengal and the Lakshadweep archipelago in the Arabian Sea. India is more like a continent than a country, with a population larger than that of Western Europe and the United States. India is also the birthplace of two of the most widely practised world religions, Hinduism and Buddhism, and has within its borders a greater number of the followers of Islam than any country of the Middle East or North Africa. India could in many ways be described as a nation of minorities, yet it is nevertheless overwhelmingly Hindu. Although Hinduism may be seen as the one unifying thread running through the country as a whole, Hinduism is not a homogeneous religion. Its centuries-old traditions have been shaped by, and have in turn shaped, several different religious and social traditions. More importantly, cultural traditions often have much deeper resonances in India than those shaped by religion.

A serious threat to India's multicultural, multi-ethnic, multi-religious polity comes from the rise of an aggressive Hindu fundamentalism which has taken political root in the last decade or so. The subcontinent has already witnessed the horrors of religious division through the experience of partition at the time of independence in 1947. Partition not only took a terrible toll of life, with an estimated 1 million victims, it also gave rise to one of the largest transfers of population in the twentieth century. The threat of Hindu fundamentalism has raised fears among the country's many different religious, ethnic and cultural minorities, regarding the future of India's democratic structures and the role of the state in ensuring the protection of minority rights. Religion is not, however, the only, or even the most significant, fault line in India's multi-layered polity. Economic transformation, and the lack of it in many cases, has led to the rise of extremism in various parts of India.

The issue of language has played an important part in shaping the modern political agenda. Pressure groups representing a range of issues – from women and the environment to trade unions and unorganized labour – have exerted, and continue to exert, pressure upon the state. Movements with a broad range of political ideologies, sometimes with a radical vision for change, have often created problems for the fragile democratic foundations of the Indian state.

This entry deals with certain broad categories of minority issues in India. The first category is that of religious minorities, and here the issue dealt with is the situation of India's Muslim minority. Christians and Buddhists, by contrast, do not suffer high levels of discrimination and are not specifically targeted as minorities. Even within the broader Hindu tradition however, many groups have suffered discrimination and persecution. A prime example of the systematic discrimination to which a group may be subjected within Hinduism is evident from the case of the Dalits. The term Dalit, which means 'the oppressed', is an assertive term of self-identity, referring to what in strict legal and constitutional terms are known as the scheduled castes. India's indigenous peoples, Adivasis, like many other indigenous peoples, may, with justification, claim that they remain victims under alien and colonial domination, even after the departure of the white colonizers. Adivasis of India cannot be treated as a homogeneous group. Nagas, although having indigenous claims, have nonetheless a distinct existence and differing political and constitutional aspirations from other Adivasi peoples. While the exploitation of Adivasis has been a historical as well as a contemporary phenomenon, and their exploitation has gained no respite from developments in post-colonial India, other ethnic and religious minorities became particular casualities of the march towards independence. The two most significant are the Kashmiris and the Sikhs; the issue of their right to existence and to self-determination has resulted in large-scale bloodshed, with tragic consequences. The entry also pays brief attention to smaller minorities – Jews, Anglo-Indians and Andaman Islanders – with a view to highlighting some of the problems these groups face as fairly marginal minority groups.

Dalits (scheduled castes)

The term Dalit means 'oppressed', 'broken' or 'crushed' to the extent of losing original identity. However, this name has been adopted by the people otherwise referred to as Harijans, untouchables, and has come to symbolize for them a movement for change and for the eradication of the centuries-old oppression under the caste system. In legal and constitutional terms, Dalits are known in India as scheduled castes. The constitution requires the government to define a list or schedule of the lowest castes in need of compensatory programmes. These scheduled castes include untouchable converts to Sikhism but exclude converts to Christianity and Buddhism; the groups that are excluded and continue to be treated as untouchables probably constitute another 2 per cent of the population.[2]

The roots of Dalit oppression go back to the origins of the caste system in Hindu religion. The philosophy of caste is contained in the *Manusmriti*, a sacred Hindu text dating from the second century BCE. 'Untouchable' outcast communities were forbidden to join in the religious and social life of the community and were confined to menial polluting tasks such as animal slaughter and leather-working. The introduction of Islam to India from about the thirteenth century AD led to widespread conversions by many low-caste and 'untouchable' groups, and by the mid-nineteenth century about one quarter of the population was Muslim.

During the struggle for Indian independence two different approaches emerged for the improvement of the situation of the people now known as Dalits. The first was led by Mahatma Gandhi, who believed in raising the status of Dalit people (or, as he preferred to call them, Harijans) while retaining elements of the traditional caste system but removing the degrading stigma and manifestations of 'untouchability'. The other approach was led by Dr Ambedkar, a lawyer and himself an 'untouchable', who believed that only by destroying the caste system could 'untouchability' be destroyed. Ambedkar became the chief spokesperson for those 'untouchables' who demanded separate legal and constitutional recognition similar in status to that accorded to Muslims, Sikhs and Christians. However, this was opposed by Gandhi and Ambedkar eventually gave up the demand. After rejecting Hindu values, in 1956 he converted to Buddhism and was later followed by a large number of converts.

After independence the Indian constitution abolished untouchability in law. Today Dalit politics largely centres around the just dispensation of the affirmative action benefits (in employment, education and electoral representation) granted to them under the constitution. However ,the Protection of Civil Rights Act 1955/1976 and the Scheduled Caste and Scheduled tribes (Prevention of Atrocities) Act 1989, both derived from the constitution, remain largely ineffective in their implementation. Many reasons lie behind this, including a lack of political will on the part of both central and state governments, a lack of commitment of upper-caste and class bureaucrats to social justice, the absence of vigilance committees of citizens to monitor the implementation process, and a lack of statutory power on the part of the Scheduled Caste/Scheduled Tribe Commission (Mandal Commission) to directly punish the perpetrators of crimes against Dalits. Affirmative government action, with regard to Dalits, is all directed at amelioration of their economic status, without liberating them from the dehumanizing effects of caste and 'untouchability'. Caste and poverty are inseparably joined together and are at the root of the Dalit socioeconomic predicament.

Dalit women have been particularly badly affected in recent times. They are discriminated against not only because of their sex but also because of religious, social and cultural structures which have given them the lowest position in the social hierarchy. The stigma of untouchability makes them especially vulnerable victims of all kinds of discriminations and atrocities. In areas of health, education, housing, employment and wages, application of legal rights, decision-making and political participation, and rural development, Dalit women have been almost entirely excluded from development policies and programmes. The national population policy, which is geared to population control and in the process targets Dalit and women for family planning programmes, does so on the grounds that they are the cause of the population 'explosion' and of poverty. No change has been made in the attitudes of society towards these women and they continue to be oppressed, marginalized, violated and all but forgotten. In the expression used often in development policies and plans they are: 'women in extreme poverty'.

Politically Dalits have not been able to break into mainstream debates and discussions despite the system of reservations that works at both national and state levels. The main reason for this has been the co-option of the Dalit agenda into that of the mainstream political parties, which are usually led by upper-caste men, with a consequent neglect of the primary demands of Dalits. In the last few years the rise of the Bhahujan Samaj Party has for the first time given Dalits a vehicle for bringing Dalit issues into the wider political arena. The success of this party in the northern states especially has given rise to hopes that the old upper-caste domination of Indian politics may finally be on the verge of giving way. Particularly significant was the experiment with a minority government led by a Dalit woman in the largest Indian state, Uttar Pradesh. Although the experiment collapsed in October 1995, with the larger coalition partner withdrawing support for the government, for the first time a Dalit party led by a Dalit woman was able to gain political control of a state government. This trend, if repeated in other states, and if eventually transferred to the national scene, would bring Dalit politics and the Dalit agenda for social transformation into the national mainstream.

Almost 90 per cent of Dalits live in rural areas. Economic exploitation remains their most acute problem. They are almost all marginal farmers or landless labourers. Large numbers migrate to cities or to labour-scarce rural areas in different parts of India. Many are in debt and are obliged to work off their debts as bonded labour, despite the fact that this practice was abolished by law in 1976. In these cases a labourer takes a loan from a landlord or moneylender and in return agrees to work for that person until the debt has been repaid. In practice such debts are difficult to repay as interest rates are high and poverty forces the labourer into deeper debt. The debt can then be passed on to the next generation and it is almost impossible to escape the cycle of bondage. In some areas many high-caste landlords pay their Dalit labourers minimum wages in cash or food, or nothing at all; resistance is frequently met by violence, sometimes resulting in the death or injury of the victim. Mob violence against Dalit communities is frequently reported, sometimes led by landlords, and has been especially noticeable in situations where Dalit workers have joined labour unions or made progress in gaining education and economic mobility.

Many Dalit families have left rural areas to live

in slums and on the pavements of the rapidly growing cities. Here they also tend to do the worst jobs for the lowest wages. However, in some cities traditional occupations such as sweepers have been organized in municipal unions and have the advantage of regular work and wages. Many Dalits work as casual day labourers, in small factories, quarries, brick kilns or on construction sites, as cycle rickshaw drivers or in petty trade. There are, however, growing numbers employed in relatively secure jobs in areas such as public service, banking and the railways, and sometimes in private industry. Those resident in the cities have some access to secondary and higher education, and a growing middle class has evolved within the Dalit community. As opportunities for education increase and aspirations rise, Dalits should become a strong and positive force for change in India in the coming decades, especially if they are able to organize themselves across barriers of language and religion.

Muslims

India's Muslim population is the third largest in the world – after those of Indonesia and Pakistan – and forms the largest religious minority in India. They are not a homogeneous group, divided as they are by language, ethnicity, culture and economic position. The great majority are Sunni Muslims, and the remainder are Shi'a and various other sects such as Bohras, Isma'ilis and Ahmadiyas. Muslims form a majority in the state of Kashmir, while elsewhere they are concentrated in particular areas. The largest numbers are to be found in the states of Uttar Pradesh, Bihar, West Bengal and Kerala. Islam was first introduced in India through the Arab invasion of Sind in CE 712 and through subsequent invasions of the eleventh and twelfth centuries. The religion firmly established itself as a force through the Mughal emperors in the sixteenth century. The Mughals generally refrained from forcible conversions to Islam, and the great Mughal Emperor Akbar granted a remarkable measure of tolerance and autonomy to non-Muslims. Although a considerable number of soldiers and officials came with the Mughals, the bulk of the Muslim population is descended from peoples of India, mainly from members of lower castes who converted to Islam as a means of escape from persecution and repression at the hands of the caste Hindus. While the concentration of Muslims was in the north-west of India (present-day Pakistan) and the east (present-day Bangladesh), there were also substantial numbers throughout the north and east.

The decline of Muslim domination of India and the ultimate dispossession of the Mughal empire had a number of consequences. While bitterly resenting the loss of the empire, Muslims had to bear the brunt of the retaliatory policies at the hands of the new colonial masters after the failed uprising of 1857. Muslims had refrained from adopting the culture and language of the British both because of their religious beliefs and out of the conviction of a lack of necessity. Consequently they made themselves ineligible for positions of influence and importance. Fearing complete and permanent submersion at the hands of the majority Hindus, at the end of the nineteenth century some more articulate Muslims began a social and cultural movement intended to inculcate a sense of consciousness and create a Muslim renaissance. Features of this movement included the educational initiatives of Syed Ahmad Khan, and Agha Khan's Simla deputation, which demanded separate Muslim political representation; it culminated in the establishment of the All India Muslim League. The Muslim League came in time to represent the aspirations of the Muslim masses in India, and ultimately spearheaded the Pakistan movement led by Mohammed Ali Jinnah and Liaquat Ali Khan. Conflict between the Muslim League and the Indian National Congress, at the helm of the movement for independence from Britain, eventually resulted in the decision to partition India and to create Pakistan.

The division of India along communal lines could not completely eradicate the religious minorities; instead it contributed to exacerbating the already existing tensions and division. The tragedy which ensued at the time of partition with Muslims, Sikhs and Hindus all victims of brutal and widespread conflict, remains one of the great catastrophes of human history. In so far as India's Muslims were concerned, the creation of Pakistan as homeland for Muslims resulted in a new minority problem for the now independent state of India. Muslim-majority regions (with the exception of Kashmir) separated to form the state of Pakistan. Muslim inhabitants of India now felt more insecure. The numerical strength of Muslims in India also decreased, from over 25 per cent of the population to about 10 per cent.

The manner of partition and the form that it took left a bitter legacy, and the perception of Muslims in India as anti-India or anti-national has done much to damage Hindu–Muslim relationships. The rise of Hindu fundamentalism as a political force, overtaking the liberal attitudes and policies that were evident in the first decades of independence, have also become an issue for Muslims to contend with. In the 1970s Indian

Muslims began to reassess their own position. The Emergency of 1975–77 proved a watershed, with Muslims in northern India particularly becoming victims of a forced sterilization campaign. The movement to demand rights for Muslims began to grow in the period following the Emergency and has gathered fresh momentum in recent times. Among the most significant of the challenges for India's Muslims have been: the Shah Bano case of 1985, where the demand for a uniform civil code was met with outright resistance from Muslim fundamentalist groups, polarizing views between the Hindu and Muslim communities; the destruction of the Babri Masjid Ayodhya (mosque) in 1992, which dealt a grave blow to the secular aspirations of the Indian state; and the movement since the late 1980s for independence in Kashmir, which has had an impact for non-Kashmiri Muslims living throughout India.

Indian Muslims are not granted the same constitutional safeguards as the scheduled castes and scheduled tribes and they are not entitled to reservations in employment and education. Although Hinduism is the majority religion, it is not an official or state-sponsored one; India is a secular state, and complete freedom of religion is guaranteed. The Minorities Commission, set up after the election of the Janata government in 1977, monitors the position of the non-scheduled caste and non-scheduled tribe minorities such as Muslims, although it has no powers to implement changes. Nor are Muslims entitled to reserved constituencies in central or state government assemblies, although all have Muslim parliamentary representatives. There have been several Muslim chief ministers and two Presidents have been Muslim, although the latter position has little real power despite high visibility.

Notwithstanding the large Muslim population of India, Muslims are strikingly under-represented in the civil service, military and institutions of higher education. At the beginning of the 1990s Muslims comprised only 2 per cent of the officers and 1.5 per cent of the clerks in the central civil service, and 3 per cent of the elite Indian administrative service. Less than 2 per cent of the army officer corps is Muslim, and Muslim representation in the higher echelons of the military is also poor. Beneath this pattern lies the issue of access to education and the general problem of large numbers of Muslims not being adequately trained or equipped to compete on equal terms at the market-place.[1]

Another problem is language. In the north of India most Muslim communities speak Urdu, which is not a recognized official language of India – largely because of the lack of a distinct majority population in a specific area. Apart from Kashmir, Muslims are everywhere in a minority in India. Uttar Pradesh, the state with the largest population in India, where approximately 15 per cent of the 110 million people are Muslims, did not recognize Urdu as an official language before 1989. Muslims campaigned for Urdu to receive the status of an official language alongside Hindi. When this was granted in Uttar Pradesh in September 1989 there were clashes between Hindu and Muslim students in which at least twenty-three people died. Urdu has also received official language status in Bihar.

While major differences exist between Hindus and Muslims in their religious, cultural and social outlook, in many cases the religious divide may be only a contributing factor to intercommunal discord. The main causes of dissension and divisiveness are equally likely to be poverty, unemployment, illiteracy, and so on. Hindu extremist groups such as the Shiv Sena and the Rashriyan Sevak Sanga consider Muslims to be disloyal to the Indian state. On the other hand, Muslim extremist groups preach a militant Islam that argues for a separate way of life for Muslims. The Shah Bano case provides a notable example of this, where an elderly Muslim woman sued her divorced husband for maintenance. Muslim traditionalists, apparently backed by the majority of Muslims, saw the court ruling in her favour as interference in the Islamic personal laws which govern the community. Less traditionalist Muslims, however, saw this ruling as an important breakthrough for the rights of women under Islam.

Muslim material expectations rose during the late 1970s and 1980s. With hundreds of thousands of Muslims working in Gulf countries, the new wealth they acquired created a sense of competition between Muslims and Hindus. The small business sector in the north has also helped bring about a slow improvement in the Muslim economic position. However, the repercussions of regional and internal conflicts have produced major setbacks for Muslims. The job market in the Gulf was seriously affected in the aftermath of the Gulf War and thousands of Muslims returned home with little prospect of regaining the same level of employment that they had enjoyed in the Middle East. In many ways Muslims are increasingly conscious of their inferior socioeconomic position, and this has given them new determination to change it. How such change is likely to come about is problematic. There is no all-Indian Muslim party, and attempts to have a common front with the scheduled castes have yet to come to fruition. There is a lack of overall direction, and as yet no appropriate forum exists through which Muslims of India can articulate their demands.

Adivasis/indigenous peoples (scheduled tribes)

Adivasis is the collective name used for the many indigenous peoples of India. The term Adivasi derives from the Hindi word *adi* which means of earliest times or from the beginning and *vasi* meaning inhabitant or resident, and it was coined in the 1930s, largely a consequence of a political movement to forge a sense of identity among the various indigenous peoples of India.[3] Officially Adivasis are termed scheduled tribes, but this is a legal and constitutional term which differs from state to state and area to area and therefore excludes some groups who might be considered indigenous. Adivasis are not a homogeneous group; there are over 200 distinct peoples speaking more than 100 languages, and varying greatly in ethnicity and culture. However, there are similarities in their way of life and generally perceived oppressed position within Indian society. There are about 69 million Adivasis, constituting 7.5 per cent of the Indian population.

Adivasis live throughout India but are primarily based in the mountain and hill areas, away from the fertile plains. The greatest concentration is in the central states of India, notably Madhya Pradesh, Orissa, southern Bihar, the Western *Ghats* (hills) of Gujarat and Maharastra, and northern Andhra Pradesh, where over 85 per cent of the indigenous population is to be found. In no central Indian state do Adivasis number more than a quarter of the population. There are smaller groups in the mountain areas of the south, notably in Kerala, Tamil Nadu and Karnataka. The other concentration is found in the north-eastern states – the 'seven sisters' (Assam, Manipur, Nagaland, Mizoram, Tripura, Megalaya and Arunchal Pradesh) – but here the situation is significantly different, as in most of these states (the exceptions are Assam and Tripura) Adivasis are a majority and are likely to remain so, since regulations restrict settlement by outsiders.

Adivasis, as their name reflects, are the earliest inhabitants of the subcontinent and once inhabited much larger areas than they do at present. Little is known of their history, although it appears that many were pushed into the hill areas after the invasions of the Indo-Aryan tribes 3,000 years ago. Indigenous peoples were not integrated into Hindu caste society, but there were many points of contact. Indigenous religious beliefs contain many aspects of Hinduism (and vice versa); Adivasis traded with settled villagers on the plains and sometimes paid tribute to Hindu rulers. In turn some Adivasi rulers conquered and ruled over non-Adivasis and some Adivasis permanently settled and entered caste society.

It was not until the unifying political rule of the British from the late eighteenth century that the government made substantial inroads into Adivasi society. British rule brought money, government officials and moneylenders into indigenous areas, beginning the process of encroachment on Adivasi land by outsiders. As a result, there were Adivasi revolts from the mid-nineteenth century in several parts of eastern India, and this forced the administration to recognize the vulnerable position of Adivasis and pass laws to protect their lands from outsiders. These laws (some of which are still on the statute book) barred the sale of indigenous lands to non-Adivasis and made provisions to restore alienated land. However, in practice most of these laws were widely disregarded, and unscrupulous merchants and moneylenders found ways to circumvent them. These problems are still encountered by Adivasis today, although their opponents are as likely to be large companies and state corporations as small traders and moneylenders. Christian missions began to proselytize in some indigenous areas, where (in contrast to Hindu and Muslim areas) they achieved a degree of success and also, most notably in the north-east, began a process of education and political awareness. Adivasis played little role in the events leading up to independence, and it was only in the north-east that they had enough political consciousness to make demands for separation or autonomy.

Under the 1950 constitution Adivasis, along with so-called untouchables, became subject to special protective provisions. The vast majority of indigenous peoples were classified as scheduled tribes. Article 341 authorizes the President of India to specify 'castes, races or tribes which shall for the purposes of this constitution be deemed to be scheduled tribes'. The first amendment to the constitution passed in 1951 allowed the state to make special provisions for the advancement of socially and educationally backward classes of citizens of the scheduled castes and scheduled tribes. The central government has a special commission for scheduled castes and scheduled tribes which issues an annual report. These reports give accounts of illegal actions against Adivasis and makes recommendations to improve their position.

There are reserved seats for scheduled tribes in Parliament and the state legislatures. In the two houses of Parliament, the Lok Sabha and the Rajiya Sabha, 7 per cent of the seats were reserved for members of scheduled tribes, and similar representation occurs in the state assemblies in proportion to the percentage of scheduled tribes in the state's population. However, since the scheduled tribe voters are always a minority (except in the north-eastern states where they are a numerical majority) in the reserved constituencies and in the legislatures as a whole, favourable legislation can be blocked by vested interests. Furthermore, the system does not encourage organization of scheduled tribes by separate parties but limits it to organization and representation by the major parties, especially the Congress Party which has been a dominant political force up until the elections of May 1996. Governments usually have ministers from scheduled tribes, including sometimes cabinet ministers, but to date there has been only one chief minister from a scheduled tribe (in Gujarat) although in the five predominantly Adivasi north-eastern states the chief minister invariably comes from a scheduled tribe.

The Bhuria Committee was set up by indigenous MPs to secure the extension of the 73rd and 74th articles of the constitution, which devolve authority to the Scheduled Areas. It presented its report in January 1995. While many consider that the Bhuria Committee process should be supported, it has been criticized because its recommendations do not extend to many indigenous areas, and because of gender insensitivity; women have long been denied political participation within indigenous areas and were poorly represented on the committee.

There have been very few attempts to found distinctive scheduled tribe political parties, apart from those in the north-eastern states. Perhaps the most notable example has been in eastern and southern Bihar, where an Adivasi regionalist movement known as the Jharkhand movement has been a factor since independence. The roots of this movement lie in the Santhal peoples of eastern Bihar and western Bengal, the scene of one of the early indigenous revolts against land alienation under British rule. Some of this area also contains India's richest mineral deposits and mining, and subsequent industrialization and deforestation have added to Adivasi grievances.

The Jharkhand Party was founded in 1950 and had as its main demands the formation of a separate state or territory in the traditional Adivasi areas of Santhal Paganas and Chotanagpur and areas in West Bengal, Orissa and Madhya Pradesh. The party went into decline after its leader joined the Congress Party but was revived in 1973 when a new party, the Jharkhand Mukti Morcha (JMM), was formed, led by a charismatic Santhal leader who worked closely with and eventually also joined the Congress Party. This split the JMM into several smaller groups, but in 1987 a new co-ordinating organization, the Jharkhand Co-ordinating Committee, was formed, with over fifty constituent organizations. This group has led a number of *bandh* (strikes) and mass demonstrations in support of its demands and also tried to set up a parallel government, albeit with little success. Both the central and state governments have consistently refused to consider any concessions regarding the creation of a Jharkhand state, although according to an agreement signed on 2 September 1992, the central and state governments formally agreed to grant a measure of autonomy to the Jharkand region. In December 1994 the Bihar state assembly passed the Jharkhand Area Autonomous Council Act, which envisages the formation of a Jharkhand Area Autonomous Council (JAAC) comprising eighteen districts in Bihar.

Over 95 per cent of the scheduled tribes still live in rural areas, and economic exploitation remains their most acute problem. Less than 10 per cent are itinerant hunter-gatherers but more than half depend on forest produce for their livelihood, many in the form of the *tendu* leaf, used for the production of *bidi* (cigarettes). From the time of the British administration, there have been laws regulating the ownership and use of the forests, and today most forest land is effectively nationalized, with large areas contracted out to private commercial interests. This has progressively deprived Adivasi communities of rights in the land, and they can be fined or imprisoned for taking forest produce which has traditionally been theirs. The ostensible reason for state intervention has been to stop the destruction of forest land which has continued throughout this century. There are a number of reasons for deforestation, although it is often blamed on the Adivasis' shifting cultivation practices; one has been the increase in demand for firewood as fuel; another is the impact of commercial, sometimes illegal, logging. A serious threat to Adivasis is large-scale dam-building, for irrigation and hydroelectricity. A number of hydro schemes have been carried out since independence, and a constitutional and political war is currently being waged over the construction of the largest dam in the Narmada basin.[4]

As with the scheduled castes, members of scheduled tribes are beneficiaries of affirmative action provisions laid down in the constitution, which reserve places in education, the civil service and nationalized industries. Problems of remoteness, poverty and prejudice mitigate against Adivasis exploiting these provisions, however. For example, in Andhra Pradesh the Adivasi literacy rate is only 11 per cent, against an all-India level of 29 per cent (in the north-east, Adivasi literacy is considerably higher). Because few Adivasis finish schooling, most are unable to use the reserved places in higher education or the civil service. Nevertheless, some Adivasis have managed to achieve positions of authority in government and education, although they continue to be under-represented in almost every field.

Some Adivasis have been organized by left-wing groups, known commonly in India as Naxalities, to press for higher wages and payments for forest produce. The Naxalite movement, which initially was a product of student-led insurrection in Bengal during the late 1960s and early 1970s, subsequently spread to regions of Bihar state, Madhya Pradesh and Andhra Pradesh. As a result, Adivasis may become victims of both Naxalite pressures and government counter-insurgency campaigns. More commonly, police, forest guards and officials frequently cheat, bully and intimidate Adivasis, and large numbers are routinely arrested and jailed, often for petty offences. In such circumstances many Adivasis prefer to bribe officials in order to escape harassment, or else flee into the jungles.

Although Adivasis are not, as a general rule, regarded as unclean by caste Hindus in the same way as Dalits are, they continue to face prejudice and often violence from society. They are at the lowest point of almost every socioeconomic indicator. The majority of the population regards them as primitive, and government programmes aim at integrating them with the majority society, rather than allowing them to maintain their distinctive way of life. While the larger tribal groups and languages will survive as a result of numbers, the destruction of their economic base and environment poses grave threats to those who are still able to follow their traditional way of life and may result in the cultural extinction of many of the smaller Adivasi peoples.

Nagas

Nagas are an Adivasi hill people numbering about 700,000 inhabiting the remote and mountainous country between the Indian state of Assam and Burma. There are also Naga groups in Burma. The Nagas are divided into sixteen main tribal groups, each with its own name and distinct language, but their sense of national identity, forged during the years of British administration and reinforced by resistance to Indian government domination, now largely overrides the differences that separate them. Nagas traditionally are tribally organized, with a strong warrior tradition. Their villages are sited on hilltops and they make frequent armed raids on the plains below. The British first came into contact with Nagas when they took over Assam and the Brahmaputra valley in the 1820s and moved into the hill areas to stop Naga raids, especially from the Angami tribe. In 1878 there was a Angami uprising, which was severely suppressed. After this the British gradually took over the whole area. However, in practice, British administration was limited. It was made a rule that no Indian official should be posted to the hills, that traders and speculators from the plains should be excluded, and that most officials were to be drawn from the Nagas themselves. Missionaries converted many Nagas to Christianity, and this facilitated literacy and the use of English, all of which encouraged a Naga sense of a separate identity.

Prior to the independence of India, Nagas presented their own case for independent statehood. However, when Assam (with other Indian provinces) was granted a large measure of self-rule in 1937, Naga areas remained under direct British administration. In the Second World War Nagas aided the British and harassed the Japanese. Nagas set up the Naga National Council (NNC) to discuss matters of future status, and in 1947 an NNC delegation led by Z.A. Phizo went to Delhi to press for Naga independence, a demand that was refused by Nehru, although he stated that autonomy for the Nagas would be considered. The NNC declared unilateral independence in August 1947 (at the time of Indian and Pakistani independence), but this was ignored by the outside world. However, the governor of Assam held talks with NNC leaders in 1948 and reached a nine-point agreement with them which recognized 'the right of Nagas to develop themselves according to their freely elected wishes', though this agreement was not to be extended or renegotiated after ten years. The Nagas interpreted this as giving them the right to opt out of the Indian union after ten years. This was not the interpretation of the Indians, however, and in practice the latter treated the nine-point agreement as a dead letter.

From 1948 the administration of Naga areas began to change. Indians took over the administration and with it the posts which in the past had been held by Nagas. After the Chief Minister of Assam had been given a hostile reception by

Nagas he ordered that a police force be placed in the hills. The Nagas again declared independence in January 1950 after they had conducted their own plebiscite, which showed an almost unanimous vote in favour of independence, but this was not recognized by the Indian government, which gave the Naga Hills a status as part of the 'tribal' areas of Assam. In 1952 Nehru visited the Naga Hills but refused to meet the NNC while he was there or to receive their demands. Nagas were suspected of being manipulated by foreigners who wished to break up the Indian union. Soon after, Baptist missionaries were expelled from Naga areas.

Nagas then launched a campaign of civil disobedience, similar to that used to achieve Indian independence, withdrawing from schools and the administration and refusing to pay taxes. NNC leaders were arrested, the sixteen tribal councils – all under the control of the NNC – were abolished; and armed police and later the Indian army were moved into the area. In 1956 the NNC proclaimed the establishment of a Federal Government of Nagaland (FGN) with its own constitution and a Naga Home Guard. From 1956 to 1958 a bitter guerrilla war was conducted in the Naga Hills, with alleged atrocities on both sides. According to government figures, 1,400 Nagas were killed against 162 Indians. Nagas and others have alleged that the Indian forces engaged in torture, rape and murder, and burnt and destroyed villages and crops. While not all these reports can be substantiated, it appears that many violations did take place.

Divisions began to emerge within the Naga movement with the formation of the Naga People's Convention led by Dr Imkongliba Ao, which favoured Indian statehood as a practical alternative to complete independence, and this received a more favourable response in Delhi, although the new state of Nagaland, at that time the smallest in India with an area of 15,360 square kilometres and a population of 350,000, came into being only in 1963. But the war continued, with the Indian army using counter-insurgency tactics of rehousing villagers away from their villages in order to separate them from the insurgents. Phizo of the NNC had managed to flee to London, where efforts on behalf of the Naga cause began to attract international attention and sympathy.

A breakthrough in the stalemate with India appeared to come with the appointment by the government of a three-man peace commission consisting of the Reverend Michael Scott, B.P. Chaliha and J.P. Narayan, which was able to negotiate a cease-fire beginning in May 1964. However, efforts to bring about a permanent settlement failed as the two sides could not agree on a formula for settlement. The cease-fire continued in name until September 1972, when it was unilaterally terminated by the Indian government, but in practice fighting had continued even while it was in force, and by the late 1960s the situation had reverted almost to what it had been before the cease-fire. Further allegations of brutalities were made against the Indian army. It appeared that the Indian forces had been strengthened, and the NNC guerrillas weakened, during these years. There were divisions within the guerrilla forces, with one breakaway group being engaged in a much publicized surrender in August 1973, and there also emerged an apparently well entrenched Nagaland state government which had joined with the Indian government and supported measures against the guerrillas. Many NNC guerrillas had taken refuge on the Burmese side of the border, while Phizo remained in exile in London. A new state government in Nagaland, the United Democratic Front (UDF), elected in 1974, attempted to negotiate a cease-fire, but this was refused by the Indian government, which was now in a position finally to defeat the much depleted NNC forces, which by 1975 were surrendering in significant numbers.

Some Nagas, while supporting the ideal of independence, nevertheless argued that the armed conflict against the full power of the Indian state could only lead to suffering for the Nagas and ultimate defeat, and therefore that resistance should be on the political plane with a search for maximum autonomy within the Indian union. The Naga Peace Council, a continuation of the body which had brought about the cease-fire of the 1960s, made contact with the underground forces. The result was the Shillong Accord, signed between the Governor and the representatives and the FGN in November 1975. The provisions of the accord stated that the signatories accepted the binding nature of the Indian constitution, that weapons would be surrendered to the peace council, that security operations would be suspended and that the curfew would be lifted. This accord reflected the strong desire for peace within Nagaland but was not accepted by all the Naga resistance forces. Phizo in London repudiated it, as did the Chinese-influenced group led by Muivah in Burma. This group became the National Socialist Council of Nagaland (NSCN) and introduced a new ideological note into the formerly heavily Christian Naga movement.

By the 1980s most of Nagaland was at peace, in contrast to other parts of north-east India, where various insurgent movements were active. The NSCN, however, was still active not only in

Nagaland but among the Nagas of neighbouring Manipur, and there were continuing clashes between the NSCN based in Burma and the Indian army, as well as allegations of human rights violations by the Indian military. Within constitutional politics there had been growing dissidence in the ruling Congress I Party (the NNC had merged with the Congress Party in 1976), but its future appeared secure when it was re-elected in November 1987. However, it lost its majority in August 1988; rather than the newly formed opposition Joint Regional Legislature Party being allowed to form a government, the legislature was dismissed and the state was placed under President's rule (direct rule from New Delhi).

Despite the many problems that the continuing insurgency has created, Nagaland's future will depend on how well any state government can fulfil the expectations of its people. Nagaland's literacy rate stands at 42 per cent, much higher than the national average, yet jobs continue to be scarce, especially outside the civil service. Nagas have successfully resisted the imposition of Hindi by the central government and have been in favour of English. Yet an adequate knowledge of Hindi is necessary to function in the north of India, and this may limit opportunities outside the state.

Sikhs

Sikhs are a religious minority in the north-western state of Punjab, where they form a majority. They are also scattered around different parts of India and the world. They number over 14 million, of whom over 1 million live outside India. Of the 13 million living in India, 80 per cent are concentrated in their home state of Punjab. The Sikh religion dates back to end of the fifteenth century and was founded by Guru Nanak (1469–1539). Dissatisfied with the teachings of Hinduism as well as Islam, he formulated an egalitarian doctrine which transcended both, and became a powerful force for change in subsequent centuries. A crucial element of this new religion was the creation of the community of the Khalsa, or Company of the Pure in 1699 during the period of the tenth Guru, Guru Gobind 1675–1708. As part of their religious injunctions they are obliged to wear the symbols called the the five Ks, taken from the words *kesh* (uncut hair), *kangha* (comb), *kirpan* (sword), *kara* (steel bangle) and *kaccha* (breeches). Sikh men are most easily identifiable through their wearing of the turban. The creation of this community marked a change of emphasis which led Sikhism away from its traditional peaceful course into a more warlike stance, and although not all Sikhs adopted the baptismal tokens, bearded and turbaned members of the Khalsa came to be recognized as guardians of Sikh orthodoxy.

For the next 150 years the Sikh Khalsa remained involved in conflict with the invading Afghans and the Muslim governors of Lahore. In 1746 the city of Amritsar was sacked, the Golden Temple defiled, and Sikh forces massacred by one such governor. Another massacre, this time perpetrated by the Afghanis, took place in 1762. In the ensuing strife and consequent power vacuum emerged Ranjit Singh. After capturing Lahore in 1799 he ruled as the Maharajah of Punjab until his death in 1839. Some Sikh states maintained a separate existence under British rule, but elsewhere in the Punjab the Sikh Khalsa remained independent. Factional infighting gave the British a chance to intervene, and after two Anglo–Sikh wars in the mid-nineteenth century the British gained control of the whole of the Punjab, and the Khalsa army was disbanded.

Sikhs played a leading role in the Indian army at the time of British colonization, and also used the opportunity provided by British citizenship to emigrate to other parts of the then British empire. Elected provincial governments began to exercise more powers in India during the years leading up to independence. As independence approached, Sikhs put forward proposals for alterations to Punjab's boundaries to exclude the largely Hindu and Muslim areas to the south-east and west or, alternatively, for increased Sikh representation in Parliament to protect their interests. These proposals were largely ignored, and the predominantly Muslim unionist party retained control over the province. During the 1940s there were increasing demands made by Muslims for a separate Muslim state after independence. Muslims urged the Sikhs to join them in the new state, but there were too few cultural and religious links between them to make this feasible. Afraid of their numbers being split between India and Pakistan, Sikh leaders in 1946 called for the creation of their own independent state of Sikhistan or Khalistan, without success. The situation deteriorated rapidly, with outbursts of violence and bloodshed in riots between Muslims on the one hand, and Sikhs and Hindus on the other.

With independence and partition the larger, western, portion of Punjab was allocated to Pakistan, now a Muslim state. In the holocaust that followed, hundreds of thousands of Punjabis were killed, and millions fled from one part of the province to the other. The Sikh community was split down the middle, and over 40 per cent were forced to leave Pakistan for India, abandoning homes, lands and sacred shrines. The majority of Sikh refugees settled in the Indian part of Punjab, although many moved to Delhi and other neighbouring regions. In 1966 the new Sikh-majority state of Punjab was created, but various complex issues remained unresolved. Firstly, the capital city of Chandigarh also doubled as the capital of the neighbouring state of Haryana. Then the water supply from the Punjab rivers was divided between them in what Sikhs saw as an unfair manner. As in 1947, many religious and linguistic groups found themselves on the wrong side of the boundary after the division, with Punjabi Hindus constituting the majority of the urban population in Punjab and a sizeable Sikh minority remaining in Haryana. Nor were the majority Sikhs politically united. The Akali Dal represented for the most part the Jat Sikh farmers, but the state Congress Party attracted many Sikh voters in addition to Hindus. Punjab was now declared a unilingual Punjabi state with safeguards for the Hindu minority.

Between 1966 and 1984 these conflicts continued to remain unresolved, which led to rising frustration amongst the Sikhs. Relations between Sikh political leaders became strained, and there were disputes between Punjab and neighbouring states, especially Haryana. These were exacerbated by Indira Gandhi's domination of the Indian political scene and her tendency to centralize power rather than grant greater autonomy to many of the country's regions, including Punjab. During the same period Punjab had undergone a remarkable agricultural and economic boom, primarily as a result of the introduction of green revolution wheat farming. Despite this economic prosperity, many Sikhs saw the contribution of Punjab to the national economy as not being sufficiently recognized. At the same time the immigration of Hindus to Punjab affected the perception of Sikhs in terms of fears of becoming a numerical minority in their own province. The influx of Hindus also meant that a significant number of young Sikhs from Rajput families were left without work in an increasingly mobile and urbanized economy at a time when military recruitment was on the decline.

The rise of an extremist Sikh movement led by the charismatic preacher Sant Jarnail Singh Bhindranwale attracted much support from within the Sikh community, and resulted in calls for an independent state of Khalistan to protect the rights and identity of the Sikhs. This movement took a violent turn and eventually led to the controversial 'Operation Bluestar' of June 1984, which saw the Indian army storm the Golden Temple, holiest of Sikh shrines, to flush out suspected terrorists sheltering in the premises. The army action caused great resentment among Sikhs generally at what was seen as the defilement of Sikh holy places and an insult to the entire community on the part of the Indian state. The ultimate act in this political tragedy was the assassination of Indira Gandhi in October 1984 by two of her Sikh bodyguards, which resulted in a wave of Hindu violence being unleashed against the Sikh community – in a number of cases with the acquiescence of the police and allegedly with the political support of Congress Party politicians throughout the country. There was massive destruction of Sikh property and at least 2,150 Sikhs, mainly males, were killed in Delhi and over 600 in other parts of India. The army took over after three days, but the killings created deep and lasting bitterness and resentment among Sikhs, not only in India but also abroad.

Following the installation of Rajiv Gandhi as Prime Minister of India in 1984, an agreement was signed (the Punjab Accord) with the leader of the Akali Dal under which Chandigarh was made the exclusive capital of the state of Punjab and the issue of the river water was to be decided by a commission. It was also agreed that Sikhs' control of their religious affairs was to be expedited and fresh investments were promised for Punjab. These measures did not go far enough for many Sikhs, and shortly after the signing of the accord the leader of the Akali Dal was assassinated. In the elections that followed, the Akali Dal was voted into power under a moderate leader, but the rise of extremism in the state continued. Eventually the government was sacked and the state placed under President's rule, with the police, and increasingly, the army being given a free hand in fighting the growing terrorist and secessionist movement. After a long period of President's rule, during which abuses of human rights were widespread, the rule of law appeared to have been restored, reflected through the state elections of 1989 (although they were boycotted by many people). The Congress government that was voted into power attempted to restore normality in the state through a combination of extreme measures in dealing with the terrorists and restoring the faith of people in a democratic system of government.

The roots of the problems that gave rise to the terrorist movement in the state have yet to be resolved, however. Demands for an investigation into the Delhi massacres have not been heeded by the central government. Moreover, the Sikh community's faith in the ability of the Indian state to protect its identity, culture and religion has been shaken by the events of the last decade. Extremism remains a problem, as was evidenced by the assassination of the Chief Minister of the state in 1995. The central government of India is likely to face a secessionist movement for an independent state of Khalistan for several more years. The numbers of people involved in the terrorist movement have, however, shrunk dramatically, and there are currently many opportunities for both the state and central government to restore popular faith in democratic institutions and processes. Yet, if these opportunities are missed or spurned, future generations of Sikhs are likely to renew calls for a secessionist movement.

Kashmiris

Kashmiris are the people living in the territory of Jammu and Kashmir, in the extreme north-west of India. Two-thirds of this territory is currently administered as the Indian state of Jammu and Kashmir and has an estimated population of 8.6 million. The remainder of the region is controlled and administered by Pakistan. The constitutional position is made complex by the fact that both India and Pakistan challenge the legality of the other's title to territory, with an effective partition of Kashmir along the cease-fire line as agreed in 1949, with some modification as a consequence of the India-Pakistan war of 1971. That part of the territory which lies within India also includes the region of Ladakh. The land and people of Jammu and Kashmir, a multi-religious, multi-ethnic and multi-cultural region, are known today for the viciousness of the conflict that has raged there for more than a decade.

The roots of the conflict go back to the partition of India in 1947. The main constitutional instrument for determining the future position of the princely states such as Kashmir was the Indian Independence Act of 1947, section 7(1)(b) of which provided that:

'The suzerainty of His Majesty over the Indian states lapses, and with it, all treaties and agreements in force at the date of the passing of this Act between His Majesty and the rulers of the Indian states, all functions execrable by His Majesty at the date with respect to Indian states, all obligations of His Majesty at the date towards Indian states or the rulers thereof and all powers, rights, authority or jurisdiction exercisable by His Majesty at that date in or in relation to Indian states, by treaty, grant usage, sufferance or otherwise'.

Despite the presence of a number of complexities surrounding the issue of succession, the strict legal position appears to be that with the lapse of the treaties and agreements with the British government, sovereignty reverted to the princely states, which then had the option of accession, merger and integration with the dominions of India or Pakistan. In practice, however, the vast majority of states decided to accede to India or Pakistan before the Indian Independence Act came into force on 15 August 1947.[5] In the case of the state of Jammu and Kashmir, the Hindu ruler of a Muslim majority state vacillated in making a decision as to whether to accede to India or Pakistan. His hesitation and indecisiveness provided the opportunity for an 'invasion' of the territory by the so-called 'Azad Kashmir Army' made up of some of the indigenous peoples of Pakistan. Under the pressure of this invasion the ruler of Jammu and Kashmir decided to appeal to India for help and acceded to India. Indian troops were rushed into the territory and stopped the advance of the indigenous army from Pakistan. The 'line of control' established as a result of this action became the border between India and Pakistan, and also the line dividing the territory of Jammu and Kashmir between the Indian and Pakistani jurisdictions. Since the accession of Jammu and Kashmir to India, it has been claimed by Pakistan that the final destination of the territory remains conditional until the people of Jammu and Kashmir themselves have had an opportunity to determine their political destiny through a referendum

Jammu and Kashmir was subsequently to become a victim of the proxy war between the states of India and Pakistan, with the Kashmiri people becoming the main victims of this conflict. A UN sponsored resolution to hold a referendum in the territory around the issue of self-determination has never been implemented, with both Indian and Pakistani governments blaming each other for lack of the necessary political will. Meanwhile political events overtook the UN resolution with first the war of 1965 between India and Pakistan, then by another in 1971, resulting in the creation of Bangladesh and the signing of the Simla agreement (1972). Under its terms it was agreed that the two countries would attempt to resolve the issue of Kashmir bilaterally, with the line of control being converted into an international border. The agreement also enabled both countries to discuss economic, social and cultural forms of cooperation for the benefit of the territory and the people. However, this has not happened as a result of endless suspicion, hostility and recriminations between the two governments. Since the late 1980s the situation in the Indian-held portion of Jammu and Kashmir has deteriorated considerably, with massive abuses of human rights, and with India accusing the Pakistan government of funding and sponsoring a terrorist war aimed at destabilizing the country. The breakdown of talks has been perhaps the most significant set-back in the search for a long-term solution to the dispute in Jammu and Kashmir.

While the case for a political settlement needs to be pursued, there is also a pressing need for India to recognize and deal with the genuine grievances of the Kashmiri people, living in Jammu, Kashmir and Ladakh. This territory has some of the most diverse peoples from India, with a mix of religions, languages and cultures. The Muslim majority population lives in the Kashmir valley, while the plains of Jammu are dominated by Hindus, who make up the largest minority in the state of Jammu and Kashmir while being in a majority in Jammu. The third largest group are Buddhist Ladhakis, who live in the region of Ladakh.

The main problem, and the starting-point for all the troubles in the territory has been the real and perceived grievances of the Muslim population. From the time of independence Kashmir has remained a poor region of India, despite being well endowed by way of natural resources and picturesque scenery which provides a natural attraction for tourists. This lack of economic development has fuelled resentment against the Indian state and has led to a hardening of view within the Muslim majority population that they were being discriminated against. Specific grievances include the fact that Urdu has not been made a nationally recognized language of India, that investment in education is among the lowest for the whole country, and that industrial investment has been virtually non-existent. The prime source of possible revenues – tourism – has become a casualty of the persistent terrorist activities and the military presence in the state.

Politics in the state of Jammu and Kashmir has tended to be dominated by the central government in New Delhi, and this has added to popular resentment against the Indian state. Devolution proposals and moves towards greater autonomy have been few and far between, and have foundered on the intransigence of Indian politicians, who have always been suspicious of Pakistani involvement in the separatist movement in Jammu and Kashmir. Another factor that has complicated the situation has been the general inefficiency and corruption of the successive state governments, especially those formed with the backing of the ruling Congress Party in New Delhi.

Ethnic diversity within the state is most notable with regard to the 3.2 million highlanders from Kashmir proper, 90 per cent of whom are Muslims, and the lowlanders from Jammu, the majority of whom are Hindus. Most of the state's industry is concentrated in Jammu, but most of the development funds are spent in the Kashmir valley, where 60 per cent of the population is engaged in horticulture, although tourism used to flourish around Srinagar Lake. The two areas compete for economic resources, and an attempt has been made to keep a delicate balance between them, reflected in the state administration moving to Jammu in winter and to Srinagar in summer. More recently there have been tensions in the remote northern area of Ladakh between the Muslims (who are a minority in the area) and the majority Buddhists. Ladakh occupies about one third of the area of Kashmir but contains only 135,000 people. Buddhist Ladakhis claim that they have not had an adequate political representation in the Jammu and Kashmir state legislature, that there were very few Ladakhis in the administration, and that commerce was dominated by traders from the Kashmir valley. In addition there have been religious tensions, fanned by the Muslim separatist feelings in Srinagar. There have been demands that Ladakh be separated from Jammu and Kashmir and be given the status of a union territory, ruled directly from New Delhi.

The future for Kashmir appears grim. Talks between India and Pakistan under the terms of the Simla agreement of 1972 probably represent the best possible hope of achieving some sort of negotiated settlement to the conflict that has dragged on and caused untold suffering, misery and hardship for the Kashmiri people as a whole.

Jews of India

There are three main Jewish communities in India, each of different origin and with different characteristics.They are the Cochinis, the Bene Israel and the Baghdadis. None has faced persecution, but they are all declining in numbers due to emigration to Israel and other countries. Malayalam-speaking Jews from the city of Cochin in Kerala claim to have arrived in the subcontinent after the destruction of the Temple, although the earliest documentary evidence dates from the ninth century. They are divided into three endogamous groups: White Jews, a mixture of indigenous Indian Jews and Middle Eastern and European Jews; Black Jews, who are in most ways indistinguishable from local Indians; and Meshuhrarim, descendants of Indian slaves who were attached to both groups. Cochin Jews maintained trading and religious links with Middle Eastern Jewish communities but, although they numbered 2,500 in 1948, emigration to Israel has reduced their numbers to a handful.

Bene Israel lived for centuries on the Konkan coast and, later, in Bombay, isolated from Jews elsewhere but maintaining some Jewish religious practices. From the nineteenth century onwards they made efforts to bring their customs into line with Orthodox Jewish practices. In 1951 there were 20,000 Bene Israel, but today there are no more than 5,000.

Compared to Cochin Jews and Bene Israel, Baghdadi Jews are relatively recent settlers in India. Originally from Baghdad, Aleppo, Yemen and Basra, they settled in Calcutta and Bombay in the early nineteenth century, when British rule was already established in India. As white non-Indians, the Baghdadis enjoyed special status and much prosperity under the British, but after independence most left for Israel or other countries, and today probably no more than 300–400 remain in India.

More recently, some indigenous groups in the north-east of India have claimed to be Jewish. These belong to the Shinlung ethnic groups, usually called Kuki in India and Chin in Burma. They claim to be the descendants of one of the lost tribes of Israel and to have maintained Jewish practices until their conversion to Christianity in the last century. These 'Manipur Jews' have established a number of synagogues and have gained thousands of converts. Some observers have seen this conversion as a way of escaping the constraints of the caste system.

Anglo-Indians

The Anglo-Indian community is the smallest officially recognized minority group in India. Article 366(2) of the Indian constitution of 1950 defines an Anglo-Indian as 'a person whose father or any of whose male progenitors in the male line is or was of European descent but who is domiciled within the territory of India and is or was born within such territory of parents habitually resident therein and not established there for temporary purposes only'.

The community originated soon after 1639 when the British East India Company founded a settlement in Madras. The community identified itself with, and was accepted by, the British until 1791, when Anglo-Indians were excluded from positions of authority in the civil, military and marine services in the East India Company. During the Indian rebellion of 1857 the Anglo-Indians sided with the British, and consequently received favoured treatment from the British government in preference to Indians, serving in large numbers in the strategic services of the railways, post and telegraph, and customs. In 1919 the Anglo-Indian community was given one reserved seat in the Central Legislative Assembly in Delhi. The English-speaking Anglo-Indians identified themselves with the British against the nationalist Congress Party, despite British attitudes of superiority.

After independence in 1947, Anglo-Indians faced a difficult choice – to leave India or to integrate. Many Indians distrusted their pro-British attitudes and Western-oriented culture. Large numbers did leave, mainly for Britain and Australia. Those who remained were allowed reserved representation in the Parliament (Article 331 – in practice one seat in the lower house), and there are similar provisions made in state legislatures. There were also stipulations for reservations in some government posts for a period of twenty years. In many ways the Anglo-Indians who remain in India are a protected and relatively well-off community. They are literate, urbanized and well represented in the military, sports and some areas of the civil service. But they are also an ageing community and declining in numbers. Most younger members emigrate, if possible, and those who remain are unlikely to have the numbers or social cohesion to continue as a dynamic community.

Andaman Islanders

There are four distinct indigenous peoples living in the Andaman Islands: Andamanese, Onges, Jarawa and Sentinelese. The Andaman Islands are a chain of over 500 islands, twenty-seven of which are inhabited, in the Bay of Bengal. Although they are closer to the South-East Asian archipelago, the islands, along with the Nicobar Islands to the south, are an Indian Union Territory, under the jurisdiction of the Home Ministry in New Delhi. Little is known about the history and development of the indigenous peoples of the Andamans, since they are small groups of hunter-gatherers, have no written language and have fallen drastically in numbers over the last two centuries. Although the islands were previously known to outsiders, the first attempts to colonize them came from the British at the end of the eighteenth century although these were soon abandoned. The islands were again colonized in the aftermath of the 'Indian Mutiny' of 1857 when a penal colony and jail were established on South Andaman, which over the years housed both political and other prisoners. In addition, people from the Indian mainland, especially from East Bengal/Bangladesh, have settled in the islands.

Today, of a total population of 180,000 on the islands, indigenous people of the four ethnic groups now number just a few hundred. They have suffered a long, and probably irreversible, decline in numbers. The Andamanese have suffered most drastically. In 1858, when the penal settlement was started, there were 4,800 of them; in 1901, 625; in 1930, 90; and in 1988, only 28. Initial casualties came from warfare with the colonizers, later ones from diseases such as pneumonia, measles and syphilis. Today the survivors have been resettled by the administration on the 603-hectare Strait Island. The Jarawa were the next group to face land colonization. At first, in desperation, they moved away from the settlements, but later they began to attack them. The British retaliated and organized punitive expeditions. The Jarawa today number about 300 and live on the 742 square kilometre Jarawa reserve in South and Middle Andaman islands. The Onge of the remote Little Andaman islands were the next to be contacted by outsiders in 1867 when they killed eight sailors. In retaliation a punitive mission took seventy Onge lives, about 10 per cent of the total population. Although friendly relations were established in 1887, the Onges were infected by disease and their numbers declined from 670 in 1901 to 250 in 1930 and about 100 in 1994. The exact numbers of the Sentinelese Islanders remains unknown but they probably number 50–150. Outsiders who have attempted contact have been met by flights of arrows and the official policy is to leave the Sentinelese alone.

Like other indigenous peoples in India, indigenous Andaman Islanders are classed as scheduled tribes and enjoy special protection under the Indian constitution. But the odds against their survival as viable peoples are overwhelming. The main threat comes from development of the islands by large-scale settlement and deforestation. The islanders' resistance continues today, especially among the Jarawa, towards those who encroach on their reserve, as happened when several road-building crew died in 1976 and two settlers died in 1985. Some attempts have been made to contact these Jarawa with gifts, and sometimes these have been successful, but anthropologists have warned that such contact is intrinsically harmful and will only result in the destruction of the few indigenous people who still survive. Recent proposals by the Indian government to give the Andaman and Nicobar Islands the status of a free port and to encourage tourism and communications development may be the final blow for the original Andaman Islanders.

Conclusions and future prospects

India, like many of the countries of the post-colonial world, remains to a great extent an artificial construct of the colonial era. Beneath the surface it is a country burdened with ethnic, religious and linguistic conflicts. There have been fears that India would meet the same fate as the former Yugoslavia or, to a lesser extent, the former Soviet Union. However, it is perhaps remarkable that a state presenting so much diversity in the character of its peoples, religions and civilizations, with an underdeveloped infrastructure and a majority of the population living in poverty, has managed to survive as a viable unit. Even so, minority issues are increasingly taking centre stage in Indian politics, whether in the form of separatist movements, demands for increased political representation, or the need to provide protection to its many religions and cultures. Many of these conflicts are yet to be resolved, and the challenge for India will be to put in place processes that enable minority problems to be discussed and resolved for the benefit of the country as a whole, while ensuring the collective survival of the many minority peoples who form an integral part of the country. A worrying feature in the last few years has been the emergence of fundamentalism in India, as elsewhere. Religious chauvinism has been on the increase and this poses a threat to future communal relations. For the promotion and protection of the rights of the minorities, the traditions of democracy and secularism that have been the characteristic of constitutional and political developments of post-independence India are virtues which need to be preserved.

Further reading

Bates, C., '"Lost innocents and the loss of innocence": interpreting Adivasi movements in South Asia', in R. Barnes, A. Gray and B. Kingsbury (eds), *Indigenous Peoples of Asia*, Ann Arbor, MI, Association for Asian Studies, 1993, pp. 103–119.

Engineer, A.A. (ed.), *Ethnic Conflict in South Asia*, Delhi, Ajanta Publications, 1987.

Joshi, B. (ed.), *Untouchable! Voices of the Dalit Liberation Movement,* London, MRG report, 1986.

Kananaikil, J. (ed.), *Scheduled Castes and the Struggle against Inequality: Strategies to Empower the Marginalized,* New Delhi, Indian Social Institute, 1983.

Lamb, A., *Kashmir: A Disputed Legacy 1846–1990,* Hertfordshire, Roxford Books, 1991.

Shackle, C., *The Sikhs,* London, MRG report, 1986.

Whitaker, B. *et al., The Biharis of Bangladesh,* London, MRG report, 1978.

Zelliot, E., *From Untouchable to Dalit: Essays on Ambedkar Movement,* New Dehli, Manohar, 1992.

Minority-based and advocacy organizations

Amnesty International, 13 Indra Prastha Building, E-109, Pandav Nagar, New Delhi 110092, India; tel. 91 11 214 5137, fax 91 11 214 5137.

Association for the Protection of Democratic Rights, 18 Madan Baral Lane, West Bengal, Calcutta 700012, India.

Centre for Social Knowledge and Action, 1 Punyashlok, Near Liberty Bus Stop, University Road, Ahmedabad 380009, India; tel. 91 272 656 0751.

Chittagong Hill Tracts, Displaced Peoples, BA/1 High School Road, Desbandhu Nagar, Baguiati, Calcutta 700059, India.

Commonwealth Human Rights Initiative, Room 507, IMA House, Indraprastha Marg, New Delhi 110002, India; tel. 91 11 331 0640, fax 91 11 331 0640.

Dalit Liberation Education Trust, 49 First Avenue, Indira Nagar, Madras 600020, India.

Gandhi Peace Foundation, 221/23 Deen Dayal Upadhyaya Marg, New Delhi 110002, India; tel. 91 11 331 7491/7493, fax 91 11 323 6734.

Human Rights Trust, 204 Ghalib Apartments, Parwana Marg Road 42, Pitam Pura, New Delhi 110034, India.

Indian Confederation of Indigenous and Tribal Peoples, 2 Masjid Lane, Bhogal-Jangpura, New Delhi 110014, India; tel. 92 11 460 3017.

Indian National Social Action Forum (INSAF), C1 Shivdham 62, Link Road, Malad (West), Bombay 400064, India; tel. 91 22 882 2950/889 8662, fax 91 22 889 8941.

Jharkhandis Organization for Human Rights (JOHAR), PO Box 3, Chaibasa, Pin 833201, Dist. Singhbhum West, Bihar, India.

Multiple Action Research Group (MARG), 113-A Shahpur Jet, New Delhi 110016, India; tel. 91 11 646 7483, fax 91 11 647 5371.

Naga Peoples' Movement for Human Rights (NPMHR), CEC Office, F-20 Ground Floor, Jankpura Extension, New Delhi 110014, India; tel./fax 91 11 462 4874.

National Front for Tribal Self-Rule, 3 Yezdeh Behram, Malyan, Dahanu Road, Thane District, Maharashtra 401602, India; tel. 91 25 282 2760.

The Other Media, K-14 (FF), Green Park Extension, New Delhi 110016, India; tel. 91 11 686 3830, fax 91 11 685 8042.

Oxfam (India) Trust, C-6/59, Safdarjung Development Area, New Delhi 110106, India; tel. 91 11 685 0318, fax 91 11 696 4611.

South Asia Human Rights Documentation Centre, 6/105 Kaushalya Park, Hauz Khas, New Delhi 110016, India; tel. 91 11 685 9622, tel./fax 91 11 686 5736.

World Chakma Organization (WCO), 3 Sambhu Das Lane, Bow Bazar, Calcutta 12, India; tel./fax 91 33 269 658.

Maldives

Land area:	298 sq km
Population:	261,310 (1995)
Main languages:	Dhivehi (national language)
Main religions:	Islam (state religion)
Main minority groups:	—
Real per capita GDP:	$2,200
UNDP HDI/rank:	0.610 (107)

The Republic of Maldives comprises a chain of 1,190 small coral islands in the Indian Ocean, lying about 675 kilometres south-west of Sri Lanka. The islands are grouped into twenty-six natural atolls (ring-shaped coral reefs) but divided into nineteen atolls for administrative purposes. The Maldivian people are of mixed Indo-Aryan, Dravidian and Arab descent. The Maldives achieved full independence from British rule on 26 July 1965 and became a republic on 11 November 1968. Under the provisions of the 1968 constitution, the President is head of state and vested with full executive powers. He is elected every five years by a two-stage process in which the Majlis (Citizens' Council) has responsibility for choosing the nominee in a secret vote; this choice must then be endorsed through a nationwide referendum. The current head of state, President Maumoon Abdul Gayoom, first came to power in November 1978 and was re-elected in October 1993 for a further five-year period following a national referendum.

The Maldivian people pride themselves on belonging to a self-reliant society, closely knit and united by religion and a single language, with no known minority concerns, yet the Maldives government cannot claim to be proud of its human rights record. In 1994 Amnesty International reported that at least fifteen possible prisoners of conscience were arrested because of their political views or religious practices. In July 1994, the Majlis passed legislation which carries a punishment of up to five years' imprisonment for anyone found guilty of involvement in 'giving religious advice that contravenes independence and government policy and the policy stated by the President'. Dozens of people were arrested and unlawfully detained in the run-up to the parliamentary elections of December 1994; some detainees, it has been alleged, were ill-treated. Further, the entire political framework in the Maldives appears to negate the principle of democratic governance. The formation of political parties is banned, resulting in an absence of any concerted opposition. Although a member of the United Nations since 1965, the country is not party to the majority of UN conventions and covenants on human rights.

Nepal

Land area:	147,181 sq km
Population:	21 million (1995)
Main languages:	Nepali (national language)
Main religions:	Hinduism (state religion), Buddhism
Main minority groups:	Buddhists 2.1 million (10%), Muslims 630,000 (3%), linguistic minorities
Real per capita GDP:	$1,000
UNDP HDI/rank:	0.332 (151)

The Kingdom of Nepal is a landlocked country surrounded by India on three sides and Tibet, a region of China, to the north. Nepal has a long and fascinating history. The spread of Buddhism, its displacement by Hinduism and the induction of the caste system are significant historical occurrences with major contemporary dimensions. The modern history of Nepal may be thought of as starting with the Gurkha ruler Pirthivinarayan Shah's conquest of Kathmandu valley in 1769, bringing under one rule the kingdoms of Patan, Bhkatpur and Kathmandu. The expansionist policies of Pirthivinarayan Shah and his successors resulted in the borders of their empire stretching as far as the River Sutlej to the west, with significant inroads in the Gangetic plains in the south. This expansion, however, brought the Gurkhas – inhabitants of the small Gurkha hill state, now part of Nepal – into conflict with China, and their subsequent defeat in 1816 at the hands of the British resulted in a peace treaty which, with subsequent minor adjustments, represents the present borders of Nepal. From 1816 to 1846 was a period of political strife and intrigue, which culminated in the seizure of power by Jung Bahadur, who adopted the prestigious title of Rana and proclaimed himself Prime Minster for life. The office of Rana was made hereditary, with Rana descendants ruling Nepal until the end of the Second World War, although the Shah dynasty continued subsequently to occupy the throne.

The British withdrawal from India in 1947 was of serious consequence to the Ranas, who were then faced with a number of movements for political reform. King Tribhuvan briefly fled into exile in India, lending his support to the anti-Rana movement. The Ranas finally yielded to India's pressure, and King Tribhuvan returned in 1951 with full powers restored to the monarchy. He established a government comprising Ranas and members of the National Congress Party (NCP), but this coalition was short-lived. Tribhuvan's son and successor, Mahendra, who succeeded in 1955, decided that partyless elections and the *panchayat* (an advisory body appointed by the King) system were the most suitable system of government. The King selected the cabinet and Prime Minister, and appointed a large segment of the National Assembly, thus retaining political power.

A wave of political unrest and dissatisfaction with the government culminated in the Jana Andolan or Peoples Movement of 1990. King Birendra, who had reigned since 1972, conceded to the demands of democracy and accountability by dissolving the cabinet, lifting the ban on political parties and inviting opposition parties to form an interim government. By November 1990 a new constitution guaranteeing free speech, human rights and a constitutional monarchy was in place. Under its provisions the King remains commander-in-chief of the armed forces but cannot make executive decisions without consulting the Prime Minister and cabinet. The old *panchayat* was replaced by a Parliament consisting of a directly elected House of Representatives and a smaller National Assembly. Since 1991 control of the government has alternated between the NCP and the United Communist Party of Nepal.

Minority and related issues

Nepal is an ethnically complex and diverse country with numerous linguistic communities including Gurung, Magar, Tamang, Rai, Limbu, Thakali, Sherpa, Tharu and Raute. The Hindu religious community can be subdivided into Hill Hindus, comprising Bahuns (or Brahmins), Thakuris, Chhettris and Newars, on the one hand, and Terai (southern-based) Hindus, comprising Maithili, Bhojpuri and Awadhi linguistic communities among others, on the other. A trend likely to be nurtured by a democratic environment is the development of stronger group consciousness and stronger demands for a share of political power and recognition of group status, whether based on ethnicity, language or both.

Nepal has traditionally been dominated by Brahmins and Chhettris, and the language and culture projected from the centre have been those of the Hindu populations of the hill and Kathmandu valley regions. Those hill peoples who speak Tibeto-Burman languages (Rai, Limbu, Tamang, Magar, Gurung and others) have been under-represented in government, while the Terai population in the south, mainly Hindus and Hindi-speakers, have also felt themselves to be poorly served in terms of the distribution of public resources. Language issues were centred on the status of Nepali as a national language, and suggestions have ranged from allowing other languages to enjoy the same status – such as Hindi for the Terai population – to abolishing Nepali as a national language and turning Nepal into a federal state with each autonomous region having its own language. The Constitution of 1990 includes the statement that 'all the languages spoken as the mother tongue in various parts of Nepal are the national languages of Nepal'.

Other prime areas of concern for minorities in Nepal are landlessness, deforestation and bonded labour. Studies indicate that people of the Limbu, Chepang and Tharu linguistic communities have lost their land rights through a combination of abrupt changes in land tenure laws, the influx of Brahmin and Chhettri settlers and the communities' lack of literacy and awareness of legal procedures.[1] In this process, land once cultivated as common land comes gradually into the hands of immigrant groups that are able to register land they initially cultivated as tenants. Land reform legislation appears to have hurt several linguistic minorities, as has the mismanagement of compulsory savings schemes, and their frequent lack of knowledge of legal and bureaucratic workings has made them vulnerable. Further, the Private Forest Nationalization Act 1957 and subsequent legislation led the way for administration of the forests to be taken over by the state. This resulted in grave injustices, largely arising from corruption among Brahmin forest administrators.[2] Linguistic minorities of Nepal have also to contend with debt bondage and serfdom. One recent study has shown that the majority of those under debt bondage, the so-called *kamaiya* system, are indeed Tharus, as are their masters.[3] To improve the situation, the study recommends advocacy aimed at establishing tenancy rights and land rights by the cultivation of barren land in the district concerned.

Conclusions and future prospects

Nepal's history of autocracy, political instability and absence of democratic institutions, when aligned with its underdeveloped infrastructure, has led to many violations of individual and collective human rights. Every section of the community has been affected, but Nepal's linguistic minorities have been particularly vulnerable and open to abuse. With democracy beginning to take root, however, a developing political consciousness and gradual assertion of group rights suggest a more hopeful future for hitherto disadvantaged and underprivileged communities.

Further reading

Hutt, M. (ed.), *Nepal in the Nineties: Versions of the Past, Visions of the Future,* London, Oxford University Press, 1994.

Skar, H., 'Nepal indigenous issues and civil rights: the plight of the Rana Tharu', in Barnes, R., Gray, A. and Kingsbury, B. (eds), *Indigenous Peoples of Asia,* Ann Arbor, MI, Association for Asian Studies, 1993, pp.173–94.

Minority-based and advocacy organizations

Amnesty International, PO Box 135, Bagbazar, Kathmandu, Nepal; tel. 977 1 231 587, fax 977 1 225 489.

Group for International Solidarity, PO Box 5690, Maharagunj, Kathmandu, Nepal; tel. 977 1 420 905, fax 977 1 226 820.

Human Rights Organization of Nepal, PO Box 224, Shreenivas, Chha 1/483, Chandol Bishalnagar, Ward No. 4, Kathmandu, Nepal.

Nepal Federation of Nationalities, PO Box 822, Kathmandu, Nepal; tel. 977 1 471 179, fax 977 1 220 082.

Nepal Tamang Ghedung, PO Box 822, Jorpati, Kathmandu, Nepal.

Pakistan

Land area:	796,095 sq km
Population:	124.9 million (1995)
Main languages:	Urdu (national language), Sindhi, Punjabi, Siraiki, Pushtu and Baluchi (regional languages)
Main religions:	Islam, Hinduism, Christianity, Buddhism, Ahmadiya
Main minority groups:	*ethnic minorities:* Sindhis 30–40 million (est., 24–32%), Pathans (Pakhtans) 16.2 million (est., 13%), Mohajirs 10–22 million (est., 8–18%), Baluchis 5 million (est., 4%); *religious minorities:* Christians 1.9 million (est., 1.5%), Ahmadiyas 1.8–4 million (est., 1.4–3.2%), Hindus 1.5 million (est., 1.2%), also Shi'is, Isma'ilis, Bohras, Parsis[1]
Real per capita GDP:	US $2,160
UNDP HDI/rank:	0.442 (134)

The Republic of Pakistan emerged as an independent sovereign state on 14 August 1947, as a result of the partition of the former British India. Today Pakistan is bounded by Iran in the west, Afghanistan in the north-west, India in the east and south-east and the Arabian Sea in the south. But at independence the Pakistani state inherited those contiguous districts of the former Indian empire that had a Muslim majority population; the result was a country divided into two wings of unequal size. Although there were significant differences between various groups of West Pakistan, these differences seemed less prominent when matched with the historical and socio-political features of East Pakistan. West Pakistan was similar in nature to the Middle East in its history, geography, culture and language, whereas East Pakistan bore greater resemblance to South-East Asia. On the other hand, whereas East Pakistan was relatively homogeneous linguistically, each of the provinces of West Pakistan had its own independent language, culture, history and tradition. East Pakistan became the independent People's Republic of Bangladesh after the Indo–Pakistan War of December 1971 (see **Bangladesh**).

Pakistan was proclaimed an Islamic republic in its first constitution, promulgated on 23 March 1956. The first general election under the constitution was due to be held in February 1959. However, Field Marshal Ayub Khan seized power in a military coup in October 1958 and ruled until March 1969, when he was ousted by General Yahya Khan. The country's first free elections were held in December 1970. Zulfikar Ali's Bhutto's Pakistan People's Party (PPP) dominated in West Pakistan, while Sheikh Mujibur Rahman's Awami League swept the polls in East Pakistan. Mujib's call for autonomy was resisted by Yahya and Bhutto, leading eventually to civil war and the creation of Bangladesh. Following the partition of Pakistan, Yahya relinquished power to the civilian government led by Bhutto.

General Zia-ul Haq deposed Bhutto in July 1977. Bhutto was tried for conspiring to murder a political opponent, sentenced to death and, in April 1979, executed. General Zia remained the leader of the country until his death in an air crash in August 1988. His death was followed by the reintroduction of democracy in Pakistan, and in the elections of November 1988, Bhutto's daughter Benazir led the PPP to victory. Benazir Bhutto was dismissed by President Ghulam Ishaq Khan in 1990 and in the elections which followed a coalition government headed by Nawaz Sharif came to power. Sharif was in turn dismissed in April 1993 amid charges of corruption and torture of political opponents. Although the Sharif government was restored by the Supreme Court, Sharif was again dismissed, President Ishaq Khan resigned, and Bhutto returned to power in the 1993 October elections. Bhutto, however, failed to hold a full term in office as Prime Minister. Her government was dismissed by President Farooq Laghari in November 1996 on grounds *inter alia* of corruption and the continued failure to prevent ethnic unrest and civil strife.

Pakistan has seen severe violations of human rights, particularly the rights of minorities, both under the various military regimes and since the restoration of democracy. Pakistan has not ratified a number of major international human rights instruments, including the International

Covenants on Civil and Political Rights (1966) and the two optional protocols, the International Covenant on Economic, Social and Cultural Rights (1966) and the Convention against Torture and other Cruel, Inhuman and Degrading Punishment or Treatment (1984). Nor has it signed the Convention on the Status of Refugees (1951) and its additional protocol (1967). Pakistan did ratify the Convention for the Elimination of All Forms of Discrimination against Women (1979) in 1996.

The issue of the rights of women in the context of an Islamic society has been the subject of intense controversy and debate. Efforts to introduce specific Islamic law have resulted in serious discrimination against women. As to the rights of ethnic, linguistic and religious minorities, two particularly worrying trends have occurred: first, the suppression of the rights of ethnic minorities such as Baluchis, Pathans and Mohajirs, all of whom have had their demands for greater autonomy met with severe government repression; and second, religious minorities such as Hindus, Christians and Ahmadiyas, whose religious freedoms have contracted as a result of harsh legislation around the issue of religious offences. Religious minorities have been targeted by extremist groups among the majority Sunni Muslims – groups that have an organizational strength disproportionate to their electoral support at the polls. Sectarianism appears to be unchecked by the government, contributing to communal clashes in addition to the ethnically rooted conflicts that have characterized Pakistan's history, recently most pronounced in Sindh province.[2]

Concern among religious minorities arises from several sources, including the practice of separate electorates, which denies the equal right to political participation. The system of separate electorates was first introduced under martial law by General Zia-ul-Haq as part of his plan to enforce an Islamic system of governance. It was based on neither the consent nor the involvement of the religious minorities but was enforced in the face of their bitter opposition. Prior to the introduction of separate electorates, non-Muslims alongside Muslim citizens were able to take part in electing members of national and provincial assemblies. Under the new arrangements non-Muslims could vote only for their own representatives in special national constituencies. This scheme both set non-Muslims apart from other fellow citizens and made the representation of their interests extremely difficult. The Sharia Act of 1991, although including an amendment stating that the constitutional guarantees for the minorities would not be affected by the Act, furthered a sense of second class citizenship among minorities, as the religious orthodox would be in a position to interpret the law in a manner best promoting their beliefs. This view was strengthened by the amendment of section 295 (c) of the Pakistan Penal Code, which made the death penalty mandatory for anyone defiling the name of the Holy Prophet Mohammed. The mere mention of the name of the Prophet by the Ahmadiyas is considered by some orthodox Muslims to constitute such defilement.

Constitutional and legislative changes of 1974 and 1984 have effectively deprived Ahmadiyas of the right to practise their religion. In the case of Hindus, victimization has occurred in the context of a backlash against the razing in 1992 of the Babri Masjid (mosque) in Ayodhya, India. No new cases of blasphemy charges against Christians have been reported since mid-1995. Frequent skirmishes have occurred between Sunnis and Shi'is – the latter a Muslim minority in need of protection on a par with the religious minorities. Government legislation and actions appear inadequate against mounting religious sectarianism and the resulting threat to minorities, whether Muslim or not.

There are four officially recognized nationalities in Pakistan: majority Punjabis, Sindhis, Pathans and Baluchis. This entry deals with the Sindhi, Mohajir, Pathan and Baluchi ethnic minority groups on the one hand, and with the Ahmadiya and Hindu religious minority groups on the other. Several other religious minority groups exist within Pakistan, including both minority Islamic groups such as Shi'is, Isma'ilis and Bohras, and also non-Islamic groups such as Christians and Parsis. All face general problems under the influence of the *sharia* system.

Sindhis and Mohajirs

Sindhis and Mohajirs are two large ethnic communities living in Sindh province. Each group regards itself as a nation and contests the other's account of its recent history and current situation. The following description comprises both a Sindhi perspective and a Mohajir one, without seeking to reconcile the evident contradictions.

According to Sindhi sources,[3] Sindhis number approximately 40 million and descend from the original Dravidian inhabitants of Sindh. In 1947, required by Britain to join India or Pakistan, Sindhis chose Pakistan, hoping to safeguard their autonomy. Sindhis maintain that successive Pakistani governments have disregarded their rights; with the creation of Pakistan, large numbers of Urdu-speaking Muslims from India were encouraged to settle in Sindh, while Sindhi Hindus were forced by state-sponsored persecution to flee to India. Property vacated by Sindhi Hindus was allocated to the immigrants (the Mohajirs), whereas Muslim Sindhis who remained were prevented by the government from buying it.

Sindhis argue that Mohajirs were given preferential treatment by the authorities. Despite the growth of the urban Mohajir population, Sindhis claim to constitute a numerical majority in Karachi and many other municipalities. They argue that before partition a highly educated Sindhi Muslim majority controlled provincial politics, but that since 1947 Sindhi-language-medium schools have been closed down or changed to Urdu-medium by the authorities, and Karachi University, formerly a major Sindhi educational institution, is now controlled by the Mohajir provincial administration, with Sindhi students denied entry.

On independence Pakistan made Urdu the national language, denying Sindhi its traditional status in Sindh. In 1972 Sindhi efforts to regain official status for their language resulted, they say, in ethnic disturbances provoked by their opponents. They blame tensions with Mohajirs on continuing illegal population transfers and on Mohajir demands for a separate homeland and accompanying violence. Sindhis accuse Mohajir militants of numerous killings and other outrages, including a wave of attacks launched in 1992, with the Pakistani army becoming involved the same year.

Sindhis see themselves as threatened by the continued immigration and urban settlement of Mohajirs and by a rural influx of Punjabis, many of them military personnel, who they claim obtain ancestral Sindhi lands unlawfully. Numerous Sindhi activists and intellectuals are reportedly in prison, some detained without trial, many tortured and denied legal or medical aid. Sindhis also consider that they are deprived of their share of irrigation water and that the province's fossil fuels are being exploited by outsiders for commercial gain, while many Sindhis suffer unemployment and poverty.

According to the Mohajir view,[4] Mohajirs (the term means 'immigrants') helped found the state of Pakistan in 1947, leaving the Indian provinces where as Muslims they had been a minority for the new homeland they had struggled to help create. They claim to have brought considerable educational attainment, skills and expertise to the new state and quickly rose to positions of prominence in commerce and the administration. Mohajirs state that this early prominence antagonized the existing feudal social order and led to the deployment of various forms of discrimination against them. Successive governments, composed in the main of feudal landowners, adopted measures that deprived Mohajirs of their political, social and economic rights as guaranteed in the constitution and available to all other citizens.

Numbering, according to their own reckoning, some 22 million people, Mohajirs claim to outnumber Sindhis and to be Pakistan's most numerous minority, constituting more than half the population of Sindh. They are concentrated mainly in Karachi and other urban centres. Mohajir nationhood has always been denied, in contrast to that of other nationalities (Punjabis, Baluchis, Pathans and Sindhis).

In the face of continuing discrimination and deprivation, in 1984 Mohajirs founded the Mohajir Quami Movement (MQM), led by Altaf Hussain, to assert their rights. The MQM claims to have won major victories in urban Sindhi in every election held since 1987. This success, Mohajirs argue, led to the launching of a military/police operation against them in June 1992 resulting in the unlawful killing and torture of thousands of Mohajirs. MQM offices throughout Pakistan have been forcibly closed, and all but three of MQM's 30 elected parliamentarians are in jail, in hiding or in exile.

Mohajirs state that the Pakistani government has waged a costly propaganda war against them and the MQM, branding them separatists and terrorists. The MQM has formulated an eighteen-point charter of demands, based on fundamental rights guaranteed in the constitution, and has been involved in negotiations with the national government. All the while, however, the state law enforcement agencies have continued their efforts to eliminate the MQM's supporters and leadership. In 1995 and 1996 the government's tactics in Sindh were condemned, Mohajirs report, by the US State Department and by international human rights organizations. The MQM participated in the general election of February 1996, achieving the third largest share of the vote.

Pathans

Of the estimated 16 million Pashtu-speaking people in Pakistan, who are known as Pathans or Pakhtuns, the vast majority inhabit the plains, whereas a minority of 2.2 million live in the highlands of the semi-autonomous Federally Administered Tribal Areas (FATA). Substantial numbers of Pathans have settled in Baluchistan, and up to 20 per cent of the total population of that province is comprised of Pathans. Due to migration to urban areas there are probably over 1 million Pathans living in greater Karachi. Pathans are, after Sindhis, the second largest ethnic community in Pakistan and belong to the Hanafi school of Sunni Islam. Pathans have an ancient history, culture and tradition often identified with the 'Pakti' kingdom as described in the writing of the classical historian Herodotus. Pathan culture and tradition were established between the twelfth and fifteenth centuries, and Pashtu folklore was ingrained and Pathan nationalism subsequently reinvigorated by the lyrics of Khushal Khan Khattack.

Pathans have a political history beset with internal strife and intrigue. Internal feuds in the Pathan-dominated Afghan regimes of the nineteenth century provided an opportunity to many outsiders, lastly the British, to interfere and subsequently divide the Pathans themselves with the establishment of the Durand line in 1893. Pathans refused to accept this boundary, and Pathan nationalists point out that it divides a 'people' with common tradition and history and continues to deprive Afghanistan of an access to the open sea. Although, by 1946, immediately prior to the partition of India, M.A. Jinnah had had a stranglehold on the affairs of the North West Frontier Province (NWFP), controversy is still generated when some Pathan nationalists highlight the fact that the referendum that had been organized by the British, and led to a 99 per cent vote in favour of joining Pakistan, could not be regarded as conclusive. They point out that the referendum did not give Pathans the option of union with Afghanistan, being limited to union with either India or Pakistan, and that a significant proportion of the Pathan population boycotted the referendum.[5]

It is equally clear that the creation of the Pakistan state was opposed by the Afghans who consorted with the Indian National Congress before partition and were led to believe they would gain the port of Karachi if the Pakistan movement failed. Such anti-Pakistan groups as Ghaffar Khan's Khudai Khidmatgas wanted a homeland for Pakhtuns and have it renamed 'Pakhtunistan'. The Afghan leaders appealed to the ethnic sensitivities of the Afghans and urged the inhabitants of the NWFP to join Afghanistan when it became clear that the British departure was imminent (see **Afghanistan**).

Many aspects of old British policy towards the Pathans have continued in post-independence Pakistan. Although the princely states of the NWFP area were abolished, there continue to be eleven designated 'tribal' areas, comprising the FATA, which remain primarily under central administration. However, they are inhabited by only a small part (18 per cent) of the total Pathan population. These 'tribal' areas retain considerable ethnic autonomy; central and provincial laws do not apply, and they are ruled by customary laws and the Frontier Crimes Regulation. After initial years of indifference to the socio-economic policies of the NWFP, the affairs of the government became highly centralized under Ayub Khan (1958–69), with West Pakistan amalgamated into one unit, which resulted in minority disaffection. After the secession of Bangladesh the provinces were reconstituted, and the 1973 constitution guaranteed considerable provincial autonomy – although in practice power was centralized even more than in previous years. The highly centralized form of government continued during the eleven-year rule of General Zia. The Zia government was initially wary of asserting its influence in the NWFP, but the Soviet military occupation of Afghanistan led to increased attempts to control the 'tribal' areas, most notably in 1985–6, with regard to heroin and arms smuggling. The presence of large numbers of refugees from Afghanistan (largely Pashtuns) also contributed to destabilizing the area. Over 3 million Afghan refugees came to Pakistan, 75 per cent to the NWFP, with a special impact on the FATA, where one out of three of the population were refugees. Apart from humanitarian and economic considerations, the refugees posed a security dilemma, as Afghan resistance groups operated from Pakistan, and *mojahedin* fighters moved freely across the border.

The economy of the NWFP is weak. What little industry exists is concentrated in the regional capital, Peshawar. Economic development is generally welcome, but some Pathan leaders have attempted to impede road construction as this would erode their own autonomy. Large amounts of opium are produced in Pathan areas and are an important economic factor; the government of Zia ul-Haq attempted a massive crackdown on opium production and consumption, with little success. There has also been severe class conflict between landlords and tenants among Pathans.

Despite the return to democracy in 1988, the political situation in the province has remained fluid. Successive provincial governments have found it difficult to stay in power. In April 1994 Bhutto's PPP succeeded in forming the provincial government. Continuing political instability, and dissatisfaction with the administration of justice and with the government's foreign policy in relation to Afghanistan, have been reflected in such incidents as the revolt of Pathan Islamists in Malakand in November 1994 in which at least 200 people died, as well as the bomb blast of December 1995 in Peshawar that resulted in the death of twenty-one people.

Baluchis

Although split between the three countries of Afghanistan, Iran and Pakistan, the majority of Baluchi people live in the Baluchistan province of Pakistan. Baluchis do not form a homogeneous group, branching out as the Makrani or western Baluchis in Pakistan and south-western Afghanistan, the Sulemani or eastern Baluchis in Iran, and the Brahuis of the central Kalat plateau of Pakistani Baluchistan. The latter speak the Brahui language, which though not related to Baluchi has certain resonances with that language. Baluchis are Sunni Muslims of the Hanafi school. Although there is considerable controversy surrounding their origins, according to popular Baluchi legend they migrated northward from Aleppo (in modern Syria) for pastureland and fresh water during the Arab conquests of the ninth century, travelling along the southern shores of the Caspian Sea and subsequently settling in what is now Iranian and Pakistani Baluchistan by the fourteenth century.[6]

Baluchi nationalists point to their largely independent history spreading over several centuries. Afghans, Persians and Sikh, all made repeated though unsuccessful attempts to establish complete control over Baluchistan. The British gained control over a considerable proportion of the region during the nineteenth century, at first through political agreements and subsidies negotiated with Baluchi leaders, and by the 1870s through direct territorial control or through influence over the princely states. Even then, Baluchis enjoyed considerable autonomy. Their customary 'tribal' law, for instance, was retained and enforced by 'tribal councils' under the authority of the Frontier Crimes Regulation (FCR).

Baluchis have experienced considerable internal strife and bitter feuds and have historically been unable to present a united political front. One key exception was in the eighteenth century, when successive rulers of the Baluchi principality of Kalat forged political unity throughout most of the Baluchi area. Since that period the Khanate of Kalat has remained a symbol of Baluchi nationalism. Indeed, prior to the independence of India there were serious possibilities of Baluchis being accorded self-rule under the inspirational leader of the Khan of Kalat. According to an agreement reached between the British and Pakistan governments on 4 August 1947: 'The Government of Pakistan recognizes the status of Kalat as a free and independent state which has bilateral relations with the British Government, and whose rank and position is different from that of other Indian states.'[7] Eleven days later the Khan of Kalat declared the independence of Kalat, a decision endorsed by the Kalat Assembly. While the newly formed government of Pakistan immediately repudiated the declaration of independence, amalgamation with Pakistan or the dismemberment of Kalat was unacceptable to the Khan.

Ignoring these political aspirations, the Pakistan authorities relied heavily on the decision of Baluchi leaders in Quetta on 29 June 1947 to merge with Pakistan, deliberately concealing the fact that these leaders had been appointed by the British, and their assembly's decision related to the small tract of land known as British Baluchistan. Baluchi rulers remained unhappy with Pakistan's interference in what they regarded as their domestic affairs, and they continued to be rebellious. Despite constant threats of coercion, and actual use of force, only in 1955 did the rulers of these independent territories formally agree to cede their states. The element of a probable claim of secession on the part of Khan of Kalat was used as a major issue which led to the abrogation of Pakistan's first constitution in October 1958, the arrest of the Khan, and the promulgation of martial law.

Recent Baluchi history in Pakistan is marked by the major rebellion of 1973–7against the government of Pakistan. This followed increasing centralization of power despite numerous assurances of devolution set out in the new Pakistani constitution of 1973, drafted following the independence of Bangladesh. The new constitution contained numerous guarantees of the rights of ethnic minorities, reaffirming their separate legal status and right to their own language and culture. The government of Zulfikar Ali Bhutto, however, disregarded these guarantees, and the provinces became increasingly subordinate to central authority. The crisis erupted when Bhutto dismissed the coalition government of Baluchistan in 1973 on the grounds of its alleged encouragement of a secessionist movement, smuggling and opposition to modernization. Opposition leaders were arrested and jailed, and in 1976 the *sardari* 'tribal chief' system was abolished. Meanwhile the war had escalated; by 1974 there were reported to be as many as 55,000 Baluchis fighting some 70,000 government troops. It is estimated that over 5,000 insurgents and 3,000 government troops were killed, and large quantities of livestock were destroyed, while the interruption of food supplies to civilians in insurgent-controlled areas caused great suffering. Some Baluchi rebels surrendered under a general amnesty; others fled to Afghanistan, where they were housed in government camps. The insurgency continued fitfully until the fall of the Bhutto government in 1977 and the subsequent release of jailed leaders of the region. Throughout the military rule of General Zia (1977–88) and the governments of Benazir Bhutto (1988–90, 1993) and Nawaz Sharif (1990–3) Baluchi demands have centred around political and economic autonomy. They demand a re-adjustment of power, with the federal government in control of only defence and foreign affairs and the province having unfettered authority over provincial matters.

Ahmadiyas

The Ahmadiya religious movement is an Islamic sect that originated in India. Its followers are sometimes referred to as Qadiyanies, from the village of Qadian where the founder, Mirza Ghulam Ahmad (1835–1908), was born. The movement has been successful in spreading to other parts of the world, with over 10 million members worldwide. Mirza Ghulam Ahmad was a Muslim revivalist who claimed to be a prophet, and this in particular alienated orthodox Muslims. In many ways the life of Ahmadiyas conforms to Islam, although the movement rejects the idea of militant *jihad* (holy war). Ahmadiyas in Pakistan follow the tradition of being a reformist Muslim sect; they consider themselves to be within Islam, although many orthodox Muslims regard them as non-Muslim. Though Qadian is in Indian territory, after 1947 the Ahmadiyas shifted their headquarters to Pakistan. Numerically a relatively small group, they have penetrated deeply all walks of life and become one of the most significant groups within Pakistan politics.

Growing Ahmadiya influence became a source of concern after independence and partition. Demands were voiced that they should be declared to be non-Muslims and should be excluded from definitions of what constituted Islam. Religious friction came to a peak in 1953 with demonstrations and violence against the Ahmadiya community. Tensions resurfaced in the early 1970s amid renewed demands on the part of Pakistan clerics to declare Ahmadiyas non-Muslims. As a result of this pressure, Ahmadiyas were declared non-Muslims in September 1974 by the Pakistan Parliament. A new clause of the constitution (clause 3 in Article 260) outlawed the group in the following terms:

'A person who does not believe in the absolute and unqualified finality of the Prophet Muhammad (S.M.) the last of the prophets, or claims to be a prophet, in any sense of the word or of any description whatsoever, after Muhammad (S.M.), or recognises such a claimant as a prophet or a religious reformer, is not a Muslim for the purposes of the constitution or law.'

Several laws in the Penal Code prohibit the exercise of Ahmadiya beliefs. Ahmadiyas are prohibited from calling themselves Muslims and from following Muslim practices.

The goal of the 1991 Sharia' law – to ensure the comprehensive Islamization of society – and the extension of the blasphemy laws have encouraged an atmosphere of religious intolerance and sectarianism in Pakistan. Ahmadiyas have found their freedom to express their beliefs curtailed and subject to arbitrary and severe punishment. The right to assembly can be restricted under section 144 of the Criminal Procedure Code, which provides for the banning of gatherings of more than four people with the intention of preventing breaches of the public peace. This provision is used most frequently against Ahmadiyas. For example, Lahore High Court dismissed in September 1991 a petition by Ahmadiyas challenging the banning of their centenary celebrations in Punjab; the court ruled that reasons of public policy, the public good and the interests of the ordinary people of the country provide a justifiable basis for banning the celebrations – adding however, that the right to profess and practise the Ahmadiya faith was not thereby infringed or violated.

Hindus and other religious minorities

The Hindu population of Pakistan makes up a small minority of about 1.5 million, or 1.2 per cent, of the total population. They live mostly in rural areas of Sindh in the lower Indus valley, many as bonded labourers, and over half are concentrated in the south-east district of Thar Parkar, which borders India. Sind at one time had a very sizeable Hindu population; however, at the time of partition large numbers migrated to the Indian side of the border. Those who decided to stay behind in Pakistan after partition had to face constitutional limitations and social stigma. One of the country's principal and primary constitutional documents, the Objective Resolution of March 1949 makes provision for non-Muslims to freely profess and practise their religion, and this tolerant spirit is reflected in the provisions of the 1956, 1962 and the 1973 constitutions. However, despite the presence of these constitutional guarantees, the Hindu community both prior to and even after 1971 has been a continual target of suspicion and has often been treated as a fifth column. Political expediency has allowed Hindus to be treated as scapegoats for the general incompetence of governments in power. While Islam has been used as the great rallying force for political ends, conversely, and for the same purposes, Hindus have been treated as anti-state and anti-Islamic elements, discriminated against and persecuted, arguably becoming victims of genocide during the secessionist war of 1971. Hindus generally lack equal access to education, employment and social advancement.

In the partyless elections of 1985 held by President Zia after the lifting of martial law, Hindus and other religious minorities were allocated separate electorates in nationwide minority constituencies. Previously the minority groups had voted in general electorates in which they resided, and members of the National Assembly subsequently elected members from the minority communities to sit in the legislature. The system of separate electorates was retained in the general elections of 1988, 1990 and 1993. Ten of the 207 seats in the National Assembly were set aside for minorities: four seats for Hindus, four for Christians, one for Ahmadiyas, and one for smaller groups such as Parsis, Sikhs, Baha'is, Jews and Kalash. Some Hindus remain opposed to the system of separate electorates, which they claim dilutes the influence of the community and paves the way for further segregation. Recent outbursts of anti-Hindu sentiment occurred in the backlash to the Babri Masjid incident of December 1992 in Ayodhya, India.

Conclusions and future prospects

Ever since its creation, Pakistan has had to face serious problems in relation to its minorities. The rather artificial nature of the national boundaries, large-scale discrimination against Bengalis and persecution of Hindus were all evident prior to the secession of East Pakistan. Since 1971, the most serious threat to the integrity of Pakistan to date has taken the form of the Baluchi insurgency of 1973–7. More recently, ethnic and sectarian violence in the urban Sindh, most prominently in Karachi, has been particularly disturbing, resulting in thousands of casualties. The actions of the law enforcement agencies and in particular the extra-judicial killings of opponents of the present government is a matter of serious international concern. Religious minorities, particularly Ahmadiyas and Christians, have also been a target for vague and potentially discriminatory legislation regarding blasphemy. There are three main areas of challenge for the future of Pakistan's many minority groups. The first arises from the growing influence of militant Islamic ideology, with its insistence on closing down areas of difference between the various faiths and cultures of Pakistan's religious minorities. The second relates to the problems of establishing democratic structures and the role of the military establishment; democracy and democratic institutions are essential if a multicultural society is to flourish. Finally, there is the challenge of economic development, to ensure that Pakistan's many peoples are adequately housed, clothed and fed. The future of Pakistan's minority peoples depends to a large extent on how these challenges are met over the next few years.

Further reading

Human Rights Commission of Pakistan, *State of Human Rights in Pakistan,* Lahore, annual reports 1991–5.

Human Rights Watch/Asia, *Persecuted Minorities and Writers in Pakistan,* New York, September 1993.

International Commission of Jurists, *Pakistan: Human Rights after Martial Law,* Geneva, 1987.

Islam, M.N., *Pakistan: A Study in National Integration*, Lahore, Vanguard, 1990.

Kamal, A., *Pakistan: Political and Constitutional Dilemmas,* Karachi, Pakistan Law House, 1987.

Nasr, S.V.R., *The Vanguard of the Islamic Revolution: The Jama'at-i Islami of Pakistan,* London, Tauris, 1994.

Wirsing, R.G., *The Baluchis and Pathans,* London, MRG report, 1987.

Minority-based and advocacy organizations

Centre for Legal Aid Assistance and Settlement, 31 Kacha Ferozpur Road, Lahore, Pakistan; tel. 92 42 759 1571.

Centre for Women in Crisis/Voice Against Torture, House 344, Street No. 97, G9/4, Islamabad, Pakistan.

Human Rights Commission of Pakistan (HRCP), 13 Sharif Complex, Main Market, Gulberg, Lahore, Pakistan; tel. 92 42 575 9219, fax 92 42 571 3078.

Human Rights Society of Pakistan, 10 Mona Shopping Centre, Chirah Road, PO Box 1761, Rawalpindi, Pakistan.

Lawyers for Human Rights and Legal Aid, 702 Mohammadi House, I.I. Chundrigar Road, Karachi 74200, Pakistan.

Sri Lanka

Land area:	64,454 sq km
Population:	18.3 million (1995)
Main languages:	Sinhala (official and national language), Tamil (national language), English
Main religions:	Buddhism, Hinduism, Islam, Christianity
Main minority groups:	Tamils 3,302,000 (18%), Muslims 1,394,000 (7.6%), Veddhas 2,000 (est., 0.01%)
Real per capita GDP:	$3,030
UNDP HDI/rank:	0.698 (89)

The Democratic Socialist Republic of Sri Lanka (formerly known as Ceylon) comprises one large, compact island and several islets, separated from the Indian subcontinent by a strip of sea which at its narrowest point is 40 kilometres wide, and centrally located in the Indian Ocean, lying off the southern tip of India. The country gained independence from British rule on 4 February 1948. The first Prime Minister, Stephen Senanayake, sought to reconcile the legitimate interests of the majority and minority ethnic and religious groups within the context of a parliamentary form of government. His United National Party (UNP) entrenched its position within a year of the gaining of independence and strengthened its hold on Parliament. The first major challenge to the UNP came from the Sri Lanka Freedom Party (SLFP), formed in 1951 under the leadership of S.W.R.D. Bandaranaike. The Mahajana Eksath Peramma (MEP, People's United Front) swept the UNP government out of power in 1956, but in September 1959 Prime Minister Bandaranaike was assassinated by a Buddhist monk. An insurrection by mainly unemployed youths in April 1971 was crushed by the United Front (UF) government of Sirimavo Bandaranaike, widow of the former prime minister. On 22 May 1972 the country was renamed the Republic of Sri Lanka. The UF lost power in the 1977 general election and the UNP administration of Prime Minister J.R. Jayawardene took over.

Jayawardene replaced the 1972 constitution and assumed unprecedented power as Executive President, becoming both head of state and head of government. He was elected to a second six-year term in October 1982, and in a referendum won a mandate to extend parliament to 1989. In late 1988, former Prime Minister Ranasinghe Premadasa was elected Executive President, and in 1989 the UNP won a large majority in parliamentary elections. On 1 May 1993, however, President Premadasa was assassinated, and was succeeded by Dingiri Banda Wijetunga. Parliamentary elections held in August 1994 saw the UNP government narrowly defeated by a coalition People's Alliance (PA), led by the SLFP under the leadership of Solomon Bandaranaike's daughter Chandrika Kumaratunga. For three months Chandrika Kumaratunga remained Prime Minister as Wijetunga held the office of President. However, in November 1994 Chandrika Kumaratunga was elected President by an emphatic 62 per cent of the vote, and she has continued to hold the office since then.

Politics in Sri Lanka over the years has been dominated by the question of resolving the rights of minorities, in particular the Tamil population. This entry looks at the Tamil issue in some detail, for the conflict between the majority Sinhalese and the Tamils has been the root cause of widespread violations of human rights and ethnic unrest. There is also a brief consideration of the Muslims (also called Moors) of Sri Lanka, and of the Veddhas (Waaniy-a-Laato, or forest-dwellers), the country's small community of indigenous peoples. The position of Veddhas merits careful analysis, for the entire community is in danger of extinction over the next few years. Apart from these groups, Sri Lanka also has other, smaller communities, including Malays and Burghers.

Tamils[1]

Sri Lanka has a plural society. The majority group, the Sinhalese, speak a distinctive language (Sinhala) related to the Indo-Aryan tongues of north India, and are mainly Buddhist. There are two groups of Tamils: 'Sri Lankan Tamils' (also known as 'Ceylon' or 'Jaffna' Tamils), the descendants of Tamil-speaking groups who migrated from south India many centuries ago; and 'Up Country Tamils' (also known as 'Indian' or 'estate' Tamils), the descendants of comparatively recent immigrants. Both Tamil groups are predominantly Hindu. The Up Country Tamils of Sri Lanka, who number about 1 million, are descended from south Indians brought to the country by the British in the nineteenth and early twentieth centuries to work on the tea and rubber plantations. At the dawn of independence they were made stateless and deprived of their political rights through the Citizenship Acts of 1948–9. Agreements with the Indian government, providing for repatriation or the awarding of Sri Lankan citizenship, were not fully implemented. This position has not changed, despite a decision in 1988 to grant all stateless persons citizenship except those who had opted for returning to India. According to the 1992 report by the Controller of Immigration and Emigration, Sri Lanka has yet to grant citizenship to 237,151 people under the terms of the Indo-Lanka Agreement of 1967. Of those opting for Indian citizenship, 80,907 still await repatriation, although the government has given assurances that it will fulfil its part of the agreement. A total of 318,058 Up Country Tamils consequently remain stateless, and Up Country Tamils thus continue to be by far the most disadvantaged minority in Sri Lanka.

The roots of the Tamil conflict go back to the years leading up to Sri Lankan independence and to assurances given to the Tamil minority by the first Sri Lankan Prime Minister, Stephen Senanayake, that they would not be discriminated against with regard to representation and legislation. However, under the two acts passed by the new government, citizenship was granted only to those persons who could prove that they had been born in Sri Lanka and who had been resident there since 1936. Since most Up Country Tamils did not have access to relevant documents, they were effectively rendered stateless. At the same time Sinhala nationalism was growing; and as vernacular education gradually replaced English, there were moves to adopt Sinhala as the official language of Sri Lanka. The *swabasha* or 'own language' movement became a central part of the nationalist cause, and the MEP government of 1956 declared that Sinhala should be the one official language of the country.

However, in view of the political pressure emanating from the Tamil Federal Party, the then Prime Minster proposed plans for preferential treatment for Tamils, and the Bandaranaike-Chelvanayakam pact of 1957 also promised 'recognition of Tamil as the language of a national minority'. The pact was never implemented, and in the years that followed positions slowly became polarized. The assassination of Bandaranaike in 1959 led to the strengthening of the Tamil Federal Party, which called for parity of status for Tamils, citizenship on the basis of residence, and the creation of one or more linguistic states. Elections held in 1960 saw the Federal Party gain the Northern province and all seats in the Eastern province. When fresh elections were held later in the year Sirimavo Bandaranaike became Prime Minister.

During the 1960s the 'Sinhla only' policy was expanded by the ruling UF government to include court proceedings, previously conducted in English. In 1964 an agreement between Sri Lanka and India provided for the repatriation of 975,000 Tamils over a period of fifteen years; 300,000 others would be granted Sri Lankan citizenship. In 1968 the Federal Party left the government and the new UF government which came to power in 1970, wrote a new constitution. This 1972 constitution established the country as a republic, severing constitutional links with the United Kingdom. While pursuing the 'Sinhla only' policy with great vigour and establishing the religious pre-eminence of Buddhism, the new republican constitution did away with the earlier constitution's safeguards for minorities. That same year a system of 'standardization' was introduced in the universities, which in practice meant that Sinhalese were given a better chance of admission than many highly educated Tamils. Tamils also felt that they were being squeezed out of positions they had occupied in the civil service; between independence and 1973 the percentage of Tamil admissions fell from 30 to 6 per cent. State-sponsored colonization schemes put many Sinhalese settlers into Tamil areas. Gradually groups from both communities moved towards extremism. The idea of a separate state became dominant in 1976 with the creation of the Tamil United Liberation Front (TULF). Among several resistance groups formed at this time was the Tamil New Tigers, later becoming the Liberation Tigers of Tamil Eelam (LTTE).

The United National Party (UNP) led by J.R. Jayawardene came to power in 1977. The TULF, now pledged to achieving a separate state, gained all 14 seats in the Northern province and 3 out of 10 seats in the Eastern province and became the principal opposition party. Relations with the UNP were at first cordial. Standardization in university admissions was abolished, and Tamil was recognized in the constitution as a national language. Talks were planned on the subject of removing discrimination in employment and education. Within a month of the elections, however, violence broke out in the north, quickly spreading to the south. The government extended legislation renewing special powers to curb the violence, and from this time on there was a steady erosion of democratic government and human rights protection which affected all communities but most particularly Tamils. During the upheavals Up Country Tamils, who had not previously been involved in the trouble, came under Sinhalese attack, and several thousand families sought refuge in the north, where they made links with Sri Lankan Tamils. Conditions on the estates had deteriorated sharply due to a slump in the export trade and rising domestic inflation. Medical and educational facilities were poor, and there was high infant mortality due partly to poor sanitation and lack of knowledge about hygiene. Nationalization of the estates in 1975 had made conditions worse rather than improving them. Many Indian Tamils were now becoming militant.

After the violence of 1977 the Tamil and Sinhalese communities were scarcely on speaking terms. A planned round table conference failed to take place, and on the Tamil side the idea of Tamil Eelam, a separate and independent state, became dominant. Yet most Tamils would probably have accepted less than this ideal: a reasonable degree of autonomy in running their own administration, and security from the fear of being dominated or overrun as a minority in their own areas through colonization. The urge to maintain their existing, though disproportionate, representation in institutions of higher education was also evident. A scheme put forward by President Jayawardene in 1981, offering Tamils some degree of autonomy under an all-island system of district development councils, was far too little to satisfy Tamil aspirations. Sinhalese hardliners opposed any concessions to Tamils, and Jayawardene instituted a series of measures which effectively curtailed civil liberties. A state of emergency and censorship of the press were imposed in 1981, while in late 1982 a referendum was used to extend the government's term of office until 1989. Extremist actions were increasing, and in July and August 1983 inter-communal violence reached a new pitch of intensity in the south when Sinhalese mobs turned on Tamils.

Tamil militant groups that had formed during the 1970s were able to consolidate their positions in the 1980s. In 1983 four such groups came together under the umbrella of the Tamil Eelam Liberation Front (TELF) with the goal of complete independence. Infighting among the Tamil groups, however, gradually led to a position of dominance for the LTTE, aided by its fanatical fighting force as well as support from India and abroad. As the government tightened its counter-insurgency campaign in the north, all Tamils were seen as suspect; thousands of young Tamil men were routinely detained and tortured.

Fighting between the LTTE and the security forces assumed greater intensity throughout the first half of 1987. In May a large-scale offensive against LTTE positions in the north-east resulted in the detention of over 2,500 Tamils and the deaths of between 200 and 1,000 people, many of them civilians. By this time there were over 130,000 Tamil refugees living in camps in Tamil Nadu, India, and the Indian government was under increasing pressure to intervene on behalf of the Sri Lanka Tamils. At talks held in New Delhi the leader of the LTTE rejected settlement proposals put forward by the Indian Prime Minister, Rajiv Gandhi. In July 1987, however, India and Sri Lanka signed an agreement which provided for regional autonomy and for the creation of newly elected provincial councils on an island-wide basis. The agreement made provision for the merging of the Northern and Eastern provinces into one provincial council, pending the outcome of a referendum to be held in the east alone to decide whether the merger should proceed.[2] Provincial councils were to be largely autonomous, and Tamil, Sinhala and English were to be given equal status as administrative languages. Hostilities would officially cease on 31 July 1987, and an amnesty would be granted to all political prisoners after the lifting of the state of emergency in mid-August. In accordance with the agreement, 3,000 Indian troops, designated the Indian Peace Keeping Force (IPKF), were sent to the north-east.

The peace proposal foundered against a backlash of Sinhala public opinion, as well as the insistence of the LTTE on independence, despite having initially agreed to accept the terms of the peace accord. The LTTE repudiated the agreement as a direct response to the failure of guarantees that Tamils would have control over the new northern-eastern provincial councils. In September 1987 Tamil groups failed to heed an Indian warning that they should stop feuding after at least 100 people had died in clashes. Indian troops launched an offensive in Jaffna against the LTTE guerrillas in October, and in one month of fierce fighting tens of thousands of refugees were made homeless. The LTTE demanded that the Indian forces withdraw to their original positions and cease patrolling the region, but instead more Indian troops were brought in. By mid-1988 an estimated Indian 70,000 troops were present, including paramilitary police, and air force, naval and support personnel. More than 1,000 civilians had died and an equal number of troops and guerrillas.

Despite the disturbances, in November 1987 a constitutional amendment created the provincial council in a unified northern and eastern region and seven Sinhalese majority regions, also granting substantial autonomy to provincial councils throughout the island. Even at the time the constitutional amendment was drafted, Tamil parties had expressed concern that it had been done too hastily, that it failed to deliver the extent of powers promised under the accord and that too much control remained in the centre. Elections to the new provincial council were held throughout 1988, the Eelam People's Liberation Organization (EPLF) winning control of the council. The councils were never allowed to work properly and were eventually overtaken by political events. The elections to the new provincial council had been boycotted by the LTTE, which had established itself as the dominant Tamil group fighting for independence. With the Sri Lankan government beset by myriad problems, including the rise of an extreme left-wing Sinhala movement, the situation deteriorated rapidly once Indian troops had withdrawn in 1990. The life of the councils was short; they were dissolved soon after the departure of the IPKF.

The coming to power of the People's Alliance government after victory in the August 1994 elections raised hopes and expectations that the long-running Tamil dispute would eventually be settled through a process of negotiation and political accommodation. The Chandrika Kumaratunga government promised fresh devolution proposals, and the LTTE called a cease-fire on 8 January 1995 to allow a process of talks to begin. However, these expectations were shattered after a few months. While the government resorted to force to coerce Tamils into submission, the LTTE called off its cease-fire, alleging that the government was not sincere in its approach resolving the dispute. War was resumed with savage intensity, and the government declared that the only way to resolve the issue was to wipe out the LTTE. Government forces launched their biggest-ever military offensive against the Jaffna stronghold of the LTTE, and the subsequent fighting has resulted in untold misery and death for Tamil and Sinhala people, and pushed further back any chance of a negotiated settlement. With the government forces' capture of Jaffna in late 1995, this long and bitter civil war appeared to reach new intensities of bloodshed and human suffering. In May 1996 official sources claimed to have established complete control over the entire Jaffna peninsula. While the situation remains volatile, there are reports of increasing repression of the Tamils and loss of life, with a mass exodus of thousands of Tamil civilians from the region.

Muslims[3]

Out of the total population of almost 1.4 million Muslims in Sri Lanka, over one third live in the north and east. The majority of these live in the east, where they constitute about a third of the population, which has roughly equal proportion of Sinhalese, Muslims and Tamils. The remaining Muslim community is dispersed throughout the urban centres of Sri Lanka. Muslims are also divided between mainly agriculturists living in the east, and traders who are dispersed across the island. The increasing radicalization of Tamil politics, especially the shift in Tamil demands from federalism to secession, drastically affected Tamil–Muslim relations. Muslims are strongly opposed to becoming a minority within a Tamil-speaking and Tamil-dominated homeland consisting of the Northern and Eastern provinces. In 1990, the LTTE began a purge of all Muslims living in the north. Muslims were the victims of attacks in the Eastern Province, which had the objective of clearing the region of non-Tamils. Muslims also became the target of gruesome massacres by the LTTE, and this led some Muslim political leaders in 1992 to discuss the needs for a *jihad*, or holy war, to defend their religion.

The formation of the Sri Lanka Muslim Congress (SLMC) in the 1980s enabled Muslims to adopt a distinct political profile. The main demand of the SLMC – in the face of Tamil separatist demands for merger of the north and east – has been the creation of a separate regional council for Muslims in the east. The devolution proposals put forward by the PA government after it came to power in late 1994 were welcomed by the SLMC, but further discussion and the implementation of these proposals cannot begin until after the war with the LTTE has ended.

Veddhas (Waaniy-a-Laato)

The Veddhas or Waaniy-a-Laato (forest-dwellers) of Sri Lanka are an indigenous group whose ancestry, according to legend, is traceable to the prehistoric inhabitants of the island. They inhabited the island before the arrival of both the Sinhalese and the Tamils. The majority Sinhalese, both as part of their culture and as a result of the island's mythical and legendary history, however, regard Veddhas as 'evil' and unwanted. According to popular legend Vijaya, the leader of the original colonists from north India, who is said to have founded the first Sinhalese kingdom, married an indigenous princess as his first wife. He subsequently cast aside his princess and their two children for another princess from south India more suited to his rank and position. As the legend goes, while the indigenous princess returned to her demon 'people', the siblings fled to the forest and upon attaining maturity married each other and became forebears of the 'Veddhas'.[4]

Veddhas are distinguished by their hunting and gathering way of life, by their unwritten language, which is closely related to but distinct from Sinhalese, by their beliefs in traditional gods and ancestor spirits, and by the importance of ancestral lands to all aspects of their life. They live mostly as nomadic forest-dwellers in the remote eastern parts of the country. The 1981 census does not provide any figures relating to the Veddha population but classifies them in the category of 'others', which is numbered at 2,000 individuals.

The numerical strength of the Veddhas is fast dwindling, primarily because many of them are being assimilated into Sinhalese and Tamil society. They have experienced drastic changes in their means of livelihood since the 1930s, when colonization schemes involving a massive influx of Sinhalese and Tamil settlers encroached on their homeland, the forests. This process has continued with large irrigation projects, the Gal Oya in the 1950s and the Accelerated Mahaweli Development Scheme in 1977. Government policies have favoured assimilation and conversion of Veddhas into settled agriculturists as a means to their economic and social enhancement and as a way to bring them into the national mainstream. The rights of the Veddhas have lately been eroded as a result of environmental policies that have involved the conversion of their traditional land into a national park.[5] On 9 November 1983 the traditional Veddha lands, comprising 51,468 hectares, were designated a combined 'catchment area' and a forest and wildlife reserve. This project, conducted under the auspices of the Department of Wildlife Conservation, has meant the exclusion and separation of the Veddhas from their own lands and the loss of their traditional hunting grounds and honey sites. Amid conflicts between the majority Sinhalese and minority Tamils, ever since the independence of Sri Lanka, the plight of the Veddhas has been all but ignored.

Conclusions and future prospects

The future of all Sri Lanka's peoples depends on resolution of the long-running civil war. The inability or unwillingness of successive governments to devise a formula guaranteeing genuine autonomy to minority groups, in particular the Tamils, has initiated communal discord and ethnic unrest, increasingly repressive measures, arbitrary detention, torture of opponents, denial of political aspirations and negation of civil and political rights of such magnitude that Sri Lanka now faces a major humanitarian crisis. Any government will need to tackle this issue by ensuring that suitable proposals are put in place and implemented so that peaceful coexistence becomes a reality in the future.

Further reading

Hannum, H., *Autonomy, Sovereignty and Self-determination: The Accommodation of Conflicting Interests,* Philadelphia, PA, University of Pennsylvania, 1990, pp.280–307.

International Work Group for Indigenous Affairs, 'Sri Lanka: Indigenous peoples and self-determination – a case study of the Wanniya-Laeto (Veddahs)', *Indigenous Affairs*, no.3, July/September 1995.

Nissan, E., *Sri Lanka: A Bitter Harvest,* London, MRG report, 1996.

Schwarz, W., *The Tamils of Sri Lanka*, London, MRG report, 1988.

Vije, M., *Where Serfdom Thrives: The Plantation Tamils of Sri Lanka*, London, Tamil Information Centre, 1987.

Minority-based and advocacy organizations

Civil Rights Movement of Sri Lanka, 16/1 Don Carolis Road, Colombo 5, Sri Lanka.

International Centre for Ethnic Studies (ICES), 8 Kynsey Terrace, Colombo 8, Sri Lanka; tel. 94 1 698 048, fax 94 1 696 618, e-mail: ices@sri.lanka.net.

Lawyers for Human Rights and Development, 225 1/1 Cotta Road, Borela, Colombo 5, Sri Lanka.

Movement for Inter-Racial Justice and Equality (MIRJ), 6 Aboe Avenue, Colombo 3, Sri Lanka.

Tamil United Liberation Front, 146/19 Havelock Road, Colombo 5, Sri Lanka; tel/fax. 94 1 595 192.

Notes

Introduction

1 Mazrui, A., 'Consent, colonialism and sovereignity', *Political Studies,* vol. 11, 1963, pp. 36–55.

2 Thornberry, P., 'Self determination, minorities and human rights: a review of international instruments', *International and Comparitive Law Quarterly*, vol. 38, 1989, pp 867–889.

3 Collins, L. and Lappierre, D., *Freedom at Midnight,* London, Collins, 1975, p 284.

4 In state reports submitted to the Committee on the Elimination of Racial Discrimination, which works under the auspices of the International Convention on the Elimination of All Forms of Racial Discrimination 1965, Pakistan, while referring to the events which led to the secession of East Pakistan, asserted: 'at no time was the imputation of racial Discrimination or differentiation a component of [the] grievances or a cause of friction between the regions of Pakistan'.

5 Barsh, R., 'Indigenous people an emerging object of international law', *American Journal of International Law*, vol. 80, 1986, pp. 369–385, 375.

6 Von Prondzynski, F., 'Law, sovereignty and democracy,' inaugural lecture, University of Hull, 1992, pp. 2–5.

7 Crawford, J., 'Democracy in international law', inaugral lecture, University of Cambridge, 1993, p. 25.

8 Seighart, P., *The Lawful Rights of Mankind,* Oxford, Oxford University Press, p. 165.

Afghanistan

1 United Nations, *Afghanistan: Operation Salam Programme for 1992*, Geneva, Office for the Coordination of UN Humanitarian and Economic Assistance Programmes relating to Afghanistan, 1991.

2 Afghanaid, *Jahrichi (Afghanaid bulletin)*, London, Afghanaid, August 1994.

Bangladesh

1 Timm, R.W., *The Adivasis of Bangladesh,* London, MRG report, 1991, p. 21.

2 Roy, R.D., 'The problem of dispossession of lands of indigenous peoples of the Chittagong Hill Tracts by government-sponsored migrants: in search of a solution', paper presented at an Open Dialogue and Seminar on the Chittagong Hill Tracts Problem and its Solution, organized by the National Committee for the Protection of Fundamental Rights in CHT, German Cultural Centre, Dhaka, Bangladesh, June 1995. See also Jumman Peoples Network in Europe (JUPNET), 'The indigenous peoples of the Chittagong Hill Tracts', briefing paper, May 1995.

3 Survival International, *Mission Witness to Genocide*, London, n.d.; Survival International, *Villages Burnt Alive in Military Attack,* London, 1992; Survival International, *Over 100 Jummas Massacred*, London, n.d.; Chittagong Hill Tracts Commission *'Life Is Not Ours': Land and Human Rights in the Chittagong Hill Tracts, Bangladesh*, London, May 1991; Timm, R.W., *The Adivasis of Bangladesh,* London, MRG report, 1992; Anti-Slavery International statement to the UN

Sub-Commission on Prevention of Discrimination and Protection of Minorities, August 1994.

4 *Pakistan Times Overseas Weekly*, 18 December 1988, p. 13.

5 Wright, T.P. Jr, 'Center-periphery relations and ethnic conflict in Pakistan – Sindhis, Muhajirs and Punjabis', *Comparitive Politics*, 1991.

6 *Herald*, November 1989, pp. 50–51.

7 *Keesings Contemporary Archives*, supplement, 1993, 1995.

8 Mohajir Quamic Movement, *Prisoners of Conscience: Stranded Pakistanis in Bangladesh*, documentary video recording.

9 'Bangla–Pakistan row over deportation', *India Abroad*, 1 December 1995; '125 more deported from Pakistan', *Bangladesh Observer*, 14 November 1995.

Bhutan

1 Amnesty International, *Bhutan: Human Rights Violations against the Nepali-speaking Population in the South*, London, December 1992.

2 See Dhakal, D.N.S. and Strawn, C., *Bhutan: A Movement in Exile*, New Delhi, Nirala Publications, 1994.

3 Amnesty International, *Bhutan: Forcible Exile*, London, August 1994.

Burma

1 Minority population statistics for Burma are all broad estimates.

2 Discussion of minorities in Burma is based largely on Martin Smith, *Ethnic Groups in Burma*, London, Anti-Slavery International, 1994.

3 US Committee for Refugees, *The Return of the Rohingya Refugees to Burma: Voluntary Repatriation or Refoulemen*, Immigration and Refugee Services of America, 1995, p.1.

India

1 See Ministry of Information and Broadcasting, *India 1993*, New Dehli, Research and Reference Division, Government of India, 1994.

2 Joshi, B.,'The case of India's untouchables', in Welch, C., Jr and Leary, V. (eds) *Asian Perspective on Human Rights*, Boulder, CO, Westview Press, 1990, 162–85.

3 Bates, C., 'Lost innocents and the loss of innocence: interpreting Adivasi movements in South Asia', in R. Barnes, A. Gray and B. Kingsbury (eds), *Indigenous Peoples of Asia*, Ann Arbor, MI, Association for Asian Studies, 1993, pp. 103–19, 103–4.

4 The case regarding the legality of the construction of the dam was still before the Supreme Court during 1996. Source of information, Survival International.

5 See Poulouse, T., *Succession in International Law: A Study of India, Pakistan, Ceylon and Burma*, New Delhi, Orient Longman, 1974, pp.30–56.

Nepal

1 Stokke, H., 'Nepal', in *Human Rights in Developing Countries Yearbook 199*, Oslo, Nordic Human Rights Publications, 1993.

2 Skar, H., 'Nepal, indigenous issues and civil rights: the plight of the Rana Tharu', in Barnes, R., Gray, A. and Kingsbury B. (eds), *Indigenous Peoples of Asia*, Ann Arbor, MI, Association for Asian Studies, 1995, pp.173–94, 186.

3 INSEC, *Bonded Labour in Nepal under Kamaiya System*, Kathmandu, 1992.

Pakistan

1 Population figures for minorities are authors' estimates based on various sources; figures for Sindhis, Mohajirs and Ahmadiyas are disputed. There has been no national census since 1981.

2 Baeher, P. *et al.*, *Human Rights in Developing Countries Yearbook 1994*, Deventer, Kluwer, 1994, pp.302–7.

3 This account is based on information provided by the UK office of the World Sindhi Congress.

4 This account is based on information provided by the UK office of the Mohajir Quami Movement.

5 Wirsing, R., *The Baluchis and Pathans*, London, MRG report, 1987, p.4. See also Mohabbat, A., 'Pakhtun national self-determination: the partition of India and relations with Pakistan', unpublished PhD dissertation, Saint Louis, MO, Saint Louis University, 1979.

6 Wirsing, R. and Harrison, S., 'Ethnicity and the political stalemate in Pakistan', in A. Banuazizi and M. Weiner, (eds), *The State, Religion and Ethnic Politics in Afghanistan, Iran and Pakistan*, Lahore, Vanguard Press, 1987, p.271.

7 Article 1; cited in Baloch, I., 'The Baluch question in Pakistan and the right to self- determination', in W-P. Zingel et al. (eds), *Pakistan in Its Fourth Decade*, Deutsches Orient-Institut, 1983, pp. 188–209.

Sri Lanka

1 See Nissan, E., *Sri Lanka: A Bitter Harvest*, London, MRG report, 1996; Hannum, H., *Autonomy, Sovereignty and Self-determination: The Accommodation of Conflicting Interests*, Philadelphia, PA, University of Pennsylvania, 1990, pp.280–307.

2 See Hannum, H. (ed.), *Documents on Autonomy and Minority Rights*, Dordrecht, M. Nijhoff, 1993, pp. 527–32.

3 See Nissan, op. cit.

4 International Work Group for indigenous Affairs (IWAF), 'Sri Lanka: indigenous peoples and self-determination – a case study of the Wanntya-Laeto (Veddahs)', *Indigenous Affairs*, no. 3, July/September 1995, pp. 13–14.

5 Tomei, M., *A Plan for the Cultural Preservation and Development of the Veddhas*, Geneva, International Labour Organization, 1993.

EAST AND SOUTH-EAST ASIA

James Chin, David Hawk and Peter O'Neill

East Asia

The future of minorities in East Asia is the touchstone for the quality of national societies across this region, and that future is intimately linked to two levels of relations: the international within the region, and the 'superpower' global level. These foreign, economic and political relations in turn revolve around the issue of the decentralization of national economic power in East Asian countries and its repercussions at regional and global level. Core issues include the degree to which minorities will share in economic advances made by urban dwellers and economic majority communities; how far their land, social, cultural and political rights will be the focus of negotiation when central governments seek increased foreign economic ties with 'democratic' neighbours and the world economic community; and how far minorities, who are often resident in remote border areas, benefit from the opening up of borders with neighbouring states, or become the victims of settlement policies through increased military presence or natural resource exploitation by government-encouraged economic migrants from the majority communities.

The situation of ethnic minorities is now often inextricably bound up with the emerging concept of economic and environmental migrants and refugees. While the United Nations' unrevised, formal conventions do not take this into account, the work of the UN High Commissioner for Refugees has to deal with the daily reality of an ever-growing number who fit into this category, particularly in border areas.

Geopolitical context

The scale of economic activity across East Asia indicates the paradoxical potential for minorities to win advantages or become further disadvantaged. The economic potential of the region as a whole remains vast, implying a further major shift in the balance of world economic power for the next century, away from Europe and the USA, towards Asia. China and Russia's decision to sign a peace treaty in April 1996 to improve security along their frontiers to avoid conflict means controlled economic expansion. India, with its borders with China and Tibet, and its proximity to the countries of former Soviet Central Asia, is the third point of this 21st-century triangle of economic power. Co-signatories of the Russian–Chinese treaty include, significantly, Central Asia's new republics of Kazakhstan, Kyrgyzstan and Tajikistan. The treaty also states that it will improve environmental conditions along the 4,300 kilometre Sino–Russian border; this is important, since many border minorities have been negatively affected by mining for fossil fuels and minerals and by nuclear experiments – key sectors where governments have shipped in large non-minority workforces who have displaced local minorities or deprived them of income from natural resource exploitation. Military control of border areas also means that minorities risk being far more controlled than city dwellers. However, the dismantling or reduction of the 'welfare state' support of the past may be less in those border areas than elsewhere, precisely to 'keep the minorities happy'.

The People's Republic of China is the dominant force in the region. Its wish to be integrated into the world economic order is the main tempering factor on its relationship with its minorities and some of its neighbours. Within China are minorities who may have been nations in their own right in the past and still consider that they should be sovereign independent states today, such as Tibetans and, perhaps, Inner Mongolians. And among China's neighbours, Taiwan, in particular, seeks to

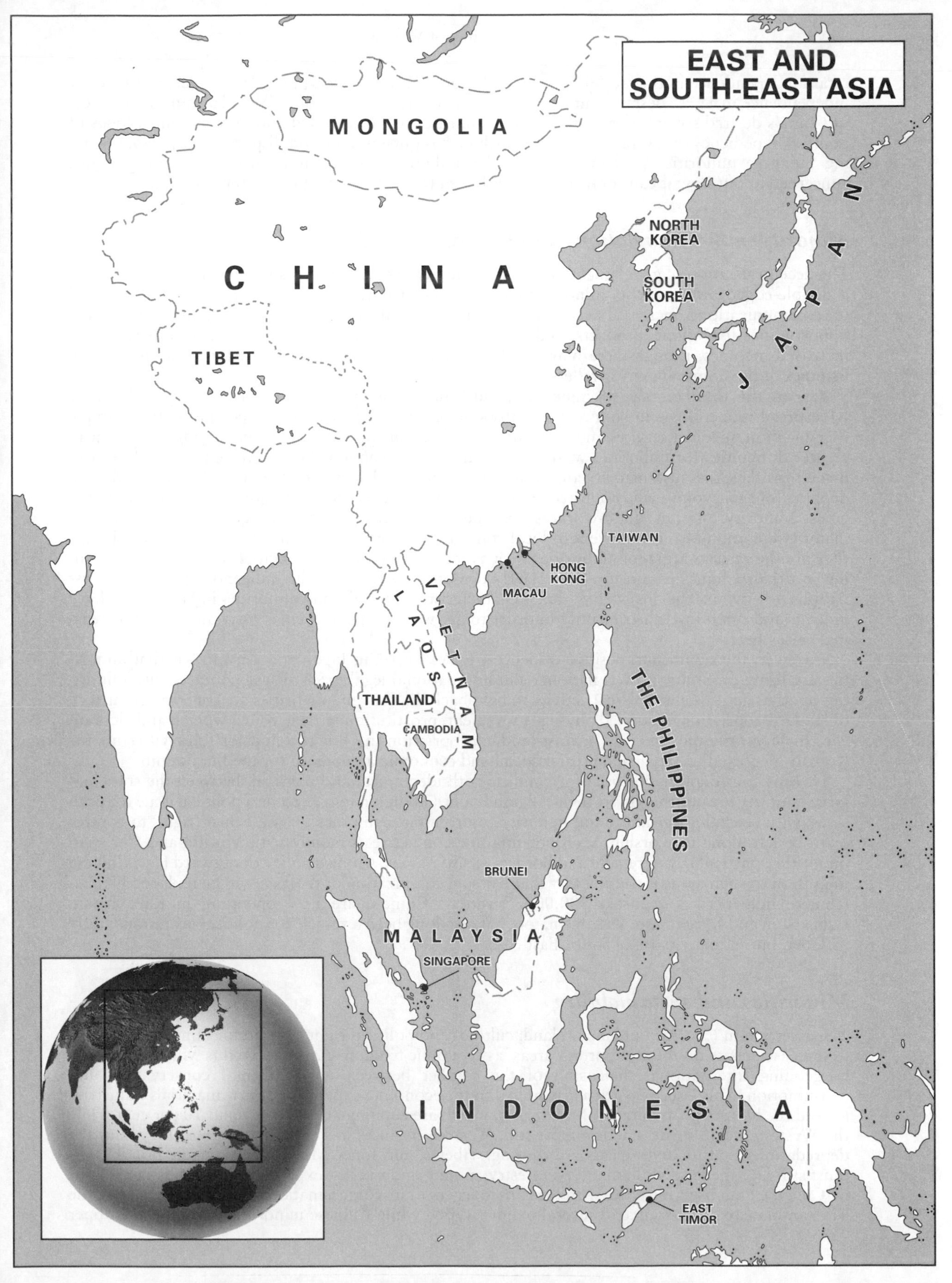
EAST AND SOUTH-EAST ASIA
MONGOLIA
CHINA
TIBET
NORTH KOREA
SOUTH KOREA
JAPAN
TAIWAN
HONG KONG
MACAU
VIETNAM
LAOS
THAILAND
CAMBODIA
THE PHILIPPINES
BRUNEI
MALAYSIA
SINGAPORE
INDONESIA
EAST TIMOR

retain independence in the face of Chinese ambitions. Taiwan's clear, presidential electoral vote for independence in 1996, despite Chinese military threats, is a case in point. With Taiwan as the object of China's desired sphere of influence, so its minorities will be affected and may become a focus of political expediency or leverage. In addition, China has outstanding land disputes with Japan, involving Japanese minorities (and including the US military presence in Japan), and China remains concerned about how it can control a divided Korea (and the US military presence there).

Majority–minority relations within states

The decentralization of government power, in economic terms, which is sweeping across East Asia is a double-edged sword for its minorities. Advantages include better transport, infrastructure and telecommunications, increased access to local and regional markets, tourism and niche marketing opportunities for 'ethnic' products, and work as economic migrants in the cities. All this results in increased incomes, though there may still be a widening gap with the simultaneously improving incomes of the dominant city dwellers.

Yet, to the disadvantage of minorities, individual economic affluence is often paralleled by widespread reductions – in both real and absolute terms – in government expenditure, for example on education, medical services and minority subsidies. Cuts to local government budgets also mean greater difficulties for minorities who fail to share in the economic boom. More freedom of movement threatens the sustainability of cultural traditions and increases the risk of 'ageing villages' deprived of their young who are forced to take on the values of distant majority communities in the cities. Minority migrant 'guest-workers' may be subject to racist-style attacks or be exploited by majority communities. In the event of local conflict, often over poor living and working conditions, they are the easiest target for authorities such as the police to harass. Much of what is now happening in urban China has already been clearly demonstrated among the indigenous peoples or first nations in Taiwan. The 'invisibility' that is characteristic of Burakumin minorities in Japan, who have hidden (and often lost) their identity in order to get work in Japan's cities, may also apply increasingly elsewhere.

However, the significant, positive evidence – for example, in Japan and Taiwan – is that minorities are using economic power, national and international legal mechanisms, contacts with minorities in other nations and political activity to fight back. In Taiwan, minorities are contesting a history of land expropriation, restricted physical movement, prostitution of their young women and alcoholism. In Japan the movement is against land expropriation in Okinawa and for full civil rights for Koreans deported to Japan and greater social and economic acceptance for the Burakumin.

There is considerable potential for conflict, both ideological and physical, between the state and large minority groups that assert their religious values. Religion may become a political issue for both sides, with central government and minority confronting each other to assert their 'right' to control or to be left alone to worship. Such potential for conflict rests mainly with Muslim and Christian minorities, particularly in remote and border-sensitive areas. China's policy of outward Han Chinese migration to such areas is causing fear that Russian colonization of the past will be replaced by Han Chinese influence. A reported 300,000 'business' Chinese are now operating in Kazakhstan, Uzbekistan and Kyrgyzstan. Buddhism, too, has also long been a vehicle for political protest, not only in Tibet, but in many parts of South-East Asia.

Minorities and sustainability

The assertion in East Asia of human, land, cultural and political rights by and for minorities is likely to increase debate on these important areas, as economic freedom expands. To this will be added the burgeoning international dimension of the conflict between environmental conservation and consumption. This issue is particularly linked to the economic expansion of raw materials industries to feed the hungry growth rates of the region, which are running at between 5 and 10 per cent while the Western world's rate stands almost still. Western business has cared too little so far about the depredations that its investments are causing. Tibetan and Inner Mongolian nomadic populations must still face the legacy of unfettered forestry, mining and nuclear experimental activity carried out by China. China itself must live with the consequences of its contamination (including nuclear) of the Tibetan plateau – the source of several major rivers – while Chinese minorities living on the upper reaches of the Yangtze face the consequences of the Three Gorges Dam project. Yet minorities can succeed in halting major development projects in remote areas, as has been proved by the World Bank's withdrawal from Arun III in Nepal, South Asia.

A further factor which, rightly or wrongly, has become an element in the conservation-versus-consumption debate is population. The bulk of minorities in East Asia, generally in rural areas, maintain a tradition of large families. China's population control policy is generally more relaxed in rural areas, although it is often invoked to control minorities in local politics. The other side of that coin is that population growth may be seen by central government as a political issue, because of fear that growing minority populations (as among Chinese Muslims or Christians, or in Tibet) are a threat to the local power of government-sponsored immigrant populations. Where the more relaxed Chinese state population policy is in place, there is some evidence that national and local government officials use the rules to 'control' minorities seeking other rights. This would seem to be the case in ethnic Tibetan areas (as opposed to the Autonomous Region based on Lhasa), as well as in regions where Muslims are more dominant than Han Chinese.

Overall, the resilience that East Asian minorities have often shown in the past, as well as more recently, should afford a hopeful outlook for their survival. That should mean an increasing contribution on their part to the economic, political and cultural diversity of the region and their majority communities. But this will depend to a degree on how far they are permitted by majority populations to assume their full civil rights and to participate in, as well as to benefit from, the general economic expansion. This in turn will be affected by the active or passive positions adopted by foreign trade partners and international rights organizations.

South-East Asia

Located between the huge populations and historic Asian civilizations of India and China, South-East Asia is one of the world's great cultural and political crossroads. Geographically, the nation states of South-East Asia constitute two broad subregions: mainland South-East Asia, comprising Burma,[1] Malaysia, Thailand, Cambodia, Laos and Vietnam; and islandic South-East Asia, comprising Singapore, the Philippine Islands, the Indonesian archipelago, Brunei, the east Malaysian provinces of Sabah and Sarawak on Borneo Island, and East Timor.

Culture and politics

Culturally, most of the countries of South-East Asia fall into two large groupings. One is the Brahmic or Hinduized, Theravada Buddhist states of mainland South-East Asia – Burma, Cambodia, Laos and Thailand – which drew their linguistic script and earliest 'high' culture and mass religion from the Indian subcontinent. The second large grouping is the 'Malay' world of peninsular Malaysia, Indonesia and the Philippines. Three states lie outside of these two broad cultural categories: Vietnam, with its Confucianist historical culture, incorporated into China for a millennium, and its mass religion of the northern, Mahayana type of Buddhism found in China, Japan and Korea; Singapore, with a population overwhelmingly derived from Chinese immigrants; and East Timor, populated by non-Malay, non-Muslimized people, which was part of the Portuguese colonial empire until the Indonesian invasion of 1975. (Because the United Nations does not recognize the Indonesian occupation, East Timor is treated as a separate entry in this *Directory*.)

Politically, except for Thailand – the only South-East Asian state never incorporated into a Western colonial empire – the countries of the region did not achieve independence until after the Second World War. For much of the post-colonial era, until the early 1990s, with the exception of Burma, South-East Asia divided into two political Cold War blocs. The former states of French colonial Indochina – Vietnam, Cambodia and Laos – were, for the most part, aligned with the Soviet Union and China. Thailand, Malaysia, Indonesia, Singapore, Brunei and the Philippines were, for the most part, aligned with the West and Japan and grouped in the anti-communist Association of South-East Asian Nations (ASEAN). However, ASEAN has since expanded to include Vietnam, and towards the end of 1996 it agreed to admit Cambodia, Laos and Burma, probably during 1997. With greater or less enthusiasm, all states in the region are adopting capitalist models of economic development. While Laos and Vietnam are still ruled by one-party, nominally Marxist-Leninist regimes, most other independent states of the region are best described as semi-democracies. Today only the Philippines, Thailand and, possibly, Cambodia can claim to be democratic societies.

South-East Asia boasts four 'tiger' economies: Malaysia, Indonesia, Thailand and Singapore. The new wealth has made these nations confident about their place in the world. Singaporean and Malaysian leaders have sought to promote the 'Asian way', based on the notion that community rights supersede individual rights. This means that minority rights are frequently not granted if this goes against the will of the majority. Many Asian nations are also suspicious of minority indigenous peoples' rights, fearing this will disrupt their nation-building process, and they fear that the promotion of minority rights may lead to independence movements and the break-up of the state. Others in the region argue that liberal democracy and 'human rights' are not suitable for their societies, since their culture, they maintain, is based on consensual decision-making and group-led behaviour. However, the rapidly growing middle class in South-East Asia is likely significantly to alter the beliefs and character of the South-East Asian political elite in the coming years. Many in the middle class support democracy, and human and minority rights. As South-East Asia industrializes, information will be harder to control, and minorities will almost certainly demand their rights and organize themselves into significant pressure groups.

Ethnicity and ethnic relations

Several broad developments have determined the ethnic composition and dynamics of South-East Asia. The earliest and most fundamental pattern of ethnicity resulted from the pre-(written) historical southern migrations of Sino-Himalayan and Sino-Tibetan peoples following the rivers that originate in the Himalayas down to the deltas and seas of South-East Asia. These migrations led to the displacement of less numerous tribal peoples, who were pushed into the forests and mountains that surround the riverine deltas of the mainland and the island coastal plains. The earliest historic pattern comprised a mainland South-East Asia of (usually warring) kingdoms based on a dominant people with 'hill-tribe' or forest minorities, and an island world with dominant people along the coastline and indigenous minorities in the interior mountains and on the more distant islands. Onto this formation were superimposed large-scale immigrant communities from the Indian subcontinent and China. Merchant traders, artisans, priests and teachers from India and China had long been present throughout South-East Asia. During the European colonial era, immigration from India and China substantially increased to include labourers, petty traders and commercial functionaries. Immigrant Indians and Chinese often came to occupy pivotal and predominant niches in the economies of the countries where they settled.

A third determinant of the ethnic map of South-East Asia was the impact of Western colonialism. With the exception of Thailand, all of the pre-existing polities of South-East Asia were incorporated into the colonial empires of Spain, Portugal, the Netherlands, the UK, France and the USA. European colonialism virtually created all the independent South-East Asian countries as we see them today. And almost everywhere in the region the relationships and decisions of the European colonial powers set the borders and boundaries of the present-day nation states. Pockets of one ethnic group were often left in the neighbouring state in which another ethnic group formed the majority. The Western colonizers pitted various ethnic groups against each other, moreover, often with disastrous results for the minorities involved.

There had always been indigenous revolts against foreign rule, but towards the end of the nineteenth century 'modern' nationalist movements took shape, particularly following Japan's victory over Tsarist Russia in 1905, and following the propagation of Wilsonian 'self-determination' and its Leninist 'anti-imperialist' corollary after the First World War. The ease of Japanese conquest of colonial South-East Asia at the outset of the Second World War, and the economic and political exhaustion of Western Europe by the end of that war, cleared the way for the successes of the region's independence movements in the 1950s, 1960s and 1970s. The rallying cry of 'self-determination' offered by nationalist political movements, however, was not considered to apply to the ethnic minority peoples of the newly independent nation states. Forging ethnic relationships became a major, and sometimes the principal, task of the political leaderships of the new nation states.

Historians have delineated five areas where ethnic relationships comprise primary factors in the newly independent states of South-East Asia – processes that are by no means complete. The first is the consolidation of geographical territory by capturing or coercing the loyalties of ethnic minorities in the mountains or outlying regions. Second, the creation of a modern economy implies accommodation with, or coercion of, ethnic minorities that play a key role in commercial relationships or occupy land on which valuable natural resources are located. Third, acquiring a nationwide cultural personality involves attitudes towards religion, language and education – matters usually tied up with ethnicity. Fourth, the independent states need to adopt policies towards citizenship and immigration – matters intimately related to existing immigrant communities. Fifth, the establishment of foreign policies by the newly independent states involves considerations with respect to pockets of minorities who are the ethnic kin of the predominant ethnic group of neighbouring states, and with respect to relationships with China, which has been perceived as a patron of ethnic Chinese minorities and political parties.

South-East Asian ethnic groupings

It may be helpful to consider briefly the situation of dominant ethnic majorities, urban minorities, rural minorities and 'tribal' minorities in South-East Asia in relation to ecological terrain, economic roles, degree of cultural development, language, education and political structures. Typically, dominant ethnic majorities (and dominant minorities) reside in the lowlands, plains, broad valleys and coastal areas. Most grow wet rice for consumption and commercial sale, engage in seaborne trade with world and regional markets, have monetary and market exchange systems and are increasingly engaged in industrial development. They have long-established scripts for writing and are Buddhist or Muslim (except for the Philippines) with national religious hierarchies. Most are monolingual, with standardized dialects resulting from nationwide primary public schools. Their polities are former kingdoms, now nation states with borders set by colonial powers, and they substantially dominate governmental bureaucracies.

Urban minorities also reside in large lowland cities and market towns, but some members may engage in itinerant trade, and they are often in specialized economic positions, particularly in commercial and financial enterprises. These groups are literate and have a world historical religion, but often different from that of the ethnic majority. Their traditions often relate to another country or era. They are frequently bilingual, sometimes possessing specialized schools. The extent of intermarriage varies. Urban minorities are usually not organized politically, but may participate in central government. Cultural loyalties cross national borders, and loyalties to nation and ethnic group are sometimes in conflict. The most prominent urban minority in South-East Asia is the ethnic Chinese. Often referred to as the 'Nanyang' (South Seas) Chinese, most came in the late nineteenth century from mainland China to escape poverty. Despite living in the region for more than a hundred years, ethnic Chinese are still regarded with fear and suspicion by most South-East Asian governments, partly because of their entrepreneurial success.

The region's rural minorities reside in more remote lowland or low-hills areas. Frequently rural minorities are subsistence wet and dry rice cultivators, or work in occupations shunned by the majority ethnic group, or in petty trading. Degrees of education vary. Their religion is frequently different from that of the ethnic majority. They may speak a dialect of the majority language, but these may not be mutually intelligible, and they are encouraged to learn the national language. Rural minorities usually have contact with the lower bureaucratic levels of government, but frequently have little communication with the central government. They are usually organized politically only at the local level, and political loyalties are often only to local leaders.

Small groups of hill-tribes people usually inhabit interior mountain areas away from rivers and coasts, in discontinuous habitats mixed in with other groups and, on the mainland, distributed irrespective of modern political boundaries. Apart from a few remaining 'hunter-gathers', hill-tribes people are frequently shifting cultivators, often of dry rice, except for small-scale terracing. Apart from the opium-growing hill tribes, these peoples are usually poorer than their neighbours on the lower hills and plains, selling forest products or crafts to itinerant traders from nearby market towns. There is very little wage work among them, and virtually no industrialization or modern agricultural production. Literacy and schooling are limited to where there has been Christian missionary activity. There is strong attachment to the local oral traditions and language, which is usually different language from that of the dominant ethnic group. Their religion is usually classified as animist, with little, if any, overlay of Buddhism or Islam. Political organization is usually only local, with contact only with the lowest bureaucratic levels of government.

Further reading

Barnes, R.H., Gray, A. and Kingsbury, B. (eds.), *Indigenous Peoples of Asia*, Ann Arbor, MI, Association of Asian Studies, 1995.

Brown, D., *The State and Ethnic Politics in Southeast Asia*, London, Routledge, 1993.

Gungwu, W., *Community and Nation*, Sydney, Allen & Unwin, 1981.

Harris, L.C., 'Xinjiang, Central Asia and the implications for China's policy in the Islamic world', *China Quarterly*, March 1993.

International Work Group for Indigenous Affairs, *The Indigenous World 1995–96*, Copenhagen, IWGIA, 1996.

Somers Heidhues, M. *et al.*, *The Chinese of South-East Asia*, London, MRG report, 1992.

Walker A.R. (ed.), *Studies of Ethnic Minority Peoples*, Singapore, Department of Sociology, National University of Singapore, 1982.

Warikoo, K., 'Ethnic religious resurgence in Xinjiang', *Eurasian Studies*, vol. 2, no. 4, Winter 1995/6.

Brunei

Land area:	5,769 sq km
Population:	295,000 (1995)
Main languages:	Malay, Chinese
Main religions:	Islam (official), Confucianism, animism, Christianity
Main minority groups:	Chinese 44,000–59,000 (est., 15–20%), Dusun 23,600 (8%), Iban 11,800 (4%), Murut 2,655 (0.9%), Kedayan (no data)
Real per capita GDP:	$18,414
UNDP HDI/rank:	0.872 (36)

Prior to colonization, the Sultanate of Brunei was a regional power, controlling large parts of Borneo and the southern Philippine islands. The wealth and power of the sultanate were based on trade. At various times Brunei was a tributary state of China and of the Hindu Majapahit of Java. The extent of the sultanate's domain was drastically curtailed by Spanish, Dutch and British imperialism. By the late nineteenth century, Brunei had shrunk to about its present size. In 1888 Brunei voluntarily became a British Protectorate. In 1929 oil was discovered off its coast, but large-scale extraction did not begin until after the Second World War. In the early 1960s, Brunei entered negotiation with Kuala Lumpur to join the Malaysian Federation. Negotiations broke down over Brunei's desire to retain control over its oil wealth, and over issues pertaining to the status of the Sultan. In the late 1950s, Parti Rakyat Brunei (the Brunei People's Party) was established and won elections on a platform of democratic reforms and federation with neighbouring states. Unwilling to share power, the Sultan called in Gurkhas and British forces. A state of emergency was declared in 1962 and remains in effect. Political opposition to the royal household is non-existent. The country is governed by the 1959 constitution, under which the Sultan is head of state with full executive authority. Half the cabinet comes from the royal family. On 1 January 1984, Brunei became a fully independent state.

Brunei's wealth is based entirely on the petroleum industry. Oil money allows the state to provide its citizens with one of the highest standards of living in Asia. More than 70 per cent of the ethnic Brunei labour force works for the government and another 10–15 per cent work for the oil and gas industries and related commercial concerns.

Chinese

Ethnic Chinese migrated to Brunei during the British colonial period and they dominate the small non-state commercial sector. Ethnic Chinese are held to be roughly 15–20 per cent of the population. Before independence Chinese in Brunei were British protected persons holding British travel documents but neither British subjects, nor subjects of the Sultan. After independence, only about 9,000 ethnic Chinese were given full Brunei citizenship. Another few thousand are permanent residents. The rest remain effectively stateless persons. In recent years, Australia has taken some of these stateless persons. In 1984 the Sultan tightened citizenship regulations, requiring applicants to have resided in the country for twenty-five consecutive years, and to meet language and cultural qualifications as well. The Sultan has declared Brunei an Islamic state, with the official national ideology of Melayu Islam Beraja (or Malay Muslim Monarchy). This has resulted in pressures on the non-Muslim population to convert to Islam and adopt Malay culture. It has reportedly been easier for Chinese to obtain permanent residency/ citizenship if they have converted to Islam. A sizeable number of the Chinese are Christians and they face problems in trying to practise their faith. The government has refused work permits for foreign priests and permission to build churches. Many Christians are forced to use shops and houses as churches. Chinese who practise traditional religions (for example, Taoism, Buddhism) face similar problems.

Dusun, Iban, Murut, Kedayan

The indigenous minority tribal groups in Brunei are the same as in the neighbouring Malaysian states of Sabah and Sarawak. Dusun constitute about 8 per cent of the population, and Murut less than 1 per cent. They are animistic migrating swidden cultivators and collectors of jungle products residing in the forested interior of the country. Iban, roughly 4 per cent of the population, live mostly along the border with Sarawak (see **Malaysia**). Kedayan are Malay-speaking and Muslim agriculturalists. Despite their language and religious affiliation with the ethnic Malay majority, Kedayan are regarded by Bruneians as closer in status to the animist, interior tribal groups. In the 1970s, mass conversions to Islam took place among the indigenous groups, after pressure from the state.

Conclusions and future prospects

The policy of the sultanate on minorities is assimilation. Given the omnipresence of the Brunei state, the process of assimilation of indigenous minorities will take place, although the pace is uncertain. The situation of stateless Chinese remains, and without citizenship papers they are easily exploitable.

Further reading

Singh, R., *Brunei 1839–1983: The Problems of Political Survival*, Singapore, Oxford University Press, 1984.

Somers Heidhues, M. *et al.*, *The Chinese of South-East Asia*, London, MRG report, 1992.

Cambodia

Land area:	181,040 sq km
Population:	10.2 million (1995)
Main languages:	Khmer (official), Chinese, Vietnamese, Malayo-Polynesian
Main religions:	Buddhism, Islam, Christianity
Main minority groups:	Cham and indigenous hill tribes 510,000 (est., 5%), Chinese and Vietnamese 510,000 (est., 5%)
Real per capita GDP:	$1,250
UNDP HDI/rank:	0.325 (156)

Cambodia lost most of the territory it once held to the growing states of Siam and Annam, now Thailand and Vietnam, after the fifteenth century when the great kingdom and civilization centred on Angkor went into steep decline. During the nineteenth century, Cambodia was almost completely swallowed up by its encroaching neighbours before this process was halted by the imposition of French colonial rule. The overwhelming majority of Cambodia's population, close to 90 per cent, is ethnic Khmer. The other 10 per cent is made up of four distinct ethnic minority groups: Cham (also known as Khmer Islam), indigenous hill tribes (also known as Khmer Leou), ethnic Chinese and ethnic Vietnamese. From the time of Cambodia's independence from France in 1953 until the 1970 coup against Prince Norodom Sihanouk only Cham (Khmer Islam) and the hill tribes (Khmer Leou) were recognized as Cambodian citizens. Ethnic Chinese and ethnic Vietnamese were regarded as overseas residents. All Cambodians suffered enormously during some twenty years (1970–91) of civil wars, genocide and foreign occupation, and some ethnic minority groups suffered extreme discrimination and even genocide under recent regimes. This has left a difficult legacy for the Cambodian government as it attempts to work out its ethnic policies.

Cambodia's brief period of stable, post-colonial rule ended in 1970 when the war between the USA and North Vietnam swept into central Cambodia. A bitter and destructive civil war ensued, augmented by massive US bombing, between the US-backed Khmer republican regime led by Lon Nol and an insurgent Chinese- and Hanoi-backed Khmer Rouge. In April 1975 the Khmer Rouge under Pol Pot won, and the new government sought to restructure Cambodian society completely. The Khmer Rouge called the new start 'Year Zero'. More than 1 million Cambodians died in the process. In 1979, the Khmer Rouge fell out with the Vietnamese communists, their former allies, and the Vietnamese successfully invaded and installed a puppet regime in Phnom Penh (1979–90). From sanctuaries in Thailand, the Khmer Rouge, joined by remnants of former royalist and republican regimes in Cambodia and backed by China, the ASEAN states and the West, waged a guerrilla war. A rough stalemate continued for a decade until 1991, when the warring factions signed a peace agreement in Paris. The United Nations Transitional Authority in Cambodia (UNTAC) took control until elections were held. In late 1993 the new government promulgated a new Cambodian constitution, based on a constitutional monarchy, and began to reformulate Cambodia's social and political order. The constitution specifically protects the rights of minorities. The Khmer Rouge remain in jungle bases along the Thai–Cambodia border, waging low-intensity armed political struggle against the government.

Cham

Originally, Cham were the inhabitants of the medieval Hindu kingdom of Champa located on the coast of what is now central Vietnam. They converted to Islam as the Muslim faith spread eastward into island and peninsular South-East Asia. After the Khmer deserted Angkor, the imperial capital of Cambodia, in the fifteenth century, the Vietnamese, expanding south from their historical base in Tonkin and Annam, conquered Champa. Preferring to live among the Hinduized Buddhist Khmer rather than the Sinoized or Confucianized Vietnamese, Cham abandoned Champa and migrated to Cambodia, settling along the rivers and the Tonle Sap lake. Ethnically and linguistically Cham are Malay-Polynesian. Before 1975 Khmer and foreign accounts numbered Cham between 150,000 and 250,000. In the Cambodian countryside, Cham live in their own villages, often directly next to Cambodian villages. In the cities, Cham are clustered in their own neighbourhoods or suburbs. Cham maintain their distinctive style of dress: women have long hair and cover their heads with scarves; men wear skullcaps and often grow beards. During the Sihanouk and Lon Nol eras, Cham, unlike ethnic Chinese and Vietnamese, were citizens. However, they were severely persecuted during the Pol Pot years (1975–9). In many areas Cham communities were sent to the countryside or executed *en masse*. Probably in response to prohibitions on the practice of their Islamic religion and the threatened loss of their Islamic identity, some Cham rebelled against the Pol Pot regime. An attempted genocide of the Cham followed. With the defeat of the Khmer Rouge, Cham were able to resume their traditional lifestyles and religious practices, rebuilding their former mosques and returning to their traditional neighbourhoods and occupations.

Indigenous hill tribes

Like all of South-East Asia, Cambodia has indigenous hill tribes, known as Khmer Leou (literally 'upper Khmer'). Khmer Leou are recognized as indigenous in the sense that like the Khmer they are deemed original inhabitants, as opposed to Cham or ethnic Chinese and Vietnamese who migrated to Cambodia only centuries or decades ago. Thus, after independence, Khmer Leou were recognized as Cambodian citizens. The Cambodian hill tribes inhabit the isolated north-east mountainous regions of Ratanakiri and Mondulkiri provinces, and also the mountainous areas of Koh Kong Province in the south-west. Many of the hill tribes continue to practise slash-and-burn subsistence farming. One tribal group, the Kuoy, have been more influenced than the rest by Khmer culture and intermarry with the Khmer. There is no consensus concerning the number or even classifications of the various hill tribes, although a UN estimate in 1992 noted six larger tribes numbering over 10,000 and twenty smaller groups of less than 3,000.

Chinese

Chinese traders have long been present in Cambodia. At the time of Cambodia's independence in 1953, the ethnic Chinese population was estimated at 400,000. While the Chinese in Cambodia maintained their own communities and dialects, they also adopted many Khmer customs and were prone to intermarriage with the Cambodian elite. Despite the high degree of assimilation, the Chinese continued to consider themselves as Chinese. After independence for the most part the Chinese were regarded as overseas residents, not Cambodian citizens. But until the advent of the Khmer Rouge, they did not face any overt hostility or discrimination. Under Pol Pot, the Chinese were identified as 'bourgeois' and many were executed or sent to the countryside to work. After the 1979 Vietnamese invasion, many surviving ethnic Chinese and Sino-Khmer fled to Thailand. Others returned to Phnom Penh and the provincial towns to resume their economic enterprises. But they were not allowed to re-establish Chinese associations or Chinese language schools or to display business signs in Chinese during the 1980s. This situation only changed recently. As of 1995, the Chinese community in Cambodia is cohesive, tolerated and integrated, and it does not face any significant levels of discrimination from the Khmer majority. Ethnic Chinese are often able to get obtain Cambodian citizenship.

Vietnamese

Ethnic Vietnamese are the one minority group in Cambodia currently at risk. Threats to the status and safety of ethnic Vietnamese derive, in part, from centuries of antagonism between Cambodia and Vietnam, and also in part from substantial Vietnamese migration into Cambodia during the 1980s, when Cambodia was under Vietnamese occupation. Historically, Vietnamese emperors had a policy of settling Vietnamese in sparsely populated areas that the Khmer regarded as part of Cambodian territory. Vietnamese rice farmers and fishers continued to migrate into Cambodia during the nineteenth and twentieth centuries; during the French colonial period France staffed much of its colonial administration in Cambodia with French-speaking Catholic Vietnamese. The French also imported Vietnamese plantation workers. In the nineteenth century Vietnam permanently took over part of Cambodia, and during one occupation of Phnom Penh attempted to impose the Vietnamese language and political structures and Sinicized or Confucianized Vietnamese cultural norms and practices on the Hinduized Therevada Buddhist Khmers. Thus, many Cambodian nationalists came to perceive Vietnamese as a threat not only to their political independence but also to the survival of the Khmer people and culture.

Under Prince Sihanouk's rule during the post-independence period, ethnic Vietnamese in Cambodia were, like ethnic Chinese, regarded as foreign residents. However, extreme Cambodian nationalists regarded ethnic Vietnamese as agents or instruments of a Vietnamese intention to take over Cambodia. Ethnic Vietnamese were severely persecuted under the successive regimes of Lon Nol (1970–5) and Pol Pot (1975–9). Almost immediately after Lon Nol's coup against Prince Sihanouk, pogroms were initiated against ethnic Vietnamese in Phnom Penh that left several thousand dead and drove more than 100,000 to flee back to Vietnam. When the Khmer Rouge came to power in 1975 perhaps as many as 150,000 Vietnamese who had not fled or been expelled during the Lon Nol years were expelled to Vietnam. Those Vietnamese who remained, often because they were married to Khmer, were massacred, along with, in many instances, the children of mixed Khmer-Vietnamese families. While Cambodia was under Vietnamese occupation, ethnic Vietnamese who had been expelled during the Lon Nol and Pot Pot regimes returned to Cambodia. Additional Vietnamese artisans entered the country in response to an economic boom that followed the signing of the Cambodian peace treaty in 1991. In the early 1990s the Khmer Rouge and some right-wing Cambodian politicians organized political assassinations of ethnic Vietnamese living in isolated fishing villages, which led to an exodus of perhaps 25,000 Vietnamese to the Cambodia–Vietnamese border. Vietnam admitted the majority of them. Anti-Vietnamese sentiments remain so strong that a new immigration law, primarily aimed at the Vietnamese, which allows for the mass expulsion of non-citizens, was passed with a large majority in the elected Assembly. Although the current Cambodian political leaders have pledged that there will be no mass expulsions, there is no guarantee that this measure will not be used by future leaders.

Conclusions and future prospects

During the period of the UN peace-keeping mission, Cambodia acceded to the major international human rights conventions: the Covenant on Civil and Political Rights; the Covenant on Economic, Social and Cultural Rights; the women's and children's rights conventions; the Convention on the Elimination of All Forms of Racial Discrimination; and the Refugee Convention and Protocol. However, when the UN left, the newly elected Cambodian government, consisting of the royalist faction and the former Vietnamese-backed regime, became embroiled in internal squabbles and in fighting the Khmer Rouge in the countryside. The elected National Assembly became paralyzed. Three of Cambodia's ethnic minority groups – Cham, ethnic Chinese and Cambodian hill tribes – can, pending the passage of a 'basic law' on associations, form associations, speak their own languages and practise their religion and customs. For the Vietnamese, however, major concerns remain, arising from the legacy of the 'citizenship' definition of the post-independence, pre-turmoil period (1953–70), when Cham and the hill tribes were regarded as full citizens while ethnic Vietnamese and Chinese were regarded as overseas residents. The Cambodian government must now face the need to regard Vietnamese and Chinese as eligible for full citizenship – despite its apparent inability, or unwillingness, to distinguish between Vietnamese whose families have resided in Cambodia for generations and who would, under international norms, be fully eligible for citizenship, and other Vietnamese who entered the country while Cambodia was under Vietnamese occupation and would have a less clear case for citizenship. Further persecution of the Vietnamese in Cambodia still remains a possibility.

Further reading

Chandler, D.P., *Cambodia*, Sydney, Asia–Australia Institute, University of New South Wales, 1993.

Hawk, D., *Minorities in Cambodia*, London, MRG report, 1995.

Somers, Heidhues, M. *et al.*, *The Chinese of South-East Asia*, London, MRG report, 1992.

Vickery, M., *Cambodia, 1975–1982*, Sydney, Allen & Unwin, 1984.

Minority-based and advocacy organizations

Cambodia League for Promotion and Defence of Human Rights (LICADHO), No. 103, Street 97, Phnom Penh, Cambodia; tel. 855 23 27626.

Cambodian Human Rights and Development Association (ADHOC), No. 1, Street 158, Boeng Raing, Daun Penh District, Cambodia; tel. 855 23 25435, fax 855 23 27229.

Cambodian Institute of Human Rights, PO Box 144, Phnom Penh, Cambodia; tel. 855 15 912 607, fax 855 23 27425.

Human Rights Vigilance of Cambodia (Vigilance), No. 57, Street 222, Boeng Raing, Daun Penh District, Cambodia; tel. 855 23 27767.

China and Tibet

Land area:	9,571,3000 sq km[1]
Population:	1,219 million (1996)[2]
Main languages:	Putonghua (Mandarin Chinese), Tibetan and more than 50 other languages
Main religions:	animism, Buddhism, Chinese folk religions, Christian sects, Roman Catholicism, Islam, Lamaism (Tibetan Buddhism), Protestantism, Shamanism, Taoism
Main minority groups:	Chuang (Zhuang) 15,489,630 (1.3%), Manchu 9,821,180 (0.82%), Hui (Huihui) 8,602,978 (0.7%), Miao (Hmong) 7,398,035 (0.62%), Uighur 7,214,431 (0.6%), Yi (Lolo) 6,572,173 (0.55%), Tujia 5,704,223 (0.48%), Mongolians 4,806,849 (0.4%), Tibetans 4,593,330 (disputed figure, 0.38%)[3] , Bouyei 2,545,059 (0.21%), Dong 2,514,014 (0.21%), Yao (Gerbao) 2,134,013 (0.18%), Koreans 1,920,597 (0.16%), Bai (Borean) 1,594,827 (0.13%), Hani 1,253,952 (0.1%)
Real per capita GDP:	$2,330
UNDP HDI/rank:	0.609 (108)

Scholars and official publications vary in their statistical analyses of Chinese society. Its constituent elements are also changing quickly because of the impact of recent rapid developments in the social, economic, cultural and political fields and because of China's foreign policy. The future of minorities in China is bound up inextricably with these recent developments.

China is situated on the west coast of the Pacific Ocean. Its topography plays an important role in the life of minority communities. Many minorities live in border regions, which are also often rich in raw materials such as coal, timber, oil and gas, and minerals. Growing border trade with other countries may benefit or hinder minorities, who are often poor. There may be conflict over land use, and great control of local populations because of significant border army, police or militia forces. With a 22,800 kilometre long border, China is linked with Korea in the east, Mongolia in the north, Russia in the north-east, Kazakhstan, Kyrgystan and Tajikistan in the north-west, Afghanistan, Pakistan, India, Nepal and Bhutan in the west and south-west, and Burma, Laos and Vietnam in the south. It has 5,000 islands, of which Hainan (at 34,000 square kilometres, slightly smaller than Taiwan) is the largest. Many of China's minorities live in remote rural and mountain areas and along the upper reaches of major rivers, so their economies suffer from poor infrastructure and the presence of government-backed migrant workers with no long-term stake in the local economy. Local people miss out on value-added benefits from primary industries (hydroelectric power, minerals, coal, oil and gas extraction).

The economy

Minorities are often severely disadvantaged by China's focus on economic liberalization. This could threaten their survival as communities. Special Economic Zones (SEZs) attract most of the money, privileges and development, and poor areas do not get the means to compete. The zones themselves do, however, put special project money into poor areas. Migrant workers from the interior are used in coastal regions as cheap labour, but they also send money back to their village. Some argue that this redistribution of wealth does at least happen, whereas government subsidies may be creamed off by the bureaucracy. But minorities are forced to become migrant workers, threatening the economic life of their villages, which have growing elderly populations.

Migrant workers are a major group. Shenzhen employs 2.1 million workers from outside the SEZ and each of them, on average, sends 3,000 yuan back to their family every year – seven times a peasant's income. There is growing poverty because of inflation running as high as 26 per cent, which means subsistence communities are facing growing difficulty earning the extra money needed to buy agricultural inputs on the open market. This is confirmed by the government's own extensive programmes to supply food and clothing to such areas. Such assistance is separate from aid sent during droughts or after floods, which can be widespread. The central government is trying to improve the social security net, but the burden of implementation is being shifted on to local authorities. In poor areas the latter cannot mobilize enough taxes to do a proper job, even though officials want to improve on the status quo. Migrant workers in Guangdong Province are estimated at 12 million (one-sixth of the local population) and they are accused of raising crime rates. They are often subcontracted by local Chinese, who have seen their income reach the levels of income earned by Hong Kong Chinese. Migrant workers are usually housed in dormitory camps, but have no resident status and, if not working illegally, are required to carry three separate identity cards. One estimate suggests that 10 per cent of the total Chinese population is now involved in migrant labour.

Because of pressure on food production, the government is arranging to move major population groups away from flood and drought zones so that communities have a better chance of improving food production and, literally, of surviving. These are not forced removals. While county towns are booming in Ningxia Province in north-west China, peasants in its rural areas seem to face a stark choice of move or starve. With annual incomes averaging 400 yuan, working the land offered them little hope. So, the government began a relocation programme in 1985, aiming to move 746,000 people from the dry south to more fertile neighbouring areas, and people welcomed this. About 176,000 had been relocated by the end of 1994.

China's wish to be a growing and officially recognized player in international trade, and to be represented in regional and global international trade bodies, could contribute to better human rights performance generally and to improved internal attitudes towards minorities. The stakes for China are enormous. In 1994, foreign trade totalled US $236,700 million, 11.5 times the volume of 1978. This was an increase of 21 per cent over 1993, ranking China eleventh in international trade. The government cannot be unaware that there is a linkage between its guarantees on basic rights (see **Hong Kong**) and foreign investment. But it can also use its cheap labour rates as a lever between foreign business owners and their governments.

Education

Despite official protestations about the preservation and development of minority languages, the individual's need to climb the official or business hierarchy results in members of minorities being forced to pursue the Chinese language and educational system as their main method of advancement and communication. Two pictures emerge of education development in remote and poorer areas where many minorities are located. Government figures say that since 1982 education for the minority nationalities has developed rapidly, yet the government itself acknowledges that there is a poor foundation for education of minorities who generally live in more backward economic areas. Before 1949, more than 90 per cent of people of minority nationalities were illiterate. Officials claim that 'many' institutions of higher learning have opened nationalities classes and preparatory courses especially for students of minority nationalities, and that secondary schools for minority students or nationalities classes have been established in the interior areas. When institutions of higher learning and secondary vocational schools enrol students, grades for entrance examinations for the students of minority nationalities are appropriately reduced, to increase access. At the same time national schools are promoting bilingual teaching.

There are now claimed to be more than 120,000 primary schools of nationalities, 11,000 middle schools of nationalities, 189 secondary teacher-training schools, 35 teacher-training colleges and universities, 12 colleges of nationalities and 107 universities and colleges in national autonomous areas. Minority nationalities now have more and more PhD and MA students overseas. The number of teachers specializing in the education of nationalities has exceeded 600,000. Though there is no independent means of verifying such figures, it is also clear that the government fully recognizes the other reality – that poverty and the need to contribute their labour prevents millions of children attending school.

China has not been backward in accepting World Bank assistance for education. It says the grant and loan system will be continually improved under the '211 Project', effectively engineering and cultivating 100 major universities. The implications for remote areas need to be considered. While a large number of children in some areas have been able to go back to school, under recent programmes this was not the case for millions of others in impoverished areas who cannot attend a school. Those attending often only receive part-time schooling, which is affected by seasonal harvest work. About 60 per cent are girls and in poor districts the attendance rate for girls is 20–30 per cent. This results in a huge population of illiterates and semi-illiterates. Though the situation is of particular concern to parents, it has been taken up as a social issue by many Chinese organizations. As a result the 'Project of Hope' was set up in 1989, and by June 1994, 549,000 children across China had been given financial aid and returned to school. Yet the number of children excluded from school has not diminished and has even increased in certain areas because simply reducing the cost of tuition does not necessarily allow children to remain at school long enough to acquire the basic knowledge they need.

In the last two decades, while urban areas have boomed economically, rural schools and their equipment have deteriorated considerably as central government has contributed nothing beyond the fixed budget, making local government responsible for its own finances and educational costs. This has put a heavy burden on impoverished districts. Migrant worker mobility, involving both teachers and family members, has created instability. In some mountainous regions certain villages have not had a school since 1949 and in some areas the number of schools has declined. The threat to minorities is clear if the suggestion is made that this system of education only serves the purpose of those people who can profit from it, while the other children (the majority) are excluded, or pushed aside, in a disguised way. The chance of a peasant child being accepted at university is practically nil.

More than half the school-age children in a recent survey in ten poor provinces did not look at or listen to media such as the written press, television and radio. Teachers have poor living standards and have extremely low salaries. Families in prosperous zones, however, can cope with the rising costs of books and equipment, while those in rural areas cannot. Educational costs in poverty zones have risen six to eight times whereas income has only doubled in the last ten years.

Politics, human rights and religion

China reflects the old dictum that a political system may be perfect in theory but not in practice. The constitution and representative system offer all the guarantees desirable, yet these do not make them a reality. The Chinese political leadership is engaged in a balancing act to maintain economic liberalization with continued political control. Minorities are being squeezed economically and may be a source of rebellion. Tibet is the focus of significant control and human rights abuses. The crackdown on the nascent pro-democracy movement in June 1989, highlighted by the Tiananmen Square massacre, was an expression of fear of loss of control.

Weaker groups, such as ethnic minorities in remote areas, do not have the physical access to institutions of power, nor easy political access to protecting their interests. However, there are committed officials and political forces seeking to ensure that the poor and minorities are not left out of the race. The structure of the country's political institutions allows for a degree of consultation which can influence the way change takes place. It should not be dismissed out of hand, since it offers an institutionalized avenue which minorities can use to argue their case. Minorities have a political role through an allocation of electoral seats. China has an elected National People's Congress (NPC) and local people's congresses. Deputies to the NPC are elected from all fifty-six officially recognized nationalities and the Eighth NPC is composed of 2,978 deputies serving from 1993 to 1998. Among them 439 represent all fifty-five national minorities, the fifty-sixth being the Han, the majority nationality. The Communist Party and its committees decide policy and effectively run the country.

More than half the population (59.2 per cent) profess no religious belief. Buddhism, Christianity and Taoism are followed by members of the majority Han population. Other significant practices include Chinese folk religions, Islam, Lamaism or Tibetan Buddhism (widespread in Tibet and Inner Mongolia), and Shamanism.[4]

Conflict between the Chinese authorities and minorities following non-approved religions has been reported: for example, arrests of churchgoers. Protestant and evangelical Christian movements have borne the brunt of persecution in the modern period in China up to the present. Evangelical movements often develop in the remote countryside among small groups of converts. They are also more likely to receive attention from foreign 'missionaries', often from the USA. These are rural areas where foreign-exchange donations from a movement's adherents in the West have a proportionately greater impact on the aspirations of the poor than they would in cities. They also expose such Chinese communities to the charges of being counter-revolutionaries and collaborating with foreign powers. There is ample international evidence of foreign intelligence agencies using missionary groups as conduits for money and local agents, a practice that exposes true believers to manipulation.

About 2.4 per cent of the Chinese population

is Muslim, spread across the country and ethnic groups. Islam, like Christianity, is a missionary and proselytizing religion, often ready to challenge the state. And it is Islam that most touches minority nationalities in China today. It has been suggested that the revival of Islam during the past two decades, alongside the relatively liberal domestic policies adopted by Deng Xiao-ping in the 1980s, has triggered a new dynamic in the role of Islamic minorities.[5] Chinese and non-Chinese scholars have produced a growing amount of research material on China's Muslims, and the wealthy Islamic governments of the Middle East have also taken interest and offered grants for scholarships and building renovations. Extended visits have been allowed to Chinese Islamic communities. This opening makes it easier for the Chinese government to monitor the Islamic community, which is certainly far more extensive than official figures indicate.

The widespread Muslim rebellions of the mid-nineteenth century in north-west and south-west China have not been forgotten. Today, the disintegration of the Soviet Union has produced new independent neighbouring republics with Islamic leanings or where the official religion is Islam. Three of these republics are across the frontier from Chinese (or Eastern) Turkestan and share with it many cross-frontier ethnic groups. They could become a source of ethnic-religious unrest. Some Muslims made their way into positions of power during the Chinese imperial period, allowing them to some degree to intervene on behalf of their co-religionists from 'within the system', especially within the military. Muslims may also adopt Chinese religious practices so that they are less conspicuous, particularly in isolated areas where being 'too Muslim' could attract attention and risk. The Chinese state remains unitarian. Muslim ideology, in turn, requires the assumption of political power, since the will of Allah has to be worked on earth by a political system. In this sense the seeds of conflict remain always ready to take root. Muslim activism erupted during the period of the Hundred Flowers announced by Mao in 1957 and in the relaxed period after the end of the rule of the Gang of Four, on the death of Mao in 1976. It could erupt again.

Population issues

The Chinese government has used coercion to enforce its one-child family policy. There are obvious repercussions – demographic change will result in a diminishing number of young people caring for an increasingly ageing population. Minorities, largely in rural areas, have been able to have two children. The authorities in Beijing initially insisted that ethnic groups with populations of less than 10 million were exempt from the one-child policy or even from family planning entirely. It is clear, however, that controls have been applied to these groups for many years, including more stringent sanctions for urban residents and 'prohibitions' on a third child. There have also been reports of controls extending to enforcement of one-child families, in particular for state employees. Currently, as with the rest of the population, specific regulations and their implementation are decided by 'Autonomous Regions and Provinces where minorities reside'.

But migration from the countryside by minorities may mean that their villages begin to die. There are reports that the policy of allowing rural areas to have a higher number of children per family is also being tightened up. Also, minorities who are attached to Muslim or Christian beliefs may become targets of discrimination by other families who are restricted in the number of children they can have, or by officials who have been set population control quotas and try to build them up by pressure on weaker groups.

There is considerable debate about the imbalance of girls to boys in China and orphan and girl infanticide. Figures on infanticides are based on various conflicting sources and reports, and the degree to which the one-child policy is a cause is not clear. The government denies that there is an official policy of allowing baby orphans to die in institutions through starvation or lack of medical care. Decentralized economic policies mean that the responsibility for funding services now falls on the shoulders of local government, and in some regions there is a severe shortage of funds.

The Chinese government officially allows large numbers of rural areas more children than the official two-child rural family. Tibet has no controls in theory, though there may be deviations from this. The Office of His Holiness the Dalai Lama in New Delhi understands that official Chinese policy on family size for Tibetans is two children per family. However, instances are reported, for example, that where a Tibetan is working as a government official and the family has a second child, they are pressured indirectly. They may lose a promotion or their salary or benefits may be affected. Further, while Tibetans are not officially bound by the one-child policy, indirect pressures are brought to stop couples having larger families. This seems to follow similar local coercion and pressure in other parts of China, for example among rural Christians, although they may be entitled under the law to more than one child because of their national minority status. There are reports of conflict between the authorities and Christian groups who are against birth control and are outside the officially recognized Catholic and Protestant churches. There may also be benefits for the one-child family which rural families do not get.

In most regions, urban couples may have only one child unless their child is disabled, while rural couples may have a second if the first is a girl. A third child is 'prohibited' in most available regulations. Regulations covering migrant women indicate that abortion is mandatory if the woman does not return to her home region. Abortion is also mandatory for unmarried women. 'Fines' in rural areas have reportedly included the demolition of the houses of people who have failed to pay the fines, or the arrest and detention of pregnant women or their relatives until a termination is agreed to.

China's minorities

Including Tibetans and Mongolians, China has fifty-six officially recognized ethnic groups or nationalities. The full list, based on 1990 official population census figures, is as follows: Han (1,042,482,187 people, 91.06% of the total), Chuang (Zhuang) (15,489,630, 1.3%), Manchu (9,821,180, 0.82%), Hui (Huihui) (8,602,978, 0.7%), Miao (Hmong) (7,398,035, 0.62%), Uighur (7,214,431, 0.6%), Yi (Lolo) (6,572,173, 0.55%), Tujia (5,704,223, 0.48%), Mongolians (4,806,849, 0.4%), Tibetans (4,593,330, 0.38%), Bouyei (2,545,059, 0.21%), Dong (2,514,014, 0.21%), Yao (Gerbao) (2,134,013, 0.18%), Koreans (1,920,597, 0.16%), Bai (Borean) (1,594,827, 0.13%), Hani (1,253,952, 0.1%), Kazak (1,111,718, 0.093%), Li (1,110,900, 0.093%), Tai (Dai) (1,025,128, 0.085%), She (630,378, 0.052%), Lisu (574,856, 0.048%), Kelao (Gelao) (437,997, 0.036%), Lahu (411,476, 0.034%), Dongxiang (373,872, 0.031%), Wa (Va) (351,974, 0.029%), Shui (345,993, 0.029%), Naxi (278,009, 0.023%), Qiang (198,252, 0.017%), Tu (191,642, 0.016%), Sibo (Xibe) (172,847, 0.014%), Mulam (159,328, 0.013%), Kirghiz (141,549, 0.012%), Daur (121,357, 0.01%), Jingpo (119,209, 0.0099%), Salar (87,697, 0.0073%), Pulang (Blang) (82,280, 0.0069%), Maonan (71,968, 0.006%), Tajiks (33,538, 0.0028%), Pumi (Primi) (29,657, 0.0025%), Achang (27,708, 0.0023%), Nu (27,123, 0.0023%), Evenk (Ewenki) (26,315, 0.0022%), Jing (18,915, 0.0016%), Jino (18,021, 0.0015%), Penglung (De'ang) (15,462, 0.0013%), Uzbeks (14,502, 0.0012%), Russians (13,504, 0.0011%), Yugur (12,297, 0.001%), Paoan (Bonan) (12,212, 0.001%), Mempa (Monba) (7,475, 0.00062%), Tulung (Drung) (5,816, 0.00048%), Oranchun (Oroqen) (6,965, 0.00058%), Tatar (4,873, 0.00039%), Goldi (Hezhen, Hoche) (4,245, 0.00035%), Gaoshan (2,909, 0.00024%), and Lopa (Lhoba) (2,312, 0.00019%).

Contemporary documentation on minorities in China is still very limited.[6] The different languages, customs of dress, food and various festivals common among all the minorities will not be detailed here. Many of these customs have been banned or repressed at various times under communist rule. Today such differences are not only allowed but encouraged. Some Chinese of Han origin are reportedly now trying to become classed as part of minority communities to take advantage of positive discrimination for various benefits, including access to college and university, or being allowed two children and getting through quota allocations. Nevertheless, the economic systems of ethnic minorities in China are still less advanced than the economy of the majority Han. Attainment of political rights involves knowledge, which in turn is conditional upon education. When 'development' merely requires minorities to adapt their traditional institutions, their values and normative systems to the specific version of modernity as idealized by the Han Chinese in order to modernize, this is nothing more than assimilation.

China's non-Chinese peoples have contributed an important physical and cultural element to the present Han population, as they have historically become assimilated into Chinese civilization. Han–minority relations since 1949 have reflected national political directions. During times of radical change, such as the period of socialist transformation and the Great Leap Forward (1956–62), as well as the Great Proletarian Cultural Revolution (1966–9), the emphasis was on rapid movement towards socialism and criticism of 'local nationalism'. The communists attempted to make these periods as shattering to the minorities' social structures as it was to the Han's. Traditional customs were criticized as wasteful superstitions. Old aristocrats were 're-educated', and class origin was taken into account when appointing new officials and party members. During the lulls (1950–6, 1963–6, 1969–75) between these periods of rapid change, more stress was placed upon regional (political) and minority (cultural) autonomy. Great Hanism (excessive centralization and ethnocentricity) was criticized and each nationality was to be guided into socialism at its own pace.

The Putonghua (Mandarin) Chinese language – a working language of the United Nations – is used by the majority Han as well as the Hui and Manchu nationalities. The other fifty-three nationalities have their own spoken languages, and twenty-three have their own written languages. (A discussion of language is dealt with below in the context of the Yi minority.)

Because of the lack of available information, and limitations of space, it is not possible here to give a comprehensive account of China's minorities. The Yi are featured as an example of the kinds of challenges faced by minority communities in China, and their responses. A discussion of the better-known case of Tibet follows. Finally, some shorter profiles of other Chinese minorities are included.

Yi (Lolo)

The problem of policies towards nationalities, development strategies and questions of cultural identity are reflected in the case of the Yi living in the Liangshan Autonomous Prefecture, established in 1952. Yi, one of China's largest ethnic minorities, live in areas of Szechwan, Yunnan, and Kweichow provinces. A small number live in Kwangsi Province. They are hill-tribe people who belong to the Tibeto-Burmese language group. They are predominantly farmers, but this activity is supplemented with hunting. There is a spoken Yi language, while the men speak and write Putonghua (Mandarin Chinese) and can write the Yi language. The Yi are animists. In the first half of the twentieth century Han and Yi fought each other mercilessly.

The social structure of the Yi was based on a two-class system: the 'Black Yi' – nobility, landowners and slave-owners – and a slave class comprising three graded castes. Controversies about rights and interest of clan members were often settled by force of arms, resulting in frequent clan feuds. Under the Communist Party comprehensive reforms became operative in 1956, when the slave system was abolished. The state deprived large owners of slaves and landed properties of their privileges; the released slaves in the Liangshan Prefecture 1952 were given land, implements, seeds and building material for houses. Yi leaders and former Yi slaves were made to participate in the reform process. From the beginning, the communists left no doubt that Yi society would not be allowed to continue in its traditional form. The reforms impeached Yi cultural identity and affected it fundamentally. Their traditional social organization was declared 'historically outdated' and the Han called for its extinction. Although the land was equally distributed among all Yi, Black Yi became integrated in the new hierarchy of the state. In the mid-1950s riots flared up in the Yi regions although they were suppressed. There has more recently been success in both increasing the earnings of Yi peasants and stimulating their readiness to perform more efficiently by their having more control over rural production units.

Changes in the written script of the Yi reveal a significant aspect of the way change has affected minorities in China. The script is more than a thousand years old. In former times, only the *bimo* (shamans) mastered the script and could write. The bulk of traditional literature that existed was intended as instruction books for the shamans, although they contained poems, tales and treatises on medicine and production techniques. During the early 1950s it was decided the scripts would be adapted to modern requirements. In the mid-1970s, at the request of many Yi, the old script was reintroduced in modified form. Today, there is a daily newspaper, a literary journal and quite a number of publications in Yi. The publishing centre for literature of national minorities also has a Yi department. Nowadays, all public announcements in Liangshan have to be bilingual, following a decree of the autonomous prefecture.

Continued changes in language strategies have not helped tackle the root problems of illiteracy among the Yi and have obstructed the implementation of an effective educational policy. Yi college students are still rare. In 1983 writings of importance were only available in the Chinese language, and publications of well-known Yi authors were in Chinese. Since 1979, illiteracy among the Yi has fallen with the help of specific instruction material in Yi script. Today every county has a special office to eliminate illiteracy. Yi script is taught in villages by teachers delegated for this particular purpose, supported by unpaid assistants. However, language development is relatively difficult. There are insufficient qualified teachers and translators available for Yi, and so linguistic underdevelopment of schools will continue. Opportunities for promotion and mobility are conditional upon the knowledge of Chinese, which remains the privileged road into higher education.

Today the Yi see the main elements of their autonomy in the use and development of their native language and its script, accelerated education within the region, protection and maintenance of customs and traditions and the promotion of education and health services. Most Yi clearly appreciate the envisaged level of autonomy, and so they are interested in having laws that would safeguard the scope of self-administration they can achieve and economic development that could accompany it.

Tibet[7]

China maintains that it has had administrative and political control over Tibet for centuries. Tibetans in exile say that China had formal relations with Tibet, not governance of it. Tibet's land area is a question of dispute between China and Tibetans in exile under the Dalai Lama. In 1949 China invaded eastern Tibet, capturing Chamdo a year later. In May 1951, a Tibetan delegation to Beijing signed a 'Seventeen-point Agreement on Measures for the Peaceful Liberation of Tibet'. This agreement was used a few months later to justify the overrunning of the capital, Lhasa, by thousands of Chinese troops. Nationwide Tibetan resistance culminated in March 1959 with the 'Tibetan National Uprising' in Lhasa. This was put down and included the massacre of thousands of children, women and men. The Dalai Lama, who had become head of state in November 1950 at the age of 16, was forced, along with 80,000 other Tibetans, to seek political asylum in India. The Dalai Lama insisted that the Seventeen-point Agreement with China was imposed under armed force, and in Dharamsala, India, he established a Tibetan government in exile.

Since China's occupation of Tibet, southern, central and part of northern Tibet have been re-designated as the Tibet Autonomous Region (TAR), while the rest, including most of the Amdo region (renamed Qingai by the Chinese), has been classified as part of China's non-autonomous administrative structures. There has been forced migration of Han Chinese into Tibet, in an attempt to change the demographic profile of the region, and thus ensure the integration of Tibet into the mainstream of Chinese politics. Tibetans are considered by the Chinese to be one of fifty-five national minorities within China, rather than belonging to a separate nation. (There are also minority groups within Tibet: Upa, Khampa and Amdo; the majority of Upas live in what Tibetans call Utsang, which covers Lhasa, and the whole of southern and central Tibet.)

The long-standing position of the Office of His Holiness the Dalai Lama (OHHDL) was formerly that there could be no negotiations with the Chinese without their recognition of the independent status of Tibet. The Dalai Lama's most recent position is that Tibetans may be prepared, as a first step, to settle for incomplete independence involving Tibetan self-government within a mutually agreed Tibet area, while the Chinese retain control of foreign affairs and defence. A linked politico-religious issue of disagreement between the Dalai Lama and the Chinese government is the designation of the second most important religious figure for Tibetans, the Panchen Lama.

In theory, Tibetans enjoy full rights under the Chinese constitution. In practice there is extensive documentation of serious human rights abuses. Reports from Tibet continue to mention widespread unlawful arrests and the torture of Tibetans – including monks and nuns – by such methods as food and sleep deprivation, electric shock and long-term shackling. There is extensive control over freedom of speech. Tibetans are subject to economic discrimination, to the advantage of Han Chinese. There are educational pressures against Tibetan language and customs and limited freedom of movement.

The Chinese say that over the past four decades they have invested the equivalent of approximately US$4,600 million sterling in Tibet, bringing improvements in the fields of agricultural production, livestock-breeding, energy, communications, education and culture. Extensive construction programmes have been undertaken, including the building of highways, oil pipelines, power stations and hotels, in order to establish an infrastructure capable of industrial development, and of exploiting the developing tourist market. OHHDL officials dispute the Chinese view that economic developments since 1959 have had any positive impact on the lives and living standards of the vast majority of Tibetans. Approximately one in four of the Tibetan population are nomads and make their living by selling wool, but they are restricted by quotas which limit the numbers of sheep, cattle and yaks they can own. Any excess is confiscated by the state. Nomads, in particular, have reportedly seen no improvement in their living standards. The majority of Tibetans remain in the countryside and are prevented from doing jobs other than labouring. The Tibet Autonomous Region (TAR) has also seen conflict between migrants and local communities, such as clashes between Tibetans and Chinese Muslims who are often at the forefront of entrepreneurial activities in border areas. About 1 million Tibetans now live in exile, the majority of them in India, 20,000 in Nepal and 1,700 in the USA and Canada. Chinese officials made strenuous efforts to prevent Tibetan participation at the Women's Conference in Beijing in 1995.

There have been increasing incentives over the years to encourage teachers, along with other professionals, to work in Tibet. A large part of the current tourist boom in Tibet is based on a hotel infrastructure funded by the business acumen of the Chinese People's Liberation Army and the militia, the People's Armed Police, who number some 65,000 in Tibet. In the TAR, official schools make very limited provision for the teaching of the Tibetan language, and printed material generally represents an adulteration of the language, history, literature and religion of Tibetans. In higher education, access to which is restricted for Tibetans, the only language of instruction is Putonghua (Mandarin Chinese). Tibetans have also been unable to pursue higher level study opportunities abroad, which is not the case for other official minorities in China. Most publications and broadcasts are in Putonghua.

The persecution of Buddhist monks and nuns forms the nodal point of human rights issues in Tibet, since the Dalai Lama is regarded as the spiritual and temporal leader of Tibetans. Mass destruction of monasteries took place after the Chinese armed occupation began. An awareness of the cultural and tourism industry losses which this has implied has led the Chinese government to change its attitude to the country's architectural heritage, and the majority of monasteries have been restored as a matter of policy. But this has been strictly controlled and is tempered by Chinese determination that restored monasteries should not become spiritual communities that can become a focus of political resistance. The Communist Party is determined that Buddhist spiritual values should not be allowed to form part of the normal schooling process. There is also friction between China's population control policy and Tibetan values about family size.

The comparatively small population of the vast TAR contrasts with enormous forestry, mineral and energy resources. These are important for the Chinese economy. A gold rush, both private and official, is said by Chinese officials to be a new growth sector for the region's economic development. Nomads are reportedly taking the opportunity to increase their incomes. Gold, panned or mined by Tibetans, is subject, however, to an informal 'gold tax', whereby they lose a significant amount of their finds. State mines on the plateau are said to be staffed by political prisoners working in concentration camp conditions. It is suspected that large-scale open cast mining on the Tibet plateau, coupled with timber clearance without adequate replanting, increases both the level of local soil loss, increasing river bed levels of the Yangtze and Yellow rivers, and downriver silting. This not only threatens nomadic pastures which are important for Tibetan pastoralists; it may also present increased flood risks for communities, many of them minorities, who base part of their income on riverine agriculture, as well as threatening their homes. The delicate ecology of grazing regions is also under threat, and the hunting of animals in Tibet for resale as elements in medicines may pose a further threat to the livelihood of nomads. While the Chinese government states that it sends significant amounts of food products into the TAR for both Tibetan and Han populations, local production of food must necessarily put pressure on pastoralists' traditional grazing areas.

The nuclear issue is an important one. The OHDDL in New Delhi says it is sure there have been serious side effects from the use of nuclear testing sites in Lop Nor and in the disposal of waste from nuclear research institutions. But there is no sure procedure by which the office can obtain accurate scientific information on the degree and extent of the problem. It is reported that India is well aware of the general nuclear risk, both short and long term, on the Tibetan plateau. This has included political and other prisoners working in hazardous nuclear mines, overexposure of local populations to radioactivity, and unreported nuclear accidents.

Within Tibet there are various populations, chiefly Upa (1.5 million), Khampa (90,000) and Amdo (50,000). Khampa are from the north-east and have their own dialect, although the script they use is common to all Tibetans. They are nomadic, grazing yak and sheep, living in *yurt*. The OHHDL aim is to preserve the entire Tibetan linguistic heritage, and Khampa in exile in India are trying to preserve their own dialect and traditions. They have distinctive dress and their cuisine leans towards meat, in contrast to that of other Tibetans. Their copious jewellery includes, gold, silver, coral and amber. The sale of this wealth brings in return televisions, videos and other consumer goods. Amdo live mainly in northern Tibet. They have specific cultural, social and economic traditions and are known as writers and poets. Although a small group, they have the highest literacy rate (around 95 per cent) in Tibet. They particularly suffered during the Chinese invasion as they were the first to be occupied from 1949 onwards. They have their own dialect which is close to that of the Khampa.

China is under constant pressure to heed international concern about its policy on Tibet, and trade pressures may help bring about a degree of change. While the Tibetan movement in exile has always used nonviolent means under the leadership of the Dalai Lama, this may not always be the case in the future in the face of Chinese refusals to negotiate and the growth of a more militant consciousness among younger Tibetans. An informal alliance committee exists comprising Muslims from Sinkiang, Mongolians from Inner Mongolia, Tibetans and Manchurians in exile (all from areas affected by Han immigration) although it does not have an office. Sinkiang Muslims and Inner Mongolians and Manchurians, who have been encouraged by the Chinese authorities as 'safe' migrants to go to the TAR, are also a source of potential supporters of Tibetan independence.

More uncertain, both for Tibetans and for Chinese, is the development of new market forces in the TAR. Many young Tibetans have embraced the chance to earn a better living from these forces and to participate in the new wave of consumerism. However, while such people might be pragmatic in their acceptance of China's presence, it is also possible that they will provide a more powerful Tibetan opposition to Chinese control should China begin to show signs of weakness. There has been an increase in crime in Lhasa involving Tibetans, and this has been accompanied by growing numbers of Tibetans including children, jailed on political grounds.

Other minorities

A large number of Chinese minorities are agriculturalists, often supplementing this activity with hunting and fishing. Many of these communities are animist by religion, and all have their own languages. Among these groups are the Chuang (Zhuang) of the central and western regions of Kwangsi Province (there are also Chuang communities in Guangdong, Yunnan, and Kweichow provinces). Their spoken language is Chuang, although most males also speak Chinese, which is also the standard written language. Chuang are animists.

There are some 10 million Manchu across China. Manchu people live in the north-eastern provinces, and in Hopei Province, Beijing and Inner Mongolia. The Manchu dynasty of emperors once ruled China, but today agriculture is the main Manchu occupation. As a result of almost total assimilation into Han culture, Manchu speak and write the Putonghua language. Only about 30,000 to 50,000 still speak Manchu; they live in Kirin and Heilungkiang provinces. The religion they profess depends on individual choice. A gathering of surviving members of the imperial family celebrated the traditional Manchu Ban Jin festival in a Beijing hotel banqueting suite in December 1995. This marked not only the 369th anniversary of the naming (Ban Jin) of the Manchus in the seventeenth century, but the largest gathering since the 1949 Communist Party takeover. Manchu were allowed to celebrate Ban Jin only after 1980.

Miao (Hmong) live mainly in Kweichow, southern Szechwan, western Hunan and north-western Hupei, with a small number also in Guangdong Province. The majority of the community have been assimilated into mainstream Chinese culture.

Uighur are a fair-complexioned Turkic people, living mainly in Sinkiang Province, with some living in Tsinghai and parts of Hunan Province. Uighur are farmers. They speak and write the Uighur language and follow Islam.

Mongolians, numbering almost 5 million, inhabit Inner Mongolia, Liaoning, Kirin, Heilungkiang, Hopei, Honan, Kansu, Tsinghai and Sinkiang. Traditionally they were nomads, although they may combine farming and nomadism. The people speak and write Mongolian, and their main religion is Lamaism.

Most of the Yao (Gerbao) people are concentrated in north-western Kwangsi, south-western Hunan, south-eastern Yunnan, and north-eastern Guangdong, while a small number live in south-eastern Kweichow. They are animists. The community speaks the Yao language, but most also speak Chinese. Yao identity appears to be strong, as reflected in the community that has migrated from China. Among Yao abroad, there have been few significant changes to their traditional culture.

Li live mainly in the mountains of the island of Hainan; some live in the foothills. They have their own Li language; men and a small number of women also speak Chinese.

Kelao (Gelao) are cultivators, hunters and fishers in Kweichow, Hunan and Shensi provinces. Most Kelao, who are animists, speak and write Chinese; very few speak Kelao.

China has numerous other minorities which are too small to be included in the list of 'official' minorities or nationalities. The Mosuo, linked to the Naxi minority, are one example. Mosuo offer, despite low incomes and an impoverished, backward infrastructure, an example of resilience, nonconformism and survival based on traditional values. Mosuo live in remote south-west China, have no notion of formal marriage, and are matriarchal in structure. Children take the mother's family name. In contrast to the Han tradition, of the female partner in a marriage living with the man's parents, they have a tradition of 'walking marriages'. After they become a couple, both the man and the woman each stay in the maternal home and visit each other. When a child is born the child is taken to both homes, so it belongs to both. This produces an extended family where uncles and aunts have as much care of the children as the 'natural' parents, and perhaps more. It also makes adoption very easy and informal. Unlike the problems connected with infanticide, families welcome both boy and girl babies without apparent discrimination. Nevertheless women are generally less educated than men, and while controlling the home and finances they also still tend to carry the main burden of domestic and agricultural work.

Conclusion and future prospects

The dominant Han Chinese view is that they are trying to move forward at a pace that will keep society together. There is certainly corruption (as in other societies), and the realpolitik of the Chinese leadership tends to imply that it would become worse were overall control to weaken. This concern on the part of Beijing – to maintain control while allowing gradual change to take place and external contacts to grow – cannot justify Chinese activities in Tibet. Nor does it make more acceptable the manipulation of family planning policies as methods of political control in remote areas. Where population growth may be one of the few means by which a minority can survive outside pressures. The benchmarks by which China should be evaluated in its approach to minorities are those that show how far it adheres to basic rights as determined by the UN. Yet the present economic change and development which the country is undergoing should also be taken into account. The Chinese people have become more independent and reflective; they now dare to challenge the status quo.

There is a danger of increased marginalization for minorities as central government reduces its role of protector and subsidizer of poor regions. Poverty may be alleviated, however, as investors seek better profit margins by relocating their production units further inland where labour is cheaper. The growth of tourism, both domestic and foreign, should also work to the economic and cultural advantage of minorities. Chinese minorities face the pressure of having to integrate themselves into the mainstream educational and language system for advancement. Rapid growth in access to national and international television will also be an influence for change, particularly in remote areas. Government schemes to promote minority language and education, greater freedom through increased income for some families, and the manifestation of cultural identity for revenue-generating tourism – all will affect the identities of minority communities. Paradoxically, what the Han Chinese attempted before 1949 and could not accomplish by force, they are now accomplishing as a by-product of a very different goal: they are encouraging respect for minority differences, while economic liberalization and the proliferation of new information media mean that minorities are becoming ever more assimilated into national political, economic, social and cultural institutions. How this double-edged process – of recognition and differentiation, on the one hand, and assimilation, on the other – will be resolved cannot be predicted.

Further reading

Bstan-dzin-rgya-mtsho, Dalai Lama XIV, *Freedom in Exile: The Autobiography of the Dalai Lama*, London, Hodder & Stoughton, 1990.

Dessaint, A.Y., *Minorities of Southwest China: An Introduction to the Yi (Lolo) and Related Peoples*, New Haven, CT, HRAF Press, 1980.

Heberer, T., *China and Its National Minorities: Autonomy or Assimilation?* (trans. Vale, M.), New York, M.E. Sharpe, *c.* 1989.

Human Rights Watch/Asia, *Detained in China and Tibet: A Directory of Political and Religious Prisoners*, New York, 1994.

Kerr, B., *Sky Burial: An Eyewitness Account of China's Brutal Crackdown in Tibet*, Chicago, IL, Noble Press, 1993.

Kumar, A., *Tibet: A Sourcebook*, New Delhi, All Party Indian Parliamentary Forum for Tibet, 1994.

Lemoine, J. and Chien, C. (eds), *The Yao of Southern China*, Paris, Editions de l'AFEY, 1991.

Lifestyles of China's Ethnic Minorities, Hong Kong, Peace Books, 1991

Ling, N., *Tibetan Sourcebook*, Hong Kong, Union Research Institute, 1964.

McCorquodale, R. and Orosz, N. (eds), *Tibet: The Position in International Law – Report of the Conference of International Lawyers on Issues Relating to Self-Determination and Independence for Tibet, London 6–10 January 1993*, Stuttgart, Hansjörg Mayer, 1994.

Schwarz, H.G., *The Minorities of Northern China*, Washington, DC, Western Washington, 1984.

Tibetan Young Buddhist Association, *Tibet: The Facts*, report prepared by the Scientific Buddhist Association for the UN Commission on Human Rights, Dharamsala, India, 1990.

Zhang, W. and Qingman, Z., *In Search of China's Minorities*, Beijing, New World Press, 1993.

Minority-based and advocacy organizations

Assembly of Tibetan People's Deputies, Gangchen Kyishong, Dharamsala 176215, Dist. Kangra, HP, India.

East Timor

Land area:	14,870 sq km
Population:	840,000 (est. 1997)
Main languages:	Tetum, Timorese (or Vaiquino), Portuguese, Bahasa Indonesia, Chinese
Main religions:	animism, Roman Catholicism, Islam
Main ethnic groups:	Timorese (mainly Atoni and Belu) 700,000 (est., 83%), Indonesians 140,000 (est., 17%), a few thousand Chinese and Malays
Real per capita GDP:	—
UNDP HDI/rank:	—

East Timor is the eastern half of the island of Timor, part of the Lesser Sundas island chain. Since 1975 it has been under military occupation by Indonesia. Nonetheless, the United Nations continues to recognize Portugal as the administrating power. The Portuguese first came to Timor in 1520; by the end of the sixteenth century Timor was under Portuguese influence, exporting sandalwood. In 1613 the Dutch began gradually to replace the Portuguese throughout the East Indies, although by the mid-nineteenth century they had conquered only the western portion of Timor. The Netherlands held West Timor until 1949, when it granted independence to all of Dutch-held Indonesia. West Timor became Indonesian, while East Timor remained the East Asian remnant of Portuguese colonialism.

Most of the population of Portuguese East Timor was apolitical, and towards the end of Portuguese rule, which came in 1974, there was no broad-based nationalist movement or armed political struggle for independence. In April 1974 the Portuguese armed forces overthrew the dictatorship of Marcello Caetano, largely in order to end Portugal's colonial wars in Africa. This quickly brought political tensions to a head in East Timor. The three small political factions in East Timor had incompatible goals: the União Democrática Timorense (UDT) advocated continuing association with Portugal; the Associação Popular Democrática Timorense (APODETI) advocated integration with Indonesia; and the Frente Revolucionária de Timor Leste Independente (FRETILIN) drew inspiration from revolutionary nationalist movements in Angola and Mozambique and advocated complete independence. The new Portuguese government sought a new Timor constitution and an election in 1976 leading to complete independence in 1978. FRETILIN partially boycotted negotiations, insisting on immediate independence. In August 1975 the pro-Portuguese UDT seized key government installations in the two main cities. The Portuguese authority fled, and the Timorese military went over to FRETILIN, which enabled it to win a brief civil war costing some 2,000 lives. Taking power, FRETILIN initiated agricultural cooperatives and a mass literacy campaign, advocating the revival of Timorese, as opposed to Portuguese, culture. On 28 November 1975, FRETILIN declared the colony to be independent and named it the Democratic Republic of East Timor. Portugal did not recognize East Timor's independence. In early December 1975, Indonesia, which had already taken over the East Timorese enclave of Oecussi in West Timor, invaded East Timor. Western nations like Australia and the USA had prior knowledge of the invasion but refused to act, apparently willing to sacrifice the East Timorese for their own perceived strategic interests.

The Indonesian invasion was accompanied by great cruelty and appalling loss of life. The Timorese population rallied to FRETILIN in opposition to the invasion, and FRETILIN fled to the interior mountains to wage guerrilla war. The Indonesians initiated Operasi Keamanan (Operation Security), which involved the destruction of arable land and crops in an attempt to coerce submission. The Indonesian invasion and initial occupation of East Timor were among the most bloody and destructive of the twentieth century. The Indonesian estimate is that 15 per cent of the Timorese population – 100,000 people – died during the invasion and first five years of occupation. Other estimates are that more than one-third of the population died from the invasion and the famines and spread of disease caused by Operasi Keamanan.

Today the Timorese population of approximately 700,000 finds itself dominated by up to 140,000 Indonesian administrators, troops and settlers. Whereas the Indonesian government regards Timorese as a 'minority' in East Timor, most Timorese do not regard themselves as such.

Timorese

The Atoni people ('people of the dry land') are believed to have been the original inhabitants, and occupy the interior highlands of East Timor and most of what is now Indonesian West Timor. They speak Timorese, also known as Vaiquino, and are thought to have migrated to Timor when the entire Indonesian archipelago was still a prehistoric land-bridge to the continent of Australia. Ethnically, Atoni are 'proto-Malay', and some bear features similar to the Australian Aborigines. The other historic and pre-colonial inhabitants are mainly the Belu peoples, who occupy the southern coastal plains of both West Timor and East Timor. Belu speak Tetum. Atoni and Belu together developed a distinct Timorese culture well before the arrival of the Europeans and often in distinction to the world of the pre-colonial Malay peoples.

Within days of the Indonesian invasion of East Timor in 1975 the UN General Assembly and Security Council had passed resolutions calling on Indonesia 'to withdraw without delay its forces from the territory in order to enable the people of the territory freely to exercise their right to self-determination and independence'. This and other resolutions since have been ignored by Indonesia, which continues to occupy the territory. In 1976 Indonesia staged an 'Act of Self-Determination' and declared East Timor to be the twenty-seventh province of Indonesia.

Owing to the continuing guerilla war, the Indonesian government has systematically excluded foreign journalists, medical teams and other independent observers from visiting East Timor. This has prevented an accurate detailed assessment of the loss of life among East Timorese resulting from military killings, injuries, famine, exposure and disease, as well as the many cases of torture and political murder. Some observers described the situation as 'genocidal'. The Indonesian army controls most of the territory, except for pockets of resistance fighters in the east. Indonesia has at least 17,000 troops in East Timor. Indonesian rule is still resented by most East Timorese; a nationwide network of clandestine opposition groups is active in the towns and villages.

In 1989 Indonesia – to show that it was in control of East Timor – tentatively began to allow East Timor a greater degree of openness, allowing more freedom of movement and communication within East Timor and between East Timor and the outside world. Prestigious and high-ranking foreign visitors, including the Pope, ambassadors stationed in Jakarta, UN officials, delegations of journalists and human rights NGOs were allowed to visit East Timor. These visits, however, became the occasion for pro-independence demonstrations by East Timorese. The demonstrators were frequently arrested, tortured and imprisoned. One such demonstration, a march to a cemetery in Dili in November 1991, led to the killing of nearly 300 people. This resulted in renewed international interest and pressure on Indonesia and an official commission of inquiry into the massacre was set up. The commission came to the conclusion that excessive force was used. Shortly afterwards, the top two officers who were in command of the troops during the Dili massacre were removed, and several lower-ranking officers were court-martialled. In 1992 the Indonesians army captured Xanana Gusmão, leader of the FRETILIN resistance organization. At his trial, he was given a life sentence (subsequently commuted to twenty years).

Since 1975 there has been significant Indonesian economic development assistance designed to promote East Timor's integration into Indonesia.

This has led to considerable immigration of Indonesian administrators, entrepreneurs, commercial agents and settlers. And this, in turn, has led to clashes between the mainly Muslim Indonesian immigrants and the Roman Catholic East Timorese, frequently over perceived insults to East Timorese Catholic nuns or religious practices. There have also been widespread demonstrations and protests. Arrests, torture, disappearances and extrajudicial killings commonly occur, and scores of Timorese have been jailed as a result of unfairly conducted trials. These recurring incidents have led to increased interest in East Timor by the growing human rights movement in South-East Asia. The Indonesian government has persuaded other South-East Asian governments to cancel or curtail several NGO conferences on East Timor in the Philippines, Thailand and Malaysia.

Chinese

Chinese trading contacts with Timor date back to the fifteenth century. During Portuguese and Dutch colonial rule, Chinese traders migrated to Timor, buying grain or coffee from Timorese farmers and selling it to Portuguese and Dutch administrators – although many ethnic Chinese took up farming alongside Timorese cultivators. Ethnic Chinese commercial domination was substantial; by the mid-1950s, of approximately four hundred retailing outlets in East Timor, all but four were owned by Chinese families. The Chinese maintained their cultural identity, speaking Cantonese or Mandarin, educating their children in Chinese schools and marrying within the Chinese community. The majority of Chinese resided in the capital of Dili and the towns of Baucau, Ermera and Bobonaro. In the early 1970s, ethnic Chinese may have accounted for some 3 per cent of the population of East Timor.

During the mid-1970s, at the time of East Timor's abortive decolonialization process, most Chinese were apolitical or tended to support the continuation of Portuguese rule, because the pro-independence party was critical of Chinese commercial domination. At the time of the Indonesian invasion, many of the wealthier Chinese feared for their future, whether in independent Timor or under Indonesian rule, and fled to Australia. Of those who remained, many were killed by the invading Indonesian army. Massacres took place in Dili, and nearly all Chinese in the towns of Liquíça and Maubara were killed. Subsequently, some Chinese sought to emigrate while others have remained to continue their trading positions. According to one estimate, the pre-1974 Chinese population of some 20,000 had been reduced to only a few thousand by 1985.

Conclusions and future prospects

The international community has largely regarded Indonesian occupation as a *fait accompli*. Annually from 1975 to 1982 the UN General Assembly reaffirmed the East Timorese people's right to self-determination and independence in accordance with the UN Charter and the 1960 General Assembly Declaration on the Granting of Independence to Colonial Countries and Peoples. East Timor is also debated annually at the UN Decolonialization Committee, and regularly since 1984 at the UN Commission on Human Rights. Because of Indonesia's close ties to the industrial democracies and its stature as a founding and leading member of the Non-Aligned Movement of developing countries, UN member states have been unwilling to use significant pressure on Indonesia to respect the resolutions of the Security Council and General Assembly. However, as Indonesia takes a more assertive and high profile role in international affairs, international criticism will be taken seriously by Jakarta. The regime's response to the commission of inquiry into the Dili massacre indicated that it does take note of international criticism, especially if the criticism is uniform. In 1995, unofficial talks began between groups of Timorese from inside and outside the country. UN-sponsored talks between Portugal and Indonesia have been held regularly without result. The East Timorese national resistance committee has drawn up a three-phase peace plan leading from a period of autonomy to an act of self-determination, but Jakarta has persisted in ignoring this.

The invasion of East Timor has been a war with no winners. Indonesia cannot coerce the East Timorese into accepting Indonesian rule; the Timorese cannot muster enough force to push out the Indonesians. Ali Alatas, the Indonesian Foreign Minister, has acknowledged that East Timor is a 'pebble in Indonesia's shoe'. The Indonesians cannot easily pull out without triggering similar independence movements elsewhere in the country, notably Aceh. Meanwhile, the Western governments which did not stop – and may even have encouraged – the 1975 invasion are paying the price for their lack of integrity. Although the award of the 1996 Nobel Peace Prize jointly to the exiled resistance leader José Ramos-Horta and to Carlos Filipe Ximenes Belo, Roman Catholic bishop of East Timor, offered substantial encouragement, the future of East Timor remains uncertain.

Further reading

Aditjondro, G.J., *In the Shadow of Mount Ramelau: The Impact of the Occupation of East Timor*, Leiden, Indonesian Documentation and Information Centre, 1994.

Cox, S. and Carey, P.B.R., *Generations of Resistance: East Timor*, London, Cassell, 1995.

Human Rights Watch, *The Limits of Openness: Human Rights in Indonesia and East Timor*, New York, 1994.

Suter, K., *East Timor and West Irian*, London, MRG report, 1982.

Hong Kong

Land area:	1,076 sq km
Population:	6.15 million (1994)
Main languages:	Chinese (Cantonese most common, Putonghua Mandarin increasing), English
Main religions:	Taoism, also Buddhism, Protestantism and Roman Catholicism, Islam and Hinduism
Main minority groups:	Filipinos 115,500 (1.9%), Thais 23,800 (0.39%), Indonesians 19,700 (0.32%), Indians 19,500 (0.32%), Malaysians 13,800 (0.22%), also former Vietnamese 'boat people' and expatriates from Canada, Japan, UK, USA
Real per capita GDP:	$21,560
UNDP HDI/rank:	0.905 (24)

A British colony until 1997, Hong Kong is the main entrepôt for East Asia and one of the world's major trading economies. China initially ceded Hong Kong Island (now the centre of business and government) to the UK in a trade agreement in the 1840s. The New Territories (the largest region, stretching to the mainland Chinese province of Guangdong, and including outlying southern islands) was leased by the UK from China for 99 years in 1898. The colony is due to be handed back to China at midnight on 30 June 1997. At present Hong Kong's minorities consist mainly of resident expatriate groups. The Filipinos represent the largest freely moving expatriate group but are perhaps the least secure. Their position (and often low financial ability to return home, or seek a new country of work) could mean they will become a minority target, after the 1997 handover, of both official and social forces looking to distract attention from other problems. The Chinese government has said that it will make adequate arrangements for such groups.

Hong Kong may be seen as a touchstone for the manner in which China intends to treat minority populations. China's present policy indicates that it seeks the political integration of Hong Kong into a structure that restrains democratic rights but is without adverse affect on commercial revenues.

There has been a flight of (mainly affluent) people and money from Hong Kong. An unspecified number have arranged entry rights to other countries but are holding them in reserve. This is due in part to the UK government's unwillingness to grant full UK citizenship to the mainly Chinese residents of the UK colony. An initial 1990 quota of 50,000 heads of family (amounting to 200,000 people, each family being deemed to consist of four people) has been taken up. It is not known how many have actually moved to the UK. In autumn 1995 the British Governor of the colony stated the position of the Hong Kong government that Britain should consider offering residence to some 3.5 million Chinese from the island. Political statements suggest this would not be countenanced by the UK government. The Portuguese government's readiness to issue Portuguese passports to residents of neighbouring Macau, due to return to China in 1999, contrasts with this position.

In mid-1995 Hong Kong voters elected a majority of politicians who were unhappy with China's determination to weaken present political and social rights. China is establishing a provisional legislature before the 1997 transfer and has been using the Preliminary Working Committee as a vehicle for this. Its successor is the Preparatory Committee, involving members from Hong Kong and China. Conflict may arise if and when China insists on the present legislature being wound up and replaced before its term, which is due in 1999.

It is not possible to estimate the future population mix, nor the attitude Beijing will have towards expatriate residents of Hong Kong or to Hong Kong Chinese. China has put forward its own Hong Kong passport, which would be issued to Chinese qualifying as permanent residents of what will be called the Hong Kong Special Administrative Region. It would need UK government agreement for holders to receive visa-free entry to Britain, which they have at present as British Hong Kong passport holders. Human rights organizations are monitoring the situation. The way China treats individual groups, for better or worse, may also be linked to China's aspirations for full integration into the world trade system. Examples would be the status of migrant workers such as Filipinos, mainly in domestic service, and the remaining former Vietnamese 'boat people', whom the present Hong Kong authorities aimed to repatriate. In May 1996 there were reported to be 18,000 'boat people' held in camps, where violent riots broke out as the Hong Kong government stepped up repatriation. The last inmates were moved by the end of 1996.

Minority-based and advocacy organizations

Asian Human Rights Commission/Asia Legal Resource Center, A Center, Pak Tin Village, Mei Tin Road, Shatin, NT, Hong Kong; tel. 852 2698 6339, fax 852 2698 6367, e-mail: alrchk@hk.super.net.

Indonesia

Land area:	1,919,440 sq km
Population:	203.6 million
Main languages:	Bahasa Indonesia (official), English, Javanese and other local dialects
Main religions:	Islam, Protestantism, Roman Catholicism, Hinduism, Buddhism
Main minority groups:	Sundanese 30.5 million (est., 15%), Chinese 6–7.1 million (est., 3–3.5%), Dayak 4.1 million (est., 2%), Acehnese 3.7 million (est., 1.8%), Minangkabau 3.7 million (1.8%), Batak 3.3 million (est., 1.6%), Balinese 2.7 million (est., 1.3%), West Irians (indigenous) 1.2 million (est., 0.6%), South Moluccans 1 million (est., 0.5%)
Real per capita GDP:	$3,270
UNDP HDI/rank:	0.641 (102)

The Republic of Indonesia is a sprawling archipelago of nearly 14,000 islands, which divides into two tiers. The main islands of the more heavily populated southern tier include Sumatra, Java, Bali and Timor. The northern tier includes Kalimantan (most of Borneo), Sulawesi, the Moluccas and Irian Jaya (the western half of New Guinea). Sumatra lies west and south of peninsular Malaysia and Singapore across the narrow Strait of Malacca. Kalimantan, the Indonesian section of Borneo, is bounded to the north by Sarawak, Sabah and Brunei. North of the Indonesian island of Sulawesi is the Celebes Sea and beyond that the Philippine Islands.

The main islands of Sumatra and Java had

flourishing pre-colonial empires and long-established commercial links with China and India, Asia Minor and Europe. In 1511, the Portuguese captured Malacca, which controlled the sea lanes between India and China. The Portuguese fought the Spanish and local sultanates to establish armed forts and trading factories in the archipelago. The Portuguese held on to East Timor until the Indonesian invasion of 1975 (see **East Timor**), but elsewhere, in the early seventeenth century, they were pushed aside by the Dutch, who set up a monopolistic trading company and empire based in Batavia (present-day Jakarta). The Dutch gained control of the coastal trading enclaves throughout the archipelago, and developed mining and plantation agriculture. The Dutch largely ignored the interiors of the islands and ruled through alliances with local sultans. Only in the late nineteenth and early twentieth centuries did the Dutch seek to unify control, greatly extending plantation agriculture, based on forced labour, and repatriating huge profits to the Netherlands. Chinese immigration was encouraged to provide intermediaries between the colonial authorities and the indigenous peoples. The Dutch were ousted by the Japanese at the beginning of the Second World War. The Japanese installed Sukarno and Hatta, leaders of the Indonesian nationalist pro-independence movement, in nominal power. In 1945, the Indonesians proclaimed independence. However, after the defeat of Japan, the Dutch sought to re-establish their rule, forcing the Java-based nationalists to fight a four-year war of independence. The Netherlands finally recognized Indonesian independence in 1949.

Indonesia's history since independence has been tumultuous, as its leaders have attempted to deal with its ethnic diversity, sheer size, lack of internal political cohesion and impoverished peasantry. Indonesia had military and political confrontations with Malaysia and the UK over the creation of the eastern Malaysian states of Sabah and Sarawak and the Sultanate of Brunei. These three states now occupy the island of Borneo along with the Indonesian province of Kalimantan. Indonesia confronted the Dutch over the forced incorporation of Irian Jaya (West Irian) into Indonesia and the Portuguese over East Timor (see **East Timor**). There have been rebellions on the Outer Island provinces of Central and North Sumatra, Irian Jaya, East Timor, North Sulawesi and the Moluccas; and recurrent outbreaks of anti-Chinese violence.

To counterbalance the political strength of the army and the militant Islamic political parties in the 1950s, Sukarno, Indonesia's first President, encouraged the re-emergence and political strength of the Communist Party of Indonesia (PKI). In 1965, the Communists attempted a coup, which was quickly suppressed by elite army units under General Suharto. The army launched a massive witch-hunt for PKI members and sympathizers, which saw the slaughter of many thousands of innocent people, including an estimated half a million ethnic Chinese. Suharto was installed as President, a position he has held ever since. Since then, the military, better known by its acronym ABRI, has retained political power, enjoying special civic rights and responsibilities, including unelected military seats in Parliament and local legislatures, in addition to its defence and security roles.

The Indonesian political system remains authoritarian. The absolute priority for the 'New Order' government, as the Suharto regime is known, is internal security and national stability. The regime has little tolerance of dissent and it is government policy that political activity should only be expressed in a harmonious and consensual manner through a government-sanctioned framework and the three officially recognized political parties. In recent years, the government has started a wave of reforms and significantly reduced its role in the economy. Today Indonesia is one of the fastest-growing economies in the region, although the benefits have largely been restricted to the Chinese minority and Suharto's immediate family and circle.

Apart from Irian Jaya, whose indigenous groups remained in isolation, the remainder of the archipelago was, over two millennia, subjected to successive waves of cultural and religious influences. The transmission and absorption of these were, however, not uniform, which has contributed to the ethnic diversity of modern Indonesia. Even so, more than 80 per cent of Indonesians are considered to be Muslim, making Indonesia nominally the largest Muslim state in the world. Indonesia is linguistically diverse. West of Jaya, the majority language group is the Malayo-Polynesian family of more than 250 languages, usually distinguished into sixteen major groups. Four of the sixteen groups of the Malayo-Polynesian family are Malayan. One of the four is Riau Malayian, the primary literary language of Indonesia, which in modernized form is Bahasa Indonesia, the official language of Indonesia.

The larger islands support several ethno-linguistic groups. Central Java is the homeland of the predominant Javanese ethnic group, members of which have migrated over time to many of the other inhabited islands in the archipelago. East

Java also contains substantial numbers of Balinese and Madurese from the islands of Bali and Madura, the Balinese being distinctive for having maintained a Hindu-based religion while the other Malay peoples of the archipelago adopted Islam. West Java also has a large Sundanese population, who are similar to the Lampung peoples of South Sumatra. Java supports more than half of Indonesia's total population. The economically important island of Sumatra contains a number of significant ethno-linguistic groups besides Javanese. These include the strongly Islamic Aceh of north Sumatra; Minangkabau, a Muslim group noted for its matriarchal structure and tradition of commerce and trading; and Batak, a half-dozen related tribes many of which have become Christianized. Kalimantan is dominated by Dayak, Murut, coastal Malay peoples and ethnic Chinese. The Moluccas are inhabited mostly by non-Malay peoples who have long resisted Javanese domination. Sulawesi is inhabited mainly by Muslim Buganese and Makasarese in the south and Christianized Minahasans and Manadonese in the north. West Irian is home to some 800,000 indigenous people divided into many hundreds of groupings. The names of smaller islands, or clusters of islands, are often coterminous with the ethno-linguistic groups.

The Indonesian independence struggle against Dutch colonial rule resulted in archipelago-wide political domination by the Javanese ethnic group. On the other hand, the mineral and agricultural resources that generate Indonesia's national income are largely found on the Outer Islands. Many of the ethno-linguistic minorities on the Outer Islands feel that they are given short shrift by the Javanese political elite, working with multinational corporations or Sino-Indonesian enterprises. Tensions between Javanese and peoples of the Outer Islands are exacerbated by the Transmigrasi (Transmigration) programme, a policy to settle landless Javanese in the Outer Islands where land is plentiful. Population density has increased significantly, particularly on Java and Sumatra, and has caused a dramatic rise in urbanization in the island of Java. The Transmigration programme was instituted to relocate more than 1 million families to underpopulated areas of the Outer Islands. Superimposed on the distinction between the dominant Javanese and all the Outer Island ethnic groups is the distinction between indigenous ethnic groups and ethnic Chinese, who, over a long period, have been subjected to sustained discrimination and ethnic violence, mainly for economic reasons.

Indonesia is not an Islamic state. One of the five principles in the state ideology of Pancasila is belief in one supreme God, not necessarily the Islamic God. Many fundamentalist groups that sought to establish a Muslim theocracy consequently feel betrayed. They view the government's commitment to Pancasila as an effort to subordinate Islam to a secular state ideology. The political divide between the state and orthodox believers caused riots and a wave of bombings and arson attacks in the mid-1980s. The Islamic revival has also caused conflicts with Indonesian Christians, deemed a threat by the fundamentalists. Many Indonesian Christians belong to minority ethnic groups such as the Batak and the Chinese. In recent years, this conflict has led to churches being burnt by more radical Muslims, incited by fiery clerics. Because Islam is a powerful weapon for the political elite, the state has slowly become a major promoter of Islamic institutions.

There are hundreds of ethnic groups and minorities in Indonesia. The precise extent of this diversity is unknown, however, since Indonesian censuses do not collect data on ethnicity. The following discussion focuses on those minorities that are politically most significant.

Sundanese

The Sundanese are indigenous to the Sunda region of western Java. Their language is incomprehensible to the Javanese. Islam is a strong presence in their life. The Sunda region was an important site for the Muslim separatist Darul Islam rebellion of 1948–62. There is still controversy over the cause of the rebellion but it is generally accepted that Islam played an important role. Although Sundanese and Javanese possess similar family structures, economic patterns and political systems, there is some rivalry between them. In general, Sundanese do not face significant levels of discrimination.

Chinese

The Chinese are the most politically important minority group in Indonesia and have suffered significant discrimination in the short period they have been in Indonesia. Small Chinese settlements have existed since the late thirteenth century, but larger-scale immigration took place under early Dutch rule when Chinese served as economic intermediaries between the Dutch East India Company and the Javanese. In the eighteenth century Chinese were encouraged to immigrate to work the tin mines of Bangka and the gold mines of western Borneo (now Kalimantan), and to continue to settle in cities and towns forming a broad arc around Singapore. Since this Chinese immigration was almost entirely male, considerable intermarriage occurred, giving rise to Sino-Indonesian communities, particularly in eastern Java, West Sumatra and West Kalimantan, which adopted many local customs, ceremonies, manners and beliefs.

With the development of extensive export agriculture in the late nineteenth and early twentieth centuries large-scale Chinese immigration resumed. Nearly all Chinese in Indonesia came from either Fujian or Guangdong provinces in southern China. The dominant languages among these immigrants were Hokkien, Hakka and Cantonese. Most were engaged in petty trading, mining or artisanship. This gave rise to the development of purely Chinese communities in Java and, in particular, in the Outer Islands, which retained Chinese language, religion and customs.

At independence, nearly half of Chinese Indonesians failed to secure Indonesian citizenship, either because of continuing loyalty to China or Taiwan, or because of the difficulties in gaining citizenship papers. Many of these people became stateless when Indonesia broke off diplomatic relations with China after the 1965 coup. The government believed that China played a major part in encouraging the coup through the Communist Party (PKI). Normal diplomatic ties only resumed in 1990. Since then, the government has enacted new regulations to expedite the naturalization of ethnic Chinese. By 1992 only about 6 per cent, or 300,000, of approximately 6 million Chinese Indonesians were considered non-Indonesians. Almost all of these people were later given Chinese citizenship by the People's Republic of China.

The assimilation of the Chinese population into the local communities in which they live has been government policy since the 1970s. Before that the Chinese were forcibly separated from their non-Chinese neighbours. Prior to 1919, Chinese had to live in separate urban neighbourhoods and could travel only with government permits. Initially, under the Indonesian government's assimilation policy, the use of symbols of Chinese identity, such as Chinese characters in shops, was banned. Chinese-language newspapers, schools and public use of Chinese names were all banned, and many Chinese were forced to take Indonesian names. In recent years, due to the policy of economic liberalism and the growth of the economy, anti-Chinese policies have been muted or relaxed. A local Chinese newspaper has started again. It can only devote several pages to Chinese, the rest must be in Bahasa Indonesia. Today Chinese Indonesians still dominate Indonesia's private sector, despite policies designed to promote indigenous entrepreneurs.

Identifying someone in modern-day Indonesia as ethnic Chinese is not easy, because the physical characteristics, language, name and lifestyle of Chinese Indonesians are not always distinct from those of the indigenous population. Census figures do not record Chinese as a separate group. There are also many people who identify themselves as Chinese Indonesians but cannot read or write a Chinese language. There are marked differences between *peranakan* (local-born Chinese, usually with some Indonesian ancestry) and *totok* (full-blooded Chinese, usually born in China). In general, the *peranakan* community's ties to their Chinese roots are more distant. *Peranakan* often speak Bahasa Indonesia as their first language and some are even Muslims, although the majority are Christians. Unlike the more strictly male-dominated *totok* Chinese, *peranakan* families recognise descent based on both female and male lines. In contrast, *totok* consider themselves as the 'real' Chinese, keeping Chinese culture and traditions alive through household shrines, celebrating Chinese festivals and private Chinese language instruction for their children.

Several hundred thousand Chinese were killed after the 1965 failed coup, and anti-Chinese riots have occurred since the 1970s. In 1974 anti-Chinese riots erupted on the occasion of the visit to Jakarta of the Japanese Prime Minister. Other anti-Chinese demonstrations and riots have broken out in Semarang, Yogyakarta and Ujungpandang, leading to the death of several hundred ethnic Chinese. The latest outbreak of such rioting took place in 1994 in the city of Medan.

Popular resentment against ethnic Chinese has continued because of their economic success. The government response has been actively to promote indigenous enterprises. Suharto's call for increased assistance to indigenous (*pribumi*) business efforts resulted in some transfer of Chinese capital to the indigenous business sector, and served to remind Chinese Indonesian business people that while they may be economically dominant they are still beholden to the indigenous political elite.

Dayak

Dayak, is a collective name for the indigenous people of Borneo who traditionally resided in longhouses in the jungle interior. Among the Dayak are Ngaju Dayak, Penan, Murut, Maanyan and Lawangan. They tend to be either Protestant or Kaharingan, a form of native religious practice viewed by the government as Hindu although by Western standards it would be regarded as a pagan religion because of its shamanic curing and rituals. Dayak make a living through shifting agriculture and as manual labourers in urban areas.

Dayak have a long history of struggle for autonomy. Since the southern coast of Kalimantan has long been dominated by the politically and numerically dominant Muslim Banjarese, Dayak sought government recognition of a Great Dayak territory in 1953. When these efforts failed, a rebellion broke out in 1956 along religious lines, culminating in the establishment of the new province of Kalimantan Tengah in 1957. After the 1965 PKI coup attempt Dayak were viewed as separatists and labelled communist. Many were slaughtered by the Indonesian army. Negotiations began again in the 1970s between the Dayak and Jakarta over recognition of the indigenous religion of the peoples of the province. This process culminated in official recognition in the 1980s.

In recent times, some Dayak in the interior of Kalimantan have been under threat from loggers who are destroying forests needed by Dayak for their livelihood. The army (ABRI) has been used to intimidate anti-logging Dayak activists and to protect the loggers. A small number of Dayak advocate total independence from Indonesia. In political terms, their numbers are still small and they do not pose a threat to the republic.

Acehnese

Acehnese are mainly found in Aceh, in the northernmost region of Sumatra. They are most famous for their devotion to Islam and their militant resistance to external rule. The Acehnese family system is based on a separation of male and female spheres of activity. Males are directed outward towards the world of trade through the practice of *merantau* – going away from one's birthplace to seek one's fortune and gain new knowledge and experience. Females are encouraged to stay at home and perform the traditional family roles. However, this practice has meant that increasing numbers of men have failed to return to the Acehnese homeland, but have instead married and settled elsewhere.

Aceh separatists have sought to establish an independent Islamic state and have combined their religious and nationalist appeal with the exploitation of social and economic pressures and discontent. Many Acehnese perceive themselves as disadvantaged in employment because of the influx of Javanese. This has led to several clashes between the military and Achenese separatists. In the early 1990s, several hundred Acehnese fled by boats to nearby Malaysia, claiming harassment from ABRI and seeking political asylum. Because Malaysia and Indonesia enjoy close political ties, the Malaysian government has refused to give them asylum. Today, the ABRI maintains a high profile in Aceh.

Minangkabau

Minangkabau live mainly along the coasts of Sumatera Utara and Sumatera Barat, in the interior of Riau, and in the northern Bengkulu provinces of Sumatra. Minangkabau are traditionally matrilineal. Thus a male has his primary responsibility to his mother's and sisters' clans. According to anthropologists, sisters and unmarried lineage members try to live close to one another, or even in the same house. Minangkabau do not suffer significant discrimination.

Batak

Batak refers to any of the several groups inhabiting the interior of Sumatera Utara Province south of Aceh – Angkola, Karo, Mandailing, Pakpak, Simelungen, Toba and others. Culturally, they lack the social hierarchy of the Balinese, and they seem to bear a closer resemblance to the highland swidden cultivators of South-East Asia, even though some also practise wet rice farming. The Batak orient themselves traditionally to the *marga*, a patrilineal descent group. This group owns land and does not permit marriage within it. The *marga* has proved to be a flexible social unit. Batak who resettle in urban areas, such as Medan and Jakarta, draw on *marga* affiliations for financial support and political alliances, reinforcing their ethnic identity. The majority of Batak are Christians and in recent times there have been reports of tension between Batak church groups and the more fundamentalist Islamic groups operating in Batak areas. However, in general, the rights of Batak are fairly well observed by the Indonesian state.

Balinese

There is probably no group in Indonesia more aware of its own ethnic identity than the Balinese.

Mainly inhabiting the islands of Bali and Lombok and the western half of Sumbawa, Balinese are often depicted as graceful and aesthetically inclined people. Although such descriptions are largely based on historical legend, this characterization is also partly based on events in contemporary Indonesia. The tourist market for traditional Balinese carvings, dance performances and paintings has, in modern times, helped create this image and reinforced Balinese identity. The contemporary Hindu religious practices of Balinese date back at least to the fifteenth century, when Javanese princes from Majapahit fled the advances of Islam and sought refuge in Bali, where they were absorbed into the local culture. Balinese have maintained a generally anti-Islamic political stance, and moves by Jakarta to convert them to Islam have largely failed. Indeed, segregation between themselves and outsiders has been an organizing factor in Balinese culture. Like Javanese and Hindu societies, Balinese society is stratified. There is a small hereditary Brahman class, as well as small groups of Vaisya and Kshatriya classes. However, the Balinese rank system involves no occupational specializations, nor does it prohibit marriage between ranks. The vast majority of Balinese, including many prominent politicians and business people, belong to the Sudra or commoner rank. Because of the tourist trade, which is a major foreign-exchange earner, the central government has helped Balinese protect and preserve their culture.

West Irians

West Irian (also known as West Papua or Irian Jaya) constitutes the western portion of the island of New Guinea. While presumed to harbour vast natural resources, much of the island is inaccessible and unexplored, its plant and animal life largely uncatalogued. West Irian is home to more than a thousand largely isolated tribal groups with different languages. With the exception of a few pygmy Negrito groups, most of the people are classified as Papuans, and share more affinity with the Melanesian world of the South Pacific than with the rest of South-East Asia.

That West Irian is a part of Indonesia is a happenstance of colonial history. In the mid-nineteenth century, in order to separate the Dutch East Indies from the South Pacific British Empire, and to avoid leaving any unclaimed areas for the potential interest of the German latecomers to European colonialism, the Dutch proclaimed anything west of 141 degrees to be Dutch territory. The part of the island which lay to the east of this line, Papua New Guinea, was mostly administered as an Australian colony on behalf of the British empire. The Dutch basically ignored Irian. But during the Indonesian independence struggle after the Second World War, the Netherlands refused to hand over West Irian to the Indonesians directly, partly because of its presumed natural resources and partly because the Dutch envisaged the need for a refuge for their Outer Island collaborators after Indonesian independence. They gave it instead in 1962 to the United Nations, predictably creating a major political issue for the Indonesian nationalists, who wanted control over the former colonial territory in its entirety. The United Nations, in 1963, handed West Irian to the Indonesians with the proviso that there would be a plebiscite in 1969 to settle its final political status. Large portions of the indigenous population may have been unaware of any of these developments, and the Indonesian-administered 1969 'Act of Free Choice' was widely considered to be such a charade that the UN only 'took note' rather than 'endorsed' the outcome.

The Indonesians have attempted to provide economic assistance and investment to Irian, which in turn has led to Javanese immigration into the area. However, Jakarta also launched Operasi Koteka to 'Indonesianize' or 'civilize' some of the indigenous peoples. The best-known example of this exercise was the unsuccessful attempt to compel the Dani people to wear clothes rather than cover their bodies in pig fat as protection against cold weather. These kinds of efforts led to a sporadic, if long-lasting, rebellion by some groups, sometimes millenarian in character, but sometimes taking the form of a modern secular national liberation movement, such as the Organisasi Papua Merdeka (OPM), the Free Papua Movement, which began in 1963, and which operates from isolated bases in Papua New Guinea. No other countries, however, want to oppose Indonesia on this issue, and the thousand-odd fighters of the OPM have little chance of success.

See also entry on **West Papua, OCEANIA.**

South Moluccans

Until the 1975 Indonesian invasion of East Timor, South Moluccans were the best known ethnic minority group in the archipelago resisting Indonesian rule. The South Moluccas consist of some 150 small islands in the eastern portion of the archipelago and are home to some 1 million people. The Moluccas are the fabled 'spice islands' of the East Indies and were first colonized by Portugal in 1512 and then by the Dutch late in the same century. Over the centuries the Dutch extensively Christianized the population and incorporated them into the colonial army.

When the Dutch sought to reassert control over Indonesia after the Second World War, they based their efforts on the Outer Islands and incorporated South Moluccans into their military actions against the Javanese-based Indonesian nationalists. During the negotiations leading to Dutch recognition of independent Indonesia, the Netherlands sought local autonomy for the Moluccans who, in turn, proclaimed a Republik Maluku Selatan, which was forcibly and quickly suppressed by Jakarta. Sympathy for the Moluccans led the Dutch to bring some 40,000 to the Netherlands, including military personnel and their families. There, the South Moluccans initially declined to integrate into Dutch society, waiting in vain for the emergence of an independent Molucca. The Dutch government can do little or nothing to accommodate South Moluccan political demands in the face of unyielding Indonesian opposition to any independent or autonomous unit within the archipelago. South Moluccans in the Netherlands now face the choice of repatriating to Indonesian Molucca or integrating into Dutch society. There is no strong separatist group operating in the South Moluccas today.

Other minorities

The Indonesian government has put increasing pressure on traditional indigenous groups to give up elaborate rituals and feasting practices, as they are deemed by the state to be 'wasteful' and 'backward'. The pressure applied is usually indirect through education and the mass media.

Conclusion and future prospects

For all its turmoil, in its five decades of independence, Indonesia has had only two leaders, Presidents Sukarno and Suharto. Future political developments and stability in the country depend on how the post-Suharto transition will be handled, when it occurs. Suharto is close to 80 years old. Almost certainly, the Indonesian armed forces will remain dominant, and with them the political determination that Indonesia remains a unitary state with little regional autonomy. Tensions between the Outer Islands and Java are also likely to remain, which means that resource, environmental and labour issues will continue to be affected by ethnic loyalties and divisions. Religious conflicts between the state and radical Islamic elements, and between Muslims and non-Muslims will also be prominent in the coming years. Indonesia has shown a willingness to respect minority rights as long as they do not interfere with the integrity of the state. Any attempts at promoting a separate state will invite harsh security measures. The future of minorities' rights, especially those of the Chinese community, also largely depend on the performance of the economy. As long as the economy is doing well, ethnic divisions will be softened.

Further reading

Hill, H., *et al.*, *Indonesia's New Order: The Dynamics of Socio-economic Transformation*, St Leonards, NSW, Allen & Unwin, 1994.

Ramage, D., *Politics in Indonesia: Democracy, Islam, and the Ideology of Tolerance*, London, Routledge, 1995.

Schwarz, A., *A Nation in Waiting: Indonesia in the 1990s*, St Leonards, NSW, Allen & Unwin, 1994.

Suryadinata, L., *Pribumi Indonesians, the Chinese minority and China*, Singapore, Heinemann Asia, 1992.

Suter, K., *East Timor and West Irian*, London, MRG report, 1982.

Vatikiotis, M., *Indonesian Politics under Suharto: Order, Development and Pressure for Change*, London, Routledge, 1994.

Minority-based and advocacy organizations

Center for Human Rights Studies (PUSHAM), Tebet Dalam III C/19, PO Box 8134/JKSTT, Jakarta 12081, Indonesia; tel./fax 62 21 830 1169, e-mail: pusham@indo.net.id.

ELSAM (Lembaga Studi & Advokasi Masyarakat), Jl. Masjid IV/4, Pejompongan, Jakarta, Indonesia; tel./fax 62 21 573 4744.

Institute for the Defense of Human Rights (LPHAM), Jl. Kramat Asem Raya 37, Jakarta 13120, Indonesia; tel. 62 21 856 3389.

International NGO Forum on Indonesian Development (INFID), Jl. Duren Tiga Selatan No. 15, Jakarta 12760, Indonesia; tel./fax 62 21 799 5400, e-mail: infid@nusa.or.id.

KOMNAS HAM (Komnisi Nasional Hak Asasi Manusia), Jl. Veteran No. 11, Jakarta Pusat, Indonesia.

LKI (Lembaga Keadilan Indonesia), PO Box 5366, Jl. Majapahit No. 18–24, Jakarta Pusat, Indonesia.

Yayasan Lembaga Hukum Indonesia (Indonesian Legal Aid Foundation), Jl. Diponegoro 74, Jakarta Pusat 10320, Indonesia; tel. 62 21 390 4227/310 5518, fax 62 21 330 140, e- mail: elawjakarta@igc.apc.org.

Japan

Land area:	377,800 sq km (excluding northern islands)
Population:	126,669,520 (1996)
Main languages:	Japanese (national language), Korean, Chinese, Ainu
Main religions:	Shintoism and Buddhism, also Protestantism and Roman Catholicism
Main minority groups:	Burakumin 1,170,410–3,000,000 (0.9–2.4%), Okinawans 1,134,668 (0.89%), Koreans 759,600 (0.6%), Chinese 141,832 (0.11%), Ainu 25,149 (0.02%)
Real per capita GDP:	$20,680
UNDP HDI/rank:	0.940 (3)

Japan is an archipelago of 3,400 islands, the main four being Honshu, Kyushu, Shikoku and Hokkaido. Forty per cent of the population lives on only 1 per cent of the land area in the narrow Pacific coastal plains, because 72 per cent of the country is mountainous, and 70 per cent of the people live in cities. Japan's 126.7 million inhabitants are concentrated in the major cities of Tokyo, Osaka and Nagoya. The Ainu minority, the earliest known inhabitants of the islands, are thought to be of Caucasian origin; many Japanese place names are Ainu words. Japan is a democracy with a parliament (the Diet) and a figurehead imperial family. Emperor Akihito is head of state. A world economic leader, Japan is touched by recession, threatening a modern national tradition of lifetime employment. Resulting economic pressures will affect minority groups. The Japanese government is particularly sensitive about the minority rights issue. There have been political and business corruption scandals in the last decade, and in 1995 nerve-gas explosions raised the possibility of disruption by extremist religious sects.

Japan has been seeking a greater role in international affairs, and has become the world's major aid donor, according to a 1995 review by the Organization for Economic Cooperation and Development, making new commitments to women in development, grassroots and non-governmental organizations. This may have a bearing on government attitudes to the weaker groups in Japan, particularly minorities.

Hierarchical traditions, which distinguished between 'acceptable' and 'unacceptable' occupations, remain the core element of conflict between majority and minority groups in Japan. There is debate among scholars about the Japanese mindset towards outsiders, which perhaps in part reflects traditional Japanese attitudes to 'lower caste' minorities. Many majority Japanese may feel that they are of one, exclusive, ethnic strand, giving them a sense of uniqueness. This is ethnologically not the case, but research into this area has been made difficult by government restrictions on access to archives by scholars. In 1996 Japan still had not signed the International Convention on the Elimination of All Forms of Racial Discrimination.

By law all citizens have equal rights; however custom can result in covert discrimination. This may be reinforced by the use of illegal lists which identify minorities, and so enable firms to avoid employing members of such groups. Another practice is examining family residence papers for proposed matrimonial suitability. While native Japanese do not have to carry identity papers, the system of family registration (*koseki*) is the main route by which ethnic origin can be identified. The registration records the address of the 'family base', *honseki*, usually the town of birth, and this is also printed on a driver's licence. Other personal details, such as divorce or naturalization, are included. The family base address is more than enough in Japanese society to indicate ethnic origin. It is rare that entry into an institution's employ or care, from company to school, can be achieved without presenting the *koseki*. Since many minorities are physically indistinguishable from majority Japanese, one technique reportedly employed by those who wish to remove traces of their ancestry is continually to change address until the original family base 'drops' off the renewed documents. This, however, entails a lifetime of denying one's roots, which may well be damaging to the self-esteem of the individual and the minority community. A significant recent increase in the number of 'mixed' marriages suggests that the younger generation of Japanese are shedding some of the subtle discrimination of older generations.

Citizenship for the Korean minority is a major issue. Many Koreans in Japan are still official aliens and have to carry a photo identity card, despite being third and fourth generation. In March 1995, the Supreme Court ruled that 'permanent resident foreign nationals' could vote in local elections, as a result of a challenge by a Korean. Some 200 municipal councils and local governments have adopted local laws to allow such voting. The industrial city of Kawasaki has put in place modalities for a representative council of foreign nationals.

In 1995 there were 1,281,644 permanent immigrants or registered aliens in Japan – from North and South Korea, Taiwan, Hong Kong, China, Brazil, the Philippines, the USA, Peru, the UK, Thailand, Vietnam and Canada. There is also a large population of illegal migrant workers.[1]

Burakumin

The history of the Burakumin is marked both by repression by the majority Japanese society and by a determination, often violent, to assert their right to a full role. Ethnically fully Japanese, Burakumin in the Middle Ages were deemed to belong to the two *senmin* or 'despised citizen' classes. These were classified as *eta* ('extreme filth'), people who performed 'polluting' tasks (animal slaughter, tanning, disposing of the dead), and *hinin* ('non-humans' – beggars, prostitutes and criminals) who had 'fallen' into the category because they had violated civil and penal codes. It is an indication of the rigidity of the system that, though *eta* status was considered the 'higher' of the two outcast groups, it was a result of birth or acquired by marriage or close association and could not be lost, irrespective of change of occupation or residence. This endures till today. On the other hand, those deemed *hinin*, or those who have transgressed social codes, can acquire another status by settling down in 'normal' communities. In some areas *eta* were forced to wear special clothing or identifying leather patches and live in districts called *dowa*. The residents of these districts and their descendants are referred to today as Burakumin. The official figures of 1.17 million Burakumin only refer to those in *dowa* districts. In reality the figure is probably in excess of 3 million.

Job discrimination on the basis of ethnicity or origin is illegal in Japan, but more than one hundred large corporations such as Mitsubishi and Nissan are known to have bought illegal lists giving the location of known Burakumin throughout Japan. Under a 1976 law, anyone seeking access to details of a person's family register is supposed to stipulate the reason, but private investigators seeking details for potential in-laws, for example, easily circumvent this. The Burakumin school dropout rate is two to three times the national average. Among Burakumin only half the national average of 35.5 per cent goes on to further education. Combined with job discrimination, this means unemployment among Burakumin is high. Employment is usually with small companies which are being hit by recession. Many still work in the leather and shoe industries. Family income is only 60 per cent of the national average. Though there have been extensive government housing programmes for minorities such as the Burakumin, they still have poorer-than-average living conditions. Burakumin often suffer two to three times more illness than the national average. The percentage of Burakumin receiving government assistance is eight (Osaka) to ten (Kagwa) times the national average.

The Buraku Kaiho Domei (Buraku Liberation League) is the leading community organization. The community has been lobbying for a new law. Based on a draft bill from 1985, it would be added to Japan's eleven 'fundamental laws' as 'A Fundamental Law for Buraku Liberation'. Central and local government would be required to eliminate discrimination, and other citizens would be obliged to cooperate. But it does not provide legal redress for individual Burakumin to take action. The bill still awaits action.

While Buddhism has stimulated reform movements among Burakumin in the past, so have anarchism and Marxism. Burakumin have also won legislative positions in elections. Some have won ownership of their tenant lands and this has created a not insignificant group of wealthy Burakumin. Trades unions have also tended to back the reform movement, but it is unclear whether the Christian churches have generally been active in supporting them.

Burakumin have also benefited from funding from central government and from individual city efforts, such as those by Osaka, Kyoto, Kobe and in large areas in the Kinki region, to improve their physical living and working conditions and to provide suitable educational inputs. There have been children-to-children programmes to break down discrimination and to increase friendship and good-neighbourly relations between majority and Burakumin families. Government expenditure following the enactment of the 1969 Law on Special Measures for Buraku Improvement Projects saw 6 billion yen spent on projects in its first thirteen years. Such budgets tailed off under its second extension in 1978. Burakumin leaders wish to develop a sense of history about their origins and see their community as a free-standing and valued component in a multi-ethnic society.

Okinawans

The geographical remoteness of Okinawa and the other seventy-seven Ryukyu Islands (only forty-seven of which are inhabited), extending up to 1,000 kilometres south of the Japanese mainland, has led to the creation of a 'minority through isolation'. In the seventeenth century the Shimazu invasion of Okinawa led to the prohibition of the people of Ryukyu from becoming 'Japanized'. They were forced to adopt Chinese fashions, and mainland Japan viewed them as being of a completely different race. In 1872, the Meiji government annexed the area and imposed Japanese education and culture on the Okinawans. Okinawa is strategically placed, almost equidistant from Taiwan and the People's Republic of China, and served as the site of the last land battle of the Second World War. Almost a third of the population died in the battle, and significant numbers were killed or forced to commit suicide by Japanese soldiers, as this was considered more honourable than surrender. Many Okinawans still feel that they were regarded as 'expendable' by the mainland.

Following Japan's surrender, Okinawa was placed under military rule, and US military bases were established on the island. These remained when the territory was returned to Japan on 15 May 1972. Today the US bases occupy 20 per cent of the best land on the island. Okinawans resent the fact that their island is subject to US–Japanese foreign policy, and are opposed to the presence of military units which other Japanese communities do not want on the mainland. They feel that much of the benefit of huge subsidies ploughed into Okinawa has gone to companies on the mainland who win the most profitable government contracts. There can also be conflict amongst Okinawans, as some are seen to profit through service industries by the presence of Americans. Cutbacks in US military spending have meant significant redundancies for Okinawans employed on the bases, with unemployment now sometimes two to three times higher than on the mainland, particularly among young workers. At times local incomes have been among the highest in Asia, but because of these unemployment factors they have also dropped well below those on the mainland. Agricultural work has been eliminated by a switch to as much as 75 per cent employment in the service sector, eroding the land-based traditions of the Okinawans. While tourism has been a major growth area, control and financing have been from mainland Japan and local people see this as a threat to the long-term exploitation of the islands.

The issue of payments by Japan for the presence and maintenance of US military bases in Okinawa has often been the focus of violent demonstration in Japan nationally. While Okinawans are free to travel to and from the mainland and are physically as Japanese as the rest of the country, there is discrimination in both employment and social life, particularly in marriage. Okinawan women are discriminated against because they are held to mix with foreigners, that is, US service personnel. Children of mixed Okinawan and US parentage also face problems of adjustment. At one stage in the 1980s there were an average of 400 mixed marriages a year, as well as common-law relationships; many ended in desertion and divorce. In the mid-1980s people in Okinawa of mixed descent were often given abusive names. The nationality status of these children has been an issue before the Japanese Supreme Court. It is unlikely that Okinawans will give up their determination to exercise all the political and legal rights of mainland Japan.

Koreans

Some 300,000 ethnic Koreans have taken Japanese citizenship through naturalization since 1952, but an estimated 759,000 remain registered as Korean nationals and are therefore aliens in legal terms. Japan's links with Korea go back many centuries. The source of present links is Japan's thirty-five-year colonization of Korea after invading it in 1910. By 1939, nearly 1 million Koreans, mostly unskilled labourers and their families, had moved to Japan and were a prime factor in boosting the prewar Japanese economy. A significant number were kidnapped in Korea and taken to Japan for use as slave labour (*kyousei renko*). (The Chinese minority in Japan were also often subject to the same enslavement.) It appears likely that many Koreans will seek compensation from the Japanese government.

Although Koreans had Japanese nationality until 1952, government regulations forced them to carry a passbook with a photo. A policy of official assimilation required them to take Japanese names and to speak Japanese in public, in order to eliminate Korean (and Chinese) ethnic consciousness and to create an underclass of productive and obedient 'lesser' Japanese citizens. By the end of the Second World War there were some 2.4 million Koreans in Japan. Most were repatriated under an Allied Powers' programme, but 600,000 Koreans and 40,000 Taiwanese stayed on. A range of subsequent legal procedures stripped the Koreans of various rights including, in 1952, their Japanese nationality. Third and even fourth generation Koreans born in Japan are still considered Korean nationals and foreigners. While there have been various negotiations between Japan and North and South Korea to try to reduce the problem of this status issue, from the age of 16 Koreans are fingerprinted. They must carry a passbook containing their photograph, which must be produced upon request. The Research/Action Institute for Koreans in Japan says this is deliberately to target Koreans for control and harassment. Children who attend Korean schools wear Korean dress, and so stand out and are a target of harassment.

While foreign nationals (and this also means long-resident Koreans) can apply for Japanese citizenship and be naturalized under the 1950 Nationality Act, they must also show 'proof of assimilation'. This can lead to pressure to change to a Japanese name. In 1987 a resident of Kyoto won a court ruling against changing their name from Korean to Japanese after naturalization.

Ainu

In the Ainu language Ainu means 'human beings'. Ainu are indigenous to the Japanese islands of Hokkaido and northern Honshu, and to the Russian islands of Kurile and Sakhalin. Some are thus 'exiled' under Russian occupation, but recent economic links may permit a change to freedom of movement for Ainu, without their having to wait for a settlement to the Russian–Japanese land dispute. Ainu were traditionally hunter-gatherers and fishers, and their religion was based on mountain spirits, trees and other living things. There is no written Ainu language, but a strong oral tradition was passed on through epic poems and stories about the laws of nature. In the Tokugawa period (1603–1867), after much military conflict, Hokkaido came under Japanese control.

Most Ainu are today concentrated in the south-eastern part of Hokkaido in villages, though a few thousand live outside the area. They were given Japanese nationality in 1870 and laws were introduced prohibiting Ainu from their traditional hunting, fishing and forestry tasks. A policy of forced assimilation into Japanese society was undertaken, with bans on Ainu customs and language, and they were ordered to register under the Japanese family register system. In 1899, the Diet passed an act to encourage agriculture among Ainu and to assimilate them through financial aid, medical and education benefits. However, the land they were given was largely barren; most of the fertile land had already been sold to Japanese buyers. Even today the law still means that Ainu owners can only transfer land with permission of the Governor of Hokkaido and subject to other restrictions. The Ainu Association of Hokkaido moved in 1982 to have the law declared discriminatory and abolished.

Under the 1899 law educational measures, including 'native schools', were introduced, but the curriculum excluded history and geography and, so, the Japanese invasion of Hokkaido. The schools were abandoned later and Ainu children were integrated into Japanese schools. As with other minorities in Japan, Ainu generally have lower educational levels of attainment than majority Japanese: in 1986, the percentage of Ainu finishing high school was 78.4 per cent (compared with 94 per cent for other households in the same municipalities) and the percentage in further education was only 8.1 per cent (versus 27.4 per cent). Since the Japanese language is used both in schools and in daily life, few young Ainu today can speak Ainu.

The Ainu Association of Hokkaido drafted a bill in 1984 to replace the 1899 law. The bill was submitted to the Japanese government in August 1988 and reportedly remains in limbo. It demands equal status under the constitution and action by the government to improve education, employment and the social status of Ainu, as well as promotion of their language and culture. It includes the establishment of a government commission containing representatives of the Ainu community.

The Ainu population may have continued to grow slightly, as it did in the 1970s, and there could be at least another 25,000 Ainu who have hidden their origins but who might eventually emerge, were social conditions to make this possible. Proposals for a tax on majority Japanese to generate more funds for Ainu projects have not been successful. However, the growing success of first nations in retrieving rights over their land, for example in Canada and Australia, may assist and ensure the survival of the Ainu in the long term, perhaps on the basis of financial and land compensation. Ainu have recently increased contact with other first nations such as those in the USA, Canada, the Nordic countries and Greenland.

Migrant workers

There are an estimated 100,000–300,000 illegal workers in Japan, most having overstayed on short-term work permits, tourist or educational visas. Many of these migrants go underground, losing access to social services. Among them are a reported 7,000–20,000 Iranians, mostly working as low-paid labour. Many women illegals from the Philippines are drawn into prostitution. A Supreme Court ruling in January 1995, that a child, half Filipino and half Japanese, whose parents had disappeared, should be given Japanese citizenship, may signal a shift of official attitude. Japanese law at present allows only a child with at least one Japanese parent to have citizenship. Recessionary pressures threaten the security of both legals and illegals.

Conclusions and future prospects

Japan's minorities will suffer if recession grows, encouraging seeds of social conflict. Minorities are asserting their rights to a full social, economic and cultural role and it is expected that this sense of assertion will develop. Recent Supreme Court rulings in favour of wider citizenship and local voting rights should give minorities greater confidence to press for this role to be strengthened and in turn fortify their position in society. The same applies to demands for the repeal of past laws which work against minority community growth. Those minorities under Russian occupation, or suffering from loss of aboriginal land rights, may be expected to gain growing support in international rights fora and to press the Japanese government to regularize historical land disputes. The growing number of mixed marriages may also slowly change discriminatory mind-sets towards minorities and reduce the need for some of their individual members to hide their origins in order to live normally in mainstream Japanese society. Japan's cultural opening to the outside world has also seen attempts by the government and official bodies to move to some form of apology and discussion of compensation for treatment meted out to foreign military prisoners during the Second World War and for forced prostitution of civilian prisoners, known as 'comfort women', for Japanese troops.

Further reading

Asia Quarterly Review, vol. 14, no. 4, 1982, special issue on Okinawa.

De Vos, G.A., Wetherall, W. and Stearman, K., *Japan's Minorities*, London, MRG report, 1983.

Hah, C.D. and Lapp, C.C., 'Japanese politics of equality in transition: the case of the Burakumin', *Asian Survey*, vol. 18, no. 5, May 1978, pp. 487–504.

Hahn, B. and Hong, S., 'The Korean minority in Japan: their problems, aspirations and prospects', *Korea Journal*, vol. 15, no. 6, June 1975.

Liberation of the Korean Minority in Japan, presented to the Division of Human Rights of the United Nations by Association Fighting for the Acquisition of Human Rights of Koreans in Japan, 1991.

The Reality of Buraku Discrimination in Japan, Osaka, Buraku Kaiho Kenkyusho, 1991.

Siddle, R.M., *Race, Resistance and the Ainu of Japan*, Sheffield, Centre for Japanese Studies, and London, Routledge, 1996.

Suginohara J., *Status Discrimination in Japan: Introduction to the Buraku Problem*, Kobe, Hyogo Institute, 1982.

Ueda, D., 'The Ainu and their present legal questions', paper presented at International Conference on Indigenous Rights in the Pacific and North America, University of London, May 1991.

Upham, F.K., 'Ten years of affirmative action for Japanese Burakumin: a preliminary report on the law on special measures for *dowa* projects', *Law in Japan*, vol. 13, no. 39, 1980, pp. 39–73.

Minority-based and advocacy organizations

Ainu Association of Hokkaido, Kita 2, Nishi 7, Chuo-ku, Sapporo, Hokkaido 060, Japan; tel. 81 11 221 0462, fax 81 11 221 0672.

Buraku Liberation League, 3–5–11 Roppongi, Minato-ku, Tokyo 106, Japan.

Buraku Liberation Research Institute, 1–6–12 Kuboyoshi, Naniwa-ku, Osaka 556, Japan.

Foundation for Human Rights in Asia, 2–28–218 Shimomiyabi, Shinjuku-ku, Tokyo 162, Japan.

International Movement Against All Forms of Discrimination and Racism, 3–5–11 Roppongi, Mintato-ku, Tokyo 106, Japan.

Japan Civil Liberties Union, 306 Atagoyama Bengoshi Building, 1–6–7 Atago Minato-ku, Tokyo 105, Japan.

Research Action Institute for Koreans in Japan, 2–3–18 Nishi-Waseda, Room 52, Japan Christian Centre, Shinjuku-ku, Tokyo 169, Japan.

Laos

Land area:	236,800 sq km
Population:	4.8 million (1995)
Main languages:	Lao, Mon-Khmer language group
Main religions:	Buddhism, animism
Main minority groups:	Lao Theung 96,000–1.44 million (est., 2–30%), Lao Soung 23,000–96,000 (est., 0.5–2%), Tai 23,000–96,000 (est., 0.5–2%), Chinese 8,000 (est., 0.2%), Vietnamese (no data)
Real per capita GDP:	$1,458
UNDP HDI/rank:	0.399 (138)

Laos is a mountainous, landlocked and poor country. Half the population consists of the lowland Lao majority. The other half is made up of nearly seventy distinct, but often related, minority groups. The majority population of Laos, called Lao Lum, or lowland Lao, live along the Mekong river and its tributaries. But nine times as many ethnic Lao are Thai citizens residing in north-east Thailand as are citizens of Laos residing within Laos's modern borders. The largest minority group, the Lao Theung, or middle Lao, live in Burma and Cambodia as well. Other hill tribes such as the Tai groups, the Hmong and several other Lao Soung, or highland Lao, inhabit and traditionally migrated between southern China, northern Vietnam, north Thailand and north Burma, as well as Laos.

During the last fifty years, Laos has been caught up in the Indochina wars, particularly North Vietnam's struggles against the French and the USA. The Western powers supported a royalist faction of the predominant lowland Lao, and also some hill tribe groups, particularly the Hmong. The North Vietnamese supported another lowland Lao faction, the Pathet Lao. Additionally, in the early 1970s huge US bombing campaigns in the areas peopled by ethnic minorities resulted in widespread internal displacement. In 1975, following the communist victories in Vietnam and Cambodia, the Pathet Lao took control, following which a tenth of the population fled to Thailand, fearful of the new government's collectivization schemes and a large-scale programme of political imprisonment and forced labour. After 1975 Laos entered a period of isolation, maintaining close relations only with Vietnam, until economic necessity forced the country to reopen in the early-1990s. There is no semblance of democracy in Laos, nor has there ever been. Its communist leadership do not permit any political opposition or activity.

Lao Theung

Lao Theung is a term now used to categorize ethno-linguistically Mon-Khmer tribes that reside on the middle elevation between the lowland Lao (Lao Loum) and those highland tribes residing on the mountain tops (Lao Soung). Consisting of some thirty to sixty different clans, depending on how they are differentiated, Lao Theung are the original inhabitants of the land whose conquest by migrating Tai peoples is still celebrated in national festivals. Some tribes in this grouping may be related to various Negrito groups in South-East Asia. Largely animist, only a few of these tribes have adopted Buddhism. Linguistically, Lao Theung are part of the Mon-Khmer language group also spoken in Cambodia and some parts of Burma, but there is no written script and the language structure is quite different from that of the lowland Lao. The largest Lao Theung tribe is the Khmu in northern Laos. Other main tribes include Sasseng, Loven, So and Bru (Brao) in southern Laos and Alak, Ataouat, Cao, Cheng, Halang, Halang Doan, Katang, Langya, Monom, Ngeh, Ngung Bo, Nha Heun, Noar, Pacoh, P'u Noi, Sapuan, Sayan, Sork, Sou, Thap, The and Ven.

Lao Soung

Lao Soung, or high mountain Lao, comprise two principal groups: Hmong (formerly called Meo or Miao) and Yao (formerly called Man). Smaller hill tribes sometimes included among the Lao Soung are Lolo, Ho and Kho (also known as Akha). Hmong and Yao are recent immigrants from southern China, who migrated to Laos after 1850. They are animists and retain southern Chinese cultural influences. Living only at altitudes above about 1,000 metres, the Hmong and Yao practise shifting cultivation. Their most important crop is opium. There is also a tradition of Hmong and Yao conflict with the Tai and Mon-Khmer who resided on the lower elevations of the same mountain ranges and often outnumbered the Lao Soung. During the Vietnam War, Hmong were armed by the US, who used them to fight the North Vietnamese and the Pathet Lao. Hmong continued to fight after the Pathet Lao took control, until they were defeated by North Vietnamese troops, after which many fled to Thailand. Many Hmong refugees resettled in the USA.

Tai and other hill peoples

Tai hill tribes live in the higher valleys and on the middle slopes of the mountains in northern Laos (and in adjacent areas of south-west China, north Thailand and north-west Vietnam). Largely self-sufficient, they cultivate rice on irrigated terraces as well as corn, wheat and beans and also engage in swidden agriculture. They are mainly animist and speak a variation of the Lao-Thai language which means they can communicate with lowland Lao and Thai peoples. Some Tai have an alphabet based on the same Sanskrit alphabet as the Lao and Thai, but their literacy rates are low. Tai tribes are usually categorized according to their traditional costumes: Tai Dam (Black Tai), Tai Khao (White Tai), Tai Deng (Red Tai). Other Tai tribes such as Tai Neua, Tai Phong, Phou Tai, Lue Tai, Yuan and Phuan, have been characterized by location or other characteristics. Tai are regarded as inferior by lowland Lao, and Tai, in turn, look down on lowland Lao for having failed to maintain Tai tradition and culture. There are other hill peoples who are not generally included within the larger categories of hill tribes, and about whom little information is available.

Chinese and Vietnamese

In the 1950s about 40,000 ethnic Chinese lived in Laos, predominantly in the capital, Vientiane, and other major towns. By 1975, estimates of their numbers varied from 30,000 to 80,000. Historically, while regarded as foreign residents, ethnic Chinese had been able to establish associations and operate Chinese schools. In 1959 the Royal Government passed an ordinance barring foreigners (except for Vietnamese) from engaging in a specified list of occupations and professions, but Chinese business owners were able to mitigate much of the effect of this policy by becoming Lao citizens or setting up Lao business fronts. Up to 90 per cent of Laos's ethnic Chinese fled to Thailand in 1975, after the communist Pathet Lao came to power. In the early 1990s Laos liberalized its economic policies and normalized relations with China and Thailand, which should improve the situation for the estimated 8,000 Chinese still living in Laos.

France brought French-speaking Vietnamese into Laos to staff the colonial administrative structures. Other Vietnamese trades-people, merchants and artisans migrated on their own. An estimated 8,000 Vietnamese resided in Laos in the late 1950s. Large numbers of Vietnamese soldiers and civilians were brought into Laos after 1975 to fight ongoing hill tribe insurgencies and to assist the new communist government. Information about the numbers or categories of Vietnamese remaining in Laos is not available, although presumably many Vietnamese officials and regular armed forces personnel have returned to Vietnam following the end of the Cold War in the late 1980s.

Conclusions and future prospects

During the war years, the Pathet Lao promised that all national minorities would be able to preserve their customs and traditional culture and join in the management of the country. The Pathet Lao recruited many minority group members to their party, and after taking power in 1975 involved tribal leaders in positions of authority, particularly at the provincial and district levels. However, the regime considered that tribal cultures included superstitions and individualistic ways that were inimical to collectivized national economic development. Many tribespeople objected to policies of conscription and forced labour, to attempted prohibitions on swidden agriculture, to the collectivization of tribal lands and to resettlement at lower elevations. Laos has changed little over recent decades. Despite attempts at economic liberalization in the 1990s, the Lao People's Revolutionary Party (LPRP) maintain tight control. Irrespective of economic policies, much of Laos's potential for economic development lies in the areas peopled by tribal minorities. Thus, Laotian tribal minorities face the prospect of the same problems that have emerged elsewhere in the developing world to threaten indigenous peoples whose lands and ways of life are being 'developed' at the behest of, and for the primary benefit of, the lowland majorities and foreign economic interests. The future of Laos's minorities appears bleak.

Further reading

Ovesen, J., *A Minority Enters the Nation State: A Case Study of a Hmong Community in Vientiane Province, Laos,* Uppsala, Sweden, Uppsala University, 1995.

Stuart-Fox, M. (ed.), *Contemporary Laos*, New York, St Martin's Press, 1982.

Zasloff, J. and Unger, L. (eds), *Laos: Beyond the Revolution*, New York, St Martin's Press, 1991.

Macau

Land area:	19.3 sq km
Population:	355,693 (resident), 403,038 (total) (1993)
Main languages:	Chinese (mainly Cantonese) and Portuguese (both official), English
Main religions:	Buddhism, Roman Catholicism and Protestantism
Main minority groups:	*by ethnicity*: Portuguese and racially mixed Macanese 10,000 (est., 2.5%); *by nationality*[1]: Portuguese 101,245 (28.5%), also British, Filipinos, Thais and others
Real per capita GDP:	$13,269
UNDP HDI/rank:	—

Macau consists of a mainland peninsula and the islands of Taipa and Coloane in the Pearl river estuary in south-east China. Under Portuguese rule since the mid-sixteenth century, Macau was originally established as a base for missionaries to introduce Christianity to China. It rapidly developed into an entrepôt for trade between China and Japan. Buddhism is the major faith, but more than 60 per cent of Macau's population profess no religion. Portugal is due to hand Macau back to China in 1999. Macau is regarded by both countries as Chinese territory under Portuguese administration. It has a governor, appointed by Portugal. The Legislative Assembly is composed of directly elected members, those elected by constituent groups and nominated members.

Portugal has issued passports to Chinese residents

of Macau, who have the right to settle in Portugal or any European Union country if they wish to after 1999. The number of those entitled to Portuguese passports has been estimated at 150,000 in 1990, rising to 200,000 by 1999. This has partly stemmed the tide of emigration. Macau will become a Special Administrative Region (SAR) of China on 20 December 1999. Under the Sino-Portuguese Joint Declaration of 1987 Macau will retain a high degree of autonomy, remain a free port and continue to be a free market economy for fifty years after the hand-over, with an unrestricted flow of capital and a freely convertible currency. The Basic Law for Macau, ratified by China in 1993, sets out its approach to democratic rule for Macau. Elections to the Legislative Assembly are due in 2000, when it will be enlarged to twenty-seven members, ten of whom shall be directly elected. What the representation of minority groups shall be remains to be seen.[2]

Malaysia

Land area:	329,749 sq km
Population:	20.2 million (1995)
Main languages:	Bahasa Melayu (official), English, Chinese dialects, Tamil
Main religions:	Islam (official), Hinduism, Buddhism, Taoism, Confucianism, Christianity, Sikhism, animism
Main minority groups:	*peninsular Malaysia* (total 16.7 million): Chinese 5.01 million (30%), Indians 1.3 million (8%), Orang Asli 86,000 (0.5%); *Sabah* (1.6 million): Kadazan-Dusun 400,000 (25%), Chinese 240,000 (15%), Bajau 240,000 (15%), Murut 64,000 (4%); *Sarawak* (1.9 million): Dayak-Iban 570,000 (30%), Chinese 551,000 (29%), Malay 399,000 (21%), Bidayuh 171,000 (9%),
Real per capita GDP:	$12,510
UNDP HDI/rank:	0.825 (53)

The Federation of Malaysia consists of the Malay peninsula (peninsular Malaysia), and Sabah and Sarawak in the north-east and north of the island of Borneo. Malacca, a major trading port on the Malay peninsula, was captured by the Portuguese in 1511 and by the Dutch in 1641. The arrival of the Europeans shattered the political cohesion of the Malay world, which broke up into clusters of sultanates lining the coastal plains of present-day Malaysia, Indonesia and the southern Philippines. In the late nineteenth century, the UK consolidated direct control over the entire peninsula. Peninsular Malaysia gained independence from the UK in 1957. In 1963 the British territories of Singapore, Sabah and Sarawak came together to form the Malaysian Federation. In 1965 Singapore left the Federation.

Before British rule, Malaya was thinly populated, with Malay fishing and rice-growing settlements along the east and west coasts, often at the mouths of rivers. Inland, forested mountainous areas were inhabited by small indigenous tribes known collectively as Orang Asli. The development of tin mining and plantation agriculture in the nineteenth century attracted large-scale Chinese and Indian immigration, particularly from 1880 to 1930. Chinese and Indian immigrants settled in separate urban and rural communities, particularly in sparsely populated western Malaysia, geographically isolated from Malays. Islam prevented intermarriage between Malays and the new arrivals. In Sarawak, Malays are considerably outnumbered by both Chinese and indigenous groups, collectively known as Dayak. In Sabah (formerly North Borneo), Malays, many of whom migrated from the Sulu sultanates in neighbouring southern Philippines, are similarly outnumbered by ethnic Chinese and indigenous tribal groups, particularly Kadazan-Dusun.

At the time of independence, there was considerable socio-economic disparity between indigenous Malays and immigrant Chinese and Indian communities. In general, Malays held political power while Chinese dominated the economy. The disparity led to riots in 1969, after which the government amended the constitution to include 'special rights' for *bumiputera* ('sons of the soil', that is, Malays and other indigenous people). Under the law, no individual or institution, including Parliament, can question the 'special rights'. The New Economic Policy (NEP) promulgated after independence discriminated against non-*bumiputera*. Under it, *bumiputera* were given preference in all social, political and economic spheres. Although the NEP was portrayed by the government as affirmative action, Chinese and Indians felt, correctly, that it made them second class citizens. The NEP expired in 1990, but its successor, the New Development Policy, retained the key discriminatory elements of the NEP.

National cultural policy is based on Malay and Islamic traditions. This has created tension with Chinese and Indians and with indigenous communities in Sabah and Sarawak, who wish to promote and retain their own cultures. The ethnic divide between Malays and non-Malays is compounded by religion. By law, all Malays are Muslims. The majority of Chinese, Indian and tribal groups in Sabah and Sarawak are non-Muslims. Under the law, Islam is the official religion although religious freedom is enshrined in the constitution. In practice, the state seeks to convert the non-Muslim population, especially indigenous peoples and Christians. Churches and temples are regularly denied building permits. In many urban areas, burial land is not made available to non-Muslims. Conversions to Islam also take place by force of law; if a non-Muslim marries a Muslim, the former must convert. Although the non-*bumiputera* community constitute about 40 per cent of the population, gerrymandering ensures that political power remains in the hands of Malays.

Like Thailand, Indonesia and Singapore, Malaysia is a 'tiger' economy with consistently high rates of economic growth.

Chinese

Ethnic Chinese constitute between a quarter and a third of Malaysia's population overall. Chinese trading communities have long been present in Malaysia, but large-scale migration only began in the nineteenth century as a result of British policy. Young Chinese males were encouraged to go to Malaysia to work in tin mining for several years before emigrating back to China with their earnings. In the early twentieth century, immigration by Chinese women increased, and settled Chinese communities developed. The increased size of the population allowed the community to build temples, schools and community and political associations. Most Chinese were found in urban areas and had little interaction with Malays and other indigenous peoples, who lived mainly in rural areas. Chinese migration to Sabah and Sarawak followed a similar pattern.

After independence, the Chinese hold on the economy became stronger. The 1969 anti-Chinese riots led to the constitutional amendments on 'special rights' and the NEP. Chinese activists and politicians who have protested against the NEP and erosion of non-Malay culture and education have been arrested, as late as 1988, and detained without trial under the Internal Security Act (ISA). Chinese education at post-primary level is available only at private schools. Although the Chinese are represented in the government, they are marginalized in the key policy decision-making process. In successive elections, the majority of Chinese votes have gone to Chinese-based opposition political parties.

Indians

The earliest Indian merchant communities brought Hindu and Islamic religious and political culture to Malaysia. With the development of the plantation economy under British rule, large-scale Indian immigration occurred. The first immigrants usually came in under the indentured labour system. Tamil-speaking labourers from southern Madras were brought in to provide labour for the booming rubber plantations. Others were brought in, often for particular economic functions, such as building and maintaining the railways. A small number of Tamils from Sri Lanka came to staff the colonial civil service. Sikhs and Punjabi Muslims arrived for police work. Chettiars from Madras immigrated to specialize in banking and moneylending. Like the Chinese, the Indian populations often lived in their own communities in their own areas. Although early Indian immigrant communities were divided along caste and geographical lines, these differences are no longer noticed by the younger generation. The only divide is religious: between Indian Muslims and non-Muslims. Indian Muslims have a high rate of intermarriage with the Malay community. Almost all the Indian community are found in peninsular Malaysia; there are few Indians in Sabah and Sarawak. The social, economic and political position of the Indian community is similar to that of the Chinese as they are classified as non-*bumiputera*. Like the

Chinese, the majority of Indians vote for the opposition.

Orang Asli

Orang Asli is the collective name for the indigenous aboriginal tribal groupings whose existence on peninsular Malaysia pre-dates the arrival of the Malay peoples. Sixty per cent live in the mountainous forests and hill areas. About 75 per cent practise traditional animist religions, about 10 per cent are Christian and 10–15 per cent Muslim. Official government policy is to convert the community to Islam, and to this end, in the past few years, government officials have demolished Orang Asli Christian churches. Linguistically, Orang Asli belong to two major language groups: Austroasiatic/Mon-Khmer (sometimes referred to as Central Aslian) and Austronesian. The nineteen Orang Asli tribal groups constitute three categories: Negrito/Semang, Senoi and Proto-Malay/Melau Asli. Negrito tribes include Kensiu, Kintak, Lanoh, Jahai, Mendruq and Bateq. They are hunter-gatherers, generally residing in the hilly forests of north and north-east Malaysia. Their language is distantly related to the Mon-Khmer language group. The Senoi tribal group language is also distantly related to the Mon-Khmer language group. They practise shifting cultivation, as well as forest hunting and gathering, mostly in the more remote areas of the central highlands. Senoi tribes include Che Wong, Jahut, Mah Meri, Semai, Semoq Beri and Temar. The Proto-Malay group are similar in appearance to Malays, but of diverse origin. They live along the Strait of Malacca and in southern Johor. Some have adopted Islam and are being absorbed into the Malay community. These tribal groups include Jakun, Orang Kanaq, Orang Laut, Selitar, Semelai, Temuan (Balandas) and Temoq.

Prior to European colonization, the Malacca sultanate was based on the naval prowess of Orang Laut sailors in alliance with Malay rulers. However, other Orang Asli were captured and enslaved by Malays, and Orang Asli used to be referred to as *sakai* meaning slave, or with the derogatory expression, *semang*. During the 1950s insurgency known as the Emergency, communist (and ethnic Chinese) guerrillas often fled to the mountainous areas inhabited by Orang Asli, some of whom cooperated with the guerrillas because of their traditional hostility towards Malays. The British established fortified settlements, often with health clinics or schools, to resettle the Orang Asli and isolate them from communist contact. A Department of Aborigines was created, which, after independence, eventually became the Department of Orang Asli Affairs. The government retains ownership of lands populated by Orang Asli, who have no security of tenure. The government has the right to appoint Orang Asli village leaders and prohibit entry into Orang Asli settlements. The best Orang Asli lands are coveted by private corporations and agencies of the state for logging or other development projects. Orang Asli remain significantly at risk.

Ethnic minorities in Sabah

In Sabah, non-Malay indigenous tribal communities are in the majority, comprising about 85 per cent of the territory's 1.6 million inhabitants. There are about thirty-nine tribal groups, the largest being the Kadazan-Dusun, Bajau and Murut. Nationally, the indigenous peoples of Sabah comprise only 6.6 per cent of Malaysia's population. Sabah Chinese and Malay account for 15 per cent and 9 per cent of the state's population, respectively. Most of the indigenous groupings are Dusunic peoples, who are largely Roman Catholic. This group includes Kadazan-Dusun and nine other identifiable tribal subgroups. There are nine tribes in the Murutic group, and six tribes in the Paitanic group. Other tribes which do not fit into these groupings include Bajau, Bengkahak (Mangkaak), Bonggi, Bugis, Ida'an, Illanun, Lundayeh, Suluk (Tausug) and Tidung.

Ethnic minorities in Sarawak

Sarawak has a population of 1.9 million, 80 per cent of whom live in rural areas. Like Sabah, Sarawak is ethnically diverse; it has about twenty-six tribal groupings. Also like Sabah, the nationally predominant ethnic Malays are considerably outnumbered both by ethnic Chinese and by indigenous non-Muslim minority groups. Non-Muslim tribal groups are collectively called Dayak and account for 45 per cent of Sarawak's inhabitants but for only 4 per cent of the total population of Malaysia. The two biggest ethnic groups within the Dayak community are the Iban and Bidayuh. Dayak who live in the interior of Sarawak are sometimes referred to as Orang Ulu, or people from the interior. Members of this group typically live in longhouses and practise shifting cultivation and engage in fishing to supplement their diet if they live near a river. Orang Ulu comprise Bisayah, Kelabit, Kenyah, Kayan,

Kedayan, Murut, Punan, Penan and others. In recent years, Dayak have staged small-scale protests against excessive logging in their immediate surroundings. The government has responded by detaining protesters and protecting the logging operations, which are covertly owned by leading Sarawak politicians. In 1994, the decision was made to build the Bakun dam, South-East Asia's largest. The dam will displace about 10,000 indigenous people.

Conclusions and future prospects

Orang Asli and smaller tribal groups in Sabah and Sarawak are at significant risk because of the concerted efforts to convert them to Islam. Tellingly, becoming a Muslim is known as 'Masuk Melayu', or becoming a Malay. The indigenous populations of Sabah and Sarawak also suffer discrimination because they do not hold political power, which is in the hands of the small Malay/Muslim community, supported by central government based in peninsular Malaysia. In the 1960s, the central government intervened politically in Sabah and Sarawak to remove Kadazan- and Iban-based state governments. Logging and other forms of economic development also threaten the survival of Malaysia's indigenous peoples. Chinese and Indian communities, due to their sheer numbers, will be better able to protect their cultural and religious autonomy.

With the 'special rights' of *bumiputera* enshrined in the constitution, the non-*bumiputera* community (Chinese and Indian) will continue to suffer significant levels of official discrimination. This tension has remained dormant since 1969 because of the country's high rate of economic growth, which has allowed the state to loosen some of its discriminatory policies and allowed non-*bumiputera* to prosper economically. The strong security apparatus of the state and its frequent use of the ISA have also ensured that minority rights advocates are kept under control. Difficulties for minorities are likely to come to a head when the economy slows down, as it did in the mid-1980s, with increased tensions between *bumiputera* and non-*bumiputera*. Mass arrests were made at that time, and many Chinese and Indian minority rights advocates were held in preventive detention.

Further reading

Hong, E., *Natives of Sarawak: Survival in Borneo's Vanishing Forests*, Penang, Institute Masyarakat, 1988.

Jesudason, J.V., *Ethnicity and the Economy: the State, Chinese Business and Multinationals in Malaysia*, Singapore, Oxford University Press, 1989.

King, V.T. and Parnwell, M.J. (eds), *Margins and Minorities: The Peripheral Areas and Peoples of Malaysia*, Hull, Hull University Press, 1990.

Lee, R., *Ethnicity and Ethnic Relations in Malaysia*, De Kalb, IL, Northern Illinois University, 1986.

Somers Heidhues, M. *et al.*, *The Chinese of South-East Asia*, London, MRG Report, 1992.

Ung-Ho Chin (Chin, J.), *Chinese Politics in Sarawak*, New York, Oxford University Press, 1996.

Minority-based and advocacy organisations

Aliran, PO Box 1049, 10830 Pulau Pinang, Malaysia; tel./fax 60 4 641 5785.

Asia Pacific Forum on Women, Law and Development (APFWLD), PO Box 12224, 9th Floor, APDC Building, Persiaran Duta, Kuala Lumpur 50770, Malaysia.

Centre for Orang Asli Concerns, 86-B Jalan SS 24/2, 47301 Petaling Jaya, Malaysia; tel. 60 3 704 2814, fax 60 3 777 2087.

Mongolia

Land area:	1,567,000 sq km
Population:	2,634,601 (1996)
Main languages:	Mongolian (incl. regional dialects), Russian
Main religions:	Buddhism (majority), traditional Lamaism, Sunni Islam, Christianity
Main minority groups (1989):[1]	Kazakh 118,000 (est., 5.9%), Durbed Mongol 54,000 (est., 2.7%), Bayad 38,000 (est., 1.9%), Buryat Mongol 34,000 (est., 1.7%), Dariganga Mongol 28,000 (est., 1.4%), others 152,000 (est., 7.6%), unknown number of Russians
Real per capita GDP:	$2,090
UNDP HDI/rank:	0.578 (113)

Mongolia is a landlocked country bordered by Russia to the north and China to the south. A large part of Siberia once belonged to Mongolia but is now part of Russia. Mongolia's southern region, now called Inner Mongolia, is a province of China. Mongolia has eighteen *aimag* (provinces) and three autonomous cities. The word Mongolia is generally first associated with Genghis Khan in the thirteenth century to define the T'atan subtribe to which he belonged, rather than a geographical area. The Mongols, of Ural-Altaic origin, were mentioned, by the Chinese, living north of the Gobi Desert between the sixth and ninth centuries. Historically there have been turbulent relations between Mongols and China. After the 1949 takeover of China by the communists, Mongolia maintained equitable relations with the Soviet Union and China. The Sino–Soviet split of the 1960s led Mongolia to side with the Soviets. It expelled thousands of ethnic Chinese, while more than 100,000 Soviet troops entered Mongolia. Many Mongolians learnt Russian and went for education to the Soviet Union. Russians set up communities in Mongolian cities. In March 1990 pro-democracy protests erupted in Ulaanbaatar, accompanied by hunger strikes. The government amended the constitution to permit multi-party elections in the same year. Communists won the elections, and freedom of speech, religion and assembly, already in the constitution, were turned into a reality. In 1991 the constitution was revised again and elections were held in June 1992, again resulting in a communist victory. In the July 1996 elections the Democratic Union Coalition won power from the communists.

Mongolia's majority culture is based on an ancient tradition of nomadism. Khalkha Mongols are the dominant ethnic group, and there are several other regional Mongol minorities. In the west of the country Kazakhs are the only major non-Mongolian ethnic group. No specific problems are reported for minority Mongols or Kazakhs. The country's small population is spread over vast areas, so the information structure is important for different groups to maintain their identity and make their views known. There is satellite broadcasting by Mongolian and Russian television. A recent vast increase in newspapers and magazines, some independent of the state or main parties, and their circulation, is countered by severe newsprint shortages and rising costs.

Conclusions and future prospects

Almost all Mongolia's food and livestock industries and a major part of manufacturing industry are now under private ownership. It is not clear how this will affect nomadic economics. Revenue from rich mineral resources will not necessarily go into services that were formerly subsidized under central government economic policy. In 1993 one-fourth of the population was classified as poor, and 29 per cent of these classified as very poor. The government has implemented a national programme of poverty alleviation in collaboration with international organizations. One reason for such poverty levels is rising unemployment. There is now also a national programme for the development of children, including measures to centralize education management, rationalize the location of secondary schools in rural areas, revise textbooks and reorganize vocational schools and further education. Foreign non-governmental agencies are concerned at the growing numbers of children forced on to the streets by extreme poverty affecting their families. The former system of boarding schools for children of nomadic groups, which was effectively free, is also breaking down due to lack of government funds.

The Mongolian tradition of living in *yurt* is still the norm. Yet the severe pressure of market forces is likely to increase the number of poor and affect nomadic lifestyles. Antipathy to Russians staying on may be expressed through resentment. The government is trying to create a social security system to protect the population, especially vulnerable minorities, but structural adjustment required by the International Monetary Fund may limit such efforts.[2]

North Korea

Land area:	122,762 sq km
Population:	23,067,000 (1994)
Main languages:	Korean, Chinese
Main religions:	Ch'ondogyo, Buddhism, Christianity, Confucianism, shamanism
Main minority groups:	Chinese 46,134 (0.2%)
Real per capita GDP:	$3,000
UNDP HDI/rank:	0.714 (83)

A unified nation for more than 1,200 years, Korea was independent except for brief periods at the height of the Mongol empire in the thirteenth century and after annexation by Japan in 1910. The Democratic People's Republic of Korea (DPRK) was created upon the defeat of Japan in the Second World War. In 1945 the USA and Soviet Union partitioned the country along the 38th parallel. Failure of reunification attempts led to elections in 1948 and the creation of the DPRK in the north, with its capital at Pyongyang, and the Republic of Korea (ROK) in the south, with US troops stationed in the ROK. The USA withdrew in 1949, and the DPRK invaded the ROK in 1950. Conflict continued until an armistice in 1953. A demilitarized zone with an electrified fence divides the two. There is a general state of alert on both sides with 40,000 US troops and 1 million South Koreans facing the fifth largest army in the world. The DPRK has maintained almost complete isolation. Its communist ideology is based on the principle of socialist self-sufficiency enunciated by its founding President, Kim Il Sung, and carried on by his son and successor Kim Jong Il. In theory the constitution offers all rights to the country's citizens.

North Korean officials claim – as do their counterparts in South Korea – that there are no natural ethnic minorities in the country, because the Korean peninsula naturally isolated the area from the outside world; they suggest the population may have its origins in immigration from Mongolia. There is no official religion; most of the population is stated to be atheist or non-religious, although covert religious practice is thought to be far more widespread than the government would admit. DPRK data made available to the United Nations Population Fund in 1989 indicate that the urban population increased by more than 10 million between 1953 and 1987. Events may indicate that the DPRK could reduce its isolationist stance. Its recent need for aid against famine and flood is one element. Another is the brokering of a deal for a modern light-water nuclear reactor, built by a consortium of US, Japanese and ROK companies. These developments could lead to an increase in trade and perhaps, later, political links between the two Koreas and other countries in the region. No specific minority rights issues have been identified.[1]

The Philippines

Land area:	300,000 sq km
Population:	68.5 million
Main languages:	Tagalog (national language), English (widely used), Bicolano, Cebuano, Hiligaynon, Ilocano, Pampangan, Pangasinan, Visayan, Waray-Waray, Chinese
Main religions:	Roman Catholicism, Islam, animism
Main minority groups:	Muslims (Moros) 3.17 million (est., 5%), indigenous peoples 2.05 million (est., 3%), Chinese 685,000 (est., 1%)
Real per capita GDP:	$2,590
UNDP HDI/rank:	0.665 (95)

The Republic of the Philippines is an archipelago consisting of more than 7,000 islands. The country is divided into three major island groups: Luzon in the north, including the capital, Manila, the largest group; the island grouping in the middle, the Visayas, the smallest; and Mindanao, in the south. The original inhabitants are believed to have been Negrito hunter-gatherers; then came waves of Malay immigrants from what are now Malaysia and Indonesia. Malays developed the agricultural and fishing life that characterized traditional Filipino society. Eleven different and mutually incomprehensible languages gradually developed, with over eighty identifiable dialects. However, about 90 per cent of the population speaks one of eight languages, all of which are part of the Malayo-Polynesian language family. Major cultural-linguistic groups include Tagalog, Cebuano, Ilocano, Hiligaynon, Bicolano, Waray-Waray, Pampangan and Pangasinan. Filipino society has been in the past, and is today, characterized by sizeable migrations: from rural areas to the capital and main provincial cities, and from the heavily populated northern island of Luzon to the Visayas and Mindanao. Long-term migrations to Mindanao have led to considerable tension and armed conflict with the Muslim and upland groups that previously dominated those islands.

In 1521 during Magellan's global circumnavigation, the Spaniards claimed the islands for Spain and named them Las Islas Filipinas in honour of King Philip II of Spain. The nearly three centuries of Spanish rule had two far-reaching effects: the introduction of Catholicism and a land-tenure system based on Spanish feudalism. Today, the Philippines is overwhelmingly Roman Catholic, the only Christian nation in South-East Asia. When the USA defeated the Spanish in Cuba in 1901, Spain ceded the Philippines to the USA. The Filipino independence movement, which had started in the mid-1800s, continued its armed struggle. The USA brutally suppressed the nationalist movement and proceeded to rule for the next fifty years. It greatly expanded education and transportation and encouraged agricultural and commercial production. Nationalists were co-opted into the political process, which was based on US constitutional practices. The Philippines became independent in 1946.

During the early independence period a communist insurgency developed in Luzon. Initially, the Huk movement was defeated in the 1950s with US assistance. But a second communist movement called the New Peoples Army and led by Huk elements along with radical students, re-emerged in the late 1960s. Simultaneously, a Muslim insurgency developed in Mindanao. These two insurgencies, and a desire to remain in office, led President Marcos to declare martial law in 1972. Marcos's authoritarian rule lasted until 1983, when opposition leader Benigno Aquino was assassinated on his return from exile in the USA. An election held shortly afterwards saw a landslide victory for his widow, Corazon Aquino. When Marcos refused to hand over power, a popular uprising, People's Power, forced him into exile in Hawai'i and Corazon Aquino became President. In 1992, Fidel Ramos became President after a closely fought election. Under the new 1988 constitution, the President can serve only one six-year term, making it much harder for another authoritarian ruler like Marcos to emerge again. Although democratic rule has been restored, Filipino politics remains based on patron–client relations and dominated by a dozen powerful elite families. All the major landholding families and political figures are *mestizo* (of Spanish-Filipino descent).

Muslims (Moros)

Moro, the Spanish name for Moor, is the name by which Filipino Muslim ethno-linguistic groups are usually known. Moros comprise roughly 5 per cent of the total Filipino population and are the most significant minority because of their long fight for independence from Manila. The main Moro ethno-linguistic groups are Maguindanao, Marano, Tausug, Samal, Bajau, Yakan, Ilanon, Sangir, Melabugnan and Jama Mapun. However, three of these groups – Maguindanaos of North Cotabato, Kudarat and Maguindanos provinces, Maranos of the two Lanao provinces, and Tausug from Jolo – make up the great majority of Moros. Despite their common differentiation from the Christian majority, Moros have not traditionally been united, and the various groups, which are divided by degrees of Islamic orthodoxy as well as by linguistic difference, are often hostile to each other. Yet Moros have shared a common hostility to the central authorities – Spaniards, Americans, and then after independence Christianized Filipinos from Luzon.

The Islamic religion came to the southern Philippine islands some two hundred years before the European colonial period. Moros developed a centralized religious, social and political system based on the Qur'an. Several sultanates emerged, similar to historical sultanates that developed in what are now Indonesia and Malaysia, with the sultans being both religious and secular leaders. These sultanates were *de facto* states, exercising jurisdiction over Muslim and non-Muslim alike. At the time of the Spanish conquest the Muslim principalities had the most politically advanced communities in the Philippines. The sultanates established on Sulu and Mindanao were the furthermost extension into Asia of the Islamic religion, and it is possible to see the Moro conflict as a 400-year struggle between Islam and Christianity, with neither side being able entirely to subdue the other. The sultanates resisted and fought Spanish authority for 300 years. After the Americans replaced the Spaniards, Moros fought the USA from 1903 to 1935, losing an estimated 20,000 lives. Since independence, Moros have sporadically waged political and armed struggle against the Philippine government based in Manila.

A long-term historical trend has been the displacement and dispossession of previously Moro territory. In the nineteenth century, the Spanish gained a foothold on Mindanao, through missionary efforts among the non-Muslim elements of the population, and through private military expeditions. Displacement and dispossession accelerated in the early 1900s as the American colonial authorities initiated policies to import homesteaders from the northern islands. The development of large-scale plantation agriculture for commercial export provided a further incentive for immigration. Policies of resettlement accelerated after the Second World War and independence, when, in response to the Huk rebellion in Luzon, tens of thousands were encouraged to migrate to farms and homesteads in Mindanao. Lowland, formerly northern Catholic Filipinos came to outnumber Moros, which led to land disputes, Christian vigilantism, and a cultural and religious reaction.

In 1968, the Muslim Independence Movement (MIM) was launched by radical Islamic leaders calling for independence from the Philippines and the creation of a Bangsa Moro, or Moro nation. This, and local 'Christian' countermeasures, led to full-scale revolt. The years 1969 to 1972, prior to martial law, were a period of indiscriminate violence between Muslims and Christians. In September 1972, Marcos cited the bloodshed and chaos in Mindanao, along with the communist New Peoples Army insurgency in Luzon, as reasons for the imposition of martial law. The result was a full-scale guerrilla war as the Moro National Liberation Front (MNLF) supplanted the MIM, and proclaimed Mindanao, Sulu and Palawan as Bangsa Moro. Radical Arab states such as Libya began to provide financial aid and Sabah (in eastern Malaysia) became a sanctuary for MNLF fighters. Fighting continued throughout the 1970s and the 1980s, causing large-scale disruptions and displacements. Through the intervention of the Organization of Islamic Conference, the MNLF and Manila held negotiations in the late 1970s and 1980s, although there was still fighting on the ground. A plebiscite following the passage of the 1987 constitution created an 'Autonomous' Region in four Muslim provinces in Mindanao (Magindanao, Lanao del Sur, Sulu and Tawi-Tawi). In the early 1990s, the MNLF split. The old faction accepted that independence was politically unviable and that the autonomous region is the best available option. The radical faction in MNLF has left and formed its own guerrilla army to fight for independence. In 1996, there was sporadic fighting between the two factions and the government.

Indigenous peoples

In some estimates there are close to a hundred indigenous groupings, exclusive of the Islamic groupings, or 3 per cent of the population. There is a great disparity of social organization and cultural expression among these minorities. Some specialize in wood-carving, basket-making, and weaving. Others are known for their embroidery, appliqué and bead-making. They range from the highly technologically sophisticated Bontoc and Ifugaos, who built the renowned rice terraces in the mountainous interior of Luzon, to groupings practising shifting cultivation or hunter-gathering. A significant number of indigenous minorities in central Luzon are Protestant Christians, having been converted by American missionaries in the early twentieth century and educated in missionary schools. For others there is a wide disparity in terms of integration with lowland Christian Filipinos. Some have intermarried. Others, such as Kalingas in Luzon, have remained isolated. There is little general agreement on the names and numbers of these indigenous minorities.

A common geographical distinction is often made between Igorot (Tagalog for 'mountaineer') on Luzon, and Lumad ('indigenous'), which is a collective name for some seventy-eight minority groups in central and southern Philippines. Reportedly, many Igorots prefer to be called by their specific group name. Ten upland tribal groups on Luzon have been identified: Ifugao, Bontoc, Kankanay, Ibaloi, Kalinga, Tinguian, Isneg, Gaddang, Ilongot and Nigrito. Ifugaos of Ifugao Province, Bontocs of Mountain and Kaling-Apayao provinces and Kankanay and Ibaloi of Benguet Province were all wet-rice farmers who have for centuries worked their elaborate rice terraces. Iankanay and Ibaloi were the most influenced by Spanish and American colonialism and lowland Filipino culture because of the extensive gold mines in Benguet, the proximity of the city of Baguio, good roads and schools, and a consumer industry in search of folk art. Other mountain peoples of Luzon include Kalinga of Kalinga-Apayao Province and Tinguian of Abra Province, who employ both wet-rice and dry-rice growing techniques. Isneg of northern Kalinga-Apayao, Gaddang of the border between Kalinga-Apayao and Isabela provinces, and Ilongot of Nueva Vizcaya Province all practise shifting cultivation. Although Negritos formerly dominated the highlands, by the early 1980s they were reduced to small groups living in widely scattered locations, primarily along the eastern ranges.

The other concentration of indigenous communities is in central and southern Philippines. The Lumad tribal groupings of Mindanao include Ata, Bagobo, Guiangga, Mamanwa, Magguangan, Mandaya, Banwa-on, Bukidnon, Dulangan, Kalagan, Kulaman, Manobo, Subanon, Tagabili, Takakaolo, Talandig, and Tiruray or Teduray. The Lumad groups of Mindanao have faced, and continue to face, long-term displacement and legalized land dispossession, a threat to other minority groups in the Philippines. The southern Philippine island groupings of Mindanao are resource-rich, and were formerly underpopulated compared to the northern island groupings of Luzon. Thus, throughout the twentieth century, there has been a steady migration of Christian lowland Filipinos into areas previously occupied and dominated by Lumad and Moros. These migrations were initially encouraged by the American authorities when the Philippines was under their rule, and were given further impetus by the development of plantation agriculture, logging concessions and hydro-electric and geothermal energy schemes. The Lumad are now outnumbered in their ancestral lands.

The Spanish crown formerly claimed rights over the islands and the authority to dispose of the land. Later, the US authorities institutionalized their legal powers to dispose of all land, and voided all the previous land grants by Moro or Lumad chiefs that had been made without government consent. Only individuals or corporations could register private claims to land ownership. This left no room for the concept of ancestral or communal land, which the indigenous Lumad had held to be sacred and not subject to individual title or ownership. Through the efforts of the Lumad of Mindanao, and their supporters among the lowland Christian Filipino community, two important provisions were written into the 1987 constitution. Article XII (5) obliges the state to 'protect the rights of indigenous cultural communities to their ancestral lands to ensure their economic, social and cultural well-being', while Article XIV (17) commits the state to 'recognize, respect and protect the rights of indigenous cultural communities to preserve and develop their cultures, traditions and institutions'. What this important step forward will mean in practice remains to be seen, in that the state also continues to maintain rights to land, and national development policies will continue to be shaped by powerful economic interests and political forces. The Lumad continue to seek the return of lands taken from them through harassment and illegal manipulation and seek the revocation of all plantation permits and logging concessions. They seek self-government within their ancestral lands with their customary laws, and the preservation of their indigenous cultures. In all these matters, the Lumad face an up-hill battle.

Chinese

Under Spanish colonial rule, the Philippines was an entrepôt for trade between China and the Spanish empire in Latin America. Ethnic Chinese in Manila managed the trade. The Chinese soon outnumbered the Spanish, who sought to control the ethnic Chinese by residential and occupational restrictions, deportations and periodic violence. Not until the mid-nineteenth century were Chinese granted freedom of occupation and residence. In the second half of the nineteenth century there was a new surge of Chinese immigration. Moving into the rural provinces, ethnic Chinese came to occupy a central position in commerce and commercial agriculture at provincial and local levels. Under US rule, Chinese immigration was sharply curtailed.

It is difficult to estimate numbers of ethnic Chinese because ethnicity is not specified in census data. Estimates vary from 600,000 to 900,000, with fewer than 150,000 being foreign-born. Under Marcos, citizenship procedures were eased, and many Chinese became citizens. There is a small-scale Chinese press, Chinese cultural associations, and private Chinese schools. Most younger Filipino Chinese, however, are more at ease with English than with their mother tongue. Although ethnic Chinese dominate the corporate world, they are still denied access to the political arena. This comes mainly from popular resentment and envy against the Chinese for their commercial success. None of the major political parties in the Philippines courts the Chinese openly, and all hide the fact that much of the campaign funds come from Chinese businesses. The Chinese are thus forced to become 'influence peddlers'. There is also pressure for Chinese to marry into prominent *mestizo* families to protect their business interests. In recent years, the Chinese have been targets of kidnapping for ransom and, in many cases, the police are involved. This has led many Chinese to send their families abroad.

During the seventeenth and eighteenth centuries, Chinese immigration to the Philippines was almost entirely male. This led to intermarriage with Malay Filipinos and the creation of a Chinese *mestizo* group. When restrictions on Chinese economic activity were lifted, many Chinese *mestizos* moved into rural landholding and agricultural development by leasing the large tracts of land owned by Spanish religious orders. By the late nineteenth century, as Chinese *mestizo* landholding increased, they became a major component of the Filipino elite, a situation that continues to the present day. Chinese *mestizos* acquired Filipino identities and contributed substantially to the development of Filipino national identity.

Conclusions and future prospects

The main threats to minority rights in the Philippines are faced by Lumad and Igorot indigenous communities, ethnic Chinese and Moros. Lumad, who unlike Moros have not resorted to armed struggle, have only recently organized to assert their rights through an umbrella organization, Lumad Mindanaw, representing seventy-eight Lumad groups. Igorot cultural groupings in central Luzon will continue to face problems with evacuations from their tribal lands and the loss of their culture. Ethnic Chinese essentially faced a problem of perception: that they are rich business owners backed by Chinese cartels who have stamped out competition from other groups. There is, however, a sizeable Chinese working class in the Philippines, and there is a sharp gap between rich and poor Chinese. As long as they are seen as 'soft' economic targets, kidnappings and extortion of the community will continue. The Muslim question is political rather than religious; solutions are complicated by the split in the Muslim leadership.

Further reading

Rodil, B.R., *The Lumad and Moro of Mindanao*, London, MRG report, 1993.

Steinberg, D., *The Philippines: A Singular and Plural Place*, Boulder, CO, Westview Press, 1990.

Timberman, D., *A Changeless Land: Continuity and Change in Philippines Politics*, New York, M.E. Sharpe, 1991.

Minority-based and advocacy organizations

Alliance of Advocates for Indigenous People's Rights (TABAK), IB Guijo Street, Project 3, Quezon City 1109, Philippines.

Amnesty International, PO Box 286, Sta Mesa Post Office, Sta Mesa 1008, Manila, Philippines; fax 63 2 924 4440.

CBHS Mindanao, PO Box 122, Davao City 9501, Philippines.

Cordillera Peoples' Alliance, PO Box 975, Baguio City 2600, Philippines; tel. 63 74 442 7008, fax 63 74 442 5347.

Ethnic Studies Development Center, PO Box 10125, Main, Quezon City, Philippines.

General Secretariat Lumad Mindanaw (GSLM), PO Box 80905, Davao City 8000, Phlippines; tel. 63 82 7994.

Indigenous Peoples' Research Center, PO Box 332, Davao City 8000, Philippines.

Mindanao Partnership for Human Development, 123 Dongallo Compound, Bishop Hayes Street, Camaman-an, Cagayan de Oro City, Philippines.

Moro People's Resource Center (MPRC), PO Box 9600, Cotabato City, Philippines; tel. 63 21 5756.

National Federation of Indigenous Peoples in the Philippines (KAMP), Room 71, Web-Jet Building, 64 Quezon Avenue, Quezon City, Philippines; tel. 63 2 712 0951, fax 63 2 922 0033.

Philippines Human Rights Information Center, Room 403, FMSC Building, 9 Balette Drive, Manilla, Quezon City, Philippines.

Tribal Cooperative for Rural Development, Calitlitan Aritao, Nueva Vizcaya 3704, Philippines.

Singapore

Land area:	620 sq km
Population:	3.1 million (1995)
Main languages:	English, Mandarin and other Chinese dialects, Malay, Tamil
Main religions:	Buddhism, Christianity, Hinduism, Islam, Sikhism
Main minority groups:	Malays 465,000 (15%), Indians 217,000 (7%), others 62,000 (2%)
Real per capita GDP:	$19,350
UNDP HDI/rank:	0.881 (34)

Virtually surrounded by Malaysia and Indonesia, the Republic of Singapore, whose population is 76 per cent ethnic Chinese, is sometimes referred to as 'a Chinese island in a Malay sea'. Singapore was founded in 1819 by Sir Stamford Raffles. His intent was to open a port under the British flag and circumvent Dutch and Spanish commercial monopolies in the Indonesian and Philippine islands. At the time of its founding, Singapore was inhabited by a small number of Malay and Orang Laut fishing peoples and about thirty Chinese planters and traders. As Singapore grew as a port and trading centre, it attracted an influx of migrants from mainland China. After the Second World War, Singapore joined the Federation of Malaysia, but the inclusion of Singapore's Chinese population upset the delicate ethnic balance in the Federation. In 1965, Singapore became independent.

Singapore is one of the original Asian 'tiger' economies. In less than three generations, it has achieved the status of an industrialized nation. This has been possible because Singapore is the most disciplined society in South-East Asia. The country is a republic with a parliamentary system of government and since independence has been governed by the People's Action Party (PAP). Although elections are fair, the political opposition is weak and not a serious threat to the PAP. The government does not recognize the concept of human rights; rather it talks of 'Asian values' based on community over individual rights.

Singapore has a Presidential Council for Minority Rights to which legislation affecting minority groups is referred. The council has been a success in Singapore because of the government's commitment to maintaining ethnic harmony. This is done through deliberate policies such as compulsory military service for all males, an education system that uses English as the medium of instruction (Malay Chinese, English and Tamil are all official languages), and a housing policy that breaks up ethnic enclaves. The idea has been to create a 'Singapore' identity. Ethnic tolerance is promoted in terms of national survival and identity. Multiculturalism is strongly promoted (along with self-discipline, austerity and respect for authority) as a matter of national identity.

Malays

Ethnic Malays constitute 15 per cent of Singapore's population and are, like the Chinese and the Indians, descendants of immigrants. They or their ancestors came from peninsular Malaya, Sumatra, Java and the other islands of the Indonesian archipelago. Malay identity was couched in religious terms, with Malay being taken almost as a synonym for Muslim, and most Malay organizations taking a religious form. Malays have conspicuously occupied the lower socio-economic scale, mainly due to their low level of educational attainment. In general, Malays do not suffer any significant level of discrimination. However, many feel that they have been left out of the 'economic miracle', and in the last few elections the majority of Malays voted for opposition parties. This has caused the government to launch several programmes especially targeted at improving the educational level of Malays.

Indians

Indians first came to Singapore in the nineteenth and early twentieth centuries. Almost two-thirds of the Indian population are Tamils. The great diversity of the Indian populace was indicated by the census category 'other Indians', who made up a substantial 19 per cent of the group, followed by Malayalis (8 per cent), Punjabis (mostly Sikh) (8 per cent), and Gujaratis (1 per cent). Like the Chinese, most of Singapore's Indians adopted English as a first language. In religion Indians are the most diverse of Singapore's ethnic categories: an estimated 50–60 per cent are Hindu, 20–30 per cent Muslim, 12 per cent Christian, 7 per cent Sikh, and 1 per cent Buddhist. The Indian Muslims tend to intermarry with Malays and are absorbed into the Malay community. Indians are represented at all levels of the occupational hierarchy in numbers roughly proportional to their share of the total population. They do not suffer any significant level of discrimination.

Conclusions and future prospects

Singapore is run as a meritocracy. As such, minorities who achieve a high level of education or technical skills will face few problems. Singapore's large Chinese majority has given its leaders the confidence to uphold minority rights.

Further reading

Hill, M. and Lian, K.F., *The Politics of Nation Building and Citizenship in Singapore*, London, Routledge, 1995.

Somero Heidhues, M. *et al.*, *The Chinese of South-East Asia*, London, MRG Report, 1992.

Tania, L., *Malays in Singapore*, Singapore, Oxford University Press, 1990.

Tremewan, C., *The Political Economy of Social Control in Singapore*, London, Macmillan, 1994.

South Korea

Land area:	99,263 sq km
Population:	45,981,913 (1996)
Main languages:	Korean
Main religions:	Buddhism, Christianity, Taoism, Confucianism, Wonbulgyo, Ch'ondogyo, Islam
Main minority groups:	—
Real per capita GDP:	$9,710
UNDP HDI/rank:	0.886 (29)

The Republic of Korea (ROK) is located in the southern part of the Korean peninsula, which has China to the north and Japan to the south. Korean scholars believe that the earliest Koreans were migrants from Mongolia. Koreans have a long history studded with cultural innovation. The ROK and the Democratic People's Republic of Korea were created in the aftermath of the defeat of Japan in the Second World War (see **North Korea**). Because of confrontation with the North, military rule tended to dominate politics in the South. The two Koreas signed a non-aggression pact in 1991, and the first civilian was elected President of the ROK in 1992.

There is no official religion, although 54 per cent of the population profess religious beliefs; the Buddhist clergy has protested at police intervention in religious affairs. According to officials in both North and South, there are no natural ethnic minorities in the peninsula. Since the division of the peninsula, the ROK has seen significant economic growth, in large measure due to foreign investment, and this has produced significant disparities in the distribution of wealth. Rising labour costs have created a demand for cheaper, immigrant workers, brought in under 'technical training programmes'. This has led to vehement trade union resistance to immigrant workers. Of an official 92,000 foreign workers, more than 59 per cent are illegals. Of 24,552 'trainees' in 1995, 9,366 were Chinese, 4,145 Vietnamese, 3,600 Filipinos, 2,060 Bangladeshis, and there are groups of around 100 each from Nepal, Pakistan, Sri Lanka and Uzbekistan. There may be social conflict and more pressure from the unions, who fear Korean workers will see their rights diminish. Riots, in support of trade union rights and pay increases, shook the country in January 1997, and confirmed this. South Korean conglomerates are also shifting production abroad to cheaper labour countries such as Britain. No further minority rights issues have been identified.[1]

Minority-based and advocacy organizations

Korea Council of Trade Unions (KCTU) [contact point for Korean human rights organizations], Cho Yong-whan, 2nd Floor, Changlim Building, Yoksam-dong 816–3, Kangnam-ku, Seoul, South Korea; tel. 82 2 567 2316, fax 82 2 568 3439.

Korea Human Rights Network, 704 Century 2 B/D 1595–2, Seocho-dong, Seocho-ku, Seoul 139–091, South Korea; tel. 82 2 522 7284, fax 82 2 522 7285.

Taiwan

Land area:	35,981 sq km
Population:	21,151,000 (1994)
Main languages:	Mandarin (official), Taiwanese, Japanese, English
Main religions:	Buddhism, Taoism, I-Kuan Tao, Christianity
Main minority groups:	Han Chinese from mainland 2,961,140 (14%), indigenous peoples (Atayal, Bunun, Tsou, Paiwan and Rukai, Puyuma, Ami, Yami, Saisiyat) 423,020 (2%)
Real per capita GDP:	—
UNDP HDI/rank:	—

Taiwan, officially the Republic of China, is situated in the western Pacific approximately 130 kilometres east of the Chinese mainland, and includes a total of eighty-six islands. Mountainous and upland areas dominate three-quarters of the country and are home to most of the indigenous minorities, who have suffered severe abuse in the past and have made accusations of genocide against the majority population. Taiwan is a constitutional democracy with all the expected rights and safeguards but it has a modern history of authoritarian structures. This is due to former military rule and because of the state of constant military readiness against mainland Chinese threats of invasion. Both Beijing and Taipei agree that Taiwan is a province of China – but both also claim suzerainty over the whole of China.

Taiwan's history has been turbulent. After the Second World War it was conceded by Japan, after fifty years of occupation, to mainland China. In 1949 the communist revolution in China forced the exiled nationalists on to the island. Martial law was proclaimed. The nationalist government claimed to represent all Chinese people at the United Nations. US support for the nationalist government had deteriorated dramatically by 1971, and Taiwan was forced to revoke its claim of representing China. Since then, Taiwan has been obliged to forge greater economic links with mainland China.

There are two groupings of Han Chinese in Taiwan: the majority who came over to the island over centuries and 2,961,140 who came after the split with Beijing post-1949. The latter are viewed differently by the centuries-old residents.

Political, cultural, social and economic freedoms are far greater for the peoples of Taiwan than for those of mainland China. Taiwan's minorities nevertheless face a range of problems, in part produced by the island's massive economic expansion into a world trading power. This has caused rural migration and a 'globalization' of urban culture with major investment over the years by US and Japanese companies. The formation of the Democratic Progressive Party (DPP) in 1986 was a challenge to the ruling Kuomintang Chinese Nationalist Party (KMT). The small but high-profile Labor Party, set up by Taiwanese professional groups on the left in 1987, has in its founding declaration a full policy to restore 'primordial people's rights'.

Indigenous peoples

Taiwan's indigenous peoples are descendants of the earliest inhabitants, who probably came from the Philippines and Malaysia. They are sometimes referred to as 'mountain peoples', a term they consider insulting. They wish to be known as Yuan Chu Min, meaning indigenous or primordial peoples. Taiwan's position on recognition and representation of minorities at the UN is ill-defined. The government ratified the International Convention Concerning the Protection and Integration of Indigenous and Other Tribal and Semi-Tribal Populations in Independent Countries in 1962 and the International Convention on the Elimination of All Forms of Racial Discrimination in 1966. In 1992 a constitutional amendment was passed to upgrade the status of indigenous people. The government does not try to play down problems facing indigenous minorities, and regards them as an important part of Taiwan's identity and as an educational resource for young Taiwanese, as well as an enhancement of the country's appeal to tourists. However, there is a significant loss of cultural identity among minority groups.

For years, the various indigenous tribes were

collectively called *shanpao* ('mountain compatriots'), which term was in the country's constitution. But many tribes wanted it changed to 'primordial' or 'indigenous inhabitants' to assert their historical origins and claims and to remove what they saw as discrimination by the Chinese. Various of the tribal names mean 'human beings', and Ami means 'guests'. They had hoped for improved social status and more legal protection and assistance from the government, so creating improved standards of living. By the end of 1995, amendments introducing the new term had been set in motion, and machinery had been put in place to create a cabinet-level post heading a Department of Aboriginal Affairs. Indigenous peoples increasingly participate in local and national politics, with indigenous people elected to the National Assembly, the Legislative Yuan, and serving in the Taiwan Provincial Assembly. Others are county councillors, magistrates of rural townships and delegates to township councils. More than 2,000 have served in government agencies at various levels, and the number is growing.

Despite such progress, Taiwan's indigenous peoples have suffered severe abuse. The recent drift to the cities may have been driven by economic change for some; but earlier they were largely deprived of their productive lands, which were declared reserves so that Han business owners could log the state-owned forests and mine state-owned mineral resources. In the 1970s there was a forced exodus from the mountains of some 40 per cent of indigenous peoples into city slums as cheap labour and rag-pickers, with a reported 40 per cent of the women forced into prostitution. Urban prostitution involving teenage indigenous girls remains widespread. Men were forced into dangerous deep-sea fishing and mining. Reaction by the indigenous peoples to this oppression surfaced in publications in the 1980s with accusations of genocide. It led to the formation of the Alliance of Taiwan Aborigines. Since the late 1980s the Yami have been running a publicity campaign against government depositing of nuclear waste near their fields. Rukai have been fighting against a reservoir which threatens to flood their lands, to supply the industrial city of Kaohsiung.

Some native traditions are still maintained, such as periodic harvest festivals, which celebrate a rich crop with singing and dancing. Most indigenous peoples have switched to Western attire, although loincloths are still common on Orchid Island. By adopting Han Chinese dietary habits, most indigenous peoples eat a much more varied diet than their forebears did. Animistic and shamanistic beliefs have largely given way to Christianity, as a result of intensive missionary efforts. The educational system is drawing more indigenous young into mainstream Han Chinese culture. However, the overall educational and income levels of Taiwan's indigenous peoples still lag behind those of other Taiwanese, and many face acute social problems such as alcoholism, unemployment and adolescent prostitution. In 1992, the Ministry of the Interior began a six-year 'Living Guidance Plan for Aborigines Residing in Cities' to promote indigenous culture, subsidized medical care, legal advice, educational guidance, employment counselling and loans for setting up businesses. At the same time, the government began improving road links to indigenous peoples' villages. The Aboriginal Administration Section of the Department of Civil Affairs of the Ministry of the Interior, which is responsible for indigenous affairs at the central government level, and an Aborigine Committee provide assistance to indigenous peoples through a number of programmes. There are also private organizations devoted to indigenous peoples' welfare such as World Vision of Taiwan (WVT) and the Taiwan Aborigine Tribal Welfare Promotion Association.

The nine major indigenous tribes in Taiwan are the Atayal, Saisiyat, Bunun, Tsou, Paiwan, Rukai, Puyuma, Ami and Yami. The early plains-dwelling indigenous Pingpu are now thought to be extinct due to assimilation. Growing determination among tribal peoples to assert their identity has led them to define their origins more accurately. In some cases the mountain tribes have been able to maintain their cultural identities by resisting intermarriage with Han Chinese. Each tribe has its own set of indigenous languages. Formosan indigenous languages (called Formosan to avoid confusion with 'Taiwanese', which is the southern Fukienese dialect of Chinese spoken widely in Taiwan) belong to the Austronesian family of languages, to which Malaysian and Hawaiian also belong. There is great diversity among the Formosan indigenous languages. Some scholars believe that Taiwan may have been the original homeland of the vast Austronesian speech community.

Tribal groupings

The largest group and mainly plains dwellers, Ami live in the valleys of the Haulien-Taitung area. Their villages are relatively large, with 200–1,000 people each. The tallest of the indigenous peoples, they can be divided into three main groups based on geography, customs and language: northern Ami, central Ami, (including coastal and Hsiukuluan groups) and southern Ami (including Peinan and Hengchun groups). Ami farm and fish; hunting is now done only for recreation. Ami society is matrilineal and the oldest woman in the extended family is generally the household head. Men exercise authority in village councils of leading men from each village ward, and their sessions are held in men's houses. A rigid authority based on age is enforced.

Atayal are distributed over a large area in northern Taiwan. Their language is divided into the Atayal and Sediq branches, and is apparently not closely related to any other indigenous language. Their main occupations were traditionally farming and hunting with some animal husbandry. Facial tattooing among both men and women for personal adornment and to ward off harm is a special feature of this tribe. Atayal generally live in nuclear families based on the husband's parental home. Leaders of several ritual groups of a community usually constituted the political authority. Atayal society was historically relatively closed and did not readily accept outsiders. The Atayal believe in *utux*, which refers to all kinds of spirits and unnamed supernatural powers, as well as spirits of the dead.

Bunun live in the mountainous regions of central Taiwan and were traditionally hunters. Patrilineal, they have extended family households in small villages. They have been relatively open to outsiders, have a strong music tradition and male and female priests for religious ceremonies and treating illness.

Tsou depend mainly on mountain agriculture, supplemented by hunting, fishing and animal husbandry. The men's meeting hut serves as the religious and political centre. Tsou speak one of three language groups: Tsou, Kanakanabu or Saaroa. Of all Formosan indigenous languages, the Tsou language has the least in common with the others.

Paiwan are divided into the Raval and Butaul tribes, the latter made up of Paumaumaq, Chaoboobol, Parilarilao and Pagarogaro groups. The main occupation of Paiwan and Rukai is agriculture. Paiwan and Rukai kinship is ambilineal. Formerly, inter-class marriage was forbidden. Butaul clans join together to celebrate a major sacrificial rite every five years called *maleveq*. Inheritance is by male primogeniture.

Dependent upon farming supplemented by fishing and hunting, Puyuma have a multilineal kinship system with ritual groups. Family inheritance goes to the eldest daughter; men and woman share kinship equality and commoners may marry children of chiefs. The men's houses are centres for the public activity of the whole village, including tribal education, warrior training and a twice-a-year harvest ceremony.

Yami live almost exclusively on Orchid Island. Culturally Yami are closely related to the inhabitants of the Batan Islands of the Philippines, and the Yami language and Ivatan dialect are mutually intelligible. Yami seems also to be closely related to the Paiwanic language on Taiwan. Fishing is central to the Yami economy. They are the only indigenous Taiwanese to practice silversmithing, and the only tribe never to have practised headhunting. There is no Yami chieftainship.

Saisiyat are numerically the smallest of Taiwan's indigenous tribes. Their language is divided into northern and southern dialect groups. They have been threatened by their Atayal neighbours, who have also influenced their culture. Early Saisiyat practised mobile slash-and-burn mountain cultivation and hunting. Among the first to be influenced by the Han Chinese and to adopt Chinese surnames, the Saisiyat have as their basic living unit the totemic clan linked by geographical and family ties. Several neighbouring settlements might unite to form a village with shared farmland and fishing areas.

Conclusions and future prospects

Taiwanese indigenous peoples' culture and lifestyles have changed because of modernization and oppression. Indigenous languages are still spoken, but native speakers are fewer and the young are more fluent in Mandarin or Taiwanese. Yet, on Orchid Island, for example, Yami is still widely spoken. Bilingual educational efforts there have been successful, and the language may be able to hold its ground. Stories and legends are being successfully published, to stop their loss as oral traditions. This situation, combined with government assistance programmes for cultural development and improved infrastructure to help local indigenous economies, may both help indigenous peoples survive, and, paradoxically, encourage further rural–urban migration. The increased numbers of young going into the Taiwanese further education system may produce a new generation with the skills and financial ability to cherish and try to rebuild indigenous languages and traditions while taking advantage of economic opportunities in the mainstream economy. Links with other first nations movements, such as those in Australia, are growing. Since the late 1980s demands have grown for the restitution of tribal land and land rights. This has been accompanied by increased participation in political activities and elections. Tourism is increasingly an important source of local aboriginal economic regeneration, but the danger of producing 'museum' groups is also a risk. This may be helped or hindered by growing trade collaboration with China and recent relaxations on China's resistance to direct flights between Taiwan and the mainland. The interests of minorities in Taiwan are best served by the development of democratic processes in recent years. However, future relations with China will affect their political movement to guarantee their identity and sustainability. Should relations with China deteriorate, progress for the minorities could be uncertain.[1]

Further reading

Jao-mei, H., 'Indigenous peoples of Taiwan', *Outsider*, MRG newsletter, no. 42, 1995.

US State Department, *Human Rights Report: Indigenous People*, Washington, DC, 1995.

Minority-based and advocacy organizations

Alliance of Taiwan Aborigines, 5th Floor, Cheng-kuong Road, Sec. 2, Yung Ho, Taiwan; tel./fax 886 2 928 6120.

Fishermen Service Center, No. 24–1 Yukang Chung 2nd Road, Chien Chen District, Kaohsiung, Taiwan; tel. 886 7 831 4875, fax 886 7 841 6870.

International Committee for Human Rights in Taiwan, 2nd Floor, 27 Hang-chow South Road, Sec. 1, Taipei, Taiwan.

Thailand

Land area:	512,820 sq km
Population:	61.1 million (1995)
Main languages:	Thai (official), Chinese, Malay, various minority languages with Tibeto-Burman, Mon-Khmer and Miao-Yao roots
Main religions:	Buddhism, Islam, Hinduism, Christianity, animism
Main minority groups:	Chinese 6–7.3 million (est., 10–12%), Malays 1.8 million (est., 3%), Mon, Khmer and highlanders 611,000–1.2 million (est., 1–2%)
Real per capita GDP:	$5,950
UNDP HDI/rank:	0.827 (59)

While still largely agricultural, the economy of the Kingdom of Thailand has expanded rapidly in recent years, earning it the designation of a 'tiger' economy. The population of Thailand, one of the most ethnically homogeneous countries in South-East Asia, is about 85 per cent ethnic Thai. Thais can be differentiated among central Thai (Siamese), Thai-Lao (north-eastern Thai or Thai Eesan), and the much smaller groupings of northern and southern Thai (Chao Pak Thai). All speak one of the Tai family of languages, though speakers can have difficulty communicating with one other, and share other cultural features, such as Theravada Buddhism. Non-Thai minority groups who speak Tai family languages include Shan, Le and Phutai. Central Thais have long dominated Thailand's government and society. Cultural differences among the groups have tended to dissipate with internal migration and the modernization of Thai society.

The ancestors of modern Thais came from southern China to the Chao Phraya river valley in the thirteenth century and established a kingdom at Sukhothai. The kingdoms at Sukhothai and later at Ayutthaya gradually gained control over other Tai areas and engaged in intermittent military struggles with neighbouring states. Following the destruction of Ayutthaya by the Burmese in the eighteenth century, a unified Thai state was established in Bangkok in 1782.

Thais take great pride in the fact that they are the only South-East Asian state never to have been under colonial rule. Nonetheless, Britain and France exerted considerable political and economic pressure on the Thai government in the nineteenth and early twentieth centuries. In 1932 a bloodless coup brought an end to the absolute monarchy and established a constitutional monarchy that continues to the present. Since then the country has been run by numerous governments, most of which were dominated by the military. In 1991, another bloodless military coup toppled an elected civilian government, abolishing the constitution and national assembly. A year later, in May 1992, the middle class combined with students to protest against continued military rule. The military fired on the protesters, creating the potential for a civil war. The King stepped in and forced the departure of the military junta. Although the King has little direct power, he is deeply revered in Thai society as the symbol of national identity and unity. The middle class revolt of 1992 has since led to two democratically elected governments. The assertiveness of the middle class suggests the gradual formation of civil groups in Thai society who will no longer tolerate military interference in politics. Most observers consider the military, discredited by the events of 1992, unlikely to return to politics for some time. With a combative free press and numerous non-governmental organizations, Thailand is among the most open societies in South-East Asia today. In recent decades Thailand has played host to thousands of refugees from Burma: Burmese, Mon, Karen, Shan and others who are fleeing government repression in Burma. These influxes have had no significant impact on Thailand's ethnic and cultural homogeneity.

Thailand's rapid industrialization is uneven, and is mostly concentrated in the region around the capital Bangkok. Rapid economic growth has caused problems such as excessive tourism and environmental degradation. In the long run, this is likely to create problems for those living in rural areas, including minorities. In recent years there have been credible reports that developers, working in tandem with local politicians, have taken land illegally from hill tribespeople for business projects. This should be seen less as an attack on minorities than as a manifestation of political corruption, which is rife in Thai politics.

Chinese

Chinese make up roughly 10–12 per cent of the population of Thailand. Because of a long history of assimilation and the difficulties of definition, precise figures are hard to ascertain. With the exception of a small minority, the majority of the Chinese are Thai-Chinese. There is also a distinct rural Yunnanese Chinese community in northern Thailand. In the nineteenth century, Thailand's Chinese were engaged in commercial activities and as labourers in industry, mines, construction and plantations. Their role was significant in the important rice export trade. In the twentieth century, successive Thai governments sought to counter what was seen as a distinct and influential Chinese community. Assimilation was promoted by the granting of citizenship to Thai-born Chinese and the placing of restrictions on Chinese language education peaked in the 1950s as part of the government's efforts to quell the Communist Party of Thailand, which included many Chinese. The creation of state-owned industries, placed in Thai hands, forced the Chinese community to diversify its economic activities and form alliances with powerful Thais.

The shift in the 1960s and 1970s to an export-oriented economy was to the advantage of Chinese businesses. Today those of Chinese or partial Chinese descent occupy all strata of Thai society, including Thailand's biggest companies outside of the agricultural sphere. More than half live in the Bangkok area and the Chinese population as a whole is largely urbanized. Involvement in the commercial sphere, whether as owners of large businesses or as small shopkeepers, remains predominant. Although traditionally the Chinese have shied away from politics, in the 1980s they became more involved. Some of today's most prominent politicians are Thai-Chinese. The Chinese in Thailand went through a re-Sinification period in the early 1980s. Today, local Chinese newspapers are sold in Bangkok, and there are several private Chinese schools. Of all the minority Chinese communities in South-East Asia, the Chinese in Thailand have assimilated most successfully with the local indigenous population.

Malays

Ethnic Malays comprise about 3 per cent of the population. Their language (Malay), religion (Islam) and culture differentiate them from the Thai majority. They live primarily in the five southernmost provinces, near the border with Malaysia. A small number also live around Bangkok as a result of a deliberate policy during the nineteenth century to move Malays out of the south. Historically, Malays have suffered from low standards of living and of educational attainment. Thais and Thai-Chinese have long dominated the local economy in southern Thailand as well as the political administration. Various Malay separatist movements, such as the United Pattani Freedom Movement, have engaged in low-level insurgency in the south. However, since the restoration of democracy in 1992, guerrilla activities have virtually ceased. The border with Malaysia is now an 'open border' with very lax controls. Bangkok has taken a soft approach to the Muslim areas, relying on economic development to persuade Malays to give up their separatist ambitions. Government policy is now to develop the southern areas within the 'Northern Growth Triangle' of Penang (Malaysia) and Medan (Indonesia).

Mon and Khmer

Mon have been settled in what is now Thailand since the ninth century BCE. Mon were receptive to Hindu and other Indian cultural influences, traces of which persist. After the eighth century, Mon became the primary conduit for Theravada Buddhism in the region. These ancestral Mon were largely absorbed into the Thai population. Many Mon now living in Thailand are descendants of those fleeing Burmese oppression from the seventeenth to the nineteenth centuries. They were welcomed by the Thai kings and settled in central Thailand. Historically they faced few difficulties in Thailand and were culturally compatible with the majority population. Today they are closely integrated into Thai society, speak Thai, and have all but lost cultural practices distinct from those of the Thai. Others are more recent refugees from Burma, who left after the Union of Burma failed to establish a Mon state.

Ethnic Khmer (Cambodians) consist of fewer than 1 per cent of the population. They live primarily in the eastern provinces of Surin and Srisaket along the Cambodian border. Many speak Thai and have intermarried with Thais.

Highlanders

Highlanders (in Thai, *chao khao*, literally 'mountain peoples') are ethnic minorities living in the mountainous areas of western and northern Thailand. Most came to Thailand in the past two hundred years from Burma, China and Laos. In the mid-1980s, their numbers were estimated at 0.5 million. As many as twenty different hill tribes may exist in Thailand, and include the Karen, Akha, Lisu, Lahu and Meo (Hmong). These groups largely continue to live as they have in the past and remain among the poorest of Thailand's populations. Their customs, religious beliefs and dress are all distinct from one another. Traditional crops include rice, corn and opium. A large influx of tourists to the Chiang Mai region since the late 1980s has brought both more money and job opportunities to the area but has also had an intrusive impact on cultural practices.

Land expansion by the Thai majority is another threat to the highlander populations. Karen number more than 250,000 and are by far the largest highland group. Many are refugees from the Karen independence struggle in Burma, which has continued since the late 1940s. Most are animist, but there is a large, well-educated Christian minority. The Karen language has its own script, modified from Burmese script, and a considerable body of written material.

Conclusions and future prospects

Thailand's small ethnic minority population exists at both ends of the country's socio-economic scale. Ethnic Chinese play a crucial role in the country's economic and urban life. At the opposite end are the highland people, who struggle to survive economically and culturally. Whether their standard of living can be raised without destroying their culture is an issue that Thailand should address. The Thai government has, by and large, respected minority rights, as long as the minority groups do not challenge Thai sovereignty or security. Since 1992 many new NGOs, mainly concerned with the environment, have been established in rural areas. These groups have a positive effect on minorities as they usually work with local peoples. Minority groups are unlikely to suffer significant discrimination as long as the civilian government is in place.

Further reading

McKinnon, J. and Bhruksasri, W., *Highlanders of Thailand*, Singapore, Oxford University Press, 1986.

Somers Heidhues, M. *et al.*,*The Chinese of South-East Asia*, London, MRG Report, 1992.

Minority-based and advocacy organizations

Asia Indigenous Peoples' Pact, PO Box 48, PO Klong Chan, Bangkok 10240, Thailand; tel./fax 66 2 918 0241.

Asian Cultural Forum on Development (ACFOD), PO Box 26, Bungthonglang, Bangkok 10242, Thailand; tel. 66 2 377 9357, fax 66 2 374 0464.

Child Rights/ASIANET, Faculty of Law, Chulalongkorn University, Phyathai Road, Bangkok 10330, Thailand; tel. 66 2 218 2065, fax 66 2 215 3604.

Forum Asia, 109 Suthisarnwinichai Road, Samsennok, Huaykwang, Bangkok 10310, Thailand; tel. 66 2 276 9846, fax 66 2 276 2183, e-mail: chalida@mozart.inet.co.th.

Vietnam

Land area:	329,650 sq km
Population:	75.5 million (1995)
Main languages:	Vietnamese, Hoa (Chinese), Khmer, Tai, Hmong
Main religions:	Buddhism, Roman Catholicism, indigenous syncretic religions, animism
Main minority groups:	highlanders (Tay, Tai, Muong, Dao and others) 7.5 million (est., 10%), Chinese (Hoa) and Khmer less than 1 million (< 1.3%)
Real per capita GDP:	$1,040
UNDP HDI/rank:	0.523 (121)

The 1989 government census found that ethnic Vietnamese (Kinh) form 87 per cent of the population of the Socialist Republic of Vietnam, the remaining 13 per cent consisting of ethnic minorities. Scholars once thought that the Vietnamese migrated initially from China. But similarities in the Vietnamese and Muong languages indicate instead that the Kinh formed a branch of the Muong people who were influenced by one thousand years of Han Chinese rule and culture. Traditionally, Vietnamese are lowlanders who in rural areas engage in intensive irrigated-rice cultivation and fishing. The Vietnamese population has always been heavily concentrated in the Red river and Mekong deltas, and the long coastal strip that connects the two. Although the state is officially atheist, Vietnam's population consists of a large Buddhist (Mahayana) majority and a small but significant Catholic minority, particularly in the south. And despite some social dissimilarities between northerners and southerners, the Vietnamese are ethnically and culturally homogeneous. They overwhelmingly control the country's political, military and economic life.

Chinese dominated the region from the first century BCE until the tenth century CE, and left an indelible mark on Vietnamese culture, language and society. Much of Vietnamese history is an account of expansion from the Red river delta to the Mekong delta, an advance not completed until the late eighteenth century. Fighting with the kingdom of Champa, which occupied what is now central Vietnam, continued for nine hundred years until the Chams, a Malay-Polynesian people, were subjugated in the late seventeenth century. Following the defeat of Champa, the Vietnamese pursued military campaigns against the kingdom of the Khmer (Cambodia) in the Mekong delta, including what is now Ho Chi Minh City. While the defeat of the Champa brought a virtual end to a distinct Cham society in Vietnam, ethnic Khmer retain an important presence in the delta area.

The expansion of Vietnam led to greater regionalism in politics. This resulted in the division of the country at roughly the 18th parallel (the line that divided North from South Vietnam from 1954 to 1976). This division continued from 1620 until 1802 when the southern emperor Gia Long, with the aid of the French, reunified the country. Sixty years later, the French began to wrest political control from the Vietnamese. The present borders of Vietnam were defined by French military action between 1858 and 1883. Except for a period of Japanese occupation during the Second World War, French colonial rule continued until defeated at Dien Bien Phu in 1954. Vietnam suffered enormous devastation and loss of life during the three Indochina wars. The first, lasting from the late 1940s until 1954, ended with independence from the French. The country was then divided into the Republic of Vietnam (South) and the Democratic Republic of Vietnam (North). During the American phase of the second Indochinese war, which lasted from the mid-1960s until the Paris Peace Accords of 1973, the country's infrastructure was virtually destroyed. The victory of North over South Vietnam in 1975 reunified the country. The third Indochinese war saw Vietnam invade Cambodia in 1978 and the Chinese invade northern Vietnam the following year. These events caused the massive departure of ethnic Chinese 'boat people' in the 1980s.

Despite considerable economic gains in recent years, the country as a whole remains one of Asia's poorest. The move towards a free market in the late 1980s was not matched by greater political freedom. The Communist Party of Vietnam (CPV) does not tolerate dissent. Freedom of movement, expression and association remain tightly constricted.

Vietnam's minorities

Unlike the largely homogeneous Vietnamese, the ethnic minorities of Vietnam consist of widely diverse peoples, occupying two-thirds of the national territory. Forty-four minority groups have been identified. Most belong to the largest groups: highlanders (Tai, Tay, Muong and others), Chinese (Hoa) and Khmer. Of these, eleven have scripts, using Latinized, Arabic or Pali characters. Some groups, such as the Khmer now living in the south-central highlands, are considered indigenous to their areas, though some of these were strongly influenced by outside Indian and Indonesian cultures. Other groups, such as the Tai, who arrived around the fifth century, emigrated from China or Laos. Most live in the highlands, though two major groups, Khmer and Cham, as well as the largely urban Chinese, live in lowland areas.

During the pre-colonial period, ethnic minorities living in the highland areas maintained autonomy from the Vietnamese state, which did not consider them a threat. However, the highland population in both the north and the south was economically exploited by the Vietnamese. During the colonial period, the highland areas were targets of French missionary education and commercial activities. The French played the Vietnamese and ethnic minorities off against one another, sometimes supporting Vietnamese settlement in highland areas, at other times prohibiting such settlement and encouraging local administration by highlanders.

Highlander reaction to the French was also mixed. Because of the economic exploitation there were a number of revolts, including a revolt by the Jarai that lasted until the late 1930s. At the same time, many hill tribe populations supported the French for the protection they gave them from the Vietnamese. 'Montagnards' especially in the south, fought alongside French and, later, US forces during successive Indochinese wars. They suffered tremendously during the fighting and have continued to do so since the communist victory in 1975. While the economy of Vietnam has grown rapidly in recent years, the areas in which ethnic minorities predominate have benefited the least, and for the most part they remain the poorest people in Vietnam. Only the Chinese population in the urban areas of southern Vietnam has benefited somewhat from Vietnam's more open economy.

Highlanders

Highlanders represent approximately 10 per cent of the population of Vietnam and inhabit the mountainous areas beyond the Red river delta in the north and the central highlands in the south. Some groups consist of significant subgroups. The South Vietnamese government sought to incorporate highlanders into Vietnamese society by providing citizenship and education, as well as by heavy-handedly imposing Vietnamese laws and administration on the highlander population. Highlander cooperation with US forces during the second Indochinese war reflected their distrust of both the South Vietnamese government and the insurgent Viet Cong, but did little to gain highlanders the greater autonomy they sought. The highlands of northern Vietnam are inhabited primarily by speakers of the Austro-Asian family of languages, such as Tay, Tai (Thai) and Muong. Tai, for instance, are differentiated as Black Tai, White Tai and Red Tai, according to the distinctive clothing worn by the women of respective groups. Tai have a complex social and political organization, a valley-based principality called a *muong*, that goes beyond the village level. Because of the great distances to markets, subsistence farming is the norm. Highlanders in the north are closer culturally to the lowland Vietnamese than those in the south, though relations between the two were historically no better than in the south.

The current Vietnamese government has adopted

a dual but often contradictory policy towards the highlander population. One objective is to respect the essential rights and customs of each minority. At the same time the government has sought to overcome what it views as backward elements and to make the lifestyles of the minorities conform more with those of the majority. Highland peoples are not fully trusted by the communist authorities. Protestants in the highlands have been subject to arrest or confiscation of property for preaching, distributing religious materials or holding house church services.

Chinese (Hoa)

Prior to 1975, Chinese in South Vietnam were concentrated in urban areas and largely engaged in commercial activities. In the late 1950s the government imposed a series of decrees that sought to weaken their economic predominance. These laws forced Chinese to take Vietnamese citizenship and prevented non-citizens from engaging in certain occupations. The Vietnamese language became required in Chinese high schools. In effect, however, the citizenship provisions actually provided the Chinese with greater access to the Vietnamese economy. Bolstered by US foreign aid during the war, the economic activities of the Chinese community thrived and expanded until the North's victory in 1975. Chinese in the North played a very different societal role to those in the South. Most lived in Quang Ninh province bordering on China and were mainly engaged in fishing, forestry and crafts. Those in the urban areas were primarily workers and technicians.

In the late 1970s the Socialist Republic of Vietnam took increasingly drastic action to transform the capitalist economy of the south into a socialist one, and Chinese were disproportionately affected. The creation of, and threatened transfer of people to, New Economic Zones led to the first wave of 'boat people', primarily from the south, beginning in April 1978. The short but bloody border war with China a year later resulted in a deliberate policy to encourage the departure of ethnic Chinese from Vietnam. In 1978–9, some 450,000 ethnic Chinese left Vietnam or were expelled across the land border with China. The decline of the Chinese population in Vietnam continued throughout the 1980s. The recent liberalization of the economy and renewed efforts to integrate Chinese into society has added new vitality to the small Chinese community. The number of ethnic Chinese leaving Vietnam by the mid-1990s was negligible, due to a strict policy of not resettling Vietnamese refugees by Western governments, who regard them as economic refugees. The majority of ethnic Chinese today live in the south and still suffer from low-level discrimination, mainly due to fear that they might dominate the economy again.

Khmer

Khmer of the Mekong delta region are ethnically and culturally close to the Khmer of Cambodia. They are the remnants of the society that existed prior to the take-over of the Mekong delta by the Vietnamese in the eighteenth century. The Mekong delta is among the poorest regions of Vietnam. Although afforded equal protection under the law, in practice the Khmer minority are treated by the majority population as second class citizens in day-to-day life. Many have moved to Cambodia in recent years in search of better employment opportunities.

Conclusions and future prospects

Although the rights of minorities are enshrined in the constitution, it is the policy of the ruling CPV to assimilate all minorities into mainstream Vietnamese culture. While ethnic minorities are represented in the government at all levels, they are under the strict control of the CPV. Unresolved issues that will directly affect minorities include the status of landownership in highland areas, the continued and in some instances increasing influx of ethnic Vietnamese into minority areas, and the migration of minority people to urban areas for economic reasons.

Further reading

Amer, R., *China, Vietnam and the Chinese Minority in Vietnam*, Uppsala, Sweden, Uppsala University, 1993.

Dournes, J., *Minorities of Central Vietnam*, London, MRG report, 1980.

Pollock, A., *Vietnam: Conflict and Change in Indochina*, Melbourne, Oxford University Press, 1995.

Notes

Contributions to this section are as follows. James Chin and David Hawk: regional introduction to South-East Asia, and entries on Brunei, Cambodia, East Timor, Indonesia, Laos, Malaysia, the Philippines, Singapore, Thailand, Vietnam; Peter D. O'Neill: regional introduction to East Asia, and entries on China and Tibet, Hong Kong, Japan, Macau, Mongolia, North Korea, South Korea, Taiwan.

The East Asian studies have drawn widely and gratefully on a large number of authors, institutions, journals, governmental, diplomatic and media sources. It has not been possible to refer to them all in the further reading and notes sections, but exemplary sources would include, for example, Thomas Heberer's work on China. Thanks are also due for additional research and editing to Uma Ram Nath, Gillian Arrindell, John Bonning, James Crombie and Mark Soole. The author, Peter D. O'Neill, has asserted his moral rights.

Introduction

1 Burma has geographical and cultural affinities with both South Asia and South-East Asia and is included in the former part of this *Directory*.

China and Tibet

1 Includes Inner Mongolia and Tibet. The Office of His Holiness the Dalai Lama (OHHDL) disputes the definition of the land area of Tibet, classified by China as the Tibet Autonomous Region (TAR). The OHHDL definition is based on ethnographic and historical residence. This has implications for population figures.

2 Includes 10.9–13.5 million inhabitants (1992–5 figures) of ethnographic Tibet, including the Tibet Autonomous Region and Qingai; 13.5 million is the OHHDL figure.

3 Ethnic groups in the Tibet Autonomous Region (TAR): Upa 1.5 million, Khampa 90,000 (0.7%), Amdo 50,000 (0.4%). The Chinese government also includes the following minorities: Hui, Moinba, Lhoba, Deng, Sharpa.

4 *The Republic of China Yearbook 1994*, Taipei, Taiwan Government Information Office, 1994.

5 Israeli, R., *Islam in China: A Critical Bibliography*, Westport, CT, Greenwood Press, 1994.

6 Sources of information used for this account include: *The Republic of China Yearbook 1994*, Taipei, Taiwan Government Information Office, 1994; World Bank, *Annual Report 1994*, Washington, DC, 1994; Jahan, R. (ed.), *Women in Asia*, London, MRG report, 1980, 1982; *Fifty-Six Nationalities*, Beijing, New Star Publishers, 1992; *The Minority Nationalities*, Beijing, New Star Publishers, 1992; *China 1995*, Beijing, New Star Publishers, 1995; Amnesty International, *China, Six Years after Tiananmen*, London, 1995; Christian Aid, *The Invisible Woman: A Report for the UN Conference on Women, Beijing*, London, 1995; Yasuko, H. and Seiko, K., *Population Policy and Vital Statistics in China*, Tokyo, Institute of Developing Economies, 1991.

7 Additional sources of information used for the discussion of Tibet include: *Tibet: Its Ownership and Human Rights Situation*, Beijing, Information Office of the People's Republic of China, 1992; Jia, S., *Freedom of Religious Belief*, About Tibet No. 8, Beijing, New Star Publishers, 1991; *Changes of Population in Tibet*, Beijing, Intercontinental Press, 1995; Amnesty International, *People's Republic of China: Persistent Human Rights Violations in Tibet*, London, 1995; International Campaign for Tibet, *Nuclear Tibet: Nuclear Weapons and Nuclear Waste on the Tibetan Plateau*, Washington, DC, n.d.; Saunders, H.H. *et al.*, *Tibet: Issues for Americans*, New York, National Committee on US–China Relations, 1992.

Japan

1 Sources of information used for this account include: Hongkong & Shanghai Banking Corporation and Barclays Bank Economics Department, *Japan Business Profile*, Hong Kong and London, 1994; The Economist, *Japan: The Economist Guide*, London, 1987; Organization for Economic Cooperation and Development, *Japan*, Paris, 1994.

Macau

1 As a result of Portugal offering passport rights.

2 Sources of information used for this account include: Roberts, E.V., Bradshaw, P. and Sum, N.L., *Historical Dictionary of Hong Kong and Macau*, Maryland, Scarecrow Press, 1993; Census and Statistics Department, *XIII Population Census*, Macau, 1993.

Mongolia

1 More recent minority population data are unavailable.

2 Sources of information used for this account include: Becker, J., *The Lost Country: Mongolia Revealed*, London, Hodder & Stoughton, 1992; Sanders, A.J.K., *The People's Republic of Mongolia*, London and New York, Oxford University Press, 1968; Nordby, J., *Mongolia*, World Bibliographical Series, Oxford, Clio Press, 1993; Academy of Sciences of the MPR, *Information Mongolia*, Oxford, Pergamon Press, 1990.

North Korea

1 Sources of information used for this account include: Eberstadt, N., *Korea: Approaches to Reunification*, Armonk, NY, and London, National Bureau of Asian Research and M.E. Sharpe, n.d.; OECD, *Economic Survey, Korea 1993–1994*, Paris, 1994; *Financial Times*, (London) 12/12/1995 and 14/12/1995; Diplomatic Missions of the DPRK in New Delhi and London (c/o International Maritime Organisation).

South Korea

1 Sources of information used for this account include: OECD, *Economic Survey, Korea 1993–1994*, Paris, 1994; Lee, C.H., *The Economic Transformation of South Korea*, Paris, OECD, 1995; Yonhap News Agency, *Korea Annual*, 32nd annual edition, Seoul, 1995; *Report on Submission by the ROK to the UN Committee on Economic, Social and Cultural Rights in South Korea: NGOs' Initial Report under Articles 16 and 17 of the International Covenant on Economic, Social and Cultural Rights*, Seoul, Korean Council of Trades Unions and other Non-Governmental Organizations, Center for Human Rights and International Solidarity, 1994; 'Status of foreign workers in Korea', *Korea Focus*, vol. 3, no. 4, pp. 70–9, Seoul, Korea Foundation, 1995.

Taiwan

1 Sources of information used for this account include: *Bibliography of Anthropological Works Published in Taiwan, 1945–82* (Chinese and English entries), Taipei, Ethnological Society of China and Resource Center for Chinese Studies, 1983; Ministry of Interior, Republic of China, *Living Guidance Plan for Aborigines Residing in Cities* (in Chinese), Taipei, 1992; Institute of Ethnology, Academia Sinca, *Studies on Taiwan Plains Aborigines: A Classified Bibliography* (Chinese and English entries), Taipei, 1988; *Republic of China Yearbook 1994*, Taipei, Government Information Office, 1994; and issues of *Free China Review*.

OCEANIA

John Connell

The islands and seas of Oceania, ranging from the vast, thinly populated continent of Australia to the tiny atolls of Micronesia and Polynesia, cover more than a third of the globe but have a population of just 25 million. Despite its small population, Oceania is exceptionally diverse in language, culture and ethnicity. A quarter of the languages on the planet are spoken in the region, and language diversity reflects geographical and cultural diversity, especially in New Guinea. New Zealand (Aotearoa) and many of the smaller islands of Micronesia and Polynesia were some of the last areas of the world to be settled; both the colonial period and decolonization were late arriving here, and a number of states remain politically dependent on colonial powers. Despite its recency, colonial contact has had a powerful impact in most parts of the region, resulting in the initial decline of indigenous populations in some areas, the disappearance of some languages and cultures, the imposition of new languages, institutional structures (including legal and political systems) and economic systems, and the migration of white settlers into the larger states. Christian missionaries have transformed belief systems, created new divisions – important in several small island states – and emphasized old differences. In the twentieth century new migration movements, including Indian labour into Fiji and postwar refugees into Australia, have transformed demographic structures, while rural–urban migration in many states and international migration from the smaller states have influenced concepts of identity, nationality and sovereignty and produced dependent economic development.

There are four conventional social divisions of Oceania. Australia is largely a nation apart, historically occupied mainly by an indigenous Aboriginal population. Aborigines had a primarily hunting and gathering economy and forms of social organization very different from those elsewhere. The largest and most complex region is Melanesia, extending from West Papua (Irian Jaya; the western half of the island of New Guinea, and a province of Indonesia) to Fiji, which shares many affinities with Polynesia. Melanesia is characterized by extreme diversity of languages, cultures and economic systems. Social systems are small scale and there is intense competition for local leadership. Colonial contact was later here than elsewhere, as recent as the postwar years in parts of highland New Guinea, hence indigenous cultures and belief systems play a more important part in everyday life. The regions of Micronesia and Polynesia are mainly composed of much smaller islands. Although the islands of Micronesia are small and resource-poor, colonial contact has been significant, especially in the Northern Mariana Islands where the indigenous Chamorro population have been reduced to a minority and are currently endeavouring to retain and restore cultural and economic identity. Social and political organization is mainly based on hierarchical, hereditary systems. Polynesia covers a vast area. Only in Hawai'i and New Zealand are populations large, but, in the first case especially, Polynesians have become a minority in their homelands. Social organization is elaborate, often formal and hierarchical, with hereditary leadership highly important; in some Polynesian states royalty remains important and social stratification is rigid. Despite various forms of modernity – from Christianity to nuclear testing – these historical social and geographical divisions retain significance in contemporary Oceania.

History

Oceania was the last part of the world to be discovered, colonized and decolonized. Only in Vanuatu (New Hebrides) was there a violent transition to independence, in 1980. More difficult political problems have arisen in the 'settler colonies' of Australia, New Zealand and New Caledonia (where colonization reduced the indigenous population to a minority), and in Guam, West Papua and Fiji, where more recent migration has had a similar effect.

By 1906 the Western powers (the UK, the USA, Germany, the Netherlands, Spain and France) had

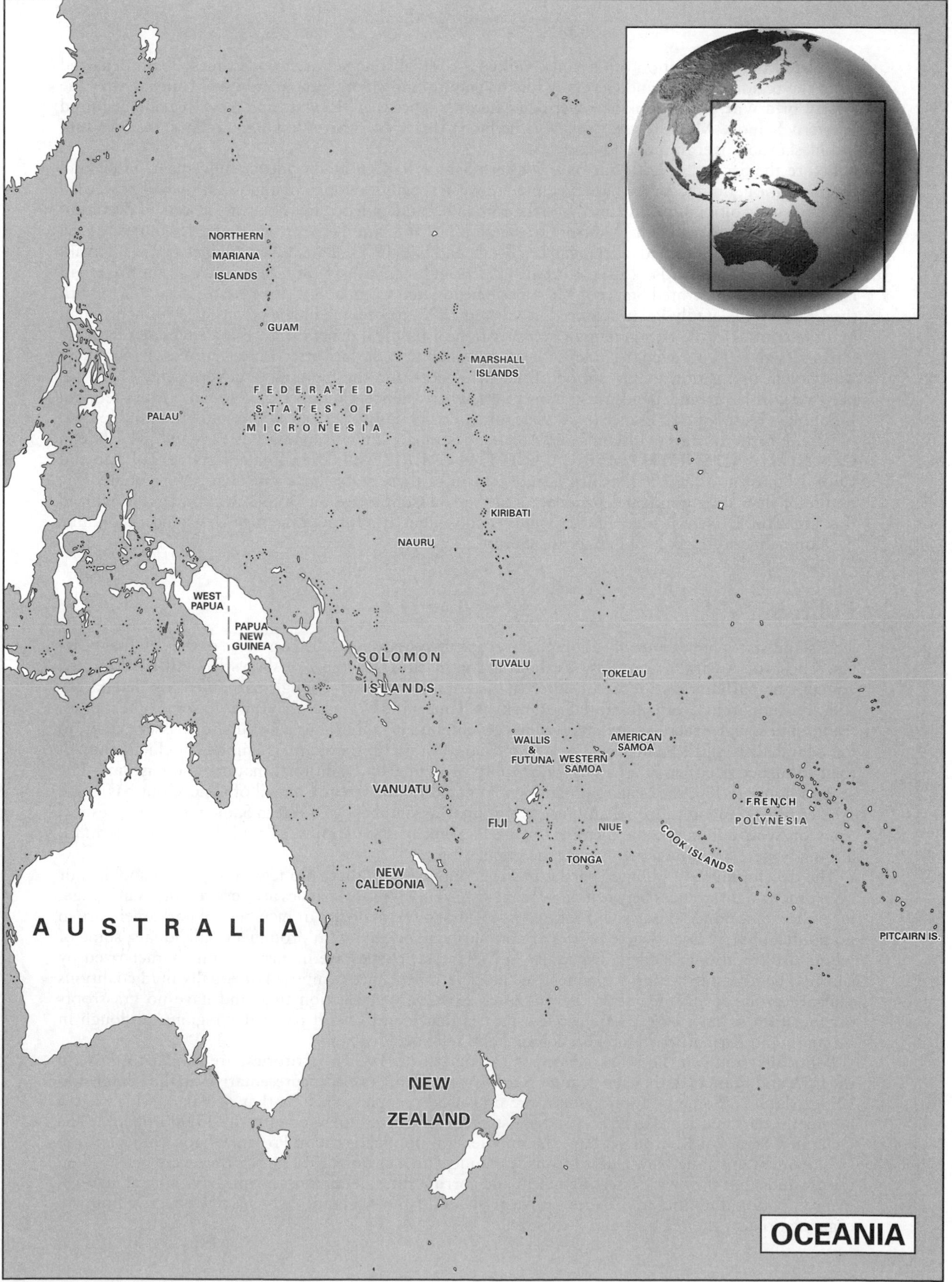
NORTHERN MARIANA ISLANDS
GUAM
MARSHALL ISLANDS
FEDERATED STATES OF MICRONESIA
PALAU
KIRIBATI
NAURU
WEST PAPUA
PAPUA NEW GUINEA
SOLOMON ISLANDS
TUVALU
TOKELAU
WALLIS & FUTUNA
AMERICAN SAMOA
WESTERN SAMOA
VANUATU
FIJI
NIUE
FRENCH POLYNESIA
COOK ISLANDS
TONGA
NEW CALEDONIA
AUSTRALIA
PITCAIRN IS.
NEW ZEALAND
OCEANIA

completed the colonization of Oceania. Colonial control changed at various times: Spain departed from the region in 1906 and Germany lost its empire (mostly in Samoa and New Guinea) after the First World War. Japan took over German Micronesia between the wars and New Zealand acquired Western Samoa. More recently, the Netherlands departed from West Papua Jaya in 1962 and Indonesia took over in the following year.

Before the Second World War only Western Samoa had an independence movement. Elsewhere fragmentation, limited economic development, weak social development and isolation had prevented challenges to colonialism. In 1962 Western Samoa became independent, but the process of decolonization was slow. Nauru emerged from trusteeship in 1968, and between 1970 and 1980 most of the remaining countries gained independence: Tonga and Fiji (1970), Papua New Guinea (1975), Tuvalu and the Solomon Islands (1978), Kiribati (1979) and Vanuatu (1980). Subsequently the Marshall Islands and the Federated States of Micronesia negotiated Compacts of Free Association (CFA) with the USA, and belatedly Palau achieved its CFA in 1993, to become independent in 1994. More than half the entities in the region remain in a situation of political dependence. France retained its three territories and discouraged the independence movements in the larger territories. In West Papua there was violent opposition to any notion of independence from the Indonesian government. There has been very little pro-independence sentiment elsewhere, hence a number of colonial powers remain: Indonesia (West Papua), France (New Caledonia, French Polynesia and Wallis and Futuna), the USA (Guam, Northern Mariana Islands and American Samoa), Chile (Rapanui/Easter Island: see **Chile** in **CENTRAL AND SOUTH AMERICA AND THE CARIBBEAN**), New Zealand (Niue, Tokelau and Cook Islands) and the UK (Pitcairn Islands). Most of these states have satisfactorily negotiated the nature of their own political dependence and the UN Committee on Decolonization has recognized this situation. Dissent is more likely to involve the extent and form of financial assistance, economic development and the role of indigenous culture.

Politics

The island states have generally adopted government systems modelled on those of the colonial powers. Those of Australia and New Zealand are even closer to the British system. All have elected councils or parliaments, but with different electoral situations. Though parliamentary democracy prevails, monarchs exert substantial authority in Tonga and Wallis and Futuna. In some other states, traditional social structures are involved in contemporary politics, but generally to a lesser extent. In the Marshall Islands, Palau, the Cook Islands and Vanuatu, there are assemblies of chiefs, though their influence is either in an advisory capacity or limited to traditional matters and customs. The second house in Fiji, the Senate, is mainly nominated by the Great Council of Chiefs, but has much greater power and authority than other 'traditional' assemblies. In Western Samoa, there are restrictions on who might become members of parliament; members must be traditional chiefs (*matai*), although these are now a majority of the population.

The development of political parties has been limited, and there are few, if any, philosophical or even practical differences between those that exist. Many political parties are very recent, as in Tonga, where the first political party was formed in 1994 and the majority of members of parliament are in no political party. Everywhere parties are primarily associated with prominent individuals, some of whom are traditional leaders. Especially in Melanesia, parties are numerous and characterized by shifting membership within parliament, while governments are composed of equally fluid coalitions that are prone to disintegration. Parties often exist only at election time and have no grassroots organization or members. There are few parties that identify with particular regions, although in Vanuatu and Kiribati parties reflect colonial and religious divisions.

Political systems in the US-associated states, and in the French territories, are similar to those in the USA and France. In the French and US territories, islanders elect representatives in the French and US legislatures. Some political systems are unusually complex, such as that of Palau, which has a bicameral national legislature and sixteen state governments for a country of 15,000 people. The Federated States of Micronesia have the only federal political system. Provincial governments were most evident in Papua New Guinea from after independence until 1995, when they were removed on the grounds that they were often inefficient and corrupt. In general, most people have no real involvement in national politics and, except in Australia and New Zealand, there are few effective political organizations at the regional and local level.

Political systems are still in transition in most places, as parties emerge and fragment, and dependent states seek out new relationships with colonial powers. Political cultures are usually personalized, involve elements of tradition and regionalism, where loyalties to social group and region override national interests, and have involved corruption in several contexts. There are growing challenges to more hierarchical political systems in both Micronesia and Polynesia. Classes have scarcely emerged in the island Pacific, and are of no significance in politics. There are few trade unions; those that exist tend to represent better paid urban workers and play little part in politics. Democracy is often qualified by ethnicity; the only coups and military government in the region (in Fiji) have been largely a result of ethnic divisions. Ethnicity has posed problems where a particular ethnic category claims sovereignty within a nation or, while not claiming full sovereignty, claims a higher degree of legitimacy. Historically this was true of white Australians and New Zealand Pakeha, but increasingly indigenous people in those countries, and also in Hawai'i (see **USA** in **NORTH AMERICA**), Fiji, Guam and New Caledonia have sought to reverse that situation and claim exclusive, or considerable, sovereignty based on the legitimacy of prior occupation.

Ethnicity

Ethnicity remains of exceptional importance in Oceania, at different scales and in different ways. It is particularly significant in the 'settler colonies' where ethnic variations were, and are, significant in social, economic and geographical terms. Ethnic divisions are also important in those Melanesian states where there are many languages, and where the nations exhibit limited national unity, as they are in a very real sense composed of minorities, rather than particular minorities being dominated by others at the national or regional level. In several cases certain ethnic categories have disproportionate power relative to their numbers because of fortuitous location near what is now the capital.

A number of island states have considerable linguistic and cultural uniformity, although in the geographically fragmented states there are greater cultural divisions. Some states make constitutional provision for political representation by ethnic category; in Fiji there are special provisions for Rotumans and Indians which, in the latter case, are discriminatory. The most critical ethnic division in the Pacific is in Fiji, between the indigenous Fijian population and Indo-Fijians, who are descendants of migrants at the start of the century (brought in by the British colonial administration to work in sugar plantations). Although the Fiji constitution, established for independence in 1970, gave both special preferences to Fijians and was designed to ensure some voting across ethnic groups, it was ultimately unable to prevent ethnic polarization becoming critical in the wake of the Fiji Labour Party gaining power in the 1987 elections. Two coups followed, more strident ethnic nationalism ensued and the new 1990 constitution guaranteed the political dominance of Fijians. Ethnic divisions in New Caledonia are also of political importance, with a high proportion (more than three-quarters) of the indigenous Melanesian (Kanak) population in favour of independence, and almost all other residents (mainly whites and Polynesians) in support of the French territory. A similar situation exists in West Papua, though the extent to which Melanesians favour independence – or other constitutional changes – or are discriminated against in particular contexts is difficult to ascertain. West Papua remains under rigid Indonesian control indigenous participation in its government is nominal and nationalist sentiment can only be expressed by guerrilla activity, for which retribution has been violent. In Australia and New Zealand, indigenous minorities have been marginalized and displaced, though in both of these states there is now progress towards a much greater degree of self-determination. Here, as elsewhere, nationalism and ethnicity are closely linked to land issues.

Throughout Oceania there is a powerful emotional (and material) attachment to land; land tenure holds social, political and economic importance; land is central to feelings of security, even for those who have long migrated from their ancestral homes, and is crucial to traditional political power. Alienation and threats of alienation have created unrest and stimulated nationalist and independence movements. Land issues remain of contemporary concern. Nauru gained compensation from Australia after launching legal proceedings in the International Court of Justice for the loss of land and royalties. In Guam, the indigenous Chamorro population voted in favour of the Guam Commonwealth Act in 1982 largely out of concern at losing control of more land to outsiders. In Papua New Guinea disputes over land compensation have resulted in violent confrontations between landowners and governments in various places.

The colonization of Oceania took little account of regional and ethnic diversity, hence decolonization stimulated nationalism and regionalism and attempts to achieve new divisions; the dismantling of the UN Trust Territory of the Pacific Islands and the secession of Polynesian Tuvalu from Micronesian Kiribati have been two successful examples. Attempts at secession have otherwise failed, typified by the ongoing seven-year rebellion in Bougainville; elsewhere there have been more fragmentary attempts at secession in the western Solomon Islands, northern Vanuatu, Rotuma (from Fiji) and elsewhere. Most states remain characterized by some degree of ethnic and regional diversity and uneven development. There are also political divisions within ethnic groups based on cultural, linguistic or regional divisions.

In some states ethnicity is influential in the structure of political parties and political alignments. This is especially so in Fiji where the minority Indian population is associated with the National Federation Party (or the Fiji Labour Party) and the Fijian population with the Soqosoqo ni Vakavulewa ni Taukei – (or Fijian Political Party) – a situation indicative of broader divisions between the two ethnic groups. In New Caledonia the pro-independence parties, most of which are involved in the Front de Libération Nationale Kanak et Socialiste, are primarily associated with Melanesians; the white population, Polynesians and Asians mainly support the anti-independence Rassemblement pour la Calédonie dans la République. Other ethnic divisions are usually less acute and political parties less structured.

Religion has often emphasized more traditional social divisions, especially in Kiribati and Vanuatu, where there are acute religious rivalries and the political parties follow these divisions. Freedom of religious expression exists virtually throughout Oceania. However, Christian missionary activities have been hampered inWest Papua, and Papua New Guinea has sought to limit the number of missions operating in the country.

Gender

In Melanesia especially, and to a lesser extent in much of Micronesia, women are disadvantaged as they are the primary agriculturalists, and subsistence agriculture continues to be important, whilst the demographic transition towards lower fertility levels has barely begun. In Polynesia men are the agriculturalists. Throughout Oceania women may contest elections and vote, though the latter right was only gained in Western Samoa in 1990. Only exceptionally, outside Australia and New Zealand, are women elected to political office, at local or national level, and they are discouraged in some countries. There are active women's organizations in much of the region. At times of political and economic crisis, such as following the Fijian coups and in contemporary Bougainville, women's rights have been ignored: they have lost jobs, been victimized and experienced various forms of violence. Sexual and physical abuse of women has increased since independence, especially in Melanesia, and notably Papua New Guinea, where domestic violence is unusually prevalent; cultural values discourage discussion of these issues and patriarchal legal and police systems prevent prosecutions. Domestic violence also exists at high levels among Aborigines and Maoris.

Conclusions and outlook

Most countries in the region are extremely small, remote and often fragmented, with limited prospects for economic development; they are heavily dependent on aid, especially where they remain politically dependent, and are politically fragile. In the past decade they have experienced political and constitutional crises, growing corruption, poverty and environmental degradation. Women's status has worsened. Colonies and colonialism remain, notably in French Polynesia, where French nuclear testing resumed from mid-1995 to early 1996. Few states have military forces, though there has been military violence in West Papua, Papua New Guinea and Fiji. However, there is a high degree of freedom of expression and movement, and the almost complete absence of political prisoners. Children are not exploited and work only in some Melanesian societies. There have been recent attempts to assert indigenous identity, as much in the large nations as in 'colonial' remnants, from Tahiti to West Papua and Bougainville.

There are various minority situations, ranging from the Melanesian states, which are effectively composed of many minorities, to Australia, where indigenous Aborigines represent little more than 1 per cent of the population. In the past few years the position and rights of indigenous people have changed significantly in many states, including Australia, New Zealand and Fiji, in terms of both land rights and historic state policies aimed at assimilation. Ethnicity has become more important, stimulating demands for land rights, secession and new political provisions; it is likely to grow in significance.

All the nations of Oceania are experiencing larger and more complex problems than the primarily domestic problems that absorbed them in the early years of independence and self-government. Ethnic, regional and cultural differences have fuelled political instability and uncertainty, even in such large states as New Zealand. The 1980s were particularly volatile – coups in Fiji, riots in Vanuatu and French Polynesia, violence associated with the independence struggle in New Caledonia, a secession bid and a guerrilla war in Bougainville (Papua New Guinea) – with most of these issues being related to minority problems. Few were effectively resolved and many have lingered on into the 1990s: new struggles for sovereignty, among Maori and Aborigines, for identity, among Chamorros particularly, and against colonialism, in French Polynesia, have added to the range of problems in the region. Nevertheless, despite the existence of discrimination, oppression and exclusion, the persistent violence that divides groups in some other parts of the world is rarely so evident in Oceania.

Note

The United Nations Development Programme has developed a South Pacific Human Development Index (SP HDI) for most of the states in the island Pacific, based on life expectancy, literacy, education and per capita income. The index and country rankings are included where they are available.

Further reading

Connell, J., 'Politics and tradition in Melanesia: beyond the struggle for Kanaky', in G. Trompf (ed.), *Islands and Enclaves*, New Delhi, Sterling, 1993, pp. 224–61.

Connell, J. and Howitt, R., *Mining and Indigenous Peoples in Australasia*, Sydney, Sydney University Press and Oxford University Press, 1991.

Crocombe, R. (ed.), *Culture and Democracy in the South Pacific*, Suva, Institute of Pacific Studies, 1992.

Douglas, N. and Douglas, N. (eds), *Pacific Islands Yearbook*, Sydney, Fiji Times, 1994.

International Work Group for Indigenous Affairs, *The Indigenous World 1995–96*, Copenhagen, IWGIA, 1996.

United Nations Development Programme, *Pacific Human Development Report*, Suva, 1994.

Weingartner, E., *The Pacific: Nuclear Testing and Minorities*, London, MRG report, 1991.

White, G.M. and Lindstrom, L., 'Oceania', in M.S. Miller and Cultural Survival (eds), *State of the Peoples: A Global Human Rights Report on Societies in Danger*, Boston, MA, Beacon Press, 1993.

American Samoa

Land area:	200 sq km
Population:	54,600 (1994)
Main languages:	Samoan
Main religions:	Christianity (mainly Christian Congregational Church)
Main minority groups:	Western Samoans, Tongans (no data)
Real per capita GDP:	$4,450 (1985)
UNDP HDI/rank:	—
SP HDI/rank:	—

The islands of American Samoa were ceded to the USA in 1900; it was administered by the US Navy until 1951 when it was transferred to the Department of the Interior. American Samoa remains an unincorporated territory of the USA. American Samoans are 'US nationals' with unrestricted entry into the mainland USA – where most live – but cannot vote for the President or for other federal candidates. The American Samoan legislature seeks greater control over administration and finance, while retaining US protection, subsidies and immigration; substantial over-expenditure in the 1990s resulted in the USA seeking greater control over the economy. Other than in the tuna canneries there is little private sector employment. Because of high wage levels there has been substantial immigration, especially from Western Samoa (but also Tonga), to the extent that locally born Samoans may be a minority. There are also some Asian migrants. Only locally born Samoans are able to obtain government employment, while almost all employment in the canneries is of migrant workers; there are no unions. Other than in access to employment there is no discrimination against minority groups.

Further reading

Sunia, F., 'American Samoa: Fa'a Amerika?', in R. Crocombe and A. Ali (eds), *Politics in Polynesia*, Suva, Institute of Pacific Studies, 1983, pp. 115–28.

Australia

Land area:	7,682,300 sq km
Population:	18.1 million (1995)
Main languages:	Aboriginal languages (about 100), English and others
Main religions:	Christianity, Islam, Buddhism and others
Main minority groups:	Aborigines 250,000 (1.4%), Torres Strait Islanders 26,000 (0.14%), South Sea Islanders 11,000
Real per capita GDP:	$18,530
UNDP HDI/rank:	0.929 (11)

The vast continent of Australia is geographically diverse and thinly populated, with most of the population concentrated in five main coastal cities. The historic indigenous populations – the Aborigines and the Torres Strait Islanders – are more evenly distributed and, despite being little more than 1 per cent of the total population, are dominant in parts of the Northern Territory and

Cape York and in some other northern and inland areas. European colonization began in 1788 and resulted in the expropriation of Aboriginal land, warfare, massacres and disease, and declining population numbers. Though most of the original colonial population was British, the sources of migration became more diverse, especially in the second half of the twentieth century. There was significant Chinese migration in the mid-nineteenth century, but after 1901 the 'White Australia' policy virtually ended Asian migration for half a century. After the war a migration programme was introduced which resulted in the enormous diversification of Australian society, especially after a non-discriminatory immigration policy was adopted in 1973. By the 1980s there were more than a hundred nationalities in Australia; many postwar migrants were from southern Europe and subsequently west and South-East Asia, though the UK has remained the single most important source of migrants. Australia's economy was long based on the export of agricultural and mining products, but though these remain of considerable importance, they have become less important than manufacturing and the service sector as a source of employment and economic growth. This evolution has contributed to urbanization and to the urban concentration of almost all recent migrants. By contrast, Aborigines and Torres Strait Islanders are more obviously located in the rural areas or small towns. The issues that concern minority groups are quite different. In the mid-1970s the policy of assimilation began to give way to a policy of multiculturalism, where all Australians had the right to express their cultural heritage (including language and religion) and to receive social justice in terms of equal treatment and opportunity (without barriers of race, ethnicity, culture, religion, language, gender or birthplace).

Aborigines

Aboriginal people have lived in Australia for at least 50,000 years and probably very much longer; they currently represent about 1.4 per cent of the population. The largest population concentrations are in urban areas, but Aborigines achieve numerical dominance in the more remote areas of Australia. In the south-east of Australia many Aboriginal populations and languages have declined or disappeared, whereas in the north and west a number of languages have more than 10,000 speakers. Although Aborigines in the south and east are more likely to be involved in the wider social and economic environment, they are no less likely to perceive themselves as Aboriginal than those who are more physically remote from large urban areas.

Before the European invasion and settlement Aborigines were migratory, often over long distances, and were primarily dependent on some combination of hunting, gathering and fishing. Social organization was complex, closely and intricately linked to the land and related to beliefs concerning the spiritual world. After 1788 such lifestyles began to change as Aborigines were displaced from land, wars were fought, women were raped and new diseases resulted in high death rates. During the nineteenth century most of the south-eastern tribes, especially in Tasmania, were fragmented and marginalized. In inland areas violent attacks on Aborigines continued until the interwar years.

The Aboriginal population declined from perhaps a million people in 1778 to no more than about 70,000 in the 1930s. It was hitherto assumed (the belief in 'Social Darwinism') that the Aboriginal population would eventually die out and the most enlightened government policies sought merely to 'smooth the dying pillow' of the indigenous population. Nevertheless population numbers grew. Aborigines took up employment in cattle stations and in urban areas, and official policy increasingly moved towards one of assimilation. Health, education and other services were slowly extended into remote areas. However 'half-castes', who were regarded by whites as quite different from 'full-bloods', were driven into white institutions by legislation preventing them remaining on reserves. 'Full-blooded' Aborigines were to be dispersed. One of the most harmful elements of the new approach was the separation of children from parents when parents, for one reason or another, but often without foundation, were regarded as unsuitable and inadequate. Such children were often permanently separated from their families, including other siblings, brought up on mission stations and by foster parents, and denied access to knowledge of their own Aboriginality, let alone knowledge of Aboriginal languages and traditions. In 1995 the Federal government mounted a Commission of Inquiry, due to report in 1997, to examine the possibility of compensation for Aborigines who had been victimized and harmed in this way.

By the 1940s Aborigines had formed their own organizations, such as the Australian Aborigines' League and Aborigines' Progressive Association, to campaign for improved status and better access to employment and services. The wartime employment of Aborigines had changed their perceptions of status and equality, as some were paid wages and shared the same accommodation and canteen facilities as whites. However, they had no legal status (and Aboriginal dispute settlement procedures were not recognized), no political status (being without the vote and denied citizenship) and were excluded from censuses, while assimilation policies denied them a separate identity. Many Aborigines, displaced from their land, with limited education and inadequate employment, were an impoverished and destitute population. Discrimination was rife in every context.

As late as 1951 the Federal and State governments officially adopted assimilation as the main objective for all facets of Aboriginal affairs, but strategies varied between governments, partly because of differences in political composition. In 1967 it was decided that the Federal government should legislate for all Aborigines, though states could also enact laws. For the first time, Aborigines were counted in censuses, and during the 1960s many discriminatory laws were repealed; Aborigines gained entitlement to state benefits and the right to vote. More attention was given to appropriate health and education policies, as their living conditions, health status and life expectancy were significantly below those of other Australians. However, Aborigines were sometimes employed for very low wages and housed inadequately, especially in rural areas. In 1966 Aboriginal stockmen at Gurindji (Wave Hill) went on strike against their exploitation by the multinational Vestey Corporation, a strike which focused widespread attention on the circumstances of the Aboriginal population and marked the start of the contemporary land rights movement. There was more radical opposition to the existing system as Aborigines gained higher educational levels and parts of white society supported human rights issues, as in the Freedom Ride of 1965 which took a group of students to a number of New South Wales towns notorious for their racist practices. Two different kinds of issues were influential in the 1960s. One was civil rights – the rights of Aborigines to attend white schools, own property, buy land, drink in hotels and generally to integrate in white society. The other was a revival of cultural identity and thus land rights. Though the two issues were away from and towards white society, because Aborigines suffered both the denial of civil rights and a separate identity, they were intertwined.

The 1970s marked a turning point in Aboriginal control of their internal affairs, following the conservative Liberal and Country Party government rejection of land rights and the establishment of an Aboriginal tent embassy outside Parliament House in Canberra. The Australian Labour government, elected in 1972, promised changes, created a National Aboriginal Consultative Committee (NACC) and set up the Department of Aboriginal Affairs, but left much unaccomplished. An important development was the Aboriginal Land Rights Act, enacted by the Liberal government in 1976, which handed over former reserve land in the Northern Territory to be held in trust by Aboriginal Land Councils: the Central and Northern Land Councils. Other land councils were formed in the 1980s. The Act provided the basis for some degree of long-term security and economic development for the Aboriginal population in the Northern Territory. During the 1970s other states sought to develop similar legislation, notably in South Australia, where the Pitjantjatjara people gained ownership of much of their land. However, conservative states, notably Queensland (which has the largest Aboriginal population in Australia), were reluctant to grant rights to Aborigines and mining interests were also often opposed. In Queensland, the Aboriginal and Islanders Act 1971 prevented Aborigines from living or visiting reserves of their choice and forced them to work for below minimum wages. Though this legislation has been repealed, the legacy of recent discrimination remains.

The Aboriginal Development Commission was set up in 1980 and brought together various government-sponsored bureaus of land acquisition and economic enterprise which gave the Aboriginal commissioners powers to act without direct ministerial interference. However, relationships within the National Aboriginal Conference (the successor to the NACC) began to deteriorate, and pressures from some State governments and the Australian Mining Industry Council drove the Federal government further away from the minimum demands of Aboriginal pressure groups (which now included the land councils and Aboriginal legal services) which centred on the implementation of a policy of national uniform land rights. There was considerable dismay when the Labour government abandoned the proposal in 1986. However, the land councils, housing associations, cooperatives and many other organizations indicated that regional management was almost entirely in Aboriginal hands. At a national level the failure of national land rights proposals emphasized that Aborigines had little more power than before; they had achieved considerable self-management but not self-determination.

The second half of the 1980s was marked by a number of institutional changes. In 1988, the bicentennial year, some 30,000 Aborigines marched through Sydney to protest against the invasion and subsequent displacement and discrimination. The Prime Minister, Bob Hawke, promised to negotiate a treaty between Aborigines and the Australian government, but the promise was never kept, and was effectively superseded by Mabo legislation (see below) and, to a lesser extent, debate over the existence of an early treaty in Tasmania. In the same year the Department of Aboriginal Affairs was replaced by a new structure, the Aboriginal and Torres Strait Islanders' Commission (ATSIC), which enabled greater indigenous participation and was intended to draw together the executive, advisory and policy-making functions of many government and non-government Aboriginal organizations. Elections for membership of the ATSIC were held in constituencies of indigenous people across Australia.

The treaty had failed to materialize, and the Federal government's Council for Aboriginal Reconciliation had produced no recommendations, when in 1992 the Mabo Judgement of the Australian High Court was passed. The High Court, following initial submissions by Eddie Mabo, a Torres Strait Islander, recognized that the people of Murray Island, in Torres Strait, held and continued to hold Native Title to their land. The Court therefore extinguished the old notion of *terra nullius*, that the land was empty and without owners until European settlement. In 1993 the Federal government accepted the implications of the Mabo Judgement for the whole of Australia, in the Native Title Act, and thus recognized the continued existence of Native Title for all areas of Crown land held by the states and the Commonwealth, where it had not been specifically extinguished. Tribunals were established in all states to determine the eligibility of Native Title claims. The act confirmed the potential to settle difficult cases by negotiation and created a land acquisition fund to meet the needs of dispossessed indigenous peoples who would not otherwise be able to claim Native Title (though financial assistance proved difficult to obtain). The Federal Native Title Act met particular resistance in Western Australia where it was perceived by the conservative State government as having the potential to restrict mining companies from operating in a large proportion of the state. The Mabo decision thus influenced debate on state rights. It has also led to some new agreements between Aborigines and mining companies. Initially Native Title has been the source of both cohesion and dispute as the opportunity of gaining title has opened up both expectations of the return of country and also tensions and wounds around connections to country, family histories and community relationships. In every way the Native Title Act is central to the process of reconciliation between indigenous Aborigines and Torres Strait Islanders and other Australians.

On every index of human needs Aborigines still fare worse than other Australians. Even in 1995 Aboriginal life expectancy was 18 years less, and infant mortality rates were three times that of non-Aboriginal Australians. Diseases which are largely absent from other populations, such as trachoma and leprosy, continue to exist, and diabetes and renal disease reach high levels. Malnutrition and undernutrition are not unusual. Twenty per cent of Aboriginal children in the Northern Territory meet World Health Organization definitions of malnutrition. Alcoholism is pervasive in both urban and rural communities, and some rural communities have banned alcohol. Petrol sniffing by youths is a problem in some remote arreas. Aboriginal housing conditions are poor, especially in rural areas, where there is also inadequate access to water supplies, health and education services. Education levels are poor, and there are disproportionately fewer high school and university graduates. Levels of unemployment are often very high, sometimes as high as 90 per cent, in small towns and remote communities where a combination of discrimination, lack of employment opportunities and sometimes an unwillingness or inability to work have led to a demoralized population. The Aboriginal unemployment rate is approximately five times the national average; most Aborigines who are employed are in lower skilled jobs and Aboriginal incomes are on average half those of other Australians. Domestic violence is above average. At the end of the 1980s Aborigines accounted for 15 per cent of the national prison population and 21 per cent of deaths in custody. The Royal Commission on Aboriginal Deaths in Custody in 1991 established that the deaths were partly a result of the tendency to arrest and place in custody young men and women for relatively trivial offences, including drunkenness, and followed the neglect of Aboriginal prisoners and, more generally, the neglect of Aboriginal lives and livelihoods. Since then there have been some reforms to the prison, legal and medical services, but the problem of Aboriginal deaths in custody has not yet been ended.

Torres Strait Islanders

The Melanesian Torres Strait Islanders have lived in the islands north of Queensland for at least 10,000 years and are closely related to the nearby Papuan people of Papua New Guinea. There is some mobility between the two areas. The present population numbers about 6,000 (in the Torres Strait Islands), has two main Melanesian languages (and a pidgin English) and is increasingly concentrated in the urban centre of Thursday Island (within the Torres Strait). In the present century there has been considerable migration to the Cape York peninsula on the mainland and to the large urban centres of Cairns, Townsville and Brisbane; about 20,000 Torres Strait Islanders live in mainland Queensland. Because of their marginal location Torres Strait Islanders largely escaped the early excesses of European invasion and settlement until well into the nineteenth century, when a pearling and trading economy began to develop. The contemporary economy is based on fishing, but much of the population is dependent on welfare services.

Islanders have experienced discrimination and inadequate access to employment and services. Land issues have posed problems in the Torres Strait and in 1982 Eddie Mabo and four other Meriam people of the Murray Islands in Torres Strait sought to confirm their traditional land rights in the High Court. They claimed continuous enjoyment of their land rights to Murray Island (Mer) and thus that these rights had not been extinguished by the annexure of the islands by the Queensland government in 1879. The case took ten years, during which time Eddie Mabo and three other plaintiffs died, but in 1992 the High Court upheld the claim. There has been growing pressure for increased self-determination and, in the late 1980s, there was pressure for self-government (along the lines of that in the Cook Islands) because of what was perceived as neglect by the Federal and Queensland State governments. Since then greater powers have been devolved to the Island Councils.

South Sea Islanders

Between 1863 and 1904 more than 55,000 Melanesians were recruited, mainly from the New Hebrides (Vanuatu) and Solomon Islands, to work in the cane fields of Queensland. After the end of the contract labour system most returned, but more than 2,000 remained in Australia, many around Mackay in north Queensland. Their descendants, who suffered less institutional discrimination than their parents, gained housing from the Aboriginal and Islander Advancement Corporation in the 1960s, but access to education was inadequate and South Sea Islanders became one of the poorest groups in Australia. Although white Australians regarded them as Aborigines, they were not eligible for the benefits given to Aborigines unless they denied their South Sea Islander origins. In 1977 a Royal Commission into Human Relationships recommended that they be given access to the same benefits that were available to Aborigines. By the 1990s there were around 11,000 South Sea Islanders, most of whom remained around Mackay, and were disadvantaged in terms of such basic needs as home ownership, health, education and employment; the unemployment rate was 28.5 per cent, two and a half times the national average, and few were employed in skilled occupations. South Sea Islanders continued to experience the outcome of a history of exploitation and racial discrimination similar to that of Aborigines and Torres Strait Islanders, but were unrecognized as a distinct group. A 1992 Inquiry by the Human Rights and Equal Opportunity Commission recommended that they be formally recognized as a distinct disadvantaged group, and that schemes comparable with those available to Aboriginal and Torres Strait Islanders be made available to them. In 1994 the government accepted these recommendations and South Sea Islanders began to move towards a new future.

Other minority populations

In the postwar years, migration into Australia has intensified and a high proportion of the population (25 per cent in 1991) has been born overseas. Only the UK, Eire and New Zealand have provided a relatively constant supply of migrants, as the dominant migration streams have shifted from Europe to Asia, accompanied by a significant increase in refugee migration, mainly from Indo-China. New restrictions were placed on migration as the desire for population growth gave way to selectivity related to skilled migration appropriate for economic development. Most contemporary migrants have settled in the larger cities, which has given these cities – and some suburbs – a cosmopolitan population.

Although many migrant groups, particularly those of recent non-English-speaking origin, are concentrated in particular areas, these are not necessarily marked by more inadequate housing and living conditions than other areas of cities. In the nineteenth century there were a few areas of migrant concentration; indeed the Chinese population on the gold fields were confined by decree to certain areas. In the postwar years there were new concentrations, where previously there had only been small centres of Chinese or Jewish settlement. More recently the location of hostels has been particularly important for the subsequent establishment of Vietnamese residential concentrations in particular areas of the state capital. The combination of an initial refugee population, limited English-speaking ability, employment-related skills, capital and income has given this recent migrant population a more distinct and localized population distribution than almost any other migrant group. A number of very small groups, such as the Hmong, have also chosen to remain close together for cultural and economic reasons. Such concentrations are emphasized by distinct ethnicity, and by the emergence of many 'ethnic businesses', mainly restaurants and stores.

The ethnic diversification of Australia in the postwar years has caused few serious social problems. Currently the Vietnamese population experience the greatest problems of access to employment and services, and the unemployment rate is particularly high. Within this population, especially in Sydney, there have been gang and drug problems that have emphasized the considerable difficulties of settlement and adjustment over a short period of time. The election in 1966 of an independent and outspoken member of parliament, Pauline Hanson, openly opposed to Asian migration, and to the funding of Aboriginal programmes, resulted in increased hostility and violence towards Asians in several cities. There have also been tensions between some migrant groups, most recently between those from the former Yugoslavia, usually associated with differences over issues relating to their home areas. To deal with the various issues of development for a diverse population Australia has sought to develop multicultural policies and institutions. In 1987 the government set up an Office of Multicultural Affairs within the Department of the Prime Minister, and State governments have set up Ethnic Affairs Commissions. Overall, despite the rapidity of recent migration, the Aboriginal population of Australia has experienced much greater social disadvantages, and these problems have attracted more political interest and government funding than those of migrants.

Cocos (Keeling) Islanders

The Cocos (Keeling) Islands are an Australian territory more than 2,750 kilometres north-west of Perth. The islands, which are coral atolls, were unoccupied until the early nineteenth century when a private copra plantation was developed and the islanders brought from Malaya as plantation labourers. About 58 per cent of the present population of about 600 are descendants of these migrants. Australian administration only effectively began in 1955, when one of the islands was purchased as a military base. In the 1970s the plantation was criticized as 'feudal' because of constraints on Islanders (who were forbidden to speak to outsiders and threatened with banishment if they left the islands) and in 1978 the islands were compulsorily purchased from their private owner. In 1984 the Islanders voted in a referendum to become Australian citizens (rejecting independence or free association with Australia), broke all ties with the former owner and requested the UN to monitor further developments on the islands. The UN recognized this act of self-determination in 1985. The islands have a limited subsistence economy, are effectively subsidized by Australia and, following a Memorandum of Understanding in 1991, are moving towards standards and conditions similar to those on the mainland.

Christmas Island

Christmas Island, some 500 kilometres from the Cocos Islands, is also an Australian territory. It was essentially uninhabited until the end of the nineteenth century, when it was developed as a phosphate mine, until mining ended in 1987 (though there have been subsequent attempts to revive mining). Constructing a hotel and casino complex subsequently began and there has been an influx of tourists from Asia. Christmas Island has no indigenous population. The population was 1,275 in 1991 (though it has subsequently grown), consisting mainly of ethnic Chinese and Malays. Since 1981 all residents have been eligible for Australian citizenship. Australia appoints an administrator and the Christmas Island Shire Council has some authority; there have been recent discussions about the extent of that authority. In 1984 an unofficial referendum was held in which 85 per cent of the population voted in favour of greater autonomy, but rejected the option of secession.

Norfolk Island

Norfolk Island is an Australian territory some 1,400 kilometres east of Brisbane, with a population of 1,900 in 1991. It was only briefly occupied until the early nineteenth century when it was settled by, among others, descendants of the original settlers of Pitcairn Island, and became a penal settlement. Its present population is primarily European, with close ties to the Australian population, and historical distinctions of dialect and custom have disappeared. Norfolk Island is now largely dependent on tourism, and some financial support from Australia, and has a considerable degree of autonomy. There have been demands for a greater degree of autonomy, but threats to reduce financial assistance have weakened these demands. Under the Norfolk Island Act 1979, Norfolk Island has moved towards greater legislative and executive government, enabling it to run its own affairs to the greatest practicable extent. A referendum in 1991 rejected proposals by the Australian government to include it in an Australian Federal electorate.

Conclusions and future prospects

Until extremely recently the history of the Aboriginal population of Australia has been painful, dominated for the most part by disease and genocide, displacement and dispossession, resistance, poverty and marginalization. Assimilation denied Aboriginal identity. The Mabo land rights legislation, despite opposition and uncertainties, has been the culmination of more concerted attempts to secure Aboriginal rights; however, access to employment and services is still inadequate and basic needs are poorly satisfied. Aborigines remain something of an internal colony within Australia. Torres Strait Islanders are similarly disadvantaged and in 1995 sought an independent commission (separate from ATSIC) that might give them greater control over their own affairs. Their future may diverge from that of Aborigines. By contrast, migrant populations, despite facing discrimination, have often established secure economic futures and places in social and political life though the most recent migrant groups, some of whom arrived as refugees, have experienced difficulties. In a range of contexts there is active, if illegal, discrimination against Aborigines and many non-English-speaking residents, despite the move to multiculturalism, and uneven social, economic and political development is likely to continue.

Further reading

Aboriginal and Torres Strait Islander Social Justice Commissioner, *Native Title Report January-June 1994*, Canberra, Commonwealth of Australia, 1995.

Beckett, J., *Torres Strait Islanders: Custom and Colonialism*, Cambridge, Cambridge University Press, 1987.

Human Rights and Equal Opportunity Commission, *The Call for Recognition: A Report on the Situation of Australian South Sea Islanders*, Sydney, Human Rights and Equal Opportunity Commission, 1992.

Jupp, J. (ed.), *The Australian People*, Sydney, Angus & Robertson, 1988.

Suter, K. and Stearman, K., *Aboriginal Australians*, London, MRG report, 1988.

Minority-based and advocacy organizations

Aboriginal Law Centre, University of New South Wales, Faculty of Law, PO Box 1, Kensington, NSW 2033, Australia; tel. 61 2 697 2256, fax 61 2 313 7209.

Aboriginal and Torres Strait Islander Social Justice Commissioner, GPO Box 5218, Sydney, NSW 2001, Australia; tel. 61 02 284 9600, fax 61 02 284 9715.

Amnesty International, Private Bag 23, Broadway, NSW 2007, Australia; tel. 61 2 211 3566, fax 61 2 211 3608.

Centre for South Pacific Studies, University of New South Wales, NSW 2033, Australia; tel. 612 2 385 3386, fax 61 2 313 6337.

Conflict Resolution Network, PO Box 1016, Chatswood, NSW 2057, Australia; tel. 61 2 9419 8500, fax 61 2 9413 1148.

National Aboriginal and Islander Legal Service Secretariat, PO Box 366, Roma Street, Brisbane, Queensland 4033, Australia; tel. 61 7 211 3522, fax 61 7 211 3234.

Cook Islands

Land area:	237 sq km
Population:	19,100 (1994)
Main languages:	Cook Islands Maori, English
Main religions:	Christianity (mainly Cook Islands Christian Church)
Main minority groups:	—
Real per capita GDP:	$3,339 (1990)
UNDP HDI/rank:	—
SP HDI/rank:	0.985 (1)

The fifteen Cook Islands have a small population spread over an area of more than a million square kilometres. The Cook Islands have been in free association with New Zealand since 1965. They are not a member of the United Nations, although in 1995 they sought membership, and largely make and implement their own foreign policy. Despite some occasional concern over limits to sovereignty, the Polynesian Cook Islanders have not sought full independence (preferring substantial aid from, and freedom of migration to, New Zealand). Other than a small number of contract workers, mainly from New Zealand, there are no minority groups in the Cook Islands.

Federated States of Micronesia

Land area:	701 sq km
Population:	105,700 (1994)
Main languages:	Pohnpeian, Chuukese, Yapese, Kosraean, Ulithi-Woleaian, Pingelapese, Mokilese, Nukuoran, Kapinga
Main religions:	Christianity (mainly Roman Catholicism)
Main minority groups:	Polynesians 5,000 (4.7%)
Real per capita GDP:	$1,700 (1992)
UNDP HDI/rank:	—
SP HDI/rank:	0.604 (8)

The Federated States of Micronesia are the most complex state in Micronesia, geographically and culturally. The territory is composed of four separate states – Kosrae, Pohnpei (Ponape), Chuuk (Truk) and Yap – each of which function as separate entities in some contexts. Some states have expressed interest in a separate political status. The relatively large extent of land on the central high islands has meant that there has been considerable migration from the outer coral islands, especially in Pohnpei and Chuuk. Outer islanders are culturally distinct from high islanders; in Pohnpei two outer islands have Polynesian populations and most outer islanders speak different languages, and have different forms of social organization, than those in the centre. Historically, outer islanders were dominated by high islanders, especially in Yap, and they are discriminated against in terms of access to employment, land, housing and other services, though they have full political rights. Most outer islanders live in distinct, often segregated, areas in the urban centres. There has been some migration from Palau and the Philippines (partly balanced by migration since 1986 to Guam and Saipan).

Fiji

Land area:	18,270 sq km
Population:	775,000 (1994)
Main languages:	Fijian, Hindi, Rotuman, English
Main religions:	Christianity (mainly Uniting Church), Hindu
Main minority groups:	Indians (Indo-Fijians) 348,000 (est., 45%), Rotumans 8,000 (1.0%), Banabans
Real per capita GDP:	$5,530
UNDP HDI/rank:	0.853 (47)
SP HDI/rank:	0.652 (5)

Fiji is one of the largest Pacific island states, consisting of about 100 populated islands, though almost 90 per cent of the population live on the two main islands. The population consists of two principal racial groups: the indigenous Melanesian population (subsequently referred to as Fijians), who now constitute a majority of the population, and the Indo-Fijian (commonly referred to as Indian) population. The remainder of the population are of diverse origins with a significant Polynesian group from the outlying island of Rotuma, and the remainder primarily Europeans and Chinese. Banabans from the Gilbert Islands (Kiribati) were settled in Fiji in the 1940s, after phosphate mining ruined their home island, and there has been some migration from many Pacific islands. Fiji has a relatively diversified economy, with one of the highest average incomes for an independent island state.

Indians (Indo-Fijians)

At the last census in 1986 the Fijian population was 329,000 (46 per cent of the total) and the Indian (Indo-Fijian) population was 348,000 (48 per cent), maintaining the numerical dominance of the Indian population that had been established after the Second World War. Indians are predominantly located in the three most developed provinces, and especially in the urban areas, despite the historic link of Indians and sugar-cane farming. Indians were first introduced to Fiji in the 1880s, and between 1879 and 1916 over 60,000 indentured labourers came from various parts of India to work in the cane plantations. Many other Pacific islanders came at the same time, but most returned. The Indian migrants remained. Opposition to Indian migration to Fiji was latent in the colonial period, but in post-independence years there was more concerted opposition, directed to the numerical dominance of Indians and their pre-eminence in commerce and some parts of the public service. Resentment has increased at times of high unemployment, and in the 1970s there were occasional thoughts of repatriation of Indians. In 1982 the Great Council of Chiefs sought to reserve two-thirds of parliamentary seats for Fijians. Indians have remained landless, dependent on leasing land from Fijians, hence many have moved into urban commerce.

After independence in 1970 the new constitution safeguarded the interests of the Fijian minority, in terms of access to land, through having a majority in the Senate and through the assurance that they would have almost half the seats in the lower house, the House of Representatives. Despite these guarantees, and despite the relative growth of the Fijian population (through differential natural increase and emigration rates), there was opposition to Indians. Political parties and elections were essentially divided on racial grounds. In 1985 the multiracial Fiji Labour Party (FLP) was formed and, led by a Fijian, Dr Timoci Bavadra, won the April 1987 election in a coalition with the Indian-based National Federation Party. Although the FLP awarded sensitive ministerial posts to Fijians, there was powerful opposition and in May 1987 a military coup led by Colonel Sitiveni Rabuka overthrew the government. When the Governor-General established a caretaker government of a coalition including FLP members, a second coup again overthrew the government. In October Rabuka declared a republic, which eventually led to Fiji being expelled from the Commonwealth, and there was violence against, and victimization of, supporters of the previous government.

Rabuka subsequently handed over power to a chosen civilian government under long-time Prime Minister, Ratu Sir Kamesese Mara, with a new constitution drawn up in 1990 by Rabuka, which gave more preferential treatment to the Fijian population, guaranteeing Fijian political supremacy, in a race-based political system, in which the majority of seats in both Houses were allocated to Fijians. Rabuka again became Prime Minister in 1994 and Mara became President. The lower house now has 37 members to represent Fijians, 27 for Indians, one for Rotumans and five for others. The Senate has 34 members, including 24 recommended by the Fijian Great Council of Chiefs. The President is also elected by the Great Council of Chiefs, hence Fijian political power is institutionalized. The principal party is now Soqosoqo ni Vakavulewa ni Taukei, usually referred to as 'the Chiefs' party'. In 1995 a two-year process of reviewing the 1990 constitution by a three-person commission began, which included a prominent Indian critic of the government, but constitutional changes must be accepted by two-thirds of the members of parliament. There is limited prospect that this will restore Indian political rights.

Other minorities

The outlying Polynesian island of Rotuma was early incorporated into Fiji. Rotuman rights were protected in the 1990 constitution; Rotumans are highly dependent on government employment in Fiji and many have migrated overseas. In the wake of the 1987 coups there was considerable interest in gaining a separate independence, and Rotumans remain concerned about the political and economic future.

Banabans were resettled on Rabi island (Vanua Levu) after 1942. While in Fiji Banabans fought a long battle for compensation against the UK because of the damage to their home island and their displacement. Attempts to revive a traditional economy in Banaba have largely failed, and most Banabans now see their future in Fiji. Many remain on the island of Rabi though others have migrated to Suva and elsewhere. Though they have become Fijian citizens, they experience some political problems and there have been disputes over the management of Rabi affairs. Banabans can also vote in Kiribati, and have a member of parliament; they have sought independence for Banaba though most wish to remain in Fiji. The 1987 coups made Banabans more aware of the limitations to their future in Fiji and they have increasingly tended to accept the provisions made for them by Kiribati.

There are other minority groups in Fiji – including the Chinese (whose numbers are not increasing) and other Pacific islanders, who are often temporary residents. There are many Pacific islanders at the University of the South Pacific, and there have been tensions between some national groups.

Conclusions and future prospects

Violence against Indians during and after the coups, the greater political power of Fijians, concern over economic growth (as tourism and other economic activities slumped) and fear for the future all led to substantial emigration of Indians, so that Fijians became a majority. Demographic projections suggest that Indians will be less than 40 per cent of the population by the end of the century.

Indians were marginalized in most spheres, though they have since regained substantial economic power, whilst the more prominent Fijian nationalist movements have lost some influence. Nonetheless the position of Indians in Fiji remains problematic; many are poor, all are landless and the present constitution is biased against them. The expiry of sugar land leases on Fijian 'native land' in 1997 poses uncertainties for Indians' rural livelihoods. At the same time Fijians remain concerned that an internationally accepted constitution would mean the loss of political control of their homeland. Provincial divisions have also become important. At a political level there are acute divisions between the two main ethnic groups, though in other areas there is some degree of harmony, despite divisions that span every facet of social life.

Further reading

Emberson-Bain, A., 'Fiji: women, poverty and post-coup pressure', in D. Robie (ed.), *Tu Galala: Social Change in the Pacific*, Wellington, Bridget Williams Books, 1992, pp. 145–62.

Kaplan, M., 'Imagining a nation: race, politics and crisis in post-colonial Fiji', in V. Lockwood, T. Harding and B. Wallace (eds), *Contemporary Pacific Societies*, Englewood Cliffs, NJ, Prentice Hall, 1993, pp. 34–54.

Naidu, V., 'Social change and the survival of neo-tradition in Fiji', in A. Robillard (ed.), *Social Change in the Pacific Islands*, London, Kegan Paul International, 1992, pp. 134–99.

Tinker, H., Duraiswamy, N., Ghai, Y. and Ennals, M., *Fiji*, London, MRG report, 1987.

Minority-based and advocacy organization

Pacific Concerns Resource Centre, 83 Amy Street, Toorak, Private Bag, Suva, Fiji; tel. 679 304 649, fax 679 304 755.

French Polynesia

Land area:	3,520 sq km
Population:	218,000 (1994)
Main languages:	Polynesian/Maohi (eight languages), French
Main religions:	Christianity (various)
Main minority groups:	Europeans 22,000 (10.1%), Chinese 8,000 (3.7%)
Real per capita GDP:	$15,000 (1990)
UNDP HDI/rank:	—
SP HDI/rank:	—

French Polynesia is the largest in population, and geographical area, of France's three territories in the South Pacific. There are five archipelagoes, each with a distinct Polynesian language, though the territory is dominated by the island of Tahiti where the majority of the population live, more than half in the capital, Papeete. European contact largely began in the late eighteenth century. France established a protectorate in the 1840s and all the present islands of French Polynesia were incorporated into the territory by 1901. Plantations were established in the 1850s in the Society Islands, leading to Chinese and European migration. In other archipelagos Polynesian society was less affected by modernization until the twentieth century.

After the Second World War, when there were military bases in Polynesia and Polynesians fought for France, there was a rapid growth of nationalism associated with a prominent local leader, Pouvanaa a Oopa, who formed the first Polynesian political party, the Rassemblement Démocratique des Populations Tahitiennes which sought greater economic, cultural and political freedom. Pouvanaa was elected to the French parliament and in 1958, as Vice-President of Government Council of French Polynesia, sought secession from France. In the following year 36 per cent of the population, mainly in the Society Islands, voted for secession. Soon afterwards Pouvanaa was arrested and jailed.

In 1960 an international airport was opened on Tahiti, and the tourist industry began to grow. In 1966 France started its nuclear testing programme on Mururoa and Fangataufa atolls in the Tuamotus archipelago. Both tourism and nuclear testing increased employment opportunities and incomes and reduced the demand for independence. New autonomist leaders and parties emerged in the 1970s and after 1977 increased autonomy was granted to French Polynesia. At the 1982 election the principal pro-independence party Ia Mana Te Nunaa gained three (out of thirty) seats, but there was no great support for independence. Opposition to nuclear testing grew, with Protestant Church support, but despite strikes and riots it continued until 1991, and then resumed from 1995 to 1996.

Oscar Temaru, who became Mayor of Fa'aa, a poor Papeete suburb, founded Tavini Huiraatira (the Polynesian Liberation Front), which also sought independence. Independence was primarily intended to focus on the development of local resources, the establishment of regional ties and the use of the Tahitian (Maohi) language, but many Polynesians perceived this as idealistic rather than pragmatic. Greater autonomy was given to French Polynesia, Tahitian became an official language (with French) and support for the pro-independence parties stagnated, until 1996 when Tavini won 10 of the 40 seats in the Territorial Assembly. In 1992 the Territorial Assembly negotiated a ten-year Pacte de Progrès (Progress Pact) to develop other sources of income, to replace the expenditure associated with nuclear testing.

The historic Polynesian population is partly assimilated with migrant Europeans; many prominent Polynesians are mixed-race (*demis*). More than 10,000 Europeans moved into French Polynesia in association with nuclear testing and the growth of the government economy. In the late nineteenth century there was significant Chinese migration and there is some hostility to the Chinese community; Chinese were not given citizenship until the 1960s. Otherwise there has been some migration from former, and present, French colonies and territories, but there are no real minority groups though, to some extent, migrants from the outer islands are minorities in Tahiti.

The resumption of French nuclear testing in Mururoa in mid-1995 resulted in enormous opposition in French Polynesia. Evidence has mounted that nuclear testing has been injurious to the health of Polynesians who have worked for lengthy periods on Mururoa, and there are concerns about the present and future disintegration of the atoll. Supporters of independence regarded the French government decision as a 'colonial decision' taken without local consultation; there was a resurgence in support for Tavini Huiraatira and considerable violence against French institutions. However, the independence movement has never gained support in the outer islands, where the prospects for economic development are exceptionally poor. French Polynesia is unlikely to attain independence in the foreseeable future.

Further reading

Aldrich, R. and Connell, J., *France's Overseas Frontier*, Cambridge, Cambridge University Press, 1992.

Weingartner, G., *The Pacific: Nuclear Testing and Minorities*, London, MRG report, 1991.

Guam

Land area:	541 sq km
Population:	147,000 (1994)
Main languages:	Chamorro, English, Filipino
Main religions:	Christianity (mainly Roman Catholicism)
Main minority groups:	Filipinos 32,000 (21.8%), Europeans 20,000 (13.6%), Koreans 4,500 (3.1%), Micronesians (no data)
Real per capita GDP:	$12,374 (1992)
UNDP HDI/rank:	—
SP HD/rank:	—

Guam is an unincorporated territory of the USA, and officially the westernmost part of the USA. It has long been a significant US military base with a considerable European population. The Guam economy is based on the military, government and tourism (mainly from Japan). The indigenous population were Chamorros, as in the adjoining Northern Marianas, with some similarities to other Micronesian populations. From the Spanish colonial era onwards there was immigration and Spanish, Filipino and American influences have transformed some elements of Chamorro culture. Guam has been under US administration since 1898; it became an unincorporated territory in 1950 when its people became US citizens. In the 1990s Guam has sought to redefine its political relationship with the USA, but the US government has opposed many of Guam's proposals, such as indigenous rights, mutual consent, local control of immigration and the return of military land. The Government of Guam took these issues to the UN Special Committee on Decolonization in 1994.

There has been extensive migration to Guam in the postwar years, especially from other parts of the USA, the Philippines and elsewhere in Asia. By 1950 the Chamorro population was a numerical minority, with the US-born population making up more than a third of the population. Since then the Chamorro population has more or less remained in a minority position while the Filipino population has grown to almost a quarter of the total. In the past decade there has been significant migration from Micronesia, especially the Federated States of Micronesia and Palau. There has been little interest in independence. By contrast, there has been an enormous recent increase in expressions of Chamorro identity. A pressure group, campaigning for the rights of indigenous people, Chamoru Nation, emerged in 1993 to appeal for stricter control of migration to Guam, because it was regarded as a threat to Chamorro culture and political and social stability.

Kiribati

Land area:	690 sq km
Population:	78,300 (1994)
Main languages:	Gilbertese
Main religions:	Christianity (Roman Catholicism and Protestantism)
Main minority groups:	Banabans 500 (0.6%)
Real per capita GDP:	$700 (1992)
UNDP HDI/rank:	—
SP HDI/rank:	0.439 (10)

Kiribati is a Micronesian state consisting of three island groups, two of which are populated, separated by 3,500 kilometres. The economy is highly dependent on remittances (from workers in Nauru or elsewhere) and overseas aid. There has been considerable migration from the outer islands to the main island of South Tarawa, where more than a third of the population live. The island of Banaba produced phosphate until closure in 1979, the same year that Kiribati achieved independence. There are divisions within the country between Protestants, mainly from the southern islands, and Roman Catholics from the northern islands, who have their own political party, the Christian Democratic Party. Political parties are not, however, of great significance.

The mining of Banaba from 1900 to 1979 resulted in the postwar displacement of the Banaban population, whose language is slightly different from that of the Gilbertese of Kiribati. The Banabans were transferred to the island of Rabi in Fiji (see **Fiji**). There has been some minority interest in returning to Banaba, and a few Banabans live there, but compensation payments made to the Banabans have been invested in Fiji, and the island has not been rehabilitated. There are no other minorities in Kiribati.

Marshall Islands

Land area:	181 sq km
Population:	54,700 (1994)
Main languages:	Marshallese
Main religions:	Christianity (mainly Protestantism)
Main minority groups:	—
Real per capita GDP:	$2,000 (1993)
UNDP HDI/rank:	—
SP HDI/rank:	0.611 (7)

The Republic of the Marshall Islands consists entirely of coral atolls and reef islands. After periods of German and Japanese colonial history the Marshall Islands became part of the postwar US-administered Trust Territory of the Pacific Islands. In the early years of this trust, the populations of Bikini and Enewetak were resettled so that the atoll could be used as a site for atomic bomb tests. These tests irradiated the island and people of the nearby atolls of Utirik and Rongelap. The 'nuclear nomads' of Bikini now mainly live on the southern atoll of Kili, and have not been able to return to their contaminated home island. Islanders from the four northern atolls have received substantial compensation payments for displacement and long-term health problems. The atoll of Kwajalein was later developed into a target range and subsequently a 'star wars' missile testing base. In 1982 the Marshall Islands signed a Compact of Free Association with the USA and became effectively independent, although the economy is exceptionally dependent on US aid. There are some tensions between the eastern and western island groups and there are a substantial number of migrants from the Philippines, Japan and, more recently, Taiwan. There is some concern over the extent of alien employment.

Further reading

Weingartner, E., *The Pacific: Nuclear Testing and Minorities*, London, MRG report, 1991.

Nauru

Land area:	20 sq km
Population:	10,500 (1994)
Main languages:	Nauruan
Main religions:	Christianity (mainly Nauru Congregational Church)
Main minority groups:	i-Kiribati 1,300 (12.4%), Tuvaluans 700 (6.7%), Chinese 600 (5.7%)
Real per capita GDP:	$25,000 (est. 1990)
UNDP HDI/rank:	—
SP HDI/rank:	—

Nauru, which became independent in 1968, is a raised coral atoll occupied by a Micronesian population, and a large number of migrant workers, mainly from neighbouring Kiribati and Tuvalu. These are mainly employed in phosphate mining, the sole element of the island economy. This has given Nauru a very high national income, though unevenly distributed, a massive dependence on imported goods (including food and, occasionally, water), the largest proportion of migrant workers in the Pacific region and serious health and environmental problems. Data on social and economic conditions in Nauru are difficult to obtain.

About two-thirds of all employment in Nauru is of migrants, though Nauruans dominate government employment. Over half (around 2,000) of all migrant workers are from Kiribati and Tuvalu, with significant numbers of Europeans, Filipinos, Chinese and other Pacific Islanders. All but Europeans and some Asians live in a single labour compound in cramped conditions. The government has opposed the migration of families, provided low wages for all expatriate workers, discouraged long-term residence (to the extent that only those born of Nauruans, or of Nauruans and other Pacific Islanders may become citizens) and offered poor conditions of employment, matters of concern in the countries of migrant origin. Some governments have discouraged their citizens from taking up employment on Nauru. Phosphate mining will end around the turn of the century, and many migrant workers will leave.

Further reading

Weeramantry, C., *Nauru: Environmental Damage under International Trusteeship*, Melbourne, Oxford University Press, 1992.

New Caledonia

Land area:	19,100 sq km
Population:	196,840 (1996)
Main languages:	Melanesian (about 32 languages), French
Main religions:	Christianity (mainly Roman Catholicism and Protestantism)
Main minority groups:	Melanesians 86,800 (44%), Polynesians 22,800 (12%), Asians 8,200 (4%)
Real per capita GDP:	$13,000 (1989)
UNDP HDI/rank:	—
SP HDI/rank:	—

New Caledonia is one of ten French overseas departments and territories. France took formal possession of New Caledonia in 1853 and, by the 1870s, three crucial themes in New Caledonia's history were already present: a nickel rush, Melanesian opposition to land acquisition and the growth of a European population at the expense of the indigenous Melanesian population, who became a minority. The extent of land alienation, the bitterness of the dispossessed and mutual incomprehension between Melanesians and Europeans provoked a sustained and bloody revolt in 1878, the longest and most violent reaction to European colonization in the island Pacific. The eventual triumph of the French emphasized the marginalization of the Melanesians, many of whom were forced onto reservations and subject to the *indigénat*, a code of 'native law'. For fifty years the Melanesian population declined, while migration from Asia and Europe emphasized their minority status.

During the Second World War, New Caledonia when it became a major US military base employing Melanesians at high wages. The war ensured rising demand for nickel and chrome, and a mining boom was matched by a commercial boom. Melanesians received more adequate wages, the *indigénat* was abolished, the agricultural sector declined, and the tertiary sector – both public and private – absorbed the bulk of the waged labour force. Continued and increased financial subsidies, especially for the bureaucracy, transformed New Caledonia into an artificial 'consumer colony', widening the gulf between urban prosperity and rural poverty. France contributes more than half of New Caledonia's budget. This situation has weakened mainly Melanesian (Kanak) demands for independence. Relative regional and ethnic economic inequalities have worsened in the past decade. Melanesians are incorporated into the periphery of the New Caledonian economy through wages, taxes, pensions, medical assistance and a variety of legal and institutional means, and there is no longer a 'traditional' self-reliant Melanesian economy.

Melanesians

The Melanesian population consists of more than thirty distinct language groups, some (in the Loyalty Islands) influenced by historical Polynesian migration. Their social organization is similar to those in the Melanesian islands to the north. Following European contact, Melanesian population numbers fell from about 50,000 to only 28,000 in 1901 and Melanesians were displaced by settlers to reservations on the east coast of the main island (the Grande Terre), though in the Loyalty Islands European settlers were absent. Population numbers began to grow in the 1930s but, as Melanesians were poised to become a majority in the 1960s, a new wave of European and Polynesian migration ensured that they remained a minority. In contrast with other ethnic groups, Melanesians are a more rural population. After more than a century of marginalization, the land is the only resource unequivocally owned by Melanesians and attitudes to the retention, expansion, exploitation and alienation of land underlie economic and political development.

After the Second World War Melanesians sought to improve their political, economic and social status. The first significant multiracial party, Union Calédonienne (UC), was founded in 1951 and attracted substantial Melanesian support. However, Melanesian frustrations with the slow pace of reform, racial discrimination and continued opposition to their aspirations towards greater autonomy produced a radicalization of politics by the 1970s. Confrontations between militant Melanesians (Kanaks) and the administration focused on land rights, and a number of wholly Kanak parties, based on regional and religious differences, broke away from UC or were spontaneously created. In opposition to the more radical Kanak parties, fragmented conservative parties consolidated into the Rassemblement pour la Calédonie dans la République (RPCR), a primarily European party.

Land issues dominated politics. In many Melanesian reserves land pressures were emphasized by natural increases which stimulated demands for land reform. Though the speed of restoring land to Melanesians increased in the 1960s and 1970s it still fell short of Melanesian expectations and needs. In the second half of the 1970s Kanaks mounted direct action and occupied alienated land. Increased amounts of land were also purchased and returned to Melanesians, but invariably too little and too late to defuse tension and political pressure, which gradually shifted to demands for independence rather than increased autonomy.

As other parts of Melanesia became independent, and a socialist government took power in France in 1981, there was renewed Kanak hope for independence. However, there was no sign that France intended to move towards independence for New Caledonia. Tension and violence mounted and Kanaks, angry that no electoral reform was proposed and there was no timetable for independence, came together in a new coalition, the Front de Libération Nationale Kanak et Socialiste (FLNKS), to demand independence. The population composition of New Caledonia consistently ensures that as long as Europeans, Asians and Polynesians vote for retention of ties with France, Kanak demands for independence are unlikely to be satisfied through the ballot box. As the Kanak position hardened, the conservative settler (Caldoche) position also became increasingly extremist.

The emergence of FLNKS heralded an escalation of conflict as Kanaks abandoned the unbalanced struggle for constitutional change and embarked on direct and violent action to secure independence. FLNKS boycotted the November 1984 elections, and undertook more direct action, briefly holding the small town of Thio and declaring a provisional government of the Republic of Kanaky, with Jean-Marie Tjibaou, the FLNKS leader, as President. Violent conservative reaction followed and Kanaks and Europeans were killed in various incidents. The military presence was strengthened, right-wing opposition to Kanak militancy grew and, without French or urban support, Kanak militants were unable to gain power. Tentative French proposals for independence in association with France were ignored and the French Prime Minister, Laurent Fabius, devised new proposals which divided New Caledonia into four regions, each with its own council responsible for a range of development planning issues. FLNKS eventually accepted the basis of this plan.

As the French government stepped up its military presence, and the RPCR organized private militias, FLNKS sought to develop a more self-reliant Melanesian society and economy in rural areas, in association with the regional councils as a basis for eventual independence. Schools were established for Kanaks and cooperative agriculture was encouraged in a futile bid to destabilize the economy of Noumea. In the 1985 elections for the regional councils FLNKS won three of the four regions, but RPCR won so comprehensively in the predominantly European Noumea region that it also retained control of the Territorial Congress. A year later, the new Prime Minister, Jacques Chirac, reversed the process of change, freezing the funds of the regional councils and concentrating power in the hands of the Territorial Congress and the French High Commissioner. Starved of finance, FLNKS effectively lost its limited power, but not support, in the regions, the only places where it had legal and constitutional authority, and was reduced to an ineffective minority in the Territorial Congress.

The French conservative government moved forward with plans to hold a referendum on independence in 1987 in the face of socialist opposition and no changes to the electoral roll. FLNKS embarked on a series of pre-referendum protests leading to strong repression from the French riot police. Although the referendum gave overwhelming support to the existing political status, more than 80 per cent of the Melanesian population boycotted it. Intermittent violence continued.

The new French socialist government of 1988 began a process of negotiation and reconciliation resulting in the Matignon Accords of August 1988; three new regional assemblies would be established, with substantial power and financial resources (especially in the least developed regions), and a referendum on independence was scheduled for 1998 (with an electorate based on those living in the territory in 1988). Despite criticisms by extremists on both sides, the Accords won support at a referendum by the majority of Melanesians, but only 40 per cent of non-Melanesians. Most non-Melanesians thus opposed any notion of independence, however distant, but militant Kanaks were impatient at the long delay, despite initially welcoming a period of peace.

The most violent expression of Kanak opposition to the Matignon Accords was the murder in May 1989 of the FLNKS President, Jean-Marie Tjibaou, and the Vice-President, Yeiwene Yeiwene, by a dissident Kanak activist. The hesitant unity of the FLNKS coalition began to disintegrate. With the death of Tjibaou there was no comparable charismatic leadership, no consistent agenda for a programme of social and economic development leading towards now distant independence and frustration with the structure of development in the regions. Discontent remained and social and economic concerns surfaced again in the mid-1990s with various pro-independence parties arguing that France had provided little support for the socioeconomic advancement of Melanesians, and demanding that structures of independence be in place by 1998.

Polynesians and Asians

In the 1930s and subsequently during the 1970s there was substantial migration, initially from Asia (Vietnam and Indonesia) and subsequently from France's other French Pacific territories, Wallis and Futuna, and French Polynesia. After the boom many migrants left, but Wallisians and Futunans generally remained because of poor development prospects in their home islands. Both Asians and Polynesians have generally supported France and French policy in New Caledonia, though in the 1990s there was some Wallisian and Futunan support for the FLNKS. Wallisians and Futunans have found it relatively difficult to obtain employment in New Caledonia – and have higher unemployment rates than Melanesians – but otherwise, like most migrants, have superior access to services than in their home countries. Asians have become established, are well integrated into commercial activities and, unlike Polynesians, are not concentrated in particular urban areas.

Conclusions and future prospects

The problems experienced by FLNKS, following the death of Tjibaou and the signing of the Matignon Accords, suggest that independence is no closer now than it was at the start of the 1980s, during the first period of Kanak militancy. Although Melanesians have achieved superior access to education, health and other services, there remain marked disparities between Noumea, where the bulk of the European population live, and the rural areas, and also within Noumea, between Melanesian housing estates and European suburbs. Melanesian incomes, life expectancy and access to services are significantly poorer than those of other groups. Access to employment has scarcely improved in more than a decade, strikes have become more common in the 1990s and frustrations over the French presence have scarcely changed. These were rekindled in 1995 with the election of Chirac as French President, the resumption of nuclear testing in French Polynesia, high unemployment and significant immigration.

Further reading

Connell, J., *New Caledonia or Kanaky? The Political History of a French Colony*, Canberra, National Centre for Development Studies, 1987.

Henningham, S., 'The uneasy peace: New Caledonia's Matignon accords at mid-term', *Pacific Affairs*, vol. 66, no. 4, 1994, pp. 519–37.

Kircher, I., *The Kanaks of New Caledonia*, London, MRG report, 1986.

Ounei-Small, S., 'Kanaky: the "peace" signed with our blood', in D. Robie (ed.), *Tu Galala: Social Change in the Pacific*, Wellington, Bridget Williams Books, 1992, pp. 163–79.

Vivier, J-L., *Mon chemin avec le FLNKS*, Paris, L'Harmattan, 1992.

New Zealand

Land area:	270,530 sq km
Population:	3,494,300 (1993)
Main languages:	English, Maori
Main religions:	Christianity (various)
Main minority groups:	Maori 430,000 (12.3%), Pacific Islanders 175,000 (5.0%)
Real per capita GDP:	$16,720
UNDP HDI/rank:	0.927 (14)

New Zealand (Aotearoa) has two main populated islands, the North Island and the South Island. It was not settled until around the eleventh century when there was significant migration from eastern Polynesia. The Maori culture largely developed in isolation from other Polynesian cultures, and from European influences. By the start of the nineteenth century traders had sought to exploit New Zealand's natural resources and missionaries had begun to evangelize the *tangata whenua* (the people of the land). There was considerable settlement before New Zealand officially became part of the British Empire in 1840.

The Treaty of Waitangi was signed in February 1840 by the Lieutenant-General-Elect, Captain William Hobson, and many of the major Maori chiefs; this treaty acknowledged Maori ownership of the land. However, the treaty did not prevent unscrupulous practice by Europeans seeking to obtain more land, and thus consequent violence. Maori disillusionment and anger at subsequent white responses to the treaty have underlain all, and especially the more recent, attempts to gain greater self-determination and power. The increasing demand of white settlers (Pakeha) for land led to considerable conflict throughout much of the nineteenth century, especially in the North Island. Sporadic contact in the 1840s was followed by the New Zealand wars of the 1860s in the central and west coast areas of the North Island. Disease, violence and displacement reduced the Maori people and by the 1890s the Maori population had reached its nadir, having declined to about 40 per cent of its pre-contact size.

During the nineteenth century New Zealand developed as a mining and increasingly agricultural economy, in which the sheep industry dominated. Despite the displacement of Maori the white population grew only slowly. Maori men were granted the vote in 1867 and in the same year received four special seats in the House of Representatives. The Maori population again grew slowly. Depressions in the 1880s and 1930s slowed economic and population growth. Between 1945 and 1970 the annual rate of population growth increased significantly following a higher birth rate and considerable immigration. Economic growth led to diversification of migration away from its British origins, to Polynesia and South-East Asia. In the postwar years the economy became more urban, with export problems for the agricultural sector, and the population shifted into urban areas. Issues that concern minority groups are increasingly experienced in urban rather than rural areas.

Maori

Maori population numbers were probably about 1 million at the end of the eighteenth century, with an agricultural and fishing economy and a social organization similar to those of Polynesians in the smaller islands to the north-east. There were differences between tribal groups and warfare between them was not uncommon. The arrival of white settlers brought rapid population decline to the extent that the Maori were believed to be on the verge of extinction towards the end of the nineteenth century, when the population had fallen to not much more than 40,000. As in Australia colonial policy towards the indigenous population was to 'smooth the dying pillow' of an inferior race.

One initial result of European contact was the introduction of guns, which resulted in the escalation of indigenous warfare between Maori tribes in the 'musket wars'. About a quarter of the Maori population died from illness, and during the wars, and there were important divisions between Maori at the time of the signing of the Treaty of Waitangi in 1840. Maori chiefs were divided over signing the treaty and were uncertain about its provisions. The English text of the treaty guaranteed Maori 'the full, exclusive and undisturbed possession of their lands', while the Maori text used the words *te tino rangatiratanga* which could be translated as 'the sovereignty of their lands'. However, the Crown was promised *kawanatanga*, a Maori translation of 'governorship'. When the treaty was signed, there were some 2,000 white settlers, about 1 per cent of the population; many were uninterested in abiding by treaty regulations. A number of Maori chiefs refused to sign the treaty, fearing that they would lose their *mana* (power) and their lands. Some, such as the Waikato Chief Te Wherowhero, were dispossessed of their lands following the 'Maori wars'.

In the 1840s, as Pakeha settlers increased in numbers, there were clashes in all parts of the country between Pakeha and Maori. Pakeha resented Maori ownership of much of the best land in the North Island and land was purchased under the terms of the Treaty of Waitangi. This process was too slow for many Pakeha and too rapid for many Maori. In 1852 the country had gained its first constitution, a parliament and six provincial councils. Maori, excluded from the electorate (as they were not individual property holders), sought to establish their own government and in 1858 elected a Maori king, Te Wherowhero. One intention of this King Movement (*Kingitanga*) was to halt the sale of land to Pakeha by placing it under the *mana* of the king, and to establish a legal administrative system in areas ignored by the British administration. Two years later the New Zealand wars began at Waitara in Taranaki province. During the wars, which lasted for twelve years, the New Zealand government sought to punish those tribes involved by confiscating their lands. Almost 3.25 million acres were confiscated, including much of the best Waikato land, the Taranaki coastland and land in the Bay of Plenty.

The wars demoralized the Maori. Even the 'loyal' Maori who had opposed *Kingitanga* and supported British troops lost land in the aftermath. In some cases it was taken in the confiscations (*raupatu*), but a variety of semi-legal means were used to dispossess tribes throughout the remainder of the century. Increasingly the government sought to assimilate the Maori but, as Sinclair (1980) recorded, 'the white man's peace was more devastating than his war' as Parliament oppressed Maori and appropriated their resources.

After the land wars there were intermittent Maori attempts to reopen discussions on the Treaty of Waitangi, and to seek the restoration of confiscated land. In 1884 the Maori King led a deputation to London, but was refused an audience with the Queen and their petition was sent back to the New Zealand government, despite repeated unsuccessful attempts to negotiate with that government. An earlier movement, *Te Kotahitanga* (the Maori unity movement) was revived late in the century; it introduced a Maori Rights Bill into the New Zealand Parliament (where Maori had four seats) in 1894, seeking Maori control over their own lands, fisheries and other food resources, which was rejected two years later.

Further attempts to restore the provisions of the Treaty were again made at various points in the twentieth century, and have remained the central theme of Maori history and political affairs. A Royal Commission's findings on *raupatu* in 1928 vindicated the Maori position, and offered the Waikato, Taranaki and Bay of Plenty tribes compensation, based on the value of their lands at the time and the degree of 'blame' that could be attached to them in the wars. Waikato refused the offer and many Maori demanded that the land and not money be returned to them. A revised offer was eventually accepted by the Waikato people in 1946, though the basic problem of land alienation was little changed.

By the time of the Second World War the Maori were still primarily a rural population, mainly in the North Island. Most lived in poor conditions, with inadequate housing, poor access to services and limited access to land, as no more than about 1 per cent of the land of New Zealand was actually owned and occupied by Maori. After the war much of the increased affluence of New Zealand escaped the Maori despite new provisions for state housing, public health, education and other services. Many Maori began to migrate to the cities in search of employment, and a future outside traditional tribal (*iwi*) areas, hence problems of race relations and inadequate economic and social status became more visible. By the 1990s more than 80 per cent of Maori lived in urban areas.

A more radical Maori protest movement began in the 1970s with the formation of *Nga Tamatoa*, a group of educated young militants, who campaigned on issues such as language teaching in schools. In 1975 they organized a Land March down the length of the North Island to the Parliament in Wellington, which created a wide public consciousness of Maori issues. There was a renewed focus on the Treaty of Waitangi, centring on claims that it has failed to protect Maori land, forests and fisheries. In 1971 Nga Tamatoa attempted to disrupt the annual Waitangi Day celebrations that commemorated the signing; such disruptions have continued for the following quarter of a century.

The establishment of a conservative National Party government in 1975 resulted in a tendency to dismiss Maori issues as merely the grievances of militant radicals; this intensified Maori opposition. In the same year, however, the Labour government had passed the Treaty of Waitangi Act which set up a tribunal to investigate land claims and related matters. A number of Maori mounted legal challenges against the government over land issues. These came before the Waitangi Tribunal that had the power to investigate new legislation for breaches of the treaty. Prominent among these cases was one in opposition to government plans to develop a fuel plant on the Taranaki coast, where Maori land had long been confiscated, that would have pumped industrial waste into coastal waters and on reefs used by the Te Atiawa tribe of Taranaki for fishing. The Tribunal concluded that the proposed outfall constituted a breach of the treaty and the Chairman of the Tribunal, Judge Edward Taihakurei Durie, stated that the tribunal itself was 'an acknowledgement of Maori existence, of their prior occupation of the land and of an intent that the Maori presence would remain and be respected. It made us one country, but acknowledged that we were two people. It established the regime not for uniculturalism, but for bi-culturalism.'

During the 1980s there was a growing demand for Maori sovereignty alongside renewed attempts to gain a public commitment from the government to honour the Treaty of Waitangi. The demand for sovereignty emphasized the necessity for the acknowledgement that New Zealand is Maori land, and that confiscated land be returned to Maori. In 1984 the Tainui of Waikato demanded that the provisions of the Treaty of Waitangi be enshrined in a constitution or bill of rights and that there be a reform of the political system. The new Labour Party government increased the powers of the Waitangi Tribunal, enabling it to consider claims that had arisen since 1840, thus enabling Maori for the first time to seek restitution and compensation for the loss of land and resources. Despite discussions of political reform no new Maori seats were created. Maori voters can choose either to be on the general electoral roll or vote for one of the four Maori seats.

The provisions of the Treaty of Waitangi and the Waitangi Tribunal met more challenges in the second half of the 1980s. In 1987 the New Zealand Maori Council successfully opposed government plans to transfer certain assets to state-owned enterprises as a prelude to privatization, arguing that if Crown lands were sold off there would be no assets left to settle Maori claims before the Waitangi Tribunal. Two years later the Tainui Maori achieved a similar success when they challenged government plans to sell off coal-mining rights in the Waikato, when the coal was under land confiscated from the Tainui. The government also experienced problems when it ignored Maori fishing rights. At a time of economic recession, with the government seeking to restructure the national economy, these developments created tension in New Zealand society. There was a backlash as many Pakeha felt threatened by the apparently increasing scope and greater militancy of Maori claims. Simultaneously Maori were critical of the continued slow progress in meeting their demands, though social changes resulted in the teaching of the Maori language and *taha Maori* (the Maori way) in schools, enabling some degree of biculturalism.

Maori participation in resource management and conservation has become increasingly prominent as the effects of the Resource Management Act (1991) and the Conservation Act (1987) have become apparent. These acts included rights of reparation for past and ongoing violations of the treaty, including the right to have Crown land (and resources) returned to traditional owners and the right of Maoridom to control and manage their natural resources according to their own cultural values. Nevertheless there was slow progress in making reparations by returning land and other resources. Few resources have been available to Maoridom to battle for the preservation and integrity of their resources. Despite a series of new statutes, laws and speeches, Maoridom had experienced little real change in practical terms; this increased the frustrations of militants and angered conservative Pakehas who believed that scarce financial resources were being wasted on ingrates.

At the end of 1994 the New Zealand government sought a 'once and for all' settlement for all Maori grievances, with a 'fiscal envelope' of NZ $1,000 million, after which all treaty claims would be deemed by the Crown to have been settled. The attempt to reduce all issues of justice for Maori to a sum of money denied the social, political and cultural impacts of colonization and sought to eradicate Maori rights as established by the Treaty of Waitangi. It defined Maori rights, and therefore *rangatiratanga*, within a colonial framework as 'limited management rights' rather than self-determination, and failed to recognize Maori spiritual attachment to their land. It was rejected by Maori activists in many places, though in December 1994 the Waikato Tainui tribe reached an agreement with the government concerning one of the largest of the 400 outstanding claims. The settlement cost the government NZ $170 million, involved the return of 14,000 hectares of land to the Waikato people and a government apology for *raupatu*. Generally Maoridom rejected the 'fiscal envelope', resulting in considerable unity in Maori society but frustration for the conservative National Party government.

During 1995 Maori demonstrators occupied a number of sites, including a public park in Wanganui and the tourist centre of Rotorua, in an ongoing series of protests over the Crown's allegedly illegal occupation of Maori land. Disputes within Maoridom over the distribution of settlement claims met conservative reaction. In May 1995 the Prime Minister, Jim Bolger, and Dame Arikinui Te Atairangikaahu, Queen of the Tainui, the largest Maori tribal federation, signed an agreement under which the government would give cash and land to a total value of NZ $170 million in full and final settlement of land grievances. Under the agreement, which concerned 500,000 hectares of land illegally seized by European settlers in the 1860s, the government handed back thousands of hectares of land which remained under government control. Activists opposed the May 1995 settlement on the grounds that it was insufficient and land would go to the wrong people. Tribes with little claim on fishing rights and urban Maori without close links to their tribes have protested that tribally based settlements may deliver disproportionate benefits to some Maori simply because of the assets available in their region, and would disadvantage urban Maori. Most of the major Maori land claims have yet to be decided on, including three-quarters of South Island and large tracts of North Island, and only 5 per cent of New Zealand is owned by Maori.

Relative to other ethnic groups in New Zealand the Maori are disadvantaged socially and economically. Developments on Maori land, still of limited extent, are limited by lack of capital. Most Maori are concentrated in areas of unskilled employment, where wages are low and unemployment rates are high. In 1995 the national unemployment rate was 8 per cent, but for Maori it was 21 per cent. Some 22 per cent of Maori graduate from high school, but the national average is 40 per cent. The Maori crime rate is high, as is the Maori percentage of the jailed population. In 1989 the Maori infant mortality rate was 19, compared with the non-Maori rate of 11, though this discrepancy has since declined, and Maori life expectancy was seven to eight years less than the New Zealand average. Poor living conditions, with inadequate housing in inner urban areas, and high rates of unemployment, have contributed to poor self-images, violence and criminal behaviour, a situation dramatically portrayed in the highly successful New Zealand film, *Once Were Warriors* (1994), based on Alan Duff's book of the same title. A major challenge facing Maoridom is to use Maori resources, and other systems, to enable development for the urban dispossessed, for whom social organizations other than the tribe (*iwi*) have greater validity.

A small group of militant Maori have continued to press for a version of sovereignty; they have proved a disruptive force at Waitangi Day celebrations, and on other occasions, have alienated Pakeha, whose views of Maori issues have otherwise become less intractable. The slow settlement of historical grievances has not yet created an economic base enabling Maori to achieve greater self-determination in terms of economic sovereignty, and there is a range of opinions on how self-determination might better be achieved. There are generational and rural–urban and regional divisions in Maori leadership but a growing acceptance of the need for Maori sovereignty. This is likely to require the government to seek out new constitutional arrangements, and it has led to considerable turbulence and fluctuation in New Zealand politics. The outcome in the first half of 1995 was greater confrontation, anger, resentment and violence, despite the progress on grievances under the Treaty of Waitangi, and considerable ongoing public expenditure.

Pacific Islanders

Since the early 1960s there has been migration from the Pacific, especially Polynesia, to New Zealand. The larger urban concentration of Pacific Islanders living outside their own countries is in Auckland, sometimes referred to as the 'Polynesian capital of the world'. By 1991 there were 167,000 Pacific Islanders – those specifying an island ethnic identity – in New Zealand, of whom half were born there. The largest group were Samoans (86,000), followed by Cook Island Maori (38,000), Tongans (23,000), Niueans (14,000) and Fijians (5,000). Islanders experience higher rates of unemployment and are mainly employed in manufacturing industries, but Islanders born in New Zealand are more likely to be employed and work in professional, managerial and technical jobs. Economic restructuring in the 1980s has tended to disadvantage Islanders, some of whom have migrated onwards to Australia and the USA. There are some concentrations of Pacific Islanders in overcrowded, impoverished inner city areas, especially in Auckland, where their residential distribution is similar to that of Maori. Formal recognition of the political significance of Pacific Islanders came in 1985 when the Labour government formed a Ministry of Pacific Island Affairs, which has an advisory council consisting of members of the six main island groups.

Other minorities

Historically most migration to New Zealand was from Great Britain but the sources of migration became more diverse in the years after the Second World War. Immigration reached a peak in the late 1950s, when more than half of all migrants were from Great Britain and most others were from northern Europe. The proportion of migrants from outside northern Europe (and, in recent decades, Polynesia) has always been relatively small. Although there has been migration from the former Yugoslavia, and considerable discrimination against non-English-speaking migrants, the most serious health, housing, educational and welfare service problems are associated with non-English speaking migrants from the Pacific, rather than migrants from Europe or Asia. Indo-Chinese refugee settlers have experienced problems, especially in access to employment; a small number have migrated onwards to Australia.

Conclusions and future prospects

Through the policy of biculturalism, and the practice of the Waitangi Tribunal, New Zealand governments have increasingly sought to enable Maori development. Maori tribes (*iwi*) have developed programmes for local development, but have often been without the land and capital to implement them; much less attention has been given to the more intractable problems of urban Maori. Obtaining redress from the government for the wrongful invasion and confiscation of land has been a slow and bitter process. Changing Maori political and cultural strategies have drawn attention away from difficulties experienced by other migrant groups, especially Pacific Islanders. Biculturalism has meant little to other minorities, mainly Asian groups, who have also sometimes been disadvantaged. Despite the willingness of Pakeha to address such issues as resource and cultural alienation associated with colonialism, and substantial changes in policy and practice, the task of achieving development, especially of Maori, is likely to remain difficult.

Further reading

Duff, A., *Once Were Warriors*, Auckland, Tandem Press, 1990.

Maaka, R., 'The new tribe: conflicts and continuities in the social organization of urban Maori', *The Contemporary Pacific*, vol. 6, no. 2, 1994, pp. 311–36.

MacDonald, R., *The Maori of Aotearoa/New Zealand*, London, MRG report, 1990.

Sinclair, K. (Sir), *A History of New Zealand*, 2nd edn, London, Allen Lane, 1980.

Spoonley, P., 'Polynesian immigrant workers in New Zealand', in C. Moore, J. Leckie and D. Munro (eds), *Labour in the South Pacific*, Townsville, James Cook University of North Queensland, 1990, pp. 155–60.

Walker, R., *Ka Whawhai Tonu Mataou: Struggle without End*, Auckland, Penguin Books, 1990.

Wilson, M. and Yeatman, A. (eds), *Justice and Identity: Antipodean Practices*, Wellington, Allen & Unwin, 1995.

Minority-based and advocacy organizations

Amnesty International, PO Box 793, Wellington, New Zealand; tel 64 4 499 3349, fax 64 4 499 3505.

Federation of Maori Authorities, 158 The Terrace, Wellington, New Zealand; tel. 64 4 472 8080.

Maori Women's Welfare League, 24 Burnell Avenue, Thorndon, Wellington, New Zealand; tel. 64 4 473 6451, fax 64 4 499 6802.

New Zealand Maori Council, PO Box 5195, Wellington, New Zealand; tel. 64 4 472 5291, fax 64 4 473 4210.

New Zealand Federation of Ethnic Councils, 25 Houghton Street, Meadowbank, Auckland 5, New Zealand; tel. 64 9 528 8257, fax 64 9 302 2434.

Programme on Racism, PO Box 9573, Auckland, New Zealand.

Niue

Land area:	260 sq km
Population:	2,000 (1994)
Main languages:	Niuean, English
Main religions:	Christianity (mainly the Protestant Ekalesia Niue)
Main minority groups:	—
Real per capita GDP:	$1,360 (1984)
UNDP HDI/rank:	—
SP HDI/rank:	0.879 (3)

Niue is an uplifted coral atoll with a declining Polynesian population. Since 1974 it has been a self-governing state in free association with New Zealand. Niue had a population of more than 5,000 as recently as 1966, but it has fallen with extensive emigration to New Zealand (where there is a population of more than 10,000 of Niuean descent). There are some Europeans and other Polynesians (mainly from Tonga and Samoa) in Niue. No minority rights issues have been identified.

Northern Mariana Islands

Land area:	470 sq km
Population:	56,600 (1994)
Main languages:	Chamorro, English, Filipino
Main religions:	Christianity (mainly Roman Catholicism)
Main minority groups:	Filipinos, Chinese, Micronesians (no data)
Real per capita GDP:	$12,850 (1992)
UNDP HDI/rank:	—
SP HDI/rank:	—

Almost the whole population (90 per cent) of the Commonwealth of the Northern Mariana Islands live on Saipan. In 1947 the islands became part of the US Trust Territory of the Pacific Islands, but in 1975 78 per cent of the population voted to become a Commonwealth of the United States. The indigenous population of the Northern Marianas are Chamorros (as in Guam), but in the nineteenth century there was a substantial immigration of Carolinians (mainly from what are now the outer islands of Yap and Chuuk, Federated States of Micronesia). In almost every context the two populations are indistinguishable though the government has a 'special assistant' on Carolinian affairs. Since the 1960s there has been a substantial migration of Filipinos, other Asians and Micronesians into the Marianas. Only 39 per cent of the population was born in the Northern Marianas. Foreign migrant workers cannot become permanent residents (much less citizens) so the citizen minority dominate business and political life and tightly regulate migration.

Palau

Land area:	488 sq km
Population:	15,600 (1991)
Main languages:	Palauan, Filipino, English
Main religions:	Christianity (mainly Roman Catholicism)
Main minority groups:	Filipinos
Real per capital GDP:	$3,564 (1992)
UNDP HDI/rank:	—
SP HDI/rank:	0.939 (2)

Palau (Belau) is the westernmost Pacific island state, consisting of high islands where most of the population live, and largely depopulated outlying coral atolls. After more than a decade of often acrimonious constitutional debate and many referenda, Palau finally implemented a Compact of Free Association with the USA in October 1994 and became the most recent independent state, the last UN Trust Territory to achieve independence. There was considerable friction over support for and opposition to a nuclear-free constitution, a factionalism and polarity which also reflected traditional divisions in Palauan society. Since the 1980s there has been a substantial growth in Filipino migration, and, to a lesser extent, of the Japanese and Korean populations. Most are employed in the private sector, including fishing, tourism and construction. There has been some resentment at the increase in Asian population numbers despite considerable Palauan unwillingness to work in other than government employment. At the end of 1993 the overseas workforce had reached around 4,600, whereas the Palauan workforce was around 4,700. Outer islanders, from the southern atolls, speak distinct languages and form something of a minority in the Palauan state. There is much political and cultural conflict and instability, alarm about immigration and concern over the extent of Palauan emigration to Guam and the USA.

Further reading

Clark, R. and Roff, S.R., *Micronesia: The Problem of Palau*, London, MRG report, 1987.

Papua New Guinea

Land area:	462,240 sq km
Population:	3,963,000 (1994)
Main languages:	Melanesian (over 800 languages), Tok Pisin, Motu, English
Main religions:	animism, Christianity (various)
Main minority groups:	Bougainvilleans 159,000 (est., 4%)
Real per capita GDP:	$2,530
UNDP HDI/rank:	0.504 (126)
SP HDI/rank:	0.138 (13)

Papua New Guinea (PNG) consists of the eastern half of the island of New Guinea plus more than a hundred populated islands to the east and north, extending eastwards to the island of Bougainville in the Solomon Islands chain. The indigenous population is almost entirely Melanesian, though there are Polynesian outliers north of Bougainville. There are significant ethnic distinctions between population groups in different parts of the country. The country is unusually fragmented, by terrain, history, culture and language. About 840 distinct languages are spoken in PNG, around a quarter of the world's stock, reflecting enormous cultural divisions. There are a small number of Asian and European migrants, some of whom are long-established settlers. In a very real sense the country is a nation of minorities.

Melanesians were established in New Guinea at least 40,000 years ago, but colonialism is largely a twentieth century phenomenon which did not occur until after the 1940s in much of the densely populated highlands. It was only in the postwar years that modern education, health services and money reached the bulk of the population. PNG gained independence from Australia in 1975, against the wishes of many highlanders who feared coastal, especially Papuan, domination of the political economy.

At the time of independence PNG had a primarily agricultural economy, though a major copper and gold mine had begun production in the island of Bougainville in 1972. Since then other major copper and gold mines and natural gas and oil fields have been opened. More than three-quarters of the population live in rural areas and the capital city has about 250,000 people.

In the 1970s a small number of coastal ethnically based sub-regional groups exerted some localized political power in bids to obtain a greater share of national economic development. The Mataungan Association sought greater indigenous (Tolai) control of political and economic development in East New Britain, following concern over the extent of land alienation. The Association opposed the establishment of a multiracial Local Government Council, claiming that the council was a device to enable Europeans to control Tolai land and affairs.

Regional dissent was also strong in central Papua, whose identity was a colonial creation. In the core areas of Papua, around Port Moresby, grievances had built up over the direction of development. Although the capital city was in Papua, much postwar economic development was in resource-rich New Guinea, and many Papuans felt they were neglected. The movement largely originated in fear and distrust of highlanders and concern over their potential influence. In 1971 a group of Papuans in the House of Assembly formed a pressure group known as Papuan Action, and used the threat of secession to press for economic development in Papua. The Papua Besena secessionists made a unilateral and symbolic declaration of independence for Papua in early 1975; from then onwards the movement lost support as the quest for secession died and the party adapted itself to the task of securing greater political spoils for Papua, but above all for Central Province. Papuans remain convinced that they have been disadvantaged politically since independence and were strong supporters of Ted Diro and the Papuan Group of members of parliament in the late 1980s.

Bougainvilleans

The principal regional problems arose in Bougainville, which is geographically, historically and culturally more closely linked to the western Solomon Islands. Only in the present century, under colonialism, have traditional social and economic links become modernized and orientated westwards. Bougainvilleans are black, a characteristic which is shared in the Pacific by only a few peoples in the adjacent Solomon Islands. For most of the colonial era, Bougainville was neglected, and Bougainvilleans have always claimed uniqueness.

Neglect of Bougainville ended in 1964 when a huge copper deposit was confirmed at Panguna, in the interior mountains. Villagers opposed exploration and land alienation, emphasizing their feelings of separateness. This attitude was promoted by the nationalist Napidakoe Navitu which sought a referendum on whether Bougainville should remain within Papua New Guinea. The administration refused to hold such a referendum, but in 1973 the island was allowed to have the first provincial government in the country as a concession to emergent nationalism. Pressure for secession continued. Almost all the prominent secessionists were Roman Catholics, and the Roman Catholic Church was closely tied to the search for an independent cultural identity. Secession was sought both in defence of identity and in search of the material rewards of mining.

The province declared its independence, on 1 September 1975, just two weeks before PNG became independent. After six months the so-called Republic of the North Solomons effectively disintegrated. Although the two key issues that had contributed to secession remained, secessionist aspirations declined in the post-independence years as mining brought considerable wealth and rapid social change. However, despite growing incomes and access to services, concern increased over the environmental damage caused by the mine and there was resentment over the distribution of mining profits, the immigration of a workforce from elsewhere in PNG, and other social problems. Secessionist sentiments were rekindled and resurfaced in dramatic form in 1989 when militant landowners opposed the Panguna copper mine. Since then the struggle for Bougainvillean secession has provided the strongest challenge ever to the basis and stability of the Papua New Guinea nation, and the most serious political and humanitarian issue in Oceania since the war.

Mounting grievances over mining in 1988 evolved into a more general pressure for secession. The police force was unable to end the militancy, a national government Peace Package was rejected, the Bougainville Revolutionary Army (BRA) emerged, led by Sam Kauona, and the mine finally closed in September 1989. In 1990 the national government announced a total blockade of goods and services to the province, a decision quickly followed by the unilateral declaration of independence of the Republic of Bougainville. By this time the BRA was in apparent control of much of the island, though in the northern island of Buka support for the rebellion was hesitant. An interim government was established on Bougainville, with Francis Ona as President. From then onwards an effective communications blackout largely limited information from the island, though there were health problems and the economy and other services were collapsing. PNG and Bougainville leaders held talks on board a New Zealand ship, the *Endeavour*, off Kieta in mid-1990 which resulted in the Endeavour Accord.

The Endeavour Accord, which stated that services to Bougainville would be restored and that the long-term political status of Bougainville would be reconsidered, did not hold. PNG troops landed on Buka in September 1990 and restored some semblance of government control, but not without force. Civil war was waged there for several months, and human rights abuses in various parts of the province were documented on both the PNG and BRA sides. By the end of 1992 most of the north and centre of Buka and parts of south-western Bougainville were under government control. The area around the Panguna mine remained under BRA control and there was sporadic violence in the marginal areas.

Government forces entered the town of Arawa in February 1993 and in 1994 the government temporarily gained control of Panguna. Further attempts were made to secure a political resolution of the crisis and services were restored to more areas of Bougainville. A change of government in August 1994 led to Sir Julius Chan giving primacy to a peace initiative for Bougainville. A ceasefire was declared, a South Pacific Peacekeeping Force was introduced and a peace conference organized at Arawa. A Bougainville Transitional Government was established in March 1995, operating through eight local interim authorities but the Premier, Theodore Miriung, was murdered in October 1996. An end to violence and a peaceful solution for the whole of Bougainville remain distant.

Though the crisis did not fragment PNG, it resulted in massive devastation in Bougainville. The economy disintegrated, hundreds of lives were lost, children missed years of education, communities and families were torn apart, new divisions and hatreds emerged and old divisions were rekindled and, after more than six years of struggle, no end appeared imminent, despite the intervention of the UN. The extensive blockade of Bougainville, the refusal to allow the International

Red Cross or medical supplies to enter for long periods of time, or to give journalists access to the island, and the difficulties placed in the way of Amnesty International led to considerable external criticism of the manner in which PNG was seeking to resolve the crisis. The crisis disturbed relations between PNG and both Australia and the Solomon Islands.

Conflicts on Bougainville are the most severe ethnic and regional issue in PNG, but there are other regional differences. Generally these are perceived to be distinctions between highlanders and other Papua New Guineans, based on social and physical characteristics and on the late development of much of the highlands. Tribal fighting remains a means of dispute settlement in the highlands. There has been substantial migration from the highlands to coastal towns and rural areas, and some conflicts between migrants (not only from the highlands) and other urban residents. Where migration has led to conflict between migrant and settled populations for land, work and services, ethnic and racial conflicts are more prevalent, often leading to attempts to displace new and different urban residents and achieve greater ethnic homogeneity. With increased unemployment, and more difficult access to resources, such tensions have increased rather than diminished.

At both national and provincial levels, there are few places where there has never been a threat of secession. Demands from the island provinces have always been more substantial. In 1994 the four island provinces (other than the North Solomons) prepared their own constitution for a five-province Federated Melanesian Republic, in their demand for greater autonomy and in opposition to proposals to reduce the power of provincial governments, but the bid faded in 1995. The most significant outcome of regional dissent around the time of independence was the establishment of a provincial government system, based on that first introduced in Bougainville, and designed to give greater autonomy to the provinces and so weaken secessionist tendencies. However, by the end of the 1980s provincial government had become costly and inefficient. In 1995 the provincial government system was removed, despite enormous opposition, especially in the islands, and some concern that this would result in an increase in secessionist aspirations.

Conclusions and future prospects

Because of the extreme fragmentation of Melanesian society, PNG has not generally been faced with long-term ethnic unrest – except in Bougainville – or class conflict, but rather faces civil unrest, crime and violence as a result of social changes and other factors. Although there have been elements of national unity, including the rapid growth of the principal *lingua franca*, Tok Pisin, the sense of national unity and purpose has been overshadowed by the pervasiveness of localism and regionalism. Ethnic and cultural identities in PNG are not quaint relics of traditional times, but contributing elements to powerful local nationalist struggles that may develop further.

Further reading

Amnesty International, *Papua New Guinea: An Agenda for Human Rights*, London, 1995.

Connell, J., *Papua New Guinea: The Challenges of Economic Growth*, London, Routledge, 1997.

Oliver, D., *Black Islanders,* Melbourne, Hyland House, 1991.

Minority-based and advocacy organizations

Australian Bougainville Support Group, 34 Darvall Road, Eastwood, Sydney, NSW 2122, Australia; tel./fax 61 2 804 7602.

Bougainville Freedom Movement, PO Box 134, Erskineville, NSW 2043, Australia; tel. 61 2 290 1620, fax 61 2 267 4746.

Pitcairn Islands

Land area:	5 sq km
Population:	53 (1993)
Main language:	English (Pitcairnese dialect)
Main religions:	Christianity (Seventh Day Adventism)
Main minority groups:	—
Real per capita GDP:	—
UNDP HI/rank:	—
SP HDI/rank:	—

Pitcairn Islanders are mainly the descendants of the mutineers of HMS *Bounty* and the Tahitian women they took to Pitcairn in 1790. There has been substantial emigration in the twentieth century, though for two decades the population has stabilized. There are no minority groups on the island.

Solomon Islands

Land area:	27,560 sq km
Population:	376,400 (1994)
Main languages:	Melanesian (about 80 languages), Polynesian (about 5 languages), Pijin, English
Main religions:	Christianity (various), animism
Main minority groups:	Polynesians 25,000 (6.6%), i-Kiribati 5,000 (1.3%)
Real per capita GDP:	$2,266
UNDP HDI/rank:	0.563 (118)
SP HDI/rank:	0.191 (12)

The Solomon Islands are one of the largest Pacific island states. This British colony became independent in 1978, has an economy based on the export of natural resources (especially, in recent years, the rapid and unsustainable exploitation of timber) and a rapidly growing, primarily Melanesian population. More than 80 per cent of the population live in rural areas and rely on a semi-subsistence agricultural economy. The central chain of high islands was historically occupied by Melanesians, while outlying islands, including coral atolls, were occupied by different Polynesian cultural groups. Many Polynesians have moved to the centre, and especially the capital Honiara, but experience some difficulties in obtaining employment there.

The Micronesian Gilbertese (i-Kiribati) were resettled in the Solomon Islands from the 1950s, when both the Gilbert Islands (Kiribati) and Solomon Islands were British colonies, because of land shortages in the Gilbert Islands. By the 1970s about a thousand Gilbertese were established in the Solomon Islands; the population has grown to around 4,000, many living in Honiara. Like Polynesians they have experienced problems of access to employment, and of access to land in rural areas. There are small numbers of other migrant groups, mainly around Honiara, including Chinese and Europeans, but numbers have fallen since independence. There are considerable cultural differences throughout the country, not only between those peoples of Polynesian, Melanesian and Micronesian (Gilbertese) origin, but between the peoples of the west and those of the east. Cultural and economic differences have resulted in secessionist sentiments in some areas.

Tokelau

Land area:	12 sq km
Population:	1,500 (1994)
Main language:	Tokelauan
Main religions:	Christianity (Roman Catholicism and Congregational)
Main minority groups:	—
Real per capita GDP:	$670 (1983)
UNDP HDI/rank:	—
SP HDI/rank:	—

Tokelau is the smallest political entity (after the Pitcairn Islands) in Oceania, consisting solely of three coral atolls occupied by a Polynesian population. It is 480 kilometres north of Samoa, only accessible by sea, and some administration remains based in Apia in Western Samoa because of the fragmentation of the territory, poor links between the atolls and some social tensions between them. Tokelau remains a non-self-governing territory under New Zealand's administration. Tokelauans are New Zealand citizens; more than half of all Tokelauans are established migrants in New Zealand but the island populations are more or less stable. There are no minority populations in Tokelau.

Tonga

Land area:	750 sq km
Population:	98,300 (1994)
Main languages:	Tongan
Main religions:	Christianity (Free Wesleyan, Roman Catholicism, Mormon and Tokakailo)
Main minority groups:	—
Real per capita GDP:	$1,350 (1992)
UNDP HDI/rank:	—
SP HDI/rank:	0.723 (4)

The Kingdom of Tonga consists of four groups of low-lying islands, thirty-six of which are inhabited by a Polynesian population. Tonga remains a constitutional monarchy and the king exercises considerable influence; nobles also have enormous political and economic power and Tonga is probably the most stratified contemporary Polynesian society. Cabinet ministers are appointed for life by the King. In 1996 two journalists and a member of parliament were jailed for twenty-six days for 'contempt of parliament' and were declared 'prisoners of conscience' by Amnesty International. The Tongan economy is predominantly agricultural but remittances from Tongans overseas are the most important element of the national economy. Because of substantial emigration, the population has remained more or less stable over the past two decades. Immigration is discouraged and the Tongan-born children of aliens are required to leave the country at the age of 21. In recent years, however, passports have been sold to aliens, and a number of these, especially from Hong Kong and Taiwan, have settled in Tonga and established businesses there. Otherwise, migrant populations have few political rights, and migrants, including passport holders, are unwelcome.

Tuvalu

Land area:	24 sq km
Population:	9,500 (1994)
Main languages:	Tuvaluan
Main religions:	Christianity (Congregational Church of Tuvalu)
Main minority groups:	—
Real per capita GDP:	$1,210 (1992)
UNDP HDI/rank:	—
SP HDI/rank:	0.652 (5)

Tuvalu is one of the smallest and least developed independent nations in the world, consisting of nine coral atolls and reef islands stretching over some 590 kilometres of the South Pacific. The Polynesian state of Tuvalu (the Ellice Islands) became independent in 1978, after separation from the Micronesian Gilbert Islands (which became Kiribati). Other than a small number of expatriate workers, there are few migrants in Tuvalu and no minority populations.

Vanuatu

Land area:	12,190 sq km
Population:	164,100 (1994)
Main languages:	Melanesian (about 105 languages), Bislama, French, English
Main religions:	Christianity (various), animism
Main minority groups:	Wallisians and Futunans, i-Kiribati (no data)
Real per capita GDP:	$2,500
UNDP HDI/rank:	0.562 (119)
SP HDI/rank:	0.424 (11)

Vanuatu, known until independence in 1980 as the New Hebrides, is part of Melanesia, although the small southern island of Futuna is to some extent a Polynesian outlier. For its population size, it has a greater linguistic diversity than any other country in the world. The constitution declares the national language to be Bislama (a pidgin English), with the official languages also including English and French. There are some seventy populated islands. Diversity is manifest in geographical, cultural and linguistic divisions.

Contemporary political divisions were shaped during the colonial years, when there were two separate colonial administrations, British and French, governing the condominium (locally referred to as 'pandemonium') alongside mission-provided education. Gaining independence was unusually complicated as Britain wished to leave but France sought to stay. There was a secessionist, anti-independence movement centred on Santo in the northern group of islands; the rebellion was ended by troops from Papua New Guinea. Vanuatu was the only country in Oceania that did not achieve independence peacefully. This has resulted in some friction between different regions and although there has been no resurgence of secessionist movements since independence, there are regional religious and political differences, especially between Francophone and Anglophone areas.

There are some recent migrant populations from other Pacific island states. During the condominium years, Wallisians and Futunans migrated to Vanuatu to take up plantation employment and their population was around 1,000 at the time of independence. Since then the number has declined because of the difficulty of obtaining work permits. From the early 1960s there was also migration of Gilbertese (i-Kiribati) and there were several hundred there in the 1980s. Like Wallisians and Futunans, they have experienced considerable difficulty in obtaining work permits and Vanuatu citizenship, despite having renounced Kiribati citizenship and having been in Vanuatu for several decades. The government discourages immigration and expatriates have been deported on several occasions, often for arbitrary reasons. The various minority populations of Vanuatu have thus declined in number since independence.

Wallis and Futuna

Land area:	124 sq km
Population:	14,400 (1994)
Main languages:	Wallisian, Futunan, French
Main religions:	Christianity (Roman Catholicism)
Main minority groups:	—
Real per capita GDP:	—
UNDP HDI/rank:	—
SP HDI/rank:	—

Wallis and Futuna are an overseas territory of France, consisting of two populated Polynesian islands, with their own languages and cultures. French is the official language of administration. The islands are divided into three administrative districts: Wallis, Alo (Futuna) and Sigave (Samoa), which correspond with established kingdoms. The hereditary kings retain considerable authority. An official from France (*administrateur supérieur*) is head of the territory and president of the Territorial Assembly, which includes the three kings and a number of elected members. There has been substantial emigration since the 1960s and about half of all Wallisians and Futunans live in New Caledonia. There have been numerous disputes on both islands between the traditional Polynesian leaders and French officials and there is an uneasy relationship between the traditional chiefly structure (the kings), the powerful Roman Catholic Church, the locally elected people's representatives and French government officials (who are not Polynesians). Other than a small number of French bureaucrats there are no minority groups, though Futunans, who represent a third of the population, are culturally distinct from Wallisians.

West Papua

Land area:	410,660 sq km
Population:	1,750,000 (1993)
Main languages:	Melanesian (many languages), Indonesian
Main religions:	animism, Christianity (various), Islam
Main minority groups:	Melanesians 1,100,000 (62.9%)
Real per capita GDP:	—
UNDP HDI/rank:	—
SP HDI/rank:	—

West Papua is the easternmost province of Indonesia, consisting of the western half of the island of New Guinea and some large offshore islands. The alternative and official name for the province is Irian Jaya, but this name is rejected by the indigenous movement. The indigenous Melanesian population is similar to that in the eastern half of New Guinea. West Papua is populated by many small social groups, separated by terrain, custom and language, of which there are about 250 in the province. Melanesians have been present in West Papua for at least 40,000 years, but European and Asian colonization was belated. Although West Papua became part of the Dutch East Indies in 1848, the Dutch devoted little attention to the island. Japan occupied West Papua during the Second World War. Many inland areas did not experience European contact until after the war when the Dutch regained control. There was Melanesian opposition to continued Dutch control, and guerrilla groups emerged in a number of areas. Considerable international debate followed over the legal status of the territory, and the Dutch belatedly made some efforts to develop it so that by the start of the 1960s a third of all government posts were held by Melanesians. Indonesia gained independence in 1949 and later claimed West Papua, formed the autonomous province of West Irian (at the same time as the Dutch formulated a separate plan for a state of Papua) and threatened an invasion. Military clashes occurred, the Dutch handed West Papua to the UN in 1962, which then passed it on to Indonesia in 1963, with the proviso that a plebiscite be held in 1969. In 1969 an 'Act of Free Choice' (officially the 'Determination of People's Opinion') was held, but through a combination of bribery and brute force, a majority of the 1,025 delegates was persuaded to accept the continuation of Indonesian rule.

See also 'West Irians' in entry on **Indonesia, EAST AND SOUTH-EAST ASIA.**

Melanesians

The majority of the Melanesian population live in rural areas, dependent primarily on subsistence agriculture with some cash cropping. Communications between many parts of the province are exceptionally difficult and service provision is very limited. Since the 1970s, mining has become of considerable importance, especially at the Mt Ertsberg gold and copper mine of the Freeport Corporation, and new mines have opened in the 1990s. Mineral products (including oil) now represent more than 90 per cent of the value of all exports from West Papua. Little of that income remains in the province and few Melanesians (less than 15 per cent at Freeport's mine) are employed in the mining industry, or in the public service or the commercial sector.

The largest and most conspicuous mine site is at Tembagapura in the most rugged area of the southern highlands. There have been bad relations between the Freeport company and the local Amungme people, whose traditional lands were appropriated when the mine began in 1967. In 1977 the Amungme people and Organisasi Papua Merdeka (OPM) guerrillas blew up Freeport's pipeline to the coast in protest against inadequate compensation and environmental degradation. The Indonesian military bombed and strafed villages and entire communities were resettled far away from the mine. From mid-1994 into 1995 there was further violence between villagers, OPM guerrillas and the Indonesian military, especially in the Tsinga valley, east of the mine site, because of the new land concessions and the destruction of the local environment and culture.

Pressure has been put on the Indonesian Commission for Human Rights to investigate the situation in the region. There are indications that there have been many other similar incidents in different parts of the province, some in association with forestry and oil palm development.

Since the early 1960s there has been considerable opposition to Indonesian rule, primarily led by the OPM, or Free Papua Movement, which was formed in 1963, and in 1971 proclaimed a Provisional Revolutionary Government of West Papua. The OPM was particularly significant in the early 1980s in response to the Indonesian government's transmigration schemes, which led to enormous repression, unrest and the flight of more than 10,000 refugees to Papua New Guinea. Some refugees have been granted asylum in Papua New Guinea, Australia, Sweden and elsewhere in the wake of massive arrests and reprisals by the Indonesian army in the late 1980s; the size and effectiveness of OPM have declined in the 1990s because of successful Indonesian military opposition, the death or migration of leaders and divisions between particular groups. The OPM has survived, but in much weakened and fragmented form, independent of regional and ideological differences. Opposition to Indonesian colonization remains considerable.

Transmigration from Indonesia has substantially changed the population composition of West Papua. The official aim of transmigration was to resettle millions of people from overcrowded central islands, especially Java and Bali, to more thinly populated, peripheral islands, such as Sumatra and West Papua. Transmigration has also been perceived as colonialism through demographic colonization, to create political stability in the periphery by overwhelming nationalist dissent. Transmigration has proved particularly difficult in West Papua because of local opposition, the limited fertility of soils and the unfamiliarity of migrants with forest environments. There has also been spontaneous migration from nearby islands, involving more than 100,000 people. Resistance to migration into West Papua has been a major cause of violence, though allegations and accounts are difficult to verify. Estimates vary but probably more than 150,000 transmigrants have moved to the coastal areas of West Papua; not all have stayed because of isolation, conflict, agricultural difficulties and the absence of services. There are some indications that transmigration has been scaled down because of opposition, environmental problems and World Bank concern. Because of various forms of migration, Melanesians now represent about two-thirds of the population of the province.

Conclusions and future prospects

In different ways the Melanesian population has been marginalized, physically displaced from new Indonesian mining, agricultural and forestry areas, and has intermittently experienced such severe problems that large numbers have been killed or become refugees. The Indonesian military forces have repressed any opposition and labelled all dissent as associated with the OPM. Despite attempts to assimilate and acculturate the Melanesian population, they remain ethnically and culturally distinct; integration has failed although assimilation remains a national policy. Disputes between villagers, the OPM and the military are likely to continue. The Melanesian population will continue to experience significant social, economic, environmental and political problems, and to maintain resistance in one form or another.

Further reading

Australia–West Papua Association, *West Papua Information Kit*, Sydney, 1995.

Suter, K., *East Timor and West Irian*, London, MRG report, 1982.

Whittaker, A., *West Papua: Plunder in Paradise*, London, Anti-Slavery Society, 1990.

Minority-based and advocacy organizations

Australia–West Papua Association, PO Box 1148, Collingwood, Victoria, 3066, Australia.

Western Samoa

Land area:	2,935 sq km
Population:	163,500 (1994)
Main languages:	Samoan
Main religions:	Christianity (various)
Main minority groups:	Niueans, Tokelauans
Real per capita GDP:	$3,000
UNDP HDI/rank:	$0.700 (88)
SP HDI/rank:	0.578 (9)

Western Samoa is one of the largest Polynesian states and in 1962 was the first Pacific island state to gain independence. Western Samoa has retained strong elements of *fa'a Samoa* (the Samoan traditional culture) in its constitution and political structure. Universal suffrage was not introduced until 1990 and only traditional chiefs (*matai*) are able to stand for election to parliament. Christian churches, as elsewhere in Polynesia, also exercise enormous authority. Village meetings have increasingly exercised authority under the 1990 Village Fono Act. Conflicts between the churches, village assemblies and parliament remain unresolved. Western Samoa was the first Pacific island state to experience significant labour immigration: to German plantations established in the second half of the nineteenth century. Most migrants were Chinese and Melanesians. There has also been historical migration from Tokelau, Niue and other Polynesian states. Most of the descendants of these migrant groups live in the capital city, Apia, and have been absorbed into the Samoan social system, although few have access to land. More recent migrants from Tokelau have experienced problems of access to scarce employment and the number has fallen since independence. Other than a very small number of Chinese, there are no other minority groups in Western Samoa.

CONTEMPORARY LEGAL STANDARDS ON MINORITY RIGHTS

Patrick Thornberry

Introduction

The *Directory* describes and investigates the world from one particular, striking perspective, observing the condition in each country of 'minorities'. Description and investigation build upon traditions from various disciplines – including history and legal studies, sociology and politics – which view the ethnic and the religious as a reality which repays investigation in its own right. The assumption is that exploring 'ethnic' issues and phenomena is capable of contributing to our understanding of the world we inhabit, illuminating the complex nature of its reality, the nature of human beings and the wellsprings of human action as individuals and through communities.

Law is a major discipline in this area, and structures the ethnic landscape in its own way. It is not and cannot be independent of currents and flows in related disciplines, but assimilates and transforms their understandings. The relevance of law lies in its claim to convert understandings into norms binding states, individuals and communities. The norms can be mutually inconsistent, hence the importance in this and other spheres of the relationship between international and municipal law: between the treaties and declarations and judgments of international law and the constitutions, statutes and judicial and administrative practices of the States. The present essay underscores the particular importance of international law for the rights of individuals and communities in the face of resistances by States. Human rights should not be conceived as antagonistic to the rights of States: the 'good State' provides security of rights for its citizens.

The *Directory* is a cartographic representation of enlightenment as well as oppression in the domestic realm. Domestic and international norms and developments influence each other. But international law declares that some State policies are legitimate, some not. It also suggests that enlightened practices which respect human rights can make the State a haven for all the people. The principal importance of this law lies in the provision of a reservoir of principles to which States, on different occasions and to various degrees, have expressed themselves as committed and bound. The principles are part idealistic and part practical. They are written in a language which is more than usually open, allowing adaptation to the specific circumstances of a nation. They are the product of a common diplomatic enterprise and reflect global or regional minimum standards. They are not the exclusive preserve or property of elites, but are our common property and imply a global readership. Their ultimate purpose is to touch the lives of human beings for the better, to restore dignity to persons and communities, or fortify it. They deserve to be better known and in some instances demand their dissemination as a legal obligation. Human rights are everyone's home ground, not a foreign field.

National self-expression and human rights

Legal comprehension of the importance of ethnic and religious bases of identity undergoes constant re-evaluation. Principles of mutual respect between peoples of different cultures and religion, between States and within States, were never entirely submerged in the Eurocentric international law of the nineteenth century. They interacted with post-Enlightenment respect for individuals, and the growth of non-European Powers to produce paternalism towards dependent peoples, and then rights for peoples and persons – those principles of self-determination and human rights which are building blocks of contemporary law. The existence of so many States in the international community owes much to nation-State doctrines of the nineteenth century and Wilsonian principles in the twentieth. The UN Charter enshrines self-determination,[1] as it enshrines human rights.[2]

Self-determination and human rights are neighbours; they are sometimes friendly, sometimes cool, and the relationship of both to ethnicity is a variable. Part of the vitality of self-determination is its tendency to assimilate, to push towards parallelism of outlooks, politics, language, culture and perhaps religion among the people of a country, whereas human rights tends towards diversity and self-expression. Neither tendency is unequivocal. Self-determination is an ideal which ought to connect with the reality – vividly illustrated in the *Directory* – of the astounding diversity and complex clustering of the world's peoples, languages and religious communities. It requires fresh readings if we are to avoid more Rwandas or Bosnias: less fascination with 'purification' of territory, secession and independence. Self-determination needs to accommodate diversity, the understanding that unity and diversity are not opposites, and the proposition that most people have multiple, sometimes divided loyalties – emotional splits are human, all too human.

Difference is not necessarily chaos. The doctrine of human rights, on the other hand, has been relatively comfortable with individual diversity but less so with the diversity of communities. Individual freedom and diversity can too easily become only the freedom of the decontextualized individual, floating free from ties of family, community, locality or belief group. The overstretching of individual rights can have deleterious consequences for many societies, including the indigenous. Some groups which comprehend individuals if not individualism, or value communal duties more than rights, may be knocked off balance by the zealotry of culturally desensitized individualism.[3] The law has only recently begun to search in earnest for appropriate normative space for diversity of communities as well as for assertive individuals.

Accordingly, it may be observed that, as successor to the League of Nations which made the protection of (mostly) European minorities into a major policy, the world order announced in the UN Charter was slow to accommodate minority rights.[4] A kind of negativism towards minorities prevailed in the early postwar years, at least in the sense of a reluctance to set out rights specifically for groups: the middle ground between self-determination and minority group rights was empty space. Minority rights were 'talked out' of key international texts. The UN Charter and the Universal Declaration of Human Rights deal with the principle of non-discrimination in the enjoyment of human rights rather than specific rights for groups. Positive action to support minorities was regarded as superfluous or even contrary to the principle on non-discrimination. The principle of non-discrimination in essence elaborates a statute of prohibited treatment, of forms of social disqualification of members of minorities; it does not systematically encode their rights.[5] The individual rights/non-discrimination principle adopted by the UN bears the strong imprint of the USA, a major actor in the drafting of Charter norms on human rights.

Global standards on minority rights

The blurring of the gaze of international law did not produce a complete myopia about minorities. The setting up of the UN Sub-Commission on the Prevention of Discrimination and the Protection of Minorities in the 1940s and the drafting of Article 27 of the Covenant on Civil and Political Rights were signposts to the eventual re-emergence of minority rights on the international agenda. Local arrangements in Europe and elsewhere for the disposition of particular minority questions continued to be made on a bilateral basis.[6] Article 27 still functions as the basic global treaty standard for minority rights:

> In those States in which ethnic, religious or linguistic minorities exist, persons belonging to such minorities shall not be denied the right, in community with the other members of their group, to enjoy their own culture, to profess and practise their own religion, or to use their own language.[7]

The Covenant does not define 'minority', and 'scientific' definitions such as those of the UN Special Rapporteur Capotorti have not been incorporated formally into the international canon: the Rapporteur defined a minority for the purposes of Article 27 as

> A group numerically inferior to the rest of the population of a State, in a non-dominant position, whose members – being nationals of the State – possess ethnic, religious or linguistic characteristics differing from those of the rest of the population and show, if only implicitly, a sense of solidarity, directed towards preserving their culture, traditions, religion or language.[8]

While retaining a universalist approach to rights, international law gradually moved in the direction of greater complexity. The general concepts of human rights have been 'stretched' to recognize the specific claims of refugees, migrant workers, children, women, indigenous peoples, adherents of religions, the stateless and myriad other groups through dedicated international instruments.[9] Non-discrimination is still axiomatic, but functions in the context of a widening range of rights addressed to multiple human groups: it is still a vital first step, if not the last word, for the protection of minorities. The texts inscribing the principle of non-discrimination, notably the International Convention on the Elimination of All Forms of Racial Discrimination, have played a key role in developing an international conscience on the socially destructive effects of practices of discrimination.[10]

International organizations have now delivered up specific rules on minority rights, transcending the non-discrimination paradigm. At the level of the United Nations, Article 27 of the Covenant on Civil and Political Rights functions as the minimum global treaty standard. Further, Article 30 of the UN Convention on the Rights of the Child of 1989 combines rights of indigenous and minority children in a text which adapts Article 27:

> In those States in which ethnic, religious or linguistic minorities or persons of indigenous origin exist, a child belonging to such a minority or who is indigenous shall not be denied the right, in community with other members of his or her group, to enjoy his or her own culture, to profess and practise his or her own religion, or to use his or her own language.[11]

The most important non-treaty text specifically devoted to minority rights is the UN Declaration on the Rights of Persons belonging to National or Ethnic, Religious and Linguistic Minorities,[12] proclaimed by the General Assembly in 1992. The implementation of this instrument is now – partly – in the hands of a new Working Group on Minorities of the UN Sub-Commission on the Prevention of Discrimination and Protection of Minorities. Without defining 'minority', the Declaration enshrines basic minority rights to existence, identity, participation and their derivatives in a formula which elaborates the rights as those of 'persons belonging to minorities', but which may be exercised individually or collectively without any discrimination. The Declaration does not recognize autonomy as a minority right, let alone self-determination which is simply not touched by its terms. One of its most important provisions commits the UN system to contribute to the realization of the Declaration's rights and principles. The importance of the Declaration was underlined for the global community in the Vienna Declaration of the World Conference on Human Rights, 1993, which reaffirmed

> the obligation of States to ensure that persons belonging to minorities may exercise fully and effectively all human rights and fundamental freedoms without any discrimination and in full equality before the law [in accordance with the UN Declaration on Minorities] . . . [and] . . . persons belonging to minorities have the right to enjoy their own culture, to profess and practise their own religion and to use their own language in private and in public, freely and without interference or any form of discrimination.[13]

There are many other references to minorities in UN texts.[14] The initial dearth of specific minority standards has been remedied, and the United Nations has acted on the concerns expressed at the time of the Universal Declaration of Human Rights in 1948 – when the General Assembly declared that the UN could not remain indifferent to the fate of minorities.[15] The UN has now committed itself to address the question of minority rights on a constant and consistent basis, at all levels.

Global standards and 'initiatives' on indigenous peoples

In the contemporary development of an 'ethnic dimension' to the human rights movement, the growth of international concern for the rights of indigenous peoples has been even more remarkable than that for minority rights. At the UN, the indigenous rights resurgence follows an initial interest in the indigenous as a discrete issue,[16] a lengthy period of neglect and then an upsurge in interest. There has been a specific indigenous code in international law under the International Labor Organization since 1957, without a counterpart in minority rights. There is also in existence what can be called 'an' or 'the' indigenous movement.

Indigenous mobilization was spurred on by the example of decolonization of the empires of the West, by the civil rights struggles of the 1960s, problems with the concept of development, an alliance (sometimes) with environmentalists and the growth of international human rights law with a sharp focus on racism. Indigenous organizations began to mobilize internationally in the 1970s and have alerted the conscience of the international community. There is now widespread knowledge and concern about the fate of the indigenous of the rainforests, of groups from the Yanomami and other rainforest dwellers[17] to the San/Basarwa, the Aboriginals of Australia, the Sami[18] and Inuit of the Arctic.[19] International consciousness has been well and truly raised. Indigenous peoples may be recognized from the 'statement of coverage'[20] in ILO Convention No. 169 on indigenous and Tribal Peoples:

> 1. This Convention applies to:
>
> (a) tribal peoples in independent countries whose social, cultural and economic conditions distinguish them from other sections of the national community, and whose status is regulated wholly or partially by their own customs or traditions or by special laws or regulations;
>
> (b) peoples in independent countries who are regarded as indigenous on account of their descent from the populations which inhabited the country, or a geographical region to which the country belongs, at

the time of conquest or colonization or the establishment of present state boundaries and who, irrespective of their legal status, retain some or all of their own social, economic, cultural and political institutions.

2. Self-identification as indigenous or tribal shall be regarded as a fundamental criterion for determining the groups to which the provisions of this Convention apply.

A key institutional actor in putting indigenous rights on the international agenda is the UN Working Group on Indigenous Populations. The Group was set up by the Economic and Social Council in 1982[21] as a subsidiary organ of the Sub-Commission on the Prevention of Discrimination and Protection of Minorities.[22] The Group, which has met annually since that year with the exception of 1986,[23] formally consists of five members of the Sub-Commission; but the proceedings are open to States, international intergovernmental and non-governmental organizations, organizations of indigenous peoples and individuals, indigenous or otherwise. Participation of indigenous representatives at the meeting is assisted by a Voluntary Fund established by the UN General Assembly of the United Nations in 1985.[24] The meetings continue and will do so unless and until the Working Group is replaced by a Permanent Forum for Indigenous Peoples. The Forum is a recent proposal, stemming from a recommendation of the World Conference on Human Rights in 1993. The relationship between these two concepts of appropriate indigenous representation at the United Nations is unclear,[25] but the survival of the Working Group has been stoutly defended.[26] The Working Group has drafted a Declaration on the Rights of Indigenous Peoples, pressing for its adoption by the UN General Assembly.[27] In the light of this goal, a drafting group of the Commission on Human Rights commenced the further 'preparation' of the draft Declaration in November 1995.[28]

There has been a spate of 'initiatives' of all kinds for the benefit of indigenous peoples at the United Nations. In the present context, it is possible only to present a sample of activities. Among examples of UN or UN-inspired work on behalf of indigenous peoples, the 1992 United Nations Conference on Environment and Development held in Rio de Janeiro devoted considerable attention to indigenous issues. Chapter 26 of its Agenda 21 is dedicated to 'Recognizing and Strengthening the Role of Indigenous People and their Communities'. Paragraph 1 of Chapter 26 set out a basis for action in underlining the link between indigenous peoples and the world's need for environmentally sensitive development:

> In view of the interrelationship between the natural environment and its sustainable development and the cultural, social, economic and physical well-being of indigenous people, national and international efforts to implement environmentally sound and sustainable development should recognize, accommodate, promote and strengthen the role of indigenous people and their communities.[29]

Questions concerning indigenous peoples feature regularly on the agendas of the UN Commission on Human Rights[30] and its subordinate body, the Sub-Commission on the Prevention of Discrimination and Protection of Minorities.[31] Relevant treaty bodies in the UN system deal with indigenous issues within the parameters of their work of implementation of standards.[32] The year 1993 was the International Year of the World's Indigenous People,[33] proclaimed by the UN General Assembly.[34] The World Conference on Human Rights, held in Vienna from 14 to 25 June 1993, went further and recommended that

> the General Assembly proclaim an international decade of the world's indigenous people, to begin from January 1994, including action-orientated programmes, to be decided upon in partnership with indigenous people. An appropriate voluntary trust fund should be set up for this purpose. In the framework of such a decade, the establishment of a permanent forum for indigenous people in the United Nations system should be considered.[35]

The Decade of the World's Indigenous People, proclaimed in 1993 by General Assembly resolution 48/163, commenced on 10 December 1994.

Issues for reflection

Minority groups, names, facts

The complexity of the situations revealed in the *Directory* highlights the relative sparsity of international standards, which reveal themselves as schematic and short on specifics. Nevertheless, for reasons outlined above, the open nature of the principles and norms should not lead to an underestimation of the potential of human rights law to act as guide to good conduct, to evaluate and judge the rightness of the local treatment of minority and indigenous groups in their home States. Scanning the mass of material presented in the *Directory*, one is struck by the variety of group types. Minorities can be scattered throughout a territory, settled compactly in particular regions, historic or new to a State, nomadic or sedentary, citizens or non-citizens of the State, have kin-States[36] or none. The various countries where such minorities are situated may treat the groups differently according to their situation – a distinction permitted by international law provided it conforms to principles of non-discrimination, equality and proportionality. Beyond this, international law provides only a platform of rights; it has not moved far in the direction of individuated rights[37] for these different group types.[38] UN practice is the most 'open' and generous in its recognition of minorities, paying little attention, for example, to the citizen/non-citizen distinction made by some States in the application of minority rights.[39]

A related issue concerns what kind of community we are dealing with. Is it a people, a minority, a religious community, an ethnic community, or a group formed on the basis of free association such as political or activist groups?[40] The most extreme mistranslation of minority rights denies the existence of the group, and the right of the group to exist is fundamental.[41] Among the international standards on minority rights is that which insists that a State cannot deflect the application of standards by misnaming[42] or deliberately undercounting minorities or indigenous peoples.[43] The existence of a minority is a question of fact, not a question of law.[44] On the whole, international law does not offer definitions of minorities, but principle suggests that facts can still be respected in the absence of definition – a 'scientific' exercise the positive effects of which can easily be exaggerated. Respect for the facts includes the fact of self-definition – exampled in Article 1.2 of ILO Convention No. 169 (above).

The reader of the *Directory* may be struck by the significance of names. Names can be disputed among States – as evidenced by the contest between Greece and (the former Yugoslav Republic of) Macedonia.[45] In the world of ethnic groups, the preferred name of a group is sometimes contested by others,[46] sometimes as part of the oppression of a group, or as an element in a political contest. Pejorative names can be used to point out a minority and stigmatize them in some way.[47] In rare cases, the pejorative name is reclaimed and taken up as an emblem of identity.[48] In other cases, members of the group have many views on an appropriate name, and views change.[49] Human rights principles are intended to promote mutuality of respect. Propaganda for ethnic hatred through the use of names or otherwise is prohibited.[50] The naming of names is also related to the fundamental right to an identity,[51] the conjoined twin of the right to existence. It is only a short step from suppressing a name to suppressing those who value it.

Our readings of international law should not blind us to the fact that the bases of identity are multiple and kaleidoscopic,[52] and that the ethnic question assumes a bewildering variety of forms in different regions. But the point remains that the attribution or denial of minority rights is not simply in the gift of States, and that groups do not compromise their aspirations by the strategic use of rights.[53] The rights are expressed simply but can be adapted to circumstances – if relevant actors decide to use them. Their application and implementation require dialogue and good faith on all sides.

Standards and policies

The *Directory* illustrates the broadest range of State policies towards minority groups. Having no policy or neglecting minorities is a policy in itself, and can be devastating. Approaches taken by States vary from the good to the atrocious: from self-determination,[54] promoting partnership and reconciliation,[55] pluralism, autonomy,[56] strategies of integration, neglect, discrimination,[57] assimilation,[58] forced assimilation,[59] segregation and slavery[60] to policies in essence genocidal to which the inappropriate term 'ethnic cleansing'[61] may or may not be applied.[62] The object for good or ill of these orientations may be the colour-visible or invisible minorities, indigenous peoples or communities, religions and sects, language groups, cultural groupings, imagined enemies of the State, etc.

There is evidence of change over time, in that fewer States explicitly commit themselves to nation-building through group destruction than was the case a generation ago. With the weakening of some strong ideologies, such as the Communist, there is less spoken about transformations in the personal sphere, of reshaping human beings,[63] though some religiously oriented governments still harbour aspirations in this direction. There is at least talk of pluralism and embracing diversity, and evidence from constitutional change,[64] which can result in a greater installation or reinforcement of ostensibly benign policies.

If there is change, movement in the sphere of international law and organization has perhaps played a part. The law provides signposts to temperate policies and warning signals on what is intolerable. International legal principles obviously rule out 'ethnic cleansing' as a 'policy', though practice does not always match principle and the resurgence of such horrors in the 'age of human rights' is a blot on our community conscience. International law rules out the separation of children from their families in order to 'civilize' them[65] – a practice which is capable of being genocidal in both the spirit and the letter.[66] The law also prohibits enforced segregation on the apartheid model.[67] It prohibits discrimination, though not distinctions which can be defended as reasonable. The attitude to assimilation and integration is more nuanced. The Organization for Security and Cooperation in Europe Copenhagen Document recognizes the right of persons belonging to minorities to express, preserve and develop their identity, 'free of any attempts at assimilation against their will'.[68] The Council of Europe's Framework Convention for the Protection of National Minorities explicitly links integration and assimilation in Article 5.2:

> Without prejudice to measures taken in pursuance of their general integration policy, the parties shall refrain from policies or practices aimed at assimilation of persons belonging to national minorities against their will and shall protect these persons from any action aimed at such assimilation.

In this formula, integration is legitimate State policy, and only assimilation against the will of those subjected to it is stigmatized. Integration is generally regarded as a 'good thing' but needs careful application if it is not to shade over into something like forced assimilation. The variety of 'integration' placed before indigenous peoples by ILO Convention No. 107 [69]was not benign but more a codeword for policies of deliberate assimilation through 'development', with indigenous cultures and identities regarded as essentially transitory and destined to be replaced.[70] The new spirit and new approach to minority rights, summed up in a variety of recent texts, is that policies of development, nation-building, reformation of State and society, and the promotion of democratic and economic security and political stability, are assumed to take place against the background of rights. The new principles try to promote the notion that government control over administration, culture, education, the media, the economy, the security and defence apparatus, land, the environment and natural resources, etc., is connected with the rights and entitlements of people, majority, minority, indigenous and otherwise.

Self-determination and autonomy

The relationship between self-determination and human rights is introduced above as one of interdependence and difficulty. Self-determination as expressed in the Charter of the United Nations, the International Covenant on Civil and Political Rights, the Declaration on Principles of International Law and many other instruments is generally viewed as one of the underpinning norms of the contemporary legal order, a principle of *jus cogens*.[71] It represents a collective right of peoples to determine their own destiny. International law has not advanced any canonical definition of peoples, as it has not advanced any for minorities. In the great rush to decolonization,[72] self-determination became identified with that process and the 'people' with the 'whole peoples' of emerging States. At one point, self-determination may have been no more than a synonym for the majority taking power within existing colonial boundaries. But self-determination cannot be easily confined in that way. 'People' is better regarded as a differentiated concept – implying some role in the ongoing self-determination process for all the constituent elements of a State, and self-determination is also 'about' human rights.[73] Accordingly, scholars have distinguished between 'external' self-determination (secession and independence) and democratic or 'internal' self-determination.

Indigenous peoples have made a bold assertion of the right to self-determination in Article 3 of the UN draft Declaration on the Rights of Indigenous Peoples:[74] in the vast majority of cases they are not seeking independence but respect for their existence and their rights and the means to continue to live as distinct peoples in their ancestral territories. The fear of minority rights developing too much in the direction of collective rights and thus self-determination and secession has preoccupied many governments. Secessions still occur in the post-decolonization era[75] and claims continue to be made.[76] On the whole, it may be said that events in Bosnia, the former Soviet Union and elsewhere have not transformed the fundamental caution of the international community into accepting secessionist claims; on the contrary, they may have hardened that caution. Most groups will have to satisfy their ambitions within the boundaries of existing States.

On the level of concept and practice, insufficiently sharp distinctions are made between minority rights, self-determination and autonomy. Even with self-determination – as with the indigenous – the direction is not inexorably towards secession and independence. Autonomy, as a creative concept for the resolution of disputes between minorities and the State, within the State, has not been accepted as a general right of minorities. Proposals on autonomy were not adopted during the drafting of the UN Declaration on Minorities. The term 'autonomy' is used in, for example, the OSCE Copenhagen Document of the Human Dimension:

> The participating States note the efforts undertaken to protect and create conditions for the promotion of the ethnic, cultural, linguistic and religious identity of certain minorities by establishing, as one of the possible means to achieve these aims, appropriate local or autonomous administrations corresponding to the specific historical and territorial circumstances of such minorities and in accordance with the policies of the State concerned.

The 'efforts' are only 'noted'; or do we detect a faint ripple of applause for using autonomy as a creative resolution of – some – minority questions? Despite the fact that, or because, autonomy is not mandated by international law, the *Directory* provides abundant evidence of creative attempts to use forms of self-regulation and self-administration including territorial autonomy within States. Forms and examples of autonomy are found within all the regional sections in the *Directory*, from the self-government of the indigenous in North, Central and South America, to the clear regionalist trends in Western Europe, to developments in Asia including China.[77] Autonomy may be grudgingly offered and ungratefully accepted[78] but it can work to civilize rival ambitions – and certainly many governments think it can. In the area of autonomy, there is the sharpest contrast between the complexity of local arrangements and the reductionism of international standards.

Culture, language, education, participation

Much of contemporary international law and domestic legislation focuses on basic issues of rights in the spheres of language and culture. Minority language rights are set out in all the major international instruments, and language is a prohibited ground of discrimination in League of Nations texts and the UN canon. Concern for minority languages has generated a dedicated international instrument in the European Charter for Regional or Minority Languages. The rights do not go far in the sense of an overriding exclusive concern for the speakers of these languages. Principles of non-discrimination and equality are always relevant in this area, as in others. In terms of the general right of freedom of expression, the Human Rights Committee observed, in the case of *Ballantyne, Davidson and McIntyre v. Canada*, that 'A State may choose one or more official languages, but it may not exclude, outside the spheres of public life, the freedom to express oneself in a language of one's choice.'[79]

The public/private distinction is a regular reference point in assessments of the scope of language rights. In the specific field of minority rights, the UN Declaration on the Rights of Persons belonging to National or Ethnic, Religious and Linguistic Minorities[80] may be taken as a standard formulation. The Declaration extends the meaning of Article 27 of the Covenant on Civil and Political Rights by making it clear that the right of members of minorities to use their own language includes its use 'in private and in public, freely and without any form of discrimination'.[81] Article 4.3 individuates a language right in providing that 'States should take appropriate measures so that, wherever possible, persons belonging to minorities have adequate opportunities to learn their mother tongue or to have instruction in their mother tongue.' The alternatives of learning through mother tongue and learning about the mother tongue are also standard. This is expressed in another way by legal formulations which try to ensure that official or State languages are not neglected in the protection of minority languages, in the interests of social integration.[82] Minority rights clearly show their human face in the personal and private language rights. Language is often a vital component of the identity of minorities through furnishing an interactive context, a shared knowledge, codes and symbols, a world-view.[83] Rights formulae become more hesitant when they seek to penetrate the spheres of public administration – as in rights to use minority languages in contacts with local authorities; hence the hesitancies of Article 10.2 of the Council of Europe's Framework Convention for the Protection of National Minorities:

> In areas inhabited by persons belonging to national minorities traditionally or in substantial numbers, if those persons so request and the request corresponds to a real need, the parties shall endeavour to ensure, as far as possible, the conditions which would make it possible to use the minority language in relations between those persons and the administrative authorities.

The ring of limitations should not obscure the value of the right for minorities in many countries.[84] Language rights are also a vital component of the standards on education, where, again, the public/private (school) distinction may be a determinant of rights. However, these standards transcend the language context to go towards the content of education for people in general and for minorities, a content which is particularly well expressed in Article 29 of the Convention on the Rights of the Child which provides that education should be directed to:

> (c) The development of respect for the child's parents, his or her own cultural identity, language and values, for the national values of the country in which the child is living, the country from which he or she may originate, and for civilizations different from his or her own.
>
> (d) The preparation of the child for responsible life in a free society, in the spirit of understanding, peace, tolerance, equality of sexes, and friendship among all peoples, ethnic, national and religious groups and persons of indigenous origin.

In minority rights, the UN Declaration on Minorities makes specific reference to education in Article 4.5:

> States should, where appropriate, take measures in the field of education in order to encourage knowledge of the history, traditions, language and culture of the minorities existing within their territory. Persons belonging to minorities should have adequate opportunities to gain knowledge of the society as a whole.

The message of the texts is similar: tolerance, mutual respect/reciprocity of esteem, groups in society learning about each other, not lapsing into entrenched, exclusive fundamentalisms. While not all minorities are linguistic minorities,[85] language rights are important for many. Languages are developed by human communities, they change, and they disappear.[86] The rights, as elsewhere on minority rights, are not attempts to retrieve the irretrievable, but attempts to give minority languages a fair chance of survival and flourishing as complex and changing contexts of expression, if speakers continue to value their unique linguistic space.[87]

A third limb of minority rights is the right to participation. In the UN Declaration on Minorities, Article 2.2 introduces the concept. Wide-ranging participation rights for minority group members are specified, including the right 'to participate effectively in cultural, religious, social, economic and public life', and the right to participate effectively in local decisions affecting them (the minorities) 'in a manner not incompatible with national legislation' – Article 2.3. Modalities of participation remain unspecified, but the development of mediating minority organizations is not excluded, since Article 2.4 states the right to establish and maintain minority associations. Participation can therefore involve the creation of ethnic, cultural and religious associations and societies, as well as political parties in the State. It is also probable that effective participation for minorities in a complex society will move in the direction of greater decentralization, towards levels of government appropriate to continuing 'effective' involvement.[88] Article 4.5 further develops the theme of participation: 'States should consider appropriate measures so that persons belonging to minorities may participate fully in the economic progress and development in their country.' This 'participation in progress' principle is important for minorities in order to avoid relegation to an economic and social backwater. Some of the themes of the UN Declaration are echoed in the Vienna Declaration and Programme of Action of the World Conference on Human Rights. The Programme of Action provides[89] that the measures to advance the rights of persons belonging to minorities where appropriate, should include 'facilitation of their full participation in all aspects of the political, economic, social, religious and cultural life of society and in the economic progress and development of their country'.

As elsewhere the *Directory* shows good and bad in terms of the contemporary standards on the 'basics' of minority rights. Rights form a network. The softening of a determined assimilation policy will find typical expression in changes in the sphere of minority language, culture and education. There are many examples of change in line with the new standards,[90] though the standards themselves need further elaboration. The complex distribution of language/dialect clusters[91] within States can hardly have the effect of compelling poor (and rich) States to treat all to the same degree. Principles of proportionality, need, numbers, wishes of the speakers and considerations of linguistic vitality and resources must be drawn upon to suggest approximate answers on what this or that State is obliged to do. Some of the practical questions can be assisted towards solution if the participation rights – at national and local levels – are given genuine expression.[92] The *Directory* reveals that the level of minority participation in national and local processes of governance in many States is extremely low or non-existent;[93] sometimes the right is reduced to little more than group participation in their own subjugation.[94]

On rights and religion

Some of the most difficult situations contemplated by the *Directory* have their origins or motive force in disputes where religion plays a role. Problems for minorities arise when religion becomes a government monopoly,[95] when it is identified as a badge of difference,[96] or subversive of social order, when it stands as a challenge to the truth or chosen path[97] of a particular faith held by great numbers of believers,[98] or whether it is regarded as pretext for interference in domestic affairs by outside powers. The approach taken by the *Directory* is broad, and not confined to minority religions which find their dominant expression within the confines of a particular State. On the contrary, many adherents of great world religions find themselves in a minority situation in many countries. In such cases, the standards of rights practised in a State where that religion dominates might be improved by the knowledge that oppression by the militant religious 'at home' can cause problems when the dominators are a minority elsewhere. Regrettably, that realization does not always sink home and reciprocity of oppression can become a temptation.

International law points to State responsibility for violations within discrete jurisdictions, and does not accept the proposition that 'we hurt your minorities if you hurt ours'. Negative reciprocity and reprisals are contrary to the spirit and sometimes the letter of humanitarian norms. Each State must answer for itself before international organizations and to its own population. The protection of the religious is a cornerstone of contemporary standards, whether from the viewpoint of general individual rights, non-discrimination, the rights of members of religious minorities, protection from genocide – which applies to religious groups as it does to others – or protection from acts of intolerance, incitement to hatred, etc. In view of this, the evidence in the *Directory* of forced conversions, the destructive activities of State-sanctioned religious missions,[99] prosecutions and executions of apostates and those alleged to blaspheme,[100] and the wholesale persecution of religious communities,[101] is evidence of a widespread disregard of solemn commitments to the international community.

On the condition of the indigenous

One of the major divides in international human rights law is between minorities and indigenous peoples. Leading texts for both 'camps' are set out above. One need not make too much of the differences in some respects. Indigenous peoples have been prime movers on the development of the international law on minority rights through the United Nations. But they claim to be 'more than' minorities and look forward to recognition by international law of a broader range of rights. In some respects, the claims made by indigenous peoples are simple.[102] They want their identities and traditions to be respected by governments and claim their future as distinct peoples. This requires the activation of international standards on the prohibition of genocide and forced assimilation.[103] They suggest that treaties and other agreements made between themselves and the States should be respected by the latter.[104] Much of their discourse is bound up with land rights, in view of the relationship, spiritual rather than exploitative, with their ancestral lands.[105] Indigenous peoples have also made claims in the field of heritage, their arts and crafts, their knowledge and intellectual endeavours, so often exploited for the benefit of others.[106]

But indigenous peoples are claiming more than such basic protection and survival rights. They also claim self-determination for themselves,[107] and some States resist this.[108] If indigenous self-determination is to be conceded by governments, the price to be paid by the indigenous may be that a sharper line will be drawn between their case and that of minorities.

There are formidable problems in assessing the presence of the 'indigenous' in many regions. It is too loose a usage to say that it must always mean the firstcomers. Questions of historical precedence are not easy for, say, Africa and Asia. The picture of the prior population and the later incomers may be easier to gauge in the Americas and Oceania. Where there is historical precedence and where not, key elements of 'indigenousness' may be some form of cultural or historical continuity with earlier societies, a wide cultural gap between the indigenous and others, specific experience of colonialism, and a particular relationship with lands and territories: the land rights question is both an issue and a defining element for many groups. The *Directory* shows many cases where the survival of the indigenous is threatened and cases where the burdens of existence have been lightened.[109] It is notable how often elements in 'progress' are bound up with the destruction of indigenous communities and habitats. Indigenous peoples continue to suffer from insensitive and crude applications of 'development' programmes. They continue to be marginalized, disenfranchised, expelled from territories – sometimes by governments turning a blind eye to or failing to deal effectively with territorial invasions by the non-indigenous.[110] Their existence is denied or 'reduced' by undercounting.[111] They continue to be victims of ethnocidal policies, or even genocide.

On a more hopeful note, the general raising of international awareness and indigenous organization may have improving effects. There have been important developments on land rights in Australia which can set precedents for other countries, and important settlements of land claims. Indigenous territories have been carved out,[112] indigenous treaties litigated.[113] Participation and representation of the indigenous in national and their own affairs have been enhanced in a number of countries. The indigenous are now recognized in the laws of many States – not only in the Americas.[114] Indigenous culture is viewed in a more positive light in many States who increasingly appreciate the indigenous contribution to the cultural, social and spiritual diversity of the nations, and the special quality of their ecological awareness. Indigenous claims perhaps succeed best when they present the positive aspects of their culture to majority populations and reserve the language of complaint for the most serious and shocking cases: insofar as they are portrayed only as victims, they compete for attention with the poor populations of poor States.[115] They offer cultural prospects of incomparable richness and variety, a way of relating to the world, the loss or further diminution of which impoverishes the humanity of all.

Coda

The *Directory*'s concern with minority and indigenous rights is not intended to obscure the privations endured by so many human beings falling into neither group. The entries follow the contours of human rights law which to some degree may be seen as narrow and over-categorized. 'Minorities' in international law are not everyone's idea of a minority. But they are groups which furnish a human dimension and context for the expression of personal identity as well as providing discrete targets for oppression. They share their oppression with other groups of vulnerable people. In places the *Directory* refers to and empathizes with the plight of women, refugees, children and others. UN parlance recognizes an ill-defined category of 'vulnerable groups'. While oppression endures for all, the reasons and motives for trampling on the rights of different groups may themselves be different, and the prospects of cure. The case of minorities and indigenous peoples is specific enough to deserve discrete treatment, and this is the idea in the mind of the law. There is an ethical limit to assessing the claim to attention of specific groups and revealing them through a directory: we reach it when the luminosity of the claims and revelations only dims the light of others.

Notes

1 In Articles 1(2) and 55, as well as implicitly in Chapters XI and XII.

2 See, for example, Article 1(3), where human rights are affirmed 'without distinction as to race, sex, language, or religion' – a formula used repeatedly in the Charter.

3 Elements of a misplaced individualism sanctioned by international organization may be found in ILO Convention No. 107, 1957, on the Protection and Integration of Indigenous and Other Tribal and Semi-Tribal Populations. The ILO has moved vigorously to correct this orientation through the adoption of Convention No. 169 on Indigenous and Tribal Peoples, 1989.

4 P. Thornberry, *International Law and the Rights of Minorities,* Oxford, Clarendon Press, 1991.

5 For reviews of the principle in international law, see N. Lerner, *Group Rights and Discrimination in International Law,* Dordrecht/Boston/London, Martinus Nijhoff, 1991; W.A. McKean, *Equality and Discrimination under International Law,* Oxford, Oxfor University Press, 1983; M. Banton, *Discrimination,* Buckingham, Philadelphia, Open University Press, 1994.

6 See P. Thornberry, *Minorities and Human Rights Law,* London, MRG Report 1991.

7 The UN Human Rights Committee issued a General Comment (No. 23) on Article 27 in 1994, designed in part to guide governments in their reading of how this article applies within their own States: UN Doc. A/49/40, 107–110.

8 *Study on the Rights of Persons Belonging to Ethnic, Religious and Linguistic Minorities,* New York, United Nations, 1991, UN Sales No. E.91.XIV.2, paragraph 568. Other definitions are discussed in both of the above cited works of the present author.

9 For a snapshot of the instruments, see I. Brownlie, *Basic Documents on Human Rights,* 3rd edn, Oxford, Clarendon Press, 1992.

10 See especially N. Lerner, op. cit.

11 Adopted and opened for signature, etc., by General Assembly resolution 44/25, 20 November 1989.

12 See A. Phillips and A. Rosas (eds), *Universal Minority Rights,* Abo and London, Abo Akademi University and Minority Rights Group International, 1995.

13 Consult P. Thornberry, 'Minority rights and the World Conference on Human Rights', in J. Patel (ed.), *Addressing Discrimination in the Vienna Declaration: A Guide for NGOs and Interested Individuals,* Tokyo, International Movement Against All Forms of Discrimination and Racism, 1995, 13–22.

14 See P. Thornberry, 'The UN Declaration on the Rights of Persons belonging to . . . Minorities: Background, Analysis, Observations and an Update', in A. Phillips and A. Rosas (eds), op. cit., pp. 13–76.

15 Resolution 217C (III).

16 See General Assembly resolution 275(III), 1949. The resolution and its fate are discussed by G. Bennett, *Aboriginal Rights in International Law,* London, Royal Anthropological Institute of Great Britain and Ireland, 1978, ch. II.

17 See for example, the *Directory*'s regional introductions and entries for Central and Southern Africa and South America.

18 Entries in section on Western Europe – Norway, Sweden, Finland.

19 Entries for Canada and the USA.

20 The term is used by the ILO to avoid universalist or *a priori* overtones attached to the word 'definition. Any general UN 'definition' which may emerge through current attempts to draft a Declaration on the Rights of Indigenous Peoples (discussed below) might well be different.

21 The creation of the Working Group was proposed by the Sub-Commission on Prevention of Discrimination and Protection of Minorities in its resolution 2(XXXIV) of 8 September 1981, endorsed by the Commission on Human Rights in resolution 1982/19 of 10 March 1982 and authorized by the Economic and Social Council in resolution 1982/34 of 7 May 1982. The first Chairman of the Working Group was Mr Asbjorn Eide of Norway.

22 For a useful general review of the work of the Sub-Commission, see A. Eide, 'The Sub-Commission on Prevention of Discrimination and Protection of Minorities', in P. Alston (ed.), *The United Nations and Human Rights: A Critical Appraisal* Oxford, Clarendon Press, 1992, pp. 211–64.

23 In 1986, a workshop on indigenous rights was sponsored by the Anti-Slavery Society for the Protection of Human Rights and the World Council of Indigenous Peoples, and chaired by the present Chairman/Rapporteur of the Working Group, Mrs Erica-Irene Daes. The fifth session of the Working Group was postponed from 1986 to 1987. The cancellation was attributed to a UN budgetary crisis. The report of the 'substitute' Workshop is contained in UN Doc. E/CN.4/Sub.2/AC.4/1987/WP.4/Add.1.

24 For the background to the Fund, its *modus operandi* and a questionnaire for applicants, see *The Rights of Indigenous Peoples,* Fact Sheet no. 9, World Campaign for Human Rights, UN Centre for Human Rights, Geneva 1990.

25 A general review of options was undertaken by the UN Secretariat in UN Doc. E/CN.4/Sub.2/AC.4/1994/11. The Chairperson/Rapporteur of the Working Group prepared a note on the question – UN Doc. E/CN.4/Sub.2/AC.4/1994/13, and the Twelfth Report of the Working Group contains an annex on Guidelines for the Establishment of a Forum also prepared by the Chairperson. The most substantial Forum proposals at the Working Group in 1994 were presented by the Government of Denmark in UN Doc. E/CN.4/Sub.2/AC.4/1994/CRP.3. Following proposals by the Sub-Commission on Prevention of Discrimination and Protection of Minorities endorsed by resolution 1995/30 of the Commission on Human Rights, a Workshop with representatives of governments, indigenous peoples and independent experts on the Forum question was held in Copenhagen on 26–28 of June. The results were presented to the 1995 meeting of the Working Group in UNDoc.E/CN.4/Sub.2/AC.4/1995/7.alsoUN Doc. E/CN.4/Sub.2/AC.4/1995/6 – a note by the Chairperson of the Working Group on its future role.

26 Notably by Working Group member Mr Miguel Alfonso Martinez in UN Doc. E/CN.4/Sub.2/AC.4/1994/10, a working paper on the 'Future role of the Working Group'.

27 The text of the draft Declaration was included in the *Report of the Working Group on its Eleventh Session,* UN Doc. E/CN.4/Sub.2/1993/29, Annex 1. See also UN Doc. E/CN.4/Sub.2/1994/2/Add.1, *Technical Review of the United Nations draft Declaration on the Rights of Indigenous Peoples.*

28 Resolution 1995/32 of the Commission on Human Rights entitled '*Establishment of a Working Group of the Commission on Human Rights to elaborate a draft Declaration in accordance with paragraph 5 of General Assembly resolution 49/214 of 23 December 1994*' – the resolution of the General Assembly encouraged the Commission to consider the draft Declaration with the participation of representatives of indigenous people.

29 Doc. A/CONF.151/26 (vol. III), 14 August 1992, 26.1.

30 For example, resolutions at the 1995 session dealt with the International Decade of the World's Indigenous People (1995/28); a Permanent Forum for Indigenous People in the United Nations System (1995/30); the Report of the Working Group on Indigenous Populations (1995/31), and the Establishment of a Working Group of the Commission to Elaborate a draft Declaration – on Indigenous Peoples (1995/32). Decisions were taken concerning the Protection of the Heritage of Indigenous People (1995/108), and the Study on Treaties, Agreements and other Constructive Arrangements between States and Indigenous Populations (1995/109) : ECOSOCOR, 1995, Supplement No.4, 51st Session of the Commission on Human Rights, UN Docs. E/1995/23; E/CN.4/1995/176.

31 The Sub-Commission adopted five resolutions on indigenous peoples at its 1995 session: on the United Nations Voluntary Fund for Indigenous Populations (1995/36); the International Decade of the World's Indigenous People (1995/37); Discrimination Against Indigenous Peoples (1995/38); the Permanent Forum in the United Nations for Indigenous People (1995/39), and Protection of the Heritage of Indigenous People (1995/40): *Report of the Sub-Commission on Prevention of Discrimination and Protection of Minorities on its Forty-Seventh Session,* UN Docs. E/CN.4/1996/2; E/CN.4/Sub.2/1995/51.

32 At its Forty-Ninth Session, the Human Rights Committee made more or less extensive references to indigenous peoples in connection with reports of three States out of seventeen – Norway, Japan and Mexico: *Report of the Human Rights Committee, Vol 1,* UN Doc. A/49/40. General Comment No.23 on Article 27 of the Covenant made a number of references to indigenous peoples – *ibid.*, Annex V.

33 See *Indigenous People, International Year 1993, Newsletter no.1*, June 1993, and *Calendar of Events*, both produced by the UN Centre for Human Rights for the International Year.

34 The Year was proclaimed by General Assembly resolution 47/75 of 14 December 1992.

35 Vienna Declaration and Programme of Action, II, 32, Doc. A/CONF.157/23, 12 July 1993.

36 See, for example, the entries for Slovakia and Romania as they concern the Hungarian minorities.

37 For a distinction between territorial and non-territorial languages with potential rights implications, see the Council of Europe's Charter for Regional or Minority Languages, 1992.

38 There was, for example, a substantial discussion of classification and categorization of minorities at the second session of the UN Working Group on Minorities in 1996, initiated by Professor Eide, the Chairman of the Group.

39 See entries for Estonia and Latvia.

40 For a complex discussion of differences between 'communitarian' sub-national associations and ethnic groups, see W. Kymlicka, *Multicultural Citizenship: A Liberal Theory of Minority Rights,* Oxford, Clarendon Press, 1995.

41 See Article 1 of the UN Declaration on Minorities.

42 Consider the use of 'communities' or 'cultural communities' for indigenous groups rather than the more generally preferred term 'peoples' – see the entry for the Philippines. On 'tribes' see, for example, the entry for India.

43 See R. Stavenhagen, *The Ethnic Question: Conflicts, Development, and Human Rights,* Tokyo, United Nations Press, 1990, on the question of 'statistical ethnocide'.

44 See General Comment no. 23 of the Human Rights Committee, on Article 27 of the Covenant on Civil and Political Rights.

45 See the respective country entries.

46 The term 'Roma' for that ethnic group is contested by the Romanian government which prefers 'Gypsy' on the grounds of (alleged) confusion between 'Roma' and 'Romanian'.

47 On the ignoble origins of 'Berber', see the entry for Algeria.

48 See the appropriate entries on the use of 'Moro' in the Philippines, the revival of 'Bushman' in Namibia, and the reclaiming of *negro* in Colombia.

49 See the various expressions of view in the section on Central and Southern Africa on San/Basarwa/Bushmen.

50 See Article 20 of the Covenant on Civil and Political Rights.

51 For a legal extension of identity rights from the person/group to the description of an area, see the provisions of the Council of Europe's Framework on the Protection of Minorities, 1994.

52 While group identity may be a fluid, changing concept, group membership may not. For an extreme example, see the entry on Iraq for the Yazidis, who claim to be different from the rest of humanity on account of their descent from Adam but not Eve.

53 One may consider here the strategic use of minority rights in international law by indigenous peoples, who claim to be 'more than' minorities. It cannot be seriously maintained that the indigenous 'lose' something by claiming the 'lesser' minority rights. The law is a resource; the use of a particular category of rights by a group is a matter of their strategy.

54 See, for example, the entry for Ethiopia.

55 For example, the section on Aboriginals in the entry for Australia.

56 See below.

57 See the entry for Brazil: the meaning in job advertisements of the phrase 'good appearance'.

58 The uneven history of assimilationist policies is well illustrated in the entries for Australia, Canada and the USA.

59 Among many, see the entries for Iran and Sudan.

60 See the Sudan entry, among others.

61 There is nothing purificatory about mass murder.

62 See the entries on countries of the former Yugoslavia; see also the section on indigenous peoples in the introduction to North America; and the Cyprus entry.

63 Introduction to the Commonwealth of Independent States, on 'Homo Sovieticus'.

64 See, among others, entries for Colombia, Bolivia, Ethiopia, Finland, Hungary, Norway and Peru.

65 See, among others, entries for Australia and Canada.

66 Article II(e) of the Genocide Convention 1948 includes 'Forcibly transferring children of the group to another group' as one of the acts which amount to genocide when committed 'with intent to destroy, in whole or in part, a national, ethnical, racial or religious group . . . '

67 The International Convention on the Suppression and Punishment of the Crime of Apartheid 1973 states in Article II that 'the term "the crime of apartheid" . . . shall include similar policies and practices of racial segregation and discrimination as practised in Southern Africa, shall apply to . . . inhuman acts committed for the purpose of establishing and maintaining domination by one racial group of persons over any other racial group of persons and systematically oppressing them' – there follows a list of acts similar in scope to the Genocide Convention, adding exclusion of racial groups from participation and development, denial of human rights, prohibition of mixed marriages, land expropriation, exploitation of labour and persecution of those who oppose apartheid. See also the preamble to the African Charter on Human and Peoples' Rights.

68 Paragraph 32. Also the Geneva Meeting of Experts on Minorities 1991.

69 Convention Concerning the Protection and Integration of Indigenous and other Tribal and Semi-Tribal Populations in Independent Countries 1957.

70 It may be observed, however, that in practice the ILO has moderated the effects of the Convention and applies it in the more positive spirit of later instruments and concepts.

71 Fundamental, peremptory norms of international law.

72 On 'colonization by kitsch', see the entry for the USA under 'Native Hawai'ians'.

73 See the various essays in C. Tomuschat (ed.), *Modern Law of Self-Determination,* Dordrecht, Matinus Nijhoff, 1993.

74 Indigenous peoples have the right of self-determination. By virtue of that right they freely determine their political status and freely pursue their economic, social and cultural development.

75 Apart from the monumental events associated with the break-up of Yugoslavia and the Soviet Union, the best known are probably those of Bangladesh from Pakistan, and Eritrea from Ethiopia. See also the section on Oceania on the secession of Tuvalu from Kiribati.

76 See discussion of the Nagas and Khalistan under the entry for India; and references to the Kurds in the section on the Middle East.

77 For a contemporary review, see H. Hannum, *Autonomy, Sovereignty, and Self-Determination: The Accommodation of Conflicting Rights*, Philadelphia, University of Pennsylvania Press, rev. edition, 1996.

78 On autonomy robbed of any meaning, see the section on the Kurds in the entry for Iraq.

79 *Report of the Human Rights Committee*, Part II, UN Doc. A/48/40 (1993), 91–109, paragraph 11.4.

80 Adopted in UN General Assembly resolution 47/135 , 18 December 1992.

81 Article 2.1.

82 Perhaps the most complex constitutional evaluation of the role of languages is that contained in the Constitution of India. See also remarks on the Constitution of the Russian Federation.

83 See T. Skutnabb-Kangas, *Language, Literacy and Minorities*, London, MRG report 1990.

84 Among many entries, see those for Estonia, Hungary, Latvia, Romania and Slovakia.

85 The linguistic elements of language rights may not be important for, say, African Americans; Irish minorities in Britain or the USA are usually not identified through their familiarity with the Irish language.

86 See the entry for Australia on the Aborigines.

87 See, for example, the entry for Cyprus on the Maronites and Cypriot Arabic.

88 For an 'extreme' example, see the remarks on village-level democracy in Switzerland.

89 Paragraph 27.

90 Including, for example, 'new' constitutional developments in many Central and South American countries.

91 See the entries for Papua New Guinea and West Papua, and remarks on the Nuba in the Sudan entry.

92 See the entry for the Sudan.

93 In some States, *general* participation and access to the levers of political power is the major problem: see, for example, the entry for Kuwait.

94 See general remarks on the level of participation and extension of the franchise in the section on the Middle East.

95 On the enforcement of prayer observance in the public domain, see the entry for Saudi Arabia.

96 See the section on the Alevis in the entry for Turkey, and their practice of dissimulation.

97 See entry for Pakistan on blasphemy laws.

98 See the section on the Baha'i in the entry for Iran.

99 See the introduction to Central and South America and the Caribbean on the New Tribes Mission.

100 See entries for Sudan, Pakistan and Saudi Arabia.

101 This is the condition of the Baha'i, particularly in Iran.

102 In essence, they are summed up in the UN draft Declaration on the Rights of Indigenous Peoples, contained in UN Doc. E/CN.4/Sub.2/1994/2/Add.1.

103 The draft Declaration on the Rights of Indigenous Peoples addresses the practices of genocide, cultural genocide and ethnocide often directed against indigenous peoples.

104 See Article 36 of the draft Declaration.

105 See, among others, entries for Australia, Bangladesh, Canada, Finland, Guatemala, Kenya, Mexico, New Zealand, Nicaragua, Norway, the Philippines, Sweden, Tanzania and the USA.

106 See E.-I. Daes, *Protection of the Heritage of Indigenous People*, UN Doc. E/CN.4/Sub.2/1995/26.

107 Article 3 of the UN draft Declaration.

108 Even if States practise 'self-determination' in domestic law, they may be reluctant to translate this into international standards – this has sometimes represented the position of the USA.

109 Consider in the aggregate the constitutional changes recorded by the *Directory* for Central and South America.

110 See the entry for Brazil.

111 See the entry for Bangladesh.

112 See the remarks on Nunavut in the entry for Canada.

113 A notable example is the Treaty of Waitangi – see the entry for New Zealand.

114 See remarks on the Russian Federation Law on Native Peoples; also the entries for Scandinavian countries, the Philippines, India and Pakistan.

115 The case of the Adivasis in Bangladesh may be considered in this perspective.

APPENDIX

Basic Documents on Minorities and Indigenous Peoples

Compiled by Patrick Thornberry

Contents

The International Bill of Human Rights

Universal Declaration of Human Rights

Adopted and proclaimed by General Assembly resolution 217A (III) of 10 December 1948

PREAMBLE

Whereas recognition of the inherent dignity and of the equal and inalienable rights of all members of the human family is the foundation of freedom, justice and peace in the world,

Whereas disregard and contempt for human rights have resulted in barbarous acts which have outraged the conscience of mankind, and the advent of a world in which human beings shall enjoy freedom of speech and belief and freedom from fear and want has been proclaimed as the highest aspiration of the common people,

Whereas it is essential, if man is not to be compelled to have recourse, as a last resort, to rebellion against tyranny and oppression, that human rights should be protected by the rule of law,

Whereas it is essential to promote the development of friendly relations between nations,

Whereas the peoples of the United Nations have in the Charter reaffirmed their faith in fundamental human rights, in the dignity and worth of the human person and in the equal rights of men and women and have determined to promote social progress and better standards of life in larger freedom,

Whereas Member States have pledged themselves to achieve, in co-operation with the United Nations, the promotion of universal respect for and observance of human rights and fundamental freedoms,

Whereas a common understanding of these rights and freedoms is of the greatest importance for the full realization of this pledge,

Now, therefore, The General Assembly, Proclaims this Universal Declaration of Human Rights as a common standard of achievement for all peoples and all nations, to the end that every individual and every organ of society, keeping this Declaration constantly in mind, shall strive by teaching and education to promote respect for these rights and freedoms and by progressive measures, national and international, to secure their universal and effective recognition and observance, both among the peoples of Member States themselves and among the peoples of territories under their jurisdiction.

Article 1

All human beings are born free and equal in dignity and rights. They are endowed with reason and conscience and should act towards one another in a spirit of brotherhood.

Article 2

Everyone is entitled to all the rights and freedoms set forth in this Declaration, without distinction of any kind, such as race, colour, sex, language, religion, political or other opinion, national or social origin, property, birth or other status.

Furthermore, no distinction shall be made on the basis of the political, jurisdictional or international status of the country or territory to which a person belongs, whether it be independent, trust, non-self-governing or under any other limitation of sovereignty.

Article 3

Everyone has the right to life, liberty and security of person.

Article 4

No one shall be held in slavery or servitude; slavery and the slave trade shall be prohibited in all their forms.

Article 5

No one shall be subjected to torture or to cruel, inhuman or degrading treatment or punishment.

Article 6

Everyone has the right to recognition everywhere as a person before the law.

Article 7

All are equal before the law and are entitled without any discrimination to equal protection of the law. All are entitled to equal protection against any discrimination in violation of this Declaration and against any incitement to such discrimination.

Article 8

Everyone has the right to an effective remedy by the competent national tribunals for acts violating the fundamental rights granted him by the constitution or by law.

Article 9

No one shall be subjected to arbitrary arrest, detention or exile.

Article 10

Everyone is entitled in full equality to a fair and public hearing by an independent and impartial tribunal, in the determination of his rights and obligations and of any criminal charge against him.

Article 11

1. Everyone charged with a penal offence has the right to be presumed innocent until proved guilty according to law in a public trial at which he has had all the guarantees necessary for his defence.

2. No one shall be held guilty of any penal offence on account of any act or omission which did not constitute a penal offence, under national or international law, at the time when it was committed. Nor shall a heavier penalty be imposed than the one that was applicable at the time the penal offence was committed.

Article 12

No one shall be subjected to arbitrary interference with his privacy, family, home or correspondence, nor to attacks upon his honour and reputation. Everyone has the right to the protection of the law against such interference or attacks.

Article 13

1. Everyone has the right to freedom of movement and residence within the borders of each State.

2. Everyone has the right to leave any country, including his own, and to return to his country.

Article 14

1. Everyone has the right to seek and to enjoy in other countries asylum from persecution.

2. This right may not be invoked in the case of prosecutions genuinely arising from non-political crimes or from acts contrary to the purposes and principles of the United Nations.

Article 15

1. Everyone has the right to a nationality.

2. No one shall be arbitrarily deprived of his nationality nor denied the right to change his nationality.

Article 16

1. Men and women of full age, without any limitation due to race, nationality or religion, have the right to marry and to found a family. They are entitled to equal rights as to marriage, during marriage and at its dissolution.

2. Marriage shall be entered into only with the free and full consent of the intending spouses.

3. The family is the natural and fundamental group unit of society and is entitled to protection by society and the State.

Article 17

1. Everyone has the right to own property alone as well as in association with others.

2. No one shall be arbitrarily deprived of his property.

Article 18

Everyone has the right to freedom of thought, conscience and religion; this right includes freedom to change his religion or belief, and freedom, either alone or in community with others and in public or private, to manifest his religion or belief in teaching, practice, worship and observance.

Article 19

Everyone has the right to freedom of opinion and expression; this right includes freedom to hold opinions without interference and to seek, receive and impart information and ideas through any media and regardless of frontiers.

Article 20

1. Everyone has the right to freedom of peaceful assembly and association.

2. No one may be compelled to belong to an association.

Article 21

1. Everyone has the right to take part in the government of his country, directly or through freely chosen representatives.

2. Everyone has the right to equal access to public service in his country.

3. The will of the people shall be the basis of the authority of government; this will shall be expressed in periodic and genuine elections which shall be by universal and equal suffrage and shall be held by secret vote or by equivalent free voting procedures.

Article 22

Everyone, as a member of society, has the right to social security and is entitled to realization, through national effort and international co-operation and in accordance with the organization and resources of each State, of the economic, social and cultural rights indispensable for his dignity and the free development of his personality.

Article 23

1. Everyone has the right to work, to free choice of employment, to just and favourable conditions of work and to protection against unemployment.

2. Everyone, without any discrimination, has the right to equal pay for equal work.

3. Everyone who works has the right to just and favourable remuneration ensuring for himself and his family an existence worthy of human dignity, and supplemented, if necessary, by other means of social protection.

4. Everyone has the right to form and to join trade unions for the protection of his interests.

Article 24

Everyone has the right to rest and leisure, including reasonable limitation of working hours and periodic holidays with pay.

Article 25

1. Everyone has the right to a standard of living adequate for the health and well-being of himself and of his family, including food, clothing, housing and medical care and necessary social services, and the right to security in the event of unemployment, sickness, disability, widowhood, old age or other lack of livelihood in circumstances beyond his control.

2. Motherhood and childhood are entitled to special care and assistance. All children, whether born in or out of wedlock, shall enjoy the same social protection.

Article 26

1. Everyone has the right to education. Education shall be free, at least in the elementary and fundamental stages. Elementary education shall be compulsory. Technical and professional education shall be made generally available and higher education shall be equally accessible to all on the basis of merit.

2. Education shall be directed to the full development of the human personality and to the strengthening of respect for human rights and fundamental freedoms. It shall promote understanding, tolerance and friendship among all nations, racial or religious groups, and shall further the activities of the United Nations for the maintenance of peace.

3. Parents have a prior right to choose the kind of education that shall be given to their children.

Article 27

1. Everyone has the right freely to participate in the cultural life of the community, to enjoy the arts and to share in scientific advancement and its benefits.

2. Everyone has the right to the protection of the moral and material interests resulting from any scientific, literary or artistic production of which he is the author.

Article 28

Everyone is entitled to a social and international order in which the rights and freedoms set forth in this Declaration can be fully realized.

Article 29

1. Everyone has duties to the community in which alone the free and full development of his personality is possible.

2. In the exercise of his rights and freedoms, everyone shall be subject only to such limitations as are determined by law solely for the purpose of securing due recognition and respect for the rights and freedoms of others and of meeting the just requirements of morality, public order and the general welfare in a democratic society.

3. These rights and freedoms may in no case be exercised contrary to the purposes and principles of the United Nations.

Article 30

Nothing in this Declaration may be interpreted as implying for any State, group or person any right to engage in any activity or to perform any act aimed at the destruction of any of the rights and freedoms set forth herein.

International Covenant on Economic, Social and Cultural Rights

Adopted and opened for signature, ratification and accession by General Assembly resolution 2200 A (XXI) of 16 December 1966

ENTRY INTO FORCE: 3 January 1976, in accordance with article 27

PREAMBLE

The States Parties to the present Covenant,

Considering that, in accordance with the principles proclaimed in the Charter of the United Nations, recognition of the inherent dignity and of the equal and inalienable rights of all members of the human family is the foundation of freedom, justice and peace in the world,

Recognizing that these rights derive from the inherent dignity of the human person,

Recognizing that, in accordance with the Universal Declaration of Human Rights, the ideal of free human beings enjoying freedom from fear and want can only be achieved if conditions are created whereby everyone may enjoy his economic, social and cultural rights, as well as his civil and political rights,

Considering the obligation of States under the Charter of the United Nations to promote universal respect for, and observance of, human rights and freedoms,

Realizing that the individual, having duties to other individuals and to the community to which he belongs, is under a responsibility to strive for the promotion and observance of the rights recognized in the present Covenant,

Agree upon the following articles:

PART I

Article 1

1. All peoples have the right of self-determination. By virtue of that right they freely determine their political status and freely pursue their economic, social and cultural development.

2. All peoples may, for their own ends, freely dispose of their natural wealth and resources without prejudice to any obligations arising out of international economic co-operation, based upon the principle of mutual benefit, and international law. In no case may a people be deprived of its own means of subsistence.

3. The States Parties to the present Covenant, including those having responsibility for the administration of Non-Self-Governing and Trust Territories, shall promote the realization of the right of self-determination, and shall respect that right, in conformity with the provisions of the Charter of the United Nations.

PART II

Article 2

1. Each State Party to the present Covenant undertakes to take steps, individually and through international assistance and co-operation, especially economic and technical, to the maximum of its available resources, with a view to achieving progressively the full realization of the rights recognized in the present Covenant by all appropriate means, including particularly the adoption of legislative measures.

2. The States Parties to the present Covenant undertake to guarantee that the rights enunciated in the present Covenant will be exercised without discrimination of any kind as to race, colour, sex, language, religion, political or other opinion, national or social origin, property, birth or other status.

3. Developing countries, with due regard to human rights and their national economy, may determine to what extent they would guarantee the economic rights recognized in the present Covenant to non-nationals.

Article 3

The States Parties to the present Covenant undertake to ensure the equal right of men and women to the enjoyment of all economic, social and cultural rights set forth in the present Covenant.

Article 4

The States Parties to the present Covenant recognize that, in the enjoyment of those rights provided by the State in conformity with the present Covenant, the State may subject such rights only to such limitations as are determined by law only in so far as this may be compatible with the nature of these rights and solely for the purpose of promoting the general welfare in a democratic society.

Article 5

1. Nothing in the present Covenant may be interpreted as implying for any State, group or person any right to engage in any activity or to perform any act aimed at the destruction of any of the rights or freedoms recognized herein, or at their limitation to a greater extent than is provided for in the present Covenant.

2. No restriction upon or derogation from any of the fundamental human rights recognized or existing in any country in virtue of law, conventions, regulations or custom shall be admitted on the pretext that the present Covenant does not recognize such rights or that it recognizes them to a lesser extent.

PART III

Article 6

1. The States Parties to the present Covenant recognize the right to work, which includes the right of everyone to the opportunity to gain his living by work which he freely chooses or accepts, and will take appropriate steps to safeguard this right.

2. The steps to be taken by a State Party to the present Covenant to achieve the full realization of this right shall include technical and vocational guidance and training programmes, policies and techniques to achieve steady economic, social and cultural development and full and productive employment under conditions safeguarding fundamental political and economic freedoms to the individual.

Article 7

The States Parties to the present Covenant recognize the right of everyone to the enjoyment of just and favourable conditions of work which ensure, in particular:

(a) Remuneration which provides all workers, as a minimum, with:

(i) Fair wages and equal remuneration for work of equal value without distinction of any kind, in particular women being guaranteed conditions of work not inferior to those enjoyed by men, with equal pay for equal work;

(ii) A decent living for themselves and their families in accordance with the provisions of the present Covenant;

(b) Safe and healthy working conditions;

(c) Equal opportunity for everyone to be promoted in his employment to an appropriate higher level, subject to no considerations other than those of seniority and competence;

(d) Rest, leisure and reasonable limitation of working hours and periodic holidays with pay, as well as remuneration for public holidays

Article 8

1. The States Parties to the present Covenant undertake to ensure:

(a) The right of everyone to form trade unions and join the trade union of his choice, subject only to the rules of the organization concerned, for the promotion and protection of his economic and social interests. No restrictions may be placed on the exercise of this right other than those prescribed by law and which are necessary in a democratic society in the interests of national security or public order or for the protection of the rights and freedoms of others;

(b) The right of trade unions to establish national federations or confederations and the right of the latter to form or join international trade-union organizations;

(c) The right of trade unions to function freely subject to no limitations other than those prescribed by law and which are necessary in a democratic society in the interests of national security or public order or for the protection of the rights and freedoms of others;

(d) The right to strike, provided that it is exercised in conformity with the laws of the particular country.

2. This article shall not prevent the imposition of lawful restrictions on the exercise of these rights by members of the armed forces or of the police or of the administration of the State.

3. Nothing in this article shall authorize States Parties to the International Labour Organisation Convention of 1948 concerning Freedom of Association and Protection of the Right to Organize to take legislative measures which would prejudice, or apply the law in such a manner as would prejudice, the guarantees provided for in that Convention.

Article 9

The States Parties to the present Covenant recognize the right of everyone to social security, including social insurance.

Article 10

The States Parties to the present Covenant recognize that:

1. The widest possible protection and assistance should be accorded to the family, which is the natural and fundamental group unit of society, particularly for its establishment and while it is responsible for the care and education of dependent children. Marriage must be entered into with the free consent of the intending spouses.

2. Special protection should be accorded to mothers during a reasonable period before and after childbirth. During such period working mothers should be accorded paid leave or leave with adequate social security benefits.

3. Special measures of protection and assistance should be taken on behalf of all children and young persons without any discrimination for reasons of parentage or other conditions. Children and young persons should be protected from economic and social exploitation. Their employment in work harmful to their morals or health or dangerous to life or likely to hamper their normal development should be punishable by law. States should also set age limits below which the paid employment of child labour should be prohibited and punishable by law.

Article 11

1. The States Parties to the present Covenant recognize the right of everyone to an adequate standard of living for himself and his family, including adequate food, clothing and housing, and to the continuous improvement of living conditions. The States Parties will take appropriate steps to ensure the realization of this right, recognizing to this effect the essential importance of international co-operation based on free consent.

2. The States Parties to the present Covenant, recognizing the fundamental right of everyone to be free from hunger, shall take, individually and through international co-operation, the measures, including specific programmes, which are needed:

(a) To improve methods of production, conservation and distribution of food by making full use of technical and scientific knowledge, by disseminating knowledge of the principles of nutrition and by developing or reforming agrarian systems in such a way as to achieve the most efficient development and utilization of natural resources;

(b) Taking into account the problems of both food-importing and food-exporting countries, to ensure an equitable distribution of world food supplies in relation to need.

Article 12

1. The States Parties to the present Covenant recognize the right of everyone to the enjoyment of the highest attainable standard of physical and mental health.

2. The steps to be taken by the States Parties to the present Covenant to achieve the full realization of this right shall include those necessary for:

(a) The provision for the reduction of the stillbirth-rate and of infant mortality and for the healthy development of the child;

(b) The improvement of all aspects of environmental and industrial hygiene;

(c) The prevention, treatment and control of epidemic, endemic, occupational and other diseases;

(d) The creation of conditions which would assure to all medical service and medical attention in the event of sickness.

Article 13

1. The States Parties to the present Covenant recognize the right of everyone to education. They agree that education shall be directed to the full development of the human personality and the sense of its dignity, and shall strengthen the respect for human rights and fundamental freedoms. They further agree that education shall enable all persons to participate effectively in a free society, promote understanding, tolerance and friendship among all nations and all racial, ethnic or religious groups, and further the activities of the United Nations for the maintenance of peace.

2. The States Parties to the present Covenant recognize that, with a view to achieving the full realization of this right:

(a) Primary education shall be compulsory and available free to all;

(b) Secondary education in its different forms, including technical and vocational secondary education, shall be made generally available and accessible to all by every appropriate means, and in particular by the progressive introduction of free education;

(c) Higher education shall be made equally accessible to all, on the basis of capacity, by every appropriate means, and in particular by the progressive introduction of free education;

(d) Fundamental education shall be encouraged or intensified as far as possible for those persons who have not received or completed the whole period of their primary education;

(e) The development of a system of schools at all levels shall be actively pursued, an adequate fellowship system shall be established, and the material conditions of teaching staff shall be continuously improved.

3. The States Parties to the present Covenant undertake to have respect for the liberty of parents and, when applicable, legal guardians to choose for their children schools, other than those established by the public authorities, which conform to such minimum educational standards as may be laid down or approved by the State and to ensure the religious and moral education of their children in conformity with their own convictions.

4. No part of this article shall be construed so as to interfere with the liberty of individuals and bodies to establish and direct educational institutions, subject always to the observance of the principles set forth in paragraph I of this article and to the requirement that the education given in such institutions shall conform to such minimum standards as may be laid down by the State.

Article 14

Each State Party to the present Covenant which, at the time of becoming a Party, has not been able to secure in its metropolitan territory or other territories under its jurisdiction compulsory primary education, free of charge, undertakes, within two years, to work out and adopt a detailed plan of action for the progressive implementation, within a reasonable number of years, to be fixed in the plan, of the principle of compulsory education free of charge for all.

Article 15

1. The States Parties to the present Covenant recognize the right of everyone:

(a) To take part in cultural life;

(b) To enjoy the benefits of scientific progress and its applications;

(c) To benefit from the protection of the moral and material interests resulting from any scientific, literary or artistic production of which he is the author.

2. The steps to be taken by the States Parties to the present Covenant to achieve the full realization of this right shall include those necessary for the conservation, the development and the diffusion of science and culture.

3. The States Parties to the present Covenant undertake to respect the freedom indispensable for scientific research and creative activity.

4. The States Parties to the present Covenant recognize the benefits to be derived from the encouragement and development of international contacts and co-operation in the scientific and cultural fields.

PART IV

Article 16

1. The States Parties to the present Covenant undertake to submit in conformity with this part of the Covenant reports on the measures which they have adopted and the progress made in achieving the observance of the rights recognized herein.

2. (a) All reports shall be submitted to the Secretary-General of the United Nations, who shall transmit copies to the Economic and Social Council for consideration in accordance with the provisions of the present Covenant;

(b) The Secretary-General of the United Nations shall also transmit to the specialized agencies copies of the reports, or any relevant parts therefrom, from States Parties to the present Covenant which are also members of these specialized agencies in so far as these reports, or parts therefrom, relate to any matters which fall within the responsibilities of the said agencies in accordance with their constitutional instruments.

Article 17

1. The States Parties to the present Covenant shall furnish their reports in stages, in accordance with a programme to be established by the Economic and Social Council within one year of the entry into force of the present Covenant after consultation with the States Parties and the specialized agencies concerned.

2. Reports may indicate factors and difficulties affecting the degree of fulfilment of obligations under the present Covenant.

3. Where relevant information has previously been furnished to the United Nations or to any specialized agency by any State Party to the present Covenant, it will not be necessary to reproduce that information, but a precise reference to the information so furnished will suffice.

Article 18

Pursuant to its responsibilities under the Charter of the United Nations in the field of human rights and fundamental freedoms, the Economic and Social Council may make arrangements with the specialized agencies in respect of their reporting to it on the progress made in achieving the observance of the provisions of the present Covenant falling within the scope of their activities. These reports may include particulars of decisions and recommendations on such implementation adopted by their competent organs.

Article 19

The Economic and Social Council may transmit to the Commission on Human Rights for study and general recommendation or, as appropriate, for information the reports concerning human rights submitted by States in accordance with articles 16 and 17, and those concerning human rights submitted by the specialized agencies in accordance with article 18.

Article 20

The States Parties to the present Covenant and the specialized agencies concerned may submit comments to the Economic and Social Council on any general recommendation under article 19 or reference to such general recommendation in any report of the Commission on Human Rights or any documentation referred to therein.

Article 21

The Economic and Social Council may submit from time to time to the General Assembly reports with recommendations of a general nature and a summary of the information received from the States Parties to the present Covenant and the specialized agencies on the measures taken and the progress made in achieving general observance of the rights recognized in the present Covenant.

Article 22

The Economic and Social Council may bring to the attention of other organs of the United Nations, their subsidiary organs and specialized agencies concerned with furnishing technical assistance any matters arising out of the reports referred to in this part of the present Covenant which may assist such bodies in deciding, each within its field of competence, on the advisability of international measures likely to contribute to the effective progressive implementation of the present Covenant.

Article 23

The States Parties to the present Covenant agree that international action for the achievement of the rights recognized in the present Covenant includes such methods as the conclusion of conventions, the adoption of recommendations, the furnishing of technical assistance and the holding of regional meetings and technical meetings for the purpose of consultation and study organized in conjunction with the Governments concerned.

Article 24

Nothing in the present Covenant shall be interpreted as impairing the provisions of the Charter of the United Nations and of the constitutions of the specialized agencies which define the respective responsibilities of the various organs of the United Nations and of the specialized agencies in regard to the matters dealt with in the present Covenant.

Article 25

Nothing in the present Covenant shall be interpreted as impairing the inherent right of all peoples to enjoy and utilize fully and freely their natural wealth and resources.

PART V

Article 26

1. The present Covenant is open for signature by any State Member of the United Nations or member of any of its specialized agencies, by any State Party to the Statute of the International Court of Justice, and by any other State which has been invited by the General Assembly of the United Nations to become a party to the present Covenant.

2. The present Covenant is subject to ratification. Instruments of ratification shall be deposited with the Secretary-General of the United Nations.

3. The present Covenant shall be open to accession by any State referred to in paragraph 1 of this article.

4. Accession shall be effected by the deposit of an instrument of accession with the Secretary-General of the United Nations.

5. The Secretary-General of the United Nations shall inform all States which have signed the present Covenant or acceded to it of the deposit of each instrument of ratification or accession.

Article 27

1. The present Covenant shall enter into force three months after the date of the deposit with the Secretary-General of the United Nations of the thirty-fifth instrument of ratification or instrument of accession.

2. For each State ratifying the present Covenant or acceding to it after the deposit of the thirty-fifth instrument of ratification or instrument of accession, the present Covenant shall enter into force three months after the date of the deposit of its own instrument of ratification or instrument of accession.

Article 28

The provisions of the present Covenant shall extend to all parts of federal States without any limitations or exceptions.

Article 29

1. Any State Party to the present Covenant may propose an amendment and file it with the Secretary-General of the United Nations. The Secretary-General shall thereupon communicate any proposed amendments to the States Parties to the present Covenant with a request that they notify him whether they favour a conference of States Parties

for the purpose of considering and voting upon the proposals. In the event that at least one third of the States Parties favours such a conference, the Secretary-General shall convene the conference under the auspices of the United Nations. Any amendment adopted by a majority of the States Parties present and voting at the conference shall be submitted to the General Assembly of the United Nations for approval.

2. Amendments shall come into force when they have been approved by the General Assembly of the United Nations and accepted by a two-thirds majority of the States Parties to the present Covenant in accordance with their respective constitutional processes.

3. When amendments come into force they shall be binding on those States Parties which have accepted them, other States Parties still being bound by the provisions of the present Covenant and any earlier amendment which they have accepted.

Article 30

Irrespective of the notifications made under article 26, paragraph 5, the Secretary-General of the United Nations shall inform all States referred to in paragraph 1 of the same article of the following particulars:

(a) Signatures, ratifications and accessions under article 26;

(b) The date of the entry into force of the present Covenant under article 27 and the date of the entry into force of any amendments under article 29.

Article 31

1. The present Covenant, of which the Chinese, English, French, Russian and Spanish texts are equally authentic, shall be deposited in the archives of the United Nations.

2. The Secretary-General of the United Nations shall transmit certified copies of the present Covenant to all States referred to in article 26.

International Covenant on Civil and Political Rights

Adopted and opened for signature, ratification and accession by General Assembly resolution 2200 A (XXI) of 16 December 1966

Entry into force: 23 March 1976, in accordance with article 49

Preamble

The States Parties to the present Covenant,

Considering that, in accordance with the principles proclaimed in the Charter of the United Nations, recognition of the inherent dignity and of the equal and inalienable rights of all members of the human family is the foundation of freedom, justice and peace in the world,

Recognizing that these rights derive from the inherent dignity of the human person,

Recognizing that, in accordance with the Universal Declaration of Human Rights, the ideal of free human beings enjoying civil and political freedom and freedom from fear and want can only be achieved if conditions are created whereby everyone may enjoy his civil and political rights, as well as his economic, social and cultural rights,

Considering the obligation of States under the Charter of the United Nations to promote universal respect for, and observance of, human rights and freedoms,

Realizing that the individual, having duties to other individuals and to the community to which he belongs, is under a responsibility to strive for the promotion and observance of the rights recognized in the present Covenant,

Agree upon the following articles:

PART I

Article 1

1. All peoples have the right of self-determination. By virtue of that right they freely determine their political status and freely pursue their economic, social and cultural development.

2. All peoples may, for their own ends, freely dispose of their natural wealth and resources without prejudice to any obligations arising out of international economic co-operation, based upon the principle of mutual benefit, and international law. In no case may a people be deprived of its own means of subsistence.

3. The States Parties to the present Covenant, including those having responsibility for the administration of Non-Self-Governing and Trust Territories, shall promote the realization of the right of self-determination, and shall respect that right, in conformity with the provisions of the Charter of the United Nations.

PART II

Article 2

1. Each State Party to the present Covenant undertakes to respect and to ensure to all individuals within its territory and subject to its jurisdiction the rights recognized in the present Covenant, without distinction of any kind, such as race, colour, sex, language, religion, political or other opinion, national or social origin, property, birth or other status.

2. Where not already provided for by existing legislative or other measures, each State Party to the present Covenant undertakes to take the necessary steps, in accordance with its constitutional processes and with the provisions of the present Covenant, to adopt such legislative or other measures as may be necessary to give effect to the rights recognized in the present Covenant.

3. Each State Party to the present Covenant undertakes:

(a) To ensure that any person whose rights or freedoms as herein recognized are violated shall have an effective remedy, notwithstanding that the violation has been committed by persons acting in an official capacity;

(b) To ensure that any person claiming such a remedy shall have his right thereto determined by competent judicial, administrative or legislative authorities, or by any other competent authority provided for by the legal system of the State, and to develop the possibilities of judicial remedy;

(c) To ensure that the competent authorities shall enforce such remedies when granted.

Article 3

The States Parties to the present Covenant undertake to ensure the equal right of men and women to the enjoyment of all civil and political rights set forth in the present Covenant.

Article 4

1. In time of public emergency which threatens the life of the nation and the existence of which is officially proclaimed, the States Parties to the present Covenant may take measures derogating from their obligations under the present Covenant to the extent strictly required by the exigencies of the situation, provided that such measures are not inconsistent with their other obligations under international law and do not involve discrimination solely on the ground of race, colour, sex, language, religion or social origin.

2. No derogation from articles 6, 7, 8 (paragraphs 1 and 2), 11, 15, 16 and 18 may be made under this provision.

3. Any State Party to the present Covenant availing itself of the right of derogation shall immediately inform the other States Parties to the present Covenant, through the intermediary of the Secretary-General of the United Nations, of the provisions from which it has derogated and of the reasons by which it was actuated. A further communication shall be made, through the same intermediary, on the date on which it terminates such derogation.

Article 5

1. Nothing in the present Covenant may be interpreted as implying for any State, group or person any right to engage in any activity or perform any act aimed at the destruction of any of the rights and freedoms recognized herein or at their limitation to a greater extent than is provided for in the present Covenant.

2. There shall be no restriction upon or derogation from any of the fundamental human rights recognized or existing in any State Party to the present Covenant pursuant to law, conventions, regulations or custom on the pretext that the present Covenant does not recognize such rights or that it recognizes them to a lesser extent.

PART III

Article 6

1. Every human being has the inherent right to life. This right shall be protected by law. No one shall be arbitrarily deprived of his life.

2. In countries which have not abolished the death penalty, sentence of death may be imposed only for the most serious crimes in accordance with the law in force at the time of the commission of the crime and not contrary to the provisions of the present Covenant and to the Convention on the Prevention and Punishment of the Crime of Genocide. This penalty can only be carried out pursuant to a final judgement rendered by a competent court.

3. When deprivation of life constitutes the crime of genocide, it is understood that nothing in this article shall authorize any State Party to the present Covenant to derogate in any way from any obligation assumed under the provisions of the Convention on the Prevention and Punishment of the Crime of Genocide.

4. Anyone sentenced to death shall have the right to seek pardon or commutation of the sentence. Amnesty, pardon or commutation of the sentence of death may be granted in all cases.

5. Sentence of death shall not be imposed for crimes committed by persons below eighteen years of age and shall not be carried out on pregnant women.

6. Nothing in this article shall be invoked to delay or to prevent the abolition of capital punishment by any State Party to the present Covenant.

Article 7

No one shall be subjected to torture or to cruel, inhuman or degrading treatment or punishment. In particular, no one shall be subjected without his free consent to medical or scientific experimentation.

Article 8

1. No one shall be held in slavery; slavery and the slave-trade in all their forms shall be prohibited.

2. No one shall be held in servitude.

3. (a) No one shall be required to perform forced or compulsory labour;

(b) Paragraph 3 (a) shall not be held to preclude, in countries where imprisonment with hard labour may be imposed as a punishment for a crime, the performance of hard labour in pursuance of a sentence to such punishment by a competent court;

(c) For the purpose of this paragraph the term "forced or compulsory labour" shall not include:

(i) Any work or service, not referred to in subparagraph (b), normally required of a person who is under detention in consequence of a lawful order of a court, or of a person during conditional release from such detention;

(ii) Any service of a military character and, in countries where conscientious objection is recognized, any national service required by law of conscientious objectors;

(iii) Any service exacted in cases of emergency or calamity threatening the life or well-being of the community;

(iv) Any work or service which forms part of normal civil obligations.

Article 9

1. Everyone has the right to liberty and security of person. No one shall be subjected to arbitrary arrest or detention. No one shall be deprived of his liberty except on such grounds and in accordance with such procedure as are established by law.

2. Anyone who is arrested shall be informed, at the time of arrest, of the reasons for his arrest and shall be promptly informed of any charges against him.

3. Anyone arrested or detained on a criminal charge shall be brought promptly before a judge or other officer authorized by law to exercise judicial power and shall be entitled to trial within a reasonable time or to release. It shall not be the general rule that persons awaiting trial shall be detained in custody, but release may be subject to guarantees to appear for trial, at any other stage of the judicial proceedings, and, should occasion arise, for execution of the judgement.

4. Anyone who is deprived of his liberty by arrest or detention shall be entitled to take proceedings before a court, in order that that court may decide without delay on the lawfulness of his detention and order his release if the detention is not lawful.

5. Anyone who has been the victim of unlawful arrest or detention shall have an enforceable right to compensation.

Article 10

1. All persons deprived of their liberty shall be treated with humanity and with respect for the inherent dignity of the human person.

2. (a) Accused persons shall, save in exceptional circumstances, be segregated from convicted persons and shall be subject to separate treatment appropriate to their status as unconvicted persons;

(b) Accused juvenile persons shall be separated from adults and brought as speedily as possible for adjudication.

3. The penitentiary system shall comprise treatment of prisoners the essential aim of which shall be their reformation and social rehabilitation. Juvenile offenders shall be segregated from adults and be accorded treatment appropriate to their age and legal status.

Article 11

No one shall be imprisoned merely on the ground of inability to fulfil a contractual obligation.

Article 12

1. Everyone lawfully within the territory of a State shall, within that territory, have the right to liberty of movement and freedom to choose his residence.

2. Everyone shall be free to leave any country, including his own.

3. The above-mentioned rights shall not be subject to any restrictions except those which are provided by law, are necessary to protect national security, public order (*ordre public*), public health or morals or the rights and freedoms of others, and are consistent with the other rights recognized in the present Covenant.

4. No one shall be arbitrarily deprived of the right to enter his own country.

Article 13

An alien lawfully in the territory of a State Party to the present Covenant may be expelled therefrom only in pursuance of a decision reached in accordance with law and shall, except where compelling reasons of national security otherwise require, be allowed to submit the reasons against his expulsion and to have his case reviewed by, and be represented for the purpose before, the competent authority or a person or persons especially designated by the competent authority.

Article 14

1. All persons shall be equal before the courts and tribunals. In the determination of any criminal charge against him, or of his rights and obligations in a suit at law, everyone shall be entitled to a fair and public hearing by a competent, independent and impartial tribunal established by law. The press and the public may be excluded from all or part of a trial for reasons of morals, public order (*ordre public*) or national security in a democratic society, or when the interest of the private lives of the parties so requires, or to the extent strictly necessary in the opinion of the court in special circumstances where publicity would prejudice the interests of justice; but any judgement rendered in a criminal case or in a suit at law shall be made public except where the interest of juvenile persons otherwise requires or the proceedings concern matrimonial disputes or the guardianship of children.

2. Everyone charged with a criminal offence shall have the right to be presumed innocent until proved guilty according to law.

3. In the determination of any criminal charge against him, everyone shall be entitled to the following minimum guarantees, in full equality:

(a) To be informed promptly and in detail in a language which he understands of the nature and cause of the charge against him;

(b) To have adequate time and facilities for the preparation of his defence and to communicate with counsel of his own choosing;

(c) To be tried without undue delay;

(d) To be tried in his presence, and to defend himself in person or through legal assistance of his own choosing; to be informed, if he does not have legal assistance, of this right; and to have legal assistance assigned to him, in any case where the interests of justice so require, and without payment by him in any such case if he does not have sufficient means to pay for it;

(e) To examine, or have examined, the witnesses against him and to obtain the attendance and examination of witnesses on his behalf under the same conditions as witnesses against him;

(f) To have the free assistance of an interpreter if he cannot understand or speak the language used in court;

(g) Not to be compelled to testify against himself or to confess guilt.

4. In the case of juvenile persons, the procedure shall be such as will take account of their age and the desirability of promoting their rehabilitation.

5. Everyone convicted of a crime shall have the right to his conviction and sentence being reviewed by a higher tribunal according to law.

6. When a person has by a final decision been convicted of a criminal offence and when subsequently his conviction has been reversed or he has been pardoned on the ground that a new or newly discovered fact shows conclusively that there has been a miscarriage of justice, the person who has suffered punishment as a result of such conviction shall be compensated according to law, unless it is proved that the non-disclosure of the unknown fact in time is wholly or partly attributable to him.

7. No one shall be liable to be tried or punished again for an offence for which he has already been finally convicted or acquitted in accordance with the law and penal procedure of each country.

Article 15

1. No one shall be held guilty of any criminal offence on account of any act or omission which did not constitute a criminal offence, under national or international law, at the time when it was committed. Nor shall a heavier penalty be imposed than the one that was applicable at the time when the criminal offence was committed. If, subsequent to the commission of the offence, provision is made by law for the imposition of the lighter penalty, the offender shall benefit thereby.

2. Nothing in this article shall prejudice the trial and punishment of any person for any act or omission which, at the time when it was committed, was criminal according to the general principles of law recognized by the community of nations.

Article 16

Everyone shall have the right to recognition everywhere as a person before the law.

Article 17

1. No one shall be subjected to arbitrary or unlawful interference with his privacy, family, home or correspondence, nor to unlawful attacks on his honour and reputation.

2. Everyone has the right to the protection of the law against such interference or attacks.

Article 18

1. Everyone shall have the right to freedom of thought, conscience and religion. This right shall include freedom to have or to adopt a religion or belief of his choice, and freedom, either individually or in community with others and in public or private, to manifest his religion or belief in worship, observance, practice and teaching.

2. No one shall be subject to coercion which would impair his freedom to have or to adopt a religion or belief of his choice.

3. Freedom to manifest one's religion or beliefs may be subject only to such limitations as are prescribed by law and are necessary to protect public safety, order, health, or morals or the fundamental rights and freedoms of others.

4. The States Parties to the present Covenant undertake to have respect for the liberty of parents and, when applicable, legal guardians to ensure the religious and moral education of their children in conformity with their own convictions.

Article 19

1. Everyone shall have the right to hold opinions without interference.

2. Everyone shall have the right to freedom of expression; this right shall include freedom to seek, receive and impart information and ideas of all kinds, regardless of frontiers, either orally, in writing or in print, in the form of art, or through any other media of his choice.

3. The exercise of the rights provided for in paragraph 2 of this article carries with it special duties and responsibilities. It may therefore be subject to certain restrictions, but these shall only be such as are provided by law and are necessary:

(a) For respect of the rights or reputations of others;

(b) For the protection of national security or of public order (*ordre public*), or of public health or morals.

Article 20

1. Any propaganda for war shall be prohibited by law.

2. Any advocacy of national, racial or religious hatred that constitutes incitement to discrimination, hostility or violence shall be prohibited by law.

Article 21

The right of peaceful assembly shall be recognized. No restrictions may be placed on the exercise of this right other than those imposed in conformity with the law and which are necessary in a democratic society in the interests of national security or public safety, public order (*ordre public*), the protection of public health or morals or the protection of the rights and freedoms of others.

Article 22

1. Everyone shall have the right to freedom of association with others, including the right to form and join trade unions for the protection of his interests.

2. No restrictions may be placed on the exercise of this right other than those which are prescribed by law and which are necessary in a democratic society in the interests of national security or public safety, public order (*ordre public*), the protection of public health or morals or the protection of the rights and freedoms of others. This article shall not prevent the imposition of lawful restrictions on members of the armed forces and of the police in their exercise of this right.

3. Nothing in this article shall authorize States Parties to the International Labour Organisation Convention of 1948 concerning Freedom of Association and Protection of the Right to Organize to take legislative measures which would prejudice, or to apply the law in such a manner as to prejudice, the guarantees provided for in that Convention.

Article 23

1. The family is the natural and fundamental group unit of society and is entitled to protection by society and the State.

2. The right of men and women of marriageable age to marry and to found a family shall be recognized.

3. No marriage shall be entered into without the free and full consent of the intending spouses.

4. States Parties to the present Covenant shall take appropriate steps to ensure equality of rights and responsibilities of spouses as to marriage, during marriage and at its dissolution. In the case of dissolution, provision shall be made for the necessary protection of any children.

Article 24

1. Every child shall have, without any discrimination as to race, colour, sex, language, religion, national or social origin, property or birth, the right to such measures of protection as are required by his status as a minor, on the part of his family, society and the State.

2. Every child shall be registered immediately after birth and shall have a name.

3. Every child has the right to acquire a nationality.

Article 25

Every citizen shall have the right and the opportunity, without any of the distinctions mentioned in article 2 and without unreasonable restrictions:

(a) To take part in the conduct of public affairs, directly or through freely chosen representatives;

(b) To vote and to be elected at genuine periodic elections which shall be by universal and equal suffrage and shall be held by secret ballot, guaranteeing the free expression of the will of the electors;

(c) To have access, on general terms of equality, to public service in his country.

Article 26

All persons are equal before the law and are entitled without any discrimination to the equal protection of the law. In this respect, the law shall prohibit any discrimination and guarantee to all persons equal and effective protection against discrimination on any ground such as race, colour, sex, language, religion, political or other opinion, national or social origin, property, birth or other status.

Article 27

In those States in which ethnic, religious or linguistic minorities exist, persons belonging to such minorities shall not be denied the right, in community with the other members of their group, to enjoy their own culture, to profess and practise their own religion, or to use their own language.

PART IV

Article 28

1. There shall be established a Human Rights Committee (hereafter referred to in the present Covenant as the Committee). It shall consist of eighteen members and shall carry out the functions hereinafter provided.

2. The Committee shall be composed of nationals of the States Parties to the present Covenant who shall be persons of high moral character and recognized competence in the field of human rights, consideration being given to the usefulness of the participation of some persons having legal experience.

3. The members of the Committee shall be elected and shall serve in their personal capacity.

Article 29

1. The members of the Committee shall be elected by secret ballot from a list of persons possessing the qualifications prescribed in article 28 and nominated for the purpose by the States Parties to the present Covenant.

2. Each State Party to the present Covenant may nominate not more than two persons. These persons shall be nationals of the nominating State.

3. A person shall be eligible for renomination.

Article 30

1. The initial election shall be held no later than six months after the date of the entry into force of the present Covenant.

2. At least four months before the date of each election to the Committee, other than an election to fill a vacancy declared in accordance with article 34, the Secretary-General of the United Nations shall address a written invitation to the States Parties to the present Covenant to submit their nominations for membership of the Committee within three months.

3. The Secretary-General of the United Nations shall prepare a list in alphabetical order of all the persons thus nominated, with an indication of the States Parties which have nominated them, and shall submit it to the States Parties to the present Covenant no later than one month before the date of each election.

4. Elections of the members of the Committee shall be held at a meeting of the States Parties to the present Covenant convened by the Secretary-General of the United Nations at the Headquarters of the United Nations. At that meeting, for which two thirds of the States Parties to the present Covenant shall constitute a quorum, the persons elected to the Committee shall be those nominees who obtain the largest number of votes and an absolute majority of the votes of the representatives of States Parties present and voting.

Article 31

1. The Committee may not include more than one national of the same State.

2. In the election of the Committee, consideration shall be given to equitable geographical distribution of membership and to the representation of the different forms of civilization and of the principal legal systems.

Article 32

1. The members of the Committee shall be elected for a term of four years. They shall be eligible for re-election if renominated. However, the terms of nine of the members elected at the first election shall expire at the end of two years; immediately after the first election, the names of these nine members shall be chosen by lot by the Chairman of the meeting referred to in article 30, paragraph 4.

2. Elections at the expiry of office shall be held in accordance with the preceding articles of this part of the present Covenant.

Article 33

1. If, in the unanimous opinion of the other members, a member of the Committee has ceased to carry out his functions for any cause other than absence of a temporary character, the Chairman of the Committee shall notify the Secretary-General of the United Nations, who shall then declare the seat of that member to be vacant.

2. In the event of the death or the resignation of a member of the Committee, the Chairman shall immediately notify the Secretary-General of the United Nations, who shall declare the seat vacant from the date of death or the date on which the resignation takes effect.

Article 34

1. When a vacancy is declared in accordance with article 33 and if the term of office of the member to be replaced does not expire within six months of the declaration of the vacancy, the Secretary-General of the United Nations shall notify each of the States Parties to the present Covenant, which may within two months submit nominations in accordance with article 29 for the purpose of filling the vacancy.

2. The Secretary-General of the United Nations shall prepare a list in alphabetical order of the persons thus nominated and shall submit it to the States Parties to the present Covenant. The election to fill the vacancy shall then take place in accordance with the relevant provisions of this part of the present Covenant.

3. A member of the Committee elected to fill a vacancy declared in accordance with article 33 shall hold office for the remainder of the term of the member who vacated the seat on the Committee under the provisions of that article.

Article 35

The members of the Committee shall, with the approval of the General Assembly of the United Nations, receive emoluments from United Nations resources on such terms and conditions as the General Assembly may decide, having regard to the importance of the Committee's responsibilities.

Article 36

The Secretary-General of the United Nations shall provide the necessary staff and facilities for the effective performance of the functions of the Committee under the present Covenant.

Article 37

1. The Secretary-General of the United Nations shall convene the initial meeting of the Committee at the Headquarters of the United Nations.

2. After its initial meeting, the Committee shall meet at such times as shall be provided in its rules of procedure.

3. The Committee shall normally meet at the Headquarters of the United Nations or at the United Nations Office at Geneva.

Article 38

Every member of the Committee shall, before taking up his duties, make a solemn declaration in open committee that he will perform his functions impartially and conscientiously.

Article 39

1. The Committee shall elect its officers for a term of two years. They may be re-elected.

2. The Committee shall establish its own rules of procedure, but these rules shall provide, *inter alia*, that:

(a) Twelve members shall constitute a quorum;

(b) Decisions of the Committee shall be made by a majority vote of the members present.

Article 40

1. The States Parties to the present Covenant undertake to submit reports on the measures they have adopted which give effect to the rights recognized herein and on the progress made in the enjoyment of those rights:

(a) Within one year of the entry into force of the present Covenant for the States Parties concerned;

(b) Thereafter whenever the Committee so requests.

2. All reports shall be submitted to the Secretary-General of the United Nations, who shall transmit them to the Committee for consideration. Reports shall indicate the factors and difficulties, if any, affecting the implementation of the present Covenant.

3. The Secretary-General of the United Nations may, after consultation with the Committee, transmit to the specialized agencies concerned copies of such parts of the reports as may fall within their field of competence.

4. The Committee shall study the reports submitted by the States Parties to the present Covenant. It shall transmit its reports, and such general comments as it may consider appropriate, to the States Parties. The Committee may also transmit to the Economic and Social Council these comments along with the copies of the reports it has received from States Parties to the present Covenant.

5. The States Parties to the present Covenant may submit to the Committee observations on any comments that may be made in accordance with paragraph 4 of this article.

Article 41

1. A State Party to the present Covenant may at any time declare under this article that it recognizes the competence of the Committee to receive and consider communications to the effect that a State Party claims that another State Party is not fulfilling its obligations under the present Covenant. Communications under this article may be received and considered only if submitted by a State Party which has made a declaration recognizing in regard to itself the competence of the Committee. No communication shall be received by the Committee if it concerns a State Party which has not made such a declaration. Communications received under this article shall be dealt with in accordance with the following procedure:

(a) If a State Party to the present Covenant considers that another State Party is not giving effect to the provisions of the present Covenant, it may, by written communication, bring the matter to the attention of that State Party. Within three months after the receipt of the communication the receiving State shall afford the State which sent the communication an explanation, or any other statement in writing clarifying the matter which should include, to the extent possible and pertinent, reference to domestic procedures and remedies taken, pending, or available in the matter;

(b) If the matter is not adjusted to the satisfaction of both States Parties concerned within six months after the receipt by the receiving State of the initial communication, either State shall have the right to refer the matter to the Committee, by notice given to the Committee and to the other State;

(c) The Committee shall deal with a matter referred to it only after it has ascertained that all available domestic remedies have been invoked and exhausted in the matter, in conformity with the generally recognized principles of international law. This shall not be the rule where the application of the remedies is unreasonably prolonged;

(d) The Committee shall hold closed meetings when examining communications under this article;

(e) Subject to the provisions of subparagraph (c), the Committee shall make available its good offices to the States Parties concerned with a view to a friendly solution of the matter on the basis of respect for human rights and fundamental freedoms as recognized in the present Covenant;

(f) In any matter referred to it, the Committee may call upon the States Parties concerned, referred to in subparagraph (b), to supply any relevant information;

(g) The States Parties concerned, referred to in subparagraph (b), shall have the right to be represented when the matter is being considered in the Committee and to make submissions orally and/or in writing;

(h) The Committee shall, within twelve months after the date of receipt of notice under subparagraph (b), submit a report:

(i) If a solution within the terms of subparagraph (e) is reached, the Committee shall confine its report to a brief statement of the facts and of the solution reached;

(ii) If a solution within the terms of subparagraph (e) is not reached, the Committee shall confine its report to a brief statement of the facts; the written submissions and record of the oral submissions made by the States Parties concerned shall be attached to the report. In every matter, the report shall be communicated to the States Parties concerned.

2. The provisions of this article shall come into force when ten States Parties to the present Covenant have made declarations under paragraph 1 of this article. Such declarations shall be deposited by the States Parties with the Secretary-General of the United Nations, who shall transmit copies thereof to the other States Parties. A declaration may be withdrawn at any time by notification to the Secretary-General. Such a withdrawal shall not prejudice the consideration of any matter which is the subject of a communication already transmitted under this article; no further communication by any State Party shall be received after the notification of withdrawal of the declaration has been received by the Secretary-General, unless the State Party concerned has made a new declaration.

Article 42

1. (a) If a matter referred to the Committee in accordance with article 41 is not resolved to the satisfaction of the

States Parties concerned, the Committee may, with the prior consent of the States Parties concerned, appoint an ad hoc Conciliation Commission (hereinafter referred to as the Commission). The good offices of the Commission shall be made available to the States Parties concerned with a view to an amicable solution of the matter on the basis of respect for the present Covenant;

(b) The Commission shall consist of five persons acceptable to the States Parties concerned. If the States Parties concerned fail to reach agreement within three months on all or part of the composition of the Commission, the members of the Commission concerning whom no agreement has been reached shall be elected by secret ballot by a two-thirds majority vote of the Committee from among its members.

2. The members of the Commission shall serve in their personal capacity. They shall not be nationals of the States Parties concerned, or of a State not Party to the present Covenant, or of a State Party which has not made a declaration under article 41.

3. The Commission shall elect its own Chairman and adopt its own rules of procedure.

4. The meetings of the Commission shall normally be held at the Headquarters of the United Nations or at the United Nations Office at Geneva. However, they may be held at such other convenient places as the Commission may determine in consultation with the Secretary-General of the United Nations and the States Parties concerned.

5. The secretariat provided in accordance with article 36 shall also service the commissions appointed under this article.

6. The information received and collated by the Committee shall be made available to the Commission and the Commission may call upon the States Parties concerned to supply any other relevant information.

7. When the Commission has fully considered the matter, but in any event not later than twelve months after having been seized of the matter, it shall submit to the Chairman of the Committee a report for communication to the States Parties concerned:

(a) If the Commission is unable to complete its consideration of the matter within twelve months, it shall confine its report to a brief statement of the status of its consideration of the matter;

(b) If an amicable solution to the matter on the basis of respect for human rights as recognized in the present Covenant is reached, the Commission shall confine its report to a brief statement of the facts and of the solution reached;

(c) If a solution within the terms of subparagraph (b) is not reached, the Commission's report shall embody its findings on all questions of fact relevant to the issues between the States Parties concerned, and its views on the possibilities of an amicable solution of the matter. This report shall also contain the written submissions and a record of the oral submissions made by the States Parties concerned;

(d) If the Commission's report is submitted under subparagraph (c), the States Parties concerned shall, within three months of the receipt of the report, notify the Chairman of the Committee whether or not they accept the contents of the report of the Commission.

8. The provisions of this article are without prejudice to the responsibilities of the Committee under article 41.

9. The States Parties concerned shall share equally all the expenses of the members of the Commission in accordance with estimates to be provided by the Secretary-General of the United Nations.

10. The Secretary-General of the United Nations shall be empowered to pay the expenses of the members of the Commission, if necessary, before reimbursement by the States Parties concerned, in accordance with paragraph 9 of this article.

Article 43

The members of the Committee, and of the *ad hoc* conciliation commissions which may be appointed under article 42, shall be entitled to the facilities, privileges and immunities of experts on mission for the United Nations as laid down in the relevant sections of the Convention on the Privileges and Immunities of the United Nations.

Article 44

The provisions for the implementation of the present Covenant shall apply without prejudice to the procedures prescribed in the field of human rights by or under the constituent instruments and the conventions of the United Nations and of the specialized agencies and shall not prevent the States Parties to the present Covenant from having recourse to other procedures for settling a dispute in accordance with general or special international agreements in force between them.

Article 45

The Committee shall submit to the General Assembly of the United Nations, through the Economic and Social Council, an annual report on its activities.

PART V

Article 46

Nothing in the present Covenant shall be interpreted as impairing the provisions of the Charter of the United Nations and of the constitutions of the specialized agencies which define the respective responsibilities of the various organs of the United Nations and of the specialized agencies in regard to the matters dealt with in the present Covenant.

Article 47

Nothing in the present Covenant shall be interpreted as impairing the inherent right of all peoples to enjoy and utilize fully and freely their natural wealth and resources.

PART VI

Article 48

1. The present Covenant is open for signature by any State Member of the United Nations or member of any of its specialized agencies, by any State Party to the Statute of the International Court of Justice, and by any other State which has been invited by the General Assembly of the United Nations to become a Party to the present Covenant.

2. The present Covenant is subject to ratification. Instruments of ratification shall be deposited with the Secretary-General of the United Nations.

3. The present Covenant shall be open to accession by any State referred to in paragraph 1 of this article.

4. Accession shall be effected by the deposit of an instrument of accession with the Secretary-General of the United Nations.

5. The Secretary-General of the United Nations shall inform all States which have signed this Covenant or acceded to it of the deposit of each instrument of ratification or accession.

Article 49

1. The present Covenant shall enter into force three months after the date of the deposit with the Secretary-General of the United Nations of the thirty-fifth instrument of ratification or instrument of accession.

2. For each State ratifying the present Covenant or acceding to it after the deposit of the thirty-fifth instrument of ratification or instrument of accession, the present Covenant shall enter into force three months after the date of the deposit of its own instrument of ratification or instrument of accession.

Article 50

The provisions of the present Covenant shall extend to all parts of federal States without any limitations or exceptions.

Article 51

1. Any State Party to the present Covenant may propose an amendment and file it with the Secretary-General of the United Nations. The Secretary-General of the United Nations shall thereupon communicate any proposed amendments to the States Parties to the present Covenant with a request that they notify him whether they favour a conference of States Parties for the purpose of considering and voting upon the proposals. In the event that at least one third of the States Parties favours such a conference, the Secretary-General shall convene the conference under the auspices of the United Nations. Any amendment adopted by a majority of the States Parties present and voting at the conference shall be submitted to the General Assembly of the United Nations for approval.

2. Amendments shall come into force when they have been approved by the General Assembly of the United Nations and accepted by a two-thirds majority of the States Parties to the present Covenant in accordance with their respective constitutional processes.

3. When amendments come into force, they shall be binding on those States Parties which have accepted them, other States Parties still being bound by the provisions of the present Covenant and any earlier amendment which they have accepted.

Article 52

Irrespective of the notifications made under article 48, paragraph 5, the Secretary-General of the United Nations shall inform all States referred to in paragraph 1 of the same article of the following particulars:

(a) Signatures, ratifications and accessions under article 48;

(b) The date of the entry into force of the present Covenant under article 49 and the date of the entry into force of any amendments under article 51.

Article 53

1. The present Covenant, of which the Chinese, English, French, Russian and Spanish texts are equally authentic, shall be deposited in the archives of the United Nations.

2. The Secretary-General of the United Nations shall transmit certified copies of the present Covenant to all States referred to in article 48.

Optional Protocol to the International Covenant on Civil and Political Rights

Adopted and opened for signature, ratification and accession by General Assembly resolution 2200 A (XXI) of 16 December 1966

ENTRY INTO FORCE: 23 March 1976, in accordance with article 9

The States Parties to the present Protocol,

Considering that in order further to achieve the purposes of the International Covenant on Civil and Political Rights (hereinafter referred to as the Covenant) and the implemenation of its provisions it would be appropriate to enable the Human Rights Committee set up in part IV of the Covenant (hereinafter referred to as the Committee) to receive and consider, as provided in the present Protocol, communications from individuals claiming to be victims of violations of any of the rights set forth in the Covenant,

Have agreed as follows:

Article 1

A State Party to the Covenant that becomes a Party to the present Protocol recognizes the competence of the Committee to receive and consider communications from individuals subject to its jurisdiction who claim to be victims of a violation by that State Party of any of the rights set forth in the Covenant. No communication shall be received by the Committee if it concerns a State Party to the Covenant which is not a Party to the present Protocol.

Article 2

Subject to the provisions of article 1, individuals who claim that any of their rights enumerated in the Covenant have been violated and who have exhausted all available domestic remedies may submit a written communication to the Committee for consideration.

Article 3

The Committee shall consider inadmissible any communciation under the present Protocol which is anonymous, or which it considers to be an abuse of the right of submission of such communications or to be incompatible with the provisions of the Covenant.

Article 4

1. Subject to the provisions of article 3, the Committee shall bring any communications submitted to it under the present Protocol to the attention of the State Party to the present Protocol alleged to be violating any provision of the Covenant.

2. Within six months, the receiving State shall submit to the Committee written explanations or statements clarifying the matter and the remedy, if any, that may have been taken by that State.

Article 5

1. The Committee shall consider communications received under the present Protocol in the light of all written information made available to it by the individual and by the State Party concerned.

2. The Committee shall not consider any communication from an individual unless it has ascertained that:

(a) The same matter is not being examined under another procedure of international investigation or settlement;

(b) The individual has exhausted all available domestic remedies. This shall not be the rule where the application of the remedies is unreasonably prolonged.

3. The Committee shall hold closed meetings when examining communications under the present Protocol.

4. The Committee shall forward its views to the State Party concerned and to the individual.

Article 6

The Committee shall include in its annual report under article 45 of the Covenant a summary of its activities under the present Protocol.

Article 7

Pending the achievement of the objectives of resolution 1514(XV) adopted by the General Assembly of the United Nations on 14 December 1960 concerning the Declaration on the Granting of Independence to Colonial Countries and Peoples, the provisions of the present Protocol shall in no way limit the right of petition granted to these peoples by the Charter of the United Nations and other international conventions and instruments under the United Nations and its specialized agencies.

Article 8

1. The present Protocol is open for signature by any State which has signed the Covenant.

2. The present Protocol is subject to ratification by any State which has ratified or acceded to the Covenant. Instruments of ratification shall be deposited with the Secretary-General of the United Nations.

3. The present Protocol shall be open to accession by any State which has ratified or acceded to the Covenant.

4. Accession shall be effected by the deposit of an instrument of accession with the Secretary-General of the United Nations.

5. The Secretary-General of the United Nations shall inform all States which have signed the present Protocol or acceded to it of the deposit of each instrument of ratification or accession.

Article 9

1. Subject to the entry into force of the Covenant, the present Protocol shall enter into force three months after the date of the deposit with the Secretary-General of the United Nations of the tenth instrument of ratification or instrument of accession.

2. For each State ratifying the present Protocol or acceding to it after the deposit of the tenth instrument of ratification or instrument of accession, the present Protocol shall enter into force three months after the date of the deposit of its own instrument of ratification or instrument of accession.

Article 10

The provisions of the present Protocol shall extend to all parts of federal States without any limitations or exceptions.

Article 11

1. Any State Party to the present Protocol may propose an amendment and file it with the Secretary-General of the United Nations. The Secretary-General shall thereupon communicate any proposed amendments to the States Parties to the present Protocol with a request that they notify him whether they favour a conference of States Parties

for the purpose of considering and voting upon the proposal. In the event that at least one third of the States Parties favours such a conference, the Secretary-General shall convene the conference under the auspices of the United Nations. Any amendment adopted by a majority of the States Parties present and voting at the conference shall be submitted to the General Assembly of the United Nations for approval.

2. Amendments shall come into force when they have been approved by the General Assembly of the United Nations and accepted by a two-thirds majority of the States Parties to the present Protocol in accordance with their respective constitutional processes.

3. When amendments come into force, they shall be binding on those States Parties which have accepted them, other States Parties still being bound by the provisions of the present Protocol and any earlier amendment which they have accepted.

Article 12

1. Any State Party may denounce the present Protocol at any time by written notification addressed to the Secretary-General of the United Nations. Denunciation shall take effect three months after the date of receipt of the notification by the Secretary-General.

2. Denunciation shall be without prejudice to the continued application of the provisions of the present Protocol to any communication submitted under article 2 before the effective date of denunciation.

Article 13

Irrespective of the notifications made under article 8, paragraph 5, of the present Protocol, the Secretary-General of the United Nations shall inform all States referred to in article 48, paragraph 1, of the Covenant of the following particulars:

(a) Signatures, ratifications and accessions under article 8;

(b) The date of the entry into force of the present Protocol under article 9 and the date of the entry into force of any amendments under article 11;

(c) Denunciations under article 12.

Article 14

1. The present Protocol, of which the Chinese, English, French, Russian and Spanish texts are equally authentic, shall be deposited in the archives of the United Nations.

2. The Secretary-General of the United Nations shall transmit certified copies of the present Protocol to all States referred to in article 48 of the Covenant.

Article 27 CCPR and the General Comment of the Human Rights Committee

ARTICLE 27 OF THE INTERNATIONAL COVENANT ON CIVIL AND POLITICAL RIGHTS

In those States in which ethnic, religious or linguistic minorities exist, persons belonging to such minorities shall not be denied the right, in community with the other members of their group, to enjoy their own culture, to profess and practise their own religion, or to use their own language.

HUMAN RIGHTS COMMITTEE. GENERAL COMMENT 23 (FIFTIETH SESSION, 1994)

[Report of the Human Rights Committee, Vol. I, GAOR, Forty-ninth Session, Supplement No. 40 (A/49/40), pp. 107–110]

1. Article 27 of the Covenant provides that, in those States in which ethnic, religious or linguistic minorities exist, persons belonging to these minorities shall not be denied the right, in community with the other members of their group, to enjoy their own culture, to profess and practise their own religion, or to use their own language. The Committee observes that this article establishes and recognizes a right which is conferred on individuals belonging to minority groups and which is distinct from, and additional to, all the other rights which, as individuals in common with everyone else, they are already entitled to enjoy under the Covenant.

2. In some communications submitted to the Committee under the Optional Protocol, the right protected under article 27 has been confused with the right of peoples to self-determination proclaimed in article 1 of the Covenant. Further, in reports submitted by States parties under article 40 of the Covenant, the obligations placed upon States parties under article 27 have sometimes been confused with their duty under article 2(1) to ensure the enjoyment of the rights guaranteed under the Covenant without discrimination and also with equality before the law and equal protection of the law under article 26.

3.1. The Covenant draws a distinction between the right to self-determination and the rights protected under article 27. The former is expressed to be a right belonging to peoples and is dealt with in a separate part (Part I) of the Covenant. Self-determination is not a right cognizable under the Optional Protocol. Article 27, on the other hand, relates to rights conferred on individuals as such and is included, like the articles relating to other personal rights conferred on individuals, in Part III of the Covenant and is cognizable under the Optional Protocol.[1]

3.2. The enjoyment of the rights to which article 27 relates does not prejudice the sovereignty and territorial integrity of a State party. At the same time, one or other aspect of the rights of individuals protected under that article – for example, to enjoy a particular culture – may consist in a way of life which is closely associated with territory and use of its resources.[2] This may particularly be true of members of indigenous communities constituting a minority.

4. The Covenant also distinguishes the rights protected under article 27 from the guarantees under articles 2(1) and 26. The entitlement, under Article 2(1), to enjoy the rights under the Covenant without discrimination applies to all

individuals within the territory or under the jurisdiction of the State whether or not those persons belong to a minority. In addition, there is a distinct right provided under article 26 for equality before the law, equal protection of the law, and non-discrimination in respect of rights granted and obligations imposed by the States. It governs the exercise of all rights, whether protected under the Covenant or not, which the State party confers by law on individuals within its territory or under its jurisdiction, irrespective of whether they belong to the minorities specified in article 27 or not.[3] Some States parties who claim that they do not discriminate on grounds of ethnicity, language or religion, wrongly contend, on that basis alone, that they have no minorities.

5.1. The terms used in article 27 indicate that the persons designed to be protected are those who belong to a group and who share in common a culture, a religion and/or a language. Those terms also indicate that the individuals designed to be protected need not be citizens of the State party. In this regard, the obligations deriving from article 2(1) are also relevant, since a State party is required under that article to ensure that the rights protected under the Covenant are available to all individuals within its territory and subject to its jurisdiction, except rights which are expressly made to apply to citizens, for example, political rights under article 25. A State party may not, therefore, restrict the rights under article 27 to its citizens alone.

5.2. Article 27 confers rights on persons belonging to minorities which 'exist' in a State party. Given the nature and scope of the rights envisaged under that article, it is not relevant to determine the degree of permanence that the term 'exist' connotes. Those rights simply are that individuals belonging to those minorities should not be denied the right, in community with members of their group, to enjoy their own culture, to practise their religion and speak their language. Just as they need not be nationals or citizens, they need not be permanent residents. Thus, migrant workers or even visitors in a State party constituting such minorities are entitled not to be denied the exercise of those rights. As any other individual in the territory of the State party, they would, also for this purpose, have the general rights, for example, to freedom of association, of assembly, and of expression. The existence of an ethnic, religious or linguistic minority in a given State party does not depend upon a decision by that State party but requires to be established by objective criteria.

5.3. The right of individuals belonging to a linguistic minority to use their language among themselves, in private or in public, is distinct from other language rights protected under the Covenant. In particular, it should be distinguished from the general right to freedom of expression protected under article 19. The latter right is available to all persons, irrespective of whether they belong to minorities or not. Further, the right protected under article 27 should be distinguished from the particular right which article 14(3) (f) of the Covenant confers on accused persons to interpretation where they cannot understand or speak the language used in the courts. Article 14(3) (f) does not, in any other circumstances, confer on accused persons the right to use or speak the language of their choice in court proceedings.[4]

6.1. Although article 27 is expressed in negative terms, that article, nevertheless, does recognize the existence of a 'right' and requires that it shall not be denied. Consequently, a State party is under an obligation to ensure that the existence and the exercise of this right are protected against their denial or violation. Positive measures of protection are, therefore, required not only against the acts of the State party itself, whether through its legislative, judicial or administrative authorities, but also against the acts of other persons within the State party.

6.2. Although the rights protected under article 27 are individual rights, they depend in turn on the ability of the minority group to maintain its culture, language or religion. Accordingly, positive measures by States may also be necessary to protect the identity of a minority and the rights of its members to enjoy and develop their culture and language and to practise their religion, in community with the other members of the group. In this connection, it has to be observed that such positive measures must respect the provisions of articles 2(1) and 26 of the Covenant both as regards the treatment between different minorities and the treatment between the persons belonging to them and the remaining part of the population. However, as long as those measures are aimed at correcting conditions which prevent or impair the enjoyment of the rights guaranteed under article 27, they may constitute a legitimate differentiation under the Covenant, provided that they are based on reasonable and objective criteria.

7. With regard to the exercise of the cultural rights protected under article 27, the Committee observes that culture manifests itself in many forms, including a particular way of life associated with the use of land resources, especially in the case of indigenous peoples. That right may include such traditional activities as fishing or hunting and the right to live in reserves protected by law[5]. The enjoyment of those rights may require positive legal measures of protection and measures to ensure the effective participation of members of minority communities in decisions which affect them.

8. The Committee observes that none of the rights protected under article 27 of the Covenant may be legitimately exercised in a manner or to an extent inconsistent with the other provisions of the Covenant.

9. The Committee concludes that article 27 relates to rights whose protection imposes specific obligations on States parties. The protection of these rights is directed towards ensuring the survival and continued development of the cultural, religious and social identity of the minorities concerned, thus enriching the fabric of society as a whole. Accordingly, the Committee observes that these rights must be protected as such and should not be confused with other personal rights conferred on one and all under the Covenant. States parties, therefore, have an obligation to ensure that the exercise of these rights is fully protected and they should indicate in their reports the measures they have adopted to this end.

Notes

1. See Report of the Human Rights Committee, GAOR, Thirty-ninth Session, Supplement No. 40 (A/39/40), annex VI, general comment No. 12(21), (art. 1), also issued in document CCPR/C/21/Rev. 1; Report of the Human Rights Committee, Vol. II, GAOR, Forty-fifth Session, Supplement No. 40 (A/45/40), annex IX, sect. A, communication No. 167/1984 (*Bernard Ominayak, Chief of the Lubicon Lake Band v. Canada*), views adopted on 26 March.

2. Report of the Human Rights Committee, GAOR, Forty-third Session, Supplement No. 40 (A/42/40), annex VII, sect. G., communication No. 197/1985 (*Kitok v. Sweden*), views adopted on 27 July 1988.

3. Report of the Human Rights Committee, GAOR, Forty-second Session, Supplement No. 40 (A/42/40), annex VIII, sect. D., communication No. 182/1984 (*F.H. Zwaan-de Vries v. the Netherlands*), views adopted on 9 April 1987, ibid., sect. C, communication No. 180/1984 (*L.G. Danning v. the Netherlands*), views adopted on 9 April 1987.

4. Report of the Human Rights Committee, Vol. II, GAOR, Forty-fifth Session, Suplement No. 40 (A/45/40), annex X, sect. A, communication No. 220/1987 (*T.K. v. France*), decision of 8 November 1989; ibid., sect. B. communication No. 222/ 1987 (*M.K. v. France*), decision of 8 November 1989.

5. See notes 1 and 2 above, communication No. 167/1984 (*Bernard Ominayak, Chief of the Lubicon Lake Band v. Canada*), views adopted on 26 March 1990, and communication No. 197/1985 (*Kitok v. Sweden*), views adopted on 27 July 1988.

Convention on the Prevention and Punishment of the Crime of Genocide

Approved and proposed for signature and ratification or accession by General Assembly resolution 260 A (III) of 9 December 1948

ENTRY INTO FORCE: 12 January 1951, in accordance with article XIII

The Contracting Parties,

Having considered the declaration made by the General Assembly of the United Nations in its resolution 96 (I) dated 11 December 1946 that genocide is a crime under international law, contrary to the spirit and aims of the United Nations and condemned by the civilized world,

Recognizing that at all periods of history genocide has inflicted great losses on humanity, and

Being convinced that, in order to liberate mankind from such an odious scourge, international co-operation is required,

Hereby agree as hereinafter provided:

Article I

The Contracting Parties confirm that genocide, whether committed in time of peace or in time of war, is a crime under international law which they undertake to prevent and to punish.

Article II

In the present Convention, genocide means any of the following acts committed with intent to destroy, in whole or in part, a national, ethnical, racial or religious group, as such:

(a) Killing members of the group;

(b) Causing serious bodily or mental harm to members of the group;

(c) Deliberately inflicting on the group conditions of life calculated to bring about its physical destruction in whole or in part;

(d) Imposing measures intended to prevent births within the group;

(e) Forcibly transferring children of the group to another group.

Article III

The following acts shall be punishable:

(a) Genocide;

(b) Conspiracy to commit genocide;

(c) Direct and public incitement to commit genocide;

(d) Attempt to commit genocide;

(e) Complicity in genocide.

Article IV

Persons committing genocide or any of the other acts enumerated in article III shall be punished, whether they are constitutionally responsible rulers, public officials or private individuals.

Article V

The Contracting Parties undertake to enact, in accordance with their respective Constitutions, the necessary legislation to give effect to the provisions of the present Convention, and, in particular, to provide effective penalties for persons guilty of genocide or any of the other acts enumerated in article III.

Article VI

Persons charged with genocide or any of the other acts enumerated in article III shall be tried by a competent tribunal of the State in the territory of which the act was committed, or by such international penal tribunal as may have jurisdiction with respect to those Contracting Parties which shall have accepted its jurisdiction.

Article VII

Genocide and the other acts enumerated in article III shall not be considered as political crimes for the purpose of extradition.

The Contracting Parties pledge themselves in such cases to grant extradition in accordance with their laws and treaties in force.

Article VIII

Any Contracting Party may call upon the competent organs of the United Nations to take such action under the Charter of the United Nations as they consider appropriate for the prevention and suppression of acts of genocide or any of the other acts enumerated in article III.

Article IX

Disputes between the Contracting Parties relating to the interpretation, application or fulfilment of the present Convention, including those relating to the responsibility of a State for genocide or for any of the other acts enumerated in article III, shall be submitted to the International Court of Justice at the request of any of the parties to the dispute.

Article X

The present Convention, of which the Chinese, English, French, Russian and Spanish texts are equally authentic, shall bear the date of 9 December 1948.

Article XI

The present Convention shall be open until 31 December 1949 for signature on behalf of any Member of the United Nations and of any non-member State to which an invitation to sign has been addressed by the General Assembly.

The present Convention shall be ratified, and the instruments of ratification shall be deposited with the Secretary-General of the United Nations.

After 1 January 1950, the present Convention may be acceded to on behalf of any Member of the United Nations and of any non-member State which has received an invitation as aforesaid. Instruments of accession shall be deposited with the Secretary-General of the United Nations.

Article XII

Any Contracting Party may at any time, by notification addressed to the Secretary-General of the United Nations, extend the application of the present Convention to all or any of the territories for the conduct of whose foreign relations that Contracting Party is responsible.

Article XIII

On the day when the first twenty instruments of ratification or accession have been deposited, the Secretary-General shall draw up a *procès-verbal* and transmit a copy thereof to each Member of the United Nations and to each of the non-member States contemplated in article XI.

The present Convention shall come into force on the ninetieth day following the date of deposit of the twentieth instrument of ratification or accession.

Any ratification or accession effected, subsequent to the latter date shall become effective on the ninetieth day following the deposit of the instrument of ratification or accession.

Article XIV

The present Convention shall remain in effect for a period of ten years as from the date of its coming into force.

It shall thereafter remain in force for successive periods of five years for such Contracting Parties as have not denounced it at least six months before the expiration of the current period.

Denunciation shall be effected by a written notification addressed to the Secretary-General of the United Nations.

Article XV

If, as a result of denunciations, the number of Parties to the present Convention should become less than sixteen, the Convention shall cease to be in force as from the date on which the last of these denunciations shall become effective.

Article XVI

A request for the revision of the present Convention may be made at any time by any Contracting Party by means of a notification in writing addressed to the Secretary-General.

The General Assembly shall decide upon the steps, if any, to be taken in respect of such request.

Article XVII

The Secretary-General of the United Nations shall notify all Members of the United Nations and the non-member States contemplated in article XI of the following:

(a) Signatures, ratifications and accessions received in accordance with article XI;

(b) Notifications received in accordance with article XII;

(c) The date upon which the present Convention comes into force in accordance with article XIII;

(d) Denunciations received in accordance with article XIV;

(e) The abrogation of the Convention in accordance with article XV;

(f) Notifications received in accordance with article XVI.

Article XVIII

The original of the present Convention shall be deposited in the archives of the United Nations.

A certified copy of the Convention shall be transmitted to each Member of the United Nations and to each of the non-member States contemplated in article XI.

Article XIX

The present Convention shall be registered by the Secretary-General of the United Nations on the date of its coming into force.

Convention against Discrimination in Education

Adopted on 14 December 1960 by the General Conference of the United Nations Educational, Scientific and Cultural Organization

Entry into force: 22 May 1962, in accordance with article 14

The General Conference of the United Nations Educational, Scientific and Cultural Organization, meeting in Paris from 14 November to 15 December 1960, at its eleventh session,

Recalling that the Universal Declaration of Human Rights asserts the principle of non-discrimination and proclaims that every person has the right to education,

Considering that discrimination in education is a violation of rights enunciated in that Declaration,

Considering that, under the terms of its Constitution, the United Nations Educational, Scientific and Cultural Organization has the purpose of instituting collaboration among the nations with a view to furthering for all universal respect for human rights and equality of educational opportunity,

Recognizing that, consequently, the United Nations Educational, Scientific and Cultural Organization, while respecting the diversity of national educational systems, has the duty not only to proscribe any form of discrimination in education but also to promote equality of opportunity and treatment for all in education,

Having before it proposals concerning the different aspects of discrimination in education, constituting item 17.1.4 of the agenda of the session,

Having decided at its tenth session that this question should be made the subject of an international convention as well as of recommendations to Member States,

Adopts this Convention on the fourteenth day of December 1960.

Article 1

1. For the purpose of this Convention, the term "discrimination" includes any distinction, exclusion, limitation or preference which, being based on race, colour, sex, language, religion, political or other opinion, national or social origin, economic condition or birth, has the purpose or effect of nullifying or impairing equality of treatment in education and in particular:

(a) Of depriving any person or group of persons of access to education of any type or at any level;

(b) Of limiting any person or group of persons to education of an inferior standard;

(c) Subject to the provisions of article 2 of this Convention, of establishing or maintaining separate educational systems or institutions for persons or groups of persons; or

(d) Of inflicting on any person or group of persons conditions which are incompatible with the dignity of man.

2. For the purposes of this Convention, the term "education" refers to all types and levels of education, and includes access to education, the standard and quality of education, and the conditions under which it is given.

Article 2

When permitted in a State, the following situations shall not be deemed to constitute discrimination, within the meaning of article 1 of this Convention:

(a) The establishment or maintenance of separate educational systems or institutions for pupils of the two sexes, if these systems or institutions offer equivalent access to education, provide a teaching staff with qualifications of the same standard as well as school premises and equipment of the same quality, and afford the opportunity to take the same or equivalent courses of study;

(b) The establishment or maintenance, for religious or linguistic reasons, of separate educational systems or institutions offering an education which is in keeping with the wishes of the pupil's parents or legal guardians, if participation in such systems or attendance at such institutions is optional and if the education provided conforms to such standards as may be laid down or approved by the competent authorities, in particular for education of the same level;

(c) The establishment or maintenance of private educational institutions, if the object of the institutions is not to secure the exclusion of any group but to provide educational facilities in addition to those provided by the public authorities, if the institutions are conducted in accordance with that object, and if the education provided conforms with such standards as may be laid down or approved by the competent authorities, in particular for education of the same level.

Article 3

In order to eliminate and prevent discrimination within the meaning of this Convention, the States Parties thereto undertake:

(a) To abrogate any statutory provisions and any administrative instructions and to discontinue any administrative practices which involve discrimination in education;

(b) To ensure, by legislation where necessary, that there is no discrimination in the admission of pupils to educational institutions;

(c) Not to allow any differences of treatment by the public authorities between nationals, except on the basis of merit or need, in the matter of school fees and the grant of scholarships or other forms of assistance to pupils and necessary permits and facilities for the pursuit of studies in foreign countries;

(d) Not to allow, in any form of assistance granted by the public authorities to educational institutions, any restrictions or preference based solely on the ground that pupils belong to a particular group;

(e) To give foreign nationals resident within their territory the same access to education as that given to their own nationals.

Article 4

The States Parties to this Convention undertake furthermore to formulate, develop and apply a national policy which, by methods appropriate to the circumstances and to national usage, will tend to promote equality of opportunity and of treatment in the matter of education and in particular:

(a) To make primary education free and compulsory; make secondary education in its different forms generally available and accessible to all; make higher education equally accessible to all on the basis of individual capacity; assure compliance by all with the obligation to attend school prescribed by law;

(b) To ensure that the standards of education are equivalent in all public education institutions of the same level, and that the conditions relating to the quality of education provided are also equivalent;

(c) To encourage and intensify by appropriate methods the education of persons who have not received any primary education or who have not completed the entire primary education course and the continuation of their education on the basis of individual capacity;

(d) To provide training for the teaching profession without discrimination.

Article 5

1. The States Parties to this Convention agree that:

(a) Education shall be directed to the full development of the human personality and to the strengthening of respect for human rights and fundamental freedoms; it shall promote understanding, tolerance and friendship among all nations, racial or religious groups, and shall further the activities of the United Nations for the maintenance of peace;

(b) It is essential to respect the liberty of parents and, where applicable, of legal guardians, firstly to choose for their children institutions other than those maintained by the public authorities but conforming to such minimum educational standards as may be laid down or approved by the competent authorities and, secondly, to ensure in a manner consistent with the procedures followed in the State for the application of its legislation, the religious and moral education of the children in conformity with their own convictions; and no person or group of persons should be compelled to receive religious instruction inconsistent with his or their conviction;

(c) It is essential to recognize the right of members of national minorities to carry on their own educational activities, including the maintenance of schools and, depending on the educational policy of each State, the use or the teaching of their own language, provided however:

(i) That this right is not exercised in a manner which prevents the members of these minorities from understanding the culture and language of the community as a whole and from participating in its activities, or which prejudices national sovereignty;

(ii) That the standard of education is not lower than the general standard laid down or approved by the competent authorities; and

(iii) That attendance at such schools is optional.

2. The States Parties to this Convention undertake to take all necessary measures to ensure the application of the principles enunciated in paragraph 1 of this article.

Article 6

In the application of this Convention, the States Parties to it undertake to pay the greatest attention to any recommendations hereafter adopted by the General Conference of the United Nations Educational, Scientific and Cultural Organization defining the measures to be taken against the different forms of discrimination in education and for the purpose of ensuring equality of opportunity and treatment in education.

Article 7

The States Parties to this Convention shall in their periodic reports submitted to the General Conference of the United Nations Educational, Scientific and Cultural Organization on dates and in a manner to be determined by it, give information on the legislative and administrative provisions which they have adopted and other action which they have taken for the application of this Convention, including that taken for the formulation and the development of the national policy defined in article 4 as well as the results achieved and the obstacles encountered in the application of that policy.

Article 8

Any dispute which may arise between any two or more States Parties to this Convention concerning the interpretation or application of this Convention which is not settled by negotiations shall at the request of the parties to the dispute be referred, failing other means of settling the dispute, to the International Court of Justice for decision.

Article 9

Reservations to this Convention shall not be permitted.

Article 10

This Convention shall not have the effect of diminishing the rights which individuals or groups may enjoy by virtue of agreements concluded between two or more States, where such rights are not contrary to the letter or spirit of this Convention.

Article 11

This Convention is drawn up in English, French, Russian and Spanish, the four texts being equally authoritative.

Article 12

1. This Convention shall be subject to ratification or acceptance by States Members of the United Nations Educational, Scientific and Cultural Organization in accordance with their respective constitutional procedures.

2. The instruments of ratification or acceptance shall be deposited with the Director-General of the United Nations Educational, Scientific and Cultural Organization.

Article 13

1. This Convention shall be open to accession by all States not Members of the United Nations Educational, Scientific and Cultural Organization which are invited to do so by the Executive Board of the Organization.

2. Accession shall be effected by the deposit of an instrument of accession with the Director-General of the United Nations Educational, Scientific and Cultural Organization.

Article 14

This Convention shall enter into force three months after the date of the deposit of the third instrument of ratification, acceptance or accession, but only with respect to those States which have deposited their respective instruments on or before that date. It shall enter into force with respect to any other State three months after the deposit of its instrument of ratification, acceptance or accession.

Article 15

The States Parties to this Convention recognize that the Convention is applicable not only to their metropolitan territory but also to all non-self-governing, trust, colonial and other territories for the international relations of which they are responsible; they undertake to consult, if necessary, the governments or other competent authorities of these territories on or before ratification, acceptance or accession with a view to securing the application of the Convention to those territories, and to notify the Director-General of the United Nations Educational, Scientific and Cultural Organization of the territories to which it is accordingly applied, the notification to take effect three months after the date of its receipt.

Article 16

1. Each State Party to this Convention may denounce the Convention on its own behalf or on behalf of any territory for whose international relations it is responsible.

2. The denunciation shall be notified by an instrument in writing, deposited with the Director-General of the United Nations Educational, Scientific and Cultural Organization.

3. The denunciation shall take effect twelve months after the receipt of the instrument of denunciation.

Article 17

The Director-General of the United Nations Educational, Scientific and Cultural Organization shall inform the States Members of the Organization, the States not members of the Organization which are referred to in article 13, as well as the United Nations, of the deposit of all the instruments of ratification, acceptance and accession provided for in articles 12 and 13, and of notifications and denunciations provided for in articles 15 and 16 respectively.

Article 18

1. This Convention may be revised by the General Conference of the United Nations Educational, Scientific and Cultural Organization. Any such revision shall, however, bind only the States which shall become Parties to the revising convention.

2. If the General Conference should adopt a new convention revising this Convention in whole or in part, then, unless the new convention otherwise provides, this Convention shall cease to be open to ratification, acceptance or accession as from the date on which the new revising convention enters into force.

Article 19

In conformity with Article 102 of the Charter of the United Nations, this Convention shall be registered with the Secretariat of the United Nations at the request of the Director-General of the United Nations Educational, Scientific and Cultural Organization.

Done in Paris, this fifteenth day of December 1960, in two authentic copies bearing the signatures of the President of the eleventh session of the General Conference and of the Director-General of the United Nations Educational, Scientific and Cultural Organization, which shall be deposited in the archives of the United Nations Educational, Scientific and Cultural Organization, and certified true copies of which shall be delivered to all the States referred to in articles 12 and 13 as well as to the United Nations.

The foregoing is the authentic text of the Convention duly adopted by the General Conference of the United Nations Educational, Scientific and Cultural Organization during its eleventh session, which was held in Paris and declared closed the fifteenth day of December 1960.

IN FAITH WHEREOF we have appended our signatures this fifteenth day of December 1960.

United Nations Declaration on the Elimination of All Forms of Racial Discrimination

Proclaimed by General Assembly resolution 1904 (XVIII) of 20 November 1963

The General Assembly,

Considering that the Charter of the United Nations is based on the principles of the dignity and equality of all human beings and seeks, among other basic objectives, to achieve international co-operation in promoting and encouraging respect for human rights and fundamental freedoms for all without distinction as to race, sex, language or religion,

Considering that the Universal Declaration of Human Rights proclaims that all human beings are born free and equal in dignity and rights and that everyone is entitled to all the rights and freedom set out in the Declaration, without distinction of any kind, in particular as to race, colour or national origin,

Considering that the Universal Declaration of Human Rights proclaims further that all are equal before the law and are entitled without any discrimination to equal protection of the law and that all are entitled to equal protection against any discrimination and against any incitement to such discrimination,

Considering that the United Nations has considered colonialism and all practices of segregation and discrimination associated therewith, and that the Declaration on the Granting of Independence to Colonial Countries and People proclaims in particular the necessity of bringing colonisation to a speedy and unconditional end,

Considering that any doctrine of racial differentiation or superiority is scientifically false, morally condemnable, socially unjust and dangerous, and that there is no justification for racial discrimination either in theory or in practice,

Taking into account the other resolutions adopted by the General Assembly and the international instruments adopted by the specialised agencies, in particular the International Labour Organisation and the United Nations Educational, Scientific and Cultural Organization, in the field of discrimination,

Taking into account the fact that, although international action and efforts in a number of countries have made it possible to achieve progress in that field, discrimination based on race, colour or ethnic origin in certain areas of the world continues none the less to give cause for serious concern,

Alarmed by the manifestations of racial discrimination still in evidence in some areas of the world, some of which are imposed by certain Governments by means of legislative, administrative or other measures, in the form, *inter alia*, of *apartheid*, segregation and separation, as well as by the promotion and dissemination of doctrines of racial superiority and expansionism in certain areas,

Convinced that all forms of racial discrimination and, still more so, governmental policies based on the prejudice of racial superiority or on racial hatred, besides constituting a violation of fundamental human rights, tend to jeopardize friendly relations among peoples, co-operation between nations and international peace security,

Convinced also that racial discrimination harms not only those who are its objects but also those who practise it,

Convinced further that the building of a world society free from all forms of racial segregation and discrimination, factors which create hatred and division among men, is one of the fundamental objectives of the United Nations,

1. *Solemnly affirms* the necessity of speedily eliminating racial discrimination throughout the world, in all its forms and manifestations, and of securing understanding of and respect for the dignity of the human person;

2. *Solemnly affirms* the necessity of adopting national and international measures to that end, including teaching, education and information, in order to secure the universal and effective recognition and observance of the principles set forth below;

3. *Proclaims* this Declaration:

Article 1

Discrimination between human beings on the ground of race, colour or ethnic origin is an offence to human dignity and shall be condemned as a denial of the principles of the Charter of the United Nations, as a violation of the human rights and fundamental freedoms proclaimed in the Universal Declaration of Human Rights, as an obstacle to friendly and peaceful relation among nations and as a fact capable of disturbing peace and security among peoples.

Article 2

1. No State, institution, group or individual shall make any discrimination whatsoever in matters of human rights and fundamental freedoms in the treatment of persons, groups of persons or institutions on the ground of race, colour or ethnic origin.

2. No State shall encourage, advocate or lend its support, through police action or otherwise, to any discrimination based on race, colour or ethnic origin by any group, institution or individual.

3. Special concrete measures shall be taken in appropriate circumstances in order to secure adequate development or protection of individuals belonging to certain racial groups with the object of ensuring the full enjoyment by such individuals of human rights and fundamental freedoms. These measures shall in no circumstances have as a consequence the maintenance of unequal or separate rights for different racial groups.

Article 3

1. Particular efforts shall be made to prevent discrimination based on race, colour or ethnic origin, especially in the fields of civil rights, access to citizenship, education, religion, employment, occupation and housing.

2. Everyone shall have equal access to any place or facility intended for use by the general public, without distinction as to race, colour or ethnic origin.

Article 4

All States shall take effective measures to revise governmental and other public policies and to rescind laws and regulations which have the effect of creating and perpetuating racial discrimination wherever it still exists. They should pass legislation for prohibiting such discrimination and should take all appropriate measures to combat those prejudices which lead to racial discrimination.

Article 5

An end shall be put without delay to governmental and other public policies of racial segregation and especially policies of *apartheid*, as well as all forms of racial discrimination and separation resulting from such policies.

Article 6

No discrimination by reason of race, colour or ethnic origin shall be admitted in the enjoyment by any person of political and citizenship rights in his country, in particular the right to participate in elections through universal and equal suffrage and to take part in the government. Everyone has the right of equal access to public service in his country.

Article 7

1. Everyone has the right to equality before the law and to equal justice under the law. Everyone, without distinction as to race, colour or ethnic origin, has the right to security of person and protection by the State against violence or bodily harm, whether inflicted by government officials or by any individual, group or institution.

2. Everyone shall have the right to an effective remedy and protection against any discrimination he may suffer on the ground of race, colour or ethnic origin with respect to his fundamental rights and freedoms through independent national tribunals competent to deal with such matters.

Article 8

All effective steps shall be taken immediately in the fields of teaching, education and information, with a view to eliminating racial discrimination and prejudice and promoting understanding, tolerance and friendship among nations and racial groups, as well as to propagating the purposes and principles of the Charter of the United Nations, of the Universal Declaration of Human Rights, and of the Declaration on the Granting of Independence to Colonial Countries and Peoples.

Article 9

1. All propaganda and organizations based on ideas or theories of the superiority of one race or group of persons of one colour or ethnic origin with a view to justifying or promoting racial discrimination in any form shall be severely condemned.

2. All incitement to or acts of violence, whether by individuals or organizations against any race or group of persons of another colour or ethnic origin shall be considered an offence against society and punishable under law.

3. In order to put into effect the purposes and principles of the present Declaration, all States shall take immediate and positive measures, including legislative and other measurers, to prosecute and/or outlaw organizations which promote or incite to racial discrimination, or incite to or use violence for purposes of discrimination based on race, colour or ethnic origin.

Article 10

The United Nations, the specialized agencies, States and non-governmental organizations shall do all in their power to promote energetic action which, by combining legal and other practical measures, will make possible the abolition of all forms of racial discrimination. They shall, in particular, study the causes of such discrimination with a view to recommending appropriate and effective measures to combat and eliminate it.

Article 11

Every State shall promote respect for and observance of human rights and fundamental freedoms in accordance with the Charter of the United Nations and shall fully and faithfully observe the provisions of the present Declaration, the Universal Declaration of Human Rights and the Declaration on the Granting of Independence to colonial Countries and Peoples.

Convention on the Elimination of All Forms of Racial Discrimination

Adopted and opened for signature and ratification by General Assembly resolution 2106 A (XX) of 21 December 1965

Entry into force: 4 January 1969, in accordance with article 19

The States Parties to this Convention,

Considering that the Charter of the United Nations is based on the principles of the dignity and equality inherent in all human beings, and that all Member States have pledged themselves to take joint and separate action, in co-operation with the Organization, for the achievement of one of the purposes of the United Nations which is to promote and encourage universal respect for and observance of human rights and fundamental freedoms for all, without distinction as to race, sex, language or religion,

Considering that the Universal Declaration of Human Rights proclaims that all human beings are born free and equal in dignity and rights and that everyone is entitled to all the rights and freedoms set out therein, without distinction of any kind, in particular as to race, colour or national origin,

Considering that all human beings are equal before the law and are entitled to equal protection of the law against any discrimination and against any incitement to discrimination,

Considering that the United Nations has condemned colonialism and all practices of segregation and discrimination associated therewith, in whatever form and wherever they exist, and that the Declaration on the Granting of Independence to Colonial Countries and Peoples of 14 December 1960 (General Assembly resolution 1514 (XV)) has affirmed and solemnly proclaimed the necessity of bringing them to a speedy and unconditional end,

Considering that the United Nations Declaration on the Elimination of All Forms of Racial Discrimination of 20 November 1963 (General Assembly resolution 1904 (XVIII)) solemnly affirms the necessity of speedily eliminating racial discrimination throughout the world in all its forms and manifestations and of securing understanding of and respect for the dignity of the human person,

Convinced that any doctrine of superiority based on racial differentiation is scientifically false, morally condemnable, socially unjust and dangerous, and that there is no justification for racial discrimination, in theory or in practice, anywhere,

Reaffirming that discrimination between human beings on the grounds of race, colour or ethnic origin is an obstacle to friendly and peaceful relations among nations and is capable of disturbing peace and security among peoples and the harmony of persons living side by side even within one and the same State,

Convinced that the existence of racial barriers is repugnant to the ideals of any human society,

Alarmed by manifestations of racial discrimination still in evidence in some areas of the world and by governmental policies based on racial superiority or hatred, such as policies of *apartheid*, segregation or separation,

Resolved to adopt all necessary measures for speedily eliminating racial discrimination in all its forms and manifestations, and to prevent and combat racist doctrines and practices in order to promote understanding between races and to build an international community free from all forms of racial segregation and racial discrimination,

Bearing in mind the Convention concerning Discrimination in respect of Employment and Occupation adopted by the International Labour Organisation in 1958, and the Convention against Discrimination in Education adopted by the United Nations Educational, Scientific and Cultural Organization in 1960,

Desiring to implement the principles embodied in the United Nations Declaration on the Elimination of All Forms of Racial Discrimination and to secure the earliest adoption of practical measures to that end,

Have agreed as follows:

PART I

Article 1

1. In this Convention, the term "racial discrimination" shall mean any distinction, exclusion, restriction or preference based on race, colour, descent, or national or ethnic origin which has the purpose or effect of nullifying or impairing the recognition, enjoyment or exercise, on an equal footing, of human rights and fundamental freedoms in the political, economic, social, cultural or any other field of public life.

2. This Convention shall not apply to distinctions, exclusions, restrictions or preferences made by a State Party to this Convention between citizens and non-citizens.

3. Nothing in this Convention may be interpreted as affecting in any way the legal provisions of States Parties concerning nationality, citizenship or naturalization, provided that such provisions do not discriminate against any particular nationality.

4. Special measures taken for the sole purpose of securing adequate advancement of certain racial or ethnic groups or individuals requiring such protection as may be necessary in order to ensure such groups or individuals equal enjoyment or exercise of human rights and fundamental freedoms shall not be deemed racial discrimination, provided, however, that such measures do not, as a consequence, lead to the maintenance of separate rights for different racial groups and that they shall not be continued after the objectives for which they were taken have been achieved.

Article 2

1. States Parties condemn racial discrimination and undertake to pursue by all appropriate means and without delay a policy of eliminating racial discrimination in all its forms and promoting understanding among all races, and, to this end:

(a) Each State Party undertakes to engage in no act or practice of racial discrimination against persons, groups of persons or institutions and to ensure that all public authorities and public institutions, national and local, shall act in conformity with this obligation;

(b) Each State Party undertakes not to sponsor, defend or support racial discrimination by any persons or organizations;

(c) Each State Party shall take effective measures to review governmental, national and local policies, and to amend, rescind or nullify any laws and regulations which have the effect of creating or perpetuating racial discrimination wherever it exists;

(d) Each State Party shall prohibit and bring to an end, by all appropriate means, including legislation as required by circumstances, racial discrimination by any persons, group or organization;

(e) Each State Party undertakes to encourage, where appropriate, integrationist multiracial organizations and movements and other means of eliminating barriers between races, and to discourage anything which tends to strengthen racial division.

2. States Parties shall, when the circumstances so warrant, take, in the social, economic, cultural and other fields, special and concrete measures to ensure the adequate development and protection of certain racial groups or individuals belonging to them, for the purpose of guaranteeing them the full and equal enjoyment of human rights and fundamental freedoms. These measures shall in no case entail as a consequence the maintenance of unequal or separate rights for different racial groups after the objectives for which they were taken have been achieved.

Article 3

States Parties particularly condemn racial segregation and *apartheid* and undertake to prevent, prohibit and eradicate all practices of this nature in territories under their jurisdiction.

Article 4

States Parties condemn all propaganda and all organizations which are based on ideas or theories of superiority of one race or group of persons of one colour or ethnic origin, or which attempt to justify or promote racial hatred and discrimination in any form, and undertake to adopt immediate and positive measures designed to eradicate all incitement to, or acts of, such discrimination and, to this end, with due regard to the principles embodied in the Universal Declaration of Human Rights and the rights expressly set forth in article 5 of this Convention, *inter alia*:

(a) Shall declare an offence punishable by law all dissemination of ideas based on racial superiority or hatred, incitement to racial discrimination, as well as all acts of violence or incitement to such acts against any race or group of persons of another colour or ethnic origin, and also the provision of any assistance to racist activities, including the financing thereof;

(b) Shall declare illegal and prohibit organizations, and also organized and all other propaganda activities, which promote and incite racial discrimination, and shall recognize participation in such organizations or activities as an offence punishable by law;

(c) Shall not permit public authorities or public institutions, national or local, to promote or incite racial discrimination.

Article 5

In compliance with the fundamental obligations laid down in article 2 of this Convention, States Parties undertake to prohibit and to eliminate racial discrimination in all its forms and to guarantee the right of everyone, without distinction as to race, colour, or national or ethnic origin, to equality before the law, notably in the enjoyment of the following rights:

(a) The right to equal treatment before the tribunals and all other organs administering justice;

(b) The right to security of person and protection by the State against violence or bodily harm, whether inflicted by government officials or by any individual group or institution;

(c) Political rights, in particular the right to participate in elections – to vote and to stand for election – on the basis of universal and equal suffrage, to take part in the Government as well as in the conduct of public affairs at any level and to have equal access to public service;

(d) Other civil rights, in particular:

(i) The right to freedom of movement and residence within the border of the State;
(ii) The right to leave any country, including one's own, and to return to one's country;
(iii) The right to nationality;
(iv) The right to marriage and choice of spouse;
(v) The right to own property alone as well as in association with others;
(vi) The right to inherit;
(vii) The right to freedom of thought, conscience and religion;
(viii) The right to freedom of opinion and expression;
(ix) The right to freedom of peaceful assembly and association;

(e) Economic, social and cultural rights, in particular:

(i) The rights to work, to free choice of employment, to just and favourable conditions of work, to protection against unemployment, to equal pay for equal work, to just and favourable remuneration;
(ii) The right to form and join trade unions;
(iii) The right to housing;
(iv) The right to public health, medical care, social security and social services;
(v) The right to education and training;
(vi) The right to equal participation in cultural activities;

(f) The right of access to any place or service intended for use by the general public, such as transport hotels, restaurants, cafés, theatres and parks.

Article 6

States Parties shall assure to everyone within their jurisdiction effective protection and remedies, through the competent national tribunals and other State institutions, against any acts of racial discrimination which violate his human rights and fundamental freedoms contrary to this Convention, as well as the right to seek from such tribunals just and adequate reparation or satisfaction for any damage suffered as a result of such discrimination.

Article 7

States Parties undertake to adopt immediate and effective measures, particularly in the fields of teaching, education, culture and information, with a view to combating prejudices which lead to racial discrimination and to promoting understanding, tolerance and friendship among nations and racial or ethnical groups, as well as to propagating the purposes and principles of the Charter of the United Nations, the Universal Declaration of Human Rights, the United Nations Declaration on the Elimination of All Forms of Racial Discrimination, and this Convention.

PART II

Article 8

1. There shall be established a Committee on the Elimination of Racial Discrimination (hereinafter referred to as the Committee) consisting of eighteen experts of high moral standing and acknowledged impartiality elected by States Parties from among their nationals, who shall serve in their personal capacity, consideration being given to equitable geographical distribution and to the representation of the different forms of civilization as well as of the principal legal systems.

2. The members of the Committee shall be elected by secret ballot from a list of persons nominated by the States Parties. Each State Party may nominate one person from among its own nationals.

3. The initial election shall be held six months after the date of the entry into force of this Convention. At least three months before the date of each election the Secretary-General of the United Nations shall address a letter to the States Parties inviting them to submit their nominations within two months. The Secretary-General shall prepare a list in alphabetical order of all persons thus nominated, indicating the States Parties which have nominated them, and shall submit it to the States Parties.

4. Elections of the members of the Committee shall be held at a meeting of States Parties convened by the Secretary-General at United Nations Headquarters. At that meeting, for which two thirds of the States Parties shall constitute a quorum, the persons elected to the Committee shall be nominees who obtain the largest number of votes and an absolute majority of the votes of the representatives of States Parties present and voting.

5. (a) The members of the Committee shall be elected for a term of four years. However, the terms of nine of the members elected at the first election shall expire at the end of two years; immediately after the first election the names of these nine members shall be chosen by lot by the Chairman of the Committee;

(b) For the filling of casual vacancies, the State Party whose expert has ceased to function as a member of the Committee shall appoint another expert from among its nationals, subject to the approval of the Committee.

6. States Parties shall be responsible for the expenses of the members of the Committee while they are in performance of Committee duties.

Article 9

1. States Parties undertake to submit to the Secretary-General of the United Nations, for consideration by the Committee, a report on the legislative, judicial, administrative or other measures which they have adopted and which give effect to the provisions of this Convention:

(a) within one year after the entry into force of the Convention for the State concerned; and

(b) thereafter every two years and whenever the Committee so requests. The Committee may request further information from the States Parties.

2. The Committee shall report annually, through the Secretary-General, to the General Assembly of the United Nations on its activities and may make suggestions and general recommendations based on the examination of the reports and information received from the States Parties. Such suggestions and general recommendations shall be reported to the General Assembly together with comments, if any, from States Parties.

Article 10

1. The Committee shall adopt its own rules of procedure.

2. The Committee shall elect its officers for a term of two years.

3. The secretariat of the Committee shall be provided by the Secretary-General of the United Nations.

4. The meetings of the Committee shall normally be held at United Nations Headquarters.

Article 11

1. If a State Party considers that another State Party is not giving effect to the provisions of this Convention, it may bring the matter to the attention of the Committee. The Committee shall then transmit the communication to the State Party concerned. Within three months, the receiving State shall submit to the Committee written explanations or statements clarifying the matter and the remedy, if any, that may have been taken by that State.

2. If the matter is not adjusted to the satisfaction of both parties, either by bilateral negotiations or by any other procedure open to them, within six months after the receipt by the receiving State of the initial communication, either State shall have the right to refer the matter again to the Committee by notifying the Committee and also the other State.

3. The Committee shall deal with a matter referred to it in accordance with paragraph 2 of this article after it has ascertained that all available domestic remedies have been invoked and exhausted in the case, in conformity with the generally recognized principles of international law. This shall not be the rule where the application of the remedies is unreasonably prolonged.

4. In any matter referred to it, the Committee may call upon the States Parties concerned to supply any other relevant information.

5. When any matter arising out of this article is being considered by the Committee, the States Parties concerned shall be entitled to send a representative to take part in the proceedings of the Committee, without voting rights, while the matter is under consideration.

Article 12

1. (a) After the Committee has obtained and collated all the information it deems necessary, the Chairman shall appoint an *ad hoc* Conciliation Commission (hereinafter referred to as the Commission) comprising five persons who may or may not be members of the Committee. The members of the Commission shall be appointed with the unanimous consent of the parties to the dispute, and its good offices shall be made available to the States concerned with a view to an amicable solution of the matter on the basis of respect for this Convention;

(b) If the States Parties to the dispute fail to reach agreement within three months on all or part of the composition of the Commission, the members of the Commission not agreed upon by the States Parties to the dispute shall be elected by secret ballot by a two-thirds majority vote of the Committee from among its own members.

2. The members of the Commission shall serve in their personal capacity. They shall not be nationals of the States Parties to the dispute or of a State not Party to this Convention.

3. The Commission shall elect its own Chairman and adopt its own rules of procedure.

4. The meetings of the Commission shall normally be held at United Nations Headquarters or at any other convenient place as determined by the Commission.

5. The secretariat provided in accordance with article 10, paragraph 3, of this Convention shall also service the Commission whenever a dispute among States Parties brings the Commission into being.

6. The States Parties to the dispute shall share equally all the expenses of the members of the Commission in accordance with estimates to be provided by the Secretary-General of the United Nations.

7. The Secretary-General shall be empowered to pay the expenses of the members of the Commission, if necessary, before reimbursement by the States Parties to the dispute in accordance with paragraph 6 of this article.

8. The information obtained and collated by the Committee shall be made available to the Commission, and the Commission may call upon the States concerned to supply any other relevant information.

Article 13

1. When the Commission has fully considered the matter, it shall prepare and submit to the Chairman of the Committee a report embodying its findings on all questions of fact relevant to the issue between the parties and containing such recommendations as it may think proper for the amicable solution of the dispute.

2. The Chairman of the Committee shall communicate the report of the Commission to each of the States Parties to the dispute. These States shall, within three months, inform the Chairman of the Committee whether or not they accept the recommendations contained in the report of the Commission.

3. After the period provided for in paragraph 2 of this article, the Chairman of the Committee shall communicate the report of the Commission and the declarations of the States Parties concerned to the other States Parties to this Convention.

Article 14

1. A State Party may at any time declare that it recognizes the competence of the Committee to receive and consider communications from individuals or groups of individuals within its jurisdiction claiming to be victims of a violation by that State Party of any of the rights set forth in this Convention. No communication shall be received by the Committee if it concerns a State Party which has not made such a declaration.

2. Any State Party which makes a declaration as provided for in paragraph 1 of this article may establish or indicate a body within its national legal order which shall be competent to receive and consider petitions from individuals and groups of individuals within its jurisdiction who claim to be victims of a violation of any of the rights set forth in this Convention and who have exhausted other available local remedies.

3. A declaration made in accordance with paragraph 1 of this article and the name of any body established or indicated in accordance with paragraph 2 of this article shall be deposited by the State Party concerned with the Secretary-General of the United Nations, who shall transmit copies thereof to the other States Parties. A declaration may be withdrawn at any time by notification to the Secretary-General, but such a withdrawal shall not affect communications pending before the Committee.

4. A register of petitions shall be kept by the body established or indicated in accordance with paragraph 2 of this article, and certified copies of the register shall be filed annually through appropriate channels with the Secretary-General on the understanding that the contents shall not be publicly disclosed.

5. In the event of failure to obtain satisfaction from the body established or indicated in accordance with paragraph 2 of this article, the petitioner shall have the right to communicate the matter to the Committee within six months.

6. (a) The Committee shall confidentially bring any communication referred to it to the attention of the State Party alleged to be violating any provision of this Convention, but the identity of the individual or groups of individuals concerned shall not be revealed without his or their express consent. The Committee shall not receive anonymous communications;

(b) Within three months, the receiving State shall submit to the Committee written explanations or statements clarifying the matter and the remedy, if any, that may have been taken by that State.

7. (a) The Committee shall consider communications in the light of all information made available to it by the State Party concerned and by the petitioner. The Committee shall not consider any communication from a petitioner unless it has ascertained that the petitioner has exhausted all available domestic remedies. However, this shall not be the rule where the application of the remedies is unreasonably prolonged;

(b) The Committee shall forward its suggestions and recommendations, if any, to the State Party concerned and to the petitioner.

8. The Committee shall include in its annual report a summary of such communications and, where appropriate, a summary of the explanations and statements of the States Parties concerned and of its own suggestions and recommendations.

9. The Committee shall be competent to exercise the functions provided for in this article only when at least ten States Parties to this Convention are bound by declarations in accordance with paragraph 1 of this article.

Article 15

1. Pending the achievement of the objectives of the Declaration on the Granting of Independence to Colonial Countries and Peoples, contained in General Assembly resolution 1514 (XV) of 14 December 1960, the provisions of this Convention shall in no way limit the right of petition granted to these peoples by other international instruments or by the United Nations and its specialized agencies.

2. (a) The Committee established under article 8, paragraph 1, of this Convention shall receive copies of the petitions from, and submit expressions of opinion and recommendations on these petitions to, the bodies of the United Nations which deal with matters directly related to the principles and objectives of this Convention in their consideration of petitions from the inhabitants of Trust and Non-Self-Governing Territories and all other territories to which General Assembly resolution 1514 (XV) applies, relating to matters covered by this Convention which are before these bodies;

(b) The Committee shall receive from the competent bodies of the United Nations copies of the reports concerning the legislative, judicial, administrative or other measures directly related to the principles and objectives of this Convention applied by the administering Powers within the Territories mentioned in subparagraph (a) of this paragraph, and shall express opinions and make recommendations to these bodies.

3. The Committee shall include in its report to the General Assembly a summary of the petitions and reports it has received from United Nations bodies, and the expressions of opinion and recommendations of the Committee relating to the said petitions and reports.

4. The Committee shall request from the Secretary-General of the United Nations all information relevant to the objectives of this Convention and available to him regarding the Territories mentioned in paragraph 2 (a) of this article.

Article 16

The provisions of this Convention concerning the settlement of disputes or complaints shall be applied without prejudice to other procedures for settling disputes or complaints in the field of discrimination laid down in the constituent instruments of, or conventions adopted by, the United Nations and its specialized agencies, and shall not prevent the States Parties from having recourse to other procedures for settling a dispute in accordance with general or special international agreements in force between them.

PART III

Article 17

1. This Convention is open for signature by any State Member of the United Nations or member of any of its specialized agencies, by any State Party to the Statute of the International Court of Justice, and by any other State which has been invited by the General Assembly of the United Nations to become a Party to this Convention.

2. This Convention is subject to ratification. Instruments of ratification shall be deposited with the Secretary-General of the United Nations.

Article 18

1. This Convention shall be open to accession by any State referred to in article 17, paragraph 1, of the Convention.

2. Accession shall be effected by the deposit of an instrument of accession with the Secretary-General of the United Nations.

Article 19

1. This Convention shall enter into force on the thirtieth day after the date of the deposit with the Secretary-General of the United Nations of the twenty-seventh instrument of ratification or instrument of accession.

2. For each State ratifying this Convention or acceding to it after the deposit of the twenty-seventh instrument of ratification or instrument of accession, the Convention shall enter into force on the thirtieth day after the date of the deposit of its own instrument of ratification or instrument of accession.

Article 20

1. The Secretary-General of the United Nations shall receive and circulate to all States which are or may become Parties to this Convention reservations made by States at the time of ratification or accession. Any State which objects to the reservation shall, within a period of ninety days from the date of the said communication, notify the Secretary-General that it does not accept it.

2. A reservation incompatible with the object and purpose of this Convention shall not be permitted, nor shall a reservation the effect of which would inhibit the operation of any of the bodies established by this Convention be allowed. A reservation shall be considered incompatible or inhibitive if at least two thirds of the States Parties to this Convention object to it.

3. Reservations may be withdrawn at any time by notification to this effect addressed to the Secretary-General. Such notification shall take effect on the date on which it is received.

Article 21

A State Party may denounce this Convention by written notification to the Secretary-General of the United Nations. Denunciation shall take effect one year after the date of receipt of the notification by the Secretary-General.

Article 22

Any dispute between two or more States Parties with respect to the interpretation or application of this Convention, which is not settled by negotiation or by the procedures expressly provided for in this Convention, shall, at the request of any of the parties to the dispute, be referred to the International Court of Justice for decision, unless the disputants agree to another mode of settlement.

Article 23

1. A request for the revision of this Convention may be made at any time by any State Party by means of a notification in writing addressed to the Secretary-General of the United Nations.

2. The General Assembly of the United Nations shall decide upon the steps, if any, to be taken in respect of such a request.

Article 24

The Secretary-General of the United Nations shall inform all States referred to in article 17, paragraph 1, of this Convention of the following particulars:

(a) Signatures, ratifications and accessions under articles 17 and 18;

(b) The date of entry into force of this Convention under article 19;

(c) Communications and declarations received under articles 14, 20 and 23;

(d) Denunciations under article 21.

Article 25

1. This Convention, of which the Chinese, English, French, Russian and Spanish texts are equally authentic, shall be deposited in the archives of the United Nations.

2. The Secretary-General of the United Nations shall transmit certified copies of this Convention to all States belonging to any of the categories mentioned in article 17, paragraph 1, of the Convention.

Right to Enjoy Culture; International Cultural Development and Co-operation

Declaration of the Principles of International Cultural Co-operation

Proclaimed by the General Conference of the United Nations Educational, Scientific and Cultural Organization at its fourteenth session on 4 November 1966

The General Conference of the United Nations Educational, Scientific and Cultural Organization, met in Paris for its fourteenth session, this fourth day of November 1966, being the twentieth anniversary of the foundation of the Organization,

Recalling that the Constitution of the Organization declares that "since wars begin in the minds of men, it is in the minds of men that the defences of peace must be constructed" and that the peace must be founded, if it is not to fail, upon the intellectual and moral solidarity of mankind,

Recalling that the Constitution also states that the wide diffusion of culture and the education of humanity for justice and liberty and peace are indispensable to the dignity of man and constitute a sacred duty which all the nations must fulfil in a spirit of mutual assistance and concern,

Considering that the Organization's Member States, believing in the pursuit of truth and the free exchange of ideas and knowledge, have agreed and determined to develop and to increase the means of communication between their peoples,

Considering that, despite the technical advances which facilitate the development and dissemination of knowledge and ideas, ignorance of the way of life and customs of peoples still presents an obstacle to friendship among the nations, to peaceful co-operation and to the progress of mankind,

Taking account of the Universal Declaration of Human Rights, the Declaration of the Rights of the Child, the Declaration on the Granting of Independence to Colonial Countries and Peoples, the United Nations Declaration on the Elimination of All Forms of Racial Discrimination, the Declaration on the Promotion among Youth of the Ideals of Peace, Mutual Respect and Understanding between Peoples, and the Declaration on the Inadmissibility of Intervention in the Domestic Affairs of States and the Protection of their Independence and Sovereignty, proclaimed successively by the General Assembly of the United Nations,

Convinced by the experience of the Organization's first twenty years that, if international cultural co-operation is to be strengthened, its principles require to be affirmed,

Proclaims this Declaration of the principles of international cultural co-operation, to the end that governments, authorities, organizations, associations and institutions responsible for cultural activities may constantly be guided by these principles; and for the purpose, as set out in the Constitution of the Organization, of advancing, through the educational, scientific and cultural relations of the peoples of the world, the objectives of peace and welfare that are defined in the Charter of the United Nations:

Article I

1. Each culture has a dignity and value which must be respected and preserved.

2. Every people has the right and the duty to develop its culture.

3. In their rich variety and diversity, and in the reciprocal influences they exert on one another, all cultures form part of the common heritage belonging to all mankind.

Article II

Nations shall endeavour to develop the various branches of culture side by side and, as far as possible, simultaneously, so as to establish a harmonious balance between technical progress and the intellectual and moral advancement of mankind.

Article III

International cultural co-operation shall cover all aspects of intellectual and creative activities relating to education, science and culture.

Article IV

The aims of international cultural co-operation in its various forms, bilateral or multilateral, regional or universal, shall be:

1. To spread knowledge, to stimulate talent and to enrich cultures;

2. To develop peaceful relations and friendship among the peoples and bring about a better understanding of each other's way of life;

3. To contribute to the application of the principles set out in the United Nations Declarations that are recalled in the Preamble to this Declaration;

4. To enable everyone to have access to knowledge, to enjoy the arts and literature of all peoples, to share in advances made in science in all parts of the world and in the resulting benefits, and to contribute to the enrichment of cultural life;

5. To raise the level of the spiritual and material life of man in all parts of the world.

Article V

Cultural co-operation is a right and a duty for all peoples and all nations, which should share with one another their knowledge and skills.

Article VI

International co-operation, while promoting the enrichment of all cultures through its beneficent action, shall respect the distinctive character of each.

Article VII

1. Broad dissemination of ideas and knowledge, based on the freest exchange and discussion, is essential to creative activity, the pursuit of truth and the development of the personality.

2. In cultural co-operation, stress shall be laid on ideas and values conducive to the creation of a climate of friendship and peace. Any mark of hostility in attitudes and in expression of opinion shall be avoided. Every effort shall be made, in presenting and disseminating information, to ensure its authenticity.

Article VIII

Cultural co-operation shall be carried on for the mutual benefit of all the nations practising it. Exchanges to which it gives rise shall be arranged in a spirit of broad reciprocity.

Article IX

Cultural co-operation shall contribute to the establishment of stable, long-term relations between peoples, which should be subjected as little as possible to the strains which may arise in international life.

Article X

Cultural co-operation shall be specially concerned with the moral and intellectual education of young people in a spirit of friendship, international understanding and peace and shall foster awareness among States of the need to stimulate talent and promote the training of the rising generations in the most varied sectors.

Article XI

1. In their cultural relations, States shall bear in mind the principles of the United Nations. In seeking to achieve international co-operation, they shall respect the sovereign equality of States and shall refrain from intervention in matters which are essentially within the domestic jurisdiction of any State.

2. The principles of this Declaration shall be applied with due regard for human rights and fundamental freedoms.

Declaration on Race and Racial Prejudice

Adopted and proclaimed by the General Conference of the United Nations Educational, Scientific and Cultural Organization at its twentieth session, on 27 November 1978

Preamble

The General Conference of the United Nations Educational, Scientific and Cultural Organization, meeting at Paris at its twentieth session, from 24 October to 28 November 1978,

Whereas it is stated in the Preamble to the Constitution of UNESCO, adopted on 16 November 1945, that "the great and terrible war which has now ended was a war made possible by the denial of the democratic principles of the dignity, equality and mutual respect of men, and by the propagation, in their place, through ignorance and prejudice, of the doctrine of the inequality of men and races", and whereas, according to Article 1 of the said Constitution, the purpose of UNESCO "is to contribute to peace and security by promoting collaboration among the nations through education, science and culture in order to further universal respect for justice, for the rule of law and for the human rights and fundamental freedoms which are affirmed for the peoples of the world, without distinction of race, sex, language or religion, by the Charter of the United Nations",

Recognizing that, more than three decades after the founding of UNESCO, these principles are just as significant as they were when they were embodied in its Constitution,

Mindful of the process of decolonization and other historical changes which have led most of the peoples formerly under foreign rule to recover their sovereignty, making the international community a universal and diversified whole and creating new opportunities of eradicating the scourge of racism and of putting an end to its odious manifestations in all aspects of social and political life, both nationally and internationally,

Convinced that the essential unity of the human race and consequently the fundamental equality of all human beings and all peoples, recognized in the loftiest expressions of philosophy, morality and religion, reflect an ideal towards which ethics and science are converging today,

Convinced that all peoples and all human groups, whatever their composition or ethnic origin, contribute according to their own genius to the progress of the civilizations and cultures which, in their plurality and as a result of their interpenetration, constitute the common heritage of mankind,

Confirming its attachment to the principles proclaimed in the United Nations Charter and the Universal Declaration of Human Rights and its determination to promote the implementation of the International Covenants on Human Rights as well as the Declaration on the Establishment of a New International Economic Order,

Determined also to promote the implementation of the United Nations Declaration and the International Convention on the Elimination of All Forms of Racial Discrimination,

Noting the Convention on the Prevention and Punishment of the Crime of Genocide, the International Convention on the Suppression and Punishment of the Crime of *Apartheid* and the Convention on the Non-Applicability of Statutory Limitations to War Crimes and Crimes against Humanity,

Recalling also the international instruments already adopted by UNESCO, including in particular the Convention and Recommendation against Discrimination in Education, the Recommendation concerning the Status of Teachers, the Declaration of the Principles of International Cultural Co-operation, the Recommendation concerning Education for International Understanding, Co-operation and Peace and Education relating to Human Rights and Fundamental Freedoms, the Recommendations on the Status of Scientific Researchers, and the Recommendation on participation by the people at large in cultural life and their contribution to it,

Bearing in mind the four statements on the race question adopted by experts convened by UNESCO,

Reaffirming its desire to play a vigorous and constructive part in the implementation of the programme of the Decade for Action to Combat Racism and Racial Discrimination, as defined by the General Assembly of the United Nations at its twenty-eighth session,

Noting with the gravest concern that racism, racial discrimination, colonialism and *apartheid* continue to afflict the world in ever-changing forms, as a result both of the continuation of legislative provisions and government and administrative practices contrary to the principles of human rights and also of the continued existence of political and social structures, and of relationships and attitudes, characterized by injustice and contempt for human beings and leading to the exclusion, humiliation and exploitation, or to the forced assimilation, of the members of disadvantaged groups,

Expressing its indignation at these offences against human dignity, deploring the obstacles they place in the way of mutual understanding between peoples and alarmed at the danger of their seriously disturbing international peace and security,

Adopts and solemnly proclaims this Declaration on Race and Racial Prejudice:

Article 1

1. All human beings belong to a single species and are descended from a common stock. They are born equal in dignity and rights and all form an integral part of humanity.

2. All individuals and groups have the right to be different, to consider themselves as different and to be regarded as such. However, the diversity of life styles and the right to be different may not, in any circumstances, serve as a pretext for racial prejudice; they may not justify either in law or in fact any discriminatory practice whatsoever, nor provide a ground for the policy of *apartheid*, which is the extreme form of racism.

3. Identity of origin in no way affects the fact that human beings can and may live differently, nor does it preclude the existence of differences based on cultural, environmental and historical diversity nor the right to maintain cultural identity.

4. All peoples of the world possess equal faculties for attaining the highest level in intellectual, technical, social, economic, cultural and political development.

5. The differences between the achievements of the different peoples are entirely attributable to geographical, historical, political, economic, social and cultural factors. Such differences can in no case serve as a pretext for any rank-ordered classification of nations or peoples.

Article 2

1. Any theory which involves the claim that racial or ethnic groups are inherently superior or inferior, thus implying that some would be entitled to dominate or eliminate others, presumed to be inferior, or which bases value judgements on racial differentiation, has no scientific foundation and is contrary to the moral and ethical principles of humanity.

2. Racism includes racist ideologies, prejudiced attitudes, discriminatory behaviour, structural arrangements and institutionalized practices resulting in racial inequality as well as the fallacious notion that discriminatory relations between groups are morally and scientifically justifiable; it is reflected in discriminatory provisions in legislation or regulations and discriminatory practices as well as in anti-social beliefs and acts; it hinders the development of its victims, perverts those who practise it, divides nations internally, impedes international co-operation and gives rise to political tensions between peoples; it is contrary to the fundamental principles of international law and, consequently, seriously disturbs international peace and security.

3. Racial prejudice, historically linked with inequalities in power, reinforced by economic and social differences between individuals and groups, and still seeking today to justify such inequalities, is totally without justification.

Article 3

Any distinction, exclusion, restriction or preference based on race, colour, ethnic or national origin or religious intolerance motivated by racist considerations, which destroys or compromises the sovereign equality of States and the right of peoples to self-determination, or which limits in an arbitrary or discriminatory manner the right of every human being and group to full development is incompatible with the requirements of an international order which is just and guarantees respect for human rights; the right to full development implies equal access to the means of personal and collective advancement and fulfilment in a climate of respect for the values of civilizations and cultures, both national and worldwide.

Article 4

1. Any restriction on the complete self-fulfilment of human beings and free communication between them which is based on racial or ethnic considerations is contrary to the principle of equality in dignity and rights; it cannot be admitted.

2. One of the most serious violations of this principle is represented by *apartheid*, which, like genocide, is a crime against humanity, and gravely disturbs international peace and security.

3. Other policies and practices of racial segregation and discrimination constitute crimes against the conscience and dignity of mankind and may lead to political tensions and gravely endanger international peace and security.

Article 5

1. Culture, as a product of all human beings and a common heritage of mankind, and education in its broadest sense, offer men and women increasingly effective means of adaptation, enabling them not only to affirm that they are born equal in dignity and rights, but also to recognize that they should respect the right of all groups to their own cultural identity and the development of their distinctive cultural life within the national and international contexts, it being understood that it rests with each group to decide in complete freedom on the maintenance, and, if appropriate, the adaptation or enrichment of the values which it regards as essential to its identity.

2. States, in accordance with their constitutional principles and procedures, as well as all other competent authorities and the entire teaching profession, have a responsibility to see that the educational resources of all countries are used to combat racism, more especially by ensuring that curricula and textbooks include scientific and ethical considerations concerning human unity and diversity and that no invidious distinctions are made with regard to any people; by training teachers to achieve these ends; by making the resources of the educational system available to all groups of the population without racial restriction or discrimination; and by taking appropriate steps to remedy the handicaps from which certain racial or ethnic groups suffer with regard to their level of education and standard of living and in particular to prevent such handicaps from being passed on to children.

3. The mass media and those who control or serve them, as well as all organized groups within national communities, are urged – with due regard to the principles embodied in the Universal Declaration of Human Rights, particularly the principle of freedom of expression – to promote understanding, tolerance and friendship among individuals and groups and to contribute to the eradication of racism, racial discrimination and racial prejudice, in particular by refraining from presenting a stereotyped, partial, unilateral or tendentious picture of individuals and of various human groups. Communication between racial and ethnic groups must be a reciprocal process, enabling them to express themselves and to be fully heard without let or hindrance. The mass media should therefore be freely receptive to ideas of individuals and groups which facilitate such communication.

Article 6

1. The State has prime responsibility for ensuring human rights and fundamental freedoms on an entirely equal footing in dignity and rights for all individuals and all groups.

2. So far as its competence extends and in accordance with its constitutional principles and procedures, the State should take all appropriate steps, *inter alia* by legislation, particularly in the spheres of education, culture and communication, to prevent, prohibit and eradicate racism, racist propaganda, racial segregation and *apartheid* and to encourage the dissemination of knowledge and the findings of appropriate research in natural and social sciences on the causes and prevention of racial prejudice and racist attitudes with due regard to the principles embodied in the Universal Declaration of Human Rights and in the International Covenant on Civil and Political Rights.

3. Since laws proscribing racial discrimination are not in themselves sufficient, it is also incumbent on States to supplement them by administrative machinery for the systematic investigation of instances of racial discrimination, by

a comprehensive framework of legal remedies against acts of racial discrimination, by broadly based education and research programmes designed to combat racial prejudice and racial discrimination and by programmes of positive political, social, educational and cultural measures calculated to promote genuine mutual respect among groups. Where circumstances warrant, special programmes should be undertaken to promote the advancement of disadvantaged groups and, in the case of nationals, to ensure their effective participation in the decision-making processes of the community.

Article 7

In addition to political, economic and social measures, law is one of the principal means of ensuring equality in dignity and rights among individuals, and of curbing any propaganda, any form of organization or any practice which is based on ideas or theories referring to the alleged superiority of racial or ethnic groups or which seeks to justify or encourage racial hatred and discrimination in any form. States should adopt such legislation as is appropriate to this end and see that it is given effect and applied by all their services, with due regard to the principles embodied in the Universal Declaration of Human Rights. Such legislation should form part of a political, economic and social framework conducive to its implementation. Individuals and other legal entities, both public and private, must conform with such legislation and use all appropriate means to help the population as a whole to understand and apply it.

Article 8

1. Individuals, being entitled to an economic, social, cultural and legal order, on the national and international planes, such as to allow them to exercise all their capabilities on a basis of entire equality of rights and opportunities, have corresponding duties towards their fellows, towards the society in which they live and towards the international community. They are accordingly under an obligation to promote harmony among the peoples, to combat racism and racial prejudice and to assist by every means available to them in eradicating racial discrimination in all its forms.

2. In the field of racial prejudice and racist attitudes and practices, specialists in natural and social sciences and cultural studies, as well as scientific organizations and associations, are called upon to undertake objective research on a wide interdisciplinary basis; all States should encourage them to this end.

3. It is, in particular, incumbent upon such specialists to ensure, by all means available to them, that their research findings are not misinterpreted, and also that they assist the public in understanding such findings.

Article 9

1. The principle of the equality in dignity and rights of all human beings and all peoples, irrespective of race, colour and origin, is a generally accepted and recognized principle of international law. Consequently any form of racial discrimination practised by a State constitutes a violation of international law giving rise to its international responsibility.

2. Special measures must be taken to ensure equality in dignity and rights for individuals and groups wherever necessary, while ensuring that they are not such as to appear racially discriminatory. In this respect, particular attention should be paid to racial or ethnic groups which are socially or economically disadvantaged, so as to afford them, on a completely equal footing and without discrimination or restriction, the protection of the laws and regulations and the advantages of the social measures in force, in particular in regard to housing, employment and health; to respect the authenticity of their culture and values; and to facilitate their social and occupational advancement, especially through education.

3. Population groups of foreign origin, particularly migrant workers and their families who contribute to the development of the host country, should benefit from appropriate measures designed to afford them security and respect for their dignity and cultural values and to facilitate their adaptation to the host environment and their professional advancement with a view to their subsequent reintegration in their country of origin and their contribution to its development; steps should be taken to make it possible for their children to be taught their mother tongue.

4. Existing disequilibria in international economic relations contribute to the exacerbation of racism and racial prejudice; all States should consequently endeavour to contribute to the restructuring of the international economy on a more equitable basis.

Article 10

International organizations, whether universal or regional, governmental or non-governmental, are called upon to co-operate and assist, so far as their respective fields of competence and means allow, in the full and complete implementation of the principles set out in this Declaration, thus contributing to the legitimate struggle of all men, born equal in dignity and rights, against the tyranny and oppression of racism, racial segregation, *apartheid* and genocide, so that all the peoples of the world may be forever delivered from these scourges.

Declaration on the Elimination of All Forms of Intolerance and of Discrimination Based on Religion or Belief

Proclaimed by General Assembly resolution 36/55 of 25 November 1981

The General Assembly,

Considering that one of the basic principles of the Charter of the United Nations is that of the dignity and equality inherent in all human beings, and that all Member States have pledged themselves to take joint and separate action in co-operation with the Organization to promote and encourage universal respect for and observance of human rights and fundamental freedoms for all, without distinction as to race, sex, language or religion,

Considering that the Universal Declaration of Human Rights and the International Covenants on Human Rights proclaim the principles of non-discrimination and equality before the law and the right to freedom of thought, conscience, religion and belief,

Considering that the disregard and infringement of human rights and fundamental freedoms, in particular of the right to freedom of thought, conscience, religion or whatever belief, have brought, directly or indirectly, wars and great suffering to mankind, especially where they serve as a means of foreign interference in the internal affairs of other States and amount to kindling hatred between peoples and nations,

Considering that religion or belief, for anyone who professes either, is one of the fundamental elements in his conception of life and that freedom of religion or belief should be fully respected and guaranteed,

Considering that it is essential to promote understanding, tolerance and respect in matters relating to freedom of religion and belief and to ensure that the use of religion or belief for ends inconsistent with the Charter of the United Nations, other relevant instruments of the United Nations and the purposes and principles of the present Declaration is inadmissible,

Convinced that freedom of religion and belief should also contribute to the attainment of the goals of world peace, social justice and friendship among peoples and to the elimination of ideologies or practices of colonialism and racial discrimination,

Noting with satisfaction the adoption of several, and the coming into force of some, conventions, under the aegis of the United Nations and of the specialized agencies, for the elimination of various forms of discrimination,

Concerned by manifestations of intolerance and by the existence of discrimination in matters of religion or belief still in evidence in some areas of the world,

Resolved to adopt all necessary measures for the speedy elimination of such intolerance in all its forms and manifestations and to prevent and combat discrimination on the ground of religion or belief,

Proclaims this Declaration on the Elimination of All Forms of Intolerance and of Discrimination Based on Religion or Belief:

Article 1

1. Everyone shall have the right to freedom of thought, conscience and religion. This right shall include freedom to have a religion or whatever belief of his choice, and freedom, either individually or in community with others and in public or private, to manifest his religion or belief in worship, observance, practice and teaching.

2. No one shall be subject to coercion which would impair his freedom to have a religion or belief of his choice.

3. Freedom to manifest one's religion or belief may be subject only to such limitations as are prescribed by law and are necessary to protect public safety, order, health or morals or the fundamental rights and freedoms of others.

Article 2

1. No one shall be subject to discrimination by any State, institution, group of persons, or person on the grounds of religion or other belief.

2. For the purposes of the present Declaration, the expression "intolerance and discrimination based on religion or belief" means any distinction, exclusion, restriction or preference based on religion or belief and having as its purpose or as its effect nullification or impairment of the recognition, enjoyment or exercise of human rights and fundamental freedoms on an equal basis.

Article 3

Discrimination between human beings on the grounds of religion or belief constitutes an affront to human dignity and a disavowal of the principles of the Charter of the United Nations, and shall be condemned as a violation of the human rights and fundamental freedoms proclaimed in the Universal Declaration of Human Rights and enunciated in detail in the International Covenants on Human Rights, and as an obstacle to friendly and peaceful relations between nations.

Article 4

1. All States shall take effective measures to prevent and eliminate discrimination on the grounds of religion or belief in the recognition, exercise and enjoyment of human rights and fundamental freedoms in all fields of civil, economic, political, social and cultural life.

2. All States shall make all efforts to enact or rescind legislation where necessary to prohibit any such discrimination, and to take all appropriate measures to combat intolerance on the grounds of religion or other beliefs in this matter.

Article 5

1. The parents or, as the case may be, the legal guardians of the child have the right to organize the life within the family in accordance with their religion or belief and bearing in mind the moral education in which they believe the child should be brought up.

2. Every child shall enjoy the right to have access to education in the matter of religion or belief in accordance with the wishes of his parents or, as the case may be, legal guardians, and shall not be compelled to receive teaching on religion or belief against the wishes of his parents or legal guardians, the best interests of the child being the guiding principle.

3. The child shall be protected from any form of discrimination on the ground of religion or belief. He shall be brought up in a spirit of understanding, tolerance, friendship among peoples, peace and universal brotherhood, respect for freedom of religion or belief of others, and in full consciousness that his energy and talents should be devoted to the service of his fellow men.

4. In the case of a child who is not under the care either of his parents or of legal guardians, due account shall be taken of their expressed wishes or of any other proof of their wishes in the matter of religion or belief, the best interests of the child being the guiding principle.
5. Practices of a religion or belief in which a child is brought up must not be injurious to his physical or mental health or to his full development, taking into account article 1, paragraph 3, of the present Declaration.

Article 6

In accordance with article 1 of the present Declaration, and subject to the provisions of article 1, paragraph 3, the right to freedom of thought, conscience, religion or belief shall include, *inter alia*, the following freedoms:

(a) To worship or assemble in connection with a religion or belief, and to establish and maintain places for these purposes;

(b) To establish and maintain appropriate charitable or humanitarian institutions;

(c) To make, acquire and use to an adequate extent the necessary articles and materials related to the rites or customs of a religion or belief;

(d) To write, issue and disseminate relevant publications in these areas;

(e) To teach a religion or belief in places suitable for these purposes;

(f) To solicit and receive voluntary financial and other contributions from individuals and institutions;

(g) To train, appoint, elect or designate by succession appropriate leaders called for by the requirements and standards of any religion or belief;

(h) To observe days of rest and to celebrate holidays and ceremonies in accordance with the precepts of one's religion or belief;

(i) To establish and maintain communications with individuals and communities in matters of religion and belief at the national and international levels.

Article 7

The rights and freedoms set forth in the present Declaration shall be accorded in national legislation in such a manner that everyone shall be able to avail himself of such rights and freedoms in practice.

Article 8

Nothing in the present Declaration shall be construed as restricting or derogating from any right defined in the Universal Declaration of Human Rights and the International Covenants on Human Rights.

Declaration on the Human Rights of Individuals Who are not Nationals of the Country in which They Live

Adopted by General Assembly resolution 40/144 of 13 December 1985

The General Assembly,

Considering that the Charter of the United Nations encourages universal respect for and observance of the human rights and fundamental freedoms of all human beings, without distinction as to race, sex, language or religion,

Considering that the Universal Declaration of Human Rights proclaims that all human beings are born free and equal in dignity and rights and that everyone is entitled to all the rights and freedoms set forth in that Declaration, without distinction of any kind, such as race, colour, sex, language, religion, political or other opinion, national or social origin, property, birth or other status,

Considering that the Universal Declaration of Human Rights proclaims further that everyone has the right to recognition everywhere as a person before the law, that all are equal before the law and entitled without any discrimination to equal protection of the law, and that all are entitled to equal protection against any discrimination in violation of that Declaration and against any incitement to such discrimination,

Being aware that the States Parties to the International Covenants on Human Rights undertake to guarantee that the rights enunciated in these Covenants will be exercised without discrimination of any kind as to race, colour, sex, language, religion, political or other opinion, national or social origin, property, birth or other status,

Conscious that, with improving communications and the development of peaceful and friendly relations among countries, individuals increasingly live in countries of which they are not nationals,

Reaffirming the purposes and principles of the Charter of the United Nations,

Recognizing that the protection of human rights and fundamental freedoms provided for in international instruments should also be ensured for individuals who are not nationals of the country in which they live,

Proclaims this Declaration:

Article 1

For the purposes of this Declaration, the term "alien" shall apply, with due regard to qualifications made in subsequent articles, to any individual who is not a national of the State in which he or she is present.

Article 2

1. Nothing in this Declaration shall be interpreted as legitimizing the illegal entry into and presence in a State of any alien, nor shall any provision be interpreted as restricting the right of any State to promulgate laws and regulations

concerning the entry of aliens and the terms and conditions of their stay or to establish differences between nationals and aliens. However, such laws and regulations shall not be incompatible with the international legal obligations of that State, including those in the field of human rights.

2. This Declaration shall not prejudice the enjoyment of the rights accorded by domestic law and of the rights which under international law a State is obliged to accord to aliens, even where this Declaration does not recognize such rights or recognizes them to a lesser extent.

Article 3

Every State shall make public its national legislation or regulations affecting aliens.

Article 4

Aliens shall observe the laws of the State in which they reside or are present and regard with respect the customs and traditions of the people of that State.

Article 5

1. Aliens shall enjoy, in accordance with domestic law and subject to the relevant international obligation of the State in which they are present, in particular the following rights:

(a) The right to life and security of person; no alien shall be subjected to arbitrary arrest or detention; no alien shall be deprived of his or her liberty except on such grounds and in accordance with such procedures as are established by law;

(b) The right to protection against arbitrary or unlawful interference with privacy, family, home or correspondence;

(c) The right to be equal before the courts, tribunals and all other organs and authorities administering justice and, when necessary, to free assistance of an interpreter in criminal proceedings and, when prescribed by law, other proceedings;

(d) The right to choose a spouse, to marry, to found a family;

(e) The right to freedom of thought, opinion, conscience and religion; the right to manifest their religion or beliefs, subject only to such limitations as are prescribed by law and are necessary to protect public safety, order, health or morals or the fundamental rights and freedoms of others;

(f) The right to retain their own language, culture and tradition;

(g) The right to transfer abroad earnings, savings or other personal monetary assets, subject to domestic currency regulations.

2. Subject to such restrictions as are prescribed by law and which are necessary in a democratic society to protect national security, public safety, public order, public health or morals or the rights and freedoms of others, and which are consistent with the other rights recognized in the relevant international instruments and those set forth in this Declaration, aliens shall enjoy the following rights:

(a) The right to leave the country;

(b) The right to freedom of expression;

(c) The right to peaceful assembly;

(d) The right to own property alone as well as in association with others, subject to domestic law.

3. Subject to the provisions referred to in paragraph 2, aliens lawfully in the territory of a State shall enjoy the right to liberty of movement and freedom to choose their residence within the borders of the State.

4. Subject to national legislation and due authorization, the spouse and minor or dependent children of an alien lawfully residing in the territory of a State shall be admitted to accompany, join and stay with the alien.

Article 6

No alien shall be subjected to torture or to cruel, inhuman or degrading treatment or punishment and, in particular, no alien shall be subjected without his or her free consent to medical or scientific experimentation.

Article 7

An alien lawfully in the territory of a State may be expelled therefrom only in pursuance of a decision reached in accordance with law and shall, except where compelling reasons of national security otherwise require, be allowed to submit the reasons why he or she should not be expelled and to have the case reviewed by, and be represented for the purpose before, the competent authority or a person or persons specially designated by the competent authority. Individual or collective expulsion of such aliens on grounds of race, colour, religion, culture, descent or national or ethnic origin is prohibited.

Article 8

1. Aliens lawfully residing in the territory of a State shall also enjoy, in accordance with the national laws, the following rights, subject to their obligations under article 4:

(a) The right to safe and healthy working conditions, to fair wages and equal remuneration for work of equal value without distinction of any kind, in particular, women being guaranteed conditions of work not inferior to those enjoyed by men, with equal pay for equal work;

(b) The right to join trade unions and other organizations or associations of their choice and to participate in their activities. No restrictions may be placed on the exercise of this right other than those prescribed by law and which are necessary, in a democratic society, in the interests of national security or public order or for the protection of the rights and freedoms of others;

(c) The right to health protection, medical care, social security, social services, education, rest and leisure, provided that they fulfil the requirements under the relevant regulations for participation and that undue strain is not placed on the resources of the State.

2. With a view to protecting the rights of aliens carrying on lawful paid activities in the country in which they are present, such rights may be specified by the Governments concerned in multilateral or bilateral conventions.

Article 9

No alien shall be arbitrarily deprived of his or her lawfully acquired assets.

Article 10

Any alien shall be free at any time to communicate with the consulate or diplomatic mission of the State of which he or she is a national or, in the absence thereof, with the consulate or diplomatic mission of any other State entrusted with the protection of the interests of the State of which he or she is a national in the State where he or she resides.

Convention on the Rights of the Child

Adopted and opened for signature, ratification and accession by General Assembly resolution 44/25 of 20 November 1989

Entry into force: 2 September 1990, in accordance with article 49

Preamble

The States Parties to the present Convention,

Considering that, in accordance with the principles proclaimed in the Charter of the United Nations, recognition of the inherent dignity and of the equal and inalienable rights of all members of the human family is the foundation of freedom, justice and peace in the world,

Bearing in mind that the peoples of the United Nations have, in the Charter, reaffirmed their faith in fundamental human rights and in the dignity and worth of the human person, and have determined to promote social progress and better standards of life in larger freedom,

Recognizing that the United Nations has, in the Universal Declaration of Human Rights and in the International Covenants on Human Rights, proclaimed and agreed that everyone is entitled to all the rights and freedoms set forth therein, without distinction of any kind, such as race, colour, sex, language, religion, political or other opinion, national or social origin, property, birth or other status,

Recalling that, in the Universal Declaration of Human Rights, the United Nations has proclaimed that childhood is entitled to special care and assistance,

Convinced that the family, as the fundamental group of society and the natural environment for the growth and well-being of all its members and particularly children, should be afforded the necessary protection and assistance so that it can fully assume its responsibilities within the community,

Recognizing that the child, for the full and harmonious development of his or her personality, should grow up in a family environment, in an atmosphere of happiness, love and understanding,

Considering that the child should be fully prepared to live an individual life in society, and brought up in the spirit of the ideals proclaimed in the Charter of the United Nations, and in particular in the spirit of peace, dignity, tolerance, freedom, equality and solidarity,

Bearing in mind that the need to extend particular care to the child has been stated in the Geneva Declaration of the Rights of the Child of 1924 and in the Declaration of the Rights of the Child adopted by the General Assembly on 20 November 1959 and recognized in the Universal Declaration of Human Rights, in the International Covenant on Civil and Political Rights (in particular in articles 23 and 24), in the International Covenant on Economic, Social and Cultural Rights (in particular in article 10) and in the statutes and relevant instruments of specialized agencies and international organizations concerned with the welfare of children,

Bearing in mind that, as indicated in the Declaration of the Rights of the Child, "the child, by reason of his physical and mental immaturity, needs special safeguards and care, including appropriate legal protection, before as well as after birth",

Recalling the provisions of the Declaration on Social and Legal Principles relating to the Protection and Welfare of Children, with Special Reference to Foster Placement and Adoption Nationally and Internationally; the United Nations Standard Minimum Rules for the Administration of Juvenile Justice (The Beijing Rules); and the Declaration on the Protection of Women and Children in Emergency and Armed Conflict,

Recognizing that, in all countries in the world, there are children living in exceptionally difficult conditions, and that such children need special consideration,

Taking due account of the importance of the traditions and cultural values of each people for the protection and harmonious development of the child,

Recognizing the importance of international co-operation for improving the living conditions of children in every country, in particular in the developing countries,

Have agreed as follows:

PART I

Article 1

For the purposes of the present Convention, a child means every human being below the age of eighteen years unless under the law applicable to the child, majority is attained earlier.

Article 2

1. States Parties shall respect and ensure the rights set forth in the present Convention to each child within their jurisdiction without discrimination of any kind, irrespective of the child's or his or her parent's or legal guardian's race, colour, sex, language, religion, political or other opinion, national, ethnic or social origin, property, disability, birth or other status.

2. States Parties shall take all appropriate measures to ensure that the child is protected against all forms of discrimination or punishment on the basis of the status, activities, expressed opinions, or beliefs of the child's parents, legal guardians, or family members.

Article 3

1. In all actions concerning children, whether undertaken by public or private social welfare institutions, courts of law, administrative authorities or legislative bodies, the best interests of the child shall be a primary consideration.

2. States Parties undertake to ensure the child such protection and care as is necessary for his or her well-being, taking into account the rights and duties of his or her parents, legal guardians, or other individuals legally responsible for him or her, and, to this end, shall take all appropriate legislative and administrative measures.

3. States Parties shall ensure that the institutions, services and facilities responsible for the care or protection of children shall conform with the standards established by competent authorities, particularly in the areas of safety, health, in the number and suitability of their staff, as well as competent supervision.

Article 4

States Parties shall undertake all appropriate legislative, administrative, and other measures for the implementation of the rights recognized in the present Convention. With regard to economic, social and cultural rights, States Parties shall undertake such measures to the maximum extent of their available resources and, where needed, within the framework of international co-operation.

Article 5

States Parties shall respect the responsibilities, rights and duties of parents or, where applicable, the members of the extended family or community as provided for by local custom, legal guardians or other persons legally responsible for the child, to provide, in a manner consistent with the evolving capacities of the child, appropriate direction and guidance in the exercise by the child of the rights recognized in the present Convention.

Article 6

1. States Parties recognize that every child has the inherent right to life.

2. States Parties shall ensure to the maximum extent possible the survival and development of the child.

Article 7

1. The child shall be registered immediately after birth and shall have the right from birth to a name, the right to acquire a nationality and, as far as possible, the right to know and be cared for by his or her parents.

2. States Parties shall ensure the implementation of these rights in accordance with their national law and their obligations under the relevant international instruments in this field, in particular where the child would otherwise be stateless.

Article 8

1. States Parties undertake to respect the right of the child to preserve his or her identity, including nationality, name and family relations as recognized by law without unlawful interference.

2. Where a child is illegally deprived of some or all of the elements of his or her identity, States Parties shall provide appropriate assistance and protection, with a view to re-establishing speedily his or her identity.

Article 9

1. States Parties shall ensure that a child shall not be separated from his or her parents against their will, except when competent authorities subject to judicial review determine, in accordance with applicable law and procedures, that such separation is necessary for the best interests of the child. Such determination may be necessary in a particular case such as one involving abuse or neglect of the child by the parents, or one where the parents are living separately and a decision must be made as to the child's place of residence.

2. In any proceedings pursuant to paragraph 1 of the present article, all interested parties shall be given an opportunity to participate in the proceedings and make their views known.

3. States Parties shall respect the right of the child who is separated from one or both parents to maintain personal relations and direct contact with both parents on a regular basis, except if it is contrary to the child's best interests.

4. Where such separation results from any action initiated by a State Party, such as the detention, imprisonment, exile, deportation or death (including death arising from any cause while the person is in the custody of the State) of one or both parents or of the child, that State Party shall, upon request, provide the parents, the child or, if appropriate, another member of the family with the essential information concerning the whereabouts of the absent member(s) of the family unless the provision of the information would be detrimental to the well-being of the child. States Parties shall further ensure that the submission of such a request shall of itself entail no adverse consequences for the person(s) concerned.

Article 10

1. In accordance with the obligation of States Parties under article 9, paragraph 1, applications by a child or his or her parents to enter or leave a State Party for the purpose of family reunification shall be dealt with by States Parties in a positive, humane and expeditious manner. States Parties shall further ensure that the submission of such a request shall entail no adverse consequences for the applicants and for the members of their family.

2. A child whose parents reside in different States shall have the right to maintain on a regular basis, save in exceptional circumstances, personal relations and direct contacts with both parents. Towards that end and in accordance with the obligation of States Parties under article 9, paragraph 1, States Parties shall respect the right of the child and his or her parents to leave any country, including their own, and to enter their own country. The right to leave any country shall be subject only to such restrictions as are prescribed by law and which are necessary to protect the national security, public order (*ordre public*), public health or morals or the rights and freedoms of others and are consistent with the other rights recognized in the present Convention.

Article 11

1. States Parties shall take measures to combat the illicit transfer and non-return of children abroad.

2. To this end, States Parties shall promote the conclusion of bilateral or multilateral agreements or accession to existing agreements.

Article 12

1. States Parties shall assure to the child who is capable of forming his or her own views the right to express those views freely in all matters affecting the child, the views of the child being given due weight in accordance with the age and maturity of the child.

2. For this purpose, the child shall in particular be provided the opportunity to be heard in any judicial and administrative proceedings affecting the child, either directly, or through a representative or an appropriate body, in a manner consistent with the procedural rules of national law.

Article 13

1. The child shall have the right to freedom of expression; this right shall include freedom to seek, receive and impart information and ideas of all kinds, regardless of frontiers, either orally, in writing or in print, in the form of art, or through any other media of the child's choice.

2. The exercise of this right may be subject to certain restrictions, but these shall only be such as are provided by law and are necessary:

(a) For respect of the rights or reputations of others; or

(b) For the protection of national security or of public order (*ordre public*), or of public health or morals.

Article 14

1. States Parties shall respect the right of the child to freedom of thought, conscience and religion.

2. States Parties shall respect the rights and duties of the parents and, when applicable, legal guardians, to provide direction to the child in the exercise of his or her right in a manner consistent with the evolving capacities of the child.

3. Freedom to manifest one's religion or beliefs may be subject only to such limitations as are prescribed by law and are necessary to protect public safety, order, health or morals, or the fundamental rights and freedoms of others.

Article 15

1. States Parties recognize the rights of the child to freedom of association and to freedom of peaceful assembly.

2. No restrictions may be placed on the exercise of these rights other than those imposed in conformity with the law and which are necessary in a democratic society in the interests of national security or public safety, public order (*ordre public*), the protection of public health or morals or the protection of the rights and freedoms of others.

Article 16

1. No child shall be subjected to arbitrary or unlawful interference with his or her privacy, family, home or correspondence, nor to unlawful attacks on his or her honour and reputation.

2. The child has the right to the protection of the law against such interference or attacks.

Article 17

States Parties recognize the important function performed by the mass media and shall ensure that the child has access to information and material from a diversity of national and international sources, especially those aimed at the promotion of his or her social, spiritual and moral well-being and physical and mental health. To this end, States Parties shall:

(a) Encourage the mass media to disseminate information and material of social and cultural benefit to the child and in accordance with the spirit of article 29;

(b) Encourage international co-operation in the production, exchange and dissemination of such information and material from a diversity of cultural, national and international sources;

(c) Encourage the production and dissemination of children's books;

(d) Encourage the mass media to have particular regard to the linguistic needs of the child who belongs to a minority group or who is indigenous;

(e) Encourage the development of appropriate guidelines for the protection of the child from information and material injurious to his or her well-being, bearing in mind the provisions of articles 13 and 18.

Article 18

1. States Parties shall use their best efforts to ensure recognition of the principle that both parents have common responsibilities for the upbringing and development of the child. Parents or, as the case may be, legal guardians, have the primary responsibility for the upbringing and development of the child. The best interests of the child will be their basic concern.

2. For the purpose of guaranteeing and promoting the rights set forth in the present Convention, States Parties shall render appropriate assistance to parents and legal guardians in the performance of their child-rearing responsibilities and shall ensure the development of institutions, facilities and services for the care of children.

3. States Parties shall take all appropriate measures to ensure that children of working parents have the right to benefit from child-care services and facilities for which they are eligible.

Article 19

1. States Parties shall take all appropriate legislative, administrative, social and educational measures to protect the child from all forms of physical or mental violence, injury or abuse, neglect or negligent treatment, maltreatment or exploitation, including sexual abuse, while in the care of parent(s), legal guardian(s) or any other person who has the care of the child.

2. Such protective measures should, as appropriate, include effective procedures for the establishment of social programmes to provide necessary support for the child and for those who have the care of the child, as well as for other forms of prevention and for identification, reporting, referral, investigation, treatment and follow-up of instances of child maltreatment described heretofore, and, as appropriate, for judicial involvement.

Article 20

1. A child temporarily or permanently deprived of his or her family environment, or in whose own best interests cannot be allowed to remain in that environment, shall be entitled to special protection and assistance provided by the State.

2. States Parties shall in accordance with their national laws ensure alternative care for such a child.

3. Such care could include, *inter alia*, foster placement, *kafalah* of Islamic law, adoption or if necessary placement in suitable institutions for the care of children. When considering solutions, due regard shall be paid to the desirability of continuity in a child's upbringing and to the child's ethnic, religious, cultural and linguistic background.

Article 21

States Parties that recognize and/or permit the system of adoption shall ensure that the best interests of the child shall be the paramount consideration and they shall:

(a) Ensure that the adoption of a child is authorized only by competent authorities who determine, in accordance with applicable law and procedures and on the basis of all pertinent and reliable information, that the adoption is permissible in view of the child's status concerning parents, relatives and legal guardians and that, if required, the persons concerned have given their informed consent to the adoption on the basis of such counselling as may be necessary;

(b) Recognize that inter-country adoption may be considered as an alternative means of child's care, if the child cannot be placed in a foster or an adoptive family or cannot in any suitable manner be cared for in the child's country of origin;

(c) Ensure that the child concerned by inter-country adoption enjoys safeguards and standards equivalent to those existing in the case of national adoption;

(d) Take all appropriate measures to ensure that, in inter-country adoption, the placement does not result in improper financial gain for those involved in it;

(e) Promote, where appropriate, the objectives of the present article by concluding bilateral or multilateral arrangements or agreements, and endeavour, within this framework, to ensure that the placement of the child in another country is carried out by competent authorities or organs.

Article 22

1. States Parties shall take appropriate measures to ensure that a child who is seeking refugee status or who is considered a refugee in accordance with applicable international or domestic law and procedures shall, whether unaccompanied or accompanied by his or her parents or by any other person, receive appropriate protection and humanitarian assistance in the enjoyment of applicable rights set forth in the present Convention and in other international human rights or humanitarian instruments to which the said States are Parties.

2. For this purpose, States Parties shall provide, as they consider appropriate, co-operation in any efforts by the United Nations and other competent intergovernmental organizations or non-governmental organizations co-operating with the United Nations to protect and assist such a child and to trace the parents or other members of the family of any refugee child in order to obtain information necessary for reunification with his or her family. In cases where no parents or other members of the family can be found, the child shall be accorded the same protection as any other child permanently or temporarily deprived of his or her family environment for any reason, as set forth in the present Convention.

Article 23

1. States Parties recognize that a mentally or physically disabled child should enjoy a full and decent life, in conditions which ensure dignity, promote self-reliance and facilitate the child's active participation in the community.

2. States Parties recognize the right of the disabled child to special care and shall encourage and ensure the extension, subject to available resources, to the eligible child and those responsible for his or her care, of assistance for which application is made and which is appropriate to the child's condition and to the circumstances of the parents or others caring for the child.

3. Recognizing the special needs of a disabled child, assistance extended in accordance with paragraph 2 of the present article shall be provided free of charge, whenever possible, taking into account the financial resources of the parents or others caring for the child, and shall be designed to ensure that the disabled child has effective access to

and receives education, training, health care services, rehabilitation services, preparation for employment and recreation opportunities in a manner conducive to the child's achieving the fullest possible social integration and individual development, including his or her cultural and spiritual development.

4. States Parties shall promote, in the spirit of international cooperation, the exchange of appropriate information in the field of preventive health care and of medical, psychological and functional treatment of disabled children, including dissemination of and access to information concerning methods of rehabilitation, education and vocational services, with the aim of enabling States Parties to improve their capabilities and skills and to widen their experience in these areas. In this regard, particular account shall be taken of the needs of developing countries.

Article 24

1. States Parties recognize the right of the child to the enjoyment of the highest attainable standard of health and to facilities for the treatment of illness and rehabilitation of health. States Parties shall strive to ensure that no child is deprived of his or her right of access to such health care services.

2. States Parties shall pursue full implementation of this right and, in particular, shall take appropriate measures:

(a) To diminish infant and child mortality;

(b) To ensure the provision of necessary medical assistance and health care to all children with emphasis on the development of primary health care;

(c) To combat disease and malnutrition, including within the framework of primary health care, through, *inter alia*, the application of readily available technology and through the provision of adequate nutritious foods and clean drinking-water, taking into consideration the dangers and risks of environmental pollution;

(d) To ensure appropriate pre-natal and post-natal health care for mothers;

(e) To ensure that all segments of society, in particular parents and children, are informed, have access to education and are supported in the use of basic knowledge of child health and nutrition, the advantages of breastfeeding, hygiene and environmental sanitation and the prevention of accidents;

(f) To develop preventive health care, guidance for parents and family planning education and services.

3. States Parties shall take all effective and appropriate measures with a view to abolishing traditional practices prejudicial to the health of children.

4. States Parties undertake to promote and encourage international co-operation with a view to achieving progressively the full realization of the right recognized in the present article. In this regard, particular account shall be taken of the needs of developing countries.

Article 25

States Parties recognize the right of a child who has been placed by the competent authorities for the purposes of care, protection or treatment of his or her physical or mental health, to a periodic review of the treatment provided to the child and all other circumstances relevant to his or her placement.

Article 26

1. States Parties shall recognize for every child the right to benefit from social security, including social insurance, and shall take the necessary measures to achieve the full realization of this right in accordance with their national law.

2. The benefits should, where appropriate, be granted, taking into account the resources and the circumstances of the child and persons having responsibility for the maintenance of the child, as well as any other consideration relevant to an application for benefits made by or on behalf of the child.

Article 27

1. States Parties recognize the right of every child to a standard of living adequate for the child's physical, mental, spiritual, moral and social development.

2. The parent(s) or others responsible for the child have the primary responsibility to secure, within their abilities and financial capacities, the conditions of living necessary for the child's development.

3. States Parties, in accordance with national conditions and within their means, shall take appropriate measures to assist parents and others responsible for the child to implement this right and shall in case of need provide material assistance and support programmes, particularly with regard to nutrition, clothing and housing.

4. States Parties shall take all appropriate measures to secure the recovery of maintenance for the child from the parents or other persons having financial responsibility for the child, both within the State Party and from abroad. In particular, where the person having financial responsibility for the child lives in a State different from that of the child, States Parties shall promote the accession to international agreements or the conclusion of such agreements, as well as the making of other appropriate arrangements.

Article 28

1. States Parties recognize the right of the child to education, and with a view to achieving this right progressively and on the basis of equal opportunity, they shall, in particular:

(a) Make primary education compulsory and available free to all;

(b) Encourage the development of different forms of secondary education, including general and vocational education, make them available and accessible to every child, and take appropriate measures such as the introduction of free education and offering financial assistance in case of need;

(c) Make higher education accessible to all on the basis of capacity by every appropriate means;

(d) Make educational and vocational information and guidance available and accessible to all children;

(e) Take measures to encourage regular attendance at schools and the reduction of drop-out rates.

2. States Parties shall take all appropriate measures to ensure that school discipline is administered in a manner consistent with the child's human dignity and in conformity with the present Convention.

3. States Parties shall promote and encourage international co-operation in matters relating to education, in particular with a view to contributing to the elimination of ignorance and illiteracy throughout the world and facilitating access to scientific and technical knowledge and modern teaching methods. In this regard, particular account shall be taken of the needs of developing countries.

Article 29

1. States Parties agree that the education of the child shall be directed to:

(a) The development of the child's personality, talents and mental and physical abilities to their fullest potential;

(b) The development of respect for human rights and fundamental freedoms, and for the principles enshrined in the Charter of the United Nations;

(c) The development of respect for the child's parents, his or her own cultural identity, language and values, for the national values of the country in which the child is living, the country from which he or she may originate, and for civilizations different from his or her own;

(d) The preparation of the child for responsible life in a free society, in the spirit of understanding, peace, tolerance, equality of sexes, and friendship among all peoples, ethnic, national and religious groups and persons of indigenous origin;

(e) The development of respect for the natural environment.

2. No part of the present article or article 28 shall be construed so as to interfere with the liberty of individuals and bodies to establish and direct educational institutions, subject always to the observance of the principle set forth in paragraph 1 of the present article and to the requirements that the education given in such institutions shall conform to such minimum standards as may be laid down by the State.

Article 30

In those States in which ethnic, religious or linguistic minorities or persons of indigenous origin exist, a child belonging to such a minority or who is indigenous shall not be denied the right, in community with other members of his or her group, to enjoy his or her own culture, to profess and practise his or her own religion, or to use his or her own language.

Article 31

1. States Parties recognize the right of the child to rest and leisure, to engage in play and recreational activities appropriate to the age of the child and to participate freely in cultural life and the arts.

2. States Parties shall respect and promote the right of the child to participate fully in cultural and artistic life and shall encourage the provision of appropriate and equal opportunities for cultural, artistic, recreational and leisure activity.

Article 32

1. States Parties recognize the right of the child to be protected from economic exploitation and from performing any work that is likely to be hazardous or to interfere with the child's education, or to be harmful to the child's health or physical, mental, spiritual, moral or social development.

2. States Parties shall take legislative, administrative, social and educational measures to ensure the implementation of the present article. To this end, and having regard to the relevant provisions of other international instruments, States Parties shall in particular:

(a) Provide for a minimum age or minimum ages for admission to employment;

(b) Provide for appropriate regulation of the hours and conditions of employment;

(c) Provide for appropriate penalties or other sanctions to ensure the effective enforcement of the present article.

Article 33

States Parties shall take all appropriate measures, including legislative, administrative, social and educational measures, to protect children from the illicit use of narcotic drugs and psychotropic substances as defined in the relevant international treaties, and to prevent the use of children in the illicit production and trafficking of such substances.

Article 34

States Parties undertake to protect the child from all forms of sexual exploitation and sexual abuse. For these purposes, States Parties shall in particular take all appropriate national, bilateral and multilateral measures to prevent:

(a) The inducement or coercion of a child to engage in any unlawful sexual activity;

(b) The exploitative use of children in prostitution or other unlawful sexual practices;

(c) The exploitative use of children in pornographic performances and materials.

Article 35

States Parties shall take all appropriate national, bilateral and multilateral measures to prevent the abduction of, the sale of or traffic in children for any purpose or in any form.

Article 36

States Parties shall protect the child against all other forms of exploitation prejudicial to any aspects of the child's welfare.

Article 37

States Parties shall ensure that:

(a) No child shall be subjected to torture or other cruel, inhuman or degrading treatment or punishment. Neither capital punishment nor life imprisonment without possibility of release shall be imposed for offences committed by persons below eighteen years of age;

(b) No child shall be deprived of his or her liberty unlawfully or arbitrarily. The arrest, detention or imprisonment of a child shall be in conformity with the law and shall be used only as a measure of last resort and for the shortest appropriate period of time;

(c) Every child deprived of liberty shall be treated with humanity and respect for the inherent dignity of the human person, and in a manner which takes into account the needs of persons of his or her age. In particular, every child deprived of liberty shall be separated from adults unless it is considered in the child's best interest not to do so and shall have the right to maintain contact with his or her family through correspondence and visits, save in exceptional circumstances;

(d) Every child deprived of his or her liberty shall have the right to prompt access to legal and other appropriate assistance, as well as the right to challenge the legality of the deprivation of his or her liberty before a court or other competent, independent and impartial authority, and to a prompt decision on any such action.

Article 38

1. States Parties undertake to respect and to ensure respect for rules of international humanitarian law applicable to them in armed conflicts which are relevant to the child.

2. States Parties shall take all feasible measures to ensure that persons who have not attained the age of fifteen years do not take a direct part in hostilities.

3. States Parties shall refrain from recruiting any person who has not attained the age of fifteen years into their armed forces. In recruiting among those persons who have attained the age of fifteen years but who have not attained the age of eighteen years, States Parties shall endeavour to give priority to those who are oldest.

4. In accordance with their obligations under international humanitarian law to protect the civilian population in armed conflicts, States Parties shall take all feasible measures to ensure protection and care of children who are affected by an armed conflict.

Article 39

States Parties shall take all appropriate measures to promote physical and psychological recovery and social reintegration of a child victim of: any form of neglect, exploitation, or abuse; torture or any other form of cruel, inhuman or degrading treatment or punishment; or armed conflicts. Such recovery and reintegration shall take place in an environment which fosters the health, self-respect and dignity of the child.

Article 40

1. States Parties recognize the right of every child alleged as, accused of, or recognized as having infringed the penal law to be treated in a manner consistent with the promotion of the child's sense of dignity and worth, which reinforces the child's respect for the human rights and fundamental freedoms of others and which takes into account the child's age and the desirability of promoting the child's reintegration and the child's assuming a constructive role in society.

2. To this end, and having regard to the relevant provisions of international instruments, States Parties shall, in particular, ensure that:

(a) No child shall be alleged as, be accused of, or recognized as having infringed the penal law by reason of acts or omissions that were not prohibited by national or international law at the time they were committed;

(b) Every child alleged as or accused of having infringed the penal law has at least the following guarantees:

(i) To be presumed innocent until proven guilty according to law;

(ii) To be informed promptly and directly of the charges against him or her, and, if appropriate, through his or her parents or legal guardians, and to have legal or other appropriate assistance in the preparation and presentation of his or her defence;

(iii) To have the matter determined without delay by a competent, independent and impartial authority or judicial body in a fair hearing according to law, in the presence of legal or other appropriate assistance and, unless it is considered not to be in the best interest of the child, in particular, taking into account his or her age or situation, his or her parents or legal guardians;

(iv) Not to be compelled to give testimony or to confess guilt; to examine or have examined adverse witnesses and to obtain the participation and examination of witnesses on his or her behalf under conditions of equality;

(v) If considered to have infringed the penal law, to have this decision and any measures imposed in consequence thereof reviewed by a higher competent, independent and impartial authority or judicial body according to law;

(vi) To have the free assistance of an interpreter if the child cannot understand or speak the language used;

(vii) To have his or her privacy fully respected at all stages of the proceedings.

3. States Parties shall seek to promote the establishment of laws, procedures, authorities and institutions specifically applicable to children alleged as, accused of, or recognized as having infringed the penal law, and, in particular:

(a) The establishment of a minimum age below which children shall be presumed not to have the capacity to infringe the penal law;

(b) Whenever appropriate and desirable, measures for dealing with such children without resorting to judicial proceedings, providing that human rights and legal safeguards are fully respected.

4. A variety of dispositions, such as care, guidance and supervision orders; counselling; probation; foster care; education and vocational training programmes and other alternatives to institutional care shall be available to ensure that children are dealt with in a manner appropriate to their well-being and proportionate both to their circumstances and the offence.

Article 41

Nothing in the present Convention shall affect any provisions which are more conducive to the realization of the rights of the child and which may be contained in:

(a) The law of a State Party; or

(b) International law in force for that State.

PART II

Article 42

States Parties undertake to make the principles and provisions of the Convention widely known, by appropriate and active means, to adults and children alike.

Article 43

1. For the purpose of examining the progress made by States Parties in achieving the realization of the obligations undertaken in the present Convention, there shall be established a Committee on the Rights of the Child, which shall carry out the functions hereinafter provided.

2. The Committee shall consist of ten experts of high moral standing and recognized competence in the field covered by this Convention. The members of the Committee shall be elected by States Parties from among their nationals and shall serve in their personal capacity, consideration being given to equitable geographical distribution, as well as to the principal legal systems.

3. The members of the Committee shall be elected by secret ballot from a list of persons nominated by States Parties. Each State Party may nominate one person from among its own nationals.

4. The initial election to the Committee shall be held no later than six months after the date of the entry into force of the present Convention and thereafter every second year. At least four months before the date of each election, the Secretary-General of the United Nations shall address a letter to States Parties inviting them to submit their nominations within two months. The Secretary-General shall subsequently prepare a list in alphabetical order of all persons thus nominated, indicating States Parties which have nominated them, and shall submit it to the States Parties to the present Convention.

5. The elections shall be held at meetings of States Parties convened by the Secretary-General at United Nations Headquarters. At those meetings, for which two thirds of States Parties shall constitute a quorum, the persons elected to the Committee shall be those who obtain the largest number of votes and an absolute majority of the votes of the representatives of States Parties present and voting.

6. The members of the Committee shall be elected for a term of four years. They shall be eligible for re-election if renominated. The term of five of the members elected at the first election shall expire at the end of two years; immediately after the first election, the names of these five members shall be chosen by lot by the Chairman of the meeting.

7. If a member of the Committee dies or resigns or declares that for any other cause he or she can no longer perform the duties of the Committee, the State Party which nominated the member shall appoint another expert from among its nationals to serve for the remainder of the term, subject to the approval of the Committee.

8. The Committee shall establish its own rules of procedure.

9. The Committee shall elect its officers for a period of two years.

10. The meetings of the Committee shall normally be held at United Nations Headquarters or at any other convenient place as determined by the Committee. The Committee shall normally meet annually. The duration of the meetings of the Committee shall be determined, and reviewed, if necessary, by a meeting of the States Parties to the present Convention, subject to the approval of the General Assembly.

11. The Secretary-General of the United Nations shall provide the necessary staff and facilities for the effective performance of the functions of the Committee under the present Convention.

12. With the approval of the General Assembly, the members of the Committee established under the present Convention shall receive emoluments from United Nations resources on such terms and conditions as the Assembly may decide.

Article 44

1. States Parties undertake to submit to the Committee, through the Secretary-General of the United Nations, reports on the measures they have adopted which give effect to the rights recognized herein and on the progress made on the enjoyment of those rights:

(a) Within two years of the entry into force of the Convention for the State Party concerned;

(b) Thereafter every five years.

2. Reports made under the present article shall indicate factors and difficulties, if any, affecting the degree of fulfilment of the obligations under the present Convention. Reports shall also contain sufficient information to provide

the Committee with a comprehensive understanding of the implementation of the Convention in the country concerned.

3. A State Party which has submitted a comprehensive initial report to the Committee need not, in its subsequent reports submitted in accordance with paragraph 1 (b) of the present article, repeat basic information previously provided.

4. The Committee may request from States Parties further information relevant to the implementation of the Convention.

5. The Committee shall submit to the General Assembly, through the Economic and Social Council, every two years, reports on its activities.

6. States Parties shall make their reports widely available to the public in their own countries.

Article 45

In order to foster the effective implementation of the Convention and to encourage international co-operation in the field covered by the Convention:

(a) The specialized agencies, the United Nations Children's Fund, and other United Nations organs shall be entitled to be represented at the consideration of the implementation of such provisions of the present Convention as fall within the scope of their mandate. The Committee may invite the specialized agencies, the United Nations Children's Fund and other competent bodies as it may consider appropriate to provide expert advice on the implementation of the Convention in areas falling within the scope of their respective mandates. The Committee may invite the specialized agencies, the United Nations Children's Fund, and other United Nations organs to submit reports on the implementation of the Convention in areas falling within the scope of their activities;

(b) The Committee shall transmit, as it may consider appropriate, to the specialized agencies, the United Nations Children's Fund and other competent bodies, any reports from States Parties that contain a request, or indicate a need, for technical advice or assistance, along with the Committee's observations and suggestions, if any, on these requests or indications;

(c) The Committee may recommend to the General Assembly to request the Secretary-General to undertake on its behalf studies on specific issues relating to the rights of the child;

(d) The Committee may make suggestions and general recommendations based on information received pursuant to articles 44 and 45 of the present Convention. Such suggestions and general recommendations shall be transmitted to any State Party concerned and reported to the General Assembly, together with comments, if any, from States Parties.

PART III

Article 46

The present Convention shall be open for signature by all States.

Article 47

The present Convention is subject to ratification. Instruments of ratification shall be deposited with the Secretary-General of the United Nations.

Article 48

The present Convention shall remain open for accession by any State. The instruments of accession shall be deposited with the Secretary-General of the United Nations.

Article 49

1. The present Convention shall enter into force on the thirtieth day following the date of deposit with the Secretary-General of the United Nations of the twentieth instrument of ratification or accession.

2. For each State ratifying or acceding to the Convention after the deposit of the twentieth instrument of ratification or accession, the Convention shall enter into force on the thirtieth day after the deposit by such State of its instrument of ratification or accession.

Article 50

1. Any State Party may propose an amendment and file it with the Secretary-General of the United Nations. The Secretary-General shall thereupon communicate the proposed amendment to States Parties, with a request that they indicate whether they favour a conference of States Parties for the purpose of considering and voting upon the proposals. In the event that, within four months from the date of such communication, at least one third of the States Parties favour such a conference, the Secretary-General shall convene the conference under the auspices of the United Nations. Any amendment adopted by a majority of States Parties present and voting at the conference shall be submitted to the General Assembly for approval.

2. An amendment adopted in accordance with paragraph 1 of the present article shall enter into force when it has been approved by the General Assembly of the United Nations and accepted by a two-thirds majority of States Parties.

3. When an amendment enters into force, it shall be binding on those States Parties which have accepted it, other States Parties still being bound by the provisions of the present Convention and any earlier amendments which they have accepted.

Article 51

1. The Secretary-General of the United Nations shall receive and circulate to all States the text of reservations made by States at the time of ratification or accession.

2. A reservation incompatible with the object and purpose of the present Convention shall not be permitted.

3. Reservations may be withdrawn at any time by notification to that effect addressed to the Secretary-General of the United Nations, who shall then inform all States. Such notification shall take effect on the date on which it is received by the Secretary-General.

Article 52

A State Party may denounce the present Convention by written notification to the Secretary-General of the United Nations. Denunciation becomes effective one year after the date of receipt of the notification by the Secretary-General.

Article 53

The Secretary-General of the United Nations is designated as the depositary of the present Convention.

Article 54

The original of the present Convention, of which the Arabic, Chinese, English, French, Russian and Spanish texts are equally authentic, shall be deposited with the Secretary-General of the United Nations.

IN WITNESS THEREOF the undersigned plenipotentiaries, being duly authorized thereto by their respective governments, have signed the present Convention.

Declaration on the Rights of Persons belonging to National or Ethnic, Religious and Linguistic Minorities

Adopted by General Assembly resolution 47/135 of 18 December 1992

The General Assembly,

Reaffirming that one of the basic aims of the United Nations, as proclaimed in the Charter, is to promote and encourage respect for human rights and for fundamental freedoms for all, without distinction as to race, sex, language or religion,

Reaffirming faith in fundamental human rights, in the dignity and worth of the human person, in the equal rights of men and women and of nations large and small,

Desiring to promote the realization of the principles contained in the Charter, the Universal Declaration of Human Rights, the Convention on the Prevention and Punishment of the Crime of Genocide, the International Convention on the Elimination of All Forms of Racial Discrimination, the International Covenant on Civil and Political Rights, the International Covenant on Economic, Social and Cultural Rights, the Declaration on the Elimination of All Forms of Intolerance and of Discrimination Based on Religion or Belief, and the Convention on the Rights of the Child, as well as other relevant international instruments that have been adopted at the universal or regional level and those concluded between individual States Members of the United Nations,

Inspired by the provisions of article 27 of the International Covenant on Civil and Political Rights concerning the rights of persons belonging to ethnic, religious or linguistic minorities,

Considering that the promotion and protection of the rights of persons belonging to national or ethnic, religious and linguistic minorities contribute to the political and social stability of States in which they live,

Emphasizing that the constant promotion and realization of the rights of persons belonging to national or ethnic, religious and linguistic minorities, as an integral part of the development of society as a whole and within a democratic framework based on the rule of law, would contribute to the strengthening of friendship and co-operation among peoples and States,

Considering that the United Nations has an important role to play regarding the protection of minorities,

Bearing in mind the work done so far within the United Nations system, in particular by the Commission on Human Rights, the Subcommission on Prevention of Discrimination and Protection of Minorities and the bodies established pursuant to the International Covenants on Human Rights and other relevant international human rights instruments in promoting and protecting the rights of persons belonging to national or ethnic, religious and linguistic minorities,

Taking into account the important work which is done by intergovernmental and non-governmental organizations in protecting minorities and in promoting and protecting the rights of persons belonging to national or ethnic, religious and linguistic minorities,

Recognizing the need to ensure even more effective implementation of international human rights instruments with regard to the rights of persons belonging to national or ethnic, religious and linguistic minorities,

Proclaims this Declaration on the Rights of Persons Belonging to National or Ethnic, Religious and Linguistic Minorities:

Article 1

1. States shall protect the existence and the national or ethnic, cultural, religious and linguistic identity of minorities within their respective territories and shall encourage conditions for the promotion of that identity.

2. States shall adopt appropriate legislative and other measures to achieve those ends.

Article 2

1. Persons belonging to national or ethnic, religious and linguistic minorities (hereinafter referred to as persons belonging to minorities) have the right to enjoy their own culture, to profess and practise their own religion, and to use their own language, in private and in public, freely and without interference or any form of discrimination.

2. Persons belonging to minorities have the right to participate effectively in cultural, religious, social, economic and public life.

3. Persons belonging to minorities have the right to participate effectively in decisions on the national and, where appropriate, regional level concerning the minority to which they belong or the regions in which they live, in a manner not incompatible with national legislation.

4. Persons belonging to minorities have the right to establish and maintain their own associations.

5. Persons belonging to minorities have the right to establish and maintain, without any discrimination, free and peaceful contacts with other members of their group and with persons belonging to other minorities, as well as contacts across frontiers with citizens of other States to whom they are related by national or ethnic, religious or linguistic ties.

Article 3

1. Persons belonging to minorities may exercise their rights, including those set forth in the present Declaration, individually as well as in community with other members of their group, without any discrimination.

2. No disadvantage shall result for any person belonging to a minority as the consequence of the exercise or non-exercise of the rights set forth in the present Declaration.

Article 4

1. States shall take measures where required to ensure that persons belonging to minorities may exercise fully and effectively all their human rights and fundamental freedoms without any discrimination and in full equality before the law.

2. States shall take measures to create favourable conditions to enable persons belonging to minorities to express their characteristics and to develop their culture, language, religion, traditions and customs, except where specific practices are in violation of national law and contrary to international standards.

3. States should take appropriate measures so that, wherever possible, persons belonging to minorities may have adequate opportunities to learn their mother tongue or to have instruction in their mother tongue.

4. States should, where appropriate, take measures in the field of education, in order to encourage knowledge of the history, traditions, language and culture of the minorities existing within their territory. Persons belonging to minorities should have adequate opportunities to gain knowledge of the society as a whole.

5. States should consider appropriate measures so that persons belonging to minorities may participate fully in the economic progress and development in their country.

Article 5

1. National policies and programmes shall be planned and implemented with due regard for the legitimate interests of persons belonging to minorities.

2. Programmes of co-operation and assistance among States should be planned and implemented with due regard for the legitimate interests of persons belonging to minorities.

Article 6

States should co-operate on questions relating to persons belonging to minorities, inter alia, exchanging information and experiences, in order to promote mutual understanding and confidence.

Article 7

States should co-operate in order to promote respect for the rights set forth in the present Declaration.

Article 8

1. Nothing in the present Declaration shall prevent the fulfilment of international obligations of States in relation to persons belonging to minorities. In particular, States shall fulfil in good faith the obligations and commitments they have assumed under international treaties and agreements to which they are parties.

2. The exercise of the rights set forth in the present Declaration shall not prejudice the enjoyment by all persons of universally recognized human rights and fundamental freedoms.

3. Measures taken by States to ensure the effective enjoyment of the rights set forth in the present Declaration shall not *prima facie* be considered contrary to the principle of equality contained in the Universal Declaration of Human Rights.

4. Nothing in the present Declaration may be construed as permitting any activity contrary to the purposes and principles of the United Nations, including sovereign equality, territorial integrity and political independence of States.

Article 9

The specialized agencies and other organizations of the United Nations system shall contribute to the full realization of the rights and principles set forth in the present Declaration, within their respective fields of competence.

The Vienna Declaration and Programme of Action, 1993, Selected Parts

THE VIENNA DECLARATION AND PROGRAMME OF ACTION

[Adopted by the World Conference on Human Rights on 25 June 1993. UN Doc.A/CONF.157/23]

Part I

* * * *

19. Considering the importance of the promotion and protection of the rights of persons belonging to minorities and the contribution of such promotion and protection to the political and social stability of the States in which such persons live,

The World Conference on Human Rights reaffirms the obligation of States to ensure that persons belonging to minorities may exercise fully and effectively all human rights and fundamental freedoms without any discrimination and in full equality before the law in accordance with the Declaration on the Rights of Persons Belonging to National or Ethnic, Religious and Linguistic Minorities.

The persons belonging to minorities have the right to enjoy their own culture, to profess and practise their own religion and to use their own language in private and in public, freely and without interference or any form of discrimination.

20. The World Conference on Human Rights recognizes the inherent dignity and the unique contribution of indigenous people to the development and plurality of society and strongly reaffirms the commitment of the international community to their economic, social and cultural well-being and their enjoyment of the fruits of sustainable development. States should ensure the full and free participation of indigenous people in all aspects of society, in particular in matters of concern to them. Considering the importance of the promotion and protection of the rights of indigenous people, and the contribution of such promotion and protection to the political and social stability of the States in which such people live, States should, in accordance with international law, take concerted positive steps to ensure respect for all human rights and fundamental freedoms of indigenous people, on the basis of equality and non-discrimination, and recognize the value and diversity of their distinct identities, cultures and social organization.

* * * *

Part II

* * * *

B. Equality, dignity and tolerance

* * * *

2. *Persons belonging to national or ethnic, religious and linguistic minorities*

25. The World Conference on Human Rights calls on the Commission on Human Rights to examine ways and means to promote and protect effectively the rights of persons belonging to minorities as set out in the Declaration on the Rights of Persons belonging to National or Ethnic, Religious and Linguistic Minorities. In this context, the World Conference on Human Rights calls upon the Centre for Human Rights to provide, at the request of Governments concerned and as part of its programme of advisory services and technical assistance, qualified expertise on minority issues and human rights, as well as on the prevention and resolution of disputes, to assist in existing or potential situations involving minorities.

26. The World Conference on Human Rights urges States and the international community to promote and protect the rights of persons belonging to national or ethnic, religious and linguistic minorities in accordance with the Declaration on the Rights of Persons belonging to National or Ethnic, Religious and Linguistic Minorities.

27. Measures to be taken, where appropriate, should include facilitation of their full participation in all aspects of the political, economic, social, religious and cultural life of society and in the economic progress and development in their country.

Indigenous people

28. The World Conference on Human Rights calls on the Working Group on Indigenous Populations of the Sub-Commission on Prevention of Discrimination and Protection of Minorities to complete the drafting of a declaration on the rights of indigenous people at its eleventh session.

29. The World Conference on Human Rights recommends that the Commission on Human Rights consider the renewal and updating of the mandate of the Working Group on Indigenous Populations upon completion of the drafting of a declaration on the rights of indigenous people.

30. The World Conference on Human Rights also recommends that advisory services and technical assistance programmes within the United Nations system respond positively to requests by States for assistance which would be of direct benefit to indigenous people. The World Conference on Human Rights further recommends that adequate human and financial resources be made available to the Centre for Human Rights within the overall framework of strengthening the Centre's activities as envisaged by this document.

31. The World Conference on Human Rights urges States to ensure the full and free participation of indigenous people in all aspects of society, in particular in matters of concern to them.

32. The World Conference on Human Rights recommends that the General Assembly proclaim an international decade of the world's indigenous people, to begin from January 1994, including action-orientated programmes, to be decided upon in partnership with indigenous people. An appropriate voluntary trust fund should be set up for this purpose. In the framework of such a decade, the establishment of a permanent forum for indigenous people in the United Nations system should be considered.

Excerpts from the European Charter for Regional or Minority Languages, Council of Europe 1992

PREAMBLE

The member States of the Council of Europe signatory hereto, Considering that the aim of the Council of Europe is to achieve a greater unity between its members, particularly for the purpose of safeguarding and realising the ideals and principles which are their common heritage;

Considering that the protection of the historical regional or minority languages of Europe, some of which are in danger of eventual extinction, contributes to the maintenance and development of Europe's cultural wealth and traditions;

Considering that the right to use a regional or minority language in private and public life is an inalienable right conforming to the principles embodied in the United Nations International Covenant on Civil and Political Rights, and according to the spirit of the Council of Europe Convention for the Protection of Human Rights and Fundamental Freedoms;

Having regard to the work carried out within the CSCE and in particular to the Helsinki Final Act of 1975 and the Document of the Copenhagen Meeting of 1990;

Stressing the value of interculturalism and multilingualism and considering that the protection and encouragement of regional or minority languages should not be to the detriment of the official languages and the need to learn them;

Realising that the protection and promotion of regional or minority languages in the different countries and regions of Europe represent an important contribution to the building of a Europe based on the principles of democracy and cultural diversity within the framework of national sovereignty and territorial integrity;

Taking into consideration the specific conditions and historical traditions in the different regions of the European States,

Have agreed as follows:

PART I
GENERAL PROVISIONS

Article 1
Definitions

For the purpose of this Charter:

a. the term "regional or minority languages" means languages that are

i. traditionally used within a given territory of a State by nationals of that State who form a group numerically smaller than the rest of the State's population and

ii. different from the official language(s) of that State;

it does not include either dialects of the official language(s) of the State or the languages of migrants;

b. "territory in which the regional or minority language is used" means the geographical area in which the said language is the mode of expression of a number of people justifying the options of the various protective and promotional measures provided for in this Charter;

c. "non-territorial languages" means languages used by nationals of the State which differ from the language or languages used by the rest of the State's population but which, although traditionally used within the territory of the State, cannot be identified with a particular area thereof.

Article 2
Undertakings

1. Each Party undertakes to apply the provisions of Part II to all the regional or minority languages spoken within its territory and complying with the definition in Article 1.

2. In respect of each language specified at the time of ratification, acceptance or approval, in accordance with Article 3, each Party undertakes to apply a minimum of thirty-five paragraphs or sub-paragraphs chosen from among the provisions of Part III of the Charter, including at least three chosen from each of the Articles 8 and 12 and one from each of the Articles 9, 10, 11 and 13.

Article 3
Practical arrangements

1. Each contracting State shall specify in its instrument of ratification, acceptance or approval, each regional or minority language, or official language which is less widely used on the whole or part of its territory, to which the paragraphs chosen in accordance with Article 2, paragraph 2, shall apply.

2. Any Party may, at any subsequent time, notify the Secretary-General that it accepts the obligations arising out of the provisions of any other paragraph of the Charter not already specified in its instrument of ratification, acceptance or approval, or that it will apply paragraph 1 of the present article to other regional or minority languages, or to other official languages which are less widely used on the whole or part of its territory.

3. The undertakings referred to in the foregoing paragraph shall be deemed to form an integral part of the ratification, acceptance or approval and will have the same effect as from their date of notification.

Article 4

Existing regimes of protection

1. Nothing in this Charter shall be construed as limiting or derogating from any of the rights guaranteed by the European Convention on Human Rights.

2. The provisions of this Charter shall not affect any more favourable provisions concerning the status of regional or minority languages or the legal regime of persons belonging to minorities which may exist in a Party or are provided for by relevant bilateral or multilateral agreements.

Article 5

Existing obligations

Nothing in this Charter may be interpreted as implying any right to engage in any activity or perform any action in contravention of the purposes of the Charter of the United Nations or other obligations under international law, including the principle of the sovereignty and territorial integrity of States.

Article 6

Information

The Parties undertake to see to it that the authorities, organisations and persons concerned are informed of the rights and duties established by this Charter.

PART II

OBJECTIVES AND PRINCIPLES PURSUED IN ACCORDANCE WITH ARTICLE 2, PARAGRAPH 1

Article 7

Objectives and principles

1. In respect of regional or minority languages, within the territories in which such languages are used and according to the situation of each language, the Parties shall base their policies, legislation and practice on the following objectives and principles:

a. the recognition of the regional or minority languages as an expression of cultural wealth;

b. the respect of the geographical area of each regional or minority language in order to ensure that existing or new administrative divisions do not constitute an obstacle to the promotion of the regional or minority language in question;

c. the need for resolute action to promote regional or minority languages in order to safeguard them;

d. the facilitation and/or encouragement of the use of regional or minority languages, in speech and writing, in public and private life;

e. the maintenance and development of links, in the fields covered by this Charter, between groups using a regional or minority language and other groups in the State employing a language used in identical or similar form, as well as the establishment of cultural relations with other groups in the State using different languages;

f. the provision of appropriate forms and means for the teaching and study of regional or minority languages at all appropriate states;

g. the provision of facilities enabling non-speakers of a regional or minority language living in the area where it is used to learn it if they so desire;

h. the promotion of study and research on regional or minority languages at universities or equivalent institutions;

i. the promotion of appropriate types of transnational exchanges, in the fields covered by this Charter, for regional or minority languages used in identical or similar form in two or more States.

2. The Parties undertake to eliminate, if they have not yet done so, any unjustified distinction, exclusion, restriction or preference relating to the use of a regional or minority language and intended to discourage or endanger the maintenance or development of a regional or minority language. The adoption of special measures in favour of regional or minority languages aimed at promoting equality between the users of these languages and the rest of the population or which take due account of their specific conditions is not considered to be an act of discrimination against the users of more widely-used languages.

3. The Parties undertake to promote, by appropriate measures, mutual understanding between all the linguistic groups of the country and in particular the inclusion of respect, understanding and tolerance in relation to regional or minority languages among the objectives of education and training provided within their countries and encouragement of the mass media to pursue the same objective.

4. In determining their policy with regard to regional or minority languages, the parties shall take into consideration the needs and wishes expressed by the groups which use such languages, They are encouraged to establish bodies, if necessary, for the purpose of advising the authorities on all matters pertaining to regional or minority languages.

5. The parties undertake to apply, *mutatis mutandis*, the principles listed in paragraphs 1 to 4 above to non-territorial languages. However, as far as these languages are concerned, the nature and scope of the measures to be taken to give effect to this Charter shall be determined in a flexible manner, bearing in mind the needs and wishes, and respecting the traditions and characteristics, of the groups which use the languages concerned.

PART III

MEASURES TO PROMOTE THE USE OF REGIONAL OR MINORITY LANGUAGES IN PUBLIC LIFE IN ACCORDANCE WITH THE UNDERTAKINGS ENTERED INTO UNDER ARTICLE 2, PARAGRAPH 2

Article 8

Education

1. With regard to education, the Parties undertake, within the territory in which such languages are used, according

to the situation of each of these languages, and without prejudice to the teaching of the official languages(s) of the State, to:

a. i. make available pre-school education in the relevant regional or minority languages; or
ii. make available a substantial part of pre-school education in the relevant regional or minority languages; or
iii. apply one of the measures provided for under (i) and (ii) above at least to those pupils whose families so request and whose number is considered sufficient; or
iv. if the public authorities have no direct competence in the field of pre-school education, favour and/or encourage the application of the measures referred to under (i) to (iii) above;

b. i. make available primary education in the relevant regional or minority languages; or
ii. make available a substantial part of primary education in the relevant regional or minority languages; or
iii. provide, within primary education, for the teaching of the relevant regional or minority languages as an integral part of the curriculum; or
iv. apply one of the measures provided for under (i) to (iii) above at least to those pupils whose families so request and whose number is considered sufficient;

c. i. make available secondary education in the relevant regional or minority languages; or
ii. make available a substantial part of secondary education in the relevant regional or minority languages; or
iii. provide, within secondary education, for the teaching of the relevant regional or minority languages as an integral part of the curriculum; or
iv. apply one of the measures provided for under (i) to (iii) above at least to those pupils who, or where appropriate whose families, so wish in a number considered sufficient;

d. i. make available technical and vocational education in the relevant regional or minority languages; or
ii. make available a substantial part of technical and vocational education in the relevant regional or minority languages; or
iii. provide, within technical and vocational education for the teaching of the relevant regional or minority languages as an integral part of the curriculum; or
iv. apply one of the measures provided for under (i) to (iii) above at least to those pupils who, or where appropriate whose families, so wish in a number considered sufficient;

e. i. make available university and other higher education in regional or minority languages; or
ii. provide facilities for the study of these languages as university and higher education subjects; or
iii. if, by reasons of the role of the State in relation to higher education institutions, sub-paragraph i. and ii. cannot be applied, encourage and/or allow the provision of university and higher education in regional or minority languages or of facilities for the study of these languages as university or higher education subjects;

f. i. arrange for the provision of adult and continuing education courses which are taught mainly or wholly in the regional or minority languages; or
ii. offer such languages as subjects of adult and continuing education; or
iii. if the public authorities have no direct competence in the field of adult education, favour and/or encourage the offering of such languages as subjects of adult and continuing education;

g. Make arrangements to ensure the teaching of the history and the culture which is reflected by the regional or minority language;

h. provide the basic and further training of the teachers required to implement those of paragraphs (a) to (g) accepted by the Party;

i. set up a supervisory body or bodies responsible for monitoring the measures taken and progress achieved in establishing or developing the teaching of regional or minority languages and for drawing up periodic reports of their findings, which will be made public.

2. With regard to education and in respect of territories other than those in which the regional or minority languages are traditionally used, the Parties undertake, if the number of users of a regional or minority language justifies it, to allow, encourage or provide teaching in or of the regional or minority language at all the appropriate stages of education.

Article 9
Judicial authorities

1. The parties undertake, in respect of those judicial districts in which the number of residents using the regional or minority languages justifies the measures specified below, according to the situation of each of these languages and on condition that the use of the facilities afforded by the present paragraph is not considered by the judge to hamper the proper administration of justice:

a. in criminal proceedings:
i. to provide that the courts, at the request of one of the parties, shall conduct the proceedings in the regional or minority languages; and/or
ii. to guarantee the accused the right to use his/her regional or minority language; and/or
iii. to provide that requests and evidence, whether written or oral, shall not be considered inadmissible solely because they are formulated in a regional or minority language; and/or
iv. to produce, on request, documents connected with legal proceedings in the relevant regional or minority language, if necessary by the use of interpreters and translations involving no extra expense for the persons concerned;

b. in civil proceedings:
i. to provide that the courts, at the request of one of the parties, shall conduct the proceedings in the regional or minority languages; and/or

ii. to allow, whenever a litigant has to appear in person before a court, that he or she may use his or her regional or minority language without thereby incurring additional expense; and/or
iii. to allow documents and evidence to be produced in the regional or minority languages if necessary by the use of interpreters and translations;

c. in proceedings before courts concerning administrative matters:
i. to provide that the courts, at the request of one of the parties, shall conduct the proceedings in the regional or minority languages; and/or
ii. to allow, whenever a litigant has to appear in person before a court, that he or she may use his or her regional or minority language without thereby incurring additional expense; and/or
iii. to allow documents and evidence to be produced in the regional or minority languages if necessary by the use of interpreters and translations;

d. to take steps to ensure that the application of sub-paragraphs (i) and (iii) of paragraphs (b) and (c) above and any necessary use of interpreters and translations does not involve extra expense for the persons concerned.

2. The Parties undertake:

a. not to deny the validity of legal documents drawn up within the State solely because they are drafted in a regional or minority language; or

b. not to deny the validity, as between the parties, of legal documents drawn up within the country solely because they are drafted in a regional or minority language, and to provide that they can be invoked against interested third parties who are not users of these languages on condition that the contents of the document are made known to them by the person(s) who invoke(s) it; or

c. not to deny the validity, as between the parties, of legal documents drawn up within the country solely because they are drafted in a regional or minority language.

3. The Parties undertake to make available in the regional or minority languages the most important national statutory texts and those relating particularly to users of these languages, unless they are otherwise provided.

Article 10

Administrative authorities and public services

1. Within the administrative districts of the State in which the number of residents who are users of regional or minority languages justifies the measures specified below and according to the situation of each language, the Parties undertake, as far as this is reasonably possible, to:

a. i. ensure that the administrative authorities use the regional or minority languages; or
ii. ensure that such of their officers as are in contact with the public use the regional or minority languages in their relations with persons applying to them in these languages; or
iii. ensure that users of regional or minority languages may submit oral or written applications and receive a reply in these languages; or
iv. ensure that users of regional or minority languages may submit oral or written applications in these languages; or
v. ensure that users of regional or minority languages may validly submit a document in these languages;

b. make available widely used administrative texts and forms for the population in the regional or minority languages or in bilingual versions;

c. allow the administrative authorities to draft documents in a regional or minority language.

2. In respect of the local and regional authorities on whose territory the number of residents who are users of regional or minority languages is such as to justify the measures specified below, the Parties undertake to allow and/or encourage:

a. the use of regional or minority languages within the framework of the regional or local authority;

b. the possibility for users of regional or minority languages to submit oral or written applications in these languages;

c. the publication by regional authorities of their official documents also in the relevant regional minority languages;

d. the publication by local authorities of their official documents also in the relevant regional or minority languages;

e. the use by regional authorities of regional or minority languages in debates in their assemblies, without excluding, however, the use of the official language(s) of the State;

f. the use by local authorities of regional or minority languages in debates in their assemblies, without excluding, however, the use of the official languages(s) of the State;

g. the use or adoption, if necessary in conjunction with the name in the official language(s), of traditional and correct forms of place-names in regional or minority languages.

3. With regard to public services provided by the administrative authorities or other persons acting on their behalf, the Parties undertake, within the territory in which regional or minority languages are used, in accordance with the situation of each language and as far as this is reasonably possible; to

a. ensure that the regional or minority languages are used in the provision of the service; or

b. allow users of regional or minority languages to submit a request and receive a reply in these languages; or

c. allow users of regional or minority languages to submit a request in these languages.

4. With a view to putting into effect those provisions of paragraphs 1, 2 and 3 accepted by them, the Parties undertake to take one or more of the following measures:

a. translation or interpretation as may be required;
b. recruitment and, where necessary, training of the officials and other public service employees required;
c. compliance as far as possible with requests from public service employees having a knowledge of a regional or minority language to be appointed in the territory in which that language is used.

5. The parties undertake to allow the use or adoption of family names in the regional or minority languages, at the request of those concerned.

Article 11

Media

1. The Parties undertake, for users of the regional or minority languages within the territories in which those languages are spoken, according to the situation of each language, to the extent that the public authorities, directly or indirectly, are competent, have power or play a role in this field, and respecting the principle of the independence and autonomy of the media:

a. to the extent that radio and television carry out a public service mission:
i. to ensure the creation of at least one radio station and one television channel in the regional or minority languages, or
ii. to encourage and/or facilitate the creation of at least one radio station and one television channel in the regional or minority languages, or
iii. to make adequate provision so that broadcasters offer programmes in regional or minority languages;
b. i. to encourage and/or facilitate the creation of at least one radio station in the regional or minority languages, or
ii. to encourage and/or facilitate the broadcasting of radio programmes in the regional or minority languages on a regular basis;
c. i. to encourage and/or facilitate the creation of at least one television channel in the regional or minority languages, or
ii. to encourage and/or facilitate the broadcasting of television programmes in the regional or minority languages on a regular basis;
d. to encourage and/or facilitate the production and distribution of audio and audio-visual works in regional or minority languages;
e. i. to encourage and/or facilitate the creation and/or maintenance of at least one newspaper in the regional or minority languages;
or
ii. to encourage and/or facilitate the publication of newspaper articles in the regional or minority languages on a regular basis;
f. i. to cover the additional costs of those media which use regional or minority languages, wherever the law provides for financial assistance in general for the media; or
ii. to apply existing measures for financial assistance also to audio-visual productions in regional or minority languages;
g. to support the training of journalists and other staff for media using regional or minority languages.

2. The Parties undertake to guarantee freedom of direct reception of radio and television broadcasts from neighbouring countries in a language used in identical or similar form to a regional or minority language, and not to oppose the retransmission of radio and television broadcasts from neighbouring countries in such a language. They further undertake to ensure that no restrictions will be placed on the freedom of expression and free circulation of information in the written press in a language used in identical or similar form to a regional or minority language. The exercise of the above-mentioned freedoms, since it carried with it duties and responsibilities, may be subject to such formalities, conditions, restrictions or penalties as are prescribed by law and are necessary in a democratic society, in the interests of national security, territorial integrity or public safety, for the prevention of disorder or crime, for the protection of health or morals, for the protection of the reputation or rights of others, for preventing disclosure of information received in confidence, or for maintaining the authority and impartiality of the judiciary.

3. The Parties undertake to ensure that the interests of the users of regional or minority languages are represented or taken into account within such bodies as may be established in accordance with the law with responsibility for guaranteeing the freedom and pluralism of the media.

Article 12

Cultural activities and facilities

1. With regard to cultural facilities and activities – especially libraries, video-libraries, cultural centres, museums, archives, academies, theatres and cinemas, as well as literary work and film production, vernacular forms of cultural expression, festivals and the culture industries, including *inter alia* the use of new technologies – the parties undertake, within the territory in which such languages are used and to the extent that the public authorities are competent, have power or play a role in this field, to:

a. encourage types of expression and initiative specific to regional or minority languages and foster the different means of access to works produced in these languages;

b. foster the different means of access in other languages to works produced in regional or minority languages by aiding and developing translation, dubbing, post-synchronisation and subtitling activities;

c. foster access in regional or minority languages to works produced in other languages by aiding and developing translation, dubbing, post-synchronisation and subtitling activities;

d. ensure that the bodies responsible for organising or supporting cultural activities of various kinds make appropriate allowance for incorporating the knowledge and use of regional or minority languages and cultures in the undertakings which they initiate or for which they provide backing;

e. promote measures to ensure that the bodies responsible for organising or supporting cultural activities have at their disposal staff who have a full command of the regional or minority language concerned, as well as of the language(s) of the rest of the population;

f. encourage direct participation by representatives of the users of a given regional or minority language in providing facilities and planning cultural activities;

g. encourage and/or facilitate the creation of a body or bodies responsible for collecting, keeping a copy of and presenting or publishing works produced in the regional or minority languages;

h. if necessary create and/or promote and finance translation and terminological research services, particularly with a view to maintaining and developing appropriate administrative, commercial, economic, social, technical or legal terminology in each regional or minority language.

2. In respect of territories other than those in which the regional or minority languages are traditionally used, the parties undertake, if the number of users of a regional or minority language justifies it, to allow, encourage and/or provide appropriate cultural activities ad facilities in accordance with the preceding paragraph.

3. The parties undertake to make appropriate provision, in pursuing their cultural policy abroad, for regional or minority languages and the cultures they reflect.

Article 13

Economic and social life

1. With regard to economic and social activities, the parties undertake, within the whole country, to:

a. eliminate from their legislation any provision prohibiting or limiting without justifiable reasons the use of regional or minority languages in documents relating to economic or social life, particularly contracts of employment, and in technical documents such as instructions for the use of products or installations;

b. prohibit the insertion in internal regulations of companies and private documents of any clauses excluding or restricting the use of regional or minority languages, at least between users of the same language;

c. oppose practices designed to discourage the use of regional or minority languages in connection with economic or social activities;

d. facilitate and/or encourage the use of regional or minority languages by means other than those specified in the above sub-paragraphs.

2. With regard to economic and social activities, the parties undertake, in so far as the public authorities are competent, within the territory in which the regional or minority languages are used, and as far as this is reasonably possible, to:

a. include in their financial and banking regulations provisions which allow, by means of procedures compatible with commercial practice, the use of regional or minority languages in drawing up payment orders (cheques, drafts, etc.) or other financial documents, or, where appropriate, ensure the implementation of such provisions;

b. in the economic and social sectors directly under their control (public sector), organize activities to promote the use of regional or minority languages;

c. ensure that social care facilities such as hospitals, retirement homes and hostels offer the possibility of receiving and treating in their own language persons using a regional or minority language who are in need of care on grounds of ill-health, old age or for other reasons;

d. ensure by appropriate means that safety instructions are also accessible in regional or minority languages;

e. arrange for information provide by the competent public authorities concerning the rights of consumers to be made available in regional or minority languages.

Article 14

Transfrontier exchanges

The Parties undertake:

a. to apply existing bilateral and multilateral agreements which bind them with the States in which the same language issued in identical or similar form, or if necessary to seek to conclude such agreements, in such a way as to foster contacts between the users of the language in the States concerned in the fields of culture, education, information, vocational training and permanent education;

b. for the benefit of regional or minority languages, to facilitate and promote co-operation across borders, in particular between regional or local authorities in whose territory the same language is used in identical or similar form.

Parliamentary Assembly of the Council of Europe

FORTY-FOURTH ORDINARY SESSION

RECOMMENDATION 1201 (1993)[1]

on an additional protocol on the rights of national minorities to the European Convention on Human Rights

1. The Assembly recalls its Recommendations 1134 (1990) and 1177 (1992), and its Orders No. 456 (1990) and No. 474 (1992) on the rights of minorities. In the texts adopted on 5 February 1992 it asked the Committee of Ministers:

i. to conclude as soon as possible the work under way for the elaboration of a charter for regional or minority languages and to do its utmost to ensure the rapid implementation of the charter;

ii. to draw up an additional protocol on the rights of minorities to the European Convention on Human Rights;

iii. to provide the Council of Europe with a suitable mediation instrument.

2. By adopting the European Charter for Regional or Minority Languages – a Council of Europe convention – on 22 June 1992, the Committee of Ministers gave the Assembly satisfaction on the first point, The charter, on which legislation in our member states will have to be based, will also be able to give guidance to many other states on a difficult and sensitive subject.

3. There remains the rapid implementation of the charter. It is encouraging that when it was opened for signature on 5 November 1992, eleven Council of Europe member states signed it straight away. But one has to go further.

4. The Assembly therefore appeals to member states which have not yet signed the charter to do so and to urge all of them to ratify it speedily, accepting as many of its clauses as possible.

5. The Assembly reserves the right to return, at a later date, to the question of a suitable mediation instrument of the Council of Europe which it has already proposed to set up.

6. It has been advised of the terms of reference given by the Committee of Ministers to the Steering Committee for Human Rights and its Committee of Experts for the Protection of National Minorities and wishes to give its full support to this work and actively promote it.

7. Through the inclusion in the European Convention on Human Rights of certain rights of persons belonging to minorities as well as organisations entitled to represent them, such persons could benefit from the remedies offered by the convention, particularly the right to submit applications to the European Commission and Court of Human Rights.

8. Consequently, the Assembly recommends that the Committee of Ministers adopt an additional protocol on the rights of national minorities to the European Convention on Human Rights, drawing on the text reproduced below, which is an integral part of this recommendation.

9. As this matter is extremely urgent and one of the most important activities currently under way at the Council of Europe, the Assembly also recommends that the Committee of Ministers speed up its work schedule so that the summit of heads of state and government (Vienna, 8 and 9 October 1993) will be able to adopt a protocol on the rights of national minorities and open it for signature on that occasion.

Text of the proposal for an additional protocol to the Convention for the Protection of Human Rights and Fundamental Freedoms, concerning persons belonging to national minorities

Preamble

The member states of the Council of Europe, signatory, hereto,

1. Considering that the diversity of peoples and cultures with which it is imbued is one of the main sources of the richness and vitality of European civilisation;

2. Considering the important contribution of national minorities to the cultural diversity and dynamism of the states of Europe;

3. Considering that only the recognition of the rights of persons belonging to a national minority within a state, and the international protection of those rights, are capable of putting a lasting end to ethnic confrontations, and thus of helping to guarantee justice, democracy, stability and peace;

4. Considering that the rights concerned are those which any person may exercise either singly or jointly;

5. Considering that the international protection of the rights of national minorities is an essential aspect of the international protection of human rights and, as such, a domain for international co-operation.

Have agreed as follows:

Section 1 – Definition

Article 1

For the purposes of this Convention,[2] the expression "national minority" refers to a group of persons in a state who:

a. reside on the territory of that state and are citizens thereof;

b. maintain longstanding, firm and lasting ties with that state;

c. display distinctive ethnic, cultural, religious or linguistic characteristics;

d. are sufficiently representative, although smaller in number than the rest of the population of that state or of a region of that state;

e. are motivated by a concern to preserve together that which constitutes their common identity, including their culture, their traditions, their religion or their language.

Section 2 – General principles

Article 2

1. Membership of a national minority shall be a matter of free personal choice.

2. No disadvantage shall result form the choice or the renunciation of such membership.

Article 3

1. Every person belonging to a national minority shall have the right to express, preserve and develop in complete freedom his/her religious, ethnic, linguistic and/or cultural identity, without being subject to any attempt at assimilation against his/her will.

2. Every person belonging to a national minority may exercise his/her rights and enjoy them individually or in association with others.

Article 4

All persons belonging to a national minority shall be equal before the law. Any discrimination based on membership of a national minority shall be prohibited.

Article 5

Deliberate changes to the demographic composition of the region in which a national minority is settled, to the detriment of that minority, shall be prohibited.

Section 3 – Substantive rights

Article 6

All persons belonging to a national minority shall have the right to set up their own organisations, including political parties.

Article 7

1. Every person belonging to a national minority shall have the right freely to use his/her mother tongue in private and in public, both orally and in writing. This right shall also apply to the use of his/her language in publications and in the audio-visual sector.

2. Every person belonging to a national minority shall have the right to use his/her surname and first names in his/her mother tongue and to official recognition of his/her surname and first names.

3. In the regions in which substantial numbers of a national minority are settled, the persons belonging to a national minority shall have the right to use their mother tongue in their contacts with the administrative authorities and in proceedings before the courts and legal authorities.

4. In the regions in which substantial numbers of a national minority are settled, the persons belonging to that minority shall have the right to display in their language local names, signs, inscriptions and other similar information visible to the public. This does not deprive the authorities of their right to display the above-mentioned information in the official language or languages of the state.

Article 8

1. Every person belonging to a national minority shall have the right to learn his/her mother tongue and to receive an education in his/her mother tongue at an appropriate number of schools and of state educational and training establishments, located in accordance with the geographical distribution of the minority.

2. The persons belonging to a national minority shall have the right to set up and manage their own schools and educational and training establishments within the framework of the legal system of the state.

Article 9

If a violation of the rights protected by this protocol is alleged, every person belonging to a national minority or any representative organisations shall have an effective remedy before a state authority.

Article 10

Every person belonging to a national minority, while duly respecting the territorial integrity of the state, shall have the right to have free and unimpeded contacts with the citizens of another country with whom this minority shares ethnic, religious or linguistic features or a cultural identity.

Article 11

In the regions where they are in a majority the persons belonging to a national minority shall have the right to have at their disposal appropriate local or autonomous authorities or to have a special status, matching the specific historical and territorial situation and in accordance with the domestic legislation of the state.

Section 4 – Implementation of the protocol

Article 12

1. Nothing in this protocol may be construed as limiting or restricting an individual right of persons belonging to a national minority or a collective right of a national minority embodied in the legislation of the contracting state or in an international agreement to which that state is a party.

2. Measures taken for the sole purpose of protecting ethnic groups, fostering their appropriate development and ensuring that they are granted equal rights and treatment with respect to the rest of the population in the administrative, political, economic, social and cultural fields and in other spheres shall not be considered as discrimination.

Article 13

This exercise of the rights and freedoms listed in this protocol fully applies to the persons belonging to the majority in the whole of the state but who constitute a minority in one or several of its regions.

Article 14

The exercise of the rights and freedoms listed in this protocol are not meant to restrict the duties and responsibilities of the citizens of the state. However, this exercise may only be made subject to such formalities, conditions, restrictions or penalties as are prescribed by law and necessary in a democratic society in the interests of national security, territorial integrity or public safety, for the prevention of disorder or crime, for the protection of health or morals or for the protection of the rights and freedoms of others.

Section 5 – Final clauses

Article *15*

No derogation under Article 15 of the Convention from the provisions of this protocol shall be allowed, save in respect of Article 10 of the latter.

Article 16

No reservation may be made under Article 64 of the Convention in respect of the provisions of this protocol.

Article 17

The States Parties shall regard the provisions of Articles 1 to 11 of this protocol as additional articles of the Convention and all the provisions of the Convention shall apply accordingly.

Article 18

This protocol shall be open for signature by the member states of the Council of Europe which are signatories to the Convention. It shall be subject to ratification, acceptance or approval. A member state of the Council of Europe may not ratify, accept or approve this protocol unless it simultaneously ratifies or has previously ratified the Convention. Instruments of ratification, acceptance or approval shall be deposited with the Secretary General of the Council of Europe.

Article 19

1. This protocol shall enter into force on the first day of the month following the date on which five member states of the Council of Europe have expressed their consent to be bound by the protocol in accordance with the provisions of Article 18.

2. In respect of any member state which subsequently expresses its consent to be bound by it, the protocol shall enter into force on the first day of the month following the date of the deposit of the instrument of ratification, acceptance or approval.

Article 20

The Secretary General of the Council of Europe shall notify the member states of the Council of:

a. any signature;

b. the deposit of any instrument of ratification, acceptance or approval;

c. any date of entry into force of this protocol;

d. any other act, notification or communication relating to this protocol.

In witness whereof the undersigned, being duly authorised thereto, have signed this protocol.

Done at Strasbourg this .... day of ...., in English and French, both texts being equally authentic, in a single copy, which shall be deposited in the archives of the Council of Europe. The Secretary General of the Council of Europe shall transmit certified copies to each member state of the Council of Europe.

Notes

1 Assembly debate on 1 February 1993 (22nd Sitting) (see Doc. 6742, report of the Committee on Legal Affairs and Human Rights, Rapporteur: Mr Worms; and Doc. 6749, opinion of the Political Affairs Committee, Rapporteur: Mr de Puig).

2 The term 'Convention' in this text refers to the Convention for the Protection of Human Rights and Fundamental Freedoms.

Framework Convention for the Protection of National Minorities, 1994

Council of Europe, Strasbourg, 8 November 1994
[Document H(94) 10]

The member States of the Council of Europe and the other States, signatories to the present framework Convention,

Considering that the aim of the Council of Europe is to achieve greater unity between its members for the purpose of safeguarding and realising the ideals and principles which are their common heritage;

Considering that one of the methods by which that aim is to be pursued is the maintenance and further realisation of human rights and fundamental freedoms;

Wishing to follow up the Declaration of the Heads of State and Government of the member States of the Council of Europe adopted in Vienna on 9 October 1993;

Being resolved to protect within their respective territories the existence of national minorities;

Considering that the upheavals of European history have shown that the protection of national minorities is essential to stability, democratic security and peace in this continent;

Considering that a pluralist and genuinely democratic society should not only respect the ethnic, cultural, linguistic and religious identity of each person belonging to a national minority, but also create appropriate conditions enabling them to express, preserve and develop this identity;

Considering that the creation of a climate of tolerance and dialogue is necessary to enable cultural diversity to be a source and a factor, not of division, but of enrichment for each society;

Considering that the realisation of a tolerant and prosperous Europe does not depend solely on co-operation between States but also requires transfrontier co-operation between local and regional authorities without prejudice to the constitution and territorial integrity of each State;

Having regard to the Convention for the Protection of Human Rights and Fundamental Freedoms and the Protocols thereto;

Having regard to the commitments concerning the protection of national minorities in United Nations conventions and declarations and in the documents of the Conference on Security and Co-operation in Europe, particularly the Copenhagen Document of 29 June 1990;

Being resolved to define the principles to be respected and the obligations which flow from them, in order to ensure, in the member States and such other States as may become Parties to the present instrument, the effective protection of national minorities and of the rights and freedoms of persons belonging to those minorities, within the rule of law, respecting the territorial integrity and national sovereignty of states;

Being determined to implement the principles set out in this framework Convention through national legislation and appropriate governmental policies,

Have agreed as follows:

Section I

Article 1

The protection of national minorities and of the rights and freedoms of persons belonging to those minorities forms an integral part of the international protection of human rights, and as such falls within the scope of international co-operation.

Article 2

The provisions of this framework Convention shall be applied in good faith, in a spirit of understanding and tolerance and in conformity with the principles of good neighbourliness, friendly relations and co-operation between States.

Article 3

1. Every person belonging to a national minority shall have the right freely to choose to be treated or not to be treated as such and no disadvantage shall result from this choice or from the exercise of the rights which are connected to that choice.

2. Persons belonging to national minorities may exercise the rights and enjoy the freedoms flowing from the principles enshrined in the present framework Convention individually as well as in community with others.

Section II

Article 4

1. The Parties undertake to guarantee to persons belonging to national minorities the right of equality before the law and of equal protection of the law. In this respect, any discrimination based on belonging to a national minority shall be prohibited.

2. The Parties undertake to adopt, where necessary, adequate measures in order to promote, in all areas of economic, social, political and cultural life, full and effective equality between persons belonging to a national minority and those belonging to the majority. In this respect, they shall take due account of the specific conditions of the persons belonging to national minorities.

3. The measures adopted in accordance with paragraph 2 shall not be considered to be an act of discrimination.

Article 5

1. The Parties undertake to promote the conditions necessary for persons belonging to national minorities to maintain and develop their culture, and to preserve the essential elements of their identity, namely their religion, language, traditions and cultural heritage.

2. Without prejudice to measures taken in pursuance of their general integration policy, the Parties shall refrain from policies or practices aimed at assimilation of persons belonging to national minorities against their will and shall protect these persons from any action aimed at such assimilation.

Article 6

1. The Parties shall encourage a spirit of tolerance and intercultural dialogue and take effective measures to promote mutual respect and understanding and co-operation among all persons living on their territory, irrespective of those

persons' ethnic, cultural, linguistic or religious identity, in particular in the fields of education, culture and the media.

2. The Parties undertake to take appropriate measures to protect persons who may be subject to threats or acts of discrimination, hostility or violence as a result of their ethnic, cultural, linguistic or religious identity.

Article 7

The Parties shall ensure respect for the right of every person belonging to a national minority to freedom of peaceful assembly, freedom of association, freedom of expression, and freedom of thought, conscience and religion.

Article 8

The Parties undertake to recognise that every person belonging to a national minority has the right to manifest his or her religion or belief and to establish religious institutions, organisations and associations.

Article 9

1. The Parties undertake to recognise that the right to freedom of expression of every person belonging to a national minority includes freedom to hold opinions and to receive and impart information and ideas in the minority language, without interference by public authorities and regardless of frontiers. The Parties shall ensure, within the framework of their legal systems, that persons belonging to a national minority are not discriminated against in their access to the media.

2. Paragraph 1 shall not prevent Parties from requiring the licensing, without discrimination and based on objective criteria, of sound radio and television broadcasting, or cinema enterprises.

3. The Parties shall not hinder the creation and the use of printed media by persons belonging to national minorities. In the legal framework of sound radio and television broadcasting, they shall ensure, as far as possible, and taking into account the provisions of paragraph 1, that persons belonging to national minorities are granted the possibility of creating and using their own media.

4. In the framework of their legal systems, the Parties shall adopt adequate measures in order to facilitate access to the media for persons belonging to national minorities and in order to promote tolerance and permit cultural pluralism.

Article 10

1. The Parties undertake to recognise that every person belonging to a national minority has the right to use freely and without interference his or her minority language, in private and in public, orally and in writing.

2. In areas inhabited by persons belonging to national minorities traditionally or in substantial numbers, if those persons so request and where such a request corresponds to a real need, the Parties shall endeavour to ensure, as far as possible, the conditions which would make it possible to use the minority language in relations between those persons and the administrative authorities.

3. The Parties undertake to guarantee the right of every person belonging to a national minority to be informed promptly, in a language which he or she understands, of the reasons for his or her arrest, and of the nature and cause of any accusation against him or her, and to defend himself or herself in this language, if necessary with the free assistance of an interpreter.

Article 11

1. The Parties undertake to recognise that every person belonging to a national minority has the right to use his or her surname (patronym) and first names in the minority language and the right to official recognition of them, according to modalities provided for in their legal system.

2. The Parties undertake to recognise that every person belonging to a national minority has the right to display in his or her minority language signs, inscriptions and other information of a private nature visible to the public.

3. In areas traditionally inhabited by substantial numbers of persons belonging to a national minority, the Parties shall endeavour, in the framework of their legal system, including, where appropriate, agreements with other States, and taking into account their specific conditions, to display traditional local names, street names and other topographical indications intended for the public also in the minority language when there is a sufficient demand for such indications.

Article 12

1. The Parties shall, where appropriate, take measures in the fields of education and research to foster knowledge of the culture, history, language and religion of their national minorities and of the majority.

2. In this context the Parties shall *inter alia* provide adequate opportunities for teacher training and access to textbooks, and facilitate contacts among students and teachers of different communities.

3. The Parties undertake to promote equal opportunities for access to education at all levels for persons belonging to national minorities.

Article 13

1. Within the framework of their education systems, the Parties shall recognise that persons belonging to a national minority have the right to set up and to manage their own private educational and training establishments.

2. The exercise of this right shall not entail any financial obligation for the Parties.

Article 14

1. The Parties undertake to recognise that every person belonging to a national minority has the right to learn his or her minority language.

2. In areas inhabited by persons belonging to national minorities traditionally or in substantial numbers, if there is sufficient demand, the Parties shall endeavour to ensure, as far as possible and within the framework of their education systems, that persons belonging to those minorities have adequate opportunities for being taught the minority language or for receiving instruction in this language.

3. Paragraph 2 of this article shall be implemented without prejudice to the learning of the official language or the teaching in this language.

Article 15

The Parties shall create the conditions necessary for the effective participation of persons belonging to national minorities in cultural, social and economic life and in public affairs, in particular those affecting them.

Article 16

The Parties shall refrain from measures which alter the proportions of the population in areas inhabited by persons belonging to national minorities and are aimed at restricting the rights and freedoms flowing from the principles enshrined in the present framework Convention.

Article 17

1. The Parties undertake not to interfere with the right of persons belonging to national minorities to establish and maintain free and peaceful contacts across frontiers with persons lawfully staying in other States, in particular those with whom they share an ethnic, cultural, linguistic or religious identity, or a common cultural heritage.

2. The Parties undertake not to interfere with the right of persons belonging to national minorities to participate in the activities of non-governmental organisations, both at the national and international levels.

Article 18

1. The Parties shall endeavour to conclude, where necessary, bilateral and multilateral agreements with other States, in particular neighbouring States, in order to ensure the protection of persons belonging to the national minorities concerned.

2. Where relevant, the Parties shall take measures to encourage transfrontier co-operation.

Article 19

The Parties undertake to respect and implement the principles enshrined in the present framework Convention making, where necessary, only those limitations, restrictions or derogations which are provided for in international legal instruments, in particular the Convention for the Protection of Human Rights and Fundamental Freedoms, in so far as they are relevant to the rights and freedoms flowing from the said principles.

Section III

Article 20

In the exercise of the rights and freedoms flowing from the principles enshrined in the present framework Convention, any person belonging to a national minority shall respect the national legislation and the rights of others, in particular those of persons belonging to the majority or to other national minorities.

Article 21

Nothing in the present framework Convention shall be interpreted as implying any right to engage in any activity or perform any act contrary to the fundamental principles of international law and in particular of the sovereign equality, territorial integrity and political independence of States.

Article 22

Nothing in the present framework Convention shall be construed as limiting or derogating from any of the human rights and fundamental freedoms which may be ensured under the laws of any Contracting Party or under any other agreement to which it is a Party.

Article 23

The rights and freedoms flowing from the principles enshrined in the present framework Convention, in so far as they are the subject of a corresponding provision in the Convention for the Protection of Human Rights and Fundamental Freedoms or in the Protocols thereto, shall be understood so as to conform to the latter provisions.

Section IV

Article 24

1. The Committee of Ministers of the Council of Europe shall monitor the implementation of this framework Convention by the Contracting Parties.

2 The Parties which are not members of the Council of Europe shall participate in the implementation mechanism, according to modalities to be determined.

Article 25

1. Within a period of one year following the entry into force of this framework Convention in respect of a Contracting Party, the latter shall transmit to the Secretary General of the Council of Europe full information on the legislative and other measures taken to give effect to the principles set out in this framework Convention.

2. Thereafter, each Party shall transmit to the Secretary General on a periodical basis and whenever the Committee of Ministers so requests any further information of relevance to the implementation of this framework Convention.

3. The Secretary General shall forward to the Committee of Ministers the information transmitted under the terms of this Article.

Article 26

1. In evaluating the adequacy of the measures taken by the Parties to give effect to the principles set out in this framework Convention the Committee of Ministers shall be assisted by an advisory committee, the members of which shall have recognised expertise in the field of the protection of national minorities.

2. The composition of this advisory committee and its procedure shall be determined by the Committee of Ministers within a period of one year following the entry into force of this framework Convention.

Section V

Article 27

This framework Convention shall be open for signature by the member States of the Council of Europe. Up until the date when the Convention enters into force, it shall also be open for signature by any other State so invited by the Committee of Ministers. It is subject to ratification, acceptance or approval. Instruments of ratification, acceptance or approval shall be deposited with the Secretary General of the Council of Europe.

Article 28

1. This framework Convention shall enter into force on the first day of the month following the expiration of a period of three months after the date on which twelve member States of the Council of Europe have expressed their consent to be bound by the Convention in accordance with the provisions of Article 27.

2 In respect of any member State which subsequently expresses its consent to be bound by it, the framework Convention shall enter into force on the first day of the month following the expiration of a period of three months after the date of the deposit of the instrument of ratification, acceptance or approval.

Article 29

1. After the entry into force of this framework Convention and after consulting the Contracting States, the Committee of Ministers of the Council of Europe may invite to accede to the Convention, by a decision taken by the majority provided for in Article 20.d of the Statute of the Council of Europe, any non-member State of the Council of Europe which, invited to sign in accordance with the provisions of Article 27, has not yet done so, and any other non-member State.

2. In respect of any acceding State, the framework Convention shall enter into force on the first day of the month following the expiration of a period of three months after the date of the deposit of the instrument of accession with the Secretary General of the Council of Europe.

Article 30

1. Any State may at the time of signature or when depositing its instrument of ratification, acceptance, approval or accession, specify the territory or territories for whose international relations it is responsible to which this framework Convention shall apply.

2. Any State may at any later date, by a declaration addressed to the Secretary General of the Council of Europe, extend the application of this framework Convention to any other territory specified in the declaration. In respect of such territory the framework Convention shall enter into force on the first day of the month following the expiration of a period of three months after the date of receipt of such declaration by the Secretary General.

3. Any declaration made under the two preceding paragraphs may, in respect of any territory specified in such declaration, be withdrawn by a notification addressed to the Secretary General. The withdrawal shall become effective on the first day of the month following the expiration of a period of three months after the date of receipt of such notification by the Secretary General.

Article 31

1. Any Party may at any time denounce this framework Convention by means of a notification addressed to the Secretary General of the Council of Europe.

2. Such denunciation shall become effective on the first day of the month following the expiration of a period of six months after the date of receipt of the notification by the Secretary General.

Article 32

The Secretary General of the Council of Europe shall notify the member States of the Council, other signatory States and any State which has acceded to this framework Convention, of:

(a) any signature;

(b) the deposit of any instrument of ratification, acceptance, approval or accession;

(c) any date of entry into force of this framework Convention in accordance with Articles 28, 29 and 30;

(d) any other act, notification or communication relating to this framework Convention.

In witness whereof the undersigned, being duly authorised thereto, have signed this framework Convention.

Done at Strasbourg, this 1st day of February 1995, in English and French, both texts being equally authentic, in a single copy which shall be deposited in the archives of the Council of Europe. The Secretary General of the Council of Europe shall transmit certified copies to each member State of the Council of Europe and to any State invited to sign or accede to this framework Convention.

Document of the Copenhagen Meeting of the Conference on the Human Dimension of the CSCE (1990)

* * * * *

Part IV

(30) The Participating States recognize that the questions relating to national minorities can only be satisfactorily resolved in a democratic political framework based on the rule of law, with a functioning independent judiciary. This framework guarantees full respect for human rights and fundamental freedoms, equal rights and status for all citizens, the free expression of all their legitimate interests and aspirations, political pluralism, social tolerance, and the implementation of legal rules that place effective restraints on the abuse of governmental power.

They also recognize the important role of non-governmental organizations, including political parties, trade unionS, human rights organizations and religious groups, in the promotion of tolerance, cultural diversity and the resolution of questions relating to national minorities.

They further reaffirm that respect for the rights of persons belonging to national minorities as part of universally recognized human rights is an essential factor for peace, justice, stability and democracy in the participating States.

(31) Persons belonging to national minorities have the right to exercise fullY and effectively their human rights and fundamental freedoms without any discrimination and in full equality before the law.

The participating States will adopt, where necessary, special measures for the purpose of ensuring to persons belonging to national minorities full equality with the other citizens in the exercise and enjoyment of human rights and fundamental freedoms.

(32) To belong to a national minority is a matter of a person's individual choice and no disadvantage may arise from the exercise of such choice.

Persons belonging to national minorities have the right freely to express, preserve and develop their ethnic, cultural, linguistic or religious identity and to maintain and develop their culture in all its aspects, free of any attempts at assimilation against their will. In particular, they have the right

(32.1) to use freely their mother tongue in private as well as in public;

(32.2) to establish and maintain their own educational, cultural and religious institutions, organizations or associations, which can seek voluntary financial and other contributions as well as public assistance, in conformity with national legislation;

(32.3) to profess and practise their religion, including the acquisition, possession and use of religious materials, and to conduct religioUs educational activities in their mother tongue;

(32.4) to establish and maintain unimpeded contacts among themselves within their country as well as contacts across frontiers with citizens of other States with whom they share a common ethnic or national origin, cultural heritage or religious beliefs;

(32.5) to disseminate, have access to and exchange information in their mother tongue;

(32.6) to establish and maintain organizations or associations within their country and to participate in international non-governmental organizations.

Persons belonging to national minorities can exercise and enjoy their rights individually as well as in community with other members of their group. No disadvantage may arise for a person belonging to a national minority on account of the exercise or non-exercise of any such rights.

(33) The participating States will protect the ethnic, cultural, linguistic and religious identity of national minorities on their territory and create conditions for the promotion of that identity. They will take the necessary measures to that effect after due consultations, including contacts with organizations or associations of such minorities, in accordance with the decision-making procedures of each State.

Any such measures will be in conformity with the principles of equality and non-discrimination with respect to the other citizens of the participating State concerned.

(34) The participating States will endeavour to ensure that persons belonging to national minorities, notwithstanding the need to learn the official language or languages of the State concerned, have adequate opportunities for instruction of their mother tongue or in their mother tongue, as well as, wherever possible and necessary, for its use before public authorities, in conformity with applicable national legislation.

In the context of the teaching of history and culture in educational establishments, they will also take account of the history and culture of national minorities.

(35) The participating States will respect the right of persons belonging to national minorities to effective participation in public affairs, including participation in the affairs relating to the protection and promotion of the identity of such minorities.

The participating States note the efforts undertaken to protect and create conditions for the promotion of the ethnic, cultural, linguistic and religious identity of certain national minorities by establishing, as one of the possible means to achieve these aims, appropriate local or autonomous administrations corresponding to the specific historical and territorial circumstances of such minorities and in accordance with the policies of the State concerned.

(36) The participating States recognize the particular importance of increasing constructive co-operation among themselves on questions relating to national minorities. Such co-operation seeks to promote mutual understanding and confidence, friendly and good-neighbourly relations, international peace, security and justice.

Every participating State will promote a climate of mutual respect, understanding, co-operation and solidarity among all persons living on its territory, without distinction as to ethnic or national origin or religion, and will encourage the solution of problems through dialogue based on the principles of the rule of law.

(37) None of these commitments may be interpreted as implying any right to engage in any activity or perform any action in contravention of the purposes and principles of the Charter of the United Nations, other obligations under international law or the provisions of the Final Act, including the principle of territorial integrity of States.

(38) The participating States, in their efforts to protect and promote the rights of persons belonging to national minorities, will fully respect their undertakings under existing human rights conventions and other relevant international instruments and consider adhering to the relevant conventions, if they have not yet done so, including those providing for a right of complaint by individuals.

(39) The participating States will co-operate closely in the competent international organizations to which they belong, including the United Nations and, as appropriate, the Council of Europe, bearing in mind their on-going work with respect to questions relating to national minorities.

They will consider convening a meeting of experts for a thorough discussion of the issue of national minorities.

(40) The Participating States clearly and unequivocally condemn totalitarianism, racial and ethnic hatred, anti-semitism, xenophobia and discrimination against anyone as well as persecution on religious and ideological grounds. In this context, they also recognize the particular problems of Roma (gypsies).

They declare their firm intention to intensify the efforts to combat these phenomena in all their forms and therefore will

(40.1) take effective measures, including the adoption, in conformity with their constitutional systems and their international obligations, of such laws as may be necessary, to provide protection against persons or groups based on national, racial, ethnic or religious discrimination, hostility or hatred, including anti-semitism;

(40.2) commit themselves to take appropriate and proportionate measures to protect persons or groups who may be subject to threats or acts of discrimination, hostility or violence as a result of their racial, ethnic, cultural, linguistic or religious identity, and to protect their property;

(40.3) take effective measures, in conformity with the constitutional systems, at the national, regional and local levels to promote understanding and tolerance, particularly in the fields of education, culture and information;

(40.4) endeavour to ensure that the objectives of education include special attention to the problem of racial prejudice and hatred and to the development of respect for different civilizations and cultures;

(40.5) recognize the right of the individual to effective remedies and endeavour to recognize, in conformity with national legislation, the right of interested persons and groups to initiate and support complaints against acts of discrimination, including racist and xenophobic acts;

(40.6) consider adhering, if they have not yet done so, to the international instruments which address the problem of discrimination and ensure full compliance with the obligations therein, including those relating to the submission of periodic reports;

(40.7) consider, also, accepting those international mechanisms which allow States and individuals to bring communications relating to discrimination before international bodies.

* * * * *

CSCE Helsinki Document 1992. The Challenges of Change

Helsinki Decisions

I Strengthening CSCE Institutions and Structures

* * * * *

High Commissioner on National Minorities

(23) The Council will appoint a High Commissioner on National Minorities. The High Commissioner provides "early warning" and, as appropriate, "early action" at the earliest possible stage in regard to tensions involving national minority issues that have the potential to develop into a conflict within the CSCE area, affecting peace, stability, or relations between participating States. The High Commissioner will draw upon the facilities of the Office for Democratic Institutions and Human Rights (ODIHR) in Warsaw.

* * * * *

II CSCE High Commissioner on National Minorities

(1) The participating States decide to establish a High Commissioner on National Minorities.

Mandate

(2) The High Commissioner will act under the aegis of the CSO [the Committee of Senior Officials] and will thus be an instrument of conflict prevention at the earliest possible stage.

(3) The High Commissioner will provide "early warning" and, as appropriate, "early action" at the earliest possible stage in regard to tensions involving national minority issues which have not yet developed beyond an early warning stage, but, in the judgement of the High Commissioner, have the potential to develop into a conflict within the CSCE area, affecting peace, stability or relations between participating States, requiring the attention of and action by the Council or the CSO.

(4) Within the mandate, based on CSCE principles and commitments, the High Commissioner will work in confidence and will act independently of all parties directly involved in the tensions.

(5a) The High Commissioner will consider national minority issues occurring in the State of which the High Commissioner is a national or a resident, or involving a national minority to which the High Commissioner belongs, only if all parties directly involved agree, including the State concerned.

(5b) The High Commissioner will not consider national minority issues in situations involving organized acts of terrorism.

(5c) Nor will the High Commissioner consider violations of CSCE commitments with regard to an individual person belonging to a national minority.

(6) In considering a situation, the High Commissioner will take fully into account the availability of democratic means and international instruments to respond to it, and their utilization by the parties involved.

(7) When a particular national minority issue has been brought to the attention of the CSO, the involvement of the High Commissioner will require a request and a specific mandate from the CSO.

Profile, appointment, support

(8) The High Commissioner will be an eminent international personality with long-standing relevant experience from whom an impartial performance of the function may be expected.

(9) The High Commissioner will be appointed by the Council by consensus upon the recommendation of the CSO for a period of three years, which may be extended for one further term of three years only.

(10) The High Commissioner will draw upon the facilities of the ODIHR in Warsaw, and in particular upon the information relevant to all aspects of national minority questions available at the ODIHR.

Early warning

(11) The High Commissioner will:

(11a) collect and receive information regarding national minority issues from sources described below (see Supplement paragraphs (23)-(25));

(11b) assess at the earliest possible stage the role of the parties directly concerned, the nature of the tensions and recent developments therein and, where possible, the potential consequences for peace and stability within the CSCE area;

(11c) to this end, be able to pay a visit, in accordance with paragraph (17) and Supplement paragraphs (27)-(30), to any participating State and communicate in person, subject to the provisions of paragraph (25), with parties directly concerned to obtain first-hand information about the situation of national minorities.

(12) The High Commissioner may during a visit to a participating State, while obtaining first-hand information from all parties directly involved, discuss the questions with the parties, and where appropriate promote dialogue, confidence and co-operation between them.

Provision of early warning

(13) If, on the basis of exchanges of communications and contacts with relevant parties, the High Commissioner concludes that there is a prima facie risk of potential conflict (as set out in paragraph (3)) he/she may issue an early warning, which will be communicated promptly by the Chairman-in-Office to the CSO.

(14) The Chairman-in-Office will include this early warning in the agenda for the next meeting of the CSO. If a State believes that such an early warning merits prompt consultation, it may initiate the procedure set out in Annex 2 of the Summary of Conclusions of the Berlin Meeting of the Council ("Emergency Mechanism").

(15) The High Commissioner will explain to the CSO the reasons for issuing the early warning.

Early action

(16) The High Commissioner may recommend that he/she be authorized to enter into further contact and closer consultations with the parties concerned with a view to possible solutions, according to a mandate to be decided by the CSO. The CSO may decide accordingly.

Accountability

(17) The High Commissioner will consult the Chairman-in-Office prior to a departure for a participating State to address a tension involving national minorities. The Chairman-in-Office will consult, in confidence, the participating State(s) concerned and may consult more widely.

(18) After a visit to a participating State, the High Commissioner will provide strictly confidential reports to the Chairman-in-Office on the findings and progress of the High Commissioner's involvement in a particular question.

(19) After termination of the involvement of the High Commissioner in a particular issue, the High Commissioner will report to the Chairman-in-Office on the findings, results and conclusions. Within a period of one month, the Chairman-in-Office will consult, in confidence, on the findings, results and conclusions the participating State(s) concerned and may consult more widely. Thereafter the report, together with possible comments, will be transmitted to the CSO.

(20) Should the High Commissioner conclude that the situation is escalating into a conflict, or if the High Commissioner deems that the scope for action by the High Commissioner is exhausted, the High Commissioner shall, through the Chairman-in-Office, so inform the CSO.

(21) Should the CSO become involved in a particular issue, the High Commissioner will provide information and, on request, advice to the CSO, or to any other institution or organization which the CSO may invite, in accordance with the provisions of Chapter III of this document, to take action with regard to the tensions or conflict.

(22) The High Commissioner, if so requested by the CSO and with due regard to the requirement of confidentiality in his/her mandate, will provide information about his/her activities at CSCE implementation meetings on Human Dimension issues.

Supplement: Sources of information about national minority issues

(23) The High Commissioner may:

(23a) collect and receive information regarding the situation of national minorities and the role of parties involved therein from any source, including the media and non-governmental organizations with the exception referred to in paragraph (25);

(23b) receive specific reports from parties directly involved regarding developments concerning national minority issues. These may include reports on violations of CSCE commitments with respect to national minorities as well as other violations in the context of national minority issues.

(24) Such specific reports to the High Commissioner should meet the following requirements:

– they should be in writing, addressed to the High Commissioner as such and signed with full names and addresses;

– they should contain a factual account of the developments which are relevant to the situation of persons belonging to national minorities and the role of the parties involved therein, and which have taken place recently, in principle not more than 12 months previously. The reports should contain information which can be sufficiently substantiated.

(25) The High Commissioner will not communicate with and will not acknowledge communications from any person or organization which practises or publicly condones terrorism or violence.

Parties directly concerned

(26) Parties directly concerned in tensions who can provide specific reports to the High Commissioner and with whom the High Commissioner will seek to communicate in person during visit to a participating State are the following:

(26a) governments of participating States, including, if appropriate, regional and local authorities in areas in which national minorities reside;

(26b) representatives of associations, non-governmental organizations, religious and other groups of national minorities directly concerned and in the area of tension, which are authorized by the persons belonging to those national minorities to represent them.

Conditions for travel by the High Commissioner

(27) Prior to an intended visit, the High Commissioner will submit to the participating State concerned specific information regarding the intended purpose of that visit. Within two weeks the State(s) concerned will consult with the High Commissioner on the objectives of the visit, which may include the promotion of dialogue, confidence and co-operation between the parties. After entry the State concerned will facilitate free travel and communication of the High Commissioner subject to the provisions of paragraph (25) above.

(28) If the State concerned does not allow the High Commissioner to enter the country and to travel and communicate freely, the High Commissioner will so inform the CSO.

(29) In the course of such a visit, subject to the provision of paragraph (25) the High Commissioner may consult the parties involved, and may receive information in confidence from any individual, group or organization directly concerned on questions the High Commissioner is addressing. The High Commissioner will respect the confidential nature of the information.

(30) The participating States will refrain from taking any action against persons, organizations or institutions on account of their contact with the High Commissioner.

High Commissioner and involvement of experts

(31) The High Commissioner may decide to request assistance from not more than three experts with relevant expertise in specific matters on which brief, specialized investigation and advice are required.

(32) If the High Commissioner decides to call on experts, the High Commissioner will set a clearly defined mandate and time-frame for the activities of the experts.

(33) Experts will only visit a participating State at the same time as the High Commissioner. Their mandate will be an integral part of the mandate of the High Commissioner and the same conditions for travel will apply.

(34) The advice and recommendations requested from the experts will be submitted in confidence to the High Commissioner, who will be responsible for the activities and for the reports of the experts and who will decide whether and in what form the advice and recommendations will be communicated to the parties concerned. They will be

non-binding. If the High Commissioner decides to make the advice and recommendations available, the State(s) concerned will be given the opportunity to comment.

(35) The experts will be selected by the High Commissioner with the assistance of the ODIHR from the resource list established at the ODIHR as laid down in the Document of the Moscow Meeting.

(36) The experts will not include nationals or residents of the participating State concerned, or any person appointed by the State concerned, or any expert against whom the participating State has previously entered reservations. The experts will not include the participating State's own nationals or residents or any of the persons it appointed to the resource list, or more than one national or resident of any particular State.

Budget

(37) A separate budget will be determined at the ODIHR, which will provide, as appropriate, logistical support for travel and communication. The budget will be funded by the participating States according to the established CSCE scale of distribution. Details will be worked out by the Financial Committee and approved by the CSO.

Excerpts from the Report of the Meeting of Experts on National Minorities, CSCE, Geneva 1991

I.

Recognizing that their observance and full exercise of human rights and fundamental freedoms, including those of persons belonging to national minorities, are the foundation of the New Europe,

Reaffirming their deep conviction that friendly relations among their peoples, as well as peace, justice, stability and democracy, require that the ethnic, cultural, linguistic and religious identity of national minorities be protected, and conditions for the promotion of that identity be created,

Convinced that, in States with national minorities, democracy requires that all persons, including those belonging to national minorities, enjoy full and effective equality of rights and fundamental freedoms and benefit from the rule of law and democratic institutions,

Aware of the diversity of situations and constitutional systems in their countries, and therefore recognizing that various approaches to the implementation of CSCE commitments regarding national minorities are appropriate,

Mindful of the importance of exerting efforts to address national minorities issues, particularly in areas where democratic institutions are being consolidated and questions relating to national minorities are of special concern,

Aware that national minorities form an integral part of the society of the States in which they live and that they are a factor of enrichment of each respective State and society,

Confirming the need to respect and implement fully and fairly their undertakings in the field of human rights and fundamental freedoms as set forth in the international instruments by which they may be bound,

Reaffirming their strong determination to respect and apply, to their full extent, all their commitments relating to national minorities and persons belonging to them in the Helsinki Final Act, the Madrid Concluding Document and the Vienna Concluding Document, the Document of the Copenhagen Meeting of the Conference on the Human Dimension of the CSCE, the Document of the Cracow Symposium on the Cultural Heritage as well as the Charter of Paris for New Europe, the participating States present below the summary of their conclusions.

The representatives of the participating States took as the fundamental basis of their work the commitments undertaken by them with respect to national minorities as contained in the relevant adopted CSCE documents, in particular those in the Charter of Paris for a New Europe and the Document of the Copenhagen Meeting of the Conference on the Human Dimension of the CSCE, which they fully reaffirmed.

II.

The participating States stress the continued importance of a thorough review of implementation of their CSCE commitments relating to persons belonging to national minorities.

They emphasize that human rights and fundamental freedoms are the basis for the protection and promotion of rights of persons belonging to national minorities. They further recognize that questions relating to national minorities can only be satisfactorily resolved in a democratic political framework based on the rule of law, with a functioning independent judiciary. This framework guarantees full respect for human rights and fundamental freedoms, equal rights and status for all citizens, including persons belonging to national minorities, the free expression of all their legitimate interests and aspirations, political pluralism, social tolerance and the implementation of legal rules that place effective restraints on the abuse of governmental power.

Issues concerning national minorities, as well as compliance with international obligations and commitments concerning the rights of persons belonging to them, are matters of legitimate international concern and consequently do not constitute exclusively an internal affair of the respective State.

They note that not all ethnic, cultural, linguistic or religious differences necessarily lead to the creation of national minorities.

III.

Respecting the right of persons belonging to national minorities to effective participation in public affairs, the participating States consider that when issues relating to the situation of national minorities are discussed within their countries, they themselves should have the effective opportunity to be involved, in accordance with the decision-making procedures of each State. They further consider that appropriate democratic participation of persons belonging to national minorities or their representatives in decision-making or consultative bodies constitutes an important element of effective participation in public affairs.

They consider that special efforts must be made to resolve specific problems in a constructive manner and through dialogue by means of negotiations and consultations with a view to improving the situation of persons belonging to national minorities. They recognize that the promotion of dialogue between States, and between States and persons belonging to national minorities, will be most successful when there is a free flow of information and ideas between all parties. They encourage unilateral, bilateral and multilateral efforts by governments to explore avenues for enhancing the effectiveness of their implementation of CSCE commitments relating to national minorities.

The participating States further consider that respect for human rights and fundamental freedoms must be accorded on a non-discriminatory basis throughout society. In areas inhabited mainly by persons belonging to a national minority, the human rights and fundamental freedoms of persons belonging to that minority, of persons belonging to the majority population of the respective State, and of persons belonging to other national minorities residing in these areas will be equally protected.

They reconfirm that persons belonging to national minorities have the right freely to express, preserve and develop their ethnic, cultural, linguistic or religious identity and to maintain and develop their culture in all its aspects, free of any attempts at assimilation against their will.

They will permit the competent authorities to inform the Office for Free Elections of all scheduled public elections on their territories, including those held below national level. The participating States will consider favourably, to the extent permitted by law, the presence of observers at elections held below the national level, including in areas inhabited by national minorities, and will endeavour to facilitate their access.

IV.

The participating States will create conditions for persons belonging to national minorities to have equal opportunity to be effectively involved in the public life, economic activities, and building of their societies.

In accordance with paragraph 31 of the Copenhagen Document, the participating States will take the necessary measures to prevent discrimination against individuals, particularly in respect of employment, housing and education, on the grounds of belonging or not belonging to a national minority. In that context, they will make provision, if they have not yet done so, for effective recourse to redress for individuals who have experienced discriminatory treatment on the grounds of their belonging or not belonging to a national minority, including by making available to individual victims of discrimination a broad array of administrative and judicial remedies.

The participating States are convinced that the preservation of the values and of the cultural heritage of national minorities requires the involvement of persons belonging to such minorities and that tolerance and respect for different cultures are of paramount importance in this regard. Accordingly, they confirm the importance of refraining from hindering the production of cultural materials concerning national minorities, including by persons belonging to them.

The participating States affirm that persons belonging to a national minority will enjoy the same rights and have the same duties of citizenship as the rest of the population.

The participating States reconfirm the importance of adopting, where necessary, special measures for the purpose of ensuring to persons belonging to national minorities full equality with the other citizens in the exercise and enjoyment of human rights and fundamental freedoms. They further recall the need to take the necessary measures to protect the ethnic, cultural, linguistic and religious identity of national minorities on their territory and create conditions for the promotion of that identity; any such measures will be in conformity with the principles of equality and non-discrimination with respect to the other citizens of the participating State concerned.

They recognize that such measures, which taken into account, *inter alia*, historical and territorial circumstances of national minorities, are particularly important in areas where democratic institutions are being consolidated and national minorities issues are of special concern.

Aware of the diversity and varying constitutional systems among them, which make no single approach necessarily generally applicable, the participating States note with interest that positive results have been obtained by some of them in an appropriate manner by, *inter alia*:

– advisory and decision-making bodies in which minorities are represented, in particular with regard to education, culture and religion;

– elected bodies and assemblies of national minority affairs;

– local and autonomous administration, as well as autonomy on a territorial basis, including the existence of consultative, legislative and executive bodies chosen through free and periodic elections;

– self-administration by a national minority of aspects concerning its identity in situations where autonomy on a territorial bias does not apply;

– decentralized or local forms of government;

– bilateral and multilateral agreements and other arrangements regarding national minorities;

– for persons belonging to national minorities, provision of adequate types and level of education in their mother tongue with due regard to the number, geographic settlement patterns and cultural traditions of national minorities;

– funding the teaching of minority languages to the general public, as well as the inclusion of minority languages in teacher-training institutions, in particular in regions inhabited by persons belonging to national minorities;

– in cases where instruction in a particular subject is not provided in their territory in the minority language at all levels, taking the necessary measures to find means of recognizing diplomas issued abroad for a course of study completed in that language;

– creation of government research agencies to review legislation and disseminate information related to equal rights and non-discrimination;

– provision of financial and technical assistance to persons belonging to national minorities who so wish to exercise their right to establish and maintain their own education, cultural and religious institutions, organizations and associations;

– governmental assistance for addressing local difficulties relating to discriminatory practices (e.g. a citizens relations service);

– encouragement of grassroots community relations efforts between minority communities, between majority and minority communities, and between neighbouring communities sharing borders, aimed at helping to prevent local tensions from arising and address conflicts peacefully should they arise; and

– encouragement of the establishment of permanent mixed commissions, either inter-State or regional, to facilitate continuing dialogue between the border regions concerned.

The participating States are of the view that these or other approaches, individually or in combination, could be helpful in improving the situation of national minorities on their territories.

V.

The participating States respect the right of persons belonging to national minorities to exercise and enjoy their rights alone or in community with others, to establish and maintain organizations and associations within their country, and to participate in international non-governmental organizations.

The participating States reaffirm, and will not hinder the exercise of, the right of persons belonging to national minorities to establish and maintain their own education, cultural and religious institutions, organizations and associations.

In this regard, they recognize the major and vital role that individuals, non-governmental organizations, and religious and other groups play in fostering cross-cultural understanding and improving relations at all levels of society, as well as across international frontiers.

They believe that the first-hand observations and experience of such organizations, groups, and individuals can be of great value in promoting the implementation of CSCE commitments relating to persons belonging to national minorities. They therefore will encourage and not hinder the work of such organizations, groups and individuals and welcome their contributions in this area.

The participating States, concerned by the proliferation of acts of racial, ethnic and religious hatred, anti-semitism, xenophobia and discrimination, stress their determination to condemn, on a continuing basis, such acts against anyone.

In this context, they reaffirm their recognition of the particular problems of Roma (gypsies). They are ready to undertake effective measures in order to achieve full equality of opportunity between persons belonging to Roma ordinarily resident in their State and the rest of the resident population. They will also encourage research and studies regarding Roma and the particular problems they face.

They will take effective measures to promote tolerance, understanding, equality of opportunity and good relations between individuals of different origins within their country.

Further, the participating States will take effective measures, including the adoption, in conformity with their constitutional law and their international obligations, if they have not already done so, of laws that would prohibit acts that constitute incitement to violence based on national, racial, ethnic or religious discrimination, hostility or hatred, including anti-semitism, and policies to enforce such laws.

Moreover, in order to heighten public awareness of prejudice and hatred, to improve enforcement of laws against hate-related crime and otherwise to further efforts to address hatred and prejudice in society, they will make efforts to collect, publish on a regular basis, and make available to the public, data about crimes on their respective territories that are based on prejudice as to race, ethnic identity or religion, including the guidelines used for the collection of such data. These data should not contain any personal information.

They will consult and exchange views and information at the international level, including at future meetings of the CSCE, on crimes that manifest evidence of prejudice and hate.

VII.

Convinced that the protection of the rights of persons belonging to national minorities necessitates free flow of information and exchange of ideas, the participating States emphasize the importance of communication between persons belonging to national minorities without interference by public authorities and regardless of frontiers. The exercise of such rights may be subject only to such restrictions as are prescribed by law and are consistent with international standards. They reaffirm that no one belonging to a national minority, simply by virtue of belonging to such a minority, will be subject to penal or administrative sanctions for having had contacts within or outside his/her own country.

In access to the media, they will not discriminate against anyone based on ethnic, cultural, linguistic or religious grounds. They will make information available that will assist the electronic mass media in taking into account, in their programmes, the ethnic, cultural, linguistic and religious identity of national minorities.

They reaffirm that establishment and maintenance of unimpeded contacts among persons belonging to a national minority, as well as contacts across frontiers by persons belonging to a national minority with persons with whom they share a common ethnic or national origin, cultural heritage or religious belief, contribute to mutual understanding and promotes good-neighbourly relations.

They therefore encourage transfrontier co-operation arrangements on a national, regional and local level, *inter alia*, on local border crossings, the preservation of and visits to cultural and historical monuments and sites, tourism, the improvement of traffic, the economy, youth exchange, the protection of the environment and the establishment of regional commissions.

They will also encourage the creation of informal working arrangements (e.g. workshops, committees both within and between the participating States) where national minorities live, to discuss issues of, exchange experience on, and present proposals on, issues related to national minorities.

With a view to improving their information about the actual situation of national minorities, the participating States will, on a voluntary basis distribute, through the CSCE Secretariat, information to other participating States about the situation of national minorities in their respective territories, as well as statements of national policy in that respect.

The participating States will deposit with the CSCE Secretariat copies of the contributions made in the Plenary of the CSCE Meeting of Experts on National Minorities which they wish to be available to the public.

VIII.

The participating States welcome the positive contribution made by the representatives of the United Nations and the Council of Europe to the proceedings of the Geneva Meeting of Experts on National Minorities. They note that the work and activities of these organizations will be of continuing relevance to the CSCE's consideration of national minorities issues.

The participating States note that appropriate CSCE mechanisms may be of relevance in addressing questions relating to national minorities. Further, they recommend that the third Meeting of the Conference on the Human Dimension of the CSCE consider expanding the Human Dimension Mechanism. They will promote the involvement of individuals in the protection of their rights, including the rights of persons belonging to national minorities.

ILO Convention No. 107 of 1957

CONVENTION CONCERNING THE PROTECTION AND INTEGRATION OF INDIGENOUS AND OTHER TRIBAL AND SEMI-TRIBAL POPULATIONS IN INDEPENDENT COUNTRIES

The General Conference of the International Labour Organisation,

Having been convened at Geneva by the Governing Body of the International Labour Office, and having met in its Fortieth Session on 5 June 1957, and

Having decided upon the adoption of certain proposals with regard to the protection and integration of indigenous and other tribal and semi-tribal populations in independent countries, which is the sixth item on the agenda of the session, and

Having determined that these proposals shall take the form of an international Convention, and

Considering that the Declaration of Philadelphia affirms that all human beings have the right to pursue both their material well-being and their spiritual development in conditions of freedom and dignity, of economic security and equal opportunity, and

Considering that there exist in various independent countries indigenous and other tribal and semi-tribal populations which are not yet integrated into the national community and whose social, economic or cultural situation hinders them from benefiting fully from the rights and advantages enjoyed by other elements of the population, and

Considering it desirable both for humanitarian reasons and in the interest of the countries concerned to promote continued action to improve the living and working conditions of these populations by simultaneous action in respect of all the factors which have hitherto prevented them from sharing fully in the progress of the national community of which they form part, and

Considering that the adoption of general international standards on the subject will facilitate action to assure the protection of the populations concerned, their progressive integration into their respective national communities, and the improvement of their living and working conditions, and

Noting that these standards have been framed with the co-operation of the United Nations, the Food and Agriculture Organisation of the United Nations, the United Nations Educational, Scientific and Cultural Organisation and the World Health Organisation, at appropriate levels and in their respective fields, and that it is proposed to seek their continuing co-operation in promoting and securing the application of these standards,

adopts this twenty-sixth day of June of the year one thousand nine hundred and fifty-seven the following Convention, which may be cited as the Indigenous and Tribal Populations Convention, 1957:

PART I. GENERAL POLICY

Article 1

1. This Convention applies to –

(a) members of tribal or semi-tribal populations in independent countries whose social and economic conditions are at a less advanced stage than the stage reached by the other sections of the national community, and whose status is regulated wholly or partially by their own customs or traditions or by special laws or regulation;

(b) members of tribal or semi-tribal populations in independent countries which are regarded as indigenous on account of their descent from the populations which inhabited the country, or a geographical region to which the country belongs, at the time of conquest of colonisation and which, irrespective of their legal status, live more in conformity with the social, economic and cultural institutions of that time than with the institutions of the nation to which they belong.

2. For the purposes of this Convention, the term "semi-tribal" includes groups and persons who, although they are in the process of losing their tribal characteristics, are not yet integrated into the national community.

3. The indigenous and other tribal or semi-tribal populations mentioned in paragraphs 1 and 2 of this Article are referred to hereinafter as "the populations concerned".

Article 2

1. Governments shall have the primary responsibility for developing co-ordinated and systematic action for the protection of the populations concerned and their progressive integration into the life of their respective countries.

2. Such action shall include measures for:

(a) enabling the said populations to benefit on an equal footing from the rights and opportunities which national laws or regulations grant to the other elements of the population;

(b) promoting the social, economic and cultural development of these populations and raising their standard of living;

(c) creating possibilities of national integration to the exclusion of measures tending towards the artificial assimilation of these populations.

3. The primary objective of all such action shall be the fostering of individual dignity, and the advancement of individual usefulness and initiative.

4. Recourse to force or coercion as a means of promoting the integration of these populations into the national community shall be excluded.

Article 3

1. So long as the social, economic and cultural conditions of the populations concerned prevent them from enjoying the benefits of the general laws of the country to which they belong, special measures shall be adopted for the protection of the institutions, persons, property and labour of these populations.

2. Care shall be taken to ensure that such special measures of protection –

(a) are not used as a means of creating or prolonging a state of segregation; and

(b) will be continued only so long as there is need for special protection and only to the extent that such protection is necessary.

3. Enjoyment of the general rights of citizenship, without discrimination, shall not be prejudiced in any way by such special measures of protection.

Article 4

In applying the provisions of this Convention relating to the integration of the populations concerned –

(a) due account shall be taken of the cultural and religious values and of the forms of social control existing among these populations, and of the nature of the problems which face them both as groups and as individuals when they undergo social and economic change;

(b) the danger involved in disrupting the values and institutions of the said populations unless they can be replaced by appropriate substitutes which the groups concerned are willing to accept shall be recognised;

(c) policies aimed at mitigating the difficulties experienced by these populations in adjusting themselves to new conditions of life and work shall be adopted.

Article 5

In applying the provisions of this Convention relating to the protection and integration of the populations concerned, governments shall –

(a) seek the collaboration of these populations and of their representatives;

(b) provide these populations with opportunities for the full development of their initiative;

(c) stimulate by all possible means the development among these populations of civil liberties and the establishment of or participation in elective institutions.

Article 6

The improvement of the conditions of life and work and level of education of the populations concerned shall be given high priority in plans for the over-all economic development of areas inhabited by these populations. Special projects for economic development of the areas in question shall also be so designed as to promote such improvement.

Article 7

1. In defining the rights and duties of the populations concerned regard shall be had to their customary laws.

2. These populations shall be allowed to retain their own customs and institutions where these are not incompatible with the national legal system or the objectives of integration programmes.

3. The application of the preceding paragraphs of this Article shall not prevent members of these populations from exercising, according to their individual capacity, the rights granted to all citizens and from assuming the corresponding duties.

Article 8

To the extent consistent with the interests of the national community and with the national legal system –

(a) the methods of social control practised by the populations concerned shall be used as far as possible for dealing with crimes or offences committed by members of these populations;

(b) where use of such methods of social control is not feasible, the customs of these populations in regard to penal matters shall be borne in mind by the authorities and courts dealing with such cases.

Article 9

Except in cases prescribed in law for all citizens the exaction from the members of the populations concerned of compulsory personal services in any form, whether paid or unpaid, shall be prohibited and punishable by law.

Article 10

1. Persons belonging to the populations concerned shall be specially safeguarded against the improper application of preventive detention and shall be able to take legal proceedings for the effective protection of their fundamental rights.

2. In imposing penalties laid down by general law on members of these populations account shall be taken of the degree of cultural development of the populations concerned.

3. Preference shall be given to methods of rehabilitation rather than confinement in prison.

PART II. LAND

Article 11

The right of ownership, collective or individual, of the members of the populations concerned over the lands which these populations traditionally occupy shall be recognised.

Article 12

1. The populations concerned shall not be removed without their free consent from their habitual territories except in accordance with national laws and regulations for reasons relating to national security, or in the interest of national economic development or of the health of the said populations.

2. When in such cases removal of these populations is necessary as an exceptional measure, they shall be provided with lands of quality at least equal to that of the lands previously occupied by them, suitable to provide for their present needs and future development. In cases where chances of alternative employment exist and where the populations concerned prefer to have compensation in money or in kind, they shall be so compensated under appropriate guarantees.

3. Persons thus removed shall be fully compensated for any resulting loss or injury.

Article 13

1. Procedures for the transmission of rights of ownership and use of land which are established by the customs of the populations concerned shall be respected, within the framework of national laws and regulations, in so far as they satisfy the needs of these populations and do not hinder their economic and social development.

2. Arrangements shall be made to prevent persons who are not members of the populations concerned from taking advantage of these customs or of lack of understanding of the laws on the part of the members of these populations to secure the ownership or use of the lands belonging to such members.

Article 14

National agrarian programmes shall secure to the populations concerned treatment equivalent to that accorded to other sections of the national community with regard to –

(a) the provision of more land for these populations when they have not the area necessary for providing the essentials of a normal existence, or for any possible increase in their numbers;

(b) the provision of the means required to promote the development of the lands which these populations already possess.

PART III. RECRUITMENT AND CONDITIONS OF EMPLOYMENT

Article 15

1. Each Member shall, within the framework of national laws and regulations, adopt special measures to ensure the effective protection with regard to recruitment and conditions of employment of workers belonging to the populations concerned so long as they are not in a position to enjoy the protection granted by law to workers in general.

2. Each Member shall do everything possible to prevent all discrimination between workers belonging to the populations concerned and other workers, in particular as regards –

(a) admission to employment, including skilled employment;

(b) equal remuneration for work of equal value;

(c) medical and social assistance, the prevention of employment injuries, workmen's compensation, industrial hygiene and housing;

(d) the right of association and freedom for all lawful trade union activities, and the right to conclude collective agreements with employers or employers' organisations.

PART IV. VOCATIONAL TRAINING, HANDICRAFT AND RURAL INDUSTRIES

Article 16

Persons belonging to the populations concerned shall enjoy the same opportunities as other citizens in respect of vocational training facilities.

Article 17

1. Whenever programmes of vocational training of general application do not meet the special needs of persons belonging to the populations concerned governments shall provide special training facilities for such persons.
2. These special training facilities shall be based on a careful study of the economic environment, stage of cultural development and practical needs of the various occupational groups among the said populations; they shall, in particular, enable the persons concerned to receive the training necessary for occupations for which these populations have traditionally shown aptitude.
3. These special training facilities shall be provided only so long as the stage of cultural development of the populations concerned requires them; with the advance of the process of integration they shall be replaced by the facilities provided for other citizens.

Article 18

1. Handicrafts and rural industries shall be encouraged as factors in the economic development of the populations concerned in a manner which will enable these populations to raise their standard of living and adjust themselves to modern methods of production and marketing.
2. Handicrafts and rural industries shall be developed in a manner which preserves the cultural heritage of these populations and improves their artistic values and particular modes of cultural expression.

PART V. SOCIAL SECURITY AND HEALTH

Article 19

Existing social security schemes shall be extended progressively, where practicable, to cover –

(a) wage earners belonging to the populations concerned;

(b) other persons belonging to these populations.

Article 20

1. Governments shall assume the responsibility for providing adequate health services for the populations concerned.
2. The organization of such services shall be based on systematic studies of the social, economic and cultural conditions of the populations concerned.
3. The development of such services shall be co-ordinated with general measures of social, economic and cultural development.

PART VI. EDUCATION AND MEANS OF COMMUNICATION

Article 21

Measures shall be taken to ensure that members of the populations concerned have the opportunity to acquire education at all levels on an equal footing with the rest of the national community.

Article 22

1. Education programmes for the populations concerned shall be adapted, as regards methods and techniques, to the stage these populations have reached in the process of social, economic and cultural integration into the national community.
2. The formulation of such programmes shall normally be preceded by ethnological surveys.

Article 23

1. Children belonging to the populations concerned shall be taught to read and write in their mother tongue or, where this is not practicable, in the language most commonly used by the group to which they belong.
2. Provision shall be made for a progressive transition from the mother tongue or the vernacular language to the national language or to one of the official languages of the country.
3. Appropriate measures shall, as far as possible, be taken to preserve the mother tongue or the vernacular language.

Article 24

The imparting of general knowledge and skills that will help children to become integrated into the national community shall be an aim of primary education for the populations concerned.

Article 25

Educational measures shall be taken among other sections of the national community and particularly among those that are in most direct contact with the populations concerned with the object of eliminating prejudices that they may harbour in respect of these populations.

Article 26

1. Governments shall adopt measures, appropriate to the social and cultural characteristics of the populations concerned, to make known to them their rights and duties, especially in regard to labour and social welfare.

2. If necessary this shall be done by means of written translations and through the use of media of mass communication in the languages of these populations.

PART VII. ADMINISTRATION

Article 27

1. The governmental authority responsible for the matters covered in this Convention shall create or develop agencies to administer the programmes involved.

2. These programmes shall include –

(a) planning, co-ordination and execution of appropriate measures for the social, economic and cultural development of the populations concerned;

(b) proposing of legislative and other measures to the competent authorities;

(c) supervision of the application of these measures

PART VIII. GENERAL PROVISIONS

Article 28

The nature and scope of the measures to be taken to give effect to this Convention shall be determined in a flexible manner, having regard to the conditions characteristic of each country.

Article 29

The application of the provisions of this Convention shall not affect benefits conferred on the populations concerned in pursuance of other Conventions and Recommendations.

Article 30

The formal ratification of this Convention shall be communicated to the Director-General of the International Labour Office for registration.

Article 31

1. This Convention shall be binding only upon the Members of the International Labour Organization whose ratifications have been registered with the Director-General.

2. It shall come into force 12 months after the date on which the ratifications of two Members have been registered with the Director-General.

3. Thereafter, this Convention shall come into force for any Member 12 months after the date on which its ratification has been registered.

Article 32

1. A Member which has ratified this Convention may denounce it after the expiration of 10 years from the date on which the Convention first comes into force, by an act on which the Convention first comes into force, by an act communicated to the Director-General of the International Labour Office for registration. Such denunciation shall not take effect until one year after the date on which it is registered.

2. Each Member which has ratified this Convention and which does not, within the year following the expiration of the period of 10 years mentioned in the preceding paragraph, exercise the right of denunciation provided for in this Article, will be bound for another period of 10 years and, thereafter, may denounce this Convention at the expiration of each period of 10 years under the terms provided in this Article.

Article 33

1. The Director-General of the International Labour Office shall notify all Members of the International Labour Organization of the registration of all ratifications and denunciations communicated to him by the Members of the Organization.

2. When notifying the Members of the Organization of the registration of the second ratification communicated to him, the Director-General shall draw the attention of the Members of the Organization to the date upon which the Convention will come into force.

Article 34

The Director-General of the International Labour Office shall communicate to the Secretary-General of the United Nations for registration in accordance with Article 102 of the Charter of the United Nations full particulars of all ratifications and acts of denunciation registered by him in accordance with the provisions of the preceding Article.

Article 35

At such times as it may consider necessary the Governing Body of the International Labour Office shall present to the General Conference a report on the working of this Convention and shall examine the desirability of placing on the agenda of the Conference the questions of its provision in whole or in part.

Article 36

1. Should the Conference adopt a new Convention revising this Convention in whole or in part, then, unless the new Convention otherwise provides

(a) the ratification by a Member of the new revising Convention shall *ipso jure* involve the immediate denunciation of this Convention, notwithstanding the provisions of Article 32 above, if and when the new revising Convention shall have come into force;

(b) as from the date when the new revising Convention comes into force this Convention shall cease to be open to ratification by the Members.

2. This Convention shall in any case remain in force in its actual form and content for those Members which have ratified it but have not ratified the revising Convention.

Article 37

The English and French versions of the text of this Convention are equally authoritative.

ILO Convention No. 169 concerning Indigenous and Tribal Peoples in Independent Countries

Adopted on 27 June 1989 by the General Conference of the International Labour Organisation at its seventy-sixth session

ENTRY INTO FORCE: 5 September 1991

The General Conference of the International Labour Organisation,

Having been convened at Geneva by the Governing Body of the International Labour Office, and having met in its seventy-sixth session on 7 June 1989, and

Noting the international standards contained in the Indigenous and Tribal Populations Convention and Recommendation, 1957, and

Recalling the terms of the Universal Declaration of Human Rights, the International Covenant on Economic, Social and Cultural Rights, the International Covenant on Civil and Political Rights, and the many international instruments on the prevention of discrimination, and

Considering that the developments which have taken place in international law since 1957, as well as developments in the situation of indigenous and tribal peoples in all regions of the world, have made it appropriate to adopt new international standards on the subject with a view to removing the assimilationist orientation of the earlier standards, and

Recognising the aspirations of these peoples to exercise control over their own institutions, ways of life and economic development and to maintain and develop their identities, languages and religions, within the framework of the States in which they live, and

Noting that in many parts of the world these peoples are unable to enjoy their fundamental human rights to the same degree as the rest of the population of the States within which they live, and that their laws, values, customs and perspectives have often been eroded, and

Calling attention to the distinctive contributions of indigenous and tribal peoples to the cultural diversity and social and ecological harmony of humankind and to international co-operation and understanding, and

Noting that the following provisions have been framed with the co-operation of the United Nations, the Food and Agriculture Organization of the United Nations, the United Nations Educational, Scientific and Cultural Organization, and the World Health Organization, as well as of the Inter-American Indian Institute, at appropriate levels and in their respective fields, and that it is proposed to continue this co-operation in promoting and securing the application of these provisions, and

Having decided upon the adoption of certain proposals with regard to the partial revision of the Indigenous and Tribal Populations Convention, 1957 (No. 107), which is the fourth item on the agenda of the session, and

Having determined that these proposals shall take the form of an international Convention revising the Indigenous and Tribal Populations Convention, 1957;

Adopts this twenty-seventh day of June of the year one thousand nine hundred and eighty-nine the following Convention, which may be cited as the Indigenous and Tribal Peoples Convention, 1989.

PART I. GENERAL POLICY

Article 1

1. This Convention applies to:

(a) Tribal peoples in independent countries whose social, cultural and economic conditions distinguish them from other sections of the national community, and whose status is regulated wholly or partially by their own customs or traditions or by special laws or regulations;

(b) Peoples in independent countries who are regarded as indigenous on account of their descent from the populations which inhabited the country, or a geographical region to which the country belongs, at the time of conquest or colonisation or the establishment of present State boundaries and who, irrespective of their legal status, retain some or all of their own social, economic, cultural and political institutions.

2. Self-identification as indigenous or tribal shall be regarded as a fundamental criterion for determining the groups to which the provisons of this Convention apply.

3. The use of the term "peoples" in this Convention shall not be construed as having any implications as regards the rights which may attach to the term under international law.

Article 2

1. Governments shall have the responsibility for developing, with the participation of the peoples concerned, co-ordinated and systematic action to protect the right of these people and to guarantee respect for their integrity.

2. Such action shall include measures for:

(a) Ensuring that members of these peoples benefit on an equal footing from the rights and opportunities which national laws and regulations grant to other members of the population;

(b) Promoting the full realisation of the social, economic and cultural rights of these peoples with respect for their social and cultural identity, their customs and traditions and their institutions;

(c) Assisting the members of the peoples concerned to eliminate socio-economic gaps that may exist between indigenous and other members of the national community, in a manner compatible with their aspirations and ways of life.

Article 3

1. Indigenous and tribal peoples shall enjoy the full measure of human rights and fundamental freedoms without hindrance or discrimination. The provisions of the Convention shall be applied without discrimination to male and female members of these peoples.

2. No form of force or coercion shall be used in violation of the human rights and fundamental freedoms of the peoples concerned, including the rights contained in this Convention.

Article 4

1. Special measures shall be adopted as appropriate for safeguarding the persons, institutions, property, labour, cultures and environment of the peoples concerned.

2. Such special measures shall not be contrary to the freely-expressed wishes of the people concerned.

3. Enjoyment of the general rights of citizenship, without discrimination, shall not be prejudiced in any way by such special measures.

Article 5

In applying the provision of this Conventions

(a) The social, cultural, religious and spiritual values and practices of these peoples shall be recognised and protected, and due account shall be taken of the nature of the problems which face them both as groups and as individuals;

(b) The integrity of the values, practices and institutions of these peoples shall be respected;

(c) Policies aimed at mitigating the difficulties experienced by these peoples in facing new conditions of life and work shall be adopted, with the participation and co-operation of the peoples affected.

Article 6

1. In applying the provisions of this Convention, Governments shall:

(a) Consult the peoples concerned, through appropriate procedures and in particular through their representative institutions, whenever consideration is being given to legislative or administrative measures which may affect them directly;

(b) Establish means of which these peoples can freely participate, to at least the same extent as other sectors of the population, at all levels of decision-making in elective institutions and administrative and other bodies responsible for policies and programmes which concern them;

(c) Establish means for the full development of these peoples' own institutions and initiatives, and in appropriate cases provide the resources necessary for this purpose.

2. The consultations carried out in application of this Convention shall be undertaken, in good faith and in a form appropriate to the circumstances, with the objective of achieving agreement or consent to the proposed measures.

Article 7

1. The peoples concerned shall have the right to decide their own priorities for the process of development as it affects their lives, beliefs, institutions and spiritual well-being and the lands they occupy or otherwise use, and to exercise control, to the extent possible, over their own economic, social and cultural development. In addition, they shall participate in the formulation, implementation and evaluation of plans and programmes for national and regional development which may affect them directly.

2. The improvement of the conditions of life and work and levels of health and education of the peoples concerned, with their participation and co-operation, shall be a matter of priority in plans for the overall economic development of areas they inhabit. Special projects for development of the areas in question shall also be so designed as to promote such improvement.

3. Governments shall ensure that, whenever appropriate, studies are carried out, in co-operation with the peoples concerned, to assess the social, spiritual, cultural and environmental impact on them of planned development activities. The results of these studies shall be considered as fundamental criteria for the implementation of these activities.

4. Governments shall take measures, in co-operation with the peoples concerned, to protect and preserve the environment of the territories they inhabit.

Article 8

1. In applying national laws and regulations to the peoples concerned, due regard shall be had to their customs or customary laws.

2. These peoples shall have the right to retain their own customs and institutions, where these are not incompatible with fundamental rights defined by the national legal system and with internationally recognised human rights. Procedures shall be established, whenever necessary, to resolve conflicts which may arise in the application of this principle.

3. The application of paragraphs 1 and 2 of this Article shall not prevent members of these peoples from exercising the rights granted to all citizens and from assuming the corresponding duties.

Article 9

1. To the extent compatible with the national legal system and internationally recognised human rights, the methods customarily practised by the peoples concerned for dealing with offences committed by their members shall be respected.

2. The customs of these peoples in regard to penal matters shall be taken into consideration by the authorities and courts dealing with such cases.

Article 10

1. In imposing penalties laid down by general law on members of these peoples account shall be taken of their economic, social and cultural characteristics.

2. Preference shall be given to methods of punishment other than confinement in prison.

Article 11

The exaction from members of the peoples concerned of compulsory personal services in any form, whether paid or unpaid, shall be prohibited and punishable by law, except in cases prescribed by law for all citizens.

Articles 12

The peoples concerned shall be safeguarded against the abuse of their rights and shall be able to take legal proceedings, either individually or through their representative bodies, for the effective protection of these rights. Measures shall be taken to ensure that members of these peoples can understand and be understood in legal proceedings, where necessary through the provision of interpretation or by other effective means.

PART II. LAND

Article 13

1. In applying the provisions of this Part of the Convention governments shall respect the special importance of the cultures and spiritual values of the peoples concerned of their relationship with the lands or territories, or both as applicable, which they occupy or otherwise use, and in particular the collective aspects of this relationship.

2. The use of the term “lands” in Articles 15 and 16 shall include the concept of territories, which covers the total environment of the areas which the peoples concerned occupy or otherwise use.

Article 14

1. The rights of ownership and possession of the peoples concerned over the lands which they traditionally occupy shall be recognised. In addition, measures shall be taken in appropriate cases to safeguard the rights of the peoples concerned to use lands not exclusively occupied by them, but to which they have traditionally had access for their subsistence and traditional activities. Particular attention shall be paid to the situation of nomadic peoples and shifting cultivators in this respect.

2. Governments shall take steps as necessary to identify the lands which the peoples concerned traditionally occupy, and to guarantee effective protection of their rights of ownership and procession.

3. Adequate procedures shall be established within the national legal system to resolve land claims by the peoples concerned.

Article 15

1. The rights of the peoples concerned to the natural resources pertaining to their lands shall be specially safeguarded. These rights include the right of these peoples to participate in the use, management and conservation of these resources.

2. In cases in which the State retains the ownership of mineral or sub-surface resources or rights to other resources pertaining to lands, governments shall establish or maintain procedures through which they shall consult these peoples, with a view to ascertaining whether and to what degree their interests would be prejudiced, before undertaking or permitting any programmes for the exploration or exploitation of such resources pertaining to their lands. The peoples concerned shall wherever possible participate in the benefits of such activities, and shall receive fair compensation for any damages which they may sustain as a result of such activities.

Article 16

1. Subject to the following paragraphs of this Article, the peoples concerned shall not be removed from the lands which they occupy.

2. Where the relocation of these peoples is considered necessary as an exceptional measure, such relocation shall take place only with their free and informed consent. Where their consent cannot be obtained, such relocation shall take place only following appropriate procedures established by national laws and regulations, including public inquiries where appropriate, which provide the opportunity for effective representation of the peoples concerned.

3. Whenever possible, these peoples shall have the right to return to their traditional lands, as soon as the grounds for relocation cease to exist.

4. When such return is not possible, as determined by agreement or, in the absence of such agreement, through appropriate procedures, these peoples shall be provided in all possible cases with lands of quality and legal status at least equal to that of the lands previously occupied by them, suitable to provide for their present needs and future development. Where the peoples concerned express a preference for compensation in money or in kind, they shall be so compensated under appropriate guarantees.

5. Persons thus relocated shall be fully compensated for any resulting loss or injury.

Article 17

1. Procedures established by the peoples concerned for the transmission of land rights among members of these peoples shall be respected.

2. The peoples concerned shall be consulted whenever consideration is being given to their capacity to alienate their lands or otherwise transmit their rights outside their own community.

3. Persons not belonging to these peoples shall be prevented from taking advantage of their customs or of lack of understanding of the laws on the part of their members to secure the ownership, possession or use of land belonging to them.

Article 18

Adequate penalties shall be established by law for unauthorised intrusion upon, or use of, the lands of the peoples concerned, and governments shall take measures to prevent such offences.

Article 19

National agrarian programmes shall secure to the peoples concerned treatment equivalent to that accorded to other sectors of the population with regard to:

(a) The provision of more land for these peoples when they have not the area necessary for providing the essentials of a normal existence, or for any possible increase in their numbers;

(b) The provision of the means required to promote the development of the lands which these peoples already possess.

PART III. RECRUITMENT AND CONDITION OF EMPLOYMENT

Article 20

1. Governments shall, within the framework of national laws and regulations, and in co-operation with the peoples concerned, adopt special measures to ensure the effective protection with regard to recruitment and conditions of employment of workers belonging to these peoples, to the extent that they are not effectively protected by the laws applicable to workers in general.

2. Governments shall do everything possible to prevent any discrimination between workers belonging to the peoples concerned and other workers, in particular as regards:

(a) Admission to employment, including skilled employment, as well as measures for promotion and advancement;

(b) Equal remuneration for work of equal value;

(c) Medical and social assistance, occupational safety and health, all social security benefits and any other occupational related benefits, and housing;

(d) The right of association and freedom for all lawful trade union activities, and the right to conclude collective agreements with employers or employers' organisations.

3. The measures taken shall include measures to ensure:

(a) That workers belonging to the peoples concerned, including seasonal, casual and migrant workers in agricultural and other employment, as well as those employed by labour contractors, enjoy the protection afforded by national law and practice to other such workers in the same sectors, and that they are fully informed of their rights under labour legislation and of the means of redress available to them;

(b) That workers belonging to these peoples are not subjected to working conditions hazardous to their health, in particular through exposure to pesticides or other toxic substances;

(c) That workers belonging to these peoples are not subjected to coercive recruitment systems, including bonded labour and other forms of debt servitude;

(d) That workers belonging to these peoples enjoy equal opportunities and equal treatment in employment for men and women, and protection from sexual harassment.

4. Particular attention shall be paid to the establishment of adequate labour inspection services in areas where workers belonging to the peoples concerned undertake wage employment, in order to ensure compliance with the provisions of this Part of this Convention.

PART IV. VOCATIONAL TRAINING, HANDICRAFTS AND RURAL INDUSTRIES

Article 21

Members of the peoples concerned shall enjoy opportunities at least equal to those of other citizens in respect of vocational training measures.

Article 22

1. Measures shall be taken to promote the voluntary participation of members of the peoples concerned in vocational training programmes of general application.

2. Whenever existing programmes of vocational training of general application do not meet the special needs of the peoples concerned, governments shall, with the participation of these peoples, ensure the provision of special training programmes and facilities.

3. Any special training programmes shall be based on the economic environment, social and cultural conditions and practical needs of the peoples concerned. Any studies made in this connection shall be carried out in co-operation with these peoples, who shall be consulted on the organisation and operation of such programmes. Where feasible, these peoples shall progressively assume responsibility for the organisation and operation of such special training programmes, if they so decide.

Article 23

1. Handicrafts, rural and community-based industries, and subsistence economy and traditional activities of the peoples concerned, such as hunting, fishing, trapping and gathering, shall be recognised as important factors in the maintenance of their cultures and in their economic self-reliance and development. Governments shall, with the participation of these peoples and whenever appropriate, ensure that these activities are strengthened and promoted.

2. Upon the request of the peoples concerned, appropriate technical and financial assistance shall be provided wherever possible, taking into account the traditional technologies and cultural characteristics of these peoples, as well as the importance of sustainable and equitable development.

PART V. SOCIAL SECURITY AND HEALTH

Article 24

Social security schemes shall be extended progressively to cover the peoples concerned, and applied without discrimination against them.

Article 25

1. Governments shall ensure that adequate health services are made available to the peoples concerned, or shall provide them with resources to allow them to design and deliver such services under their own responsibility and control, so that they may enjoy the highest attainable standard of physical and mental health.

2. Health services shall, to the extent possible, be community-based. These services shall be planned and administered in co-operation with the peoples concerned and take into account their economic, geographic, social and cultural conditions as well as their traditional preventive care, healing practices and medicines.

3. The health care system shall give preference to the training and employment of local community health workers, and focus on primary health care while maintaining strong links with other levels of health care services.

4. The provision of such health services shall be co-ordinated with other social, economic and cultural measures in the country.

PART VI. EDUCATION AND MEANS OF COMMUNICATION

Article 26

Measures shall be taken to ensure that members of the people concerned have the opportunity to acquire education at all levels on at least an equal footing with the rest of the national community.

Article 27

1. Education programmes and services for the people concerned shall be developed and implemented in co-operation with them to address their special needs, and shall incorporate their histories, their knowledge and technologies, their value systems and their further social, economic and cultural aspirations.

2. The competent authority shall ensure the training of members of these peoples and their involvement in the formulation and implementation of education programmes, with a view to the progressive transfer of responsibility for the conduct of these programmes to these people as appropriate.

3. In addition, governments shall recognise the right of these peoples to establish their own educational institutions and facilities, provided that such institutions meet minimum standards established by the competent authority in consultation with these peoples. Appropriate resources shall be provided for this purpose.

Article 28

1. Children belonging to the peoples concerned shall, wherever practicable, be taught to read and write in their own indigenous language or in the language most commonly used by the group to which they belong. When this is not practicable, the competent authorities shall undertake consultations with these peoples with a view to the adoption of measures to achieve this objective.

2. Adequate measures shall be taken to ensure that these peoples have the opportunity to attain fluency in the national language or in one of the official languages of the country.

3. Measures shall be taken to preserve and promote the development and practice of the indigenous languages of the peoples concerned.

Article 29

The imparting of general knowledge and skills that will help children belonging to the peoples concerned to participate fully and on an equal footing in their own community and in the national community shall be an aim of education for these peoples.

Article 30

1. Governments shall adopt measures appropriate to the traditions and cultures of the peoples concerned, to make known to them their rights and duties, especially in regard to labour, economic opportunities, education and health matters, social welfare and their rights deriving from this Convention.

2. If necessary, this shall be done by means of written translations and through the use of mass communications in the languages of these peoples.

Article 31

Education measures shall be taken among all sections of the national community, and particularly among those that are in most direct contact with the peoples concerned, with the object of eliminating prejudices that they may harbour in respect of these peoples. To this end, efforts shall be made to ensure that history textbooks and other educational materials provide a fair, accurate and informative portrayal of the societies and cultures of these peoples.

PART VII. CONTACTS AND CO-OPERATION ACROSS BORDERS

Article 32

Governments shall take appropriate measures, including by means of international agreements, to facilitate contacts and co-operation between indigenous and tribal people across borders, including activities in the economic, social, cultural, spiritual and environmental fields.

PART VIII. ADMINISTRATION

Article 33

1. The governmental authority responsible for the matters covered in this Convention shall ensure that agencies or other appropriate mechanisms exist to administer the programmes affecting the peoples concerned, and shall ensure that they have the means necessary for the proper fulfilment of the functions assigned to them.

2. These programmes shall include:

(a) The planning, co-ordination, execution and evaluation, in co-operation with the peoples concerned, of the measures provided for in this Convention;

(b) The proposing of legislative and other measures to the competent authorities and supervision of the application of the measures taken, in co-operation with the peoples concerned.

PART IX. GENERAL PROVISIONS

Article 34

The nature and scope of the measures to be taken to give effect to this Convention shall be determined in a flexible manner, having regard to the conditions characteristic of each country.

Article 35

The application of the provision of this Convention shall not adversely affect rights and benefits of the peoples concerned pursuant to other Conventions and Recommendations, international instruments, treaties, or national laws, awards, custom or agreements.

PART X. FINAL PROVISIONS

Article 36

This Convention revises the Indigenous and Tribal Populations Convention, 1957.

Article 37

The formal ratifications of this Convention shall be communicated to the Director-General of the International Labour Office for registration.

Article 38

1. This Convention shall be binding only upon those Members of the International Labour Organisation whose ratifications have been registered with the Director-General.

2. It shall come into force twelve months after the date on which the ratifications of two Members have been registered with the Director-General.

3. Thereafter, this Convention shall come into force for any Member twelve months after the date on which its ratification has been registered.

Article 39

1. A Member which has ratified this Convention may denounce it after the expiration of ten years from the date on which the Convention first comes into force, by an act communicated to the Director-General of the International Labour Office for registration. Such denunciation shall not take effect until one year after the date on which it is registered.

2. Each Member which has ratified this Convention and which does not, within the year following the expiration of the period of ten years mentioned in the preceding paragraph, exercise the right of denunciation provided for in this Article, will be bound for another period of ten years and thereafter, may denounce this Convention at the expiration of each period of ten years under the terms provided for in this Article.

Article 40

1. The Director-General of the International Labour Office shall notify all Members of the International Labour Organisation of the registration of all ratifications and denunciations communicated to him by the Members of the Organisation.

2. When notifying the Members of the Organisation of the registration of the second ratification communicated to him, the Director-General shall draw the attention of the Members of the Organisation to the date upon which the Convention will come into force.

Article 41

The Director-General of the International Labour Office shall communicate to the Secretary-General of the United Nations for registration in accordance with Article 102 of the Charter of the United Nations full particulars of all ratifications and acts of denunciation registered by him in accordance with the provisions of the preceding Articles.

Article 42

At such times as it may consider necessary the Governing Body of the International Labour Office shall present to the General Conference a report on the working of this Convention and shall examine the desirability of placing on the agenda of the Conference the question of its revision in whole or in part.

Article 43

1. Should the Conference adopt a new Convention revising this Convention in whole or in part, then, unless the new Convention otherwise provides:

(a) The ratification by a Member of the new revising Convention shall *ipso jure* involve the immediate denunciation of this Convention, notwithstanding the provisions of Article 39 above, if and when the new revising Convention shall have come into force;

(b) As from the date when the new revising Convention comes into force this Convention shall cease to be open to ratification by the Members.

2. This Convention shall in any case remain in force in its actual form and content for those Members which have ratified it but have not ratified the revising Convention.

Article 44

The English and French versions of the text of this Convention are equally authoritative.

African [Banjul] Charter on Human and Peoples' Rights

Adopted June 27, 1981, OAU Doc. CAB/LEG/67/3 rev. 5, 21 I.L.M. 58 (1982), entered into force October 21, 1986

Preamble

The African States members of the Organization of African Unity, parties to the present convention entitled "African Charter on Human and Peoples' Rights";

Recalling Decision 115 (XVI) of the Assembly of Heads of State and Government at its Sixteenth Ordinary Session held in Monrovia, Liberia, from 17 to 20 July 1979 on the preparation of a "preliminary draft on an African Charter on Human and Peoples' Rights providing *inter alia* for the establishment of bodies to promote and protect human and peoples' rights";

Considering the Charter of the Organization of African Unity, which stipulates that "freedom, equality, justice and dignity are essential objectives for the achievement of the legitimate aspirations of the African peoples";

Reaffirming the pledge they solemnly made in Article 2 of the said Charter to eradicate all forms of colonialism from Africa, to co-ordinate and intensify their co-operation and efforts to achieve a better life for the peoples of Africa and to promote international co-operation having due regard to the Charter of the United Nations and the Universal Declaration of Human Rights;

Taking into consideration the virtues of their historical tradition and the values of African civilization which should inspire and characterize their reflection on the concept of human and peoples' rights;

Recognizing on the one hand, that fundamental human rights stem from the attributes of human beings, which justifies their national and international protection and on the other hand, that the reality and respect of peoples' rights should necessarily guarantee human rights;

Considering that the enjoyment of rights and freedoms also implies the performance of duties on the part of everyone;

Convinced that it is henceforth essential to pay particular attention to the right to development and that civil and political rights cannot be dissociated from economic, social and cultural rights in their conception as well as universality and that the satisfaction of economic, social and cultural rights is a guarantee for the enjoyment of civil and political rights;

Conscious of their duty to achieve the total liberation of Africa, the peoples of which are still struggling for their dignity and genuine independence, and undertaking to eliminate colonialism, neo-colonialism, *apartheid*, Zionism, and to dismantle aggressive foreign military bases and all forms of discrimination, particularly those based on race, ethnic group, colour, sex, language, religion or political opinions;

Reaffirming their adherence to the principles of human and peoples' rights and freedoms contained in the declarations, conventions and other instruments adopted by the Organization of African Unity, the Movement of Non-Aligned Countries and the United Nations;

Firmly convinced of their duty to promote and protect human and peoples' rights and freedoms taking into account the importance traditionally attached to these rights and freedoms in Africa;

Have agreed as follows:

Part I

RIGHTS AND DUTIES

Chapter I. Human and Peoples' Rights

Article 1

The Member States of the Organization of African Unity parties to the present Charter shall recognize the rights, duties and freedoms enshrined in this Charter and shall undertake to adopt legislative or other measures to give effect to them.

Article 2

Every individual shall be entitled to the enjoyment of the rights and freedoms recognized and guaranteed in the present Charter without distinction of any kind such as race, ethnic group, colour, sex, language, religion, political or any other opinion, national and social origin, fortune, birth or other status.

Article 3

1. Every individual shall be equal before the law.
2. Every individual shall be entitled to equal protection of the law.

Article 4

Human beings are inviolable. Every human being shall be entitled to respect for his life and the integrity of his person. No one may be arbitrarily deprived of this right.

Article 5

Every individual shall have the right to the respect of the dignity inherent in a human being and to the recognition of his legal status. All forms of exploitation and degradation of man particularly slavery, slave trade, torture, cruel, inhuman or degrading punishment and treatment shall be prohibited.

Article 6

Every individual shall have the right to liberty and to the security of his person. No one may be deprived of his freedom except for reasons and conditions previously laid down by law. In particular, no one may be arbitrarily arrested or detained.

Article 7

1. Every individual shall have the right to have his cause heard. This comprises:
   (a) the right to an appeal to competent national organs against acts violating his fundamental rights as recognized and guaranteed by conventions, laws, regulations and customs in force;
   (b) the right to be presumed innocent until proved guilty by a competent court or tribunal;
   (c) the right to defence, including the right to be defended by counsel of his choice;
   (d) the right to be tried within a reasonable time by an impartial court or tribunal.
2. No one may be condemned for an act or omission which did not constitute a legally punishable offence at the time it was committed. No penalty may be inflicted for an offence for which no provision was made at the time it was committed. Punishment is personal and can be imposed only on the offender.

Article 8

Freedom of conscience, the profession and free practice of religion shall be guaranteed. No one may, subject to law and order, be submitted to measures restricting the exercise of these freedoms.

Article 9

1. Every individual shall have the right to receive information.
2. Every individual shall have the right to express and disseminate his opinions within the law.

Article 10

1. Every individual shall have the right to free association provided that he abides by the law.
2. Subject to the obligation of solidarity provided for in Article 29 no one may be compelled to join an association.

Article 11

Every individual shall have the right to assemble freely with others. The exercise of this right shall be subject only to necessary restrictions provided for by law in particular those enacted in the interest of national security, the safety, health, ethics and rights and freedoms of others.

Article 12

1. Every individual shall have the right to freedom of movement and residence within the borders of a State provided he abides by the law.
2. Every individual shall have the right to leave any country including his own, and to return to his country. This right may only be subject to restrictions, provided for by law for the protection of national security, law and order, public health or morality.
3. Every individual shall have the right, when persecuted, to seek and obtain asylum in other countries in accordance with the laws of those countries and international conventions.

4. A non-national legally admitted in a territory of a State party to the present Charter, may only be expelled from it by virtue of a decision taken in accordance with the law.

5. The mass expulsion of non-nationals shall be prohibited. Mass expulsion shall be that which is aimed at national, racial, ethnic or religious groups.

Article 13

1. Every citizen shall have the right to participate freely in the government of his country, either directly or through freely chosen representatives in accordance with the provisions of the law.

2. Every citizen shall have the right of equal access to the public service of his country.

3. Every individual shall have the right of access to public property and services in strict equality of all persons before the law.

Article 14

The right to property shall be guaranteed. It may only be encroached upon in the interest of public need or in the general interest of the community and in accordance with the provisions of appropriate laws.

Article 15

Every individual shall have the right to work under equitable and satisfactory conditions, and shall receive equal pay for equal work.

Article 16

1. Every individual shall have the right to enjoy the best attainable state of physical and mental health.

2. States parties to the present Charter shall take the necessary measures to protect the health of their people and to ensure that they receive medical attention when they are sick.

Article 17

1. Every individual shall have the right to education.

2. Every individual may freely take part in the cultural life of his community.

3. The promotion and protection of morals and traditional values recognized by the community shall be the duty of the State.

Article 18

1. The family shall be the natural unit and basis of society. It shall be protected by the State which shall take care of its physical health and moral.

2. The State shall have the duty to assist the family which is the custodian of morals and traditional values recognized by the community.

3. The State shall ensure the elimination of every discrimination against women and also ensure the protection of the rights of the woman and the child as stipulated in international declarations and conventions.

4. The aged and the disabled shall also have the right to special measures of protection in keeping with their physical or moral needs.

Article 19

All peoples shall be equal; they shall enjoy the same respect and shall have the same rights. Nothing shall justify the domination of a people by another.

Article 20

1. All peoples shall have the right to existence. They shall have the unquestionable and inalienable right to self-determination. They shall freely determine their political status and shall pursue their economic and social development according to the policy they have freely chosen.

2. Colonized or oppressed peoples shall have the right to free themselves from the bonds of domination by resorting to any means recognized by the international community.

3. All peoples shall have the right to the assistance of the States parties to the present Charter in their liberation struggle against foreign domination, be it political, economic or cultural.

Article 21

1. All peoples shall freely dispose of their wealth and natural resources. This right shall be exercised in the exclusive interest of the people. In no case shall a people be deprived of it.

2. In case of spoliation the dispossessed people shall have the right to the lawful recovery of its property as well as to an adequate compensation.

3. The free disposal of wealth and natural resources shall be exercised without prejudice to the obligation of promoting international economic co-operation based on mutual respect, equitable exchange and the principles of international law.

4. States parties to the present Charter shall individually and collectively exercise the right to free disposal of their wealth and natural resources with a view to strengthening African unity and solidarity.

5. States parties to the present Charter shall undertake to eliminate all forms of foreign economic exploitation particularly that practised by international monopolies so as to enable their peoples to fully benefit from the advantages derived from their national resources.

Article 22

1. All peoples shall have the right to their economic, social and cultural development with due regard to their freedom and identity and in the equal enjoyment of the common heritage of mankind.

2. States shall have the duty, individually or collectively, to ensure the exercise of the right to development.

Article 23

1. All peoples shall have the right to national and international peace and security. The principles of solidarity and friendly relations implicitly affirmed by the Charter of the United Nations and reaffirmed by that of the Organization of African Unity shall govern relations between States.

2. For the purpose of strengthening peace, solidarity and friendly relations, States parties to the present Charter shall ensure that:

(a) any individual enjoying the right of asylum under Article 12 of the present Charter shall not engage in subversive activities against his country of origin or any other State party to the present Charter; (b) their territories shall not be used as bases for subversive or terrorist activities against the people of any other State party to the present Charter.

Article 24

All peoples shall have the right to a general satisfactory environment favourable to their development.

Article 25

States parties to the present Charter shall have the duty to promote and ensure through teaching, education and publication, the respect of the rights and freedoms contained in the present Charter and to see to it that these freedoms and rights as well as corresponding obligations and duties are understood.

Article 26

States parties to the present Charter shall have the duty to guarantee the independence of the Courts and shall allow the establishment and improvement of appropriate national institutions entrusted with the promotion and protection of the rights and freedoms guaranteed by the present Charter.

Chapter II. Duties

Article 27

1. Every individual shall have duties towards his family and society, the State and other legally recognized communities and the international community.

2. The rights and freedoms of each individual shall be exercised with due regard to the rights of others, collective security, morality and common interest.

Article 28

Every individual shall have the duty to respect and consider his fellow beings without discrimination, and to maintain relations aimed at promoting, safeguarding and reinforcing mutual respect and tolerance.

Article 29

The individual shall also have the duty:

1. to preserve the harmonious development of the family and to work for the cohesion and respect of the family; to respect his parents at all times, to maintain them in case of need;

2. To serve his national community by placing his physical and intellectual abilities at its service;

3. Not to compromise the security of the State whose national or resident he is;

4. To preserve and strengthen social and national solidarity, particularly when the latter is threatened;

5. To preserve and strengthen the national independence and the territorial integrity of his country and to contribute to its defence in accordance with the law;

6. To work to the best of his abilities and competence, and to pay taxes imposed by law in the interest of the society;

7. To preserve and strengthen positive African cultural values in his relations with other members of the society, in the spirit of tolerance, dialogue and consultation and, in general, to contribute to the promotion of the moral well-being of society;

8. To contribute to the best of his abilities, at all times and at all levels, to the promotion and achievement of African unity.

Part II

MEASURES OF SAFEGUARD

Chapter I . Establishment and Organization of the African Commission on Human and Peoples' Rights

Article 30

An African Commission on Human and Peoples' Rights, hereinafter called "the Commission", shall be established within the Organization of African Unity to promote human and peoples' rights and ensure their protection in Africa.

Article 31

1. The Commission shall consist of eleven members chosen from amongst African personalities of the highest reputation, known for their high morality, integrity, impartiality and competence in matters of human and peoples' rights; particular consideration being given to persons having legal experience.

2. The members of the Commission shall serve in their personal capacity.

Article 32

The Commission shall not include more than one national of the same State.

Article 33

The members of the Commission shall be elected by secret ballot by the Assembly of Heads of State and Government, from a list of persons nominated by the States parties to the present Charter.

Article 34

Each State party to the present Charter may not nominate more than two candidates.The candidates must have the nationality of one of the States parties of the present Charter. When two candidates are nominated by a State, one of them may not be a national of that State.

Article 35

1. The Secretary-General of the Organization of African Unity shall invite States parties to the present Charter at least four months before the elections to nominate candidates.

2. The Secretary-General of the Organization of African Unity shall make an alphabetical list of the persons thus nominated and communicate it to the Heads of State and Government at least one month before the elections.

Article 36

The members of the Commission shall be elected for a six-year period and shall be eligible for re-election. However, the term of office of four of the members elected at the first election shall terminate after two years and the term of office of three others, at the end of four years.

Article 37

Immediately after the first election, the Chairman of the Assembly of Heads of State and Government of the Organization of African Unity shall draw lots to decide the names of those members referred to in Article 36.

Article 38

After their election, the members of the Commission shall make a solemn declaration to discharge their duties impartially and faithfully.

Article 39

1. In case of death or resignation of a member of the Commission, the Chairman of the Commission shall immediately inform the Secretary-General of the Organization of African Unity, who shall declare the seat vacant from the date of death or from the date on which the resignation takes effect.

2. If, in the unanimous opinion of other members of the Commission, a member has stopped discharging his duties for any reason other than a temporary absence, the Chairman of the Commission shall inform the Secretary-General of the Organization of African Unity, who shall then declare the seat vacant.

3. In each of the cases anticipated above, the Assembly of Heads of State and Government shall replace the member whose seat become vacant for the remaining period of his term unless the period is less than six months.

Article 40

Every member of the Commission shall be in office until the date his successor assumes office.

Article 41

The Secretary-General of the Organization of African Unity shall appoint the Secretary of the Commission. He shall also provide the staff and services necessary for the effective discharge of the duties of the Commission. The Organization of African Unity shall bear the costs of the staff and services.

Article 42

1. The Commission shall elect its Chairman and Vice-Chairman for a two-year period. They shall be eligible for re-election.

2. The Commission shall lay down its rules of procedure.

3. Seven members shall form the quorum.

4. In case of an equality of votes, the Chairman shall have a casting vote.

5. The Secretary-General may attend the meetings of the Commission. He shall neither participate in deliberations nor shall he be entitled to vote. The Chairman of the Commission may, however, invite him to speak.

Article 43

In discharging their duties, members of the Commission shall enjoy diplomatic privileges and immunities provided for in the General Convention on the Privileges and Immunities of the Organization of African Unity.

Article 44

Provision shall be made for the employments and allowances of the members of the Commission in the Regular Budget of the Organization of Aftrican Unity.

CHAPTER II. MANDATE OF THE COMMISSION

Article 45

The functions of the Commission shall be:

1. To promote Human and Peoples' Rights and in particular:

(a) to collect documents, undertake studies and researches on African problems in the field of human and peoples' rights, organize seminars, symposia and conferences, disseminate information, encourage national and local institutions concerned with human and peoples' rights, and should the case arise, give its views or make recommendations to Governments;

(b) to formulate and lay down, principles and rules aimed at solving legal problems relating to human and peoples' rights and fundamental freedoms upon which African Governments may base their legislations.

(c) Co-operate with other African and international institutions concerned with the promotion and protection of human and peoples' rights.

2. Ensure the protection of human and peoples' rights under conditions laid down by the present Charter.

3. Interpret all the provisions of the present Charter at the request of a State party, an institution of the Organization of African Unity or an African organization recognized by the Organization of African Unity.

4. Perform any other tasks which may be entrusted to it by the Assembly of Heads of State and Government.

Chapter III. Procedure of the Commission

Article 46

The Commission may resort to any appropriate method of investigation; it may hear from the Secretary-General of the Organization of African Unity or any other person capable of enlightening it.

Communication From States

Article 47

If a State party to the present Charter has good reasons to believe that another State party to this Charter has violated the provisions of the Charter, it may draw, by written communication, the attention of that State to the matter. This communication shall also be addressed to the Secretary General of the Organization of African Unity and to the Chairman of the Commission. Within three months of the receipt of the communication, the State to which the communication is addressed shall give the enquiring State, written explanation or statement elucidating the matter. This should include as much as possible relevant information relating to the laws and rules of procedure applied and applicable, and the redress already given or course of action available.

Article 48

If within three months from the date on which the original communication is received by the State to which it is addressed, the issue is not settled to the satisfaction of the two States involved through bilateral negotiation or by any other peaceful procedure, either State shall have the right to submit the matter to the Commission through the Chairman and shall notify the other State involved.

Article 49

Notwithstanding the provisions of Article 47, if a State party to the present Charter considers that another State party has violated the provisions of the Charter, it may refer the matter directly to the Commission by addressing a communication to the Chairman, to the Secretary-General of the Organization of African Unity and the State concerned.

Article 50

The Commission can only deal with a matter submitted to it after making sure that all local remedies, if they exist, have been exhausted, unless it is obvious to the Commission that the procedure of achieving these remedies would be unduly prolonged.

Article 51

1. The Commission may ask the States concerned to provide it with all relevant information.

2. When the Commission is considering the matter, States concerned may be represented before it and submit written or oral representations.

Article 52

After having obtained from the States concerned and from other sources all the information it deems necessary and after having tried all appropriate means to reach an amicable solution based on the respect of human and peoples' rights, the Commission shall prepare, within a reasonable period of time from the notification referred to in Ariticle 48, a report stating the facts and its findings. This report shall be sent to the States concerned and communicated to the Assembly of Heads of State and Government.

Article 53

While transmitting its report, the Commission may make to the Assembly of Heads of State and Government such recommendations as it deems useful.

Article 54

The Commission shall submit to each ordinary Session of the Assembly of Heads of State and Government a report on its activities.

Other Communications

Article 55

1. Before each session, the Secretary of the Commission shall make a list of the communications other than those of States parties to the present Charter and transmit them to the members of the Commission, who shall indicate which communications should be considered by the Commission.

2. A communication shall be considered by the Commission if a simple majority of its members so decide.

Article 56

Communications relating to human and peoples' rights referred to in Article 55 received by the Commission, shall be considered if they:

1. Indicate their authors even if the latter request anonymity;
2. Are compatible with the Charter of the Organization of African Unity or with the present Charter;
3. Are not written in disparaging or insulting language directed against the State concerned and its institutions or to the Organization of African Unity;
4. Are not based exclusively on news disseminated through the mass media;
5. Are sent after exhausting local remedies, if any, unless it is obvious that this procedure is unduly prolonged;
6. Are submitted within a reasonable period from the time local remedies are exhausted or from the date the Commission is seized of the matter; and
7. Do not deal with cases which have been settled by these States involved in accordance with the principles of the Charter of the United Nations, or the Charter of the Organization of African Unity or the provisions of the present Charter.

Article 57

Prior to any substantive consideration, all communications shall be brought to the knowledge of the State concerned by the Chairman of the Commission.

Article 58

1. When it appears after deliberations of the Commission that one or more communications apparently relate to special cases which reveal the existence of a series of serious or massive violations of human and peoples' rights, the Commission shall draw the attention of the Assembly of Heads of State and Government to these special cases.
2. The Assembly of Heads of State and Government may then request the Commission to undertake an in-depth study of these cases and make a factual report, accompanied by its findings and recommendations.
3. A case of emergency duly noticed by the Commission shall be submitted by the latter to the Chairman of the Assembly of Heads of State and Government who may request an in-depth study.

Article 59

1. All measures taken within the provisions of the present Chapter shall remain confidential until such a time as the Assembly of Heads of State and Government shall otherwise decide.
2. However, the report shall be published by the Chairman of the Commission upon the decision of the Assembly of Heads of State and Government.
3. The report on the activities of the Commission shall be published by its Chairman after it has been considered by the Assembly of Heads of State and Government.

Chapter IV. Applicable Principles

Article 60

The Commission shall draw inspiration from international law on human and peoples' rights, particularly from the provisions of various African instruments on human and peoples' rights, the Charter of the United Nations, the Charter of the Organization of African Unity, the Universal Declaration of Human Rights, other instruments adopted by the United Nations and by African countries in the field of human and peoples' rights as well as from the provisions of various instruments adopted within the Specialized Agencies of the United Nations of which the parties to the present Charter are members.

Article 61

The Commission shall also take into consideration, as subsidiary measures to determine the principles of law, other general or special international conventions, laying down rules expressly recognized by Member States of the Organization of African Unity, African practices consistent with international norms on human and peoples' rights, customs generally accepted as law, general principles of law recognized by African states as well as legal precedents and doctrine.

Article 62

Each State party shall undertake to submit every two years, from the date the present Charter comes into force, a report on the legislative or other measures taken with a view to giving effect to the rights and freedoms recognized and guaranteed by the present Charter.

Article 63

1. The present Charter shall be open to signature, ratification or adherence of the Member States of the Organization of African Unity.
2. The instruments of ratification or adherence to the present Charter shall be deposited with the Secretary-General of the Organization of African Unity.
3. The present Charter shall come into force three months after the reception by the Secretary-General of the instruments of ratification or adherence of a simple majority of the Member States of the Organization of African Unity.

PART III

GENERAL PROVISION

Article 64

1. After the coming into force of the present Charter, members of the Commission shall be elected in accordance with the relevant Articles of the present Charter.

2. The Secretary-General of the Organization of African Unity shall convene the first meeting of the Commission at the Headquarters of the Organization within three months of the constitution of the Commission.Thereafter, the Commission shall be convened by its Chairman whenever necessary but at least once a year.

Article 65

For each of the States that will ratify or adhere to the present Charter after its coming into force, the Charter shall take effect three months after the date of the deposit by that State of its instrument of ratification or adherence.

Article 66

Special protocols or agreements may, if necessary, supplement the provisions of the present Charter.

Article 67

The Secretary-General of the Organization of Aftrican Unity shall inform Member States of the Organization of the deposit of each instrument of ratification or adherence.

Article 68

The present Charter may be amended if a State party makes a written request to that effect to the Secretary-General of the Organization of African Unity. The Assembly of Heads of State and Government may only consider the draft amendment after all the States parties have been duly informed of it and the Commission has given its opinion on it at the request of the sponsoring State. The amendment shall be approved by a simple majority of the States parties. It shall come into force for each State which has accepted it in accordance with its constitutional procedure three months after the Secretary-General has received notice of the acceptance.

Adopted by the eighteenth Conference of Heads of State and Government of the Organization of African Unity, June 1981 – Nairobi, Kenya.

Economic and Social Council Technical Review

E/CN.4/Sub.2/1994/2/Add.1
20 April 1994

Original: ENGLISH
COMMISSION ON HUMAN RIGHTS
Sub-Commission on Prevention of Discrimination and Protection of Minorities
Forty-sixth session
Item 15 of the provisional agenda

DISCRIMINATION AGAINST INDIGENOUS PEOPLES

Technical review of the United Nations draft declaration on the rights of indigenous peoples

Addition

DRAFT DECLARATION AS AGREED UPON BY THE MEMBERS OF THE WORKING GROUP AT ITS ELEVENTH SESSION

Affirming that indigenous peoples are equal in dignity and rights to all other peoples, while recognizing the right of all peoples to be different, to consider themselves different, and to be respected as such,

Affirming also that all peoples contribute to the diversity and richness of civilizations and cultures, which constitute the common heritage of humankind,

Affirming further that all doctrines, policies and practices based on or advocating superiority of peoples or individuals on the basis of national origin, racial, religious, ethnic or cultural differences are racist, scientifically false, legally invalid, morally condemnable and socially unjust,

Reaffirming also that indigenous peoples, in the exercise of their rights, should be free from discrimination of any kind,

Concerned that indigenous peoples have been deprived of their human rights and fundamental freedoms, resulting, *inter alia*, in their colonization and dispossession of their lands, territories and resources, thus preventing them from exercising, in particular, their right to development in accordance with their own needs and interests,

Recognizing the urgent need to respect and promote the inherent rights and characteristics of indigenous peoples, especially their rights to their lands, territories and resources, which derive from their political, economic and social structures and from their cultures, spiritual traditions, histories and philosophies,

Welcoming the fact that indigenous peoples are organizing themselves for political, economic, social and cultural enhancement and in order to bring an end to all forms of discrimination and oppression wherever they occur,

Convinced that control by indigenous peoples over developments affecting them and their lands, territories and resources will enable them to maintain and strengthen their institutions, cultures and traditions, and to promote their development in accordance with their aspirations and needs,

Recognizing also that respect for indigenous knowledge, cultures and traditional practices contributes to sustainable and equitable development and proper management of the environment,

Emphasizing the need for demilitarization of the lands and territories of indigenous peoples, which will contribute to peace, economic and social progress and development, understanding and friendly relations among nations and peoples of the world,

Recognizing in particular the right of indigenous families and communities to retain shared responsibility for the upbringing, training, education and well-being of their children,

Recognizing also that indigenous peoples have the right freely to determine their relationships with States in a spirit of coexistence, mutual benefit and full respect,

Considering that treaties, agreements and other arrangements between States and indigenous peoples are properly matters of international concern and responsibility,

Acknowledging that the Charter of the United Nations, the International Covenant on Economic, Social and Cultural Rights and the International Covenant on Civil and Political Rights affirm the fundamental importance of the right of self-determination of all peoples, by virtue of which they freely determine their political status and freely pursue their economic, social and cultural development,

Bearing in mind that nothing in this Declaration may be used to deny any peoples their right of self-determination,

Encouraging States to comply with and effectively implement all international instruments, in particular those related to human rights, as they apply to indigenous peoples, in consultation and cooperation with the peoples concerned,

Emphasizing that the United Nations has an important and continuing role to play in promoting and protecting the rights of indigenous peoples,

Believing that this Declaration is a further important step forward for the recognition, promotion and protection of the rights and freedoms of indigenous peoples and in the development of relevant activities of the United Nations system in this field,

Solemnly proclaims the following United Nations Declaration on the Rights of Indigenous Peoples:

PART I

Article 1

Indigenous peoples have the right to the full and effective enjoyment of all human rights and fundamental freedoms recognized in the charter of the United Nations, the Universal Declaration of Human Rights and international human rights law.

Article 2

Indigenous individuals and peoples are free and equal to all other individuals and peoples in dignity and rights, and have the right to be free from any kind of adverse discrimination, in particular that based on their indigenous origin or identity.

Article 3

Indigenous peoples have the right of self-determination. By virtue of that right they freely determine their political status and freely pursue their economic, social and cultural development.

Article 4

Indigenous peoples have the right to maintain and strengthen their distinct political, economic, social and cultural characteristics, as well as their legal systems, while retaining their rights to participate fully, if they so choose, in the political, economic, social and cultural life of the State.

Article 5

Every indigenous individual has the right to a nationality.

PART II

Article 6

Indigenous peoples have the collective right to live in freedom, peace and security as distinct peoples and to full guarantees against genocide or any other act of violence, including the removal of indigenous children from their families and communities under any pretext.

In addition, they have the individual rights to life, physical and mental integrity, liberty and security of person.

Article 7

Indigenous peoples have the collective and individual right not to be subjected to ethnocide and cultural genocide, including prevention of and redress for:

(a) Any action which has the aim or effect of depriving them of their integrity as distinct peoples, or of their cultural values or ethnic identities;

(b) any action which has the aim or effect of dispossessing them of their lands, territories or resources;

(c) Any form of population transfer which has the aim or effect of violating or undermining any of their rights;

(d) Any form of assimilation or integration by other cultures or ways of life imposed on them by legislative, administrative or other measures;

(e) Any form of propaganda directed against them.

Article 8

Indigenous peoples have the collective and individual right to maintain and develop their distinct identities and characteristics, including the right to identify themselves as indigenous and to be recognized as such.

Article 9

Indigenous peoples and individuals have the right to belong to an indigenous community or nation, in accordance with the traditions and customs of the community or nation concerned. No disadvantage of any kind may arise from the exercise of such a right.

Article 10

Indigenous peoples shall not be forcibly removed from their lands or territories. No relocation shall take place without the free and informed consent of the indigenous peoples concerned and after agreement on just and fair compensation and, where possible, with the option of return.

Article 11

Indigenous peoples have the right to special protection and security in periods of armed conflict.

States shall observe international standards, in particular the Fourth Geneva Convention of 1949, for the protection of civilian populations in circumstances of emergency and armed conflict, and shall not:

(a) Recruit indigenous individuals against their will into the armed forces and, in particular, for use against other indigenous peoples;

(b) Recruit indigenous children into the armed forces under any circumstances;

(c) Force indigenous individuals to abandon their lands, territories or means of subsistence, or relocate them in special centres for military purposes;

(d) Force indigenous individuals to work for military purposes under any discriminatory conditions.

PART III

Article 12

Indigenous peoples have the right to practise and revitalize their cultural traditions and customs. This includes the right to maintain, protect and develop the past, present and future manifestations of their cultures, such as archaeological and historical sites, artefacts, designs, ceremonies, technologies and visual and performing arts and literatures, as well as the right to the restitution of cultural, intellectual, religious and spiritual property taken without their free and informed consent or in violation of their laws, traditions and customs.

Article 13

Indigenous peoples have the right to manifest, practise, develop and teach their spiritual and religious traditions, customs and ceremonies; the right to maintain, protect, and have access in privacy to their religious and cultural sites; the right to the use and control of ceremonial objects; and the right to the repatriation of human remains.

States shall take effective measures, in conjunction with the indigenous peoples concerned, to ensure that indigenous sacred places, including burial sites, be preserved, respected and protected.

Article 14

Indigenous peoples have the right to revitalize, use, develop and transmit to future generations their histories, languages, oral traditions, philosophies, writing systems and literatures, and to designate and retain their own names for communities, places and persons.

States shall take effective measures, whenever any right of indigenous peoples may be threatened, to ensure this right is protected and also to ensure that they can understand and be understood in political, legal and administrative proceedings, where necessary through the provision of interpretation or by other appropriate means.

PART IV

Article 15

Indigenous children have the right to all levels and forms of education of the State. All indigenous peoples also have this right and the right to establish and control their educational systems and institutions providing education in their own languages, in a manner appropriate to their cultural methods of teaching and learning.

Indigenous children living outside their communities have the right to be provided access to education in their own culture and language.

States shall take effective measures to provide appropriate resources for these purposes.

Article 16

Indigenous peoples have the right to have the dignity and diversity of their cultures, traditions, histories and aspirations appropriately reflected in all forms of education and public information.

States shall take effective measures, in consultation with the indigenous peoples concerned, to eliminate prejudice and discrimination and to promote tolerance, understanding and good relations among indigenous peoples and all segments of society.

Article 17

Indigenous peoples have the right to establish their own media in their own languages. They also have the right to equal access to all forms of non-indigenous media.

States shall take effective measures to ensure that State-owned media duly reflect indigenous cultural diversity.

Article 18

Indigenous peoples have the right to enjoy fully all rights established under international labour law and national labour legislation.

Indigenous individuals have the right not to be subjected to any discriminatory conditions of labour, employment or salary.

PART V

Article 19

Indigenous peoples have the right to participate fully, if they so choose, at all levels of decision-making in matters which may affect their rights, lives, and destinies through representatives chosen by themselves in accordance with their own procedures, as well as to maintain and develop their own indigenous decision-making institutions.

Article 20

Indigenous peoples have the right to participate fully, if they so choose, through procedures determined by them, in devising legislative or administrative measures that may affect them.

States shall obtain the free and informed consent of the peoples concerned before adopting and implementing such measures.

Article 21

Indigenous peoples have the right to maintain and develop their political, economic and social systems, to be secure in the enjoyment of their own means of subsistence and development, and to engage freely in all their traditional and other economic activities. Indigenous peoples who have been deprived of their means of subsistence and development are entitled to just and fair compensation.

Article 22

Indigenous peoples have the right to special measures for the immediate, effective and continuing improvement of their economic and social conditions, including in the areas of employment, vocational training and retraining, housing, sanitation, health and social security.

Particular attention shall be paid to the rights and special needs of indigenous elders, women, youth, children and disabled persons.

Article 23

Indigenous peoples have the right to determine and develop priorities and strategies for exercising their right to development. In particular, indigenous peoples have the right to determine and develop all health, housing and other economic and social programmes affecting them and, as far as possible, to administer such programmes through their own institutions.

Article 24

Indigenous peoples have the right to their traditional medicines and health practices, including the right to the protection of vital medicinal plants, animals and minerals.

They also have the right to access, without any discrimination, to all medical institutions, health services and medical care.

PART VI

Article 25

Indigenous peoples have the right to maintain and strengthen their distinctive spiritual and material relationship with the lands, territories, waters and coastal seas and other resources which they have traditionally owned or otherwise occupied or used, and to uphold their responsibilities to future generations in this regard.

Article 26

Indigenous peoples have the right to own, develop, control and use the lands and territories, including the total environment of the lands, air, waters, coastal seas, sea-ice, flora and fauna and other resources which they have traditionally owned or otherwise occupied or used. This includes the right to the full recognition of their laws, traditions and customs, land-tenure systems and institutions for the development and management of resources, and the right to effective measures by States to prevent any interference with, alienation of or encroachment upon these rights.

Article 27

Indigenous peoples have the right to the restitution of the land, territories and resources which they have traditionally owned or otherwise occupied or used, and which have been confiscated, occupied, used or damaged without their free and informed consent. Where this is not possible, they have the right to just and fair compensation. Unless otherwise freely agreed upon by the peoples concerned, compensation shall take the form of lands, territories and resources equal in quality, size and legal status.

Article 28

Indigenous peoples have the right to the conservation, restoration and protection of the total environment and the productive capacity of their lands, territories and resources, as well as to assistance for this purpose from States and through international cooperation. Military activities shall not take place in the lands and territories of indigenous peoples, unless otherwise freely agreed upon by the peoples concerned.

States shall take effective measures to ensure that no storage or disposal of hazardous materials shall take place in the lands and territories of indigenous peoples.

States shall also take effective measures to ensure, as needed, that programmes for monitoring, maintaining and restoring the health of indigenous peoples, as developed and implemented by the peoples affected by such materials, are duly implemented.

Article 29

Indigenous peoples are entitled to the recognition of the full ownership, control and protection of their cultural and intellectual property.

They have the right to special measures to control, develop and protect their sciences, technologies and cultural manifestations, including human and other genetic resources, seeds, medicines, knowledge of the properties of fauna and flora, oral traditions, literatures, design and visual and performing arts.

Article 30

Indigenous peoples have the right to determine and develop priorities and strategies for the development or use of their lands, territories and other resources, including the right to require that States obtain their free and informed consent prior to the approval of any project affecting their lands, territories and other resources, particularly in connection with the development, utilization or exploitation of mineral, water or other resources. Pursuant to agreement with the indigenous peoples concerned, just and fair compensation shall be provided for any such activities and measures taken to mitigate adverse environmental, economic, social, cultural or spiritual impact.

PART VII

Article 31

Indigenous peoples, as a specific form of exercising their right to self-determination, have the right to autonomy or self-government in matters relating to their internal and local affairs, including culture, religion, education, information, media, health, housing, employment, social welfare, economic activities, land and resources management, environment and entry by non-members, as well as ways and means for financing these autonomous functions.

Article 32

Indigenous peoples have the collective right to determine their own citizenship in accordance with their customs and traditions. Indigenous citizenship does not impair the right of indigenous individuals to obtain citizenship of the States in which they live.

Indigenous peoples have the right to determine the structures and to select the membership of their institutions in accordance with their own procedures.

Article 33

Indigenous peoples have the right to promote, develop and maintain their institutional structures and their distinctive juridical customs, traditions, procedures and practices, in accordance with internationally recognized human rights standards.

Article 34

Indigenous peoples have the collective right to determine the responsibilities of individuals to their communities.

Article 35

Indigenous peoples, in particular those divided by international borders, have the right to maintain and develop contacts, relations and cooperation, including activities for spiritual, cultural, political, economic and social purposes, with other peoples across borders.

States shall take effective measures to ensure the exercise and implementation of this right.

Article 36

Indigenous peoples have the right to the recognition, observance and enforcement of treaties, agreements and other constructive arrangements concluded with States or their successors, according to their original spirit and intent, and to have States honour and respect such treaties, agreements and other constructive arrangements. Conflicts and disputes which cannot otherwise be settled should be submitted to competent international bodies agreed to by all parties concerned.

PART VIII

Article 37

States shall take effective and appropriate measures, in consultation with the indigenous peoples concerned, to give full effect to the provisions of this Declaration. The rights recognized herein shall be adopted and included in national legislation in such a manner that indigenous peoples can avail themselves of such rights in practice.

Article 38

Indigenous peoples have the right to have access to adequate financial and technical assistance, from States and through international cooperation, to pursue freely their political, economic, social, cultural and spiritual development and for the enjoyment of the rights and freedoms recognized in this Declaration.

Article 39

Indigenous peoples have the right to have access to and prompt decision through mutually acceptable and fair procedures for the resolution of conflicts and disputes with States, as well as to effective remedies for all infringements of their individual and collective rights. Such a decision shall take into consideration the customs, traditions, rules and legal systems of the indigenous peoples concerned.

Article 40

The organs and specialized agencies of the United Nations systems and other intergovernmental organizations shall contribute to the full realization of the provisions of this Declaration through the mobilization, *inter alia*, of financial co-operation and technical assistance. Ways and means of ensuring participation of indigenous peoples on issues affecting them shall be established.

Article 41

The United Nations shall take the necessary steps to ensure the implementation of this Declaration including the creation of a body at the highest level with special competence in this field and with the direct participation of indigenous peoples. All United Nations bodies shall promote respect for and full application of the provisions of this Declaration.

PART IX

Article 42

The rights recognized herein constitute the minimum standards for the survival, dignity and well-being of the indigenous peoples of the world.

Article 43

All the rights and freedoms recognized herein are equally guaranteed to male and female indigenous individuals.

Article 44

Nothing in this Declaration may be construed as diminishing or extinguishing existing or future rights indigenous peoples may have or acquire.

Article 45

Nothing in this Declaration may be interpreted as implying for any State, group or person any right to engage in any activity or to perform any act contrary to the Charter of the United Nations.

ACKNOWLEDGEMENTS

MRG gratefully acknowledges all organizations and individuals who gave financial and other assistance for this project.

Funding organizations

Bilance
European Human Rights Foundation
Norwegian Foreign Ministry
Overseas Development Administration (UK)
United States Institute of Peace

The opinions, findings and conclusions or recommendations expressed in this publication are those of the authors and do not necessarily reflect the views of the United States Institute of Peace.

Sources of information, advice and assistance, including referees and reviewers

Eric Abitbol
Natalia Ablova
Hugh Adamson
Shapan Adnan
Africa Directory
African Rights
Afrika-Studiecntrum, University of Leiden
Sangeeta Ahuja
Shirin Akiner
Yusif Al Khoei
Al Khoei Foundation
Alaskan Intertribal Council
Anthony Alcock
Robert Aldrich
S. Aliyeva
Tim Allen
American-Arab Anti-Discrimination Committee
Amnesty International Netherlands
Amnesty International United Kingdom
Rob Angove
Marija Anteric
Antisemitism World Report
Arab Association for Human Rights
Bernard Arachi
Istavan Arnold
Bojana Asanovic
Asian American Federation
Association for the Study of Nationalities
Association of Slovak Writers and Artists in Hungary
Assyrian Cultural and Advice Centre
Nicholas Atampugre
Jonathan Aves
Khudoberdiev Aziz
Hannelore Baier
Baluch Research and Cultural Association
BBC Summary of World Broadcasts
Hugh Beach
Somsri Berger
Lucie Bernier
Anna-Maria Biro
Jutta Blauert
G. Bordyugov
Hamit Bozarslan
Brida Brennan, Transnational Institute, Netherlands
Teddy Brett
Bojan Brezigar
British Embassy, Belgrade
Natalie Brown
Carmel Budiardjo
Rob Buijtenhuij
Bulgarian Embassy, London
O. Cao
Peter Carey
Joji Cariño
Cindy Carlson
Carnegie Endowment for International Peace
Richard Carver
Carles Castellani
Central European University
Eyad Abu Chakra
Roger Chennells
S. Chervonnaya
Christian Clerk
Jonathan Cohen
Helen Collinson
Commission for Racial Equality
Committee for Defending the Rights of the Bidoon

Cultural Survival
Sally Cummings
Current Digest of Post-Soviet Press
Plaid Cymru
Stefanie D'Orey
Farhad Daftary
John Darby
Darién J. Davis
Murray Dawson-Smith
Dennis Deletant
Maria Delgado
Democratic Association of Hungarians in Romania
Cosmas Desmond
Deutsches Gymnasium fur Nordschleswig
Panayote Elias Dimitras
Mike Dottridge
Amaro Drom
Peter Duncan
Sheena Duncan
Karlis Eihenbaumns
Steven Ellis
Pierre Englebert
Europa World Year Book
European Bureau for Lesser Used Languages
James Fairhead
Abbas Faiz
Basil Fernando
Don Flynn
Françoise Fonval
Former Federal Ministry for Minorities, Belgrade
Deirdre Fottrell
Mike Franklin
Adrian Fraser
Jane Freeland
P. Goble
Sarah Graham-Brown
Duncan Green
Vibeke Greni
Ordesse Zubeir Hamad
Han Juo-mei
Sidney Harring
Neil Harvey
Helsinki Foundation for Human Rights, Poland
John B. Henriksen
Patricia Higgins
Monica Higuera
Gerard Hill
Martin Hill
Manfred Hinz
Robert Hitchcock
Frank Horn
Rosaleen Howard-Malverde
Human Rights Internet Reporter Masterlist
Human Rights Watch
Humanitarian Law Center, Belgrade
Hungarian Embassy, London
Anthony Hyman
Ibn Khaldoun Center for Development Studies
Infotag, Moldova
Institute for Ethnic Studies, Ljubjana
Institute of Jewish Affairs
Institute of Race Relations
Institute for War and Peace Reporting
Institute of Ethnography, Russian Academy of Sciences
Institute of Isma'ili Studies
Inter Ethnic Initiative for Human Rights
International Alert
International Alliance of the Indigenous-Tribal Peoples of the Tropical Forests
International Labour Organization
International Labour Review
Ashir Ioliev
Yvette Isaac
Pauline Jones
Ka Lahui Hawai'i
Alan Kaitoukov
Mansur Kardosh
Shereen Karmali
Anni King-Underwood
Lesley-Anne Knight
Eva Konig
P. Konings
Martin Kovats
Helen Krag
Laith Kubba
Yurii Kulchik
Kurdish Cultural Centre
Paul Lall
Gara LaMarche
Charles Lane
Aingeru Larrayoz
Latin America Bureau
Martin Lau
Ian Leggett
Katrin Legrain
Joe Llantos
Virginia Luling
Martin MacEwen
Bronwen Manby
Milena Mahon
Reynaldo Mariqueo
Alvidas Medalinskas
Pauline Martin
Marco Martiniello
Marianne Menjívar
Mehtab Ali Shah
Alessandro Michelucci
Claire Miller
B. Mililani Trask
Mischa Mills
G. Mirsky
Mohaijir Quami Movement
Richard Moorsom
Glenn T. Morris
M.M. Moshoeshoe-Chadzingwa
Minority Rights Group Finland

Minority Rights Group France
Minority Rights Group Greece
Minority Rights Group Slovakia
Minority Rights Group Sweden
NACLA *Report on the Americas*
Phil ya Nangoloh
Clemens Nathan
National Council of La Raza
National Spritual Assembly of the Baha'is of the United Kingdom
Anne Nelson
William Nicholls
Armin Nickelsen
Elizabeth Nissan
Hoshang Noriaee
Office for National and Ethnic Minorities, Hungary
OMRI
Open Media Research Institute, Czech Republic
Organization of Africans in the Americans
Eva Orsos-Hegyesi
Oxfam
Elfi Pallis
Angelika Pathak
Jenny Pearce
Mark Percival
James Pettifer
Giovanni Pezzoli
Kate Phillips
Liz Phillipson
Yves Plasseraud
Tomas Prader
Terence Ranger
Nora Rathzel
Filip Reyntjens
Peter Richardson
Claire Ritchie
Romanian Embassy, UK
Madge Rondo
Valentina Roslin
Stephen Roth
Chandra Roy
Royal Institute of International Affairs
Don Rubenstein
Russian Ministry of Nationalities and Regional Policy
Denis Samutt
Aram Sarbast
Igor Savin
George Schopflin
Bill Seary
Issa Shivji
Michael Shuttleworth
Rachel Sieder
Rickey Singh
Wendy Singh
Slovak Embassy, London
Malcolm Smart
Sergei Sokolovskii
Doug Soutar
Sia Spiliopoulou Akermark
Paul Spoonley
Bill Standish
Zoran Stankovic
Nick Stockton
Kristina Stockwood
Surya Subedi
Keith D. Suter
Saul Takahashi
Yash Tandon
TAPOL Indonesian Human Rights Campaign
Axel Thoma
V. Tishkov
Frédéric Tomesco
Pramod Unia
United Nations High Commissioner for Refugees
Unrepresented Nations and Peoples Organization
US Committee for Refugees
Lydia van de Fliert
Nick van Heer
Blanca Vazquez
Shams Vellani
K.S. Venkateswaran
Verification Technology Information Centre
Verkehrsburo, Leichtenstein
Bert Verstappen
Miranda Vickers
Rosângela Maria Vieira
Alex Vines
David Waller
Elizabeth Watson
Fiona Watson
Kieran Williams
Anne Wilson
Richard Wilson
Andrew Wilson
Marvin Wingfield
Rob Witte
James Woodburn
World Rainforest Movement
World Sindhi Congress
Wuokko Knocke, Istitutet for Arbetslivforskning
Albert Yelda
Helen Yuill
Mitja Zagar

NOTES ON CONTRIBUTORS

Bridget Anderson is research fellow in sociology at the University of Leicester, and an associate research fellow at the Centre for Race and Ethnic Relations at the University of Warwick. She acts as consultant to the Catholic Institute for International Relations and is author of *Britain's Secret Slaves: The Plight of Overseas Domestic Workers in Britain* (1993) and other articles and reports.

James U.H. Chin PhD teaches contemporary South-East Asian politics at Middlesex University, London. He has published on Sarawak, Sabah, Malaysian, Singaporean and Fijian politics and is author of *Chinese Politics in Sarawak* (1996). Prior to an academic career, he worked as a journalist in Singapore and Malaysia.

John Connell was educated at University College London, and has worked at the Institute of Development Studies, University of Sussex, and the Department of Economics, Australian National University. He is currently an associate professor in the Department of Geography at the University of Sydney. His numerous publications on Pacific history, population, migration and social issues include *Migration, Employment and Development in the South Pacific* (1987), *New Caledonia or Kanaky? The Political History of a French Colony* (1987) and *Papua New Guinea: The Struggle for Development* (1997).

Patrick Costello has worked on and in Latin America since 1987. He was formerly an electoral observer with the UN Observer Mission in South Africa, a human rights observer with the UN/OAS Mission in Haiti, and Guatemala coordinator with the Central America Human Rights Committee. He is co-author of *Literacy and Power: The Latin American Battleground* (1990) and other articles, papers and briefings. He has worked as a freelance researcher on human rights and Latin America, providing research papers to UNHCR. He is currently an adviser on foreign affairs to the Socialist Group of MEPs in the European Parliament.

Lindsey Crickmay has a PhD in Amerindian Studies and teaches Amerindian culture and history and Quechua in the Department of Social Anthropology at St Andrews University. She has spent several years in Latin America, principally the Andean countries, where her research focused primarily on weaving practice among highland Quechua and Aymara.

Chris Dammers is a consultant in social and economic development and writer on human rights and development issues. He has worked for the European Commission, the United Nations, Oxfam UK-I and a variety of non-governmental organizations.

James Ferguson is a researcher/writer at the Latin America Bureau, London, specializing in the Caribbean region. His publications for LAB include studies of the Dominican Republic, Grenada and Venezuela. He is also the author of *The Traveller's Literary Guide to the Caribbean* (1997).

David Hawk is a human rights researcher, formerly of Amnesty International. He is convenor of the Cambodia Documentation Commission and edited the MRG report *Minorities in Cambodia* (1995).

Miles Litvinoff is head of programmes at MRG.

David McDowall is a consultant and specialist writer on the Middle East. He has written MRG reports on the Kurds, the Palestinians and Lebanon and the MRG books *The Kurds: A Nation Denied* (1992) and *The Palestinians: The Road to Nationhood* (1995). He is the author of *A Modern History of the Kurds* (1996) and also *Europe and the Arabs: Discord or Symbiosis?* (1992).

Anna Matveeva graduated from Moscow State University and completed her PhD studies at the Institute of Oriental Studies, Russian Academy of Sciences. After coming to the UK in 1991, she worked at the International Relations Department, London School of Economics, first as a research assistant, then as a research officer. She currently works at International Alert as former Soviet Union project officer and is a visiting lecturer at the University of Westminster.

Julia Maxted studied geography at St Catherine's and Nuffield colleges, Oxford. A former research fellow at the Centre for Research in Ethnic Relations, University of Warwick, she currently teaches in the Black Studies and Sociology Department at the University of California, Santa Barbara. Her research interests focus on processes of social and spatial exclusion.

Neil J. Melvin received his DPhil from St Antony's College, Oxford University. He has been a research fellow of the Russian Research Center, Harvard University, and the Royal Institute of International Affairs, and was a British Academy postdoctoral fellow in the Government Department of the London School of Economics. He is currently a lecturer in Russian and Central Asian politics at Leeds University. He is the author of *Russians beyond Russia: The Politics of National Identity* (1995), a study of the Russian diaspora in the former Soviet Union, and has travelled widely throughout the region.

Peter O'Neill BA joint hons, MPhil, undertook his higher education in Durham, Bradford, Paris, Cambridge, Moscow and New Delhi. He began his career as a Reuter correspondent in Europe and South Asia. Author and co-editor of a number of books, he has worked on previous MRG publications, been a consultant to a number of UN agencies and rapporteur for international conferences on issues such as migrant workers and refugees. He is founder editor of EEC: Third World (TWEEC) news features and research agency (est. 1980).

Suzanne Pattle has an MA in contemporary Soviet and East European studies from the School of Slavonic and East European Studies, University of London. She worked on Central and Eastern European and former Soviet Union issues for MRG between 1991 and 1995.

Martyn Rady is senior lecturer in Central European history at the School of Slavonic and East European Studies, University of London. His previous publications include *Romania in Turmoil: A Contemporary History* (1992) and (as co-editor) *Towards a New Community: Culture and Politics in Post-Totalitarian Europe* (1993). His articles on minorities and rights in Central and Eastern Europe have appeared in the journals *Slavonic and East European Review* and *Ethnic and Racial Studies*.

Javaid Rehman LLM PhD has been teaching in various areas of international law for a number of years and has also practised as a human rights and constitutional lawyer. His specialized areas of research include the study of comparative constitutional laws and the rights of minorities and indigenous peoples of South Asia.

Alex Roslin is a writer, editor and publisher living in Montreal, Canada. He co-founded *The Nation*, a magazine serving the James Bay Cree Native Americans, and regularly writes for *The Montreal Gazette and Windspeaker*, a national Aboriginal newspaper, on the environment, First Nations and other political issues.

Nikhil Roy has worked at the International Secretariat of Amnesty International, London, since 1988 as Asia development coordinator, and worked with MRG for fourteen months in 1994–5. Formerly based in New Delhi, he has been associated with numerous human rights groups. After finishing his postgraduate studies at Delhi University, he worked with indigenous peoples in the Indian states of Madhya Pradesh and Bihar.

David Sogge studied at Harvard and also holds degrees from Princeton and the Institute of Social Studies, The Hague. Involved professionally in Africa since 1965, and today based in Amsterdam, he has served as adviser and staff member for agencies supporting development and human rights initiatives in Southern Africa. He is the author of *Sustainable Peace: Angola's Recovery* (1992) and of articles and reports stemming from assignments in Angola, Mozambique and South Africa.

Bogdan Szajkowski is Professor of Pan-European Politics and Director of the Centre for European Studies at the University of Exeter. A leading authority on the former communist countries, his research interests include ethnic minorities and social, political, economic and religious conflicts. His most recent books are *Encyclopaedia of Conflicts, Disputes and Flashpoints in Eastern Europe, Russia and the Successor States* (1994), *Political Parties of Eastern Europe, Russia and the Successor States* (1995) and, as co-editor, *Muslim Communities in the New Europe* (1996).

Patrick Thornberry is Professor of International Law and Director of the Centre for Minority Rights at Keele University. His publications include *International Law and the Rights of Minorities* (1991). He is an MRG Council member and was a consultant to MRG on the UN Draft Declaration on Minorities at the UN Human Rights Commission in 1991. He has acted as an expert adviser to the European Union, the Council of Europe, UNDP, OSCE and the British Foreign Office.

Carl Wilson is a Canadian-born freelance writer, editor and musician. He is a correspondent for *The Nation* in New York City and former editor of *This Magazine* in Toronto and conducted research for the award-winning Wildheart Productions documentary *Rwanda: The Dead Are Alive*. He writes a weekly column for Montreal's *Hour Magazine*.

Abebe Zegeye has written extensively on society and the environment in Africa and is currently a visiting professor at the University of California, Santa Barbara. His latest publication is *Ethiopia in Change* (1996). He is co-editor of *Social Identities: Journal for the Study of Race, Nation and Culture*.

INDEX

This is an index of names of minority groups; contexts where a group is dominant have not been indexed. Alternative names are given in [square brackets]. If a group is seen as a subgroup or branch of a larger grouping, this is shown in (parentheses).

Cross-references have been used to show *either* such relationships *or* where one name is preferred to another. Preferred terms and spellings follow those in the text as far as possible, and the more pejorative terms have been excluded.

Group names indicate ethnic or national origin, except where the group identity comes primarily from religion, language or culture. Place-names may be political, cultural or simply geographical. Names are included in this index to help users of the *Directory* and they do not represent any opinion about sovereignty or the status of a minority group.

Where the text concentrates – for a few lines or possibly a few pages – on one group, page numbers are shown in **bold**.

index prepared by
Gerard M-F Hill